# BIBLICAL AND TALMUDIC MEDICINE

*by*

**JULIUS PREUSS**

*translated and edited by*

**FRED ROSNER, M.D.**

A Jason Aronson Book

ROWMAN & LITTLEFIELD PUBLISHERS, INC.
*Lanham • Boulder • New York • Toronto • Oxford*

A JASON ARONSON BOOK

ROWMAN & LITTLEFIELD PUBLISHERS, INC.

Published in the United States of America
by Rowman & Littlefield Publishers, Inc.
A wholly owned subsidary of The Rowman & Littlefield Publishing Group, Inc.
4501 Forbes Boulevard, Suite 200, Lanham, Maryland 20706
www.rowmanlittlefield.com

PO Box 317
Oxford
OX2 9RU, UK

British Library Cataloguing in Publication Information Available

**Library of Congress Cataloging-in-Publication Data**

Preuss, Julius, 1861–1913.
  [Biblisch-talmudische Medizin.  English]
  Biblical and Talmudic medicine / Julius Preuss [translated and
edited] by Fred Rosner.
      p.  cm.
  Originally published: New York : Sanhedrin Press, c1978.
  Includes bibliographical references and index.
  ISBN 1-56821-134-1
  1. Medicine in the Bible. 2. Medicine in rabbinical literature.
I. Rosner, Fred. II. Title. III. Title: Biblical and Talmudic medicine.
R135.5.P7413  1994
220.8'61—dc20                                              93-33952

Printed in the United States of America

Dedicated to my loving wife
*Saranne*
and to my cherished children
*Mitchel, Miriam, Aviva and Shalom*

# Table of Contents

**CHAPTER 1. THE PHYSICIAN & OTHER MEDICAL PERSONNEL   11**

The general practitioner, the obstetrician-gynecologist, specialists, military physicians, salaried physicians, education of the physician, the title "physician," physicians in the Talmud, the physician's license to heal, faith-healing, the physician's responsibility and liability, physicians' fees, the bloodletter, the circumciser, the midwife, the veterinarian.

**CHAPTER 2. THE PARTS OF THE BODY & THEIR FUNCTIONS   41**
**(ANATOMY & PHYSIOLOGY)**

Introduction; *The External Body Form:* the head, the neck, the shoulders, the arm, the hand, the fingers, the lower extremity, the loins, the abdomen, the 248 limbs; *The Organs of Sensation:* the eye, eye socket, eyebrows and eyelashes, tears, physiology of the eye, vision in old age; the nose and its anatomy and its functions, sneezing; the ear, earrings; skin color, incisions and tattooing; hair, hair-growth, the beard; *The Viscera; Organs of Digestion:* mouth, lips, spittle, the tongue, the palate, speech defects, the teeth, internal organs, the esophagus, the stomach, the intestines, *libba,* physiology of digestion, the liver, the gallbladder, the spleen; *Organs of Respiration:* mouth, nose and larynx, the lungs, physiology of the lung, the voice; *Organs of Blood Circulation:* the heart, the great vessels, the "hairy heart," heart as the seat of psyche, *leb, tzippar nephesh; Urogenital System:* the kidneys, urine, male genitalia, penis, testicles, the sperm, female sex organs, the hymen, menstruation, identification of menstrual blood, red stains, puberty; *Nervous System:* the brain, the spinal cord, peripheral nerves, sleep and wakefulness, soporifics, dreams.

**CHAPTER 3. ILLNESS & ITS HEALING   139**
**(GENERAL PATHOLOGY & THERAPY)**

Definition of a patient, demons causing illness, astrology and the evil eye, causes of disease, diagnosis of disease, illness and death, incantations, amulets, healing by magic, medical therapeutics.

**CHAPTER 4. SICKNESSES & THEIR TREATMENT   151**
**(SPECIAL PATHOLOGY & THERAPY)**

Epidemics, plague (pestilence), plague of the Philistines, *askara,* fever, *yerakon,* hydrops, podagra (gout), heatstroke; mouth odors, mouth abscess, *tzafdina;* diseases of the throat, diseases of the lung, diseases of the heart, diseases of the digestive tract: dysentery, large bowel ailments, bulimia, the illnesses of King Jehoram, Antiochus and

Herod, hemorrhoids, worms, the bile, the spleen, miscellaneous, death through fright or disgust.

depilatories, facial make-up, cosmetics, embrocations, soaps, perfumes and cosmetics.

# FOREWORD

by Dr. Immanuel Jakobovits, Chief Rabbi of the British Commonwealth of Nations

Dr. Rosner's monumental undertaking in rendering Preuss's masterly work into English marks a significant milestone, and fills an acute void, in the landscape of contemporary Jewish literature and culture.

*Biblisch-Talmudische Medizin,* though first published over six decades ago, is still unsurpassed, and likely to remain so, as the authoritative study in this field. Felicitous in its style, comprehensive in its scope, and impeccable in its scholarship, this remarkable book has served generations of scholars as the principal guide to the highly-developed concepts of medical knowledge and practice so profusely dispersed in Biblical and Talmudic literature. Its only limitation has been its publication in a language which, with the destruction of German Jewry in the Holocaust, is now alas all but archaic as a vehicle of Jewish thought. Its availability to English-speaking readers will therefore bring new life to Preuss's immortal heritage.

Medicine has, of course, advanced in giant strides since Preuss's days. But the role of the Bible and the Talmud in the history of medicine, and particularly in nurturing the Jewish proclivity to the healing art and the Judaic sensitivity to its ethical ramifications, remains as notable as it ever was. Modern medical progress, however brilliant, will never outshine the insights of the ancient Hebrew luminaries with the mysteries of life and death, of disease and healing, as revealed in these fascinating pages. Whether studied in depth or just cursorily perused, this volume is bound to open up entirely new vistas on the long, intimate and creative association between Judaism and medicine.

I hope that the welcome, indeed overdue, appearance of this work in the language now most widely spoken among Jews, and in the Western world generally, will deepen the appreciation for the legacy of Israel. It should also help to renew the partnership between Jewish spiritual and physical healers which contributed so significantly to the advance of medicine through the ages and its emergence as a rational discipline to promote the conquest of disease, the sanctity of life and the preservation of health.

Immanuel Jakobovits

# PREFACE

This book represents a complete English translation of Julius Preuss' classic work on Biblical and Talmudic medicine. A biography of Julius Preuss and a complete bibliographical listing of his writings as well as a description of this, his *magnum opus,* follow in the Introduction. An updating of Preuss' book, and a critical commentary on it, remain a desideratum.

A few words regarding the philosophy of translation in general seem appropriate here. There are two major types of translations. The first is where an attempt is made to render, as faithfully as possible, the language, intent and sense of the original work. The other is where one tries, in a looser manner, to present the content of the original work, but where one follows more closely the syntax and style of the language into which one is translating. The present translation follows the former philosophy, attempting to remain as literal as possible while imparting all of Preuss' thoughts and ideas clearly and comprehensibly.

Words and phrases in numerous parentheses in Preuss' original work have been faithfully translated but, for the sake of clarity, the parentheses have been omitted wherever possible. Biblical quotations are printed in italics. Foreign words (Greek, Latin, Hebrew, etc.) are also in italics. Some words or phrases italicized by Preuss for special emphasis have also been italicized in the English translation.

Some paragraphs appear indented from the main text. These paragraphs were published in smaller print in the original German edition. They are really extended notes dealing with some matters of detail and for this reason were reduced in size so as not to disturb the continuity of the main text. This device of Preuss enables the reader to distinguish the principal text from what are meant to be only marginal observations. I have added titles or headings to all the subsections within each chapter to help the reader more easily find a specific topic. The reader familiar with Hebraica will recognize that the word "Jerushalmi" in the footnotes refers to the Jerusalem Talmud. If not otherwise stated, all Talmudic citations are from the Babylonian Talmud.

I am indebted to Chief Rabbi Dr. Immanuel Jakobovits for supplying the Foreword and for his helpful suggestions and advice, to Mr. William Wolf for editing and correcting the manuscript, to Dr. Basil Tatsis and Mrs. Adina Feldstern for technical assistance, and to Mrs. Sophie Falk and Mrs. Miriam Regenworm for secretarial assistance. Only three small portions of this English translation have been published before: the chapters on Otology (April 1975 issue of the *Journal of Laryngology & Otology*), Neurology (April 1975 issue of the *Israel Journal of Medical Sciences*), and Dentistry (June 1975 issue of the *Bulletin of the History of Dentistry*). Permission has been granted by these journals to reprint these portions in the present book and for this I am grateful.

To my loving wife, I express my sincere appreciation for her understanding and unselfish support, and to my cherished children, I affirm my love and devotion and voice my deepest thanks for their extreme patience during the long hours of painstaking work. It is to them that this book is dedicated.

*New York City*
*June 1977*

*FRED ROSNER*

**FIGURE 1.** PHOTOGRAPH OF JULIUS PREUSS
*(COURTESY OF MR. JACOB PREUSS, HERZLIYA, ISRAEL)*

# PREFACE TO THE REPRINTED EDITION

In 1978, the Sanhedrin Press of the Hebrew Publishing Company in New York published my English translation of Julius Preuss's *Biblical and Talmudic Medicine*. This classic work was previously only available in its original German version. In view of its wide appeal to the English-speaking world, the book was quickly sold out. A second printing in March 1983 by the Hebrew Publishing Company was also exhausted within a few years. Continuing requests for the book to the publisher and to me personally over the past several years made clear the need to reprint this classic book once more.

Jason Aronson, Inc., has now accomplished that goal and made available in an attractive format the rich medical literature from the Bible, Talmud, and other early Jewish sources, as originally compiled in the German edition of 1911 by Julius Preuss, the master Jewish medical historian. An introductory chapter on the life and writings of Preuss enhances the reader's understanding of this remarkable man and his remarkable book, which is the authoritative work in its field. It is still unsurpassed, as briefly discussed by Lord Immanuel Jakobovits in his Foreword.

*New York City*
*Summer 1993*

*FRED ROSNER*

# INTRODUCTION:
# JULIUS PREUSS AND HIS CLASSIC BOOK

The oldest known Hebrew medical writing is that of Asaph, which dates from the seventh century (1). Since the ancient Hebrews left us no specific medical texts, our only sources of their knowledge on this subject are the medical and hygienic references found in the Jewish sacred, historical and legal literatures. The difficulty of gathering this information has been great, for the material is scant and its meaning often uncertain; the period which these sources cover is very long. Much of the material is "popular medicine"; most, if not all, was transmitted by laymen.

The first systematic studies of the medicine of the Bible were published early in the seventeenth century, among the first fruits of the study of the Bible awakened by the Reformation. These early works dealt only with the Old and the New Testaments (with the single exception of the dissertation of Gintzburger of 1743), and it was not until the nineteenth century that studies included the Talmud and other ancient Hebraic writings (2).

The literature that has grown up during the past three centuries is very extensive; much of it deals with special subjects, much embraces studies limited to single works such as the Talmud. As would be expected, these studies reflect the scientific spirit of their period, the uncritical or the critical attitude of the Biblical scholars, and the current views on medicine.

The writers have, for the most part, been students of the Bible; others were students of medical history; there are few who were both.

Thus, for instance, two of the most important works on Biblical and Talmudic medicine were written by a layman (Wunderbar, *Biblisch-Talmudische Medizin*, 1860), and by a great physician who was unfamiliar with the Semitic language and literature (Ebstein, *Die Medizin im Alten Testament*,1901; *Die Medizin im Neuen Testament und im Talmud*, 1903). What this means can hardly be appreciated by someone who knows nothing of the Hebrew or Arabic tongues — their briefness, conciseness and force (3). It was not until the publication of Julius Preuss' *Biblisch-Talmudische Medizin* in 1911 that we acquired a reliable, comprehensive, and scholarly exposition of the subject by someone who, on the one hand was a first class physician, who made the history of medicine his life's study, and on the other, was a thorough semitic philologist (3).

Julius Preuss (Figure 1) was born on September 5, 1861, in the small village of Gross-Schoenbeck near Potsdam, in Uckermark, Germany (3-17). His was the only Jewish family in the village. Young Preuss attended the public schools in the town of Angermunde and then entered the *Gymnasium* in Prenzlau, where he distinguished himself by his brilliant scholarship. Upon graduation, he went to study medicine at the University of Berlin, completing the course of study in 1886. Preuss' doctoral thesis was entitled, "Concerning Syphilis as the Etiology of Tabes Dorsalis and Dementia Paralytica." The newspapers contained an interesting account of the brilliant young doctor who achieved the rare feat of having passed Rudolph Virchow's examination with the highest marks (3, 15). Virchow, the founder of cellular pathology, was a

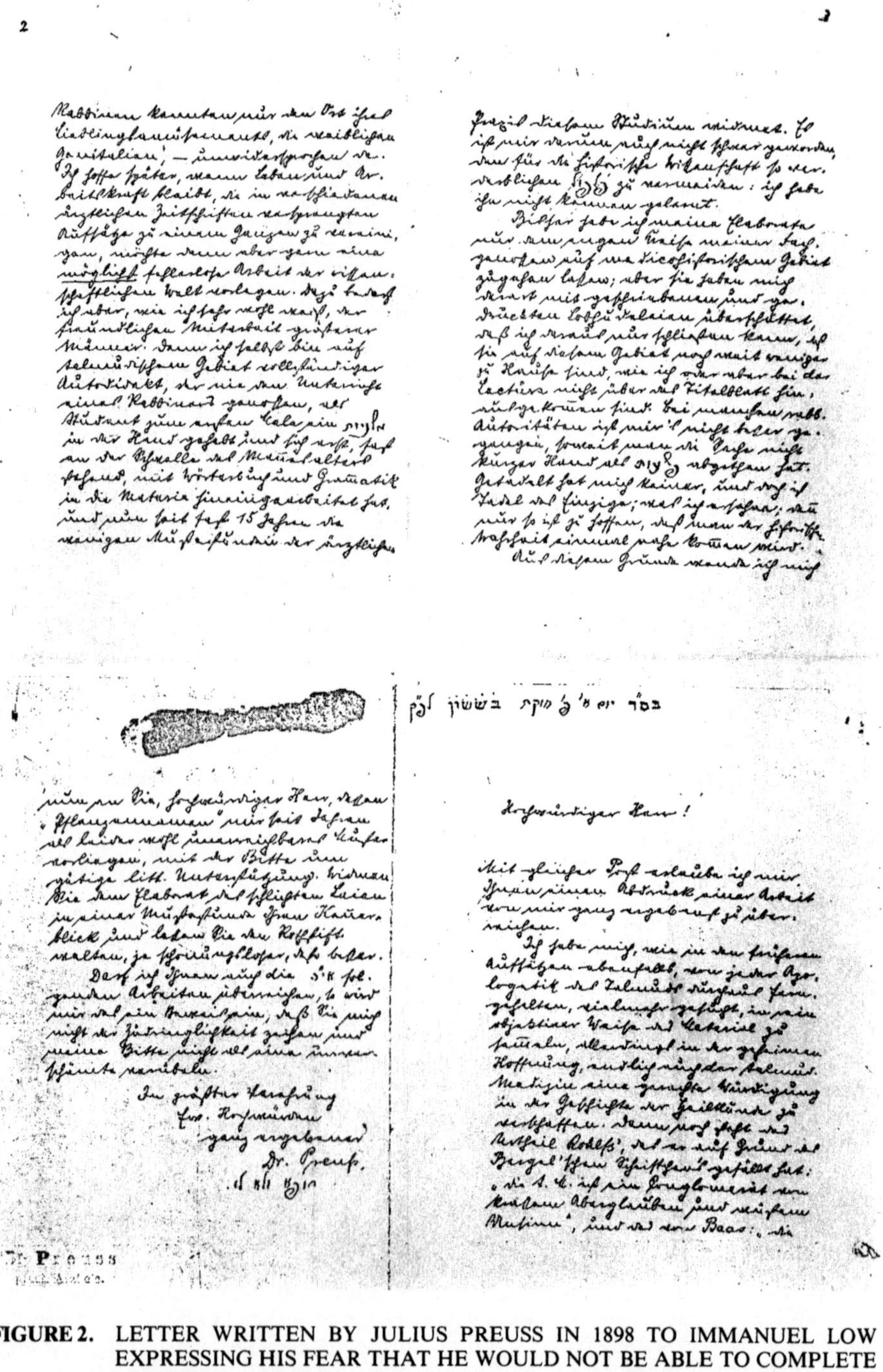

בס״ד יום ד׳ ו׳ מקץ בשׁושון לבן

Hochwürdiger Herr!

**FIGURE 2.** LETTER WRITTEN BY JULIUS PREUSS IN 1898 TO IMMANUEL LOW EXPRESSING HIS FEAR THAT HE WOULD NOT BE ABLE TO COMPLETE HIS WORK BECAUSE OF ILL HEALTH. THE LETTER IS SIGNED: DR. PREUSS, *ROPHE VELO LO* ("PHYSICIAN, BUT NOT FOR HIMSELF").

highly versatile personality known for his uncompromisingly exacting standards. He paid Preuss the extreme compliment of telling him that his way of thinking was that of a true physician: *sie koennen medizinisch denken.* Preuss returned to his native town to practice medicine, but in 1891 went back to Berlin where he lived as a general medical practitioner and where he studied and wrote.

According to Muntner (4,6), Preuss lived in an age which saw the resurgence of the critical approach in scientific as well as historical research. He was a part of the century which gave to the Jewish world Solomon Judah Rapoport (1790-1867) and Leopold Zunz (1794-1886), the pioneers of the "Science of Judaism"; the literary historians Leopold Dukes (1810-1891) and Abraham Berliner (1833-1915); scholars like David Cassel (1818-1893), Abraham Geiger (1810-1874), Moritz Guedemann (1835-1918), David Kaufmann (1852-1899), Mayer Moritz Kayserling (1829-1905), Isidore Loeb (1839-1892) and, of course, Heinrich Graetz (1817-1891), the author of the classic history of the Jews. Towering above all these luminaries was Moritz Steinschneider (1816-1907), the Orientalist and bibliographer who, in addition to other ancient source material, unearthed a wealth of data on the history of Jewish research in the sciences, including medicine.

Historical literature in the field of medicine could boast of a number of impressive works, including those of Haeser, Henschel, Neuburger and Pagel. Sadly lacking, however, was reliable and critical research in the field of Jewish medicine. To be sure, continues Muntner, there was no dearth of general essays on medicine in Biblical and even Talmudic times, but most of these were superficial, unscientific and, occasionally, like those written by Carmoly (1802-1875), of dubious authenticity. Even the few outstanding works that appeared, such as those of Bergel, Holub, Rabinowitz, Wunderbar and Ebstein, fell far short of the analytical approach which characterized the writings of Julius Preuss (4).

Preuss was a physician of fine training and wide experience, a learned scholar in Hebrew literature as well as in medical and general history. He studied Talmud with Rabbi Biberfeld and the famous Rabbi Ritter, later Chief Rabbi of Rotterdam, never having attended a Jewish school in his youth. Preuss' unusual Hebraic background, his vast knowledge of Jewish thought and Hebrew literature and his scientific method, make his book *Biblisch-Talmudische Medizin* the authoritative work on the subject to this very day.

In 1961, to commemorate the one-hundredth anniversary of the birth of Julius Preuss and the fiftieth anniversary of the appearance of his *magnum opus,* a variety of meetings and lectures were held, and numerous articles and essays were published (5-11). Leibowitz (7) decries the lack of available detailed information concerning the life of Preuss. Leibowitz points out that Rabbi Joseph Carlebach, last Chief Rabbi of Hamburg and Preuss' son-in-law, said that Preuss used to read the book of Psalms and study the *Mishnah* when he travelled to and from his patients in neighboring towns, so that after a while he learned them by heart. Preuss turned to the renowned Rabbi Hildesheimer for legal Judaic opinions concerning medical matters, such as remuneration for Sabbath visits to the sick. Preuss' return to Berlin in 1891 was precipitated either by his desire to be surrounded by learned scholars and academicians (3), or by the great difficulties in the observance of traditional Judaism which he encountered in his small native village.

Preuss was a very successful physician and his practice grew considerably. He married Martha (Rachel) Halberstadt from Hamburg late in 1899 or early in 1900. His wife Martha was an enormous help to her husband in proofreading all his writings and in assisting in any other possible way. The Preusses had three children, two daughters and one son. One daughter and her husband, Rabbi Carlebach, were killed in the holocaust of World War Two; two daughters of this couple now reside in Israel, one son lives in England and one son lives in New York. A second daughter of Preuss,

ב"ה        Berlin, 18. Mai 05.

Niemand soll mir eine Leichenrede, einen Nachruf o. dgl. halten, weder im Hause noch auf dem Friedhofe, weder bei der Beerdigung noch später, weder ein be-zahlter Redner noch sonst irgend jemand.

Niemand soll aus Anlaß meines Sterbetages [...] fassen. —

Ich wünsche, daß mein Grabhügel eine Einfassung erhält und mit einer Platte aus Granit, wie solcher zu [...] Verwendung findet, bedeckt wird. Diese Platte soll folgende Inschrift erhalten:

יוחנן בן יצחק הלוי אצל י"ל
י"ו מיכל ולא [...] לו :

Dr. Julius Preuß.

aber weiter keine Zusätze, [...] Daten u. dgl.
Falls die Anbringung der Inschrift von der Verwaltung ver-weigert wird, soll ein Stein wie der meines Vaters [...] gesetzt und auf diesem die obige Inschrift angebracht werden.

Das Grab soll keinerlei Schmuck noch [...] oder dgl. er-halten.

married to Felix Goldschmidt of Jerusalem, died in 1966 leaving five children, all residing in Israel. Julius Preuss' son, Jacob Preuss, lives with his wife in Herzliya, Israel. Their four children are also residents of the Jewish state. Julius Preuss' wife died in Israel in 1960.

Preuss himself became ill in 1911 when his *Biblisch-Talmudische Medizin* first appeared, although he had already written to Immanuel Löw in 1898 expressing his fear that he would not be able to complete his work because of ill health (Figure 2). His illness is variously described as "a lung abscess which probably could have been controlled by chest surgery and/or antibiotics which were not available in his lifetime" (7) or "cancer of the throat, complicated by tuberculosis and bronchiectasis." (4) Details of his fatal illness were described by Leibowitz (7). Preuss died on September 23, 1913 at the young age of 52 and was buried in the "Adath Israel" cemetery in Berlin. He was not eulogized at his funeral, in accordance with his own wishes. In his last Will & Testament, dated May 18, 1905 (Figure 3), Preuss said, in part, "no one should deliver a funeral oration, memorial address or the like for me, not at home nor at the cemetery not at the interment nor later, not a paid speaker nor anyone else. No one should be motivated to fast on the day of my death. . .the grave should not be preserved with any type of ornament or ivy or the like." His tombstone bears the simple epitaph: *rophé, velo lo,* "Physician, but not for himself." The humility of Preuss is also exemplified by the title which appears beneath his name in all editions of his book: Julius Preuss, *Arzt in Berlin,* "physician in Berlin." Lengthy eulogies did appear in the press, however, following Preuss' death including those by Karl Sudhoff *(Münch. Med. Wchschr.* Jan. 13, 1914), Edward Biberfeld *(Der Israelit.* Oct. 1, 1913), Joseph Carlebach *(Jüdische Presse* 1913, p. 397), David Macht (3), and many others.

Sudhoff said the following about Preuss (15):

"In the one hour we were together, Preuss permitted me, the non-Jew, to see so deeply into his soul, that I knew his hope was to be a classical philologist — this man, whose practical course of life made his dream impossible because he was a Jew. He had become a physician and his remarkable talent for historical and philological investigation directed him to the study of the history of his specialty as an avocation, and in particular to that branch which inevitably attracts every Jewish physician of the old stamp, namely, Biblical and Talmudic medicine. . .

"Julius Preuss never lacked in his work either the inspiration or the devotion so essential to thorough accomplishment. But from inspiration he derived only the incentive which spurred him on to the mastery of difficulties. Never did he permit it to obscure his historical judgement in its incorruptible service toward the establishment and enunciation of truth. Cool to the very heart he was; love of the people of Israel did not cloud his view. Enthusiasm for their superior viewpoint did not make him see the straight line as crooked. For these very reasons, Dame History has laid laurels upon his grave, as a memorial to him, the master of historical criticism. . ."

The original manuscript of Preuss' *magnum opus* is today housed in the manuscript and archives section of the Jewish National and Hebrew University Library (Ms.Var. 443 #14-14) in Jerusalem (Figure 4). In the Friedenwald collection of medica-judaica in the same library, there is an item called "Notes on Preuss" (rare book division Fr.812B), in which the late Dr. Harry Friedenwald of Baltimore took copious notes in English on Preuss' book, chapter by chapter.

Preuss' writings on Biblical and Talmudic medicine began with an article entitled *Der Arzt in Bibel und Talmud* (The Physician in the Bible and Talmud), which was published in 1894 in the prestigious *Virchow's Archiv* and was soon reprinted in Hebrew translation in the periodical *Ha-Measseph.* Numerous other essays on various aspects of Biblical and Talmudic medicine followed in a variety of scientific and literary journals. (A complete bibliography is to be found at the end of this Introduction.) The two previously published bibliographies of Preuss' writings (2,4,11)

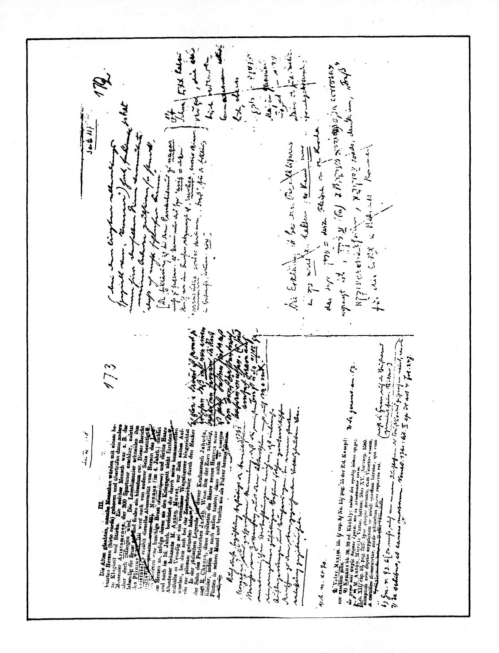

**FIGURE 4.** PHOTOGRAPH OF PAGES ONE-HUNDRED-SEVENTEEN AND ONE-HUNDRED-EIGHTEEN OF THE ORIGINAL MANUSCRIPT OF PREUSS' *BIBLISCH-TALMUDISCHE MEDIZIN* SHOWING NOTES AND COMMENTS BY OBERRABBINER DOV RITTER (P.118 MIDDLE RIGHT), OBERRABBINER DR. IMMANUEL LOW (P.117 MIDDLE RIGHT AND BOTTOM), JULIUS PREUSS HIMSELF (P.118 BOTTOM AND MIDDLE) AND JULIUS PREUSS' WIFE MARTHA (P.117 TOP 5 LINES).

are incomplete and contain several errors. Both Friedenwald (2) and Muntner (4,11) cite an anonymously written English article entitled "The Medicine of the Bible," published in *Medical Magazine* (London, volume 23 #4 pp 232-244, April 1914). It seems highly unlikely that Preuss wrote this paper, since he did not write in English (17) and the article was published a year after he died. Copies of several unpublished articles of Preuss, kindly supplied to me by Mr. Jacob Preuss of Herzliya, Israel, are also included in the bibliography. The article entitled "Ueber die Veranderungen der Zähne bei der Kieferrachitis des Schweines" (Concerning Changes of the Teeth in Rickets of the Jaw in the Pig), published in the *Archiv fur Wissenschaftliche und Praktische Tierheilkunde* (Berlin, vol. 35 #6 pp 562-581, Sept. 27, 1909), was written by a veterinarian named Dr. Julius Preuss, but he is not the same Julius Preuss of *Biblisch-Talmudische-Medizin* fame (17).

Preuss' book is not without imperfections. As Gordon (5) points out, the Jerusalem Talmud was not compiled by Rabbi Yochanan, as Preuss asserts, because many of the sages mentioned therein lived much later than Rabbi Yochanan. Rav Ashi is also not the last of the compilers of the Babylonian Talmud, as stated by Preuss. The listing of physicians in the Talmud enumerated by Preuss is incomplete. Numerous other "minor" criticisms are cited by Gordon. For certain errors, Preuss cannot be faulted. For example, he states that the earliest Hebrew medical writing is that of Donnolo from the tenth century. Recent research by Muntner (1) has shown that the text of Asaph Harofe antedates Donnolo by several centuries. Finally, the indices in Preuss' book, particularly the general index, are very sparse.

In preparing this English translation of Preuss' classic book, I, too, have found numerous minor errors. For example, in chapter 12, Preuss states that Tractate *Negaim* has 10 chapters whereas in fact there are fourteen. In chapter 17, he erroneously attributes a Talmudic statement to Rabbi Akiba instead of Rabbi Eleazar and, in chapter 6, he does the reverse. In the first appendix to chapter 5, Preuss gives the dates of birth and death of Maimonides as 1131 and 1205; the correct dates are 1135 and 1204. In chapter 4, Preuss incorrectly speaks of the "daughter" of the Shunamite woman instead of her "son." He says the Hebrews have no word for coughing, like the *su'al* of the Arabs; yet he overlooked the Hebrew word for cough which is *she'ul*. He says that *yerakon* and *shiddaphon* always occur together in Bible and Talmud. There is an exception, however, in Jeremiah 30:6. Numerous other minor errors of this nature could be cited. Furthermore, there are more than a score of incorrect bibliographic citations from Bible and Talmud. These amount, however, to less than a fraction of one percent of the many thousands of references which Preuss quotes.

The above shortcomings do not detract from the enduring value of Preuss' work. Every major medical library, public or private, possesses at least one copy of *Biblisch-Talmudische Medizin* in the original German. The creation of the state of Israel in 1948, and the renaissance of the Hebrew language, have awakened new interest in Biblical and Talmudic writings and the grandeur of Preuss' contribution to medical research is being more and more appreciated by modern scholars. An updating and revision, with correction of errors, of Preuss' *magnum opus* remains a *desideratum* to this very day. Only four pages of Preuss' work (pages 515 to 519) and a few excerpts have ever been published in English translation (18,19), prior to the present volume. Karl Sudhoff, the most illustrious figure in the field of the history of medicine in Preuss' day, hailed Preuss' work as one of the most important contributions to the history of medical scholarship in the preceding half century (15). Nothing has happened in the nearly seven decades since then to change that assertion. It remains an indispensable work for the student of Hebrew medicine.

I would like to call attention to several little known yet important articles of Preuss which antedated his Biblical-Talmudic work. The first, which was never published, was written in 1885 and is entitled *Ueber Untersuchungen des Blutes Zu Diagnostischen Zwecken* (Concerning the examination of blood for diagnostic purposes). In this paper, Preuss gathered material from the major books and medical journals on pathology, therapy and diagnosis. His purpose was to provide practical diagnostic guidance to the practicing physician about bleeding from any body orifice, including the mouth, nose, urethra, anus, vagina, navel and venipuncture site. This lengthy paper already shows his systematic organization of source material and its presentation in a clear and lucid manner, qualities characteristic of his subsequent writings.

Another little-known major article of Preuss, entitled *Vom Versehen den Schwangeren* (Concerning fright in pregnant women), was published in two different periodicals in 1892 (see Bibliography). In this detailed critical-historical study with 211 references, Preuss discusses the possible effect on her unborn child of a pregnant woman's psychic or psychological impressions during coitus. Can such psychic influences partially or completely alter the development of the unborn fetus? This erudite paper was published in 1892 and already clearly demonstrated the depth and precision with which Julius Preuss approached a subject.

Another brief article, entitled *Zur Pathologie der Zunge* (On the pathology of the tongue), describes two patients, one of whom was a baby with a tumor on the lingual frenulum and the other a woman with chronic superficial glossitis. Other unpublished articles by Preuss include papers on quackery and secret remedies, domicile hygiene, the position of the woman in Judaism and the duty of Jewish physicians (see Bibliography).

There follows a brief description of Preuss' *Biblisch-Talmudische Medizin*. It is an anthology of all his articles published over many years in a variety of scholarly journals (see Bibliography), beginning with his pioneering study entitled *Der Arzt in Bibel und Talmud* which appears in *Virchow's Archiv* in 1894. Originally published in Berlin by S. Karger in 1911, it was reprinted unchanged in 1921 and 1923 by the original publisher, and in 1969 by Gregg Publishers in England. In 1971, the Ktav Publishing House in New York reprinted the book unchanged for the fourth time but added an introduction, biographical sketch and bibliography of Julius Preuss by Suessmann Muntner, and a Hebrew and Aramaic register which was prepared in handwritten copy by Adolph Löwinger several years after the original 1911 publication. An English translation of this register by Samuel Paley was also included.

In chapter one, entitled "The Physician and Other Medical Personnel," Preuss defines the term physician, *rophé* in Hebrew and *asya* in Aramaic. He describes the position of the physician in antiquity, his fees and his responsibilities to his patients. In Judiasm, a physician is regarded as a messenger of God. If he intentionally injures a patient, the physician is obviously liable; otherwise he is held blameless. Physicians served as expert witnesses in civil court cases and in the evaluation of a criminal in terms of his capacity to tolerate disciplinary flogging. The physician was and still is consulted regarding the severity of an illness which involves the need to desecrate the Sabbath or the Day of Atonement for the patient.

Preuss describes the education of a physician in ancient times which was accomplished either by the apprenticeship method or in official schools of medicine. He also lists some of the physicians mentioned in the Talmud, such as Theodoros, Tobiya, Bar Girnte, Bar Nathan, Rabbi Ammi and, of course, Mar Samuel, the most illustrious of all.

In chapter two, Preuss describes the anatomy and physiology of the various body organs and limbs as mentioned in the Bible and Talmud by dividing them into external organs (head, face, chin, neck, shoulder, axilla, elbow, forearm, hand, fingers, thumb, fist, nail, foot, heel, toes, knee, thigh, hips, back and abdomen), organs of sensation (eye, nose, ear, skin) and internal organs. The latter include organs of the digestive system (lips, teeth, esophagus, stomach, liver, gallbladder and spleen), respiratory system (lung and voice box), circulatory system (heart and aorta), genito-urinary system (kidneys, urinary bladder and male and female genitalia) and nervous system (brain and spinal cord). He attempts to identify the 248 limbs, mentioned throughout early Jewish writings, which are said to correspond to the 248 positive commandments of Judaism.

Preuss begins chapter three by defining a patient. He then discusses the belief in ancient Judaism that demons cause illness. For example, the Talmud states that a mad dog is possessed by an evil spirit. Preuss talks of astrology and the evil eye, of magic and incantations and amulets to ward off disease. Astrological reasons were especially decisive for the selection of days appropriate for bloodletting, not only in Talmudic times, but throughout the centuries and millennia. Rarely found in Talmudic writings is the medieval concept of the four body humors (black bile, yellow bile, phlegm and blood), whereby diseases are thought to occur by a disequilibrium of these humors with one or the other predominating in the body or in a specific organ.

The fourth chapter, called "Sicknesses and Their Treatment," begins with a lengthy discussion of plague or pestilence. Preuss lists all the epidemics described in the Bible and Talmud, and concludes that, because of the dearth of symptomatology mentioned, it is not possible to establish with certainty whether or not the numerous Biblical and Talmudic diseases referred to as *magepha, deber, nega* or *negeph,* represent bubonic plague, cholera, dysentery, typhus or some other epidemic illness. *Askara* seems to be epidemic diphtheria since it afflicts primarily children, and the major symptoms are referable to the throat.

Preuss discusses acute and chronic fevers and describes various remedies, mostly from folk medicine, for quotidian, tertian and quartan fevers. He also lists the causes and remedies for hydrops (dropsy), podagra (gout), heatstroke and *yerakon* which is the Biblical and Talmudic expression for jaundice and/or anemia.

Biblical and Talmudic descriptions of lung maladies, such as perforations, defects, lumps, cysts, fistulae and adhesions, as well as citations of digestive tract illnesses such as dysentery, colic, bulimia, hemorrhoids, and intestinal worms are provided by Preuss in this chapter. Finally, the five types of heart ailments are discussed: pain, weakness, heaviness, palpitations and pressure of the heart.

Chapter five is devoted to surgery and deals primarily with injuries and malformations. Preuss begins with a discussion of surgical instruments, such as the small drill for opening the skull, the knife for circumcision, needles to remove splinters, and others. He then describes various types of injuries such as sword or other stab or puncture wounds, burn wounds, broken bones, dislocations and sprains, and amputations for gangrene. Also described are injuries inflicted by animals, such as the bite of a mad dog, snake bites, insect bites and worm infestation. The signs of a mad dog as mentioned in the Talmud are as follows: its mouth is open, its saliva is dripping, its ears flap, its tail hangs between its thighs and it walks on the edge of the road.

There are two appendices to this chapter. The first deals with circumcision. Preuss discusses some of the boundless literature on the theories of the origin of circumcision, the covenant of Abraham, the importance, technique and timing of circumcision and reasons for its postponement, i.e. illness, the instrumentation used and circumcision practiced by other peoples. The recognition by the sages of the Talmud of a bleeding disorder, probably hemophilia, and its genetic transmission is astounding. The Talmud rules that if two children of a woman exsanguinated as a result of circumcision, the third child should not be circumcised. Furthermore, if two sisters each had a son who died of bleeding following circumcision, then the third sister should not circumcise her son. Although later Jewish codes assumed that hemophilia can also be transmitted through the baby's father, the second century Talmud correctly recognized the sex-linked nature of this disease, i.e. only males have the disease but females are carriers and transmit it to their male offspring.

The second appendix deals with bloodletting, either for therapeutic reasons or as a preventive measure. The Talmud discusses the frequency, amount, site of bloodletting, and the instrumentation used, including a lancet, a nail or other pointy objects, and cupping glasses. Dietary factors in relation to bloodletting are considered important. Mar Samuel said that a person to be bled should be fasting; after the bloodletting, the patient should tarry a little, then arise and eat a little before going out. The consumption of nourishing foods after bloodletting is essential. Venesection on animals is also discussed.

Surgery on the eye is not at all considered in the Bible or Talmud, but eyeglasses, eye prostheses, artificial eyes and eye make-up are described in some detail.

In chapter seven, which deals with dentistry, Preuss discusses toothaches, cavities, loose teeth and artificial teeth. Sour fruit is said to be good for toothache. The vapors of a bathhouse are harmful to the teeth. Vinegar causes loosening of teeth. Preuss points out the emphasis which Oriental people place on beautiful teeth.

In the very brief chapter on otology, Preuss describes anatomical defects of the ears, piercing of ears and other injuries, whether intentionally inflicted or not, pain in the ear, remedies for ear ailments and deafness and its causes.

In an equally brief chapter on disorders of the nose, he describes various abnormal shapes and disfigurements of the nose, mostly secondary to leprosy. Nasal polyps are discussed, as well as remedies for nosebleeds, mostly from folk medicine.

Chapter ten is devoted to neurological disorders. About a third of the chapter deals with epilepsy and hysteria. Love-sickness was thought in antiquity to be a type of hysteria. Also discussed in this chapter are headache, plethora and migraine, paralysis, strokes (apoplexy), sciatica and the tremor of old age. The Talmud recommends that one rub the head with wine, vinegar or oil to treat a headache. Numerous remedies are prescribed for migraine including many from folk medicine.

Mental disorders are covered in chapter eleven. Preuss discusses in detail the mental illness of King Saul of Israel. After considerable deliberation, he concludes that Saul was a "melancholic in the psychiatric sense;" today we would say that he suffered from a paranoid psychopathia. His raving and ranting, his affliction with evil spirits and the stripping off of his clothes, are interpreted by Preuss to represent epilepsy or an epileptic equivalent. Visual and auditory hallucinations, insanity, "possession by demons or spirits," and exorcism are all described by Preuss from Bible and Talmud. An imbecile is considered to be mentally deficient and is equated with a minor and a deaf-mute in Jewish law: he cannot testify in court, his contracting of marriage is invalid, etc. The Talmud defines someone who is mentally ill: "He who goes out at night alone, and he who spends the night in a graveyard, and he who tears his garments, and destroys everything that is given to him" (Chagigah 3b). Someone mentally ill is distinguished from a drunk or intoxicated person in that the latter behaves like a madman.

In the chapter on skin diseases, Preuss points out that an enormous number of books and treatises have been written about the thirteenth chapter of the book of Leviticus which deals with an illness called *tzaraath,* probably leprosy. As a result, says Preuss, "one might think that every detail would have been clarified and every linguistic and archaeological problem solved. However, just the opposite is the case." He discusses the fundamental law of *tzaraath,* and describes the various skin lesions, scabs, boils, scars, eczema, burn wounds and the like, as mentioned in the Bible and Talmud. The diagnosis, treatment and cure of leprosy are discussed. Leprosy was thought to represent punishment for the sin of slander. The illness *shechin* and its various forms, the *shechin* of Egypt, and the sicknesses of Job and King Hezekiah (possibly leprosy, elephantiasis, syphilis, diphtheria, variola or some other malady) are also discussed. Preuss concludes that *shechin* is a collective name comprising many types of skin diseases including inflammatory and traumatic lesions.

There are two appendices to this chapter. The first deals with gonorrhea, its causes and mode of transmission, and the Jewish ritual laws pertaining to someone afflicted with it. In the second appendix, which concerns cosmetics in the Bible and Talmud, Preuss describes hair-cutting instruments, haircuts and hair styles for both men and women, hair hygiene, depilatories and wigs. Also discussed are embrocations, oils, perfumes, cosmetics, soaps and facial make-up.

A brief chapter on gynecology deals primarily with menstruation and its ritual implications, vaginal bleeding and its causes and treatment, and castration in the female. Most remedies are from folk medicine; for example, "Give the woman with vaginal bleeding Persian onions boiled in wine or cumin, safflower and fenugreek boiled in wine, and exclaim to her: 'Cease your discharge' ".

Chapter fourteen is devoted to obstetrics. The first half of the chapter deals with normal physiological events surrounding pregnancy, including the recognition and duration of pregnancy, the fetus and fetal development, sex determination, multiple births, premature births, parturition, the birthstool, the placenta, postpartum ritual purification, the newborn infant, washing, salting and swaddling of the newborn, lactation and suckling, wet-nurses and nursing from an animal or bottle. Of particular interest is the recognition by Mar Samuel in the Talmud that a fetus begins to assume form and shape at 40 days after conception. Prior to that time, it is "mere fluid." Also of interest is the "preserving stone" which women carried with them to insure normal pregnancies. Furthermore, the concept of superfecundation, that is one woman becoming pregnant from two men, was accepted in the Talmud.

The second half of the chapter on obstetrics deals with pathological occurrences. Among the subjects discussed are sterility, oral contraception by means of a "potion of herbs," abortion and the abortus, moles, monster births and the *sandal* fetus, false pregnancy, difficult labor and embryotomy, sorcery in obstetrics, cesarian sections and puerperal illnesses. Numerous methods of contraception are discussed in the Talmud, but perhaps the most interesting is the "potion of herbs," also known as the "cup of roots." This remedy is prepared from Alexandrian gum, liquid alum and garden crocus, powdered and mixed with beer or wine (Shabbath 110a).

In chapter fifteen, which is entitled "Materia Medica," Preuss first discusses the plant remedies which the Talmud recommends as abortifacients, emetics, purgatives, digestives, etc., as well as various types of plasters, compresses, poultices, and bandages and the like, and their various medicinal ingredients. Also discussed are animal remedies, such as honey, goat's milk, crushed pearl, animal dung and urine, and the great theriac. Non-medicinal remedies can be exemplified by the Talmudic suggestion that for abdominal pain, one should place warm clothes on the abdomen or a hot cup or bottle on the navel. Sunbathing is said to heal a variety of ailments. Certain foods should be avoided for certain illnesses. The final part of this chapter is devoted to a discussion of Jewish hospitals in antiquity (or the lack thereof) and the visiting of the sick. The traditional Jewish concept of visiting the sick is that it is not a social call but rather a visit in which to help the patient by cooking or cleaning for him, or by assisting him in some other manner.

Chapter sixteen is very lengthy and deals with sex ethics in the Bible and Talmud. The subjects discussed by Preuss in this chapter are: chastity, marriage, procreation, genealogy in marriage, conjugal duties, cohabitation, impotence, unnatural coitus, *coitus interruptus,* abstention from procreation, times when cohabitation is prohibited, cohabitation and sexual desire, aphrodisiacs, the *duda'im* or mandrakes, conceptions *sine concubito,* proscribed marriages, punishment for incest, rarity of punishment infliction, the incest of Lot and his daughters, Amnon and Tamar, Levirate marriage, adultery, lustful thoughts, the *sotah* or suspected adulteress, rape, seduction, virginity, prostitution, the street of harlots, harlots in Biblical times, their skills, their attire and their hire, the *jus primae noctis,* Hegemonian coitus, masturbation, pederasty and homosexuality, transvestism, sodomy and bestiality, tribady and lesbianism.

In chapter seventeen, Preuss discusses the Jewish dietary laws, ritual slaughtering and the Biblical prohibitions of blood and certain fat. He then describes the laws of ritual purity and impurity known as *tumah* and *taharah* of the human body, utensils and clothing, and the rules of defilement relating to the Temple, priests, cadavers, people afflicted with leprosy and/or gonorrhea, and the purification process including the ritual immersion. Even though these rules may serve a hygienic purpose, they are not meant to be "hygienic laws" but are Divine commands. The importance of washing and bathing in ancient times is emphasized by Preuss.

Preuss also discusses death and dying in this chapter. In Jewish law, a dying person may not be touched or moved lest his death be hastened. The recognition of death required the cessation of respiration and the absence of a heartbeat. Furthermore, one must be certain that the person has not just fainted or fallen in a swoon. The perfuming and embalming of the dead are then described. The five Biblical cases of suicide are mentioned, including those of Saul, Ahitophel and Omri. Remarkable Biblical and Talmudic descriptions of marble and wooden coffins are given. Graves were either in the ground or in natural or man-made caves. Biblical and Talmudic discussions of the sepulchres of the Patriarchs, and of burial, cremation and the decomposition of bodies, conclude the section on death and dying.

The final chapter, entitled "Dietetics," deals with the rules which a healthy person should follow in order not to become ill. Preuss asserts that dietetics refers not only to nutrition, as the modern usage of the word connotes, but also includes the entire mode of life of an individual, since residence, clothing, sports, work and many other things have certain influences on health, and hence belong in the word "diet."

The general rules of health and nutrition, among others, are: eat moderately, eat simply, eat slowly and eat regularly. Chronic alcoholism, a rare disorder among Jews, is mentioned because of the juridical difference in Jewish law between a *shattuy* (tipsy or fuddled) and a *shikkor* (drunk or intoxicated). Regarding exercise, Rabbi Yohanan said: "Do not sit too much, for sitting provokes hemorrhoids; do not stand too much, for standing is harmful to the heart (or stomach); do not walk too much, for (excessive) walking is harmful to the eyes" (Kethuboth llla). With regard to domicile, it is said that it is healthy to live in an open city, and harmful to live in a fortified or closed city. In the latter, houses are built close together, but in the former there are gardens and parks and the air is good.

How does one find words to emphasize the enormity of the contribution to medicine and Judaica of Preuss' book? I believe that an editorial written by J. O. Leibowitz, in the May 1961 issue of the Hebrew periodical *Koroth,* devoted to the memory of Julius Preuss, expresses it best as follows:

". . . Preuss was one of the greatest Jewish historians of medicine, endowed with intimate insight in the field of early Hebrew medicine, outstanding in his critical approach, wide knowledge and unbiased honesty. Dear to our heart, his memory may serve as a shining and stimulating example for present and future historians."

# References

1. Muntner, S. *Introduction to the Book of Asaph the Physician.* Geniza. Jerusalem 1957. 174 pp (Hebr.)
2. Friedenwald, H. *The Jews and Medicine.* 1944 Johns Hopkins Univ. Press. Baltimore. Vol. 1. pp 99-145
3. Macht, D.I. In Memoriam — Dr. Julius Preuss. *Johns Hopkins Hosp. Bull. 25* #277 March 1914
4. Muntner, S. Julius Preuss — Father of Hebrew Medical Research. in J. Preuss' *Biblisch-Talmudische Medizin.* Ktav, New York 1971, pp VII-XII
5. Gordon, H. L. The Centenary of the Birth of Dr. Julius Preuss. *Harofe Haivri* (The Hebrew Physician) Vol. 1-2 pp 196-204, 1961 (Hebr.)
6. Muntner, S. Julius Preuss as a Founder of Research on the Field of the Ancient Hebrew History of Medicine. *Koroth* (A Quarterly Journal Devoted to the History of Medicine & Science). Jerusalem-Tel Aviv. Tenth Year. Vol. 2 #9-10 pp 410-413, May 1961 (Hebr.)
7. Leibowitz, J. O. Julius Preuss & the Medico-Historical Research in Bible & Talmud. *ibid* pp 414-425 (Hebr.) and I-III (Eng.)
8. Moeller, J. My Memories of Julius Preuss. *ibid* pp 404-406 (Hebr.).
9. Sudhoff, K. Julius Preuss. *ibid.* pp 407-409 (Hebr.)
10. Margalith, D. Obituary. Dr. Yitzhak (Julius) Preuss. Sept. 5, 1861 to Sept. 23, 1913. *ibid* pp 479-480 (Hebr.)
11. Muntner, S. Bibliographie der Schriften Von Julius Preuss *ibid.* pp XIII-XV
12. Kagan, S. R. *Jewish Medicine.* Medico Historical Press. Boston 1952 p. 562
13. Margalith, D. *Physician Forerunners of Modern Israel.* Jerusalem Academy of Medicine. Tel Aviv. 1973 pp. 163-164
14. Margalith, D. *The Way of Israel in Medicine.* Jerusalem Academy of Medicine. Jerusalem 1970 pp 348-349 (Hebr.)
15. Sudhoff, K. *Essays in the History of Medicine.* New York, Medical Life Press 1926 pp. 351-353
16. Pagel, J. L. *Biographisches Lexicon Hervorragendor Aerzte des Neunzehnten Jahrhunderts.* Berlin & Vienna. Urban & Schwarzenberg 1900-1902, XXXII & 1983 p.
17. Preuss, Jacob. personal communication, August 31, 1974
18. Rosenthal, R. The Care of the Sick in the Bible and the Talmud. Translated from Julius Preuss (1861-1913) in *Victor Robinson Memorial Volume*—S.R. Kagan, Editor. Froben Press, New York, 1948 pp 353-358
19. Snowman, J. *A Short History of Talmudic Medicine.* London 1935. John Ball, Sons & Danielsson, Ltd. p. 94

# BIBLIOGRAPHY OF THE WRITINGS
# OF JULIUS PREUSS

1. *Ueber die Syphilis als Aetiologie der Tabes Dorsalis und der Dementia Paralytica.* Inaugural Dissertation welche zur Erlangung der Doctorwuerde in der Medicin und Chirurgie, mit Zustimmung der Medicinischen Facultaet der Freiedrich-Wilhelms Universitaet zu Berlin am 6 Februar 1886 nebst den angefuegten Thesen oeffentlich verteidigen wird der Verfasser JULIUS PREUSS aus Gross-Schoenebeck (Mark). Opponenten: Herr Dd. med. M. Birnbaum, Herr Dd. med. J. Lazarus, Herr Cand. med. M. Caro, Cursist. A. Itzkowski 1886. 30p. l.l. 8°.
2. Vom Versehen der Schwangeren; eine historisch kritische Studie. *Berl. Klinik* Vol. 4-5 (Heft 51): 1-50, 1892-1893
2a. *ibid, Deutsche Medizinal Zeitung* #79:924-926 (Oct. 3) 1892
3. Zur Pathologie der Zunge. *Centralblatt fur Chirurgie 20*(9): 203-205 (March 4) 1893
4. Der Arzt in Bibel und Talmud; Eine Historische Studie. *Virchow's Archiv fur Patholog. Anat. und Physiol. und fur Klin. Med. 138:* 261-283, 1894. Hebrew translation by Kahan published in Volume 1 of *Ha-Measseph*. ed. Rabbinowitz pp 79-91
5. Die Askara Krankheit im Talmud. Ein Beitrag zur Geschichte der Diphterie. *Jahrbuch fur Kinderheilkunde.* New Series *40:* 251-257, 1895
6. Zur Geschichte der Aderlasses. *Wien. Klin. Wochenschrift 8*(34): 608-611 (Aug. 22) 1895 and *8*(35): 625-629 (Aug. 29) 1895
7. Neuere Arbeiten uber Biblisch-Talmudische Medizin. *Israelitische Monatsschrift.* Berlin. Nov. 26, 1896
8. Schriften uber Medicin in Bibel und Talmud. Ein Nachtrag nebst einigen Berichtungen zu Steinschneider's Artikel. *Brody's Ztschr. fur Hebr. Bibliographie* Vol. 2, Part 1, p. 22, 1897
9. Das Auge und Seine Krankheiten nach Bibel und Talmud. Eine Historische Studie. *Wiener Medizinische Wochenschrift 46*(49): 2151-2156, 1896; *46*(50): 2201-2203, 1896; *46*(51): 2245-2249, 1896; *46*(52): 2295-2298, 1896; *46*(53): 2341-2343, 1896; *47*(1): 38-40, 1897; *47*(2): 79-82, 1897; *47*(3): 121-124, 1897
10. Die Beschneidung nach Bibel und Talmud. *Wiener Klin. Rundschau 11*(43): 708-709 (Oct. 24) 1897 and *11*(44): 724-727 (Oct. 31) 1897
11. Die Mundhöhle und ihre Organe nach Bibel und Talmud. *Deutsche Medizinal Zeitung 18*(16): 143-144 (Feb. 25) 1897; *18*(17): 151-152 (Mar. 1) 1897 and *18*(18): 169-170 (Mar. 4) 1897
12. Die Männlichen Genitalien und ihre Krankheiten nach Bibel und Talmud. *Wiener Mediz. Wochenschrift 48*(12): 569-572, 1898; *48*(13): 617-619, 1898; *48*(14): 661-663, 1898; *48*(15): 709-712, 1898; *48*(24): 1193-1195, 1898; *48*(25): 1239-1240, 1898; *48*(26): 1285-1289, 1898
13. Materialien zur Geschichte der Alten Medicin. Die Organe der Bauchhohle nach Bibel und Talmud. *Allg. Med. Central Ztg.* (Berlin) *67*(39): 489-490 (May 14) 1898; *67*(40): 502 (May 18) 1898; *67*(41): 514-515 (May 21) 1898; *67*(42): 526-527 (May 25) 1898; *67*(43): 538-539 (May 28) 1898; *67*(44): 551 (June 1) 1898; *67*(45): 564 (June 4) 1898; *67*(46): 575 (June 8) 1898
14. Materialien zur Geschichte der Talmudischen Medizin. Das Nervensystem. *Deutsche Medizinal Zeitung. 20*(37): 416-418 (May 8) 1899 and *20*(38): 428-430 (May 11) 1899
15. Nerven und Geisteskrankheiten nach Bibel und Talmud. *Ztschr. fur Psychiatrie* etc. #56: 107-137, 1899
16. Materialien zur Geschichte der Talmudischen Medizin. Die Organe der Brusthohle. *Allg. Med. Central Ztg.* (Berlin) *68*(61): 740-741 (Aug. 2) 1899; *68*(62): 752-753 (Aug. 5) 1899; *68*(63): 764-765 (Aug. 9) 1899; *68*(64): 777-778 (Aug. 12) 1899
17. Materialien Zur Geschichte der Talmudischen Medicin. Nase und Ohr. *Allg. Med. Central Ztg.* (Berlin) *68*(76): 921-922 (Sept. 23) 1899; *68*(80): 970-971 (Oct. 7) 1899; *68*(81): 981-983 (Oct. 11) 1899
18. Chirurgisches in Bibel und Talmud. *Deutsche Zeitschrift fur Chirurgie* (Leipzig) *59*(5-6): 507-534 (May) 1901

19. Materialien zur Geschichte der Talmudische Medicin. Der Tote und seine Bestattung. *Allg. Med. Central Ztg.* (Berlin) *71*(25): 294–295 (March 26) 1902; *71*(26): 306–307 (March 29) 1902; *71*(27): 320–321 (April 2) 1902
20. Biblisch-Talmudischen Pathologie und Therapie. *Ztschr. fur Klin. Medicin* (Berlin) *45* (5–6): 457–489, 1902
21. Die Strafrechtliche Verantwortlichkeit des Arztes im Altertum. *Muncher Medizin. Wochenschrift.* *49*(12): 489–490 (March 25) 1902
22. Die Medizin der Juden in *Handbuch der Geschichte der Medizin* Ed. M. Neuburger & J. Pagel. Jena. 1902 Gustav Fisher Verlag. Vol. l pp 110–118
23. Malum Malannum. *Medicinische Blätter.* (Vienna) *26*(24): 404–405 (June 11) 1903. Reprinted in Jubilee Volume Honoring the 70th Birthday of A. Berliner. Berlin 1910
24. Materialien Zur Geschichte der Biblisch-Talmudischen Medicin. Die Erkrankungen der Haut. *Allg. Med. Central Ztg.* (Berlin) *72*(21): 431–434 (May 23) 1903; *72*(22): 455–457 (May 30) 1903; *72*(23): 474–477 (June 6) 1903
25. Angina Lacunaris and Kali Chloricum (Vergiftungsfalle) *Deutsche. Med. Ztg.* (Berlin) *24*(1): 447–448 (May 21) 1903
26. Waschungen und Bäder nach Bibel und Talmud. *Wiener Mediz. Wochenschrift 54*(2): 83–86, 1904; *54*(3): 137–140, 1904; *54*(4): 185–188, 1904; *54*(7): 327–329, 1904; *54*(9): 397–400, 1904; *54*(10): 439–442, 1904
27. Schwangerschaft, Geburt und Wochenbett nach Bibel und Talmud. *Zeitschrift fur Geburtshulfe und Gynäkologie* (Stuttgart) *53*(3): 528–573, 1904
28. Materialien zur Geschichte der Biblische-Talmudische Medicin. XVI. Die Weiblichen Genitalien. *Allg. Med. Central Ztg.* (Berlin) *74*(5): 96–98 (Feb. 4) 1905; *74*(6): 115–118 (Feb. 11) 1905; *74*(7): 135–137 (Feb. 18) 1905
29. Die Pathologie der Geburt nach Bibel und Talmud. *Zeitschrift fur Geburtshulfe und Gynäkologie* (Stuttgart). *54*(3): 448–481, 1905
30. Sexuelles in Bibel und Talmud. *Allg. Med. Central Ztg.* (Berlin) *75*(30): 571–573 (July 28) 1906; *75*(31): 589–592 (Aug. 4) 1906; *75*(32): 608–610 (Aug. 11) 1906; *75*(33): 625–627 (Aug. 18) 1906; *75*(34): 642–643 (Aug. 25) 1906; *75*(35): 659–661 (Sept. 1) 1906
31. Prostitution und Sexuelle Perversitäten nach Bibel und Talmud. *Monatshefte fur Praktische Dermatol.* (Hamburg). *43*(6): 271–279 (Sept. 15) 1906; *43*(7): 342–345 (Oct. 1) 1906; *43*(8): 376–381 (Oct. 15) 1906; *43*(9): 470–477 (Nov. 1) 1906; *43*(10): 549–555 (Nov. 15) 1906
32. Biblische und Talmudische Bezeichnungen der Gesichtsfarbe. *Festschrift zum Vierzigjährigen Amtsjubiläum des Herrn Rabbiners Dr. Salomon Carlebach in Lubeck.* July 16, 1910. Gewidmet von Freunden und Verwandten. Published by Von Moritz Stern. Berlin 1910. Printed by H. Itzkowski, Auguststrasse 69
33. *Biblisch-Talmudische Medizin. Beiträge Zur Geschichte der Heilkunde und der Kultur Uberhaupt.* Berlin. S. Karger. 1911 pp 735, 8°. Reprinted unchanged by S. Karger in 1921 & again in 1923. Reprinted unchanged by Gregg Internation. Publishing Co., Ltd., Westuread, Farnborough, England in 1969. Reprinted unchanged by Ktav Publishing House (New York) in 1971 but with an Introduction by Suessman Muntner and a Register of Hebrew & Aramaic Terms by Adolph Löwinger, translated & edited by Samuel Paley.

# Unpublished Articles

34. Ueber Untersuchung des Blutes zur Diagnostischen Zwecken, 1885
35. Kurpfuscherei und "Geheimmittel" 1893 (Lecture delivered to the Handwerker-Verein, Berlin 1893)
36. Frauenlob. (undated)
37. Eine Aufgabe fuer Juedische Aerzte. (undated)
38. Wohnungshygiene. (undated)

# BIBLICAL
## and
# TALMUDIC
# MEDICINE

# PREFACE

The present work, which covers the entire subject of Biblical-Talmudic medicine, is a first for two reasons: it is the first composed by a physician, and the first in which the material is directly derived from the original sources. Wunderbar, who completed his *Biblisch-Talmudische Medizin* in 1860, was a layman. Ebstein, whose writings appeared in 1901 (*Die Medizin im Alten Testament*) and 1903 (*Die Medizin im Neuen Testament und im Talmud*) was dependent upon the use of available fragmentary translations. Other works concerning the total subject of Biblical-Talmudic medicine do not exist. Concerning only Talmudic medicine, we only have the small collection of excerpts of Rabbinowicz (Paris 1880) and the small work of Bergel (Leipzig 1885).

For this reason alone, it is unlikely that, dealing with this subject for the first time, I should have avoided mistakes. In spite of this, I do not ask for the customary indulgence; for as pleasant as generous overlooking of errors might be for the author, historical truth — which should be the only concern — can only be arrived at by way of objections. *I will, therefore, even in the future, be thankful for every notification of deficiencies or errors.*

The number of commentaries, textbooks and individual works on the Bible is certainly very much larger than the number of letters contained in the Bible. No one would be able to read them all, even if he reached the age of ancient men, and even if he were familiar with all languages, and dedicated every minute of his life to this study. It is indeed a certainty that one cannot articulate a single thought concerning any Biblical subject, or give any clarification, which is not already contained in one of these innumerable writings. That which was just said about the Bible also holds true for the Talmud, but in a much smaller measure. I gladly relinquish any claim to priority, whether in the area of the subject matter or in the area of language, particularly since the glory of discovery properly belongs to the person who first thought a thought, and not to the one who first established it through printer's ink. On the other hand, one should not overlook the fact that to the one who lives and feels at home in this literature, many things are self-evident which impress an occasional visitor as being a great discovery. It is self-evident that I have nowhere intentionally plagiarized anything.

My previous works have been criticized as being "cool all the way up to the heart". I hope and pray that one can say the same about this book. To be sure, one cannot do without love while working on anything, and certainly the attraction for the subject of this book never left me. But never did I lose sight of the teaching of Rabbi Simeon ben Eleazar, or according to Genesis Rabbah Rabbi Simeon ben Yochai, that "love disregards the rule of dignified conduct" (Sanhedrin 105b), which means it muddies the clear decision. Otherwise, I would not have devoted to these studies every leisure hour that my medical practice would allow throughout twenty years. This objectivity and constant skepticism is indeed one of the reasons why I did not understand many things which were completely clear to my predecessors; that I only arrive at a *non liquet* where others felt with great certainty that a decision could be reached.

1

The foundation and first requirement of historical research into antiquity is philological minutiae. It was already stated by the ancient Epictetus that "every understanding of sources begins with a study of the words". Unfortunately, a physician is as little concerned with philological research as with mathematical formulae — grammar and logarithmic tables are equally disgusting to him. The most scholarly treatise on Aramaic names of plants or the use of the aorist leaves him as cold as the most ingenious study of irrational numbers and the quadrature of the segments of a parabola. I have, therefore, limited my purely linguistic remarks to the most essential ones and have reproduced them in smaller print* so that the physician can easily skip over these sections. The expert will recognize that these represent the more important and more difficult part of the entire work.

For the revision of a large part of the manuscript, I am gratefully indebted to Chief Rabbi Dr. Ritter of Rotterdam and Dr. Löw of Szegedin.

Julius Preuss

Berlin, on the twenty-fifth
anniversary of my graduation
from medical school.

* indented in this English translation

# INTRODUCTION

Ancient Jewish literature begins with the Pentateuch (the Torah), to which are added the other books of the Bible in the form of chronicles or poetry.

I have everywhere based myself on the traditional, so-called Masoretic text of the Bible. This might be considered unscientific today, but, for our purposes, I considered it the only practical way. There is no dearth, moreover, of conjectures and question marks in this book.

In addition to the Bible, the "Written Law", there is the "Oral Law", which serves as an explanation of and supplement to the former. According to tradition, the latter, too, was revealed to Moses at Sinai. It was handed down from generation to generation through oral transmission, enriched by exegesis and Rabbinic ordinances, until, at the end of the second century of the Common Era, Rabbi Judah HaNasi collected and edited this voluminous material together with already existent individual private collections.

His work is called *Mishnah*. Another similar type of collected material is the *Tosefta* (or "additional" *Mishnah*). Attached to these writings (i.e. *Mishnah* and *Tosefta*) one finds detailed discussions, with digressions into all areas of knowledge, as well as fables and legends, as they pertain to the specific legal matter under discussion, which are in turn related to the individual statements in the *Mishnah*. The totality of these discussions is called the *Gemara*. The editor of the first completed collection, the Palestinian *Gemara*, known as *Jerushalmi* for short, was Rabbi Yochanan, at the beginning of the third century. The editor of the Babylonian Talmud, the *Babli*, was Rabbi Ashi in the fifth century. The *Mishnah* and Babylonian *Gemara* are together called "Talmud." Other collections, which are called *Midrashim*, comprise only written expositions which are arranged according to the sequence of the Biblical passages — either expositions of the law (*Halachic Midrashim*), which are the original form of Halacha teachings, or ethically motivated meditations similar to short sermons (*Aggadic Midrashim*). They were written during various periods, and came to us from various times and climes. Some are very ancient.

Among the ancient *translations of the Bible,* the most famous are the Aramaic (*Targumim*) and the Greek, the Septuagint, both older than the *Gemara*; also the later Latin translation, the Vulgate. I have compared these translations throughout, as well as the writings of Josephus, because they all provide important information concerning the elucidation of the Biblical text of that time. Otherwise, I exclusively held fast to the original text, because "a completely satisfactory translation of the Torah is impossible"[1].

Among the ancient *commentators* on the Bible and Talmud, the most important are Rabbi Solomon Yitzchaki (*Rashi*) of Troyes in France (died 1105), who still based his commentary on the direct transmissions from the Babylonian Rabbinical colleges; Rabbi Chananel of Kairouan in North Africa (approximately 1015-1050); and, among

---

1. Soferim 1:7

the Spaniards, Abraham Ibn Ezra in about 1174, Rabbi Moses ben Nachman (Nachmanides), physician in Gerona (1194-1260), and Moses ben Maimon (Maimonides, 1131-1205)[2]. The latter is also well-known to medical historians.

The citations in the footnotes refer to the following works:
1. The Bible with *Targumim* and Commentaries: *Mikra'oth Gedoloth*, Warsaw, 1885 ff.
2. Apocrypha, Septuagint and Vulgate: Polyglot Bible of Stier and Theile. Bielefeld & Leipzig, 1891 ff.
3. *Das Neue Testament* (The New Testament). Greek and German. Stuttgart, 1853. Bibelanstalt.
4. *Mishnah.* ed. Orgelbrand. Warsaw, 1878 ff.
5. *Tosefta.* ed. Zuckermandel. Pasewalk, 1881.
6. Babylonian Talmud. ed. Romm. Vilna, 1880 ff.
7. Palestinian Talmud. ed. Krotoschin, 1866. The commentary thereon is according to the Pietrikow edition, 1897.
8. *Mechilta.* ed. Friedman. Vienna, 1870.
9. *Sifra.* ed. Weiss. Vienna, 1862.
10. *Sifre.* ed. Friedmann Vienna, 1864.
11. *Midrash Rabbah.* ed. Romm. Vilna, 1885.
12. *Midrash Tanchuma. Pesikta de Rab Kahana, Midrash Tehillim* (Psalms). ed. Buber.
13. *Yalkut.* ed. Warsaw, 1876.

There does not exist a work from Jewish antiquity devoted exclusively to medicine; nor even a compendium of natural history, such as that of Plinius. The Torah and the Talmud are primarily law books, and medical matters are chiefly discussed only as they pertain to the law. To be sure, in legal debates in the Talmud, medical matters are discussed a little more thoroughly. However, the main point is not the medical information, but the juridical, religious and sanitary aspect of the question, although they may have been based on hygienic considerations and experiences. There is thus nowhere to be found a systematic treatment of medicine throughout the Talmudic literature. Perhaps the only exception is a collection of prescriptions arranged according to the parts of the body[3]. There are always individual, mostly coincidental remarks on medicine found scattered throughout the Talmud. *Any systematical arrangement in the present book is, therefore, artificial,* produced by us solely for the purpose of clarity, and not based on the arrangement in the original sources. To this unusual form of the source material must be added the fact that undoubtedly only the smallest fraction of Talmudic Rabbis were professional physicians — proof for this contention will be cited later — so that the majority of pronouncements belong to folk medicine.

*There is, therefore, no "medicine of the Talmud", which might perhaps be compared to*[4] *the medicine of Galen or of Susrutas.* There is also no Jewish medicine in the sense that we speak of an Egyptian or a Greek medical science. The first Jewish physicians who occupied themselves with the literary aspect of medicine, as far as we know, are Arabic physicians, who also wrote in the language of their mother-country. The oldest fragment of a medical work in the Hebrew language is that of Donnolo, an Italian Jew of the tenth century,[5] who produced a collection of prescriptions[6].

---

2. Maimonides was actually born in 1135. (F.R.)
3. Gittin 68b and 69a
4. literally: placed in parallel with
5. not entirely correct; the Hebrew work of Asaph dates from the seventh century. See

Muntner S. & Rosner, F. *The Book of Medicines of Asaph the Physician.* in press (F.R.)
6. Steinschneider. *Virchow's Archiv* Vol. 38 p. 65ff

The "Propadeutic for Physicians," attributed to Isaac Israeli, was probably written by a different author in the twelfth century[7].

## II

The arena of Talmudic medicine is the Near East. Here in the pasture lands between the Euphrates and the Tigris, a nomadic nation grazed its herds approximately 2000 years B.C.E., and later moved westward to Canaan, where the Nomads lived next to the native Canaanites and Philistines. During times of famine, they temporarily moved their tents to Egypt, with which they had apparently been in touch for a long time; for Abraham already had an Egyptian maidservant. It is possible that in those days the Egyptians lived on the other side of the Red Sea, on the west coast of Arabia, so that direct traffic was easier.

After one of the Hebrews in Egypt rose to the rank of chancellor, the entire tribe followed him there and remained domiciled in that land for 400 years. Egypt at that time was already a monarchy with an advanced culture in which medical science also flourished, as evidenced by the *Papyrus of Eber*, which dates from that time (1550 B.C.E.). It is uncertain as to how much the Jews learned therefrom. Considering, as related in the Biblical books, that the Jews were at first disdained and shunned as plain shepherds, or not valued any higher than day laborers, whereas culture and science were the privileges of the completely secluded Priestly caste, one cannot assume that direct borrowing of Egyptian learning by the Jews occurred. Much later, after Palestine was already an independent kingdom, the relationships with Egypt did not cease. King Solomon married an Egyptian princess (about the year 1018), and commercial connections between the two lands were constantly active. In spite of this, however, not one of the three major elements of Egyptian dietetics and prophylaxis, namely, enemas, sneezing and vomiting[8], is found in the Talmud.

Approximately 300 years later, the involuntary relationships with Media and Assyria began. In the year 597, after the conquest of Jerusalem, 10,000 inhabitants were deported to Babylon where they remained for 80 years. Assyria, too, at that time was a country with a highly developed culture. From the year 650 we know of the surgeon Arad Nana from the court of King Asarhaddon, and his direct reports, and "his unfriendliness toward his colleagues with lesser titles than he, very much as in modern times"[9]. When Assyria came under Persian domination, Judea became a Persian province, until the year 330, when Alexander the Great incorporated both Persia and Judea into his world empire. At that time, Greece had already passed its prime, and Rome gradually began to dominate the world. Under Titus, the Jewish state was destroyed for all times; many inhabitants left the land, some voluntarily and others as slaves captured in war, and were scattered throughout the entire world.

A large segment of the Jews remained in Persia, to which, since the time of Cyrus, Babylon also belonged, and more or less willingly accepted Persian views. Whether medical teachings were also included must remain undecided, in view of the paucity of reliable source material from that time. On the other hand, numerous notations in the Talmud prove with certainty that Babylon was the land of origin of Talmudic medical teachings. At a much later date (after Christ), the Jews in Babylon even developed their own schools of higher learning in which instruction in medicine was given.

The influence of Alexandria, the commercial city founded by Alexander the Great at the western mouth of the Nile, was, perhaps, even greater. From there the Jews

7. D. Kaufmann. *Magazin für die Wissenschaft des Judenthums*, 1885 Vol. 11
8. *Prokatalamvanome- noi klysmois Kai nesteiais Kai emetois.* They are seized by diarrhea and fasting and vomiting.
9. See Oefele, in Neuburger-Pagel's *Handbuch der Geschichte des Medizin.* Jena 1902 Vol. 1 p. 94

derived their education, for here they lived in full equality with the Greeks. It is known that the Ptolemaic kings were particularly favorably inclined towards physicians, and even allowed vivisection of female criminals, so that in reality, the foundation of anatomy and of scientific medicine was laid in Alexandria. The history of these Alexandrians has certainly not been sufficiently investigated, and the part that the Jews played in the aspirations and the achievements of these physicians is totally unknown. It is quite possible that some of these physicians were in fact Jews; however, at the present time, we cannot but conjecture on this point. Moreover, we cannot even draw conclusions from their names, because it was not at all rare for Jews to have Greek names. There is, however, no question at all of any influence of Galen on the Rabbis, some of whom were older than he was, while others were contemporaries of his. Furthermore, teachings of science did not travel through the ancient world, as they do today.

The history of medical science is part of the history of culture. Every culture, however, has evolved: as soon as it becomes incorporated into the writings or other monuments of a nation, it has already undergone development, which is rarely purely esoteric. Indeed, every nation has possibly at some time or other come into contact with another, and the result has certainly been an exchange of cultural elements. Such relationships between the Jews and other peoples is quite obvious: "the sense of beauty of the Greeks was nurtured in the tents of Shem"[10]. On the other hand, they also actively participated in the spiritual development of these peoples, either directly or as a cultural mediator. I remind you only of the *Judaei emplastrum, fracto capiti accomodatum* and the *Judaei composito,* both of which are found in Celsus[11], and later in Aetius[12], and of the *ad splenem remedium singulare* of the Patriarch Gamliel in Marcellus Empiricus[13]. Which teachings in the Talmud are generally Semitic, which are exclusively the property of the Hebrews, and which were borrowed from others must in each individual case be investigated and shown. This is the question of the original sources of Talmudic medicine.

Naturally, it is pure folly to assert that the *société savante de la Talmud n'a rien emprunté à aucune école de ce temps, pas plus aux Grecs qu'aux Romains, ou qu'à toute autre médecine de leur époque.*[14]

It will be only briefly indicated here that care must be taken in this investigation of sources. When the hieroglyphic texts became legible after the year 1830, through Champollion, the conclusions made by that discovery were used to "prove" earlier assumptions, namely that all Biblical laws originated from *Egypt.* In 1836, Nork recognized that *"India* is the country of origin of the Hebrews and their fables"[15]. The *Assyrian* Babel-Bible uproar of our days is still remembered by all.

## III

According to Comte's "positivism," every cultural cycle goes through three phases of development: the theological, the metaphysical and the positive. One can also express the doctrine in a less scholarly, but just as correct a manner, as follows: the development of the human spirit leads from belief to superstition, and from there to knowledge. The history of medicine must also demonstrate this evolution for its own special sphere, and the history of medical science of a particular nation must be

---

10. Megillah 9b
11. Book V, Chapt. 19:11 and chapt. 22:4
12. *Tetrab.* IV. Sermo III. 14 col. 934 of the Ed. Lugdun 1549
13. *De Medicamentis* lib. 23;77
14. *L'Origine de la Médecine.* Paris 1877 p. 12 by Handvogel
15. *Braminen und Rabbinen.* Meissen 1836

demonstrated similarly for that nation. Along with scientific medicine, there is folk medicine, which is constantly influenced by scholarly learning, and which, more or less, slowly accepts the teachings of the former (i.e. scientific medicine). On the other hand, folk medicine may impart suggestions, methods and data to science. A history of the medicine of the Talmud, which is comprised of both scholarly, scientific medicine and folk medicine intimately intermingled, must be considered in the framework of two rotating spheres which, in general, are concentric, but which have numerous points of contact, so that the one which represents science takes precedence, more or less, over the other. Whereas scientific medicine has already reached a positive state, having arrived at certain facts by rational observation and the evaluation of one fact against the other, folk medicine is still tied down to metaphysics.

However, this separation of Talmudic medicine into scholarly medical science and folk medicine, which is absolutely essential for an exact description, and even more so for a proper appreciation of the material, encounters serious difficulties. To be sure, it is easy to demonstrate, for example, how from the belief in direct Divine intervention as a cause of illness, one came to believe in demons, the evil eye etc., and then to the simple view of the connection of phenomena (the *terefoth* teachings, pneuma, cold). However, as soon as we begin to separate science from folklore, we search in vain for criteria whereby this separation can be accomplished. Most Talmudic teachings came down to us anonymously through tradition, and where the name of the author is mentioned, we often learn nothing of his profession and his life. Or, coincidentally, the name of a physician may be mentioned, but nothing is stated about his medical teachings. For the Torah and the Talmud, as must be reiterated, are primarily legal sources, and not medical textbooks.

We should also mention two other difficulties. Although the *Mishnah* was completed in the second century, the *Gemara* in the fourth to sixth centuries, and some *Midrashim* much later yet, still the teachings of individual authors in part extend back to 100 years and more before Christ, so that the Talmud embraces a time span of at least 600 years. One must assume with certainty that medical views changed over such a long time period, which is much longer yet if one includes the time span of the Bible. The Talmud itself admits this in regard to anatomical nomenclature[16]. Since, in general, we do not know the originator of individual teachings, it is only rarely possible to date them, and, therefore, we lack the means with which to consider the appropriate conditions which were contemporary with the teaching, within whose framework a real picture can be elucidated. For undoubtedly — we do not have to go into detail — medical science is influenced by the actual conditions of the culture, just as it exerts its own influence on the fashioning of many outward life situations.

The second difficulty lies in the peculiarity of the sources. Most of those who are concerned with the Bible read it as a religious work and not as a historical document. To the devout person, it is repugnant to find views in the Bible which contradict our modern notions, and he attempts to clarify and justify opposite statements in the Bible and Talmud by introducing modern views. On the other hand, the non-devout person seizes the welcome opportunity to discredit the Divine origin of the Holy Scriptures by accentuating the disharmony between individual Biblical and modern views. Thus originate the classes of apologists and mockers — for even those who consider themselves to be pure objective historians can be more or less counted among one of these two classes, depending upon their religious viewpoint. Both are not always completely honest, due to the nature of this matter, even if many lack *dolus*[16a]. Both often violate the simple meaning of a historical tradition.

In general, that which applies to the Bible also applies to the Talmud. This

---

16. Shabbath 36a          16a. Latin: malice (F.R.)

collective work of ancient Jewish scholarship is generally considered to be a religious work by the few who still study it. Depending upon one's religious convictions, one person finds in the Talmud the sum total of modern scholarship, whereas another perceives limited and long outdated false statements. *For historical research, however, religious sentiments should play no role at all*; only the facts must speak for themselves. Where the sources are too meager to permit a clear picture, and where one is forced to establish a relationship through conjecture, one should not offer the product of one's own imagination as historical fact. Furthermore, there is no reason for apology or refutation of the Talmud; this would mean that our various views represent immutable, absolute truth! It is equally foolish to criticize the physicians in Talmudic times for not using ophthalmoscopes, as it is for us to use scholastic ingenuity to prove their acquaintance with bacteria, from incidental remarks concerning demonic influences (*mazzikin*).

# IV

Once a civilization was at its acme, it did not vanish without leaving traces of its existence for a certain period of time and over a certain geographic area, whether these traces resemble rapidly developing and rapidly vanishing circular waves which occur when one hurls a stone into water, or whether they are like brooks and streams which originate from a live well and continually and inexhaustibly feed the large waters into which they flow. So, too, it seems certain that the medical teachings which the Jews created themselves, or borrowed from others, did not vanish without a trace.

Church fathers and monks were students of Jews[17]. Numerous Jews, well versed in the Talmud, were physicians who had non-Jewish students. It is certainly no coincidence that the number of limbs of the human body in the writings of the illustrious Arabic physicians Avicenna and Abulcasem is not based on Galen, but rather coincides with the number given in the *Mishnah*, that is 248. It is also no coincidence that a Talmudic remedy for the treatment of worms in the brain emerges again in a Gothic pharmacopoeia[18]. It is further no coincidence that the story of the white children of a Moorish king, which until the last century was found in many writings, is already related in the *Midrash*[19].

Admittedly, all these represent only circumstantial evidence, and although quite weighty, are not conclusive. Only rarely is it possible to prove the relationship with certainty, as in the case of a Jew who fled to America from Russia because of persecution. After a physician mistreated him by giving him digitalis for urinary retention, he followed a remedy recommended in the Talmud; he placed a live insect in his urinary passageway, and he was promptly relieved[20].

The Jews had a most distinctive opportunity to carry their scholarship to all parts of the world; there is surely scarcely a place to which they were not coerced to wander. Even if it is an exaggeration to draw an ethnographic parallel, as does Mallery[21], between the Israelites and the Indians, or between the Masai in German East Africa and the Israelites, as was most recently done by Captain Merker[22], it still seems certain that an exact investigation would reveal traces of the Jews where such traces were

17. The priest Hiernonymus, for example, learned Hebrew from a *frater qui ex Hebraeis crediderat*. Ep. 125:12. Migne 1:1079.
18. Kethuboth 77b and Oefele. *Archives de Parasitologie* 1901 p. 87
19. Preuss. Vom Versehen der Schwangeren. *Berliner Klinik* 1892. Book 51, note 6

20. *The Times and Register*. Vol. 21, No. 16 p. 362, Oct. 18, 1890 and Gittin 69b
21. Garrick Mallery. *Israeliten und Indianer*. German by Krauss, Leipzig 1891.
22. M. Merker. *Die Masai. Ethnographische Monographie eines ostafrikanischen Semitenvolkes*. Berlin 1904, particularly p. 294

previously unsuspected. To them (Mallery and Merker) Bastian's teaching concerning the thoughts of nations was foreign.

It was my wish not only to give completely accurate citations as they relate to the contents, but to consider each individual teaching in its milieu, according to its sources and its later development, in order to construct a part of the cultural history in this manner; particularly because it seems impossible, for the above-mentioned reasons, to provide a collection of biographies with more or less detailed extracts from the writings of individual authors as a substitute for a section from the history of the development of ideas. Even today, I am not ready to assert that the implementation of this plan is impossible, in spite of all the aforementioned difficulties. The Talmud itself teaches that the formula "we have not yet observed it" (consequently it is impossible) "is not a logical conclusion"[23]. I must regretfully admit that I was not successful in the realization of my goal in spite of my sincere efforts. I can also say of myself only what Rabina thought of himself in wise resignation: "I am not a prophet (who views the truth through lofty inspiration), nor a Sage (who ascertains the truth by his own discernment) — I am only a collector and organizer"[24].

---

23. For example Eduyoth 2:2          24. Pesachim 105b

# CHAPTER I

## *THE PHYSICIAN AND OTHER MEDICAL PERSONNEL*

### PART I
### THE PHYSICIAN

#### I   The General Practitioner

Whereas in Egypt, according to the report of Herodotus[1], every physician was a specialist or an "eminent doctor," his Jewish colleague, the *rophé* or *asya,* was an "ordinary practicing physician", who, like ourselves, served all needs. As an *internist,* he prescribed warm animal milk for a patient with consumption[2], and cured a desperately ill Persian king with the milk of a lioness[3]. As a *neurologist,* he examined a young man afflicted with love-sickness and asserted that the patient could only be healed if the woman who was the object of his affection would be permitted to him; however, the Rabbis did not consider this therapeutic advice to be even worthy of debate[4].

The Jewish physician is also expected to heal *diseased eyes.* Tobit traveled to physicians because of corneal erosions, but they could not help him[5]. If a patient suffers from eye illnesses, he pays money to the *rophé,* although it is doubtful whether he will heal him[6]. A woman whose eyelashes fell out as a result of excessive crying had an eye salve prescribed by the *asya*[7]. He must also serve as a *dentist.* He would drill the tooth of his slave[8], and provide information to Rabbi Jassa as to why the teeth of his fellow student were falling out[9].

Surgery and all it encompasses also fell into his sphere of activity. During an operation, the *rophé* wears a leather apron[10], straps the patient tightly to the table[11], and makes use of a bandage box *(thruntik)* with several compartments containing writing stylus, scissors and knife[12]. The *rophé* heals wounds with all types of herbs that God produces[13]; he is called from one place to another to suck out snake bites [14], and

---

1. II, 84: *mies nosou ekastos ietros esti* — For every disease there is one physician
2. Baba Kamma 80a
3. Midrash Psalms on 39:2
4. Sanhedrin 75a
5. Tobit 2:10
6. Kethuboth 105a
7. Lamentations Rabbah 2:11 fol 23b
8. Kiddushin 24b
9. Jerushalmi Shabbath 6; 8c
10. Kelim 26:5
11. *Tosefta* Shekalim 1:6
12. Kelim 16:8, according to the commentary of Maimonides, which, however, is only valid for his own time
13. Genesis Rabbah 10:6; see also Sirach 38:4
14. Yoma 83b; *Tosefta* Shabbath 14:14

to prescribe certain dietary regulations for injured people[15]. If someone falls off the roof, the *rophé* is summoned and applies plaster to his head, his hands and his feet and all other limbs, until the patient is all plaster[16]. He opens abscesses skillfully "as the physicians do"[17], opens the skull with the physician's drill[18], splits the brain[19], and closes the defect with pumpkin peel[20]. As early as the time of the Temple, amputation of diseased limbs was already carried out by the *rophé*, not only on lepers[21], but also for other indications, possibly referring to serious lymphangitis[22]. He also cut away gangrenous parts[23].The treatment of bone fractures was also his task. Rabbi Meir says that a person who sees his friend more than a year after a death occurred in the latter's family and begins to console him regarding his loss is comparable to a *rophé* who meets a person with a healed bone fracture and says to him: I will break your leg anew and then heal it again to make you recognize that my therapeutic measures are effective[24]. An operation which is particularly frequently carried out by the *rophé,* although not only by him, is ritual circumcision[25]. It was expected that the qualified physician understand the use of the scalpel and internal medications: one who studies in his youth is compared to a physician who has both instruments and medications, but one who begins to study during his old age is like a physician who knows only the knife[26].

In contrast to his Greek and Roman colleagues, the Jewish physician was spared one aspect of the surgical specialty: unlike the former, he did not have to heal people who were injured by torture, for Jewish law does not ever impose torture or other body mutilation as punishment for wrongdoing[27]. Nevertheless, this did not prevent Herod, disregarding the law, from making abundant use of torture and then, seized with a sense of justice, allowing the tortured people to be healed[28]. The Talmud has no expression to correspond to the Greek *basanizein* (torture).

The prophet reproached the people as follows: *the diseased animal have ye not strengthened, neither have ye healed that which was sick, neither have ye bound up that which was broken*[29]. In this rebuke there is certainly no indication of the separation of physician from surgeon. The Psalmist extols God: *He healeth the broken in heart, and bindeth up their wounds (atzvotham)*[30].Those who insist on separating the surgeon from the general physician must propose a correction of the text to read *atzmotham,* meaning "their bones".

## II   The Obstetrician-Gynecologist

There is not much mention of the gynecological expertise of the physician in all of antiquity. Among the Greeks, women were treated by female physicians, *iatrinai*[31], or midwives, *maiai* (in Greek), who examined the female genitalia and communicated the results to the physicians[32]. These are the *gynaikeious iatrous* mentioned by Soran, and it was they who treated gynecological disorders[33]. It was no different among the Jews. A woman who discharged peculiar matter from her genitalia asked the Sages in regard to her ritual impurity. The Sages submitted the question, and, perhaps, also "the

15. Baba Kamma 85a
16. Exodus Rabbah 27:9
17. *Tosefta* Eduyoth 1:8
18. Oholoth 2:3
19. Levit. Rabbah 22:3
20. *Tosefta* Oholoth 2:6
21. Kerithoth 3:7
22. Jerushalmi Sanhedrin 9; 27a; *ibid,* Nazir 9; 58a
23. Chullin 77a; *Sifra Emor* p.94a
24. Moed Katan 21b
25. Abodah Zarah 26b; Genesis Rabbah 46:10

26. Aboth de Rabbi Nathan 23:4
27. We will later discuss Deut 25:12
28. Josephus. *The Jewish War.* Book 1; Chapt. 30:4
29. Ezekiel 34:4. Compare *ibid* 34:16
30. Psalms 147:3
31. Galen. *De Locis Affectis* 6:40 (Kühn 8:414). The son of a *iatrina* is also mentioned by Josephus, *Vita* 37
32. *ibid* p.433
33. Chapt. 47. ed. Ermerins p.191

matter" to the opinion of "the physicians" for their advice[34]. During the time of Jesus, a woman with prolonged vaginal bleeding consulted numerous physicians[35].

However, nothing is mentioned about the examination or treatment of a woman. It seems hardly likely that the genitalia of even a sick woman were explored by a physician. The following story may serve to prove the point. The importance of establishing puberty in the ancient world is well-known. Mar Samuel, who enjoyed the reputation of being a great physician, wished to be able to pass judgment by personal observation, and therefore he examined the change of the female breast through puberty on his maidservant. He paid her four *zuz* as "shame money", since only her work, but not her shame, belonged to him[36]. Here one should remember that in the concept of heathen antiquity, a maidservant was altogether not considered as a person, but as a mere object, *res*!

An *obstetrician* in the modern sense of the word did not exist either. Böttiger has already proven this for classical antiquity[37]. Most probably, the physician was only called when the midwife encountered a transverse or pelvic presentation or any other deviation from the norm, where natural spontaneous completion of birth was considered impossible. Then the physician came in his capacity as a surgeon, to dismember the baby in order to extract it. The turning of the feet, which Celsus recommends in addition to the usual turning of the head, in the case of a dead fetus[38], remained totally unknown. Hence, in every *surgical procedure* of antiquity and the Middle Ages, one finds a chapter: *qua ratione partus emortuus ex utero excutiatur.*

From *Kiddushin 24b,* one cannot conclude anything about male obstetricians[39]. For according to Biblical law, a master who blinds an eye, or knocks out a tooth or destroys any other important organ (for example a finger, or the hearing) of his heathen servant must give him his freedom[40]. Since, in the opinion of most Sages, the fetus is an appendage of the mother[41], he is considered as one of her "important organs". That is, not only his totality but his individual organs are entitled, in respect to liability, to the same dignity as those of the mother who is carrying him. Most Talmudic commentators assume that regarding liability, premeditation on the part of the owner of the slave is required. Thus, if the "owner of a maidservant inserts his hand in her womb in order to deliver the child, and thereby blinds it" (deprives the child of an eye), he is not liable, because premeditation was not present, and therefore the maidservant need not be given her freedom.

It is clear that from an emergency case of that kind, one can certainly draw no conclusions regarding the *professional* practice of midwifery.

The responsibility of the physician for bodily injuries is discussed in the *Tosefta,* in various places, as we will mention later. In this connection, his liability in specific cases where "he dismembers the fetus in the womb of the mother" is established[42]. It does not follow, however, that for Jews, any more than in Egypt, midwifery was distinct from medicine[43]; nor must one conclude therefrom that there existed a category of embryotomists separate from the class of *rophé* (physician). According to Jewish law, which is not however absolutely undisputed, an *error in objecto* is not actionable similar to today's German

34. Niddah 22b
35. Matthew 9:20
36. Niddah 47a
37. C.A. Böttiger. *Klassiche Schriften Archaeologischen und Antiquarischen Inhalts.* ed. Sillig. Dresden 1838 Vol. 3 p.6
38. Celsus. Book 7 Chapt. 29
39. The case involves a man who inserts his hand in his bondmaid's womb and blinds the child within her.
40. Exodus 21:26
41. Chullin 58a & passim
42. *Tosefta* Makkoth 2:5; *Tosefta* Baba Kamma 6:17; *Tosefta* Gittin 4:7
43. Oefele, in Pagel-Neuburger. *Handbuch der Geschichte der Medizin* 1:82

law[44]: a person who intended to kill person A, but actually killed person B, cannot be punished for murder or for manslaughter[45]. If the mother, then, dies during the dismemberment of her fetus through the fault of the physician, and if the exemption from liability in a case of *error in objecto* is considered admissible, then the operator would normally be exempt from punishment according to this principle, since he was not intent on harming the mother. However, this is *not* the accepted rule; rather the teaching of the minority prevails that the fetus is not considered an appendage of the mother but is, at least during the birth process, considered to be a separate being[46], and the operator, according to the principle of *aberratio ictus,* should be punished with banishment like anyone who killed a person without having had any intention of hurting him[47]. The general rules applicable to the *rophé* are reiterated, not because there existed a class of embryotomists separate from the *rophé* and for whom separate laws had to be enacted, but rather because a different juridical construction of offense was possible.

Accordingly, the threefold division of medical practitioners into physician, surgeon and magician, which according to Oefele, "was always and everywhere found in antiquity"[48] cannot be authenticated in Jewish antiquity.

## III  Specialists

Whatever else is reported about *specialists* among the Jews is based on error. Ben Achiya acted in the Temple for the priests who frequently fell ill as a result of walking barefoot on the stone floor and depending excessively on a meat diet[49]. He was known as Ben Achiya "for intestinal ailments" but nowhere is he addressed by the title *rophé.* It is likely, as reported in the Palestinian Talmud, that he was a priest "who knew which wine was beneficial for the intestines and which was not"[50]. In the list of Temple officials which is given in the *Tosefta*[51], a physician is not mentioned at all.

The priests and Levites were examined in a separate room in the Temple for their suitability to serve[52]. We do not know who performed the inspection.

It has been suggested that one might find a reference in the *Midrash* to an eye surgeon[53]. One should probably translate the *Midrash* as follows: "Woe to the city in which the physician suffers from podagra and from whom one eye has been removed". One is concerned here with the meaning of the word *ikoteta.* (Variants are found in Friedmann)[54]. According to *Mathnath Kehunna (a.l.),* it refers to an eye surgeon. Derivation from *katat* is linguistically impossible, and the root *dakat* (Buxtorf) does not exist. Levy[55] and Fürst suggest the Greek *akestor* which is only poetic, however; and Krauss suggests the Greek *akestos.* Both words mean simply "healer" without the connotation of specialist.

It cannot be doubted that the specialization concerning whose prevalence Pseudo-Galen so bitterly complained[56] is totally strange to Biblical-Talmudic literature.

A *rophé* who is also a *chaver,* that is who belongs to the fraternity which devotes

44. Olshausen. *Strafrecht* sub No. 211 p.789
45. Rabbi Simeon in Sanhedrin 9:2 and Maimonides, *Hilchoth Rotzeach* 4:1
46. On the basis of today's penal code, Liszt considers the fetus to have independent status from the beginning of labor onwards; Olshausen, *loc. cit;* Oppenhoff. *Strafgesetzbuch* p.508
47. Numbers 35:11 ff
48. *loc. cit.*
49. Shekalim 5:1-2
50. Jerushalmi Shekalim 5; 48d
51. *Tosefta* Shekalim 2:14-15
52. *Tosefta* Chagigah 2:9
53. Levit. Rabbah 5:6
54. *Das Blinden-Institut auf der Hohen Warte bei Wien.* Vienna 1873 p.138, note 104
55. *Neuhebräisches und Chaldäisches Wörterbuch.* Leipzig 1876-1889
56. *De Part. Artis Med.* Chapt. 2. ed. Charter. 2:182b

itself to an extraordinarily strict way of life, is mentioned in the Palestinian Talmud[57]. Perhaps the Essenes are meant, just as are the *ropheim* whose custom it is to eat their bread with barley puré[58], as well as the physician in Sepphoris who wished to divulge the Tetragrammaton[59] to Rabbi Pinechas Bar Chama.

It is unlikely that *mesan* should have the meaning "physician", as claimed by the commentary of the Cracow edition and others: "Chinena was a *mesan* and threw his wife a bill of divorce. When the neighbor came running as a result of her screams, he tore the document away from her"[60]. The meaning which best applies is: "quarrelsome, hot tempered".

In Leviticus Rabbah 32:5, the Israelites are praised for not having changed their names in Egypt. "Judah did not call himself *rophé* nor Reuben Luliani". However this reading is false; it should correctly read: "Reuben did not call himself Rufus nor Judah Julian", as is evident from the commentary of D. Luria and the proper textual reading in Song of Songs Rabbah 4:12 fol 28c. Naturally, one is dealing with a ridicule of the conditions current in the Greco-Roman era.

The Samaritans twice slavishly translate the name of the giant people, the *rephaim*[61], with the word *asain,* physicians; probably also Genesis 15:20[62].

## IV   Military Physicians

I have nothing to report concerning *military physicians* in Jewish antiquity. One cannot draw any conclusions from the Biblical remark that King Joram had to return to his homeland from the battlefield to be healed[63], because seriously wounded generals were probably always evacuated from the battlefield if they were capable of being transported. Since the time of King Saul, Jewish kings, in addition to their personal guards and royal princes, had a standing army as well as a militia[64]. Also, in post-exilic times, there existed a peacetime army; and military expeditions are repeatedly described in the Bible. Yet there is no mention of military physicians.

To be sure, the sanitation services of the Romans are a much later development, even if perhaps high ranking personalities took their private physicians along to the battlefield[65]. The soldiers, however, bandaged each other as best they could, and carried bandages themselves for this purpose[66]. On the other hand, in Greece, military physicians were incorporated early into the armies, at least on marches, and also in war[67]. The essence of military medicine in Rome first developed at the beginning of the time of the Caesars, approximately at the time of the birth of Christ[68].

During the Jewish War, Rabbi Yochanan ben Zakkai requested and received physicians from Vespasian (69 C.E.) for Rabbi Zaddok, who was near death from fasting[69]. This might serve as proof that the Jews had no physicians of their own, but relied on Roman physicians, unless one wishes to assume that the Jewish physicians had already all been killed. It is therefore not possible to ascertain where Josephus, who broke his joint at the wrist (fracture of the radius) when he fell off a horse, "sent for physicians"[70], since this occurred *prior* to his capture by the Romans.

57. Jerushalmi Demai 3; 23b
58. Jerushalmi Nedarim 4; 39b
59. Jerushalmi Gittin 1; 43b
60. Jerushalmi Yoma 3; 40d
61. Deut. 2:20
62. Kohn in *Frankels Mschr.* 1867 p.177
63. Second Kings 8:29; 9:15 Second Chronicles 22:6
64. First Samuel 13:2
65. Plutarch *Cato Minor* Chapt. 70

66. Rosenbaum-Sprengel 1:199, note
67. *ibid* p.322
68. Marquardt. *Römische Staatsverwaltung* 2:554 ff; Iwan Bloch, in Pagel-Neuburgers *Handbuch* 1:586
69. Gittin 56b
70. *Vita* No. 72; *metapempsamenos iatrous,* he sent for physicians

After the cessation of the Jewish state (70 C.E.), no Jewish army continued to exist.

## V   Salaried Physicians

It is also doubtful whether Jewish sources were familiar with *physicians* who were *paid a lump sum as salary from the communal treasury.* In other countries, such an arrangement had been known for a long time. In Egypt, according to the report of Diodorus[71], physicians were generally paid from communal resources, *misthon ek tou koinou,* and received no extra honorarium during wartime. Charondas in Athens, according to the same author (Diodorus), by promotional education and philosophy, acted more wisely than some legislators who engaged public-salaried physicians, *demosio misthoo*[72]. Democedes of Croton, who healed the sprained foot of Darius and thereby achieved great fame, was engaged for one year each, first by the Aeginetans then by the Athenians and then by Polycrates of Samos, receiving a raise in salary each year, which probably accounted for his changes of residence[73]. The Gallic Massiliotes took physicians from Greece. These were partly paid by individual people, and partly by the joint municipalities[74].

While the Talmud advises not to live in a city that has no *rophé*[75], there is no indication of any distinction between the communal physician, the *demosiewon,* and the private practitioner, the *idioteuon*[75a].

In Rome, these community physicians later developed into the *archiatri municipales,* whose circumstances were definitely regulated by Valentinian in the year 370 C.E. Such a Roman district physician is also mentioned in a parable in the *Midrash*[76]:"The son of an *archiater* (prominent physician) came across a quack[77] and greeted him: *kyrie* (master), my lord, my father. At this, the real father felt insulted and said: let him no longer see my face since he now calls a quack his father. When the son became ill, however, he asked that his father come to visit him....So too Israel speaks to God: and now that we are in trouble, Thou art our father''[77a]. The *archiater,* however, was not known in the Jewish city and state constitution.

It is possible that physicians also served as *expert witnesses in court.* Concerning restitution claims for bodily injuries[78], and concerning the administration of corporal punishment[79], the Talmud speaks of an "appraisal" of the bodily harm, as well as the ability of the body to tolerate such corporal punishment. The fact that the physician is not explicitly mentioned in this regard is perhaps only a coincidence.

In the methods of work, one can distinguish two groups: one is the group of theoreticians (book-learned), such as Rabbi Yochanan, who, when asked to demonstrate the location of kidney fat, answered: "I am no butcher, nor did I grow up among butchers, but I remember having heard such and such"[80]. The other group consisted of natural scientists in the modern sense; they studied the facts objectively, such as Rab, who spent 18 months with a shepherd in order to study eye diseases of animals at first hand[81], or such as the disciples of Rabbi Ishmael, who performed a dissection on a prostitute.

Some are directly called *askan bidebarim,* or experimenters. Thus Rabbi Simeon ben Halafta, in order to convince Rabbi Judah that a plucked hen need not necessarily die, plucked a hen, placed it in an oven and wrapped it in the apron of a blacksmith.

---

71. Diod. Sic. 1:82,3
72. *ibid* 12:13,4
73. Herodotus 3:129
74. Strabo 4 Chapt. 1,5
75. Sanhedrin 17b
75a. Plato, *Gorgias.* 70 E fol 514
76. Exodus Rabbah 46:3
77. *samardakos,* imposter

77a. Isaiah 64:7
78. for example Sanhedrin   78a-b
79. for example Makkott 3:11
80. Chullin 93a. A similar example is that of Rabbi Judah. Chullin 45b
81. Sanhedrin 5b. He actually learned to distinguish transient from permanent blemishes in animals (F.R.)

The result was that it grew feathers even larger than the original ones[82]. Rabbi Assa experimented with raven fledglings[83], and Rabbi Simeon with a *dukipath* (heath cock)[84]. Experiments with ants are also mentioned[85].

Just like the physician generally in antiquity, the *rophé* simultaneously served as his own pharmacist. A *narthex* is described into which all remedies were placed[86], as well as a metal basket and a tower, *migdal*[87], which, as the commentaries would have it, contained not only instruments but also medicaments *(armarium*, Arabic *almansor)*, and which, perhaps, represents a hand apothecary, a type of pocket case. Such medicament boxes from the followers of Hippocrates are also known, and in fact some have come down to us[88]. A physician said to a woman with an eye illness: "paint your eye with *my* salve!"[89] *Theriak,* that peculiar composite mixture of antiquity, was prepared by the physicians themselves using wondrous ingredients[90]. "The large ladle of the physicians"[91] is used by the physician in his capacity as a pharmacist.

## VI   Education

We have no information at all concerning the physician's training. Puschmann's presumption seems most likely, "that the essential professional training occurred through the personal instruction of the student by a teacher who was experienced and knowledgeable in medical therapeutics"[92]. At least there is mention of the disciple of a physician who "was already taught all teachings of medicine"[93], as well as a physician who possessed a *narthex* full of remedies, which he gave over to his son when the latter established himself in medical practice[94]. This form of instruction was probably in addition to the empiricism which was originally customary among *all* nations.

It is probable that medical matters were also discussed in Jewish schools of higher learning, even if not in systematic courses as in our universities.This is so because they were necessary for the understanding and application of the laws, and because every judge was expected to be familiar with all scientific fields, including medicine[95]. Thus, Rabbi Yochanan expounded *(darash)* at his Sabbath discourse, *pirka*[96], in the house of study[97], on a remedy for *tzafdina* which he had learned from a Roman lady. Rabba also taught in Mehoza about a general salve he had compounded (compress for all pains)[98]. So too, Emperor Antoninus asked Rabbi Judah (Rebbe)[99] to send one of his disciples when one of the Emperor's servants was seriously ill and on the verge of dying[100].

In Rome, during the era of the Emperors, it was customary for the physician to take his disciples with him when he visited his patients, evidently for purposes of instruction, even if, as Martial so amusingly pictures it[101], the examination by so many hands is not always desired by, or pleasant to, the patient. There is no direct proof of this type of *"polyclinic"* in the Talmud, but it seems to be implied in the frequent references to *"physicians"* in situations where in our opinion a single physician would have sufficed. To decide the question as to whether certain bones belonged to the same

82. Chullin 57b
83. Levit. Rabbah 19:1
84. *ibid* 22:4
85. Chullin 57b
86. Jerushalmi Berachoth 5; 9b
87. Kelim 12:3 and 15:1
88. Guhl and Koner. *Leben der Griechen und Römer* 2:297
89. Lamentations Rabbah 2:15 fol 23b
90. Song of Songs Rabbah 4:5 fol 25d
91. Kelim 17:12
92. *Geschichte des Medizinische Unterrichts* 1889 p.26

93. Deut. Rabbah 6:13
94. Jerushalmi Rosh Hashana 1; 57b
95. Maimonides *Hilchoth Sanhedrin* 2:1
96. Abodah Zarah 28a
97. Jerushalmi Abodah Zarah 2; 40d
98. Shabbath 133b
99. Rabbi Judah the Patriarch
100. Levit. Rabbah 10:4
101. Epigr. 5:9 *Languebam: sed tu comitatus protinus adme/ Venisti centum, Symmache, discipulis/Centum me tetigere manus aquilone gelatae:/Non habui febrem, Symmache, nunc habeo*

skeleton, Thodos the physician "and all the physicians" came to the house of study of the Rabbis in Lydda[102]. To diagnose doubtful blood flow from a woman "physicians"[103] were called. A love-sick young man[104], a pious person with a chest disorder[105] and the sick Rabbi Jacob Bar Acha consulted "physicians". According to Biblical law, someone who injures another must pay the physicians' fee[106]. Josephus obligates him to replace *asa tois iatros edoken,* whatever the injured person gave to (i.e. paid) the physicians[107]. The *Midrash* states that it is the norm "as all people die",that the patient lies on his bed and is visited by physicians[108]. Some of these sources are reminiscent of the Roman *Collegium medicum,* the physicians' guild.

Naturally, I do not here include the notices of sick kings who, such as Hezekiah, sought healing "from the physicians"[109], or of the Persian king for whom "the physicians" prescribed the milk of a lioness[110]; for it is likely that even in those days, people in high office, and others who aspired thereto, were not satisfied with their own house physician when they themselves became ill.

Nor do the descriptions of patients such as Tobit, who "traveled to the physicians"[111], or who "went to all the physicians"[112], or who "gave all their money to physicians", such as the bleeding woman in the gospel[113], belong here. For the patient's endurance is always rapidly exhausted, and moreover, it is understandable that those who are not cured fast enough by a *single* physician seek out another one.

## VII    The Title "Physician"

The Bible first uses the term *physicians, rophim,* for the Egyptian servants of Joseph, who embalmed his father Jacob. The Septuagint translates *rophim* as *entaphiastai,* or gravediggers[114].

The original text evidently chose the expression *rophim* because embalming of the dead was not practiced by the Hebrews, and the Hebrew language did not possess a specific term for an embalmer. One cannot therefore conclude from the word *rophé* that embalming of corpses constituted a part of the medical practice of the Hebrews.

Physicians are not mentioned in the detailed Biblical rules concerning leprosy[115]. Even if we assume that the Hebrew *priests,* like those in other civilizations, possessed medical knowledge, there is still no proof that they practiced medicine as a profession. The assertion of Friedreich[116], as well as the identical statement of Israels[117], that "healing was a function of the priests as mediators between God and the people", is devoid of any support. There is no mention at all of a *curandi methodus sacerdotum.* The priest only declares what is ritually clean or unclean, and observes "if the plague of leprosy be healed in the leper"[118]. Nowhere do we find the slightest hint of any therapeutic counsel given by a priest. The position of the priest in ancient Judaism is most easily compared to the present-day English health officer. According to the

102. *Tosefta* Ololoth 4:2
103. Niddah 22b
104. Sanhedrin 75a
105. Baba Kamma 80a; see also *Tosefta* Baba Kamma 8:13 where *rophé* is in the singular
106. Exodus 21:19, *Targum*
107. *Antiquities.* Book 4, Chapt. 8:33. Also the Vulgate has: *impensas in medicos*
108. Numbers Rabbah 18:12
109. Second Chronicles 16:2
110. Midrash Psalms 39:2
111. Tobit 2:10
112. Song of Songs Rabbah 2:3 fol 14c

113. Matthew 2:20
114. Genesis 50:2.Ritter says that Joseph did not have his father embalmed by the usual *entaphiasters,* but rather by his personal physicians. As Ibn Ezra points out in his handwritten commentary, they are also called "servants of Joseph", as were all Egyptians other than the Pharaoh.
115. Leviticus 13:1 ff
116. *Zur Bibel* I p.196
117. *Collect. Gynaec. ex Talmud Babli.* p.3-4
118. Leviticus 14:3

statement in the *Mishnah,* his function is purely a formal one: "Anyone can decide whether a skin eruption is unclean or clean (that is, leprosy or not); the priest shall only pronounce the word "unclean" in the case of uncleanliness"[119]. The Jewish tradition knows so little of any medical functions of the priests that in an allegory in the *Midrash,* a competent physician was called to treat an epileptic priest[120]—not a priestly colleague, which would have been much easier.

That all noblemen of Israel were *medendi artis periti*[121] is an assumption which, as far as Biblical antiquity is concerned, is completely without sound foundation, even if a legend incidentally recorded by Josephus about Solomon, the wisest of all kings, ascribes to him the knowledge of the entire healing apparatus, including exorcism, etc.[122] But even to designate Ezra and Nehemiah too as physicians is, at the least, naive; then one might well go as far as Börner who gives the title of medical doctor to almost every male person named in the Bible[123]. The ancient bibliographies list a large series of medical writings which are even traced back to the progenitors of the human race. The episcopal library of Mayence is said to contain *ampli de Medicina Commentarii* of Shem, the son of Noah[124].

We have been aware for a long time that this entire "pseudo-epigraphic literature" is, on the one hand, nothing more than a large conglomeration of falsifications and mystifications, and on the other hand, writings whose authors could scarcely have surmised that later elaborators, following the general custom of their time, would give these books the strangest titles, and then judge them by these titles without taking cognizance of their contents. The *Antidotum Esdrae Aut Prophetae Doctoris,* which haunts the Middle Ages in the *Compendia* from the time of Aetius[125], the "prophet's salve" *tou prophetou ygrokollourion* which is described by Alexander of Tralles[126], and many similar items, should probably also be included in this listing.

On the other hand, it is unquestionable that some of the *prophets* possessed some knowledge of medicine and the natural sciences. One need only remember the treatment of an apparently dead child by Elisha[127], or the healing of King Hezekiah by the prophet Isaiah[128], or the improvement of the drinking water by Elisha[129]. However, they are never designated as physicians, although the name *rophé* for a physician was already in use at that time. Jeremiah thought it unbelievable that no physician resided in Gilead[130]. It is related that King Asa sought the aid of physicians[131], and Job called his friends "physicians of no value"[132].

## VIII    Physicians in the Talmud

In the Talmud, only the following people are explicitly given the title "physician":
1) The physician Thodos or Theodoros[133]. To be sure, one cannot prove that he is identical with Theodas the empiricist who is mentioned by Galen[134], or with Theydas, whose commentators are mentioned by Suidas[135], and that he is one of the 20 Theodori whom Diogenes Laertius enumerates[136]. There are numerous citations in the Talmud

119. Negaim 3:1
120. Levit. Rabbah 26:5
121. Sigism. Cohn. *De Medicina Talmudica.* Vratislav 1846 p.3
122. *Antiquities.* Book 8, Chapter 2:5
123. *De Statu Medicinae Apud Veteres Hebraeos.* Witteberg 1775
124. *ibid* 18 p.16
125. see Pagel. *Allgemeine Zeitung des Judentums* 1898 No. 12
126. Ed. Puschmann 2 p.47
127. Second Kings 4:18 ff
128. *ibid* 20:7
129. *ibid* 2:21
130. Jeremiah 8:22
131. Second Chronicles 16:12
132. Job 13:4
133. *Tosefta* Oholoth 4:2
134. *De Meth. Med.* 2:7; Kühn 10:142
135. Suidas 2:173. Ed. Bernhardy p.1132
136. Liber 2:8. Aristipp. ed. Cobet. p.57. Number 17 in the list is an *iatros* or physician who is a disciple of Athenäus.

which seem to support the assumption that he studied in Alexandria. These citations, perhaps referring to autopsy, relate that every sow and every cow, prior to being exported from Alexandria, was castrated in order to prevent propagation of what they considered the best breed of pigs and cows outside the native country of Egypt[137]. We are also told that he came to the house of study in response to an inquiry by the Rabbis, either in Tarsis[138] or in Lydda[139], and explained that the several vertebrae and skulls placed before him did not derive from the same skeleton. This knowledge too seems to indicate an Alexandrian origin for Thodos.

In the Talmud, a "Roman Thudos" is mentioned many times[140]. There is also a Thudos in Acts 5:36. In Bechoroth 4:4, the Berlin Maimonides manuscript has Thurdos instead of Thudros, no doubt due to a copying error[140a].

2) Nothing is known about the physician Tobiya[141] except his name.

3) The physician Bar Girnte[142] lived at the time of Rabbi Jeremiah about 200 C.E.

To identify his name with the Greek *geronta* (old man)[143] is as superfluous as the derivation of the name Ben Achiya from the Greek *ygios* (healthy)[144]. Girnte is supposed to be an old man and, therefore, could justify the permissibility of using a sedan chair on the Sabbath when visiting the sick. This is what the text speaks about.

4) The physician Manjome, or Benjamin, a contemporary of Rabba, lived in the year 280 C.E. He maintained that all kinds of fluids are detrimental to the ear except the fluid of kidneys[145]. When Rabba once publicized a universal bandage, the school of Benjamin left Mahoza in great dismay for fear that their medical practice might become smaller[146]. Significant is the fact that these "children of the physician Benjamin" were disbelievers (Epicures) in that they used to say "of what use are the Rabbis to us?"[147] — an ancient illustration of the opposition between physicians and theologians.

5) Rabbi Ammi *asya*[148], later than Rabbi Jeremiah.

6) A Physician called Bar Nathan[149], at the time of Rabbi Joseph about 300 C.E. Brüll[150] identifies him with Manjome because we know nothing about him.

The apostle Paul too concludes his letter to the Colossians with *Luke, the beloved physician*[151], *greets you*[152].

Whether or not Luke was born Jewish is uncertain. For evidence concerning his medical practice, see Winckler. *Diss. de Luca Evangelist Medico.* Lips. 1736, B.G. Clauswitz. *De Luca Evangelist Medico.* Hal. 1740, and Ad. Harnack, *Lukas der Arzt,* Leipzig. 1906 p. 11 and 122 ff.

While it must remain doubtful whether the above-mentioned individuals were physicians in the modern sense, that is, persons whose profession was therapeutics, even though they carried the title "physician", there is no doubt at all about several others whom the Talmud calls *rophé mumche,* meaning "experienced or skillful physician"[153], yet some were merchants, such as Rabbi Yochanan (the later rector of the school of higher learning in Tiberias), or manufacturers, such as Rabbi Abahu.

---

137. Bechoroth 4:4 and 28b; Sanhedrin 93a
138. Nazir 52a
139. *Tosefta* Oholoth 4:2; Jerushalmi Berachoth 1; 3a
140. Berachoth 19a; Pesachim 53b; Betzah 23a
140a. It is possible that Preuss intended Thudos. (F.R.)
141. Rosh Hashanah 1:7
142. Jerushalmi Betzah 1; 60c
143. Schorr, *Hechaluk.* 9:1 p.6
144. *ibid* p.76
145. Abodah Zarah 28b
146. Shabbath 133b
147. Sanhedrin 99b
148. Jerushalmi Berachoth 2;4c
149. Pesachim 52a, according to the commentary of Rabbi Chananel and *Alfasi*
150. In his *Jahrbuch Für Jüdische Geschichte und Literatur.* 1874 p.225
151. *o iatros* in Greek
152. Colossians 4:14
153. Abodah Zarah 28a; Shabbath 119a

In yet other instances, the designation *rophé* is not used, and yet the Talmud considers such a person to be almost an authority in medical matters. This is particularly true of the Babylonian Mar Samuel about 200 C.E., who was given the professional title of *yarchinai*, or astrologer. He was the rector of the school of higher learning in Nehardea in Babylon. A large number of medical teachings originate from him, and in the succeeding pages we will often encounter his name. As an astronomer he was able to say about himself that the streets of heaven were as familiar to him as those of his hometown[154]. But as early as in his studies in Palestine, we already see him as the personal physician of the Patriarch Rabbi Judah. When he cured the latter from an eye ailment, the convalescing Rabbi Judah wished to bestow the title ''Rabbi'' upon him, as one would today give a medal or bestow the title ''Professor''. However, as the *Gemara* laconically remarks, ''it did not come to pass''[155]. Like every physician, he was not spoiled by excessive thanks from the patient, and he consoled his well-wisher Rabbi Judah by saying: ''Let it not grieve thee, for I have seen written in the book of Adam (i.e. it is written in the books of destiny) that I will be called *''chacham''* or sage[156], but not ''Rabbi''.

Rabbi Chiya, who went to heal his colleague Rabbi Yochanan and felt the latter's pulse[157], probably possessed medical expertise, as did Rabbi Ishmael and his disciples, who conducted a post-mortem examination on a female corpse, and Mar Bar Rav Ashi, who performed plastic surgery on the penis[158].

As a result of the aforementioned, it seems that the names *rophé* and *asya* in the Talmud do not denote one's profession in the modern sense, but possibly encompass the term ''learned physician'' and certainly also ''lay practitioner''. Thus one should be careful to translate the word *rophé* as ''healer'', and not as ''physician''.

This *license to practice* made it necessary that one express the warning that no one should engage in the practice of medical therapeutics unless he really understands it, and even then only if there is none more skilled than he. Otherwise the healer could easily become a murderer[159].

On the other hand, it is likely that the expression *rophé umman*[160] refers to a certified physician. From here we derive the teaching that the ''healer who is commissioned to heal by the administrative authority'', referring to the municipal physician, as we thought above, is *always* designated as *rophé umman*. For the assumption is that one would demand a certificate of competency from a person who is engaged to perform a municipal function requiring civil service qualities.

The circumstances of the Jews in those times were quite similar, on the one hand, to those of the Egyptians, if the expression of Homer *iatros de ekastros*[161] is true, and as reported by Plinius[162] concerning the Romans: *in hac artium sola evenit, ut cuicunque medicum se professo statim credatur* — and, on the other hand, to the conditions of the Greeks. The latter had to testify who their teachers were[163] before they could be considered as candidates for the position of municipal physician.

However, the majority of medical statements in the Talmud belong to folk medicine. The most prominent representative thereof is Abaye with his innumerable prescriptions that he heard from his nursemaid or mother. There were probably frequent occurrences in which a person vainly sought help from the physicians, and

---

154. Berachoth 58b
155. Baba Metziah 85b
156. perhaps this title was already in customary use at that time for a physician in the Orient. See Rappaport. *Bicc. Haitt.* 1827 p.14
157. Berachoth 5b
158. Yebamoth 75b

159. Yoreh Deah 336:1
160. Sanhedrin 91a; *Tosefta* Makkoth 2:5; *Tosefta* Baba Kama 6:17; Jerushalmi Shabbath 14; 14d, ed. princeps; ed. Sitomor and Pietrkow: *neeman*
161. *Odyssey* 4:231
162. *Hist. Natur.* 29:8
163: Rosenbaum in *Sprengel* p.319, note

was recommended a simple "home remedy" by a layman[164] — perhaps someone who, like Rabbi Chanina, "was knowledgeable in healing remedies"[165]. To be sure, we do not learn whether or not this "simple remedy" helped the patient. We will not include here the case of a person suffering from hair loss, who sought the advice of his barber[166].

The number of such healers at the beginning of our era was certainly not negligible, even in small places of those countries. During the time of the Roman emperors, every village in Egypt had its physician and its *iatreion*[167]. If the person who injured another offers to bring a physician from a distant place, the injured person can object, saying: "If the physician is a long way off, the eye will be blind (before he arrives)"[168]. There must have thus been physicians everywhere. We have already mentioned above that it was considered the "norm" for physicians to visit the sick. A common maxim is: "he who has pain should consult a physician"[169]. In spite of this, it could happen in those days, as today, that the patient had to wait for hours to see the physician:

"A patient being treated by physicians (plural) waited: when will the physician come? At four or five or six or seven o'clock — he did not arrive. It is eight, nine and ten o'clock and he still has not arrived. Finally, at dusk his wagon was heard in the distance. Then the patient said to the physician: had you tarried just a little bit longer, my soul would have left (my body.) So too does Israel speak with the Psalmist when it must bear the oppression of other nations: *but, O Lord, how long?*[170] Thou art my physician, but Thou delayest coming to me"[171]!

## IX  God the Healer and the Physician's License to Heal

At the time of the first mention of a medical act in the Bible, circumcision, the era of pure empiricism, which was undoubtedly considered to be the original condition of medical therapeutics, was finished, and the age of theology was upon us. Comte, as far as medicine is concerned, incorrectly designates it as the first stage of culture. Circumcision was in fact carried out by Abraham at the direct command of God, and, with the giving of the Law at Sinai, theocracy was fully developed: *out of the mouth of the most High proceedeth both evil and good*[172]; *I kill and I make alive, I wound and I heal; and there is none that can deliver out of My hand*[173]; *for He maketh sore and bindeth up, He woundeth and His hands make whole*[174]; *if thou wilt diligently hearken to the voice of the Lord thy God, and wilt do that which is right in His eyes, and wilt give ear to His commandments, and keep all His statutes, I will put none of the diseases upon thee, which I have put upon the Egyptians, for I am the Lord that healeth thee*[175]. The latter phrase implies also prophylactic medicine[176]. The Talmud states that "no man bruises his finger here on earth unless it was so decreed against him in heaven"[177], and that "a snake only bites a person when a command from heaven forces it to do so"[178]. *Nothing is outside God*[179]; even sorcery is successful only if He wills it[180]. "God sends his word and heals mankind and delivers them from their own destructions"[181]. For this reason, a person convalescing from illness should recite a prayer of thanks[182].

---

164. Song of Songs Rabbah 2:3 fol 14c
165. Yoma 49a
166. Eccles. Rabbah 5:6 fol 4a
167. Haeser 1:90
168. Baba Kamma 85a
169. Baba Kamma 46b
170. Psalms 6:4
171. Midrash Psalms 6:5
172. Lamentations 3:38
173. Deut. 32:39
174. Job 5:18
175. Exodus 15:26
176. On the other hand, Jesus teaches: *not the healthy (ygiainontes) require a physician; but the sick.* Luke 5:31
177. Chullin 7b
178. Jerushalmi Peah 1; 16a
179. Deut. 4:35
180. Chullin 7b
181. Psalms 107:20
182. Berachoth 54b

In its consequences, this theory of Divine providence and predetermination of human destiny is in agreement with the theory of fatalism as taught by the Stoics in antiquity, by Islam in later times, and by the mechanistic world outlook, as found in the materialism of *modern* times. "The atoms can only fall in *one* manner."

Only in one respect does theocracy take a fundamentally different position. Fate, and even more so mechanism, as a law of nature, are unalterable. A Divine decree, however, can be modified by prayer and by a related activity, repentance of the sins committed. For although "suffering as a sign of God's *love*" is known in Judaism, it appears that in the great majority of cases, sickness is a *punishment* for having committed a transgression. The Lord says: *if I send pestilence among my people, and if my people . . . turn from their wicked ways . . . I will forgive*[183]. In reference to the Ninevehites[184] Scriptures emphasize: *And God saw their works, that they turned from their evil way*[185]. In this manner does Rabbi Meir explain the observation that two people may become ill with the same sickness, yet one recovers, but the other does not[186]. Not only should the patient himself ask God for mercy, but others have the obligation to do likewise on his behalf.

One also fasts for a sick person, so that he should recover[187]. Hence King David fasted and cried when the child of Bathsheba became ill: *who can tell whether God will be gracious to me, that the child may live*[188]? According to a report by Josephus[189], sacrifices were even offered for the expulsion of an illness. As far as I am aware, the Talmud does not know of this custom. However, it does mention pledges and contribution of generous donations to the poor for the same purpose[190]. If someone is sick for more than one day, he should publicize it so that others will pray for him[191]; *for God fulfills the desire of them that fear Him; He also hears their cry, and saves them*[192]. The brief fervent prayer of Moses for his sick sister "God, I beseech Thee, heal her now"[193] was immediately answered. The prayers of certain individuals were believed to be particularly efficacious. Thus, Rabbi Chanina ben Dosa concluded that if his prayer was fluent in his mouth without hesitation or error, the prayer was granted and the patient would recover[194]. It is also written in the Jacobus document: if someone is sick, he should invite the elders of the community and have them pray for him and anoint him with oil in the name of the Master; and the faithful prayer will help the patient[195].

*In none of these systems is there a place for a physician* — neither in providence, nor in fatalism nor in materialism. The course of the world of mechanism cannot be changed by anyone. Concerning fatalism, the Stoics teach: *Si fatum tibi est, ex hoc morbo convalescere, sive medicum adhibueris, sive non, convalesces*[196]. In the *Mishnah,* an unknown Sage teaches that "the best of physicians are destined to go to hell"[197], or expressed in the positive sense, the physician is counted among the seven types of professions whose members have no share in the eternal bliss[198], because he is the accomplice of the patient who should leave his destiny to the decree of the Lord. Medical healing and physicians are considered to be superfluous in the consistent philosophy of fatalism. In consistent religious fatalism they are considered to be an annoyance[199] and sinful. The author of Chronicles is of the same opinion in that he criticizes King Asa for having sought the help of physicians to cure his illness rather

183. Second Chronicles 7:13-14
184. Jonah 3:10
185. Taanith 2:1
186. Rosh Hashana 18a
187. *Tosefta* Taanith 3:2
188. Second Samuel 12:22
189. *Antiquities* Book 3 Chapt. 9:4
190. Baba Bathra 10b
191. Berachoth 55b

192. Psalms 145:19
193. Numbers 12:13
194. Berachoth 5:5
195. Jacobus 5:14
196. *Cicero de Fato* 13
197. Kiddushin 4: 14
198. Aboth de Rabbi Nathan 36:5
199. L. Löw. *Ben Chananja* 3:546, 1860; *Gesammelte Schriften* 3:371

than turning to God[200]. It is possible that this opinion was also shared by those who indicated that King Hezekiah was to be praised for having eliminated the use of "the Book of Remedies"[201]. Rabbi Acha too is of the opinion that, in reality, people do not have the right to heal, but this is a habit with them[202]. This point of view would also perhaps explain the fact that the *Mishnah* and the *Beraitha*, which describe regulations concerning the responsibilities of various officials exactly as does the *Tosefta,* seem to intentionally omit the physician, and take no notice at all of his existence[203].

These same perceptions of the *Mishnah* seem to be espoused by the Septuagint which also excludes the physician from resurrection. They express their opinion about the godlessness of physicians in the phrase *iatroi ou me anastesousin* (physicians shall not rise)[204].

The Septuagint believed the physicians to be godless and here agree with the Vulgate by astonishingly substituting *rophim* (physicians) for *rephaim* (ghosts) and thus the Psalmist asks: *shall the physicians arise and praise thee*[205]? In another place, they translate *rephaim* directly with the word *aseveis* (disrespectful of God)[206]. Here the Vulgate did not follow suit.

A small faction in antiquity was of the opinion, which I cannot, however, prove from the Talmud, that seeking the aid of physicians is a sign of an unmanly character and therefore of weakness, as exemplified by the philosopher Seneca; or people refrained from using physicians for special reasons such as the ancient Cato, who hated Greek physicians, and who even insinuated that they had made common cause, *barbaros necare omnes medicina*[207]. Even the Talmudic Sages only allowed heathen physicians to heal Jews with certain precautions; tragic experiences gave rise to this insulation from Gentile physicians[208].

It seems very doubtful whether the proponents of the above theories ever translated them into practice when it came to their own persons. Even the most obstinate Stoic, if he should see blood spurting from a wound, would try to stem the flow by exerting pressure with his finger. He would also certainly not resist the application of a bandage, rather than let fate run its course. Indeed, Stoics helped themselves in very skillful ways, by arranging for the physician and his skill to be integrated with fate: *tam est fatale, medicum adhibere, quam convalescere!*

These systems are completely inapplicable to the life of a community or a state. The Talmud gives an example of this: If court witnesses were allowed to console themselves by saying: "though a plague (epidemic) may last seventy years, no one dies before his time (through a possible miscarriage of justice)[209]; thus, our declaration does not change fate" — anarchy would follow, and men would swallow one another alive[210].

In the medical sphere, the Bible, in the ordination of liability for personal injuries, specifically decrees that every person who injures another must cause him to be healed (*faire guérir*)[211]. From this Scriptural text, the school of Ishmael logically deduces that *the Bible therewith gave specific sanction to a physician to heal*[212]. This latter interpretation is *the prevailing one* in the Talmud. The *Gemara* does not at all comment on the *Mishnaic* statement that "the best of physicians is destined to go to hell". In regard to many questions of civil and criminal law, and in cases of doubts of a purely ritual nature, the opinion of the physician is sought and respected. The

200. Second Chronicles 16:12
201. Pesachim 56a
202. Berachoth 60a
203. For example Makkoth 2:4 and *Tosefta* Makkoth 2:5
204. Isaiah 26:14 usually translated: they shall not rise.
205. Psalms 88:11
206: Isaiah 26:19
207. Plinius 29:1
208. *Tosefta* Abodah Zarah 3:4
209. Sanhedrin 29a
210. Aboth 3:2
211. Exodus 21:19
212. Berachoth 60a

physician, as already mentioned at the beginning of this chapter, was consulted for all branches of medical skill, without opposition from the Rabbis. In fact, they too consulted physicians.

The *Midrash* relates the following[213]: "in a certain neighborhood there lived a physician. If a person was injured, the physician would heal him; if the patient was ill internally, the physician would heal him. When the physician moved out of the neighborhood, the inhabitants exclaimed: Woe!" It is "normal" that not only good friends[214] but also physicians[215] visit the sick and the dying. The recognition of the physician in the Talmud is seen in the fact that in order to carry out his prescriptions, the laws of the Sabbath and the laws of kosher foods were set aside[216]. Furthermore, his assurance that an amulet had healing powers was accepted without question[217]. Sirach correctly states: *the skill of the physician exalts him, and he is admired among the great (enati megistanon)*[218]. Indeed, it is directly counseled that no learned person should live in a city where there is no *rophé* and no bloodletter[219].

The remarks which ostensibly speak against the *social* value of the physician only *seem* to do so. It is suggested that one not live in a city where the mayor is a physician[220]. The reason underlying this recommendation, however, as already noted by Rabbi Samuel ben Rabbi Meir (about 1150), is the fear that the physician, because of his preoccupation with his patients, might not be able to adequately devote his attention to municipal matters. The rule that a person who owns a multidwelling building should not lease an apartment to a physician or a bloodletter[221] is based upon the fact that one tries to protect the residents from the noise of their neighbors[222], since social welfare patients might use the front steps and make noise. For this reason a tanner and a town scribe (or teacher) are discussed next to the physician and bloodletter[223].

The admonition: "honor your physician *before* you have need of him"[224] only demonstrates that one could not believe the physician to be without human weakness. That one occasionally transferred one's dislike of sickness to the person of the physician was only natural. Sirach said that *the man who sins in the sight of his Maker may fall into the hands of the physician*[225]; and the *Midrash* asserts that "the door that is not opened for good deeds will be opened for the physician"[226].

The Biblical commentaries of the Middle Ages are not satisfied with the unconditional recognition of the physician.

Ibn Ezra (about 1170) is of the opinion that "license to heal", granted to the physician by the Bible, refers only to cases analogous to the verses in the Bible, that is for bodily injuries and for other external illnesses. However, internal illnesses may not be healed by the physician[227]. Very astonishing is the perception of Nachmanides (about 1200) that the above scriptural phrase (*and heal he shall heal*)[228] does in fact give the physician permission to heal. However, the patient may not seek healing from the physician, for the truly God-believing person will not consult a physician. Indeed, the pious will not be placed in the position of needing to do so, for "piety" means nothing more than the observance of God's commandments. God promises to bless the

213. *Tanchumah Beshallach* p.29 Buber's ed.
214. Nedarim 39b
215. Numbers Rabbah 18:12
216. Yoma 83a
217. Jerushalmi Shabbath 8b
218. Sirach 38:3
219. Sanhedrin 17b
220. Pesachim 113a, according to the version of *Rashbam*. Rabbenu Tam in *Tosafoth* Baba Bathra 110a *s.v. velo*, and others, interpret *assi* as a proper name instead of *asya* or physician.

221. Baba Bathra 21a
222. *Choshen Mishpat* No. 156:1
223. One may not lease the apartment to any of these types of individuals for fear of their constant visitors disturbing the other tenants.
224. Jerushalmi Taanith 3; 66d
225. Sirach 38:15
226. Song of Songs Rabbah on 6:11, fol 35b
227. Ibn Ezra on Exodus 21:19
228. Exodus 21:19. Also translated: *and cause him to be thoroughly healed*

bread and the water of the pious and to take sickness away from their midst[229], so that they do not find it necessary to be given prescriptions concerning their bread and water (i.e. dietary rules about eating and drinking)[230]. This teaching is even more astonishing in view of the fact that its author (Nachmanides) was himself originally a practicing physician.

The opinions of the *Mishnah* commentators are expressed in their remarks on the assertion that "the best physician is destined to go to hell". *Rashi* (about 1050) compiles all the bad things which people say about physicians, which the *Tosafist* Rabbi Yitzchak Sen summarizes in the pithy words "they cause the death of the patient". Rabbi Samuel Edeles (in the year 1630) is of the opinion that the condemning judgment (of going to hell) applies only to the physician who considers himself to be the best, and who haughtily refuses to consult with others. When Joshua Falk, in reiterating some of these views, concludes "may the Lord God protect us from physicians"[231], he is only saying what Diodorus asserted about the famous Egyptian physicians: "we wish that we should not have need for any one of them"[232].

There is no dearth of other explanations of the above expression (that the best of physicians should go to hell). In 1724, Chr. Reinecke wrote a separate book on the subject. Buxtorf[233] and Schenkel[234] interpret it to mean a general deprecation of physicians, whereas Israels[235] considers it a vote of censure of physicians who are followers of Greek philosophy, *omnibus nugis religiosis Rabbinicis non obtemperabant*. Landau[236] states that the phrase refers to the sect of Essenes, although the entire *Mishnah* only speaks of different professions, etc.

The Christian Bible commentators found themselves in the same dilemma as the Jews, although Jesus himself repeatedly teaches that the sick require physicians[237]. During the time of Luther, a Dr. Carlstadt zealously preached against the use of a physician[238]. More than 100 years later (in 1656) Des Marets had to prove with detailed assertions "that a Christian person, when he is ill, is permitted to seek a physician"; not as the Belgians did during the plague, where every individual had to piously await his destiny[239]. Even in our own times, an ecclesiastic complains about health insurance[240] which is in opposition to the providence of God. "Whomever God decreed to be sick must bear the sickness and not attempt to set aside divine punishment"[241]. The followers of Christian Science treatment in America, and the "peculiar people" in England with their opposition, on principle, to allowing a physician to visit the sick, may serve as modern proof for the eternal cycle of culture.

## X   Faith Healing

The philosophical attempts at mediation between glaringly contradictory points of view in the Talmud date back to the time before Christ. The Sirachites, in particular, found the correct path. Thus they teach: *The Lord has created medicines out of the earth and a sensible man will not despise them*[242]; and "with them the physician heals the wound and the apothecary compounds his salves"[243]. They also admonish *And seek the advice of a physician; he too prays to the Lord that He guide him to bring relief and effect a cure and restore health*[244]. This is the point of view which, in actual

---

229. Exodus 23:25
230. Nachmanides on Levit. 26:11
231. In his commentary *Binyan Yehoshua* on Aboth de Rabbi Nathan 36:5
232. Diodorus 12:13
233. *Lexicon Chaldaic. s.v. rophé*
234. *Bibellexikon* 1:252
235. *op. cit.* p.29
236. *Bicc. Haitt.* 1824 p.59
237. Matthew 9:12; Mark 2:17; Luke 5:31
238. Luther *Tischreden*. Ed. Irmischer No. 1411

239. Sam. Maresius. *An possit et debeat Homo Christianus in suis Morbis Medicum Adhibere*. Groningen 1656.
240. literally: treasury for the sick
241. Wehberg. *Enthaltsamkeit von Geistigen Getränken*. 1897 p.35
242. Sirach 38:4
243. Genesis Rabbah 10:6
244. Sirach 38:12-14

practice, became the only authoritative one: the patient turns to the physician, and the latter ministers to the best of his ability. *The success of the cure and its blessing, however, come from God, and one must pray for it.* There is no restriction in this matter, as is usual for the Catholic moral theologians, who permit the physician to be consulted only in cases of serious disturbances of health which do not respond to simple remedies[245].

Even youthful enthusiasm for a good cause should not lead to considering every prayer of a sick person to be quackery or to ridiculing a pious Catholic who publicly declared in a newspaper "the Virgin Mary miraculously helped her ill son whom the physicians had already abandoned". Only in the eyes of the superficial observer do faith healing and similar frauds have something in common with *religious* matters. A person who has been a physician for a long time, and who critically evaluates the results of his therapeutics, readily becomes convinced that, at the present time, we are far from being able to replace the omnipotence of God with the "omnipotence" of the physician.

On the other hand, the following statement of Rabbi Yanai is valid: "A man should never stand in a place of danger and say that a miracle will be wrought for him"[246]. It also refers to one who believes that one should count on being cured by a direct intervention by God without the patient having a hand therein. In a parable the *Midrash* relates as follows:

Rabbi Ishmael and Rabbi Akiba were walking through the streets of Jerusalem in the company of a peasant. A sick man approached them, and they responded to his request for medical advice. The peasant said: "you are dealing in a matter which is not your concern. God afflicted him with illness and you wish to heal him?" They answered him: "don't you as a farmer do the same? Although God created the earth, you have to plow and till and fertilize and weed if you wish it to yield produce. Don't you know what is written: *As for man, his days are as grass*[247]. The body is the tree (the grass), the medicine is the fertilizer, and the physician is the tiller of the earth"[248].

*The physician, therefore, is considered to be the messenger of the Lord, the one who accomplishes the Divine will.* It therefore follows that it is his obligation to respond to every call of a sick person, even if the patient has someone else who can heal him; for not every patient can be healed by every physician; for not every physician is the proper messenger for a particular patient[249].

## XI    The Physician's Responsibility and Liability

Although the physician is thus an instrument in the hand of the Creator, he has the right of self-determination, as does every person. This conflict between providence and free will, as taught in Judaism, poses one of the most difficult problems in the philosophy of religion. Attempts at reconciling these two views can not be discussed here. But since a person is morally free, he has to bear the responsibility for his conduct.

For an understanding of the following paragraph it must be stated that Jewish law does not recognize double punishment for the same offense; for example, legal punishment and restitution for damages. One penalty excludes the other. In general, in cases of bodily injuries, restitution for damages must be made. The question of premeditation or carelessness generally plays no role in the ruling[250]. The compensation for damages is accomplished in a five-fold manner: *rippuy* or

245. Capellmann. *Pastoralmedizin.* p.38, according to Scavini
246. Shabbath 32a
247. Psalms 103:15
248. Midrash Samuel. par. 4 Ed. Venet. 1546 fol 52a
249. Jerushalmi Kethuboth 13; 35d
250. Baba Kamma 2:6

healing costs (physician and medicines); *shebeth* or compensation for lost income due to inability to work (sick benefits); *tza'ar* or monetary compensation for pain; *bosheth* or damages for the shame incurred as a result of the injury; and *nezek* or compensation if the injury has permanent consequences such as the loss of an eye. It is not possible to describe in detail here the principles upon which the estimation of the specific amounts of compensatory damages are based. For the healing costs and the sick benefits (or loss of time), a lump sum is paid in advance[251], and deposited with the court. In this manner, the injured person avoids the temptation of dragging out his healing and of neglecting it[252]. It is known that even in our times important voices have been raised for the one-time monetary settlement in cases of accidental injury.

The legal rules governing the responsibility of the physician are as follows:

If he intentionally injures a patient, he is obviously liable. On the other hand, if the injury occurs following an error on the part of the physician, then, in contrast to other people, the physician is held blameless "because of the public good"[253]. For it is evident from the often-cited Biblical law (he who strikes a person must pay the physician's fee), that the Divine arrangement of the world requires and presupposes the existence of physicians. If one were to hold the physician liable for every error, it is likely that no person would wish to engage in the profession of medicine. Thus does the commentator David Pardo explain[254]. In the Bible, the physician is thus granted that privileged position which we today also attempt to provide for him, but admittedly without success[255].

It must be conceded, however, that this exceptional position of the physician also has its dangers, and that the determination of error or negligence is not always easy to establish. It was perhaps motivated by this, that another rule states that, although the earthly court may hold the physician innocent, his definitive judgment is reserved to Heaven[256].

Furthermore, this exceptional position in regard to blamelessness in case of error only applies to a "*rophé umman* (experienced or expert physician), who heals at the request of the authorities", whom we consider to be the licensed community physician[257]. The non-licensed physician is subject to the general law. In *our* courts, as is well known, error and ignorance apply as grounds for excuse of the quack only.

If a physician injures a patient more than is necessary, then *negligence* has been demonstrated and the physician is liable[258]. He must also free his slave if he blinded his eye while treating it[259].

If someone is permanently employed by the community as an official, and acts very negligently, he should be summarily dismissed. To be sure, among medical personnel, only the bloodletter is specifically mentioned[260]. Rabbi Papa also speaks of the dismissal of a circumciser[261]. There can be no doubt, however, that the physician is also included in this regulation.

The intentional wounding of a person for therapeutic reasons, *lege artis,* such as "if someone says: blind my eye because it is harming me; or cut off my hand because it is harming me", is exempt from punishment[262], although the surgical operation, as

---

251. Baba Kamma 91a
252. *Choshen Mishpat* 420:18
253. *Tosefta* Gittin 4:6
254. *Chasde David.* Livorno 1776 & 1789. I am grateful to Professor Berliner for calling to my attention the existence of this commentary.
255. Virchow *Ges. Abhandlung* 2:514
256. *Tosefta* Baba Kamma 6:17
257. see section V above

258. *Tosefta* Baba Kamma 9:11
259. Kiddushin 24b
260. Baba Bathra 21b
261. Shabbath 133b
262. see *Tosefta* Baba Kamma 9:32; when the Jerushalmi Baba Kamma 8; 6c holds the surgeon in this case to be liable, the phrase "it is harming me" probably does not refer to bodily damage

our modern penal judges can already deduce from the Talmud, contains all the criteria for premeditated bodily injury[263]. It seems that this immunity from punishment also applies where the patient did not consent to the operation, but where it can be recognized with certainty that the physician was acting solely to save the life or the health of the patient.

On the other hand, if someone who is not ill[264] says to another: "blind my eye, cut my hand off, break my leg! I will not hold you responsible", then the person who carries out this request is nevertheless liable, because he should have known that, in reality, no person wishes to be maimed[265].

If one person says to another: "blind the eye of so and so; in case you are held responsible, I will pay for the compensation", then the person who carries out the act is himself liable and the accord is not valid. For no one can become the legal agent of another to commit an illegal act[266]. However, even the agent who commissioned the illegal act is a villain (i.e. liable), because he caused a "blind" man to stumble, and strengthened the hands of a law breaker[267].

Furthermore, only in a case of property damage is the case settled as soon as he pays for the damages. However, in the case of personal injury, the guilty person is also required to ask forgiveness of the injured person[268].

If a patient dies as a result of the treatment, and this result had been intended, the physician is obviously a murderer and is dealt with accordingly. If the death, however, occurred as a result of an oversight, then the physician, like any person who accidentally killed someone without intending to harm him, must be exiled to one of the cities of refuge[269], where he has to stay until the death of the High Priest. For the Biblical regulation that *if a man come presumptuously upon his neighbor, to slay him with guile, thou shalt take him from Mine altar, that he may die*[270] specifically excludes a physician if he accidentally causes the death of the patient, a father or a teacher who hits a child who dies as a result, and a bailiff who administers flogging to a sinner who collapses and dies[271]. For even though they deliberately inflicted corporal damage, they had no evil intentions, no *dolus*[272]. It would not enter anyone's mind to hold the physician liable if the patient did not follow all his instructions[273].

According to Maimonides, the father who inadvertently slays his son, the teacher who beats his pupil, and the court official who inadvertently kills the litigant during a court-prescribed flogging are all exempt from going into exile, for this punishment is only applicable where one did not act while performing a duty[274]. The same should apply to the physician, at least when "he treats at the request of the municipality", i.e. the municipal physician. Nevertheless, the requirement for him to be exiled is ordained in the Codes, based upon the above-cited *Tosefta*[275].

Greek law does not at all recognize liability of the physician, even for the premeditated killing of a patient. The defending attorney of an accused physician can state "Even if the patient died at the hand of the physician, the latter is legally not a murderer, because the law considers him innocent"[276]. Accordingly, Philemon, with

---

263. Sanhedrin 84b
264. perhaps this refers to the young Christian ascetics (see Matthew 5:29). Democritus blinded himself in order not to be prevented by outside influences from philosophizing. *Gellius* 10:17
265. Baba Kamma 8:7 and 93a
266. Baba Kamma 8:7
267. Maimonides *Hilchoth Chovel Umazik* 5:13
268. *ibid* 5:9
269. *Tosefta* Makkoth 2:5

270. Exodus 21:14
271. *Yalkut* on Exod. 21:14
272. *Mechilta* on Exod. 21:14 p.87, ed. Weiss
273. *Pesikta de Rab Kahana* 14 p.118a, Buber's ed.
274. *Hilchoth Rotzeach* 5:5-6
275. *Yoreh Deah* 336:1
276. *Ei d'eti kai ypo tou iatrou apethanen, o men gar iatros ou phoneus autou estin, o gar nomor apolyei auton. Antiphon Tetral.* 3:3 par. 5 ed. Blass p.49

complete justification, asserts that only the physician has the right to cause death, but not to be killed[277]. The same is mentioned by Plinius for Rome[278]. Perhaps with regard to this regulation, the *Tosefta* found it necessary to explicitly decree that this heathen regulation should *not* take effect in Judaism, and that for premeditated acts the general laws of crime and punishment should apply equally, or even more so, to the physician[279].

Hammurabi's much extolled "humanitarianism" is evident also in his rules concerning the physician. In paragraph 218 of his law book, severance of the physician's hands is decreed if death of the patient follows bloodletting, or if blindness follows cataract extraction. On the other hand, Plato, in his system of legal philosophy, decreed the immunity of the physician for inadvertently causing death[280].

In addition to these responsibilities which are prescribed by law and for whose violation the law metes out punishment, there are those which we designate as "moral". The compassion which a physician feels towards his patient is one of the most noble of these responsibilities. The *Midrash* strongly criticizes the prophet Isaiah for having directly stated to King Hezekiah: *set thine house in order, for thou shalt die (of this sickness)*[281]. Even if the physician observes that his patient is near death, he should still prescribe for him "eat this and do not eat that; drink this and do not drink that; but do not tell him that his end is near"[282]. When the Syrian Ben Hadad sent to ask Elisha whether he (Ben Hadad) would recover from his illness, Elisha answered the messenger: *Go, say unto him, thou mayest certainly recover*[283]. In reality, however, God had revealed to Elisha that Ben Hadad would die.

It is perhaps no coincidence that, as far as can be ascertained, only the Hebrew language derives the name of the physician, *rophé,* from a root which means "alleviate, assuage". The designations in other languages, insofar as they do not identify the physician with a magician, derive his name from the root meaning "knowledge".

*Magician (sorcerer):*
Sanscrit: *blishay;* Persian: *bizashik;* Armenian: *pjishg;*[284] Celtic: *leigis,* from *lepagi,* conjurer[285]; Gothic: *leikeis;* Ancient German: *lahhi;* Middle Ages German: *lachenaere,* jester[286]; Arabic: *tebib;* Ethiopian: *saraja,* heal and conjure[287]; Greek: *iatros,* from *ios* meaning *pharmakon,* magic herb[288], perhaps also "physician" from (the Greek) *erdein, facere sc. sacrificium;* according to Grimm 1:577, however, it is derived from *archiatros.* The Syrian *asja* and the Assyrian *asu* also belong to this derivation.

*Knowledge:*
Egyptian: *sun(suen) von sa;* Coptic: *saein;* Sanscrit: *vaidja* from *vid;* Latin: *medicus,* from *medh,* to be wise; Arabic: *chakim, sapiens.*

Gesenius already has the assertion[289] that *rophé* means tailor, our Heavenly mender as Luther said, since to the Arabs the word *rapha* means "to sew" (from whence the *raphe* of our anatomists), and because the Egyptian embalmer, the *paraschist,* is also called *rophé* in the story of the Patriarchs. Neither proof is

---

277. *apokteinein men, opothneskein de me.* Stobäus Florileg 6a,ed. Meineke 4:2
278. *Histor. Natur.* 29:8. *Medico tantum hominem occidisse impunitas summa est.* cf. Cassiodorus, Book 6, epistle 19
279. *Tosefta* Gittin 4:6
280. *Leges* 9:865, ed. Schneider.Paris 1852 fol 427
281. Second Kings 20:1
282. Eccles. Rabbah 5:6
283. Second Kings 8:10

284. Pictet in Kuhns *Ztschr. f. Vergl. Sprachforschg.* 5:24
285. Holder. *Alt-Celtischer Sprachschatz.* Leipzig 1904, 2:170
286. Klug. *Etym. Wörterbuch der Deutschen Sprache.* Strassburg 1910 p.24
287. Fränkel. S. *Die Aram. Fremdwörter im Arab.* Leiden 1886 p.260
288. Curtius, *Griechische Etymol.* p.384
289. *Thesaurus.* ed. 2 Vol. 3:1301

valid. The *paraschist* literally is "the one who slits open". This activity alone is his important one, not the sewing, for it is uncertain whether or not the latter (i.e. sewing up a corpse after embalming) was done at all. Noldeke has shown[290] that *rophé* in the sense of physician is a general Semitic term that has been in use for quite some time and from which the individual Semitic roots have not yet been differentiated. Can it be believed that in those ancient times, suturing of bloody wounds was already known and said to be the professional function of the physician *kat'exohen*?

The limits of human (medical) skill were certainly recognized. The Lord Himself threatened the disobedient people of Israel with punishment, consisting of illnesses from which there is no cure[290a]. Chronic illness makes light of the physician, says Sirach[291]. When a braggart offered to straighten the hump of a hunchback, the latter retorted in ridicule: if you could do that, you would be called a great physician *(rophé umman)* and command large fees.[292]. Even the skilled physician who achieves palliation in his patient is powerless when it comes to illness of his own body. When Rabbi Chanina was ill, he lamented: "when I was outside (healthy), I could be a surety (helper) for others, but now that I am myself in trouble, I must seek others to help me"[293]. A Talmudic saying in regard to the physician is: "a prisoner cannot free himself from jail"[294]. And a proverb exhorts the one who sees a splinter in the eye of another, but not a beam in his own eye: "physician, (first) heal your own lameness"[295]. In Jesus' time the phrase was: "physician, heal thyself (first)"[296]. The physician tolerated this inevitable situation with dignity, and one physician suffering from profuse lacrimation said with grim humor: "one of my eyes is crying for the other"[297].

## XII   Physicians' Fees

In those days of simple and straightforward thinking, it went without saying,that the physician's work called for payment. The often-cited Biblical phrase *and cause him to be thoroughly healed*[298] is interpreted by the translations of *Onkelos* and *Jonathan*, the Septuagint and the Vulgate (and thence also Luther): "he must pay the physician's fee". If the offender in a case of personal injury tells the injured person to be healed in the (free) "public clinic", the latter may retort: "A physician who heals for nothing is worth nothing"[299]. An agreement for lump sum payment for future services of a physician is also mentioned in the Talmud. According to the advice of Rabbi Yochanan, heirs who are obligated to provide medical care for their constantly-ill widowed mother can make an agreement with a physician for an all-inclusive fee for which the latter will constantly treat the patient[300]. I can find no mention in the Talmud of a difference in the fee paid to a physician for treating free people, slaves or freed persons, as is the case in the Code of Hammurabi.

Hammurabi has special prices varying between two and ten *shekels,* depending upon whether the case involves minor or major surgery, and according to whether the patient is a free man, or an inmate of a poorhouse, or a slave[301]. Fees for the treatment of internal illnesses are not specified, and, as far as I am

290. *Zeitschr. Deut. Morg. Gesellschaft* 40:723
290a. Deut. 28:27
291. Sirach 10:10
292. Sanhedrin 91a
293. Song of Songs Rabbah 2:16. fol 19a. Romm
294. Berachoth 5b
295. Genesis Rabbah 23:4
296. Luke 4:23; Cf. Sirach 18:20
297. Lamentations Rabbah 1:16 fol 18b Romm
298. Exodus 21:19
299. Baba Kamma 85a
300. Kethuboth 52b
301. Paragraphs 215, 216, 221-223, 227

aware, are not even mentioned. For the failure of an operation, the hands of the physician were cut off in the case of a free person[302]; a slave had to be replaced.

A person who possesses remedies which his neighbor urgently requires should not charge him more than the usual price. If, during his time of need, the patient agreed to an excessive price, because the remedy was otherwise not available, he still only has to pay the normal price. If under such circumstances, however, the physician asked for a very large fee, then the acquiescence of the patient is binding, although the conduct of the physician is not proper. For the object of the sale is the knowledge and skill of the physician, and this cannot be appraised in monetary terms[303].

In general, in antiquity, it seems to have been customary to pay the physician's fee in advance. When David prays: *Be gracious unto me, O God, according to Thy mercy*[304], he resembles a person who has a wound on his hand. The physician says: "You cannot be healed; for the wound is large and your money bag small!" To which the patient replies: "Take everything that I possess; the remainder supplement with your own, but have mercy upon me"[305] The Psalmist prays further: *Against Thee only have I sinned. . . that Thou mayest be. . . in the right when Thou judgest*[306]. Here he resembles a person who broke a limb and who says to the physician who looks amazed at the extent of the injury: "I have only injured myself so greatly so that you can earn much money from me"[306a]. Whosoever has pain in the eyes should pay the physician money in advance, although the patient's cure is still uncertain[307].

It is not possible to ascertain whether the intent was to criticize Greek or Roman circumstances, because, as already mentioned, the custom of payment in advance was general[308]. The father of Aspasia could not afford the payment in advance for the elimination of a *phyma mohtheron* (nodule?). Therefore the physician refused to administer the treatment, and the commentator does not complain at all about the lack of humanitarianism[309]. Hippocrates advises physicians, for purely practical reasons, not to stipulate the fee before undertaking the treatment of a patient; for the fear that the physician can simply let the patient lie in his sickbed, if no agreement is reached regarding the fee, is not without influence on the success of the treatment. Nevertheless, he is sufficiently liberal to advise that the physician take into consideration the financial circumstances of the patient, and to occasionally treat *gratis* a *xenos* (guest or foreigner) or a poor person[310]. His answer to the Abderites proves nothing[311]. In Rome, too, payment in advance for the physician's services was the rule. Plinius[312] speaks of the greedy monetary demands made in Rome by immigrant Greek physicians even before the termination of the illness: *ne avaritiam quidem arguam rapacesque mundinas pendentibus fatis.*

In the Middle Ages we find the same thing in the case of the Salernitans. In the famous didactic poem, we find the following: *dum dolet infirmus, instanter quaerat nummos vel pignus habere*[313]. Probably according to this standard, Isaac Judaeus writes: determine your fee when the illness increases.[314]

Concerning the amount of the fee charged by the Talmudic physicians, there are no statements. If one wishes to draw an analogy from the situation in Greece, the fees were barely sufficient. The budget of an aristocratic gentleman, as recorded by

302. Paragraph 218
303. *Yoreh Deah* 336:3
304. Psalms 51:3
305. Midrash Psalms and *Yalkut, ad. loc.*
306. Psalms 51:6
306a. Midrash Psalms and *Yalkut, ad. loc.*
307. Kethuboth 105a
308. See also L. Freidländer. *Sittenge-schichte Roms.* 1:305 Leipzig 1881
309. Aelian. *Var. Hist.* 12:1. Ed. Hercher Vol.

2 p.117; Cf. Achilles Tatius 4:15. Ed. Jacobs p.97
310. *Praecept.* Ed. Littre. Vol. 9 p.255 No. 4 and 6
311. *ibid* p.327
312. *Hist. Natur.* 29:8
313. Chapt. 5. See Pagel. *Deontologie.* Berlin 1897 p.12
314. *Magazin für die Wissenschaft des Judentums.* Vol. 11. 1885 No. 39

Diogenes Laertius, allows one to draw a conclusion from circumstances similar to ours: "for the cook 200 *thalers,* for the physician 5 *pennies,* and for the courtesan 1400 *thalers*"[315].

Naturally, individual physicians who were exceptionally prominent received higher fees. Charmis relieved a patient of 200,000 *sesters.* The surgeon Alcon, under Claudius, could pay a fine of 10 million *sesters* and he earned as much in the course of a few years[316].

The handling of the question of fees in post-Talmudic times is rather unusual. It is taught[317] that every person must be of assistance to another in the return of a lost object, which also includes the restitution of one's lost health. A person is thus fulfilling an obligation for which he should expect no earthly reward, just as the judge or teacher of the Divine word (receives no payment). However, already during the time of the Temple, when the official functions became so numerous that the judges had to be in court constantly, they were given a stipend from the Temple revenues, because *"nolens volens* they required something for their sustenance"[318]. Later, each community established a separate treasury account for this specific purpose[319]. Teachers of religious subjects too were granted this privilege of accepting remuneration. For if they were required to seek a livelihood from other trades, it is possible that teaching and learning might completely cease, because of the anxiety for the provision of the daily bread[320].

These considerations were also applied to the medical profession. It could not be demanded of any person that he renounce every occupation by means of which he could earn his daily bread, in order to serve suffering mankind, and to respond to every call, disregarding inclement weather and the time of day (or night), even disregarding his own physical condition. Therefore, it was necessary to permit the physician to accept remuneration, not for the advice given to the patient, but for the loss of time during which the physician could have been earning a living by other means.

# PART II
# THE BLOODLETTER

Whereas the physician in Judaism is considered to be a scholar, a *chakim,* the bloodletter, as his Talmudic name *umman* or *ummana* connotes, is an artisan. Sometimes he is also called *gara*[321], which is exactly what the late Latin expression *minutor* connotes.

Latin *gara* is *minuens sanguinem;* in Syriac *minuens barbam,* the cutter or barber. To consider that *umman* refers to (the Greek) *aimon* which means "shedder of blood" (i.e. murderer)[322] is sheer nonsense. Obadya of Bertinoro (the famous *Mishnah* commentator) also mentions the interpretation "blacksmith".

---

315. Book 6:5. Crates. p.15. ed. Cobet: *Tithei mageiro mnas thek'iatro thrahmen/Kolaki talanta pente, symvoulo kapnon/Porne talanton, philosopho triovolaon.* Give to the cook ten *mnas;* to the physician one *drachme;* to the courtesan five *talanta;* to the advisor *kapnon;* to the prostitute one *talanton* and to the philosopher one *triovolon*

316. Plinius 29:8. Cf Herodotus 3:131 and Friedländer. *op. cit.*

317. *Yoreh Deah* No. 336
318. *Tosafoth* on Bechoroth 29a *s.v. mah*
319. *Choshen Mishpat* 9:3
320. *Tosafoth loc. cit.* & Lipman Heller on Bechoroth 4:6
321. Kiddushin 82a; Kelim 12:4; Derech Eretz Zutta 10:2 In Syriac, *gara* refers only to cutting, not *minuere.* Löw
322. Bergel. *Die Medizin der Talmudisten* 1885 p.4

Other than his function as a bloodletter, the *umman* was also sometimes referred to as a circumciser[323]. He had no other occupation. As already proven earlier, the surgeon throughout Talmudic times was only the *rophé*. The functions of the barber were served by the *sappar*. This seems to be undoubtedly evident from the combination (or juxtaposition) of the two designations, *ummana* and *sappar*[324]. Jost and others[325] assert that the barber also served as a bloodletter but they overlooked the fact that their authority (i.e. Maimonides) explicitly speaks of "cupping of this (his) time"[326].

Even in documents from the Middle Ages, the *minutor* is differentiated from the *rasor* and also from the *chirurgicus,* although occasionally it happened in a cloister that a monk would execute all three functions simultaneously[327]. Even the physician did not perform bloodletting, and the Persian physician even today considers this operation to be below his dignity[328].

We have already spoken above about a *rophé umman*. This expression does not refer to the *medicus venam secans* or the surgeon who performs the most difficult type of surgery, as opposed to the barber-surgeon, as Kotelmann claims[329]. *Libellar umman* is a skillful writer, as opposed to a calligraphist[330]. Even the professional wood-gatherer is called *umman*[331].

In the Derenbourg edition (of the *Mishnah),* the word *chagamin* of the Arabic text is translated as *sapparim*; more correct would be the older translation *makkizim (bekeren* or bloodletters).

In the Jerusalem Talmud[332], it is reported that the workers in lamp factories *(ummanim)* used to singe the burners, so that they burn reliably. From this, Levy deduces that "the servants of the hairdressers singe our hair"[333].

Socially, the *umman* stood far below the physician. He was in fact considered to be an artisan, just as Johann Busch counts the *minutor* among the *officia mechanica,* together with the shoemaker and the tailor, the shepherd and the swineherd[334]. Moreover, his bloody profession — in legal matters he is often mentioned together with a butcher[335] — did not gain him particularly great sympathy. This in spite of the fact that among those who were born under the planet Mars (and therefore according to the Talmud[336], were predestined to shed blood), he, like his fellow sufferer, the ritual circumciser, had chosen a more noble profession, instead of becoming a killer of men or beasts. The rector of the school of higher learning in Pumpaditha was so modest that he "did not even summon a bloodletter to come to him"[337].

There are very few complimentary things which the Talmud says about an *umman*. He may not be appointed as leader of a community, or as an administrator *(epitropos)*[338]; nor may he be elected king or High Priest, not because he is inherently unsuited, but because his profession was held in low esteem. He becomes haughty

323. Shabbath 130a and 139b
324. Baba Metzia 97a
325. *Jüdische Geschichte* Vol. 2:24; notes
326. Commentary on Kelim 24:5
327. The convert Mercilius De Ysela, for a period of 40 years in the Windesheim cloister, was *fidelissimus fratrum infirmarius, rasor et minutor chirurgicusque expertissimus.* Busch. (1400-1475), *De Orig. Devot. Modern.* Chap. 28. (Geschichtsquellen der Provinz Sachsen. Vol. 19 p.318)
328. Stern. *Medizin, Aberglaube and Geschlechtsleben in der Türkei* Berlin 1903. 1:198
329. *Virchow's Arch.* Vol. 84 p.175.
330. Shabbath 133b
331. *Tosefta* Moed Katan 1:10. Additional

examples of this usage for *umman* are found in Löw. *Gesammelte Schriften* 3:376, notes
332. Jerushalmi Shabbath 2; 55a
333. Levy. *Neuhebräisches und Chaldäisches Wörterbuch.* Leipzig 1876-1889. 2:110b
334. In the Bodike Cloister *omnia officia mechanica hàbere probantur, videl. sartores, sutores...opiliones, subulcos, rasores, minutores et cetera similia officia eis necessaria.* Busch. *De Reformat. Monast.* Book 1, Chapt. 32. (Geschichtsquellen der Provinz Sachsen. Vol. 19 p.491. The same about the Molenbeke Cloister. *ibid.* Chapt. 33 p.493)
335. Baba Metzia 97a and 109a
336. Shabbath 156a
337. Berachoth 64a
338. Derech Eretz Zutta 10:2

because people place their lives in his hands. He becomes accustomed to eating much and well in his patients' houses, and thus he develops into a miser and a gourmet. His desire to be very busy awakens his jealousy against those who are constantly healthy. Finally, his necessary contacts with women during the course of his occupation make him suspect of committing immorality and theft[339].

Also disdained was the scarifier *(al-chagim)* of the Arabs, who was equivalent to the bloodletter of the Jews. It was an insult to call someone "the son of a lady scarifier". Three occupations were always practiced by the most base people: weaving, scarifying and tannery. "Arabs are all of equal value; only the weaver and the scarifier are not equal to their tribal brethren"[340].

Even in the Occident, the followers of the ancient bloodletter, the surgeon-barber, were not highly respected. Until the cabinet-council of Kaiser Wenzel (1406), they (bloodletters) were considered dishonest. In Germany, until the last century, no one would take a young man as an artisan's apprentice if he could not produce an affidavit attesting to the fact that his parents were honest, and that he was not related to any barber or surgeon-barber or shepherd or knacker[341].

Naturally, there were exceptions to this rule. The Talmud expressly describes the merit of a bloodletter named Abba[342], who not only had separate rooms for men and women, but who also insisted that women wear a special garment he had (which was slit at the shoulder) so that only the site of bloodletting was exposed[343]. Outside of his consultation room, he had a special place, a box into which the patients deposited the fees which he would charge. Those that could afford it put their fees there, and those who could not pay were not put to shame. If a scholar consulted him, he would not accept a fee from him. If he saw (after the bloodletting) that a person was poor, he would give him some money and say to him: "Go, strengthen yourself!"

The fees which were paid to the *umman* were certainly not very high. Whereas in the *sostrum* of the physician, the expression "money" *(mamon)* is used[344], the bloodletter was paid with *p'schite* (pennies). Rab (in the year 200 C.E.) determined as an assessment *(ekerysse* in Greek) that to bleed 100 cupping glasses full should cost only one *zuz*[345].

One hundred cupping glasses must have probably been used for a family bleeding. The fee is not so small if one realizes that for two *zuz* one could buy a fat kid (or goat)[346].

# PART III
# THE CIRCUMCISER

The obligation for the performance of circumcision rests primarily with the father of a child, and, in the era of the Patriarchs, with the leader of the tribe (Abraham)[347]. Nevertheless, women were always considered to be entitled (but not obligated) to perform circumcision. The Pentateuch in fact describes this act being performed by Zipporah, the wife of Moses, a woman who cut off the foreskin of her son[348], although

339. Kiddushin 28a
340. Goldziher in *Globus.* Vol. 66 No. 13
341. Möhen. *Gesch. d. Wiss. in d. Mark Brandenburg.* Berlin 1783 p.292 ff
342. Taanith 21b
343. This garment was certainly not used as a protection against the cold as suggested by Brecher (*Prager Med. Wochenschrift* 1876 p.228) since the text explicitly states "in

order not to see her exposed body".
344. Kethuboth 105a
345. Shabbath 129b according to Rabbi Chananel and *Aruch* and Rabbenu Tam. Rashi has a different explanation.
346. Berachoth 44b
347. Genesis 21:4
348. Exodus 4:25

the father was present. During the era of the Maccabees, Antiochus had two women killed because they circumcised their children[349]. According to Josephus[350], the children were also killed. There is no talk at all of punishing the father.

Even in Talmudic times, circumcision by the mother, perhaps as a residue from the ancient Matriarchate, was not a rare occurrence[351]. As a rule, however, the father would engage a technically skilled male proxy, a man emotionally less involved. Indeed this person was either the physician *(rophé)*, particularly for the performance of the circumcision of an adult[352], or more rarely the bloodletter, *umman,* who was probably properly licensed (to perform this operation), because the possibility of his dismissal is discussed[353]. Moreover, a type of lay specialist, the *mahola (mohel* in modern Hebrew) seems to have existed, concerning whose technical skills we find nothing laudable[354].

Furthermore, the *gozer, scindens sc. praeputium,* is probably an analogue of the *mohel* of our times; that is, he was a lay person. The Palestinian Talmud even speaks of a "street of circumcisers".

Rabbi Judah *ha-gozer*[355]; Rabbi Judah, Rabbi Judan *gazora*[356]; *gizra*[357]. Löw says *gazora* is correct since *gizra* is impossible. The "Street of Circumcisers"[358]. According to Moses Margolis[359], it should be "street of lumberjacks". The meaning of *chuldath ha-molim*[360] is also uncertain.

The opinions of the Rabbis were divided as to whether or not, in the absence of a Jew, a non-Jew is permitted to perform a circumcision[361]. The "most tolerant" Sages, however, demanded heathen physicians in general to be trustworthy (this does not apply to lay heathens). For experience had shown that the average heathen practitioner was feared; "he could press too hard with the scalpel" and intentionally inflict damage by incising the urethra. In practice, the perception of circumcision is that it is primarily a religious act, and it was (and still is) a strict rule, that the circumciser should not only be a Jew outwardly but he should consider the performance of circumcision as a religious duty. As a result, any circumciser who asked for a fee has been abhorred for centuries.

In an ancient handwritten *mohel* book in my possession, the following is written: "Israel Isserlein took a bath when invited to hold a child for circumcision; the *mohel* should also first take a bath because he is compared to a priest serving in the Temple". Although one can disagree with the underlying reason, this rule can only result in good.

# PART IV
# THE MIDWIFE

The obstetrical skill of the physician in antiquity, as already mentioned, was quite modest. The midwife, therefore, played a major role in childbirth. In the Bible, she is called *meyaledeth* or birth helper. During the time of Egyptian slavery, two are

349. Second Maccabees 6:10
350. *Antiquities.* Book 12 Chapt. 5:4
351. Shabbath 134a in the story of Rabbi Nathan.
352. King Izates. Josephus' *Antiquities.* Book 20 Chapt. 2:4 *(iatros)*
353. Shabbath 133b
354. *ibid* 135a concerning the child of Ada bar Ahaba
355. Shabbath 130b and Jerushalmi Shabbath 19; 16d
356. Jerushalmi Rosh Hashana 3; 59a and

Jerushalmi Megilla 1; 71a
357. Jerushalmi Kethuboth 5; 30a
358. Jerushalmi Erubin 5; 22d
359. *loc. cit.*
360. Jerushalmi Yoma 1; 38c and Jerushalmi Megilla 4; 75c
361. Jerushalmi Shabbath 19; 17a. Rabbi Jose says: circumcision requires no (religious) intent. Even a Samaritan may circumcise in honor of Mount Gerizim which he considers holy.

mentioned by name, Shiphra and Puah. They were instructed to carry out the order of Pharaoh, namely, to kill all newborn male infants of the Hebrews[362]. According to Talmudic tradition, these midwives were Jochebed, the mother of Moses, and Miriam, her daughter; or Elisheva, her daughter-in-law. The names Shiphra and Puah were said only to indicate their occupations: Shiphra because the midwife cleaned the baby *(shafar)*[363], and Puah because she only had to call *(po'ah)* the woman in labor and the child came forth[364].

Rabbi Chananel, a tenth-century Arabic commentator, remarks that in his time the Moslems used to whisper a magic incantation into the ears of pregnant women before they gave birth. We know from Plato that, in antiquity, one attributed such powers and knowledge to midwives. He quite seriously reports that "midwives could provoke labor pains by medical means or by magical incantations, and if they so desired could make the pains subside"[365].

Such designations of names, as just mentioned in the case of midwives, are quite common in the Talmud. The Preacher says: "a good name is better (more precious) than oil"[366].

The Bible commentators found it surprising that there should only have been two midwives for a population of at least one million people (600,000 adult men alone). They assume that either every woman served as her own midwife, as conjectured by the Aramaic translator[367], or alternatively, the two midwives listed by name, for whom "God made distinguished houses", were, according to Egyptian custom, the leaders of an entire caste system of midwives and were therefore the ones who received orders directly from the king. Ibn Ezra himself saw similar circumstances in many places[368]; he lived in Spain in 1150. According to Josephus, only Egyptian midwives could help deliver Hebrew women in response to the decree of Pharaoh, because only then could one expect strict compliance with the royal decree[369].

A midwife is also mentioned at the confinement of Rachel, which occurred on the road between Bethel and Bethlehem. This midwife was probably summoned from one of these two places. She talked to the pregnant Rachel until the latter died in childbirth[370]. During the twin birth of Tamar, the midwife tied a red thread to the hand of the child that put its hand out first, in order to assure it its primogeniture[371]. She must thus have recognized the presence of twins. "Women" stood around the wife of Phinehas, daughter-in-law of the high priest Eli[372]; a midwife, however, is not mentioned.

In the *Mishnah*, the midwife is mostly known by the name *chachama*, "the wise woman", just as the "weise Frau" of modern Germany and the "Sage femme" of the French. Rabban Gamliel the Elder ordained easing of the laws in regard to distances that a midwife is permitted to travel on the Sabbath[373]. Later, it was generally permitted for a pregnant woman on the Sabbath to call a "wise woman" from one city to another[374], irrespective of the distance. Occasionally in the *Mishnah*, the expression *chaya* is used for midwife; a *chaya* is described[375] who examined a pregnant woman whose baby had died.

In the *Gemara*, the name *chaya*, or *chayeta* in Aramaic, is used not only for midwife, but also denotes the pregnant woman as well as the parturient woman. Rarely do we find the Aramaic word *molada*[376], which is equivalent to the Hebrew

---

362. Exodus 1:15
363. Sotah 11b
364. Eccles. Rabbah 7:1
365. Plato *Theätet* 149C ed. Firmin-Didot fol 114
366. Eccles. 7:1
367. on Exodus 1:19
368. see his commentary on Exodus 1:15

369. *Antiquities.* Book 2 Chapt. 9:2
370. Genesis 35:17
371. *ibid* 38:28
372. First Samuel 4:20
373. Rosh Hashana 2:5
374. Shabbath 18:3
375. Chullin 4:3
376. Abodah Zara 26a

*meyaledeth*. For her own confinement, a midwife needs another midwife[377]. The expectation that a three-day-old baby could distinguish its mother's breast from that of another was ridiculed by Mar Samuel, who said he should then also remember the midwife who brought him into the world[378].

Among the requirements enumerated for a place where a scholar (who is probably already married) should take up residence is the presence of a physician[379]. A midwife is not listed, however. In reality, in the place where Bar Kappara lived, there was no midwife and "a maid servant went to deliver a woman"[380]. A proverbial saying is "while the midwife and the pregnant woman are quarreling, the child is lost"[381]. The attestation of a midwife during a twin birth: "this one came out first", is believed forthwith, if no objection is raised by anyone[382]. This is one of the rare instances where the testimony of a woman in court is recognized.

It is sad that one has to recommend extreme caution in the use of heathen midwives. A heathen should only render external birth help to a Jewish woman; not internally, however, lest she crush the infant in the womb[383]. In the absence of a surgeon, where embryotomy is indicated, a midwife can carry out the task. Under no circumstances, however, should one allow a heathen midwife to perform an embryotomy because one must be fearful lest she commit murder, i.e. the unnecessary killing of a live child[384]. Rabbi Meir is also of the opinion that such a midwife can intentionally kill a newborn infant by pressing on the fontanel, so that the killing can not later be recognized. Such a midwife, who was often hired to deliver Jewish women, boasted that she saw to it that the blood of her parturient patients flowed like a foaming river[385] The *Mishnah*[386] does not yet mention this exceptional rule, so that one can assume that bad experiences led the Rabbis in the *Gemara* to impose the ban on using heathen midwives. The Palestinian Sages had no misgivings about a heathen midwife, if she was generally known to be trustworthy[387]. But, the Babylonian Sages recommended that the heathen midwife not be left alone with the woman in labor[388].

A fee for a midwife is mentioned in a legal case. If a person accidentally strikes a pregnant woman so that she aborts, according to Biblical law, the one responsible must pay to the husband a fine determined by the court, as well as the expenses incurred[389]. According to the teaching of Rabbi Jose, the fee for the midwife is to be deducted from this estimate of the sum to be paid, since her husband would ordinarily have to pay this fee for a normal delivery. It appears that even for abortions, at least a *midwife* was engaged; whether a physician was also consulted remains undecided. Women who considered themselves clever believed that for an abortion they could forego even a midwife[390].

# PART V
# THE VETERINARIAN

Among animal physicians, the *Midrash* first mentions the Roman institution of horse surgeons who took on the designation *hippiatros*. The *hippiater* (or veterinary surgeon) cauterized a sick she-ass[391]. During the time of the Temple, persons were

377. Sotah 11a
378. Jerushalmi Kethuboth 5; 30a
379. Pesachim 113a
380. Jerushalmi Shabbath 18: 16c
381. Genesis Rabbah 60:3
382. *Tosefta* Baba Bathra 2:2
383. Jerushalmi Abodah Zara 40c
384. *Tosefta* Abodah Zara 3:4
385. Abodah Zara 26a
386. Abodah Zara 11:1
387. Jerushalmi Abodah Zara 40c
388. Abodah Zara 26a
389. Exodus 21:22
390. Baba Kamma 59a
391. Numbers Rabbah 9:5

engaged for a salary[392] to examine firstborn animals who were to be sacrificed. Prominently mentioned among these people are Ila[393] and Imla[394] from Yabneh. It is not clear from the sources whether they also healed sick animals.

The shepherd (or herdsman) is the birthhelper for animals; "as the shepherd places his hand in the womb of the animals and draws out the offspring, so too did God take Israel by force out of Egypt"[395]. The *Mishnah* already mentions the case of a herdsman who places his hand in the womb of an animal whose fetus had died[396].

Hammurabi mentions a cattle or donkey physician who charged fees and had liability for operations[397].

---

392. Jerushalmi Shekalim 6; 48a
393. Bechoroth 4:5
394. *Tosefta* Bechoroth 4:11

395. Midrash Psalms 107:4
396. Chullin 4:3
397. Code of Hammurabi No. 224-225

# CHAPTER II

## *THE PARTS OF THE BODY AND THEIR FUNCTIONS*
### (ANATOMY AND PHYSIOLOGY)

## INTRODUCTION

Knowledge of the structure of the human body was derived by the ancients from four sources:

1) From observation of external body parts.

2) From conclusions by analogy to observations made at the slaughter-house, in the kitchen and at the altar.

It is true that the Talmud explicitly warns against carrying over to human beings information learned from animals[1]. Nevertheless, there is no doubt at all that such conclusions were in fact drawn[2].

3) From incidental observations on remains of corpses that were found in the desert, and perhaps not infrequently, particularly in water-rich Babylon, in and near water.

In the Orient even today drowning is one of the death penalties, and the Code of Hammurabi is rather generous therewith. Furthermore, Galen states that the following are among the subjects of the above observations: unburied criminals, killed highwaymen, abandoned children, killed enemies, people thrown to wild animals, and patients with deep wounds and sores[3].

4) [From autopsies]. It is totally uncertain as to when a corpse was first dissected for scientific purposes. As a rule, the external parts of slaves and the internal organs of animals (apes) were displayed, as was done by Rufus[4]. The report of ɩ Plinius concerning Egyptian kings who performed autopsies[5] (*regibus corpora mortuorum ad scrutandos morbos insecantibus*) is usually thought to be apocryphal. However, the story is also found in an ancient part of the Talmud: Rabbi Ishmael related that Cleopatra, the queen of Alexandria, brought her pregnant slaves who were sentenced to death to the king, who cut them open and found that a male fetus was completely formed at forty days and a female fetus at eighty days of gestation[6].

---

1. *Tosafoth,* Chullin 42b; Zebachim 116a
2. for example Sanhedrin 78a
3. Galen. *De Admin. Anat.* Book 3 Chapt. 5, Kühn 2:385
4. Rufus. *De Appellat. Part.* ed. Daremberg and Ruelle p.134; Galen *loc. cit.*
5. Plinius. *Histor. Natur.* 19 Chapt. 27. Harduin 3:588
6. *Tosefta* Niddah 4:17. Even if one attempts to equate *lamelech* here with *lamalchuth* of the *Gemara*, the singular *karathan* would remain unexplained.

Naturally, the assertion of Plinius is not herewith proven as fact. However, one observes from the identical reports of two separate authors who were contemporaries but certainly independent of each other — Rabbi Ishmael was a Palestinian — that that story in the first century of the common era had many adherents. Certainly, one would not interpret the "Egyptian king" to represent a Pharaoh from the time of the hieroglyphics. All the evidence points much more to an Alexandrian regent, as is expressly stated in the narration of the Babylonian Talmud: "from Alexandria in Egypt"[7]. Indeed, in all probability, Alexandrian physicians can be regarded to be the first anatomists. One would not be in error if one agrees with Pagel[8] that Herophilus was the founder of human anatomy. It is therefore not surprising that, under such circumstances, even an Alexandrian king once dabbled in anatomy.

To make use of criminals condemned to death for anatomical studies is a custom which can be traced even into the eighteenth century. Some of the details concerning this matter can be found in Hyrtl[9].

The dispute as to whether these investigations involved the dissection of corpses or whether vivisection of live people was carried out, as Herophilus is alleged to have done[10], is of no great importance. There is no evidence in the Talmud *pro* or *contra* in this matter.

It is not easy to give a precise answer to the question as to whether or not the Jews performed autopsies altogether in antiquity. One of the numerous discoveries with which the flowery fantasy of Carmoly has blessed scientific knowledge is the statement that Rab, a Talmudic sage of the third century, "bought corpses and dissected them"[11]. The Talmud makes no mention thereof. On the other hand, it is incorrect to assume that it was impossible for the Jews to occupy themselves with anatomy because of the law, found throughout the Talmud, that anyone who touches a corpse becomes ritually unclean. It is true that touching a corpse makes one unclean for seven days and then a purification ceremony is required; in fact, if one only enters a tent or room in which a corpse is lying, one already becomes unclean even without touching it[12]. Nevertheless, the touching of a corpse is nowhere prohibited in Jewish law; on the contrary, the interment of the dead is considered to be a holy *duty* incumbent upon *every man*. One could only absolve oneself from this obligation in a place where a burial society, *chaburetha,* was active[13]. The priest, however, had certain restrictions[14]. Nevertheless, for his closest relatives, he too *had to* defile himself. The wife of Joseph the priest died on the eve of Passover, and he did not wish to touch her corpse so that he could still function as a priest on Passover. His fellow priests, however, pushed him against the corpse and called out to him that the matter of her burial was not up to his decision but was an obligation[15]. Even in the case of a stranger — for example, a corpse found in the field, *meth mitzvah* — if no lay people were available, the High Priest was legally bound to bury the deceased[16]. Indeed, the literal interpretation of Deuteronomy 34:6 is that God buried Moses with His own hands[17].

In order to bring the Paschal offering, everyone had to be ritually clean; for those who were "defiled by a corpse" — an *accidental* touching is not what is meant here — and could therefore not bring the offering, a separate, second Passover was

---

7. Niddah 30b
8. Pagel. *Geschichte der Medizin.* Berlin 1898 p.89
9. Hyrtl. *Lehrbuch der Anatomie des Menschen.* Vienna 1884 p.66
10. Celsus. *Praef.* p.7 of the edition of Almeloveen; Galen, *Admin. Anat.* 3:5, Kühn 2:385; Tertullian, *De Anima,* Chapter 10, Migne 2, Col. 703.
11. Carmoly. *Histoire des Médecins Juifs.* Brussels 1844 p.12. One should not blame Richard Landau (*Geschichte der Jüdische Aerzte.* Berlin 1895 p.15) for not recognizing this falsification in spite of its unwieldiness.
12. Numbers 19:11-14
13. Moed Katan 27b
14. Levit. 21:1-3
15. Zebachim 100a
16. *Sifre, Naso* 26 p.9a, ed. Friedmann
17. *Rashi loc. cit.*

instituted[18]. This would certainly not have been done if defilement through touching a corpse were considered sinful.

In reality, the restraint among Jews in performing autopsies was due to the aversion of *wounding* a corpse, because, in all circumstances, this would be considered a desecration of the dead, *nivul hameth*. The following Talmudic passage, important also for other reasons, shows how far the Jews applied the law of prohibiting the desecration of the dead and how strictly this law was observed. An example is used to illustrate that, in passing judgement, a court must be guided by obvious probabilities and daily experiences, and not by a theoretical possibility. In this connection, the following is stated: in a court trial concerning murder, the objection was raised that the alleged victim might have been ill and died a natural death. When the suggestion was made that the corpse be examined, it was prohibited because the body would thereby be mutilated. Even if one would argue that in order to save a life (i.e. the life of the accused) we should be allowed to mutilate the body, the answer is that, were it not for the fact that we follow the usual occurrence, there is always the rare possibility that there had been a mortal wound in the place where the victim was struck by the sword[19].

Similarly, even in a civil court case, it was not permitted to exhume a body only to observe the corpse, because exhumation is considered to constitute a desecration (*nivul*)[20]. The law prohibiting the mutilation of a corpse also hinders the performance of embalming of the dead among the Jews; embalming is not possible without damaging the corpse. Furthermore, according to the report of Diodorus Siculus[21], the Egyptian *paraschist* who cut open the abdomen of a corpse had to flee, because the people threw stones at him as a mutilator of the dead; they were of the opinion that he who inflicts a wound on a corpse, *somati traumata poiounta,* is deserving of such hatred.

Performing a Caesarian section on a recently deceased pregnant woman is not considered a mutilation of the dead. The *Mishnah* already requires or suggests that this procedure be carried out[22]. Consideration for the dead must be set aside, when there is the possibility, however remote, of saving a life (i.e. that of the unborn baby).

One passage in the Talmud seems to contradict the prohibition of the dissection of the dead: "once the disciples of Rabbi Ishmael, in the year 100 C.E., cooked — I will presently discuss the term "cooked" — the body of a prostitute who had been condemned by the king to be burnt to death, in order to ascertain the number of limbs of the human body"[23]. It is noteworthy that Rabbi Ishmael himself did not participate in the autopsy in view of the fact that he was of priestly descent[24] and because it is emphasized that he was not even informed if the corpse was a male or a female. If one assumes that the case concerned the corpse of a *heathen* prostitute, then all difficulties fall away.

The above case concerned *the cooking* (or boiling — *shalak*) *of the corpse.* This method of anatomical preparation, particularly for the study of bones, was used by anatomists of the Middle Ages, and among them, above all, Vesalius (born 1514). In those days, the usual procedure to exhibit the bones consisted of placing the body in lime for eight days; then one put it into a swift-flowing river where the lime and the macerated pieces of flesh were washed away. Vesalius correctly states that with such preparations the fine details of the forms of bones cannot be recognized, not to mention the difficulty of the method. He therefore recommends that corpses be cooked

---

18. Numbers 9:10
19. Chullin 11b
20. Baba Bathra 154b
21. Siculus. Book 1 Chapt. 91, ed. Dindorf
  and Müller. *Sammlung.* Firmin-Didot. Paris

1878 Vol. 17 p.73
22. Arachin 1:4
23. Bechoroth 45a
24. Chullin 49a

and he gives precise instructions therefor[25]. Nevertheless, he is not the discoverer of this method; his contribution consists merely in the fact that he converted a procedure which had been practiced by lay people for many centuries into a scientifically useful method. Long before him, the bones of the knights who came to Italy with German troops were cooked in order to remove the flesh from them so that they could be returned to their native land for burial, until an edict by Pope Boniface VIII in the year 1301 put an end to this indecency[26].

It is very difficult to decide whether or not this type of bone preparation was already practiced in antiquity. Galen only states that a cooked lower jaw (*epsomenon*) separates into two parts[27], and that the structure of the vertebrae can be clearly recognized when the three or four parts of the sacrum become separated by cooking (*yph epseseos*)[28]. However, these citations could equally well refer to kitchen (i.e. animal) anatomy, especially since Galen's objects of observation were animals (usually monkeys). Further evidence for cooking of corpses in antiquity is not found even in the writings of the scholar Jacob Philip Hartmann[29]; such does not therefore seem to exist. If the cooking of *human* corpses had been portrayed anywhere in the writings of the ancients, Vesalius would certainly not have failed to point it out, and Galen himself would not have been satisfied with only an allusion.

Thus, the expression in the above-cited Talmudic passage is even more striking. It appears completely without emphasis or explanation. One could hypothesize that it refers to a report of the Alexandrian physicians, were not Rabbi Ishmael, whose disciples originated the citation, a Palestinian. Unfortunately, we also know very little about the Alexandrian physicians and their methods. Other than the already-mentioned report of Celsus concerning the vivisection practiced by Herophilus, only Galen speaks of the activity of this great anatomist, but he only uses the expression *anatemno* (i.e. dissector)[30].

For the preparation of foods, particularly meat, the Hebrews have the designations: *tzalah* meaning to roast, *shalak* (only in the Talmud) meaning to steam or to stew, and *baschal* meaning to cook in water[31]. The corresponding expressions of the Greeks are *aptao, pesso, (pepto)*, and *epso*[32]. The last expression, meaning to bake, is used by Galen, as mentioned above. For this reason, his procedure cannot be identical with that of the Talmud.

In order to resolve this difficulty, the dictionaries, following the precedent of Schönhak, offer an additional meaning for the word *shalak:* "to cut, to split, to dissect". Since only the Syrian (Aramaic) *schelak* (and not *selak*) can be considered to be equivalent to the Hebrew *shalak,* then the Arabic analogue can only be *salak,* which has as little equivalence to the above-suggested meaning "to dissect" as the Arabic *schalak*. The allusion to the Aramaic *tzalak* is not acceptable. Löw states that the Assyrian *schlk* which, according to Delitzsch[33], has the meaning "to cut out, to cut open, to slit open", cannot be used for comparison. I remain firm with the basic interpretation "to cook". I therefore assume that the corpses were "cooked" — *shalak* is a stronger type of cooking than *baschal*.

---

25. Vesalius. *De Corporis Hum. Fabrica.* Book 1 Chapt. 40 ed. Boerhave. Lugd. Bat. 1725 fol. 131
26. Haeser. *Geschichte der Medizin* 1:735; Hyrtl, *Lehrbuch des Anatomie* p.50
27. Galen. *De Ossibus ad Tiron.* Chapt. 6, Kühn 2:754
28. *ibid* Chapt. 11. Kühn 2:762
29. Hartmann, *Disquis. Hist. De Re Anat. Veterum.* Regiom. 1693. New edition by

Kurella, Berlin 1754 p.368. Professors Ritter von Töply and Pagel were also unable to provide me with additional proofs
30. Galen. *De Uteri Dissect.* Chapt. 5 & 9. Kühn 2:895,900
31. See contrasts in Nedarim 20b & *Tosefta* Betzah 2:1
32. In Plutarch: *ephtha kai opta kai pepta.*
33. Delitzsch. *Wörterbuch* No. 666

The report in the Talmud must therefore remain unexplained.

# PART I
# THE EXTERNAL BODY FORM
## I   The Head

Concerning the *head, rosh,* the king of limbs[34], one distinguishes between the hairy part and the countenance, the *panim.* That part of the hairy portion of the head which corresponds to the location of the anterior fontanel[35] is called the *kodkod* or crown. Absalom was very handsome: *from the sole of his foot to the crown of his head there was no blemish on him*[36]. The Lord will smite the disobedient nation of Israel with leprosy *from the sole of the foot to the crown of the head*[37]. Satan smote Job with bad leprosy *from the sole of his foot to the crown of his head*[38]. In certain poetic settings, the word *kodkod* is used parallel to "head"[39].

According to the teaching of the school of Rabbi Yannai, the *kodkod* is the place on the head where *tefillin* (phylacteries) should be worn. Since a fontanel no longer exists on the skull of an adult and its former position is marked only by the point of intersection of the coronary and sagittal sutures, one must return to the earliest time in infancy to determine its size. In general, the size of two fingerbreadths is probably correct. Rabbi Samuel, who is of the opinion that there is sufficient room on the *kodkod* to wear two *tefillin*[40], probably carries over the childhood size of the fontanel to the skull of an adult, which means the size that the fontanel would be in an adult if it grew along with the skull.

The *kodkod,* therefore, corresponds to the *bregma* of the Greeks. Aristotle says of it that it is the last bone of the body to become hard[41]. The word "fontanel" originated in the Middle Ages. In Plinius, the site is called *vertex palpitans*[42]. The Talmudic Sages call it "the place where the brain of a child is soft"[43] or "pulsating"[44]. As a result, the Aramaean translator directly translated the word *kodkod* of the text as *mocha* meaning brain[45].

The Greek translators of the Bible, however, never translate *kodkod* as *bregma,* but use the term *koryphe*[46]. This word means summit, whence is derived *koryphaios* meaning one who stands on top, a choir leader and the like. To us today, a *koryphae* is a very important person. This Greek word *(koryphe)* corresponds exactly to the Talmudic "*gobah* (elevation or highest point) on the head"[47]. To the anatomists, *koryphe* is the hair whorl, which lies in the middle of the *lissoma* of the hair, as stated by Aristotle[48]. This expression can also be found in the Bible in the words of the Psalmist *kodkod se'ar*[49].

The word *partzof*[50], equivalent to the Greek *prosopon,* is rarely used to designate *the face,* instead of the usual Hebrew *panim,* with which it is sometimes connected. A corpse can only be identified with certainty if the face *(partzof panim),* together with the nose, is clearly recognizable[51]. The first man, Adam, is said to have had a double

---

34. Aboth de Rabbi Nathan 31:3
35. Menachoth 37a
36. Second Samuel 14:25
37. Deut. 28:35
38. Job 2:7
39. for example Genesis 49:26
40. Erubin 95b
41. Aristotle. *Histor. Anim.* 1:7
42. Plinius. *Histor. Natur.* 7:1
43. Menachoth 37a; Löw states that the textual reading *rophes* should be abandoned
44. Jerushalmi Erubin 10; 26a
45. Second Samuel 14:25
46. In addition to Job *loc. cit.,* they freely translate thusly in Isaiah 3:17; Jeremiah 2:16 & 48:45
47. Menachoth 37b
48. Aristotle *Hist. Anim.* 1:7
49. Psalms 68:22
50. Löw states that it should not be vocalized *partzuf*
51. Yebamoth 16:3

face, and Eve was created from one of these two faces, not from one of his ribs[52]. When a human artist wishes to create a large number of figures, he makes one form according to which he fashions all the figures, each of identical form and appearance. Not so the Lord; no person is exactly like another. The appearances of all people are different so that a person can not appropriate the wife or property of another[53].

Faces, even of idolatrous images, were also engraved into signet rings or were fashioned thereon as embossed work[54], or were even embroidered into fabrics[55]. Fountains which led water to the cities were also adorned with faces (heads) and these were therefore called *partzafoth*[56].

The upper part of the face is the forehead or *metzach,* called *paddachath* in the *Mishnah.* The obstinate one has a brass forehead[57], and the defiant one has a hard forehead[58]. To have "the forehead of a whore"[59] is a designation of shamelessness and insolence. The author of the Apocalypse recognizes a characteristic mark on the forehead of the Great Prostitute, *tes pornes tes megales*[60]. This indicates her profession.

On both sides of the forehead are located the *temples, rakka,* from *rak* meaning the thin parts of the skull[61]. The Talmudic expression for temple is *tzida.* The term *tzida,* which is called *kilkul* in the *Mishnah,* must be distinguished from *bath tzida,* the *andiphi*[62]. The former is said to be the upper larger part, and the latter the lower-smaller, thin, hairy portion of the temple which women epilate by painting lime thereon. It probably refers to the whiskers of a woman. The "corner of the head", the circumferential cutting off of which is forbidden by the Bible[63], is also said to refer to the temples, the "end of the head"[64].

The word *lechi,* which refers to the jaw, may also mean the cheek. With a new jawbone which Samson found, he slew a thousand Philistines[65]. To strike someone on the cheek is a great insult[66]. Rabbi Akiba thought that Bar Kochba was the Messiah. However, Rabbi Yochanan said: even when *bilchayeka* grass will grow, the true Messiah will not yet have arrived[67]. If the upper jaw of a priest protrudes over the lower jaw or vice-versa, he is unfit to serve in the Temple because of his unsightly appearance, irrespective of whether or not there is a bone contained therein[68]; it matters not whether the defect is a malformation of the jaw or an abnormally large development of the lip. If the lower jawbone of an animal is gone, one can maintain the animal alive by stuffing food into its gullet[69]. If one desires to use a flowery expression to denote the jaw of an animal, one calls it the "bone of the mouth"[70] or "in the mouth"[71].

The Aramaic translation of *lechi* is *loa,* both for man as well as for animal. For a donkey that has an injury, one makes a "neck ladder" (probably a type of jaw bar) or a jaw receptacle (*be loa,* a mouth basket), so that it not turn its head backwards and chafe the wound afresh[72].

Another synonym in the *Mishnah* is *leseth.* The author of Lamentations states that it is good that a man bear a yoke in his youth and become accustomed to insult early in life and stretch out his cheek (*listha*) to one who strikes him[73]. According to the

52. Berachoth 61a
53. Jerushalmi Sanhedrin 4; 22b
54. *Tosefta* Abodah Zarah 5:2
55. *Tosefta* Shekalim 3:14
56. *Tosefta* Abodah Zarah 6:6
57. Isaiah 48:4
58. Ezekiel 3:7
59. Jeremiah 3:3
60. Apocalypse 17:5
61. Judges 4:21
62. Shabbath 8:4. The explanation of the word given by Krauss is unsatisfactory. Löw states

it is *metopion.*
63. Levit. 19:27
64. Makkoth 20b
65. Judges 15:15
66. Job 16:10
67. Jerushalmi Taanith 4; 68d
68. Bechoroth 40a
69. Chullin 55b
70. Bechoroth 6:10
71. Bechoroth 40b
72. Shabbath 54b; *lo'a,* Proverbs 23:2
73. Lamentations 3:30

translation of Jonathan, the report in the Bible concerning the aged Moses[74] — the usual interpretation is: *his freshness (turgor) did not abate* — means: "the teeth of his jaw were not loosened". The nose and the cheeks can be sufficient to identify a mutilated corpse[75]. The cheeks are required, together with the forehead, eyebrows, eye, ear and "depression of the beard", in order to differentiate the head of a human premature birth from that of an animal[76].

The renowned allegory of old age: *Rejoice, o young man, in thy youth*[77] *before the sun and the light and the moon and the stars become darkened*[78], is interpreted by the Talmud[79] as follows: rejoice before the forehead and nose and soul and cheeks become darkened from old age. The *Midrash* has a better interpretation: the sun is the bright countenance, the light is the nose, i.e. the seat of respiration and of life, the moon is the forehead, and the stars are the cheekbones which become prominent in old age[80].

The Talmudic expression *lugma* is the same as the Arabic *lukma,* but not *lygmos,* which the Greeks use to designate the ability to swallow. The usual Talmudic textual reading is *melo lugmav,* which means "full cheeks" or "a mouthful". The amount referred to, according to one opinion, is as much as one can hold in *one* cheek or in *one-half* of the mouth[81]. According to the other opinion, *melo lugmav* refers to a true mouthful which, on the average, amounts to one-quarter *log,* which is approximately one-sixth of a liter[82].

"One gulp" is called *gemiah, gemiyah* or *gemi'ah*[83].

The *chin* is designated as *santer.* He who walks with his chin sideways or has his turban turned backwards, or sits cross-legged belongs to the haughty of spirit[84]. When Rebbe yawned, he placed his hand on his chin so that one should not see his open mouth[85].

Immanuel Löw[86] already doubts the justification of the translation of *santer* as *anthereon* as found in many dictionaries. To me, in addition to the phonetic difficulty (it should at least be called *santher*), the fact of the matter is that the Greek word (*anthereon* ) is only used by poets and as a professional term by physicians, whereas the general populace uses the term *geneion.*

It is highly unlikely that the word *maktesch*[87] refers to any sort of anatomical designation. If one accepts the interpretation of *Rashi* and others that it means the "tooth alveolus", one must presuppose that a tooth fell out from the donkey's jawbone when the Philistines were struck by it. Even then, the definite article is striking. Much more likely is the translation of Levi ben Gerson (*Ralbag* ): "The Lord cleaved the hollow-like rock (crater) which was located in a place called *Ramath lechi*"[88].

Josephus also has the term "rock"[89].

## II   The Neck

The skin of the neck, *tzavar,* is normally smooth. Rebecca placed the skin of the kid on the "smooth of the neck" of Jacob so that his father could not distinguish him from the hairy Esau[90]. A beautiful neck is like the tower of David[91] or like a tower of

---

74. Deut. 34:7
75. Jerushalmi Yebamoth 16; 15c
76. Jerushalmi Niddah 3; 50c
77. Eccles. 11:9
78. *ibid* 12:2
79. Shabbath 151b
80. Eccles. Rabbah 12:2
81. Jerushalmi Yoma 8; 44d
82. Yoma 80a
83. Compare Shabbath 77a

84. Derech Eretz Rabbah 11:15
85. Berachoth 24b
86. in Krauss. *Lehnwörter. s.v. santer*
87. Judges 15:19
88. see verse 17
89. *kata tinos petras.* Josephus, *Antiquities,* Book 5, Chapter 8:9
90. Genesis 27:16
91. Song of Songs 4:4

ivory[92]. Victorious generals placed their feet on the necks of the (captured) enemy as a sign of victory, not in order to kill the enemy[93]. A yoke was placed on the neck of the conquered[94]. The Egyptian king hung a gold chain on the neck of the newly appointed regent Joseph[95]. A father has "his hand on the neck of his son", meaning he has control over him, as long as he is young[96].

There are divided opinions in the Talmud as to whether one should first marry a wife and then study Torah or vice-versa. Those who support the first opinion offer the reasoning that a married man is not disturbed in his Torah study by his evil inclination. Those of the latter opinion are concerned that household worries would impede proper concentration: with a millstone around the neck[97], can one study Torah? Both parties finally agree that one cannot lump all people together but must individualize[98].

In general, the nape of the neck, *oreph,* is used in the figurative sense. Moses repeatedly calls the people of Israel "stiffnecked"[99], obstinate (headstrong), as we too use this term figuratively. Those who flee are said to turn their backs[100] to their enemies[101].

The Talmudic translation for *oreph* is mostly *kedal* or *kedala*[102]. The head covering of Rabbi Meir was blown off by the wind when he ran rapidly, so that the passersby could see his *kedal* from behind[103]. Those who were jealous of Moses thought that the building of the Tabernacle was to his advantage. They said: "look at his obese neck!" Therefore Moses gave them detailed accounts and called the Tabernacle[104] "the Tabernacle of the testimony" (evidence for computations)[105].

The Biblical and Talmudic *maphreketh* is the vertebra *(perek)* in the cervical portion of the vertebral column, and therefore not the *o notos* of the Septuagint, which means back. Rather, *maphreketh* refers to "cervical", as the Vulgate correctly translates. Severance of the *maphreketh* leads to death in both man[106] and animal[107].

The *Targum* translates *maphreketh* as *perikta* or *afkutha.*

*Parkedan* is someone who is lying on his back. When eating, one should not lie on one's back, but recline on the side according to Oriental custom, supporting oneself on the left elbow[108]. One should not lie on one's back while praying because it is contrary to proper decorum[109].

## III   The Shoulders

In the narrowest sense of the word, some people interpret *shoulder* to refer only to the prominence produced by the deltoid muscle; others consider it to be the rounding of the muscles on the head of the upper arm. Shoulder properly refers to the whole section bounded by the clavicle and posteriorly by the ridge of the shoulder blade. One can thus distinguish between an anterior and a posterior shoulder. One can carry loads on either part depending on the type of load. An elongated object such as a pole is carried on the anterior part of the shoulder, whereas a round object such as a sack of grain is carried on the posterior part of the shoulder. Biblical Hebrew distinguishes both parts and calls the anterior part *kathef* and the posterior part *shekem.*

When Abraham walked with Isaac to the latter's offering, he (Isaac) took the wood of the burnt offering[110], like someone who — according to Roman custom —

92. *ibid* 7:5
93. Joshua 10:24
94. Jeremiah 28:10
95. Genesis 41:42
96. Kiddushin 30a
97. in that the head is stretched through the central opening of the stone
98. Kiddushin 29b
99. Exodus 32:9; 34:9 etc.
100. literally: nape of the neck
101. Joshua 7:8
102. Löw. *Mishnah; Mechilta* Deut. ed. Hoffmann Vol. 1 Chapt. 4:13
103. Jerushalmi Betzah 5; 63a
104. Exodus 31:18
105. Exodus Rabbah 51:6
106. First Samuel 4:18
107. Chullin 113a
108. Pesachim 108a
109. Berachoth 13b
110. Genesis 22:6

carries the stake on which he is to be executed, upon his shoulder (*kethefo*)[111]. So too, the members of the family of Kohoth carried the holy vessels on their *kathef*, the anterior part of the shoulder[112], after these vessels had been placed by the priests on the special carrying stretchers[113].

While bathing in the wells of Tiberias, a person would place his hand on the shoulder of the person who stood before him in order to support himself[114]. In Babylon, captured Jews had sacks of sand placed on their shoulder (*kathef*), until they were stooped over[115]. When the dispersed Israelites eventually reassemble in their native city of Jerusalem, *they will bring their sons in their chotzen*, the bosom created by closed arms, *and their daughters will be carried upon their shoulders*[116]. The ambiguous poetic portrayal of Benjamin, the favorite of God, resting "*ben kethefav*"[117], which is usually translated "between the shoulders" is explained in the same way. It obviously also means carrying between the anterior shoulders (similar to *chotzen*); thus, "he rests on his neck", or "on his bosom", as a nurse carries the suckling babe on her bosom (*chek*)[118].

On the other hand, the professional porter carries his load on the posterior shoulder; *he bows his shoulder to bear*[119]. A water bottle was also carried on this part of the shoulder[120]. The same was done to the pitchers into which young maidens drew water[121].

Shem and Japheth placed a garment on their posterior shoulders, *shekem*, and walked backwards towards their father Lot, who had disrobed in his drunkenness. In this manner, they were able to drop the cover on the nakedness of their father without having to look at it[122].

The expression of the poet who wrote the book of Job, who generally displays much medical knowledge, is very exact. Job states: *if I have lifted up my hand against the fatherless. . .then let mine "kathef" fall out of its "shekem"*[123], which means precisely: "let my head of the humerus fall out from the posterior shoulder (the shoulder blade)".

Against this distinction, it cannot be very important that in post-Biblical Hebrew a porter is called *kattaf* or *sabbal*, whereas no such trade designation exists for *schechem*. Löw states that since the latter word has no Aramaic support, it disappeared from the *Mishnah*.

The *axilla* or armpit is referred to as *beth hashechi*, meaning "the site of flexure", or simply *shechi*. According to general Oriental custom, women removed the hair from their armpits. Rabbi Yochanan forbids men from doing this act because it is a practice of women[124]. Rabbi Ammi said: many popular customs are noteworthy in that one should beware of them. For example, one should not place coins in the mouth, nor place food under the bed, nor carry bread under the armpits, because it is unappetizing[125]. It appears, however, that this advice was not generally followed[126].

## IV     The Arm

*Zeroa*, in the strict anatomic sense, refers only to the *shaft* of the upper arm, while the head of the humerus is considered to be part of the shoulder. Job states: if I lifted mine arm against an orphan, let it be broken off from its tube, i.e. the forearm[127]. The

---

111. Genesis Rabbah 56:3
112. Numbers 7:9
113. *ibid* 4:15
114. Jerushalmi Shabbath.1; 3a
115. Midrash Psalms on 137:3, p.262a
116. Isaiah 49:22
117. Deut. 33:12
118. Numbers 11:12
119. Genesis 49:15
120. *ibid*   21:14.   Pictorially   shown   by

Benzinger & Frohnmeyer in *Bilderatlas zur Bibelkunde*. Stuttgart 1905 No. 289
121. *ibid* 24:15
122. Genesis 9:23. *Onkelos & Jonathan:kethaf*
123. Job 31:21-22
124. Nazir 59a
125. Jerushalmi Terumoth 8;.45d
126. Jerushalmi Sanhedrin 6; 23c
127. Job 31:21-22

term *zeroa* or arm is very often used to portray power and might. God will break the arm of the wicked[128]. The *man of the arm*[129] is a mighty man. The arm of a person serves as a support for his friends; thus, women carry their friend in labor to the birthstool[130]. Similarly, the shepherd carries the lambs in his arm[131], and the Lord is our arm (i.e. support) every day[132]. The Lord brought Israel out of the land of Egypt *with a mighty hand and with an outstretched arm*[133].

The Torah decrees that a person *bind the laws of God on his hand*[134]. According to tradition, this site is the *kibboreth*[135], which is translated by *Rashi* as *badron* and explained by Rabbenu Tam[136] as the "elevation of the flesh (eminence) between the axilla and the elbow". It refers to the "prominence of the arm"[137], i.e. the belly of the biceps muscle which lies against the heart when the arm is placed flush against the thorax, so that these Divine words are literally *on thine heart*[138].

The connection between the upper arm and the forearm is effected by the *elbow joint,* the *atziley yedehen* in Hebrew or *marpek* in Aramaic. According to tradition, the admonition of Ezekiel that priests should not gird themselves "with sweat"[139] (i.e. in places where there is much sweat secretion) means "not below the loins (i.e. in the groin flexure) and not above the elbows (i.e. in the axilla) — in both places there is much sweat secretion — but at the height of the elbow and the lower ribs"[140]. It is considered to be an offense against the rule of revering the Holy Scriptures to place the unfolded scroll of the Torah on one's knees and to secure it with one's elbow while reading therefrom[141].

If someone vows to donate "the weight of his hand" in gold or the like to the Temple, Rabbi Judah says the amount is measured as follows: one inserts the arm up to the elbow into a vessel filled with water up to the top, whereby a certain amount of water is expelled. One then puts a quantity of the flesh of an ass with its bones and tendons into the vessel until it is full again to the top. One then removes this flesh and weighs it and this weight is the amount the man has to give to the Temple. Rabbi Jose, however, states that not all types of flesh and bones and tendons are alike in weight, volume for volume, and hence it is sufficient to estimate the approximate weight of the hand[142].

*Kaneh* is the *forearm*. This word, transferred from names of plants to bones[143], is also found again as *kanna* in the Indo-Germanic languages. It is naturally also found with the anatomists of the Middle Ages, to whom this word was probably simply transcribed from the Hebrew or from the corresponding Arabic word. Since every tube, including the lumen of bones, was called *kaneh,* one later differentiated the ulna or *kanna major* from the radius or small tube. In the Hebrew version of Avicenna, the bone of the upper arm (humerus) is called the *kaneh hazeroa*[144], the shinbone (tibia) is called "the large *kaneh* ", and the fibula is called "the small *kaneh* "[145].

*Kaneh* in the sense of forearm is rarely found in the *Mishnah*[146]. In Coelius Aurelianus, it is often used to denote "windpipe", such as *kanna gutturis*[147], as well as with the addition *quam arteriam (sc. asperam) vocant*[148].

---

128. Psalms 10:15
129. Job 22:8
130. Shabbath 129a
131. Isaiah 40:11
132. *ibid* 33:2
133. Deut. 26:8
134. Deut. 6:8
135. Menachoth 37a
136. *Tosafoth loc. cit.*
137. *Sifre* on Deut. 6:8
138. Deut. 6:6
139. Ezekiel 44:18
140. Zebachim 19a. Where the elbow naturally touches the body.
141. Soferim 3:11
142. Arachin 5:1
143. Löw states: for the history of the wanderings of this word, see Hehn's *Kulturpflanzen und Haustiere.* 6. Auflage 300
144. Hyrtl. *Das Arabische* p.9
145. *ibid* p.67
146. Probably only in Oholoth 1:8
147. Aurelianus *Acut.* Book 2 Chapter 16 p.115
148. Aurelianus. *Chronic.* Book 2 Chapter 12 p.396

The ell or *amma,* from the earliest part of antiquity up to the present time, was, and is, used to denote a measure of length, and not only for measuring draperies. Originally one designated an *amma* as the length of the forearm bone which one can easily, in its entire length, palpate on a live person, i.e. the ulna.

A similar measure of length in the Bible is *gomed,* and in the Talmud, *gurmida.* I cannot, however, prove that these refer to the ulna.

## V   The Hand

The word *yad* which, in the exact sense always refers to the hand, is also used to denote the entire arm — just like *cheir* of the Greeks[149] — perhaps only dialectically, somewhat in the same manner that the Germans use the expression that the entire foot hurts "from the toes up to the hips".

It is considered to be a "heathen practice" (i.e. superstition) to believe in a "lucky hand"[150]. Rabbi Meir taught: "when a person enters the world, his hands are clenched as if to say, 'The whole world is mine, I shall conquer it'; but when he takes leave of the world, his hands are spread open as if to say that he has acquired nothing from the world"[151]. For an oath, one raised one's hand in order to invoke God to serve as a witness[152]. The same image is used in reference to God Himself[153].

The *palmar surface* of the hand or *kaph,* actually the flatness above the curved palm, is distinguished from the back of the hand or *gab ha-yad* or *achar yad*[154]. The virtuous housewife gives a begger bread from her open palm, but to a deserving, needy person stretches out her closed hand[155]. During the crowning of a king, people clap their hands with joy; (more precise than the German *Klatscht in die Hände*)[156]. Rivers also clap their hands[157], as do the trees in the fields[158], when they pay homage to the Lord King. The Aramaic translation portrays the poet's picture by saying that the trees rustle their branches.

One also claps hands as a sign of ridicule and gloating[159], as well as for a "promise through a handshake". The epigrammatic poet warns: *do not be one of them that strike hands, or of them that are sureties for debts*[160]. Only a person without understanding shakes hands and becomes a security for another person[161]. The cupbearer placed the cup on the palm of the hand of his royal master, the Pharaoh[162].

A physician who visits his patient takes the latter's palm[163], obviously to palpate the radial pulse, while a visitor grasps the hand of the patient in order to help raise him in the bed[164]. During prayers, a person stretches out his palms towards God[165], just as the heathen turns his palms to the sun. "The raising of the palms" or *nesiyath kappayim* is the usual expression for the priestly blessing[166].

Perhaps the following is based on observation: it is reported in Scripture that only the skull and the feet and the palms of the hands of the corpse of Jezebel were found in the field[167], and that the wild dogs left undisturbed the *palmae manus* because of the taut texture of the palm.

In later writings, in addition to *kaph,* the terms *pas* and *pissath yad* are also used in the same sense, often as a translation of *kaph*[168]. When the flaming writing of *Mene*

149. Rufus. *De Appellat. Part.* ed. Daremberg p.144
150. *Tosefta* Shabbath 6:12
151. Eccles. Rabbah 5:14
152. Genesis 14:22
153. Exodus 6:11
154. Baba Kamma 8:6; Jerushalmi Betzah 5; 63a
155. Proverbs 31:20
156. Second Kings 11:12
157. Psalms 98:8
158. Isaiah 55:12
159. Nahum 3:19
160. Proverbs 22:26
161. *ibid* 17:18
162. Genesis 40:21
163. Midrash Psalms 73:1
164. Berachoth 5b
165. Exodus 9:29; First Kings 9:38; Psalms 44:21
166. for example Megillah 4:7
167. Second Kings 9:35
168. for example Yoma 87a. Also in the *Targum.*

*tekel* appeared on the wall of Belshazzar's palace, the king saw *pas yeda,* the palm of the hand in silhouette[169]. From a mere handful of grain which a person brings from the field, he supports himself as well as his family[170].

## VI   The Fingers

The *fingers*[171] of a person, *etzba,* like the nails, are pointed so that if he hears something unfit to be heard, he can plug his ears with his fingers[172].

The following parts of a finger are identified: 1) the *ikarim*[173] or roots of the finger, which refer to the sites of transition between fingers and metacarpals. The same meaning is attributed to *kesher* or knot[174]; 2) the joint (knuckle) or *perek;* 3) the fingertips or *rashim*[175].

Individual fingers are named as follows: the *index finger* is called *etzba* without further addition. The *middle finger* is called *amma* meaning ell (ulna), as if it were a continuation of the latter bone. It is also called the *etzba tzereda,* the snapping finger. In order to keep the High Priest awake on the night of the Day of Atonement, "the young priests snapped with this finger"[176] against the large finger of the right hand[177], so that with it and the thumb they elicited the well-known snapping sound. According to the commentaries, the nail side of the bent *index finger* was pressed against the end of the thumb and both were struck smartly against the palm of the other hand. According to a third tradition, the finger was struck against the mouth[178], perhaps in the same manner that our children strike their lower lip with their fingers to produce a loud sound.

The *ring finger* is called *kemitza;* and the *little finger* is called *tzereth* and also *etzba ketannah.* If someone only looks at the little finger of a woman with lustful intent, it is considered just as punishable as if he gazed at "that" place (i.e. her genitalia)[179].

When Rehoboam became king, the people petitioned him for a lightening of their burdens. Just as for every newly enthroned king, the people who were attracted to him were *the young men that were with him*[180]. They convinced him to be strict in that they told him to say: *my little finger is thicker than the loins of my father*[181]. The result was a splitting of the entire kingdom in 978 B.C.E.

According to *Rashi,* the word *batda*[182], or *batra* as in the *Aruch,* is the index finger. Others mistakenly consider it to refer to the Arabic *bintir* or ringfinger[183].

For the *thumb,* the Bible only uses the expression *"bohen" of the hand* in portraying the consecration of a priest[184]. The Aramaeans use the word *alyon* for thumb. When Nebuchadnezzar attempted to coerce the Israelites "at the rivers of Babylon" to play for him at a banquet the songs which they once played in the Temple, they placed the thumbs of their hands in their mouths and crushed them. Then they stretched out their mutilated thumbs to the king and cried out: "How can we play the song of the Lord"[185]? For toothache, a folk remedy is to bind a stalk of garlic on the thumbnail and place it on the side where the tooth aches[186].

---

169. Daniel 5:5
170. Kethuboth 111b
171. see I. Löw's "Die Finger in Literatur und Folklore der Juden". *Gedenkbuch für David Kaufmann.* Breslau 1900 p.61 ff.
172. Kethuboth 5b
173. Nazir 50b
174. Jerushalmi Nazir 7; 56b
175. for example Negaim 6:7
176. Yoma 1:7
177. *Tosefta* Yom Hakippurim 1:9
178. Jerushalmi Yoma 39b
179. Shabbath 64b

180. First Kings 12:10
181. *ibid*
182. Chullin 50b
183. Lewysohn. *Zoologie des Talmud.* p.34, notes; and Levy-*Neuhebräisches und Chaldäisches Wörterbuch.* Leipzig 1876-1889 *s.v.* On the other hand, see Fleischer *ibid.* 1, 284b.
184. Exodus 29:20
185. Midrash Psalms on 137:5; p.524, Ed. Buber
186. Gittin 69a

Rarely, and perhaps only when associated with matters of magic — the origin of magic, as is known, was in Babylon — the word *zakpha* is used for thumb. He who fears the evil eye should place his right thumb in his left hand and his left thumb in his right hand — just as in the exorcism of demons[187] — while he recites the magical incantation[188].

The usual designation for thumb, which is also often used in measuring, is *gudal* or *agudal*. An especially famous singer in the Temple choir was Ugdas[189] or Hagrus[190] the Levite, who understood the *perek beshir,* perhaps the modulation of singing. Even in the times of the *Gemara,* there were no longer any direct witnesses who heard or saw Ugdas sing and, thus, reports about his singing ability are greatly embellished, particularly the more recent reports. It is related of him that he could produce many different types of song (*zemer*) by placing his thumb in his mouth, so that his delighted colleagues in the choir nodded their heads in applause[191]. According to another undoubtedly later report, he placed his thumb in his mouth and placed a finger between his teeth[192]. Finally, according to the *Midrash,* he placed one thumb in his mouth, placed the other on the floor of the mouth *(karka?),* and the finger between his teeth. As a result, he produced all melodies (*neima*) and could deliver all songs, so that his colleagues retreated in amazement[193].

For our term *handful,* the Bible has two expressions: *melo chophnav* and *melo kumtzo.*

In the former case, one probably more or less bent both hands with the two small fingers firmly apposed to each other and thus created a single open mold from both palms. Evidence for this is the constant dual usage of the word; further evidence is the parallel with *kaph,* the palm of the hand: *better is a "kaph" with quietness, than both hands full with travail and vexation of spirit*[194]. For this reason, the Cherub in the vision of Ezekiel could place the fire in the *chophnayim* of the man clothed with linen[195], because his hands were open. During the sacrificial service on the Day of Atonement, the High Priest took *his hands full* of the especially finely pulverized incense[196].

Distinct from this type of drawing of an offering, known as *chaphina,* is the *kemitza,* which is exemplified by the practice used in preparing the meal offering or *minchah.* Here, the priest only takes out *his handful*[197], so that he only grasps half of the amount that he grasps in the case of *chaphina*[198]. According to the tradition, this occurred in such a way that "he bends his three fingers until he reaches the palm of his hand and then takes a handful; thus his thumb faces upwards and his little finger faces downwards"[199]. The Talmudic remark that this *kemitza* was one of the most difficult services in the Temple[200] can only refer to this unusual placement of the fingers, for a *kemitza* was also performed by the general populace[202a], as was the *chaphina*[201].

God says: I prefer a handful of the flour of the free-will meal-offering of a poor man to the two handfulls of the incense of the High Priest[202], both of which are brought for expiation[203].

A third Talmudic expression for "handful", *malé pissath yad,* has already been mentioned above.

---

187. Pesachim 110a
188. Berachoth 55b
189. *Tosefta* Yom Hakippurim 2:8
190. Yoma 3:11
191. Jerushalmi Shekalim 5; 48d
192. Yoma 38b
193. Song of Songs Rabbah 3:5:6
194. Eccles. 4:6
195. Ezekiel 10:2
196. Levit. 16:12

197. Levit. 2:2
198. Genesis Rabbah 5:7
199. Menachoth 11a
200. *ibid*
200a. *ibid*
201. Yoma 47b
202. Levit. Rabbah 3:1
203. The former had an expiatory effect, the latter did not.

The Biblical *scho'al*[204] (*Targum: sha'ala* or *she'ola*), which really only refers to the palm of the hand, also has the meaning "handful", both meanings of *drax* of the Septuagint.

The clenched *fist* is called *egroph*. One person hits another with his fist[205]. The wicked smite with the fist of wickedness[206]. The "men of fists" are the men of violence. At first, the custom existed to collect the skins of sacrifices and divide them every evening among the priests of the officiating division; however, when "men of the fist"[207] seized more than their share by force, the custom had to be changed. Rabbi Simeon ben Chalafta said[208]: from the day the fist of flattery[209] prevailed, no judge is unbiased, no conduct is without blemish and no person can say to his neighbor: my conduct is better than yours.

*Egroph* always refers to the *empty* fist; *malé egroph*[210] does not mean "a full fist", but "a space (hole in the wall) which a fist would fill".

For the *Targum*, the meaning "fist" for the Midrashic *kurmeza* seems to be assured[211].

Every finger has a *nail* or *tzipporen,* known in Aramaic as *tuphra*. Every organ that has a nail also has a bone[212]; the reverse is obviously not true.

Long nails usually interfered with one's work and were therefore cut short. Even in this minor matter, a person's character becomes apparent: a wicked man throws his cut-off nails away without considering whether or not someone walking barefoot might be hurt as a result; a righteous man (*tzaddik*) buries them; and an especially pious man (*chassid*) burns them[213]. Interesting is the remark of Nathan ben Yechiel[214] on this citation[215]: the piety and consideration in burning the nails consists in the fact that fingernails and all other wastes of a human being are harmful to the person from whom they originate, as stated in the Talmud[216]; the truly pious individual, however, thinks not of himself when he can prevent his neighbor from being harmed.

A person in mourning does not cut his nails[217]. So too, a woman captured in war lets her nails grow[218] as a sign of mourning for her relatives that died in the war[219]. The nails of the emotionally disturbed King Nebuchadnezzar, who lived with the animals in the field, became like birds' claws[220]; that is, not only long, but curved like claws. Rabbi Chiya was graced by God with the fact that even in his old age he looked young and his nails were lustrous and rosy like those of a child[221].

To test whether a slaughtering knife is completely notch-free, it is prescribed that it be examined with the nail and the fingertip[222].

The first man in Paradise had a skin made of a naily substance — Immanuel Löw compares it to the legend of the horny Siegfried; after the fall of Man, this skin was removed from him and "he noticed that he was naked"[223]. The *kothnath or,* with which the first people (Adam and Eve) were provided *after* the original sin, is interpreted in this manner[224].

---

204. First Kings 20:10; Isaiah 40:12; Ezekiel 13:19
205. Exodus 21:18
206. Isaiah 59:4
207. thus in Jerushalmi Peah 2; 20c; however in Pesachim 57a it states "men of arms", and in *Tosefta* Zebachim 11:16 & *Tosefta* Menachoth 12:18 it states "the large ones of the priesthood".
208. Sotah 41b
209. *egropha,* allusion to Agrippa
210. Kelim 17:12
211. Nöldeke. in Levy. *opus cit.* 2:537, as opposed to Fleischer. *ibid* p.457
212. Niddah 6:2
213. Niddah 17a
214. *Aruch s.v. schalosch*
215. cited by *Tosafoth* and *Tosafoth Rosh* in Niddah 17a
216. Shabbath 75b
217. Moed Katan 18a
218. Deut. 21:12
219. Rabbi Akiba in *Sifré. loc. cit.*
220. Daniel 4:30
221. Jerushalmi Rosh Hashana 2; 58b
222. Chullin 17b
223. *Pirké de Rabbi Eliezer* No. 14
224. Genesis Rabbah 20:12 and *Yalkut op. cit.* 1:No. 34

## VII    The Lower Extremity

The word *regel,* which properly refers only to the *foot,* is also used to denote the leg, as the *Gemara* explicitly deduces[225], particularly in the Palestinian-Aramaic dialect. A similar situation in regard to the word *yad* for hand (or the entire arm) has already been mentioned above.

In water-poor Egypt, it was necessary to "water the land with one's foot"[226] just as for a vegetable garden; this means one used foot-driven machines such as well-wheels, as still observed by Niebuhr in Egypt[227].

Hillel used to say: "to the place that I love, there my feet lead me" (i.e. mechanically direct me). Rabbi Yochanan said: "A man's feet are his surety; they lead him to the place where he is destined to die"[228]. A certain heathen once asked of Hillel that he teach him the entire Torah while he (the heathen) stood on one foot (*stante pede*). Hillel answered him: "what is hateful to you, do not do unto your neighbor; that is the whole Torah; all the rest is the commentary thereof, go and learn it"[229]!

The Psalmist sings that God will carry you Israel on His hands, so that you *not dash your foot against a stone*[230].

Just as in the hand, in the foot one distinguishes between the sole, *kaph,* and the dorsum of the foot, *gab.* The sinful Israelites are warned that they will find no resting place for the soles of their feet among the nations[231]. The extremely spoiled and delicate woman never attempts to place the sole of her foot on the ground[232], but always lets herself be carried in a sedan chair.

The post-Biblical term *pissath ha-regel* also refers to the sole of the foot, just like the corresponding expression for the hand (*pissath ha-yad* ).

The *toe,* like the finger, is called *etzba,* just as the Greek *daktylos* and the Latin *digitus* are also used for both meanings. It is a sign of haughtiness to amuse oneself with a flock of pigeons, to fan oneself with his hands, to stump with the feet or to walk on tip-toe[233].

The *heel* is called *akeb.* It is probable that the word *akeb* was also used in the Bible to denote pudenda[234], without necessarily referring to the genitalia. The Talmud accepts this meaning as correct[235].

Next on the foot, if one proceeds upwards, is the *ankle joint,* known as *karsol* or *kartzol.* God strengthens my steps so that my joints do not wobble[236]. The well-known allegory of the "preacher" that in old age the almond forsakes its service[237] is interpreted by the *Midrash* to refer to the foot joints[238].

When the ancient Bible translators render our word as *talus* in Latin or *aphyron* in Greek, this definition is correct insofar as the ankle bone itself connects the foot with the lower leg. It cannot be established with certainty whether or not *karsol* refers to the ankle *bone* itself and not to the joint. Perhaps this is the explanation of the above-cited Midrashic interpretation of almond i.e. *karsol.* In any event, the similarity of the ankle bone with an almond is just as great and just as small as with the dice of antiquity which were called *talus* in Latin and *astragalos* in Greek, and which were oblong and had eyes on four sides. To be sure, in later times, one also played with cubic dice; these, however, were called *kybos* in Greek or *cubis* in Latin[239] or *kubya* in the Talmud.

225. Yebamoth 103a
226. Deut. 11:10
227. Rosenmüller. *Morgenland.* Vol. 2:303
228. Sukkah 53a
229. Shabbath 31a
230. Psalms 91:12
231. Deut. 28:65
232. *ibid.* 28:56
233. Derech Eretz Rabbah 2:8
234. Jeremiah 13:22
235. Niddah 20a
236. Psalms 18:37
237. Eccles. 12:5
238. Levit. Rabbah 13:1
239. Hyrtl. *Das Hebr. und Arab. in der Medizin.* p.83

According to the traditional explanation of *Rashi,* the expression *isthewara* also refers to the "connection between foot and leg" i.e. the ankle joint[240].

The *Targum* and commentaries also understand the poetic *aphsayim*[241] in the same sense, referring to the duality of the two ankles.

The *lower legs* (i.e. below the knee), including the feet, are called *kera'ayim* in the Bible, and the anterior surface (i.e. the shinbone) is called *"lechtha* of the lower leg"[242].

According to *Rashi,* the Talmud is referring to a person "whose foot is reversed, so that he walks on the upper side of the foot", i.e. club-foot. Therefore, *kara* must here refer only to the foot. According to Kazenelson, it denotes "someone who walks on the edges of the soles", i.e. *pes varus* or *pes valgus*[243]. But where does the word *kara* mean sole of the foot? Löw states that *lechta* cannot be separated from the Syrian *lachtha.* In Syriac it means the palm, and in Hebrew it refers to the middle of the sole *or* the back (dorsum) of the foot. The latter view is the traditional opinion of *Rashi.*

It is uncertain whether or not the term *shok* has a precise anatomical meaning. It could refer to the whole leg, or only the upper or lower leg. The word is also used in relation to muscle power; as a result, one usually interprets it in the sense of "calf" of the leg. His *"shokayim" are as pillars of marble*[244] is a portrayal of overwhelming exuberance. The Lord does not delight in the strength of the horse, nor does He take pleasure in the legs of a man, but rather in them that fear Him[245]. It is a practice of prostitutes to uncover the legs[246].

The *knees, birkayim,* are bent in prayer before the Lord. God says: *every knee bows and every tongue swears unto Me*[247]. Daniel kneeled three times daily (*barek*) to pray[248]. One also bends down on one's knees (*kara*) in order to drink water from rivers[249]. Out of fear, hands become feeble and knees "go (flow) like water", i.e. loosen[250]. When the Lord's judgement approaches, knees rattle (*phik*) and the loins tremble[251]. The Lord, however, strengthens weak hands and makes firm, feeble knees[252].

Babes are dandled upon the knees of their mothers[253]. Delilah treacherously allowed Samson to fall asleep on her knees, so that the Philistine lying in ambush could cut off his (Samson's) locks in which his strength resided[254]. A woman in labor used the knees of a man or another woman as a live birthstool[255].

The word *arkubba* is used to denote both the human knee[256] as well as the knee of animals. On the *arkubba* of an animal, two parts are distinguished: an upper part with the curvature posteriorly and a lower part with the curvature toward the front[257]. It was correctly recognized that the joint which one ordinarily calls "knee" is the ankle joint of ruminants, and that the real knee joint is located very high up, directly at the end of the abdomen. That which was thought to be the lower leg in reality represents the long stretched-out foot bones. The upper, anatomical knee joint has its "curvature" (popliteal space) posteriorly; the lower one (anatomically the ankle joint) has its curvature anteriorly. The Talmudic Sages thus remained free of the error of the ancient scientists such as Aristotle[258].

240. Menachoth 33a and Yebamoth 103a
241. Ezekiel 47:3
242. Yebamoth 103a
243. Kobert. *Historische Studien.* Vol. 5, 1896 p.214
244. Song of Songs 5:15
245. Psalms 147:10-11
246. Isaiah 47:2; Berachoth 24a
247. Isaiah 45:23
248. Daniel 6:11
249. Judges 7:6
250. Ezekiel 7:17
251. Nahum 2:11
252. Isaiah 35:3
253. Isaiah 66:12
254. Judges 16:19
255. More detailed discussion in chapter on obstetrics
256. for example Daniel 5:6 and Yebamoth 12:1
257. for example Chullin 76a
258. Aristotle. *Hist. Anim.* 2:1

It is important in *halachah* that the *arkubba* only has bones and sinews but no flesh[259]. A soldier carries his sword on the upper leg (or thigh), *yarech*[260]; and as a rule, on the left side. Only Ehud, who was ambidextrous, could gird it on his right thigh without being hindered in its use[261], and was thus able to conceal it from Eglon, whom he intended to kill.

One "smites upon the thigh" as evidence of repentance[262] and of mourning[263]. The "thigh" is also used as a euphemistic expression for the penis. The expression "those who issued from the thigh of Jacob[264] or Gideon"[265] refers to their children. Later, this expression was also used to denote the womb of a woman in that one said: "that woman is envious of the other woman's thigh", i.e. her large number of children[266].

In taking an oath in the times of the Patriarchs, a servant would "place his hand under the thigh of his master"[267]; he thus expresses an oath without having to repeat the words or the contents of the oath. With the above-cited meaning of the word *yarech* as referring to phallus, which was already accepted in ancient times, the aforementioned practice is explained as follows: the slave placed his hand on the phallus of his master[268] because the sign of the circumcision on his penis was considered to be the highest and perhaps only symbol of his racial or religious community. A similar form of oath-taking is still found among certain primitive peoples even today.

In the history of the Patriarchs, this manner of taking an oath occurred twice: once Abraham had his servant swear in the specified manner; the other time Jacob demanded the oath from his son Joseph with the same words[269]. In the latter instance, many commentaries apparently consider it shocking to assert that the son (Joseph) grasped the phallus of his father, while Ham and Japhet were already cursed because they only *gazed* upon the nakedness of their father[270]. These commentaries therefore lack any explanation of this word (*yarech*) in the story of Jacob. Only pseudo-Jonathan in his translation does not take offense at such an interpretation. It is further noteworthy that in the first case, it specifically states: *and the servant put his hand under the thigh of Abraham his master*[271], whereas in the case of Joseph it only says: *and he swore unto him*[272] without further addition.

In Josephus, the taking of an oath by a slave is portrayed as follows: "they both put their hands under the thigh (*ypo tous merous allelois tas cheiras epagagones*) and called God as a witness"[273]. Concerning Jacob, Josephus has no such notation.

To me, the explanation of Ibn Ezra is the most enlightening of all. He says that the subject placed his hand under the loins of his master as a sign of his obedience.

## VIII   The Loins

The area above the crest of the ileum posteriorly towards the sacrum, perhaps including the soft tissues covering the ileum, comprises the *loins* or *mothnayim*. It is that part of the trunk where one wears a belt. A belt is put on when one sets out on a journey; therefore, to "gird one's loins"[274] means the same as "to prepare oneself for a journey".

---

259. Chullin 128b
260. Psalms 45:4
261. Judges 3:16
262. Jeremiah 31:18
263. Ezekiel 21:17
264. Genesis 46:26
265. Judges 8:30
266. Megillah 13a
267. Genesis 24:9
268. Genesis Rabbah 59:8
269. Genesis 47:29
270. Genesis 9:22 ff (Actually only Ham was cursed, not Japhet, F.R.)
271. Genesis 24:9
272. Genesis 47:31
273. Josephus. *Antiquities* Book 1, Chapt. 16:1
274. for example Second Kings 4:29

A writer carries *an inkhorn on his loins*[275] or on his belt. A mourner places a sack on his loins[276]. If someone is wearing something on his loins which constrains him (i.e. which must be laced up), he has the feeling as if he were brought into a net[277]. The priestly breeches extended from the loins up to the thighs[278].

The posterior portion of the loins next to the sacral bone, often including the latter, is the site of labor pains in most parturient women. *Therefore are my loins filled with convulsions*[279] (*chalchala,* from *chal* meaning to rotate i.e. labor pains). *And the knees smite together and convulsions are in all loins*[280].

*Chalatzayim* or *chartza* seem to have the same meaning as *mothnayim*[281]. Nevertheless, *to gird one's chalatzayim* [282] means to prepare for battle. Because of fright, the joints *(kitre)* of the loins of Belshazzar loosened[283]. The expression *and kings shall come out of thy loins*[283a] is used in the same sense as the above-mentioned *to come forth from his thigh.*

The *back* is designated as *gab, gav* or *geb*. *A whip for the horse, a bridle for the ass, and a rod for the fool's back*[284]. Transgressors cast the Lord behind their back[285], i.e. disdain Him; the Lord Himself, however, *casts all mine sins behind His back*[286], i.e. forgives them.

Rabbi Saul Ben Nachman said[287] that God initially created the first man with two faces; He then split him and formed two backs, one back for each side, so that in this manner man and woman came into being.

The advantages of man over animals is a favorite theme of ancient preachers. Teleologically, of course in a naive manner, every part of the body was subject to a specific way of thinking, and this observation was then related to the Biblical text. In the Biblical narration of the creation of the first woman, it states that God took one of the ribs of the sleeping man *and closed up the place with flesh instead thereof*[288]. This phrase is explained by Rabbi Chanina bar Yitzchak: "God provided the man with a fitting outlet for his nether functions, that his modesty might not be outraged, like an animal" — the anus and the process of defecation in man are covered by the *nates* (buttocks). Rabbi Yannai said: God made him a cushion so that he should not suffer pain when he sits[289]. These are popular enunciations of the fact that man has an advantage over the animals in that he is able to sit. Similar ways of thinking were widely displayed by the church fathers.

Where a more precise term is not applicable, the *buttocks* are designated as *agaboth*[290].

The Biblical narrative of creation states: *and God created man... as a nephesh chaya*[291] which might mean: "He created him as an animal". Man originally had a tail, *zanab*[292], or caudal vertebra, *ukab,* like an animal. Later, however, God removed it because of man's dignity[293]. I fight the temptation to interpret this remark of Rabbi Judah in the sense of the modern theory of evolution. Most probably we have here the reflection of the legends of tailed men.

The commentators have divided opinions concerning the Biblical terms *miphsa'ah*[294] and *sheth*[295], which both probably have the same meaning. Some

---

275. Ezekiel 9:2; compare L. Löw. *Graphische Requisien* 1 p.184
276. Genesis 37:34
277. Psalms 66:11
278. Exodus 28:42
279. Isaiah 21:3
280. Nahum 2:11
281. *Rashi* on Jeremiah 30:6
282. Job 38:3
283a. Genesis 35:11
283. Daniel 5:6
284. Proverbs 26:3
285. Ezekiel 23:25
286. Isaiah 38:17
287. Genesis Rabbah 8:1
288. Genesis 2:21
289. Genesis Rabbah 17:6
290. Berachoth 24a
291. Genesis 2:7
292. Erubin 18a
293. Genesis Rabbah 14:9
294. First Chronicles 19:4
295. Second Samuel 10:4

consider these terms to be designations for the buttocks; others, for the genitalia. One can draw no conclusions from the text itself. In both Biblical places, it is related that the Canaanite King Hanun had the garments of David's messengers — who came to console him concerning the death of his father — cut off in the middle, down to the *miphsa'ah* or *sheth,* in order to ridicule them.

## IX    The Abdomen

The words *beten* in the Bible, *keres* in the Mishnah, and *karsa* in the Talmud all have the same meaning of *abdomen*, i.e. they refer to the abdominal wall as well as the abdomen in its totality, i.e., the viscera together with the abdominal wall.

The strength of the Behemoth animal resides in the sinews of its loins[296]. Two nations are in the abdomen (i.e. womb) of the pregnant woman[297]. In case the suspected adulteress is guilty, her abdomen swells after she drinks the testing water[298].

When the rich and the poor meet, the Lord makes them all equal[299]. If the rich man says to the poor man: "why do you not go and work to earn your bread? Look at those hips *(shokayim)*! Look at that thigh! Look at that abdomen"!, then the Lord will say: "It is not enough that you have not given him anything of yours, but you do not even grant him that which I have given him"[300].

A legal case in the Talmud is the following: in a house the lower floor began to sink into the ground so that the owner desired the upstairs tenant to move out, while the house was being rebuilt. The tenant however said: "I am quite comfortable, flatten your belly to get in and flatten it again to get out of your rooms"[301]. Naturally, the final legal ruling is not in the manner suggested by the tenant[302].

The word *tabbur* for the navel is only used in the Bible in the sense of the *navel of the earth*[303], i.e. its middle point, just as the Greek poets speak of *omphalos oures.* Otherwise, the term for navel is *shor;* later one also used the words *tibbur, shorar* or *sharar.*

The comparison with a ditch *(bor)* indicates that one considered the deep-lying type of navel to be the most common one[304]. The poet in his love song calls it a bowl filled with wine.

The teaching of Abba Saul that an embryo in its mother's womb develops from its navel[305] was widely disseminated among the Rabbis, and even advocated by some Greek philosophers[306]. The navel is the central point of intrauterine life and is also of importance after the baby is born. If one finds a dead man slain in the field by an unknown hand, the members of the highest court shall measure to ascertain which city is closest to the corpse[307]. According to one opinion, they begin to measure from the nose which is the identification mark on the face; according to another view, they begin to measure from the navel which is the site of origin of intrauterine life[308].

If a man is buried in a pile of rubble, one should clear the debris even on the Sabbath up to his nose which is the "site of respiration" (i.e. life). Another opinion says: up to his navel which is the source of life[309].

The seat of the Sanhedrin is in the middle of the Temple, like the navel in the middle of the abdomen[310]. Israel sucks its "life" from the wisdom of this learned body of men, as a child sucks its life in the mother's womb through the navel[311].

---

296. Job 40:16
297. Genesis 25:23
298. Numbers 5:21
299. Proverbs 22:2
300. Levit. Rabbah 34:4
301. Literally: make your belly flat, *shuph akresek,* Baba Bathra 7a
302. see *Choshen Mishpat* 164:2
303. Ezekiel 38:12

304. Aboth de Rabbi Nathan 31:3
305. Sotah 45b
306. Plutarch. *De Placit.* 5:17
307. Deut. 21:1 ff
308. Jerusalmi Sotah 9; 23c
309. Yoma 85a; Jerusalmi Yoma 8; 45b
310. Numbers Rabbah 1:4
311. Song of Songs Rabbah 7:3

# PART II
# THE 248 LIMBS

Man is composed of body and soul; if the soul departs, only the body or *geviyah* remains[312] and there is no longer an advantage of man over animals[313].

The body has 248 limbs (or members), corresponding to the days of the lunar year, and 365 sinews, corresponding to the days of the solar year[314]. Abraham was first called Abram[315] (the letters of the name have the numerical value of 243); later he was called Abraham because God gave him mastery over the five important limbs (the extra letter "h" added to his name has the numerical value of 5): the two eyes, the two ears and the genitalia. Thus, he had mastery over all 248 limbs of the body[316]. In a similar manner, the "248 limbs" are often spoken about[317], not only in discourses as in the two above-mentioned places, but also in law. The question of the number of limbs, therefore, also has practical meaning.

For according to Biblical decree, everything which is found in a closed room (tent) in which there lies a corpse is ritually unclean[318]. According to an often-mentioned Talmudic legislative rule, a fraction more than one-half may be considered equal to one. In our case, even a portion of the corpse which encompasses more than half the limbs (in connection with the existence of such a "partial" corpse) has the same effect, and renders unclean just like the entire corpse[319].

According to the explicit definition of the *Tosefta* with which all the commentators agree, the term "limb" includes bones, sinews and flesh, so that the human body, according to the Talmud, has 248 *bones*. The teeth cannot be included in the count since they have no flesh. The same applies to the auditory ossicles.

There is no doubt at all that *in everyday speech* the term "limb" or *eber* also includes boneless organs. It would be peculiar not to consider, for example, the organ which is called the *kat, exohen* "limb", or *eber* (membrum), i.e. the procreative organ or penis, among the "organs" (or limbs). Furthermore, in ritual law, the "tips of organs (or limbs)" are mentioned, and among these organs are the ears (i.e. the earlobe), the penis and the nipples of the breast, all boneless organs which are enumerated as "limbs"[320]. In addition, in the aforementioned *Aggadic* story about Abraham, the eyes are counted as "limbs".

Opinions differ in the definition of "limb (torn) from a living animal" which *halachically* is equated with the "limb (torn) from a dead animal"[321]. Rabbi Akiba also includes the knee although it has no flesh; Rabbi Jose the Galilean considers a "limb" to be an organ which cannot be replaced such as the kidneys and the lips, i.e. also boneless parts of the body. Only Rabbi Judah requires bones, sinews and flesh (to define a "limb")[322].

Whether a definition of the term "limb" (or "organ") existed elsewhere in antiquity is unknown to me. Plinius speaks of the "eight organs of the face, more or less" (*decem aut paulo plura membra*)[323], but he doesn't specify the organs to which he

---

312. Concerning man: First Samuel 31:10; concerning animals: Judges 14:8
313. Eccles. 3:19
314. Makkoth 23b
315. Genesis 17:5
316. Nedarim 32b
317. Moed Katan 17a; Genesis Rabbah 69:1 and elsewhere. *Tanchuma, beshallach* p.34. Buber

318. Numbers 19:14
319. Oholoth 2:1; Bechoroth 45a
320. Negaim 6:7
321. Oholoth 2:1
322. Chullin 128b
323. Plinius. Book 7 Chapt. 1.

refers. Aristotle asserts that certain body parts which cannot be homogeneously dissected, such as the head, thigh, hand, arm and thorax, are not only called "parts" but also "limbs" (*ou monon mere alla kai mele kaleitai*)[324]. Similarly, Avicenna calls "partes" *corpora ex proxima humorum commixtione concretioneve progenita*[325].

*In actuality,* the human skeleton has 240 bones if one counts the breastbone and the coccyx as simple bones and includes the teeth and auditory ossicles but disregards the various sesamoid ones. Without the 32 teeth and 3 auditory ossicles, the number is 205 and if one considers the breastbone and coccyx to have four parts each, the total number would be 211 *bones.* According to the *Tosefta,* a skeleton can have 200 to 280 bones[326].

The *Mishnah*[327] enumerates the 248 bones in the following manner:

| | |
|---|---:|
| In the foot, *pissath ha-regel* | |
|     with 6 in each toe (i.e. 6 x 5 = 30) | 30 |
| in the ankle, *kursal* | 10 |
| in the lower leg, *shok* | 2 |
| in the knee, *arkubba* | 5 |
| in the upper leg, *yarech* | 1 |
| in the *kotlith* | 3 |
| ribs | 11 |
| in the hand, *pissath ha-yad* | |
|     with 6 in each finger (i.e. 6 x 5 = 30) | 30 |
| in the forearm, *kaneh* | 2 |
| in the elbow, *marpek* | 2 |
| in the upperarm, *zeroa* | 1 |
| in the shoulder, *katheph* | 4 |
| | 101; for both sides 202 |
| Then add vertebrae | 18 |
| in the head, *rosh* | 9 |
| in the neck | 8 |
| in the heart-key, *maphteach ha-leb* | 6 |
| in the openings, *nekabim* | 5 |
| | 248 |

We do not know by which method this data was derived — in the only Talmudic case where it possibly speaks of the boiling of a corpse[328], 251 limbs were found. We also do not know whether the above rendering of the anatomical terms correctly corresponds to our names. If it does, the majority of the quoted numbers are as untrue as the asserted total number of bones. Comparison with the teachings of the contemporary heathen physicians leaves us in the lurch, because their osteology, as is known, rests on very weak grounds. Galen only speaks of "more than 200 bones"[329], but is careful not to give a specific number. Concerning that part of medical science, namely the determination of the number of bones, the scholar Foes says[330]: *non adeo exacte a veteribus fuit exculta aut exornata.*

---

324. Aristotle. *Hist. Anim.* beginning
325. Avicenna. *Canon.* Book 1 Sect. 1, Doct 5. beginning. fol 25b edition of Plempius. Lovanii 1658
326. *Tosefta* Oholoth 1:7
327. Oholoth 1:8
328. Bechoroth 45a
329. Galen. *De Foet. Form.* Book 6. Kühn 4:694
330. In his edition of Hippocrates. Geneva 1657 fol. 326b

Hippocrates has very vague numbers: "hand 27, foot 24, neck 7, loins (*osphyos*) 5, spine 20, head 8, together 91, with the nails, *syn onyxi'n,* 111"[331].

As already mentioned in the introduction to this book, the great Arabic physicians assert the number of bones of the human skeleton to be 248, although Galen, whom they otherwise follow slavishly, mentions no specific number at all. Since they were geographically and ethnically closely related to the Jews — in fact, some of them were Jews — the Jewish tradition, and not Galen, was probably the source from which they derived this number. This seems probable for the additional reason that they only adopted the Talmudic number of 248 as a base number, in order to correct it by additions. Avicenna (died 1037) also teaches 248 bones: *demtis iis exiguis ossibus, quae sesamoeidea vocantur quodque a lambdae literae graecae similitudine dicitur lambdoeides*[332]. One hundred years later, Abulcasem (died 1106) wrote: *numerus ossium totius humani corporis est 248 ossa, praeter os gutturis quod simulatur litterae lambda graece, et praeter os cordis et praeter parva ossa, de quibus plenae sunt concavitates juncturarum, quae dicuntur sisamina vel Alaniaht, et praeter duo ossa rotunda genuum, quae sunt in capite genu, quod dicitur oculus genu*[333].

Naturally there was no dearth of attempts to vindicate the assertions of the *Mishnah.* Rabbinowicz[334] "corrects" individual numbers in that he includes the *points d'ossification* (he means the epiphyses); however, he does this totally arbitrarily, where he pleases, just as he arbitrarily determines the number of bones in the head and includes the nostrils and auditory canal in the "openings", contrary to the linguistic usage of the Talmud.

Kazenelson[335] studied this question systematically. As is known, a person is not born with fully developed bones. The latter develop much more from separated bony parts long after birth, and are tied by cartilaginous portions, so that only much later do bones become totally ossified and unified. Kazenelson assumed that the corpse of a 16-year-old person was boiled for such a long time that the cartilage dissolved, the result of which was a higher number of bones than that of a fully developed adult. These individual arguments have only two serious weaknesses: firstly, the age limits for ossification of bones are not as constant as Kazenelson asserts. For example, he states that the lower end of the upper arm (humerus) ossifies at age 18, whereas Bardeleben[336] assumes the age 16 or 17; such variations occur for most bones. Even if one assumes that the time of final ossification of bones is certainly subject to individual variations, and, therefore, the ages cited by Kazenelson might occasionally be correct, the second very serious objection remains, that even if one accepts this assumption, he still finds himself forced to speak of "certain inexactitudes which are the result of the inexperience of investigators and the imperfections of the investigative methodologies"[337]. Such an "incorrectness" is the assumption that there is *one* bone in the femur, whereas there are in fact two sites of ossification there; there are other incorrectnesses[338]. In other words: Kazenelson first arranged his hypothesis; whenever the facts did not coincide with his hypothesis, he did not abandon or even modify his assumptions; rather he ascribed the error to his source, whereas the real guilty one, naturally, was he. As a result, his entire work, so painstakingly prepared, loses its validity and reliability.

---

331. Hippocrates. *De Ossium Natura. ibid* fol. 274
332. Avicenna. Book 1 Sect. 1 Doct. 5. Sum 1. Oap.30a. fol 46a Plempius
333. Alsaharavii. *Liber Theoriae.* Tract. 4, Chapt. 1 fol 111a. Kgl. Bibl. Berlin. B. Diez 95
334. Rabbinowicz. *La Médecine du Thalmud.* Paris 1880 p.192
335. Kazenelson. Die Normal und Pathologische Anatomie des Talmud. Kobert's *Historische Studien.* Vol. 5, 1896 p.164 ff
336. Eulenburg's *Real-Encyklopädie* 11:149
337. Kazenelson. *loc. cit.* p.191
338. *ibid.* p.196

Besides, I offer the following thought: since the ossification of a cartilaginous joint does not occur suddenly, perchance in a day or a week, therefore, long before the ossification is completed, so much osseous tissue has developed that a separation of the bone by boiling can no longer occur. One must also still investigate whether or not the laws of ossification apply equally to all races; they may have no validity at all for the Orient. I have discussed this question with Privy Counsellor R. Waldeyer, who attaches great significance thereto.

We thus cannot extricate ourselves from a *non liquet:* in simple language, the *Mishnah* remains unexplained.

There remains only to describe several concepts of the *Mishnah* which have not been discussed heretofore.

The bone of the thigh is called *kulith* by the Rabbis and is equivalent to the Biblical *yarech*. It is related that knife-handles were made from the *kulith* of a dead person[339]. The marrow of the *kulith*[340], particularly of young lambs, was considered to be a delicacy[341]. Rabbi Isaac ben Eleazar once saw a *kulith* (thighbone) washed up from the sea on the shores of Caesarea[342]. According to the opinion of probably all peoples of antiquity, the "marrow" is the site of the strength of human beings; as a result, legend relates that the marrow of the *kulith* of the "giants" was eighteen cubits long[343]. It was debated whether or not the flesh outside the bone can be restored from the marrow within[344].

*Kaph* refers to any round object that has a flat area on its curvature; for example a bowl, pan and the like. Accordingly, *kaph ha-yad* means the palm of the hand, *kappa de mocha* refers to the skull of an animal[345], and *kaph ha-yarech* really means the hip-pan (i.e. socket of the hip joint). However, tradition interprets this term to refer to the *head of the femur*. It is this bone which the Patriarch Jacob dislocated during his wrestling with the angel according to the Biblical story[346].

In Aramaic, the term for head of the femur is *pethe yarka,* and the Talmud uses the expression *buka de atma*[347]. The corresponding expression used by the Arabic physicians, *chuk al-wark,* means both head of the femur and hip socket[348].

The "sinew of the thigh", the ligamentum teres, is called *nib* in the Talmud. A luxation is considered to be a life-threatening situation for an animal[349].

The term *kotlith* occurs only once in the Talmud, namely in our *Mishnah*. The commentaries also consider it to refer to the head of the femur. Only Maimonides states that the term *kotlith* also includes "that which hangs thereon in an upward direction".

The dictionaries derive *kotlith* from the Greek *kotyle* (head of the femur). More precise is the Arabic *al-kitnah*, which is the translation found in Maimonides. To the Arabic physicians, however, *katan* always refers to the region of the loins, particularly when combined as follows: *charaz-al-katan* meaning lumbar vertebrae[350]. This is probably what Maimonides means when he says "that which hangs from above the femur". Freytag thus correctly translates *katan* as *quod inter duas est coxas*. It does not refer to the perineum as suggested by Johan Jacob Reiske, doctor of medicine and professor of Arabic in Leipzig, in his remarks on Rhazes; rather it (i.e. *katan*) refers to the region of the loins or perhaps the sacrum.

---

339. *Tosefta* Oholoth 4:3
340. *Tosefta* Uktzin 2:4
341. *Tosefta* Pesachim 4:10
342. Genesis Rabbah 10:7
343. Genesis Rabbah 26:7
344. Chullin 125a

345. Chullin 54a
346. Genesis 32:36
347. Chullin 42b
348. De Koning. *opus. cit.* p.817
349. Chullin 54b
350. for example in Rhazes, ed. Koning p.16

Arabic anatomists call the sacrum *aguz.*

The head of the femur lies in the *kliboseth* or *klibusta,* the sacral hollow of the pelvis.

During old age, these bones become especially prominent[351], either because of the leanness of the body or because of the more or less stooped-over posture (of old age). The word is not equivalent to *kollops*[352].

According to Mar Samuel[353], "the fat of the *kliboseth*" is the same as the "fat which is on the kidneys which is by the *kesalim* "[354]; it is designated by the Bible as part of an offering, and it is embedded posteriorly. As a result, the Biblical term *kesalim* also refers to the bones of the pelvis.

The Septuagint has *meria* (buttocks); the Vulgate has *ilia;* the *Targum* has the imprecise term *gisa* which simply means "side", certainly also including the side of the thorax[355]. *Rashi* has the translation *hanka* which is equivalent to *ancha* whose anatomical meaning is uncertain[356].

The Arabs call the hipbone *etzem al varak* (equal to the Hebrew *yarech* ).

The assertion of the *Mishnah* "five (bones) in the knee" is amplified in the *Tosefta:* "two on each side and the knee cap, *phika,* in the middle"[357]. These probably refer to the condyles of the tibia and the femur which were apparently thought to be autonomous bones.

On the other hand, in the elbow joint, the *marpek,* only two bones are listed while an additional three bones, namely the two condyles of the humerus and the olecranon, are easily palpable.

The "cooking theory" provides no explanation for the above. According to most authors, the *capitis radii* and its diaphysis first coalesce during the 16th to 18th year of life. Thus, if one cooks this bone of a sixteen-year-old, it might still loosen and separate[358].

The *Mishnah* only enumerates eleven *ribs,* because it is thought that the twelfth rib which ends unattached (to the rib cage), should not be counted[359]. This reason, naturally, is not valid; for the eleventh rib also does not reach the breastbone nor is it attached to another rib. According to Rabbi Yochanan, only "the large ribs" contain marrow[360]. The joint connection between the ribs and the vertebrae is compared to a mortar and pestel, *bukna be asitha*[361].

Hippocrates only mentions seven ribs[362]; and Aristotle describes eight on each side[363]. I find nothing mentioned about a difference between true and false ribs.

To create the first woman *the Lord God caused a deep sleep to fall upon Adam*[364], and He then took one of his ribs and closed up the site with flesh. "Mine rib" is thus the dialectic term for "mine wife"[365]. The Hebrew word *tsela*[366] is spoken of as *ala* in Aramaic.

Nowhere is it stated that this rib defect of the first man was transmitted to his descendants so that men would have one less rib than women. The word "rib" in the Biblical story of creation is given many different meanings in the *Midrashim.*

To the assertion of the *Mishnah* that the head has nine bones, the *Tosefta* adds that the jaw (*lechi*) is included in this number[367]. This addition was perhaps motivated

---

351. Shabbath 152a
352. Löw in Krauss *s.v.*
353. Chullin 93a
354. Levit. 3:4 and elsewhere
355. Niddah 48b
356. Hyrtl. *Das Arabische* p.26-27
357. *Tosefta* Oholoth 1:6
358. Contrary to Kazenelson p.193
359. *Yoreh Deah* 54:1
360. Chullin 52a

361. *ibid*
362. Hippocrates. *De Locis.* ed. Foes. fol. 410 No. 23
363. Aristotle. *Hist. Anim.* Book 1. Chapt. 15 No. 56
364. Genesis 2:21
365. Kiddushin 6a
366. Daniel 7:5 and Nazir 52a
367. *Tosefta* Oholoth 1:6

by the fact that to the physicians of antiquity, and naturally to the Arabs, it was general custom to consider the bones of the jaw separate from those of the head.

If one assumes that the *Mishnah* refers to the seven cervical vertebrae and the lingual bone when it speaks of "the eight bones of the neck", the statement about the "eighteen vertebrae" (*chulyoth*) is easily explained: twelve thoracic and six lumbar vertebrae. Even if the normal number of lumbar vertebrae is only five, in exceptionally tall individuals one can also observe six[368].

Hippocrates correctly lists the number of cervical vertebrae[369]. Concerning the total number of vertebrae, he has the astonishing assertion: "some have more and some have less; those who have more, *pleonas*[370], have twenty-two"[371]. Galen has the correct numbers $(7 + 12 + 5)$[372] and so do the Arabs[373]. The number eighteen is later found in the Middle Ages among the Salernitans, based upon an unknown source, but perhaps from the Jews whose number and prestige in Salerno was not inconsiderable. As shown above, this assertion need not be "one of the many and monstrous anatomical errors of that era"[374].

At the end of the eighteen vertebrae, there is a bone[375] which resembles an almond[376] and which the legend of the Talmud calls *luz*. King Hadrian once asked Rabbi Joshua ben Hananiah: from which part of the body will man in the world to come sprout forth? He answered: the *luz* of the spinal column. As proof of the indestructibility of this bone, he placed one in water but it was not dissolved; he let it pass through millstones but it was not ground; he put it on an anvil and beat it with a hammer; the anvil was flattened out and the hammer was split, but the *luz* remained undamaged[377]. Only the deluge, by which God meant to *annihilate* mankind[378], also destroyed the *luz* of the vertebral column[379].

This unusual little bone, which can only refer to the coccyx, was sought in various sites of the body by anatomists of the Middle Ages without their being able to find it[380]. Höfler assembled German fables concerning the "little Jew bone"[381].

Legends concerning the indestructibility of individual parts of the body were also known in heathen antiquity. The great toe of King Pyrrhus was also said to be incombustible (*hunc cremari cum reliquo corpore non potuisse tradunt* )[382], as was the heart of Germanicus and that of all poisoned people[383].

The vertebral column and the ribs together form what the Talmud calls *sheled* or *sheladda*[384]. A corpse can be burned[385] or become macerated by lying in water[386], but the *sheled* remains intact. Such a skeleton can lie diagonally across the street so that no one can pass[387], or it may be placed in a coffin for transporting it from one place to another for burial[388]. A crawling creature (i.e. reptile) can also dry up in the same manner[389].

The word *sheled* is not equivalent to the Greek *skeleton*.

The "heart-key" mentioned in the *Mishnah* might be interpreted to have the same

368. Hyrtl. *Anatomie.* p.345
369. Hippocrates. *De Oss. Nat.* beginning. Foes. fol. 274 No. 5
370. Foes erroneously translates *pauciores* instead of *plures*
371. Hippocrates. *De Locis.* Foes fol. 410 No. 21
372. Galen. *De Ossibus* 7. Kühn 2:755
373. De Koning. *op. cit.* p.17 Rhazes; p.123 Haly; 478, 82,86 Avicenna.
374. Hyrtl. *Das Arabische.* p.166
375. *Artuch. s.v. luz*
376. Eccles. 12:5
377. Levit. Rabbah 18:1 and Eccles. Rabbah on 12:5

378. Genesis 6:7
379. Genesis Rabbah 28:3
380. Hyrtl. *Das Arabische.* p.167
381. Höfler. *Deutsches Krankheits-namenbuch.* Munich 1899 p.381 & 252, *s.v. Jungfer.*
382. Plinius 7:2
383. *ibid* 11:71
384. *Yoreh Deah* 345:8
385. Niddah 28a
386. Lament. Rabbah on 4:17
387. Baba Kamma 31b
388. Moed Katan 25a
389. Niddah 56a

meaning as the *kleis* of the Greeks and the *clavicula* of the anatomists of the Middle Ages, namely the clavicle. To be sure, it does not have six parts as stated in the *Mishnah*.

The commentators on the *Mishnah* consider the heart-key to be the same as the *chazeh* of the Bible; and, as far as I can see, there is no dispute aş to its meaning, i.e. "breast". According to the *Tosefta, chazeh* is "that part of the standing animal which faces the ground and which reaches up to the neck, anteriorly and down to the abdomen posteriorly. In a slaughtered animal this piece is cut out from the space between the two sides"[390]. The cut is thus not made on the breastbone but inside the ribs, perhaps in the mammillary line. The removal of this piece resulted in the production of a large hole (window) in the body of the animal[391].

The *chazeh* is one of the allowances given to the priests[392], and *for this special purpose* one always cut out the breast together with one or, more likely, two pairs of ribs (probably the upper ones). By contrast, when an *entire* animal sacrifice was divided among the priests, these two pairs of ribs remained attached to the *neck* portion of the animal[393].

It is, therefore, untrue that "the ancient Hebrews interpreted the breastbone or heart-key to be the *os sterni cum pare primo costarum* "[394]. This is only correct in the special case quoted whereby the number of ribs is also still in dispute. Furthermore, one would only obtain the form of a key if one completely excises the breastbone and the two upper ribs which would represent the grip of the key together with the vertebrae attached thereto, after one has removed the shoulder — certainly not a simple task!

*Rashi* notes that the two small upper ribs which one excises for the priestly allowance (one on each side) "are situated around the windpipe and are called *furcile* ".

Apparently *Rashi* refers to the same thing which later anatomists called *furcula,* namely the bifurcation formed by the breastbone and the two clavicles, which was considered to be an analogue of the wishbone of birds. It was well-known to *Rashi* that cattle have no clavicles.

Hyrtl[395] asserts that the name *furcula* in the modern sense was first used in the Latin translations of Avicenna. Since Avicenna died in 1037[396] and *Rashi,*in 1105, the word *furcula* as an anatomic term, at least in the ancient French form, had probably already been known previously. The dictionaries use *fourcil, fourcelle, forcel* only as lay terms in the sense of *estomac, poitrine* (chest), etc. Godefroy cites from a translation of Galen edited in 1609: *"les clavicules ou forcelles"*.

The "openings" (mentioned in the *Mishnah*) are constantly referred to in the Talmud as thè anus and the urethra. "To have need of one's openings" is an expression which is synonymous with "nature is calling", meaning one has need to relieve oneself. *Beth nekuba* is the area of the anal opening (in an animal)[397] and *beth hanekeb* is the opening in the trousers opposite the anus[398].

In only *one* place in the Talmud does the term "openings", according to the commentaries, refer to the *nose* and the anus[399].

One might consider that the "five bones of the openings" refer to the five sacral vertebrae, were it not for the fact that the bones of the anterior "opening", the urethra, would then be lacking. Furthermore, Galen[400] and, therefore, also the

390. *Tosefta* Chullin 9:13
391. Tamid 4:3
392. for example Levit. 7:31
393. Tamid 4:3
394. Kazenelson p.199
395. Hyrtl. *Das Arabische.* p.122 No. 60

396. Preuss erroneously has 1073 (F.R.)
397. Pesachim 7:1
398. Niddah 13b
399. Shabbath 151b
400. Galen. *De Ossibus* Chapter 11. Kühn 2:762

Arabs[401], only list three sacral vertebrae, which is correct for some animals, but not for man.

The following assertion by Kazenelson is a complete fabrication: "the statement about the eighteen vertebrae once became adopted in Hebraic tradition...and the authors of the fragment (i.e. our *Mishnah*), in order not to conflict with the tradition (of eighteen vertebrae), counted the first sacral vertebra as one of the lumbar vertebrae, and considered the other four sacral vertebra and the coccyx to comprise a separate grouping (of bones) concerning which the fragment (i.e. *Mishnah*) states: *quinque in foraminibus*"[402]. There is nothing at all known about such a tradition which must have preceded the *Mishnah*.

Remarkable is the fact that Maimonides (died 1204) understands "openings" to refer to penis *and testicle*; he doesn't even mention the anus. His authority was accepted by Rabbi Asher ben Yechiel in 1328 and Rabbi Obadya from Bertinoro in 1500.

# PART III
# THE ORGANS OF SENSATION

The apparently common knowledge that a person has five senses is as new and as recent in Jewish literature as the acquaintance of the latter with philosophy in general. There is also lacking in the Hebrew language a word to describe the scientific concepts of the senses[403] because everything transmitted to us from Hebraic writings of antiquity is based on legal sources and not on philosophical meditations. However, the commentaries of the Middle Ages, beginning with Saadia, endeavored to show that Scripture already enumerates the five sense organs in succession.

It is completely self-evident that these organs and their functions were *known* in earliest times, despite the absence of systematic physiology and philosophy. In the following sections, we have assembled the remarks found in the Bible and Talmud concerning the individual organs.

## THE EYE

### I  Anatomy of the Eye

The eye is called *ayin* from a root which means "to flow"; for this reason the same word *ayin* is also used to denote a well of water. Simple observation can distinguish the white or *laban* and the black or *schachor* of the eyeball. According to the opinion of Rabbi Jose son of Rabbi Bun, in man, the white is predominant whereas in animals the black is dominant[404]. It was of course well known that the black part makes vision possible. Rabbi Yochanan, in a sermon, said: "The eye is white; the black sits in the middle; should one not properly see through the white? And yet it is not so"[405]!

A folk-legend relates that the white originates from the white sperm of the father, and the black from the seed of the mother[406]. In the black of the eye, one saw human beings on a markedly reduced scale. According to this portrayal, people were called "dolls"; actually "little men", *ishon*[407]. The expression "daughter of the eye", *bath*

---

401. De Koning. *opus cit.* p.129. Haly: 487, Avicenna
402. Kazenelson p.201
403. D. Kaufmann. *Die Sinne*, Leipzig, 1884 p.35
404. Jerushalmi Niddah 3; 50c
405. *Tanchuma, Tetzavch.* Ed. Buber p.49a.
406. Niddah 31a
407. Deut. 32:10 and Proverbs 7:2. Usually translated "the apple of his eye".

*ayin,* is also used[408]. The term *baba* as a pet name or word expressing fondness is found both in Hebrew and in Arabic writings in the same sense[409] and is sometimes used by the Aramaic translators for *ishon.* Similar designations for the pupils also exist in other languages. *Baba* can be compared to the English word "baby" and *bath ayin* to the Greek *kore* (girl) which the Septuagint uses for *ishon*[410] and to the word *parthenos* (virgin) in Aretäus. Further terms for pupil are *pupa* and *pupilla. Ishon* can be compared to the Arabic *insanu-l-ajni* etc.

*Rashi*[411] interprets *ishon* as an expression for darkness (equivalent to blackness) based on the meaning of the word conveyed in the Proverbs[412]. His grandson Rabbi Samuel ben Meir erroneously explains[413]: "*ishon* is the flesh which curves over the eye, i.e. *palpèbre,* and, since it covers and darkens the eye, it is called *ishon".*

The Rabbis call the pupil *galgal* meaning the round globe or that which rotates. They also call it *ukkama* meaning the black part[414]. The *galgal* is round in humans and oblong in animals[415]. Only the snake has a round pupil[416].

Nevertheless, it is undeniable that the word *galgal* also refers to the eyeball since, in certain legends of the Talmud, the meaning "pupil" would be nonsensical. Abba Saul relates: "I buried dead people; once a burial cave opened beneath me and I stood in the *galgal* of the eye of a corpse up to my nose. When I returned, I was told that it was the (insatiable) eye of Absalom"[417]. It is related in a fable that 300 barrels of oil were drawn from the *galgal* of a fish[418]. The generation of the flood was haughty with the *galgal* of the eye which resembles water (*ayin* means both "well of water" and "eye"); therefore God judged them with water which resembles the eye[419].

The corium (of the white) is considered by the Rabbis to be a fatty substance[420]. Aristotle also calls this eye skin *pion* (pus) and *steatodes* (fatty)[421].

The term *sira* either refers to the iris or the corneal-scleral fold.

According to *Rashi, sira* is "the round (of the sphere) which surrounds the black, *la prunelle"* i.e. the iris[422]. Maimonides explains "*sira* is the margin of the white because the skins of the eyeball envelop the eye all around except for the white; the latter encircles the cornea on all sides around the black of the eye; that is around the site which is subject to different variations in color: black or blue"[423]. Thus, *sira* refers to the corneal-scleral fold.

According to Rabbenu Chananel, *cirya,* which is the same as *sira,* is the red (clearness) which encircles the black (the pupil) i.e. the iris[424].

One *Mishnah,* attributed to Samuel the Small, has its own nomenclature in considering the eyeball to be a *microcosmus* of the world! The world is comparable to the eyeball of a person: the white therein is the ocean, which encircles the entire world, the black therein is the earth, the *komet* of the black (the pupil) is Jerusalem, and the face *(partzuf* being equivalent to *ishon)* in the *komet* is the Temple[425].

The teaching of microcosm is already found in the writings of Aristotle[426], in Plato and in writings of the Stoics[427], and it is possible that Samuel the Small, who

408. Lament. 2:18 and Psalms 17:8
409. Zechariah 2:12
410. Deut. 32:10; Psalms 17:8; Proverbs 7:2 & 20:20
411. on Deut. 31:10
412. Proverbs 7:9 and 20:20
413. on Deut. 32:10
414. Bechoroth 40a
415. Jerushalmi Niddah 3; 50c
416. Niddah 23a
417. *ibid* 24b
418. Baba Bathra 73b
419. *Tosefta* Sotah 3:9
420. Bechoroth 38b
421. Aristotle. *Hist. Anim.* Book 3 Chapt. 18 No. 89
422. *Rashi* Bechoroth 38a, end
423. Maimonides' Commentary on Bechoroth 6:2
424. *Aruch. s.v. tzar.* 4
425. Derech Eretz Zuta 9:13
426. Zeller. *Philosophie der Griechen.* Vol. 2:2 p.488
427. Eisler. *Wörterbuch der philosophischen Begriffe.* Berlin 1904 Vol. 1 p.670

lived around the year 100 C.E., got it from them. The Talmudic writings also speak elsewhere of microcosm: "God created in man everything that He created in the world. The forests correspond to the hair, wild (carnivorous) animals to the entrails, aroma to the nose, the sun to vision, foul-smelling water to nasal mucus, salt water of the sea to tears, a brook to the urinary stream, gates to the lips, doors to the teeth, sweet water to spittle, and the stars to the cheeks"[428].

Of course, the writers who wrote specifically on microcosm[429] make no mention of either Samuel the Small or any other Talmudic teaching thereon.

## II    The Eye Socket

The eyeball lies in a hollow or *chor,* the fat content of which is responsible for the protuberance or sunkenness of the globe. The eyes of prosperous wicked people *stand out with fatness*[430]. The *Midrash* also states[431] that man's eyes become sunken from poverty and hunger. The sons of Korach complained: *mine eye languishes because of affliction*[432] and David states: *mine eye is consumed because of grief*[433].

*Rashi* here explains that vision becomes weak so that a person feels as if he is looking through a glass which is held before his eyes. This statement is evidence that *Rashi* was not yet familiar with spectacles. He died in 1105 and the invention of spectacles cannot be assumed any earlier than the end of the thirteenth century[434].

The boundaries of the eye socket are curves, *gubbah* in Arabic, upon which are located the eyebrows, *gabboth* in Mishnaic Hebrew and in Aramaic. A leper must shave off the eyebrows as well as other hair before he takes the ritual cleansing bath which allows him to reenter the company of the healthy[435].

As certified by Aristotle[436], in elderly people, the eyebrows sometimes become so bushy *(dasynontai)* that they have to be shorn off. The Talmud also relates that when Rabbi Yochanan became old, his *gebinim* (eyebrows) were overhanging, whereupon he spoke to his disciples: "lift mine eyes up so that I can see Rabbi Kahana". They lifted up his eyebrows with silver cosmetic pincers[437].

## III    Eyebrows and Eyelashes

The eyeball is protected by the *afapayim* which, in the Bible, refer both to the lids as well as the eyelashes[438]. The *Beraitha,* however, speaks of "the hair on the *afapayim"*[439], so that only the eyelids can be meant. In the Aramaic translation, the term mostly used therefor is *thimura,* which is identical with the Biblical *ap.eir. shemura*[440] which means "the watchman or the protector"[441].

Every creation in nature has a purpose. Why is the *thimura,* the long lower eyelid of a chicken, bent upwards? Because it dwells among the rafters, and if dust (or the smoke from the chimney) entered its eyes, it would go blind[442].

The *Mishnah* uses the designation *ris,* which cannot be identified either with the Greek *ophrys* (eyebrow)[443] or with iris[444], because the Greeks call the iris *ragoeides chiton.*

---

428. Aboth de Rabbi Nathan 31:3
429. for example Adolf Meyer in *Berner Studien zur Philosophie.* Vol. 25, 1900
430. Psalms 73:7
431. Midrash Psalms *loc. cit.* ed Buber p.164
432. Psalms 88:10
433. Psalms 6:8
434. Hirschberg. *Mitteilungen zur Geschichte der Medizin.* Vol. 6 p.221
435. Leviticus 14:9
436. Aristotle. *Hist. Anim.* 3:11 No. 74
437. Baba Kamma 117a
438. Psalms 11:4; Proverbs 6:4; Job 16:16
439. Shabbath 109a
440. Psalms 77:5
441. Löw states that he cannot agree in this matter with Barth & others.
442. Shabbath 77b
443. Perles. *Etymolog. Studien.* p.58
444. Kohut's *Aruch. s.v. charatz* 3:502

The term *ris* also refers both to the lids, "the external wall of the eye"[445], as well as the eyelashes. According to German linguistic use, "*zuckt die Wimper*" refers to the twitching movement of the eyelids and not that of the lashes. The eye is clearly visible "between the lids", and its expression betrays one's opinion.

An orphaned child once asked whether the orders of one's father or one's mother take precedence if the parents are divorced. Rabbi Joshua answered: "from the *risé* of your eyes one can recognize that you are a widow's son (who never knew his father or the love between a father and son; otherwise you would not have asked this question)"[446].

*Ris* occurs most often in the sense of "eyelashes". In old age, *the eyes are heavy (or dim) from old age*[447] which means, according to the explanation of the *Midrash*[448], that the *risé* of the eyes are heavy and stick together. According to the opinion of Rabbi Jose the Galilean, a leper need not shave off the *risé* of his eyes[449] as he has to do for the other hair on his body, perhaps because it is harmful to the eyes[450]. Here we can readily recognize that *risé* means eyelashes, the "external seam of the eye, which is called *pestañas* in a foreign language (Spanish)"[451].

Priests and kings are anointed between the *risé* of the eyes[452]. According to Pseudo-Jonathan's translation, the site where Scripture prescribes that the commandments be bound *between thine eyes*[453] denotes "between the *risé* of your eyes". According to the two latter citations, it appears that *ris* was also used to denote the eyebrows. Tradition, in fact, confirms this interpretation for the first citation[454].

If one does not wish to assume that the usage of the word changed with place and time — which we cannot prove — then it is probably correct to assert that in folk language *ris* is a designation for the eyelids as well as the hair on the eyes (eyelashes and eyebrows). The *Torah* and the Sages, as so often stated[455], use the language of the people.

*Rashi* has the term *"baba"* for the *ris* which means eyelid, and "hair on the *baba"* for the *ris* which means eyelash. In Plinius, the term *palpebra* is equivalent to eyelid and illness of the eyelid[456].

The secretion of the lacrimal glands accumulates if it is produced in large amounts, such as overnight, in the inner corner of the eye, and dries out there, together with the secretion of the conjunctiva, occasionally in a more or less solid mass. The Rabbis call this mass *liphluph* meaning sticky[457]. The Greeks call it *leme* and more recently *glamia (gramiae)*. Maimonides rightly considers this secretion to be unhealthy[458].

## IV    Tears

It is an often-repeated statement that manifestations of emotion were more

---

445. Bechoroth 38a; *Aruch* has *charitz,* derived from *charatz* meaning "to be sharp" or "to cut"; the same textual reading is found in Gittin 56a for the *dokin* of our text. Maimonides (*Biyath Hamikdash* 7:4) asserts that the Biblical *charutz* (Levit. 22:22) refers to an animal with one of the specified eyelid defects. The commentaries, without reference to the Talmud, explain *charutz* as "wounded in the leg" *(Ibn Ezra)* and the like. According to Kohut, *charitz* is the same as the Arabic *charidah* which means *puella.*
446. Kiddushin 31a
447. Genesis 48:10
448. *Pesikta Rabbah* 8. *op. cit.*
449. *Tosefta* Negaim 8:4

450. This is evidenced by the Scriptural demand that *he shave the eyebrows* or *gabboth;* therefore not the eyelashes.
451. Abraham ben David, in the year 1150, in his commentary on *Sifra Emor* 6:7. Ed. Weiss p.98c
452. Horayoth 12a
453. Exodus 13:16; different in Deut. 6:8 and 11:18
454. Maimonides. *Keley Mikdash* 1:9
455. for example Berachoth 31b
456. Plinius. *Hist. Natur.* 28:18
457. Mikvaoth 9:2 and 9:4; Niddah 67a
458. Maimonides Commentary on Mikvaoth *loc. cit.*

natural in antiquity than in recent times. As proof for this assertion, one points to the "florid tears" of heroes of the time of Homer. If one delves into the Biblical books, one comes to the conclusion that we can readily explain each episode of crying that is mentioned in the Pentateuch. In later times, when Jews were threatened with loss of political independence or when catastrophe had already struck or when oppression and persecution did not allow those persecuted to enjoy life, it is only natural that tears should flow profusely. However, we will not here consider "the language of tears" any more than the "silent language of the eyes"[459].

It is taught that there are six types of tears[460]; three are beneficial and three are harmful. The tears caused by smoke, tears of mourning and tears in the privy (from diarrhea or from straining at defecation) are harmful, but tears over the loss of a grown-up child are the worst of all. Tears produced by a medication or by mustard or by an eye-salve are beneficial, but tears of joy are the best of all.

Proverbs states: *as vinegar for the teeth and as smoke to the eyes, so (harmful) is the sluggard to them that send him*[461]. "Tears in the privy" is naturally interpreted by modern (Western) scholars to refer to the effect of ammonia (disinfectant) on the conjunctiva. The Oriental person, however, who is plagued with dysentery cries because of the pain of tenesmus.

Vision is dependent upon crying. The prophet bemoans: *mine eyes do fail with tears*[462]. Legend relates that when a daughter of Rabbi Chanina died, he forcibly withheld his tears, whereupon his wife asked him critically: have you just sent out a fowl from your home? He answered: "shall I suffer two evils; losing children and blindness are siblings"[463]!

The expression of the preacher that in old age *clouds occur after the rain*[464] is interpreted in one place in the Talmud[465] to refer to the clouding over and darkening of the eyes due to constant crying by a person over all the grief that he experiences. It is also possible that the weakness of vision of elderly people has been attributed to the fact that they shed so many tears. For this reason, Samuel teaches that crying in a person past 40 years of age is particularly harmful[466].

If one places a finger in the eye, the latter tears; as long as the finger is in the eye, new tears continue to form[467].

Daily experience teaches that tears are salty. If they trickle on cracks in the skin, they produce pain; they can even cause erosions on the skin of the cheeks. Rabbi Simeon ben Yochai hid in a cave buried up to his neck in sand for twelve years to escape his persecutors. When he emerged, his son-in-law took him into the baths and massaged him, thereby noting that there were clefts on his body from the sand. As a result, his son-in-law wept and when the tears fell on the skin into the clefts, Rabbi Simeon ben Yochai cried out in pain[468]. When the enemy entered the Temple, they seized the young men and bound their hands behind their backs so that their tears could not be wiped. The tears ate themselves into their cheeks like the scar of a boil[469].

Teleologically, a reason was sought and found for the saltiness of tears. The *Midrash* is of the opinion[470] that if tears were not salty, a person would continually cry for a deceased individual and he would soon become blind. The saltiness, however, burns his eyes and reminds him to cease.

---

459. Compare M. Friedmann. *Der Blinde im biblischen und rabbinischer Schrifttume.* Vienna 1873 p.86 ff
460. Lament. Rabbah on 2:15; Variants in Aboth de Rabbi Nathan 41:5 and Shabbath 151b
461. Proverbs 10:26
462. Lament. 2:11
463. Shabbath 151a
464. Eccles. 12:2
465. Shabbath 151a
466. ibid
467. Niddah 13a
468. Shabbath 33b
469. Lament. Rabbah 1:25
470. Numbers Rabbah 18:22

In microcosm salty tears correspond to the salty ocean water of the large world[471].

Fables and legends often speak of crying that does not involve human beings. A calf which ran away from the slaughterer fled to Rabbi Judah and cried[472]. When Rabbi Abbahu died, the columns of Caesarea cried[473].

## V    Physiology of the Eye

When the prophet puts these words into God's mouth: *make the heart of the people fat and make their ears heavy and shut their eyes lest they see with their eyes. . . .*[474], he is referring to the often-emphasized fact that it is not the external organ but the faculty of perception which sees. This interpretation is even more clearly recognizable in the words of the same prophet: the people are blind although they have eyes, and deaf although they have ears[475].

In later times, it was even assumed that there is an anatomical relationship between the eyes and the heart or psyche. The Talmud states: "the *shuryane* of the eye is connected to the chamber (*obantha*) of the heart"[476]. It is possible that this assertion is based on the teaching of Aristotle in which, by a misunderstanding of the papillary muscles, all nerves of the body are said to originate from the heart. This assertion in the Talmud also explains the Talmudic concept that many eye illnesses are dangerous to life.

The word *shuryane* is also found in Arabic writings in the sense of arteries and nerves. According to Fraenkel[477], it is a foreign word derived from Aramaic. The Rabbis derive the word *obantha* from *bin* meaning "to understand" and they therefore explain: "eyesight is dependent upon the understanding of the heart" i.e. perception is a matter of comprehension.

Only a human being, but not an animal, has the capacity to see what is happening on the sides even when his eyes are directed straight ahead[478]. For this reason, in most birds, the eyes are fixed on the sides of the head[479].

According to Rabbi Simeon ben Eleazar, one can close the eyelids of a dead person if one blows wine in his nose and places oil between the eyelashes or *rise*[480].

If a dead animal, after the forced slaughtering, still blinked its eye (*riphreph*), it cannot be concluded that it was still alive when it was slaughtered and hence permissible for human consumption. This blinking is thought to represent the "fleeing of life"[481], meaning the movement following the relaxation of muscle tone. It is known that movement of the eyelids is not only produced from the bulb but also occurs on the freshly decapitated head of cattle[482].

While it sleeps, a gazelle keeps one eye open and the other tightly closed[483].

## VI    Vision in Old Age

With advancing age, the visual ability of the eye decreases. When the Patriarch Isaac became 123 years old, *his eyes were dim*[484]. According to the *Midrash*, this diminution of visual acuity was a special blessing from God so that Isaac did not have

471. Aboth de Rabbi Nathan 31:3
472. Baba Metzia 85a
473. Moed Katan 25b
474. Isaiah 6:10
475. *ibid* 43:8
476. Abodah Zara 28b. *Rashi's* rendering is: the nerves of the eye affect the fat around the heart; *Tosafoth* interprets: the eyesight is connected with the mental faculties.
477. Fraenkel. *Die Aramaeischen Fremdwörter im Arabischen*. p.261
478. Genesis Rabbah 8:11
479. Niddah 23a
480. *Tosefta* Shabbath 17:19
481. *Tosefta* Chullin 2:12; Chullin 38b and *Baer Hetev's* commentary on *Yoreh Deah* 17, note 4
482. Dembo. *Das Schächten*. Leipzig 1894 p.11
483. Song of Songs Rabbah 8:14 and *Targum* on Song of Songs 8:14. See also Bochart *Hierozoicon*. ed. Frankfurt 1:926
484. Genesis 27:1

to see the misdeeds of his son Esau[485]. It is emphasized as being exceptional that Moses was 120 years old and *his eye was not dim, nor his natural force abated*[486]. Such findings of dim vision and body frailty are the usual occurrences at such an age. Concerning Eli the priest and later judge, we are told that at age 98 *his eyes began to wax dim*[487] and shortly thereafter *his eyes were dim* (ceased to function) *that he could not see*[488].

Just as later generations lived for shorter periods than earlier generations, so too the organs of man in the course of time cease to function. Only Jacob was 147 years old when *his eyes were dim for age, so that he could not see*[489]. I do not know how old Achiya was when *his eyes were set by reason of his age*[490].

Rabbi Simeon ben Chalafta said: the eyes which once could see at a distance cannot now in old age even see near[491]. *Nor the clouds return after the rain*[492] is interpreted to refer to an old man who cries very lightly and his eyes overflow uncontrollably with tears[493].

## THE NOSE

### I   Anatomy of the Nose

From the word *aph* which is the term for nose, one derives the dual *appayim* for nostrils, as in the case for the names of all paired organs. The term *nechirayim* is also used for nostrils. Only the Talmud uses the terms *apputha* and *chotem*[494] with the plural *chotamin* (for *ala nasi* and the septum?). The term *tarpha dinechira*, or membrane of the nose, is also used for nostrils[495]. The expression *osya*[496] is uncertain; the Greeks did not use the term *ousia* in the sense of "nose".

The nose determines the facial expression. As a result, the definitive identification of a corpse can only occur if the nose is still intact on the face[497]. The inhabitants of Sepphoris were persecuted during the time of Ursicinus. They tried to make themselves unrecognizable by pasting plaster on their noses; nevertheless, they were betrayed and collectively imprisoned[498].

The eyes of an embryo are like two drippings of a fly which are far removed from one another. The two nostrils are like two drippings of a fly which are near one to another[499].

We do not understand the compliment that the shepherd is paying to his Shulamith when he compares her nose to *the tower of Lebanon which looketh toward Damascus*[500]. The term *gobah aph* has the meaning and the sense of haughtiness (i.e. nose in the air)[501]. It is uncertain whether or not the Talmudic expression *ba'al hachotem*[502] also refers to haughtiness.

After the fall of Jerusalem, a Roman official was sent to arrest Rabbi Gamliel, and came to the house of study and announced: "I am searching for a *ba'al hachotem*". Perhaps the expression also has a derogatory second meaning. The *bene nasati* were considered to be especially experienced as in the *Ars amandi*[503].

485. Genesis Rabbah 65:10
486. Deut. 34:7
487. First Samuel 3:2
488. *ibid* 4:15
489. Genesis 48:10
490. First Kings 14:4
491. Levit. Rabbah 18:1
492. Eccles. 12:2
493. Levit. Rabbah 18:1
494. This is the proper vocalization according to Judaic tradition. Buxtorf correctly has *chotem*. *Chotam* is not correct. Compare *ozen, bohen, chomesh*, etc...Löw

495. Berachoth 55b
496. Shabbath 66a, in a magical incantation about the nose of an animal
497. Yebamoth 16:3
498. Jerushalmi Sotah 9; 23c
499. Niddah 25a
500. Song of Songs 7:5
501. Psalms 10:4
502. Taanith 29a
503. See Hagen. *Sexuelle Osphresiologie.* Charlottenburg 1901 p.15; Levy. *Neuhebraisches und Chaldäisches Wörterbuch.* Leipzig 1876-1889 Vol. 2:538a."*Trotznasige*"

The secretion of the nose is called *mé ha'aph*[504] or *ha-yotzeh min ha-chotem*[505], *quod ex naso exit*. It is also called *tzoah* or excrement[506]. The secretion is offensive. The *Midrash* describes a reason therefor, namely when a person inhales a bad aroma he would immediately die were it not for the fact that the offensive water of the nose arrests the external aroma[507]. If nasal secretion is present in a small amount, it is beneficial; in large amounts, it is harmful[508].

## II    Functions of the Nose

The nose is the organ of respiration. God breathes the breath of life into the nostrils[509] which remains in the nose as long as the soul is in a person's body[510]. It is typical of graven images (or idols) that they do not breathe with their nose[511].

The nose is also the organ of smell. Only idols have noses, yet cannot smell[512]. The apostle considers man's sense of smell to be essential: *if the whole body were hearing, where would the smell be?*[513] Only the soul and not the body derives benefit from an aroma[514]; if the latter is sufficiently intense, it can revive a person who fainted[515].

An angry temperament is recognizable in the face by the vibration of the *ala nasi*. One sees fumes emanating from the nostrils of the angry Behemoth[516]. As a result, during antiquity, the nose was thought to be the organ of anger and its name — usually *aph* but later also *nechartha*[517] — was simply used to denote "anger". A person who quickly becomes angry is a *ba'al aph*[518] and someone slow to anger is called *erech appayim* which literally means "having a long nose". As opposed to a forbearing person, there is the *ketzar appayim* or hot-tempered individual[519]. For this reason, Rebbe interpreted the dream of Bar Kappara — that his nose fell off — to mean that God had removed His anger from him[520].

In post-Biblical times, it was taught that the seat of anger is in the liver[521].

## III    Sneezing

Sneezing was considered a noteworthy occurrence by the ancients. Aristotle explains it as a holy, Divine sign which has great significance: *ton Ptarmon theon egoumetha einai*[522]. He simultaneously raises the question[523] as to why the other types of air which emanate from the body[524], flatus and ructus, are not considered to be holy. He answers that only sneezing comes from the principal and most Divine organ. Already in Homer, Penelope is happy that her son Telemachus sneezes when she expresses a wish[525]. When someone sneezed at the precise moment that Kleanor declared that the situation of the 10,000 was not hopeless, the entire army *mia orme* offered prayers to the god on high[526].

The belief that an assertion has validity if someone "sneezes on it" is widespread even today. In the Talmud, it is considered to be a favorable omen if someone sneezes

504. *Tosefta* Shabbath 8:28
505. Machshirim 6:5
506. Baba Metzia 107b, from the Syrian *tzaa* meaning "to be dirty".
507. Numbers Rabbah 18:22
508. Baba Metzia 107b
509. Genesis 2:7
510. Job 27:3
511. Wisdom of Solomon 15:15
512. Psalms 115:6. The nose of *Pe'or*. Jerushalmi Sanhedrin 10; 28d
513. First Corinthians 12:17
514. Berachoth 43b
515. *ibid* 57b

516. Job 41:12
517. Genesis Rabbah 67:10
518. Proverbs 22:24
519. Proverbs 14:17
520. Berachoth 56b
521. *ibid* 61b
522. Aristotle. *Problem Sect.* 33:7
523. *ibid. problem.* 9
524. So too in *Hist. Anim.* 1 c.11, where Aubert and Wimmer misunderstood the word *pneumaton* of the text.
525. Homer. *Odyssy* 17:545
526. Xenoph. *Anab.* 3 Chapt. 2:9

while he is praying. It is a sign that just as God looks favorably towards him here on earth so too they look favorably toward him in heaven[527].

A second line of interpretation in antiquity connects sneezing with the presence of great danger. The Jews call out: I wish you *marpé* ("be healed")[528] or *chayim* ("life")[529] or *chayim tobim* ("good life")[530] to a person that sneezes. In Greece, the person who sneezed would cry out: *Zeu soson* ("Zeus, help us")[531]. From Rome, Plinius[532] reports: *sternuentes salutamur*. He relates that when the Emperor Tiberius, otherwise the *tristissimus, ut constat hominum*, sat on a wagon, he would call out this greeting to the passersby[533]. Even Mohammed instructed that someone who sneezes should be wished luck[534].

The ancient historians such as Sigo[535] and Urbini[536], as well as clerics[537], report that the origin of this use of sneezing as a sign of great danger is the bubonic plague which raged in Rome in the year 590 and in which people suddenly died while sneezing or yawning. Pope Pelagius also died in this epidemic. As a result, it became customary to call out *"deus te adjuvet"* to someone who sneezed. A Jewish chronicler of the sixteenth century, David Gans, also fell victim to this assertion[538]. The much older usage of this belief that sneezing heralds great danger is mentioned by Caesar Baron[539], who cites as proof the aforementioned quotation from Plinius. From the report of the Dutch physician Isbrand Van Diemerbroeck who describes the plague in Nijmegen, one might perceive that the above narrative (of Plinius) might nevertheless be based on a true occurrence: *cum crebris sternutationibus neminem evadisse vidimus*[540].

Dioscorides also reports that during the time of Valerius Flaccus cases were known in which epilepsy occurred following copious sneezing. Naturally, the modern German "bacteria-fanatic" knows that sneezing is "an attempted reaction of the nasal membrane against penetration by microbes". To him, the traditional *"prosit"* or *"zur Gesundheit"* ("bless you") is equivalent to saying to the person: "I wish you luck and hope that you rid yourself of the bacillus or bacilli"[541]!

Among the Jews, there exists the legend that originally there was no illness in the world at all; rather, wherever a healthy person found himself, if his time to die had arrived, he sneezed and his soul left him through his nose. Thus, when Jacob began to bless his sons, he began to sneeze, and in anticipation of his imminent death, prayed: *I have waited for thy salvation, O Lord*[542]! He said: give me enough time to bless my sons. Thus, when a person sneezes, he is obligated to thank God that he remains alive[543]. This narrative is also of recent date.

Monotheism in antiquity considered this salutation of "bless you" to someone

---

527. Berachoth 24b
528. i.e. bless you. *Tosefta* Shabbath 7:5
529. *Pirke de Rabbi Eliezer* 52
530. *Aruch* from *Yelamdenu*. Not found in our edition
531. Ammianos ridicules a Proklos who had such a long nose that he did not call out *Zen soson* when he sneezed because he didn't hear it since his ear was too far away. *Florileg. Divers. Epigramat. Vet.* ed. Henry Stephanus. Book 2 c.13 p.141.
532. Plinius. *Hist. Natur.* 28:5
533. *ibid.*
534. see Hammer. *Fundgruben des Orients* 1:161
535. Carol. Sigonu. *Historiar. de regno Italiae.* Book 15 Basel 1575 p.31. *ad anum* 590
536. Polydorus Vergilius Urbinatus. *De*

*Rerum Inventoribus.* Book 8. Amsterdam 1671. Elzevir (preface in August 1499). Book 6 c.11 p.410
537. Guil. Durandus. *Rationale Divinor. Officior.* Lugdun. 1605. Book 6 c.102 p.393.
538. D. Gans. *Tzemach David.* Sedilkow 1834 p.51b:until the year 590
539. Baronius. *Annales Ecclesiast.*:until the year 590. ed. Theiner. Vol. 10 p.451 b.
540. Diemerbroeck. *De Peste.* Amsterdam 1665 p.101
541. Rivinus who is the same as Dr. Franz Bachmann. *Was ist Krankheit?* Birnbaum 1892 p.24
542. Genesis 49:18. This passage is lacking in the sources (*Yalkut* Genesis No. 78; *Yalkut* Job No. 927; *Pirke de Rabbi Eliezer* 52) but must be restored for proper understanding.
543. *Pirke de Rabbi Eliezer* 52

who sneezes as a superstition and, therefore, prohibited it, as did the school of Rabban Gamliel[544]; others didn't wish to interrupt their study by wishing good health to someone who sneezed[545]. These Rabbis who tried to prohibit the saying of "bless you" following sneezing had no success. In fact, one observes that the above-cited *Midrash* considers the Patriarch Jacob to be the originator of this custom. In addition, Augustine also decreed: *Illas non solum sacrilegas, sed etiam ridiculosas sternutationes considerare et observare nolite*[546], but he too was not to be pleased with the results.

Sneezing at the table was considered to be a particularly evil omen[547]. Even those who are otherwise averse to offering "good wishes" might here be inclined to do so. As a result, it was necessary to specifically forbid the exclamation of *jjs*[548] during meals because of the feared danger of choking[549], given the general prohibition extant against speaking while eating[550].

Sneezing occurs forcibly and involuntarily[551]. A concealed eavesdropper once revealed his presence thereby[552]. Sometimes a sneeze is released by a strong external stimulus such as the fumes of frankincense[553]. Among the signs in a woman "about to menstruate" are: "she yawns or sneezes"[554]. After a suspected adulteress drinks the "testing waters", she sneezes until her body becomes unsettled (spasmodic sneezing)[555].

Although the later legend of the ill patriarch[556] considers sneezing to be a bad and feared omen, the older teaching of the *Gemara* states that the same phenomenon is prognostically a good sign in a patient[557] and indicates healing. *His sneezing signifies the light of healing*[558]. The son of the Shunamite woman who appeared to have died from sunstroke sneezed seven times and opened his eyes[559]. Even in modern times, Jonathan Hutchinson reports[560] that he has never observed a seriously ill patient sneeze.

According to Hippocrates, sneezing prior to or following a lung illness is dangerous. Otherwise, it is beneficial, even in patients with fatal illnesses[561]. Celsus considers sneezing during convalescence from illness to be a beneficial sign[562]. Noteworthy is the fact that the same belief is still extant among the Zulus, as described by Tylor[563], who also provides us with abundant ethnographic material on our subject. Furthermore, the term *ittush* is used for sneezing as well as being an expression for flatus[564].

---

544. *Tosefta* Shabbath 7:5
545. Berachoth 53a
546. Augustine. Sermo 278 de Auguriis. Migne Vol. 39, p.2269; also Vol. 40 p.1172
547. Plinius 28:5
548. This word is unintelligible. The word *iasis* (healing) mentioned by the dictionaries, was not used by the Greeks. *Aruch* has the equally unintelligible textual reading *zt* which the author Kohut interpreted to mean *zeto* ("live long"). But *zeto* was not said (to someone who sneezed). The exclamation *zethi* ("live long") for sneezing is mentioned by Olympiodor (Scholia in Platonis *Phaedon*. ed. Finckh p.30) but to equate *zt* with *zethi* is impossible. Perhaps it is an imperative of *asi*, to heal.
549. Jerushalmi Berachoth 6; 10d
550. Taanith 5b

551. Berachoth 24b
552. Jerushalmi Yoma 3; 40d
553. Jerushalmi Sukkah 5; 55b
554. Niddah 9:8
555. Numbers Rabbah 9:21
556. Genesis 48:1
557. Berachoth 57b
558. Job 41:10
559. Second Kings 4:35
560. *Sheffield Med. Journal.* April 1893 p.254
561. Hippocrates. *Caoc. Praenot.* No. 399, fol. 181 & *Prognos.* fol. 41:22 of the Foes edition.
562. Celsus, *Med.* 2:3
563. Tylor. *Anfänge der Kultur.* 1:98 of the German edition. Leipzig 1873
564. Berachoth 62a; Jerushalmi Berachoth 3; 6d.

# THE EAR

## I   Anatomy and Function of the Ear

The ear is called *ozen* or *udna* and consists of the cartilage, *thenuch ozen*[565] or the height of the ear known as *rum udna* or *gobah shel ozen*[566] and *bedal ozen*[567] and (also in humans) *chashus*[568], as well as the earlobe *alyah* (tail) or *milath*[569]. Sometimes, the fold in the cartilage is called "the middle railing of the ear"[570].

The priest is anointed on the right ear cartilage[571]. The ear cartilage of a patient convalescing from *tzara'ath* is wetted with sacrificial blood[572]. The school of Rabbi Ishmael taught as follows: why is the entire ear hard and only the lobe (the *alyah*) is soft? So that if a person hears something unworthy, he folds his earlobe inwardly and thus effectively closes it[573]. For the ear is not in the power of man; he must hear even that which he doesn't wish to hear[574], even blasphemy[575]. The "water of the ears" (cerumen) provides a certain degree of protection. Providence selected a fatty liquid for this purpose; otherwise, if a person were to receive a bad (distressing) piece of news, it would be maintained in his ear by a hard substance and the person would die. However, the soft liquid (cerumen) brings the news into one ear and out the other[576]. In a small quantity, "the dirt" *(tzoah)* of the nose and the ear is beneficial; in large amounts, it is dangerous[577].

"Double ears" (rolled-together pinnae) are repulsive, and represent a beauty blemish in a woman[578].

The ear is opened[579] and implanted[580] by God. Its relationship to the body is like that of a cooking plate upon which pots are placed. If one lights a fire under the plate, every pot senses it[581]; so too the ear transmits words to each of the 248 limbs of man[582] in that it separates individual words[583]. Not every ear hears, however; rather *the hearing ear and the seeing eye — the Lord hath made both of them*[584].

The sense of hearing is part of the contribution made by God in the formation of an embryo, whereas the bodily parts originate from the parents[585]. The Lord must first open the ear so that it can hear[586]. Nevertheless, it happens that one hears with the ears but does not understand[587]. When the prophet speaks in the name of the Lord: *make the heart of this people obstinate and their ears heavy and their eyes dull, so that they not see with their eyes, nor hear with their ears*[588], it appears that the ear doesn't actually hear, but the power of recognition, i.e. the heart, discerns.

If one wishes to hear precisely, one must incline[589] or bend[590] the ear; these images are probably based on the observation of animals that actively move their pinnae or tips of the ears. Even then, two sounds cannot simultaneously penetrate one ear[591] and one cannot therefore hear the utterances of two people who are speaking simultaneously.

---

565. for example Levit. 8:23
566. Kiddushin 21b
567. Amos 3:12
568. Bechoroth 40b; *sachus* is a corrupt form
569. *ibid* 37b
570. *Sifra* on *tzav* 42a, Weiss; *Targum Jonathan* on Levit. 8:23 & elsewhere
571. Exodus 29:20
572. Levit. 14:14
573. Kethuboth 5b
574. Genesis Rabbah 67:3
575. *Tanchuma, Toledoth* p.71a. Buber
576. Numbers Rabbah 18:22
577. Baba Metzia 107b
578. Nedarim 66b
579. Psalms 40:7
580. *ibid* 94:11
581. *Pesikta de Rab Kahana* 14 p.117a, Buber.
582. Deut. Rabbah 10:1
583. Job 12:11
584. Proverbs 20:12
585. Niddah 31a
586. Isaiah 50:5
587. Mark 4:12
588. Isaiah 6:10
589. Isaiah 55:3
590. Song of Songs Rabbah 1:8
591. Jerusalmi Megillah 4; 74d

In old age the ears become heavy (i.e. hard of hearing)[592]. "The near becomes distant" means: the ears which earlier heard following a single call now do not hear even after the hundredth time of speaking[593]. Thus, when Barzillai was eighty years old, he thought it was natural that he was no longer able to hear the voice of male and female singers[594].

There are also people, however, who intentionally stop up their ears in order not to hear[595]. But, whoever stops up his ears at the cry of the poor will himself cry out to God but will not be heard[596]. Nevertheless, there are warnings which are so frightening that "the ears"[597] or "both ears"[598] of anyone who hears them quiver (tingle). As a war stratagem, Joshua advised the spies to feign deafness so that the enemy would then not hesitate to discuss their plans in their presence[599].

According to Jewish tradition, a person does not become "complete" until after circumcision. Therefore the prophet scolds: *Behold, their ear is uncircumcised and they cannot hearken*[600].

With the destruction of the Temple, songs of joy ceased in Israel. As a result, Rab said that the ear which listens to singing at a festive banquet is worthy of being torn off[601].

To-and-fro movement of the ears of an animal is a sign of vitality, thereby still rendering its slaughtering permissible[602].

## II   Earrings

Because of vanity, young girls pierce their ear lobes and place a chip through the opening so that it not heal and can later serve to hold colored threads or earrings[603]. The latter are indispensable parts of the female toilette. In ancient times, women wore a colored flock of wool which even had its own handle[604]. Various artisans would carry the signs of their profession on the ear; this was perhaps a primitive forerunner of the modern living advertisement: the pen of the writer[605], the chip of the carpenter, the mark of the painter, the denar of the money changer[606], the wool flock of the weaver[607].

The ear is also mentioned in various *proverbs*. Our maxim "the walls have ears" is already found in the *Midrash* in precisely those words[608]. For this reason, Jacob had his women go out into the field so that he could speak with them privately[609], and the Medes would only deliberate in an open field[610]. A somewhat drastic form of a modern *vox populi* or maxim is the following: "if someone tells you that you have donkey ears, pay no attention; but if two people say it, order a halter"[611]. Another proverb warns the insatiable person: "when the camel went to demand horns, they cut off its ears"[612].

592. Shabbath 152a
593. Levit. Rabbah 18:1
594. Second Samuel 19:36
595. Zechariah 7:11
596. Proverbs 21:13
597. Jeremiah 19:3
598. First Samuel 3:11
599. Ruth Rabbah 2:1. muteness: *cheresh*. Joshua 2:1
600. Jeremiah 6:10
601. Sotah 48a
602. Chullin 38a

603. Shabbath 6:6
604. Shabbath 6:5 and Jerushalmi Shabbath 6; 8c
605. Jerushalmi Shabbath 1; 3b
606. *Tosefta* Shabbath 1:8
607. Shabbath 11b
608. *oznayim la-kothel*, Eccles. Rabbah on 10:20
609. Genesis Rabbah 74:2
610. Berachoth 8b
611. Genesis Rabbah 45:7
612. Sanhedrin 106a

# THE SKIN

## I   Skin Color

The poet portrays the development of a person in the mother's womb as follows: *God poured me out like milk, curdled me like cheese, clothed me with skin and flesh, hedged me with bones and sinews and granted me life*[613]. The resurrection of the dead bones which the prophet saw in his vision is described in a similar manner: *behold...I will lay sinews upon you, and will bring up flesh upon you, and cover you with skin, and put breath in you, and ye shall live*[614].

The skin of Semitic people normally has the yellowish color of box-tree wood and is intermediate in color between that of Germanic people and that of the Moors[615]. It becomes dark-black when the sun burns it[616]. It also becomes black-like *(koder)* even without the sun[617] as a result of anxiety and grief. Finally, the skin becomes discolored and wrinkled *like a bottle in the smoke*[618]. Legend relates that Ham, the son of Noah, had black skin as punishment for immorality[619]. His descendants, the Moors *(kushi)* (Ethiopians?), are also black. The prophet scolds that a Moor can no more change his skin nor a leopard his spots than a person who is accustomed to doing evil who suddenly wishes to do good[620] (i.e. he is unable to do so).

Immoral sovereigns *hate good and love evil, they pluck off the skin* (from the citizens) *and the flesh from their bones*[621]. For material goods, a person would give *skin for skin,* but for his life he would give everything that he possesses[622].

The skin of Moses shone like (polished) horns *(karan)* from the glow of divine splendor which he saw for forty days while on Mount Sinai[623]. Ibn Ezra quotes with displeasure the statement of a commentator called Chawi who explains the Biblical expression to mean that the face of Moses was pale like a horn because of his forty-day fast. How enraged Ibn Ezra would have been if he had known that Aquila and the Vulgate speak of actual horns on Moses' face: *viderunt cornutam Moysis faciem* (Rabbi Samuel ben Meir calls this "nonsense"). This translation, horns, is the reason that Michelangelo portrays Moses with horns.

## II   Skin Incisions and Tattooing

Expressions of emotions by Oriental people are much more intensive and explosive than those of the "cooler" Westerners; during times of grief, Orientals not only cry and lament, but strike themselves with their fists on the thigh[624], and scratch themselves until the blood flows, not only for a death but also "if one's house collapsed or if one's ship sunk in the ocean"[625]. Where the fingernails are insufficient, they use a knife to *make cuttings in the flesh for the dead*[626]. It is a sign of irreverence if one doesn't cut oneself during mourning[627], and if there are not cuttings on all the hands[628]. The author of the *Apocalypse* also alludes thereto[629].

However, the Bible would not have prohibited such a folk custom as strongly as it does[630] were it not for the fact that this "cutting oneself", *serita* and *gedidah,* was also

---

613. Job 10:10-12
614. Ezekiel 37:6
615. Negaim 2:1
616. Song of Songs 1:6
617. Job 30:28-30
618. Psalms 119:83
619. Sanhedrin 108b
620. Jeremiah 13:23
621. Micah 3:2
622. Job 2:4

623. Exodus 34:29 and *Ibn Ezra, loc. cit.*
624. Ezekiel 21:17
625. Makkoth 20b
626. Levit. 19:28
627. Jeremiah 16:6
628. *ibid* 48:37
629. Apocalypse 13:16 and 14:1
630. Levit. 19:28

a cultic practice of the heathens. It is related about the priests of Ba'al on Mount Carmel that *they cut themselves with swords and lancets after their manner, till the blood gushes out upon them*[631]. For this reason, the Bible motivates its prohibition with the allusion: *Ye are the children of the Lord your God*[632], and especially enunciates this prohibition again to the priests[633].

Another idolatrous practice whose extirpation is one of the duties of Judaism is the custom of tattooing or *kethobath kaka*[634]. The skin used to be inscribed with ink *(deyo)*, with eye-paint *(kuchla)*, or any other material that makes a mark *(roshem)*, and then the skin was pricked with a needle or a knife[635]. According to Bar Kappara, one is only liable if one inscribed the name of an idol in this manner. Other Sages, however, interpret the prohibition quite generally and include liability even if he "tattooed his slave, so that he not flee"[636]. This "stigmatization" was widely practiced in heathen antiquity. In Rome, soldiers had the name of their leader or another sign of their army unit etched into their skin. Some Sages were even careful not to sprinkle any black fireplace ashes *(epher miklah)* on a wound, whereas others permitted it because the presence of the wound or the scar, even if it became colored, clearly indicates that no idolatry is intended (by sprinkling powder or medication thereon)[637].

Simple writing on the skin without tattooing is completely permissible in Jewish law. One even used to write documents on the hand of a slave and send the "live letter" (i.e. the slave) to the addressee[638]. Some people wrote the divine name on their skin and covered it with reeds *(gemi)* when they took a bath to protect it from erasure[639]. Ben Stada exported witchcraft from Egypt tattooed on his skin, because the Egyptians did not allow the export of magic texts; the Sages called him a fool[640].

## III   Hair

The general term for hair is *se'ar,* mostly in the collective sense like our "hair". For a single hair, the name *sa'ara* is used. The Talmud also uses the names *nima, bintha* and *mazia;* the first is also used to denote individual hairs of the tail of a cow or a horse. Pork bristles are called *ziphin*[641] and *maksha*[642].

The full (unsheared) hair on the head is called *pera*[643]. In Assyrian it is *pirtu*. The *machalaphoth* of Samson[644] and probably also the *tzitzith* of Ezekiel[645] were tresses (tufts) of hair. The *kevutzoth, rehatim* and, perhaps, also *dalla* are locks in the Song of Songs[646].

Isaiah portrays the pubes with the term *sa'ar haraglayim,* meaning "hair of the feet"[647], just as urine is generally called "water of the feet" in post-Biblical writings. The Talmud calls pubic hair *zakan ha-thachton, barba inferior,* meaning the "lower beard", but even more often *sa'ar beth ha'erva, crines loci pudoris,* meaning hair of the genitalia. These represent the only sign of puberty in males and, for matters concerning laws of marriage, two ripe pubic hairs are sufficient proof of male puberty. Once the hair has grown around the *mons veneris,* the lad has become a man and he is of a responsible age (i.e. subject to all commandments enjoined upon adults)[648].

The normal color of hair on Semites is black[649] and *no man can make a single hair black or white*[650]. Red-haired people were feared as being bloodthirsty. Thus, Esau

631. First Kings 18:28
632. Deut. 14:1
633. Levit. 21:5
634. Levit. 19:28
635. Makkoth 3:6 and 21a
636. Gittin 86a
637. Makkoth 21a
638. Gittin 2:3
639. Shabbath 120b
640. *ibid* 104b

641. *Tosefta* Shabbath 9:1-2
642. Shabbath 90a
643. Numbers 6:5
644. Judges 16:13
645. Ezekiel 8:3
646. Song of Songs 5:2 & 7:6
647. Isaiah 7:20
648. Sanhedrin 8:1 and Niddah 6:11
649. Levit. 13:31
650. Matthew 5:36

was *admoni,* reddish[651], like a murderer. When the prophet Samuel[651a] saw that David was *admoni,* he feared that David too would be a shedder of blood, like Esau; whereupon God said: he is in fact ruddy, but "with public approval"[652], implying that Esau killed by his own impulse, whereas David would only slay on the sentence of the court[653]. Exceptionally it would happen (only in a cow?) that the root of a hair is black but the tip is red, and vice-versa[654].

In old age, hair becomes white. A miracle happened to Rabbi Eleazar ben Azariah that at eighteen years of age he suddenly developed eighteen streaks of white hair, perhaps as a result of the marked excitement of his totally unexpected election to the rectorship of the Rabbinic Academy, so that he exclaimed of himself: I appear like one who is seventy years old[655]. It is prohibited as a womanly custom to pluck out white hairs that are found among the black ones[656]. A man married two women, a young one and an old one. The young wife plucked out his white hairs so that he should appear young like her, and the old wife plucked out the black hairs — finally he was totally bald[657]!

## IV   Hair Growth

For every hair on the human body, the Lord created a separate groove, *guma* or *kos* (the hair follicle), so that two hairs should not suck from the same groove, for in that case they would impair the sight of man. Thus states the *Aggadah*[658]. In the *Halachah,* however, cases are described in which two hairs grow in the same groove, both in humans[659] and in animals[660]. The latter viewpoint is the correct one, even though, as a rule, hair follicles split deep in the skin and only reunite on the surface.

The *Midrash* also teaches that a separate source was created by God for each hair; if it dries up, the hair also dries[661]. The *Midrash* is probably referring to the vessels of the hair follicles.

Opinions are divided concerning the growth of hairs. It was debated whether hair grows from the tips, perhaps like young shoots of plants, or from the roots, in that fresh hair substance develops at the base of the hair and the old, already-present hair is pushed ahead of the new hair. The final proofs cited to support the correctness of the latter viewpoint, i.e. that hair grows from the roots, are the observation that wool on sheep which is painted a bright color grows colorless again underneath the marking, and that the beards of old men who dye them gradually grow white again at the *roots*[662]. Aristotle also found it necessary to note that a hair which is cut does not regrow from the site it was cut, but from the root[663].

## V   The Beard

On the head, the hair on the top is differentiated from the hair of the beard. The latter is called *zakan* in Hebrew and *dekan* or *dikna* in Aramaic. The boundary is the joint of the jaw, *perek shel lechi,* the condyle of the lower jaw. If one stretches a thread from ear to ear, then above the thread is considered the hair of the head and below the thread is the beard. Posteriorly, the hair of the head reaches up to the *pika shel pirka,* "up to the slit[664] of the vertebra", i.e. up to the end of the neck ridge. That which lies below this level is considered to be part of the body (and not head) skin, even if it has

---

651. Genesis 25:25
651a. Preuss erroneously has Saul (F.R.)
652. First Samuel 16:12
653. Genesis Rabbah 63:8
654. Parah 2:5
655. Berachoth 28a
656. Shabbath 94b
657. Baba Kamma 60b

658. Baba Bathra 16a
659. Niddah 52a
660. Parah 2:5
661. *Tanchuma, thazria* p.18b on Job 38:25
662. Nazir 39a
663. Aristotle. *Hist. Anim.* 3:11
664. for this translation, see *Rashi* on Chullin 134b *s.v. pika*

hair on it. Anteriorly, the beard stretches down to the cartilage of the throat, *chulya shel gargereth,* the thyroid cartilage. That which is below this level, even if it has hairs on it, is considered to be part of the body skin[665].

On a head that is bald, one differentiates anterior baldness, *gabbachath,* from posterior baldness, *karrachath*[666]. Posterior baldness is defined as absence of hair from the vertex *(kadkad* or *kodkod)* sloping to the rear, and anterior baldness, from the vertex sloping anteriorly[667]. The *Mishnah* gives the following definition: *karrachath* is the absence of hair from the crown sloping to the rear as far as the *pika* of the neck[668], which Maimonides interprets to mean the first cervical vertebra *(al-unk).*

The presence of a beard is proof that a male is of age to be obligated to fulfill all the commandments of the Torah. We do not appoint a trustee to supervise the affairs of a bearded person, *diknane* (as we do for a minor)[669]. Some people, such as Rabbi Nachman, only have a few bristles of hair as their beard, *sikke dikna,* so that they might be (mistakenly) considered to be eunuchs[670]. The latter have no beard at all.

Folklore teaches that a thin-bearded man *(zaldekan)* is very wise *(kurteman)*; a thick-bearded man *(abdekan)* is a fool *(siksan)*; he who blows away the froth from his glass is not thirsty; he who asks: what shall I eat with my bread? — take the bread away from him (he is certainly not hungry); he who has a parting *(mabartha)* in his beard will be defeated by none (because of his cunning)[671].

Rab Huna did not allow a thin-bearded male *(zaldekan)* to recite the priestly blessing, although everyone in his home town knew that the latter was a grownup. However, strangers who came for the pilgrimage festivals might be able to relate: we saw a young lad recite the priestly blessing[672].

# PART   IV
# THE VISCERA

## A. THE ORGANS OF DIGESTION

### I   The Mouth

The mouth is called *peh* in Hebrew and *pum* or *puma* in Aramaic. The word *peh,* just like the Greek *stoma,* refers both to the opening made by the lips as well as the oral cavity up to the pharynx[673]. The function of the mouth is subjugated to the will of man, as is the function of his hand and foot.

Rabbi Levi said: six organs serve man; three are within his power and three are not. Eye, ear and nose are not dependent upon his will: he sees, hears and smells even that which he doesn't wish to. Mouth, hand and foot are dependent upon him; he can speak pious things or slander and blasphemy; his hand can fulfill the command of God or can steal and kill; his feet can take him to the theater and the circus or to the house of worship and the house of study[674]. The only exception is the transgressor Bileam[675] in whose mouth God put a word so that he only spoke that which the Lord willed.[676]

---

665. *Tosefta* Negaim 4:12
666. Levit. 13:42
667. *Tosefta* Negaim 4:9
668. Negaim 10:10
669. Baba Metzia 39a
670. Yebamoth 80b
671. Sanhedrin 100b

672. Jerushalmi Taanith 67b
673. Rufus. *De Appellat. Part.* ed. Daremberg
     p.139
674. Genesis Rabbah 67:3
675. Numbers 22:35
676. Numbers Rabbah 20:18

One eats with the mouth. Ezekiel said: *I have not eaten of that which dieth of itself*[677]. Daniel also did not eat meat or drink wine when he was among the heathens[678].

One also breathes with the mouth: the breath from the mouth of the Lord causes transgressors to vanish[679]. Idols have no breath in their mouths[680].

One also yawns with the mouth[681].

One also speaks with the mouth. The Psalmist prays: *let the words of my mouth...be acceptable before thee, O Lord, my strength and my redeemer*[682]. The mouth of the Lord also speaks[683], but only with Moses did He speak *mouth to mouth*[684]. Rabbi Simeon ben Yochai said that if he had stood at Mount Sinai, he would have asked God to give every person two *pumim* (mouths) — one to be occupied with learning Torah and the other for all other necessities[685]. When Moses said he was not eloquent in speaking[686], God rebuked him by saying: did not I create all the mouths *(piyoth)* in the world[687]? To be "the mouth of someone"[688] means to speak in his stead or to be his spokesman[689].

One also kisses with the mouth. The *Midrash* teaches that all kissing is indecent except in three cases: the kiss of high office, the kiss of reunion and the kiss of parting[690]. For this reason Samuel kissed Saul after he anointed him king[691]. Moses kissed his brother Aaron when he was reunited with him[692], and Orpah kissed her mother-in-law when she bade her farewell[693]. When people saw Jacob kissing Rachel, they said: "what type of new immorality is he introducing among us?" This accusation motivated Jacob to cry[694]. The people did not know that Rachel was a relative of Jacob and a kiss among relatives is permitted[695].

Legend relates[696] that when Jacob was reunited with his son Joseph whom he believed to be dead, *he fell on his neck and wept on his neck a good while*[697], because the father did not kiss his son or tolerate his kiss. Jacob said to himself: since Joseph who *had a beautiful countenance and was goodly to look at*[698] was thrust into a strange environment from his ancestor's house, the women of Egypt must certainly have forced themselves upon him. Therefore, Joseph suppressed the desire of his heart in favor of the will of God which requires the preservation of chastity under all circumstances. Later, however, Jacob became convinced of the legitimacy of the two sons of Joseph and therefore kissed the children[699], but not Joseph himself. Jacob correctly conjectured that Joseph did not remain completely cold to the wife of Potiphar, even though he never allowed the relationship to reach the point of adultery. Only after Jacob's death does Joseph throw himself on his father's body and kiss him[700] saying: for 39 years I was not allowed to kiss my father, and now I should bury him without a farewell kiss[701]?

Apparently, Jacob was not so strict with his uncle Laban, although it was well-known that the latter kissed pictures of idols and whores (probably Temple prostitutes). Jacob allowed himself to be kissed by Laban, but to be sure, not on the

---

677. Ezekiel 4:14
678. Daniel 10:3
679. Job 15:30
680. Psalms 135:17
681. *Tosafoth*, Niddah 63a *s.v. mephaheketh; phahak* also in Niddah 9:8 and Berachoth 24a-b
682. Psalms 19:15
683. Isaiah 1:20
684. Numbers 12;8
685. Jerushalmi Berachoth 1;3b
686. Exodus 4:10
687. Exodus Rabbah 3:15
688. Exodus 4:16

689. *Targum* on Exodus 4:16 and Exodus Rabbah 3:16
690. Genesis Rabbah 70:12
691. First Samuel 10:1
692. Exodus 4:27
693. Ruth 1:14
694. Genesis 29:11
695. Genesis Rabbah 70:12
696. Kallah Rabbathi 3:19 fol. 53a
697. Genesis 46:29
698. Genesis 39:6
699. *ibid* 48:10
700. *ibid* 50:1
701. Kallah Rabbathi 3:19

mouth — only the *piel* or the intensive form has this meaning, whereas the Biblical text *(vayishak)*[702] has the *kal* form[703]. Another legend relates that Laban only simulated a kiss. Since Jacob came without any baggage, his uncle thought that he was carrying his precious gems concealed in his mouth, and he, Laban, attempted to steal them using the pretext of a kiss[704].

Esau fell on his brother's neck when they met, and embraced him and kissed him[705]. The *Midrash* relates that Esau's intent was to wound his brother fatally with a bite. However, when he attempted to sink his teeth into Jacob's neck, "they became like wax"[706]. Others are of the opinion that the neck of Jacob became hard like ivory so that Esau's teeth broke[707], for the Psalmist says: *the Lord breaketh the teeth of transgressors*[708].

Samuel kissed Chanan bar Abba on the mouth for having told him a teaching of Rab[709]. Rabbi Gamliel kissed Rabbi Chananya on the head when the latter was a child, out of joy for an intelligent response[710]. Amram kissed his daughter Miriam when the whole house became filled with light with the birth of Moses, concluding from this that her prophecy — that Moses would be the redeemer of Israel — would be fulfilled[711]. Simeon the Just kissed a Nazarite whose vow rejoiced him on the head[712]. Only devout Orientals kiss the feet as an expression of profuse thankfulness[713].

Through the kiss of God — the mildest of the 903 types of death that were brought into the world[714] — Moses, exceptionally beloved and distinguished by God, died[715]. Rabbi Akiba said: I admire three things practiced by the Medes: they only cut their meat on the table but not on the hand as is done by most Orientals; they only conduct their deliberations in an open field because "the walls have ears"; and they only kiss on the hand out of deference, as the commentaries explain, thereby sparing the person to be kissed from contact with their spittle[716]. It is very prosaic for Saadiya to derive the "sweetness" of a kiss from the "water under the tongue" i.e. sweet spittle[717].

According to Ibn Ezra, *nashak*, in the accusative, means to kiss "on the mouth", but the dative implies the hand, shoulder or cheek.

The mouth of an embryo is closed and resembles a barley kernel[718]. When a child sees the light of day (i.e. is born), an angel comes and strikes it on the mouth so that it forgets all the knowledge it was born with[719]. This legend seems to vividly remind us of the platonic *mathesis anamnesis*. Rabbi Ammi considers the aversion of the people against placing coins in their mouths to be well-founded[720]. Maimonides remarks that it is possible that spittle from people suffering from contagious illnesses might have dried on the coins, or, perhaps, human sweat may have dried thereon, and the *Gemara* teaches that the latter is poisonous[721].

## II   The Lips

The slit of the mouth is formed by the lips or *sephathayim*. The upper border is called the red of the lip, *ha-odem shebesaphah*[722]. The shepherd sings to the shepherdess: *thy lips are like a thread of scarlet*[723]. Shulamith replies: *your lips are like lilies, dropping sweet-smelling myrrh*[724].

702. Genesis 29:13
703. Kallah Rabbathi 3:19
704. Genesis Rabbah 70:13
705. Genesis 33:4
706. Kallah Rabbathi 3:19
707. Genesis Rabbah 78:9
708. Psalms 3:8
709. Jerushalmi Berachoth 1;3d
710. *Tosefta* Niddah 5:15
711. Sotah 13a
712. Nedarim 9b
713. Jerushalmi Kiddushin 1;61c
714. Berachoth 8a
715. Baba Bathra 17a
716. Berachoth 8b
717. *Ibn Ezra's* commentary on Song of Songs 1:1
718. Levit. Rabbah 14:8
719. Niddah 30b
720. Jerushalmi Terumoth 8;45d
721. Maimonides *Hilchoth Rotzeach* 12:4
722. *Tosefta* Negaim 2:13
723. Song of Songs 4:3
724. *ibid.* 5:13

During speech, the movements of the lips are most noticeable since they are more visible than the organ of speech. Job vows: as long as I live, *my lips shall not speak wickedness*[725]. The word *saphah* is used directly to mean "speech". *A man of lips*[726] is a boaster, and *words of the lips*[727] refer to gossip.

Among the Hebrews, a person only becomes complete when he is circumcised. Thus, when he said of himself that he had *uncirumcised lips*[728], Moses meant to imply that he was an awkward speaker[729]. During the announcement of a famine, *the lips of the prophet quivered*[730]. The lips of a teacher move even in the grave if, during a discourse, his teachings are quoted in his name[731] as is required by law[732].

A split lip (harelip) imparts a grotesque look to the mouth. As a result, Rabbi Yochanan, who had poor vision because of old age, thought that Rabbi Kahana, who was sitting before him and was afflicted with such a lip *(parteh sephathayim),* was laughing at him[733]. A poetic expression of the Psalmist for "they ridicule" is: *the transgressors split their lips*[734]. Those who scorn are called *maphtiré sephathayim* meaning "who split the lip"[735]. Linguistically (and perhaps even phonetically: *parat* is equivalent to *patar* which is equivalent to *rapat*), one should also here mention the Talmudic expression: "the lips of the aged are split" *(mithraphtoth)*[736], meaning the lower lip hangs loosely down.

The Biblical expression *to split open the mouth concerning someone*[737] has nothing to do with our subject. *Petzah peh* means "to scoff" i.e. either to curse someone aloud, or to gesticulate quietly as an imitation of an idiotic face. *To make one's mouth large (thagdal peh)*[738] means to "tightly close the lips", or "to pucker the lips", *karatz sephathayim*[739], the gesticulation of spiteful people, i.e. malicious joy.

## III   Spittle

The oral cavity is kept moist by spittle which is constantly, albeit unknowingly, swallowed. Job complains: *Thou doesn't let me alone* (free of suffering long enough) *till I swallow down my spittle*[740]. Orientals consider expectoration in front of another person to be offensive and a sign of contempt; the perpetrator is not prosecuted by an earthly court but punishment will be meted out later by Heaven[741]. A woman spits before her brother-in-law[742] who refuses to marry her *(to build up his brother's house)*[743].

The cultivated Greek strongly emphasized that the Persians consider it loathsome to spit or to blow one's nose *(aischron men gar eti kai nyn esti Persais kai to apoptyein kai to apomyttesthai)*[744]. It is possible that the perception that spitting before another person is a terrible insult is the underlying reason why there is no trace at all in the Talmud[745] of the widespread practice among Greeks and Romans to *ptyen eis kolpon* (spit into a container) at the sight of an epileptic[746].

A student commits a sin if he spits before his teacher. The Talmud states that no one may spit before one's teacher unless one has eaten gourds *(kara)* or groats *(dasya)* which are as difficult to digest as a lead wire[747]. According to Resh Lakesh, such a

725. Job 27:4
726. *ibid.* 11:2
727. Second Kings 18:20
728. Exodus 6:12
729. Targum *loc. cit.*
730. Habakkuk 3:16
731. Yebamoth 97a
732. Megillah 15a
733. Baba Kamma 117a
734. Psalms 22:8
735. Derech Eretz 2:1
736. Shabbath 152a; Löw states that the word

is derived from the Syriac *raphad* or *raphath*
737. Lament. 2:16 & 3:46
738. Obadiah 1:12
739. Proverbs 10:10
740. Job 7:19
741. *Tosefta* Baba Kamma 9:31
742. Deut. 25:9
743. Chagigah 5a
744. Xenophon. *Cyrop.* 1:2:16
745. Job 30:10 cannot be cited here
746. Proof in Becker-Göll, *Charikles* 1:213
747. Tamid 27b

pupil is worthy of being killed[748]. It is also related of the Persians: *nec ministranti famulo hiscere vel loqui licet vel spuere*[749].

*Spitting* was considered to be one of the most outrageous types of insult. If a father spits on his daughter in her face, *should she not be ashamed for seven days*[750]? The offense is so outrageous that this type of shaming is punished by an earthly judge with a 400 *zuz* fine to be paid to the insulted person. For a blow on the ear, the fine is only half this amount[751]. For this reason, also, one should not spit on the Temple Mount or in the House of the Lord, because it is equivalent to spitting God in the eye[752] and His eyes are there perpetually[753]. A proverb states: If a man spits into the air, the spittle falls on his face, and when the kettle boils over, it pours the boiling water on its own side[754]. He thus punishes himself for his violent temper.

It is possible that this view of spitting as being offensive is related to the tradition that ritual uncleanness is transmitted through spittle. If a person with a flux spits on a clean person, the latter must wash his clothes[755]. If, during a conversation with an Arab, a jet of spittle splashes on the clothes of a High Priest, he cannot perform his duties on the Day of Atonement[756].

If a person spits or expectorates[757] on the ground, he is liable if another person is injured as a result (by slipping and falling)[758].

According to a *Midrash*[759], the water (i.e. saliva) of the mouth is sweet because a person sometimes eats a food which his stomach does not accept. Were it then not for the sweet water of the mouth, the person would vomit and his soul would not return (i.e. he could easily die). Here the chemical purpose of the spittle is described. In another *Midrash*[760] the physical purpose is described, namely that spittle (or esophageal mucous) makes the food soft and slippery so that the intestines not become injured thereby.

Onions and *gargishtha* (i.e. red clay) stimulate profuse salivation[761]. Blood expectoration is also mixed with spittle, unless one is dealing with a hemorrhage[762].

The precise term for spittle is *mé ha-peh,* literally: water of the mouth. When it flows out of the mouth, it is called *rir*. When it is spit out, as was the custom among the Arabs and as is still done today by sailors, it is called *tzinnora*[763] or, more exactly, *tzinnora shel rok*. A term which is very commonly used already in the Bible is *rok*, which actually means expectoration or sputum, and thus connotes something pathological. For this reason, it is taught that if *rok* accumulates in the mouth, one should not walk four cubits without expectorating it[764].

The term *mosheke ha-rok,* literally "those who draw out the spittle"[765], probably refers to "lickspittle" (or sycophant), and not to haughtiness[766].

## IV    The Tongue

The following organs in the oral cavity are of importance: the tongue, the palate and the teeth. I have been unable to ascertain designations which, in all probability, would refer to the tonsils or uvula.

---

748. Erubin 99a
749. Ammian. 23:6
750. Numbers 12:14. Compare Isaiah 50:6
751. Baba Kamma 8:6
752. Berachoth 62b
753. First Kings 9:3
754. Eccles. Rabbah 7:9
755. Levit. 15:18
756. Yoma 47a; a similar case is found in Niddah 33b
757. i.e. sputum or spittle, according to the

explanation of *Choshen Mishpat* 384:1
758. Baba Kamma 3b
759. Numbers Rabbah 18:22
760. Exodus Rabbah 24:1
761. Yebamoth 106a
762. *ibid*. 105a
763. Yoma 47a
764. *Tosefta* Erubin 11:8
765. *Tosefta* Sotah 14:8
766. as *Rashi* suggests in Sotah 47b

The tongue, known as *lashon,* is an organ of taste, *ta'am.* A Jew not only tastes food but also tastes reasons[767] (as a result, the generally used term for "reason" is *ta-am*) and the good of the Lord[768]. The Jew also tastes cohabitation[769], sin[770], sleep[771], and death[772]. In old age, the sense of taste decreases. I am 80 years old today, said Barzilai to the king; can I discern between good and evil? or do I taste what I eat and drink[773]? For in the Talmud[774] it is thought that the lips of the elderly become loose. Rab considered the 80-year-old Barzilai to be a liar, for in the house of Rebbe[775] there was a 92-year-old cook[776] who could still taste dishes. Raba said that Barzilai was steeped in lewdness and "old age hastens (comes suddenly) upon whoever is steeped in lewdness"[777] i.e. *senectus praecox.*

The tongue speaks: therefore the Hebrew *lashon,* like the Latin *lingua* and the Greek *glossa,* also means "speech". *The remnant of Israel shall not do iniquity nor speak lies, neither shall a deceitful tongue be found in their mouth*[778]. The Talmud says that the kidneys advise, the heart discerns, the tongue cuts (articulates) and the mouth completes (the enunciation of the words). These are the characteristics of the popular physiology of speech[779]. The movable portion of the tongue is the "speaking" part. If a considerable portion thereof is missing in an animal, it is unsuited to be offered as a sacrifice[780].

The tongue is a small organ, yet it does great things[781]. Both glory and disgrace come from speaking, and a man's tongue is his downfall[782]. Smooth-tongued people, *machaliké lashon,* are cursed[783]. All organs of the human body stand erect, only the tongue lies down surrounded by two walls, one of bone (the jaw) and the other of flesh[784]. The tongue is arranged in numerous folds in the mouth, and a water (i.e. saliva) channel passes beneath it, but it still causes many conflagrations[785]. What then would an erect tongue cause[786]? The "evil tongue", *lashon hara* in Hebrew, and *lishschana bischa* in Aramaic, is the expression for slander used in many admonishments and warnings. *Hilshin* means to slander, and *malshin* is the slanderer.

## V  The Palate

The palate is called *chek* in Hebrew, which the Septuagint often renders *pharynx.* In Aramaic it is *chikka, chinka* and *chekka,* and in Arabic *chanak.* Since the floor of the mouth was apparently considered to be a lower palate, the dual term *chanikayim* evolved. The *Targum* usually translates this term as *moriga*[787], which is identical with *morak,* which is the designation for threshing barrel, and which means "grater". The expression *malkochayim*[788], which actually means "pincers", *fauces* "because it holds

---

767. Sotah 21b: he makes his words tasty (plausible) to the judge before the opposing litigant appears. This is prohibited.
768. Psalms 34:9; *Taste* (*Targum:* convince yourselves) *and see that the Lord is good.*
769. In Sanhedrin 19b the phrase from Second Samuel 3:16: *her husband went with her to bachurim* is interpreted to mean that they both became like young *bachurim* (unmarried youths) who have not yet tasted the pleasure of marital relations
770. Pesachim 87a: youths who have not yet tasted sin
771. Jerushalmi Sukkah 5; 55b; during the entire time of the festivities of the drawing of the water, they did not taste sleep.
772. Yoma 78b; Samuel said that he who wishes to have a taste of death should sleep in his shoes.
773. Second Samuel 19:36

774. Shabbath 152a
775. Preuss erroneously has Rab (F.R.)
776. Preuss erroneously states 93–year-old (F.R.)
777. Shabbath 152a
778. Zephaniah 3:13
779. Berachoth 61a
780. Bechoroth 6:8
781. James 3:5
782. Sirach 5:13
783. Derech Eretz Rabbah 2:3
784. Arachin 15b
785. Levit. Rabbah 16:4
786. Psalms 120:2-3
787. also the Talmud in Berachoth 55a states that the consumption of palates of animals (Shabbath 81a adds: unsalted) leads to hemorrhoids.
788. Psalms 22:16

the food like pinchers''[789], is poetically *ap.eir*. It is highly likely that the "palate" here refers only to the hard palate.

The palate too is an organ of taste. The fruit of the beloved is sweet to the palate of her lover[790]. Job asks: *does not the palate taste food*[791]? Plinius also teaches: *intellectus saporum est caeteris in prima lingua, homini et in palato*[792]. In actuality, it is at least uncertain whether the hard palate is able to taste.

The palate makes speech possible. The epigrammatic poet says: *for my palate shall speak truth*[793]. In the destroyed city of Jerusalem, *the tongue of the sucking child cleaveth to the roof of his mouth for thirst*[794] and the tongue of the nobles out of reverence, when Job walked about in the days of his splendor[795].

It is a well-known custom among the Arabs[796] to rub the palate *(chanak)* of newborn infants with a chewed date as a symbolic act of initiation for their entire lives. This practice is only undertaken by honorable people, often by Mohammed himself. Thence, the denomination *chanak* not only refers to *palatum fricuit* but also has the meaning: "to initiate someone in the ways of life by practice and experience". There is nothing to authenticate the former meaning, together with the practice which gave rise to it, in the corresponding Hebrew verb *chanak*.

The wise wife of Rabbi Papa described the pain of defloration to her husband with the sentiment: "like hard bread on the palate''[797]. He had to decide in a legal case of rape whether or not the perpetrator, in addition to receiving the other punishments, must also pay for the pain he inflicted[798]. In antiquity, the story is often told of an animal — by the Indians an elephant, in the Talmud[799] an ox — that had pain in the palate (toothache?), and drank a whole barrel of beer and became intoxicated so that it was relieved of its pain.

# VI   Speech Defects

After describing the organs of speech, it seems appropriate to describe a few items concerning speech defects. It is generally known that the Ephraimites, mentioned in the Bible,[800] pronounced the "*sh*" sound as "*s*". Our word *shibolith* is derived from that story. Rabbi David Kimchi[801] observed the same speech defect among the French and among Lithuanians one still finds it even today. Aristotle calls this speech defect *traulotes* (stuttering); *traulos,* according to his definition, is he who cannot properly enunciate certain letters[802].

From a pathological standpoint, the above problem might be spoken of as a type of stuttering in which one sound is replaced by another similar one, either as a result of awkwardness of the speech organ or because of a faulty hearing perception. However, our case of the Ephraimites only deals with "physiological stuttering", since a pathological basis is lacking and the problem is not one of a speech defect but a dialectic speech characteristic. It has nothing to do with sigmatism[803].

When Moses calls himself a man with *a heavy mouth and a heavy tongue*[804], he means that he is not eloquent and that his speech is not fluent in his mouth. *Targum*

---

789. Midrash Psalms *loc. cit.* ed. Buber p.97a has the addition: and that is the palate. Classically, however, pincers (or pliers) are called *melkachayim* (Isaiah 6:6).
790. Song of Songs 2:3
791. Job 12:11
792. Plinius. *Hist. Natur.* 2:37
793. Proverbs 8:7
794. Lament. 4:4
795. Job 29:10
796. Fleischer in Levy's *Neuhebräisches und Chaldäisches Wörterbuch.* Leipzig 1876-1889

Vol. 2:206b
797. Kethuboth 39b
798. *ibid*
799. Baba Kamma 35a
800. Judges 12:6
801. *Radak's* commentary on Judges 12:6
802. Aristotle. *Problem.* 11:30
803. This entire paragraph is a personal communication from the speech specialist, Professor Dr. Albert Leibmann.
804. Exodus 4:10

*Jonathan* states that Moses was *chigger pum* or mouth-lame, and the Septuagint states he was *ischnophonos* (i.e. of weak voice). According to Aristotle, *ischnophonia* is a condition in which a person cannot rapidly articulate one syllable after another. He correctly notes that this condition occurs more often at a young age, because then a person does not yet have sufficient control of his other limbs either[805]. He also notes that *ischnophonia* and dumbness occur only in human beings[806].

Legend relates that the reason why Moses had a "heavy tongue" is that his tongue was burned in his youth. When the child Moses was saved from drowning, the astrologers said to Pharaoh: this is the one who will once steal your crown. They advised him to kill Moses. Jethro (later to become the father-in-law of Moses), however, said: it is an ordinary child; test him by placing before him a gold vessel and live coals and see which he takes. Like a child, Moses took the live coals and thrust his hand with the live coal into his mouth so that his tongue was burnt[807].

On the other hand, the *illeg* of Isaiah[808] corresponds to the *psellos* (lisp) of Aristotle, "one who leaves out syllables or letters"[809]. When the Redeemer will come, "the tongue of the stutterer will be able to speak rapidly and clearly". Since a foreign language is usually not spoken fluently but broken or stammeringly, the Arabs and Aramaeans consider *ilug* and *lo'eg* to be a foreigner, a *barbarus,* as noted in the Aramaic translation[810]. The Palestinian Talmud and the *Midrash* simply adopt the Greek term *psellos*. The *Midrash* makes the prophet Amos into a "tongueless person"[811] because, as is deduced etymologically, he was heavy *(amus)* of tongue (i.e. a stammerer). The Talmud[812] sharply differentiates these speech defects from characteristics of dialect.

The faltering language of constraint *(megamgem)* is not related to our present subject matter.

## VII   The Teeth

A tooth is called *shen* in Hebrew, *schinna* in Aramaic and *sinn* in Arabic. The dual term *shinnayim* is modeled after the name of all paired organs (i.e. the two rows of teeth). In the Talmud, the word *shen* is mostly used as a specific designation for the sharp incisor teeth (from *shanan* meaning to sharpen), whereas the molars are referred to as *kakké.*

Mostly, the terms occur together: *shinné ve-kakké.* "Someone bought an ox; later it was found that the animal had no teeth, and, therefore, it died"[813]. The teeth of cattle usually fall out at 12 to 15 years of age[814].

Raba dreamed that his teeth fell out, and this was interpreted to him to mean that his children would imminently die[815].

When the lion was still 300 parasangs away, it gave out such a roar that people's teeth fell out because of fright[816].

*Rashi* translates *kakké* as *gencives* (gums), an interpretation which *Tosafoth* correctly question[817]. The latter more correctly translate *kakké* as *machelière*.

In the Aramaic Bible translations, the term *kakké* is repeatedly used for the word *shen* of the Biblical text, and it is used in parallel with the poetic *methaloth*[818] meaning

805. Aristotle. *Problem.* 11:30
806. *ibid.* 10:30
807. Exodus Rabbah 1:26
808. Isaiah 32:4
809. Aristotle. *Problem.* 11:30
810. Psalms 114:1
811. Eccles. Rabbah 1:2
812. Jerushalmi Nedarim 1; 37a

813. Baba Metzia 42b
814. Fischöder. *Fleischschau.* p.19
815. Berachoth 56a
816. Chullin 59b
817. Gittin 69a and Abodah Zara 28a
818. Job 29:17; Joel 1:6; Proverbs 30:14.
    Transposed *maltha'oth* in Psalms 58:7

denture. The latter is called *nibé* in the *Targumin*. The Talmud only uses the term *nibé* for animal teeth, both the canine teeth of ruminants as well as the incisors of dogs. (Arabic *naba*).

Concerning canine teeth, the Talmud[819] states that the assertion of the *Tosefta*[820] that animals which chew the cud have no upper teeth is not correct. One can draw no conclusion from the camel, because the latter at least has canine teeth, but young camels do not even have canines[821]. The opposite is probably correct: every quadruped that has no upper teeth chews the cud and has split hooves.

Concerning incisors, the Talmud relates[822] that a dog once barked at a woman as a result of which her fetus tore loose (i.e. she aborted). The owner of the dog called out too late to her that she need not be afraid since the dog's incisors had been removed etc...The *Midrash* relates[823] that God made Potiphar into a castrate so that he would not be able to practice pederasty with Joseph. Similarly, a man had the tusks removed from his she-bear so that it not kill his children[824].

The meaning of the Biblical *"nib" of the lips*[825] is uncertain. The *Gemara*[826] seems to understand it in the sense of "wind or breathing". This interpretation is impossible in view of another *Gemara*[827] where it is said that the *nib* of the lips has no bone, and yet another *Gemara*[828] which states the following: Bar Kamtza made a blemish on the *nib* of the lips of an animal to be offered as a sacrifice. The Jews consider this blemish to render the animal unfit to be offered, whereas the Romans do not. *Rashi* interprets *nib* of the lips to be the upper lip.

In an animal, the *Mishnah* differentiates between the outer *chutin* (incisors) and the inner ones, which Rabbi Chanina ben Antigonos calls "twin teeth" (bicuspids)[829].

The milk tooth of a child is called *shen de chalab* or "milk tooth"[830]. Hippocrates teaches that it arises *apo tou galaktos*[831]. In poetry, the milk teeth are called *tochanoth*, meaning grinders or millers[832], and the denture of the mythical Leviathan is called the "double bridle"[833].

A miracle happened to Rabbi Chaggai in that his teeth grew back when he was 80 years old as a reward for his untiring efforts to effect the burial of Rabbi Huna[834].

The teeth are hard[835]; they serve for biting and for chewing. When the false prophets bite with their teeth, they falsely proclaim peace[836]. God gives idle (or clean) teeth during times of hunger[837]. Rab says that when a person's teeth fall out, i.e. when he becomes old, his livelihood becomes smaller (i.e. more difficult to acquire)[838]. Rabbi Chanina said that when Judah, the son of Jacob, became angry, he pulverized iron plates with his teeth[839]. The grinders[840] cease work in old age because there are few of them[841].

Rabbi Meir said: "chew well with your teeth and you will find (the food) in your

819. Chullin 59a
820. *Tosefta* Chullin 3:20
821. see Plinius 11:37. *camelus in superiori maxilla primores non habet*
822. Shabbath 63a
823. Genesis Rabbah 86:3
824. see also Baba Kamma 23b
825. Isaiah 57:19
826. Baba Kamma 60a and Berachoth 34b
827. Chullin 128b
828. Gittin 56a
829. Bechoroth 4:4 & 39a
830. Kiddushin 24b; *Mechilta* Mishpatim 9, beginning

831. Hippocrates. *De Carnibus*. Sect. 3:251:49 Foes.
832. Eccles. 12:3
833. Job 41:13
834. Jerushalmi Kilayim 9; 32c
835. Abodah Zara 28a
836. Michah 3:5
837. Amos 4:6
838. Niddah 65a
839. Genesis Rabbah 93:6
840. literally: mill maids
841. Eccles. 12:3

steps''[842], which corresponds to our maxim "well chewed is half digested". The tooth is used elsewhere in popular sayings: 60 (i.e. many) pains reach the teeth of him who hears the noise made by another man eating, while he himself does not eat[843]. The expression "if an inhabitant of Naresh has kissed you, then count your teeth''[844] is meant as a warning to beware of the well-known thievery of the people of Naresh. It could happen even today that a man who considers himself to be quite intelligent does not know how many teeth he has[845]. Even Plinius remarks that women have fewer teeth than men[846].

## VIII    Internal Organs

Although we find numerous statements in Bible and Talmud concerning external organs in humans, and specifically the oral cavity which can be directly observed, such statements about internal organs are extremely sparse. The main reason for this, as already mentioned by Aristotle, is the fact that "the inner organs of man are mostly unknown", *agnosta gar esti malista ta ton anthropon*[847]. It is thus necessary to rely on the examination of animal organs whose structure is similar to that of man.

To be sure, this honorable admission on Aristotle's part did not prevent him from constructing such comparisons from fantasy, as, for example, when he says that the human spleen looks like that of swine[848]. Later writers, particularly Galen, were not so honest. That which they actually observed in animals was deceptively stated to have been seen in humans. The Rabbis remained free of such temptation; they had no occasion to write about human anatomy since their observations and communications relate nearly exclusively to slaughtered animals, i.e., animals for Temple offerings and ruminant animals for human consumption: cows, sheep and goats. Their reported observations are therefore totally comparable to those of their contemporary heathen anatomists.

The Hebrew designation for entrails (or viscera), *kereb*, has no precise anatomic meaning. It generally refers to the "insides of the abdomen", irrespective of which specific part is referred to. However, its meaning is much more comprehensive than that of the Greek *koilia*, which is the most closely comparable term. The word *kereb* is found especially often in regard to perceptions whose seat (or source) is said to lie within "the insides" of man, without any consideration as to the anatomic site of such a seat: *Bless the Lord, O my soul, and all that is within me, bless His holy Name*[849].

Only occasionally is the word *kereb* used in the exact sense of stomach, perhaps stomach including the intestines; for example, in the laws of sacrifices, where *the fat that covereth the inwards (kereb)*[850], referring to the omentum, is declared to be an obligatory part of the offering. Furthermore, Aristotle also uses the word *koilia* in the sense of stomach[851].

The terms *me'ayim* and *benei me'ayim* for entrails (or viscera), which are used much more often in the Talmud (and already in the Bible)[852], are probably also used as a precise designation for "intestines" *(me'aya)*.

## IX    Esophagus

The digestive tract begins from the "place of swallowing", *beth ha-beliyah*[853] or the site of the soul (life?), *beth ha-naphesh*[854]. If a person places forbidden fat (or

---

842. Shabbath 152a
843. Baba Kamma 92b
844. Chullin 127a
845. Sanhedrin 39a
846. Plinius. *Hist. Natur.* 7:15
847. Aristotle. *Hist. Anim.* Book 1 Chapt. 16:64
848. *ibid* 17:81
849. Psalms 103:1

850. for example Levit. 3:3
851. Aristotle. *loc. cit.* No. 73
852. Second Samuel 20:10
853. Zabim 5:19 and the numerous parallels
854. *Sifra. Acharey* Chapter 12, 85a. Concerning the other places in our edition which have the textual reading *beth ha-nephesh,* see the corrections of Weiss on *ibid,* Chapt. 7, 83a.

meat) in the mouth of another, he is liable if the latter swallows it, but not if the forbidden meat got stuck in the *beth ha-beliyah,* because swallowing there is no longer under voluntary control, even though in rare cases one is able to dislodge and expel the food by strong retching[855].

In front of the esophagus or *veshet* is the *tharbatz ha-veshet* or *atrium esophagi* which, according to Rabbi Zera, is identical with the aforementioned "site of swallowing". If one makes a transverse incision through the neck of an animal, according to Mar Samuel, the neck (i.e. gullet) opens wide but the foodpipe itself (i.e. pharynx) remains as it was. Thence, the "vestibule of the esophagus" refers to that part of the throat which lies behind the larynx in front of the fifth cervical vertebra, i.e. the *cavum pharyngolaryngeum.* If the incision is made below the larynx, as is usually done in slaughtering, the piece which remains attached to the head has the property of being folded and lumenless — the other piece immediately retracts deep within the upper thoracic opening — whereas the *tharbatz* itself remains as it was, unaffected by the incision[856].

Inferiorly, the esophagus reaches to the stomach whose mucous membrane in ruminants appears as if bordered with short bristles. According to Rab, in cattle, these bristles reach far into the esophagus.

Rabbah states that the esophagus has two membranes; the outer (muscular) one is red, the inner (mucous membrane) is white[857].

Rabbi Yochanan states that one should not eat while speaking since the windpipe might get in front of the foodpipe and the speaker might choke, thus endangering his life[858]. For the same reason, one should not drink while lying on one's back[859].

The explanation of this correct observation, which is important and applicable even today, is found in the investigation of Mendelsohn and Gutzmann who showed that the complete closing of the nose and larynx occurs in every body position. But this closure only opens during respiration, particularly during speaking ("primary swallowing" the wrong way). Furthermore, when a person is lying down, foods, and even more so beverages, leave the midline and produce severe irritation of the lateral parts of the pharyngeal wall, as a result of which premature respiratory movements occur ("secondary swallowing" the wrong way)[860]. Indeed, one might think that Oriental people, who normally consume food and beverage while lying on their left side, have accustomed their pharynxes to the passage of food in this manner. According to the above warnings of the Talmud, however, this seems not to be the case.

## X    The Stomach

The *Mishnah*[861] lists four designations for the (four) portions of the stomach of ruminants. Since these are generally well-known, they were not further explained. Tradition gives them the following names in sequence: *keres ha-penimith* (paunch), *beth ha-kosoth* (reticulum), *hemses* (omasum) and *kebah* (abomasum).

a) *Keres ha-penimith,* the *ventriculus internus* (*keres* meaning abdomen), corresponds to the first stomach of ruminants, the rumen or paunch. Already at the time of the *Tosefta,* this designation was no longer in active use, so that Schila, the chief slaughterer of Sepphoris, was consulted for clarification. He gave the popular

---

855. Kethuboth 30b; Niddah 42a; Jerushalmi Nazir 3; 52d
856. Chullin 43b. The circular fibres on the internal plane of the muscular coat of the gullet cause it to contract when cut, but these are not found in the pharynx.
857. *ibid.* 43a

858. Taanith 5b
859. Pesachim 108a
860. Mendelsohn & Gutzmann. Untersuchungen über des Schlucken in Verschiedenen Körperlagen. *Deutsche Med. Wochenschrift.* 1899 No. 44-77
861. Chullin 3:1

designation *sanya dibe*. The explanations of an identical term which are found in all the commentaries and dictionaries since Rabbenu Gersom (in the year 1000 C.E.), are not understandable to us[862].

The Sages of the Babylonian Talmud consider the "inner *keres*" *(sanya dibe)* to refer to the narrow hard part of the rumen, the *stomachos* of the *keres* (entrance of the rumen), as explained by Rabbi Ishmael[863]. One must also be aware that the term *stomachos* is also used for foodpipe. Samuel explains that the *sanya dibe* is that part of the rumen which has no downy lining (*milath,* the bristles of the rumen), as opposed to the remainder of the rumen.

In the schools of Palestine, the inner rumen was said to be the *entire* rumen, as opposed to the "outer *keres*" or simply *keres,* the abdominal wall[864], similar to the Roman *ventriculus* and *venter*.

b) *Beth ha-kosoth,* literally means a basket for goblets[865]; the latter does in fact have similarities to the reticulum (or second stomach of ruminants). Modern veterinarians compare its appearance to that of honeycombs.

c) *Hemses,* or perhaps more correctly *ha-masas,* means that which crushes the food, i.e. the omasum. This designation corresponds to the post-Augustinian *omasum* of the Romans which the annotators explain as a foreign Gallic word. It seems more likely to have had a Semitic origin.

d) *Kebah,* the rennet bag (i.e. abomasum), has a side with sinews and another curved side, *yathra* and *kashta (curvatura minor* and *major).*

In birds, the *hemses* corresponds to the stomach or *kurkeban,* in front of which, in a ritually clean bird, is the crop or *zephek* or anterior stomach. It is lacking, for example, in the eagle[866]. The inner membrane of the stomach, the *kis* (literally: sac) is easily peeled off in clean birds. Whether the Biblical term *murah*[867] refers to the crop or the stomach (i.e. gizzard), was already uncertain in antiquity[868].

It is noteworthy that the *Gemara* also speaks of a *kurkeban* in human beings[869]. The original meaning of the word, as seems evident from the Arabic *kurkub,* was both "abdomen" and "stomach".

## XI   The Intestines

The small intestines, called simply *dakkin* meaning thin, follow the stomach. In the Aramaic dialect, they are called *hadura de kantha,* encirclements (or slings) of the *kantha,* i.e. the mesentery. In later times, they were known as *keruka ketina,* the small wrapping (or coil), as opposed to *keruka abya,* the thick wrapping, i.e. the large intestine. The end of the intestines is formed by the *chilcholeth, karkesha* in Aramaic, later called *patruka,* which refers to the rectum.

After the destruction of the Temple, under the influence of the times and the dispersion of Jews among other peoples, certain words took on different meanings, as the Talmud itself reports[870]. Thus, during the time of Abaye (300 C.E.), the name for the organ *hablila* (or *hublila*) changed to *beth hakosoth* (in the East Aramaic dialect: *bé kisé*) and vice-versa. One source of confusion thus occurred under these circumstances.

862. *"disliked by wolves"* or "where the detested (food digest) drops", neither of which are true about the paunch of ruminants. I do not know whether modern scholars using the term "mucous sieve" refer to the paunch. One might think of the Greek *syndiabe* but I cannot prove this contention.
863. Chullin 50b
864. for example, Celsus *Medicina.* 4:1 p.182 and 4:5: *faucibus subest stomachus.*
Alexander of Tralles 1 p.204 Puschmann, compare Aristotle *Hist. Anim.* Book 1 Chapt. 16 No. 69
865. Kelim 16:2
866. Chullin 61a
867. Levit. 1:16
868. *Sifra. loc. cit.*
869. Shabbath 152a; Aboth de Rabbi Nathan 31:2
870. Shabbath 36a

This confusion increased through the ages. Thus, in collections of sermons (*Midrashim*), where lay people speak, there are certainly numerous errors concerning the location and designation of organs. We still find such errors every day[871]. Finally, copyists have also perpetuated errors.

Therefore, we should not be astonished if we cannot understand the path described in the *Midrash* that food takes through the various organs in the body of an animal. One also cannot carry over that which happens in ruminants and consider that it also applies to the pigeon and even to man. It remains undecided whether the fault lies with the author or with the copyist or with us.

The *Midrash* notes[872] that when Moses was with God and did not eat or drink, he overcame ten rulers of man (the organs of digestion): mouth, esophagus, *hemses*, *kebah*, *stomachos*, small intestine and large intestine, the *kantha di-me'aya*, the rectum and the *izketha*. The latter is known as a "ring" in Aramaic (anus, anulus) similar to the Hebrew *tabba'ath*.

In another transmission of the same story[873], the fourth stomach *(beth kisé)*, not mentioned above, as well as the enigmatic *sanya dibe*, are also listed. In reality, therefore, there are 12 "rulers", as already noted by Wolf Einhorn in his commentary on this *Midrash*. A third version, which speaks of the pigeon, has a different listing of digestive organs[874].

## XII Libba: Heart or Stomach?

Throughout the Aramaic dialect, the word *libba* is used for the stomach of human beings. However, just like the Greek *kardia* and the Assyrian *kibbu*, this word also refers to the heart. We also still speak of cardialgia and cardiac asthma. The expression *alibba rekana*, which is found in innumerable writings on nutrition and medicine, undoubtedly means "on an empty stomach". However, it is totally uncertain whether *ke'eb leb* means heart pain or stomach pain, and whether *chulsha de libba* means heart weakness or stomach weakness. The fact that we think of stomach as the more likely meaning of the word *libba* proves nothing about the ancient interpretation of this word.

## XIII Physiology of Digestion

The stomach of a human being, *kebah*[875], serves two functions: to grind the food and to bring on sleep. In old age, the sound of the grinding is low[876] because the stomach no longer grinds[877]. The nose counteracts the sleep-inducing property of the stomach in that the nose awakens. If the functions become reversed so that the sleep-inducing organ awakens and the awaking organ induces sleep, then the person slowly dies. If both induce sleep or if both awaken, the person dies forthwith[878].

This theory is reminiscent of that of Aristotle. According to him, vapors which develop from the nourishment in the stomach ascend to the head and induce drowsiness by their accumulation there[879].

In the explanation of the process of digestion, we find in the Talmud, as we do so often, proponents of various viewpoints. One group considers the action of the stomach to be purely mechanical, i.e. grating and grinding, in agreement with the Alexandrians, particularly the school of Erasistratus. Another group believes the

---

871. It is said that an eagle once tore the liver out from the left side of the Promethean Giordano Fa Presto in the house of Maurits in the Hague.
872. *Yalkut* 2:906
873. Eccles. Rabbah 7:3
874. Levit. Rabbah 3:4
875. Berachoth 61b; Eccles. Rabbah 7:20d substitutes the work *hemses* for *kebah*. It also adds *kurkeban* (as a separate part of the stomach?).
876. Eccles. 12:4
877. Shabbath 152a
878. Berachoth 61b
879. Aristotle. *De Somno* 3:16

action is a chemical one, specifically a putrescence [i.e., *pepsis*], as believed by the dogmatic school, in opposition to Hippocrates[880].

According to Rabbi Yochanan, the digestion (*ikkul* meaning burning or consumption) of food in the body lasts until one becomes hungry again — according to Resh Lakish, as long as one is thirsty on account of the meal, although it depends on the size and the type of meal one has eaten[881].

Maimonides does not adopt any of these assertions in his code of Jewish Law[882], but later authors do[883].

A dog only receives scanty amounts of food; the treatment of dogs by humans in the Orient even today is different from that in the West; therefore God makes it retain its food in its entrails for three days[884], so that it is maximally utilized. Birds and fish however, only retain food for 24 hours, and, according to Rabbi Simeon, only as long as it would take for the food to be burned in a fire[885]. Digestion is equivalent to burning.

Drops from the *kebah* (i.e. rennet) make milk flow[886]. For that reason, one then used and still today uses the abomasum for the preparation of cheese, in that one either adds rennet to the milk[887] or places the milk directly in the abomasum[888].

*Masas* is not equivalent to *hemses*. See Buxtorf, *s.v. masas,* and Löw in Krauss[889]. Löw states that the Arabic *masath* refers to *lait caillé* (rennet)[890].

# XIV   The Liver

The arrangement of the liver in the sequence of digestive organs, like the entire "systematic" of this book, is artificial, since it is not substantiated in the Biblical and Talmudic sources. According to the Talmud, the liver is the source of blood[891]. To the general population, it is the organ of anger. If a drop of gall falls into the liver, the anger is assuaged[892]. Later scholars consider the gall to be the site of jealousy[893].

A young man is strongly attracted to the prostitute *till a dart strike through his liver*[894]. Delitzsch remarks[895] that this statement reminds one of the *jecur ulcerosum* of Horace[896] and the *morbus hepatarius* interpretation of love as described by Plautus[897]. Galen also considers the liver to be the seat of love[898].

That the liver is the seat of anger was already known to the poetry of cuneiform writings:

*kabittaki lipschachu* means: may your liver become flattened, i.e. let your anger be assuaged. The translation of Zimmern "temperament" barely reflects the sense of the expression[899]. The Arabs also state: "even if you are hostile and hard towards me, my liver nevertheless feels pain about that which bites your liver (i.e. that which causes you pain)"[900].

The only appellation of the liver is *kaved*, meaning *gravis* or heavy, i.e. the heaviest of the viscera. According to Rabbi Yochanan, the liver and the gallbladder are

880. Celsus. *Medicina.* Book 1 Preface p.6
881. Berachoth 53b
882. *Hilchoth Berachoth* 2:14
883. Karo. *Orach Chayim.* 184:5
884. Shabbath 155b
885. Oholoth 11:7
886. Genesis Rabbah 4:7
887. Abodah Zarah 2:5
888. Chullin 8:5
889. Krauss. *Lehnwörter* 2:345a
890. Steinschneider. *Heilmittel der Araber.* No. 1815
891. Bechoroth 55a
892. Berachoth 61b
893. Levit. Rabbah 4:3
894. Proverbs 7:23
895. Delitzsch. *System der Biblischen Psychologie* p.268
896. *Od.* 1:25:15
897. Plautus. *Curculio* 239
898. Galen. *De Placitis* Book 6 Chapt. 3 Kühn 5:521
899. Zimmern. *Babylonische Busspsalmen.* Psalm 1:10
900. *Altarabische Gedichte in der Hamasa.* ed. Freytag p.351 v.4. Communication from Professor Barth.

attached to the fifth rib[901]; here, in the *chomesh*, Abner pierced Asahel[902] and Joab pierced Abner[903] with the spear, so that the spear came out behind them and they died. In both places, the *Targum* translates *chomesh* as *setar yarkeh*: the side of the loins.

*Yothereth hakaved* is probably the *caput extorum* of the ancient anatomists, the *lobus caudatus* of our modern veterinarians. In Jewish sources, it is only mentioned as a part of animal livers.

The *Mishnah* uses two synonyms for it: the Hebrew *etzbah ha-kaved*[904] and the Syrian *chitzar* or *chitzer*[905], both of which literally mean "finger (of the liver)" because this part of the liver protrudes from the right liver lobe like a finger or, more precisely, like the thumb from the hand. The Assyrians also describe a portion of the liver which they call "finger", *ubanu*[906].

The Aramaic Bible translations, throughout, use the term *chitzar* to designate *yothereth*, and from here it was carried over into the language of the *Mishnah*. Immanual Löw first called attention to the fact that Hai Gaon (died 1038 C.E.) already recognized the Syrian designation for "finger" in this word[907]. One should not here consider the Hebrew word *chatzer* which means atrium; and pointing out that Hippocrates uses the term *pyle* (i.e. gate) for the lobe of the liver (thence *vena portarum*) is not accurate for the above reason.

The Septuagint and Josephus[908] have the translation *lobos* for the part of the liver in question, as well as for the earlobe, since the latter can also be compared to the *lobus caudatus* of the liver. This word was used by Greek physicians for every part of the liver; however, as proven by Moore from numerous sources[909], it was especially used by soothsayers to denote the caudate lobe.

*Yothereth* literally means something superfluous or something extra, such as *etzbah yetherah* which means "the superfluous finger" and refers to the back toe of birds[910]. This comparison could also be applied to the tail-lobe (i.e. caudate lobe of the liver).

The Arabic translations have *zayida* or *ziyada*, etymologically corresponding to *yothereth* (*zad* is equivalent to *yathar* meaning superfluous or supernumerary). The Arabic meaning is defined by Avicenna[911] as follows:

"The liver has *zawaid* (plural); therewith it embraces the stomach just as something held in the fingers is embraced. The largest of these *zawaid* is called *zayida* in the narrow sense[912]. The gallbladder lies therein. There are four or five such *zawaid*"[913].

This description, obviously based on Greek sources, refers to the human liver. The original Arabic dictionaries describe the *ziyada* as the caudate lobe or cord of the liver. (Moore).

The literature of cuneiform writings explains that *kabittu kablitu* refers to the caudate lobe[914].

---

901. Sanhedrin 49a
902. Second Samuel 2:23
903. *ibid* 3:27
904. Tamid 4:3
905. Yoma 8:6
906. *Mitteilungen zur Geschichte der Medizin.* Vol. 7:4 No. 28 p.389
907. Löw. *Aramäische Pflanzennamen.* p.9 note 2
908. Josephus. *Antiquities.* Book 3 Chapter 9:3

909. Moore. *Oriental Studien.* Theodore Nöldeke for his 70th birthday p.761-769
910. for example Chullin 61a
911. Avicenna. *Canon. Fen.* 14, beginning
912. The 1523 venice Latin translation of the Canon is senseless: *et majus additamentorum ejus est additamenti!*
913. The 1496 Hebrew translator of the Canon translates *ziyadah* as *yothereth*.
914. *Mitteilungen zur Geschichte der Medizin.* Vol. 7:4 No. 28 p.389

Jacob Philip Hartmann[915] already conjectured that this portion of the liver was removed purely for technical reasons. In the animals in question, cows, goats and sheep, particularly the latter, the extending portion of the liver (i.e. caudate lobe) is only attached to the rest of the liver by a stalk and lies deeply and firmly embedded in the fat capsule of the kidneys, which must also be removed and offered in the Temple, so that a special preparation was necessary in order to remove it together with the rest of the liver. In the rabbit, this lobe often tears off if one bruskly removes the liver.

The interpretation that *yothereth* is the caudate lobe of the liver is not totally incontestable. According to the wording of the Biblical text, the priest shall remove the *yothereth* which is over (*al*) the liver with (*al*, literally: on) the kidneys (plural)[916]. No part of the liver, however, including the caudate lobe, lies near both kidneys and, thus, the right kidney is always the one referred to. One could certainly agree with Ibn Ezra's translation: "the *yothereth together* with the kidneys". Such a usage of the word *al* is also found elsewhere[917]. However, the obligation of offering both kidneys of the animal was already explicitly stated immediately above[918], and a repetition would be totally purposeless, irrespective of the fact that it is impossible to remove this lobe of the liver and both kidneys together as a single unit. Ibn Ezra's interpretation also does not address itself to the linguistic difficulty of the use of the same preposition (i.e. *al,*) in two different senses for two juxtaposed words (liver and kidneys).

It is probably as a result of these deliberations that Hieronymus and the Vulgate give the translation "reticulum", whence Luther has "net".

The translation "reticulum" (the Vulgate once has *arvina jecoris*)[919] which, according to Castelli, is the term used later to describe the former term omentum, is perhaps based on a Jewish source which we find again in *Rashi's dophen ha-masak*[920], meaning "wall of the covering", although his further statement "in Aramaic it is called *chitzera* and in old French *fibres*"[921] does not seem to fit in. *Fibres* means "lobes of the liver", just as *fibrae* to the Romans and *hebras*[922] to the Spaniards. We have already discussed *chitzera* above. Furthermore, objectively, the explanation "reticulum" is impossible because, although the reticulum lies on the liver, it does not lie on the kidneys. Moreover, it must already have been previously removed if one wishes to peel off the fat which covers the stomach system (i.e. four stomachs) and the intestines.

I would also like to mention the report of Callaway[923] that the Zulus offer frankincense together with the fat of the reticulum of the slaughtered animal in order to prepare pleasant aroma for the spirits of their people. "The pleasant aroma" strongly suggests *mission* because it is borrowed verbatim from the Bible[924].

Elsewhere[925], *Rashi* gives the interpretation *tarpescha*. This expression is found twice in the Talmud. In one place[926], there is a discussion of the danger to life in the situation where the liver is totally torn away from its surroundings so that it dangles free and only remains attached by its *tarpescha de kavda*. According to Maimonides, the *tarpescha* here refers to the diaphragm: "the separating wall in the middle of the abdomen which separates the digestive organs from the respiratory organs — it is that part which has to be cut open (in a hanging animal) before the lungs can be seen"[927].

---

915. Hartmann. *De Orig. Anatomiae.* ed. Kurella. Berlin 1754 p.20 ff
916. Levit. 3:4
917. for example Exodus 35:22
918. Levit. 3:4
919. Levit. 3:15
920. Levit. 3:4
921. Ed. Berliner has *ibres,* "insufficiently explained". p.349

922. see the commentary of *Kimchi* on Levit. 3:4
923. Tylor. *Anfänge der Kultur.* Leipzig. 1873 Vol. 2 p.383
924. for example Levit. 1:9
925. Exodus 29:13 and Berachoth 44b
926. Chullin 46a
927. Maimonides *Hilchoth Shechita* 6:10

Unfortunately, this definition of *tarpescha* as diaphragm is not applicable for the "*tarpescha* of the heart"[928], which is also discussed in the Talmud[929]. It is said to refer to the fat which sits on the heart like a cap. For objective reasons, I do not believe that it refers to cardiac fat; rather (*tarpescha* of the heart) is the cardiac sac (i.e. pericardium) which Aristotle also calls *ymenen pimelodes*[930].

Wounds of the heart are considered to be serious injuries, "even if they are sealed off by the *tarpescha de libba*". Wounds of the heart, however, must always penetrate the pericardium and usually produce hemorrhage between the heart muscle and the pericardium. In case of adhesions, sealing off can certainly only occur through the (peri-) cardiac fat.

In spite of the uncertainty of the meaning of the word *tarpescha*, it has interesting cultural and historical ramifications. It is derived from the root *taphash* meaning thick or fat, and, in this form, through the not infrequently used term of cuneiform writings *tapashu*[931], it was guaranteed to be truly Semitic. The Aramaic dialect inserted the "r" (or fused *tapaschu* with the synonym *rapaschu*) and, with this modification, produced *tarpascha* (in Syriac *tarpaschtha*) or *trapasa*, which is equally possible in view of the absence of vocalization and diacritical signs in the writing of our text. The latter word travelled to the Orient as the Greek *trapeza* and represents one of the countless names of those parts of the liver whose alleged importance in sacrificial offerings led to the designation hepatoscopy. The term *jecinora* was used for *victima*.

Theophilus explicitly declares[932] that it was one of the *mathematikon iatron* (physician-mathematicians) who gave the lobe of the liver a variety of names, of which the first was *trapeza*. We know from Sextus Empiricus[933] and others that the phrase "mathematicians and astrologers" simply refers to the Chaldaeans and vice-versa[934].

I cannot determine to what the term *trapeza* refers in relation to sacrifices. Naturally, I do not believe that *trapeza* here means table. Nicander[935] speaks of the outermost (or pointed) lobe of the liver which emanates from the *trapeza* and which lies adjacent to the gallbladder and the other lobes of the liver.

## XV    The Gallbladder

The *Mishnaic* term *mara*, which literally means bitter, is used to denote bile and the gallbladder. The Biblical terms *merora* or *merera* only refer to the liquid bile. Scripture, as well as popular usage even today, considers bitterness, poison, and gall to be derived from the above term.

## XVI    The Spleen

The data in the Talmud concerning the spleen, its functions and its illnesses are very sparse when compared to the extensive knowledge thereof in heathen antiquity. The Bible does not even mention the spleen.

The spleen is called *techol* in Hebrew and *tichal* in Arabic. Its convex side is called "the breast (or *dad* meaning mamma) of the spleen". The fatty capsule is referred to as the skin or *krum*, and the vessels of the hilum are called "strings" or *chutin*[936].

Although the spleen looks like blood, it is not. Rather, it is a fatty type of substance, *shumna*, and is therefore permitted to be eaten[937]. On the other hand, the

---

928. The stomach is discussed immediately above
929. Chullin 49a
930. Aristotle. *Histor. Anim.* Book 1 Chapt. 17 No. 75
931. Zimmern. *Babylonische Buss-psalmen.* Leipzig 1885 No. 8; 46 & p.99; Guyard, *Journal Asiatique.* 1883 Vol. 2 p.184

932. Theophilus. (Protospatharius) *De Hominis Fabrica.* Paris 1555 p.33
933. Sextus Empiricus. *Advent. Mathemat.* 4.2. Ed. Bekker p.728
934. Cicero. *De Divinatione* 1:1
935. Nicander. *Theriaca* 559
936. Chullin 93a
937. i.e. kosher. *ibid* 111a

blood which flows from the vessels of the spleen is prohibited under penalty of flogging[938].

According to the Talmud, the spleen produces laughter[939]. The Spaniard Judah Halevi (*circa* 1100 C.E.), better known as a poet than a physician, explains, in accord with Plato[940] and Aretäus, that the function of the spleen is to protect the black bile from turbidity due to condensation, and, as a result of this cleansing, the spleen produces joy and laughter[941]. It is also noteworthy that Q. Serenus Samonicus, who wrote in the year 250 C.E., stated that people with swollen spleens have a foolish laughter. If one extirpates the splenic tumor, laughter ceases and such people always have a serious demeanor:

> *Splen tumidus nocet, risum tamen addit ineptum.*
> *Dicitur exsectus faciles auferre cachinnos.*
> *Perpetuoque aevo frontem praestare severam*[942].

Plinius, the source of the prose of Serenus, also cites this last assertion[943].

According to the previously-cited *Mishnah*[944] which details the teachings of microcosm, the spleen in the body of man is like the laws of the world, i.e. the regulator.

*Nimosin* is the usual Hebraicized plural of the Greek *nomos*. The commentator Joshua Falk derives this word from *masas* meaning liquefy, without an acceptable sense[945]. Löw states that the word *nimosin* meaning "law" is never written defectively without a *vav*. The meaning is "soft and liquefied", just like the consistency of the spleen. Similarly, Galen calls the spleen *chaunos* meaning loose or spongy.

Rufus speaks of the spleen succinctly: it is without use and without function: *apraktos kai anergetos*[946].

# B.   THE ORGANS OF RESPIRATION

## I   Mouth, Nose and Larynx

The first organs of respiration are the mouth and the nose[947]. Next is the throat or *garon*. The poetic books of the Bible only describe the *garon* as the organ of speech.

In the prosaic writings, *garon* is not found. In Isaiah 16:6 and in Ezekiel 16:11, the word *garon* is used in the sense of stretching the neck in a haughty manner, or ornamenting it with a chain.

The windpipe, called *kaneh* meaning pipe, or *gargereth* meaning gullet, insofar as its membranous portion is concerned, is similar in construction to the vertebral column in that it consists of cartilaginous rings, *chulyoth*, which are connected by membranous bands, *bar chulya*[948]. It runs up to the larynx, the *pika shel gargereth* or *prominens tracheae*[949]. The latter contains the only cartilage in the entire system which totally encircles the *kaneh*, the *taba'ath ha-gedolah* or *anulus maximus* or cricoid cartilage. The thyroid cartilage sits on the latter like a helmet, *koba*. The latter has a sharp pointy part on the top, *chudda de koba*, and from there it slopes downward in a slanting

---

938. Kerithoth 21b
939. Berachoth 61b
940. *Timäus.* ed. Stephen. 3:72
941. Judah Halevi. *Kuzari* 4:25
942. Q. Serenus Samonicus Chapter 23 v. 25
943. Plinius. *Hist. Natur.* 11:80
944. see part 3:1 of this chapter re: the eye
945. Aboth de Rabbi Nathan 31:3

946. Rufus Ed. Daremberg-Ruette p.176
947. see mouth and nose described earlier in this chapter
948. Chullin 50a, according to the interpretation of *Rashi*. More appropriately Rabbi Gersom there interprets *chulya* to be the cricoid cartilage and *bar chulya* the cartilage of the windpipe.
949. Chullin 134b

fashion, *shippuy koba*. The cricoid cartilage ends posteriorly in two round cartilages, the "granules" or *chitte*[950].

The Santorini cartilages are what is meant here. The arytenoid cartilages are considered part of the cricoid cartilage. The prescribed incision in the neck during ritual slaughtering, if it involves the inside of the larynx—the inside of the windpipe is also acceptable—must in any case lie completely within the interior of the *anulus maximus*. It may be diagonally placed so that the dorsal incision line passes into the "granules" of the cricoid[951].

The precise meaning of *kaneh* is *geschling* in German (gullet and lung): "he who buys a *kaneh* from a butcher is not also entitled to the heart"[952].

In the Biblical book of Proverbs, only the word *gargeroth* (plural) is mentioned. It is used as a designation for the outside of the neck where jewelry is affixed.

Inferiorly, the windpipe bifurcates into two large channels, *simpona rabba* (the major bronchi), which then break up into smaller channels (the bronchial tree).

## II   The Lungs

The lungs of an animal[953] are divided into two separate rows, *arugoth*, which were later called *kanphe de reah*, wings of the lung[954]. Each half of the lungs (i.e. each lung) is further subdivided into a number of *unne* or lobes. The right lung has three lobes and the left has two. The lobes are separated from each other by indentations or *chittuke*. In addition, the right lung of ruminants also has the *inunitha de warda* or that which the butcher calls "the rose lobe", which refers to the median lobe of the lung in modern veterinary medicine. Particularly the anterior (superior) lobe on both sides is often divided by a more or less deep indentation which has no pathological significance.

Hippocrates erroneously states that each lung, even in humans, has an upper, middle and lower lobe[955]. According to Galen, there is unanimity of opinion among anatomists that the lobes of the lungs in all living beings are paired, i.e. two on the left and two on the right. However, exacting scientists know that an additional small lobe is present on the right side, *oion apoblastema ti thaterou toin dyoin*[956]. Thus, in actuality, there is no living being that does not have one more lobe on the right side than on the left, even if the numbers are not precisely two and three as in humans[957]. The fact that Galen thinks that the median lobe of ruminants is also present in humans is evidence that he never actually dissected a human corpse.

The controversy between Hippocrates, who states that the lungs have three lobes each, and Galen, who states that they have two lobes each, was, naturally, quite painful for scholars in the Middle Ages. However, Ludwig Duret[958], and probably many others with him, easily reconciles the problem by assuming that the earlier generations (during the time of Hippocrates) had stronger vitality and therefore had more advanced development of their organs. His contemporary, Vesal[959], instead of

950. Chullin 18a–b
951. Chullin 18b
952. Baba Bathra 5:5
953. Unless otherwise stated, the source for the section on lungs is Chullin 46a ff.
954. Levit. Rabbah 18:1
955. Hippocrates. *Coac. Praenot.* No. 400 fol. 181 of the Foes edition.
956. Galen. *De Administ. Anat.* 7:2; Kühn 2:625
957. Galen. *De Usu Partium* 6:4. Kühn 3:421
958. Ludovici Dureti. *Interpretationes et*

*Enarrationes in Magni Hippocratis Coacas Praenotiones.* Ed. Chouet. Lugdan. Batav. 1737. Book 2 No. 16, 31 fol. 258: *sed priscorum hominum thoracis amplitudo major fuit ex amplificatione calcoris vivifici at capitis magnitudine.*
959. Vesal. *De Humanis Corporis Fabrica.* 6:6 fol. 581 of the Basel edition of 1543: *Lobum autem, qui in cainbus simusque cavae venae caudicem suffulcit, nusquam in homine observavi, et hunc illo destitui certo certius scio.*

reading books, made use of the dissecting knife and taught about the anatomical differences between the lungs of humans and those of ruminants.

On the surface of the lung of animals, the Talmudic Sages differentiate an outer and an inner membrane; the former, called *kittuna de warda* or "coat of roses", corresponds to the pulmonary (or visceral) pleura, and the latter depicts the outer wall of the alveoli. The parietal pleura[960] is not mentioned at all.

## III   Physiology of the Lung

Concerning the physiology of the lung, a Talmudic tradition from the time of the *Mishnah* teaches that the lung absorbs all types of liquids[961], totally in accord with Plato[962], who, as reported by Haeser, only repeats the opinion of educated lay persons of that era. According to the communication of Gellius[963], Erasistratus was the first to demonstrate that liquids do not go into the lungs.

In reality, the followers of Hippocrates have already provided the experimental evidence for this. They assert: if one gives a very thirsty animal blue- or red-colored water to drink and slits the throat (*ton laimon*) of the animal while it is still drinking, one finds the colored water in the throat. The fluid which enters the windpipe fortuitously is expelled by the glottis. Indeed, the heart absorbs fluids from the lungs and converts it into serum[964]. Nevertheless, Plutarch considers Hippocrates to be the originator of the Platonic viewpoint, as stated by Gellius.

## IV   The Voice

The voice emanates from the lungs[965] but the larynx brings it out[966]. The voice of castrates is soft and the voice of an *aylonith*, a girl whose genitalia remained in an infantile stage of development, is thick (i.e. coarse)[967]. The voice of a mad (rabid) dog is not heard when he barks[968]. In order for a "rebellious son" to be sentenced to death, it is required that the tone (literally: color) of the voice of both parents be identical. This requirement by itself is already sufficient to make the application of the law of the rebellious son impossible[969]. Three things restore a person's good spirits: sounds (i.e. a call), sights, and aromas[970].

The voice of a woman leads one astray and deflects one's thoughts. For this reason, a woman should be silent in the house of God[971]! If a woman is a screamer or *kolanith* and speaks so loudly in her house[972] that the neighbors can hear it, the husband should abruptly divorce her because her behavior is un-Jewish[973]. To be sure, according to a homily of Rabbi Joshua, a woman's voice is by nature louder than that of a man[974]; however, the voice should nevertheless be sweet[975]. A thick (coarse) voice is a blemish[976].

---

960. literally: rib membrane of the pleura
961. Berachoth 61b & later also found in Levit. Rabbah 4: 4 & Eccles. Rabbah on 7:19
962. Plato. Timaüs. ed. Stephan 3:70: *to te pneuma kai to poma dechomene*. According to Gellius, the poet Alkaios already said this!
963. Gellius 17:11
964. Hippocrates. *De Corde*. fol. 268 ed. Foes
965. Levit. Rabbah 18:1
966. Berachoth 61a
967. Yebamoth 80b
968. Yoma 83b
969. Sanhedrin 71a
970. Berachoth 57b
971. Berachoth 24a. This is probably also the original meaning of *Let your women keep silence in the churches*. First Corinthians 14:34
972. According to Kethuboth 72b, this only refers to talk of immorality
973. *Tosefta* Kethuboth 7:7
974. Genesis Rabbah 17:8
975. Song of Songs 2:14
976. Kethuboth 75a

# C.    THE ORGANS OF THE BLOOD CIRCULATION

## I    The Heart

In the book entitled *De Corde*, the disciples of Hippocrates already demonstrate a thorough knowledge of the heart and its activity. They describe the two heart chambers, the larger left one and the smaller right one, as well as the appendages or auricles which they call the "heart ears" or *ota*[977], with their independent pulsations. They also describe the method, still in use today, for testing the closing ability of the heart valves by pouring water into the heart.

The teaching of the two chambers remained firm, and is later found in the Talmud[978], which also uses the term *chalal* (hollow space) which corresponds to the Greek expression *koilia*. This teaching is also found among the Alexandrians, among whom Rufus surprisingly explains that the right chamber is the larger one[979], and among the Arabs. Among the latter, Rhazes (died 930 C.E.) speaks of two ventricles and two auricles (ears, *udn*)[980]. Haly, in the tenth century, specifically disputes the existence of a third ventricle[981]. On the other hand, Avicenna still reproduces[982] the erroneous teaching of Aristotle[983] concerning the three cavities, whereas Maimonides[984] correctly distinguishes only a larger left and a smaller right chamber[985].

Galen recommends[986] that to study the heart of an animal one should pull firmly with the fingers or with a hook on the xiphisternum and then cut out all the soft parts of the body wall in a circular manner. This remarkable method was obviously derived from sacrificial cults or from heathen priests. We conclude this from the fact that the *Mishnah*[987] prohibits any type of benefit that one might derive from "animal skins from which the hearts were removed" (*oroth lebubin*, rarely *lebuboth*)[988]. According to Rabbi Simeon ben Gamliel, these refer to skins which have a circular hole in the area of the heart, as if the heart were removed for a heathen cult. Such a skin may not be used as a parchment upon which to write a Torah scroll[989]. The reason for this prohibition is that one used to tear out the hearts of live animals in this manner to offer them to idols[990]. Regino even relates of the Huns: *Corda hominum, quos capiunt, veluti pro remedio devorant*[991]! Celsus finds it necessary to declare it an extreme cruelty to cut open the abdomen or chest of a living person[992].

In the fibrous ring at the base of the aorta of ruminants, one finds two different large flat bones which serve as points of insertion of the semilunar valves. In horses, there is a corresponding heart cartilage which only ossifies in old animals. These bones were already known to Plinius[993] and to Galen[994], but are

---

977. In French and in English the auricles are called, respectively, *oreillettes* and auricles.
978. Chullin 45b
979. Rufus. ed. Daremberg p.151. Concerning the same assertion of Aristotle in his *Histor. Anim.* 1:17, see the comment of Aubert & Wimmer in their edition 1:238
980. *Trois Traités d'Anatomie Arabes*. Ed. De Koning p.65
981. *ibid* p.345
982. Avicenna. Canon. Book 3 Part 2 treatise 1 Chapter 1: *et in ipso (corde) sunt tres ventres, scil. duo ventres magni et venter quasi medius, quem Galenus nominavit foveam aut meatum, non ventrem.* According to the Venice edition of 1523
983. Aristotle. *Histor. Anim.* 1:17 and *De Partibus* 3:4

984. Maimonides *Mishneh Torah. Hilchoth Schechita* 6:5
985. Nevertheless, Rabbi Joseph Karo, in his code of Jewish Law, *Yoreh Deah* 40:1 again speaks of three chambers.
986. Galen. *De Administ. Anat.* 7:6, Kühn 2:603
987. Abodah Zarah 2:3
988. Sefer Torah 1:2
989. Soferim 1:2
990. Jerushalmi Abodah Zarah 41b
991. Regino. *Chronicon ad Annum 889* in Pertz. *Monum.* 1:600
992. Celsus. *Praefat.* p.11 of the Rotterdam edition of 1750
993. Plinius. *Histor. Natur.* 11:70
994. Galen. *Admin. Anat.* 7 Chapt. 10; Kühn 2:618

nevertheless not mentioned in the Talmud. On the other hand, they play a much greater role in post-Talmudic writings spanning a long time period. The question is always discussed as to whether these bones perhaps penetrate by force from the outside (thus rendering the animal unfit for consumption i.e. *terefah*) or whether they arise because of some illness or whether they are physiologically there as part of nature[995].

According to the Jewish viewpoint, a person removes all repulsive and evil things from his body when he undergoes circumcision. Similarly, in pictorial language, the evil people of Israel are asked to *circumcise the foreskin of the heart*[996], meaning to abandon evil. The *Midrash* remarks that this phrase cannot be interpreted literally, and that when Abraham was told to circumcise himself[997] without a specific body part being identified, the heart is excluded because a wound in this organ would have killed him[998].

The Biblical *tropos* of the *foreskin of the heart* did not slip by the *Latino-Barbari*; they designate the pericardium as the *praeputium cordis*[999].

## II   The Great Vessels

The "pipe of the heart",. *kaneh haleb*, or *aorta*[1000], looks like a cord of fat which lies on the walls of the lungs. According to the generally accepted teaching of Rab, the slighest perforation of this organ (the aorta) is fatal. According to Mar Samuel, only larger injuries are fatal[1001]. Perhaps the latter considered the aorta to be an *arteria*, that is an air-containing vessel, whereas Rab seems to have been aware of the true situation.

Amemar points out the teaching of Rabbi Nachman that in actuality there exist three "heart vessels": one leads to the heart (aorta), one to the lungs and one to the liver (inferior vena cava). The difference of opinion between Rab and Samuel, however, only pertains to the vessel of the heart, *kat' exochen*, the aorta[1002].

In *Rashi*, one finds the following explanation: "after the windpipe enters the chest, it divides into three branches, one of which leads to the heart". Ritter suggests that one compare this with Isaac Lampronti's commentary[1003]. It is a repetition of the ancient Aristotelian teaching, according to which air comes to the heart from the windpipe[1004]. This interpretation does not follow from the wording in the Talmud.

Maimonides states that "the two pulsating vessels in the neck adjacent to the windpipe are called *varidin*"[1005]. The slaughtering of an animal should be accomplished by a single cut in the neck perpendicular to its longitudinal axis and not from the side, so that both of these vessels, the carotids, are severed[1006]. In other places, these same vessels are called *mizrakim* meaning squirting[1007].

It is not clear how Kazenelson can consider the *varidin* to be veins[1007a]. The jugular veins are only exceptionally severed in the usual incision for slaughtering since they are located far laterally in the neck.

Job laments: *my bones are pierced in me in the night season* (because of my misfortune) *and my "orekim" do not sleep*[1008]. As *Rashi* remarks, according to

---

995. See the commentaries on Karo's *Yoreh Deah* 40:3
996. Deut. 10:16 and Jeremiah 4:4
997. Genesis 17:23
998. Genesis Rabbah 46:5
999. Hyrtl. *Anatomie*. p.1006
1000. According to Maimonides. *loc. cit.* *kaneh haleb* is the pulmonary artery. In his commentary on Chullin 3:10 he seems to identify *kaneh haleb* with the auricles
1001. Chullin 45b

1002. *ibid.*
1003. Lampronti. *Pachad Yitzchok.* lit. 51 p.53
1004. Aristotle. *Hist. Anim.* Book 1 Chapt. 16:71
1005. Maimonides' commentary on Chullin 2:1
1006. Chullin 2:1
1007. Chullin 93b; *Rashi* on Pesachim 74b
1007a. Kazenelson. *loc. cit.* p.264
1008. Job 30:17

Dunasch ibn Labrat, the Arabs interpret the word *irk* to mean "artery" (to the physicians it nevertheless refers to "vein"); therefore the same meaning is presumed to apply here: "my arteries pulsate so strongly that I cannot sleep".

Löw points out that one cannot invoke a parallelism to *nakar*. One can only postulate that *irk* may be related to the Syriac *arik,* meaning "whose flesh is gnawed off from the bone", or *uraka,* meaning *erosio ossium*, or *arrukutha* meaning *sordes dentium* (dental caries).

## III   The "Hairy Heart"

The ancients believed that some people are born with a hairy heart *(hirto corde)* and therefore excel over others in intelligence and in strength. An example of such a person was Aristomenes, who killed 300 Spartans but was finally captured. The Lacedaemonians cut his chest open while he was still alive and found a hirsute heart. This report of Plinius[1009] is also confirmed by others[1010]. Aristotle describes the same abnormality about the heart of Leonidas[1011]. Nonnus, in the fourth century, stated that the Sabirers have hairy chests *(dasysternon)* and thick hairs on the heart, as a result of which they do not fear the god of war[1012]. In addition, in the sixteenth century, Antonius Muret, known for his homosexual escapades, reported that, when he was residing in Venice, a robber-knight was sentenced to death and a *cor pilosum* was found by the executioner who dissected him[1013].

In Jewish legend, such a powerful person is Judah, the son of the Patriarch Jacob. According to Rabbi Chanin, when Judah became enraged, the hair of his heart would pierce through his clothes and protrude exteriorly. He then took iron plates in his mouth and expectorated them, ground to powder[1014].

The opinion enunciated by Morgagni in 1761[1015] confirms this narrative, in that most reports of hairy hearts from antiquity are not based on anatomical observation. Rather a single fortuitous finding of such pericardial growth and proliferation in a strong person probably gave rise to the above folk belief.

## IV   The Heart as the Seat of the Psyche

In the Bible, the heart is not an organ of the blood circulation, but the seat of the psyche. The anguished Professor of Medicine Johann Antonius Van De Linden[1016] writes:

"I am angry at Galen whenever I think *(irascor Galeno, quoties cogito)* that he is responsible, because of his arrogance, that physicians have serious disputes concerning the purpose of the heart. And to abandon the *Majorum beneplacita, ab Hebraeis profecta, ratione suffulta, sensibus probata,* Galen's motive was no different from that of the person who forced Herostratus to set fire to the Temple of the prostitutes in Ephesus".

He then gives a well-organized overview of all pertinent Biblical citations — an overview which one would certainly not find in a modern textbook of physiology — in

1009. Plinius. *Histor. Natur.* 11:70
1010. *Valer. Maxim.* Book 1 Chapt. 8:15 p.55 of the Kempf edition: *cor exectum pilis*
1011. Aristotle. *De Generatione.* Note 52
1012. Nonnus. Book 26:92. ed. Kochly: *toisin eni kradie lasiai triches, on charin ai ei psychen tharsos echousi kai ou ptossousin enyo.*
1013. M. Anton. Muret. *Variar. Lection.* Libri 15, Antwerp 1580. Book 12 Chapt. 10, p.315: *ipse quoque memini, cum Venitus essem, sumptum esse capitis supplicium de*

*nobili quodam latrone, qui cum a carnifice dissecaretur, corde admodum piloso repertus est.*
1014. Genesis Rabbah 93:6. Ritter states that since the *Midrash* is not referring to a penetration of the thorax, the hair on Judah's chest must be the hair referred to.
1015. Morgagni. *De Sedibus, et Causis Morborum.* Venice 1761. Book 2 Ep. 24, art. 4., fol. 247
1016. Van de Linden. *Medicina Physiologica.* Amsterdam 1653 p.186

order to prove that the heart is the seat of the psyche, contrary to Galen. Most of these citations are generally known to the Jews, since the view that the heart is the seat of one's temperament is familiar to us. A good heart and an evil heart, a hard heart and a soft heart and many other similar expressions are of Biblical origin without our being conscious thereof.

In the Talmud, the conception of the function of the heart is the same as in the Bible. Nevertheless, there are supporters of the Galenic viewpoint, and the expression "it appears to me (or it is apparent) that you have no brain in the skull" as a coarse answer to an opposing viewpoint[1017], already shows the correct conception of the function of the heart in the minds of the people.

The argument about the seat of intelligence was not settled even in the Middle Ages[1018]. Avicenna[1019] attempted to mediate the positions of Aristotle (heart) and Hippocrates (brain)[1020]. Modern science knows the heart only as a muscle. All emotional faculties reside in the central nervous system.

## V  "Leb" meaning Heart and Stomach

The word *kardia,* as specifically emphasized by Galen[1021], refers not only to the heart, but also to *to stoma tes koilias,* the mouth of the stomach. On the other side, the chambers of the heart are called *gasteres* (stomach chambers)[1022]. The Romans also use the term *ventriculus* to denote both the stomach and the cardiac chamber. Thus, even today, when we speak of *hypertrophia ventriculi* we refer to an abnormal condition of half of the heart; however, the term *carcinoma ventriculi* refers to cancer of the stomach. When we speak of cardialgia we think of the stomach, whereas *asthma cardiacum* refers to the heart. Also, the Ebers Papyrus describes "remedies which enable the heart to take in nourishment"[1023]. Furthermore, the Assyrians use the word *libbi* in the sense of heart and stomach. This double sense of the word is exceedingly confusing when reading ancient authors.

It is undoubted, at least in post-Biblical times and perhaps even in the Bible itself[1024], that the Hebrew word *leb* or *libba,* which ordinarily means "heart", is also used, like *kardia,* as a designation for stomach. The expression *alibba rekana* can only mean "on an empty *stomach*". According to Abaye, all medicinal potions should be taken *alibba rekana*[1025]. According to Rabbi Judah, the skin of an animal that eats three shekels of asafoetida *alibba rekana* falls off, unless it is immediately placed in water[1026]. If one excessively eats or drinks *alibba rekana,* the *thalya de libba* are torn off, i.e. the strings of the heart or the stomach[1027]. In other places, too, one is forced to interpret *leb* as stomach rather than heart. For example, it is related that a person once ate earth *(gargishtha)* and then ate cress seeds; the latter grew in the stomach and these seeds then pierced him in his *leb* so that he died[1028].

## VI  "Leb" meaning Chest Cavity

*Leb* is not only the name for heart and stomach, but also serves as the designation

---

1017. Menachoth 80b; Yebamoth 9a; Jerushalmi Yebamoth 1;2c

1018. See D. Kaufmann. *Die Sinne.* Leipzig 1884 p.62 ff

1019. see Landauer. "Psychologie des Ibn Sina." *Zeutschr. Deutsch. Morgen. Geselschaft.* Vol. 29: 402, 1875.

1020. Hippocrates *De Morbo Sacro* No. 45. Ed. Foes. Sect. 3 fol. 310,12 *cor neu̯trum prudentiae jus habet, sed horum omnium cerebrum autor est.*

1021. Galen. *De Locis* 5:2. Kühn 8:302

1022. Hippocrates *De Corde.* ed. Foes. fol. 268

1023. Ebers Papyrus. Ed. Joachim. p.70

1024. Psalms 104:15. *And wine maketh glad the heart of man...and bread which supports (nourishes) the lebab of man*

1025. Gittin 70a

1026. Chullin 59a

1027. *ibid*

1028. Erubin 113b. (no such reference exists F.R.) see also above "stomach" in this chapter.

for part of the chest cavity. The priest tears the clothing of a suspected adulteress[1029] according to the prescribed procedure *until he uncovers her "leb"*[1030]; however, he ties a string of willow fibres[1031] above her bosom so that her clothes not fall to the ground[1032]. Similarly, as a sign of mourning following the death of one's mother or father, one tears one's garment on the left side until the *leb* is exposed, whereas for other relatives the tear on the right side need only be one handbreadth in length[1033]. This *leb* is sometimes seen, sometimes not, according to whether or not it is covered by clothes. For that reason, Israelites should not desire to be "like a signet-ring[1034] on the *leb*"[1035] but should strive[1036] to be "like a (permanently visible) crown in the hand of the Lord"[1037]. Children wore a "breast hide" *(or haleb)*, a type of bib, to protect the clothes from becoming soiled[1038].

From all these Talmudic citations, it follows that *leb* cannot refer to the left lower part of the chest cavity, but more likely corresponds to the middle. It is hard to know how this word came to have such a meaning. The ancients knew very well where the heart is situated[1039]. When Galen misplaces the heart precisely in the middle of the chest, at the point of intersection of the sagittal and vertical axes[1040], it is to him only the consequence of teleological speculation, in spite of his customary tone of infallibility. Otherwise, this hardly occurred to anyone. The Talmud also has the correct conception. In order for the laws of God, according to the Biblical command, to be *on your heart*[1041], one should place them (in a capsule or phylactery box) on the inner surface of the middle of the left forearm[1042]. Naturally, the word of the preacher that a wise man's heart is on the right side but that of a fool is on the left side[1043] is not an anatomical teaching.

## VII  Tzippar Nephesh

Both the meaning of the word *tzippar* and the sense of the phrase *"tzippar nephesh"* (literally: *tzippar* of the soul, soul meaning life) are uncertain. This much is certain: a part of the body is referred to, injury to which is fatal. The Talmud asks: "how should the court know without interrogating witnesses whether the accused smote the victim on the thigh (a relatively minor injury) or on the *tzippar nephesh*[1044]? This question must be directly asked of the witnesses[1045].

The strap of the flogging whip should be short so that it not hit the *tzippar nephesh* of the criminal and he die as a result[1046]. The *Mishnah* prescribes that the strap should reach "to the beginning of the abdomen" when the convicted criminal is

---

1029. Numbers 5:11-31
1030. Sotah 1:5; *Tosefta* Sotah 1:7
1031. This is according to most commentaries. Jerushalmi Sotah 1;17a however, states: "Egyptian string because she behaved in an Egyptian manner" i.e. immorally. Levit. 18:3. Based on this, see Maimonides' *Mishneh Torah, Hilchoth Sotah* 3:11. Josephus (*Antiquities* 3:11) does not mention this part of the procedure.
1032. *Tosefta* Sotah 3:4
1033. Moed Katan 22b
1034. Such signet rings were originally worn on a string on the breast. See Genesis 38:18
1035. Song of Songs 8:6
1036. Song of Songs Rabbah 8:6 fol. 39d
1037. Isaiah 62:3
1038. Kelim 26:5, according to the

commentaries of Maimonides & Rabbi Asher. Others, however, interpret: a breast plate to protect against cat scratches. *Tosefta* Kelim 4:8 *or haluph.*
1039. Correctly stated by Aristotle. *Histor. Anim.* Book 1: Chapt. 17
1040. Galen. *De Usu Partium* 6:2; Kühn 3:415: since one can feel the pulsation of the left ventricle in the left mammillary line, it follows that not the entire heart lies on the left side, etc.
1041. Deut. 11:18
1042. Menachoth 37a
1043. Eccles. 10:2
1044. *Tosefta* Sanhedrin 12:3
1045. *ibid* 9:1
1046. *Tosefta* Makkoth 5:15

being flogged transversely across the back,[1047] that is approximately up to the axillary line[1048]. According to this, the *tzippar* refers to the "cartilage opposite the heart", as *Rashi* states, referring to the xiphoid process of the sternum (in the "pit of the heart"). Less likely is the explanation of *Aruch* that *tzippar* is "the place below the neck, above the breast" (the jugular fossa).

To the Arabs, *tzaphar* means to leap or to jump, so that the meaning is probably "the finishing blow", the *punctum saliens* (or *coup-de-grâce*).

According to Islamic folk belief, after death, the soul of a person flies about in the form of a bird[1049]. In the Talmud, there are also statements about this perception of "soul birds"[1050], but I am unable to relate it to the concept of *tzippar nephesh*[1051].

# D. THE UROGENITAL SYSTEM

## I   The Kidneys

Only the Aramaic and south-Semitic dialects have the singular term *kolya* or *kolyitha* for kidney. The term generally used (also in Canaan) is the plural *kelayoth*, not a dual term, as ordinarily is the case in the names of other paired organs. The designation *tuchoth* is only poetic[1052] and may not even refer to the kidneys.

The hilum of the kidney is called *charitz* or indentation. The "white below the loins" i.e. the calyces and pelvis of the kidney, connect to the inner parenchyma[1053]. Whether or not the "white of the kidney" is included in the Biblical concept of forbidden tallow is disputed[1054]. The kidney is covered by a double membrane; the outer one, the fat capsule, is prohibited as fat. The other, the *capsula fibrosa*, contains abundant fibres. The *fat which is on the kidneys* which must be offered in the Temple[1055] lies outside both membranes.

Aristotle[1056] and Plinius[1057] emphasize that animals have the most fat in the area of the kidneys. For this reason *the sword of the Lord is filled with the blood... of the fat of the kidneys of rams*[1058].

Rabbi Yochanan disputes the possibility of an animal's being born with *one* kidney, but Rabbi Chiya states that an animal may have one or even three kidneys on a congenital basis[1059]. He was thus familiar with the solitary kidney and the accessory kidney.

---

1047. Makkoth 3:13. According to the *Mishnah*, he is to receive one-third of the stripes "from the front"; since the convicted criminal stands bent over a block (*the judge shall cause him to lie down*. Deut. 25:2) it seems incorrect to adopt the understanding of some commentators who state that the chest of the criminal is flogged, exclusive of the fact that one is warned against injuring the *tzippar nephesh*. I therefore believe that the bailiff inflicted one-third of the flogging from the front side of the criminal and for this he (the bailiff) naturally had to leave his higher position on a stone behind the criminal.
1048. According to the commentaries: up to the navel. However, the word for navel is *tabbur*. The actual words of the text are: *ad*

*pi kereso*. One can draw no parallels from Isaiah 6:7.
1049. Geiger-Deremburg. *Jüdische Zeitschrift Für Wissenschaft und Leben*. 1867 Vol. 5 p.169 & Vol. 6 p.292. Goldziher, *Globus.* Vol. 83, 1903 Part 19 p.301.
1050. Sanhedrin 91a
1051. the Hebrew word for bird is *tzippor*
1052. Psalms 51:8 and Job 38:36
1053. Chullin 55a
1054. *ibid* 92b
1055. Levit. 3:4 and elsewhere
1056. Aristotle. *Histor. Anim.* Book 3 Chapt. 17:88
1057. Plinius. *Histor. Natur.* 11:81
1058. Isaiah 34:6
1059. Bechoroth 39a

In the Bible, the kidneys are thought to be the seat of sensation and lust. According to the epigrammatic poet, *the kidneys rejoice when the lips speak right things*[1060]. Because of yearning, Job's kidneys withered within him[1061]. The Lord places wisdom in the kidneys[1062], and tests the heart and the kidneys[1063]. The Lord, however, is near the mouth of the wicked and far from their kidneys[1064].

In the Talmud, the kidneys are the advisors of the heart[1065]. According to legend, since Abraham could not learn wisdom from his father and since he had no teacher, his kidneys played the role of teacher[1066], and he developed the recognition of the truth about God from within himself.

In the sense of the Talmud, therefore, the arrangement of the kidneys in the urogenital system is false. However, it should be energetically stressed that the already-cited, generally well-known Biblical phrase *test the heart and kidneys* presupposes a knowledge of the interrelationship of these two organs.

## II  The Urine

Urine is known by numerous names: *sheten*, transcribed as *ketannim* meaning *parvi* or "needs", *tzorech* meaning "need"; the usual name is *mémé raglayim* meaning "foot water"[1067]. The latter is also interpreted by the Masoretes to be the same as the Biblical *schayin* (or *schen*)[1068] since that word is considered to be indecent[1069].

Concerning the physiology of urine — if such an expression is permissible — one author (Rabbi Shesheth?) is of the opinion that the urine of horses and camels is not thick and not similar to milk; it is merely water coming into the body and water going out. However, in the case of the urine of an ass, which is thick and resembles milk, it is uncertain whether the urine drains from the body of the ass itself and thus contains parts of the body, or whether it too is merely water coming and water going out, and the thickness is due to the exudations of the body. The question of concern is whether or not the urine of this animal may be used as a medication, although the animal itself may not be eaten, since "that which goes forth from the unclean is unclean". Some authors consider this distinction among the various animal species as totally unacceptable[1070].

I do not know of any word from ancient Jewish writings which definitely refers to the *urinary bladder,* although it seems impossible that the Rabbis of the Talmud were unfamiliar with this organ, considering their scrupulous examination of slaughtered animals. Evidently, an injury of the urinary bladder in a slaughtered animal was not observed, as might be conjectured *a priori* from the protected location of the organ.

One cannot doubt that in Syriac the term *shalpuchtha* is used in the sense of urinary bladder. Also, in post-Talmudic times, the "*shalpuchith* into which the urine collects" is mentioned[1071]. In the Talmud itself, however, this word, according to the commentary of *Tosafoth*[1072], only refers to the uterus.

---

1060. Proverbs 23:16
1061. Job 19:27
1062. *ibid* 38:36
1063. Jeremiah 11:20 & elsewhere. The following strained apologetic interpretation is reported by the physician E. Altschuhl (*Litteraturblatt des Orients* 1845 No. 29) as an example of this (Divine) warning: From the singular *keli,* vessel (which only occurs in the sense of "organ" and not "artery"), the plural is *kelayoth.* (The correct plural of *keli* is *kelim*.) Thus the Lord tests "the heart and its vessels"! A better explanation yet is given by Dr. Feitel (*ibid.* No. 44): a person tests the pulse and the urine in order to indirectly conclude things about the condition of the

heart & kidneys; the Lord, however, (directly) tests the heart & kidneys! (Both these explanations of Jeremiah 11:20 are absurd F.R.).
1064. *ibid* 12:2
1065. Berachoth 61a
1066. Genesis Rabbah 61:1
1067. Machshirim 6:5. This term is also used for liquid stool, if the textual reading is correct.
1068. Isaiah 36:12
1069. Megillah 25b
1070. Bechoroth 7b
1071. for example Karo's *Yoreh Deah* 45:2
1072. *Tosefoth* on Chullin 48a

## III   The Male Genitalia

The Bible usually employs the designation *ervah,* nakedness, for the genitalia. Only once, in a legal matter, is the term *mebushim,* pudenda, used[1073] as follows: *When men strive together one with another, and the wife of the one draweth near for to deliver her husband out of the hand of him that smiteth him, and putteth forth her hand, and taketh him by the secrets* (*mebushim* i.e. pudenda). *Then thou shalt cut off her hand ...* according to tradition[1074], the latter refers to a monetary punishment (not, literally, the severance of the hand). Only poetically is the term *ma'or,* from *ur*[1075], used to denote the genitalia.

The Talmud uses the euphemistic name *panim shel mattah* meaning *facies inferior*[1076]. It is prohibited by the Torah law[1077] to expose the nakedness of one's father. Ham, who saw the nakedness of his father Noah, when the latter was uncovered during an episode of drunkenness, was cursed because of this, together with his offspring[1078]. The same rebuke concerning the uncovering of one's father's nakedness was levelled by Ezekiel at the immoral city of Jerusalem[1079]. Only while drunk does a man totally bare himself[1080].

Whereas, ordinarily, a single garment such as a *chiton* suffices, the priests had linen leg garments (i.e. trousers) *(michnasayim)* prescribed for them: *to cover their nakedness from the loins even unto the thighs they shall reach*[1081]. They were also forbidden to go up steps to the altar (but walked up a ramp) so that their nakedness not become uncovered thereby[1082].

## IV   The Penis

In the writings of all nations, the number of designations for the male organ is very large, obviously because of bashfulness "to name the thing by its proper name". For this reason, paraphrases and intimations are used in order not to talk in obscene terms. The nomenclature also differs, depending upon whether a term is used, as so often in the Talmud, by jurists or by physicians or by the ordinary people.

In the Bible, the usual designation for penis is *basar,* meaning flesh[1083]. Only once is the term *shophcha* meaning effusion, i.e. urinary passage, used[1084]. In the Talmud, the generally used term is *eber* meaning *membrum*[1085]; less often, one finds *etzba* meaning finger[1086], like the *digitus* of the Romans, or *gid* meaning nerve, or *amma* meaning canal[1087], or *shammash* meaning to serve[1088]. Another name is *geviyah* meaning *corpus*[1089]. The word *guph* when used alone also has the same meaning; for example: *orlath haguph,* the foreskin[1090].

In the Talmud[1091], among the prominences of the body, there is also listed the "tip of the penis", *rosh ha-geviya.* See also elsewhere[1092]. The term *rosh ha-geviya* is also used to denote the penis itself i.e. *prominentia corporis*[1093]. See also the commentary of *Tosafoth Yom Tob*[1094].

---

1073. Deut. 25:11
1074. Baba Kamma 28a
1075. Habakkuk 2:15
1076. Shabbath 48a. Used in reference to man but even more often in relation to a woman.
1077. Levit. 18:7. derived in the *Gemara* (Sanhedrin 54a-b) from the prohibition of *copula carnalis* with any wife of one's father, not only one's own mother. Levit. 18:8 requires that one honor one's father's wife even after her death.
1078. Genesis 9:22 ff
1079. Ezekiel 22:10
1080. Habakkuk 2:15
1081. Exodus 28:42
1082. Exodus 20:23

1083. for example Genesis 17:13 and Ezekiel 16:26
1084. Deut. 23:2
1085. Baba Metzia 84a
1086. Pesachim 112a. Löw says it refers to the middle finger, the *impudicus*
1087. Shabbath 108b
1088. Niddah 60b
1089. Jerushalmi Abodah Zara 3; 43a and Moed Katan 24a.
1090. Levit. Rabbah 25:6
1091. Negaim 6:7
1092. Kiddushin 25a
1093. Nedarim 32b
1094. *Tosafoth Yom Tob* on Negaim 6:7

The meaning of *petuma* is uncertain. One commentator considers it to be the penis, another thinks it means "body". One cannot arrive at a definitive conclusion from the citation which follows: "Hadrian inspected the corpse of the rebel Bar Kochba and found that a snake was wrapped around his *petuma* and was responsible for his death"[1095]. Löw states that it refers to *ptoma* meaning a cadaver.

The word *parmaschthak*[1096] probably does not mean penis but rather "very large", as shown by Schneckendorf[1097]. The Talmudic citation should therefore be translated as follows: "Pharaoh was only one ell tall and his *ancestor* was one ell tall and the tallest of his family was only one ell and a span tall". This interpretation also fits better in the Biblical citation than the explanation of *Rashi*. Fleischer, in Levy's work[1098], also states: "the Persian *parmischtak* means *extensus*". It remains puzzling why a word was taken from a foreign language for the concept of "large".

Specifically Hebrew, i.e. without analogues in other languages, is the designation *mila*, meaning *circumcisio*, and *membrum circumcisum*, meaning the penis.

During erection, the penis is designated as an *eber chay* or *membrum vivum*, as opposed to *eber meth* or *membrum mortuum*.

The protruding posterior border of the penis is called *atara*[1099] meaning crown or corona, from which our anatomical term *corona glandis* is derived.

The Rabbis of the Talmud teach as follows: there are two channels in the penis of man, one for the discharge of urine and the other for sperm. Between the two, there is a separating membrane as thin as an onion peel. If a person does not respond to the call of nature (i.e. to urinate) and one of these ducts perforates into the other, that man becomes infertile[1100]. In Pumpeditha, a man's spermatic duct *(gubtha)* closed, and the sperm came out from the site of urine (spermatorrhea). Rabbi Bibi bar Abaye declared this man to be fit to be married, whereas Rabbi Papa disagreed, saying that sperm can only fertilize if it "ripens" in its normal site[1101].

Actually, the term is "cooked", like *concoquere*. Concerning this matter, see Galen[1102] who says: *semen genitale, quod nec ipsum aliquamdiu extra propria vasa, si modo suas vires servabit, morari patitur.*

What is the reason underlying this false conception which was propagated by physicians throughout the Arabic era until the Middle Ages, namely that there exist two separate excretory channels and openings to the surface of the body for sperm and for urine? The Arabic physicians even described a third one for the secretions of the prostate. Vesal, who corrects this error in 1543[1103], is of the opinion that an Arabic physician saw homogeneously dark blood flowing from the corpora spongiosa and the urethra in a man whose penis was cut transversely, and incorrectly interpreted this observation. It seems more likely, however, that the Arabs were misled by a case of hypospadius. Vesal himself, indeed, describes as exceptional the case of a student in Pavia who "in fact had two meatuses at the tip of the glans, *unum semini, alterum urinae paratum*". Perhaps one was also misled by the frequent occurrence of periurethral passageways.

Brecher[1104] calls attention to Talmudic descriptions of the use of the penis for

1095. Jerushalmi Taanith 4; 69a
1096. Moed Katan 18a and *Yalkut* 2:1062
1097. in Buxtorf ed. Fisher. 1875. *s.v. parmaschthak.*
1098. Levy. *Neuhebräisches und Chaldäisches Wörterbuch.* Leipzig 1876-1889 Vol. 2:229a
1099. Shabbath 137a
1100. Bechoroth 44b
1101. Yebamoth 75b & 76a

1102. Galen. *Meth. Med.* 7:6. Ed. Kühn 10 p.474
1103. Vesal. *De Corporus Humanum Fabrica.* Book 5 Chapt. 14 fol 454 of the edition of Boerhave
1104. Brecher. *Das Transcendentale, Magie und magische Heilarten im Talmud.* Vienna 1850 p.146

purposes of heathen cults. These refer to Biblically prohibited magical practices. When *Onkelos* translates *yidoni*[1105] as *shael bizkuru,* one cannot fail to recognize the lingam oracle[1106]. Rabbi Simeon says[1107] that a *me'onen*[1108] brings seven types of lingam over his eyes[1109]. The *ba'al ob* also uses lingam for his necromantic practices[1110], and Bileam also conducted his sorcery with the use of lingam[1111].

This phallus cult is already mentioned in the Bible. King Asa, in his zealousness against idolatry which had found root in Israel, dethroned his own mother because she had made a *miphlezeth* for the idol Ashtaroth[1112] which, according to Rabbi Joseph in the Talmud[1113], was a phallus with which she committed immorality. Ezekiel, in his reprimand against the godless nation of Israel, states even clearer: *thou hast also taken jewels and gold and silver which I had given thee, and madest to thyself phallus images (tzalme zachar) and didst commit whoredom with them*[1114]. Idolatry and immorality (here meaning masturbation) always go hand in hand.

A recognized, or even only tolerated, cult of the phallus never existed among the Jews, as it did in Egypt, Assyria, Greece, India, the Nordic and perhaps even in transoceanic lands.

In ruminant animals, the penis skin ends in a very long prepuce, the sheath. In the *Mishnah,* this sheath is called *zoben*[1115] and in the *Tosefta* it is known as the "sac of the organ"[1116]. *Rashi* explains it as the *narthex* (or sling) in which the penis lies. *Aruch* considers it to be the organ from which the *smegma praeputii* flows; *zobhen* being derived from *zob,* to flow. Rabbi Jose ben Ha-Meshullam related that, in a place called En-Bul, a wolf once tore off the long prepuce of an animal but it grew back[1117].

It was left undecided as to whether or not a cattle breeder whose animal caused damage by knocking something with its penis must make restitution[1118].

Rabbi Judah is of the opinion that all species of water animals whose testicles are external give birth to live offspring, whereas those with internal testicles lay eggs. Mar Samuel disagrees saying: instead of testicles, substitute penis, *zachruth*[1119].

## V   The Testicles

In the Bible, the testicles are called *eshek*[1120], and in an animal *pachad*[1121], both terms *apax leg* (in Greek).

In the Talmud, the term used to denote both testicles and ovaries is *betzah,* plural *betzim,* meaning eggs. Only rarely is the expression *kubasin* used, and its meaning is uncertain as follows:

"If a landlord raises the rent of his tenant at the beginning of the winter, when everyone, of necessity, requires lodging, it is considered a brutality, just as if he is holding him by the *kubasin* in order to snatch away his overcoat"[1122]. The same word is found elsewhere in the Talmud[1123].

The scrotum is called *kis* meaning sac, and the spermatic cord is called *chuté ha-*

---

1105. Deut. 18:11
1106. Löw states that *zekuru* has no relationship to *zakar* meaning "male"
1107. Sanhedrin 65b
1108. Deut. 18:10
1109. *Rashi* states: seven types of sperm.
1110. Sanhedrin 65b
1111. *ibid.* 105a
1112. First Kings 15:13 and Second Chronicles 15:16
1113. Abodah Zara 44a
1114. Ezekiel 16:17

1115. Bechoroth 6:5
1116. *Tosefta* Bechoroth 4:6
1117. Bechoroth 39b
1118. Baba Kamma 19b
1119. Bechoroth 8a i.e. those whose penis is outside give birth but those with the penis inside lay eggs.
1120. Levit. 21:20
1121. Job 40:17
1122. Baba Metzia 101b
1123. Shebuoth 41a

*betzim* meaning "the threads of the eggs". In addition to the *kis,* each testicle has two separate vascular skins or *tunicae propriae,* just like the brain.

The Talmud states[1124]: "five skins are forbidden to be eaten: that of the spleen, the loins and the kidneys because of the prohibition of fat, and that of the testicles and the brain because of the prohibition of blood". Concerning testicles as nourishment, see Oribasius[1125].

The beginning of sperm formation in the testicles of lambs is characterized by the occurrence of red threads (small arteries) in the *tunica propria.* These threads are sometimes visible prior to the thirtieth day of life of the animal[1126].

# VI   The Sperm

In the Bible, the emission of sperm, whether *intra coitum* or not, is called *schichbath zera* meaning *depositio seminis.* Pollution is called *mikreh* or *kareh*[1127]. In the Talmud, it is called *keri,* which literally means "occurrence". *Ra'ah keri* means "to see an occurrence", which is equivalent to nocturnal pollution. It was considered praiseworthy never to have had pollution[1128].

According to Biblical command, if a man emits sperm, he should wash his entire body in water and he remains ritually unclean until evening. Every garment and every skin upon which sperm has come should be washed in water and is unclean until evening[1129]. In times of war, such a man should not return to the camp until he has bathed[1130]. This law was still adhered to during the time of the Jewish kings. When David was missing from the royal court, King Saul assumed that the reason for David's absence was that *something had befallen him so that he is not clean*[1131]. According to Josephus[1132], David "was not yet clean following intimacy with his wife". More details concerning the implementation of these baths will be provided later under "bathings and washings"[1133].

For the diagnosis of an "occurrence" of sperm emission for the purpose of being obligated to take the prescribed baths, the following is of note[1134]. If dribbling or opaque fluid comes out only at the beginning of urination, the man is clean, because the opaqueness is not due to an "occurrence" but from retained urine. All sperm remnants, according to the commentaries, had been previously emitted through micturition. It is also possible that the opaqueness is due to gonorrhea which the man may have. If the dribbling or opaque fluid comes out in the middle or at the end of urination, the man is unclean; but if from beginning to end, he is clean, because the man probably has catarrh of the bladder. White thread-like fluid makes a man unclean as do thick drops exuding from the urethra, because these probably represent sperm. If a *pollutus* bathes without first having urinated, he becomes unclean again as soon as he urinates, because sperm remnants are then emitted. According to Rabbi Jose the latter rule is only applicable to the ill and to the elderly; not, however, to healthy, strong people, because, in the latter, ejaculation occurs with great power so that nothing remains[1135].

According to Rabbi Yochanan, there can be no ejaculation without admixture of urine[1136].

During the time of the *Mishnah,* one of the miracles that occurred in the Temple is the circumstance that on the Day of Atonement the officiating High Priest never

1124. Chullin 45a. Compare *ibid* 93a
1125. Oribasius 2:34. Ed. Daremberg 1:100
1126. Chullin 93b
1127. Deut. 23:11
1128. Moed Katan 25a
1129. Levit. 15:16
1130. Deut. 23:11

1131. First Samuel 20:26
1132. Josephus *Antiquities.* Book 6 Chapt. 11:9
1133. Chapter 17, Part 4
1134. Mikvaoth 8:2-4
1135. *ibid*
1136. Jerushalmi Shabbath 1; 3d

suffered from pollution[1137], although he was separated from his wife for the previous seven days[1138]. On the eve of the Day of Atonement he was not given a large meal to eat because "eating brings on sleep" and one did not allow the High Priest to sleep on that night for fear of an "occurrence". For this reason, he avoided eating the following foods (tradition is a little vague here): lentils, lemon juice and lemons, aged and white wine, seasonings, fat meat, milk, cheese, barley bans, fishbrine and the five items which, according to experience, "induce uncleanness in people": onions, garden cress, portulace, eggs and hedge mustard. In spite of all these precautionary measures, an "occurrence" once happened to a High Priest on the Day of Atonement so that his substitute was unexpectedly called upon to officiate[1139]. Particularly dangerous *quoad pollutionem* is excessive eating following a prolonged fast[1140].

Pollution is one of the six things which are good prognostic signs in ill people. The other five are: sneezing, perspiration, normal bowel movements, sleeping and dreaming[1141].

Ejaculation only impregnates if "the entire body feels it" (orgasm). Mar Samuel said: "sperm which doesn't shoot forth like an arrow doesn't fertilize"[1142]. On the other hand, through energetic diversion, one can avoid ejaculation; one should bore his fingernails into the ground until it (the penis) dies (becomes soft)[1143].

Interesting is the following pertinent description of a medico-legal case and its adjudication in the Talmud: in the Egyptian village of Schechanya, a man wanted to divorce his wife. In order not to be accused of being the guilty party responsible for the divorce, he invited his friends to his house, made them drunk and placed them in bed next to his wife. He then placed egg-white between them and came to court with the alleged *corpus delicti*. In court, Baba ben Butha (from time of Herod)[1144] recalled the teaching of the old Schammai: egg-white retracts when near light (or fire) whereas sperm spreads in the cloth in light. Investigation confirmed this teaching and the man was flogged and sentenced to pay damages[1145].

## VII   The Female Sex Organs

The prophets often compare wicked peoples and lands, and also immoral Jerusalem, to a woman practicing harlotry who "reveals her nakedness" and who is threatened with the following punishment: "the Lord will throw the train of her dress over her face so that her nakedness is uncovered". The terms used: nakedness *(ervah)* and shame *(cherpah, kalon, nabluth, ma'ar* and *nechosheth)*[1146] do not refer specifically and only to the genitalia. An expression used very often in legal matters relating to cohabitation with a woman whom one is prohibited from marrying is "to uncover her nakedness *(ervah)*"[1147]. The word *bassar* meaning flesh is also used to denote both the genitalia of a woman[1148] and those of a man.

Other designations for the female genitalia relate to the function of these organs in pregnancy and birth. The Bible states that in the abdomen (i.e. womb), *beten*, of the matriarch Rebekah there are two nations[1149] or twins[1150]. God blesses the fruit of the *beten*[1151]. A person emerges naked from the *beten* of his mother[1152]. A child is the fruit of the womb, *peri beten*, of both the mother and the father[1153]. However, the

---

1137. Aboth 5:5
1138. Yoma 1:1
1139. Yoma 18a–b and Jerushalmi Yoma 1;
    39a
1140. Aboth de Rabbi Nathan 8:8
1141. Berachoth 57b
1142. Niddah 43a
1143. Shebuoth 18a; cf. Sotah 36b
1144. Baba Bathra 4a

1145. Gittin 57a
1146. Ezekiel 16:36 according to Niddah 41b
1147. Levit. Chapt. 18 & 20
1148. Levit. 15:19
1149. Genesis 25:23
1150. *ibid* 28:27
1151. Deut. 7:13
1152. Job 1:21
1153. Michah 6:7

meaning of the word *beten* is a general one, similar to the German word *leib* (meaning abdomen, belly, womb, body, trunk, waist, etc.). Thus, the epigrammatic poet states: *the righteous eateth to the satisfying of his soul, but the beten of the wicked shall want*[1154].

A similar situation exists with the use of the word *me'ayim* (bowels), which is chiefly used to denote *koilia* (abdomen), whereas *beten* is more often understood in the sense of "abdominal *wall*"[1155]. Children emerge both from the *me'ayim* of women[1156] and from the *me'ayim* of men[1157].

The word *rechem* is often used synonymously with *beten*[1158], but is distinguished from it in that *rechem* is *only* used to denote the womb. God opened the *rechem* of the barren Leah[1159]. In the house of Abimelech, He closed the *rechem* of everyone so that the women could not bear children[1160]. *Peter rechem,* "that which opens the womb", is the usual expression for the firstborn of man and animal[1161]. *Rechem mashkil* is a miscarrying womb[1162]. It is uncertain whether the designation *mashber*[1163], which in post-Biblical Hebrew refers to birthstool, also designates the womb.

According to the Biblical narrative, in his excitement, Phinehas pierced the Midianite woman and her lover in their *kobah*[1164]. According to the Talmud, Phinehas surprised her *inter coitum,* that is to say in the position of *Venus obversa* of Leonardo Da Vinci, and his spear pierced the genitalia of both of them[1165]. The word *kobah* is interpreted as *keba,* which elsewhere in the Bible[1166] refers to the abomasum of ruminants[1167].

One Talmudic interpretation of the phrase *and tzirim came upon the parturient woman*[1168] is that *tzirim* refer to two organs of the body which were even observed during post-mortem examinations[1169]. The Bible uses the same term in relation to man[1170], where *tzirim* are said to be made of flesh and can be easily overlooked. Nevertheless, the entire Talmudic discussion seems to indicate that *tzirim* do not refer to an anatomical entity. The usual interpretation of *tzirim* is labor pains, as a result of which the parturient woman twists and turns like a door on its hinges. The word *tzir,* plural *tzirim,* is also used elsewhere in the sense of door hinges[1171]. On the other hand, in the Bible, the word *poth* undoubtedly refers to both "door hinges"[1172] and "female genitalia"[1172a].

Moreover, I do not think that the interpretation of *tzirim* as "labor pains" is absolutely certain. In the Bible, the word *tzirim* is found next to the word *chabalim,* which is the term for "labor pains"[1173]. The *Targum* generally translates *tzirim* as *aka,* which is the general term for pain and anxiety.

The expression *I am come into my garden*[1174] is considered to be a euphemism for *copula carnalis* (the word *gan* meaning garden being equivalent to the vulva), and *a garden shut up*[1175] is said to refer to virginity[1176]. In the same sense, the Romans and Greeks used the terms *hortus* and *kepos* (garden), respectively[1177].

---

1154. Proverbs 13:25
1155. Job 40:16 and Song of Songs 7:3
1156. Genesis 25:23
1157. *ibid.* 15:4
1158. Compare for example Jeremiah 20:17 with Job 3:11
1159. Genesis 29:31
1160. *ibid* 20:18
1161. for example Numbers 18:15
1162. Hosea 9:14
1163. Second Kings 19:3 and Isaiah 13:3
1164. Numbers 25:8
1165. Sanhedrin 82b
1166. Deut. 18:3

1167. Chullin 134b
1168. First Samuel 4:19
1169. Bechoroth 45a
1170. Daniel 10:16
1171. Proverbs 26:14
1172. First Kings 7:50
1172a. Isaiah 3:17
1173. Isaiah 13:8
1174. Song of Songs 5:1
1175. *ibid* 4:12
1176. *Mechilta, Bo.* par. 5 p.5a. Friedmann on Song of Songs 4:12 Cf. Yoma 75a
1177. Rosenbaum. *Lustseuche.* p.69 Note 1

# VIII

Precise anatomical data are provided by the Talmud in discussions concerning individual cases of vaginal bleeding where the question is decided as to whether or not the bleeding originates in "the fountain" (i.e. the uterus). If it does, the woman is unclean, according to Biblical precept. In the explanation of these Talmudic statements, one must always keep in mind that the "examination of women", of which the Talmud speaks, is, with rare exception, always performed by the woman herself. Only rarely is it performed by another woman. Therefore, the Talmud is absolutely not speaking of a "pelvic examination" in the modern sense, as performed by gynecologists. The woman herself finds a spot of blood either on her body or on her undergarments, or she surmises the presence of blood on or in her genitalia and she dabs it with a cloth wrapped around her finger. This is the "examination" spoken of in the Talmud. Other than the external genitalia, only the vagina can be explored in this manner. The anatomical conditions of the internal genitalia of women in those days was, and certainly remained, unknown to them, as it is to today's women. These facts have to be taken into consideration because these laws were meant for domestic practice, not only for aristocratic women but also for the simplest woman. The expression "blood which is found in such and such a place", therefore, always *refers only to this method of "examination"*.

The *Mishnah* which introduces these rules states as follows[1178]: The Sages used figurative terms in describing the woman: *cheder* (inner chamber), *prosdor* (vestibule) and *aliyah* (upper chamber). Only the blood of the *cheder* is unclean; the blood of the *aliyah* is clean. If blood is found in the *prosdor,* however, its origin is uncertain and therefore it is unclean since ordinarily blood found here originates from "the fountain" (i.e. uterus).

It can be assumed with reasonable certainty that *cheder* refers to the uterus, that *prosdor* is the vulva, and that *aliyah* is the vagina. In practice, it is most often correct, with very rare exceptions, if one surmises that blood found in the *spatium interlabiale* originated from the uterus (thus rendering the woman unclean) and not from the urinary bladder. The incorrectness of the proper sequence in the listing of the individual organs — one would have expected *prosdor, aliyah, cheder* — has other parallels in the *Mishnah*[1179].

In the house of study of Rabbi Huna, which flourished in the third century in the town of Sura in Babylon, the above *Mishnah* was explained as follows: the *cheder* is within, the *prosdor* is without, and the *aliyah* is built above both of them. Between the *aliyah* and the *prosdor* there is a communicating *lul* (or duct; alternatively "an open *lul*"). Blood found from the *lul* inwards is certainly unclean; from the *lul* outwards, there is doubt (whether or not it originated from the uterus), and it is therefore deemed unclean[1180].

The *lul,* which is open between the vagina and the vulva, is certainly the vaginal (or cervical) orifice. In fact, instead of *lul,* the Palestinian Talmud simply says "opening of the *aliyah*"[1181]. Here, too, it is taught in the name of Samuel that the *aliyah,* the vagina, lies near the *cheder,* the uterus, and reaches to half of the *prosdor,* the middle of the vulva[1182].

Abaye considers the distinction between blood found outside or inside the vaginal (or cervical) orifice to be worthless, since movements by the woman can cause the blood to move to various sites[1183].

---

1178. Niddah 2:5
1179. Chullin 3:1. The stomachs of ruminants.
1180. Niddah 71b

1181. Jerushalmi Niddah 50a
1182. *ibid.*
1183. Niddah 17b

# IX

The *Mishnah* thus compares the female genitalia to the parts of a house and derives their designations therefrom. The *cheder* is the concealed inner chamber of the house (thus a very appropriate designation for uterus); the epigrammatic poet speaks in a similar manner of the *chadré beten*, the innermost concealed chambers or compartments of the human body which the Lord investigates[1184].

In front of, or inside, large buildings, there is a separate forecourt or vestibule which serves as a waiting room. The Greeks call it *prothyron* and the *prosdor* of the Talmud may be derived from this word, unless one prefers the other traditional textual reading *prosdod*. In this word, Löw recognizes the *prosthas* (*prosthad-os*) of the Greeks[1185]. According to the often-cited description of a Greek residential house by Vitruv[1186], a portico or *peristyl* has columns on three sides and two widely separated corner pillars on the south side. The space between these pillars, perhaps also the entire portico, was called *prosthas*. It can be considered to be the vestibule of the diagonally-built chambers, particularly the dining room, the *triclinium*. Here, in the *prostas,* the guests assembled before the meal began. Thus, the famous maxim of Rabbi Jacob: "this world is like a *prosdor* (vestibule) to the world to come (i.e. eternal bliss); prepare thyself in the *prosdor* that thou mayest enter into the *triclinium* (or banquet-hall)"[1187].

The Hebrew equivalent of *prosdor* is *chatzer* which, like *prostas*, is an inner court or waiting room of a house. This word too is used to portray the external genitalia, as opposed to *triclinium* which is used for the inner parts[1188].

On the flat roof of Oriental houses there is an upper chamber which serves various purposes. Only in extreme need is it used as a residence[1189]. According to Josephus, it was used as a sick room[1190]. It is often mentioned in the Bible as *aliyah*. A passageway, *lul*, led from the *chatzer*, the inner or forecourt, up to the *aliyah*[1191], just as the vaginal orifice connects the vulva to the vagina itself. The Talmud also speaks of this *lul* which goes "from the house to the *aliyah*"[1192]. It is deduced that *lul* is a winding staircase from the consonance with *luleoth*, the designation for loops of the curtains of the Tabernacle[1193]. But this is mere guesswork. Furthermore, one's vivid imagination can fantasize a similarity between a winding staircase and the diagonal folds of the *introitus vaginae* and the vagina itself. In the Talmud, however, the word *lul* cannot mean "step" because this term is used *in addition to* the word *kebesh*. The latter undoubtedly means "ramp". In the Talmudic citation[1194], *lul* is a deep ditch in the stone floor, between the altar and the altar step, into which one threw disqualified bird offerings.

# X

I cannot reconcile my attempt at explaining the individual terms with the explanation of the above *Mishnah* given in the Talmud by the school of Rabbi Huna. The same doubt exists for blood found in the *lul*, the vaginal orifice, as for blood found in the *prosdor* or vagina itself, i.e. does it originate from "the fountain" (uterus)? This incomprehensibility of terms is shared by *all* assertions of antiquity concerning the anatomy of female genitalia. Even in recent times, a historian of

---

1184. Proverbs 18:8 and 26:22
1185. In Krauss' *Lehnwörter s. v. prosthas.*
1186. Vitruv. 6:7
1187. Aboth 4:16
1188. *Tosefta* Niddah 8:4
1189. Aboth de Rabbi Nathan 25:5: "There are three whose life is not worth living and they are: he who must look to the table of another for sustenance, he who lives in an

*aliyah* (attic or upper chamber) and whoever is dominated by his wife." The statement is somewhat different in Betzah 32b.
1190. Josephus. *Antiquities* Book 18, Chapt. 8:2
1191. First Kings 6:8
1192. Menachoth 34a
1193. Exodus 26:4
1194. Pesachim 34a

gynecology decries the fact that the descriptions of the female sex organs by Soran, an author who specialized in writings about illnesses of women, are no longer understandable. The same applies to the writings of Galen[1195]. The same is also true of Moschion and his book on obstetrics, not only for the internal organs, but also for the external genitalia, which Rufus, a professional anatomist, also dismisses with few words[1196].

The above seems even more surprising in view of the fact that in Rome and Greece, one paid no attention to the modesty of slaves; servants functioned while completely naked in the baths of private houses, irrespective of whether men or women were bathing. Much less blame should therefore be attached to the vaguenesses of the anatomical descriptions in the schoolhouses of the Rabbis. Even Vesal, the great student of anatomy, states that the neck of the bladder empties into the vagina: *vesicae cervicis pars, uteri cervici inserta, ac urinam in illam projiciens*[1197].

# XI

There is no dearth of attempts to explain the above *Mishnah*. The discussions of Maimonides, the renowned Arabic-Jewish physician of the twelfth century, shall be mentioned first. There are two such discussions: one is very detailed and is found in his commentary on the *Mishnah*, which is now available even in the Arabic original[1198]; the other is a briefer version in his "Fourteen Books" of Jewish law. One should begin by stating that neither of them transmits correct anatomical information. I cannot determine whether or not they correspond to the viewpoints of Arabic physicians of that era since the assertions of Maimonides' contemporary Avicenna are unclear[1199], and those of Rhazes and Ali, which Koning has only recently publicized[1200], are too aphoristic. One should be reminded that the ancient physicians, who only repeated the opinions of the Arabs, call the vagina and uterus *ystera*, and thus *to stoma tes ysteras* means the vaginal (or uterine) opening. Our "external cervical os" is their inner os, *to endron stoma*, or *to stoma ton ystereon*, because they always assumed that the uterus is a double organ. They call the vagina *collum* (cervix) *uteri* in Latin, *auchen* or *trachelos* in Greek[1201] and *unk al-rachim* in Arabic. At least according to Avicenna, it is certain that the *vasa spermatica*, the *expulsorium* of the translator (*al-mukasiph*), flows into the *collum uteri* i.e. the vagina.

Maimonides writes as follows[1202]: "*cheder* refers to each of the two cavities of the uterus (*rechem*), because the uterus has two of them. *Prosdor* is the neck (*unk*) of the *rechem* (*collum uteri* which is equivalent to vagina), and *aliyah* are the two additions which resemble horns and which lie on the nape (*rakab*) of the uterus. The two eggs (ovaries) lie before them. This is the portrayal as found in the anatomy books".

"There are blood vessels connected to the fundus (*karka*) of the uterus through which menstrual blood flows; it streams in the uterus and exits through the neck of the uterus which is called *prosdor* (vagina). Other blood vessels are connected to the two uterine horns and the two eggs (ovaries) — which together are called *aliyah* — and are nourished like the other vessels of the body, but do

1195. Kossmann. *Allgemeine Gynäkologie.* Berlin 1903 p.39 & 46
1196. Ed. Daremberg p.147
1197. See the picture No. 27 on fol. 409 of the edition of Boerhave.
1198. Maimonides' Mishnah Commentary. ed. Darenbourg, Berlin 1887
1199. Avicenna. *Fen.* 21 Book 3 tract 1 Chapt. 1

1200. Koning. *Trois Traités d'Anatomie Arabes.* Leiden 1903 p.391 & 87
1201. Cf. Fr. B. Osiander. *Annalen der Entbindungs-Lehranstalt.* Vol. 2:1 Gottingen 1801 p.384
1202. Maimonides' Commentary on the Mishnah, Niddah 2:5

not remove anything superfluous. If one of *these* vessels breaks, blood flows out from it onto the neck of the *rechem* (vagina). This is ritually *clean* blood, however, because it is just like blood from the nose or from hemorrhoids"[1203].

"From this it seems evident that blood of the *cheder* is unclean whereas that of the *aliyah* is clean. If blood is thus found in the neck of the *rechem* which is the *prosdor*, the following ruling applies: if it is found in a site between the two uterine horns and the cavity of the *rechem*, it is unclean, and we do not consider that it might have reached there from the *aliyah*, because most blood at such a site is menstrual blood".

"However, if the blood is found in the *prosdor*, the neck of the *rechem*, between the site of the two uterine horns and the opening of the *rechem* which is close to the outside of the body (i.e. the vaginal introitus), the following ruling applies: if it is found "above", that is to say, toward the head of the woman when she is standing, referring to the place called by the Talmud "roof of the *prosdor*", the blood is clean because it originates from a blood vessel which broke *there* and we assume it came from the *aliyah*"[1204].

"If, however, the blood is found "below", that is to say toward the feet of the standing woman, referring to the "floor of the *prosdor*", the blood is unclean because of the uncertainty as to whether it originated from the *cheder* or from the *aliyah*".

"Both uterine horns which I have mentioned. . . . do not refer to the entire horns, because they also have a wide part (*aratz*). I refer only to their tips, because the heads of each horn resemble the tip of the human breast (nipple). From the connection between these two tips and the eggs, there develops the picture of a hole in the upper portion of the *prosdor* and this is called the *lul* of the *aliyah*".

"Whoever is familiar with practical anatomy will understand all that we have discussed and whoever pictures these matters in his mind knows them thoroughly because we have explained them in great detail"[1204a].

I (Preuss) believe I have fulfilled the above two conditions of Maimonides; nevertheless I have not achieved the result which he promised.

The other discussion (of the female genitalia) by Maimonides[1205] is as follows:

"The *rechem* (womb) in which the fetus is formed is called *makor* (the fountain). From it issues the blood of menstruation and of *zaba* (flux); it is also called *cheder* (the chamber) since it is situated in the innermost region".

"The neck of the *rechem* is the long part whose tip contracts during pregnancy so that the fetus does not fall out, and which opens wide at the time of birth. It is called *prosdor*, that is to say the antechamber to the womb".

"During coitus, the penis enters the *prosdor* but does not reach its tip but remains somewhat distant from it, according to the size of the penis"[1206].

"Above the *cheder* and the *prosdor*, and between them, is the place where the two eggs (ovaries) of the woman are situated, as well as the passages (tubes) in which the sperm of the woman ripens. This place is called the *aliyah* (upper chamber). From the *aliyah* to the roof of the *prosdor* there is a kind of orifice, and the Sages call this orifice the *lul*. During coitus, the penis enters beyond the *lul*"[1207].

---

1203. *ibid.*
1204. *ibid.*
1204a. *ibid.*

1205. Maimonides. *Hilchoth Issurei Biyah* 5:3
1206. *ibid* 5:4
1207. *ibid.*

## XII

*Modern* physicians also struggle considerably to explain our *Mishnah*. Probably misled by the explanations of Maimonides, Israels[1208] interprets *aliyah* to represent *spermatica muliebria*, that is to say, the Fallopian tube. Rosenbaum[1209] considers *aliyah* to be the *ligamentum lata* together with the adnexa. In my opinion, if one cannot explain the *Mishnah*, there is no reason why one should hold it responsible for the undoubtedly erroneous interpretations of the Arabic physician. The one thing that is certain is that the *Mishnah* is describing bleedings which *flow externally* (i.e. vaginal bleeding). Should one assume that the *Mishnah* is referring to hematosalpinx which spontaneously emptied itself? One would have avoided considering the *prosdor* to be the *collum uteri* and the latter to be the *cul-de-sac*, if one had remembered the ancient meaning of the *collum uteri*.

The author of the *Aruch* dictionary defines *aliyah* as "the site of urine excretion". Probably as a result of misinterpreting this statement, Rabbinowicz[1210] and Kazenelson[1211] interpret *lul* as urethra and *aliyah* as urinary bladder. *Aruch* certainly didn't mean this, because, in that case, he would have used the Hebrew terms *shalpuchith, shalchupith*, and the like.

Bleeding from the bladder undoubtedly occurs and, probably, more often in the Orient than elsewhere, but how should one interpret "bleeding from the *lul* (i.e. urethra) inwardly" which the woman who performs a *self-examination* finds?! The explanation is no more probable if one considers "inwardly" to mean "posteriorly", because it seems extremely impractical to think that one attributes the totally concealed urethral opening — the examination was performed by the sense of touch without direct vision — to be the point from which the blood came!

I wish to mention here that Rabbi Gersom surprisingly considers "the fountain" of the *Mishnah* to be a separate organ which lies near the *cheder*[1212].

Difficult for any type of interpretation of our *Mishnah* is the often-stated assertion of the Talmud that mammals have no *prosdor*. It is taught that an animal is to be considered "born" as soon as the head is born. On the other hand, a child only develops rights of inheritance when it is born alive *in toto*. The difference is said to be the fact that an animal has no *prosdor*[1213]. The *Tosafoth* (in the Talmud) explain that one can assume that the *prosdor* of a woman also includes the interfemoral space which can hinder the further egress of the child after the head is already born; such is not the case with animals. I question whether this explanation is based upon any factual experience.

I am naturally cognizant of the fact that, in contrast to humans, animals are lacking a manifest portion of the vagina.

## XIII

Other than the aforementioned *Mishnah* about female genitalia, there are very sparse data in the Talmud. The genitalia are usually referred to euphemistically as "that place". The Romans also used the terms *loci* or *loca* for the female genitalia, and Janss. Ab Almeloveen, in his "Notes on Caelius Aurelianus", provides considerable

1208. Israels. *Collect. Gynecol. ex Talmud Babylon.* Groningen 1845 p.37
1209. Rosenbaum. *L'Anatomie et la Physiologie des Organes Génitaux de la Femme.* Frankfurt 1901 p.58 ff
1210. Rabbinowicz. *La Médecine du Thal-mud.* Paris 18 1880 p.79
1211. Kazenelson. *Die normale und pathologische Anatomie des Talmud.* p.278
1212. Commentary of Rabbi Gersom on Baba Bathra 24a
1213. Bechoroth 46b and Shabbath 86b

evidence therefor[1214]. Other individual terms in the Talmud are *beth ha-thorpa*[1215] or *thorpath*[1216] and *beth bosheth*[1217] or *beth ha-bosheth*[1218] meaning "the site of shame". The term *ekeb*, which is the usual term for heel, is also euphemistically used for vulva, "which is situated opposite the heel"[1219].

In opposition to the infrequently used word *cheder*, the *locus internus*, for the uterus, is the common use of the term *beth ha chitzon, locus externus*, for the vagina[1220]. This *locus externus*, the site of cohabitation, reaches up to *ben ha-shinayim*, literally "between the teeth", meaning between the labia, i.e. up to the vulva. Nevertheless, some Sages interpret the *locus externus* to include the vulva itself[1221].

*Beth ha-rechem* are the genitalia, whose "walls", according to some Sages, can withhold menstrual blood[1222]. The term *sephayoth* meaning "lips" is also used to describe the labia[1223]. The striking plural construct (instead of the expected dual) term to distinguish the *labia majora* from the *minora* is difficult to understand because the same term (*sephayoth*) is also used for the lips of the mouth[1224]. A rare term for uterus, perhaps only for the pregnant uterus, is *keber*[1225], which elsewhere means "grave". Since the root of the word means "to heap up", one must assume that the comparison of grave and uterus refers to the enlarged uterus which, during pregnancy, can be felt and also sometimes seen, even by lay people. Or is it that the fetus was believed to be enclosed in the uterus like a corpse in the grave?

In the *Midrashim*, we first find the Greek word *metra*, even declined, used for uterus. Legend relates that the women in the Biblical stories who were barren for a long time and yet who gave birth in their old age originally had no uterus (*mitrin* in Latin, *metran* in Greek) and God had to mold (*galaph* in Hebrew and *glypho* in Greek) such an organ for them. This happened to Sarah[1226], Rebekah[1227], and Ruth[1228]. According to another legend, Esau, because of malice, cut his mother's womb (*mitrin*) out at his birth (i.e. castrated her) so that she could not bear any more children after him[1229]. This brings to mind the fact that the Rabbis were familiar with the excision of the uterus in female breeding cattle, a common practice in Alexandria[1230].

A premature birth is only considered to be a child (regarding ritual uncleanness of the mother) if the head of the fetus is round like a *pika*, a coil of thread. Some Sages are of the opinion that it already suffices if the *tephiphiyoth* (variant: *kephiphiyoth*) are visible during birth. This word is explained as follows: like a mule which kneels to urinate and it has the appearance of a *pika* (coil) coming forth out of a *pika* (coil)[1231]. What this means is the following: if a fetus is no longer so small that it easily slides out *in toto* during birth, then it appears, before the head has totally emerged, like a coil (i.e. the fetal head has visible ring-like formations) in another coil (i.e. the stretched vaginal walls). I cannot verify from other sources the comparative situation[1232] in the mule which the Rabbis often use in analogies.

During the reign of King Rehoboam, Susak of Egypt is said to have had statues exhibiting female genitalia (*aidora gynaikon*) erected in Palestine, as related by

1214. Almeloveen. *Noten zu Coelius Au-relianus* Ed. Amman. Amsterdam. 1722 p.625
1215. Niddah 8:1
1216. *ibid* 20a
1217. Jerushalmi Yebamoth 6; 7b
1218. Chullin 9:2
1219. Niddah 20a
1220. Niddah 5:1
1221. Jerushalmi Yebamoth 6; 7b
1222. Niddah 3a

1223. Jerushalmi Yebamoth 6; 7b
1224. Jerushalmi Kethuboth 5; 30a
1225. for example Niddah 21a and Shabbath 129a
1226. Genesis Rabbah 47:2
1227. *ibid*. 63:5
1228. Ruth Rabbah 8:14 on 4:13
1229. *Tanchuma. Ki Theze*. Buber p.18a
1230. Bechoroth 28a
1231. Bechoroth 22a. cf. Oholoth 7:4
1232. i.e. visible wrinkles on the vagina.

Josephus[1233], following Herodotus. These statues served as a sign of cowardice[1234] and were meant to ridicule the Jews.

According to some Sages, the ornament called *kumaz* in the Bible[1235] was an image of female genitalia (*beth ha-rechem*); according to others it was a picture of the female breast[1236].

The "*erya* of the female animal" probably refers to the labia[1237].

## XIV    The Hymen

The hymen is the subject of extensive and passionate discussion among physicians. Hippocrates and Celsus consider it to be an abnormal growth. Soran[1238], and later Moschion, both gynecologists by profession, dispute its existence altogether. For the Middle Ages and the following several centuries, Albrecht Van Haller provides us with a comprehensive list of supporters and opponents of the physiological existence of the hymen. Haller himself, however, states: *ego in omnibus virginibus reperi neque puto a pura virgine abesse*[1239]. In spite of Haller, the dispute remained far from settled. Correct concepts did not develop until the end of the eighteenth century[1240].

Naturally, explanations were sought for those who dispute the existence of the hymen. Haller is of the opinion that the ancient anatomists only dissected animals in whom the hymen is in fact lacking, or female criminals: *sceleratae vero feminae raro sunt virgines*. The latter assertion is not very intelligible if one reflects on how rapidly a female slave could become *scelerata*. More important is the statement of Vesal in which he complains about the destruction of the hymen often performed by mid-wives[1241]. Least of all can the negation of the hymen represent "a picture of the depravity of ancient Rome", as Lachs states[1242]. Equally unacceptable is the chauvinistic assertion of Johann David Michaelis[1243] that "in France, debauchery reached such a level that few virgins remained".

If one examines the reports of the ancients, such as the above-mentioned one by Soran, in the original, one quickly notes that the dispute often only involves the interpretation of the word for hymen, but the fact of its existence is unanimously accepted. He very clearly only controverts the teaching that a delicate skin such as a diaphragm of the vagina exists (*lepton ymena diaphrassonta ton kolpon*). Regner De Graaf even draws a picture of a hymen, but denies its existence, and only speaks of *rigositates membranosae circumcirca vaginae orificium*[1244].

The opinion of the Bible and the Talmud in this controversy cannot be decided. The bleeding of defloration, *dam bethulim,* was well recognized, but we do not know whether it was thought to be due to tearing of a separate membrane, the hymen, or whether it was due to bleeding from blood vessels in the vagina. The Talmud speaks of a wound, *makka,* which must heal[1245]; it also speaks of the "falling off" or "falling out" of the *bethulim* with the same expressions used to denote the falling off of a leaf from a tree or the falling out of hair through a depilatory[1246]. However, a final

---

1233. Josephus. *Antiquities.* Book 8 Chapt. 10:3

1234. Herodotus 2:102 & 106

1235. Exodus 35:22 and Numbers 31:50

1236. Shabbath 64a and Jerushalmi Shabbath 6; 8b

1237. Bechoroth 6:5

1238. Soranus, ed. Ermerins p.17; Oribasius, Book 24:32 Vol. 3:380

1239. Haller. *Elem. Physiol.* Vol. 7 p.2, Book 28 No. 26 p.1-95

1240. Placzek. in Neuburger-Pagel's *Handbuch* 3:747

1241. Vesal Book 5 Chapt. 15 fol. 457. Ed. Boerhave.

1242. Lachs. Gynäkologie Des Soran. Volkmann's *Sammlung Klinische Vortrage.* No. 335 p.8

1243. Michaelis. *Moses' Recht* 2:148

1244. De Graaf. *De Mulierum Organis.* Lugdunam- Batavia 1668 p.189

1245. Niddah 10:1

1246. Shabbath 63b and Jerushalmi Kethuboth 1; 25a

decision concerning the Talmudic opinions about the presence or absence of a hymen cannot be ascertained from here or elsewhere in the Talmud[1247].

## XV   Menstruation

Menstruation is one of the important physiological functions of the female genitalia and, as in all law books of antiquity, is covered in the Bible with special laws pertaining thereto.

Menses are called *derech ha-nashim* meaning the custom or manner of women[1248]. As a result, the climacteric is described as follows: *she ceased to be after the manner (orach) of (young) women*[1249]. Because of the law of menstruation which I will soon describe, one also speaks of "the time of separation" or "the time of being removed", *eth niddathah,* which *Targum* renders *richuk* meaning distant[1250]. During this time, the woman herself is called *dava,* the sick one[1251], just as we today say she is "unwell". Sporadically, a regularly menstruating woman is also called *zaba*[1252], one with an issue, or *nidda*[1253]. In the Talmud, however, the latter term is the one generally used.

The Biblical law concerning a menstruating woman is as follows:

*And if a woman have an issue, and her issue in her flesh* (i.e. genitalia) *be blood, she shall be in her impurity seven days; and whosoever toucheth her shall be unclean until the evening* (i.e. the end of the day)[1254]. Everything that she sleeps on or sits on is unclean[1255]. Whoever touches her bed or anything that she sits upon *shall wash his clothes and bathe himself in water and be unclean until the evening*[1256]. *And if any man lie with her, and her impurity* (literally: separation) *be upon him, he shall be unclean seven days, and every bed upon which he lieth shall be unclean*[1257], in addition to the legal penalties resulting therefrom, which will be discussed below.

The duration of menstrual impurity is thus always seven days, even if the bleeding is of much shorter duration. According to the wording of Scripture, the impurity ceases forthwith at the end of the seven days. However, tradition requires a complete ritual bath to conclude menstrual impurity as it does for *any* situation of impurity, as is explicitly prescribed in the Bible after a pollution[1258]. One can also forthwith assume, if one wishes to make an analogy to modern times, that if the person who was secondarily infected[1259] had to take a ritual bath, then certainly the primary carrier of the infection should require no less.

It must be constantly emphasized that the "impurity", *tumah,* imposed by the Bible only has relevance to the usage of things which were designated for Temple use, primarily priestly dues, which may not be touched by any ritually unclean person. No other impurity, irrespective of the source, has any other legal consequences. Thus, shortly after the destruction of the Temple, the meaning of all these laws ceased to have practical significance for daily life. Only the extremely pious, who are hopeful for the imminent rebuilding of the Temple, continue to observe these laws without alteration.

Even Roman women did not set foot in the Temple during the time of their menstruation. This explains an astonishing interpretation of a Biblical phrase by Josephus. Laban searched the tents of Jacob and the latter's wives for the graven images which had been stolen from him (Laban)[1260]. When he came to the tent of Rachel, she excused herself in that she could not rise for her father for "the

1247. Jerushalmi Berachoth 2:6 & Kethuboth 9b
1248. Genesis 31:35
1249. *ibid* 18:11
1250. for example Levit. 15:25
1251. Levit. 20:18
1252. *ibid* 15:19
1253. Ezekiel 18:6
1254. Levit. 15:19
1255. *ibid* 15:20
1256. *ibid* 15:21-23
1257. *ibid* 15:24
1258. Levit. 15:16
1259. Levit. 15:20
1260. Genesis 31:33

manner of women" was upon her[1261]. And Laban searched no more in that tent because, according to Josephus, he believed that his daughter would not be near the graven images in her condition[1262].

On the other hand, the prohibition of cohabitation with a menstruating woman is independent of time and place: *and if a man shall lie with a woman having her sickness, and shall uncover her nakedness — he hath made naked her fountain, and she hath uncovered the fountain of her blood — both of them shall be cut off from among their people*[1263]. In abbreviated form, elsewhere in Scripture we find the following: *and thou shalt not approach unto a woman to uncover her nakedness, as long as she is impure by her uncleanness*[1264].

The "elimination" of both concubants (since both consented) is not carried out by an *earthly* court; the latter only imposes flogging[1265]. As is usual in law books, the reason for the above prohibition is not mentioned. The general belief in antiquity, which is also shared by the Talmud[1266], that such cohabitation results in leprous or otherwise malformed infants, could hardly have been the basis for the ancient Jewish position on this matter.

According to the Jewish view, *copula menstruationis tempore* is a *peccatum mortale* — to use a Christian expression — for which there is no exception. On the other hand, most Catholic moralists only consider it to be a *peccatum veniable ob indecentiam* and hence permitted *si accedit aliqua causa cohonestans*; for example, if one thereby hopes to have children or to avoid wrongdoing[1267].

Roman persecutors well knew how severe a blow they were dealing Jewish married life when they demanded "that Jews should cohabit with menstruating women"[1268], i.e. they prohibited the use of ritual baths.

The Pentateuch considers such cohabitation as an immoral heathen practice[1269], whose extermination is an obligation upon Jews by Biblical law. Therefore, the observance of this law for every Israelite (to remain separate from a menstruous woman) is a holy obligation[1270]. However, when immorality prevailed in Jerusalem, like many other laws, it too was transgressed[1271]. It presupposes a particularly strong attraction to cohabit with a menstruating woman, an unusual *gourmandise*, so that the prohibition can hardly be an expression of the general esthetic repugnance to this practice.

A "separation", i.e. exclusion of women from the outside world, as dictated in the laws of Zoroaster and as still practiced by many primitive peoples even today, is first mentioned in the *Mishnah*. The latter speaks of "a house of unclean women"[1272]. The same *Mishnah* states that, in these "places of uncleanness", Samaritan women used to bury their abortions with the intention of later throwing them out in the field where they would be dragged off by wild animals[1273]. Married women would wear old (i.e. worn) clothes during the time of their menses[1274].

The Bible prescribes no other laws concerning menstruation. The Bible and, as might be anticipated, the Talmud too, make no mention of the superstitious conceptions which antiquity, and even more recent times, attach to menstruation. At best, one might mention the (possible heathen) practice of "putting menstrual blood away for the cat"; this custom nevertheless was certainly not widely accepted because it

1261. *ibid* 31:35
1262. Josephus. *Antiquities*. Book 1 Chapter 19:10
1263. Levit. 20:18
1264. *ibid* 18:19
1265. Makkoth 3:1
1266. Levit. Rabbah 15:5
1267. Capellmann. *Pastoralmedizin* p.177
1268. Meilah 17a
1269. Levit. 18:3
1270. Ezekiel 18:6
1271. *ibid* 22:10
1272. Niddah 7:4. cf. *Tosefta* Negaim 6:3
1273. *ibid*
1274. Kethuboth 65b

was assumed that whoever set aside menstrual blood for that purpose became ill[1275]. Examples of such superstitions are found in flagrant forms in Plinius[1276]; compilations for later times up until our own era are those of Strack[1277] and Ploss[1278].

## XVI

The Talmud describes the practical implications of the above Biblical laws. The menstruating woman is called *nidda*, throughout. In some areas, the dialect *galmuda* is used[1279], and in Persian *daschtona*[1280]. Menses is called *madve* meaning "to be unwell", but is most often simply referred to as *dam* meaning blood. Menstruation is called *roah dam* meaning "she sees blood". *Veseth* often only denotes the symptoms which accompany menstruation but not the bleeding itself[1281].

Normal menstruation seems to have begun during the twelfth year of life, which is not too early for the Orient. Nevertheless, regular bleeding was already reported in much younger children. But the term "menstruation" or *veseth* was only used when the bleeding occurred repeatedly and at regular intervals; otherwise, it was called an "occurrence" or *mikreh*. Such "occurrences", that is to say atypical bleeding, were observed even in very young infants, and such observations have also been made in modern times.

On the other hand, it is also possible that in an otherwise normal menstruating girl, the menses cease for three months without her being pregnant[1282]. Today, such occurrences are quite frequent in girls with chlorosis and with illnesses of exhaustion.

In most women, menstruation occurs at completely regular intervals: "the guest comes at the proper time"[1283]. In many women, it is even regular to within a few hours[1284]. The intervals between menstrual periods vary in different individuals, but in most women the interval from the beginning of one period to the beginning of the next period (the middle *onah*) is thirty days[1285]. The shortest interval between the end of one menstrual period and the beginning of the next is said to be eleven days[1286]. Any interval shorter than this is not called menses but a blood flow, *ziba*, that is to say an illness. The Bible says that the maximum duration of bleeding which can still be considered to be a normal menstrual period is seven days; longer than that is thought to be due to the *ziba* illness of which we will speak more later.

According to Rabbi Meir, one should not marry a woman who has never menstruated[1287]. If one, however, did marry such a woman, one must divorce her and she loses all her rights[1288]. She is not allowed to marry another man because she is incapable of procreation. Josephus reports that the Essenes, for this reason, only married their fiancées after they had menstruated three times[1289]. Aristotle also considers amenorrheic women to be sterile but admits to individual exceptions[1290]. Some Sages of the Talmud are of the opinion that through marriage, that is to say regular sexual activity, this anomaly can often be overcome[1291], an opinion which is obviously correct in some cases. The Talmud does not here consider the situations in

---

1275. Shabbath 75b. The statement of Levy (*Neuhebräisches und Chaldäisches Wörterbuch.* Leipzig 1876-1889. Vol. 1:537b), *s.v. zakrutha* from Jerushalmi Shabbath 14; 14d, concerning menstrual blood as a medication is false. See the commentaries there. — The citation of Nachmanides in his commentary on Genesis 31:35 is not found in our editions of the Talmud.
1276. Plinius 7:13
1277. Strack. *Das Blut im Glauben und Aberglauben der Menschheit.* p.28
1278. Ploss. *Das Weib.* 1:267

1279. Sotah 42a
1280. Abodah Zara 24b
1281. for example Niddah 9:8
1282. Niddah 9b
1283. *ibid* 64a
1284. *ibid* 63b
1285. *ibid* 15a
1286. *ibid* 72b
1287. *ibid* 12b
1288. e.g. usufruct, maintenance, *kethubah* etc.
1289. Josephus. *The Jewish War* 2:8
1290. Aristotle. *Hist. Anim.* 7:2
1291. Niddah 12b

which the absence of menses is due to infantile female genitalia since it explicitly speaks of these elsewhere. Such a woman is called *aylonith* meaning barren.

In most women, menstruation is heralded by a series of mostly objective symptoms: the woman yawns or sneezes (or "has ructus") or has pain in the middle of the abdomen or at the lower part of her abdomen or has a (non-bloody) discharge or is suddenly seized by a type of shivering and the like[1292]. The *Gemara* adds the following symptoms to those of the *Mishnah*: heaviness in the head, heaviness in the limbs, coughing or trembling[1293]. Aristotle only recognizes *"pnigmoi,* seizures, and *psopsos, sounds* in the womb" as subjective signs of menstruation[1294]. It is not clear to what the latter term *(psopsos)* refers; there are no "sounds in the uterus". Perhaps he means flatulence.

# XVII

Every woman who bleeds from "the fountain", either spontaneously or as a result of an external stimulus, is ritually unclean. The woman senses that something is becoming loose and flowing out. This sensation, however, differs from that of micturition.

The "external stimulus" can be one of many things: jumping, carrying a heavy load, being mishandled by her husband, various illnesses[1295], psychological excitement such as a sudden fright[1296], sexual excitation such as the observance of animals engaged in coitus, lust for cohabitation called *chimmud*[1297], or the anticipation of the latter[1298]. Hippocrates has already mentioned that girls nearing their marriage bleed more heavily[1299]. The consumption of garlic or onions or the chewing of pepper can bring forth bleeding in some women[1300]. Albrecht Van Haller also lists *plantae acres* among the things which accelerate menses[1301]. On the other hand, fear of long duration, such as during imprisonment or while in hiding from robbers, can withhold menses: "fear constricts (like vinegar) whereas sudden fright loosens"[1302].

The bleeding must originate "from the fountain", that is to say from the normal uterus. Bleedings due to injuries do not render the woman unclean[1303]. It is debated in the Talmud whether or not injuries even within the uterus are also included in this ruling.

According to the above-mentioned Biblical law, the results of this ritual uncleanness are that a woman was not allowed to touch objects which were to be employed in the Temple, and marital intercourse with her husband was prohibited for seven days. Nevertheless, in order to avoid all doubts which might arise from the laws of menstruation and "bloodflow", Jewish women already in the time of Rabbi Zera (230-300 C.E.) considered themselves to be *zaba* following any bleeding, whether typical or not. They would, therefore, wait for seven "clean", i.e. bloodless days, before they took their ritual bath. This practice has become Talmudic prescriptive law since the fourth century[1304]. A woman who demands cohabitation during her menses must be divorced by her husband and she loses her right to sustenance[1305].

Since numerous difficulties for sexual relations occur as a result of this law, it is understandable that criteria were sought to differentiate "blood from the fountain" from that originating elsewhere.

---

1292. Niddah 9:8
1293. *ibid* 63b
1294. Aristotle. *Histor. Animal.* 7:2
1295. *Tosefta* Niddah 9:1
1296. Niddah 71a and Megillah 15a
1297. Niddah 20b
1298. *ibid* 66a
1299. Hippocrates. *Quae ad Virgin. Spect.* ed.

Foes fol. 562
1300. Niddah 63b
1301. Haller. *Elem. Physiol.* Vol. 7 part 2 p.155
1302. Niddah 71a
1303. *ibid* 16a
1304. Niddah 67b
1305. Kethuboth 72a

Blood in the stool is ritually clean. By contrast, blood that comes before or after urethral emptying is unclean[1306]. Blood which issues forth together with the urine (naturally, not during the time of menstruation) is considered to be clean, that is to say not of uterine origin, because we do not assume that "urine returned to the fountain and brought back blood with it"[1307]. In the post-Talmudic casuistry, the confusion between urinary gravel and blood is often mentioned, and it is correctly pointed out that often there is true blood found in "concrements in the urine"[1308]. Maimonides already traces the cause of blood in the urine to illnesses of the bladder or the kidneys[1309].

One must also remember, in regard to the above and in regard to what follows, what I mentioned at the outset, namely, to establish ritual impurity in a woman there were no physical examinations performed by physicians according to modern medical practice. What usually happened was as follows: when a doubt about the "cleanness" of a woman arose, the bloody undergarment was presented to an independent judge for adjudication. On the basis of the object itself, usually without the benefit of a "medical report", and always without a physical examination of the woman, the judge had to decide whether or not the blood originated in the uterus. Gradually, some of the Sages of the Talmud became quite skilled in the identification of various types of blood and did not allow themselves to be deceived when someone tested them by bringing insect blood to them as if it were human blood. They also felt that different blood types could be identified by their aroma. Rabbi Zera and Rabbi Eleazar were known as "specialists" in this area[1310].

## XVIII   Identification of Menstrual Blood

Only the Samaritans consider that every "blood", that is to say, every issue, renders a woman unclean[1311]. To the Sages of the Talmud, the blood which is undoubtedly of uterine origin and, hence, unclean is that which is: red like the blood of a wound, black like ink, reddish like the color of saffron[1312], the color of (earthy) water which is poured over the earth from the valley of Beth Kerem (sealed or Lemnian earth), or like the color or a mixture of two parts of water and one part of wine of Sharon[1313]. The School of Shammai add the color of the juice of fenugreek and the color of the juice of roasted meat.

Apparently, we are here dealing with various nuances of the color red. Concerning the "black like ink" color, the Talmud itself makes the correct observation that black is actually altered red which initially did not have the (black) shade. The black color first develops when the blood comes forth from the mucous membrane. Today, we know that the admixture of blood with vaginal secretions brings about the color change.

There is no unanimity of opinion concerning the color *yarok*, which refers to all shades of yellow and green. The perception and understanding of *yarok* elsewhere in the Bible and Talmud is also not unanimous, and this is not astonishing in regard to the precise determination of colors. Thus, it was correctly recognized that the shade of color of a wine mixture differs depending upon the material of the glass utensil which is used as the test object. It is therefore mandatory that a "non-ornate glass utensil from Tiberias" be used. Rabbi Zera also calls attention to the fact that the color of menstrual blood differs in women from various lands (i.e. there are ethnic differences). He lived in Palestine; when he came to Babylon he refused to diagnose blood (as to its

---

1306. *Tosefta* Niddah 7:9
1307. Niddah 59b
1308. *Yoreh Deah* 191a
1309. Maimonides. *Hilchoth Issurei Biyah* 5:17

1310. Niddah 20b
1311. Niddah 4:1
1312. Löw. *Pflanzennamen.* p.215
1313. Niddah 19a

origin) saying: I do not understand the nature of this land (and its inhabitants); how can I render judgements regarding its blood[1314]?

The type of lighting is also of importance in declaring vaginal blood clean or unclean. That which appears "clean" during the day may appear "unclean" at night. Therefore, some Sages only examine blood using artificial light, whereas others, only in sunlight under the shadow of one's hand. Fresh blood obviously looks different than dried blood[1315]. Naturally, a weak (literally: sick) eye can provide an erroneous opinion.

Demetrius also distinguishes various types of colored issues from the body. Some come from the whole body, others only from the uterus, and yet others from various other parts of the body[1316].

## XIX    Red Stains: Blood or Dye?

Particularly difficult was the task of determining whether a red spot represented a blood stain or a dye stain. The microscope, the testing of Teichmann and spectral analysis were unknown in those days. Such a spot was treated with seven reagents[1317]:

1) *Rok taphel,* the tasteless spittle of a person who had not eaten nor spoken since the previous night.

2) *Mey grisin*, water (or soup) of the hulled grains of a certain type of bean, or the gruel obtained by chewing these beans. The designation of the type of bean involved differs in the *Mishnah* and the *Tosefta*. It is not mentioned whether this substance is to be applied moist or dried on the suspicious stain.

3) Fermented urine.

4) *Nitron*, the mineral alkaline salt, *al-kali* of the Arabs.

5) *Borith*, vegetable alkali made from the ashes of burned salt plants, potash.

6) *Kamonia*, alkali-rich argillaceous earth from Kimolos.

7) *Ashleg, leontopetalon,* soapwort.

These alkalis are applied on the stain in that one rubs each of the substances three times on the stain between one's hands, just as when one washes a garment. Before each new drug application, one must rinse the spot but does not have to dry it[1318]. If the stain disappears or becomes lighter, it is a blood stain; if not, it is a dye stain. The reagents must be applied on the stain in the proper sequence and not all together. The last five of the above-mentioned substances were generally used to wash clothes[1319]. One must, therefore, have used very good, authentic dyes in those days since they did not fade by the above test.

The explanations of the *Gemara* only complicate the instructions of the *Mishnah*.

According to Resh Lakish, "tasteless spittle" must be part of each of the other substances[1320], since only the "breath of the mouth" makes them effective.

According to Rabbi Judah, the bean soup must be used hot, and salt must first be added thereto[1321].

The *nitron* is said to be Alexandrian nitron and not that of Antipatris (in Judaea)[1322].

The urine should be such that it has fermented for three days. According to Rabbi Yochanan, for the sake of exactness, one should also specify whether the urine is that of a child or of an old man, of a man or of a woman, whether it was uncovered or

---

1314. Niddah 20b
1315. *ibid*
1316. Soran. Chapt. 50 p.223
1317. Niddah 9:6-7
1318. *Tosefta* Niddah 8:10

1319. Shabbath 89b
1320. Niddah 63a
1321. *ibid.*
1322. *ibid* 62a. According to Krauss, it refers to *aphronitron*.

covered during the fermentation, and whether it fermented in the summer season or in the rainy (i.e. winter) season[1323].

According to Rabbi Judah, *borith* is the species of salsola called *ahala* or *chol*[1324]; according to others, it refers to sulphur. Both opinions are rejected by the *Gemara*, since *borith* and *ahala* are not identical, but are different types of alkali[1325].

The *ashleg* plant is found, as Samuel learned from the seamen, between the cracks of pearls, from which it is extracted with an iron nail[1326].

Rabbi Judah explains *kamonia* or *kimolia* to be *sheloph dutz,* whose meaning is unknown.

To wash out the stain (without ascertaining whether it is blood or dye) one must not use the substance *tzapon* which also makes dye stains disappear or become much lighter. This word was interpreted to refer to *sapon* in Latin, i.e. soap[1327].

The validity of this type of examination, it appears, with all its details, was gradually cast into doubt and, therefore, in post-Talmudic times, it was not considered to be applicable[1328].

The difficulty in removing menstrual blood from clothing was also known in heathen antiquity. According to Plinius[1329], the blood-stained garments of a menstruating woman could only be cleansed by using the woman's own urine.

## XX   Puberty

Most ancient legislative systems determine that the legal boundary between minority and majority is puberty. The *puber* and *impuber* of the Romans corresponds to the Hebrew *katan* (boy) or *ketanna* (girl) or *tinoketh* (child) and *gadol* (adult male) or *na'ara* (mature girl) or, after marriage, *isha* (woman). It can no longer be determined with certainty whether or not there was ever a time in Talmudic law in which the presence of the pubes alone was juridically authoritative as was the case in Greek[1330], Roman[1331], and German[1332] law. In general, to come to maturity requires not only the signs of sexual maturity, but also the attainment of a certain age, in boys thirteen complete years and in girls twelve[1333].

Naturally, a physical examination was necessary to determine maturity. The Romans called this examination *indagatio corporis*. It was abolished by Justinian in the year 530 C.E. Ancient German law also speaks of this practice. As already mentioned, in the Talmud these examinations of pubertal girls were performed exclusively by elderly women, whose declaration was then accepted as authoritative in court. Rabbi Eliezer entrusted the examination to his wife and Rabbi Ishmael, to his mother[1334].

For the determination as to whether or not a young girl is *menstruating*, the following general rule applies: before puberty the daughters of Israel are definitely in a condition of presumptive cleanness and no examination is necessary. Later, however, when they reach puberty, they are examined by the elder women but not with their fingers because they might injure them and thus *cause* bleeding; rather the women dab the girls with oil within[1335] and wipe it off from without and they are thus self-examined[1336].

1323. *ibid* 63a
1324. According to variations in Shabbath 90a, cf. Löw, *Pflanzennamen* p.43. Zebachim 88a. *Aruch* substitutes *chol* for the *ahel* of our text.
1325. Niddah 62a
1326. *ibid*
1327. *ibid*
1328. *Yoreh Deah* 190:31
1329. Plinius 28:23
1330. Heineccius. *Antiquit. Rom.* 1:233
1331. Schilling. *Geschichte des Römischen Privatrechtes* 2:134
1332. Wackernagel. *Die Lebensalter.* Basel 1862. Note 317
1333. Löw. *Lebensalter.* p.142 ff
1334. Niddah 48b and *Tosefta* Niddah 6:8-9
1335. the word "within" is correctly omitted in *Tosefta* Niddah 4:4
1336. Since at puberty an application of oil induces the menstrual flow. Niddah 10b

At the onset of puberty, the body changes[1337] and the upper sign, i.e. the breast, and the lower sign, i.e. the pubes, develop. The prophet portrays it as follows: *thy breasts are fashioned and thine hair is grown*[1338]. This physical maturation does not always correspond to the age of the individual. Sometimes the signs develop earlier because of unusual strength of the body, and sometimes they develop later because of weakness[1339].

The signs of puberty in a girl are as follows: the appearance of a wrinkle beneath the breast (*dad*) or at least the appearance of a shallow furrow which is visible when she raises the breast[1340]; the breasts incline forward; the nipple (*pitometh*) becomes black (in brunettes!); in some women it turns silvery (that is to say like oxidized silver) which is interpreted by some to be a sign of old age. If one places a finger on the tip of the nipple, *ukatz*, it sinks in and slowly returns when the finger is released[1341]. The surface of the breast appears wrinkled[1342].

Among village women, "the upper sign" (i.e. the breast) develops earlier because they move their arms back and forth as they grind with millstones[1343]. Among the daughters of the rich, the right-hand side develops earlier because it constantly rubs against their scarves, *aphikarsuth*, which hang down from their heads up to the breast and are worn very close to the body[1344]. Among the daughters of the poor, the left side develops earlier because they draw water and carry the jars and their younger siblings on that side[1345]. These Sages thus consider the occupation and the clothing of a woman to have a certain influence on the development of the female breast. According to some Rabbis, the left side always develops earlier than the right, but Rabbi Chanina, Rabbi Joshua's nephew, is of the opinion that this is only an exceptional occurrence[1346].

In men, there is no "upper sign" of puberty. Breasts which lie (or hang) like those of a woman are considered to be an abnormality in a man, and they render a priest unfit to serve in the Temple[1347].

The beauty of the *female breast* has been praised by poets throughout the ages in a variety of ways. The poets of the Orient are particularly lavish in their portrayals. A famous analogy in the Bible states: *thy breasts are like two fawns that are twins of a gazelle which feed among the lilies*[1348]. Unsightly is a marked difference in size of the two breasts, or an excessive development of both breasts as was once observed by Rabbah bar Bar Hana who saw an Arab woman who flung her breasts over her back and nursed her child[1349].

It is considered to be an advantage in humans over animals that in the former the breast is situated "in an intelligent place" (i.e. over the heart), so that the newborn does not have to view the mother's genitalia when it nurses[1350]. This thought is also found in the work of Ali Ibn Abbas[1351].

The "lower sign" of puberty is the development of the *mons veneris* and the pubes. Above "that place", i.e. the vulva, there is an elevated eminence (*tapuach*) which gradually softens[1352] and expands[1353] as the girl grows older. It is called *kaph*; perhaps also *gab*[1354].

The pubes develop earlier in a woman than in a man[1355]. The "lower sign" can develop before the "upper sign" appears, but not the reverse[1356]. In exceptional cases,

---

1337. Kiddushin 16b
1338. Ezekiel 16:7
1339. Baba Bathra 155b
1340. Niddah 47a
1341. Niddah 5:8
1342. Niddah 47a
1343. Niddah 48b
1344. Levit. Rabbah 2:4
1345. Niddah 48b
1346. *ibid*
1347. Bechoroth 7:5

1348. Song of Songs 4:5
1349. Kethuboth 75a
1350. Midrash Psalms 103:3
1351. Ali Ibn Abbas. *Anatomie*. Chapt. 25 p.419. Koning
1352. Niddah 47b
1353. Jerushalmi Sanhedrin 8; 26a
1354. Niddah 47b & 52b
1355. Niddah 5:9
1356. *ibid* 6:1

the pubes may fall off or be removed[1357]. Therefore, for forensic purposes, an examination of the upper sign suffices, and the court in Yavneh always followed this rule[1358]. Furthermore, in all these discussions, one has reference not to lanugo hairs but to fully developed pubic hairs which have follicles at their roots[1359].

According to Rabbi Simeon ben Gamliel, the pubes develop earlier in townswomen than in village women because the former regularly take hot baths[1360].

# E. THE NERVOUS SYSTEM

## I    The Brain

The brain lies in the bony skull like marrow in long bones. Both the brain and bone marrow, therefore, have the same name: *moach*, rarely *mokra*[1361]. Thus, the Rabbis either thought that bone marrow is a nerve substance or, more likely, that the brain, the spinal cord and bone marrow are histologically equivalent. Aristotle did the same in that he called the spinal cord: *ygrotes myelodes*[1362].

According to Bar Kappara, the "brain" comprises the total contents of the skull, which includes the encephalon as well as the other parts of the brain which lie in the cranial fossa. At the point at which it begins to elongate, it is counted as the spinal cord. At the boundary, there are two bean-shaped protuberances (*polin*) that lie at the entrance of the cranium (the foramen magnum). He was uncertain whether to consider these to be part of the brain or the spinal cord. He thought it more reasonable, however, to view them as part of (i.e. within) the cranium. Rabbi Jeremiah also found these bean-shaped protuberances at the entrance to the cranium of a bird[1363].

It is clear that these "beans" cannot refer to the *apophysis ossis occipitis* (i.e. occipital condyles) as suggested by Gintzburger[1364]. It seems more likely that they refer to the cerebral hemispheres, and perhaps also, in the bird, to the optic lobes.

In sheep, one can remove the brain from the skull without breaking a single bone[1365]. The commentaries add: "by using a splinter through the nose", that is to say in the same manner used in Egypt to embalm corpses. However, the cells of the ethmoid bones, and often the nasal cartilages, have to be broken during this procedure. The Palestinian Talmud gives a more correct interpretation in that it states the removal of the brain from the skull can occur without any damage to the bones if it is drawn out through the auditory canal[1366]. Furthermore, the *foramen opticum* in the posterior wall of the orbital cavity would be the most convenient site.

It cannot be ascertained how much the Rabbis knew about the *cranial nerves*. One can obviously draw no conclusions from the silence of the sources in this regard since they only discuss injuries to animals which are considered dangerous to life (hence rendering the animal unfit for consumption, *terefah*).

Inside the skull, the brain is enveloped in two membranes, an outer (literally: upper) and an inner (literally: lower) (dura and pia). A corresponding anatomic situation is more easily recognizable in the testicles (i.e. the double membrane) because of their accessibility[1367]. The inner membrane, the pia, is soft (*rak* in Hebrew; *lepte* in Greek). Thus, if one presses with one's finger tip through the mouth of the bird against

1357. Niddah 48a
1358. *Tosefta* Niddah 6:4
1359. Niddah 52a
1360. *ibid* 48b
1361. Chullin 93a
1362. Aristotle. *Hist. Anim.* Book 3 Chapt. 8 No. 61

1363. Chullin 45a–b
1364. Gintzburger. *Medicina ex Talmude illustr.* Goettingen. 1743 p.10
1365. Pesachim 84b
1366. Jerushalmi Pesachim 7; 35a
1367. Chullin 45a

the gums and observes movement of the bird's brain through a hole in the dura, it does not prove that the *soft* membrane (i.e. the pia) was also pierced, because the pia stretches because of its softness[1368]. In water fowl, even the dura is soft, so that it does not protect the brain, and every skull fracture is thus a life-threatening situation for the bird.

The arachnoid is not mentioned by either the Rabbis or anyone else in heathen antiquity or by the anatomists of the Middle Ages. The discoverers thereof are believed to be the anatomists of Amsterdam in the seventeenth century.

According to Rabbi Yannai, the site where one places the phylacteries, according to the Biblical command of God: *and for frontlets between thine eyes*[1369], is where the skull of a babe is soft (*rophes*)[1370] and pulsates (*ropheph*). Once a rooster in Jerusalem which thought this pulsation of the fontanel in an infant to be the movement of an edible insect, pecked out the brain of the infant. The rooster was stoned to death[1371]. During the time of Abaye, the wicked Roman government once decreed that anyone who dons phylacteries should have his brains pierced through[1372].

In their fury, cruel conquerors did not spare infants. Rabbi Yochanan relates that following the conquest of the town of Bethar by Hadrian in the Bar-Kochba war, 300 brains of children were found on a single rock[1373]. The Psalmist wishes upon despots who robbed the Israelites of their land that the despots' infants be captured and dashed against the rocks[1374].

The skin of the brain and of the testicles is rich in blood vessels and is, therefore, prohibited, just as blood itself[1375]. The brain of the *shibbuta* fish, the turbot (a type of flounder)[1376], is said to taste like the flesh of swine; because for everything that the Torah has forbidden us it has permitted us an equivalent[1377], so that everyone who lives according to Biblical law is not deprived of anything.

## II   The Spinal Cord

The usual name for the spinal cord is *chut ha-shedra* meaning "string of the vertebral column". In poetic allegory, it is called the *silver cord*[1378], an expression which was preserved by the anatomists of the Middle Ages as *funis argenteus*[1379].

From the lower part of the vertebral canal, there emerge "the partings" or *parashoth*, that is to say the lumbar, sacral and coccygeal nerves (the cauda equina), from various parts of the spine. The demonstration of these anatomic relationships is difficult, and it is related that Rabbi Judah was unable to do so on an animal for Rabbi Dimi ben Isaac[1380].

Samuel said in the name of Rabbi Chiya: "if a man breaks the neck bone of an animal after it has been slaughtered, but before the life departed from it, he thereby makes the meat heavy, and robs mankind (i.e. consumers)[1381] because he causes the blood to remain in the limbs of the animal"[1382]. Modern times have proven the correctness of this teaching by experimental verification[1383]. This "breaking of the

1368. *ibid* 56a
1369. Exodus 13:16
1370. Menachoth 37a, if the textual reading is correct. See above at the beginning of this chapter.
1371. Jerushalmi Erubin 10; 26a
1372. Shabbath 49a
1373. Lamentations Rabbah 2:4 fol. 21c. The Talmud in Gittin 58a has: "400 *kabs* of brains".
1374. Psalms 137:9. Compare Second Kings 8:12; Joshua 13:16 and Hosea 14:1
1375. Chullin 93a
1376. thus according to Löw, *Aramäische*

*Fischnamen* in *Orientalische Studien..* Nöldeke Festschrift. p.10
1377. Chullin 109b
1378. Eccles. 12:6
1379. Hyrtl. *Das Arabische*, . . . p.98
1380. Chullin 45b
1381. when he sells the meat, it contains more than the usual amount of blood (F.R.)
1382. Chullin 113a
1383. Dembo. Verhandlung der physiologische Gesellschaft zu Berlin. Session of 26 January 1894; also Dembo. *Das Schächten* Leipzig 1894 p.38

neck" of an animal, which was customary in Greece as part of "religious ceremonies"[1384], and is occasionally still practiced by butchers even today, refers to the sharp stab of the slaughterer between the atlas and the tabular part of the occipital bone, thus severing the cervical spinal cord. This is not the same as the "neck breaking" in man, which involves the tooth of the epistropheus of the medulla oblongata. As a result, vasoconstriction, whose control lies in the medulla oblongata, is abolished, blood vessels dilate, and during the killing of the animal (the stab in the neck only paralyzes it[1385] just like curare) the blood does not flow out of the small and medium-sized vessels. The meat is thus heavy and the buyer is defrauded because he has to pay the high price of the fleshy (i.e. muscular) part of the meat even for the blood contained therein.

A widespread belief in antiquity was that the spinal cord of a person after his death turns into a snake. This is reported by Ovid[1386] and Aelian[1387] who, indeed, questioned the truth of the matter, and Plinius[1388]. In the Talmud, this belief is used to inculcate the Israelites with a religious precept: the spinal cord of a person, after seven years, turns into a snake only if that person does not bow during prayers where prescribed[1389].

An essay on Talmudic psychology is a discussion in a *Midrash* which seems to belong to a later date: "the soul of a person resembles a type of winged grasshopper that has a chain bound to its foot; it hangs on the spinal cord. When the person sleeps, his soul leaves him and roams about in the world, and these are the dreams which a man sees. For this reason, one can call a sleeping person innumerable times without his answering; he answers immediately, however, when one touches him"[1390].

## III    Peripheral Nerves

Nothing from antiquity can be considered as absolutely certain in regard to peripheral nerves, because the *nervus* of the Romans and the *neuron* of the Greeks and the *gid* of the Hebrews and the *irk* of the Arabs not only refer to nerves, but also to tendons and ligaments. Even arteries are also called *neura*[1391]. Herophilus, who was well known as an anatomist, interprets the report of Rufus to state that nerves that control voluntary movements originate from the brain and spinal cord; other nerves go from bone to bone, some from muscle to muscle and some attach to the joints[1392]. The "sinewy" fist in our language refers to one with many sinews.

Only *gid ha-nashe* can be identified more precisely. According to continuous tradition of the Jews, it refers to the sciatic nerve. The Arabs (even their physicians)[1393] call it *irk al-nasha*. It was already customary during the era of the Patriarchs not to eat this nerve[1394]; later, consumption thereof was prohibited by law. The Talmud gives precise instructions as to the removal of the sciatic nerve from the flesh of slaughtered animals[1395].

On the other hand, the *tzometh ha-gidin* in animals is a system of *tendons*, either in the (anatomic) popliteal space or at the ankle joint (*arkubba*). In animals, it is falsely designated to be the knee joint[1396]; the ankle joint is the place "where the butcher hangs up the animal"[1397], that is to say the outside of the joint. In the latter case, the

---

1384. Oribasius 24:3
1385. and does not also render it senseless, as suggested by Galen in Oribasius, *loc. cit.* and believed by many even today.
1386. Ovid. *Metam.* 15:389
1387. Aelian. *Hist. Anim.* Book 1 Chapt. 51
1388. Plinius. *Hist. Natur.* 10:86
1389. Baba Kamma 16a
1390. Midrash Psalms 11:6

1391. Rufus. *De Appellat. Part.* ed. Daremberg-Ruelle p.163
1392. *ibid* p.185
1393. Abulcasem. *Chirurgie.* ed. Channing p.75
1394. Genesis 32:33
1395. Chullin 89b ff
1396. see above Chapter 2. Part 1:7
1397. see *Yoreh Deah* 56:4

Achilles tendon is referred to, and this would be in agreement with the teaching of the *Mishnah* that a serious injury of this structure may be threatening to the life of the animal. The only assertion which does not fit this interpretation is the statement that this tendinous structure consists of three cords[1398].

## IV   Sleep and Wakefulness

Asceticism is foreign to the original world of Judaism: a Nazarite who vows not to drink wine for thirty days must bring a sin offering because he sinned against himself[1399]. Abstinence from sleep is considered in the same manner, as follows: Rabbi Chanina ben Chakinai said: "he that stays awake at night imperils his own life"[1400], because sleep is enforced by nature[1401]. Rabbi Judah explains: "the night was only created for sleep", and Rabbi Nachman bar Isaac says: "we humans are day workers". When someone said to Rabbi Zera: "your teachings are very ingenious" he replied, "they are the result of day study"[1402]. If someone swears not to sleep for three days, he is flogged and his oath is not valid[1403].

To be sure, one should not indulge excessively in a good thing either. *Yet a little sleep, a little slumber, a little folding of the hands to sleep* (thus does the lazy one excuse himself) — *so shall thy poverty come as a runner*[1404]. The master must always work. "Ten measures of sleep descended to the world; nine were taken by slaves, and only one by the rest of the world"[1405]. For this reason, Bigthan and Teresh, the royal servants, complained that from the day that Esther came to the palace, their eyes had seen no sleep[1406]. A priest on duty in the Temple may not sleep, and if the patrol finds him to have fallen asleep, he is awakened harshly by a blow with a stick[1407]. During the Rejoicing at the Water Drawing, the Levites did not sleep; at most they dozed for a moment on one another's shoulders[1408].

He who was sufficiently careless to have become a surety for another must work indefatigably and may not give *sleep to his eyes nor slumber to his eyelids*[1409] until he has fulfilled his obligation. In general, no one should believe that if he does not *walk in the counsel of the wicked...nor sit in the seat of the scornful*[1410], that is to say, if he avoids theatres and circuses (in their meanings in antiquity), that he can then go and sleep. Rather only when *he delights in the law of the Lord*[1411] has he fulfilled his obligation[1412], just as in general the positive "doing of good" must be combined with the negative "avoidance of evil"[1413].

Only for God does sleep not exist[1414] for *Behold! He that keepeth·Israel doth neither slumber nor sleep*[1415]. For this reason, Johanan Hyrcanus abolished the wakers who used to sing the words of the Psalmist in the Temple[1416]: *Awake, why sleepest Thou, O Lord*[1417]?

At midday, Oriental people return to their homes in order to sleep, as did Ishbosheth *who lay on a bed at noon*[1418]. So too, Abraham *sat at the door of his tent in the heat of the day*[1419], and David didn't arise from his bed until evening[1420]. The

---

1398. Chullin 76a ff
1399. Taanith lla interpreting Numbers 6:11
1400. Aboth 3:4. Alternate translations: "forfeits his own life" or "sins against himself"
1401. Tamid 28a
1402. Erubin 65a
1403. Nedarim 15a
1404. Proverbs 6:10-11
1405. Kiddushin 49b
1406. Megillah 13b. i.e. they had to constantly serve King Ahasuerus.
1407. Tamid 28a

1408. Sukkah 53a
1409. Proverbs 6:4
1410. Psalms 1:1
1411. *ibid* 1:2
1412. Abodah Zara 18b
1413. *ibid* 19b
1414. Sotah 18a
1415. Psalms 121:4
1416. Maaser Sheni 5:15
1417. Psalms 44:24
1418. Second Samuel 4:5
1419. Genesis 18:1
1420. Second Samuel 11:2

shepherd also lets his flocks rest at noon[1421]. Only an extremely zealous person allows himself to be consumed by the heat during the day and the cold by night while sleep flees from his eyes[1422].

This daytime heat in the Orient makes it necessary that work begin early in the morning. Rabbi Dosa[1423] ben Harkinas said: "sleep in the morning and wine at midday drive a man from the world"[1424]. One frequently cited the example of Abraham who arose early in the morning[1425]. This example was even followed by the heathen prophet Bileam[1426] and by many others before and after him[1427]. It is considered to be the custom of princes to arise during the third hour of the day[1428]. Only King David is said to have been awakened by his harp at midnight at which time he arose[1429], as he himself sings: *I will awaken the dawn*[1430], and not the reverse.

Gradually, abstention from sleep developed into a type of asceticism, in that one tried, as much as possible, to faithfully carry out the Psalmist's admonition *to meditate in God's law day and night*[1431]. One of the twenty-four qualifications for acquiring the Torah is moderation in sleep[1432]. Rabbi Nachman bar Isaac says that the disciples of the Sages who banish sleep from their eyes *in this world* will be rewarded with the resplendence of the Divine Presence in the future world[1433], and their wives, who also chase sleep from their eyes while waiting for their husbands to return from the house of study, will be similarly rewarded by God[1434].

Rabbi Eliezer and Rabbi Yochanan ben Zakkai were both praised because they never slept or dozed in the house of study throughout the entire week, other than on the Sabbath[1435]. Legend also relates of the Patriarch Jacob that during the entire fourteen years that he spent in the house of study of Eber, he never slept[1436]. The Lord draws a chord of loving-kindness by day over whoever occupies himself with the study of Torah by night[1437]. A house in which no words of Torah are also heard at night will be destroyed by fire[1438]; otherwise it is protected against any damage[1439]. Resh Lakesh says that the moon was created only so that there should be light in the house of study at night[1440]. One should study Torah early and late[1441], because, according to Rabbi Chisda, one can sleep sufficiently after one is dead[1442].

Nevertheless, during the day one should not sleep longer than a horse, that is to say 60 respirations[1443]; the latter number, according to Babylonian linguistic usage, refers to a short, unspecified period of time[1444].

Asceticism is methodically developed in the New Testament. The Apostle Paul exhorts the Corinthians[1445] to prove that they are *ministers of God in labors, in watchings (em agrypniais) and in fastings*; he himself was in danger *in weariness, in many watchings (agrypniais pollakis) and in much fasting*[1446].

---

1421. Song of Songs 1:7
1422. Genesis 31:40
1423. Preuss erroneously has Rabbi Jose (F.R.)
1424. Aboth 3:10
1425. Genesis 22:3
1426. Numbers 22:21
1427. The Concordances enumerate 19 such places in the Bible.
1428. Berachoth 1:2. The time from sunrise until the stars appear is divided into twelve "daytime hours" which are of varying duration depending on the season of the year.
1429. Berachoth 3b
1430. Psalms 57:9
1431. Psalms 1:2
1432. Aboth 6:6
1433. Baba Bathra 10a

1434. Kethuboth 62a
1435. Sukkah 28a
1436. Genesis Rabbah 68:11
1437. Chagigah 12
1438. Sanhedrin 92a
1439. Erubin 18b
1440. *ibid* 65a
1441. Levit. Rabbah 19:1
1442. Erubin 65a
1443. Sukkah 26b
1444. A traveler in Arabia observed that 60 respirations in a horse are more than a half-hour in duration. See the various opinions in Ch. M. Margolis' commentary on *Orach Chayim* 4:16
1445. Second Corinthians 6:5
1446. *ibid* 11:27

One used to constantly prick oneself with a thorn to remain awake[1447]. The High Priest was to remain awake the entire night prior to the Day of Atonement. To accomplish this, if he began to fall asleep, they made him walk to and fro on the cold marble floor[1448], or the young priests snapped their fingers before him[1449].

The sleep of an intoxicated wicked man is undisturbed, and this sleep is of benefit to him and of benefit to the world,[1450] since the world is spared his wickedness. Otherwise, however, the conscience of the wicked does not allow them to sleep; thus, sleep fled from the eyes of King Ahasuerus[1451] and King Darius after he threw Daniel into the den of lions[1452].

A sick person cannot rest because of pain. Job complains:[1453] *When I lie down, I say: "When shall I arise?" But the night is long and I am full of tossings to and fro unto the dawning of the day.* The Pentateuch threatens evil people with the following punishment: *In the evening, thou shalt say, would it were morning*[1454]! The Psalmist also laments that God keeps his eyelids open at night[1455], so that he moistens his bed every night with his tears. For this reason, sleep and dreaming are good signs for an ill person[1456]. If he sleeps, he will get well[1457].

Sleep and death are in principle similar. They are only different in degree, in that individual organs function more feebly: sleep is one-sixtieth (i.e. one piece) of death[1458], almost as if sleep were a premature fruit which fell from the tree and death were the ripe fruit[1459]. It is more than questionable whether the deepest sleep resembling death, called *tardemah marmita,* which no one knew or awakened from[1460], really represents *dormities mortis,* as suggested by Wolf Einhorn.

Legend relates of Choni the miracle worker, that he once saw a man plant a carob tree. The man went to sleep and when he awoke, the tree bore fruit. The man had slept for seventy years[1461].

In reference to a Scriptural phrase[1462], post-Talmudic writers have determined that eight hours of sleep are necessary, in general, but that the amount varies according to the nature of an individual person[1463]. Maimonides also requires eight hours of sleep (per night for the average person)[1464].

## V   Sleep Inducers (Soporifics)

The stomach when full induces sleep[1465]; tiredness after a meal is a well-known phenomenon[1466]. However, only *moderation* in eating brings healthy sleep; by contrast, the anguish of sleeplessness, of nausea, of abdominal pain in the unsatisfiable,[1467] *and the abundance of the rich do not allow one to sleep*[1468]. The fisherman Adda[1469] said to Rab: "after eating fish, cress and milk, occupy your body (i.e. go for a walk) and not your bed"[1470]. Rabbi Joshua ben Levi cursed those who sleep while lying on their backs[1471] because erections might easily result therefrom.

It is dangerous to sleep in one's shoes. Samuel teaches[1472]: he who wishes to taste

---

1447. Gittin 84a
1448. Yoma 1:7
1449. See above chapter 2 Part 1:6
1450. Sanhedrin 72a
1451. Esther 6:1
1452. Daniel 6:19
1453. Job 7:4
1454. Deut. 28:67
1455. Psalms 77:5
1456. Berachoth 57b
1457. John 11:12
1458. Berachoth 57b
1459. Genesis Rabbah 17:5. *mormoton* in Greek. Theodor's commentary.
1460. First Samuel 26:12
1461. Taanith 23a
1462. Job 3:12
1463. Commentary of *Ba'er Hetev* on *Orach Chayim* 1:2
1464. Maimonides. *Mishneh Torah. Hilchoth Deoth* 4:4
1465. Berachoth 61b
1466. Yoma 18a
1467. Sirach 34:20
1468. Eccles. 5:11
1469. Preuss erroneously has Abba (F.R.)
1470. Moed Katan 11a
1471. Berachoth 13b
1472. Yoma 78b

death should put on his shoes and go to sleep[1473]. An old man sleeps lightly; even a bird wakes him up[1474].

The best *soporific* is physical activity. The preacher teaches: the sleep of a laboring man is sweet, whether he ate little or much[1475]. Then one begins to place one's hand on the forehead as a "step towards sleep"[1476]. Otherwise, in order to be able to sleep, one has to wear the tooth of a fox; it has to be from a live fox, because if it is derived from a dead fox, it tends to keep one awake[1477]. Sick people often fall asleep if one extinguishes the light in their room[1478], or if one makes a soft sound like siphoning water from a vessel and letting it drip out drop by drop from the thin, pointed end of the siphon (pipette) onto a metal plate[1479]. It is possible that a mechanical device is being described, perhaps a type of water gauge which one could naturally also use to awaken sleeping people. In a similar manner, Alexander of Tralles, in the sixth century, recommended that in a sickroom water should be allowed to run from one vessel into another because this soft sound (*metrios psopsos*) of the water induces sleep[1480]. Celsus, (approximately at the time of Jesus), suggested as a tranquilizing remedy for phrenetics the use of a *silanus juxta cadens* or *saliens*, a fountain in the vicinity of the patient, *maximeque lecti suspensi motus*, a swinging cradle[1481]. Casaubonus (about the year 1600) adds: *ut nostrorum liberorum*.

On the other hand, it is prohibited to ask someone to "place a holy book or phylacteries on my child" to induce sleep[1482], obviously because it is considered to be a superstitious misuse of holy objects.

## VI   Dreams

In all of antiquity, great importance was attached to dreams, and dream interpretation became a fully developed "science" whose founder, according to legend, was Prometheus[1483]. The oneirocritic and oneiroscope of the Greeks[1484] correspond to the *pathora* of the Northern Semites. The Hebrews call a dreamer or dream interpreter a *ba'al ha-chalomoth*[1485] or *ish ha-chalom*[1486] or *ba'al ha-chalom*[1487]. Many wise men practiced dream interpretation incidentally and gratis. The professional dream interpreters, however, demanded a fee. For an appropriate honorarium, one received a favorable (i.e. propitious) interpretation; without a fee, one received an unfavorable interpretation. Raba and Abaye tested this numerous times on the (Babylonian or Arabic?) interpreter Bar Hedya. It appears that the latter occasionally insured that his interpretations came true by a *corriger la fortune*: he once told Raba that "the king's treasury will be broken into, and you will be arrested as a thief". And so it happened[1488].

The dream interpreter carries his "dream book" or *siphra* with him just as his Greek colleague carries his *pinax*[1489]. During the time of Rabbi Bana'ah, there were 24 dream interpreters in Jerusalem[1490]. They looked down on the foolish (*tipsha delibba*)

---

1473. The context does not allow one to interpret death to mean "deep sleep".
1474. Shabbath 152a
1475. Eccles. 5:11
1476. Pesachim 112a
1477. Shabbath 67a. The Talmud actually has the reverse of Preuss as follows: "a living fox's for one who sleeps too much, a dead fox's for him who cannot sleep"(F.R.)
1478. Shabbath 2:5
1479. *Tosefta* Shabbath 2:8; Erubin 104a; Jerushalmi Erubin 10; 26d. The textual reading and the meaning of the words are uncertain.
1480. Alexander of Tralles. ed. Puschmann.

Vol. 1 p.361
1481. Celsus, *Medicina* 3:18 p.153.
1482. Jerushalmi Erubin 10; 26c
1483. Aeschylus. *Prometheus* 486
1484. Compare B. Büchsenschütz. *Traum und Traumdeutung im Altertum*. Berlin 1868; Becher-Goll. *Charikles*. 1:215
1485. Berachoth 10b
1486. *Tosefta* Maaseroth 2:5
1487. Sanhedrin 30a
1488. Berachoth 56a
1489. *ibid*. This *siphra* confirms the assertion of Büchsenschütz that the *pinax* was also a dream book.
1490. Berachoth 55b

Samaritans with disdain[1491]; however, it remains uncertain whether or not the *Midrash* refers to a general aversion to this religious sect without singling out dream interpreters. It is prohibited as a heathen superstition to wear one's shirt reversed or to sit on a broom in order to dream[1492].

The people adamantly believed in the significance of the dream; "even if the dream interpreter tells a man that on the morrow he will die, he should certainly pray to God for mercy"[1493]. Furthermore, Rabbi Eleazar of Cyprus asserts, there is no dream without meaning[1494]. Rabbi Chisda said: a dream which is not interpreted is like a letter which is not read[1495]. Dreams in the morning are particularly meaningful[1496], and heathen oneirocritics would not interpret any other kind.

The overwhelming majority of Rabbis, however, are skeptical about dream interpretations. Rabbi Abahu says: dreams are of no value and of no harm[1497]. The prophet says: *dreams speak vanity*[1498], and Sirach asserts: "fools rely on dreams"[1499]. A dream cannot be used as evidence in court[1500]. One atones for "bad dreams" — the Talmud more carefully states "a dream about which one is distressed" — by going to three people who will pray for the dreamer, or one prays for oneself[1501]. In Greece, libations and other offerings served the same purpose[1502].

To here describe the extensive dream casuistry of the Bible and the Talmud[1503] is naturally pointless. However, it is interesting to see in what rational ways the Talmud explains the undoubtedly very common occurrence that the dream interpretation comes true. Above all, one should mention the fundamental rule of Rabbi Jonathan: "a man is shown in a dream only what is suggested by his own thoughts; he never sees in a dream a date palm of gold or a camel going through the eye of a needle"[1504]. In particular, pictures which occupy one's mind during the day appear in a dream, as already reported from Persian sources by Herodotus[1505]. In this manner, Rabbi Joshua ben Hananiah and Samuel were able to predict the content of the dreams of high officials; the affected officials thought the whole day about certain things and then dreamt about them[1506].

In addition, just as a dream can, in a certain sense, be the result of a suggestion, so too *the fulfillment of the dream depends on the suggestion of the interpreter*. All dreams follow this pattern and thus 24 interpretations of a single dream can all be "correct", and all may be fulfilled[1507]. This conception is very clearly exemplified in the story where the disciples of Rabbi Eleazar, in the absence of their teacher, interpreted a dream for a woman by telling her that her husband would die. On hearing this, Rabbi Eleazar reproachingly taught them: you have caused a man to die[1508].

I do not know of any theories mentioned in the Talmud about the origin of dreams other than those cited above. According to Galen[1509], a dream is a diathesis of the body and, therefore, dependent upon nutrition and time. However, experience teaches that some dreams foretell the future, in the view of Galen.

---

1491. Lamentations Rabbah 1:14-18
1492. *Tosefta* Shabbath 6:7
1493. Berachoth 10b
1494. *Sifré Korach* 119 p.39b of the Friedmann edition
1495. *ibid*
1496. Berachoth 55a
1497. Gittin 52a
1498. Zechariah 10:2
1499. Sirach 31:1
1500. *Tosefta* Maaser Sheni 5:9
1501. Berachoth 55b

1502. Aeschylus. *Perser* 206 ff
1503. Berachoth 55a ff; Jerushalmi Maaser Sheni 4; 55b ff; Genesis Rabbah 89:8; Lamentations Rabbah 1:14-18
1504. Berachoth 55b
1505. Herodotus 7:16
1506. Berachoth 56a
1507. *ibid* 55b
1508. Jerushalmi Maaser Sheni 4; 55c
1509. Galen. *De Dignot. ex Insomniis*. Kühn 6:832-833

# CHAPTER III

## *ILLNESS AND ITS HEALING*
### (GENERAL PATHOLOGY AND THERAPY)

### I   Definition of a Patient

The "popular expression" for a sick person is *choleh*. When "the illness (or demon of illness?) attacks him", he is said to be "dangerously ill", and is called a *shechib mera*[1]. The Syrian dialect designates a patient as *kecira,* and *ketzur arsa*[1a] is one who is completely bedridden[2]. When generalized debility begins, the patient is called a *gossess* or dying person, since such patients die[3].

During the morning hours most patients appear improved: the day rises, the patient rises[4]. For this reason, one should not visit the sick either during the first three hours, or during the last three hours of the day; the former because one might consider the patient's condition to be better than it actually is, and no longer consider intensive care to be needed, the latter because then one considers the illness to be more serious than it really is[5].

A patient has a sorrowful (bad or *ra'im* ) countenance[6].

### II   Demons As a Cause of Illness

The rearing of the Jewish people in pure monotheism, the belief in a single God, "who alone controls everything", was the responsibility of the leaders among the people. This task was extraordinarily difficult, and was never completely accomplished. We repeatedly find lamentations concerning the return of Jews to idolatry. The Pentateuch already bemoans the fact that Jews sacrificed unto devils or *shedim,* who are not gods, and did not recognize the true God[7]. These lamentations are repeated in every section of the Bible. As in all superstitious beliefs of the Jewish people, one must distinguish between the vestige of idolatry, and the external influences and viewpoints of foreign peoples which penetrated the Jews. To the Jews, the former originates from the pre-monotheistic period, before the separation of the individual Semitic tribes; so that certain forms of idolatry only represent a return to old habits. Whether or not the entire teaching about demons is in fact such a local vestige, rather than an expression of a generalized conception of the people, has not been investigated because the belief in evil spirits is widespread throughout the world, no matter to which race the people of any country belong[8]. This belief was certainly also prevalent among the Jews during all

---

1. Jerushalmi Gittin 6; 48d
1a. Targum on Job 29:15
2. Jerushalmi Peah 3; 17d
3. Kiddushin 71b
4. Baba Bathra 16b

5. Nedarim 40a
6. Nehemiah 2:2
7. Deut. 32:17
8. Tylor. *Anfänge der Kultur.* 2:135 ff

periods, even though the wretched figure of the public prosecutor, namely Satan, belongs to a later era. Concerning the group of illness demons, all indications are that this is a Babylonian import. The Talmud itself cites Babylonia as the source of the name of angels[9].

Whereas the Canaanites considered a rabid dog to be mad *(keleb shoteh),* the Babylonian Mar Samuel states that an evil spirit rests upon him[10]. The *Mishnah* describes this evil spirit as a being outside of the human body which causes a lonely wanderer to go astray[11] and misleads him into going beyond the Sabbath limit[12]: it is attracted by a light[13]. The rationalist Maimonides considers fear "of the evil spirit" to simply represent melancholy[14]. The Book of Tobit mentions that the liver and the heart of fish contain substances with which one should fumigate a person in order to rid him of a demon or an evil spirit[15].

These spirits or *ruchoth,* which certainly differ from *shedim* and *mazzikin* in nuances only, came to play an important role in the folk medicine of the Talmud. Their number is exceedingly large; they no longer remain outside the human body, but penetrate into it, and make the affected person "possessed", *daimonizomenois.* Such occurred to large assemblages of people in the gospel, a noteworthy observation about which we will say much more later. Among physicians, Hippocrates demanded from the midwives of Sóran that they give up their belief in demons and become *adeisidaimones.* The results of this demand did not give pleasure to either one (i.e. they failed to comply).

Patients already ill have to be especially guarded from demons[16], because the Satan accuses at a time of danger[17].

It is known that Varro and Columella, in the first century of the common era, attributed illnesses to small animals that live in the swamps and are inhaled by human beings. These "animals" should not be placed in parallel with *mazzikin,* any more than with microorganisms in today's understanding of illness.

## III    Astrology and the Evil Eye

Babylonia is also the homeland of *astrology.* The name Chaldaean was already so commonly used in Rome to denote magicians and astrologers, that Cicero had to explicitly indicate[18] that Chaldaean is the designation of a tribe of people and not of a profession. As far as can be ascertained from their writings, Greek physicians rather rejected the concept of astrology. The book *De Significatione Vitae et Mortis*[19], attributed to Hippocrates, and the *Isagoge in Artem Medici* of Sorani Ephesii[20], which are full of astrology, originated much later. Plinius states[21] that only the Massiliote physician Krinas made use of astrology. Even the great Galen is not free thereof[22]. On the other hand, later physicians, beginning with Peter Von Albano, until the last century, delighted in their thorough consideration of constellations.

This belief in astrology also gained acceptance among the Jews, and, in particular, it is again the Babylonian Mar Samuel who is involved therein. He did not, however, accept it unconditionally. His statement that even Israelites are under the influence of the planets is most vehemently opposed in the Talmud[23]. According to legend, when

9. Jerushalmi Rosh Hashana 1; 56d
10. Yoma 83b
11. Taanith 22b
12. Erubin 4:1
13. Shabbath 2:5
14. Commentary on above *Mishnah*
15. Tobit 6:8. From here, as well as Tobit 6:15 and 8:3, it is apparent that the text is dealing with someone who is "possessed".
16. Berachoth 54b
17. Jerushalmi Shabbath 2; 5b; see also

Brecher. *Das Transzendentale* p. 47 ff
18. *De Divinat* 1:1; *Chaldaei, non ex artis sed ex gentis vocabulo nominati*
19. in the edition of Van der Linden. Lugdana. Bat. 1668 p. 422 ff
20. in the collection of Albert Torino. Basel 1528 folio 9
21. *Histor. Natur.* 29:1
22. Galen. *De Diebus Decretoriis.* Book 3 Chapt. 5. Kühn 9:910 ff
23. Shabbath 156b

Abraham said: "I have seen in the stars that I will only have one son", God retorted: "leave your astrology; for Israel, there are no stars!"[24] The prophet has already spoken: *do not dread the signs of heaven, like the heathens, who fear these signs*[25]. A decision is not reached, however.

The disciples of Rabbi Chanina stated: "it is not the planetary constellation of the day which decides one's fate but the stars at the moment of birth". Thus is created another particular type of *fatum*. Therefore, neither an illness with which a person is afflicted, nor his death, occurs by chance[26]. Astrological reasons were especially decisive for the selection of days appropriate for bloodletting, not only in the time of the Talmud, but also throughout the centuries and millennia, until our own times. Perhaps the aged and experienced Carl Wenzel is not totally incorrect in his opinion that our "genius epidemicus" is basically equivalent to the "sovereignty of the stars", and only an in-depth investigation would teach us the influence of occurrences in space on our bodies[27]. It is not necessary to first prove that the mechanistic philosophy must unconditionally accept such an influence.

Another widespread belief by all peoples of antiquity, and of more recent times, is the belief that the evil eye or *ayin hara* can be the cause of disease. The *Mishnah* states that "the evil eye, the evil inclination and hatred of one's fellow creatures put a man out of the world"[28]. Rab and Chiya are of the opinion that 99 percent of all people die through the evil eye, and only one percent die of natural causes. Both lived in Babylonia, "where the evil eye was extremely prevalent"[29]. Even this belief, therefore, originated in Babylonia. When Scriptures state: *and the Lord will take away from thee all sickness*[30], it refers to the evil eye[31], from which the Israelites would be immune. One is protected from the evil eye by placing the right thumb in the left hand, and the left thumb in the right hand[32]. Similarly, during the Middle Ages, the German averted the effect of the evil eye by putting his thumb in his right hand, and closing the hand tight[33]. Similarly, the Italians, even today, believe that they can protect themselves from the *jettatura* with the *fica*.

It is easy to make enemies, but difficult to make friends; it is easy to ascend to heights but difficult to descend therefrom; most difficult of all is the ability to combat the effect of one's own evil eye[34].

## IV  Causes of Diseases

In the course of the development of culture, the stage of *positive knowledge* follows metaphysics. I refer to the straightforward observation of nature. As far as the causes of sicknesses are concerned, even to us, this scientific observation of nature is still in a bad state, and we can certainly not expect any better from earlier times. According to Rabbi Chanina, the most common cause of illness and of death is a cold, perhaps the cold representing a lack of natural body warmth, over which even Heaven has no control[35]. His son, Rabbi Jose, considers secretions (*tzoah*) to be responsible for illness, particularly aural and nasal ones. Rabbi Eleazar states that gall causes illness of the entire human body. According to Mar Samuel, all illness is caused by the wind or *ruach;* this could refer to pneuma, but in the sphere of Samuel, it more likely refers to a demon[36].

Rabbi Ishmael is of the opinion that 99 percent of people die of sunstroke (or

24. Nedarim 32a
25. Jeremiah 10:2
26. Baba Kamma 2b
27. Wenzel. *Alte Erfahrungen im Lichte der Neuen Zeit Uber die Enstehung von Krankheiten* Wiesbaden 1893 p. 53.
28. Aboth 2:11
29. Jerushalmi Shabbath 14; 14c

30. Deut. 7:15
31. Baba Metzia 107b
32. Berachoth 55b
33. Scheffel, Ekkehard. p. 120
34. *Yalkut* 1:845
35. Baba Metzia 107b
36. *ibid*

fever? Hebrew: *sarab*), and only one percent dies by the hand of Heaven. Bold is the statement of Rabbi Acha that it depends upon the person himself, as to whether or not he becomes ill. Also bold is the assertion of the Rabbis that 99 percent of all people have themselves to blame for their deaths[37]. The commentaries explicitly state that the guilt lies in the deviation from the normal regimen of health. A change in one's usual life habits is considered by Mar Samuel to be dangerous, and the beginning of illness[38]. The *Midrash* relates that as long as the Jews were in Palestine, they only drank water from cisterns *(mey nozelim)* and wells; when they were exiled to Babylon, they drank from the waters of the Euphrates, and many of them died[39]. Here we see that the influence of drinking water was also well-known.

One must admit that we have not made much progress in the general recognition of the causes of diseases in the past 2000 years.

The teachings of antiquity concerning the body humors and temperaments are rarely found in Talmudic writings. At best the expression "I, blood, am the cause of all illnesses"[40], i.e. an excess of blood, might be reminiscent of the teaching by Galen concerning plethora, and its detrimental consequences. The cause of dropsy is said to be an abnormal mixing of water and blood in the body[41]. Otherwise, as far as we can recognize names of illnesses, the Talmud speaks mostly of the afflictions of individual organs.

I know of no definite example in the Talmud where heredity is given as the cause of disease. Crzellitzer is of the opinion that:

"the Bible does not speak without a deep and valid reason about the fourth generation when it states: *God is a jealous God, visiting the iniquity of the fathers upon the children unto the third and fourth generation*[42]. Apparently this observation is based upon the fact that inheritance of any illness or malady strikes family members up to the fourth generation, that is, from the great-grandparents to the great-grandson. Even we modern physicians are only familiar with a few instances of pathological inheritance which can be traced further back than to the great-grandfather"[43].

Although the Biblical text: *and unto the fourth generation* adds: *of them that hate Me,* which, according to the translation of the *Targum,* clearly means "if the children sin according to the example of their father"; and, although another explicit Biblical teaching states: *neither shall the children be put to death for the fathers, but every man shall be put to death for his own sin*[44], a very justified doubt remains as to whether or not the Bible is at all speaking of a physical condition. It is much more likely that Scriptures refers to a moral condition. Such examples could be cited in large numbers.

The Bible and Talmud are collective works, comprising the teachings of many different people and times. It is therefore not surprising that opinions which belong to various types of cultures are juxtaposed.

## V    Diagnosis of Disease

For the general *diagnosis* of disease in those days, there existed a helpful substance, which is unknown to us today. It was the *betza tormita* or *tromita* (i.e. a well-boiled egg). Samuel said that "the work required to prepare one is worth a thousand

37. Jerushalmi Shabbath 14; 14c and Levit. Rabbah 16:8
38. Baba Bathra 146a
39. Midrash Psalms 137:3
40. Baba Bathra 58b
41. Levit. Rabbah 15:2
42. Exodus 20:5
43. Crzellitzer. *Ueber Sippschaftstafeln Med. Reform.* 1908 #48 p. 575
44. Deut. 24:16

denars. For the egg must be placed a thousand times in hot water and a thousand times in cold water until it is small enough to be swallowed whole. If an illness is present in the person, it is attracted to the egg, and when the egg is passed out per rectum, the physician knows which medication is required for the patient and how to treat him"[45]. The word *tromita* is explained by the Palestinian Talmud[46] as *rapheton oon,* the usual term of Greek cooks for soft eggs. The *tromita* of the Talmudic text, therefore, corresponds to the *trometa* of the Greeks, an expression also used by Galen for soft eggs[47].

Samuel is said to have examined himself with *kulcha* which weakened him so that his household tore their hair as a sign of mourning[48], for they thought he was dead[49]. The commentator Rabbi Nissim was not sure what this *kulcha* is: he thought it was a substitute for the *tromiton* egg to whose use Samuel was not accustomed. *Aruch* considers it to be a cabbage-stalk which was swallowed by the patient to be examined.

Palpation of the pulse by the physician is first mentioned in a later *Midrash:* a physician came to visit a patient. He took the patient's hand (the palmar surface of the hand, at the site of the radial artery) and told those caring for him: give him whatever he wishes to eat, for he will die of this illness[50]. On the other hand, Rabbi Yochanan and Rabbi Chanina would only extend their hands to a patient in order to help him stand up[51], as described by the commentator Samuel Edeles. In yet other cases, the physician would take hold of the patient's hand and raise him, as support for a verbal suggestion, as was done to the febrile mother-in-law of Simon, the apostle[52].

The Jews were intimately familiar with the diseases and blemishes of animals, because painstakingly careful examination of animals and their organs after slaughtering is required by Jewish law. It was therefore tempting to immediately apply the knowledge gained from animals to human beings. Therefore, it was explicitly taught that conclusions from analogy were not even permissible in case of animal wounds, and certainly not from animals to humans. A hole in the liver has a different implication for life than a hole in the lung[53]. Nevertheless, this rule was often disregarded, just as modern medical science unhesitatingly equates a kilo of healthy rabbit with a kilo of a sick human being.

## VI    Illness and Death

An illness that terminates in *recovery* of the patient is first mentioned from the time of King Hezekiah[54] or the prophet Elisha[55]. Illness is an affliction from God so that the patient repent from sin and, after his recovery, continue to lead a penitent life[56]. In earlier places in Scripture, we only learn that "he died"; or, if the text is speaking of an illness, as in the case of Jacob[57], the report of his death is found immediately adjacent[58]. Legend relates that only in the town of Luz, *which exists to this very day*[59], the angel of death has no power; rather, when the aged in the city note that their intelligence is waning, they go outside the city walls and die[60].

According to Rabbi Joshua ben Korcha, when a man reaches his parents' age (of death), for five years before and five years after he must fear death[61]. Rabbi Simeon

---

45. Nedarim 50b
46. Jerushalmi Nedarim 6; 39c
47. *Tormita* contrasts with a *betza megulgeleth,* or hard boiled egg. The latter is also included in the term *mebushal* or cooked; but not *tormita.* Jerushalmi Nedarim 6; 39c
48. Yebamoth 116b
49. Nedarim 50b
50. Midrash Psalms 73:1
51. Berachoth 5b

52. Mark 1:30
53. Chullin 48b
54. *Pirke de Rabbi Eliezer* #52
55. Sanhedrin 107b
56. Genesis Rabbah 65:9
57. Genesis 48:1
58. *ibid* 49:33
59. Judges 1:26
60. Sotah 46b
61. Genesis Rabbah 65:12

ben Jehozadah stated that God brings people into the world as individual families[62] and brotherhoods. If one member of the family dies, the whole family should become apprehensive[63]. In a very similar manner, Rabbi Yochanan asserts that if one brother in a family dies, all the other brothers should fear death; if one of a company *(chabura)* dies, the whole company should fear[64].

The usual duration of an illness which ends fatally is five days, but which type of illness is referred to cannot be stated with precision. The child whom the wife of Uriah bore to David died on the seventh day of illness[65]; the cause is unknown. According to Rabbi Chananya ben Gamliel, death following pestilence characteristically occurs after one day of illness. The Lord proclaimed to the prophet Ezekiel that He would take away the *pleasure of his eye* through pestilence, and the next morning, as he spoke to the people, his wife became ill and died the same evening[66].

The expressions for sudden death and for death after only one day's illness are already incomprehensible to the *Tosafists*[67]. Rabbi Chiya bar Abba asserts that the miracle of recovery that is wrought for a sick person is greater than the miracle which saved the three men[67a] from the fiery furnace. For the latter were only spared from an earthly fire which anyone could have extinguished, whereas the fire (fever) of a patient is the fire from heaven, which no mortal can extinguish; nevertheless the patient recovers[68].

Favorable *prognostic* signs for a patient are the following: sneezing, perspiration, open bowels, seminal emission, sleep and a dream[69]. For each of these, there is a supporting Biblical verse. In the case of open bowels, it is a prerequisite that the patient in question not be suffering from diarrhea[70].

Illness cleanses the body, so that the person not only becomes cleansed of sins, but is also cleansed in the literal sense[71]. This concept is still currently accepted by the Jewish people. It is also stated: "when He heals all your illnesses, He also forgives all your sins"[72].

## VII   Incantations to Heal the Sick

The treatment of a disease, in all generations, was dependent upon the understanding of the cause thereof. *To treat the cause of the disease has been the desire and goal of therapists since times immemorial.* As long as one believed that the illness was caused by the presence of a perilous evil spirit (demon, Satan) in the patient, it was natural to attempt to drive it out of the patient, in order to cure the sickness. It is noteworthy that the Talmud does not at all refer to actual exorcism. However, the word "incantation" *(lachash)* is used very often, which we interpret to represent a very mild form of exorcism.

Concerning the basic question as to whether or not incantation is "a heathen practice", as is true of most aspects of superstition, and should therefore be prohibited, one can find supporters of both positions in the Talmud. Among the ancient Sages of the *Mishnah,* the *Tannaim,* there is not a single one who allows incantation, even if no names of idolatry are invoked during the incantation, and even if Biblical verses with God's name are recited. They declare that if someone "whispers a spell over a bodily illness" and says: *I will put none of these diseases upon thee, which I have brought upon the Egyptians, for I am the Lord that healeth thee*[73], he is

---

62. Hebrew: *gilin,* meaning coevals, those born under the same planetary influence
63. Ruth Rabbah 2:8
64. Shabbath 105b
65. Second Samuel 12:18
66. Ezekiel 24:16–18
67. Moed Katan 28a
67a. Hananiah, Mishael & Azariah
68. Nedarim 41a
69. Berachoth 57b
70. *Pesikta Rabbati* #33. Ed. Friedman p. 152a
71. Jerushalmi Berachoth 2; 4c
72. Explanation of Psalms 103:3
73. Exodus 15:26

deprived of everlasting bliss (i.e. the world to come). These Sages further prohibit one person from calling another to recite a Biblical verse to calm a frightened child, or to place a Bible or phylacteries on the child, in order that he fall asleep[74].

However, Rabbi Yochanan, the most prominent Palestinian Sage of the period of the *Amora'im* (sages of the *Gemara*), is not familiar in principle with this objection incantation. In fact there exists a small but significant number of magical incantations from his Babylonian contemporaries, in which are even contained Biblical verses with God's name therein[75]. It seems very doubtful, however, that these incantations originated with the Rabbis. In view of the numerous materials with cuneiform characters, it seems probably correct to assume that the Rabbis simply took them over from their heathen environment. Wherever necessary, the names of idolatrous deities seem to have been replaced with monotheistic designations.

Since incantation belongs to an occult science, the formulas used are mostly comprised of phrases unintelligible to us. Only the names of the patient and his mother are included in all incantations of antiquity. In some such incantations, the medicine-man expectorated, and this spitting out occurred before or after a Biblical verse was recited which contained God's name. This practice was considered to be particularly offensive[76].

The use of incantations is a very ancient heathen custom. In Homer[77], blood flow is said to have been stopped in this manner. Cato is said to have bequeathed an incantation which is said to be helpful for dislocations[78]; Marcus Varro has an incantation against podagra[79]. The Druids sang (incantations) for the Gauls[80] and the Alrunes for the Teutons. In Jerusalem, the 91st Psalm was sung as a *shir shel pega'im* or *shir shel nega'im*[81], as protection from evil spirits[82]. In the "center of intelligence", even today, one can observe "incantations of the rose" recited by the most intelligent people.

One "whispered a spell" to ward off snakes and scorpions, and to guard against them, and for the healing of eye illnesses[83]. It is related that Rabbi Meir used to hold discourses on Sabbath evenings, which were also attended by women. One husband, angry because his wife stayed out so late, swore that his wife could not return to the house unless she spat in the face of the speaker. When Rabbi Meir learned of this, he feigned an eye illness and asked that an intelligent woman *(chachama)* who understood the "whispering of spells" be brought. Such a woman was brought and she spat seven times in his face. Domestic peace was thus restored among the aforementioned couple[84].

Evidently, even in those days, women, in particular, made use of incantations[85], although the Talmudic Sages themselves were not frightened away from practicing this art. Thus, Rabbi Chanina went to visit the febrile Rabbi Yochanan and "uttered an incantation over him" whereby he was healed[86].

The use of incantations by physicians of antiquity is extolled by no less an authority than the great Galen. He states:

"some people believe that incantations are equivalent to fairy tales of old women. I, too, thought this way for a long time. As time passed, however, I became convinced of the value of incantations, because of their apparent efficacy. I learned of their use for scorpion bites, and also for bones which

---

74. Jerushalmi Shabbath 6; 8b
75. Shabbath 67a
76. Sanhedrin 101a
77. *Odyssey* 19:475
78. *De Re Rust.* 160
79. Plinius 28:3
80. Cic. de Divin. 1:49

81. Shebuoth 15b
82. Jerushalmi Shabbath 6; 8b
83. *Tosefta* Shabbath 7:23
84. Jerushalmi Sotah 1; 16d
85. Aboth 2:7; Jerushalmi Sanhedrin 7:25d
86. Song of Songs Rabbah 2:16

remained stuck in the throat, and which became immediately dislodged following the enunciation of an incantation, *di'epodes*. The incantation formulas fulfill their purpose"[87].

Incantation for a bone stuck in the throat, *bil'a,* is also mentioned in the Talmud, and the disciples of Jesus revealed the power of their master to be *soter* or healing, in that, as the Talmud itself asserts, they whispered spells, using his name, with good results[88].

A special form of incantation includes the "placing of one's hands" on the patient. This is also a heathen custom. When the Syrian general Naaman came to Elisha in order to be healed of his leprosy, he thought that the prophet would stand before him and move his hand up and down over the leprous site, so that the leper (Naaman) would recover[89]. Naaman did not expect a direct placing of the hand on his body, because touching a leper renders a person ritually unclean.

Placing the hands over a patient also played an important role in the legends about Jesus in which he healed the sick.

Wolzendorff[90] cites as proof that the miraculous healing of the people effected by Jesus was the result of "suggestion", the fact that his cures were not successful in Galilee; because there, he and his family were known[91]. Jesus himself complained: *a prophet is not without honor, but in his own country, and among his own kin, and in his own house*[92].

Maimonides quotes the Talmudic decrees concerning incantations as follows: "if one was stung by a scorpion or a snake, it is permitted to whisper a spell over the affected part, so as to soothe the patient and give him reassurance. Although the procedure is absolutely useless, it has been permitted because of the patient's dangerous condition, so that he should not become distraught. One who whispers a spell over a wound, at the same time reciting a verse from the Torah, or one who recites a verse over a child to save it from fright or one who places a Torah scroll or phylacteries on an infant, to induce it to sleep, are not only considered in the category of sorcerers and soothsayers, but are also included among those who repudiate the Torah itself; for they use its words to cure the body, whereas the Torah is only medicine for the soul..."[93].

## VIII    Amulets to Ward off Sickness

Incantations only provide help when the tragedy has already occurred, or when the illness has already taken hold. However, a person who imagined that he was constantly surrounded by evil spirits which lie in wait for him required an additional protective device; and he believed that amulets which he constantly carried with him provided such protection. The use of such amulets is quite ancient. Beginning with the wing-case of the holy beetle which the Egyptians of the earliest times cut into their precious stones, amulets have maintained their powers unabatedly throughout millennia by all peoples, in spite of the prohibition of their use by church councils, and in spite of the decree of Charles the Great. Even today, amulets demonstrate their triumph over worldly wisdom and Divine teachings in their existence as four-leaved clover pendants which adorn our women.

To the Jews, the amulet was known by the name *kemiya*. It was a protective device for human beings and animals[94], and consisted either of a written parchment or of roots[95] or herbs[96]. It was worn on a small chain, or in a signet-ring or in a tube[97]. A

---

87. In *Alexander of Tralles*. ed. Puschmann. 2:474 from a writing called "üeber die aerztliche Behandlung bei Homer"
88. Jerushalmi Shabbath 14; 14d
89. Second Kings 5:11
90. *Gesundheitspflege und Medizin der Bibel. Christus als Arzt.* Wiesbaden 1903 p. 59

91. Mark 6:3; St. Matthew 13:58
92. Mark 6:4
93. *Hilchoth Akkum* 11:11-12
94. *Tosefta* Shabbath 4:5
95. *ibid* 4:9
96. Jerushalmi Shabbath 8b
97. *ibid*

*kemiya* was considered proven in its efficacy (*mumcha* meaning *probatum*) if it had been helpful on three occasions. An assurance by a physician who prescribed or made such an amulet was accepted as credible without question[98]. For in antiquity, amulets were considered part of the legitimate therapeutic armamentarium of the physician. Galen describes their use by the physician Archigenes[99].

An example of "holy" signs and amulets originating even in later times is the following: in a vision, the prophet Ezekiel hears the Lord saying: *set a mark (thav) upon the foreheads of the men that sigh and that cry for all the abominations.... These shall slay the others, but do not touch those with the mark*[100]. The Septuagint correctly translates this *thav* as *semeion* (sign or mark), but the Vulgate translates *signa Thau super frontes,* and, since the latter is the translation officially recognized by the Christian church, one interpreted this *Thau*, which is equivalent to the Greek *Thav,* as a cross. Thus, not only did the hog of the holy Antonius of Padua appear as a prophylactic against pestilence, together with the *Tau* cross of the Bible but they were mentioned again in 1437 on the amulets which represent the Holy Sebastian as the patron of the plague[101].

There was no objection in Jewish religious law against the use of amulets; they were apparently deeply rooted in popular belief. It became a basic principle to allow any measure for healing a patient other than idolatry, incest and murder. No prohibition was imposed on any remedy, even if it was recognized as encompassing superstition, if the patient believed in its therapeutic efficacy, as long as none of the three aforementioned factors was involved[102]. Amulets could therefore not contain heathen matters. It was considered to be a punishment from Heaven that among the Maccabees, those men who fell in battle wore under their shirts small amulets of the idols of Jamnia, which were forbidden to Jews to wear[103]. It was specifically prohibited to make amulets from the frankincense of idols, or from the trees of Ashtaroth, even though these were thought to have extraordinary healing powers[104]. When the febrile Rabbi Acha was given well water from a "holy grove"[105], he refused to drink it.

Nevertheless, one observes that ill people made pilgrimages to idols and returned healed. Such, however, was thought to be coincidental, as follows:

Zunin once said to Rabbi Akiba: "we both know in our heart that there is no truth in idolatry. Nevertheless, we see people enter a shrine crippled and come out cured". Rabbi Akiba gave a parable in reply: "a trustworthy man lived in a city, and all his townsmen except one used to deposit their money in his charge without witnesses. This man, however, came to deposit his money with witnesses, but on one occasion he forgot and made his deposit without witnesses. The wife of the trustworthy man suggested to her husband that he deny the deposit. The man answered her: 'Because this man acted in an untrustworthy manner, shall I destroy my reputation for trustworthiness?' When God afflicts a person with illness, he immediately determines when the afflictions come and when they shall depart, on which day, at which hour, through whom and through which remedy. On the day when the illness was supposed to depart, the patient perchanced to go to an idolatrous shrine. God should now punish him by not ending the affliction. But should God change the predetermined course of nature because of this fool?" (obviously not!)[106].

---

98. *ibid*
99. *De Compos. Medicam.* Book 2. Kühn 12:573
100. Ezekiel 9:4–6
101. see Hoefler. *Janus* 1902 p. 235; Abbildung der Pestblätter. *Mitteilungen zur Geschichte der Medizin.* Vol. 6 p.540.
102. Shabbath 66a
103. Second Maccabees 12:40
104. Exodus Rabbah 16:2; see also Pesachim 25a and Abodah Zarah 28a–b
105. or "from the phallus of Doron"?, the place in the text (Jerushalmi Shabbath 14d) is mutilated
106. Abodah Zarah 55a

This assertion of Rabbi Akiba is noteworthy in many respects, particularly in his great respect for the laws of nature, in contrast to the belief in miracles which was so prevalent during his era (approximately 17 to 130 C.E.).

Illegal sexual intercourse is also prohibited as a therapeutic modality. When a man was once deathly ill as a result of an unhappy love affair, and the physicians stated that the only cure would be for him to cohabit with the coveted woman, the Rabbis categorically asserted that he should rather die. They would not even allow him an unchaste look at the forbidden woman[107].

The prohibition of murder as a therapeutic method seems rather strange to us. The Talmud bases this prohibition on the fact that "your blood is not redder than that of your neighbor"[108]. But the customs of antiquity explain the origin of this decree. One is reminded of the report of Plinius[109] that when an Egyptian king contracted leprosy, the illness became *populis funebre,* because baths containing human blood were used for his healing. The same was reported also from Egypt by Marcellus Empiricus[110]. Furthermore, Aeschylus put these words into Clytemnestra's mouth that: "a bath in blood is alien to me"[111].

There is also a report of this horrifying procedure in Jewish writings. When the king of Egypt became leprous, his astrologers promised him a cure if he would bathe in the blood of 150 children, mornings and evenings. Scripture calls him "dead"[112] because "a leper is considered equivalent to a deceased person"[113]. The king snatched Jewish children for this purpose, until God had mercy on the Jews and healed him. Thus relates the *Midrash*[114]. This terrible procedure was also later found in the history of Pope Innocent VIII, King Constantine, and at the hand of Heinrich Von Hartman Von Der Aue, as he advised the Salernitans[115]. Rabbi Chisda is probably expressly fighting against this practice when he raises an otherwise unintelligible question in Talmudic law, namely whether or not one may save the life of an important person by sacrificing the life of a lesser person[116]. He obviously energetically answers in the negative. The only case in which, even today, a homicide is allowed is when it is necessary to destroy the fetus in the mother's womb to save the life of the mother. This case is mentioned in the *Mishnah*[117] with the restriction that if the head of the fetus has already been born, an embryotomy on the living child is no longer permitted.

All other laws of Judaism are set aside in the face of danger to life, whether they are laws pertaining to healing on the Sabbath, or dietary laws. The latter is especially noteworthy, because, in the medical writings of the Arabs, who are kinsmen of the Jews, whenever a recipe requiring wine as one of its ingredients is mentioned, the author always notes: "wine is forbidden to us by Allah. If it is the patient's fate to recover, he will recover even without wine"[118]. In fact, in a case of danger to life, one must be stricter in doing everything needed to save that life than in the observance of ritual laws[119].

Particular attention should be paid to the laws for a seriously ill patient on the Day of Atonement. Ordinarily, the consumption of food and beverage on this day is prohibited in the Bible and punishable by death at the hand of heaven. The *Mishnah*

107. Sanhedrin 75a
108. Pesachim 25b
109. *Hist. Natur.* 26:1
110. *De Medicina.* Chapt 19 ed. Cornar 1536 fol. 130
111. *Agamemnon.* translation of Wolzogen p. 23
112. Exodus 2:23
113. Nedarim 64b
114. Exodus Rabbah 1:34
115. Proof is found in Friedreich's *Zur Bibel*

1:225, note 4; Strack's *Blutaberglaube,* p. 36 ff; Freytag's *Mitteilungen zur Geschichte der Medizin* Vol. 7:452. An attempted explanation is that of Magnus in *Organ und Bluktherapie* p. 51
116. Jerushalmi Shabbath 14; 14d
117. Oholoth 7:6
118. For example in Abulcasem. Ed. Channing p. 371
119. Chullin 9b: *Sakanta chamira me'issura*

states as follows: a seriously ill patient is fed on the Day of Atonement according to the judgement of experts. If none are available, the patient's own request for food is heeded until he says "enough"[120]. The *Gemara* explains the *Mishnah* in the name of Rabbi Yannai: if the patient says: "I need" food and drink and the physician says: "he does not need it, and fasting will not harm him", one follows the patient's assertion, because *the heart knoweth his own bitterness*[121], even though the physician perhaps objectively knows better. However, if the physician says "the patient needs food", but the patient says "I do not need it", then the physician's words are heeded, because the patient is perhaps delirious. There is no difference whether one physician or a hundred physicians give their opinion; decisive is the opinion of the one who votes for alleviating the patient's illness[122].

Similarly, it is considered to be false piety and punishable, if someone observes the Sabbath laws thereby neglecting the needs of a seriously ill patient. Everything required for this patient should be done on the Sabbath without hesitation, not by servants or gentiles, but even by the greatest rabbis of Israel who have the *obligation* to teach by example, so that no human life is placed in danger because of ignorance of the law. "He who is zealous in desecrating the Sabbath for a seriously ill patient is praiseworthy"[123].

## IX  Healing by Magic

Incantations and amulets do not exhaust the number of magical remedies used in healing. There also exist many things which, like the aforementioned ones, enjoy universal and permanent acceptance. Among these is the efficacy of knotted knots (i.e. garland plants) which were already used in love magic by Vergil[124], and which found prominent use as thread knots in the Middle Ages and later. In the Talmud, their efficacy is described differently: "three knots arrest the illness, five heal it, and seven help even against magic"[125]. One here observes, according to heathen custom, *numero deus impari gaudet,* the use of numbers three and seven which were also holy to monotheism, and the use of the number five which, as a pentagon, was a symbol of Hygieia to the Pythagoreans.

During the time of Abaye (300 C.E.), it was recommended that some amulets and "medicaments", particularly those against fever, be worn around the neck, on a braid of hair, whereas the *Tosefta* still prohibits "the tying of a thread on a person" as a heathen superstition[126].

The nail from the crucifix of an executed person is efficacious against the illness called *ababitha*[127]. Plinius states that such a nail, wrapped in wool and tied around the neck, cures fever; and a chip from the gallows is a good talisman for modern intelligent women[128].

Folk remedies are thus preserved, in spite of enlightenment, although they alter their form. If, during the era of mesmerism, one accepted the healing and protective powers of amulets as being proven, and explained their action by electric currents[129], the cunning quacks of our times need only designate any metal plate as being electrified or magnetized. The person who imagines himself to be highly intelligent and enlightened would thus wear an ingenious amulet identified as a galvanized crucifix, and would derive therefrom the same efficacy as that felt by the derided simple people of the distant past.

120. Yoma 8:5
121. Proverbs 14:10
122. Yoma 83a
123. *ibid* 84b
124. Ecl. 8:77
125. Shabbath 66b
126. *Tosefta* Shabbath 7:11
127. Jerushalmi Shabbath 6; 8c
128. Plinius. *Histor. Natur.* 28:4
129. Ennomoser, *Magnetismus* p. 200

The New Testament also speaks of various types of magic. From the skin of the Apostle Paul, *one brought handkerchiefs and aprons unto the sick, so that the diseases departed from them and the evil spirits went out of them*[130]. Sick people were carried onto the streets and placed on beds and couches, so that when Peter came by, his shadow might pass over some of them[131].

Judges are supposed to acquire a knowledge of magic *ex-officio,* in order to be able to appropriately adjudicate a criminal case involving magic[132]. Although the physician is often called to testify as an expert witness in the Talmud, the magician never attained such status or recognition for his art.

## X    Medical Therapeutics

The number of remedies and therapeutic measures mentioned in the Talmud which one can ascribe to the *period of positivism* is relatively small. This should not be surprising, if one remembers that the Talmud is not a medical text. Furthermore, after the use of legal-medical therapeutics, as opposed to magic, had been sanctioned, a discussion of the individual remedies which are employed is outside the scope of the Talmud. At the most, there might be a discussion as to whether or not one or another remedy which was prohibited by dietary laws, such as the liver of a rabid dog or donkey urine, were acceptable as therapeutic measures. As already mentioned, however, these are permitted as medical remedies.

Superstitions were, of course, not defensible; to apply the fat of an executed ox on a wound as a therapeutic measure is forbidden, although the offense is not punishable[133]. Totally isolated, and purely a personal view, is the opinion of those who refused all medical therapeutic measures. They might be considered as forerunners of the modern "natural cure" proponents. For example, Rabbi Chiya advised his son: drink no *samma* and do not let any of your teeth be extracted[134].

What should be designated as "medicine in the positive sense" must be measured by the standard of antiquity, although many of the most ancient remedies, such as cockroaches, are again utilized in the therapeutic armamentarium of modern times.

---

130. Acts 19:12
131. *ibid* 5:15
132. Sanhedrin 17a
133. Pesachim 24b
134. *ibid* 113a

# CHAPTER IV

## *SICKNESSES AND THEIR TREATMENT*
### (SPECIAL PATHOLOGY AND THERAPY)

### PART I
### EPIDEMICS

#### I  Plague (Pestilence)

According to the definition of Galen[1] which remained unchanged by physicians until the sixteenth century[2], plague is an illness which kills many people in a short period of time. According to the *Mishnah*[3], which, as a law-book, requires exact numbers, pestilence or *deber* is spoken of if in a city such as Amiko which can furnish five hundred foot soldiers — the aged, women, and children are not included in the count[4] — three men die within three consecutive days (i.e. one man per day)[5]. For a large city, such as Akko, which has 1500 young men, the same proportion applies i.e. nine deaths over three consecutive days. The deaths, however, should not all occur on the same day (because it would then suggest death by poisoning or, according to *Rashi,* it would be considered to be a chance occurrence).

Nothing is mentioned about the direct causation of plague. However, there are numerous allusions thereto: large aggregations of people, particularly during a time of lack of nourishment, promote outbreaks of epidemics. *And I will bring a sword upon you...and when ye are gathered together within your cities, I will send the pestilence among you*[6]. *The sword is without and the pestilence and the famine within*[7]. This reason for the occurrence of plague in association with the counting of the people, however, as is generally accepted, is *not* valid; because the counters went to the individual tribes and required ten months to complete their task[8]. Thus an "assemblage of masses of people" never took place at all in such a case.

The dissemination of epidemics is a fact which is well-known. When Mar Samuel heard that pestilence was raging in the far-away place called Be Hozae, he ordained a fast of supplication because he feared its spread to his town since an active caravan

1. Galen. *De Acut. Morb. Victu* 1:8; Kühn 15:429
2. Puschmann. *Wiener Med. Wchschr.* 1895 Col. 1553
3. Taanith 3:4
4. Jerushalmi Taanith 3; 66d *Tosofoth Yom*

*Tob's* commentary on the *Mishnah*
5. Taanith 21b
6. Levit. 26:25
7. Ezekiel 7:15
8. Second Samuel 24:8 and Exodus 30:12

traffic *(sheyara)* existed between the two places which the pestilence accompanied[9].
One cannot rely on a river to prevent the plague from crossing, because we cannot take
away the peoples' ferryboats. Rabbi Judah also believed in the possibility of
dissemination of plague by swine, because when he heard that pestilence was raging
among the swine, he also ordained a fast, because "their intestines are like those of
human beings"[10].

Whether or not *bubonic plague* can be spread by swine is still disputed today; on
the other hand, there can be no doubt about the association between terrestrial
revolutions (earthquakes) and outbreaks of pestilence. Even the pestilence mentioned
in the Bible[11] was preceded by a sudden splitting of the earth into which the rabble of
Korach sank. Concerning the Indian pestilence, Sticker reports[12] that the
overwhelming majority of infections originated from the lower extremities. Hence, in
spite of their uncleanliness, the Mohammedans, who wore shoes, had no more
pestilence than the barefoot, but very clean, Hindus. It is perhaps this observation
which prompted Rab to make a statement which, at first glance, seems exaggerated:
one should sell even the beams of one's house to provide money with which to buy
shoes for one's feet[13].

Naturally, these remarks *do not by far* give one the right to interpret the epidemics
mentioned in the Bible and Talmud to have been bubonic plague. In the sources, the
terms *deber, magepha, nega* and *negeph* seem to be used interchangeably[14]. *Mothana,*
even to the Assyrians, refers to "the great death", just as *mothan,* which is said to be
the explanation of the Biblical *behala*[15], is "an illness which rapidly kills creatures"[16].
However, it is not possible, because of the dearth of the symptomatology throughout,
to establish for certainty whether or not the Biblical or Talmudic diseases mentioned
refer to bubonic plague, cholera, dysentery, typhus or some other epidemic illness.
Thus, according to Rabbi Nachman, *magepha,* which is the disease from which the
scouts died[17], refers to *askara,* which is epidemic croup[18]. The description of the
plague which the prophet Zachariah threatened as punishment on the nations that
would wage war on Jerusalem is to be taken in the poetic sense and is indeterminate:
*their flesh shall consume away while they stand upon their feet, and their eyes shall
consume away in their holes, and their tongue shall consume away in their mouth*[19].
The *Midrashim*[20] consider this to be a portrayal of leprosy.

Epidemics are nearly always fatal wherever they occur: in the time of Korach
14,700 died; at the *Ba'al Peor* 24,000 died[21], and after the already-mentioned counting
of the people by David, 70,000 people died. One should nevertheless not forget that in
each instance, the plague involved an entire population that was either travelling or at
war.

The most assured remedy against an epidemic is flight: *he who remains in the city
shall die by the sword, and by the famine and by the pestilence; but he that goeth out,
...he shall live...sayeth the Lord*[22]. This fact that one can, so to speak, flee the decree
of God, was a considerable embarrassment to the church fathers already; and Luther
could not easily get over it[23]. Among the Turks, the Ulema in 1837 declared every

9. Taanith 21b
10. *ibid*
11. Numbers 17:46
12. Sticker. *Wiener Klin. Rundschau* 10,98
13. Shabbath 129a
14. *negeph* is equivalent to *magepha:* Numbers 17:11 and 17:13; Isaiah 22:17 is equivalent to Numbers 25:9; *magepha* is the same as *deber:* Second Samuel 24:21
15. Levit. 26:16
16. *Sifra* fol.111c
17. Numbers 14:36
18. Sotah 35a
19. Zechariah 14:12
20. *Tanchuma Thazria* ed. Buber. p.21b; Yalkut *loc.cit.*
21. Numbers 25:8
22. Jeremiah 21:9-10
23. Anastasius Sinaita. quaest. 114. *Maxim. Bibl. Vet. Patr.* Vol.9. Lugdanae 1677. Diemerbroeck. *De Peste.* Amstelod. 1665 fol 127

precautionary measure against pestilence to be sinful. Nevertheless, a Mufti soon thereafter declared that a Moslem does not commit a sin if he leaves a place devastated by pestilence to move to another place, provided that he appeals for the grace of Allah[24]. But the fact remains, and for us requires no further explanation.

During an epidemic of plague, Raba used to close his window shutters[25], because the prophet laments: *For death is come up unto our windows*[26]. According to an ancient tradition, if there is pestilence (or famine) in the town, "gather your feet" (i.e. withdraw to a safe place, flee)[27]. "When dogs cry (or howl), the angel of death has come to the town"[28] is an assertion in which the Arabs also believe[29], and which is widely accepted in the Orient even today.

During the time of the *Mishnah,* when an epidemic broke out, a fast was decreed as penitence for transgressions committed, because pestilence comes on that account[30], and the ram's horn *(shofar)* is blown[31]. Whether the latter was a type of supplication[32], a plea for help to the Lord, or, as the rationalists in the Talmud suggest, the horn was sounded to call for human help and to alert people to the danger[33], or whether it was a simple signal as was used in the Temple in Jerusalem, cannot be established[34].

During the epidemic that followed the rebellion of Korach, as soon as the high priest noticed the outbreak of the pestilence, he took fire from the altar onto his censer, and placed incense thereon and stood between the living and those who had already died of the pestilence, and the pestilence was restrained[35]. Even this bringing of incense by the high priest has not escaped the fate of being considered a disinfectant measure; no more so than the ceremony of the ashes of the red heifer[36] and many others. One certainly cannot deny that the burning of incense, whose composition we know, produces vapors of ether-like oils which have antiseptic properties. Nor can it be doubted that "the entire original matter is rich in potassium and sodium salts", and that the added cedar-wood and hyssop are also rich in volatile oils[37]. However, would anyone believe, even if he only had the most superficial knowledge of bacteriology, that one can render an infected person aseptic by just *sprinkling a few drops of liquid* on him, even if it is the strongest antiseptic? Or can one restrain a serious epidemic by producing some resin vapors on a coal burner? Our mothers and nurses may be forgiven for harboring such beliefs; they imagined to have made the sickroom germ-free by spraying phenol water. However, men of science should not be misled, in their zealousness to find the most modern viewpoints and methods in the Bible, into believing such nonsense; because *instead of glorifying the Holy Scriptures,* which is their intent, *they make them and themselves laughable.* Among readers, only a small minority has the inclination and the ability to verify the original sources, and therefore readers accept as historical tradition what is in reality only the fantasy of the author. One *must* accept the fact that a religion is not just concerned with the *physical* well-being of its adherents. The Bible, too, is primarily a religious document, and not a handbook of medicine or hygiene. At best, the fact that the priest "stood between the living and the dead", i.e. somehow separated the sick from the healthy, can be considered to be a useful hygienic measure.

24. Stern, Bernhard. *Medizin. Aberglaube und Geschlechtsleben in der Turkei.* 1903. Vol 1:227
25. Baba Kamma 60b
26. Jeremiah 9:20
27. Baba Kamma 60b
28. *ibid*
29. Lane. *Thousand & One Nights* 2:56
30. Aboth 5:12
31. Taanith 3:4
32. Numbers 10:9
33. as in Ezekiel 33:6
34. Taanith 19b
35. Numbers 17:10-13
36. *ibid* 19:1 ff
37. Nossig. *Sozialhygiene der Juden.* 1894. p.41; Baginsky. Ad. *Die Hygienische Grundzüge der Mos. Gesetzgebung.* Braunschweig 1895 p.23

## II    The Plague of the Philistines

In their victory over the Israelites, the Philistines captured the Holy Ark and placed it in Ashdod. *And the hand of the Lord was heavy upon them of Ashdod, and He destroyed them, and He smote them with "ophalim"*[38]. And they sent the Ark to Gath. However, here too *the Lord was against the city with a very great destruction, and He smote the men of the city, both small and great, and "ophalim" cracked open in them*, or, according to another textual reading, *"ophalim" occurred in their secret parts*[39]. They sent the Ark to Ekron, the third main city, but, just as in the earlier two cities, there occurred a *deadly destruction throughout all the city. And the people that did not die were smitten with "ophalim", and the cry of the city went up to heaven*[40].

After the Ark had been in the land of the Philistines for seven months, their priests and diviners who were consulted advised that the Ark be returned, together with five golden *ophalim* and five golden mice[41]. The transfer to the Levites occurred in Beth-Shemesh, and there the transport cart and the kine which pulled the cart were burned and the Ark was placed on a large stone[42]. And the Lord smote 50,070 men of Beth-Shemesh, *because they had looked into the Ark of the Lord*[43].

This incident occurred approximately in the year 1000 B.C.E.

The word *ophalim,* other than in the above narrative, occurs only once more in ancient Hebrew writings, namely in a warning in the Bible concerning punishment for sin: *The Lord will smite thee with the botch of Egypt and with "ophalim" and with "garab" and with "cheres", from which thou canst not be healed*[44]. Etymology, admittedly the weakest help in archaeological investigations, teaches that, to the Canaanites, *ophel* refers to a mountain or hill. To the Arabs, as Lane proves with innumerable citations, *aphalah* refers to *res in pudendis feminae vel camelae, herniae in viris similis*[45], i.e. perhaps vaginal prolapse. Also, in Assyrian, *ublu* perhaps means "boil or swelling"[46]; according to Jensen[47], it should be read *uplu* and means "venereal ulcer"(?). The common meaning of the root of this word is therefore probably *tumuit* (swelling). Therefore, *ophalim* could refer to every round structure of the human body, whether it is a normal one such as the *nates, edra* or *edrai,* as the Septuagint regularly translates the word, or illness-related swelling of round form such as buboes, hemorrhoids, etc.

In the aforementioned warning of punishment, however, the word is obviously written in parallel with other names of sicknesses: *schechin, garab, cheres* — Geiger very capriciously eliminates the copulative *vav* —[48] and therefore itself probably designates the name of an illness. If the *nates* are referred to, then one would have expected the definite article: "and *the ophalim* cracked open in them".

The Masoretes ordinarily substituted for *ophalim,* the less obscene *techorim*[49], which to the Syrians means *nates*[50]. The Aramaic translators use only the word *techorim.*

They even interpret: *And the Lord smites His enemies in their hinder parts*[51] to refer to *techorim;* thus: *He smites them on their buttocks.* The word is derived

38. First Samuel 5:6
39. *ibid* 5:9
40. *ibid* 5:11-12
41. *ibid* 6:1-4
42. *ibid* 6:14-15
43. *ibid* 6:19
44. Deut. 28:27
45. so too Freytag. S.V.
46. Delitzsch. *Wörterbuch.* Leipzig 1895 p.7
47. Jensen. *Theologische Litteratur Zeitung.*

1895 col. 250
48. Geiger. *Urschrift.* p.408
49. Megillah 25b
50. Bocharti. *Hierozoicon.* Frankfurt 1675, 1:365 ff. *techara* in Hebrew, *techora* in Syrian, equivalent to *tenesmos* in Greek; constipation in Hippocrates. Nöldeke, *Beiträge.* 32. Löw
51. Psalms 78:66

from *techar* meaning to press and is translated as "hemorrhoids or swellings on the anus which protrude during tenesmus"[52], as if they were the oppressors rather than the oppressed.

In the narration of the Bible, one can thus recognize the picture of an epidemic which spread through the transporting of the Holy Ark from town to town, the results of which were simulated in votive offerings. From the report from Ekron *(vide supra),* it follows that, under certain circumstances, death can occur before the boils have yet developed. The boils usually develop in those parts of the body which are concealed by clothing.

With great probability, one can assume that this portrayal of the illness calls for the assumption of *bubonic plague.* It is known as a deadly pestilence; many die of lung pestilence before they develop buboes; others develop buboes in the concealed areas of the body, particularly in the groins and axillae.

Josephus uses the name *dysenteria* to describe this illness, but his assertion that the patients concomitantly had severe vomiting[53] makes us suspect that he really meant Asiatic cholera. An objection to his explanation may arise from the aforementioned linguistic difficulty from Deuteronomy. On the other hand, *nates* as votive offerings are just as strange as buboes or a phallus.

Probably misled by Aquilas' translation *tes phagdaines elkos* (eroding ulcer), a large number of commentators, headed by Haeser, advocate the opinion that the epidemic was due to syphilis. Syphilis is always mentioned in medical historical studies where definitive concepts are lacking. Friedreich[54] also adopts this viewpoint and supports his contention in that: "Buxtorf, considered to be a reliable author, translates the Hebrew word *efolim* as *mariscae.*" Even if one could admit that an epidemic of syphilis could affect such a large number of people in the space of seven months, it is unacceptable that syphilis could kill people in such *epidemic proportions* as is portrayed here.

Another series of commentators, particularly from ancient times, considers *ophalim* to be hemorrhoidal tags. This, however, is not an epidemic sickness, and one cannot simply do away with this fact, in that Mussaphia teaches: *hämorrhoides caecae, interdum morbus epidemius*[55].

It remains striking that none of the ancient commentators mentioned our assumption that the epidemic was one of bubonic plague. The knowledge concerning the form of this illness must have gradually but completely become extinct in the tradition, and this apparently occurred because there were no opportunities for renewed observation, since bubonic plague never again occurred in the Near East. Only Rufus speaks of buboes, and mentions that "the so-called epidemic buboes *(oi loimodeis kaloumenoi boubones)* are particularly lethal and acute; they are mentioned mostly in the area of Libya, Egypt and Syria. They are mentioned by Dionys the hunchback, and in greater detail by Dioscorides and Poseidonius in their writings concerning pestilence in Libya"[56]. These aforementioned physicians lived at about the time of Christ's birth[57] and there is thus a thousand year span between them and the plague of the Philistines, during which nothing is recorded concerning the occurrence of the plague. In this manner, we can also answer the question posed by Michaelis[58] as to why the Bible has no laws against the plague as it does concerning leprosy and

52. Genesius. *Wörterbuch.* S.V.
53. Josephus. *Antiquities.* Book 6 Chapt. 1:1 and *War of the Jews.* Book 5 Chapt. 9:4
54. Friedreich. *Zur Bibel* 1:245
55. Benjamin Mussaphia. alias Dionysii dicti: *Sacro-Medicae Sententiae.* Hamburg 1640 on 5:6 Sent. 18

56. Oribasius. *Coll.* Book 44:17. Ed. Bussemaker & Dar. 3:607 & the note on p.708
57 Fuchs in Puschmann's *Handbuch* 1:336, note 314; Hirsch. *Histor. Geogr. Pathol.* Vol. 1:349
58. *Mos. Recht.* 4:290

gonorrhea; because it does not testify to a wide view "if we are to assume that temporary decrees, and not permanent ordinances, were made for an illness which strikes suddenly".

The offering of figures portraying sick parts of the body, as thanks for one's healing, or as a sin offering, was originally a heathen custom, and is demonstrable among all peoples of antiquity. The Christian Church also mentions it since the fifth century. It was unknown among the Jews.

We do not know what the votive offering of the golden mice represents. The Septuagint and Josephus state that it was simply a present to thank for the repulsion of an additional plague of mice, as suggested by the phrase of the text: *mice that mar the land*[59]. Others think that the mice were considered in the sense of *musculi*, i.e. the muscles of the buttocks[60]. In recent times, Sticker indicates that experience has shown that a large epidemic of rat deaths — the Hebrew word *achbor* also means rat[61] — precedes an outbreak of bubonic plague, and that this association was already recognized by the Philistines, and they therefore also brought golden mice as a votive offering[62]. This opinion cannot be refuted.

On the other hand, Aschoff points out that the mouse in general is the picture of destruction[63]. The pestilence-sender Apollo is called *Smintheus* after the mouse; on certain coins he menaces with a mouse which is held in the right hand, whereas the left hand shows an advancing arrow[64]. It is also noteworthy that, although the Biblical narrative describes a pestilence among the troops of Sennacherib[65], Herodotus relates that a large horde of mice destroyed the troops[66]. On the other hand, the postscript of Peypers that "in the Temple of Thebes, Ptah, the god of destruction, is holding a mouse in his hand"[67], is in error. "Ptah is not the god of destruction, and Ptah was not idolized in Thebes. I do not know of any god in Egypt that is holding a mouse. Sett is the evil god, and this animal head was for a certain time thought to be the head of the jerboa (which is not a mouse, however, in the zoological sense)"[68].

It is difficult to explain how the mouse came to be the symbol of pestilence in spite of Aschoff's assertion that "terrible mouse plagues are in general a symbol of epidemics"; for locusts would seem to be a more logical symbol. Perhaps the animals which come forth in hordes from underground holes in the fields — obviously field mice — and which originally were interpreted to be a sign of underground deities which bring evil on mankind, gave the heathens their justification for eating mice which they offered as sacrifices in order to "sanctify themselves and purify themselves from sin"[69].

It is doubtful whether the plague at Beth Shemesh is to be considered in the above manner. According to Josephus, 70 people were killed by a lightning flash because they had touched the Holy Ark, and they were not priests[70]. A cunning writer at the end of the eighteenth century, in all seriousness, deduced from this passage that the Holy Ark was only a very large Leyden jar so that it could very easily kill a large number of people at one time — half a million, according to the Biblical text. To the same author, the entire Jewish Tabernacle is nothing more than a collection of electric

59. First Samuel 6:5
60. Wunderbar. Heft 3 p.19
61. Lewysohn. *Zoologie des Talmuds*. p.107. Erroneous. Löw
62. Sticker. *Wiener Klin. Rundschau.* 1898 No. 10-11
63. Janus 5:611
64. Klausen, Rud. Heinr., *Aeneas und die*

*Penaten.* Hamburg & Gotha. 1839, 1:72
65. Second Kings 19:35
66. Herodot. *Histor.* 2:141
67. Janus. *loc. cit.* notes
68. Mitteilungen von Oefeles 16-7-02
69. Isaiah 66:17
70. Josephus. *Antiquities.* Book 6 Chapt. 1:4

apparatuses[71]. Similar discoveries were made by Axmann[72] and Gesell[73] in our own critical century.

## III   Askara

*Askara* is a punishment for slandering. Just like slander, *askara* begins in the insides of the body and ends (afflicts last) in the mouth[74]. It affects primarily children[75], often in night attacks; adults are also afflicted, as were the scouts in the wanderings of the Jews in the desert[76] and the large number of disciples of Rabbi Akiba who were killed in an epidemic between Passover and Pentecost[77]. Whereas, ordinarily, the trumpets are sounded, as mentioned above, to announce the outbreak of an epidemic only after three deaths have occurred therefrom, *askara* is an illness that was so feared that even after one death, the above measure (of blowing the trumpets) is implemented[78]. Death occurs by asphyxiation[79]; it is the hardest death of the 903 types of death that exist. Death by *askara* is like tearing out threads of wool from thorns that lie under ferns, or like forcing a ship's cable through a narrow hole in the mast[80]; this is how difficult the death throes are, and with what difficulty the soul leaves the body[81]. He who eats lentils once a month, and uses salt on every solid food, and adds water to every beverage, keeps *askara* away from his house[82].

It is likely that the illness known as *serunke* or *sirvanke*[83] is similar to the sickness *askara*.

Rabbi Joseph said: although the *Sanhedrin* is no longer in existence (and capital punishment cannot be decreed by Jewish courts), the four forms of capital punishment still exist. He who would have been sentenced to strangulation is either drowned in the river, or dies of *serunke*[84], or is captured by heathens who strangle him. Rabbi Ishmael ben Rabbi Jose is of the opinion that immediate bloodletting is indicated in this illness[85].

*Askara* is thus an exceedingly feared epidemic illness which afflicts primarily children, has its seat in the mouth (throat), and after a difficult "fight with death", kills the affected individual by asphyxia. Of all the illnesses known to us, this description only fits *diphtheria* and especially *diphtheritic croup*.

We cannot be certain about the exact date of our citation. However, we are probably not far from the truth if we propose the second century C.E.

From the often-cited description by Aretäus of the *Aigyptia kai Syriaka elkei*[86],

71. L. Bendavid. "Ueber die innere Einrichtung der Stiftshütte. Ein Beitrag zur Geschichte der Elektrizität." *Berlinisches Archiv der Zeit und Ihres Geschmackes*. 1797 Vol. 2 p.341
72. Axmann. *Himmel und Erde*. 1904 Vol. 16 p. 505. Aus der Naturwiss. Technik d. Altertums
73. Gesell. "Kannte Moses das Pulver?" Altona. 1907. cf. *Mitteilungen zur Geschichte der Medizin und die Naturwissen.* Vol. 7, 1907 No. 1 p.70
74. Shabbath 33a
75. Taanith 27b
76. Sotah 35a
77. Yebamoth 62b. Here 12,000 pairs of disciples are mentioned; so too Yalkut Eccles. on 11:6 (p.1094 a 24, Warsaw). However, Genesis Rabbah 61:3 & Eccles.

Rabbah on 11:6 fol 29b have 12,000 and *Tanchuma Chaye Sarah* p.61b Buber has 300
78. Tosefta Taanith 2:9; Jerushalmi Taanith 2; 66 d
79. Levit. Rabbah 18:4
80. Berachoth 8a. This is the translation according to the interpretation of *Aruch*. This and other portrayals of the flight fight with death are found in Moed Katan 28b; Levit. Rabbah 4:2; Eccles. Rabbah 6:6 fol 17b; *Tanchuma Mikketz* p.100b. Buber; *Midrash Psalms* on 11:7 p.516. Buber
81. Berachoth 40a
82. *ibid*
83. *Halachoth Gedoloth* p.117, end
84. i.e. suffocation or croup. Kethuboth 30 ab
85. Yoma 84a
86. Aretäus 1:9 ed. Ermerins p. 15

which today is unequivocally accepted as being diphtheria[87], we know that diphtheria existed in that time, at least in Syria which adjoins Palestine. The above-mentioned remark, that *askara* begins in the insides of the body and finally afflicts the mouth, also finds its analogue in the theory of Aretäus; unless one simply attributes the manifestations related to the gastrointestinal tract (vomiting, etc.) to the diphtheria itself which, like many other infectious diseases, can initiate them. According to him, this disease is initiated by the consumption of cold or raw things, etc. "If the inner organs, intestines, esophagus and chest organs become ill, then the throat, the tonsils and the surrounding parts are also affected through spitting".

The weak side of the entire diphtheria question was (and, in spite of antitoxic serum, is) the therapy. Not only do the Rabbis argue whether or not bloodletting is a therapeutic remedy, but many physicians in antiquity from Hippocrates[88] and on ask the question as to where and when to perform phlebotomy. The necessary information can be found in Coelius Aurelianus[89]. Even in modern times, after a long interval, voices are being heard in favor of bloodletting for the treatment of diphtheria[90].

The lentils that Rabbi Yochanan recommends as a prophylactic against *askara* have disappeared from the therapeutic armamentarium of modern times. They played a much greater role in the diet and therapy of antiquity. Galen[91], Dioscorides[92], and Plinius[93] devote separate chapters to a discussion of lentils. The gargling solution which Aretäus recommends for angina[94] contains lentil water, in addition to other ingredients. Hippocrates[95] and Plinius also report that the juice of cooked lentils is useful for ulcerations of the mouth.

The word *askara* was first identified by Michael Sachs[96] as a transcription of the Greek *eschara*. Abraham Hartog Israels[97] indicates that, by this name, Aretäus portrays a sickness which corresponds in its symptoms to the Talmudic *askara*. Since then, the assertion of Sachs has been generally accepted as proven. Nevertheless, it is very striking that the Greek word *eschara* is not found in the writings of any other medical author, other than in Aretäus, as the name of an illness. Naturally, I do not refer to the *eschara* meaning scab on a wound[98]. Furthermore, proof is lacking for even a possible popular use of the word in the above sense. It would, therefore, be most unusual that such a singular designation by an individual writer, who moreover was barely known in antiquity[99], should find such wide acceptance in the language of another people, and even in lay circles. Therefore, one might conjecture that Aretäus, who is explicitly speaking of an illness common to the Orient, with his otherwise rather remarkable expression: "the illness is *eschara* and is also so-called" *(eschara to pathos kai esti kai kaleetai),* meant the following: the illness is named according to the country in which it occurs in greatest frequency; so that the reverse is true i.e. the designation *eschara* of Aretäus is in fact a transcription of the Hebrew *askara.*

Purely from the philological viewpoint, against which one cannot argue, it

87. Bretonneau. *Arch.Gén. de Med.* 1855 Vol. 1 p.5; Hirsch. *Hist. Geogr. Path.* 3:31; Haeser. *Epidemischen Krankheiten* p.429, etc. etc.
88. Hippocrates. De Victus Rat. in *Morb. Acut.* ed. Foes 1657 fol 396
89. *Acut. Morb.* Book 3 Chapt. 4
90. *The Times & Register.* Jan. 27, 1894 p.59
91. Galen. *De Alimentorum Facultatibus* 1:18. Kühn 6:525
92. Dioscorides. *Peri Yles Iatrikes* 2:129. Sprengel 1:249

93. Plinius. *Histor. Natur.* 22:70
94. Aretäus. *Thérapie* 1:7 p.186
95. Hippocrates. *Epidemiarum* 7:26
96. Sachs. *Beiträge zur Sprach und Altertumsforschung.* Berlin 1852 No. 2 p.41 Note 48
97. Israels. *Nederl. Tydschr. vor Geneeskd.* 1861 fol. 205
98. cf. Gorräus. *Definitiones Med.* Paris 1622. fol. 225
99. Pagel. *Geschichte der Medizin.* Berlin 1898 p.108

has been established that *askara* is not a semitic word, but of a different derivation, specifically from the Greek *eschara*[100]; we must therefore be satisfied with the constatation of the above-mentioned remarkable fact.

Löw[101] considers the attempt of the Talmudists to derive *askara* from *sakar,* obstruction, to be an "etymological joke". According to them *askara* means obstruction, similar to the use in related languages of the same picture, i.e. the closure of the throat, strangulation, to designate *angina suffocans:* Syriac *chanoke* and Arabic *chunak* or *al-chavanik.*

I agree with Buxtorf that the designation *serunke* refers to the Greek *synagche*[102]. As is known, the disciples of Hippocrates included in this term any difficulty in swallowing, even that in which the patient reaches the point of asphyxia due to respiratory deficiency — without regard to the cause of the illness. Synanche is thus a more comprehensive designation than *askara.*

*Rashi* translates the word *askara* with *estranglement* or *estranguillon,* whenever according to his concept, it is a fatal illness. As a name for the illness, he selects the designation *bon malan,* the interpretation of which has been the subject of much effort. It is really a euphemism for *mal malan,* which occurs often, particularly in the Latin form *malum malannum.* I have written in detail on this matter[103].

The interpretation of the more recent writers Fürst[104] and Dalmann[105] that *askara* refers to *skirros* is naturally nonsense, because there never existed an epidemic scirrhus. Kraus combines the word *askara* with *esch,* fire[106]. The explanations of Lederer and Jeiteles *(askaris,* from which: a worm illness), and of Voitiez[107], (i.e. hypochondria and hysteria), together with their curious discussions and derivations, are correctly described by Israels[108] as a "type of etymological nonsense". The authors who espouse *askaris* have been called "absurd" by Horschetzky[109].

Buxtorf generally explains *askara* as "angina, *synagche, unde vulgus medicorum dicit squinantia*". Against the interpretation of Rabbinowicz[110] that *askara* means "le muguet" (fungus, thrush) speaks the deleterious character already ascribed to *askara* in the Talmud. The correct interpretation (croup) is found in Wunderbar[111], except that there is no mention of "the coughed out polypoid masses" in the Talmud. The explanation of Kohut (Kohut, *Aruch Completum,* s.v.) that *askara* is scarlet fever is under no circumstances correct, even though he had it certified to by two physicians.

According to Rosenbaum[112], the sores described by Aretäus are said to be a result of fellatio *(coitus in os).*

During the time of the Temple, the priestly divisions fasted every Wednesday so that *askara* should not attack children[113]. The Karaitic prayer book[114] contains the following passage in the Wednesday prayers: "and *askara* which you have bound to

100. Prof. Nöldeke. Strassburg. in a letter dated Nov. 24, 1894 Löw. in *Festschrift zum 70 Geburtstage A. Berliner.* Berlin 1903. p.299
101. *loc. cit.*
102. Löw. *loc. cit.* is in doubt on this point
103. Preuss. *Medizinische Blätter.* Vienna 1903 No. 24
104. Fürst. *Glossar. Graeco-Hebr.* Strassburg 1890. s.v.
105. Dalmann. *Aram-Neuhebr. Wörterbuch.* Frankfurt. 1901 s.v.
106. Kraus. *Krit. Etym. Med. Lexicon.* Göttingen 1844

107. Ben Chananya. *Monatsschrift* of L. Löw 1859 p.72, 170
108. *loc. cit.*
109. Note 107 p.322
110. Rabbinowicz. *La Médecine du Thalmud,* Paris, 1880, p.133
111. Wunderbar. *Biblisch-Talmudische Medizin,* Riga & Leipzig, 1852 Part 3 p.7
112. Rosenbaum. *Geschichte der Lustseuche im Altertum,* p.227
113. Taanith 27b
114. mentioned by J. Löwy in *Ben Chananya,* 1859 p.72

this day[115] — protect the children of thy people therefrom, that it not come in their mouths".

# PART II

## FEVER

The commentators debate whether or not the names of diseases which are mentioned in the Pentateuch as warnings of punishments altogether refer to human rather than grain illnesses: *and ye shall sow your seed in vain, for your enemies shall eat it*[116]. It is not possible to resolve this question since we only have the names, and are dependent on etymology, the weakest help in archaeological investigations. All the names are derived from a common root which means "to burn", such as *pyr* and *pyretos* which mean fire and fever. Those who are of the opinion that the illnesses named in the Bible are human sicknesses consider *kadachath, daleketh* and *charchur*[117] to be types of fever. Even for *shiddaphon,* which is always mentioned together with *yerakon* (anemia), this assumption seems to be the most plausible.

*Daleketh* must be a strong fever, because a pious man who was afflicted therewith, sat with a water bottle on the Day of Atonement in order to cool the heat of the fever[118]. The illness arises from drinking-water that was left uncovered. According to Ibn Ezra[119], *kadachath* is daily fever and *daleketh* is tertian or quartan fever.

Naturally, to the ancients, fever is an illness in and of itself, and not just a symptom: "the father of Publius suffered from *pyretois kai dysenteria* (fever and dysentery)"[120], not from feverish dysentery as we would say.

In the Talmud, the terms *chamma* and *shimsha,* both of which ordinarily refer to "the sun", are common designations for fever: the *Midrash*[121] expounds the famous sentence in Genesis: "as long as the earth exists, frost and heat from fever will not cease". A pun states that "at the side of warm bread, there is fever"[122]. Patients ill with fever used to drink a lot; hence, Hagar exhausted the supply of water in the bottle, when she traveled with the feverish Ishmael in the desert[123]. If a day-worker becomes ill with fever, the employer must compensate him for the time prior to and up to his illness[124].

If a baby develops fever, the circumcision is postponed until thirty or seven days after his complete recovery[125]. Fever is a more severe illness in the winter than in the summer, the analogy being a cold oven[126]. A great deal of firewood is needed to warm up an oven in the winter; so too, it requires a great deal of illness-producing material to evoke heat of fever in the cold body in the winter. Since a person with fever takes little or no nourishment, yet nevertheless lives and defecates and urinates, it was assumed that "the fever nourishes". If the head of a baby is born but the remainder of the body becomes stuck, then the child would starve if it were not nourished by the fever of the mother[127]. According to legend, there was no fodder for the lions in Noah's ark; they too were nourished by fever. Nevertheless, one cannot live from fever for more than thirteen days[128].

---

115. based on an interpretation of Genesis 1:14
116. Levit. 26:16
117. *ibid* & Deut. 28:22
118. Jerushalmi Terumoth 8; 45c
119. in his commentary on Deut. 28:22
120. Acts 28:8
121. Genesis Rabbah 34:11
122. Jerushalmi Shabbath 1; 4b
123. Genesis Rabbah 53:13
124. Tosefta Baba Metzia 7:3
125. Shabbath 137a & Jerushalmi Shabbath 19; 17b
126. Yoma 29a
127. Yebamoth 71b
128. Sanhedrin 108b

Raba said: when fever is not a forerunner of the angel of death, it is as salutary to the body as thorns of a palm tree and as theriac, to which Rabbi Nachman ben Isaac retorted: I want neither the fever nor the theriac[129]. It is not difficult to find here approval of the modern suggestion that fever is an expression of self-defense of the body against the illness. — According to Rabbi Judah, bathing is dangerous for a patient with fever which accompanies the sting of a wasp, the prick of a thorn, a furuncle or a sore eye[130].

Since speaking is harmful to a patient with fever, one should not visit him until after the fever has subsided[131].

In the treatment of fever, people distinguish various stages of the illness. This advice originated with Abaye's mother[132]: if the fever exists for one day, give the patient only a glass of water (perhaps they heard that the methodologists had their patients with fever fast); if it lasts two days, bloodletting is necessary; after three days, give the patient very red meat and diluted wine — probably equivalent to the *oinos ydatodes* of Galen and his disciples. For a chronic fever, *shimsha attika,* complicated remedies are required: take a black hen, tear it crosswise, shave the middle of the head of the patient, and place the hen thereon and leave it there until it begins to smell. Then the patient should get up and stand in water up to his neck until he gets weak[133], then swim to the dry land, get out of the water and sit down. Or, more simply, he should eat leek and then make that somewhat heroic water procedure. Another remedy is as follows: for fever, one should eat very red meat and diluted wine; for a chill *(thalga,* from *sheleg* meaning snow), one should eat very fat meat and undiluted wine. Rabbi Joseph used to work at the mill in order to cure the shivers by developing a sweat, and Rav Shesheth by carrying heavy beams, in that he said: work is a wonderful thing to make one warm[134]. Finally, a folk remedy recommends *chema le-chamma,* radish against (hot) fever and mangold against cold (i.e. cold fever); the reverse is dangerous[135].

It appears that the term *ischshatha bath yoma* refers to intermittent or quotidian fever. For the treatment of that illness, superstitious remedies by all nations even unto our own times are in their fullest bloom. Most are "cures through sympathy", which to most peoples even today enjoy more favored status than quinine.

From the folk medicine of the Talmud, the following recommendations from the mother of Abaye should be mentioned: take a white coin and go to a salt factory, take the weight of the coin in salt and tie (both?) to the nape of the neck with a twisted cord — or, sit at a crossroad, and when one sees a large ant carrying something, take it and throw it into a brass tube and close it with lead, and seal it with sixty seals. Then shake the tube, lift it up and say to it: "thy burden be upon me, and my burden be upon thee". Since another man may have already found that ant and cast his illness upon it, the patient with fever should rather say: "my burden and thy burden be upon thee". Another remedy is for the patient to go to the river with a new pitcher and say: "O river, O river, lend me a pitcher of water for a guest that has chanced to me". Let him then wave the filled pitcher seven times about his head, throw it behind his back and say: "O river, O river, take back the water thou gavest me, for the guest that chanced to me came in its day and departed in its day"[136].

When Rab died, the people took dust from his grave as a remedy against quotidian fever[137]. It is not stated how the dust was used. Samuel explicitly sanctioned this practice, although it is otherwise forbidden to make use of

---

129. Nedarim 41a-b
130. Abodah Zarah 28b
131. Nedarim 41a
132. Gittin 67b
133. i.e. stand in river water up to his neck till

he is faint and then swim out and sit down
134. Gittin 67b
135. Abodah Zarah 28b
136. Shabbath 66b
137. Sanhedrin 47b

anything which belongs to a corpse (for example, even his clothes), perhaps specifically to negate such superstitious therapeutic measures[138]. It is likely, however, that Samuel believed in the therapeutic efficacy of dirt from a grave.

Carmoly[139] and his transcribers interpreted, from the above citation, that the people disturbed the grave of Rab out of anger concerning his dissection of the dead (also "discovered" by Carmoly), whereas it seems much more apparent that the people were paying homage to Rab as a saint.

Rab Huna recommended the following against tertian fever, *ischshatha thiltha:* take seven leaves of seven palm trees, seven chips from seven beams, seven pegs from seven bridges, seven heaps of ashes from seven ovens, seven mounds of earth from under seven doorsockets, seven samples of pitch from seven ships, seven kernels of cumin, and seven hairs from the beard of an old dog; tie all these together and wear them on the nape of the neck with a white twisted cord[140].

One glance at Plinius[141] shows that Talmudic folk medicine abundantly found its match in the Roman medicine of its time, as far as superstition is concerned.

The illness of Rav Assi which (it appears, rapidly) led to his death, is probably pyemia, and not intermittent fever: "he became ill; from cold he became hot and from hot he became cold (shaking chills?), and so Rav Assi died"[142].

One type of physiological fever in animals is produced by rut and by brooding. Thus, when rams attack each other and thereby groan, the latter is due to heat *(tzimra)* that has taken hold of them and is not due to any type of possible injury[143]. If a brooding chicken leaves its nest, its heat *(tzimra)* remains intact for three more days[144]. The Talmud also speaks of a pathological *tzimra* and, in fact, an internal and an external type. In the often-mentioned collection of remedies[145], the following is recommended against internal inflammation: take seven handfuls of mangold from seven beets, together with the earth of their roots, and cook and eat them, and then drink *adra* leaves in beer or grapes from a vine trailed on a palm tree in water. For external *tzimra,* take three measures of date-stones and three measures of *adra* leaves and boil each separately, sit between them, and put them in two basins, and bring a mug and sit on it; then stand up from one and sit on the other; then stand up again and sit on the former one, until the vapors enter the patient; then bathe therein; when he drinks thereof, as is usual after a hot bath, he should drink only of the water of the *adra* leaves but not of that of the date-stones, because they cause infertility.

A separate type of fever, perhaps just another dialectical designation for an already-mentioned type, is *eschshatha tzemirtha,* a burning fever, perhaps the *kaysos phlagodes* of the ancients. It is considered to be a dangerous illness, on account of which the Sabbath laws were set aside, according to Rabbi Yochanan[146]. Rabina also rubbed his daughter, suffering from this burning fever, with the juice of figs *(goharke)* whose use was prohibited (as *orlah)* during the first three years of their growth[147].

A procedure of exorcism against this illness was the following[148]: Rabbi Yochanan said: for *eschshatha tzemirtha,* take an all-iron knife, go where there are thorn-hedges, and tie a white twisted thread thereto. On the first day he must slightly notch it and recite: *and the angel of the Lord appeared unto him* (with the illness)[149]. On the following day, he again makes a small notch and recites: *And Moses said, I* (the illness) *will turn aside now, and see*[150]. On the third day, he makes another small notch

138. Maimonides. *Hilchoth Abel* 4:14
139. Carmoly. *Histoire des Médecins Juifs.*
    Brussels 1844 p.12
140. Shabbath 67a
141. Plinius *Hist. Natur.* 32:38 & especially
    28:66
142. Nedarim 36b
143. Chullin 51a

144. Pesachim 55b
145. Gittin 69b
146. Abodah Zarah 28a
147. Pesachim 25b
148. Shabbath 67a
149. Exodus 3:2
150. *ibid* 3:3

and recites: *God spoke: do not draw nigh hither* (O, illness!)[151]. And when the illness has left him, he should cut off the thorn over the ground and say: "O thorn, O thorn, not because thou art higher than all other trees did the Lord cause His majesty to rest upon thee, but because thou art the lowliest of all trees. And even as thou once sawest the fire *(eschtha)* in the fiery oven into which the three men (Hananiah, Mishael and Azariah) were thrown, and didst flee from before them, so shall the fire *(eschtha* i.e. fever) of so and so, son of so and so look at thee and flee from thee".

*Tzemirtha* or, as more correctly stated by *Rashi, tzamartha,* is also the name of an extraordinarily painful urinary tract illness, perhaps a bladder stone[152]. I cannot determine whether or not one associated this illness with the above-discussed fever.

One of the premonitory signs of normal menstruation is "a type of *tzemarmoroth* with which the woman is seized"[153], probably a sense of heat or stranguria. However, this word is also used as the name of an illness against which one used a remedy which contained either a phallus or water from one of the sacred idolatrous wells. *Both* remedies are prohibited[154].

Rarely the term *ababith*[155], in Syriac *kababitha*[156], is used to denote a type of fever. The preacher states: *he that increaseth knowledge increaseth sorrow*[157]. Did you ever hear anybody say: this ass has caught a cold fever *(tzina)?* Or — he is suffering from *chamma ababith?* Where is suffering prevalent? With human beings[158]. Ishmael was afflicted with *chamma* and *ababith* on the way, so that the water in his water sack was quickly exhausted because he drank so much[159]. The illness *akbitha*[160] is interpreted by the commentators to refer to "injury by a thorn", and hence is not identical with our *ababith*.

Finally, a last type of fever is *achilu,* a designation which was not in common usage. The *Gemara* itself gives the explanation: "fire (fever) of the bones". For the Babylonians, it was even necessary to translate this term into their own dialect, although the prophet already cries out that the Lord sent *fire into his bones*[161]. Pains in the bones *(atzamoth)* are considered to be milder than pains in the whole body[162]. The dictionaries derive the word *achilu* from *chil,* meaning to shake or to quiver, or from *chalah,* meaning to be sick.

The cause of this illness is thought to be abnormally prolonged standing[163] or intemperance in eating. Rabbi Joshua ben Levi said: if a man eats beef with turnip and lies awake in the moonlight on the nights of the fourteenth and/or fifteenth of Tammuz (July), he will be afflicted with *achilu.* A more ancient tradition teaches: if one gorges himself with anything which is otherwise harmless, he will develop *achilu.* Rabbi Papa remarks: this applies even to dates which satisfy and warm and promote defecation and strengthen, yet do not weaken[164].

The remedy for *achilu* is provided by the mother of Abaye: all medicines are to be taken either three days or seven days or twelve days, but with this illness, he must continue until he is cured; all medicines are taken on an empty stomach, but this one only after he has eaten and drunk and relieved himself and washed his hands. Bring a measure of lentil cakes and a measure of strong vinegar and mix them together. Let the patient eat this and then wrap himself in his cloak and lie down (to perspire). No one

---

151. *ibid* 3:5
152. Baba Metzia 85a. In Syriac, *tzamartha* or *tzemara* refers to strangury, particularly if caused by a stone. Löw·
153. Niddah 9:8. Syriac *tzemarmara.* Maimonides' commentary on this *Mishnah* has the singular *tzemarorith.* ed. Derenbourg
154. Jerushalmi Shabbath 14; 14d. The textual reading and its interpretation are uncertain.
155. Genesis Rabbah 19:1

156. Löw. in *Theodor. loc. cit.*
157. Eccles. 1:18
158. Genesis Rabbah 19:1
159. Genesis Rabbah 53:13
160. Jerushalmi Shabbath 6; 8 c
161. Lamentations 1:13
162. Erubin 54a
163. Berachoth 32a
164. Gittin 70a

should awaken the patient until he wakes up by himself. When he awakens, he should immediately remove his cloak; otherwise the illness will return[165].

Elsewhere, the Talmud states that cohabitation in a standing position is the cause of this illness, and the remedy is lentil flour in wine. The Talmud continues in the name of Samuel: all other remedies are taken on an empty stomach but this one can also be taken if one is satiated; all other remedies must be taken while standing on the floor, but this one can also be taken even if one has one foot on the floor and one on a bed; all other remedies should be taken three, seven or twelve times but this one until the patient recovers[166].

The Biblical name *shachepeth*[167] probably refers to "consumption", or phthisis, in the sense of the ancients. (*Shachaph* is equivalent to *phthio*.) The *Sifra* states[168] that no person afflicted with any illness maintains his flesh (corpulence); however, with this illness (phthisis), the body dries out completely.

In post-Biblical times the term *shachuph* refers to *impotens coeundi (et generandi)*[169]. The prophet calls such a person: *a dry tree*[170]. Rabbi Ishmael explains the Biblical term *meroach eshek*[171], the castrate, to refer to *shachuph*[172], a man who cannot cohabit with a woman[173]. According to the *Midrash*[174], Shashgas, the eunuch of the Persian king Ahasverus, was a *shachuph* and, hence, the guard of the harem.

If someone drinks white *tilia,* the worst type of the 60 extant types of wines, he will develop *withek*. The same occurs to one who sits by the fire on the mornings of the month of Nissan (April) and rubs himself with oil, and then goes out and sits in the sun. If a man lets blood and immediately has marital intercourse, or if a man returns from a journey and immediately has marital intercourse, his children will become ill with *withek,* if his wife becomes pregnant from this intercourse[175]. Fleischer considers the word to be the same as the Greek *ektikos* (hectic), which is equivalent to *kachektikos* (cachectic). This interpretation is as unlikely as the reading *phthisike*. The correct meaning seems to be that of *Rashi's* translation: "weakness".

# PART   III

## I   Yerakon

It is debated among the commentators as to whether the name *yerakon,* in the places it is mentioned in the Bible, refers to a human illness or a disease of crops. The majority apparently incorrectly lean to the latter interpretation. In the warnings of punishment for sin in Deuteronomy[176], the punishments which afflict the human organism, among them *yerakon,* are first enumerated (*chereb,* in the text, according to Ibn Ezra, also refers to an illness); and then are listed those conditions such as droughts, etc. which harm man indirectly. Furthermore, the words of the prophet[177] are that *God smote you with shidaphon and yerakon* — both expressions always occur together in the Bible and *Mishnah* —[178] *and with hail in all the labors of your hands.* Sometimes the two expressions represent an explanation of *deber,* the word for

---

165. *ibid*
166. Kallah Rabbati 1:52 a 31. Kallah 50d, end
167. Levit. 26:16 and Deut. 28:22
168. *loc. cit.* p.111c
169. Maimonides. *Hilchoth Sota* 1:1
170. Isaiah 56:3
171. Levit. 21:20
172. Sotah 26b

173. Tosefta Bechoroth 5:4
174. Midrash Rabbah on Esther 2:14
175. Gittin 70a
176. Deut. 28:22
177. Haggai 2:17
178. Preuss perhaps overlooked the one exception in Jeremiah 30:6 (F.R.)
179. for example: First Kings 8:37. Compare Amos 4:9

pestilence[179]. This is the interpretation of *Ralbag*. The *Mishnah* also considers *shidaphon* and *yerakon* to be epidemic disorders because when they occur the blowing of the *shofar* is required[180]. In addition, in the *Gemara*, a prayer for deliverance from *shidaphon* and *yerakon* ends with the supplication to God:"Blessed are Thou, who stayest the plague" *(otzer hamagephah)*[181].

Although one cannot exclude with certainty the possibility that in all these places, the disease in question is one of grains rather than a human affliction, the latter is certainly the case in those places of the *Gemara* which list the remedies for *yarkona*.

Since the symptoms of this disease are not described anywhere in the Bible or Talmud, we are dependent upon conjectures based on the meaning of the word.

The interpretation of the root word *yarak,* as with all color identifications from antiquity, is fraught with difficulty.

Firstly, it is certain that the word *yarak* all by itself, contrary to the assertion of the *Tosafists* that *yarak* is yellow, means "green", like the *green of the field*[182]. In the Talmud too, the usual expression for green vegetables is *yerek*. *Yeroka* on the surface of water (water-weed, duck-weed) is used as a burning medium (or wick for a lamp)[183]. Rabbi Eliezer compares the *yerakrak* of the Bible[184] to the color of wax and *kurmal*[185], and Symmachos compares it to the color of the wing of a peacock, or the leaf of a palm tree[186]. It is disputed whether this *yerakrak* means dark green or light green. In the *Midrash,* dark green is considered to be black: if a spring of water flows into a vegetable garden *(ginnath yerek)* the vegetables turn black *(maschchir)*[187].

Sometimes *yarak* also means "blue". When a suspected adulteress drinks the "testing water", her eyes protrude, she becomes full of *gidin*[188], and tendrils become green *(morikin)* on her[189]. These "nerve tendrils", which develop rapidly[190], apparently represent prominent veins which are not green but blueish. Compare also *Tosafoth*[191] where *yarak* is interpreted as indigo or sky blue.

Concerning humans, the *yerakon* which occurs from fear or fright is the pallid or blanched facial appearance[192]. In the Talmud, *yarak* refers to the opposite of the red color of health, whether this pallor occurs from sickness as in the case of the suspected adulteress[193], or from hunger[194], or from fright; and it designates the color of a dead person *vis-à-vis* the bright red of a live person[195]. Most important is the following report of Rabbi Nathan: three children of the same woman died following circumcision. The fourth son[196] was brought to him. He examined it and saw that it was red; so he recommended that circumcision be postponed "until the blood of the baby would become absorbed". In another case, he saw that the baby's flesh was *yarak*. In spite of careful examination, he saw no blood in the baby and recommended that circumcision be postponed "until the baby becomes full-blooded"[197]. According to this citation, there can be no doubt that *yarak* refers to *pallor of the skin due to blood lack. Yarak* is thus a true portrayal of the Greek *chloros.* Pythagoras also portrays it as the opposite of red, and it thus represents the

---

180. Taanith 3:5
181. Kethuboth 8b
182. Isaiah 15:6; Job 39:8; Proverbs 15:17
183. Shabbath 2:1. Thus *yarak* alone means green, contrary to *Tosafoth* Niddah 19b
184. Levit. 13:49 and 14:37; Psalms 68:14
185. variant *kurman,* perhaps also *karmulin.* Löw. *Pflanzennamen.* p.354 No. 299
186. Tosefta Negaim 1:5
187. Levit. Rabbah 15:3
188. nerves in the ancient sense. Sotah 3:4

189. *Sifré. loc. cit.*
190. Numbers Rabbah 9:31
191. in Chullin 47b
192. Jeremiah 30:6
193. Numbers Rabbah 9:21
194. Ruth Rabbah 3:6
195. Kethuboth 103b and Abodah Zarah 20b
196. actually the third (F.R.)
197. Shabbath 134a and Tosefta Shabbath 15:8

color of young crops (grass green) and all shades of color through the facial coloration of a pallid individual, the chlorotic, whose pallor often has a tinge of green in it; the British speak directly of "green sickness". Therefore, *yerakon* is *pallor of the face, and this is the name for anemia;* it is a malady which is more frequent and distinct in the Orient than with us.

Of the ancient Bible translations, only the Septuagint has this interpretation in that they translate *yerakon* in the above citation from Deuteronomy as *ochra* (yellow). Otherwise one finds *ikteros* in Greek, and *aerugo* or gold color in the Latin translations, corresponding to the jaundice of some Talmudic commentaries. Today's Arabs are said to call jaundice *yerakon*[198]. It is difficult to determine where this conception originated. To be sure, *yarak* is also the color of egg yolk[199], just as *chloros* also designates the golden yellow color of honey. There also exists a post-menstrual discharge which is *yarok* and concerning which it is uncertain whether or not it imparts ritual uncleanness[200]. The milk of an unclean (i.e. non-kosher for consumption) animal is said to be *yarok* compared to the white color of a clean animal[201].

However, if one wishes to adopt the view of those who interpret some of the Biblical citations of *yerakon* to represent a disease of crops, one should reflect on the fact that turning yellow is a sign of ripening and thus a blessing, and that withering and barren ears of grain are faded and pale and not golden yellow. The latter sooner resemble silver, whose Arabic name *warak* is the equivalent of the Hebrew *yarak*.

One possibility for explaining the apparent contradictory interpretations of *yerakon,* which I do not even consider debatable, should at least be mentioned. Rabbi Ishmael, in the *Mishnah*[202], states that the skin color of Semites is in between that of Ethiopians and that of Germanic people. He compares it to the color of boxwood. For Semites with such facial coloration, pallor would truly appear to be a yellowing of the skin. However, as already mentioned, this "explanation" is not at all debatable. As a refutation thereof, it suffices to point out the admonishment: one should not make one's neighbor's face turn white (pallid) by shaming him in public[203]. This is literally equivalent to shedding blood, because such shaming causes the ruddiness (i.e. blood) to depart and the white (i.e. pallor) to supervene[204].

According to the Sages, the human sickness of *yerakon* occurs as Divine punishment for causeless hatred[205]. It is said to occur by the withholding of urination[206]. Perhaps the pallor is that which occurs secondary to kidney diseases, where, in one of those numerous confusions of causes and effects, a diminution of urine was considered the cause of the illness.

There are numerous remedies mentioned for this malady. Dioscorides[207] considers the imbibition of ass urine to be helpful for kidney diseases. This remedy is prohibited to Jews, to whom products derived from an unclean animal are forbidden[208]. The same applies to the flesh of an ass which is recommended by Rabbi Mattia ben Cheresh[209]. The following are also remedies for *yerakon*[210]: the head of the *shibuta* fish (turbot), salted and cooked in beer; or three measures of Persian dates, three measures of melted wax, three measures of red aloe, cooked in beer and imbibed; or

---

198. Stern. *Türkei* 1:238
199. Chullin 47b
200. Niddah 2:6
201. Abodah Zarah 35b
202. Negaim 2:1
203. Aboth 3:11
204. Baba Metzia 58b

205. Shabbath 33a
206. Bechoroth 41b
207. Dioscorides 2:99
208. Bechoroth 7a
209. Yoma 84a
210. Shabbath 109b-110a

roasted animal head in ashes, cooked in beer; or sharp leeks; or two cups of *akarin* which, according to the prescription of Rabbi Yochanan, is prepared by cooking Alexandrian gum, alum and garden crocus in beer — the patient is cured of his jaundice by the latter potion but becomes impotent. Or again, use water from the spring of palm trees; this is a strong purgative.

The following are external measures against *yerakon:* rubbing oneself with the juice of locusts or the species *nakure* in a warm bathhouse. If the latter is not available, one performs the rub in one's own house between the oven and the wall. Alternatively, one places the fetus of an ass on the shaved head of the patient so that the blood flows on his head. One must protect his eyes, however, so that the patient does not become blind. Another remedy is to place the cut-up heart of a speckled swine on the patient's heart (near the stomach). Rabbi Yochanan said: if one wishes to warm a patient with *yarkona*, rub him with his sheet. Rabbi Kahana successfully treated a colleague in this manner[211].

## II  Hydrops (Dropsy)

The bodies of those who indulge in sin become covered with weals and wounds and, in addition, they are punished with *hadrokan* which, according to Rabbi Nachman bar Yitzchak, is a sign of sin. Therefore, the abdomen of an adulteress becomes swollen, as explained by Josephus[212], *ten koilian yderon katalabontos,* while the thighs fall away[213].

The Sages distinguish three types of this illness: the thick one *(abbah)* which is a punishment for sin, the swollen one *(thapuach)* which is caused by hunger, and the thin one *(dak)* which is caused by magic[214]. The Sages also teach that three types of people die suddenly while they are conversing: one who suffers from bowel diseases, a woman in confinement and one afflicted with dropsy *(hadrokan)*[215]. According to Rabban Simeon ben Gamliel, the illness arises from the withholding of one's bowels[216].

A notice in the *Midrash* —in fact the only one in the entire Talmud, which, as far as I can see, is a teaching of the body temperaments — seems to be describing a type of theory of humoral-pathology modeled on Job 28:25 as follows: healthy man is evenly balanced, half of him is blood and the other half is water. When he is deserving, the water does not exceed the blood, nor does the blood exceed the water; but when he sins, then the water either gains over the blood and he becomes a sufferer from dropsy *(adripikos* or *adropikos)*[217], or the blood gains over the water and then he becomes leprous[218].

The word *adripikos* is naturally the *hydropikos* of the Greeks, and the *hadrokon* of the *Gemara* perhaps represents the abbreviated form of this word in popular usage. Furthermore, physicians use the Greek word *yderos* (watery) in the same sense. As regards the three types of dropsy mentioned above, the first type probably represents the usual form of dropsy, the third type may refer to the leukophlegmasia of the ancients, and the second type might refer to that type of hydrops-illness mentioned by an Alexandrian (Demetrius from Apamea), in which the skin *sine ulla humoris infusione sed sola inflatione turget*[219]. The methodologists consider the latter case, in which one speaks of hydrops without water, as pure nonsense.

The occasional sudden death in a patient with hydrops can be explained by the often-accompanying heart disease. To explain the assumption that the withholding of

211. *ibid*
212. Josephus. *Antiquities* Book 3 Chapt. 11:6
213. Numbers 5:21
214. Shabbath 33a
215. Erubin 41b
216. Berachoth 25a

217. *Yalkut* and *Tanchuma* on *Thazria*.
    p.18b in Buber have *istenis* in Hebrew or *asthenes* in Greek
218. Levit. Rabbah 15:2
219. Coelius Aurelianus 3:8 p.468

the bowels is a cause of dropsy, one might mention the observation of a Hippocratic aphorism[220]: "if powerful diarrhea occurs in a patient with leukophlegmasia, the illness dissolves". The sins for which *hadrokan* is the punishment seem to be lewdness in the sexual sphere[221].

Nowhere (in the Bible or Talmud) is the treatment of dropsy mentioned. The Evangelist describes a certain man with dropsy of whom Jesus took hold and healed and let go[222]. The expounders did not rest until they discovered cases in which dropsical swellings were made to disappear by a strong emotional influence[223].

## III   Podagra (Gout)

King Asa reigned happily for 41 years, but in his old age he became ill in his feet[224]. Rab is of the opinion that the illness was podagra. Mar Zutra explains: podagra is like a needle in the raw flesh[225]. Some fanciful exegetes may consider this to refer to uric acid needles.

The Palestinian Talmud[226] also interprets the word *tzinith* of the *Mishnah*[227] to refer to podagra. The Babylonian Talmud considers *tzinith* to be "a daughter of the earth" (a growth caused by the soil) i.e. a callus on the sole of the foot. Both explanations are probably correct because, as remarked by Aretäus[228], pain in all limbs, no matter what the cause, was called arthritis, except for pain in the feet, which was called podagra. Coelius Aurelianus expresses himself in the same manner[229]. He perhaps offers an additional explanation of the Talmudic "daughter of the earth", in that he combines podagra with *ager* or *agrios: siquidem omne, quod immite fuerit, abusive agreste vocamus.*

One used to place a coin on such bunions whereby, as the *Gemara* concludes, the hardness and the roughness of the imprint on the coin and the exudation caused by the metal *(schuktha)*[230] produce healing. One should therefore not substitute for the coin either a hard shard, or a smooth metal plate from one's head ornaments *(tas)*, or a cut piece of wood *(pulsa)*[231].

An extraordinary confusion was here produced by Arabic commentators. The coin which was applied was the Palestinian *sela*. However, Arabic physicians use the expression *sala* for *fissura pedis,* somewhat similar to the *tzinith* of the *Mishnah*. Hence, one would have to place a bunion on a bunion.

The *Midrash* relates [232] there was once a man who suffered from his feet and who went around to all the physicians to be healed but they could not cure him, till at last one came and said to him: "if you want to be cured, there is a very easy way of doing it; plaster your feet with the excrement of cattle". This is a method which I have personally seen used by the Brandenburg farmers (warm cow dung), with positive results.

## IV   Heatstroke

In the tropics, heatstroke is a not infrequent illness. Even there, it occurs particularly often in the harvest season, and primarily affects young people, just as

---

220. Hippocrates. *Aphorisma* 6:13
221. Yebamoth 60b
222. Luke 14:2-4
223. Friedreich 1:276
224. First Kings 15:23
225. Sotah 10a
226. Jerushalmi Shabbath 6; 8c
227. Shabbath 6:6
228. Aretäus. *Chronicles* 2:12

229. Coelius Aurelianus. *Chronicles* 5:2
230. *schuktha* in syrian means either sediment or *morbus cutis, eruptio pustularum,* erysipelas. Löw
231. Shabbath 65a. Since all three properties are required: hardness, roughness of the imprint and corrosive action, and only a coin possesses all three
232. Song of Songs Rabbah on 2:3

enunciated by Celsus[233]: *inimicior senibus hiems, aestas adolescentibus est*. The Biblical books describe two such cases.

1) In the Book of Judith[234], it is related that Manasseh, the husband of Judith, died in the days of the barley harvest. For as he stood in the fields during the binding of the sheaves, the heat struck his head, he became ill and died in Bethulia, and they buried him with his forefathers.

2) The second case is described in greater detail[235]: the late-born child of an elderly couple in Shunam — according to legend, the woman was already climacteric[236] — at three years of age[237], went one day to his father to the reapers. And he called to his father: *my head, my head*. The father had the child carried to its mother where it sat on her knees until noon and then died. Here, the naive Parson Schmidt interpolates[238]: "if an intelligent physician had been called in a hurry, he would have used bloodletting, vesicatoria or blister inducers, all types of ointments and rubbings, strong-smelling volatile and sneeze-inducing things, or other remedies which are employed for similar cases". The mother, however, calls to the prophet Elisha, who first sends his servant Gehazi.

The child did not speak, nor did it respond when called or stimulated; it tolerated a stick placed on its face without resistance[239]. In the meantime, Elisha came, locked himself in with the child and prayed. He then went up on the bed, and lay upon the child, and *put his mouth on his* (the child's) *mouth, and his eyes on his eyes and his hands upon his hands,* and he stretched himself until the body of the child became warm. He then walked back and forth in the room and again stretched over the child. Finally, the child sneezed seven times and opened his eyes.

Rabbi Manna explicitly states[240] that this was a case of heatstroke. He remarks as follows in relation to the above story: "accidents occur during the harvest season, because the sun inflames[241] the head of people". The Rabbis also raise the possibility of the child's having been bitten by a poisonous snake hidden among the crops. Such snakebites certainly occur more often in the tropics[242] than do blind worm bites among our own reapers. The wording of the text, however, makes the former interpretation (i.e. sunstroke) much more likely.

It is difficult to explain the attempts at resurrecting the child. The Mesmerists consider it to be a transference of their animalistic magnetism[243]. Schreger is of the opinion that the prophet applied a form of artificial respiration to the child[244].

Another similar story of sickness, where lack of detail does not permit a precise diagnosis, is the following[245]: the son of a widow in Zarephath became ill, and his illness became very severe until there was no breath left in him. Scripture then uses the following expression concerning the prophet Elijah who healed the child: *and he stretched three times over the child*[246]. According to the interpretation of the Septuagint: he blew on it, *anephysese,* and, according to the Vulgate: *expandit se atque mensus est super puerum.* The *Targum* has a similar meaning. The commentators attempt to equate the procedure of "stretching" by Elijah with that of Elisha described above.

---

233. Celsus 2:2
234. Judith 8:2-3
235. Second Kings 4:18 ff
236. *Pirke de Rabbi Eliezer* 33
237. Thus is the calculation of Schmidt. *Biblicus Historicus* p.411
238. Schmidt. *Biblicus Medicus* p.483
239. see Mussaphia *loc. cit: apoplexia percussi an vivant mortuine sint, virga ad os apposita statim detergit, quippe ea non motitatur defuncto homine.*
240. Jerushalmi Yebamoth 15; 14d
241. The *Tosofoth* in Yebamoth 116b erroneously have *kodachath* meaning inflammation instead of *kophachath* meaning "strikes" as in the *Aggadah*
242. A case of fatal snakebite during harvest time is described in the text of Yebamoth 116b
243. Ennemoser. *Magnetismus.*.p.442 ff
244. in Friedreich. *Zur Bibel* 2:173
245. First Kings 17:17
246. *ibid* 17:21

One of the three nonsensical questions that "the men of Alexandria" asked Rabbi Joshua[247] ben Hananiah is whether or not the (dead) son[248] of the Shunamite woman could convey ritual uncleanness. He answered that only a dead person conveys ritual uncleanness[249]. The child was thus considered to be alive and only appeared to be dead[250]. On the other hand, it is assumed that the child from Zarephath was truly resurrected by the prophet in that he prayed for the keys of resurrection which the Lord keeps in His hand and does not entrust to an agent. Elijah's prayer, however, was answered[251]. This interpretation is already found in Sirach[252].

Related to our subject are the narratives of the Evangelists concerning the resurrection by Jesus of the daughter of Jairus who was thought to be dead by her neighbors. Jesus recognized that the child was not dead but was sleeping; he took her by the hand and the damsel arose[253]. It is difficult to conjecture about the nature of her illness since no details are given at any of the citations. In the case where Paul awoke Eutychus who fell out of a window *and was taken up dead*[254], the Apostle also realized that "his soul was still in him". He was thus only stunned temporarily. It is difficult to ascribe a rational meaning to the awakening of Tabea[255], the lad in Nain[256], and Lazarus[257].

# PART   IV
# DISEASES OF THE ORAL CAVITY

## I   Mouth Odors

The normal mouth does not emit an odor: *bene olet, quod non olet*. Therefore, any "aroma from the mouth", *re'ach hapeh*, is offensive. The giant Goliath had a bad odor emitting from his mouth[258]; the same occurs to an adulteress[259]. Undoubtedly, the following perception plays a role: *sangius animam quoque vitiat, et inde os hominis incipit foetere*[260]. If a man marries a woman with the condition that she be free of physical defects, and later it is found that she suffers from *foetor ex ore,* the marriage is invalid[261], similar to the Prussian provincial law regarding betrothals[262]. Lengthy fasting can produce *foetor*[263], as can the daily consumption of lentils, according to Rabbi Yochanan[264]; this is a teaching which was also promulgated by Greek cooks[265].

According to Rabbi Yitzchak, one should not converse with people who eat raw vegetables before the fourth hour of the day, because they emit a bad odor from the mouth[266]. If one doesn't walk at least four ells after eating before one lies down to sleep, the food putrefies without being digested, and this is the beginning of *foetor ex ore*[267]. Even Mar Samuel had no remedy for this situation[268].

A man cannot force his wife to spin flax, because this work makes the lips fissure (or become eczematous) and causes the mouth to emit a foul odor[269]. According to the

247. Preuss erroneously has "Jose" (F.R.)
248. Preuss erroneously has "daughter" (F.R.)
249. Niddah 70b
250. *Rashi loc. cit.* interprets otherwise
251. Sanhedrin 113a
252. Sirach 48:5
253. Matthew 9:24-25; Mark 5:41; Luke 8:52-55
254. Acts 20:9
255. *ibid* 9:37
256. Luke 7:15
257. John 11:44. see Friedreich. *loc.cit.*
258. Song of Songs Rabbah 4 fol 24d
259. Numbers Rabbah 9:21

260. Antonius Musa. *Fragmenta.* Bassani 1800 p.107
261. Kethuboth 75a
262. *Allgemeines Landrecht.* Thome 2 Title 1 No. 103. Koch-Hinsshius *loc. cit.*
263. Aboth de Rabbi Nathan 6:3 and Genesis Rabbah 42:1
264. Berachoth 40a
265. Pherecrates in Athenäus 4, 15th ed. Casaubon 1657 fol 159: *en ge trage tis, tou stomatos oze kakon*
266. Berachoth 44b
267. Shabbath 41a
268. Baba Metzia 113b
269. Tosefta Kethuboth 5:4

*Gemara,* only Roman flax has this harmful effect[270]. The spinning of wool, however, is harmless[271].

To improve the odor from one's mouth, one places pepper in the mouth[272], or chews on mastic[273], as the Greeks[274] and Orientals do to this very day for the same purpose. Alternatively, one rubs[275] the teeth with a dry powder[276]. Furthermore, ginger and cinnamon, which "a woman places in her mouth"[277], have the same effect (of making the breath pleasant).

## II    Abscess in the Mouth

The following is stated about an illness which, as its name *chinké* (from *chinka)* implies, refers to an ailment of the gums[278].

"For *chinké,* Rabbi Yochanan recommends pyrethrum and *mamru* (and the roots of pyrethrum are better than *mamru)*[279]. Both are placed in the mouth in order to overcome the illness."

The words *chomthi ki mamru* in the text are explained by *Rashi:* the former is as effective as the plant *mamru.* The meaning of both words is uncertain[280].

According to the dictionaries, *chomthi* is the translation of pyrethrum[281].

The text[282] continues: "to soften it (or ripen it) one takes bran from the top of the sieve, and lentils with the earth still on them, and fenugreek and hemlock flowers, and takes about the size of a nut thereof into one's mouth. To make it burst, someone should blow white cress (lepidium, *kardamon)* into the patient's mouth through a wheat straw. To raise the site of the opening to its previous niveau, one takes earth from the shadow of a privy and kneads it with honey and eats it. This is effective *(probatum est)".*

From these remedies, it appears that *chinké* must refer to an abscess in the mouth. It cannot be decided however whether it is an abscess of the tonsils, the soft palate, or the gums.

*Rashi* explains *chinké* to mean: "pus boils which grow in the throat; a type of *malan; estrangoilon* in Latin and *étranglement* in French". *Malan* or *malannus* is the name of every knob or boil-like elevation of the skin or mucous membrane[283].

If someone had pain in or around the mouth, he would hold a cloth in front of his mouth when he went out on the street[284].

## III    Tzafdina (Stomatitis)

An illness named *tzafdina (tzifdana* or *tzifdona)* is mentioned in the Talmud from which Rabbi Yochanan[285] and Rabbi (Rebbe)[286] are said to have suffered. The

270. Kethuboth 61b
271. Kethuboth 5:5
272. Shabbath 9:6 and 6:5 and fol. 90a and fol. 65a
273. Tosefta Shabbath 12:8
274. Dioscorides 1:90 *stomatos euodian poiei*
275. thus according to the textual reading of Maimonides; Shabbath 21:24; according to Tosefta Shabbath 12:8, one trickles it *(yatiph)* on the teeth
276. *Sam yabesh,* perhaps a special tooth powder
277. Shabbath 65a
278. Gittin 69a
279. perhaps later glosses
280. Löw. *Pflanzennamen.* p.260, note 1
281. *Aruch; Rashi: pilatro* meaning pellitory
282. Gittin 69a
283. See above Chapter 4, Part 1, Section 3
284. Jerusalmi Moed Katan 3; 82d

285. Abodah Zarah 28a and Yoma 84a
286. Baba Metzia 85a: a calf that was being taken to be slaughtered broke away and fled. It hid under Rabbi's coat and pleaded: Rabbi, save me. He, however, retorted: "Go, for this wast thou created." For this sin he suffered for seven years from *tzafdina. (summun jus summa injuria).* Once when his maid wanted to kill a young weasel, he stopped her by saying: *and His tender mercies are over all His works* (Psalms 145:9); and then Rabbi's suffering ceased. The *Midrashim* further embellish this legend of sheltering animals. The text here has *tzipparna* whereas the manuscripts have *tzafdina* (Kohut). The *Aruch* also has the latter word. This variant may be derived from Jerusalmi Kilayim 9; 32b where it says: he lived in *tzipporin* (Sepphoris) for 17 years etc.

following sign (*semeion,* symptom) is mentioned as being characteristic: if one places anything on the molar teeth (*kakké*), blood exudes from the gums (*mibbé daré*)[287]. The illness is dangerous, begins in the mouth and ends in the intestines (i.e. affects the intestines last). Etiologically, it is said to be caused by eating very cold wheat foods, very hot barley pap or remnants of fish stew. Rabbi Yochanan was cured of this illness by a Roman woman — perhaps the daughter of Domitian[288] — who kept her remedy secret, but revealed it to him. When he announced it in one of his Sabbath discourses, she hanged herself. The exact nature of the remedy is debated in the Talmud, but from the various items mentioned, one can conclude that a variety of materials were used by the general populace: leaven (or water of leaven), olive oil and salt; and goose fat applied with a goose feather[289].

Abaye tried all the above on himself without finding the cure, until an Ishmaelite recommended: take the stones of unripe olives, burn them on a new shovel[290], and sprinkle (actually; fasten) them on (or in) the gums. This was effective. Finally, in a later version, the prescription is as follows: take date stones or Nicolaos-stones[291], burn them to half their volume, add barley shells and dried children's dung, pulverize (all these ingredients) and apply this remedy on the teeth.

According to the above symptomatology, there can be no doubt that *tzafdina* refers to stomatitis, perhaps scorbutic stomatitis, which also occurs sporadically. As usual, one can draw no conclusions from the etiology or therapy (mentioned in the Talmud). It remains undecided whether or not the word *tzafdina* is derived from the Greek *sepedon.* (Buxtorf).

Dioscorides[292] has the following: *stomaton elkoseis kai sepedones aidoion*[293].

Buxtorf's source, Pollux, is not faultless: *sepedon* is a white sore *(nome)* with a bad odor. The explanation "which especially affects the mouth so that sometimes teeth and bones are lost" is an addition of Henry Stephanus.

The ancients certainly considered *tzafdina* to be an illness of the teeth or gums, as is clearly evident from numerous parallels in the *Midrash*[294].

# PART V
# DISEASES OF THE THROAT

If someone suffers from an ailment of the throat, *garon,* he gargles with oil. Gargling is defined as taking a liquid in one's mouth, shaking it to and fro and

---

287. Yoma 84a

288. Thus states Jerushalmi Shabbath 14; 14d. It could not, however, refer to the Roman emperor Domitian because he was murdered in the year 96 C.E. and Rabbi Yochanan wasn't born until 170 C.E. In the parallel passage in Jerushalmi Abodah Zarah 2; 40d, the following is found: "from *thimtinis* (*timetes* in Greek, assessment commissioner?) in Tiberias" where Rabbi Yochanan taught

289. Yoma 84a: "feather-fat" as a technical term. *Rashi:* marrow from a small bone from the head of the bird's wing; she (the Roman matron) rubbed this on his temple

290. cf. Plinius 23:51

291. *nikalbas:* according to Buxtorf, the type of date which August named after Nicolaos from Damascus, from whom he received them. Löw (*Pflanzennamen* p.110) agrees

with this interpretation. Compare with Puschmann's *Alexander of Tralles* 2:139, note 4. The assertion of Suida (s.v. *Nikolaos*) that it refers to *plakountas* (placentas, crusts) is thoroughly refuted by Bernhardy. Dried (*yebesha* or *neguba,* see Machshirim 3:5) human excrement, called *botryon,* was a famous secret remedy of the Athenian Aeschines, who used it to treat illnesses of the throat. see Plinius 28:10

292. Dioscorides 3:6

293. ulcers of the mouth and bad sores of the vulva

294. The above legend of Rabbi is found in Genesis Rabbah 33:2 and 96:2; Eccles. Rabbah on 11:2; *Pesikta de Rabbi Kahana* ed. Buber p.946. In all places it states: "he (Rabbi) suffered in his teeth", i.e. he had a toothache.

then spitting it out. The Hebrew term for gargling, *irer*[295], is therefore onomatopoetic, as is the Greek word *gargarijo* with the same meaning. In Berachoth 36a, the second "r" is missing. In the Zuckerman edition of the *Tosefta*[296], the word *je'arennu* of earlier editions is changed to *jirdeno*.

*Girger* is equivalent to the Arabic *gargar: cum murmure per guttur demisit potum*[297], somewhat similar to our commonly used expression: to gurgle. He who empties his glass in one gulp is called a *gargeran*[298], *gulosus* in Latin; he does not put his lip to the glass but pours the beverage into the open mouth[299] and gulps it all down at once.

Rabbi Mathia ben Cheresh says: if someone suffers from an ailment in the throat, one may place medications *(sam)* in his mouth even on the Sabbath because there is the question of danger to life (for which Sabbath laws are suspended)[300].

In the *Gemara*, this *Mishnah* is reported as follows: "he who has pain in (or around) his mouth". *Alfasi* and Rabbi Asher have the same textual reading but *Bertinoro* has "toothache"[301]. The above story of the *tzafdina* of Rabbi Yochanan is found adjacent to this discussion of sore throat[302]. Maimonides' commentary on this *Mishnah* states: "putrefaction of the mandible which, if untreated, leads to putrefaction of the gums."

When Esau learned from his father that Jacob not only took his birthright but also his father's blessing, he (Esau) became hoarse out of anger: he began to rumble with his throat like a person who coughs to expectorate sputum *(rok)* from his mouth in order to clear his throat[303].

# PART VI
# DISEASES OF THE LUNGS

## I

1) Blood that comes from the mouth should be examined with a wheat straw; if the blood sticks, it comes from the lungs and can be cured, but if not, it comes from the liver and cannot be cured[304]. To be sure, defects of the liver are less dangerous than those of the lungs, but when it comes to bleeding — actually: "when the liver comes from the mouth" — the entire liver must already be damaged (dissolved). The remedy for lung bleeding is as follows: take seven handfuls of hashed mangold (beta vulgaris), and seven handfuls of mashed leeks and seven handfuls of jujube berry and three handfuls of lentils and one handful of cumin and one handful of *chabla* and (place it in?) a quantity equal to all these of the large intestine of a first-born animal. Cook this mixture and eat it and then drink strong beer *(shikra)* made in the month of Tebeth[305].

2) The Arabic physicians interpret *barsam* to be pleuritis, and they painstakingly differentiate it from *sarsam* meaning phrenitis[306].

The Talmud relates the following of the illness called *barsam*[307]:

295. Tosefta Shabbath 12:10; Jerushalmi Shebiith 8; 38a; Jerushalmi Maaser Sheni 2; 53b
297. Fr. 1:262b
298. Pesachim 86b
299. Maimonides, in his Commentary on Para 9:4
300. Yoma 8:6
301. Bertinoro and Tosafoth Yom Tov, in their commentaries on this *Mishnah*.
302. Yoma 84a
303. Genesis Rabbah 67:4 to explain *haki;* Genesis 27:36
304. Gittin 69a
305. *ibid*. Does it refer to a specific type of beer? Löw
306. In the *Kuzari* 5:14, the word *barsam* is explained as "a wound in the head", to which Cassel, in his work p.403, correctly points out that it must be a copyist's error.
307. Chullin 105b

Abaye said: at first I thought the reason why one does not drink foam is because it is unappetizing. However, my Master told me it is because it can easily cause *karsam*[308]. One may not blow the foam away because it is harmful to the head, nor skim it off with the hand because it may lead to poverty. Rather, one should wait until it settles by itself. For *karsam* contracted from drinking the foam of wine, one should drink beer, for that from beer one should drink water, and for that from water, there is no remedy. This bears out the popular saying, "poverty follows the poor" (since they can only drink water)[309].

In the often-mentioned collection of remedies which is systematically arranged according to the parts of the body[310], the following is recommended against *barsam:* take about the size of a pistachio of gum ammoniac, and about the size of a nut of sweet galbanum, and a spoonful of white honey, and a Machuzan *natla*[311] of clear wine, and cook these together. When the gum ammoniac boils, the remedy is ready. Alternatively, take one quarter *log* of milk of a white goat, drip it on three stalks of carob and stir it with a piece of stem of *marmehin* (marjoram)[312]. When the marjoram stem boils, the remedy is ready. Or take the excrement of a white dog and knead it with *natopha* (a type of resin). If at all possible, however, do not eat the dog's excrement because it unsettles the body.

3) The breathing of individual people differs, all according to *the spirit for which God maketh a weight*[313]. Some people have a long (projecting) breath whereas others have a short breath; the latter, if he is possessed with *ruach katakton*[314]. A woman in labor has difficult breathing[315]. God did not allow Job, who was full of bitterness, to regain his breath[316].

The Hebrew word *katakton* refers either to the Greek *katakton, fragilis,* or, according to the textual reading of *Aruch: katariton,* equivalent to the Greek *katarryton* meaning catarrhal. It is very unlikely that *katakton* is a reduplication of the word *katan* meaning small. According to S. Fränkel, in *Aruch,* the word *metriton,* which is equivalent to the Greek *metreton* meaning measured or shortened breath, is the *translation* of the Hebrew word *mishkal* of the text. (Löw).

4) It is linguistically difficult to explain *goneach milibbo,* one who groans or moans from his *leb*[317]. It is related that Rabbi Judah ben Baba suffered from this illness and, in order to drink warm animal milk as prescribed by his physician[318], tied a goat to the posts of his bed and drank directly from the udder, as was perhaps also done by hungry shepherds[319]. He did so in spite of the fact that in Palestine, the maintenance of small cattle as pets was prohibited in order to avoid disputes concerning damage done during illegal pasturing of the animal.

The *Midrash* relates that Noah "coughed blood" in his ark because of the cold[320]. This assertion makes the statement of Nathan ben Yechiel (1100 C.E.) appear more plausible: people made sounds like *su'al* (Arabic meaning cough).

The use of goats' milk was considered highly efficacious in antiquity[321], and milk cures for chronic cough were always held in high esteem since the time of the Knidisch school[322].

---

308. This is the way the text reads. *Rashi* interprets *karsam* and *barsam* to be sniffles. A derivation from *koryza* cannot be assumed.
309. Chullin 105b
310. Gittin 69a
311. the measure of one *natla* as it was defined in the town of Machuza
312. Löw. *Pflanzennamen* p.252
313. Job 28:25
314. Levit. Rabbah 15:2

315. Isaiah 42:14
316. Job 9:18
317. *leb* means either heart or stomach
318. Thus in the Tosefta, Baba Kamma 8:13. The *Gemara,* however, has "the physicians". Baba Kamma 80a
319. Yebamoth 114a
320. Genesis Rabbah 32:11
321. proof is found in Bochart. *Hieroz* 1:629
322. examples in Daremberg in his edition of *Oribasius* 1:604

The Hebrews do not have a word for "coughing" like the *su'al* of the Arabs[323]. Were not lung ailments observed (by the ancient Hebrews)? In modern times, Liebermeister[324] and, even earlier, Tobler[325] praise the efficacy of living in Palestine for the healing of phthisis.

## II

The discussions in the Talmud concerning illnesses and injuries of the pleura and lungs *in animals* are very extensive indeed. The obligatory examination of meat which was prescribed following the slaughtering of animals, including those slaughtered in a private house, included in all cases a careful examination of the organs of the chest. In this manner, over the years, wide experience with such animal illnesses was acquired.

A discussion of the general question as to which illnesses of slaughtered cattle the Talmudists were familiar with, and the significance of their examination of the meat, from the modern viewpoint, for the health of the population, must remain for a later discussion. Here, we will only describe the anatomical findings concerning the lung and pleura, as far as these are mentioned in the Talmud. The numerous post-Talmudic special regulations which developed from the practice of daily living — since the examination of slaughtered meat has always been practiced by the Jews — will not be dealt with here.

1) Perforations or defects of the lung are declared by the *Mishnah* to be life-threatening. According to Rabbi Simeon, the perforation must extend into a bronchus. The *Gemara*[326] demands that, in any event, "both skins" (pleura) must be perforated and therefore a pneumothorax was or is present. Opinions are divided as to the definition of a defect: the conclusion is that injuries which lie within the organ without extending to the surface thereof, that is without there being a recognizable change on the surface, are not thought to be immediately fatal to the animal.

To diagnose the presence of a perforation, the generally used test is to inflate the lungs from the trachea (thus presupposing a knowledge of the condition of the organ in an unopened thorax). If one hears a hissing sound when the lung is inflated and if the opening of the perforation can be located, then one places a feather or a straw or some spittle on that spot; if it (any one of the three items) moves, it indicates there is a perforation (and the animal is not *kosher*). If one cannot locate the opening, one places the lung in a basin of lukewarm water — hot water would cause the lungs to shrivel up and cold water would cause a hardening of the lung; the lung is then inflated and if it bubbles, this indicates the presence of a perforation.

In these examinations, a prerequisite is that the pleura must also be perforated. If, in spite of the integrity of the outer membrane (pulmonary pleura), the lung bubbles, it is because air has entered between the two membranes (lung surface and pleura) and this is not a life-threatening injury.

One must be careful not to confuse a fibrin film or a crust with the outer membrane because "a membrane which formed on the lungs as a result of an illness is not a proper membrane"[327], and has no influence concerning the severity of the injury. Possible injuries caused by the fingers of the butcher during the removal of the lungs from the chest are easily recognizable as such. Small perforations of the surface, next to which one finds *murana* worms, are said to have occurred post-mortem by the crawling out of the worm. I do not believe that these worms refer to any type of

---

323. This statement of Preuss is hard to understand. The Hebrew word for cough is *she'ul* (F.R.)
324. *Deutsch. Med. Wchschr.* 188 No. 20 p.1025

325. *Beitrag zur Medizinischen Topographie von Jerusalem*. Berlin 1885 p.42
326. Chullin 46a-b
327. *ibid* 47b

strongiloidae[328] or liver fluke or lung nematode (*pseudalius ovis*), because these parasites do not leave the parenchyma of the lung after the death of the patient.

If a doubt exists as to whether an injury was already present when the animal was still alive or whether it first occurred after its death, one should *produce* a similar injury — according to others, in another animal of the same type — and compare them. If both injuries are identical, it naturally speaks for a post-mortem occurrence.

2) According to Rabbi Nachman, a fistulous communication between two adjacent bronchi is a life-threatening situation; the same does not apply to two loops of intestines that have a mesentery (*haduré de kantha*). The latter case is used as a striking example to illustrate the rule that in regard to injuries, abnormal conditions in various parts of the body cannot be analogously compared to each other[329].

3) According to Rabbi Yochanan, Rabbi Eleazar and Rabbi Chanina, a needle (or any other pointed object) that is found in the lung does not prove the presence of a dangerous injury, because it could have fortuitously been aspirated through the trachea. Other Sages, however, consider such an animal to be *terefah,* since the probability is that the needle entered the lung through a perforation of the lung membrane from the outside[330].

4) If the contents of the lung cavity in the case of intact pleura pour out like from a jug, it is a non-harmful situation (bronchiectasis or cysts), according to Rabbi Yochanan. Raba[331], however, requires that the bronchi remain intact, which proves he knows of the seriousness of ulcerous cavities. To make the diagnosis, one pours the liquid into a glazed basin; if there are any white pieces seen, it is considered to indicate a dangerous process, otherwise, it is a non-dangerous condition[332].

5) If, in the case of an otherwise normal appearance of the external surface, there occurs an obstruction *(atum)* in the lung, so that the latter does not expand when inflated, one must cut into the wall of the lung at the site of the obstruction. If viscous fluid *(mugla* i.e. pus) is found, then it is clear that the obstruction was caused by the pus. Otherwise, a feather or some spittle is placed over the obstruction; if one inflates the lung and the feather or spittle moves, it indicates free passage of air and hence indicates the presence of (non-dangerous) atelectasis[333].

6) Rafram said that a lung which is like a block of wood *(uphtha)* is *terefah.* The *Gemara* debates wherein the comparison lies: some explain, like wood in color; others like wood to the touch. The former mean that it looks bloated (lustreless, white) and the latter mean it feels hard like wood. A third opinion is that it is "a lung which is smooth because it has no fissures marking the lobes". The condition referred to here is obviously peripneumonia *(boum)*[334].

7) If a portion of the lungs becomes so dry that it crumbles when scratched by a nail — according to Raba — the animal is *terefah* (probably referring to caseation); not so, however, if it bleeds when pierced, for in the latter case, healing is still possible, because the external air has no access thereto. In the case of an organ exposed to the air, however, (for example, the ear lobe) such necrotic parts do not heal any more, even if they still bleed when pierced[335].

One should also mention here the related case of the obscure teaching concerning the dried-up (atrophic?) animal *(charuta)* whose lungs are completely shrivelled up on

---

328. Strongyloides filaria and micrurus occur in ruminants. *Murana* is derived from the Greek *myraina* and is so named because of its eel-like shape. Löw *Fischnamen* No. 6
329. Chullin 48b. Rav Ashi said...an animal may be cut in one place and die, and in another place and live.
330. *Rashi:* the windpipe swallows nothing. Therefore, the needle must have entered the alimentary canal and from there perforated the intestine (and the diaphragm) and thus penetrated the lung.
331. Preuss erroneously has Rab (F.R.)
332. Chullin 47b
333. *ibid*
334. *ibid*
335. *ibid* 46b

all sides (dried up, sunken in, *tzemukah*). Raba, the grandson of Chana, came upon such rams in the desert. Two types of this anomaly were recognized: one caused by an act of man and the other by an act of God (natural, spontaneous)[336]. To distinguish the two types, one places the lungs to be examined in water for 24 hours — in the summer in a white basin with cold water, in the winter in a dark basin with warm water; if the lungs return to their normal state, it is a sign that it was caused by an act of God and is not life-threatening. Otherwise, the fault lies in a human act and the animal is *terefah*[337]. It remains incomprehensible how the latter effect is to be interpreted. It is easier to understand that an animal parched with thirst (in the desert) should also have shrivelled-up lungs.

8) Individual blisters on the *pleura* of the lung, irrespective of their size, which contain air, clear water or a honey-like substance (*kande*, actually jugs), are of no significance, according to Rabbi Nachman, for the life of the animal. Simple cysts are probably meant. Also of no significance are small solid vegetations *(tzemachim)* or individual rock-hard lumps, *tinnare*[338].

9) According to Raba, if two such cysts *(bu'e)* are separate but contiguous no examination thereof can avail (i.e. there must have been an underlying perforation) and the animal is *terefah*. If one is in doubt as to whether or not two contiguous cysts are separated from each other, one should take a thorn and pierce one from the side; if mucous runs from one into the other, it is a *single* cyst and the situation is not dangerous[339].

10) Particular attention is devoted to the pathologic importance of cord-like or band-like adherence of the two pleural membranes, *sirka*. This is always to be considered an abnormal situation. The conceptualization of ancient anatomists that these simply represented *ligamenta spuria* is thoroughly foreign to the Talmud. *"Sirka does not ever occur if the serosa is intact." (En sirka beli nekeb).*

To examine such an adhesion, the lung is separated from the chest wall with a sharp knife. If a pathological change is found on the chest wall, then we assume the adhesion was caused by the wall (and the animal is not *terefah*). Otherwise, we assume that it (the perforation leading to the adhesion) was caused by the lung pleura, even if it cannot be demonstrated by the above-mentioned test of inflating the lungs; and the animal is naturally *terefah*[340]. The post-Talmudic responsa literature regarding individual regulations concerning *sirkoth* is extraordinarily extensive.

According to Raba, if two lobes of the lungs adhere to each other, no examination thereof is necessary, and the animal is *terefah*. The *Gemara,* however, limits this rule to the case where the lobes were not in their proper order *(shelo kesidran)* (i.e. lobe one adhered to lobe three)[341]. Already the ancient commentaries of the Talmud are of varied opinions as to the meaning of this passage. It is likely that it refers to constrictions of lobes by pleuritic cords.

According to Raba, if the outer membrane of the lung (the pleura) was peeled off, whereas the inner membrane (alveolar wall) remained intact, so that the lung now resembles a red date, it is not a life-threatening situation to the animal[342]. Kazenelson[343] considers this to be a case of epithelial desquamation as a result of *pleuritis sicca.*

---

336. I accept the opposite as by the teaching of castrates *(saris)*. The explanation given by all the commentators since Rabbi Gersom is totally unintelligible: the animal was frightened, in the former case by a person or another animal, and in the latter case by an act of Heaven such as thunder and lightning. Ritter says that the above explanation of the text is untenable according to the Talmud.

337. Chullin 55b
338. *ibid* 48ab
339. *ibid* 47a
340. *ibid* 48a
341. *ibid* 46b
342. *ibid*
343. Kazenelson *op. cit.* p.254

11) The identification of color designations from antiquity, as is known, is fraught with considerable difficulty, reasons for which need not be described here. As a result, the following assertions of the Talmud are extremely difficult for us to understand.

Raba said: if only a portion of the lungs turned red, it is not a dangerous condition, but not so if the entire organ became red (then the animal is *terefah* ). Nevertheless, the final decision is that even an alteration in the latter (i.e. partial return of the normal color) makes the illness capable of being cured (hyperemia?).

Raba further distinguishes nuances of colors of eye make-up (*kuchla,* stibium) from those of ink. If the lungs are the color of ink, the animal is *terefah,* because this black color was originally red (blood which turned black as a result of disease)[344]. A fortuitously present (inhaled) pigment cannot be what Raba is referring to. He correctly recognized that such "black or otherwise colored *multiple spots" (ukkame ukkame)* are an incidental finding. Rather, he is probably describing a hemorrhagic infarct.

The color *yarok,* as already explained above, is equivalent to the Greek *chloros* and entails all the nuances from the pallid appearance of chlorotics to the yellow of honey and the dark green of green crops. If the lung is leek green, it represents a harmless condition; however if it resembles shades of hops, or the crocus or the yolk of an egg, the animal is afflicted with a serious illness[344a].

If the lung is liver-colored, it is of no significance; not so if it resembles the color of meat.

Tradition conceives of the above remark of Rabbi Kahana as follows: "if like liver, it is *kosher;* if like meat, it is *terefah".* Naturally, the point of comparison could be something other than the color.

# PART   VII
# DISEASES OF THE HEART

## I

The ancients do not speak much of heart diseases. According to Aristotle, the heart can never become seriously diseased, because if the major part, *e arche,* becomes diseased, there is no hope any longer for the other organs of the body[345]. Aretäus states that when the heart becomes diseased, *(e men kardie pathe),* death supervenes rapidly[346]. Hippocrates already has the same assertion[347]. According to Plinius, the heart is the only internal organ which does not become afflicted by any disease, and remains free of the sufferings of life[348]. The only illness I can mention with certainty is palpitation of the heart *(palmos tes kardias).* Galen, apparently considering this to be a symptom of organic disease, correctly observed that people suffering from palpitations die between forty and fifty years of age[349].

We will speak more later about the illness *kardiakos* which is also mentioned in the Talmud by this name. The entity *kardiogmos* certainly refers to a stomach ailment[350], and the same is true of *kardialgia.* Concerning *kardioponos,* we only know its name and a remedy therefore[351].

344. Chullin 47b
344a. *ibid*
345. Aristotle. *De Partib.* 3 Chapt. 4 fol. 260 ed. Firmin-Didot.
346. Aretäus. Book 2 Chapt. 1
347. Hippocrates. *De Morbis* 4:33. Foes fol. 504
348. Plinius. *Hist. Natur.* 11:69
349. Galen. *De Locis* 5:2; Kühn. 8:305
350. Hippocrates. *Coac. Praenot.* No. 142 and the remark of Foes thereon. fol. 138
351. Galen, in *Remed. Parab.* 3; Kühn 14:550, recommends: place rue, lentil seeds and cabbage *kata ten kardian*

## II

From the Talmudic literature, the following names of illnesses are noteworthy:
1) *Keeb-leb,* pain of the heart, *kardialgia.* Rab said: "I can tolerate any illness, but not an illness of the bowels; any pain, but not heart pain; any ache, but not headache; any evil, but not an evil wife"[352]. It remains undecided whether the *keeb-leb* which affects a person who draws out his prayer and meditates on it[353] refers to an abdominal cramp or, as seems more likely, an affection of the heart (psyche). The Biblical expression in Isaiah 65:14 suggests that the latter meaning is the correct one (i.e. vexation of spirit or psychological heart pain). To protect oneself against heart pain, one used *ketzach* or black cumin, although the opinions concerning the value of this substance are divided. In any event, smelling the aroma thereof is harmful, and the mother of Rabbi Jeremiah who used to sprinkle cumin on her bread scratched it off before she distributed it[354].

The addition of cumin to bread could not be tolerated by the spirits of illness of the Germanic people, and it thus served to drive away illnesses[355]. Perhaps it played the same role with the Semites. The use of black cumin, *gith,* in baking is also mentioned by Plinius[356]: *gith gratis sime panes condiat.* The same is said of *melanthion* by Dioscorides[357].

2) *Chulsha de libba,* weakness of the *libba.* This condition affects mostly people who are hungry, such as Rabbi Chisda and Rabba Bar Huna who sat all day engaged in their function as judges[358]. Rabbi Zera could not deliver his scholarly discourse because he suffered therefrom[359]. Rabbi Awia was afraid of developing this bad condition if he should go on an empty stomach to hear the lengthy discourses of Rabbi Joseph[360]. If one takes mustard *(chardel)* once a month, one keeps certain sicknesses away. If one consumes it every day, however, one easily develops *chulsha de libba*[361]. To cure this condition, the mother of Abaye recommended the following folk remedy: roast the meat of the right flank of a male beast over the excrement of cattle cast in the month of Nissan; or roast it over a fire of willow twigs. Let the patient eat this meat and drink some wine thereafter[362] — evidently an emetic.

3) *Jukra de libba,* heaviness of the *libba.* A remedy therefor consists of three shekels of asafetida *(chiltith)* dissolved in cold or warm water, consumed on three consecutive days. Premature termination of the therapy is considered dangerous[363]. Are we here speaking of the above-mentioned *kardioponos?* Naturally, this ailment could also refer to *barythymia* (depression or melancholy). Another remedy is as follows: eat three barley cakes streaked with less than three-day-old sauce *(kameka)* and wash them down with diluted wine[364].

4) *Pircha de libba,* opposite of the former, refers to "fluttering (i.e. palpitations) of the heart". The remedy is to eat three cakes of wheat streaked with honey, followed by strong (undiluted) wine[365]. This remedy is specifically identified as an emetic.

5) For *kircha de libba,* one should consume the size of three eggs of ammi *(ninya)*[366], a measure of one egg of cumin and the same of sesame[367].

The Syriac *tzarach* means *arsit, inflammavit.* The *Targum*[368] translates the word *charchur* as *kircha de libba;* i.e. referring to "inflammation or excitement of the heart".

---

352. Shabbath 11a
353. Berachoth 55a
354. *ibid* 40a
355. Hofler. *Janus* 1902 p. 305
356. Plinius 20:71
357. Dioscorides 3:93
358. Shabbath 10a
359. Taanith 7a
360. Berachoth 28b
361. *ibid* 40a
362. Erubin 29b
363. Shabbath 140a
364. Gittin 69b
365. *ibid*
366. See Plinius 20:58. *Ammi.... Inflammationes et tormina discutit*
367. *Ibid*
368. *Targum Jerushalmi* Deut. 28:22

In the systematically organized enumeration of remedies according to the parts of the body (Gittin 69ab), the remedies suggested for the latter three conditions mentioned above are listed just before intestinal ailments. Hence, the assumption that *libba* refers to stomach becomes even more likely.

# PART VIII
# DISEASES OF THE DIGESTIVE TRACT

As already mentioned, the expressions *leb* and *libba*, as well as the *kardia* of the Greeks, apply equally well to both heart and stomach. It is possible that some of the ailments discussed under "Diseases of the Heart" more properly belong here. Therefore, in the following section, we will only consider those conditions which definitely refer to the intestines.

## I   Dysentery

*Choli me'ayim,* or intestinal illness, is one of the illnesses people were afraid of. All types of digestive disturbances are included in this term, but particularly dysentery. He who passes stool excessively is ill in his intestines and should do something for it before the ailment worsens[369]. This ailment may also occur in association with fever. The father of Publius lay sick with fever and dysentery[370]. Some bedridden patients with this condition have swollen *(thapuach)* abdomens[371]. Because of their pain, patients with intestinal disease are forgiven for their sins on this earth, and therefore do not go to hell[372]. Therefore, it is a good omen for a deceased person *(quoad vitam aeternam)* to have died of *choli me'ayim* because most pious people suffer from it[373]; and Rabbi Jose wished it upon himself[374]. Whenever Scriptures uses the expression *gawa,* he died, the cause of death was *choli me'ayim*[375]. Three people die (suddenly?) while they are speaking (while fully conscious?): one who is ill in his intestines, a woman in confinement (of pulmonary emboli?), and a person with dropsy[376].

The disease is very painful, and Rab would rather suffer from any illness but not *choli me'ayim*[377]. Tears in the privy (following strongly forced stool evacuation) are not good tears[378].

This illness has different causes. Priests who walked barefoot on the stone floor of the Temple and ate much meat and washed it down with water suffered greatly from this illness[379]. As a result, a specialist was engaged in the Temple to treat these sick priests[380]. According to Mar Samuel, any change in one's life style heralds the beginning of *choli me'ayim*[381]. Therefore, the words of the epigrammatic poet are: *all the days of the afflicted are evil*[382], because even festivals are spoiled for him if he eats rich foods thereby developing bowel ailments[383]. Even a regular but deficient nutritional intake can lead to this illness. He who eats without drinking eats blood (i.e. consumes his own body, or becomes lean), and this is the beginning of *choli me'ayim*[384]. Therefore, one who swills down his food with plenty of water does not

369. Sotah 42b
370. Acts 28:8 8:8
371. Aboth de Rabbi Nathan 41:1
372. Erubin 41b
373. Kethuboth 103b
374. Shabbath 118b
375. Genesis Rabbah 62:2
376. Erubin 41b

377. Shabbath 11a
378. Lamentations Rabbah 2:15
379. Jerushalmi Shekalim 5; 48d
380. *ibid* 5:2
381. Nedarim 37b
382. Proverbs 15:15
383. Sanhedrin 101a
384. Shabbath 42a

develop *choli me'ayim,* and, according to Rabbi Chisda, the proper measure of water is one cupful per loaf of bread or other food[385].

Very few remedies for this illness are mentioned in the Talmud. Frequently, external measures are recommended such as rubbing the abdomen with a mixture of oil and wine[386], or applying warm towels on the abdomen. It was probably also a folk custom to place an open basin with hot water on the abdomen; however, this practice was prohibited by the Rabbis because of the danger of scalding oneself[387]. One also used to "place a cup on the navel"[388], perhaps in the same way that people even today "place a glass" of any type on the abdomen for abdominal pain. One can at least divert attention from the pain by engaging in intensive mental activity[389].

Among internally taken medicaments, very old (70 year old) apple wine helps many patients with dysentery[390]. Very old grape juice is also good for the intestines, as opposed to fresh juice[391]. According to legend, a king who drank lemonade made from the citrons which, as is known, are used in the ritual of the Festival of Tabernacles, was cured of his dysentery[392]. The following is recommended as a medication for pain in the abdomen *(ke'eb me'i):* use 300 kernels of long pepper, 100 daily in wine. Rabin from Naresh gave the daughter of Rabbi Ashi 150 kernels of our (the usual Palestinian) pepper, and she was cured[393]. Fresh *sison* (camomile) also serves as an astringent if it is cooked in water; dried camomile has a purgative action. The mnemonic is: "with *moist* rushes one blocks the river"[394].

In the diet, one naturally paid attention to the influence of individual foods on the intestines, as shown by the already-mentioned suggestion of drinking a lot of water during meals. In addition, one attempted, as in folk medicine in general, to strengthen individual organs. According to one source, leek is good for the intestines but bad for the teeth; the reverse is true of spleen. Therefore, one should chew spleen and spit it out; hashed leek, however, should be swallowed without chewing[395]. A broth of mangold *(tardin,* beta vulgaris) is good for the stomach (or heart), and good for the eyes; and needless to say it is good for the intestines; Abaya, however, requires that it be well-cooked[396]. The same properties are present in wine made from cabbage sprouts (asparagus), if one glass of it is imbibed early in the morning on an empty stomach, as long as one does not become intoxicated therefrom[397].

Rab was sick with his intestines (seasick?) following a trip from Palestine to Babylon and was appropriately furious at Mar Samuel because the latter misused his medical knowledge and served Rab wheat bread, fish brine and beer all of which have a strong purgative effect on the intestine, without showing him the privy[398]. Rabbi Chiya said: if someone wishes to prevent becoming ill with *choli me'ayim,* he should accustom himself to eat bread immersed in vinegar or wine in both summer and winter; if nature calls, pull yourself away from a delicious meal and do not tarry but go to the privy immediately[399].

It is a religious obligation to visit the sick; however, one should not visit someone suffering from an intestinal ailment or someone with headache or someone with an eye disorder. The reason for the first is because of embarrassment from the diarrhea, the reason for the latter two is because speech is injurious to them[400]. Originally, incense was only placed under corpses of people that died of *choli me'ayim* (to neutralize the

385. Berachoth 40a
386. Shabbath 134a
387. *ibid* 40b
388. *ibid* 66b
389. This sense is found in Erubin 54a in the sentence: he who suffers in his intestines should occupy himself with Torah.
390. Abodah Zarah 40b
391. Nedarim 9:8

392. Levit. Rabbah 37:2
393. Gittin 69b
394. *ibid*
395. Berachoth 44b
396. *ibid* 39a
397. *ibid* 51a
398. Shabbath 108a
399. Gittin 70a
400. Nedarim 41a

odor); as a result, live patients with this illness were ashamed and, therefore, it was decreed that incense should be placed under *all* corpses, irrespective of the cause of death[401].

## II   Large Bowel Ailments

The illness *kolos* is dangerous. When Rabbi Joshua ben Levi became ill with *kolos,* Rabbi Chanina suggested that he pulverize cress, place it in aged wine, and speedily drink it so that his life not become endangered[402].

The later Talmudic-Aggaddic texts have *kolom.* It probably refers to an ailment of the colon which first occurred during the reign of Tiberius (14-37 C.E.). The first casualty therefrom was the emperor himself, and the name of the illness was completely unknown to the general populace when it first appeared in the "Bulletin"[403]. It remains undecided whether this word is identical to *kolikos,* as asserted by Mussaphia.

When Rabbi Jacob suffered from *pika,* Rabbi Ammi recommended the following[404]: place seven kernels of purple-red colored alkali (salsola); wrap them in the collar of a shirt, tie it with a white thread; dip it in white naphtha and burn it and then apply the ashes on the slit in the rectum. While preparing this, take a blackberry and apply its split *(pika)* side on the *pika.* That is so only for an upper *pika;* for a lower *pika* one melts the fat of a goat which has not yet born any young and applies it. Alternatively, one can take three melon leaves which were dried in the shade, roast them, and sprinkle the ashes on the sore; or one can take the shells of purple snails[405]; or one can take wax-oil[406] and apply it in summer with a linen rag and in winter with cotton wool.

*Pika* means "cleft". According to Rabbenu Chananel, it refers to the site of the lower part *(thachtoniyoth)* of the body (the glutei) that splits i.e. the *rima ani;* according to *Rashi,* it is the anus. The blackberry which had been deprived of its stem might be interpreted in folk fantasy as resembling the *nates cum ano* — hence the therapy. "The upper *pika*" probably represents the real anal cleft, and "the lower *pika*" the flesh in the middle. The illness was probably a type of eczema or the like.

## III   Bulimia

If someone is stricken with bulimia, he may be given even forbidden foods, until his eyes light up[407], that is until he can distinguish between good and evil, meaning until he regains his senses. According to another source, he should be given honey and other sweet things. Mar Samuel recommended fat meat, whereas another Sage said fine flour in honey. Rabbi Papa even suggests coarse barley flour in honey. Rabbi Yochanan plucked a fig for himself from the eastern side of the fig tree where the figs are the sweetest. Rabbi Judah once stole a piece of bread from a shepherd because of bulimia. When Rabbi Jose entered a city while he suffered from bulimia the people rushed to greet him with all sorts of food[408].

According to the *Tosefta*[409], the Egyptian man who was given a piece of a fig cake and two raisin cakes[410] had an attack of bulimia. The *Gemara* disputes this assertion because he had not eaten nor drunk any liquids for three days and was therefore only

401. Moed Katan 27b; Tosefta Niddah 9:16
402. Jerushalmi Shabbath 14; 14d and Jerushalmi Abodah Zarah 2; 40d
403. Plinius 26:6
404. Abodah Zarah 28b
405. *mischkede* or *mischkere chalzone;* according to *Rashi: limin* i.e. snails. *Aruch,* following the *Teshuboth Hageonim* (Kohut 5:282b) states: "frogs which split and become frogs" (tadpoles). Mussaphia disputes this interpretation.
406. *Rashi:* wax and oil melted together
407. Yoma 8:6
408. Yoma 83b
409. Tosefta Shabbath 8:30
410. First Samuel 30:12

simply faint. We can also draw no conclusions about the effect of honey for bulimia from the assertion of Jonathan: *see how mine eyes have become light (after fasting), because I tasted a little honey*[411].

As is quite apparent, the craving in bulimia is to be understood as an intense (oxlike) hunger. Alexander of Tralles[412] said: "As the name implies, bulimia is an intense hunger, *megas loimos*". The Alexandrians also mention *boulimiontes* who were found faint on the roads or elsewhere[413]. They state that bulimia consists of a cooling of the stomach caused by lack of nutrition, and weakening as a result of external cold. Hunger only occurs at the outset; it does not become persistent, however, once it has been satisfied[414]. Here lies the difference between bulimia and *orexis kynodes* (dog's appetite) which is *fames canina*. The *latter* is usually confused with bulimia but these patients are constantly *(apaystos)* hungry; coldness of the stomach also makes them hungry, and they should be given wine and fat meat to consume[415]. On the other hand, for bulimia, one separated the jaws of the patient and pulled his hair and ears up, measures which are employed in folk medicine even today. In the case of bulimia, the ravenous hunger, the craving for food occurs very often and is abnormally strong; however, it is always fleeting. In the case of *fames canina,* the patient never has the feeling of satiation, even after the ingestion of a large amount of nourishment.

He who yields to "bulimia of immorality" *(lahut)* will eventually still his hunger with his own flesh and blood, as happened to Lot and his daughters[416].

## IV    The Illness of King Jehoram

The prophet threatened King Jehoram[417] with the following punishment: the Lord will bring a great *maggepha*[418] upon your people and your children and your wives and all your goods. And you will be punished, however, with much suffering, with disease of your bowels, until your bowels fall out as a result of the sickness day by day (from time to time). Neighboring nations will conquer all the possessions of the king and carry away all his belongings, together with his wives and sons. *And after all this the Lord smote him in his bowels with an incurable disease. And it came to pass, that in the process of time after the end of two years, his bowels fell out by reason of his sickness, and he died of severe afflictions*[419].

All of the above speaks for the hypothesis that this 40-year-old man was afflicted with rectal cancer from which pieces broke off from time to time. Following two years of severe suffering, the illness led to the patient's death.

Nearly all ancient commentators consider the illness to be dysentery although, already in 1672, Bartholin objected against this diagnosis, saying: *dysenteria longus morbus non est.* He could have added that the "falling out of bowels" does not occur in dysentery; one might sooner think of *enteritis membranacea.*

## V    The Illnesses of Antiochus and Herod

In the second book of Maccabees[420] the following is related: "God, the all powerful Lord, struck down Antiochus with an incurable and externally visible sore[421]. He had hardly finished his speech when he was seized with an intolerable pain in his bowels and strong internal suffering[422]. He still did not desist from his insolence and gave orders to hasten his journey. But it happened that he fell out of his chariot as

411. *ibid* 14:29
412. Ed. Puschmann 2:25a
413. Oribasius 6:36. Vo. 5:315 ed. Daremberg.
414. *idem. Eupor.* 3:10 Vol. 5:668
415. *idem. Synops* 9:10. Vol. 5:476
416. *Yalkut* on Genesis 19:30 part 1 No. 86
417. Septuagint writes Joram

418. Septuagint has *plege* meaning sore
419. Second Chronicles 21:14-18
420. Second Maccabees 9:5 ff
421. *aniato kai aorato plege*
422. *anekestos ton splagchnon algedon kai pikrai ton endon basanoi*

it was rushing along, and dislocated *(apostreblousthai)* all the limbs in his body from the serious fall. He now lay flat on the ground and had to be carried in a litter. Worms grew from the abdomen of this godless creature, and while he was still alive, wracked with pain and torment, his flesh fell off. The entire camp was burdened with the stench from his body. He finally repented from his sins, appointed a successor, and died".

The story allows two interpretations: the acute pain in the intestines is already a symptom of the illness which led to his death, in which case one can assume that it was a case of perforation of the gut with peritonitis and subsequent abscess formation. The fall from the wagon aggravated the condition to such an extent that "the flesh fell off", meaning that pieces of the abdominal wall which were gangrenous fell off. Alternatively, as suggested by Friedreich, the abdominal pain was a separate illness in and of itself, and everything that followed could be attributed to the fall. The wounds and bruises became gangrenous, whole pieces fell off, and an intolerable stench developed[423].

The "worms" would mean the same according to both the above interpretations. Since no one could carry the patient because of the unpleasant stench emanating from him, the maintenance of the cleanliness of the wounds undoubtedly left much to be desired. As a result, maggots developed — Rust's *ulcus verminosum*. One should also here mention the complaint of Job: *my flesh is covered with worms (rimma)...my skin is broken and dissolving*[424].

The story of the Apostles[425] also relates that Herod Agrippa was eaten by worms *(skolekobrotos)* while he was alive, and he died therefrom. No precise details are given concerning the type of his illness. From the report of Josephus[426] that Herod died within five days of severe abdominal pain *(tes koilias algema),* Sir Ridson Bennet concludes[427] "that the cause of death was perforation of the bowel by intestinal worms, which produced ulceration and acute peritonitis". This diagnosis is not convincing since it can only be made with assurance by opening the corpse, and no such information is available from antiquity. Equally unlikely is the hypothesis that Herod's illness was an abdominal abscess which emptied externally and whose pus contained mawworms. One could sooner agree with Renan[428] that Herod died of poisoning.

Legend relates about the scouts that their tongues *that did bring up the evil report upon the land*[429] became so long that they extended to the navel and that maggots *(thola'im)* then came out from the tongue and entered the navel and from the navel to the tongue[430]. Similar stories are related by Cedrenus concerning the death of Diocletian[431], and the observation of such an occurrence might well represent a portrayal of lung cancer.

It is debated in the Talmud as to whether the worms which "come from living people" are actually parts of the person, perhaps somewhat altered because of the disease, or whether they only represent secretions *(pirsha,* literally: separations) of his body. Rabbi Eliezer concludes that the former interpretation is correct, whereas Rabbi Judah espouses the second opinion. The recognition that these "worms" entered the wound from the outside came much later.

It is with great pleasure that some authors who dislike the people they write about state that the latter were eaten by worms. Numerous examples of this can be found in the work of Bochard and Geber[432], concerning kings and tyrants in antiquity, and church fathers and world rulers during the Middle Ages. One should also here mention

423. Friedreich. *Zur Bibel* 1:235
424. Job 7:5
425. Acts 12:23
426. Josephus. *Antiquities* Book 19 Chapt. 8:2
427. Bennet. *The Diseases of the Bible* p.173
428. Renan. *Die Apostel.* Leipzig 1866 p.269
429. Numbers 14:37
430. Sotah 35a
431. Bochart. *Hierozoic* 1675, 2 col 620
432. Eulenburg. *Real-Encykl.* s.v. pediculosis

the Talmudic narrative of a priest from the hostile sect of Sadducees from whose nose worms extruded, until he died[433].

I do not know who first proposed the hypothesis that Antiochus and Herod died of phthiriasis. Bartholin in 1672 already speaks of this as being a widespread theory. In modern times, Trusen energetically supports the theory of pedicular disease. For his assumption, he gives no reason other than that this illness was very prevalent in antiquity. In fact, the innumerable places in ancient writings cited by Geber, and the meticulous register of writings of Huber[434] show how widespread the belief in this disease was; however, one can bring no proof therefrom concerning an individual case (such as Antiochus and Herod). In addition, the text specifically states worms, *skolekes,* and even if one deprecates the ability of lay people to observe phenomena of nature, it is at least audacious to think that they would confuse worms with lice. I will only mention in passing that the number of people who still believe in pedicular disease in the ancient sense is very small, if there are indeed any at all who so believe.

## VI   Hemorrhoids

1) The Talmudic name of the illness *tachtoniyoth* is translated as hemorrhoids, although the word itself only means *inferiores.* Support for this interpretation comes only from the commentaries. When *Rashi* translates the word as *figues,* we cannot assume that he means syphilis, because this expression did not refer to condylomata at that time (1100 C.E.). The first physician to explain *tachtoniyoth* as hemorrhoids was an anonymous contemporary of *Rashi* from Saxony[435].

The Talmud makes the following assertions concerning this illness: Rabbi Yochanan said: "do not sit excessively because *tachtonim*[436] might develop; do not stand excessively because that is harmful to the heart (or stomach, *leb* ); do not run excessively because that is harmful to the eyes; rather divide your activities equally[437]. When the Lord of the disobedient people of Israel threatens them with "failing of the eyes and suffering of the heart"[438], the illness referred to is *tachtoniyoth* (bleeding which leads to collapse?)[439]. According to an ancient teaching[440], ten things lead to *tachtoniyoth:* eating the leaves of reeds or of vines, or unsalted animal palates, or fish bones, or insufficiently cooked food, or salted fish, or drinking wine lees, or wiping one's anus with lime, potter's clay or pebbles used previously. According to some Sages, hemorrhoids also occur if one strains (or stands) unduly (literally: hangs oneself) in the privy.

It seems easy to find an allusion to all ailments of the anal region in this register including fistulas, condylomas and prolapse.

Concerning remedies for this condition, it is only mentioned that dates are helpful for three ailments: for bad thoughts (melancholy), for diarrhea *(choli me'ayim)* and for hemorrhoids *(tachtoniyoth)*[441].

2) It is also only on the authority of the commentaries that we discuss the illness known in the Talmud as *rushcheta* together with *tachtoniyoth. Aruch* has the textual reading *shichta.* The Talmud itself only mentions the name of the ailment[442] and one remedy therefor. The meaning of the details of this remedy are also uncertain: for *rushcheta* take gum arabic juice and aloe and white lead *(aspidka)*[443] and lead gloss

433. Jerushalmi Yoma 1; 39a
434. Huber. *Klinische Entomologie.* Part 1 pp.22-24; Küchenmeister. *Parasiten* p.550
435. Mitteilungun aus einer Handschrift Sammlung. in *Magazin für die Wissenschaft des Judentums.* 1885. p.185 No. 3
436. masculine; i.e. intestine and rectum to parallel the "heart" and "eyes"
437. Kethuboth 111a
438. Deut. 28:65
439. Nedarim 22a
440. Berachoth 55a and Shabbath 81a
441. Kethuboth 10b
442. *shichta* in Syriac means rust or dirt; allegedly leprosy. Löw
443. Cerussa; according to *Aruch,* it refers to *argentum vivum,* quicksilver

(*martika*, litharge) and malabathrum berries[444] and glaucium[445]; place all these ingredients in a thin rag in the summer, or in cotton wool in the winter[446]. The commentaries add: and apply it there to the site of the ailment, i.e. on the anal region. The *Gemara* concludes: alternatively, drink diluted beer.

If someone finds pleasure in studying how this *remedy* is concluded to refer to lues as the sickness involved, he may do so[447].

3) *Burdam* or *burdas*[448]. Rabbi Yochanan said: one should not visit someone with *burdas* nor mention his name because, according to Rabbi Eleazar, it is like a gushing well, and from that it derives its name (*bor dam* meaning "a well of blood"). According to Rabbi Asher ben Yechiel, one should not visit the patient (with *burdam* i.e. bloody diarrhea) in order not to shame him, and according to *Rashi,* in order not to catch it. Because of the former reason, one does not mention his name in the presence of others, because "it is not clean"[449]. Perhaps this description refers to a patient with bloody diarrhea or with profusely bleeding hemorrhoids.

# VII    Helminths

1) One of the thirteen favorable effects attributed to a morning snack is that it kills "worms in the intestines"[450]. There was unanimity of opinion in antiquity[451] that garlic has the same effect[452]. In both traditions, these worms are called *kinnim*. In the Biblical narrative of the ten Egyptian plagues, the plague of *kinnim* is usually interpreted to refer to lice.

2) Various types of worms are apparently included in the designation *kukyane*. Barley flour is said to give rise to them[453], in the same way that our mothers think that children get worms from eating bread. Another source says that only "barley flour which is more than forty days old" (since it was ground) is capable of giving rise to worms. The latter are identified with the helminths known as flour worms (larva of *Tenebrio molitor*) as proven by the variant of the text which states: "they (the *kukyane*) arise from barley flour *in the barrel,* if forty days have elapsed". A remedy therefore is to take marjoram and seven black dates[454], as also recommended elsewhere in antiquity[455]. Finally, a third Talmudic citation asserts that *kukyane* in animals enter from the outside, although they are not found in the digestive tract of the animals. For when the animal sleeps, the worms ascend into its nose[456]. These probably refer to sheep horseflies which are otherwise called "*darné* of the head"[457]. *Dura* is also the name of the worm which the Lord made develop as a result of excessive meat ingestion in the bowels of those who grumbled about the manna[458].

3) In the often-mentioned collection of remedies in Gittin 69b, among the remedies listed against a variety of abdominal illnesses, there are also those against *kirtza* and white *kirtza*. According to the commentaries, these names of ailments refer to worms in the intestines, perhaps, as suggested by Lewyson[459], the usual brown and the white mawworms. The remedy for *kirtza* is one quarter *log* (approximately 60

---

444. *chumarta de pilon, phyllon* in Greek; Löw. *Pflanzennamen* No. 209 p.269
445. one should read: *sheyapha demamita* meaning glaucium, Löw. *Pflanzennamen* p.205. *Aruch:* radish; *Rashi:* pigeon or chicken dung — Both have: *dechamimta.*
446. Gittin 69b
447. Fischer, in his edition of Buxtorf's *Wörterbuch* 1:93, Note 213
448. Löw: the manuscript only attests to *burdas.*
449. Nedarim 41b
450. Baba Metzia 107b
451. for example Coelius Aurelianus 4 p.540;

Celsus 4:17 and others. Garlic enemas are still thought highly of even today. From Indian legend: Cassel, *Mischle Sindbad* p.138
452. Baba Kamma 82a
453. Berachoth 36a
454. Shabbath 109b
455. Hyssop is recommended for *lumbricus lati* by Celsus 4:17
456. Chullin 67b
457. Shabbath 54b
458. Numbers Rabbah 7:4
459. Lewyson. *Zoologie des Talmud* No. 476

grams) of wine with laurel leaves; for white *kirtza,* take hedge mustard seeds — which, according to Plinius[460], also kill all *bestiolas* living in the body — wrap them in a rag, soak them in water and drink this broth. Be very careful with the kernels themselves because they can easily injure the intestines.

4) The name *arketha*[461], which is only found once in the Talmud[462], is explained, according to the concept of the commentaries, to refer to the *liver fluke.* Schonhak (in *Hamashbir* s.v.) derives the word from the Aramaic *arketha* meaning strap, and hence considered it to be the tapeworm. Mussaphia's explanation: *morbus arquatus* (jaundice) is false[463].

This illness occurs if one eats raw or fat meat or beef or certain cabbage seeds[464] on an empty stomach and then drinks water. As a remedy, the *yo'ezer* plant is recommended. The latter is identified in the Babylonian *Gemara* as *puthnak,* and in the Palestinian *Gemara* as polytrichon. The use of the latter drug *(herba adiantus, quam Latini capillum Veneris vocant)* is also mentioned by Coelius Aurelianus for *Morbus arquatus* but he advises against its use[465], whereas Dioscorides[466] recommends it.

Additional remedies are as follows: swallow white cress; or roast fat meat on coals, then suck a piece of it and then sip vinegar. Some people advise against the vinegar because it is harmful to the liver. Or take shavings of thorns which were pared from above downward, but not the reverse, because otherwise the *arketha* would come out through the mouth[467]; cook this in beer in the evening and imbibe it. In the morning, one should restrain the stool, but when it comes one should defecate on a palm branch(?).

If the liver is wormy *(hitlia)* — full of worms, distoma? — the capacity of the liver is not thereby endangered. The recognition of this teaching at the college at Yabneh was only effected by the *bnei asya* after much struggling[468].

## VIII   The Bile

Eighty-three illnesses arise from bile, and when Scripture promises that *the Lord will take away from thee all choli sicknesses*[469], according to Rabbi Eleazar, it refers to the various types of biliary sicknesses[470]. A good gall remedy is *mé-dekarim,* literally: spear water, because, according to the *Aggadah,* "it spears or pricks the gall". The *Gemara* explains it to refer to Egyptian *zythos* whose ingredients are cited by Rabbi Joseph: three parts of barley (according to Rabbi Papa: wheat), three parts of safflower[471], three parts of salt. Soak and burn and grind these ingredients; it is best to take this remedy between Easter and Pentecost. *Zythos* is dangerous for ill people and for pregnant women: "it loosens that which is solid and solidifies that which is loose"[472]. The latter sentence is explained by the commentaries as follows: "it helps for constipation and diarrhea". The wording, however, seems to indicate a prescription in the sense of the methodologists. As is known, they assumed that illnesses occur as a result of an increase or a decrease of the normal degree of tension (tonus) of individual organs, producing either a *status strictus* or a *status laxus. Mé dekarim* was thus thought to have the property of healing both conditions, in effect a universal remedy.

When a patient is on the verge of death, the angel of death stands over the patient's head with a sharp sword in his hand upon which hangs a drop of gall. When

460. Plinius. *Hist. Natur.* 20:49
461. *Aruch* has *aarketha*
462. Shabbath 109b
463. Löw, in Krauss, *Lehnworte* 2:134b
464. *gire de rubya,* according to Löw. *Aruch* wavers between lentil seeds and grapevine.
465. Aurelianus. *Chronicles* 3:5
466. Dioscorides 4:134
467. this seems to be an animal parasite
468. Tosefta Chullin 3:10
469. Deut. 7:15
470. Baba Metzia 104b; Baba Kamma 92b. The word *choli* is apparently equated with the Greek *chole* meaning gall.
471. *Kurtema,* carthamus tinctorius
472. Shabbath 110a and Pesachim 42b

the patient sees him, he opens his mouth because of fright, and the angel lets the drop of gall fall into the patient's mouth. It is from this that the patient dies, his face turns greenish (*morekoth,* like the color of gall) and his body develops a bad odor[473].

## IX    The Spleen

The *Gemara* reports several remedies for ailments of the spleen, *techala,* as all-comprising a concept as the *lienositas* of the heathen contemporaries of the Talmud[474]: take seven water worms *(bene de maja;* leeches?) and dry them in the shade and every day drink two or three in wine. Alternatively, take the spleen of a she-goat which has not yet born offspring and stick it inside the oven and stand by it and say: "as this spleen dries, so let the spleen of the patient dry". In the absence of an oven, stick it between the walls of a new house and repeat the same words. A very similar treatment "through sympathy" is reported by Plinius[475] to have been used by magicians.

Or again, look for the corpse of a man who died on the Sabbath and take his hand and put it on the spleen of the patient and say: "as this hand is withered, so let the spleen of the patient wither"[476]. This "stroking with the dead hand" was also strongly relied upon elsewhere in antiquity[477]. From personal knowledge, I am aware of this unfailing remedy being used in the Uckermark against chronic eczema.

Or again, take a *binnita* (carp)[478] and fry it in a smithy and eat it in the water of the smithy and wash it down with the water of the smithy. A certain goat which drank from the "smithy water" was found, on being killed, to have no spleen[479]. Here, too, we are dealing with a remedy which the physicians of antiquity employed[480], and which still plays a role in today's folk medicine. In the Brandenburg Mark I daily observed how mothers washed out the mouths of their children ill with aphthae with "charcoal water" which they either obtained from the smithy or which they prepared themselves by immersing a glowing-hot smoothing iron into water (i.e. an iron medication).

Finally, for ailments of the spleen, open a barrel of wine for the patient and let him drink a lot therefrom. Said Rabbi Acha ben Rabba to Rav Ashi: if he has a barrel of wine, he will not come to you; the wine will protect him. The patient with a splenic ailment should accustom himself to eat regularly in the mornings, as this is good for the whole body[481].

Marcellus Empiricus describes a *Ad splenum remedium singulare, quod de experimentis probatis Gamalielus patriarcha proxime ostendit*[482]. The Talmud makes no mention of it.

## X    Miscellaneous

1) *Tashnuk.* In the town of Shinar in Babylon, people "died of *tashnuk* without light and bath"[483]; without light because they have no olive oil, and without a warm bath because allegedly no cypresses grow there. The latter were first transplanted to Shinar from Palestine at a much later date[484]. The word is derived from the Aramaic *shanek* meaning to choke, and hence it means that those people "suffocated".

---

473. Abodah Zarah 20b
474. Gittin 69b
475. Plinius 30:17
476. Gittin 69b
477. Plinius 8:11. *Immatura morte raptorum manu strumas, parotidas, guttura tactu sanari affirmant*
478. thus according to Löw. *Aramäische Fischnamen.* No. 3
479. Gittin 69b. Congenital absence of the spleen in animals is mentioned by Aristotle, *De Generatione* 4:66, and in humans by Landois, *Physiologie* p.201

480. Coelius Aurelianus. *Chronicles* 3:4 p.452: *dicunt specialiter lienem deducere, in quibus est...aqua ex lacu, in quo saepissime candens ferrum fabricatores tingunt*
481. Gittin 69b
482. Empiricus. *De Medicam.* Chap. 23:77. The patriarch Rabbi Gamliel of Yabneh died approximately in the year 118 C.E. Marcellus Empiricus belongs to the school of Bordeaux from the fourth century on. The "proxime" is thus an error.
483. Jerushalmi Berachoth 4; 7b
484. Pseudo-*Rashi* on Genesis Rabbah 37:4

2) Ecclesiastes states that: *by much slothfulness the rafters sink in*[485]. The *Midrash*[486] explains that if a person is negligent and doesn't properly cover his head, the framework of his house (i.e. his upper part) will decay; that is, he will develop rheumatism (*reumatikos* in Greek).

3) *And the Lord will take away from thee all sickness*[487] is interpreted by the *Midrash*[488] to refer to *shirpa*[489] or bloodflow[490].

4) The people who complained about the constant diet of *manna* were warned that they would eat meat *until it becomes a zara to you*[491], i.e. loathsome, as in the usual translation. In the *Midrash*[492], Rabbi Huna expounds: a *zarana* and *butna;* Rabbi Abithar says: until it becomes *karda* or "I will send *dura* in their bowels". These are said to be names of illnesses as follows: *butna* is the explanation of *zarana*[493] and means "distention of the abdomen". *Karda* or *kadra* has a similar meaning since the word *kader* meaning "the pot" also occurs in the Talmud[494] in the sense of "abdomen"[495]. *Dura* is said to refer to "intestinal worms", unless the textual reading *deraria* (Greek *diarroia*) meaning diarrhea is correct.

5) Solomon says: *there is a sore evil which I have seen under the sun*[496], to which the *Midrash* asks: does then a good evil exist[497]? The answer is obviously an example of "bad evil", a particularly unfortunate situation. However, in view of the uncertainty of the textual readings, it is hard to explain and impossible to decide whether the words *diglum* or *diglus* and *patragus* are names of illnesses, as is stated by Wolf Einhorn, or whether one should accept the translation of D. Luria: "an example of a bad evil is the man Diglus who had four misfortunes *(tetragos),* namely poverty, weakness, nakedness and hunger".

## XI    Death Through Fright or Disgust

The Talmud relates: "a man hated veal. Once, without knowing it, he ate some veal. Someone called out to him: that was veal! He became disgusted *(ithkal'as)* and died"[498]. Further, "donkey drivers once ate lentils at an inn; the second portion which they ordered did not taste so good. The host explained to them that the backbone of a snake was found in the cooking pot from which the first portions were served and that he therefore had misgivings about serving them again from the same food. They became disgusted *(ithkalasun)* and died"[499].

The meaning of *kales* is unclear. Levy[500] and Fleischer[501] substitute *bales* for *kales;* either it refers to *la'as* meaning to chew, with a "b" at the beginning of the word, or to *bala* meaning to swallow, with an "s" at the end of the word. Thus, one is led to believe that the donkey drivers "choked" on the food because of the fright, or they vomited and aspirated some of the vomitus and choked thereon.

The commentary *Pneh Moshe* explains: they were terribly frightened and died of fright. Kohut agrees with him[502]. According to the contents of the story, this explanation seems to be the most logical one. I have no judgments regarding the linguistic permissibility of this interpretation. As shown by Löw[503], the word means "to be disgusted".

485. Eccles. 10:18
486. Levit. Rabbah 19:4
487. Deut. 7:15
488. Levit. Rabbah 16:8 *Aruch* s.v. Kühn 8:169
489. not *sirpa,* since *shirpa* has no relation to *saraph* meaning to burn
490. Niddah 10b
491. Numbers 11:20
492. Levit. Rabbah 18:4 and Numbers Rabbah 7:4
493. Einhorn. *op.cit.*

494. Shabbath 33a
495. S.J. Askenazi. *op. cit.*
496. Eccles. 5:12
497. Eccles. Rabbah on 5:12
498. Jerushalmi Terumoth 8; 46a ff.
499. *ibid*
500. Levy. *Neuhebräisches und Chaldäisches Wörterbuch.* Leipzig 1876-1889, 1:236b
501. *ibid* 286b
502. *Aruch Completum.* Vol. 2:100b
503. Löw. *Aramäische Schlangennamen,* in Harkavy's *Festschrift.* p.31, note 8

# CHAPTER V

## INJURIES AND MALFORMATIONS
### (SURGERY)

### I  Introduction

Although occasionally a Samaritan may have poured oil and wine on the wound of an injured person, and taken him to an inn, and there taken care of him, as depicted in the Gospels[1], the binding of wounds and surgery, at least in post-Biblical times, and probably even earlier[2], was primarily the function of the physician, *rophé,* as already explained above. A separate specialty of surgery did not exist.

The Biblical *chobesh* proves nothing. If a man says to another: *thou hast a mantle* (art a dignified figure); *be thou our katzin (ruler), and let this machshela (ruin of the city) be under thy hand*[3], the answer he gets is: *I will not be a chobesh, for in my house is neither bread nor a mantle. Ye shall not make me ruler of the people*[4].

Ibn Ganach and David Kimchi, as well as the *Targum,* interpret the word *chobesh* in the sense of "ruler", as a precise answer to the *katzin* of the previous verse. Even if one interprets *chobesh* in the not infrequently used sense of binding together or binding up of wounds — i.e. "I will not bind together the *disjecta membra (machshela)* of the city" or "I will not be the binder up or healer of its smashed body" — this does not prove the existence of a *professional* wound binder in those days.

### II  Surgical Instruments

The small drill of physicians (trephine), called *makdeach*[5], for opening the skull, is specifically mentioned as a "medical instrument". Other instruments are as follows: the *sakkin,* a large knife used for circumcision and post-mortem cesarian section[6]; and the *izmel,* a small knife used for circumcision[7] and also for general surgery[8]. We do not know whether one or more of the innumerable cutting instruments otherwise

---

1. Luke 10:34
2. Jeremiah 8:22; *Is there no balm (tzori) in Gilead? Is there no rophé there?* The balsam of Gilead was the most famous wound remedy at that time
3. Isaiah 3:6
4. *ibid* 3:7

5. Oholoth 2:3. To the Arabs (for example Abulcasem 2:23), *mikdach* is the cataract needle. To Maimonides and writers after him our *makdeach* refers to a lancet.
6. Arachin 7a
7. Jerushalmi Shabbath 19;16 d
8. for example Exodus Rabbah 26:2

**191**

mentioned in the Talmud[9] were used for surgical purposes. According to the commentaries, the *thrunthek*[10] is said to have been a surgical tool.

A splinter *(silva)* or thorn *(kotz)* is removed with a "hand needle" (sewing needle)[11]. Probably the operator is mostly a lay person[12]. For this purpose warm water for compresses is useful, whereas cold compresses or a bath are dangerous[13]. It is mostly not possible to remove a splinter without making a wound. For this reason, a son is not permitted to remove a splinter from his father's skin, if another equally competent operator is available[14], for bodily injury of parents by children is a transgression punishable by death[15].

A newborn infant whose anus is not visible should be rubbed with oil and held in the light. The skin is cut crosswise with a barley grain where it shows transparent; but not with a metal instrument because that causes inflammation[16]. This was especially considered to be true of iron[17]. A barley grain is also used to lacerate the edges of a penis fistula, if one is attempting to heal it[18]. Here we are probably dealing with an assertion of folk medicine. The fear of the inflammatory effect of iron was widespread throughout antiquity[19]. In spite of this, however, this material, iron, is used in nearly all surgical instruments.

Also known, but not for medical purposes, was a mouth bar, "an iron pincers", with which one opened the mouth of someone sentenced to death by burning, in order to pour the hot molten lead which will cause his death into his mouth[20]. This instrument was also used in the Biblically-prescribed proceedings of the "bitter water"[21] in a case of a suspected adulteress[22]. Also known was the *chakkah* or hook which heathen governments placed in the mouth of a criminal sentenced to death so that he should not be able to curse the king[23]. The learned Scribe Eleazar had his mouth forced open so that he would eat pork; he spat it out and was executed[24].

## III   Types of Injuries

The general expression for injury or trauma is *makka*. The different types of *makka* are as follows:

1) A sword wound or a puncture wound is called *petza* or *pida*. According to legend, when Cain killed Abel, he inflicted many wounds and blows because Cain knew not whence the soul departs until he reached Abel's neck[25]. What does a person get from raising monkeys (the beloved "toy" of Roman women) and other wild animals in his house? Injuries, bites and scratches![26] A drinker receives wounds and blows for no reason[27]. Even while carving meat, one can cut one's hand.[28] Rab also considers wounds on the back of the hand and back of the foot to be dangerous[29].

The Babylonian physician Mar Samuel considers a wound inflicted by a Persian lance to be absolutely fatal because, as the commentaries explain, this weapon was poisoned. It might be possible, however, to keep the patient alive long enough for him to set his house in order by giving him strong stimulants such as undiluted wine and fat meat roasted on coals[30]. Mar Samuel also considers dangerous a *pidatha* or wound inflicted by a weapon, perhaps, again, because of the already-mentioned fear of iron[31].

9. Kelim Chapter 13
10. *ibid* 16:8
11. Shabbath 17:1
12. Parah 7:11
13. Abodah Zara 28b
14. Sanhedrin 84b
15. Exodus 21:15
16. Shabbath 134a
17. Chullin 77a
18. Yebamoth 76a
19. Proof can be found in Winer. *Bibl. Realwörterb.* p.185

20. Sanhedrin 52a
21. *Tosefta* Sotah 2:3
22. Numbers 5:2ff.
23. Erubin 19a
24. Second Maccabees 6:18
25. Sanhedrin 37b
26. Eccles. Rabbah 6:11
27. Levit. Rabbah 12:1
28. Jerushalmi Niddah 9; 41c
29. Abodah Zarah 28a
30. Gittin 70a
31. c.f. *Orach Chayim* 328.7

For stopping bleeding, one applies cress with vinegar; for bringing on flesh, scraped root of cynodon and the paring of the bramble[32]. These are measures which, as already demonstrated by Löw[33], were also used by heathen physicians for the same purpose.

2) A burn wound is called *kewiya* or *michva*. It is only called by this name if it results from a burn from coals or red-hot ashes. On the other hand, more or less severe injuries of the skin caused by wood, stone, olive cakes (which served as heating material) or by the hot springs of Tiberias, or by hot air, or by unslaked lime are considered as skin disorders in the category of *schechin*. A third type of skin inflammation is mentioned in the Talmud by the name *kedach*[34].

These definitions, however, are not the same in all the sources[35]. It is also difficult to conceive of them as technical *medical* terms. Burn wounds "flow" or ooze if they have produced more than just reddening of the skin. The skin *(kerum)*, which occasionally develops "like an onion skin" — probably a layer of fibrin, as is so often seen in atonic wounds, such as on the lower leg — refers to the Biblical *tzarebeth*[36], whereas the wound covered with a scab which heals well is called *tzeleketh*[37]. If someone burned his hand while cleaning an oven, he puts his finger in his mouth[38].

It once happened that a red-hot, portable stove fell on the lower leg of a woman and she thus fell prey to the angel of death[39]. Rabbi Chiya bar Abba was gladly willing to die for his God, but he asked only that he not be martyred as were Jews during the persecution under Hadrian. They used to take iron discs and make them red hot and place them under the armpits of the martyrs until they died. Or they brought needles and stuck them under their nails until they expired[40]. According to Rabbah, if a person places red-hot coals on a neighbor's heart and the latter dies, the former does not receive the death penalty (because he assumed that the latter would simply push off the coals). If he places the coals on his neighbor's garment, however, and the neighbor is burned to death, then the perpetrator receives the death penalty[41]. On the other hand, he must pay for the pain he caused even if he only burned his fingernail with a spit, although no wound can be inflicted on a fingernail[42].

3) A *chabbura,* according to the definition of the *Tosefta,* is "a *makka* from which blood exudes, even if it cannot be expelled to the outside"[43]. It is thus a suffusion or bruise. It might soften and become fluid[44], or it might be a *chabbura* which does not recur if the blood therein gathers (i.e. flows) together[45]. The wound of defloration is also called a *chabbura*[46].

4) A *sheber*[47]. It is uncertain whether this word really refers to a broken bone as the literal translation of the word would indicate (*shabar* meaning to break). For it would not have been necessary to explicitly exclude a priest with a broken arm or leg from officiating in the Temple[48]. Perhaps it refers to a fracture which healed in a deformed manner, because the Talmud includes in the word *sheber* all different types of deformity of the hand and foot[49]. It is also uncertain whether the "setting of a fracture"[50] really refers to the setting of a bone fracture or the reduction of a dislocation.

---

32. Abodah Zarah 28a
33. *Aram. Pflanzennamen* p.184
34. Negaim 6:8
35. *Tosofoth Yom Tob* on Negaim 6:8
36. Levit. 13:28
37. Negaim 9:1; *Sifra Thazria* 6:5 p.64b and 7:3 p.65a, Weiss
38. Kelim 8:10
39. Chagigah 4b
40. Song of Songs Rabbah 2:7
41. Baba Kamma 27a. The neighbor may have thought that the perpetrator would have to replace the burned clothes and, therefore,

neglected to extinguish the fire.
42. Baba Kamma 8:1
43. *Tosefta* Shabbath 8:23
44. Psalms 38:6
45. Shabbath 107b
46. *Tosefta* Kethuboth 1:1
47. According to *Midrash* Psalms 51:3, *sheber* is equivalent to *makka.*
48. Levit. 21:19
49. Bechoroth 45a
50. literally: returning to the *sheber.* Shabbath 22:6

According to legend, when Noah came out of the ark, a lion pushed him so that he limped. The same was done to the King of Egypt by a golden lion when he sat upon Solomon's throne; he did not understand the mechanism[51]. In the fight for the *shamir* worm, a bone of the demon King Asmodai was broken[52]. When Eli the priest learned that his two sons were killed in the battle against the Philistines and that the Ark of God was captured, he fell backwards off his chair and broke his neck; *for he was an old man, and heavy*[53], and old age is a particularly dangerous time of life[54]. In a younger man, a fall from a chair would not have such serious consequences. It once happened, however, that a young man fell down in the dark and broke his neck, *maphreketh,* when the host removed the ladder to the attic in which the young guest was spending the night. He was still able to speak before he died[55].

A rib fracture which is not externally visible is only mentioned in regard to cattle[56]. A fracture of the forefoot or hindfoot of an animal renders it unfit to be offered as a sacrifice[57]. A "broken" (i.e. lame) stag, because it cannot flee, is considered like a lost article[58].

5) A dislocation or sprain; both are not always distinguishable by lay people even today. Job curses himself in his well-known manner[59]: *if I have lifted up my hand against the fatherless, then let mine arm fall from mine shoulder blade, and mine arm be broken from the bone.* An injury was fomented in cold water[60]. In a certain case, it appears as if certain hand manipulations, not further identified, produced healing of a dislocation. The text, however, only speaks of a case where there was a "change" of the hand[61]. Dislocation of the jaw (or mouth bone) hinders the use of an animal as a sacrifice[62].

6) A pus blister or abscess. The Biblical term *mazor,* which actually means to squeeze out[63], is later expressed by the name *mursa*. It is healed either by making an opening, *peh,* therein, in order to express the pus[64], or one peels it. Physicians do both[65]. Obviously, the meaning here is a simple incision (*diairesis* in Greek) as opposed to the peeling off (*periairesis* in Greek) of the abscess; they were also distinguished by Alexandrian physicians in the treatment of abscesses. They considered peeling off to be indicated for a soft or dead abscess membrane[66]. The following medicinal remedies are recommended for the healing of a *mursa:* a cup of wine in purple reddish soapwort *(ahala)*[67]. It is not certain whether this medicine was to be used internally or externally.

"*Simta* is a forerunner of fever", i.e. it is followed by fever or occurs simultaneously with fever. The remedy for it is to snap sixty times with the thumb next to it and then to cut it open crosswise, if it has not been brought to a white head; but if its head is white, no steps are needed[68]. According to this, *simta* refers to a furuncle, as *Rashi* explains: *un clou*. Elsewhere we find a magical incantation to heal *simta:* "let your color remain, let your seat be within you (i.e. not spread), let your seed be like a *kalut* (*contractus,* an animal which cannot reproduce), and like a mule that is not fruitful and does not increase; so be thou not fruitful nor increase in the body of so-and-so"[69].

7) A wound or *makka,* in the narrow sense of the word, either refers to a *makka teriyah* which is a sprouting, granulating wound[70], or a *makka nachla*[71] and *makka anusha,* a flabby or atonic wound *which does not heal*[72].

---

51. Eccles. 9:2
52. *Midrash* Psalms 78:12, Buber
53. First Samuel 4:18
54. Chullin 21a
55. Kallah Rabbathi 9 fol. 54 d 70
56. *Sifra* 98c
57. Bechoroth 6:8
58. Baba Metzia 1:4
59. Job 31: 21-22
60. Shabbath 22:6
61. *ibid* 148a

62. Bechoroth 6:10
63. Hosea 5:13
64. Eduyoth 2:5
65. *Tosefta* Eduyoth 1:8
66. Oribasius 44:8. ed. Daremberg Vol. 3: 577
67. Gittin 69b
68. Abodah Zarah 28b
69. Shabbath 67a
70. Isaiah 1:6
71. Jeremiah 14:17
72. *ibid* 15:18

The wound heals in that a *theala* or mound develops[73] whereby the "flesh heaps up". This occurs differently in different people[74], more rapidly in children than in adults[75]; finally there develops a scar which is paler than the original wound *(Kehah)*[76]. Such a scar which, for example, originated from a dog bite, can be very disfiguring for the patient[77]. It was uncertain whether or not the bone marrow contributed to the healing of the flesh overlying the bone[78]. If the patient is handled inappropriately, there develops *garguthni,* a wound surface which resembles basket wickerwork[79], probably a serpiginous wound.

8) *Nomé.* Should someone who developed a *nomé* on his foot cut if off and remain alive in comfort, or should he leave it on and suffer pain[80]? A prepuce is such a *nomé,* and the heathen King Isates immediately acquiesced to the circumcision of his son when he was told that a *nomé* existed on the foreskin and the physician recommended circumcision[81].

A *nomé* occurred on the foot of Joseph ben Pakses and the physician came to excise it. He said to the physician: when you have severed its attachment down to only a hair's breadth, let me know; for after complete severance it is considered "a limb from a living being", which ritually defiles anyone who touches it[82]. From this request of the patient, to inform him of the stage of the operation, one might conclude that the latter was painless — there is no mention of any narcosis — and that the diseased leg was devoid of sensation and became gangrenous from *lepro anesthetica.* The ostensible *nomé* on the son of Isates could naturally represent a wound with another causation, since in antiquity, the name *nomé* was used to denote any type of serious, rapidly enlarging wound[83]. Thus, Josephus states that for putrid fever *(sepomenou somatos),* one cuts off the diseased limb, in order to prevent the occurrence of a further *nomé*[84]. Paul also speaks of a *gaggraina nomé* in the figurative sense[85].

The Mishnah also mentions cases of amputation for mutilating leprosy. On the eve of Passover, those unfortunate patients would go to the physician to amputate their dead limbs. The physician cut the limb off but left a hair's breadth loosely attached; that patient would then thrust the limb upon a thorn on a wall thus severing it completely, and swiftly withdraw from it. Thus, neither the patient nor the physician touched "a limb severed from a live being" and both were able to bring the prescribed Passover offering in purity[86]. In small earthern mounds near cemeteries, women used to bury their abortions and lepers their arms[87].

## IV   Injuries Inflicted by Animals

1) *The Bite of a Mad Dog.* Among the feared injuries from animals is the bite of a *mad dog.* The following are the signs of madness (i.e. rabies in a dog) as enumerated in an ancient source: its mouth is open, its saliva is dripping, its ears flap, its tail hangs between its thighs, and it walks on the edge of the road. Some say it also barks without its voice being heard (i.e. it is hoarse). The cause of the illness is unclear. The Palestinian *Mishnah* only describes the mad i.e. rabid dog *(keleb shoteh).* The Babylonians considered it bewitched by witches or possessed by an evil spirit[88]. Even if the dog only rubs against a person, he is already endangered and should remove and destroy the clothes which the dog touched and then run away. Also, one should kill the dog by throwing something at it to avoid direct contact with the hands[89].

73. *ibid* 30:13
74. Baba Kamma 84a
75. Shabbath 134b
76. Nahum 3:19
77. Kethuboth 75a
78. Chullin 125a
79. Baba Kamma 85a
80. Abodah Zarah 10b
81. Genesis Rabbah 46:10

82. Jerushalmi Nazir 7; 55d
83. Kiddushin 30b
84. *War of the Jews.* Book 6 Chapt. 2:9
85. Second Timothy 2:17
86. Kerithoth 3:8
87. Kethuboth 20b
88. Yoma 83b
89. *ibid*

To treat the bite of a mad dog, the heathen physicians of antiquity, in general[90], as well as many primitive peoples even today[91], gave the patient certain pieces[92] of the liver of the mad dog to eat. This is a medicament which corresponds to a type of antitoxin therapy in modern times[93]. Among the Rabbis, only Rabbi Mattia ben Cheresh, who lived in Rome, recommends this therapy. The other Rabbis of the *Mishnah* consider it ineffectual (and hence prohibited, since a dog is an "unclean" animal)[94]. The compiler of the *Mishnah,* Rabbi Judah the Patriarch, himself saw this remedy tried on his Germanic slave, but in vain[95]. There is also no dearth of voices stating that *any* treatment for such a bite is hopeless[96]. Nevertheless, among the masses of people, there naturally circulated all kinds of remedies, particularly amulets:

"Take the skin of a male otter and write thereon: I, so and so, the son of that and that woman, write upon the skin of a male otter *kanti kanti kloros, God, God, Lord of Hosts, Amen, Amen, Selah.* Then let the bitten patient take off his clothes and bury them in a grave for twelve months. Then he should take them out and burn them in an oven and scatter the ashes at the crossroads. During these twelve months he should only drink water from a copper tube, lest he see the picture of the mad demon and be endangered. The mother of Abba ben Minyumi made for him a tube of gold for drinking purposes and he was healed"[97].

Only Aristotle teaches that people who are bitten by a mad dog do not become ill[98].

Among other quadrupeds, injury by a mule was greatly feared[99]. It was also considered fatal, particularly if it was caused by a white animal[100] or one with white knees. In this situation, even Rabbi Chanina, who otherwise was "knowledgeable in healing remedies", admits his helplessness[101]. A donkey once bit off the hand of a child[102].

2) *Snakebites.* By far the most dangerous animals for Oriental people are *snakes.* The desert is particularly rich in snakes, and the *saraph* snake and the scorpion are among the most dangerous of all[103]. According to Mar Samuel, all crawling animals possess a poison, *eres* (virus), but only the poison of snakes is lethal[104]. Snakebite is considered to be one of the miracles whereby no one bitten by a snake or a scorpion during the time of the Temple was harmed[105].

An animal that has inflicted injury or damage may only be killed after an orderly court-proceeding; for example, an ox that gores. However, a snake should be killed wherever one finds it[106]; even if it looks harmless, one should crush its brain[107]. Death from a snakebite resembles death from the pouring of molten lead into the body[108]. The danger from snakes existed everywhere: a thirsty maiden descended to a well to

---

90. Dioscorides 2:49 (Sprengel p.185); Galen *Fac. Spl. Med.* 11:10 (Kühn 12:335). Both recommend it be given roasted., Plinius 29:32; Plinius *Valerian.* Book 3 Chapt. 50; Sextus Papyrensis Chapt. 9 *de cane* tit. 21
91. for example the Haussa. *Ztschr. f. Ethnol.* 1896 Verhandlung p.31
92. namely the *chatzar hakabed.* See above Chapter 2
93. Calvary. *Münchener Med. Wochenschrift* 1897 p.537
94. Yoma 8:6. Maimonides, in his commentary on this Mishnah, calls this (liver) therapy a sympathetic therapy *(segula),* a view which is not supported by practical knowledge or experience.
95. Jerushalmi Yoma 8; 45b
96. Jerushalmi Berachoth 8: 12b; Yoma 84b
97. Yoma 84a
98. *Histor. Anim.* 8:22; Aubert-Wimmer Vol. 2: 183
99. Chullin 7b
100. Jerushalmi Berachoth 8; 12b
101. Yoma 49a
102. Baba Kamma 84a
103. Deut. 8:15
104. Abodah Zarah 31b
105. Aboth 5:8
106. Sanhedrin 1:4
107. Jerushalmi Kiddushin 4; 66c
108. Sotah 8b. One of the forms of capital punishment.

drink. When she placed her hand on the stone wall, a snake emerged and bit her, and she died of the bite[109].

During the journey from Mount Hor, the Israelites were bitten by *saraph* snakes (fiery serpents) and many of the Israelites died. Thereupon, Moses made a *saraph* snake out of brass and placed it upon a pole. Whoever was bitten would look at it and remain alive[110]. Hezekiah destroyed this snake because the Israelites began to worship it as an idol[111]

Bartholin[112] and, more recently, Küchenmeister and others[113] interpret the fiery serpent to be the medina worm. To be sure, the Hebrews could have equally well called the approximately one-meter-long worm *nachash,* just as Rufus calls it *ophis* (snake)[114] in his description which was discovered by Ivan Bloch[115]. One need not place any weight on the fact that the Arabs, at the time of Rufus, already knew of the transmission of this medina disease through water, whereas the Bible only speaks of a "bite". Nowhere, however, in Arabic writings is there mention of large numbers of deaths from filaria, as depicted in the Bible. Until the studies of Fedschenkos (1869-74), it was nearly universally accepted that the worm penetrates through the skin of a person from the outside. Therefore, the matter rests with the simple explanation "snakes".

Which type of snakes are here referred to can only be guessed at. The Septuagint translates *thanatountes,* the Vulgate, *ignitos,* hence the "fiery snakes" of Luther. Lewysohn has assembled several conjectures on this subject[116].

There also exists a large number of interpretations of the brass snake which can naturally only be considered as suppositions. It was even thought to be a sign similar to the Red Cross seen in a field hospital! The *Mishnah* categorically asserts: the brass snake neither killed nor brought back to life; rather if those bitten were reminded to serve God by looking at the snake, they would remain alive[117]. So, too, in the Wisdom of Solomon, it states: "They saw a picture of deliverance which reminded them of the judgement of God, for if someone turned to Him, he is not saved by the looking at the picture but by the Savior and Redeemer of all mankind"[118].

It seems quite certain that the fear of snake poison, particularly in the Orient, resulted in the rational rule of prohibiting the drinking of water that was left uncovered. If one nevertheless drank some by oversight, one should quickly drink a cup of strong wine[119]. One should also not wash one's face, hands or feet with such water that was left uncovered. Others, however, are of the opinion that the latter rule only applies if wrinkles exist on the skin which would prevent the water *(sirta)* from immediately flowing off[120]. For the same reason, one should not walk without shoes in a house in which there is a cat; the latter spits out the bones of a snake which it has consumed, and it is dangerous to step on such a bone[121]. The cat itself is immune from snake poison[122].

The prohibition of *giluy* (i.e. drinking from water that was left uncovered) is also found among the Arabs: "When night falls, cover your vessel"[123].

For baking purposes, it is permitted to use water that was left uncovered, because snake poison is destroyed by fire. For this reason, Mar Samuel only drank water which had been heated. In general, boiled water was permissible even after it cooled. It was thought that a snake does not drink from this type of water and, therefore, does not

109. Aboth de Rabbi Nathan 17:6
110. Numbers 21:4-9
111. Second Kings 18:10
112. *De Morbis Bibl.* Chapt. 6
113. E. du Bois-Reymond. *Reden* 2:494
114. ed. Daremberg-Ruelle p.216
115. *Allg. Med. Central. Ztg* 1899 No. 60
116. *Zoologie des Talmud* p.239

117. Rosh Hashana 3:8
118. Wisdom of Solomon 16:17
119. Gittin 69b
120. *Tosefta* Terumoth 7:14
121. Pesachim 112b
122. Abodah Zarah 30b
123. see Hammer. *Fundgruben des Orients.* I fol. 375

discharge its poison therein[124]. Did practical experience convince the people of antiquity that water becomes wholesome after it is boiled? This seems to be the case for the Persians, since Herodotus[125] relates that: "at the royal table of Cyrus, only water from the river Choaspes which was boiled *(ydatos apepsemenou)* was used and it was carried in silver utensils to the battle field". Obese Romans were able to drink with impunity water which had remained uncovered since they constantly ate crawling animals including snakes and worms resulting in their bodies becoming warm[126], meaning they became immune to poison. Hermippon asserts that Pythagoras' warning about snake water *(dipsas* means snake) was derived from the Jews[127].

It was forbidden to eat flesh from an animal that was bitten by a snake, even if the meat was cooked, because of the danger to life[128]. Plinius designates such meat as being harmless[129], perhaps because his experience related to different types of snakes than those in the Talmud. Similarly, one should not eat figs, grapes, cucumbers or gourds that have holes, because of fear that the holes were made by a snake and that these foods, therefore, contain poison. In the same vein, it is prohibited to sell a person a pair of sandals made from leather of a dead animal claiming they were made from leather of a slaughtered animal; firstly, because it is untrue, and secondly, because it is dangerous[130]. The commentaries explain that the danger lies in the possibility that the dead animal might have been killed by snake poison, and that remnants of the poison might still be found in the leather. With our present-day knowledge of anthrax, this latter disease seems to be a more likely explanation.

Snakebites occur primarily during harvest time[131], and some people are of the opinion that the child of the Shunamite woman[132] did not die of heatstroke, but rather became comatose secondary to a snakebite[133]. A person who sits naked in an outdoor privy is in danger of being bitten and killed by a snake[134], for it even wraps itself around the penis[135]. If someone is bitten by a snake, he jumps up suddenly[135a], and "to jump up as if bitten by a snake" was an expression used in antiquity in the same sense as our "stung by a tarantula"[136].

Generally, the bite kills rapidly. However, it also occurs that a person first notices that he was bitten when the wound swells[137] and the patient comes home[138]. This swelling is an invariable sign of a snakebite. When the Apostle Paul was bitten by a snake *(echis)*, the people waited for him to swell up *(pimprasthia)* and fall down dead[139]. It once happened in a place called Zalmon that a certain man called out: "I was bitten by a snake and I am about to die"; when they reached him, they could no longer recognize him[140].

If someone was fortunate enough to have been bitten by a snake and survive, he later fears even a string or thread[141] because it resembles a snake.

Already in Biblical times, one guarded against snakes through swearing[142]. Sirach states: "Who pities a snake-charmer when he is bitten, or all those who have to do with wild animals?"[143] During the time of the *Tosefta,* a physician was called for a man who was bitten by a snake; (prior to the arrival of the physician?), a hen was dismembered for him and a leek was cut for him[144], obviously the well-known

124. Jerushalmi Terumoth 8; 45d
125. Herodotus Book 1 Chapt. 188
126. Abodah Zarah 31b
127. Josephus. *Against Apion* 1:22
128. Terumoth 8:6
129. *Histor. Natur.* 29:18
130. Chullin 94a
131. Yebamoth 116b
132. Second Kings 4:18
133. Jerushalmi Yebamoth 14; 14d
134. Genesis Rabbah 10:7
135. Jerushalmi Taanith 4: 69a
135a. Soferim 3:13
136. Menachoth 32b
137. Exodus Rabbah 31:6
138. Tanchuma *Shemini* p.13a
139. Acts 28:6
140. Yebamoth 16:6
141. Eccles. Rabbah on 5:1
142. Jeremiah 8:17
143. Sirach 12:13
144. *Tosefta* Shabbath 15:14

antidote. The physician's duty was "to heal the patient with his tongue"[145], i.e. to suck out the wound, a method known since antiquity. Plinius relates[146] that the Ophiogenites "healed snake bites with their spittle". In folk medicine, the fetus of a healthy white ass was dismembered, and the person bitten by a snake sat thereon[147]; or (squashed?) gnats were applied on the wound[148].

I note that in Coptic, the same word means both ass and gnat, just as the Arabic *sakina.*

A unique trick is related in the following legend: Nebuchadnezzar had a snake *(tannin)* which swallowed up everything thrown to it. He was very proud of it and thought it invincible. Daniel hid nails in straw and threw it to the snake. The snake swallowed the nails and they lacerated its bowels[149]. In the story of the "Bel and the dragon", Daniel made a cake of pitch, fat and hair and placed it in the dragon's mouth.

Only healing of snakebites by invoking a foreign cult is prohibited. Our Sages preferred death to the recognition of "foreign deities"[150].

If someone swallows a snake, he should eat cuscuta and run for three *mils;* then the snake will be excreted in strips[151]. Perhaps, this "snake" refers to a tapeworm!

3) *Insect Bites.* The following insects were considered harmful to human beings: the scorpion, the hornet and the bee.

A man placed a scorpion in a fruit basket and warned the sweet-toothed maid servant not to open the basket. She did so, nevertheless, was bitten by the animal, and called out: "now I must die[152]!" Folk medicine has a large number of remedies against scorpion bites, naturally referring to the large Oriental species *scorpio afer:* drinking the gall of a white *daya* (stork) in beer[153]; a black and white lizard cooked together and the resultant ointment applied on the bite[154]; a quarter measure of 40-day-old urine[155]. Rabbi Judah recommended warm compresses[156].

For a bee sting *(zibbura),* a wise woman recommended that the patient drink creepers of a palm tree in water[157]; Rabbi Judah advises cold compresses. If the wound is associated with fever, a bath is dangerous[158]. Rabbi Idi Bar Abin considered a person who swallowed a bee to be lost. He should quickly drink one quarter measure of strong vinegar in order to at least be able to set his house in order[159]. A man who was stung on the penis by a bee died of this wound[160].

Large swarms of hornets can smite fleeing troop units and destroy them[161]. They can also make enemies of the Jews powerless in that they can enter any hiding place in which the enemies try to conceal themselves[162]. A hornet sting in the eye or scrotum can make a person blind or sterile[163]. As an antidote, squashed flies were applied to the site of the sting[164].

Ibn Ezra considers the *tzira* of the Bible to be an illness equivalent to *tzaraath.* On this point, see Bochart[165].

4) *Worms.* One should not place one's mouth at a waterpipe *(solen)* and drink, because it is dangerous. Wherein lies the danger? — The swallowing of an *aluka*

145. Numbers Rabbah 20:14
146. *Hist. Natur.* 7:2
147. Shabbath 109b
148. *ibid* 77b
149. Genesis Rabbah 68:13
150. *Tosefta* Chullin 2:22
151. Shabbath 109b
152. Aboth de Rabbi Nathan 1:8
153. Kethuboth 50a
154. Shabbath 77b
155. *ibid* 109b
156. Abodah Zarah 28b

157. Kethuboth 50a
158. Abodah Zarah 28b
159. Gittin 70a
160. Moed Katan 17a
161. Exodus 23:28; Joshua 24:12; Wisdom of Solomon 16:19
162. Deut. 7:20
163. Sotah 36b
164. Shabbath 77b
165. *Hierozoicon.* Book 4 Chapt. 13. Frankfurt 165 T. Vol. 2 Col. 534 ff

(leech). The Rabbis further state: because of the danger of swallowing an *aluka,* one should not drink water from rivers or from pools directly with his mouth or with the hand; he who does so — his blood shall be upon his head![166]If one swallows such an animal, swelling of the abdomen occurs. This swelling, however, is different from that which occurs from intentional withholding of micturition where urination is not disturbed[167].

The *Gemara* identifies the *aluka* (or *alka*) with the *nima shel mayim,* the "water filament"[168]. If a person has swallowed one, one may warm water even on the Sabbath for him, because it is dangerous. Until the water is hot he should drink vinegar[169]. The *pishpash* or *bug* serves as a remedy against *alukta*[170].

According to tradition, *aluka* and *nima* both mean leech. In antiquity, this animal was thought to be poisonous, so that it was placed in warm water before being applied[171]. The use of bugs as a remedy for swallowed leeches is also mentioned by Marcellus Empiricus: one should place a bug on hot coals and inhale the fumes; then the leech will surely emerge[172]. It cannot be established with certainty whether or not the Talmudists were of the same opinion.

It is related that a Persian who thrust Rabbi Eleazar out of the privy was bitten in the intestine by a *darkon* so that he died[173]. The same happened to a Roman field marshal ("it tore his gut out")[174]. The *darkon* is the animal which God has prepared to bite a (pregnant) wild goat in the latter's genitalia to ease the delivery of her offspring[175].

Linguistically, the *darkon* of the Talmudists is naturally identical with the *drakon* of the Greeks and the *draco* of the Romans. Undoubtedly, however, this name does not refer to any zoological entity. Aristotle[176], Plinius[177], and Aelian[178] interpret it as a larger animal, perhaps a type of snake, whereas the Greek physicians are unequivocally describing filariasis under the term *drakontiasis*. They reserve the term *drakon* for the guinea pig[179]. The above citation from the Talmud makes the former interpretation appear to be the correct one (i.e. a type of snake), but a decision is difficult. The aforementioned "water filament" or "water hair" can also be interpreted as filaria, since the latter more closely resembles a filament than the thicker leech, and the infestation that occurs from drinking water was already known to Rufus in Arabia as the major cause of the illness[180].

## V   Moles and Nevi

As far as I know, the only body tissue that is ordinarily classified as a tumor is the *shuma* or mole. It occasionally occurs on all members of a family *(gil)*. It was debated whether a mole can be used to identify a corpse, since some are of the opinion that a mole undergoes a change after one's death whereas others dispute this contention[181]. Apparently the two schools of thought are referring to different nevi. For example, a hairy mole is mentioned in the Talmud whose presence on the face of a woman makes her dreadfully disfigured[182]. If it is located on the genitalia of a child, it might be

166. Abodah Zarah 12b
167. Bechoroth 44b
168. The above warning against drinking from "brooks, rivers and pipes" is also found in *Derech Eretz Rabbah 11:5* where the word *nima* is substituted for *aluka.*
169. Abodah Zarah 12b
170. Jerushalmi Berachoth 9; 13c
171. Details are found in Daremberg in his *Oribasius-Ausg.* 2: 790
172. Lewysohn. *Zoologie des Talmud.* p.328, notes

173. Berachoth 62b
174. Gittin 57a
175. Baba Bathra 16b
176. *Hist. Anim.* 8:131
177. *Hist. Natur.* 29:20
178. *Hist. Anim.* ed. Hercher 14:12 and elsewhere
179. Proof in Bloch. *Allg. Med. Central Ztg.* 1899 No. 60
180. *ibid*
181. Yebamoth 120a
182. Kethuboth 75a

mistaken for pubic hair[183]. The son of the Priest Zaddok once recognized his sister by a mole on her shoulder when they were both in prison[184]. Most probably *Rashi's* identification of *shuma* with a wart is incorrect.

## VI  Gigantism and Dwarfism

People whose body development in length is considerably greater than the normal[185] are considered to be giants. The Bible[186] attests to their existence in prehistoric times. Later, the Anakites appeared as giants to the scouts that Moses sent to explore the land[187]. Naturally, their report is not to be considered as an objective one. The *rephaim*, who lived in Palestine before the Israelites immigrated there[188], are also ordinarily viewed as "giants". Among them, at the time of Moses, there still existed King Og of Bashan, himself a giant. He required an iron bed that was nine ells (cubits) long and four ells wide.

Josephus reports on giants in Hebron[189], and Plinius describes bodies of giants that were found[190]. People of such dimensions are not known in later times. It is possible that just as the duration of life of human beings diminished already during the period of the description of the book of Genesis, so, too, the bodies of humans may have decreased in size. Only the Philistine Goliath[191] still had the respectable height of six cubits and a span, approximately three meters[192]. Legend describes many things about him[193].

The Talmud interprets the Biblical *sarua*[194] to refer to abnormal growth of a single limb (acromegaly) which renders a priest unfit to serve in the Temple. Such an illness can be simulated if a person is unusually strong in one arm and unusually weak (atrophy) in the other[195]. The *Mishnah* mentions a man by the name of Ben Batiach who had an unusually large fist[196]. It was also said of Rabbi Ishmael ben Kamchith that he was able to grasp four *kabs* in one hand[197].

The opposite of a giant is the *nannas* in Hebrew or *nannos* in Greek, the dwarf. Both cannot serve as a priest[198]. An abnormally tall man should not marry an equally tall woman, lest their offspring be like a mast. A male dwarf should not marry a female dwarf, lest their offspring be a thimble (i.e. dwarf of the smallest size)[199].

From the words of the Lord in relation to Nebuchadnezzar that he was the smallest of all people ever to be appointed as a ruler over a kingdom[200], the *Midrash* concludes that Nebuchadnezzar was a dwarf[201].

## VII   Head Injuries in the Bible

Three cases of head injury are recorded in the Bible.

1) *Sisera,* the commander-in-chief of the forces of King Yabin, fled to the tent of a friendly people before the persecution, and was concealed under a blanket by Jael, who lived in that tent. *Then Jael took a tent pin, and took a hammer in her hand, and went softly unto him, and smote the pin into his temples, and it pierced through unto the ground; for he was in a deep sleep; so he swooned and died*[202]. The narcosis

183. Niddah 46a
184. Lamentations Rabbah 1:46
185. Perl in *Magyar Zsido Szemle* 1908, No. 4, concludes from a "legion of evidence" that the height of the Jews at the time of the Talmud varied between 1.60 and 1.70 meters. Ref. in Grunwald's *Mitt. z. Jüd. Volkskd.* Heft 32 (1909. Heft 4) p.127
186. Genesis 6:4
187. Numbers 13:33
188. Deut. 3:11
189. *Antiquities.* Book 5 Chapt. 2:3
190. *Hist. Natur.* 7:16
191. First Samuel 17:4
192. The "small Egyptian cubit" equals 6 handbreadths (Kelim 17:9)
193. Sotah 42b
194. Levit. 21:18
195. Bechoroth 3b
196. Kelim 17:12
197. Yoma 47a
198. *Sifra Emor* p.3 p.95c
199. Bechoroth 45b
200. Daniel 1:14 (This reference of Preuss is not correct, F.R.)
201. *Yalkut* 11:1062
202. Judges 4:21

*(nirdam)* was as deep as that which affected Adam, the first man on earth upon whom *the Lord caused a deep sleep (thardema) to fall*[203], a sleep so deep that He was able to remove one of his ribs and to fashion a woman therefrom.

The story is depicted somewhat more clearly in the triumphal song of Deborah: *Jael put her (left) hand to the tent pin, and her right hand to the workman's hammer; and with the hammer she smote Sisera; she smote through his head. Yea, she pierced and struck through his temples. At her feet he sunk, he fell, he lay;...where he sunk, there he fell down dead*[204].

Jael obviously slid towards the sleeping Sisera on her knees, so that his head lay in the direction "between her feet". When he received the terrible injury, he attempted to get up. Since his head was fixed on the ground, however, he could only "bend his knees" and, at most, slightly raise the upper torso. Then, however, he fell back, perhaps with spasms[205], and remained motionless until he died[206].

2) A certain woman cast an upper millstone from the tower of the wall on the head of Abimelech and broke his skull *(gulgaltho)*[207]. He hastily called his armor bearer and asked him to slay him so that it not be said that Abimelech was killed by a woman[208]. This, he did not immediately lose consciousness through the injury.

3) David smote Goliath in his forehead with a stone from his (David's) slingshot, *and the stone sank into Goliath's forehead and he fell upon his face to the earth*[209]. The power of the little stone was not sufficient to throw the giant backward, but he was only stunned by the forcible impact — *karothenta*, as stated by Josephus[210] — and fell forward unconscious on the ground, so that David could easily kill him[211].

One needs here to mention the Talmudic warning: "a Jew should not walk downstairs in front of a heathen and not bend down before him because the latter might smash the Jew's skull *(gulgaltho)*"[212].

## VIII   Jaw Dislocation and Lockjaw

In the Talmud[213], Rabbi Chanina says it is permitted to "raise the ear to its proper position" on the Sabbath because delay therein might be dangerous and directs that this can be accomplished either with a medicament or even directly by hand. The latter, however, might produce a wound of the earlobe.

Among the commentaries, *Rashi*, who still had many orally transmitted traditions at his disposal, is of the following opinion: the sinews of the ears sometimes go downwards and dislocate the jaw so that they must then be raised again. Lipschitz is also of the opinion that the case refers to subluxation of the jaw secondary to yawning, which can be corrected by lifting the patient off the ground by his ears. It is difficult to comprehend how a dislocated jaw can be reduced in this manner. To reduce a dislocated jaw, the Alexandrians used a characteristic bandage which they called *lagoos syn otiais* meaning hare with *ears*, or *syn otiatis* for short. Oribasius described it very precisely[214]. The Talmudic commentators may thus be correct in their interpretation of the case as referring to dislocation of the jaw, although "the ears" which they believed are those of the patient, are in fact the bandages which resemble ears.

It is also possible that this case refers to "raising the ears and hair" *(trichas e ota an ateinontes)* which the Alexandrians, for example, recommended for bulimia[215], and

203. Genesis 2:21
204. Judges 5:26-27
205. The reason for assuming that *naphel* means spasms is explained later in the story of Balaam
206. This is the Talmudic explanation of this Biblical passage. See Yebamoth 103a
207. Judges 9:53
208. *ibid* 9:54

209. First Samuel 17:49
210. *Antiquities.* Book 6. Chapt. 9:5
211. First Samuel 17:50
212. *Tosefta* Abodah Zarah 3:4
213. Abodah Zarah 28b
214. Oribasius: *Coll.* 48:15; 48:27 and 49:27. Pictures Vol. 4 fig. 19
215. Oribasius. *Synops.* 6:36 (Vol. 5:315)

which I have personally observed many times by the peasants in the mark. Furthermore, elsewhere in the Talmud[216] Rabbi Chanina's statement is as follows: "one raises *the bone of the head*", *etzem shel rosh,* with the explanatory addition: "one raises the daughters of the ears", *benoth oznayim.*

Since the time of Hippocrates, lockjaw was considered to be dangerous. Hippocrates taught that if the luxation is not reduced, the patient falls into a deep sleep, vomits, and mostly dies on the tenth day[217]. This served as absolute truth until Fabricius ab Aquapendente destroyed its validity, as well as the validity of the backward luxation as invented by Wilhelm of Saliceto. He explains that *ego horum nihil vidi licet plures curaverim.* If Hippocrates stated it, however, it was probably so at that time, for Fabricius considers Saliceto to be among the *chirurgici anatomes imperiti*[218]. Moreover, long before him, Maimonides already considers this questionable injury not to be dangerous[219].

I do not know how one conceived of a medicinal therapy for lockjaw at that time.

## IX   Brain Injuries

According to Rab and Samuel, perforation of the *dura mater*[220] is an injury which entails danger to life, whereas the other Sages do not believe a fatal outcome occurs as long as the pia mater is not damaged[221]. The former opinion seems to have been the prevalent one in antiquity. Aristotle[222], as well as Plinius[223], states that a severed dura does not heal any more than the membrane of the bladder or the heart, and that a tear in either of the two meningeal membranes is fatal[224].

Softening of the *brain, hamraka,* so that "it flows out from the skull as from a jug", is fatal for the animal, as is *masmasa,* when the "brain cannot stand straight but shows quivering motions on its surface"[225]. Elsewhere, the term *masmasa* is used to designate putrefied flesh "which the physician scrapes off in order to reach healthy flesh"[226]. Thus, *masmasa* of the brain seems to represent a type of gelatinous degeneration.

Whereas *masmasa* is a pathological-anatomical diagnosis, *mazmaza* is a clinical concept. It is not likely, as Rabbi Gersom suggests, that it refers to a herniation (rupture) of the brain, but rather to a concussion of the brain, *commotio cerebri,* since *masmes* or *mizmez* should be understood, according to the analogy of the Arabic *mazmaz,* in the sense of *huc illuc movit et agitavit.* This is not a life-threatening condition. When Levi once observed a man in the bathhouse fall and strike his head[227], he said: his brains were agitated *(nithmazmez)* as a result of the fall. Abaye believes that such an injury is not fatal but obliterates one's power of procreation[228]; it is not clear whether he refers only to the *potestas generandi* or also to the *coëundi.*

It appears that Abaye assumed that sperm arises from the brain, as Aristotle had already taught[229]. According to Hippocrates, sperm is transported to the testicles via the arteries behind the ears; if one, therefore, opens these arteries (such as during bloodletting), the person becomes sterile[230]. Alkmäon considers sperm to be part of the brain substance *(egkephalou meros)*[231], whereas Plato designates sperm as a liquid which originates from the spinal cord[232].

216. Jerushalmi Shabbath 14; 14d
217. Hippocrates. *De Articulis,* fol. 798 H ed. Foes
218. *Opp. Chirurg.* Book 5 Chapt. 3 Col. 354 of the Ed. Lugden. Bat. 1723
219. *Mishneh Torah. Hilchoth Shabbath* 2:10
220. literally: hard brain membrane
221. Chullin 45a
222. *Histor. Anim.* 3:13. *diakopeis on symphyetai*
223. Plinius 11:83 *cicatrice non solidescit*
224. *alterutram rumpi mortiferum est*
225. Chullin 45b
226. *ibid* 53b
227. this is the interpretation of *Aruch*
228. Chullin 45b
229. Aristotle *Problem* 10:7
230. Hippocrates *De Aëre et locis* 106; Foes, fol. 293:21
231. Plutarch *De Placit. Philos.* Book 5 No. 3
232. *ibid*

To determine whether an injury has occurred in the meninges of the brain of a bird, Rabbi Shizbi used to examine the bird by the light of the sun; Rabbi Aha bar Jacob used to examine it with a straw; Rabbi Yemar used to examine it with water[233]. According to the commentators, he poured water into the hole of the skull and after a few moments poured it into a basin; if the water now appeared opaque, it means that some of the brain matter escaped and mixed with the water thus indicating an injury of the meninges.

If a person strikes his slave on the brain so that water (spinal fluid?) escapes and covers his eyes, then the master must free his blinded slave[234]. This was the opinion until the eighteenth century; namely, it was believed that water flowing from the brain into the concave optic nerve would destroy the latter and give rise to the gray star, (whence the term "cataract" of the Salernitans, from *katarrea*). There is even a legend which relates that the eyes of a person struck on the head fall out[235]. This striking on the head, the "splitting of the brain", is mentioned not infrequently in folk justice: if a priest arrogantly serves in the Temple in uncleanness[236], he is not brought to court, but his young colleagues take him out of the Temple court and split his skull open with logs (or wooden clubs)[237]. Moses smote the Egyptian[238] with a clay shovel on the head so that his brains fell out and he died[239].

When the prosecuting angel approaches the Lord to accuse the Israelites of wrongdoing, the defense angel speaks up saying: "didn't their enemies split their skulls open because of their (the Israelites) belief in God?"[240] Hired assassins from Rome are said to have split open the skull of Trojan with wooden clubs[241]. A prince was enraged when rules were promulgated for him to follow as to the manner in which he should serve the idol *Peor;* he hired people who with wooden clubs[242] split open the skulls of those who made the rules. A resolute woman is said to have split open the skull of a lover who forced himself upon her:

A Roman woman once asked Rabbi Jose bar Chalaphtha: "with what does your God occupy himself, since He completed the creation of the world?" He answered: "He matches men and women;" to which she retorted: "I can do the same." She summoned a thousand of her male and female servants, stood them in lines, assigned each male to a female and matched them for one night. The next morning the male slaves came to her, one with a split-open skull, the other with gouged-out eyes, etc.[243].

Raba had a dream that his head split and his brains hung out[244]. Greek sources describe the well-known procedure of tying criminals between two trees curved towards each other and rapidly releasing the trees so that the criminal's "head splits". This practice is also mentioned by the Talmud as a Roman custom[245]. If the bone of the brain is broken and the brain cast out, then it (i.e. the skull) is "a useless container", which serves no more purpose[246].

# X    The Final Illness of Titus

In numerous places in Talmudic writings, there is a story which, in the main, reads as follows: When Titus landed on dry land after the destruction of the Temple in Jerusalem, a gnat flew into his nose, ascended into his head and knocked against his

233. Chullin 56 a–b
234. *Tosefta* Baba Kamma 9:27
235. Sotah 13a
236. *Tosefta* Kelim 1:6
237. Sanhedrin 9:6
238. Exodus 2:12
239. Exodus Rabbah 1:29
240. Lamentations Rabbah 2:3

241. Taanith 18b
242. *Sifre Balak* No. 131 p.48a and Jerushalmi Sanhedrin 10; 28d
243. Levit. Rabbah 8:1
244. Berachoth 56a
245. *ibid*
246. Levit. Rabbah 19:6 on Jeremiah 22:28

brain for seven years. One day as he was passing by a smithy, the gnat heard the noise of the hammer and stopped knocking. After thirty days, however, it became accustomed to the noise and again began to knock. After Titus died, they opened his skull and found there something like a sparrow (swallow), two *selas* in weight. Legend states that the mouth (beak) of this "something" was made of copper and its nails (claws) of iron[247]. According to another source, at the request of the pain-plagued Titus, his skull was split open and something like a dove was drawn forth. When the latter changed, he also changed; and when it flew away, his soul also flew away[248].

David Gans (died 1613) already remarks[249] that the Roman historians attribute the death of Titus to a high fever, and Gans mentions the opinion of some people that these historians "intentionally suppress the truth in order not to make the acts which Titus did to the Jews appear worthy of punishment". This possibility finds analogies even in the recent histories of royal courts[250]. This moral teaching, without doubt as to the authenticity of the story, is already mentioned in the *Midrash*[251]. Lampronti also mentions it[252]. Asaria de Rossi[253] goes through all the details of the story in order to arrive at the conclusion that it is only a moral poem to illustrate the teaching that the Lord can destroy even the mightiest ruler with one of His smallest creatures.

Of interest also is the report of the Turkish Kamûs (s.v. *sakhina*) concerning gnats in the nose of Nimrod. The details of this report given by Arabs are identical to the above story of Titus, except that Nimrod is the principal character[254]. The natural suggestion that we here have a pan-Semitic legend in which every Semitic nation has its own national villain, remains purely an assumption, if one does not find an identical story concerning the legend of the Assyrian Nimrod. The legends known to-date make no mention thereof[255].

If we wish to extract the medical essence from this story, we observe a man who had been plagued by severe headaches for many years, who was only temporarily deafened by the noises of the world around him, and in whom, on post-mortem examination, a brain tumor was found. According to the other version, through trepanning of the skull, the patient lost his life and the tumor was found. Both versions are plausible. Among the innumerable autopsies which the Alexandrians, who lived near the Jews, conducted, it is possible that they also came across a brain tumor. In addition, it is well known that trepanning was a very common operation in antiquity, even though Galen's assertion that he observed myriads of trepanned patients[256] is probably one of his beloved exaggerations. It can also now be demonstrated to have been practiced by a large number of primitive peoples[257]. Ancient Talmudic sources also describe, as already mentioned, a skull borer[258]; they also report the case of a trepanation on a person for *En Bul*[259]; the skull defect was later covered with the dried shell of a pumpkin, as is done today by island dwellers using coconut shells[260].

247. Gittin 56b
248. Genesis Rabbah 10:7
249. *Zemach David*. Prague 1592 p.25a
250. Bodenstedt. *Erinnerungen aus Meinem Leben*. 1:67. "According to the official Russian history, Kaiser Paul was not murdered but died of a dangerous fever".
251. *Pirkei de Rabbi Eliezer* 49
252. *Pachad Yitzchak s.v.*
253. *Meor Eynayim* ed. Cassel, Vilna 1866 p.214 Chapt. 16
254. The author of the book Malem (Ibn Batrik?) and the *Lebab* thereto. cf. *Zedler Univ. Lexikon. s.v.* Nimrod
255. Jeremias. *Izdubar-Nimrod*, Leipzig 1891, and G. Smith, *Die Chaldäische Genesis*,

Leipzig 1876. Also in the Abraham-Midrash, where the story of Abraham's struggle with Nimrod is related (Jellinek. *Beth Hamidrash* 1:25 ff), there is no mention of this legend.
256. Oribasius 46:20
257. Ploss. *Das Kind* 1:329. Excavations in Peru and New Caledonia have shown that trepanation was already practiced in prehistoric times.
258. Oholoth 2:3
259. *Tosefta* Oholoth 2:4
260. *Deutsche Med. Ztg.* 1896 p.67. Serbic folk surgeons also used pumpkin shells to cover trepanning defects. See Stern, *Turkei* 1:191

One can be misled to the assumption that the brain tumor developed from an insect which entered the nose and grew enormously from the often-mentioned finding even in the Talmud[261] of gadflies in the nasal passages of sheep, whose significance for the health of the animal was known. The change from a sparrow to a dove, as occurs in the *Midrash,* is probably directed against the Samaritan sect[262]. Finally, if one wishes to explain the copper beak and the iron claws, one might consider the former to be old (dried) blood and the latter perhaps as lime deposits.

## XI   Malformations of the Head

All conspicuous abnormalities of the external body form of a priest render him unfit to serve in the Temple. The *Mishnah*[263] enumerates a long list of malformations for recruiting purposes. The individual technical terms were obviously familiar to the officials who recruited the priests for Temple service. These terms, however, were never part of the vernacular and had probably already disappeared from common usage in Talmudic times and, therefore, required elucidation. Hence, our task of comprehending these terms is doubly difficult because even many of the explanations of the *Gemara* are no longer clear to us, so that nothing remains but to accept the interpretations of the commentaries who at least had many early sources at their disposal.

The following priests are unfit to serve:

1) The *kilon.* According to the *Gemara,* this refers to a man "whose head has the shape of a keg cover"[264]. According to the commentaries: the head is pointed at the top and wide on the bottom, and has the form of an egg which has the point slanting upwards[265]. The *cilo* of Roman scholiasts, to which one might also give some thought, is also an abnormal headshape, but *cui frons est eminentior ac dextra sinistraque velut recisa videtur.*

2) The *liftan.* The person's head resembles a head of turnip, wide at the top and becoming narrow downwards. In the Galenic schema[266], *kilon* is that form in which the transverse diameter of the head (from ear to ear) is conspicuously small; and *liftan* is a person who resembles a rachitic child.

3) The *makkaban* or *makban.* The person's head resembles a hammer with a markedly protruding forehead and occiput, whereas the sides of the head remain even i.e. a large sagittal diameter.

4) A person whose head is angular "towards the front", as added by the *Gemara*[267]. According to the commentaries, this refers to a head in which part of the forehead seems to be lacking (receding forehead) or one which seems to lie on the breast[268].

5) The *sefikas*[269], opposite of the previous one, as if the hinder part of the head is missing. To these unqualified priests one must add those "with receding necks", as if the neck lies between the shoulders, as well as those with large conspicuous necks. The former are not those with an apoplectic habitus, but those with a bulging (kyphotic) habitus.

Crookedness (hunchback), *akmuth,* is also mentioned in the Talmud. When someone boasted: "I will straighten out your hunchback *(akmuth)*", the scornful retort was: "in that case you must be a very excellent physician and could command

261. Shabbath 54b
262. cf. Chullin 6a
263. Bechoroth Chapter 7
264. Bechoroth 43b
265. Maimonides. *Biyath Hamikdash* 8:1
266. Oribasius 3:195
267. Bechoroth 43b
268. latter phrase is unclear in Preuss' book (F.R.)
269. the correct textual reading, according to Löw, is *schekifas*

large fees"[270]. Josephus also mentions a certain Mathias *o kyrtos,* the bent one[271], among his ancestors.

6) The *ba'al ha'chataroth* or *ha-chatotereth,* the hunchback. Since he is only unfit to serve in the Temple because of an unsightly appearance[272], this case probably refers to one who has a marked elevation of the flesh on his back, as the *Gemara* also points out[273], "a hump in which there is no bone". Otherwise, *chatereth* is the usual expression for the camel's hump[274].

Repulsive, but of no consequence to the priest, is the round shape of the head *(segalgal)*[275]. Round heads were typical of Babylonians because, according to Hillel, they have no skillful midwives[276]. The relationship to "skill of midwives" is clarified by the familiar notice of Hippocrates concerning the artificial shaping of the skull by midwives (microcephaly). This is a bad habit whose widespread use, as stated in the profuse material of Ploss[277], is totally unbelievable.

If serious body blemishes develop after a person's marriage, he should, according to Rabbi Simeon ben Gamliel, agree to a divorce. An example *(kophiach)* of such a blemish is mentioned by Rabbi Jeremiah[278]. The meaning of this word *kophiach* is unclear. *Peneh Moshe* considers it to be the name of a place. *Korban Ha-edah* explains that "*kophiach* is equivalent to *gibbeach,* a person who is long and thin and whose face seems to markedly protrude anteriorly, making him unsightly". This would thus refer to a person with a hump (caries) of the upper vertebral column by virtue of which the head protrudes forward. This condition could certainly have first developed after consummation of the marriage.

*Kippeach* or *kippuach*[279] and *kippeach*[280] are the opposite of *nannos* or dwarf, and hence refer to a giant or a very tall person *(geboah),* as is explained in the *Gemara*[281]. Concerning the objection that tall people are handsome and would, therefore, not be excluded from serving as priests in the Temple, one answers that the disqualified tall people are those who have "looseness" *(shemita).* Rabbi Gersom explains that there are "very tall, thin people, whose faces appear to jump forward" (i.e. the height is out of proportion to the breadth and thus the person sags and his joints seem to be "loose"). They are thus identical with the *kophiach* mentioned above. See also *Rashi* on Berachoth 58b. The *ha-darnikos* mentioned in the *Gemara*[282] refers to a giant without any physical defects.

The only correct textual reading is *kippeach,* although the Leiden manuscript has *kophiach* (Ritter). The *geboa* of the *Gemara* is a faulty correction for *gibbeach;* this is demonstrated by *Aruch,* Rabbenu Nissim, and also the *Targum*[283]. This *gibbeach* has nothing to do with the Biblical *gibbeach*[284]; rather it is the Babylonian-Aramaic form of the *Mishnaic* term *kippeach* (Löw).

# XII    Injuries of the Spinal Cord

An animal whose "thread of the spinal column", *chut hashedrah* (i.e. spinal cord) has been severed in any place, either as usually happens by a fracture of the spinal

---

270. Sanhedrin 91a
271. *Vita* No. 1
272. *Tosefta* Bechoroth 5:2
273. Bechoroth 43b
274. for example Chullin 9:2
275. Nedarim 66b
276. Shabbath 31a
277. *Das Kind* 1:306ff
278. Jerushalmi Kethuboth 7; 31d

279. *Tosefta* Berachoth 7:3 and Jerushalmi Berachoth 9; 13b
280. Bechoroth 7:6 and Berachoth 58b
281. Bechoroth 45b
282. the philological riddle of this word is still not solved. Löw in Krauss 2:222b
283. *Targum Jonathan* 2 on Levit. 21:20
284. Levit. 13:41

column or following any other cause, is considered to be a *terefah,* that is, it will die in a short period of time[285]. It is sufficient for the severance of the cord to only involve the major part of the circumference. On the other hand, the statement of Rabbi Jacob, that a perforation of the cord is just as dangerous to the animal as transverse sectioning, is not accepted. Another group of Sages adopts the view of Rab and Rav Huna[286] which attributes no significance at all to injury to the medulla of the cord, but considers injury to the membrane which envelops the cord to be the determining factor. Elsewhere in antiquity, injury to the membrane of the spinal cord was also considered to be lethal.

Plinius teaches:[287] "what applies to the brain also applies to the spinal cord, *quoniam praetenui ejus membrana modo incisa statim exspiretur"*. Experimentalists of modern times too have observed anatomic and physiologic regeneration of a severed spinal cord, even in mammals[288], thus lending support to the teaching of Rab and Rav Huna.

In regard to illness, what is valid for the brain is also valid for the spinal cord, that is to say, softening even to complete liquefaction and gelatinous degeneration are life threatening, whereas *commotio* is not[289].

## XIII    Injuries and Malformations of the Mouth

Thick lips in a woman are only a beauty blemish[290].

A priest in whom one lip protrudes beyond the other lip is unfit for Temple service because of his unsightly appearance[291]. An animal whose lips are pierced, split or otherwise injured is unsuited for use as a sacrifice[292] because only animals without a blemish may be offered[293].

"A split lip" (harelip) gives the mouth a scornful twist. As a result, Rabbi Yochanan, who was old and weak, thought that Rabbi Kahana, who was afflicted with such a harelip, was laughing at him[294].

If the mouth of an animal is *balum,* it is under certain circumstances unfit to be used as a sacrifice[295].

The variations of the text can be reconciled as follows:

1) If the mouth is *balum (constrictus* i.e. breathing is short) as a result of breathing[296] — that is as a result of shortwindedness (difficult breathing without anatomical substrate) — it is not considered a blemish. If the shortwindedness occurs as a result of the mouth itself *(atzmo)* — that is as a result of a malformation of the mouth — it is considered a blemish.

2) If the mouth is contracted (literally *constrictus*) in the space between the lips[297] — that is as a result of abnormalities of the soft parts of the mouth — it is not considered a blemish; but if it is as a result of the bone *(etzem),* then it is considered to be a blemish.

Jewish penal law and, as far as I am aware, folk justice, do not employ excision of the tongue as a punishment for wrongdoing. When the vile Nicanor fell in battle, the victorious Maccabees chopped off his head and cut out his tongue[298] — their enemy was thus *not alive* at the time. On the other hand, among the brutal acts which Antiochus inflicted upon the Jews was his order to cut out the tongue, tear off the skin,

285. Chullin 3:1
286. Chullin 45b
287. *Histor. Natur.* 11:62
288. Ziegler. *Path. Anat.* 2:608
289. Chullin 45b
290. Nedarim 66b
291. Bechoroth 7:5
292. *ibid* 6:4
293. Levit. 22:20

294. Baba Kamma 117a
295. Bechoroth 40b and *Tosefta* Bechoroth 4:13
296. *ruach;* this is according to most *Aggadists* and Maimonides
297. *rewach;* this is according to most annotators
298. Second Maccabees 15:33

and chop off the limbs of the eldest of the seven brothers who refused to eat swine's meat[299]. According to the law of Hammurabi, an illegitimate child who says to his foster-father or foster-mother: "you are not my father, you are not my mother" must have his tongue cut out[300].

An illness called *urdana* is said by the Talmud to be dangerous[301]. The word *urdana* is the Aramaic translation of the Hebrew *tzefardea* meaning frog. This name is not used to designate an illness but refers to *rana* or *ranula* of the Romans and *batrachos* or *ypoglossios* of the Greek physicians who do not consider the illness to be dangerous, but count it among the aphthae[302].

It is completely uncertain as to what *akshemunitha* refers to; this illness is also considered to be dangerous.

In a parallel passage[303], the word is *akshebunitha*. The Biblical *akschub*[304] refers to a type of snake and has its parallel in the word *nachash*. The Septuagint has *aspis* (viper) and Romans[305] has asps. See also Bochart[306]. The *Targum*, however, has *akubitha* meaning spider or araneid *(Rashi)*; hence, our word *akshemunitha* has been interpreted to refer to "a spider". Levy has: "perhaps a crab!" It is not very plausible, however, that even ordinary people, who would not confuse a viper, a spider, and a crab — even a child knows how to differentiate between them — would use the same word for all of these. See also Löw[307].

# XIV   The Death of Jesus

There exist more writings concerning the *"stab in the side of Jesus"* than the number of words in the original report of the Evangelist: "they saw that Jesus was already dead. . .one of the mercenaries pierced his side *(enyxe ten pleyran)* with a spear, and forthwith there came out blood and water"[308]. The controversy mainly concerns the question as to whether this stab was a so-called *coup-de-grâce* to kill a dying person, or whether it was a method to determine whether or not Jesus was already dead. The supporters of the former opinion assume that the stab wound pierced the heart; blood and water (serum) apparently flowed out in succession.

Aside from the needs of religion, the death of Jesus has been portrayed in an endless number of artistic productions, and it was interesting to us to see the conception of the artists in the above controversy. Although the attention given to the gross anatomic facts may sometimes be somewhat lax — I know of two, perhaps three, Promethean scenes in which the eagle tears the liver out from the left side —[309] it seems a fair assumption that in pictures of Jesus all details would be carefully considered. In the overwhelming majority of pictures that I have seen, the stab wound is portrayed on the left side; only rarely is it seen on the right side. Mr. V. Oefele taught me in Neuenahr that the basis for this lies in dogmatic differences of opinion.

I found nothing on this subject in the writings of the special archaeologists[310]. Glückselig incidentally mentions: "according to the oldest custom of the middle ages, a mercenary pierces the Lord with his spear on the right side"[311]. Long before him

---

299. *ibid* 7:4
300. Code of Hammurabi No. 192
301. Jerushalmi Shabbath 14; 14d
302. Aetius 2 Serm. 4 Chapt. 37 fol. 470. Ed. Lugd. 1549; Theoph. Nonnus. Chapt. 117 Vol. 1 p.355. Ed. Bernard
303. Jerushalmi Abodah Zarah 2; 40d
304. Psalms 140:4
305. Romans 3:13
306. Hieroz. 2 Col. 379
307. *Aramaische Schlangennamen* No. 15

308. John 19:34
309. One is Giordano Fa Presto in Mauritshius in the Hague, another is Ribera in Cassel, and the third perhaps is the sculpture on the front of the new royal stables in Berlin
310. for example, Herman Fulda. *Das Kreuz und die Kreuzigung.* Breslau 1878 p.214
311. Glückselig. *Christus-Archäologie.* Prague 1863 p.163. A similar statement is found in J.E. Wessely, *Ikonographie Gottes und der Heiligen.* Leipzig 1874 p.17.

(1743), the clergyman Schmidt remarked: "the opening is, contrary to that generally portrayed by painters, most likely to be represented on the left side"[312].

In actuality, in *ancient* portrayals, the stab wound is more often seen on the right side: for example, in pictures in Mass books of the 14th and 15th centuries, on ancient sculptures in the Cathedral of Mayence, and from time to time on pictures of a wide variety of painting schools, as for example, P.P. Rubens and Van Dyck (about 1600). From modern times, I am only aware of one interment of Ihlees in Cassel about 1850. Otherwise, as already mentioned, the left side was the rule. Where the wound is portrayed on the left side, it is placed so low that it would be very difficult for the spear to have reached the heart, even if the crucified one was not hanging so high that the lancer standing below could not at all have driven the lance between two ribs. The right-sided portrayal places the stab wound mostly two ribs below the nipple, so that the liver was most likely pierced. Sometimes — for example, on the old stone crucifix on the bridge in Kreuznach — the stab wound is even shown outside the rib cage, in the right hypochondrium; and that which is supposed to portray blood gushing forth looks more like prolapsed netting.

The cause of death during the crucifixion is also in dispute. It probably occurred as a result of exhaustion; perhaps also from hypostasis as a result of impeded breathing. Martyrologists relate that crucified people have lived for three or more days on the cross. An example of recovery following prolonged hanging on a cross is also cited by Josephus[313]. According to the *Mishnah,* the blood of a slain person "gushes out"[314] or "gushes on the wood"[315] (probably as a result of damming up) when one pierces the body, such as is portrayed, for example, in the crucifixion of Giotto (wound on the right!), whereas blood from a corpse flows out drop by drop[316].

## XV    Injuries Which Render an Animal Terefah

The *visceral-surgical* material of the next few sections refers nearly exclusively to animals. Moreover, in the overwhelming majority of instances, the cases deal not with clinical but with pathological-anatomical data as to whether or not a certain injury which is discovered during the prescribed examination of a slaughtered animal would have been fatal for this animal, had it not been slaughtered. If such were the case, the animal is *terefah* and one is prohibited from eating it.

## XVI    Tracheotomy

If the trachea is perforated by a transverse wound which encompasses more than half the circumference of the windpipe, the animal's life is threatened. On the other hand, longitudinal wounds, even with larger dilatation, were not considered dangerous[317]. The commentator explains that in the former case, the lung pulls down and the neck pulls up, so that the tear extends and does not heal. In the case of a longitudinal wound, however, the slit closes itself the more the neck is stretched; hence, it heals. Other injuries are only considered dangerous, rendering the animal *terefah,* if the defect is at least the size of an Italian *issar*[318]. It is undecided whether or not this

---

312. Schmidt, *Biblischer Medicus* p.252
313. *Vita* No. 75
314. The Jewish law, "hanging", — *thalah,* which, according to tradition (Sanhedrin 35a) is identical to *hoka* (Numbers 25:4) — is only known as a strengthening of the punishment of an already executed male criminal; (Deut. 21:22) perhaps supported by an ancient folk custom, cf. Joshua 10: 26-27. The Bible only mentions it as a method of

execution among the Persians (Esther 7:10, *on the gallows,* literally: on the wood) and among the Egyptians (Genesis 40:19). The Talmud always uses the expression *tzalab,* "to nail", for the Roman punishment of crucifixion.
315. Niddah 71b
316. Oholoth 3:5
317. Chullin 44a
318. small coin. Chullin 54a

size also applies to intentional injuries. Rabbi Jose ben Nehorai relates the case of a lamb whose windpipe was cut; the hole, according to the commentary, resembling a window. After they inserted a tube of reed *(keromith shel koneh)* to close the hole, it recovered[319]. As far as is now known, *this is the oldest record of tracheotomy in Semitic sources.* The report dates from the second century of the common era, and, perhaps, refers to Alexandrian physicians, who probably were familiar with such experiments. Our knowledge of the Alexandrians and this notice in the Talmud are not sufficient, however, to make this assumption any more than just that.

The artificial opening of the windpipe had been known for a long time. Asklepiades (B.C.E.) is said to have performed this operation for synanche, but was censured for this by methodologists[320]. It was later often practiced by Antyllus in the third century of the common era, perhaps as early as the year 140[321], as described by Paulus Aegineta[322], and later copied by the Arabs. None of the latter either saw or themselves performed a tracheotomy, although Abulcasem stitched up the transected windpipe of a maiden who attempted suicide, and she recovered[323]. Ibn Zohr even tracheotomized a goat *experimenti causa* and it healed [324]. Only tumors were considered an indication for this operation. All authors theoretically recommended a transverse incision through the third or fourth tracheal ring *(inter duos circulos),* being careful not to injure the cartilage, an injury which had been thought to be incurable since the time of Hippocrates. As already shown above, the Talmudists did not share this erroneous opinion.

Fabricius ab Aquapendente cut the soft parts vertically but opened the trachea transversely. Heister was the first to also cut through a cartilaginous ring[325]. The first attestable tracheotomy on a human being was performed by Brassavolo[326].

## XVII Esophagus

Perforation of both skins (membranes) of the esophagus (but not one of the two) threatens the life of the animal, even if the holes in the two membranes are not àt the same level, because during eating or bellowing of the animal, the foodpipe contracts and expands[327] and it could happen that one hole might coincide with the other and food might possibly be expressed into the mediastinal cavity. The stomach of a bird remains at rest and an analogous situation need not be feared. This is the generally-accepted opinion of Rav Ashi. The opposite opinion is that of Rav Papa who considers peristalsis of the stomach (i.e. gizzard) of a bird to be significant b̀ut not so the contracting waves of the esophagus of an animal[328].

Injuries of the esophagus *in human beings* are equally dangerous. Whereas, in cases of manslaughter, Scripture requires that the murder tool, if made of stone or wood, be *capable* of killing someone[329], no such requirement is stated of iron instruments, because the latter *qua talis* are automatically considered to be

---

319. *ibid* 57b
320 Coelius Aurelianus. *Acut.* 3:4 p.193: *Asclepiades a veteribus probatam approbat arteriae divisionem, ob respirationem faciendam, quam laryngotomiam, varie ac multipliciter peccans*
321. Ivan Bloch, in Neuberger-Pagels *Handbuch* 1:483
322. Paulus Aegineta 6:33: *in angina reprobamus chirurgiam,* etc.
323. Abulcasem 2:43 p.227. he found the maiden *mugientem ut mugit hostia jugulata.*
324. Abhomeron Abynzoar. Book 1, tract 10. Chapt. 14 fol. 15d: *Cum discipulus eram in*

*hoc arte, volui perscrutare dicta modernorum hujus artis...sumpsi capram unam et incisi corium et pelliculam, quae est subtilis, et de canna pulmonis aliquid minus lupino...Sed cum meo tempore non vidi aliquem, qui hanc fecisset, propter hoc eam nolui primo ordinare.*
325. Helfreich in Neuburger-Pagel's *Handbuch* 3:168
326. Heymann, *ibid* p.580
327. literally: shortens and lengthens
328. Chullin 43a
329. Numbers 35: 17-18

"dangerous". Even a needle or a small hook is dangerous since it may enter the esophagus and kill a person[330].

A newborn baby whose esophagus is obstructed *(atum)* (i.e. obliterated) cannot survive; however, a baby with a perforated esophagus *(nakub)* can survive[331].

I do not know the significance of "congenital perforation of the esophagus". In Maimonides[332], the term *nakub* is lacking; see also the *Keseph Mishneh* commentary there. If *nakub* were only a rhetorical opposite of *atum,* then it should have said *pathuach* (meaning open instead of *nakub* meaning perforated). Kazenelson considers *nakub* to refer to *fistula colli congenita*[333], but bronchial fistulae do not communicate with the esophagus!

Something stuck in the throat, *bela,* was considered to be so dangerous that all Sabbath laws may be set aside on account of it. It seems that a favorite remedy[334] was the recitation of a magical incantation which, for this purpose, was not considered to be an idolatrous practice. The earliest followers of Jesus showed the miraculous powers of their master as *soter,* specifically in the results of their magical incantations in these cases[335]. Also, as already mentioned, Galen praises the use of a magical spell, *epode* (hymn), for someone in whom a bone remains stuck in the throat[336].

If a piece of meat gets stuck in the throat ("meat chokes a person"), one should attempt to wash it down with water[337].

Rabbi Joshua ben Levi said: it is permitted to lift the *onklai* on the Sabbath because it is a dangerous sickness. What does *onklai* mean? Rabbi Abba said: the *stomachos* of the *libba!*[338].

What is the remedy for it? Take pepper-cumin *(kamona),* caraway *(karvya, carum carvi), ninya* (ammi), wormwood (asafetida, *agdana),* saturea *(tzathra),* and the *abartha* type of hyssop. For the *libba,* these should be taken in wine — as a mnemonic, note that *Wine maketh glad the heart of man*[339] — for the illness *rucha* (defective breathing?) in water, and for *kuda* (a woman in childbirth) in beer[340].

Rav Acha bar Rabba ground all these together and took a fistful of the mixture and drank it. Rav Ashi ground each one separately and took a full pinch of it with his thumb and little finger in wine.

Rav Papa tried all these but without results, whereupon an Arab advised him: fill a new jug with water, add a spoonful of honey which stood overnight under the stars, and drink the contents the next day. He did this and was cured[341].

The identification of this illness is totally unclear, since we can conclude nothing from the recommended remedy. We cannot even clarify the meaning of the name of the illness. One might suspect that *onklai* is similar to *agkyle,* if this word did not mean joint stiffness (ankylosis). The term *onklai* was apparently no longer in common usage during the time of the Talmud, so that its identification as *stomachos* of the *libba* was necessary. *Libba,* which means both "heart" and "stomach", is here explained by Rabbi Chananel to refer to stomach, *al-ma'idah. Onklai* might thus be the same as the *anatropai tou stomachou* of Galen[342], or the *thlipsis stomachou* of Aetius[343]. Unfortunately, neither gives a

330. Jerusalmi Sanhedrin 9; 27a and *Sifré Massé* 160 Ed. Friedmann p.61a
331. Niddah 23b
332. *Mishneh Torah. Issurey Biah* 10:11
333. *Normale und Pathologische Anatomie des Talmuds* p.291
334. Shabbath 67a
335. Jerusalmi Shabbath 14; 14d. *bela* may be extracted on the Sabbath. The grandson of Rabbi Joshua ben Levi suffered from *bele* i.e. a bone stuck in his throat. Someone came and uttered a magical incantation in the

name of Jesus and he recovered. In Eccles. Rabbah 10:5 fol. 26c of the Romm edition, the censors removed the name of Jesus.
336. Chapter 3, Section 8 of Preuss' book
337. Berachoth 45a
338. see below for explanation
339. Psalms 104:15
340. Abodah Zarah 29a
341. *ibid*
342. Oribasius. *Synops.* 9:10. Vol. 5:483
343. *ibid* Vol. 4 557

definition of the "turning of the stomach", but it is also healed by medicaments.

*Rashi* has two explanations: *onklai* is the fleshy wall below the heart or stomach, the diaphragm *(tarpesche),* or it is "the cartilage opposite the heart (or stomach), *nibla* in French. Sometimes it bends forwards and hinders normal breathing". *Nibla* meaning uvula[344] is not very likely. *Rashi* probably means the sense of distention, the gaseous accumulation in the stomach of an infant which the mother combats by "stroking" (i.e. burping) the baby.

## XVIII    Injuries of the Gastrointestinal Tract

If the first[345] stomach *(keres ha-penimith)* of a ruminant is pierced, or if the greater portion of the outer covering (serosa) is torn, the animal is *terefah*. The *halachah* or final ruling is in accord with Rabbi Jose[346], that the part of the stomach wall which corresponds to the *keres* is the "outer wall", and, therefore, an extensive injury of the stomach wall is considered to be dangerous to the life of the animal, since the *keres* fills nearly the entire abdomen.

If the omasum (third stomach) or recticulum (second stomach) have perforating injuries which go through to their outer surfaces (i.e. into the abdominal cavity), the animal is *terefah*. A fistulous communication between these two stomachs, however, is of no consequence[347].

Greatly debated is the case in which a needle or any other pointed object became lodged in the wall of the reticulum. Such a swallowed object would ordinarily become enveloped in the enormous amount of fodder in the ruminant's paunch (first stomach), without reaching the wall of the organ or producing any injury. On the other hand, by the nature of its form, the reticulum promotes the attachment and penetration of hard, pointed objects. In this respect, the construction of the omasum might make it even more dangerous than the reticulum for the animal to swallow a pointed object. However, the food digesta does not reach the omasum until after the cud has been chewed, i.e. after it has passed through the esophagus and pharynx twice. For this reason, perforations in the stomach complex of ruminants ordinarily occur in the reticulum.

If a needle is found lying transversely in the wall of the reticulum, and the stomach wall is perforated through and through, then the animal is *terefah,* but not if the perforation only extends through part of the diameter of the wall. Even in the former instance, the animal is only *terefah* if there is a blood spot at the opening of the perforation, because this finding proves that the injury was already present prior to the slaughtering of the animal, *intra vitam.* Otherwise, we assume that the injury occurred after the slaughtering and the animal is permitted. If the wound has a crust on it *(higlid),* the perforation occurred three days prior to the slaughtering; otherwise the age of the injury is uncertain and the animal is also *terefah*[348].

A perforation in the abomasum (fourth stomach of ruminants) is not dangerous to life if it is covered with fat and is on the venous side, i.e. the lesser curvature. Perforations of the greater curvature, however, always threaten the animal's life[349].

Holes in the intestine render the animal *terefah* if they communicate with the abdominal cavity. If the hole in an intestinal loop which is covered by a mesentery communicates with another similar loop *(haduré de kantha),* according to Rabbi Nachman, the animal is in no danger[350].

According to Rabbi Simeon ben Gamliel, even intestinal perforations that communicate with the abdominal cavity are not dangerous if they are covered with a

---

344. Landau, *Marpé Lashon s.v.*
345. literally: inner
346. Chullin 52b
347. *ibid* 3:2

348. Chullin 50b
349. *ibid* 50a
350. *ibid* 48b

sticky liquid *(lechah)*. This stickiness refers to the liquid of the intestine *(shirka de me'aya)* which is expressed if one squeezes it. It probably refers to the phlegm of the intestine and not to chyle or lymph[351]. Obstruction of perforations by fat can also render such wounds harmless.

Wounds of the rectum are usually sealed by the surrounding muscles (of the hip, *yeraichayim*) so that fecal material does not extravasate into the surrounding area. Where such a "seal" *(debek)* is lacking, the animal becomes *terefah* by the slightest perforation, and even the fat which lies thereon does not serve as a seal for the perforation[352].

If one wishes to summarize all the details of these rules, one would say the following: *every injury of the gastrointestinal tract as a result of which food or fecal material can extravasate into the abdominal cavity and neighboring tissues* (mediastinum or pelvis), *is a threat to the affected individual's life* (because it can cause peritonitis or suppuration). This statement is still indisputable to this very day.

If a doubt exists concerning a perforation found in the intestines as to whether it was already present prior to the slaughtering or whether it first developed post mortem, Rabbi Shimi bar Chiya recommends that another perforation be made next to it and the two perforations compared[353]. Rabbi Mesharsheya first squeezed and handled *(memashmesh)* the newly-made perforations saying: how many hands have handled the original perforation before it was brought to me![354] Even modern histologists should occasionally remind themselves of this ancient practical assertion.

If the entrails protruded (i.e. prolapsed) but spontaneously returned into the abdomen, no danger to the animal exists, because, by their spontaneous return, they did not become twisted. If they were manually replaced, however, then it depends whether or not they were twisted when put back. If so, the animal is *terefah,* even if no perforation occurred; because a complete reposition of the original situation is no longer possible if a change has occurred in the bowels as they were replaced, and the Lord has designated specific places in the body for each individual organ which may not be changed without endangering the individual's life[355].

In connection with the above rules, the following story is told[355a]: a gentile once saw a man fall from the roof to the ground so that his abdomen burst open and his entrails protruded. The gentile thereupon brought the son of the victim and made believe that he was slaughtering him in the presence of his father[356]. As a result, the father fainted, sighed deeply and drew in his entrails, whereupon the gentile immediately stitched up his belly without touching the entrails. The injured patient was certainly better off, in spite of this somewhat gruesome procedure, than if the operator, who was perhaps also only a lay person, had pushed the entrails back with his hands, as was generally done by heathen physicians of those times — the scene probably took place in the second century of the common era.

## XIX    Penetrating Abdominal Injuries

The second book of Maccabees describes the case of an *abdominal injury* sustained in a suicide attempt[357]. Razis, one of the Elders of Jerusalem, in order not to

---

351. In Pesachim 6:1, the scraping off (squeezing: *michuy*) of the entrails is distinguished from the rinsing off of the bowels. The former is explained by Rabbi Chiya in Pesachim 68a to refer to "the removal of the viscous substance *(shirka)* of the intestines which comes out through the pressure of the knife", i.e. removal of the phlegm.
352. Chullin 49b

353. If the two are alike in appearance the animal is permitted, because it is clear they both were made after the slaughtering.
354. Chullin 50a
355. *ibid* 56b
355a. *ibid*
356. actually "he killed him by covering his eyes", i.e. an optical illusion
357. Second Maccabees 14: 39-46

fall into the hands of his persecutors alive, thrust his sword through his abdomen. In the excitement, however, he missed his stroke. He then threw himself off the wall and fell on his stomach. Still fully alive and fired with anger, he arose and, with his blood gushing out, and though severely wounded. . .losing the last of his blood, he pulled out his bowels with both hands and hurled them at the crowd, and thus expired.

The left-handed Ehud thrust his sword[358] into the belly of Eglon, King of Moab. The handle also went in after the blade, and the fat of the very obese Eglon closed upon the blade, so that Ehud could not withdraw the sword from Eglon's belly. The latter also defecated[359]. Death must have occurred rather rapidly because the servants, listening at the door, heard no suspicious sounds, and when they opened the door that evening, they found their master dead on the ground[360]. Perhaps the abdominal aorta was pierced. According to Josephus, Ehud pierced Eglon's heart with a dagger[361].

A case of an abdominal *operation* is mentioned in the Talmud. Rabbi Eleazar and Rabbi Ishmael were so obese that when they stood waist to waist, a yolk of oxen could pass below them. The former was given a sleeping potion, taken into a marble chamber, and had his abdomen opened; many basketfuls of fat were removed from him[362]. Plinius also describes a very similar "heroic cure for obesity": the son of the Consul L. Apronius had fat removed and thus his body was relieved of a disgraceful burden[363]. In the year 1190, a surgeon cut open the abdomen of Count Dedo II of Groig in order to remove the excessive fat from him[364]. Such cures are still employed today by primitive races[365]. The science of modern surgery has also rediscovered this ancient method of treating adiposity[366].

## XX    Injuries of the Heart

A Hippocratic aphorism[367] asserts that wounds of the heart are fatal. The *Mishnah*[368] is more precise because it states that a fatal outcome is restricted to those wounds which reach into the cavity of the heart (i.e. penetrating wounds). According to Galen[369], death occurs secondary to exsanguination, and, indeed, more rapidly if the injury involves the left ventricle. In the Talmud, Rabbi Zera asks whether the *Mishnah,* which states that a perforation which pierces the heart as far as the cavity thereof is fatal, refers to the large or the small cavity[370]. Galen considers non-penetrating wounds too to be fatal; nevertheless, such an injured person can still live until the next day. Plinius, on the other hand, states that death occurs immediately after any injury of the heart[371].

## XXI    Injuries of the Spleen

The *Mishnah* states that an animal whose spleen has been removed is viable[372]. The same is stated by Plinius[373]. A clean cut in the spleen is also not fatal. The situation, however, is different with holes in the spleen. If the spleen has a hole at its

---

358. *Targum: cereb;* Septuagint: *machaira;* Josephus: *xiphidion*
359. Judges 3: 21-22. Thus the Targum and the Vulgate. Another textual reading is: the sword pierced the rectum (Sachs). The Septuagint and Josephus interpret *parshedona* as the designation for a cavity: *prostas.*
360. Judges 3: 24-25
361. *Antiquities,* Book 5 Chapt. 4:2
362. Baba Metzia 83b-84a
363. Plinius 11:85; *tradunt...detractos adipes levatumque corpus innobili onere*
364. Hyrtl, *Anat.* p.25

365. Bartels *Medizin der Naturvölker* p.305
366. Schulz C. (Brest-Litovsk): *Eine operative Behandlung der Fettleibigkeit. Grenzgebiete der Medizin und Chirurgie.* Jena 1908 p.776. An earlier case is that of Demars & Marx. *ibid* 1890
367. Aphorisms 6: 18
368. Chullin 3:1
369. *De Locis* 5:2; Kühn 8:304
370. Chullin 45b
371. *Histor. Natur.* 9:69
372. Chullin 3:2
373. *Histor. Natur.* 37:11

thick end, the animal is considered non-viable and is prohibited. If the base of the hole still has as much substance as the thickness of a golden *denar,* the animal is permitted (abscess?). A hole in the thin (or flat) end of the spleen is of no consequence at all[374]. According to the commentary of Rabbi Gersom (about 1000 C.E.), this teaching of Rabbi Awira means that only a hole in the cleft (hilus) of the spleen is fatal, but not a hole in the body of the spleen.

That which the *Mishnah* asserts, that extirpation of the spleen is not fatal, also applies to humans, according to the *Gemara*[375]. The runners of Adonijah[376] had their spleens removed and the soles of their feet partly cut off, so that they might be fleet of foot. Coelius Aurelianus also mentions that some ancient non-methodologists dared to recommend the removal of the spleen. He considers it only to have been a theoretical recommendation since he never heard of its actually being carried out[377]. The story of the harmfulness of the spleen for fast runners is also found in Plinius[378], and this belief is still widespread among the masses even today[379].

Celsus excised prolapsed portions of the liver, spleen or lung from abdominal wounds[380].

## XXII    Injuries of the Liver

An animal whose liver is gone is viable if a remnant the size of an olive remains. According to one sage, this remnant must be located in the region of the gallbladder, whereas another sage states that it must be located in the place where it receives its power of life (i.e. where it normally grows). The latter is interpreted by some sages to be the site where the liver is reflected onto the kidney, and by other sages to be the site where it attaches to the diaphragm *(tarpescha)*[381]. In this case, a *restitutio ad integrum* is still possible[382]. Nowhere is the above teaching disputed.

Amemar said in the name of Rabbi Nachman: there are three main vessels *(kanim):* one leads to the heart[383], one to the lung[384], and one to the liver[385]. For the vessel of the liver, the same applies as to the liver itself, i.e., large defects are not necessarily fatal[386]. Injuries of the vessel leading to the lung are considered like the lung itself, that is, even the smallest perforation is a life-threatening situation[387]. Mar bar Rabbi Chiya teaches exactly the opposite: any injury to the liver vessel is dangerous whereas the lung vessel can tolerate extensive injuries. Did he personally observe such abnormalities in pulmonary cavities?

According to Rav Ashi, if a needle is found in the liver, one must see if the head of the needle lies downward towards the abdominal cavity, for then it must have pierced the intestine. But if the head of the needle is inside, the animal is permitted, because the needle must have entered via the liver vessel *(simpona)*[388]. However, this is the rule only in the case of a large needle[389].

## XXIII    Injuries of the Gallbladder

Perforation of the gallbladder is a life-threatening situation for an animal[390].

---

374. Chullin 55a-b
375. Sanhedrin 21b
376. First Kings 1:4
377. Coelius Aurelianus. *Chron.* 3:4 p.453: *quidam etiam decidendum vel auferendum lienem ordinare ausi sunt, quod quidem voce dictum, non officio completum accipimus.*
378. Plinius 26:83: "it hinders runners"; and 11:80: *quamobrem inuritur cursorum laborantibus*
379. See for example the runner Halsbandt in Reuters *Dörchläuchtung*
380. Celsus Book 5 Chapt. 26 p.295
381. Chullin 46b
382. *Tosefta* Chullin 3:12
383. aorta
384. trachea or pulmonary artery
385. inferior vena cava
386. Only if it is completely missing is the animal *terefah.*
387. Chullin 45b
388. via the common bile duct ?
389. Chullin 48b
390. Chullin 3:1

According to Rabbi Yochanan, this is only so if the hole is not completely covered by the liver[391]. Once a date stone (*keshite,* gallstone?) was found in the gallbladder of an animal. Said Rav Kahana: it must have gradually entered via the liver tube (or vessel)[392], although it cannot now pass through this vessel to be expelled. An anonymous author is of the opinion that a palm stone can reach the gallbladder via that tube, but an olive stone can only penetrate the gallbladder through a perforation from the outside[393].

## XXIV    Injuries of the Kidneys

The *Mishnah*[394] declares an animal with *both* kidneys removed to be viable. This teaching is also considered as absolutely reliable in tradition, and cannot be simply eliminated by assuming a false textual reading. The explanation of this obvious error probably lies in the paucity of knowledge throughout antiquity of the function of the kidneys. Thus, the followers of Asklepiades of Bithynia completely disavow the connection between the kidneys and the bladder and taught that many things in nature, including the kidneys, were created without a function *(maten)*[395].

The Talmud, however, teaches that viability of an animal may be encroached upon by *illnesses* of the kidneys[396]. If a very small kidney is found — the size of a bean in the case of goats and sheep and the size of a wineberry (i.e. grape) in the case of large cattle —[397] the animal is non-viable. One commentator (Rabbenu Nissim, about the year 1050) points out that wrinkling of the capsule indicates contraction (i.e. shrivelling up) of the kidney whereas smoothness indicates aplasia.

An animal is also *terefah* if only *one* kidney became like putrefied flesh so that it becomes pulp and disintegrates (like the lung) when one touches it, provided that the infection extended to the "white of the kidney", (i.e. calyces).

Pus *(mugla)* in the parenchyma of the kidney renders the animal *terefah,* but not a watery liquid, if it is clear and does not have a foul aroma.

One cannot live with pierced kidneys. When Job complains[398] that the archers of the Lord pierced his kidneys, it is only to be understood in the figurative sense[399].

The post-Talmudic codes first record the observation of a kidney stone in an animal[400].

According to Rabbi Jose the Galilean, regeneration of a kidney does not occur[401].

## XXV    Injuries of the Penis

According to Biblical command, a *"keruth shophcha" shall not enter into the assembly of the Lord*[402], that is, he shall not marry, because he is incapable of procreation. The expression *keruth shophcha* has two possible meanings: "a man whose penis is cut off", *abscisso veretro* in Latin, *apokekomenos* in Greek, without further clarification, corresponding to *mechabbel* of the *Targum,* as found in ancient translations — and "a man whose penis is cut into".

Prohibition against marriage for the first group of men, according to tradition, only applies to those men who are lacking more than the glans penis. If, however, there

---

391. *ibid* 43a
392. portal vein ?, bile duct ?
393. Chullin 49a
394. Chullin 3:2
395. Galen. *De Nat. Fac.* Book 1 Chapt. 14: Kühn 2:35
396. Chullin 55a-b
397. David Luria calls attention to the fact that the wineberries of Palestine are much larger than ours

398. Job 16:13
399. Chullin 43a
400. *Yoreh Deah* 44:4, according to Rabbi Eleazar of Worms. (beginning of 13th century)
401. Chullin 128b
402. Deut. 23:2

are still remnants of the corona around the penis "even if only as much as a hair's breadth", then the man is nevertheless able to be married[403].

Much discussed in all ages and by all peoples is the procreative ability of the second group, men with hypospadias or epispadias. The *Tosefta* teaches[404]: "a man with an abnormal hole (no matter in which place) is not capable of marrying, because then the sperm flows without 'shooting like an arrow' which is considered necessary for fertilization". Seemingly identical is the statement of Rav Huna: "a man who urinates at two points — that is, from the normal urethra and from another abnormal opening — is incapable of procreation"[405]. The Alexandrians have the same teaching: "all men with hypospadias (without exception) are incapable of procreation without an operation, because the sperm flows next to the vulva (instead of into the vaginal canal)"[406]. The Arabs have the same teaching[407].

The assertions of the *Gemara* are more precise: a hole distal to the corona is not a hindrance for fertilization because, as already mentioned, the entire glans without the corona must be lacking for inability to procreate. However, a hole in the corona itself (at the small ligament) and a fistula which traverses the penis obliquely, beginning at the frenulum and flowing centrally from the corona, are hindrances to normal procreation. Naturally, a hole in the shaft of the penis, no matter where, renders a man non-marriageable. According to Mar Samuel, if the hole was closed up, the man is still unfit to marry since it will reopen during ejaculation. If not, he is fit. In order to ascertain whether ejaculation would reopen the hole, Rabbi Joseph recommends that warm barley bread be placed on the man's anus to induce ejaculation. Abaye suggests that women's colored garments be dangled before him[408].

The ancients took no offence at such remedies. One should bear in mind that for the same purpose Albrecht Van Haller in France until 1677 still recommended that the patient be given a tincture of Spanish flies, and that the test of his procreative capability, i.e. coitus with his accusing marriage partner, be carried out in court in the presence of witnesses.

Since the sexual *desires* of a *keruth shophcha* are usually normal, yet marriage is forbidden to him, he seems to be dependent on illegal sexual enjoyment i.e. unchastity. Probably to prevent this, the Sages permitted him to marry a female proselyte (which is a heathen woman who converted to Judaism) or a freed female slave, since both of these were never considered to be fully valid members of the "assembly"[409].

*In practice,* all these discussions of marriage rights have little significance, since one distinguished those "injuries inflicted by human hands" from those inflicted by "the hand of Heaven" (i.e. secondary to illnesses or congenital). The final ruling is, according to the statement of Samuel[410], that the former constitute a hindrance to marriage whereas the latter do not[411].

In connection with the above discussions, a type of plastic surgery for such a "hole" in the penis seems to be alluded to in the Talmud. Abaye said: one scratches the rims of the fistula with a grain of barley until it is bloody. Tallow is then rubbed on. Then one takes a big ant and allows it to bite in, and then one severs its head. It must be a barley kernel because an iron instrument would cause inflammation. This procedure, however, only applies to a small perforation; a large one would reopen[412].

403. Yebamoth 8:2
404. *Tosefta* Yebamoth 10:4
405. Yebamoth 76a
406. *pararreontos.* Oribasius 50:3; Daremburg 4:464
407. Abulcasem. *Chirurgie.* ed. Channing p. 269
408. Yebamoth 76a
409. Yebamoth 8:2
410. Yebamoth 75b
411. Maimonides. *Mishneh Torah. Hilchoth Issurey Biah.* 16:9 and Karo *Eben Haezer* 5:10
412. Yebamoth 76a

This peculiar method, but without the preceding freshening-up of the edges of the wound, is later reported by Abulcasem[413] as an ancient practice *(thakribah)* especially suited for healing fresh intestinal wounds. The insect used by him is the same as the one employed by the Talmudists.

*Gimla* or *namila:*[414] "one takes *nimulim,* lets them bite and cuts them off".
*Korban Ha'edah* explains this phrase as follows: "one takes small knives (wide needles?), pulls the skin of the penis forward so that it covers the hole, and cuts the skin where it is now double (distal to the hole)". This seems to be a plastic procedure by stretching the foreskin. He obviously prefers the word *moshekin* (one pulls) to the word *menashkin* (*hiphil* tense of the verb *nashak,* to bite) of our text in the Babylonian Talmud.

A similar stitching of wounds of the anterior abdominal wall is practiced even today as part of Serbian folk medicine: one places squashed strong beetles on the edges of the wound, and one cuts their back parts off after they have firmly clawed into the wound[415].

Aside from the already-mentioned penis with a fistulous type of opening, two other types of abnormality are described. Rab Huna teaches that a man whose glans penis is cut away and looks like a reed pen *(calamos)* is able to marry; if it looks like a gutter *(marzeb)* or an inverted *calamos (kulmus haphok),* he is unfit to marry, for in the latter case the air penetrates whereas in the former it does not. Rabbi Chisda teaches the opposite: if the penis is cut like a gutter, the man is fit to marry; if it has the shape of a reed pen, he is unfit, for in the first case it scratches — according to the commentary, friction is produced against the vaginal wall when the sperm leaves the man's body, so the ejaculate shoots in a stream — whereas in the latter it does not. Rabba rules like Rav Huna since scratching (friction) is not necessary for ejaculation. If one loosens the plug of a filled barrel, the contents shoot out by itself in a stream[416].

It seems undoubted that these are cases of extensive fissure formation of the penis, particularly if one accepts the traditional view that the above discussions refer to the *shaft* of the penis. As can be deduced, the *glans* penis can be totally lacking without affecting the procreative capability of the man. In the case of *calamos,* the channel lies below (hypospadius) and in the case of *marzeb* it lies above (epispadius).

Mar bar Rav Ashi (in the year 400 C.E.) in the town of Mechasia on the Tigris, once "smoothed" the penis of a person with a fissure into the shape of a *calamos* and then declared the man to be fit to marry[417]. This operation seems to be identical with one performed by his Alexandrian contemporary Antyllus. The latter recommended that, in such cases, the entire glans be resected, not with a vertical incision in the longitudinal axis, but with an incision *periglyphe omoian,* so that a protuberance remains in the form of the glans. The expression *calamos,* however, is neither used by him (i.e. Antyllus) nor by Paulus of Aegina[418]. He considers a central opening from the frenulum to be incurable. Resection of the glans is of no consequence regarding procreative ability, since during coitus it does not touch the *orificium uteri,* and copulation takes place in the vagina, and yet the sperm is still able to enter the womb because the non-pregnant uterus is always open[419].

## XXVI   Injuries of the Testicles

An animal that has no testicles or that has only one testicle is considered to have a blemish and is, therefore, unfit to be offered as a sacrifice in the Temple. The same applies if both testicles lie in a scrotum which has no septum. According to Rabbi

413. Abulcasem. *De Chirurgia* 2 sect. 85. ed. Channing p.392
414. Jerushalmi Yebamoth 8; 9b
415. Stern. *Medizin...in die Turkei* 1:189
416. Yebamoth 75b
417. *ibid*
418. Paulus 6:54
419. Oribasius. *Coll.* 50: 3 Vol. 4:464

Ishmael, the latter abnormality does not occur: if there are two testicles, there are also two sacs *(kissin);* if an animal has only one *kis,* it has only one testicle. According to Rabbi Akiba, one must also exclude cryptorchidism as follows: one sets the animal on its buttocks and one squeezes (on the abnormally-situated testicles, *ba-betzim)*[420]; if a testicle is there it will finally come out. Once, however, this procedure was carried out but no testicle came forth; yet when the animal was slaughtered, the testicle was found cleaving to the loins[421]. This, therefore, represents a case of *retentio testis lumbalis.*

According to Rabbi Judah, an animal which has one testicle as large as two normal sized ones is also not suited to be offered as a sacrifice. The Sages, however, do not agree with him.

# XXVII

A priest who is a *meroach ashech,* according to Biblical law[422], is considered like a person with a physical blemish and is, therefore, unfit to serve in the Temple. The *Mishnah*[423] interprets the defect to be the absence of one or both testicles; the Septuagint also translates *monorchis.* According to Rabbi Ishmael, it refers to a man whose testicles are softened[424], i.e. a castrate. According to Rabbi Akiba, it refers to a man "who has air in his testicles"[425], that is, a defect which Paulus of Aegina calls *pneumatokele*[426]. Paulus interprets it to be an abnormality analogous to the break of a varicose vein (i.e. varicocoele) composed solely of pneuma-containing vessels. According to the *Tosefta*[427], Rabbi Akiba uses the word *kletis,* obviously equivalent to the Greek *keletis* referring to someone with a break, *kele,* in a more general sense than the pneumatocoele of the *Mishnah.*

The following amusing example is a reflection of what goes through the mind of even famous philologists: Levy[428] considered *kletis* to correctly be *keletes* but he translates our passage: "it is a man with a fractured leg, in whose testicles the wind enters". Fleischer[429] corrects Levy as follows: instead of "the wind", write "the winds", i.e. flatulence (in the intestines)!

A *me-ushkan* is also unfit to serve in the Temple[430]. According to the *Beraitha*[431], it refers to a *kayan,* a man with long testicles where they hang down to the knees (*scrotum pendens* or a large testicular hernia).

The expression *shaabze* is used by the *Targum* to translate the word "testicles"[432].

# XXVIII

The Bible ordains[433] that an animal that is *ma'uch,* or *kathuth,* or *natchuk,* or *karuth* should not be offered as a sacrifice in the Temple. There is no doubt that these are abnormalities of the genitalia.

1) *Ma'uch* means crushed; the Septuagint has *o thladias.* The procedure of the *thlasis,* among the Arabs[434], consisted of softening the scrotum of the person to be operated upon by soaking it in warm water, and then the testicles are crushed subcutaneously. (Vulgate has *contritis testiculis.*)

2) *Kathuth* means smashed, *ektethlimmenos* in Greek and *tusis testiculis* in Latin.

---

420. *Tosefta* Bechoroth 4:8
421. Bechoroth 6:6
422. Levit. 21:20
423. Bechoroth 7:5
424. from the word *marach,* meaning to soften, as in Isaiah 38:21; perhaps, the softening in a warm bath for the purpose of castration. The *Targum* has *meres pachdin* meaning smashed or crushed testicles
425. *Sifra Emor* p.35a
426. pneumatocoele. Paulus 6:64
427. *Tosefta* Bechoroth 5:4
428. *Neuhebäisches und Chaldäisches Wörterbuch,* Leipzig 1876-1889, 4:261b
429. *ibid* 480b
430. Bechoroth 7:5
431. *ibid* 44b
432. Genesis 39:1; Job 40:17
433. Levit. 22:24
434. Abulcasem p.313

The same procedure as above is followed but without the preceding softening of the testicles by hot soaks.

3) *Nathuk* means cut, *o ekthomias* in Greek and *sectis testiculis* in Latin. This refers to the subcutaneous cutting of the spermatic cord whereby the testicle itself remains in the scrotum. It is the *al-sharik* of the Arabs.

4) *Karuth* means cut off, *apespasmenos* in Greek and *ablatis testiculis* in Latin; the removal of the testicle from the scrotum or together with the latter, *alkitah*.

According to Rabbi Eleazar ben Jacob, similar appearances can occur in animals without damaged genitalia: normal testicles (and scrotum) can shrink (contract, shrivel up, retract inside) and resemble crushed testicles, or they can hang and appear as if they were cut[435].

In the Talmud[436], only Rabbi Judah supports the opinion that all four expressions concern the testicles. According to Rabbi Eleazar (ben Jacob), they refer to mutilations of the penis, and according to Rabbi Jacob, the first two expressions refer to the testicles and the last two refer to the penis.

5) The Bible also states[437] that a *petzua dakah shall not enter into the assembly of the Lord,* i.e. shall not marry an Israelite woman.

The Septuagint has *thladias,* so that *petzua dakah* would mean "crushed soft".
The Talmud is of the same opinion: "*petzua dakah* is a person in whom one or both testicles are crushed *(niphtza)*"[438]. The Vulgate has: *eunuchus attritis vel amputatis testiculis.*

A case of injury of a testicle secondary to a fall from an olive tree is reported from the time of Rabbi Yochanan ben Nuri (about 100 C.E.)[439]. According to the *Tosefta*[440], *petzua dakah* is also that condition where one or both testicles become soft or are pierced or are totally missing. It is disputed, however, whether or not piercing of the testicles eliminates one's procreative ability. Once, a man climbed a palm tree, and a thorn pierced his testicles so that his semen issued like a thread of pus *(chut de mugla,* semen canal?), and despite that he begot children. Mar Samuel, however, doubted their legitimacy[441]. Did he observe necrosis of the testicles after such a perforation-injury?

It is also possible that the genitalia of a fetus within the mother's womb become torn off[442]; this probably occurs where there is a pelvic presentation and an unusually rough midwife.

A *restitutio ad integrum* is considered possible for a *petzua dakah,* but not for a *keruth shophcha,* a man with a cut-off or fistulous penis; and this is "one of the rules (teachings?) of physicians" (a citation?)[443], a fact recognized by medical science.

Testicles which are crushed subcutaneously in the scrotum *(be'e chashilatha* or *chalishatha)* still retain some of their vitality; since no air can get into them, they do not putrefy[444].

The procreative ability of a man with one testicle was in dispute. The rule of the *Mishnah,* as already described, is to forbid such a man from marrying. In later times, Rabbi Emme also subscribed to this opinion. However, the renowned physician Mar Samuel was opposed to this disqualification (of a monorchid man), and the disciples of Jamnia agreed with him[445]. Rabbi Judan bar Chanina insisted that it must be the *right* testicle which remains[446]. There was no unanimity of opinion on this matter even in

435. Bechoroth 39b
436. *Sifra loc. cit.* & Bechoroth 33a
437. Deut. 23:2
438. Yebamoth 8:1
439. *Tosefta* Yebamoth 10:3
440. *ibid*
441. Yebamoth 75b
442. Jerushalmi Yebamoth 8;9d

443. *Sifre loc. cit.* & Jerushalmi Yebamoth 8; 9b
444. Chullin 93a-b
445. Yebamoth 75a
446. Jerushalmi Yebamoth 8; 9b; nevertheless, the exact textual reading cannot be established. *Tosafoth* Yebamoth 75a

post-Talmudic times[447]. Even among medico-legal physicians in the Occident, the question of the procreative ability of a man with one testicle is a favorite topic of discussion even into our own century. One should also mention the decree of Pope Sixtus V (1585), that all marriages in which the man does not have two testicles in the scrotum should be dissolved[448].

That which applies to the testicles also applies to the "strands of the testicles", the spermatic cords. Crushing or cutting the latter also makes a man unfit to marry[449].

## XXIX   Castration

The abnormalities of the genitalia enumerated here are individual cases of the commonly practiced abomination called *serus,* meaning castration.

Besides the usual expression *saris* for the castrate, one rarely finds the term *gawzah,* probably with an additional despicable meaning, *shelipha*[450]. For the castration of an animal, in addition to the usual term *saras,* one occasionally finds the expression *gannach*[451].

The custom is a very ancient one in Egypt[452], in Ethiopia[453], in Media and in Persia[454], in Babylon[455], and even in Israel; the Bible calls them "eunuchs". They function as harem watchers, as in Persia; as servants of the Egyptian kings; and in the court of Jezebel[456] and Jehoiachin[457]; and even as supervisors of military personnel in Jerusalem[458]; sometimes in columns with a chief, *rab* or *sar,* at the head[459]. They can also become married, (for example Potiphar in the Bible) so that rules regarding their widows are recorded[460]. Even among the Mohammedans, all *aghawat* (eunuchs) of the mosques are married[461].

However, it cannot be established with certainty whether or not all these cases really involved castrates, or whether the term *saris* gradually came to denote servants or officials in general. Certainly the heathen Orient with its many harems also had a great need for eunuchs. This might also have been the case in Israel during the time of the kings, although, specifically, in the court of the many-wived Solomon, eunuchs were lacking. In post-Biblical times, however, many wives were no longer taken by any man even though a specific prohibition never followed, so that there was no more need for eunuchs as harem watchers. The *sarseja* has the job of a brew-master[462]. The *gawahs* seems to have been a type of attendant who stood ready to serve the presiding officer of the courts[463]. One also cannot readily accept that Rabbi Idi, who is called the *saris* of the blind Rabbi Shesheth[464], was a eunuch[465].

The publisher of the Krotoschin edition of the Jerusalem Talmud surmises that "Levi sarisa" who disagrees with the Persian Ablat[466] is really "Levi bar Sisi".

For the Jews, to all this must be added the strict prohibition in the Bible against castration: an animal which is *ma'uch, kathuth, nathuk* or *karuth*[467] — *thou shalt not offer unto the Lord, nor shalt thou perform any such (castration) in your land!*[468]

---

447. *Eben Haezer* 5:7 and all the commentaries
448. Placzek in Neuburger-Pagel's *Handbuch* 3:747
449. Yebamoth 75b
450. Shabbath 152a
451. Baba Metzia 90b
452. Potiphar, Genesis 39:1,; the court baker and the cup-bearer *ibid* 40:2
453. Jeremiah 38:7: *Ebed Melech, a eunuch from Ethiopia;* Acts of the Apostles 8:27
454. Esther
455. Isaiah 39:7
456. Second Kings 9:32
457. *ibid* 24:12
458. *ibid* 25:19
459. Daniel 1:3
460. *Tosefta* Yebamoth 2:5-6
461. Hurgronje Snouck, *Mekka* 2:24, note 2
462. Baba Metzia 42b; Kiddushin 52b
463. Megillah 28a; Kiddushin 33a and *Rashi, loc. cit.*
464. Bechoroth 31b
465. Rather the word *saris* means attendant
466. Jerushalmi Shabbath 3;6a and Jerushalmi Betzah 2;61c
467. see above
468. Levit. 22:24

Some Sages are even of the opinion that this law already existed in pre-Sinaitic times[469]. Although this prohibition was stated in relation to animals fit for offering in the Temple, the Talmud interprets the prohibition in a very general sense: "anyone who castrates a human being or a domesticated or wild animal or a bird, whether large or small, male or female, is punishable"[470]. One should not even maim in this manner animals which may not be eaten (i.e. "unclean" animals), or a dog, the proceeds of whose sale one cannot use to bring an offering[471]. Furthermore, "the castration of a castrate" is punished with disciplinary flogging[472]; for example, if someone removes the testicles of a man whose spermatic cord has already been cut. An impolite answer was given to the question as to whether or not a person who castrates his slave must give him his freedom, which would mean that the owner is also liable from the standpoint of civil law[473]. The answer was thought to be generally known; hence, the questioner was jeered.

The questioner was Hamnuna. They answered him: your name should really be *karnuna* (horned one)!

The prohibition of castrating breeding animals must have had some inconvenient consequences for Jewish farmers because bulls — these are the main animals to be considered — are not well-suited to be beasts of burden because of their ferocity. The calves of bulls which were not to be used for breeding were, therefore, sold. It also happened, however, that friendly heathens would "steal" the calves, castrate them, and then return them to their owners. Naturally, the Rabbis did not approve of this "deceitful" evasion of the law[474].

Abulcasem writes: "Although our religion *(sharyathina)* prohibits castration, I still wish to discuss it because a physician must also understand it when he is questioned about it, and because we are often called to castrate animals"[475]. No religion other than Judaism prohibits castration; neither Buddha, nor Confucius, nor Jesus, nor Muhammed considered it to be an offense, so that it appears that Abulcasem should be considered a Judaic-Arabic physician. Egypt, Babylonia, Rome and Greece are totally silent on this subject.

In Matthew, in addition to eunuchs *which were so born from their mother's womb,* and eunuchs *which were made eunuchs by other men,* there are listed those *who made themselves eunuchs for the kingdom of Heaven's sake (oitines eunouchisan eautous dia ten basileian ton ouranon)*[476]. It is known that a serious dispute arose from these words of Matthew: one group led by the church father Origen (185-254) took the words literally and cut off their own genitalia. The others understood it to refer to an admonition to celibacy (sexual abstinence) which, contrary to Judaic teaching, was considered to be especially pleasing to God. The Valerian sect adopted the view of Origen and, in spite of persecution by Emperors Constantine and Justinian in the fourth century, this view has not vanished to this very day, as proven by the Russian Skoptics.

Josephus calls these self-mutilators *galloi,* derived from the Priests of Cybele from the Phrygian river Gallus, who cut off their own genitalia. Josephus says of them: one should stay away from them and flee from their company because they remove their own manlihood *(to arren)* and their procreative ability which God has given us to increase our offspring. They should be banished like those who killed their children before the latter were even born. It is obvious that their body, like their soul, is womanish[477].

469. Sanhedrin 56b
470. *Tosefta* Makkoth 5:6
471. Deut. 23:19; Chagigah 14b
472. Tosefta Bechoroth 3:24
473. Kiddushin 25a

474. Baba Metzia 90b
475. *opus cit.* Book 2, Sect. 69 p.313
476. Matthew 19:12
477. Josephus. *Antiquities* Book 4 Chapt. 8:40

## XXX    Eunuchs

A *saris chamma* or "sun castrate"[478] is distinguished from a "human castrate". I consider this expression to be parallel to the Egyptian phrase "castrated by Ra", the sun-god. I find support for this interpretation in the *Gemara* which uses the phrase "castrated by God, *biyde shamayim*", instead of "sun castrate"[479].

If one became a eunuch[480], there was a time when he was potent; although he is presently sterile, there was a time in which he was able to procreate, unless his genitals were forcibly excised. For a congenital eunuch[481], there was never such a time. A congenital eunuch can be healed, whereas if one became a eunuch, there is no cure[482]. Rabbi Eliezer stated (about the year 50 C.E.) that such congenital eunuchs were healed in Alexandria in Egypt[483]. The cause for congenital eunuchs is that the mother baked or ate in the heat of the day, or of the oven, during her pregnancy.

*Chamma* means both sun and heat; hence, *Aruch* renders *saris* as (hot) fever.

The following are the signs of a eunuch: he has no beard, his hair is soft, his skin is smooth, his urine is not excreted in an arch, the urine does not bubble because the power of the stream is lacking, and, according to some Sages, it does not ferment, and the semen is thin like water. According to some Sages, his skin does not perspire even if he bathes in cold water during the rainy season. Rabbi Simeon ben Eleazar adds: his voice is soft, so that it cannot be distinguished from that of a woman[484]. If a man has no beard or pubic hair by 20 years of age, one must assume that he is a congenital eunuch[485].

Obviously only two situations can explain the above:

1) Congenital absence of the testicles (anorchidism), whether due to true absence or due to a simulated displacement of the testicles (ectopia) in which the organ then shrivelled up. According to this viewpoint, the disciples in Yabneh could also include a one-testicled man in the group called "sun castrates"[486].

2) Alternatively, there may be an arrest of the development of the testicles at an infantile stage, a growth suppression, as observed particularly often in the Orient following leprosy[487]. I am not aware of any reports from other sources concerning the healing of such situations in Alexandria.

It was debated into which group one should classify those who became "castrates" secondary to extrauterine illnesses. It is mentioned that a man can also become a *saris* if *chatatin* occurred on his scrotum and he then scratched or tore them off[488]. *Chatatin* are small "furrows" or holes or wounds, or, as probably correctly stated by Buxtorf, *fossulae a scabie maligna erosae.*

Cohabitation with ejaculation can occur even if a man's testicles are in an advanced state of degeneration. However, the ejaculate fluid contains no spermatozoa[489]; it is also usually not opaque but clear as water, so the assertion that a sun castrate can cohabit but not beget children[490] is probably quite correct.

The *potestas coëundi* is also not invariably preserved in all eunuchs; it is lacking, for example, in the so-called "black eunuchs", all of whose genitalia, including the penis, are cut off. However, the libido might still be active in such a person; even if he is "a dry wood"[491], he may still have the desire to ravish a young maiden[492], but he

478. i.e. natural or congenital eunuch
479. Yebamoth 80a
480. literally: man-made *saris*
481. literally: sun *saris*
482. Yebamoth 8:4
483. *ibid* 80a
484. *ibid* 80b
485. *Tosefta* Yebamoth 10:6
486. Jerushalmi Yebamoth 8; 9a

487. Glück. *Arch. f. Derm. u. Syphilis* 52:2
488. Jerushalmi Yebamoth 8; 9b
489. Englisch. in Eulenburg's *R.E.* Vol. 9:545
490. Jerushalmi Yebamoth 9b
491. Isaiah 56:3
492. Sirach 20:2 "A man who would do violence in court is like a eunuch who ravishes a girl that he is supposed to protect"

only embraces her and groans[492a]. Although it is known that he is harmless, if a married man sees that a castrate is kissing his wife, he becomes angry[493]. A *Midrash* puts it more drastically. .when he sees that his wife embraces a statue[494].

Gradually *saris* became the general expression for *impotens coëundi,* whereas the term *akar* remains for *impotens generandi.*

A eunuch is unfit to serve as a priest[495]; he is, however, acceptable to be a civil judge but cannot judge criminal cases, just like anyone who has no children or had no children[496]. It was debated as to whether or not he can serve as a prayer leader, notwithstanding the fact that he has no beard[497]. The Biblical proceedings against a "rebellious son"[498] may not be utilized on a eunuch[499] since he is lacking the physical signs through which the responsible age for punishment can be established. He is not free, however, from the ordinances of religious ceremonials[500].

It is also mentioned that a cock can be castrated (i.e. rendered impotent) by cutting off its crest. But Rav Ashi said: it only loses its proud courage and is, thereby, only rendered psychologically impotent since it refuses to copulate[501]. Bees can be made sterile by offering them mustard[502]. The hornet is said to have the ability of not only blinding people but also of rendering them impotent (by a sting in the eye or the testicles)[503].

## XXXI  Female Castrates

Corresponding to the male *saris*[504], a parallel abnormality in the woman is said to be rare and is designated as *aylonith*[505], a she-goat resembling a ram. It was recognized that castration of females in antiquity belongs to mythology, and there only remain "*aylonith* by heavenly hands", that is, women whose genitalia are totally rudimentary or are in an infantile stage of development.

The etymology of the word *aylonith* is unclear. The explanation "ram-like" of Rabbi Nachman bar Yitzchak in the Talmud[506], i.e. *dukranith,* from *dukar,* equivalent to *zakar* meaning male, is said by himself to represent only an *Aggadah* (legend). Since *ilan* means tree, the reading *ilanoth,* meaning like wood of a tree, would also be acceptable (Kohut). Brüll[507] interprets *ayala* meaning doe, whose genitals, according to a Talmudic legend[508], are also narrow. L. Löw considered *yleen* (in Greek, with a Hebrew ending)[509] which is only a poetic term, however, and only means "wooden" or "grown over with wood".

The following are the signs of an *aylonith:* she has no breasts and suffers pain during copulation. Rabbi Simeon ben Gamliel says: she has no *shippule me'ayim* like normal women. Rabbi Simeon ben Eleazer says: her voice is thick (deep) so that one cannot distinguish whether it is that of a man or a woman. Even when reaching twenty years of age, she has no pubic hair and is not capable of procreation[510].

492a. *ibid* 30:20. "This is the way with a rich man who is afflicted by the Lord; he sees things with his eyes and groans therefore; and he is like a eunuch embracing a girl", *perilambamon parthenon kai stenazon.*
493. Jerusalmi Betzah 2; 61c. Numbers Rabbah 2:15
494. Exodus Rabbah 43:7
495. *Tosefta* Bechoroth 5:2
496. *Tosefta* Sanhedrin 7:5
497. Soferim 14:7
498. Deut. 21:18
499. Yebamoth 80a
500. *Tosefta* Berachoth 5:14; *Tosefta* Rosh Hashanah 4:1; *Tosefta* Megillah 11:7, etc.
501. Shabbath 110b
502. Baba Bathra 80a
503. Sotah 36a
504. the Biblical phrase *there shall not be a male or female barren among you* (Deut. 7:14) is interpreted by the *Midrash* (Deut. Rabbah 3:6) to mean: no *saris* and no *aylonith*
505. Yebamoth 119a
506. Kethuboth 11a
507. in his *Jahrbuch* 1879 p.11
508. Baba Bathra 16b
509. *Lebensalter* p.296, note 5
510. Yebamoth 80b

*Shippul* or *shippula* is the name of the lower seam (i.e. the train), for example, of a dress[511], or of a mountain[512], etc., derived from the word *shaphal* meaning "low" or "at the bottom". The *shippule me'ayim* thus refer to the labia (according to *Rashi: mons veneris*). As a subjective sign of menstruation, among others, the following is mentioned: the woman has pains around her navel and her *shippule me'eha,* and *Rashi* has the explanation: "genitalia", *beth-harechem*[513]. Thus the case here refers to the rudimentary development of the labia and the fat cushion of the *mons veneris.*

Aristotle also mentions men and women who are hairless and incapable of begetting children as a result of stunted growth (or atrophy) or mutilation *(perothenai)* of the genitalia[514].

No one should marry an *aylonith* woman, unless he already has a wife and children. According to Rabbi Judah, even then he should not do so; for she is nothing but a concubine for the man, assuming she is capable of cohabitation. According to Rabbi Meir[515], a minor girl should not be able to contract levirate marriage because later she might be found to be incapable of procreation *(aylonith),* although this does not happen in the vast majority of cases[516]. If a woman was married unconditionally, and it turns out that she is an *aylonith,* the marriage is invalid[517]; not so, however, if the man knew of the defect in the woman prior to the marriage[518].

A man who violates or seduces an *aylonith* is punished in the same manner as the law requires for other women; that is, for seduction he has to pay the Biblically prescribed[519] fine. In addition, he must pay a penalty for the shame he caused, and compensation for the diminution of her personal worth calculated as a maid servant. If he violates her, he is exempt from marrying her[520] which, in other cases, is part of his punishment; but he still has to pay money for the pain he inflicted. However, opinions are divided in the Talmud as to whether or not an *aylonith* can at all be included in the Biblical concept of *naara* (maiden) for juridical purposes. On the other hand, there is no question that a complaint of *virginitas laesa* can be lodged against her[521].

## XXXII   Hermaphrodites

There are two other types of abnormalities, of the genitalia mentioned in the Talmud which have given difficulties in interpretation to the Sages of all generations:

1) The *androginos* (in Hebrew), *androgynos* (in Greek); i.e. the hermaphrodite or hybrid. He is one of a separate class of creatures concerning which one cannot decide whether he is a man or a woman[522]. Even the Talmudists assume that the same hermaphrodite can both menstruate as well as ejaculate[523], although many of them only see "white (i.e. sperm) *or* red (i.e. menstrual blood)"[524]. Nowhere, however, is the possibility raised in the Talmud that the hermaphrodite is capable of simultaneously being pregnant and making pregnant, something that was seriously believed to be true by medical science as recently as the last century[525].

Legally, the hermaphrodite is in an unfavorable position. He has all the

511. Shabbath 98b
512. *Targum* Joshua 11:17
513. Niddah 9:8
514. *Hist. Anim.* Book 7 Chap. 1:6
515. Yebamoth 61a-b
516. According to Biblical law, (Deut. 25:5) the brother of a man who died without having had children should marry the widow *(Yebama)* of the deceased brother, provided, however, that this widow is capable of procreation.
517. *Tosefta* Kethuboth 1:3

518. Kethuboth 11:6
519. Exodus 22:15
520. Deut. 22:28
521. *Tosefta* Kethuboth 1:3; Kethuboth 35b and 36a
522. *Tosefta* Bikkurim 2:7
523. *Tosefta* Zabim 2:2 and Niddah 28a
524. *ibid* and *Tosefta* Niddah 1:3
525. see Haller. *Vorlesungen über die gerichtliche Arzneiwissenschaft.* Bern 1782 Vol. 1 p.205

obligations of a man but not all his rights; he does not receive a portion of inheritance from his father as do his brothers, nor is he supported from the inheritance as are his sisters. As a woman, he is not able to testify in court; if he is of priestly descent, he cannot partake of priestly gifts and allowances; he is also unfit to serve as a priest. He has all the religious (ceremonial) obligations of a man[526]. On the other hand, perhaps to contrast with his legal status in other nations[527], Judaism intentionally emphasizes that he is to be considered as a human being throughout. If someone kills him intentionally, the killer is executed by strangulation; if unintentionally, the killer goes into exile[528]. On the other side, he himself is stoned if he curses his parents[529].

His legal advantages are minor; he cannot be sold as a slave and is not required to make the three yearly pilgrimages to Jerusalem. Cohabitation with him cannot be punished as incest[530]. However, the law of pederasty (death by stoning) is applied[531].

He is subject to circumcision on the eighth day of life[531a]; his marriage with a woman is legally binding and must be dissolved by formal divorce proceedings just as for the case of a normal man. On the other hand, marriage with another man is not allowed[532].

The rules of a firstborn do not apply to a firstborn hermaphrodite animal. The owner may use it for himself, i.e. shear it, or use it for labor or for consumption[533].

Scripture states of the first man: *male and female He created them*[534]. Thus, asserts Rabbi Jeremiah ben Eleazar: Adam was an *androgynos*[535].

2) The *tumtum,* or sealed one, or pasted-over one.

Derived from *tum* or *tamam* meaning sealed over. The assumption of Mussaphia that *tumtum* is *tmetos* (cut or circumcised?) is very intriguing (one should then have the reading *tumtos,* just as *lesteis* is consistently written *listim*); however, neither *tmetos* or *atmetos* (not cut), which would be more likely in our sense, is found in Greek sources.

A *tumtum* is *not* a hermaphrodite, but either male *or* female. However, his self is only recognizable after he is "split" (cut open). Before that occurs, he is incapable of procreation or of bearing children. In the town of Bairi, a *tumtum* was once placed on a chair (or "on his abdomen", *abey kurseh*) and operated upon; after that he begat seven children. Rabbi Judah, nevertheless, questioned their legitimacy[536]. In some *tumtums,* testicles are recognizable externally (perhaps in the flexure of the groin)[537], but not in the majority of them. A *tumtum* is thus a *cryptorchid.* It is generally accepted that a *tumtum,* even if he turns out to be a male after being "cut open", can still be a congenital eunuch[538]; that is, the testicles which one finds are rudimentary or degenerated.

One, therefore, assumed either that testicular ectopia implies impotence *qua talis,* as already conjectured by the congenital eunuch, or the concept of *tumtum* also includes a malformation of the *penis* which can be corrected by the operation of

---

526. *Tosefta* Berachoth 5:14; *Tosefta* Rosh Hashanah 4:1; *Tosefta* Megillah 2:7; *Tosefta* Parah 5:7; Arachin 1:1; Parah 12:10. For animals: Bikkurim 1:5; *Tosefta* Bechoroth 7:7; *Tosefta* Temurah 1:9 and others. The frequency of occurrence of hermaphrodites (in man and animal) cannot be deduced from the frequency with which the subject is mentioned in the Talmud; a category of individuals once established is consequently discussed in all areas of law.
527. for example, Constantine the Great enacted a law which required the drowning of all hermaphrodites because they signify bad luck; Haller *loc. cit.* p.206.

528. *Tosefta* Bikkurim 2:6
529. Sanhedrin 66a
530. *Tosefta* Bikkurim 2:5
531. *Tosefta* Yebamoth 10:2
531a. Shabbath 19:4
532. *Tosefta* Bikkurim 2:4; *Tosefta* Yebamoth 2:5
533. Bechoroth 6:12
534. Genesis 5:2
535. Genesis Rabbah 8:1 fol. 21b
536. Yebamoth 83b
537. Chagigah 4a; Yebamoth 72a
538. literally: sun-*saris*

"splitting". Support for the latter contention comes from the assertion of Resh Lakish that the question of the sex of a *tumtum* only occurs in relation to a human being, since his male and female parts are in the same place. In the case of an animal, one need only observe from which place it urinates to establish whether it is a male or a female animal. According to Rabbi Eleazer (or Rabbi Ilay) this test is not reliable, since a *tumtum* animal urinates from the place where normally the female genitalia are found, even if it is a male animal[539].

It is rather obvious that these items (relating to a hermaphrodite i.e. *androgynos*, and to one of indeterminate sex i.e. *tumtum*) have nothing to do with the fantasy of the ancients concerning humans, *qui sexum mutaverunt*.

Legally, the *tumtum* and *androgynos* are generally equal[540].

The striking fact that Abraham and Sarah first had a descendant after many years of marriage is explained by Rabbi Ammi[541] as follows: they were both[542] of doubtful sex *(tumtumin)* and first had to be split.

## XXXIII    Bladder Stones

Rabbi Judah the Prince suffered for thirteen years from *tzemirtha* (bladder calculi) and when he went to the toilet, his screams of pain were so loud they could be heard at the seashore.

These pains are portrayed in a flowery manner as follows: the horse steward of Rabbi was wealthier than King Shapur (i.e. he had more horses to oversee than the king). When he gave fodder to the horses, their neighs could be heard for three miles. He always fed the horses when Rabbi went to the toilet, but Rabbi's voice lifted in pain was louder than that of the horses, so that even seafarers heard it[543]. The illness was a punishment for the fact that once a calf, who was being taken to the slaughter, broke away and sought refuge with Rabbi, and the latter dismissed it saying "go, for this wast thou created" *(summum jus)*[544].

Against *tzemirtha,* the folk medicine of the Talmud recommends the following:[545] take three drops[546] of pitch sediment, and three drops of leek juice, and three drops of pure wine, and pour it on the membrum of a man or on the *locum illum* (i.e. the vulva) of a woman. Or use a louse in the same manner. Or take the ear of a bottle *(una de zika?)* or a thread which was spun by a woman of ill-repute[547] who is the daughter of a woman of ill-repute, and hang it on the membrum of the man or the breasts of the woman. When the patient urinates, he (or she) should do so on dry blackberry thorns *(sisna)* near the threshold of the house, and he should pay attention to the stone that issues from him, for it is good for all fevers[548].

In any event, the illness *tzemirtha* obviously refers to complaints relating to the bladder and, if tradition with its interpretation of *chumartha* as "stone" is correct[549], then *tzemirtha* is dysuria secondary to bladder concrements. The first two remedies apparently are intended to exert a strong irritating effect on the mucosa which reflects on the bladder muscle.

I am in the position of being able to state with absolute and unquestionable

---

539. Bechoroth 42b
540. an exception is found in Baba Bathra 126b
541. Yebamoth 64a
542. it should be: "only Sara", not both, since the legitimacy of Ishmael is certainly not in doubt. The *Tosafoth* point out another difficulty
543. Baba Metzia 85a
544. *ibid*
545. Gittin 69b

546. Preuss erroneously has: 2 drops (F.R.)
547. *duma,* from *dum* meaning a woman about which one is "silent", a euphemism for "one about whom one speaks"
548. Concerning *tzimra,* see above Chapter 4, Part 2. It is unclear how our *tzemirtha* is interpreted to mean "dysuria". Buxtorf & Levy mention the Syrian *tzemara* which has this meaning.
549. *chumartha* is equivalent to stone, bundle and, in general, anything round

certainty from modern times that the louse which is the strangest part of both remedies, can, in reality, have this effect. Under the heading "The Third Plague of Egypt as a Diuretic", an American physician relates, laughingly, that he was called to see a man who suffered from urinary retention for two days and who, following an infusion(!) of digitalis, went on his way. The next day, the physician learned that when two spoons of his remedy had not yet produced emptying of the bladder, the people in the house put a *pediculus corporis* (louse, "a subject of the Emperor of Russia"), into the urethra of the patient and "it did come, blessed be the Lord", after three minutes[550].

In view of this therapeutic performance of a physician at the end of the nineteenth century, we should not criticize the Talmudic folk medicine for not recommending a catheter for urinary retention, although the contemporary heathen physicians had known it well since the time of Erasistratos. Our people, too, still apply folk medicine.

This use of an insect *(kinna)* for urinary retention was quite prevalent among Roman *veterinarians*. Vegetus writes as follows: *cimicem* (bug) *etiam vivum in aurem animalis mittunt, alium super naturam, qua mingit, confricant; certissimum dicitur*[551]. Pelagonius has the same statement, nearly word for word[552]. It was, therefore, natural that in case of need, the same remedy was used for human beings.

## XXXIV    Urination and Defecation

Urination and defecation early in the morning is to the body what hardening is to iron[553], and a person who "defers his bodily functions" transgresses the Biblical command:[554] and *ye shall not make yourselves detestable*[555]. For this reason, teaches Rabbi Yochanan, it is permitted to urinate even in the presence of others. Once, during a discourse, Mar Samuel needed to urinate. They spread a cloak as a screen between himself and the audience; however, he asked Rabbi Abahu to inform the audience that the use of such a screen is only required where it is readily available; otherwise, people will think it is always necessary and thus endanger their health. A person who withheld his urine developed a swollen abdomen and was later only able to empty his bladder drop by drop[556].

It is related that a large number of men became impotent as a result of long discourses, particularly those of Rav Huna, in that they did not wish to leave the discourse out of reverence for their teachers. During such a discourse of Rav Huna, Rabbi Acha bar Jacob was attacked by *suskintha*[557] and when he was supported (literally: hung) on a cedar tree of the learning house, there issued from him a discharge like a green (or yellow) palm shoot[558].

According to the contents of the story, it appears that the affliction was a form of stranguria. One cannot prove that it refers to the Greek *syschinthe* as may seem plausible. The dictionaries follow the *Aruch: sasgonitha*. Since the Biblical *tachash* is rendered *sasgon* by the *Targum,* they consider it "an illness in which the body assumes different colors". It certainly does not refer to scarlet (fever) as suggested by Levy[559].

*Scheeltoth No. 145* has *subsintha;* from a manuscript, the commentaries give the textual reading: *sakantha* meaning "danger", which is probably the correct interpretation. One should compare the following to the "hanging"

---

550. *The Times & Register.* Vol. 21 No. 16 p.362, Oct. 18, 1890
551. Vegeti Renati. *Mulomedicina* 2:79 No. 21. Ed. Lommatzsch. Leipzig 1903 p.169
552. Pelagonius. *Art. Vet.* ed. Ihm. Leipzig 1892 No. 153 P.63
553. Berachoth 62b, *schena* means urine

554. Levit. 11:43
555. Makkoth 16b
556. Bechoroth 44b
557. dysuria or stone. see below
558. Yebamoth 64b
559. *Neuhebräisches und Chaldäisches Wörterbuch.* Leipzig 1876-1889

treatment: he who hangs himself in the privy develops hemorrhoids[560] to which *Rashi* explains: he only bends his knees but does not sit down — Ritter.

If the feces return to[561] the body, the person develops dropsy[562]; if urine[563] is suppressed, the person develops anemia[564]. Raba Bar Rav Huna expresses it as follows: much feces (where feces accumulate and are not excreted), much dropsy, much urine, much anemia[565].

Elderly people have to press hard when they urinate; as a result it could happen that feces[566] are excreted before the urine[567].

## XXXV　Lameness

If someone's bones are inhibited from normal movement, he is either a limper, *tzolea*, actually "one who is bent to one side", like the Patriarch Jacob after he wrestled with the angel[568]; or is like Levi bar Sisi after he demonstrated the *kidah* to Rabbi Judah the prince, i.e. that bow in which one bends the upper part of the body forward with stretched knees until the tips of the fingers touch the ground[569]. Whereas in the former case, the disturbance of movement was soon eliminated—at least nothing is later mentioned thereof—in the second patient, the abnormality, probably caused by a distortion of one of the hip joints, remained permanently[570].

Stuttering and stammering are considered to be "limping with the tongue"[571]. Alternatively, the patient is called a *pisse'ach,* and in the Talmud *chigger*[572]. Mephibosheth, the son of Jonathan, was *lame in his feet.* He was five years old when his nurse, in the haste of fleeing, let him fall from the arm (or "from the shoulders")[573]; as a result he became lame[574]. He remained lame on both his feet and, therefore, as a helpless person, was fed at the table of King David[575]. Since the servant did not saddle the ass, Mephibosheth could not go to meet the king, because he was lame[576]. It is probably more correct to assume that he was lame perhaps from an injury of the spinal cord secondary to a partial dislocation of the vertebral column which he suffered earlier in his youth.

If one of the parents is a *chigger,* then the Biblically prescribed regulations concerning a rebellious son[577] cannot be carried out, because the parents shall *bring him out unto the elders of his city*[578] which they (cannot do if they are lame but) could readily accomplish if they are only limping. A *chigger* is thus a lame person; the meaning of the word is a "bound" person in the sense of a "limp" person, *paralytikos.* Such an individual is not obligated to fulfill the law of pilgrimages to Jerusalem[579] for the festive occasions[580]. The *Gemara* interprets such a person to be "lame on one foot"[581]. He is unfit to serve as a priest[582], irrespective of whether he is lame on one foot or on both feet[583]. A lame animal may not be offered as a

560. Berachoth 55a
561. *ammud* meaning a pillar refers to feces. The usual word for feces is *tzo'ah*
562. *hidrakon.* see above Chapter 4, Part 3:2
563. *silon* is equivalent to *solen* (in Greek) meaning "tube". Here only it refers to urine.
564. *Yerakon.* see above Chapter 4, Part 3
565. Bechoroth 44b
566. *gelalim* meaning "round" fecal balls
567. Levit. Rabbah 18:1 as an explanation of the ancient allegory in Eccles. 12:2 *clouds return after the rain.*
568. Genesis 32:32
569. Taanith 25a; instead of *tzala,* the Talmud has the Aramaic *tala*
570. Jerushalmi Berachoth 1; 3c
571. Micah 4:6; Zephaniah 3:19; *Targum Jonathan* on Exodus 4:10

572. In Peah 8:9, the terms *chigger* and *pisseach* are found side by side; the former is said to mean "lame in one foot" and the latter "lame in both feet". Ritter
573. *apo ton omon.* Josephus' *Antiquities* Book 7 Chapt. 5:5
574. Second Samuel 4:4
575. *ibid* 9:13
576. *ibid* 19:27
577. Deut. 21:18
578. *ibid* 21:19
579. Deut. 34:23
580. Chagigah 1:1
581. *ibid* 3a
582. Levit. 21:18
583. *Sifra, Emor.* per 2 par. 3 No. 7 p.95b

sacrifice[584]; if it is stolen, however, four-fold restitution of a healthy animal must be made, just as for a normal animal[585]. A lame shepherd cannot run fast enough after the fleeing goats; it is only at the gate of the pen that he catches up with them, and there the accounting takes place[586]. A lame person is the usual watchman of a cucumber field[587] and the lowest paid messenger. According to legend, Bileam was lame on one foot and Samson on both feet[588]. When the Redeemer will come and the barbarians will be defeated, even the lame will run and be able to take part in the plundering[589].

The angels told Rabbi Yochanan ben Dahabai that the cause for lameness is unnatural cohabitation[590]. An old beggar's trick was to feign lameness or limping. However, if someone is neither *chigger,* nor blind, nor *pisse'ach* but pretends to be as one of these, he will not leave this world until he actually becomes like one of them[591] — a punishment through habit!

## XXXVI   Abnormalities of the Lower Extremities

In the rules concerning the recruiting of priests for Temple service, a number of defects of the lower extremities are enumerated which render a priest unfit to serve. They are found in three Talmudic collections: the *Sifra*[592], (identical citations as the *Yalkut*)[593], the *Tosefta*[594] and the *Mishnah*[595], and occur in individual sources with many variations. The list of the *Sifra* is based on the Bible and is probably the original one.

According to Biblical law[596], the following are unfit to serve as priests:

1) The *pisse'ach*, the limper. The *Sifra* and *Tosefta* also add "of the foot" (*regel; Tosefta: parsa* meaning sole of the foot).

(a) hollow — *chalula*     (b) crooked — *akuma*     (c) resembles a sickle

I do not know how these three differ from one another. They all probably refer to *talipes calcaneus.*

Maimonides[597] mentions only two types in that he combines (b) and (c). The foot is hollow, *chalula,* when the middle portion is high above the ground, so that the person stands on his heels and on his toes; or the foot is *akuma,* resembling a sickle in which the ball of the foot and the heel resemble a bow or *kesheth.* The combination of the two is explained as follows: *"akum* resembling a sickle" means like a bent palm branch[598].

2) The *sarua,* "whose hip *(yarech)* is torn off", and "who, therefore, drags his leg"[599]. In addition, the *Sifra, Tosefta* and *Mishnah* give the other explanation of *sarua:* "a person in whom one part of the body is larger than the corresponding part on the other side":

(a) "if a swelling *(pika)* protrudes from the large toe", i.e. formation of an outgrowth, exostosis.

(b) "when the heel goes backward", bunion ?

(c) "when the sole of the foot is broad (or flat, *rechaba*) like that of a goose" where a web is not necessarily present: i.e. flat-footed. Africans have this type of feet because, according to Hillel, "they live in watery marshes"[600]. The observation is correct, but the reasoning is debatable. Equating the flat feet of the Negro with a flat-

584. Malachi 1:8
585. *Tosefta* Baba Kamma 7:15
586. Shabbath 32a
587. *Tosefta* Baba Kamma 9:2
588. Sotah 10a
589. Isaiah 33:23
590. Nedarim 20a. literally: they overturned their table, *recumbente viro*
591. Peah 8:9

592. *Sifra, Emor* per 2 par. 3 No. 7 p.95b
593. *Yalkut* 1: 631 p.195c. Warsaw 1876
594. *Tosefta* Bechoroth 5:9
595. Bechoroth 7:6
596. Levit. 21:18
597. *Hilchoth Biyath Hamikdash* 8:13
598. Sukkah 32a
599. *Sifra.* Ibn Ganach. *s.v.*
600. Shabbath 31a

footed person[601], although morphologically inadmissible, is commonplace even today.

3) The *Sheber regel,* actually "leg fracture". It is difficult to give *sheber* such a "precise" meaning, as already mentioned above[602]. The *Sifra* and *Tosefta* here include the following:

(a) the *kashan* or *kishan (Tosefta: yakshan)* which, according to the *Mishnah,* refers to one "whose ankles or knees knock together" *(hamakish).* The former represents the abnormality called *genu varum,* the latter, *genu valgum,* both well-known malformations of the lower extremities.

(b) the *iklan* or *ikal,* "one whose knees do not touch when the soles of the feet are placed together" *(hamakiph).* Whereas in the case of the *kishan,* the anomaly is only noticeable when the individual walks or stands—it is correctly observed that the abnormality vanishes when he sits—in the case of the *iklan,* one can see the abnormality even when he sits. It thus refers to a bowing of the lower leg (*akal* means crooked) (i.e. bandy-legged).

(c) the *kulban (Sifra)* or *kalban (Tosefta)* or *kilban*[603]. The meaning of this term was already no longer known to Rabbi Gersom. *Rabad* (on *Sifra*) thinks it refers to a bowing of the thigh. The Greek *kolobos* means "deprived of a limb".

Rickets is undoubtedly one of the forms of the illness *ikal* and we thus have additional evidence that this disease already existed in antiquity. Its existence among Greeks and Romans cannot be doubted anymore[604].

Another abnormality is found in the *Tosefta* and *Mishnah* (but not in *Sifra*) by the name of *ba'al hapikon (Tosefta)* or *ba'al pika (Mishnah).*

Variations are as follows: in the *Tosefta: ba'al hakkupin;* in the *Mishnah: hapikim, hapika, pikum;* in the *Gemara: hakipin;* probably errors of transcription.

In the *Gemara,* Rabbi Yochanan gives the meaning: *"ba'al hapikim* is one who has many *kesathoth* (cushions), and *shuphnar* is one without any *kesathoth".* *Schuphnar* is considered to be a separate abnormality in the *Tosefta (schiyuphad, schiyuphzad).*

The commentaries are here divided into two groups:

1) Those who assume that *pika* is an abnormality of the *malleolus.* Maimonides[605] states as follows: *pika* is the round bone above the heel anteriorly. It resembles the *pika* which is the spindle which women use in spinning. Rabbi Gersom accepts the definition of Rabbi Yochanan: "it appears as if the person had many calves", that is "double joints" (i.e. rickets). Pseudo-*Rashi* has: "the *isthevira*[606] is very large".

2) By contrast, the *Tosafoth* state that "cushions" refers only to flesh and does not imply any bony abnormality. *Rabad* (on Maimonides) considers *kesathoth* to be identical to *agaboth, the gluteal muscles,* and specifically translates it as glutei, i.e. *gloutos* (in Greek)[607], in that he adds: *"pika* is a very large round body; the Adam's apple is also called the *pika* of the throat". He thus considers a *ba'al pika* to be a man with large buttocks, steatopygia.

*Schuphnar* remains unexplained by both groups. There does not exist a man without calves or without buttocks.

The *Tosefta* adds the following:

(a) a man "whose lower leg stands in the middle of the foot". (Maimonides combines this abnormality with one "whose heel protrudes posteriorly").

601. Albert *Lehrbuch der Chirurgie.* Vienna 1885 Vol. 4:503
602. beginning of this chapter
603. Bechoroth 45a
604. W. Ebstein. *Janus* 1900 p.332; Aschoff *ibid* 1901 p.207
605. *loc. cit.*
606. see above Chapter 2, Part 1:7
607. I do not understand the foreign word of the *Keseph Mishnah: tudiloir*

(b) "one who is *makkish* from above and *maphsia* from below" (?)

(c) "one who has no toes, only stumps", *gedumoth,* perhaps as a result of lepra mutilans(?)

(d) "one whose large toe is crooked", *akuma,* perhaps the *hallux valgus* of Stromayer.

(e) "one whose toes override each other", *murkaboth*[608].

(f) "one whose toes or fingers are grown together distal from the knob" (the first phalangeal joint). In mild cases, one can cut them apart, in which case the priest is fit. The separation of webbed fingers *in utero,* or later by ulceration, is also mentioned by Galen[609], Paulus of Aegina[610], and Celsus[611].

(g) "supernumerary" fingers and toes can be amputated. Often these extra digits contain no bone. The Bible mentions a case of polydactyly in a Philistine from the time of David: *a large man* (according to Josephus[612] he was six cubits tall) *that had six fingers on each hand and six toes on each foot, twenty-four in number*[613]. Rabbi Tarfon considered this abnormality to be an advantage, whereas Rabbi Jose thought it to be hideous[614]. Supernumerary digits are also mentioned by the aforementioned physicians, as well as by Plinius[615].

Incidental reports from the Talmud are as follows: "he who walks on the back of his feet" *(lachtra dekareh)*[616], probably club-foot. It is said that Rav Ashi's foot became "reversed" as a result of fright and lamenting, so that this abnormality developed[617]. Perhaps it was an apoplexy.

A priest who has a defect on his hands or on his feet should not recite the priestly benediction, because people would gaze at him[618]. To this prohibition is also added one whose hands (or fingers)[619] are deformed; either *akumoth,* deformed like a bow, or *akushoth*[620]. The former perhaps refers to contracture of the palmer aponeurosis and the latter to contracture by scarring of an individual finger. A man of the latter type is called *akshan* in the *Tosefta*[621].

In the Temple, when priests were appointed to serve for that day, the procedure was for them to each raise one or two fingers which were then counted[622], *one* finger if the priest was healthy and two if he was sick[623]. This could only refer to a local defect in which he cannot protrude one finger by itself without protruding the finger next to it.

## XXXVII    Abnormalities of the Upper Extremities

To be deprived of one's hand or foot can occur either as a result of *lepra mutilans* or from trauma. It may happen that, in order to save the life of an injured person, the physicians may recommend amputation of the hand[624]. It can also happen that a child may put his hand in a moving cylinder *(ma'agila)* and the hand becomes squashed[625]. Cutting off the hand by the executioner's ax is one of the punitive measures of antiquity and it is still employed today in the Orient. In the Code of Hammurabi, this punishment is inflicted on a son who strikes his father[626], on a physician whose patient dies or becomes blind as a result of surgery[627], a surgeon who burns "the sign" into a

---

608. *Sifra* and the *Mishnah* also list this abnormality
609. *Meth. Med.* 14:17; Kühn 10:1013
610. Paulus 6:43
611. Celsus Book 7 Chapt. 32 p.497
612. *Antiquities.* Book 7 Chapt. 12:2
613. Second Samuel 21:20
614. Bechoroth 45b
615. *Histor. Natur.* 11:99
616. Yebamoth 103a
617. Moed Katan 25b
618. Megillah 4:7; *Tosefta* Megillah 4:29

619. Jerushalmi Megillah 4; 75b
620. Megillah 24b
621. *Tosefta* Bechoroth 5:9. ed. Vienna; ed. Zuckermandel has *yakshan.*
622. Yoma 2:1
623. *ibid* 23a
624. Jerushalmi Nazir 9; 58a
625. Jerushalmi Makkoth 2; 31c
626. Code of Hammurabi. ed. D.H. Müller, Vienna 1903 No. 195
627. *ibid* No. 218

slave without having been mandated to do so[628], and the tenant farmer who steals the seed[629].

It is in dispute whether or not Jewish law ever used this punishment. In the only case mentioned in the Bible[630], a woman seizes the genitalia of a man who was attacking her husband in order to save him. Although the Bible says *thou shalt cut off her hand,* tradition interprets the punishment to be a financial penalty and even then, only if there was another way for the woman to have saved her husband[631].

In the book of Judges[632], it is related that Judah and Simeon cut off the thumbs and the great toes of the captured King of Bezek in Canaan. The king himself said: *three score and ten kings having their thumbs and great toes cut off gathered under my table (their gleanings). As I have done, so God hath requited me*[633]. It is thus a heathen war practice which the Jewish generals imitated. So, too, when Josephus had the hands of the mutineers cut off[634] or forced them to cut their own hands off[635], he only had Cicero's word: *silent leges inter arma* as an excuse. It was certainly not a case of legal infliction of punishment. At the command of David, the hands and feet of the murderers of Ishbosheth were cut off, but only after they were already dead[636]. The biblical expression "cut off the arm" (*gada,* not *katzatz*) has the meaning "to break the might of"[637].

According to Talmudic law, if someone cuts off the hand of his fellow man, he must not only pay the usual penalties but also a fine for the pain he inflicted. To determine the amount of the latter, we estimate how much a man, condemned by "a written decree" of the Roman government to lose an arm, would pay to be given the choice between having his arm cut off with a sword — the usual type of punishment — and having it taken off by means of a medication *(ben sayif lesam)*[638]. Since the latter form of *oblatio manus* was thought to be a painless type of amputation, one must assume that it was performed under narcosis, using a *samma de deschinta*[639].

When Rabbi Chiya bar Ba once saw an offensive book, he said: the hand that wrote this book should be cut off! Only later did he learn that the author was his own father. But his word was fulfilled[640], just as *an error which proceedeth from the ruler*[641] is carried out. Here, either the mutilation occurred as a result of an accident, or by a judgement and execution thereof by the Romans, since the Jews in those days (200 C.E.) no longer had their own jurisdiction.

The Hebrew language has a special term to denote someone whose hand was cut off: *giddem;* a footless person is called *kittea*[642]. The former term is used in relation to an animal which has been deprived of the tail and the ears[643].

A handless person cannot function as a judge[644], nor can he offer testimony as a witness[645] because, if the defendant is sentenced to death by stoning, *the hands of the witnesses shall be first upon him to put him to death*[646]. If the man or the woman is handless, then the prescribed procedure for a suspected adulteress[647] cannot be carried out[648]. If a man loses a hand or a foot, according to an isolated opinion, the woman is entitled to ask for a divorce[649]. Although footless and leprous persons have no

---

628. *ibid* No. 226
629. *ibid* No. 253
630. Deut. 25:12
631. Sanhedrin 29a
632. Judges 1:6
633. *ibid* 1:7
634. Josephus. *The Life* No. 30
635. *ibid* No. 34
636. Second Samuel 4:12
637. First Samuel 2:31
638. Baba Kamma 85a
639. Baba Metzia 83b
640. Jerushalmi Shabbath 16; 15c

641. Eccles. 10:5
642. An apparent exception is *Rashi* in Berachoth 58b *s.v. kitta;* but *chigger* is certainly not a footless individual.
643. Chullin 79a
644. Jerushalmi Sanhedrin 8; 26b
645. Sanhedrin 45b
646. Deut. 17:7
647. Numbers 5:11 ff.
648. Sotah 27a; nevertheless Rabbi Chiya, in Jerushalmi Sotah 3; 18c, states that the waving of the offering is performed.
649. Jerushalmi Kethuboth 7; 31d

personal worth as slaves, their value can be dedicated to the Temple[650]. If a person sees one who is blind or lame or mutilated, he should resist the temptation of considering this to be an injustice of the Lord but should state: Blessed be the true Judge![651]

If a person strikes his friend on the hand so that the hand is thereby lost, the guilty one must pay the usual five types of compensations: if it only swells, compensation for diminution in the personal value of the injured person need not be paid[652]. If the injured person is a slave, the master naturally receives the compensatory monies; however, it is obligatory upon the master to first provide for his handless slave prior to caring for an uninjured one[653]. According to the wording of the Biblical law, the procedure to follow *before the court* should be in accordance with the principle: *an eye for an eye, a hand for a hand*[654]. However, states the *Mishnah,* what an injustice it would be if a one-handed person would cut off the hand of a normal person! And if the criminal had no hands, how could one at all satisfy the requirements of the law?[655]. Therefore, tradition is unanimous in its interpretation that the above law is not to be understood literally *an eye for an eye* but refers to financial remuneration for the eye or the hand.

If someone strikes another on the arm so that the life of the latter can only be saved by amputation of the arm, then the striker must pay restitution for the arm[656], whereas the usual fundamental rule is as follows: "liability depends on the usual and natural result of the punishable offense (in concreto, the death of the injured person)"; the striker is thus only liable for a criminal offense but not also for a civil offense. The juridical deduction of this decision is not germane here.

If a healthy person asks another: blind my eyes, cut off my hand, or break my leg, then the person who carries out the request is liable because he should have assumed that the request was not a serious one, since no man intentionally renounces the possession of important limbs[657]. Naturally, if someone strikes (i.e. injures) a person or an animal for therapeutic reasons, for example for bloodletting, he is not liable[658]. It is not certain whether or not this immunity from liability also applies if the wounding was performed without the foreknowledge or acquiescence of the patient.

A minor mutilation was the loss of fingers; nevertheless, the affected person was no longer suited for certain professions such as flax or silk spinning[659], even if only one finger was missing[660]. Legend relates that when one attempted to coerce the Children of Israel to play a "Song of Zion" on the harp at the streams of Babel, they bit off their thumbs and then showed the stumps to their captors saying: how can we play the song of the Lord?[661]. Bar Kochba is said to have had an army of 200,000 soldiers each of whom cut off one of his own fingers to demonstrate his courage[662].

The Talmudists considered injuries of the back of the hand and back of the foot to be particularly dangerous[663].

If a man became submerged in the sea *shilsheluhu layam* — perhaps for the purpose of net fishing[664] — and one only recovers one of his feet, then one cannot declare him legally dead because one cannot exclude the possibility that he is nevertheless alive somewhere on land, or was rescued by a ship. If the leg together with

---

650. *Tosefta* Arachin 1:2; one can thus dedicate the value of a footless individual to the Temple.
651. Berachoth 58b
652. Jerushalmi Baba Kamma 8; 6b
653. *ibid* 8; 6c
654. Exodus 21:24
655. Jerushalmi Baba Kamma 6; 6b
656. Jerushalmi Sanhedrin 9; 27a; with numerous digressions also in Jerushalmi Nazir 9; 28a

657. Baba Kamma 8:7
658. Sanhedrin 84b
659. Song of Songs Rabbah on 8:11 *s. v. kerem*
660. *Midrash* Psalms 8:2 p.37b Buber
661. *Midrash* Psalms 137:4
662. Jerushalmi Taanith 4; 68d; Lamentations Rabbah 2:4 fol. 21a
663. Shabbath 109a; Jerushalmi Shabbath 14; 14d
664. as mentioned in *Tosefta* Yebamoth 14:6; see also *Eben Haezer* 17:32. Ritter

the knee is found, (this is decisive), then the man is considered to be dead and the widow can remarry after twelve months[665].

## XXXVIII    Prostheses

There is no report from antiquity as to the fate of a person who has lost an extremity, either from leprosy or due to some external act. Only Herodotus[666] relates about the prophet Hegesistratos from Elis that the latter, having fallen into a trap, was advised to have his foot cut off and, in order not to be tortured to death, cut off his own foot *(apetame ton tarson)* and fled to Tega. After the wound healed, he had a wooden foot made for himself *(prospoiesamenos xylinon poda)*. Plinius relates of M. Sergius that the latter, who lost his right hand in battle, had a right hand of iron made for himself, attached it to his arm and fought therewith[667]. The physicians Hippocrates, Galen, Celsus and Oribasius, however, make no mention of artificial limbs.

Thus, the repeated mention thereof in the *Mishnah* is all the more remarkable. An amputee, *kittea,* is permitted to go out on the Sabbath with his *kab* because the latter serves like a shoe. In the *kab* one can either place rags as padding *(kethinin),* or it is specially constructed to receive such foot cushions (i.e. it has a *beth kibul kethinin)*[668]. According to the explanation of *Rashi,* who is portraying the conditions in his time (eleventh century), the *kab* is a leather capsule for the upper leg, whose inner padding protects the stump from pressure, but does not serve as a support. For support during walking, stilts are tied to the thighs and hand crutches are used[669]. Nevertheless, the following explanation seems to me more likely than that of *Rashi:* in the case of Herodotus, a replacement was made for the missing anterior half of the *foot* — the *tarsos,* according to Pollux is the anterior part of the foot, including the toes[670] — and a *kab* seems to be a similar prosthesis; firstly, because gangrene of the toes due to leprosy was certainly not rare and the affected individual sought immediate temporary remedies, and secondly, because if *kab* referred to a knee stilt or even a crutch, it would certainly have been compared to the cane of a blind man[671]. A *kab* in *our* sense of the word, however, might correctly be compared to a shoe.

Some such amputees wrapped the stumps of their arms and legs with thick, soft rags, *semukoth*[672], in which they could also appear in public, in case of need. Finally, a person who can no longer use his knees for locomotion, used a stool, *kissé,* for that purpose. The commentary explains that he sits on a low stool which is attached to his body. When he wishes to move, he supports himself on his hands with small benches, lifts his body from the ground, propels himself forward and then sits down on his stool again[673].

The preparation of such prostheses was probably the work of professionals; for it is related that an unskilled worker once hollowed out a *kab* from a log of wood[674].

A prosthesis for an animal is also mentioned in the Talmud: Rabbi Simeon ben Chalafta once prepared a tube of reed as a support for a hen whose hip was dislodged or torn out, and it recovered[675].

## XXXIX    Injuries of the Hips and Ankles

In the history of the Patriarchs, it is related that a man wrestled with Jacob all

665. Yebamoth 16:4
666. Herodotus 9:37
667. *Histor. Natur.* 7:29
668. Shabbath 6:8
669. *Rashi* in Yebamoth 102b
670. Is it possible to tear off a bone if only one's foot is strangulated? Even if one could tear off a bone in such a case, can one still walk in spite of the fear of death?
671. *Tosefta* Betzah 3:17
672. Baba Bathra 20a mentions a *semikta* which is a thick, soft rag used by a bloodletter to cleanse the wound
673. Shabbath 6:8; Yoma 78b; Yebamoth 102b and 103a; Chagigah 3a
674. Shabbath 11b
675. Chullin 57b
676. Genesis 32:25

night[676]. *And when he saw that he prevailed not against him, he touched the "kaph" of his thigh, and the "kaph" of Jacob's thigh loosened, as he wrestled with him*[677]. *Kaph* is something with a curved surface; for example, the palm of the hand, the sole of the foot, a socket and a shell. Hence *kaph* probably refers to the hip socket (acetabulum). One needs no proof that this was not a case of hip-joint dislocation; for with a dislocation, Jacob should not have been able to drag himself onward, even if he had to "limp on his hip". On the other hand, he "remained alone", so that apparently no "medicine-man" of the Bedouin people would have been able to reduce his dislocated hip. It is much more likely, that the "loosening of the hip socket", in Canaan, refers to the same thing that the Arameans reported about Balshazzar when he was frightened by *Mene Tekel: the joints of his hips were loosened, and his knees smote one against another*[678].

Then the story of Jacob ends as follows: *therefore, the Children of Israel do not eat the "gid hanasheh" which is upon the hollow of the thigh, unto this day; because he touched the hollow of Jacob's thigh in the "gid hanasheh"*[679]. It is interesting that commentators from time immemorial have deduced from this concluding sentence that Jacob suffered an injury of the sciatic nerve. One cites as particular proof for this contention the fact the the word *nasheh,* which does not occur elsewhere in Hebrew, means "the nerve of the hip" in Arabic. One is also reminded that *ischion* can refer both to "the sinew of the hollow" as well as to the entire joint[680]. One can hardly anticipate results from a discussion of the meaning of Jacob's malady from archaeological findings in view of their paucity. As far as I am aware, no commentator has yet clarified the obvious question as to why the grip on the hips is set down as the *ultima ratio* of the wrestling match. *And when he saw that he prevailed not against him,* only then did the angel grasp Jacob's thigh.

A particularly important role in antiquity was given to injuries of the *Achilles tendon.* As is well known, Hippocrates, and probably the general populace, believed that such injuries were invariably fatal. Similar opinions are also found among the Jews. The war of extermination between humans and snakes takes place, in the words of Genesis, in that man steps on the head of the snake and the latter bites man in the heel[681]. The Psalmist laments: *evildoers lie in wait for my heels, as if they watch for an opportunity to kill me*[682]. For this reason, the noose (of decay) of sinners grasps at their heels[683]. According to legend, Moses injured Og, King of Bashan, on his foot joint *(bekarsuleh)* and, thereby, killed him[684]. Accordingly, it is possible that in the already above-mentioned *Mishnah* which portrays people as microcosms, the heels of people are represented as corresponding to the angel of death[685].

The *legal scholars* of the Talmud did not share the opinion of the absolute lethality of a wound in the Achilles tendon. They decreed that no one should be considered dead until death has been established through the testimony of witnesses, even if it is definite that he was seen with severed sinews *(meguyod)* or crucified[686]. For Rabbi Simeon ben Eleazar believed that the wound can be cauterized and might heal[687], and a crucified person might be cut down by a passing matron and live[688]. It is decided as law that the final will and testament of such an injured individual with severed arteries or crucified is equivalent to that of a perfectly healthy person and is, therefore, legally valid[689].

Severing sinews was probably also one of the ancient measures of war to render

---

677. *ibid* 32:26
678. Daniel 5:6
679. Genesis 32:32
680. *to neuron to pros ten kotylen kai olon to arthron.* Rufus. *De Appelat.* Ed. Daremberg p.148
681. Genesis 3:15
682. Psalms 56:7
683. Job 18:9
684. Berachoth 54b
685. Aboth de Rabbi Nathan 31:2
686. Yebamoth 16:3
687. *Tosefta* Yebamoth 14:4
688. Yebamoth 120b
689. Jerushalmi Gittin 7; 48c and *Tosefta* Gittin 7:33

one's opponent incapable of fighting[690]. The sinews of one's opponent's horses were also severed[691]. According to the report of Josephus, Saul had the sinews of his oxen cut, and warned all the people that the same would be done to whoever does not report for military duty[692]. A special expression was used therefore: *akker* (in Hebrew) and *neurokopein* (in Greek). A gruesome tradition was to sever the sinews of the royal horse at a king's funeral so that no one else could ride on it, a practice that is explicitly designated as cruelty to animals[693]. Rabba Bar Bar Chana once saw a violently angry Arab cut the sinews of his camel. The latter cried from pain, until it died[694].

This gruesomeness is also known to Nordic legend. King Nidung had the sinews of both feet of his blacksmith Weland, whom he wished to retain for himself, severed. As long as Weland lived after that, his feet were useless for walking[695].

## XL    Narcosis

During the above-described abdominal operation[696], Rabbi Eleazar was given a *samma deschinta*, a sleeping potion[697], of an unknown type. Also, in another already-cited place[698], familiarity with narcosis seems to have been present. One should also remember that painless operations were also known in heathen antiquity and occurred primarily following the internal consumption of mandragora[699] or by local anesthesia using *lepis memphiticus*[700].

A person being led to his execution is given a piece of frankincense in wine, in order to benumb his senses[701] according to the admonition of the epigram: *give strong drink unto him that is ready to perish, and wine unto the bitter in soul*[702]. The delivery of those beverages was the privilege of noble women in Jerusalem[702a]. Jesus, too, received wine and myrrh, *esmyrnisemon oinon,* to drink before the crucifixion[703].

## XLI    Treatment of Wounds

In Biblical times, wounds were treated by pressing, bandaging, and oil fomenting[704]. The wound balsam (balm) of Gilead is also mentioned[705].

We learn more of the treatment of wounds from the time of the Talmud, in connection with which one should not forget that the word *makkah* (wound), as already demonstrated earlier, refers to any type of trauma, not just tissue separation. A lesson which still retains its importance to this day warns against touching a wound because *"the hand causes inflammation"*[706]. To treat a wound, one applies *moch* (cotton or lint) and sponge, as well as garlic and onion peels, which are secured with a thread. Alternatively, one skillfully applies a bandage, *eged*[707]. The function of the sponge is not to suck out the wound but to protect it[708]. Rushes, *gemi*, were also used[709]. These were attached to the injured finger with a small belt, *ciltzul*[710]; or flocks of wool, *pokarion* (in Greek) were applied[711]. Chewed wheat kernels[712] and caraway[713] are also healing in their effect. It was prohibited to sprinkle wood ashes on

690. *Sforno* on Genesis 49:19
691. Joshua 11:6
692. Josephus' *Antiquities*. Book 6 Chapt. 5:4. He is at variance with the Biblical account in First Samuel 11:7.
693. Abodah Zarah 11a
694. Yebamoth 120b
695. V.D. Hagen. *Altdeutsche und Altnordische Heldensagen*. Breslau 1855. 1:93
696. section 19 of this chapter
697. Baba Metzia 83b
698. Section 37 of this chapter
699. Plinius 25:94
700. *ibid* 36:11

701. Sanhedrin 43a
702. Proverbs 31:6
702a. Sanhedrin 43a
703. Mark 15:23
704. Isaiah 1:6
705. Jeremiah 8:22
706. Abodah Zarah 28b
707. *Tosefta* Shabbath 5:3-4
708. Levit. Rabbah 15:4
709. Erubin 10:13
710. *ibid* 103b
711. Shabbath 50a
712. Kethuboth 103a
713. Shabbath 19:2

wounds because one did not wish to give the impression that one was tattooing the skin[714], which, as is known, is not permitted in Biblical law[715]. Oil maintained its Biblical renown[716]. According to Mar Samuel, a wound should always be treated with oil and warm water[717]. For bandaging, one naturally also used rags; but only new rags heal *(kethithin)*[718].

People also used pieces of manure from dung heaps as bandaging material[719].

This is according to Rabbi Chananel. I have personally seen in the villages of the Brandenburg Mark that people apply cow dung on fresh wounds "to pull out the heat therefrom", and they thereby caused very serious cellulitis.

I was only able to find mention of cauterization of a wound in humans in relation to injuries of the Achilles tendon *(meguyad)*[720]. It is doubtful whether or not cauterization of ulcerated leprous lesions[721] was employed for therapeutic reasons. An animal with a complicated bone fracture can be saved if the wound is cauterized[722]. The Hippiater once cauterized a sick she-ass, and the baby was born with a brand mark on it[723].

An animal which rubs itself so hard that it produces a wound is treated by the application of honey[724] or squashed snails[725]. The animal is also given putrefied honey to eat[726]. If it broke a foot, then wooden rods *(keshishin)* are applied[727].

If someone knocks his hand or his foot, he foments it with vinegar or wine. Rav Ashi did this when a donkey once trod on his foot[728]. To rub the wound, one used oil, particularly oil of roses[729]. The latter was also applied with cotton *(moch)* or with rags[730].

During antiquity, the regulation of one's diet was also part of the treatment of wounds. Such a diet had to be adhered to by the injured person if he wished to collect disability money. If the injured person disobeys the orders of the physician and eats honey and other sweet substances which are all harmful to wounds[731], and if *garguthne* (ulcers or fistulae) develop in the wound, then the offender does not have to pay the medical bills of the patient[732]. Among the costs of healing in general is the additional expenditure for the nourishment of the injured person. For the latter could say: when I was healthy I ate lentils and green vegetables; now, however, I can only tolerate eggs and chicken[733].

In an allegory, a man applies a plaster on the wound of another and says: as long as the plaster is on the wound, eat and drink whatever you wish, bathe in cold or in warm water without fear. If you remove it, however, then a *nome* will develop from the wound[734]. This "wonder plaster" is obviously the Torah.

714. Makkoth 21a
715. Levit. 19:28
716. *Tosefta* Demai 1:18
717. Jerushalmi Shabbath 9; 12a
718. Shabbath 134b
719. Abodah Zarah 28a
720. *Tosefta* Yebamoth 14:4
721. Negaim 7:4
722. *Tosefta* Chullin 3:6
723. Numbers Rabbah 9:6
724. Shabbath 8:1 and Baba Metzia 38b
725. Shabbath 77b
726. *ibid* 154a

727. *ibid* 53b
728. Shabbath 109a
729. *ibid* 14:4
730. *Tosefta* Shabbath 12:12
731. In Astrachan, a carbuncle is called "the sweet sickness" because the patient shuns sweets, according to popular belief. Münch. *Die Zaraath der Hebraischen Bibel.* Hamburg p.144
732. Baba Kamma 85a
733. Jerushalmi Baba Kamma 8; 6b
734. *Sifre* on Deut. 11:18 p.82b

# *APPENDIX I*
## CIRCUMCISION

The literature on circumcision (Hebrew: *milah*) is nearly boundless but it does not need to be considered here since our book is only a collection of ancient Hebraic source materials. In their hypotheses, the various authors attempt to elucidate the intentions of the inventor of this operation and to ascertain the identity of the inventor; or they discuss the dogmatic obligation of the ceremony; or they propose alterations in the technical execution of circumcision.

Ordinarily, Herodotus is credited with the assertion that the Jews learned circumcision from the Egyptians, without anyone considering that even elsewhere Herodotus is not a faultless historian, exclusive of the fact that he lived many centuries after the institution of circumcision and, therefore, describes his own opinions or others which he heard. Even if the Egyptians already practiced circumcision very early, as seems to be supported by recent studies of mummies, this is no proof at all that the Egyptians served as teachers of circumcision to the Jews. Andree is also of the opinion that it is likely that the Jews already practiced circumcision prior to and independent of the Egyptians[735].

According to reports of ancient and more recent writers, circumcision is much more frequently found among a large number of primitive peoples (for example, in Mexico)[736] who certainly did not learn it from the Egyptians, either directly or indirectly (i.e. from the Jews), so that the most likely hypothesis is that certain considerations or perhaps practical experiences of various peoples originally led to the removal of the foreskin. The type of conceptions that led thereto can also only be a matter of hypothetical speculation. From the fact that, originally, circumcision was only practiced in hot climates, one inferred that perhaps local illnesses secondary to processes of decay of the foreskin sebum or of the sperm residue occurred, and stimulated the practice of circumcision. There is no dearth of other hypotheses. The only certain thing is that we have no unequivocal reports concerning the reasoning behind the institution of this operation, and it is a serious violation of a cardinal rule of historical criticism to interpret the concepts of antiquity through the eyes of our modern knowledge.

## I   Introduction

According to the Biblical account[737], God commanded Abraham to circumcise all male children who are eight days old as a sign of the covenant between God and Abraham. *And the uncircumcised male (arel) whose flesh of his foreskin is not circumcised, that soul shall be cut off (by God) from his people; he hath broken my covenant.* Then Abraham[738], at the age of 99 years circumcised himself, his thirteen year old son Ishmael and all his male servants. Later, he also circumcised Isaac at eight days of age[739]. The Bible is silent about circumcision of the Hebrews during their sojourn in Egypt. According to the *Midrash*[740], they abolished *Milah* after the death of Joseph, in order to be like the Egyptians. Only the tribe of Levi (i.e. the priests)

---

735. *Arch. fur Anthropologie.* 1881 Vol. 13 p.67

736. according to tradition (*Rashi* on Genesis 18:1), the Canaanites of Mamre gave Abraham suggestions about circumcision.

737. Genesis 17:10-15

738. According to Zunz' *Zeittafel* in the year 1941 B.C.E.

739. Genesis 21:4

740. Exodus Rabbah 1:8

741. Exodus Rabbah 19:5 In the report of Joshua, it is emphasized that Joshua circumcised the sons of "the warriors". The Levites, however, were not obligated to serve in the army. Weyl. in *Israelit.* 1909 No. 15

retained it[741]. One can, therefore, readily explain that Moses, whose parents belonged to the tribe of Levi[742], was nevertheless circumcised as a child, so that the daughter of Pharaoh was thereby able to recognize him as *one of the children of the Hebrews*[743].

The story in Exodus 4:24ff. is exegetically so difficult that it is best not to consider it at all. One can only assume with certainty· that Moses had not circumcised his infant son, (it is debated as to which of the two lads is involved in the story), and that both the child and he, himself, were in danger. According to Rabbi Jose[744], Moses postponed the *milah* because of fear of the dangers of the journey.

It was only during the Exodus that Moses made up for the neglect of his other co-religionists (i.e. he had them circumcised) since *milah* is a prerequisite for the partaking of the Passover offering[745]. In this manner, the assertion in the book of Joshua, that all the people who left Egypt were circumcised[746], is vindicated.

Because of the hardships of the journeying through the desert, *milah* was again omitted after the Exodus, and only later did Joshua circumcise all those born in the desert, before they celebrated the Passover. The phrase spoken by the Lord: *today I have removed the shame of Egypt from you,* according to the aforementioned assertion of the *Midrash,* would mean that the Egyptians gave the privilege of circumcising themselves to the priestly and military castes but not to the "dishonest shepherds".

In the systematic treatment of laws in Leviticus, the duty of circumcision is only mentioned incidentally[747].

*Milah* is the sign of the covenant between God and Israel; therefore, all uncircumcised males were considered as profane, and the name *arel* gradually became a contemptible epithet[748]. Antiochus Epiphanes, who tried to convert his Jewish subjects to heathendom, forbade them to perform circumcision[749]. Violation of his edict was brutally punished; the mothers who circumcised their male children were led publicly through the streets with their children hanging at their breasts and were then thrown down from the top of the city wall[750]. In the time of the Talmud, as well, prohibitions against circumcision were not infrequent[751]; nevertheless, the pious families still practiced it secretly[752]. Mattathias reestablished the general practice of circumcision[753].

During the beginning of Christianity, circumcision was discussed at length, until, finally, converted heathens were exempted from this obligation[754]. On the other hand, among Jewish sects, the obligation of *Milah for all future generations, as an everlasting covenant*[755] was never questioned. It is, perhaps, the only point in ceremonial law concerning which the Samaritans and Israelites, Sadducees and Pharisees, Karaites and Rabbinites are all in agreement, even though they might perhaps show certain minor differences in *technicalities.*

742. Exodus 2:1
743. *ibid* 2:6
744. Nedarim 31b
745. Exodus 12:18
746. Joshua 5:5
747. Levit. 12:3
748. Particularly the "uncircumcized Philistines". Judges 14:3; First Samuel 17:26; see also Ezekiel 31:18; Isaiah 52:1 etc.
749. First Maccabees 1:48
750. Second Maccabees 6:10 and Josephus' *Antiquities* Book 12 Chapt. 5:4 and his *Jewish Wars* Book 1 Chapt. 1:2
751. The *Mishnah,* in general, speaks simply of a "time of danger". Shabbath 19:1
752. First Maccabees 1:63
753. *ibid* 2:46; and Josephus' *Antiquities* Book 12 Chapt. 7:2
754. Acts. Chapt. 15
755. Genesis 17:7

## II   The Execution of Circumcision

The Bible contains no statements concerning *the execution of milah* and, hence, the *Mishnah* is quite detailed in this regard[755a]. One should take notice, however, that the Talmudic statements are not intended to provide technical rules governing circumcision — these were assumed to be generally known[756] — but only to provide directions in instances where the rules of circumcision might conflict with the laws of the Sabbath. Then, as is usual in the Talmud, practical suggestions regarding the bandage, etc. are interspersed.

"Requisites of *milah*", which must even be performed on the Sabbath, are classified in the *Mishnah* as four actions:

1) The removal of the foreskin, *milah* in the narrow sense of the word (post-talmudic: *chittuch*).

2) The denudation of the glans penis until the corona is uncovered, *periyah*, by the tearing of the inner preputial membrane[757]. According to the explanation of the text, this act (of *periyah*) was established by Joshua[758]. According to the hypothesis of Reggio, it first originated in the time of the Maccabees, because in Jerusalem they built gymnasia in the heathen fashion, and the young Jewish men, in order not to be ridiculed during play, "reconstructed foreskins for themselves"[759]. They did this either by a type of plastic surgical operation, as described by heathen surgeons of that time[760], or by stretching the remnant of their foreskin (*epispasten*, Hebrew *mashuk*).

If this act of *periyah* is omitted or incorrectly performed, so that the larger part of the corona remains covered, according to the *Mishnah,* the circumcision is invalid, and the uncovering, "the removal of the hindering threads" *(hilkut),* must later be carried out. According to Mar Samuel, a child who is obese from "excess flesh" must at least appear circumcised at the time of an erection of his infantile penis in order for the circumcision to be valid.

It is only a more recent *Midrashic* work[761] which mentions the rule of covering the severed foreskin with sand. Here, too, is mentioned the custom of providing an "honorary chair" for the prophet Elijah who was thought to be present at every circumcision, and of preparing a godfather called *sandikus (syndikus* or *synteknos)* who holds the baby on his knees during the circumcision[762]. In another source, the godfather is called *sindiknus*[763].

For a circumcision *instrument,* Zippora, on the journey, used a stone *(tzor)*[764]. According to the Biblical narrative, Joshua also used *tzurim* which the Aramaic translation calls "sharp" knives and the *Midrash* interprets as "stone knives"[765]. In the Talmud[766], the principle is enunciated that every sharp-edged object is suitable for circumcision; only a sharpened tube of reed *(calamos)* should not be used because it

---

755a. Sources for that which follows, where no others are indicated, are the following: Shabbath Chapter 19 and the Babylonian & Palestinian *Gemaras* pertaining thereto; *Tosefta* Shabbath 15. For the post-Talmudic time: Maimonides. *Hilchoth Milah; Orach Chayim* No. 331 and *Yoreh Deah* No. 260ff.

756. The Koran makes no mention at all of circumcision, and yet it is one of the most important religious commands of the Mohammedans.

757. It is already mentioned in *Yalkut* II: 723 that one uses the (cut tip of the) thumbnail for this purpose. Abulcasem 2:57 also considers the nails to be best "because the disadvantages of iron are thereby avoided", and he only circumcised older people.

758. Yebamoth 72b explains the wording of the text in Joshua 5:2 in this manner; *he again circumcised the children of Israel, shenith* (twice). According to Yoma 28b, Abraham already practiced *periyah*.

759. First Maccabees 1:15

760. Celsus 7:25

761. *Yalkut* on Joshua 5:2

762. *ibid* II: 723 on Psalms 35

763. *Midrash* Psalms 35:2 p.124b

764. Exodus 4:24

765. Genesis Rabbah 31:8. *galbin de tinare.* The Vulgate translates *cultros lapideos.* The Septuagint combines both meanings: *machairas petrinas akrotomous.*

766. Chullin 16b

splits easily. One is reminded that the ancients, in order to sever the umbilical cord, also used a piece of wood, glass, sharp reed or a hard bread crust[767]. In practice, "iron instruments" were always used. The knife is either called *keli,* meaning simply "instrument", or *sakin (sakina* in Aramaic[768]), or *izmal* which, according to the dictionaries, is equivalent to *smile,* the designation by Greek surgeons for their scalpels.

Today a double-edged knife is often used. In addition, the foreskin prior to excision is usually clamped with a split plate (or shield); and, in order to prevent inadvertent cutting of the glans, an erection of the penis is stimulated by mildly rubbing the foreskin. During the time of Abulcasem; the Mohammedans made use of a certain thimble *(al-phalkah)* into which they placed the penis, a practice which Abulcasem correctly rejected as irrational.

3) Sucking or *metzitzah.* This procedure, as the previous two, was obviously generally known, so that very few details are given concerning its implementation. According to Rav Papa, the omission of *metzitzah* is dangerous for the baby, and, therefore, an *umman* (circumciser) who does not suck the wound (as might well have occurred) should be removed from office. The *Gemara* explains that the *metzitzah* does not remove already extravasated blood, but makes a new wound, probably by opening deep-seated blood vessels. It thus appears that the intent of this procedure is to cause cessation of bleeding by producing contraction of the bleeding vessels.

*Metzitzah* as such is no longer part of the religious act of circumcision, no more so than the application of the bandage. If our aforementioned assumption is correct, *metzitzah* is used purely for healing purposes. As a result, its omission does not make the circumcision invalid (as does omission of *periyah*), and the *Midrashim* which discuss *milah* as a religious ritual[769], only mention the first two acts[770]. Therefore, one cannot deduce from this that either *metzitzah* or the application of a bandage were omitted.

Neither Maimonides nor *Shulchan Aruch* have any more detailed discussions concerning the performance of *metzitzah.* According to tradition, the *mohel* (ritual circumciser) takes a sip of red wine in his mouth, then sucks the wound with his mouth, and spits the wine out. In Germany and certain other countries, in order to avoid a possible infection of the child (or the *mohel*), one inverts a glass tube with a piece of bandage cotton on one end and a mouthpiece at the other end on the circumcised penis and then sucks through the mouthpiece.

4) After warm water has been trickled on the wound, one applies a bandage. "One places *ispelanith (splenion* in Greek) and ground caraway on the wound"[770a]. A mixture of wine and oil was also used in those days, but we do not know whether for compresses or for some other purpose. Then a "small shirt" *(chaluk)* was pulled over the penis, that is, a small cloth with a hole in the middle for the glans to protrude, a *longuette,* obviously to prevent the remnant of the foreskin from sliding over the glans. It is designated as practical to wrap the seam of this "small shirt" from above so that threads not stick to it and damage the penis when they are torn off. For this reason, the mother of Abaye used a little bag *(kisthata)* which reached to the middle of the penis.

Fibers of wool or linen (lint) are also mentioned as bandage materials. In cases of need, a soft cloth[771] could substitute for the "small shirt". According to Abaye, one

---

767. Soren. Chapt. 27 p.117
768. Abodah Zarah 26b
769. Song of Songs Rabbah fol. 12b; Yalkut II: 723
770. removal of the foreskin and uncovering the glans penis, *milah* and *periyah,* respectively.

770a. *kammon,* from which is derived cuminum, *kyminon* in Greek, caraway
771. *semartut* or *blita,* from *marat* and *bala,* respectively, meaning corroded or decaying

should wrap the threads of the edges of such a cloth internally and then doubly externally. — Today the *Mohel* makes a more or less totally antiseptic bandage.

The baby is washed or bathed both before and after the operation. This, too, according to the *Mishnah,* belongs to the "requirements of circumcision", which must even be carried out on the Sabbath.

Maimonides (1135-1204)[771a] already is undecided concerning the custom of bathing the infant; at all events, he does not consider its omission to be dangerous. During the time of Joseph Karo (about the year 1550) the child was bathed neither immediately before nor after the circumcision. In Germany, in the time of Isserles, the child was regularly bathed before the circumcision, but after the operation only if there was a specific reason. There is no unanimity of opinion on this matter even today.

We know nothing of the further treatment of the baby. According to Rabbi Eleazar ben Azariah, the child should be bathed on the third day after circumcision (perhaps to remove the bandage?), because then, as the Pentateuch relates of the Schechemites[772], pain occurs (wound fever?). The *Gemara* questions whether or not one can apply to newborn infants the experience of these adults whose healing is much slower. Proselytes are first instructed to bathe (the ritual immersion bath for conversion) after complete healing of their circumcision, because water might aggravate the wound[773].

## III  Timing of Circumcision

Normally, circumcision should take place on the eighth day of life, even if it falls on a Sabbath. This was known to every person in the nation[774]. No specific hour of the day is prescribed; however, the zealous fulfill God's command as early in the day as possible, according to the example set by Abraham who *rose early in the morning*[775]; nevertheless, circumcision before sunrise is not permissible[776]. According to Rav Papa, one should not perform circumcision or bloodletting on a cloudy day or when the south wind blows *(yoma deshutha);* but already in his time, the response given by many was "the Lord watches over the simpletons"[777].

An essential requirement for all these regulations is that the child be healthy. *A sick child is not circumcised until it becomes healthy.* If the child suffers from a mild illness such as mild eye pain, then circumcision can take place as soon as the illness subsides. In the case of a serious illness in which the entire body also suffers, including a severe eye illness (blenorrhea?), the child is given seven extra days after the illness subsides to regain his strength. According to Mar Samuel, if the child has a feverish condition, even if it only lasts for one hour, one should wait for thirty[778] days.

An exception is made in the case of a leper *(metzorah),* irrespective of whether the patient is first being secluded (isolated) for observation because of the suspicion of leprosy or whether the patient has already been definitely declared to be a leper. Here, the foreskin should and must be removed on the eighth day[779], in spite of the Biblical warning to set aside untouched a leprosy spot before an opinion is rendered thereon by the priest[780].

Since we can no longer identify with certainty which skin illness *tzaraath* or

---

771a. Preuss incorrectly gives the dates 1131-1205 (F.R.)

772. Genesis 34:25. *And it came to pass on the third day* (after circumcision), *when they were sore.* According to the commentators, including the *Targum:* it was the climax of the pain. According to Rabbi Eleazar and Rabbi Yochanan, the third day following childbirth is also critical for the parturient woman

773. Yebamoth 47b

774. Niddah 42b. This was known even to John, see John 7:22

775. Genesis 22:4

776. Megillah 2:4

777. Yebamoth 72a

778. Jerushalmi Yebamoth 8; 9a

779. *Tosefta* Negaim 3:6; Shabbath 132b

780. Deut. 24:8

*bahereth* refers to, the above ruling is today meaningless. That which today's *mohelim* consider to be *mila betzaraath* is probably harmless herpes of the foreskin or even totally harmless pieces of foreskin sebum.

Circumcision must also be postponed if the child is still abnormally red, meaning until the blood is absorbed from the inner organs; that is, until the circulation of the blood is properly regulated. Furthermore, noticeable pallor of the child, which has already been described above as anemia or *yarkona*[781], is also a cause for postponement "until the child develops sufficient blood". In post-Talmudic times, the greatest caution was advocated specifically in these two situations, because one can always circumcise a child at a later date, but one can never restore a baby to life.

If two children of the same mother, according to Rabbi Judah, or three according to Rabbi Simeon ben Gamliel, died as a result of circumcision, then circumcision of a third or fourth child, respectively, should not be performed. The same applies in the case of three sisters; if one son of each sister died as a result of circumcision, then the son of the fourth sister may not be circumcised. The definitive decision therefore is: "if two children of the same mother or one child each of two sisters died as a result of circumcision, circumcision of the third child must be omitted".

It appears certain that we are here dealing with the oldest observations concerning a blood disease (hemophilia). This opinion is in accord with the Talmudic comment that in regard to circumcision, there are families in which the blood is loose *(raphi)* and others in which the blood is held fast (*kamit,* easily congealed)[782]. This is further in agreement with the knowledge that hemophilia nearly always occurs in males, but is nearly always transmitted only through the female member of the family.

According to Maimonides and *Shulchan Aruch,* in such cases, the circumcision should only be postponed "until the child is grown and becomes healthy". Ezekiel Landau emphasizes that for this rule there is no source at all to be found in the *Gemara*[783]. He points out that the *Mishnah* speaks of a priest, obviously an adult, who remained uncircumcised *(arel)* because his brothers died as a result of circumcision[784]. The *Tosafoth* also agrees with his view[785].

In the case of Goldmann[786] and Karewski (hemorrhage in a child from a hemophilic family in which two other children died of the same cause i.e. circumcision)[787], the *mohel* obviously committed a grievous offense against the law.

There can be no doubt that in a known family of bleeders, even the circumcision of the first child should at least be postponed.

For anatomic reasons, a true circumcision cannot be performed in the case of one who was "born circumcised" *(nolad mahul),* and in the case of an already circumcised proselyte (Arab or Gibeonite)[788]. The majority of Talmudists, however, are of the opinion that a true congenital absence of the foreskin does not occur, and that most cases are those of "squeezed-in foreskin". In such a case, as a sign of the covenant, one should "express one drop of blood (from the glans)".

During the examination of a baby as to whether a foreskin exists, one should use extreme care and also the utmost prudence to only examine with one's hands and eyes, but not with an iron instrument, in order not to produce pain in the child. If one is not sure about something, one should rather wait and postpone circumcision; for the

781. Chapter 4, Part 3 Section 1
782. Yebamoth 64b
783. *Noda Biyehuda* on *Yoreh Deah* No. 165
784. Yebamoth 8:1
785. Zebachim 75a
786. Gräfe and Walther's *Journal fur Chirurgie.* Vol. 13 Part 2

787. Short report in Löwenstein. *Die Bechneidung* 1897 p.41
788. Abodah Zarah 27a where it states the dark *gabnuni;* in Yebamoth 71a the word is *giboni.*

Talmud has already related the case of the infant son of Rabbi Ahaba Shaba that was born circumcised and which the father took to thirteen ritual circumcisers, and after much pressing[789], the infant's testicles were squashed. According to another version, the urethra was injured during attempts to "bring out the drop of blood of the covenant".

In spite of the report of Dr. Levy (Stettin) who states that he and his four brothers were all born without a foreskin[790], at present, I do not believe in the occurrence of congenital absence of the foreskin. On the other hand, in cases where the urethral meatus is not located exactly at the tip of the glans but lies in a small furrow on the undersurface of the glans (glans hypospadius), one observes that the foreskin does not hang over the penis in a cylindrical manner but is attached to the lips of the abnormal opening. In general, the free edge of the foreskin does not reach the tip of the glans but only to the middle of the glans and is firmly attached thereto, but can be loosened with a vigorous tug, so that the upper part of the glans, and, if one is inattentive, the entire glans, appears to be lacking a foreskin.

Such an observation is probably the origin of the expression "squeezed-in foreskin", orla kebusha. So, too, can be explained the advice of Soran[791] that in newborns who appear to be without foreskins, leipodermon (in Greek), one should gently pull the foreskin down. This was part of the cosmetic of Greek children.

The Talmud, as well as later commentators and law teachers, debate how one proceeds with the circumcision of a child that has two foreskins and what conditions are in general associated with such a duplication of the foreskin. Cases of double penis[792] and double glans[793] were certainly observed. — Of ritual interest, only, is the further controversial issue as to whether or not a baby born by cesarian section (yotzeh dophen) and a hermaphrodite may be circumcised on the Sabbath. A case where circumcision became necessary before the eighth day of life "because of danger to the life of the baby" (abnormal phimosis?) is first mentioned in the post-Talmudic responsa.

As already mentioned above, when Greek gymnasia were established in Jerusalem, attempts were made throughout the ages to make one's circumcision unrecognizable by methodically pulling the foreskin to the front. Josephus states that "the Jews covered the circumcision of their penis, so that even when they were naked, they could not be distinguished from the Greeks"[794] — particularly since it appears that a long foreskin was considered to be a great pride among heathens[795]. Naturally, strong protests were lodged by those loyal to the Jewish law against such practices: "if someone voids the covenant of Abraham, he has no share in the world to come (everlasting bliss)"[796]. Accordingly, the legends of Esau[797] and of Achan in the book

---

789. thus according to the version in Jerushalmi Shabbath 19; 17a

790. Virch. Arch. Vol. 116, 1889 p.539. Extraordinary is his assertion that "during puberty the prepuce was always being pushed over the glans during walking"; the prepuce was not existent

791. Soran Chapt. 34 p.160. Ermerins. Long after the above was written, I noticed that 100 years ago Autenrieth mentioned that there were as many circumcised Christian children born as Jewish children, i.e. with hypospadias. See his and Reil's Arch. fur die Physiologie Vol. 7, 1807 p.296

792. for example Centralblat fur Chirurgie 1896 p.387

793. ibid 1895 p.1106

794. Josephus. Antiquities. Book 12 Chapt. 5:1

795. see Pesikta de Rav Kahana p.190a: if God grants a heathen a son, he pulls the latter's foreskin etc. In Sinbad, p.573 ed. Cassel, someone wishes that his entire body should be foreskin at the request of his wife!

796. Aboth 3:11; Jerushalmi Peah 1; 16b adds: "these are the epispastics". See also Lamentations Rabbah 1:20 fol. 12d where the criticism of Jeremiah 11:15, they have the holy flesh from thee, is said to refer to the epispastics. The Apostle Paul also does not want those called circumcised (converted Jews) "to generate a foreskin". First Corinthians 7:18: peritetomenos me epispastho.

797. Tanchuma Toledoth p.64a. Also in Epiphanias (4th century) De Mens. et Ponder. Chapt. 16

of Joshua are made into horrible examples of such *"epispastics"* (from *epispao,* to pull towards)[798].

During the time of Hadrian (131-136 C.E.), when many Jews thought that Bar Kochba was the Messiah, the epispastics also hurried to have themselves circumcised again, without any harm occurring to their health or their procreative ability, thus contradicting the assertion of Rabbi Judah that to recircumcise an epispastic is dangerous[799]. The Talmud requires that all those who drew their foreskins to cover the corona or those in which this occurred spontaneously be recircumcised.

## IV    Importance of Circumcision

From time immemorial, *milah* has served as a holy commandment of Judaism. It is as important as all the other commandments combined[800]. Thirteenfold is the covenant which God made with Abraham[801]. Circumcision has been preserved like all other commandments for which Jews martyred themselves[802] during times of persecution[803].

"The tithe is given from the soil; so too part of the body must be sacrificed"[804]. Only after his circumcision is Abraham called "complete"[805]. With the apparent intent to make all Jewish folk heroes appear to be perfect, the legend states that even Abraham himself was born circumcised![806].

Lack of circumcision represents a portrayal of imperfection. Thus one also speaks of uncircumcised lips[807], ears[808], and heart[809]; and Moses demands that the *foreskin of the heart be circumcised*[810].

One can readily assume that the occurrence of such an important event as circumcision in a family was celebrated with appropriate festivities. Just as in Biblical times one spoke of the wedding week of the betrothed[811], during the time of the Talmud one spoke of "the week of the son" *(shebua haben).* The expression *chathan* (bridegroom) used by Zippora for her newly circumcised son is also used by the *Mishnah*[812] and the *Gemara*[813]. The Arabs before Mohammed, and, perhaps, even later[814], use the term *chathan,* which means "betrothed" to the Hebrews, only in the sense of "circumcise".[815] So, too, at a circumcision feast *(bé mehola)* Rabbi Chabiba sang the hymn "blessed is he in whose dwelling there is joy"[816]. These feasts were apparently openly announced (in the synagogues?) and then, as is frequently still the custom among Orientals today, the baby's parents kept open house, sometimes late into the night[817], unless the government prohibited both circumcision and its

798. Sanhedrin 44a
799. Yebamoth 72a
800. Nedarim 32a
801. The word "covenant" *(bris)* occurs 13 times in the 17th chapter of Genesis.
802. *Mechilta. Jithro* p.61. fol. 68b; see also Gerim 1:1 "one tries to frighten a proselyte from converting to Judaism by telling him how many Jews were killed because of their circumcisions".
803. Shabbath 120a
804. Deut. Rabbah 3:5
805. *Tosefta* Nedarim 2:5
806. David: Sotah 10b; Moses: *ibid* 12a: Abraham: Genesis Rabbah 47 fol. 96d; etc. See also Aboth de Rabbi Nathan 2:5 and *Midrash* Psalms on 9:6 p.42b. The Sunna of Islam also mentions the same of Mohammed. Risa. *Die Rituelle Beschneidung Vornehmlich im Osmanischen*

*Reiche.* Volkmann's *Sammlung Klinische Vorträge* No. 438
807. Exodus 6:12
808. Isaiah 6:10
809. Levit. 26:41
810. Deut. 10:16
811. Genesis 29:27
812. Niddah 5:3
813. Nedarim 32a
814. Ibn Ezra on Exodus 4:25: "women have the custom of calling a circumcised child *chathan"*
815. The attempts of philologists to explain this connection philologically is not germane here. In later times, the Arabs, such as physicians, used the term *tahir, purificare,* for "circumcise".
816. Kethuboth 8a
817. Deut. Rabbah 9:1

celebration[818]. In non-religious homes, this celebration degenerated into drinking orgies[819]. The performance of circumcision in the synagogue during the time of the *Mishnah* can be excluded with certainty, and in the time of the *Gemara,* with extreme likelihood[820].

Special benedictions for the circumciser, the father, and the "assembled people" were already known in ancient times[821]. On the other hand, there is no trace in the Talmud of the custom of naming the child at the occasion of the circumcision, as the Gospels report of the child Jesus[822], and as became the general custom in later times.

Perhaps it is an imitation of the Roman custom whereby a girl was given a name on the eighth day and a boy on the ninth day of life with extraordinary festivities. — The Catholic church celebrates the first of January as the day of circumcision of Jesus; it is debated when this custom was first instituted[823].

## V   Surgical Circumcision

All the discussions in the Talmud mentioned until now refer only to ritual circumcision. The *Gemara* also mentions a circumcision of heathens, i.e. adults, because of *morana*[824]. This word is used elsewhere in the Talmud to designate a worm[825] and perhaps has the same meaning here. Attempts at explaining this "foreskin worm" which makes circumcision necessary are without merit, however.

Finally, the *Midrash* speaks of a "*noma* on the flesh" (i.e. on the penis) which makes circumcision necessary[826].

# *APPENDIX II*
# BLOOD-LETTING

## I   Introduction

The ancients used blood-letting for one of two reasons: either as a therapeutic remedy for illnesses or as a measure to preserve health.

Indications for venesection for the first reason are quite sparse in the Talmud. It was also debated by the Sages[827], as by their contemporary heathen physicians[828],

---

818. Baba Bathra 60b: from the day that the government issued cruel decrees against us and does not allow us to enter into the "week of the son", we should bind ourselves not to marry and beget children. (This course of action is rejected in the *Gemara*). See also *Tosefta* Sotah 15:10. — Sanhedrin 32b: when a handmill grinds in the town of Burni, it is an announcement of a "week of the son" (since any other announcement was prohibited). See also Baba Kamma 80a and Jerushalmi Kethuboth 1; 25c.

819. Jerushalmi Chagigah 2; 77b: Abahu, father of Elisha, was one of the prominent men of Jerusalem. When a child had to be circumcised, he invited all the prominent people of Jerusalem and set them down in one room, and Rabbi Eliezer and Rabbi Joshua in another room. The former ate and drank, beat time with their hands and danced whereas the latter uttered religious prayers. — Ruth Rabbah *s.v. lini:* these sang Psalms, the others alphabets (Greek songs).

820. *Tosafoth* on Shabbath 19:1: "One may bring the circumcision knife to the child on the Sabbath, but not the child to the knife, because one cannot expect him to be transported, nor to be separated from the mother for so long". One should also keep in mind that the synagogue was mostly separated from one's dwelling.

821. *Tosefta* Berachoth 7:12

822. Luke 2:21

823. See Chr. Fr. Wintzler. *Historische Untersuchungen der Beschneidung Jesu Christi.* Wittenburg 1753.

824. Abodah Zarah 26b

825. Chullin 49a

826. See above, section 3 at the beginning of this chapter.

827. Yoma 84a

828. Coelius Aurelianus, *Acut.* 3 Chapt. 4:34 p.193

whether or not one should phlebotomize for synanche. If a fever is present for one day, one lets the patient go hungry (one only gives him a glass of water). On the other hand, a fever *(chamtha)* that is present for two days is an indication for venesection[829]. At the height of the fever, however, blood-letting is dangerous[830]. This is totally in accord with the teaching of Celsus, that the most suitable time for blood-letting is the second or third day of the illness, and that blood-letting during the acme of the fever is equivalent to murder[831]. An anonymous author in the Talmud considers phlebotomy for pain in the eyes to be dangerous[831a]. One venesects an animal that is "overtaken by blood" (i.e. has plethora), although one thereby creates a body blemish thereby rendering it unfit to be offered as a sacrifice[832].

Much more is mentioned in the Talmud concerning the use of phlebotomy as a hygienic or prophylactic measure. Most of the following Talmudic assertions refer to venesection, *quae more fit.* Today, we can no longer conceptualize the extent to which blood-letting was used in antiquity, and we can only understand the capacity of those generations to withstand such vigorous encroachment on their organisms if we assume that just as anemia and nervosity are the stigma of modern times, plethora and inflammability were the signs of ancient generations. To say that such a blood-thirsty method was not indicated in therapy in those days would be as untrue as to maintain that it should still be applied today[833].

Nevertheless, the belief that blood-letting may come to light again from today's oblivion has not yet died out[834]. If the ancient philosopher is correct with his *panta rei,* then one can expect that a generation frenzied to performing venesection will once again occur. Perhaps different climates and modes of life influence one's attitude toward venesection. Asklepiades paid attention to this fact, *utrum regio adjutorium phlebotomiae permittat adhiberi,* and he phlebotomized patients ill with pleuritis in Parium and Hellespont with good results, whereas in Rome and Athens the same procedure was harmful to the patients[835]. Even elsewhere in earlier times, there occurred variations of opinions concerning the tolerance of patients to venesection. Whereas P. Guignes simply states as fact concerning his Carthusians: *quinquies minuimur,* P. Masson remarks thereon 500 years later (1687); *si autem tale quid istis temporibus attentaremus, omnes fere Monachos in brevi necaremus,* and fully documents it by the general diminution of the strengths of people through generations[836]. A similar statement is made by Jacob Emden to certain relevant remarks of the Talmud: "our climate is not like that in the Orient, and the nature of modern man cannot be compared to that of ancient times"[837].

Nebuchadnezzar chose for himself young people *without blemish*[838], which the Talmud explains: "there was not even a lancet puncture on their bodies"[839] — that is how rare it was to find a person without venesection scars. In Sodom, if someone injured another and he bled, the judges decided that the injured person had to pay the offender the money that he (the injured person) saved since he no longer required venesection[840]. The Sages teach that a learned man should not live in a town that has

829. Gittin 67b
830. Abodah Zarah 29a
831. Celsus *Med.* 2:10 *in ipso febis impetu sanguinem mittere hominem jugulare est.*
831a. Abodah Zarah 29a
832. *Tosefta* Bechoroth 3:17; cf. Jerushalmi Pesachim 1; 28b
833. Pelman. *Nervosität und Erziehung.* Bonn, 1888, Introduction
834. Wenzel. *Alte Erfahrungen im Lichte der Neuen Zeit.* Wiesbaden 1893. See also the modern treatment of chlorosis with venesection. In America, loud voices of phy-

sicians are again heard in favor of venesections for plethora, congestion etc. See the *Times and Register.* January 12, 1895.
835. Coelius Aurelianus, *Acut.* 2 Chapt. 22: 129 p.131
836. *Annales ord. Cartusiensis v. Junoc.* Le Masson. Correriae. 1687 Book 1 Chapt. 39 fol. 73
837. See his commentary on Shabbath 129b; see also *Tosafoth* on Moed Katan 11a
838. Daniel 1:4
839. Sanhedrin 93b
840. *ibid* 109a

no blood-letter[841], and a *minutor* belongs to the *officia necessaria* of a well-staffed cloister in the Middle Ages[842]. At least in Palestine, venesection is included among the costs that a husband is obligated to pay for the continuing necessary medical treatment of his wife[843].

One can assume that it was known that every person sensed pain during venesection. The deceased Rabbi Nachman appeared to Raba in a dream and told him that in dying he had no greater pain than during venesection[844]. The daughter of Chisda described the pain of defloration to her husband with the same words[845]. If someone dreamed of venesection, it was considered to be a propitious sign[846]. The color of venesected blood was also generally well-known and could be used for comparisons[847].

The omission of blood-letting was thought to be disadvantageous and under certain circumstances was even considered to be dangerous. As recently as the eighteenth century, Höfer gives a whole list of illnesses which were thought to occur as a result of the omission of blood-letting[848]. The Talmud states "much blood, much leprosy" *(schechin)*[849].

Among the opponents of venesection, one can distinguish three groups:

1) those who tried to prevent venesection for certain medical indications, as is reported by Galen concerning a few physicians of his time.

2) those who interpreted it to be a sign of unmanly pampering; Roman soldiers were only allowed to be venesected for *ignominiae causa*[850].

3) individuals who considered the performance of blood-letting to be a transgression of a religious law. For in the Bible, it is prohibited to make any cuts in the skin[851], and Rabbi Bibi bar Abin is of the opinion that although this prohibition was originally only a remonstration against this practice as a heathen sign of mourning, it also encompasses the venesection lancing[852].

## II   Frequency of Venesection

The question as to how often a healthy person should have blood let in order to remain healthy was a matter of lively controversy. In general, in the Talmudic viewpoint, venesection is one of those things which is harmful if excessive, but useful if it is performed in an appropriate amount[853]. Mar Samuel, a Jewish physician of the third century, advises that blood be let at 30–day intervals. At a later stage in life — according to *Rashi* after 40 years of age and *Aruch* after 50 years of age — one should decrease the frequency. At an even more advanced age (20 years more), one should further decrease the frequency of blood-letting[854]. Maimonides altogether prohibits routine phlebotomy after the age of 50 years[855].

Mar Samuel does not state at what age one should begin venesection. According to the report of Prosper Alpinus, in Egypt, children less than one year of age were already venesected, particularly by cutting a blood vessel in the leg or behind the ear[856]. Hippocrates already mentions this bad habit and attributes the infertility of the Scythians to it[857]. Galen prohibits blood-letting before 14 years of age, and only allows it in people past 60 years of age in case of need[858]. In later times, this regulation of

841. *ibid* 17b
842. see Preuss' essay in *Wiener Klin. Wochenschrift.* 1895 No. 34 Note 10
843. Kethuboth 52b
844. Moed Katan 28a
845. Kethuboth 39b
846. Berachoth 57a
847. Niddah 19b and Machshirim 6:5 ff.
848. J.W. Hoefer. *De Morbis ex Intermissa Venaesect.* Halae Magd. 1732 particularly No. 12 p.37

849. Bechoroth 44b
850. Gellius *Noct. Att.* 10:8
851. Levit. 19:28
852. Makkoth 21a
853. Gittin 70a
854. Shabbath 129b
855. *Mishneh Torah. Hilchoth Deoth* 4:18
856. *De Med. Aegypt* 2:7 p.50
857. Hippocrates. *De Aere. locis et aquis.* ed. Foes 1657 fol. 293
858. Galen. *De Venaesect.* Kühn 19 p.520:26

Galen was no longer heeded. Celsus states that experience has shown that neither age nor pregnancy, but body strength, determines whether or not venesection should be carried out. "An energetic young person and a robust elderly person can certainly tolerate this procedure"[859].

Trincavella reports from the beginning of the sixteenth century that in Venice and Padua even frail children were venesected[860]; and 100 years later V. Sanden collected and reported on 23 cases of venesection on children by quoting contemporary authors[861]. Chemnitz even recommends blood-letting from newborns by delaying for a considerable period of time the tying of the severed umbilical cord[862].

## III    Instruments for Blood-letting

"To let blood" is usually called *hikkiz,* from *nakaz* meaning to prick, in the same double sense as our "blood-letting"; namely, to have one's blood let by someone else or to let the blood of someone else; the blood-letting itself is called *hakkaza.* Very rarely the terms *sekar* or *sebar*[863] are used, (wherefrom *sibura* or *sikura,* the blood-letting). Without exception, the commentaries interpret *hakkaza* to refer to blood-letting from the shoulders i.e. the cephalic vein; only once[864] does *Rashi* consider it to refer to bleeding by cupping glasses. Where the sense is absolutely clear as to the method of blood-letting, a euphemistic expression is used as is customary in the Talmud for all unesthetic things[865]: *abad miltha,* or *rem facere.*

The following instrumentation is mentioned in the Talmud for blood-letting:

1) *Kusultha,* the lancet, perhaps also *scariffum,* a small knife to cut the skin which has been made hyperemic by the cupping glass. The skin wound produced by the *kusaltha* is called *ribda.*

Rabbenu Chananel explains *kusaltha* as the Arabic *machgama,* which is incorrect, because the latter word only means *cucurbitula* (not scarificator, as Kohut asserts). To be sure, the plain term "cupping glass" probably refers to the bleeding cupping glass, so that the interpretation of *Aruch* that *ribda de kusaltha* means "glass cupping glass" is quite understandable. *Rashi* translates it as *pointure de flieme,* prick of the lancet[866].

2) *Masmar*[867], literally a nail, at any rate a pointed instrument; according to Maimonides *mibda-l-faced, scalpellum venam secantis.*

In *Aruch* one finds once the term *tharpetha*[868] whose meaning is uncertain. Also linguistically difficult is the statement of Rabbi Muna: "the hand which touches the *chasuda* deserves to be hewn off"[869], because one can thereby spill someone's blood or cause his death[870]. The ancient commentators *Rashi* and *Rabbenu Chananel* consider *chasuda* to be the wound of venesection[871].

Rabbi Joseph owned a small grove of date trees under which cuppers used to sit and let blood. Ravens used to come and drink the blood and then used to fly on to the date trees and damage the dates[872]. One thus sees that one used to let the blood flow on

---

859. Celsus 2:10
860. Trincavellus. *DeRat. Cur. Partic. Hum. Corp. Aff.* Book 2 Chapt. 10, Venice 1575, fol. 42c
861. V. Sanden. *Diss. Sistens Sanit. Conservat. ex Venaesectione.* Königsberg 1737 p.23
862. Chemnitz, Mart. *De Sang. Miss. Infantibus, neonatis, debilibus et noxia et salutari.* Giessen 1776
863. Abodah Zarah 29a. Also *Aruch* interprets Pesachim 112a as *sekar*
864. Gittin 67b

865. Pesachim 3a-b
866. *"Lanceola est ferrum subtile cum qua vena aperitur, gallice flieme".* La Curne de St. Palaye in *Dict. Hist. de l'ancien lang. franç* 6:236. The transcription "flame" is only correct in this sense.
867. Kelim 12:4
868. Kethuboth 39b
869. Shabbath 108b
870. Kallah 1:52a
871. see also *Orach Chayim* 4:4
872. Baba Bathra 12a

the ground, as still occurs today in Bokhara, so that the streets where the Bokharian physicians live resemble slaughter houses, because everywhere there are pools of blood[873]. Otherwise, the blood was collected in a vessel which could not be used again: in the "worthless *kaddin* of the blood-letter"[874] or in a potsherd, *chispa de umana*[875], or in a dirty earthenware vessel, which was otherwise unusable[876]. One also let the blood flow onto old rags, *semikta*[877].

A scab develops on the venesection wound; this scab is first soft and is firmly adherent to the skin. From the third day on, however, it begins to become loosened from the underlying tissues[878]. The post-venesection treatment of the patient requires only very minor therapeutic measures; nevertheless, Rabbi Judah would not even allow a lancet puncture to be healed by a heathen[879].

3) Another method for blood-letting is by the use of *cupping glasses*. As is known, originally, horns of young cows were used for cupping. This is proven by the findings in Egyptian mummies and is attested to by Prosper Alpinus for Egypt from a much later time (approximately 1550)[880]. The cow horn being used for this purpose even in modern times was observed by Doughty[881] among the Bedouins and by Tobler[882] in Jerusalem. According to Stern[883], cupping with horns is still customary today throughout the Orient. Bartels states that this practice is also used by primitive peoples[884]. Glax gives the details of the use of cupping horns in Croatian folk baths in our times[885]. The tip of the horn was cut off and the cupper sucked at this opening with his mouth, whereas the other opening was placed on the skin of the patient. The mouth side was then sealed with wax, as described by Celsus[886]; or with an eggshell skin that was loosened with spittle, as did the Egyptians[887]; or with the finger, as described by Antyllus[888] which seems to be the most natural way.

The Arabic designation for cupper, *al-chagim,* which actually means the sucker, proves that this method was used in ancient Arabic times. The Talmudic expression for cupping glass is also *keren* or *cornu* (i.e. horn), although it is established that they were (also?) made of glass[889]. Drinking from a cupping glass is considered to be a punishable crudeness[890]. Cupping vessels which are spherical in form and mostly constructed of metal were found in Pompeii and are illustrated by Von de Renzi[891]. In addition to the cupping horn, Antyllus mentions cupping vessels made of glass, bronze *(chalkai)* and silver in a variety of forms.

Zehnpfund (according to the explanation of V. Oefeles) has described the Babylonian *zukapiku,* an instrument which resembles a scorpion spine and which was used for scarification[892].

## IV    Conditions of Blood-letting

There are differing opinions as to the amount of blood which should be let. Galen does not consider it appropriate to mention a single amount for all situations. Everything depends on the constitution and age of the patient, the time of year, and the location. He observed venesections up to six pounds, *ita ut febris protinus*

873. Flöricke, in *Zeitgeist* 1897 No. 2
874. Levit. Rabbah 10:5
875. Gittin 69a
876. Baba Bathra 20b
877. *ibid* 20a
878. Niddah 67a
879. Abodah Zarah 27a
880. Prosper Alpinus. *De Medic Aegypt.* 2 Chapt. 13, Venice 1591 p.63
881. Doughty — *Travels in Arabia Deserta.* Cambridge 1888 Vol 1 p. 492
882. Tobler. *Medizinische Topographie Jerusalems.* Berlin 1855 p.6
883. Stern. *Türkei* 1:195
884. Bartels. *Medizin die Naturvölker* p.270
885. Glax. *Zeitschrift fur Balneologie* etc. Vol 2, 1910 No. 23
886. Celsus 2:11 Ed. Daremberg p.55
887. Prosper Alpinus. *loc. cit.*
888. Antyllus, in Oribasius. *Coll.* 7:16 Vol. 1 p.62
889. Shabbath 154b
890. Makkoth 16b
891. in his essay on Celsus. Neapel 1852 p.123
892. *Beiträge zur Assyrologie* by Delitzsch-Haupt. Vol. 4 p.220 ff. Leipzig 1902

*extingueretur,* without harm to health. Some patients, on the other hand, barely tolerate the removal of half a pound of blood[893]. According to the Talmud, the minimum amount of blood necessary to sustain human life is *one-quarter log* (approximately 250 grams)[894]; therefore, it is considered dangerous to bleed down to this limit, because then even a minor stimulus such as a chill, which is ordinarily not harmful, might bring the person's life to an end[895]. Thus, the maximum amount of blood that one may remove is unfortunately not mentioned.

The first blood which flows from blood-letting or from cupping can be distinguished from the subsequent blood, and it is very significant in certain illnesses. On the other hand, one requires a skilled eye to distinguish the nuances of venesected blood, *quae more fit;* we can, therefore, not reproach Rav Ashi and Mar Zutra for not claiming to possess that *visus eruditus*[896].

There are many factors which influence the decision as to which days are suited for blood-letting. We can, therefore, reasonably acquiesce to the regulation that one should not perform this operation on a cloudy day if one could equally well carry it out by the light of a clear day[897]. We can also understand that certain days when certain wind directions prevail might be dangerous for blood-letting[898], as was later also warned against[899]. However, from our modern standpoint, we cannot agree with all the mystical views which are so abundantly interwoven into blood-letting. Astrological notions, in particular, have exerted their influence for thousands of years, not only on the lay public but also on physicians. Even if, in respect to this point, we find certain rules enunciated in the Talmud by Mar Samuel — rules which were first mentioned by physicians in the Occident a thousand years later — one should not forget that the native country of innumerable Talmudic traditions is Babylonia which is considered the birth place of astrology. Here, in Babylonia and in Assyria, one finds the beginning of the blood-letting schedules[900], which were widely disseminated throughout the Occident from the time of the calendar of Dr. Thurneysser, physician of Johann George, the elector of Brandenburg. Blood-letting and astrology absolutely belonged together, and it is reported that Archbishop Theodor of Canterbury, in the year 650, declared that it is dangerous to venesect during the waxing moon, *quando et lumen lunae et rheuma Oceani incremento est*[901].

The relevant Talmudic regulations concerning blood-letting are as follows:[902] Samuel said that the correct time for blood-letting is on a Sunday, Wednesday and Friday, but not on a Monday or Thursday because on the latter days the Heavenly Court and the human court are both in session, and the general rule is that "the accuser *(satan)* accuses during time of danger". Why not on Tuesday? Because the planet Mars, which was feared by astrologers in all ages as the planet of murder[903], rules during even-numbered hours of the day. But on Friday, too, it rules at even-numbered hours? Since the multitude was accustomed to blood-letting on Fridays, *the Lord preserveth the simple*[904].

Samuel further stated: a fourth day of the week (i.e. Wednesday) which is the fourth, fourteenth or twenty-fourth of the month, as well as a Wednesday which does not have four more days to the end of the month — are all dangerous for blood-letting.

893. Galen. *De Cur. Rat. Per Venaes.* Chapt. 14 ed. Charter. Vol. 10 fol. 444
894. Shabbath 31b
895. Shabbath 129a
896. Niddah 20a
897. Yebamoth 72a
898. Shabbath 129b and Yebamoth 72a
899. Arnaldi Villanovi *opp.* ed. Taurellus. Basel 1585 fol. 767
900. taboo tablets; i.e. days on which certain acts are taboo or prohibited

901. Beda, *Hist. Ecclesiast.* 5:3 fol. 374
902. Shabbath 129b
903. *Mars in octava (significat) interfectionem et abscisionem manuum et pedum* etc. *Lib. Regum de Signific. Planetar.* Prague 1564. Cap. de Marte. Poetically in Gabirol in his "Royal Crown".
904. Psalms 116:6

On the first and second days of the month, blood-letting causes weakness; on the third day, it is dangerous. On the eve of a festival, it causes weakness. On the eve of Pentecost it is dangerous and, therefore, blood-letting was prohibited on the eve of every festival. One can assume that this latter prohibition was based on the consideration that the preparations for the festival and the accompanying exertions of people would so affect them that any additional weakening through blood-letting would not be considered to be harmless. Later, blood-letting schedules (taboo tablets) were compiled from such warnings against blood-letting on certain days, for astrological reasons.

The above dates of Mar Samuel are not in accord with the declarations of the cuneiform inscriptions. Only the fourteenth day of the month, the usual day of the full moon, remained as an unlucky day throughout the millennia. Otherwise, the "taboo" calendar of Samuel is changed and more complicated than the original prototype. I can see no reason for this change. In ancient Babylon, the seventh, fourteenth, nineteenth, twenty-first and twenty-eighth day of leap-Elul were considered to be unsuited for blood-letting. Other "taboo tablets" have not yet been studied[905].

## V    Nourishment and Blood-letting

There is an exceptionally large number of Talmudic statements regarding dietary factors to which one should pay attention in relation to blood-letting. Just like other physicians in antiquity, as well as lay people, Mar Samuel requires that the person to be bled should be absolutely fasting. He does not go so far as the others, however, who require an *evacuatio per clystera* prior to blood-letting. Samuel said: if one eats wheat grains and then lets one's blood, he has bled only for the wheat, but the sick body obtains no benefit therefrom[906], providing one performed the blood-letting for therapeutic purposes. But if it was done to ease one, it does accomplish this purpose even if one ate something beforehand[907]. Fifteen hundred years later, Zedler remarked as follows: if one venesects immediately after eating, then pure nourishment juice comes from the wound, but not blood[908]. This statement further clarifies the assertion of Samuel.

The consumption of vinegar and small fish, as well as cress, prior to blood-letting, is considered to be dangerous[909]. It is also necessary that venesection always be performed in a room with walls of equal thickness. Samuel was accustomed to be bled in a house whose walls were seven and a half bricks thick. One day he was bled and felt himself weak; the wall was examined and was found to be lacking half a brick[910]. This was probably a white lie of the barber-surgeon who looked for excuses to explain possible failures of blood-letting. It is sensible to warn against letting blood from a patient who is in a standing position: "five types of people are nearer to death than to life; namely, one who eats or drinks, or sleeps, or lets blood or cohabits in a standing position"[911].

Concerning the procedure after the blood-letting, Rab and Samuel teach as follows: *qui rem facit,* the patient should tarry a little, then arise and eat something before walking about. Otherwise, any fright might be disastrous for him. Nevertheless, it is advisable to wait as long as it would take to walk 1000 ells before eating. On the other hand, the venesected patient may drink immediately[912]. The question as to whether or not it is permitted to sleep immediately after blood-letting, which is discussed in all medical writings since Avicenna, is not mentioned at all in the Talmud.

905. Oefele. *Wiener. Med. Blat.* 10, 1902; Oefele. *Mitteilungen zur Geschichte der Medizin.* Vol. 6 p.151
906. i.e. bleeding immediately after a meal serves only to lighten one of that meal, but has no wider effects
907. Shabbath 129b
908. Universal-Lexicon 1:493
909. Abodah Zarah 29a
910. Shabbath 129a
911. Gittin 70a
912. Shabbath 129a–b

It is prescribed that one should wash one's hands after blood-letting; he who omits it will be frightened for seven days[913]. The punishment warning of this otherwise purely rational rule is probably based on the influence of Persian demonology.

The danger of exposing oneself to a draught after blood-letting has already been mentioned. Shivering after phlebotomy was thought to be a symptom requiring immediate relief. The following decree of Samuel is mentioned: for someone who lets blood and catches a chill, a fire is made on the summer solstice[914] so that he becomes warm. In connection with this rule, it is related that in certain cases of chill following blood-letting, where other firewood was not available, even expensive furniture was thrown into the fire[915]. Bathing after blood-letting was also considered to be dangerous[916].

It was considered absolutely essential to the Sages to partake of nourishing food after blood-letting. "He who fasts after blood-letting takes his own life in his hands."[917] An Indian physician similarly states: *qui phlebotomatus et qui expurgatus est, is unum per mensem ne abstineat cibo, ut robustus fiat*[918].

The Talmud further states that if one makes light of the meal after blood-letting, his nourishment will be made light of by Heaven[919]. One should sell even the beams of his house and buy shoes; but if one has let blood and has nothing to eat, let him sell the shoes from off his feet and provide for the requirements of the post-phlebotomy meal therewith. What are these requirements? According to Rab: meat, for meat from a strong animal adds to one's strength; and according to Samuel: wine, because red wine makes red blood[920]. In an anonymous book on blood-letting from the early Middle Ages, we find the following: *du solt dich speisen mit supteiler speise do vo sich dz plut bessert und edelt un lauteren wein trincke*[921]. The blood-rich spleen is also recommended by Samuel as a food. The advice of drinking wine after blood-letting was strictly adhered to, and, in the language of exaggeration of the Orientals, it is related that Rabbi Joseph drank wine until the wine flowed out from the venesection wound, and Rabbi Yochanan drank wine until the smell of wine emanated from his ears, and Rabbi Nachman drank wine until his spleen swam in wine[922].

The consumption of meat was taken equally seriously. When Rabbi Seira came to Palestine, he had blood let and then went to buy meat[923]. Rabbi Nachman bar Yitzchak said to his disciples: on the day of blood-letting, tell your wives that I am coming to dinner so that they prepare substantial meals[924]. Although all insidiousness is forbidden, he permitted poor people who could not afford to buy wine after blood-letting to go into numerous stores and present a coin which was not in circulation and to thereby mislead the storekeeper into letting them taste a little wine, and to repeat this maneuver until they had drunk the necessary quantity of one-sixteenth of a liter[925]. If he does not even possess such a coin, let him eat seven black dates, rub his temples with oil, and lie down in the sun to become warm[926]; for the effect of dates is equated with that of wine: a teacher who has eaten dates should not teach[927], and a priest who ate dates should not enter the Temple[928]. Oribasius considers sweet dates *(glykeis phoinikes)* among stimulating foods *(osa thermainei)*[929]. Plinius asserts that fresh fruits of the palm tree intoxicate and produce headache[930].

913. Pesachim 112a
914. literally: dog days
915. Shabbath 129a
916. Abodah Zarah 28b, according to the textual reading of Rabbenu Chananel
917. Derech Eretz Rabbah Chapter 11
918. Susrutas 2 Chapt. 39. ed. Hessler 2:201
919. Shabbath 129a
920. ibid
921. *Hie vohet an ein büchelin von alle odern zu lossen* etc., s.l. et anno. Kgl. Bibl. Berlin 1 W 420
922. Shabbath 129a
923. Jerushalmi Berachoth 2; 5c
924. Shabbath 129a
925. This quantity is otherwise thought to be intoxicating. *Tosefta Pesachim* 1:28
926. Shabbath 129a
927. Kethuboth 10b
928. Maimonides. *Biyath Hamikdash* 1:3
929. Oribasius. *Coll.* 3:31 Vol. 1:249
930. Plinius. *Hist. Natur.* 23:51

Eating fowl after blood-letting is considered to be inappropriate. Samuel said: "he who eats fowl after phlebotomy — his heart will flutter like a bird"[931]. Pickled meat is also not recommended. The consumption of fish was also considered contraindicated. It was well-known that if someone sent an errand boy to market to buy meat, the errand boy would certainly not buy fish if the meat stores were empty, if he knew that the person who sent him had just been phlebotomized. It was also known that one who had blood let should not eat of those things whose initials spell the mnemonic Hebrew word *chagbasch:* milk, cheese, onions and cress; the first two are obviously too light for the post phlebotomy meal and the latter two are too irritating to the empty stomach and weakened body[932]. Legend relates that Rabbi Eleazer ben Pedath was very poor; once, after being bled, he had nothing to eat. He took the skin of an onion (or garlic) in his mouth and fainted[933].

If someone nevertheless ate one of the *chagbasch* foods, according to Abaye, he should drink one quarter measure of vinegar and one quarter measure of wine — the latter is in any event useful after phlebotomy[934] — and the damage will be rectified. Nevertheless, the smell of his stools after having eaten such foods is quite intense and is easily harmful to the patient. Eggs are also not recommended after blood-letting. One is especially warned, however, against eating cress after blood-letting, because the face of someone who eats it develops a yellowish-green appearance[935]. Rather similar directions are given in the above-mentioned anonymous book on venesection[936]: *nach dem oderlossenn soltu dich höten vor speise die stopffet als essig bieren keise durre fleisch gesalzte und ir gleich wan sie schedlich seint.*[937].

Before and, even more so, after phlebotomy, one is directed by the Talmud to avoid all exertion, particularly travelling and cohabitation[938]. Rabbi Simeon ben Yochai says that he who cohabits following blood-letting has his blood on his own head[939]. If a man has intercourse immediately after being bled, he will have cachectic children; if intercourse took place after both husband and wife had been bled, then the children will be *ba'ale raathan*[940]. Catholic moralists also consider *copula post balneum et post sectionem venae* to be prohibited, because the latter is *notabiliter periculosa*[941]. The reason for this danger is not mentioned. In the Middle High German poem *Der Schüler von Paris,* the disciple goes to the daughter of a citizen immediately after he was bled. During the night when they are together, the wound bursts open, he exsanguinates and dies[942].

Furthermore, the Sages also consider blood-letting to be one of the things which diminish the sperm, particularly if the venesection is carried out on the lower extremities. Nevertheless, it is said that "as it is doubly bad below, it is doubly useful above" whereby the dividing line between above and below is established to be the genitalia[943].

The divergent opinion of Hippocrates in this regard has already been mentioned; but he referred to blood-letting of children. Abulcasem declares that coitus after scarification is not harmful, *quando adhibetur necessario;* however, if it is performed unnecessarily, it weakens the spine, enfeebles the kidneys and loosens their fat, *minuit etiam coitum*[944]. According to Arnold of Villanova, coitus during the first few days

931. Meilah 20b
932. Nedarim 54b; Abodah Zarah 29a
933. Taanith 25a
934. according to *Rashi* this only applies to bloodletting from the shoulder
935. Abodah Zarah 29a
936. see note 921
937. after phlebotomy, avoid food which constipates, such as vinegar, beer, cheese, hard and salted meat and the like, since they are harmful.

938. Gittin 70a
939. i.e. he forfeits his life. Niddah 17a
940. See Chapter 12, Part 2:8
941. Capellmann p.188
942. P. Cassel. *Aus Literatur und Symbolik.* Leipzig 1884, p.99
943. Gittin 70a
944. Abulcasem. *de Chirurgia* 2:96. Ed. Channing p.495

after phlebotomy is definitely not salutary. However, he explains this statement as an *imprudenter dictum, sicut et omne dictum absolutum de convenientia et inconvenientia alicujus medicinae salubris ad sanibile corpus,* since one must consider individual differences[945].

## VI   Blood-letting in Animals

Just as in human beings, venesection was also practiced on animals[946]. Even venesection in birds is mentioned[947]. Although it is ordinarily strictly forbidden to injure a first-born animal and to thereby render it unfit to be offered as a sacrifice, it is specifically decreed that such an animal may be phlebotomized if the intent is to help the animal[948]. The amount of blood withdrawn from an animal was normally not very great. As a rule, one did not let the blood flow until one came down to the last blood which is sustaining life (i.e. the soul), as was no doubt done in human beings.

The Bible and Talmud strongly prohibit the consumption of blood in any form or manner. It is, therefore, understandable that even in the rare case where one might imbibe some of this rich blood — the "life blood" — it was also explicitly prohibited[949]. Concerning the diagnosis of this "venesected blood with which the soul departs", there are divergent opinions. In the *Tosefta*[950], the following definition is given: "which is the life blood? As long as it gushes forth". This opinion is accepted by Rabbi Yochanan in the Talmud[951]. Resh Lakish, however, believes that life blood is that which flows from the black drop onward, irrespective of whether or not it gushes forth in an arc. One can explain these differing opinions as follows: the *Tosefta,* which is not specifically speaking of venesected blood, had in mind arterial blood which can in fact be considered to be the life blood of the individual. On the other hand, Resh Lakish is discussing the situation of blood-letting and he thinks that when the black (venous) blood, whose removal is the task of the venesection[952], has flowed out, then the subsequent blood which flows can be considered to be the life blood of the person, so that additional blood-letting would endanger the life of that individual.

---

945. *op. cit.* fol. 910
946. Shabbath 144a
947. *Tosefta* Moed Katan 2:11
948. *Tosefta* Bechoroth 3:17
949. Kerithoth 5:1
950. *Tosefta* Zebachin 8:17
951. Kerithoth 22a

952. "Thick and black blood is defective; therefore it is advantageous to remove it. If blood is red and clear, it is good, and then blood-letting is more harmful than helpful and should therefore be immediately stopped".

# CHAPTER VI

## *DISEASES OF THE EYES*
## (OPHTHALMOLOGY)

### I  Blemishes of the Eye

Certain physical defects render priests unfit to serve in the Temple. The same defects, if found on first-born animals, allow their secular use. Such animals, if healthy, would have to be offered as sacrifices in the Temple. The same disqualifying defects, if found on a woman, can result in invalidation of her marriage. Thus, if a man married a woman on the condition that she have no physical blemish, the marriage is invalid if any malady is discovered in the woman which is not externally noticeable and which, if present in a priest, would render him unfit to serve in the Temple[1]. In all such cases, it makes no difference whether these defects are permanent, or only temporary[2], wherein "permanent" is a juridical concept and is not equivalent to "incurable"[3]. Only practical observation on live beings can provide one with a proper evaluation of the individual defects, and Rab relates that for this purpose he spent eighteen months with a shepherd[4]. After death, such an examination is misleading for the defects in the case of an eye change in appearance, and an exact identification is no longer possible. For this reason, the use of a slaughtered first-born animal was prohibited, if the owner first slaughtered it and only afterwards brought it to an expert for examination[5]. The same is true of an animal which *in vivo* was seen to have a manifest blemish, thus rendering it unfit for offering as a sacrifice, even if after the slaughtering the blemish is no longer visible or appears different from the way it had looked during life[6].

The disqualifying blemishes of the eye will now be discussed; first, however, an observation:

In the identification of names of illnesses from antiquity, particularly from folk medicine — this may be a generally valid observation — one should always accept only the simplest possible concept. It is highly likely that people in former times also suffered from retrobulbar neuritis or albuminuric retinitis, but these illnesses were certainly not diagnosed. One should not seek to identify afflictions which are not forthwith recognizable with the naked eye, even if one believes one has seen them mentioned. On the other hand, it is unquestionable that the ancients sensed pain, photophobia and disturbances of vision just as we do; but to them, these individual symptoms were considered to be separate diseases.

---

1. *Tosefta* Kethuboth 7:9
2. Bechoroth 7:1
3. *Tosefta* Bechoroth 38b
4. Sanhedrin 5b
5. Betzah 27a
6. *Tosefta* Bechoroth 3:6

## II

The Bible decrees that any man who is a descendant of Aaron, the High Priest, and who has a physical blemish shall not serve in the Temple. Among these is a *"gibben" or "dak" or "teballul" in his eye*[7].

1) *Gibben*, according to the explanation of the *Mishnah*, is a person who has no eyebrows *(gebinim)*, or has only one eyebrow. According to Rabbi Dosa, *gibben* is a person whose eyebrows hang down over the eyes[8], for which another source uses the term *shakbana* or *shekanya*[9]. The *Gemara*[10] also interprets *liphin (lophin)* to be a priest with thick eyebrows.

Accordingly, the explanation *lippus* (Mussaphia), meaning quivering eyes *(Rashi)*, is unacceptable, as in *lipos* meaning fat, since nowhere does it refer to "someone who has extremely fat eyelids"[11]. For *gibben*, the Septuagint has *kyrtos*, and the Vulgate has *gibbus*, corresponding to the opinion of Rabbi Chanina ben Antigonos in the above-cited *Mishnah*. The "falling out" of the eyebrows is a well-known early symptom of leprosy.

2) *Dak* is clouding of the cornea[12].

Actually, *dak* means *tenuis*, as it is used elsewhere in the Bible[13]. Only Ibn Ezra explains it in this ·sense to mean "short of stature" or small; and *Targum Jonathan* translates it as *nannos* or midget. However, the Talmudic literature concurs that the words *in his eye*[14] refer to the preceding word *dak*, as being derived from *dok* meaning a thin veil, or nubecula, in the eye[15]. The Septuagint translates *dak* as *ephelos*, which has the same sense as that used by Aelian[16]. The Vulgate has *lippus*, which is certainly not correct; because "gauze in the eye" can only be understood to mean clouding of the cornea, and not watery-eyed. *Rashi* interprets *dak* as *tela*. *Kimchi* translates *dak* as "skin", as people even today use the expression "film on the eye".

*Dak* produces a diminution in visual acuity. If the cloudiness disappears after 30 days of observation, it is considered to be a "temporary *dak*" and the priest is fit for Temple service, and the animal is suitable to be sacrificed. The *Tosefta*[17] defines *dok* (sometimes *rok*) to refer only to that which floats on the eye, meaning a superficial coating, as opposed to the "deep cloudiness" the *ypochysis*, which is also a disqualifying blemish, but which is not called ·*dok*. A *Beraitha*[18] warns against confusion between the film which floats on the eye, and the corneal nubecula which is sunken within the substance of the eye. Later scholasticism perceived the contrast of both teachings, and resolved the contradiction by stating that the decision regarding opacifications is based primarily on their color (pigmentation); also on the possibilty of removing them from the eye, and finally on whether or not they are superficial or deep: only a black spot which is sunken in the eye, or a white spot which is floating is considered to be a *mum* (disqualifying blemish)[19]. The former perhaps refers to corneal cicatrice with umbilication, whereas the latter might represent nubecula[20].

---

7. Levit. 21:20
8. Bechoroth 7:2
9. *Tosefta* Bechoroth 5:2 cites Bechoroth 44a where Rabbi Gersom reads *shakabya*
10. Bechoroth 44a
11. Levy. *Neuhebräisches und Chaldäisches Wörterbuch.* Leipzig 1876-1889
12. popularly translated as cataract
13. Genesis 41:3
14. Levit. 21:20
15. Bechoroth 6:2 and 38a. *Sifra* edit. Weiss p.95c, according to Isaiah 40:22
16. *Nat. Anim.* 15:18. *Tous ophthalmous achlys katechei kai epheloi ginontai —* *Ephelos* is the speckle found on the skin of the face i.e. freckle, and on the pupil: *ephelides echon eis ten opsin.*
17. *Tosefta* Bechoroth 4:2
18. *ibid* 38b
19. *ibid*
20. Maimonides, in his commentary on Bechoroth 6:2, also interprets the former case as an "indentation", and the latter case as "white which superficially covers the black", probably a staphyloma of the cornea. "When, however, a black berry occurs in the black of the eye (prolapse of the iris), it is also called *dok*, but it is not a disqualifying blemish", because the latter is a purely dogmatic concept.

Rabbi Eliezer allowed an animal afflicted with *dokin* to be offered as a sacrifice[21]. Concerning the Passover sacrifice, there are numerous opinions[22]. Those who considered *dokin* to represent disqualifying blemishes began to comment on the requirements of the sacrifice thirty days before the Passover festival, so that everyone should observe whether or not the nubecula on his animal disappeared[23]. Rabbi Yochanan was of the opinion that there was nothing intrinsically objectionable to offering these blemished animals to idols, since, in the Jewish legal sense, they cannot serve as sacrifices to God. However, since it represented idol worship, it was not permitted[24].

3) *Teballul.* "*Teballul* in his eye" (or in one eye) is actually *mixtus in oculo suo,* whereby, according to the explanation of the *Mishnah,* "the white crosses over the (dark) border and mixes into the black". Whereas, therefore, *dak* is only the thin gauzy cloudy dimness, *teballul* is the opaque corneal spot which extends over the iris into the pupil and simulates an extension of the sclera. Rabbi Jose sees an allusion to this affliction in the phrase from Psalms: *their eyes stand forth from fatness*[25], where the "fat of the eye" is understood to refer to the sclera[26] just like the *pion* and *steatodes* of Aristotle[27].

According to the principle that there should not be a disqualifying blemish in the white of the eye, in the above sense, the opposite situation, in which the black extends into the white (coloboma), was not considered to be a disqualifying defect. Noteworthy is the opinion of Raba[28] that such a spot on the cornea does not impair vision. *Rabad* shared this opinion[29]: "*teballul* is not the result of an illness, but is inborn, so that the white expands and extends internally from the rim (*sira* or corneal-scleral notch)[30], and first reaches the outermost black", (as opposed to the "black in black", the pupil)[31]. He thus leaves the pupil unaltered.

Kotelman[32] correctly points out that *teballul* must here refer to an affliction of only one eye, since an opaque cloudiness on both eyes which extends into the pupil would render the individual blind, and the Bible has already excluded a blind priest from Temple service[33].

The *Targum* translates our word *(teballul)* as *chiliz* (*Targum Jonathan* has *yechalzeva*), which ordinarily serves as a variant of the word *chilzon*[34]. According to Kohut, it is equivalent to the Arabic *chalis* which means *cujus albus color nigro commixtus est,* and is consequently very appropriate. The Vulgate has *albuginem habens in oculo suo.* The Septuagint has *ptillos tous ophthalmous,* meaning without eyelashes; this is contrary to tradition.

4) An animal which is afflicted with *yabeleth* should not be brought as a sacrifice[35]. This word occurs often in the Talmud, and is always used in the sense of an excrescence, whether there is bone-like material therein or not. The latter is also called *dildul* or *pendula cutis* (*Rashi* has *verrue* meaning verrucous). A *yabeleth* can occur on any part of the surface of the body. According to Rabbi Chanina ben Antigonos, if a wart occurs on the eye of an animal, it renders the animal unfit to be offered as a sacrifice[36]. Ibn Ezra equates the Biblical word *yabeleth* with *teballul,* but his

21. Zebachim 9:3 and 85b. Actually it was Rabbi Akiba. (F.R.)
22. Abodah Zarah 5b
23. *ibid* 51a
24. Jerushalmi Pesachim 9; 36d and *Tosefta* Pesachim 8:11
25. Psalms 73:7
26. Bechoroth 38b
27. *Histor. Anim.* Book 3 Chapt. 18 No. 89
28. Bechoroth 44a
29. on *Sifra* p.95c
30. see above Chapter 2, Part 3:1

31. Aristotle. *Hist. Anim.* 4:80. *To melan kai to entos melanos, ten kaloumenen koren* meaning: the black & the center of the black, the so-called pupil.
32. *Die Ophthalmologie bei den Alten Hebräern.* Hamburg 1910 p.210
33. Levit. 21:18
34. *vide infra*
35. Levit. 22:22. The Vulgate has *impetiginem habens.* The Septuagint has *myrmekionta,* meaning warty. See Celsus 5.
36. Bechoroth 6:10

postscript: "in general we rely on tradition and not upon our own deficient knowledge" seems to indicate that he was not satisfied with his own explanation. Rabbi Chanina is plainly of the opinion that *yabeleth* is a wart of the eyelids or the like[37]. The *Gemara* explains[38] that since a bony *yabeleth* does not occur on the eye, it must refer to an outgrowth from the white of the eye. The *Gemara* also distinguishes between a *yabeleth* which has hair on it and one that is hairless[39]. The former might refer to a dermoid, as Bayer portrays in the *bulbus* of a cow[40].

Karna[41] gave a foolish answer to Samuel, to which the latter retorted: "May a horn *(karna)* grow between your eyes"[42]! Has such a case ever been seen?

In addition to the above-mentioned Biblical blemishes, the *Mishnah*[43] enumerates several others, namely:

5) *Chalazon* and 6) *Nachash*. The *Mishnah* and *Tosefta* consider these two names to represent different diseases, whereas the *Gemara* and later commentators consider them to have identical meanings. Rabbah, the grandson of Chana, said[44]: Rabbi Yochanan told me: an old priest who lived in our neighborhood once showed me a first-born animal and said to me: this *chalazon* which you see on this animal is that which the Sages called *nachash*.

Accordingly, *chalazon* is the popular name, and *nachash* is the technical term.

There can be no doubt that Benjamin Mussaphia, physician in Hamburg about 1650, is correct in his explanation that *chalazon* is the Greek *chalazion*. Indeed, to the Greek physicians, *chalazion*, even today, refers only to the illness of the meibomian glands known by this name; hence a disease of the eyelids and not of the eyeball, as in the *Mishnah*, where this blemish is mentioned. But this explanation becomes acceptable if one interprets *chalazon* to refer to pterygium, as does Maimonides[45]. Folk medicine may have considered it to be a sty on the eye.

Since *chalazon* (*chilzon;* Arabic *chilzuna*) is a frequent designation for the snake, and since *nachash* to the Talmudists means snake, the non-physician commentators interpreted the above two expressions to refer to an illness where the eyeball is covered with a white or sometimes snake-like film similar to that seen on items over which a snake crawls[46].

7) *Enab,* meaning grape, corresponding to the Greek *staphyloma,* according to the explanation of Galen[47], refers to that condition where the pupil swells, because of a tumor and dolor, and takes on a form resembling a grape, but with a white color. Celsus[48] has *acino similis,* and *Rashi* has *maille* meaning a speck in the eye[49].

---

37. ibid
38. Bechoroth 40b
39. see *Tosefta* Bechoroth 4:2 and the commentaries thereon.
40. *Bildl. Darstellung des Gesunden und Kranken Auges unsere Haustiere.* Vienna 1892. Plate 14 Figure 2
41. literally: horn
42. Shabbath 108a
43. Bechoroth 6:2
44. Bechoroth 38b
45. "if excessive flesh sprouts out of the eye (excrescence) and enlarges until it covers part of the black. This affliction is known among physicians by the name *taphara*". According to Gauhari, *zaphara* refers to: *cutis parva oculum tegens.* See also Rabad's commentary on Maimonides' *Biyath Hamickdash* 7:5: "*chalazon* is a red wall, which extends onto the black". According to Kohut, *nachash* is equivalent to the Arabic

*nahz,* which to Gauhari means: *caro compacta et pulposa,* and which others render: *quando sub aut infra oculum magna moles est carnis prominentis.*
46. Rashi and Rabbenu Gersom state that *chalazon* is equivalent to *limace* meaning snake. Rabad on *Sifra* p.95c states that *chalazon* has the form of a snake. *Tosefta* Bechoroth 4:2 only states "*chilzon* as is known, *nachash* as is known".
47. Introduct. 16. (Kühn 14:775). To the Arabs *inabah* means *bacca uvae* as well as *tuberculum, pustula membris humani adnascens.* The variant *eceb* is a copying error.
48. Celsus 7:7
49. Thusly according to the dictionaries. In Littré, however, *maille* is equivalent to "*masche, espace circonscrit par des capillaires ou d'autres elements anatomiques, ramifiés et entrecroisés*".

*Enab* is probably related to the Talmudic *enabatha*[50]. The Talmud states that: "*enabatha* (a berry-like excrescence?) is a forerunner of the angel of death. What is the remedy for it? Rue[51] in honey[52], or celery in *tila* wine[53]. While this is being prepared, one should take a wine berry (i.e. grape) resembling it in size and roll it over the *enabatha,* a white berry for a white *enabatha* and a black berry for a black *enabatha*".

The older commentators interpret *enabatha* either as an *ababua* meaning pustule, *malandre (Rashi)*[54], or as "a blister which sprouts on a person's body. If it is black, it heralds danger" *(Rabbenu Chananel).* One might consider that it refers to a fungoid glioma of the retina, or to a sarcoma of the choroid, either of which could serve as "the forerunner of the angel of death". One can naturally not draw any conclusions from the recommended therapy, as is true of folk medicine in general.

8) *Chawarwar*[55]. Since *chiwar* means white, *chawarwar* probably again refers to a type of corneal clouding, perhaps, as *Rashi* suggests, a type of punctate keratitis. The *chawarwar* is called chronic (or persistent) if it lasts uninterruptedly for 80 days. According to Rabbi Chanina ben Antigonos, one must examine the patient three times during this period, because this affliction usually comes and goes.

9) *Mayim,* water (in the eye). All of antiquity and the Middle Ages until the beginning of the eighteenth century believed that a grey cataract resulted from the fact that water from the brain flowed through the optic nerves, which were thought to be hollow, into the eyeball, and settled there between the iris and the lens. In this sense, the Egyptians speak of the "ascent of the water"; the Arabs speak of the "flowing of the water"[56]; and the Greeks and Romans, respectively, speak of *ypochysis* and *suffusio oculorum.* The *mayim* of our citation[57] probably has the same meaning.

If someone strikes his slave on the brain and water is expressed therefrom and covers his eyes, the owner must give his slave his freedom[58].

Our term "cataract" originated with the Salernitans in the eleventh century, and was unknown in antiquity in the sense that we know it today. It also includes the concept of "flowing downward".

The Talmudists consider this malady to be persistent (or chronic) if the animal first received fresh and then dry grass from a wet meadow for its fodder, without the cloudiness of the cornea disappearing[59]. Rabbi Simeon ben Eleazar is of the opinion[60] that when an eye tears, it is a sign that "the water" is transient. The cessation of the secretion of tears, however, indicates a persistent affliction. He thus obviously holds that a condition of irritation of the eye is a favorable prognostic sign, — or the diagnosis is in doubt.

10) If the eyelid or *ris* of a firstborn animal is pierced or defective or slit, then it is considered to be a disqualifying blemish[61], perhaps because one held the opinion, with Aristotle[62], that wounds of the lid are not curable (*an diakipe ou symphyetai,* meaning: if you cut it, it doesn't heal). A priest is unfit for Temple service if his eyelashes have

50. Abodah Zarah 28a
51. *tigna* which is *teganon* equivalent to *peganon*. Peganum Harmala, ruta. Löw. *Pflanzennamen* p.372
52. see Plinius Valerius. Book 1 Chapt. 16: *ad lacrymosos oculos: ruta sicca et melle Attico aequis ponderibus mixta oculos inungues: certum est.*
53. strong wine, i.e. an excitant remedy
54. see Preuss' essay concerning "Malum malannum" in *Wiener Med. Blätter* 1903, 24
55. The textual reading is extraordinarily faltering. *Targum Jonathan* considers our word to be equivalent with the Biblical *sanverim* or blindness. (Genesis 19:11)

56. for example Abulcasem 2:23 ed. Channing p.168
57. i.e. water in the eye
58. *Tosefta* Baba Kamma 9:27
59. In the *Gemara* and the *Tosefta* and in the commentaries, one finds the reasons for this test, with contradictory interpretations. This test is not perceived as a form of therapy *(Tosafoth)*
60. *Tosefta* Bechoroth 4:4
61. Bechoroth 6:2
62. *Hist. Anim.* Book 3 Chapt. 11:69

fallen out completely, or if only the stumps remain (the former is called a *thamir*), because he is repulsive to look at[63].

According to Pseudo-Galen[64], a person without eyelashes (*blepharides* in Greek) cannot see straight ahead, and has no distance vision. Instead of *thamir,* the *Tosefta*[65] substitutes *thimuz* or *thimiz;* (Rabbi Gersom and *Aruch* have *thiman*). The *Gemara* also has this textual reading, as derived from its *Aggadic* etymology: *thammu ziphin*. Maimonides does not make a distinction, as does the *Gemara,* between completely, or only partially, missing eyelashes. This distinction must have originated from a time during which the meaning of individual concepts was no longer well-known.

This falling out of eyelashes occurs most often as a result of (chronic blepharitis following) excessive weeping. According to legend[66], Leah's eyelashes fell off[67] when she wept over rumors that she would be given to Esau as his wife.

Rabban Gamliel once heard a woman weeping all night for her son who had just died. Rabban Gamliel wept in sympathy with her until his eyelashes fell out[68]. The Talmud continues that "on the morrow, his disciples discerned this and removed the woman from his neighborhood". *Rashi* remarks that this falling out of the eyelashes in one night seems most unusual, and therefore explains it as follows: "the hair on the eyelids fell down and lay curved over the eye". The preacher in the *Midrash* does not consider it dignified for a patriarch (or prince i.e. Rabban Gamliel) to cry solely out of sympathy for a simple woman; therefore the *Midrash* is of the opinion that he wept "because of the destruction of the Temple", when he heard her lamentation[69]. The same source[70] also describes "a woman who cried during the night for her attractive son who had just died, until the *risé* (lids) of her eyes fell out".

In addition to the above defects which disqualify humans as well as animals from Temple service, the following apply only to humans (priests):

11) If both eyes of a priest are higher or lower than normal, or if one is higher and (or) one is lower, or if (he is cross-eyed so that) he can see the room and the ceiling simultaneously, he is unfit to serve in the Temple[71]. The *liniz*[72] is also a person who is cross-eyed, even if in a different manner, as is the *zivar*[73].

12) *Sachi shemesh* or one who covers his eyes from the sun is also unfit to serve in the Temple. According to the *Tosefta,* he is equivalent to the aforementioned cross-eyed priest. According to Rabbi Joseph[74], the expression is a euphemism for *sani shemesh,* meaning one who hates the sun or has photophobia.

13) A *zablegan* should not function as a priest because of his unsightly appearance, unless he is known in his neighborhood, so that the townspeople are not disturbed by his appearance[75]. According to the commentaries, *zablegan* is one whose eyes run; to the Arabs, *sebel* is equivalent to *pannus*[76].

14) *Zugdus (sagdis, zagdan,* etc.) is explained in the *Gemara* as follows: any pair whose components are unequal is called *zugdus;* for example one large eye and one small eye[77], or one black eyebrow and one white eyebrow[78].

---

63. Bechoroth 7:3
64. introd. 10; Kühn 14 p.702
65. *Tosefta* Bechoroth 5:9
66. Baba Bathra 123a
67. Genesis 29:17
68. Sanhedrin 104b
69. Lamentations Rabbah 1:24 fol. 13d
70. *ibid* fol. 23b
71. Bechoroth 7:3
72. *Tosefta* Bechoroth 5:9
73. Bechoroth 44a; according to Fleischer from the word *zur* meaning to deviate or to turn sideways; Arabic *izwar.*

74. *ibid*
75. Megillah 24b; Bechoroth 43b; *Tosefta* Bechoroth 5:2
76. For example Abulcasem 2:18 p.161
77. In such a case even an animal would be unfit for Temple service. The difference must be visible to the naked eye, however, and not be established only after measuring the size of the eyes. (Bechoroth 6:10)
78. According to Levy (*Neuhebräisches und Chaldäisches Wörterbuch.* Leipzig 1876-1889) *zugdus* is derived from *zeugos* (couple) and *dis* (twice). This explanation is difficult

15) The meaning of a *ciran* is completely uncertain. According to *Aruch* and *Rashi*, it refers to a person with round orbital cavities. Maimonides, supported by a *Beraitha*, interprets *ciran* to mean lacrimating eyes[79]. The latter explanation is more appealing, since one can now place the terms in parallel: the eyes which tear to different degrees: *domoth* (from *dima*, tear), *dolephoth* (from *deleph*, eaves droppings), and *tordoth* (according to *Rashi* in the same sense).

16) If the eyes of a priest are as large as those of a calf, or as small as those of a goose[80], he is unfit to serve in the Temple.

# III

Concerning the above-mentioned forms of *dak*, the *Gemara*[81] states: "a mnemonic sign (by which to remember which of the affections of the eye is considered a disqualifying blemish) is *barka*". The commentaries interpret this to be a special designation for one type of corneal clouding[82]. Hoffmann points out[83] that the Samaritans translate the "veil of Moses"[84] as *barkaah*. Following the new dictionaries which derive *barka* from the well-known Punic word for lightning[85], we consider the Talmudic designation to· be one of many euphemisms for blindness, just as Hippocrates calls the shiny-white corneal cicatrice *paralampais*[86]. We are thus inclined to explain the above Talmudic citation as follows: *dak* only serves as a *vitium*, if it leads to blindness[87]. A denominative of *barak* is found in the legal ruling[88] that if someone rents a donkey and the latter is suddenly struck with blindness *(hibrikah)*, he is liable for damages. Even so, the explanation of this word *(hibrikah)* among the Talmudists was in dispute[89].

The Talmud repeatedly mentions an eye malady called *barkith* or *brukti*, which may be identical with the malady called *barka*. Thus one is warned against drinking water from a bowl because one can thereby easily develop this eye malady[90]. In another place[91], a remedy from folk medicine is described for this malady: dry (and pulverize) a sevenfold colored (old) scorpion in the shade; then mix one portion of scorpion powder with two portions of stibium, and drop three paintbrushfuls into each eye — not more, lest his eye split. It is also recommended[91a] that the blood of a partridge (or woodcock) be applied to the eye for the same purpose[92], whereas the blood of the bat[93] is helpful for the *yarod* malady of the eye. As a sign of this: "within

---

to accept, as is that of Kohut who derives it from the word *cagdid* meaning "the glance of the dog", since these eyebrows should be different from each other. In the writings of Aristotle, (*De Generate Anim.* 5:1 Ed. Bekker p.144 & others) an animal with eyes of different colors is called *eteroglaukos*.

79. *Targum Jonathan* also translates the word *rakot* of the Bible (Genesis 29:17) as *zirnaythan*.

80. Bechoroth 7:4

81. Bechoroth 38a

82. *Rashi* explains it as *maille* as stated above under *enab*.

83. *Israelitische Monattschrift* 1893 p.30

84. Exodus 34:33

85. the same meaning is also found in the other Semitic languages.

86. Hirschberg. *Geschichte der Augenheilkunde*. Leipzig 1899 p.29

87. This perception, however, produces great difficulties according to the above-mentioned explanation of Maimonides.

88. Baba Metzia 6:3 and 78b

89. some say it means "struck by lightning", whereas others prefer "paralysis of the feet"

90. Pesachim 111b. *Rashi:* "loss, disappearance of vision". See Deut. 28:65

91. Gittin 69a

91a. *Tosefta* Shabbath 8:8

92. On the other hand, the Talmud states the following about the blood of the same animal (Gittin 68b): "For migraine one should take a partridge (According to Lewysohn, *Zoologie des Talmuds* No. 267: heathcock) and slaughter it over the side of the head where there is pain, taking care that the blood does not blind him!" The same is said of ass's blood which is helpful against jaundice (Shabbath 110b).

93. *Krusthina*. In the parallel passage in the Jerusalem Talmud, Shabbath 8:11b, the word *ataleph* appears. *Rashi* also identifies it as such (*talpa* or mole; see Lewysohn no. 136). The *ataleph* of the Bible (Levit. 11:19) is translated by the Septuagint as *nykteris*, meaning bat. According to Rabbi Chananel, *krusthina* is the chicken.

for within, and without for without"[94]. Accordingly, *yarod* probably refers to the amblyopia of the Greeks, and, accordingly we interpret the various textual readings and explanations of commentaries[95] to mean that bat blood was also considered to be efficacious for a variety of other eye illnesses. Since time immemorial, this animal (the bat) and its blood have played a major role in the therapy of diseases among other peoples. It served as a specific remedy against trichiasis[96] and it is still used in folk medicine to this very day[97].

In the Apocryphal book of Tobit[98], the following is related from the times of Shalmaneser, king of Syria: and when I opened my eyes, the swallows' (or sparrows, *strouthia*) hot droppings *(thermon)* fell into my eyes and produced white spots *(leukomata)* on my eyes; and I went to physicians, but they could not help me. The angel Raphael was then sent[99] to help Tobit, and the son of the patient applied the gall of a fish which had jumped at him out of the Tigris on his father's eyes[100]. Since the gall stung, however, the patient rubbed his eyes and the white spots peeled off from the inner corners of his eyes and his vision was restored[101]. He was fifty years old[102] (or fifty-eight) when he lost his sight, and he recovered his vision eight years later[103].

As far as we are able to determine facts from the "fairy-tale book of Tobit", the eye illness referred to probably represented an erosion of the cornea with a resultant nontransparent corneal cicatrice. Manchart, who wrote a separate treatise on "The Leukoma of Tobit", attempts to prove that the corneal opacity was of that type which the Greeks call *paralampais* (flashing by), *nonnullis margarita oculi, Gallis le grand nuage*[104]. We will leave to the exegetes the dispute concerning the exact identification of the fish which provided the gall with the healing power. They all point out that, in general, fish gall was frequently used in antiquity to heal eye diseases[105].

Creighton[106] claims that one must "read between the lines", since gall in and of itself is ineffectual. He states that the corneal spots were punctured and then rubbed (tattooed) with a powder made from the gall and the heart of the fish: *kai dechtheis diatripsai,* "after the spot was punctured it was rubbed!" He concludes that it had to be a "powder", because the organ could not have been transported in any other form. A case of tattooing is found in Galen's writings.

Tattooing obviously does not improve visual acuity; the patient would not have regained his vision as a result thereof. Since we do not know what type of fish was involved, we cannot make any statement regarding the efficacy of its gall. Perhaps it worked like jequirity or like the gunpowder which the hunters blow into the eyes of their hunting dogs to treat corneal opacities.

Scripture relates that the eyes of Leah were *rakkoth*[107], which the Septuagint

---

94. the blood of a bird which lives within the house, i.e. a bat, is good for an illness which is within the eye. Shabbath 78a.
95. Rabbi Chananel says that *"yarod* is equivalent to *chawarwar,* whereby the black of the eye becomes white"; Rashi says *"yarod* means *teballul"; Aruch* says "skin on the eye"; Professor Pagel derives *yarod* from *yarad,* to descend, and explains it as *descensus* meaning cataract (Personal communication).
96. Papyrus Ebers. ed. Joachim. p.100; Galen. *Spl. Fac.* 10:2, Kühn 12:258; Plinius 30:41
97. "If one paints the eyes with bat blood, then one can see at night just as well as one can see during the day". Buck. *Medizinische Volksglauben aus Schwaben.* p.44. In Scotland, pigeon blood or urine of the patient are both used in identical ways for medicinal purposes *(Glasgow Medical*

*Journal* 7:1895). The latter was also recommended by Galen. *(De Comp. Ned.* 4:8; Kühn 12:796)
98. Tobit 2:10
99. Tobit 3:17
100. Tobit 6:2 ff and 11:7 ff.
101. *Kai elepisthe aop ton kanthon ton ophthalmon autou ta leukomata* meaning: the whites of the inner part of the eye came out.
102. or fifty-eight
103. Tobit 14:2
104. According to Winer. *Biblisches Realwörterbuch.* p.220:2. The original was not available to me.
105. Dioscorides 2:96; Plinius 32:36; see also Bochart. *Hierozoic.* Ed. Frankfurt 2: col 748 ff
106. *Janus* 6:357
107. Genesis 29:17

translates as *astheneis* (weak) and the Vulgate renders *lippi* (fatty). According to *Rashbam, rakkoth,* as in its usual Biblical connotation means "tender", but in the sense of pale-eyed[108]. According to an often-repeated legend in the Talmud[109], *rakkoth* means pale from crying; that is, after she heard that Rachel was to marry Jacob, Leah feared that she would have to marry Esau, since she did not recognize the intent behind the deceit perpetrated by her father (Laban), and therefore she cried until her eyelashes dropped off.

According to *Rashi,* the word *rakkoth* means the same as the Talmudic words *trutoth* and *thrutoth.* Someone who wished to test the patience of Hillel asked among other things: why are the eyes of the Palmyreans *thrutoth* (bleared)? Answer: because they live in sandy places (and the wind blows the sand into their eyes)[110]. A bride who has beautiful eyes need not be examined for blemishes; if her eyes are *trutoth* (bleared), however, then her body should be examined[111], for such eyes are not beautiful[112]. The above-mentioned *ciran* of the *Mishnah* can also be identified with our word *rakkoth*[113]. It is uncertain what is meant thereby. The commentators are in agreement that it means "round". *Aruch* concludes from the first citation that it refers to people who squeeze their eyes shut, have photophobia, and wink.

According to Buxtorf, the word *taruth* is equivalent to *teres, longum et rotundum.* Ibn Ezra on Genesis 29:17 states: "Ephraim already thought that *rakkoth* means *arukoth*" (long eyes). Maimonides[114] explains the epithet *trutoth* of the steps in the Temple as "long". Levy[115] draws attention to the Arabic *tarit* which means "to blink". Perhaps it refers to *oculi torti,* although in classical Latin *oculos torquere* only means "to roll one's eyes".

Otherwise, the expression for "blinking" is *nud,* which actually means to move back and forth. The reason why inhabitants of Mahoza on the Tigris river blink their eyes is that they live in dark houses[116]. The people of Shinar do so because they suffocate, without a light and without a bath[117].

## IV   Diseases of the Eye

The eye of a maidservant in Mar Samuel's house once became inflamed on the Sabbath[118]; she cried but no one attended her (thinking it was not serious enough to warrant desecrating the Sabbath), and her eye burst[119]. As a result, Mar Samuel propounded that an eye which waters may be treated (painted) on the Sabbath.

In our Talmudic text[120], the word is *maredah.* Buxtorf has:"*videtur commode exponi posse per fluere, stillare, saniem eructare ex significatione verbi radah. Unde Syriac 'marditha dedama': fluxus sanguinis.* Mark 5:25." Moist eczema is called *moredeth. Aruch* has the variant *marera,* from *rir,* meaning "to flow". See also the commentary of Rabbi Shimshon on Negaim 6:8. According to Kohut, in Hebrew as well as in Arabic, there is a separate verb *marad* meaning

---

108. His explanation literally translated is as follows: "*rakkoth,* beautiful; French *vers* (green), black eyes are not as beautiful as white". Neither white nor green ones exist; therefore both words are designations of nuances of colors, as one first learns by degrees to distinguish the quantity from the quality of light; see the works of Geiger & Magnus. *Geschichte Entwicklung des Farbensinnes.* Leipzig 1877.
109. *Targum Jonathan* on Genesis 29:17; Baba Bathra 123a; Genesis Rabbah 70:16; *Tanchuma* ed. Buber p.152.
110. Shabbath 31a
111. Taanith 24a
112. Nedarim 66b
113. *Tosefta* Bechoroth 5:3; Bechoroth 44a
114. Commentary on Middoth 2:5
115. *Neuhebräisches und Chaldäisches Wörterbuch.* Leipzig 1879-1889
116. Berachoth 59b
117. Genesis Rabbah 37:4; see also Shabbath 26a regarding the lack of oils for lighting in Babylonia.
118. Abodah Zarah 28b
119. *phaka.* See also Abodah Zarah 65a: Raba once said to Bar Sheshak, a Persian sovereign: "May the eye burst that wishes to see our evil", and the eye burst.
120. Abodah Zarah 28b; Jerushalmi Shabbath 14; 14d

"to flow". The *Tosefta*[121] enumerates eyes which are *merodaniyoth* (quivering) among the disqualifying blemishes.

*Rashi* derives our word from *marad*, to be rebellious: "an eye which tries to emerge, just like a person who is rebellious and steps out". See also Celsus[122]: *nonnunquam ingens inflammatio tanto impetu erumpit, ut oculos e sua sede propellat: proprie enim "proptosis" id, quoniam oculi procidunt, Graci appelant.* In Plinius[123] we find: *procidentia oculorum.* See also Abulcasem 2:20 p. 165.

Examples of dangerous eye ailments (or of danger-threatening symptoms) are given by Rabbi Judah[124]:

1. *Rira* (discharge). *Rir* is elsewhere also known as mucus spittle, and hence *rira* represents an intense mucus discharge from the conjunctivae, perhaps the blennorrhea of later writers. According to *Rashi*, it is *bave* (noam); if continuous crusts develop, it is called *xere*, like the term *xerophthalmia* used by Celsus for chronic blepharitis. Maimonides has the variant *tzir*[125], which in the Talmud refers to the juice of fish, etc.

2. *Diza*, from *duz* meaning pricking, i.e. shooting pains in the eye. *Rashi* has *espoint.* The word is lacking in Maimonides.

3. *Dama*, blood or bloodshot eyes, like the *amalops* of the Greeks. Rabbi Chananel and *Aruch* have "blood in the eye". Later writers considered *dama* to be real bleeding from the eye. The *Midrash* also relates[126]: when Judah became angry, blood flowed from his right eye.

4. *Dimatha*, tearing, epiphora.

5. *Kidcha (kidchatha)*, from *kadach* meaning to bore; hence "inflammation". The Biblical word *kadachath*, meaning inflammation or high fever[127], is derived therefrom. In our case, *kidcha* probably means "eye inflammation" in the broadest sense, similar to the *ophthalmia* of the Greek physicians.

6. *Ukla*, from *akal* meaning to eat (compare *rodens*). The meaning is unclear. According to *Rashi*, it means illness in general (but the term is never used in this sense elsewhere). Levy[128], based on Buxorf, has: consumption, tabes. Kohut translates *ukla* as self consumption, cancer.

Additional dangerous situations are the following:

7. *Ajma* of the eye[129] which, according to Margolis, based on the *Targum* of Levit. 13:6, means weakness. According to Levy, *ajma* is derived from *um* meaning "to quiver" or from *amam* meaning "to darken".

8. *Simuka*, meaning reddening. There is a difference of opinion among the commentaries as to whether it refers to reddening of the eye, or whether it refers to the wounds on the hands and feet which are also mentioned there[130]. Because of the danger, it is permitted to seek a scorpion spine on the Sabbath for the patient.

In the Talmud, by far, the most commonly used designation for an eye ailment is the expression *chash* or *choshesh be'aynav*, corresponding to the term used in folk medicine.

In practical religious terms, with the passage of time, there developed the recognition that a precise determination from the Talmud as to which eye ailment constitutes a dangerous situation is no longer possible. Although, therefore, one reverently accepted verbatim the names from the Talmud into the Codes[131], it was still

---

121. *Tosefta* Bechoroth 5:3
122. Celsus Book 6, Chapt. 6:8
123. Plinius 34:50
124. Betzah 22a
125. *Hilchoth Shabbath* 2:4
126. *Yalkut* Job 897

127. Levit. 26:16 and Deut. 28:22
128. *Neuhebräisches und Chaldäisches Wörterbuch.* Leipzig 1876-1889
129. Jerushalmi Abodah Zarah 2; 40d
130. Jerushalmi Shabbath 14; 14d
131. *Orach Chayim* 328:9

found necessary to decree that "for any illness which the physicians (or even only one physician of several) designate as dangerous, one is obligated when necessary to desecrate the Sabbath"[132]. This decree has its source already in the Talmud[133].

## V Etiology of Eye Diseases

The Talmudists, as do the ancient sages, tell of the influence of the mode of living of pregnant women on the development of their offspring[134]. Thus, if a woman eats garden cress *(thachle)*, she will have bleary-eyed children; if she eats fish brine[135], the children will have unsteady, blinking[136] eyes. One who eats eggs will have children with big eyes[137].

Demons also play a role in the causation of eye diseases.

The Rabbis teach[138] that one should not drink water from rivers or pools at night, and if someone nevertheless drinks, his blood is on his own head because of the danger of the demon *shabrire* (blindness)[139]. Folk medicine also differentiates between a daytime and a nighttime *shabrire* (according to Bergel[140], Hemeralopia and Nyktalopia) and recommends the following therapy:

Against the day *shabrire* one takes seven pieces of red meat; (spleens) from the insides of animals and places them on the shards of blood-letters. The patient sits inside the house, another person outside. The latter then calls out: "Blind one, give me something to eat!" Whereupon the former answers: "Seeing one, sit down and eat!" After he has eaten, he breaks the shards; otherwise he would be afflicted with the illness[141].

Against the night *shabrire,* one ties the end of a cord made from hair to the foot of the blind person. The other end is tied to the leg of a dog. Children should rattle potsherds behind him saying (the unintelligible words): "old dog, stupid cock." One should then take seven pieces of raw meat from seven houses, the meat having been hanging from the doorposts before, and let the dog eat them on the dung pile of the town. Then, the patient should untie the cord from his foot and say: "*shabrire* of so and so, son of the woman so and so[142], leave so and so, son of the woman so and so". And he should blow into the dog's eye[143].

If someone is thirsty at night and might therefore be tempted to drink from a river, he should, if possible, speak to another person and say: "I, so and so, son of so and so, am thirsty for water". If no one else is around, he should speak to himself and say: "You, so and so, my mother told me: beware of *shabrire, berire, rire, ire, re.* I drink water from a white goblet"[144].

One can here easily recognize the folk-beloved "cure through sympathy", as well as the *abracadabra*.

*Bath melech*[145] was also thought to be an eye demon, and is driven away with

132. *ibid* 328:10
133. Yoma 84b
134. Kethuboth 60b
135. or *monine* fish. This name is not listed in Löw's *Aramäische Fischnamen*. According to *Rashi* "small fish"
136. *Aruch* has "small eyes"
137. Kethuboth 61a
138. Pesachim 112a
139. The word is derived from *barar,* to light, and thus means "lightness" as a euphemism for blindness; just as the Biblical word *sanverim,* derived from *nur,* is translated by

Onkelos (Genesis 19:11 and Second Kings 6:18) as *shabrire.*
140. *Medizin der Talmudisten* p.51
141. Gittin 69a
142. the name of the mother was always used in magical incantations. Compare Goldziher. *Zeitschr. Deuts. Morgen. Gesellsch.* 48:360, 1894
143. Gittin 69a. To understand this magical incantation see Blau, *Das Altjüdische Zauberwesen* Strassbourg 1898 p.82
144. Pesachim 112a
145. literally: king's daughter or princess

stibium[146]. The following legal rule speaks against the aforementioned meaning: if a master strikes his slave on the brain so that the *benoth melech* (princesses) are driven out and the slave becomes blind as a result, his master must give him his freedom[147]. The artificial explanations of Brüll[148] and Kohut[149] are not satisfactory. According to Rabbi Chananel, *bath melech* is equivalent to *beth chorin* (the nobleman's daughter).

# VI    Blindness

All travelers to the Orient are in agreement that the number of blind people in that part of the world is comparatively very high. The conditions in antiquity for the occurrence of eye diseases were also not favorable — only at the time of the giving of the Torah were there no deaf or dumb individuals[150] —, and we thus find many descriptions of blind people in the Bible and Talmud, in fables and in legends[151], and in medical and legal expositions.

The Bible calls a blind person *iver*[152]; the Talmud also uses the term *suma*. *Suma* includes both someone born blind "who has never seen light"[153], as well as someone who became blind, either in one eye[154], or in both eyes. The opposite is known as a *pikeach liriyah*[155]. The Talmud then differentiates someone whose eyesight is dull *(keha)*, from someone whose eyesight is dark *(choshech)*, and from someone who is totally blind[156]. The word *suma* is also used in a figurative sense like "misled" or "deluded" or "hidden from sight" (invisible)[157] as follows:

"See the blindness of usurers. If a man only calls his neighbor 'wicked', he cherishes a deep-seated animosity against him; whilst they bring witnesses, a notary, pen and ink, and record and attest: 'so and so has denied the God of Israel' "[158]. Elsewhere, the Talmud states[159]: "see how blind are the eyes of those who take a bribe. If a man has pain in his eyes, he pays money to the physician, although he may or may not be cured; yet usurers take what is only worth one penny and blind their eyes therewith"[160]. The term *suma* is also not infrequently used in the sense of "blinded"[161]. Examples are Second Kings 6:18; Chullin 139b; Ibn Ezra on Genesis 19:11; Genesis Rabbah 53:14; in all these cases, the individuals are only blind until God opens their eyes, as He did to Hagar[162].

According to religious belief, the cause of blindness, — at least a remote cause — is a transgression committed by the affected person; the blindness is thus a Divine punishment[163]. The Bible warns sinful people[164]: *The Lord shall smite thee with madness, and blindness, and astonishment of heart; And thou shalt grope at noonday,*

---

146. Shabbath 109a
147. *Tosefta* Baba Kamma 9:27
148. to his *Jahrbuch* 1:157
149. *s.v. bath melech* 2:211
150. for "all the people saw the thunderings". *Midrash Lekach Tov* on Exodus 20:15
151. for example Sanhedrin 91a & b and 105a; Exodus Rabbah 36:2; Second Samuel 5:6; naturally the lustreless eyes of an individual with *bulimia* (Yoma 8:6) or the eye failing of someone exhausted from hemorrhoidal bleeding (Nedarim 22a) has nothing to do with blindness.
152. the word *sha'a* (Isaiah 29:9 and 32:3) meaning "smear" or "paste" is only poetic
153. Megillah 4:6
154. Chagigah 2a
155. Exodus Rabbah 3:15. Someone with perfect vision.

156. *Sifra* on *Thazria* fol 63c
157. Taanith 8b: "blessing is only possible in things hidden from sight, *samuy min*", based on Deut 28:8
158. Baba Metzia 71a. Such a person transgresses the Divine commandment (Exodus 22:24) prohibiting usury
159. Kethuboth 105a
160. literal translation of Exodus 23:8 *for a gift blindeth those who have sight.*
161. *Rashi* states: psychologically blind.
162. Genesis 21:19
163. Exodus 4:11: *who hath made man's mouth? or who maketh a man dumb, or deaf, or seeing, or blind? is it not I the Lord?* Even during the return from the exile, Jeremiah (31:7) prophesies that the blind and the lame will also participate in the march.
164. Deut. 28:28; see also Zechariah 12:4

*as the blind gropeth in darkness.* According to the Talmud[165], this means that there will be no one else able to see, so that he might guide the people back onto the correct path. Thus, the disciples of Jesus found it natural to ask their master: *who did sin, this man, or his parents, that he was born blind?*[166]

Legend relates[167] that Nahum[168] was blind in both his eyes, his two hands and legs were mutilated and his whole body was covered with boils. He brought all this upon himself because he once postponed giving food to a poor man until he (Nahum) returned, and the poor man died of hunger. Rabbi Yochanan ben Dehabai is of the opinion that people become blind if they gaze at the *locum illum* (i.e. vulva)[169]. A man did not prevent his son from uttering anti-religious mockery in the Temple; within three years, the entire family died out except for one pair of brothers, one blind and lame, the other mad and wicked[170]. He who feigns blindness, or a swollen abdomen, or a wounded thigh, will not leave this world until he actually develops these afflictions[171]. Even more explicit is the following parallel: he who wraps rags over his eyes or about his loins, and cries out: "help the blind! help the leper!" will in the end cry so in earnest[172]. Therefore, if one sees a blind person, one should say "blessed be the true judge![173"]

The Talmud also relates[174] that the eyes of anyone who looks at three things become dim: at the rainbow, at the regent, and at the priests during the benediction, (because the Divine majesty is mirrored in all three). See also the legends in Baba Metzia 85b.

In regard to the *causae proximae*, some writers cite appropriate directives in the Talmud which obviously point to a pure hygienic or pedagogic reason for blindness, and state that the warning against committing sins which might cause blindness is only a warning. Thus, it is taught: "Why did the Rabbis rule that washing the hands after a meal is obligatory? Because there exists a certain Sodomitic salt that causes blindness"[175]. We must remember that in antiquity one ate with one's fingers, and the Rabbis considered the consumption of salt after the meal to be proper[176]. One should also mention the statement of Rabbi Muna, that the unwashed hand that touches the eye in the morning is worthy of being cut off for it leads to blindness[177], and the assertion of Mar Samuel that untidiness (neglect) of the head leads to blindness[178]. Finally Rabbi Joseph states[179] that three things cause defective vision: combing one's head when it is dry, drinking the drip-drop of wine from the barrel, and putting on shoes while the feet are still damp.

Furthermore, an interpretation of Exodus 23:28 ascribed to Resh Lakish states[180] that the hornet did not cross the Jordan with the children of Israel, but remained by the bank, and injected its gall into the enemy and blinded their eyes[181].

A legend relates[182] that the she-ass of Rabbi Jannai ate a certain herb and turned blind. She then ate another herb and regained her sight. A similar *Midrash*[183] concerns two people; one was blind and one was able to see. They both ate of the herbs of the field. The blind one regained his sight and the one who had been able to see turned blind. Such tales, in which the same substance makes healthy people sick and heals sick

165. Megillah 24b
166. John 9:2
167. Taanith 21a
168. with the cognomen *gam zu* meaning "also this (is sent from the Lord)."
169. Nedarim 20a
170. Numbers Rabbah 4:20
171. *Tosefta* Peah 4:14
172. Aboth de Rabbi Nathan 3:1
173. Berachoth 58b
174. Chagigah 16a

175. Erubin 17b
176. Berachoth 40a
177. Shabbath 108b
178. Nedarim 81a
179. Pesachim 111b
180. Sotah 36a
181. Concerning this property of hornet gall see Bochart, *Hieroz.* 2, Col. 537
182. Levit. Rabbah 22:4
183. Numbers Rabbah 18:22

people, can be thought of as the beginnings of homeopathy. The ancient non-Jewish literature is also rich in such stories[184].

Finally, one should mention trauma as a cause of blindness. Even today, it is not unthinkable that a person should break an arm and a leg and lose his eyesight through a fall from a coach[185], or that a resolute woman should knock out the eye of her obtrusive lover[186]. Another *Midrash* relates[187] that when the children of Israel came out of Egypt, the vast majority of them had some form of blemish, because they had been working with clay and bricks. Either a stone fell and cut off the worker's hand or some clay got into his eyes and he was blinded. A blow to the brain is also thought to be one of the causes of blindness[188].

A first-born animal whose eye is blinded is unfit to be sacrificed[189]. — Why are the antennae of a grasshopper soft? Because it dwells among hard reeds. If its antennae were hard, it would hit some object and go blind[190].

Concerning traumatic blindness, one should also mention the barbaric custom of heathen peoples of putting out the eyes of prisoners. This is what the Philistines did to Samson[191]. Nahash the Ammonite made a condition of surrender for the besieged people in Jabesh Gilead that they allow their right eyes to be put out[192], thus rendering them incapable of waging war, since the left eye was covered by the soldier's shield[193]. Nebuchadnezzer put out the eyes of King Zedekiah[194]. In the latter case, it is not possible to ascertain whether the equally barbaric custom of burning the cornea with a red-hot iron, which was methodically used in Greek royal palaces[195], was employed[196]. Blinding of subjects as a sign of brutality of a heathen king is also described in the *Midrash*[197]. Such violence on the part of Jewish soldiers is not mentioned anywhere, and it has no place in Jewish law[198], as is the case in Hammurabi[199]. An exilarch once threatened an accused murderer with blindness[200] but did not carry out the threat, particularly because the Jews in those days no longer had their own jurisdiction over such matters. On the other hand, it is reported as fact that Herod put out the eyes of Baba ben Buta with hedgehog bristles[201]. Indeed, this descendant of heathens (Herod) was not deterred from committing even worse acts of violence and brutality.

Concerning the law of premeditated inflicted physical wounds[202], concerning false

184. Cassel. *Sindbad* p.120
185. Levit. Rabbah 31:4
186. Levit. Rabbah 8:1. A Roman lady asked Rabbi Jose ben Halafta: What has your God been doing since he finished creating the world? He answered: He is joining couples! To which she said: this I can also do. She sent for a thousand male slaves and a thousand female slaves, placed them in rows, designated one female slave for each male slave, and let them consort together one night. In the morning they came to her; one had a wounded head, another had an eye taken out, etc.
187. Numbers Rabbah 7:1
188. *Tosefta* Baba Kamma 9:27. In Sotah 13a it is stated that Esau tried to prevent the burial of Jacob. Joseph then took a club and struck Esau on the head so that his eyes fell out and rolled to the feet of the corpse of Jacob.
189. Bechoroth 5:5
190. Shabbath 77b
191. Judges 16:21
192. First Samuel 11:2
193. Josephus' *Antiquities.* Book 6 Chapt. 5:1
194. Second Kings 25:7
195. Andreae. *Alteste Geschichte der Augenheilkunde.* p.71
196. The expression used here is *iver;* otherwise it is *nakar* meaning to bore or to dig.
197. Exodus Rabbah 30:11
198. The word *nakar* in the figurative sense means "to lead astray": Numbers 16:14 and Rosh Hashana 14b. Animal blindness in the figurative sense is recorded in Baba Kamma 52a: when the shepherd is angry with his flock, he appoints an animal which is blind *(samutha)* to be the leader; i.e. God gives bad leaders to a sinful community. Yoma 69b records the case of the blinding of a demon
199. *Code of Hammurabi* No. 197, 198 & 199 where free people, inmates of poor houses, and slaves are differentiated.
200. Sanhedrin 27a. The commentaries do not interpret the threat literally. see Rabbi Chananel and *Aruch s.v. kah*
201. Baba Bathra 4a
202. Levit. 24:19

witnesses[203], and concerning the unintentional wounding of a pregnant woman[204], the Bible decrees "an eye for an eye". Whether or not this decree was ever interpreted literally cannot be established anymore. The Talmud is categorically opposed to such an interpretation, and states that the literal execution of such a decree would lead to great injustices. What should one do, for example, if a blind person blinded a person who was able to see? And if the offender, as a result of the court-imposed blinding, were to die, one would have exacted a life and an eye, for an eye (contrary to the law)! The phrase can, therefore, only refer to pecuniary compensation for the eye[205].

If someone totally blinds (*chatat*) the eye of his slave which was already partially blind (*sammaya*), the slave goes out free on that account, for the master robbed him of one of his organs[206]. During the persecution of the Jews under Trajan, the eyes of a Roman mocker were finally gouged out[207]. *The eye that mocketh at his father, and despiseth to obey his mother, the ravens of the valley shall pick it out, and the young eagles shall eat it*[208].

The cases in which individual people were miraculously "stricken with blindness"[209] or where "darkness fell on him"[210] are only mentioned here for the sake of completeness.

A specific therapy for blindness does not exist. Only when the redeemer will come: *then the eyes of the blind shall be opened*[211]. And when God will come to heal the world, He will first heal the blind, for there is no greater affliction and no greater torment than blindness of the eyes[212].

## VII   The Lot of the Blind

Following the Oriental custom of designating unesthetic things with virtuous expressions, the Hebrews, in cases where the legal sense is not involved, called the blind *sagi nehora*[213] or *ma'or eynayim*[214], meaning clear-sighted; also *mephatcha*[215], *apertus* or *roeh shemesh*[216], one who sees the sun. In particular, no other epithet is used to describe the blind Rabbi Shesheth. Nevertheless, it is possible that this designation is an expression of tender consideration for the helpless. Before a bride, one sings the following hymn — in Babylon: "beautiful and graceful bride"; in Palestine: "no powder, no makeup and no wave in the hair, and still graceful" (refrain?)—whether she is lame or blind[217], without regard to the Biblical command: *keep thee far from a false matter*[218]. In a legend, it is related that even Asmadai, king of the demons, did not act violently against a straying blind man, but put him back on the proper path[219]. If one's teacher is blind, one should not say to him "master, the sun has set", but rather "your prayer is ascending"[220].

Elsewhere, the lot of a blind person is a sad one: he is as good as dead[221]. After Samson was blinded, he was led about by the hand by a young lad[222]. An official who

203. Deut. 19:16
204. Exod. 21:22
205. Baba Kamma 84a
206. Kiddushin 24b
207. Semachoth 8:15
208. Proverbs 30:17
209. Genesis 19:11 and Second Kings 6:18
210. Acts 13:11
211. Isaiah 35:5 and 42:7
212. *Midrash* Psalms 146:8
213. Jerushalmi Peah 4; 19a and Jerushalmi Kethuboth 11; 34b. In Genesis Rabbah 30:9, it states that Noah was righteous only in his generation (relative, not absolute): in the street of the totally blind, the one-eyed man (*avira*, equivalent to the Arabic *awaru*, one-eyed) is called clear-sighted

214. Chagigah 5b
215. Jerushalmi Shabbath 1; 3a and Jerushalmi Shekalim 2; 47a
216. Petuchowski on Nedarim 3:7, according to *Dikduké Soferim*
217. Kethuboth 17a
218. Exod. 23:7
219. Gittin 68b
220. Kallah Rabbathi 2:16
221. Nedarim 64b: "four are considered as dead: a poor man, a leper, a blind person and one who is childless". One is reminded of the assertion of Melchthal: dying is nothing; but living without being able to see, that is a tragedy.
222. Judges 16:26

is blind and poor must be led about by his wife as a beggar[223]. It is natural that people were doubly generous with such a doubly unlucky person. If the (poor and blind) individual was a learned man, a prominent person probably involved himself to help him secure a larger income. The blind person then thanked him with kind words: "you have been gracious to one who is seen but who cannot see. May the One Who is not seen but Himself sees be gracious unto you"[224]! It is therefore quite understandable why a woman whose eye was or is in danger offered a sacrifice in the Temple[225].

Vicariously, the other senses of a blind person become much more sensitive. Thus, according to Rav Ashi, a blind child knows its mother's breast by the smell and the taste[226]. From the sound of mortar and pestle, the blind Rabbi Shesheth could recognize what was being pounded[227]. They once placed a small bone in his soup so that he should choke on it; he felt it and quietly wrapped it in his napkin[228].

Peculiar is the viewpoint of Rabbi Joseph which affirms that blind people eat without becoming satisfied; for Rabbi Assi said that one cannot compare one who sees what he eats with one who does not see what he is eating[229]. The *Midrash*[230] finds the same thought in Eccles. 5:10: *what advantage is there to the owner of goods save the beholding of them with his eyes?* The following Talmudic passage remains, for the moment, without explanation: "for every hair, a separate groove was created, so that if two hairs should suck from the same groove, they would make a man go blind"[231].

# VIII    The Blind in Jewish Law

Very early attempts were made in Jewish jurisprudence to protect the blind because of their helplessness[232]. The Bible prohibits one from placing a stumbling block before a blind person, and if you think that no one sees it, *fear thy God, I am the Lord (who sees it)*[233]. On Mount Ebal, the Levites cried out the curse with loud voices upon anyone *that maketh the blind to wander out of the way. And all the people shall say, Amen*[234]. Stones should be thrown in the middle of the road, not on the sides where the blind walk[235]. Someone who insults his blind fellow is liable for damages of indignity just as if he wounded someone with normal vision[236].

In later times, one attempted to make life as easy as possible for blind people: a priestly woman who is able to see helps one who is blind[237]. According to Rabbi Judah, a blind person is exempt from all religious commandments which call for action[238]; in particular, he is exempt from participating in the pilgrimages to the Temple, he does not have to go into exile if he killed someone unintentionally[239], and a blind woman suspected by her husband of having committed adultery does not go

---

223. Jerushalmi Kethuboth 11; 34b. Rabbi Jose the Galilean divorced his wife because she conducted herself improperly. She then married a senator. The latter became poor and blind, and she led him from door to door to beg etc.

224. Jerushalmi Shekalim 5; 49b; see also Chagigah 5b: When Rebbe and Rabbi Chiya came to a town, they were told: here lives a young scholar who is blind. Rebbe visited him against the advice of Rabbi Chiya who said that he (Rebbe) should not lower his princely dignity. When they were taking leave of the blind man, the latter said: you have visited one who is seen but who cannot see. May you be granted to visit Him who sees but is not seen!

225. Menachoth 64b

226. Kethuboth 60a

227. Gittin 23a

228. *ibid* 67b

229. Yoma 74b. Enlightening is the additional statement of Abaye that one should therefore eat only in the daytime when it is light.

230. Genesis Rabbah 65:13

231. Baba Bathra 16a

232. in Pesachim 108a, the blind Rabbi Shesheth is called *asthenes*

233. Levit. 19:14

234. Deut. 27:18

235. *Tosefta* Baba Kamma 2:13

236. Baba Kamma 8:1. The opinions differ in the *Tosefta* and *Gemara*

237. Niddah 2:1

238. Baba Kamma 87a. For religious ceremonies see *Tosefta* Berachoth 3:14 and *Tosefta* Megillah 4:28

239. Makkoth 2:3

through the ordeal prescribed in the Bible for a suspected adulteress[240]. In fact, according to Rabbi Judah, the death penalty or judicial flogging cannot be imposed upon a blind person. No one supported Rabbi Judah in his contention, however[241]. Furthermore, the opinion of Rabbi Meir that a man cannot claim not to have found virginity in his blind wife does not prevail[242], because she would eventually surrender helplessly to her husband's libel, as soon as she or her parents would be denied the appeal of the court. On the other hand, one was fearful that a blind maiden would be less strict in preserving her virginity if she knew she was free of liability[243]. No Rabbinic law can dispense with an obligation that is based upon a Biblical prohibition (i.e. adultery). For the same reason, a blind man cannot go out on the Sabbath with his cane[244], a seemingly harsh rule.

However, in spite of all humanitarianism, in order not to neglect the proper administration of justice, a blind person was considered to be physically inferior because of his disability. Thus, a blind person cannot testify in court about things which require visual identification. Naturally, this rule is not changed if he by chance has regained his sight at the time of the court proceedings[245]. Indeed, according to Talmudic law, the opposite case is also true, that is, if the witness was able to see at the time the event occurred but was blind during the time of the court proceedings (he is disqualified as a witness). However, if someone was blind between these two times, but was able to see both at the time the event occurred and at the court proceedings he is permitted to give evidence[246]. The same is true of the one who writes or delivers a bill of divorce. He must be able to see both at the time he receives it and at the time he delivers it to the woman in order to be able to establish with certainty the identities of the parties involved[247]. For the same reason, legal proceedings against a "rebellious son" cannot be undertaken if one of the parents is blind[248], and a blind husband cannot bring court action against his wife for infidelity[249].

A blind judge is under no circumstances permitted to render decisions. A judge blind in one eye is only allowed to render a decision as part of a three judge panel which is judging a case involving monetary strife[250]. Even if once in a lifetime "a blind man finds the window" (successfully without falling)[251], one can never count on it. A blind or one-eyed priest is also unfit to serve in the Temple[252]. In particular, he may not examine any spots on people, clothing or houses to determine whether or not they are leprous. For the latter purpose, even only weakness of vision is sufficient ground to disqualify the priest[253].

Blindness is listed among the severe disabilities. According to some ancient authors, if the husband became blind, the wife should be entitled to claim a bill of divorce as well as the previously stipulated widow's jointure. Some even tried to force the husband to do so, even if the wife was opposed to it. In later times, when divorces

240. Sotah 27a
241. *Tosefta* Makkoth 2:9
242. *Tosefta* Kethuboth 1:5
243. Jerushalmi Kethuboth 1; 25c
244. *Tosefta* Betzah 3:17
245. Maimonides. *Hilchoth Eduth* 9:12
246. Baba Bathra 128a & *Tosefta* Sanhedrin 5:4
247. Gittin 2:5. The question raised by the *Gemara* (Gittin 23a) that a blind man should therefore not be permitted to cohabit with his wife (nor a normal man at night) is resolved by the answer that he can recognize her voice.
248. Sanhedrin 8:4 and 71a. because they must say to the court "this our son" (Deut. 21:20)
implying that they see him. Physical blemishes on the parents weaken their pedagogic influence and partially excuse their son's behavior. See D. Hoffmann's commentary on this *Mishnah,* note 41
249. Sotah 27a
250. Sanhedrin 34b, in opposition to Rabbi Meir. See *Bertinoro* on Niddah 6:4
251. Baba Bathra 12b is equivalent to the phrase "even a blind cock finds one grain"
252. Levit. 21:18 where both the blind and the one-eyed priest are meant. *Sifra* on *Emor* 2:3 fol. 95b. The Arabic *awaru* only means "one-eyed".
253. Negaim 2:3

became more and more restricted, it was decreed that the woman, if she so desired, was permitted to leave her blind husband, but was not entitled to collect the widow's pension, because she shared happy times with him and is now deserting him as a result of his misfortune[254].

If an individual intentionally blinds another, he is liable for damages; acquiescence in advance by or a request from the blinded person is legally invalid and the perpetrator is still liable[255] — unless it was done for healing purposes and at the request of the patient[256]. Restitution is to be made according to the general principles set down for physical injuries. If a man intentionally strikes out the eye of his slave and blinds him, or if he strikes a partially blinded eye and renders it totally blind, then he must give his slave his freedom. If the blinding occurred as a result of carelessness, the punishment for the owner is the same, since the owner is obligated to prevent any harm from coming to his slave. Therefore, even a physician who in treating his slave accidentally blinds him, must give him his freedom[257].

# IX   Therapy

The therapeutic remedies mentioned in the Talmud for eye disorders can be divided into three large groups: liquids, salves and non-medical measures. All of these are used locally[258]. Dealing first with the last category, one placed green leaves on inflamed eyes for cooling purposes, as is done even today; kusbartha (coriander) was particularly favored for such compresses; however, it was considered by some to be injurious to the eye[259]. Also used for eye compresses were the various types of gourds, with the exception of the species truza which was exclusively used for medicinal purposes and therefore prohibited on the Sabbath[260], and gargira which is eruca sativa (garden rocket), which Plinius also praises[261]. Rabbi Huna said: if one finds (gargir) garden rocket he should eat it, if he can; and if not, he should pass it over his eyes[262]. Rabbi Papa warns against eating gargira metzranaah. The Biblical oroth[263] is the same as gargir, and is so named because it enlightens the eyes[264].

It must also have been considered therapeutic to "place a vessel over the eye", as was once done for Rabbi Akiba when he was afflicted with eye pain[265], for the Rabbis even permitted it on the Sabbath. Rashi explains this therapy by pointing out that even in his own time it was customary to place a metallic object, such as a knife or a bowl, on the eye in order to cool it. Alternatively, a metal ring was placed around it[266].

It is uncertain to what extent the aforementioned plants were designated as "eye remedies".

Surgery on the eye was not at all considered in the Talmud. The proverbial expression "first cast out the beam from your eye and then cast out the toothpick from your brother's eye"[267] is only a maxim. The miraculous healing of the blind by placing one's hands on[268] or touching the eyes[269], and the advice that if your eye offends you, pluck it out and cast it from thee[270] are only mentioned here for the sake of

---

254. Kethuboth 7:7 and 77a; Maimonides' Hilchoth Ishuth 25:11
255. Baba Bathra 8:7 because it must be assumed that the acquiescence was only given in hastiness
256. Tosefta Baba Kamma 9:32
257. Kiddushin 24b
258. Tosafoth on Shabbath 109a, opposed to Rashi
259. Shabbath 109a. Kusbartha, according to Löw, Pflanzennamen p.209, is coriander. Galen used to place green wine leaves on the forehead. De Comp. Med. 4, Kühn 12:79

260. Rabbi Chananel cannot provide a more precise identification of truza, nor does Löw
261. Hist. Natur. 20:49
262. Yoma 18b
263. Second Kings 4:39
264. or means light
265. Jerushalmi Shabbath 14; 14c
266. Sanhedrin 101a
267. Baba Bathra 15a, known from Matthew 7:5 and Luke 6:42
268. Acts 9:17
269. Matthew 9:29 and 20:34
270. Matthew 5:29 and Mark 9:47

completeness. A magician took his eye out, placed it in his hand, and then put it back in its normal place[271].

Among liquid eye remedies, Samuel said that, in general, all liquids used for dissolving collyrium heal, but simultaneously darken the eye and weaken one's eyesight, except water, which heals without darkening the eye. The Babylonian Jews otherwise considered the use of plain water[272], as was done in Galilee, to be a last resort, because of poverty[273]. Galen's complaint: *populos remedia* (prescriptions) *cupit*, and the empirical principle of the wise Plinius: *minus credunt, quae ad salutem suam pertinent, si intelligunt*[274], are valid for all times.

Among other liquids (used to dissolve collyrium), one should mention wine in which one also dipped pieces of bread in order to use them as compresses[275]. In all of antiquity, spittle was considered to be especially potent therapeutically for the eye, particularly if it was derived from a prominent person. Well-known is the story related by John[276] that Jesus healed a man who was born blind (*typhlon ek genetes*), in that he (Jesus) *spat* (*ptysas*) *on the ground, and made clay of the spittle, and anointed the eyes of the blind man with the clay*. Also renowned is the report of Mark[277] that Jesus restored the sight of a blind man by spitting in his eyes. Roman historians describe a similar miraculous effect of the spittle of Vespasian[278]. The Jews did not have sovereigns at their disposal anymore, and had to be satisfied with (the spittle of) lower echelon, but nevertheless outstanding, personalities, namely the firstborn, who were originally destined to be priests[279]. Thus, relates Rabbi Chanina, when people came to Abuha, he told them: "go to my son, for he is a firstborn and his spittle heals"[280].

In England and France today, the spittle of the seventh son of the same couple is said to have extraordinary efficacy[281]. In England, spittle belongs to the midwives' household remedies, and there resulted from its use many chronic cases of *ophthalmia neonatorum*[282]. Human milk, together with the spittle of both mother and father, was also utilized in Steiermark to treat blenorrhea of the eyes[283]. From personal observation of the customs of old women in the Mark of Brandenburg, I know that they used to lick people's eyes when they deemed them diseased, particularly the eyes of children.

The spittle of a fasting person (*saliva jejuna*) was thought to be particularly efficacious[284]. He who is so inclined can see therein an antiseptic treatment of eye maladies; for, as Edinger reports[285], spittle of a fasting person contains a large quantity of potassium sulfocyanide which has an antibacterial effect. In any event, there never existed a doubt as to the healing power of spittle, and even up to this century it is praised by serious therapeutists.

By far, the most widely used form of eye remedy was the paste which was called collyrion, after the form of the bread known as *kollyra*. In later Greek, collyrion became *kollourion* (for example in the Septuagint), from which developed the Talmudic *kilur* and Aramaic *kilurith*. In cases of need, these pastes, together with some

271. Jerushalmi Sanhedrin 6; 23c
272. as opposed to wine or milk
273. Shabbath 78a
274. *Hist. Natur.* 29:8
275. Shabbath 109b
276. John 9:6
277. Mark 8:23
278. Tacit. *Hist.* 4:81; Sueton *Vespasian* 7; *Dio Cass.* 66:8
279. *Rashi* on Numbers 3:12
280. Baba Bathra 126b. According to *Rashi* it refers to the healing of eye illnesses but according to Rabbi Gersom the case is one of leprosy or other wounds. For *lichenas*

*leprasque,* saliva jejuna is also helpful. Plinius 28:7; Galen. *Fac. Simpl. Med.* 10:2
281. *Nederl. Tydschr. voor Geneeskd.* 1898, 2:467
282. Becherton, in *Liverpool Med. Surg. Journal* 1897 Jan. p.85
283. Fossel. *Janus* 1899 p.538
284. Plinius 28:22; *St. Mark Emp.* Chapt 8, etc. Shabbath 108b: "Samuel says: saliva jejuna may not be applied to the eyes on the Sabbath".
285. *Deutsche Medizinische Zeitung* 1895 p.294 and 1898 p.243b; also *Berl. V. fur Innere Medizin* 18 March 1895

liquid, were rubbed into an ointment[286]. For the application (literally: rubbing) of these pastes, one used either water[287] or a liquid to which one ascribed some healing properties, such as wine[288], human milk[289], dew[290] and eggwhite[291].

The Talmud gives no details concerning the ingredients of the paste itself. It is only mentioned that a collyrium to which flour was added, does not have to be destroyed before the Passover festival[292], as does all other sour dough. Also mentioned is a collyrium that contained bitter substances, so that a stew later cooked in the same utensil still has the bitter taste of the collyrium[293]. All we know about the famous "collyrium of Mar Samuel"[294] is its name. Some heathens even had the custom of tasting the collyrium before applying it to the eye[295].

It was uncertain whether or not the poison which heathens were suspected of adding to a collyrium had any local or generalized effect. Rab thought that the poison was drawn into and discharged from the mouth[296]; it could be eliminated by gargling. On the other hand, the eye illness (dimatha) already produced by the poison remains and might lead to blindness. Levi doubts that the poison can be eliminated in the above manner: "he who wishes to die should have his eyes anointed by a heathen"[297].

The most rarely used of eye remedies is the xerocollyria or powder, sam in Hebrew and samma in Aramaic. It is related that Mar Samuel was Rebbe's personal physician[298]. When the latter contracted an eye disease, Samuel said: "I will fill the eye with samma". He answered: "I cannot bear it". "Then I will apply an ointment to it," said Samuel. "This too I cannot bear," objected Rebbe. So Samuel placed a phial of chemicals under his pillow, and he was healed. The last part of this story has been the subject of many unsatisfactory interpretations. Rashi is of the opinion that "the strong power of the sam traversed the skull and the brain up to the eyes". Oppler thinks that the use of a phial indicates the use of a remedy in spray form[299]. The closest to the truth is probably cure by the power of suggestion.

The use of collyria belongs to a later period in which the influence of Greek customs on the life style of the Jews is clearly manifest. During earlier times, powders were used instead. To the Semitic peoples such a powder was called kchl[300]. The vocalization of this word changed, according to the various branches of languages and dialects: Hebrew kochel or kechol, and Aramaic kuchla. The Talmud rarely uses the designation kchl for an eye remedy. It is mostly used in the sense of a cosmetic[301].

---

286. The Arabic shajapha which designates an eye salve is the same as the Aramaic shaj'pha (Chullin 111b), from shuph, which is used as the technical term for the application of the collyrium
287. Shabbath 8:1
288. Rabbi Meir once declared a red spot on the garment of a woman to be blood, thus rendering the woman ritually unclean, although he could have said it originated from a collyrium made with red wine. (Niddah 19b). A blood-red kilur is also mentioned in Niddah 20a
289. Tosefta Shabbath 8:8; See also Plinius 28:21: De lactis usu oculo ab ictu cruore suffuso et in dolore aut epiphoris si immulgeatur, plurimum prodest...Eum qui simul matris filiaeque lacte inunctus sit, liberari omni oculorum metu in totam vitam affirmant. Galen. Comp. Med. 4 (Kühn 2:795) prescribes the following for severe pain in the eye: Koriou chylos meta gynaikeiou galaktos, an emulsion containing woman's milk

290. Jerushalmi Shabbath 8; 11a
291. Shabbath 77b
292. Tosefta Pesachim 2:3. The flour and wine which are used must naturally first have the various legally required dues discharged. Tosefta Demai 1:25; different in Jerushalmi Demai 1; 22a
293. Chullin 111b
294. Shabbath 108b
295. Jerushalmi Abodah Zarah 2; 40d
296. was he familiar with the nasolacrimal ducts?
297. Niddah 55b
298. Baba Metzia 85b
299. Rohlf's Archiv. f. Geschichte der Medizin 4:66
300. Including the Egyptians from whom it probably originated
301. Also as a coloring material for (prohibited) tattooing (Makkoth 3:6); and in case of need for the prescribed (Levit. 17:13) covering of blood. (Chullin 88b).

Rabbi Nachman said that until the age of forty years *kuchla* improves the eyesight; thereafter it only preserves but does not improve it, even if one were to take a weaver's pin as a paint stick (for the eye salve)[302]. "Here one clearly recognizes the illness trachoma which is endemic in the Orient, and which most often causes few symptoms during the prime of life, but which produces visual difficulties related to a corneal film during the course of the years"[303].

Finally, one should certainly mention the not-too-certain report of an eye prosthesis, a golden eye:

"If a man swears not to marry a certain woman because she is ugly, and later it turns out that she is beautiful, he is still permitted to marry her in spite of his oath, because his original assumption was erroneous. According to Rabbi Ishmael, this rule is even valid if the woman was indeed ugly at the time he swore, but later corrected her beauty blemish. In such a case, he (Rabbi Ishmael) took the maiden in question to his house, had a gold tooth made to replace a missing one and an *eye of gold,* and then gave her in matrimony to the man". This is the report of the Jerusalem Talmud[304]. In the Babylonian Talmud, however, only the golden tooth is mentioned, not the golden eye[305].

That *to us* a golden eyeball is at least as undesirable as a markedly shrunken one, naturally does not bear much weight. The fact that we use large gold fillings in incisor teeth or gold crowns on various teeth is equally only a matter of custom.

Hirschberg has "set aside" the mention of the golden eye in the Jerusalem Talmud with the assumption that a stupid scribe erroneously wrote twice "a tooth of gold"; then a clever copyist, remembering the Biblical apposition of tooth and eye[306], made the golden tooth into a golden eye. In support of his hypothesis is the absence of the conjunction "and"[307].

Nothing conclusive emerged from the controversy following Hirschberg's report[308]. The fact that mummies had artificial eyes inserted, and that many mummy coverings contain artificial eyes in the face mask, is no proof at all for our case. Greeks and Romans decorated their statues with artificial eyes, but did not use them on the living, as is evident from Martial's mockeries.[309] Furthermore, the commentator *Korban Ha'edah* (in the Jerusalem Talmud) prefers to omit "the golden eye" from the text.

The first reliable report concerning the use of artificial eyes of silver or gold is that of Ambroise Paré[310].

## X   Eyeglasses

All attempts to discover eyeglasses in the Talmud must be said to prove unsuccessful.

1. *Ispaklaria* or mirror (*specularium*)[311] does not represent eyeglasses, because one can make one from a bowl (*thamchoy*) and a bowl can be used as an

---

302. Shabbath 151b
303. Hirschberg. *Geschichte der Augenheilkunde* p.30
304. Jerushalmi Nedarim 9; 41c
305. Nedarim 66b
306. Exodus 21:24
307. *Centralblat für Augenheilkunde* 1906 p.356, according to the assertion of Mittwoch
308. Kotelmann, *Mitteilungen zur Geschichte der Medizin.* Part 22, Vol. 6:3 p.243;

Mittwoch, *ibid.* Part 24 p.514. Kotelmann *Die Ophthalmologie Bei den Alten Hebraern.* Hamburg 1910 p.366 ff.
309. Epigr. 12:23: *Dentibus atque cornis nec te pudet untero emtis? Quid facies oculo, Laelia? non emitur*
310. ed. Malgaigne. Vol. 2:603: "artificial eyes made from lustrous gold having a color resembling the natural one"
311. Yebamoth 49b

*ispaklaria*[312]. It is a foreign word for the classic *mareh*, a concave mirror.

2. Rabbi Gamliel had a tube (*shephophereth*) through which he could see at a distance of two thousand cubits across the land, and a corresponding distance across the sea[313]. This was perhaps a telescope, but certainly not eyeglasses.

3. *Okselith*[314] (*haklisim, aksilin, akseli*) is a foreign word which cannot be identified with certainty. It is variously thought to represent eyeglasses[315], eye bandages[316] and — cattle shed[317]!

## XI   Eye Make-Up

Whether the use of make-up (cosmetics) on the face was already customary among Jewish women in Biblical times is still a controversial issue among archaeologists. Nevertheless, it is completely unquestionable that even in those days, women attempted to correct nature in that they "placed *puch* on their eyes"[318]. This *puch* is said to correspond to the Greek *phykos* or *fucus* and it represents antimony sulfide. The Septuagint and Vulgate translate it as *stimmi*, meaning stibium; and the *Targum* (Syriac) translates it as *cedida*.

According to Hirschberg, "the *puch* of the Bible refers to black eye paint, not cheek rouge, like *fucus*"[319]. There is no statement in the Talmud concerning the color of *puch*. However, since there is convincing evidence from the *Midrash*[320] that it is identical with *kochol*, we can conclude that both also have the same color. *Kochol, however, was not black.* "Blood that is black as ink" is differentiated from that which is of lighter color, even as light as *kochol*[321]. A lung which resembles *kuchla* may be eaten[322]. Therefore *kochol* cannot be a dark black color. According to *Rashi* it refers to a transparent color (glaze), and not *chloros* (green) or black. Later writers[323] explain *kochol* as blue. On the other hand, the *presently* used *kochol* in the Orient, according to Hille[324], is black.

The Talmud only mentions *puch* once, but as an eye remedy, not as a cosmetic[325].

If we understand the expression of Jeremiah correctly: *that thou enlargest thine eyes with puch*[326], by applying *puch* to the eyes, one makes the eyes (palpebral fissure) look larger than they really are. Dioscorides[327] uses the epithet *platyophthalmon* (large eye) for *stimmi*, because, as Plinius says[328], it dilates the eyes of women who admix it with their eye make-up (calliblepharis). It certainly does not mean dilatation of the pupil.

In ancient days of various cultures, liquids were stored in an animal horn which served as a cup[329]. Similarly, stibium was stored in a *keren* or *cornu*. One of Job's daughters was called *Keren Hapuch* meaning cosmetic horn[330]. In later times, one used

312. Kelim 30:2; see also Ehrentreu. *Jahrbuch d. Jüdischen Lit. Ges.* 6:92
313. Erubin 43b
314. *Tosefta* Kilayim 5:26
315. Rosenzweig. *Das Auge in Bibel und Talmud*, Berlin 1892 p.25
316. Levy *Neuhebräisches und Chaldäisches Wörterbuch*. Leipzig 1876-1889
317. Kohut in his *Aruch s.v.*
318. Second Kings 9:30. See also Isaiah 54:11 and First Chronicles 29:2
319. *Geschichte der Augenheilkunde* p.30
320. *Pesikta de Rab Kahana* p.135a
321. Niddah 19a
322. Chullin 47b
323. *Yoreh Deah* 38:4; the eyelids were painted dark blue with *kochol* (Jacob. *Beduinenleben* 48); To the Syrians the color of the sky is equivalent to the Arabic *kuchli* (Bar Bablul

467); *Kuchli* is a very deep color, comparable to that of *kochol* (Mullet. *Essai sur le Minérologie Arabe.* p.37, Löw); concerning eye make-up in ancient Egypt, see the evidence in Kotelmann's *Die Ophtholmologie bei den Alten Hebraërn.*-Hamburg 1910 p.33, note 271
324. *Zeits. Deut. Morgenl. Gesel.* 1851 p.236
325. Shabbath 109a
326. Jeremiah 4:30
327. Dioscorides 5:92
328. *Histor. Natur.* 33:34
329. Ink was similarly stored...see L. Löw *Graph Requisiten* 1:185
330. Job 42:14 which the Talmud (Baba Bathra 16b) explains: "like *kurkama reshaka*" (see this expression in Löw's *Pflanzennamen* p.216); in any event, it does not mean "black".

"a tube which one cut in order to hold stibium"[331], a holder for a kohl-stick, *beth makchol*[332], or a *gubtha dekichla*, a cosmetic tube[333].

The act of painting and anointing the eyes for therapeutic purposes is designated *kachal* in semitic languages[334]. Even today, the Turks, Persians and Arabs call an eye doctor and his medicament *kohol*[335]. The make-up was effected, as we know from other sources, by drawing a cosmetic-impregnated crayon (or stick) horizontally between the closed eyelids. In the *Mishnah*, the name of the cosmetic stick, *makchol* (Arabic *mikhal* or *mikhol*) is also mentioned. It had one pointed (*zachar*, meaning virile membrum) end, and one rounded (*kaph*, meaning *vola manus*) end[336]. It is generally accepted that the latter served as an earspoon; nevertheless, the designation *ha-mekabel* meaning "which receives" (*recipiens*) used by the *Tosefta*[337] leads us to conclude that it was used as a spoon to remove the make-up from the holder[338]. It is reasonable to assume that the cosmetic stick was manufactured of various substances, depending upon the financial status of the buyer; a silver *makchol* is mentioned during the era of Rabbi Yochanan[339].

The cosmetic stick was placed in a holder called *shephophereth*; both were kept together by women in a case, *thek* or *theke*[340]. *Shephophereth* and *makchol* were also used as vaginal speculum and obturator for gynecological diagnostic purposes[341].

Painting of the eyes is totally unknown in the ancient Biblical books. Even in the times of the kings of Israel, it was done only by women with questionable morals[342], and strongly condemned by the prophets[343]. The *Mishnah*, without dispute, already recognized, however, — although somewhat disapprovingly — that it was a generally accepted natural custom[344]. *Ce que femme veut, Dieu le veut*[345]. For a man, the use of cosmetics is an offense strictly prohibited because it transgresses the Biblical command: *neither shall a man put on a woman's garment*[346]. There is no more discussion as to whether or not a woman is allowed to apply cosmetics; to be sure, there are voices which permit a woman to paint herself even on the Sabbath, although she thereby commits an act of dyeing prohibited on this day[347]. It is considered to be one of the necessary adornments of a woman which was completely permitted during the intermediate days of the Passover or Sukkoth festivals[348]. The custom of using cosmetics was so much engrained in the national consciousness that *Targum Jonathan* interprets the phrase: *the sons of God saw the daughters of men that they were fair*[349] to refer to eye paint and facial rouge. Even the early Christian communities, which, like the Essenes from which most were derived, strongly leaned towards asceticism,

---

331. Kelim 17:17
332. *ibid* 16:8
333. Berachoth 18b
334. Already in the Bible; Ezekiel 23:40
335. Stern. *Turkei* 1:164
336. Kelim 13:2. "I have only lost as much learning as the ocean loses, if someone dips the *zachar* of a cosmetic crayon into it" (Song of Songs Rabbah 1 fol 6c). See also Aboth de Rabbi Nathan 25:3 where it states that the disciples of Rabbi Eliezer only learned from him as much as the cosmetic crayon takes from the cosmetic tube.
337. *Tosefta* Kelim B. M. 3:5
338. see also *Rashi* on Gittin 69a: *makchol* is a quill or a wide, thin, wooden spoon with which one takes make-up and applies it to the eye
339. Baba Kamma 117a
340. Kelim 16:18
341. see also Chapter 13 on gynecology. See

also Makkoth 7a: Rabbi Tarfon and Rabbi Akiba said: if we would sit in judgement in court, we would never sentence anyone to death. For example, in a case of incest, they would ask the witnesses: did you see the offenders as intimate as the *makchol* and *shephophereth*? (Baba Metzia 91a)
342. such as Jezebel, Second Kings 9:30. See also Ezekiel 23:40
343. Jeremiah 4:30. See *Pesikta de Rab Kahana* 17 p.132a on Isaiah 3:16 *the daughters of Zion walk with wanton eyes*, which Resh Lakish interprets to mean: "they painted their eyes with red collyrium"
344. *Tosefta* Sotah 3:3 "The Sotah painted her eyes, therefore they are now popping out"
345. God wants what a woman wants
346. Deut. 22:5
347. *Tosefta* Shabbath 10:13; Shabbath 95a
348. Moed Katan 1:7
349. Genesis 6:2

allowed their women to use cosmetics; and the vanity of women triumphed over the anger of the church fathers.

Cyprian (3rd century, Bishop of Carthage) said: *illi (sc. peccatores et apostatae angeli) et oculos circumducto nigrore fucare et genas mendacio rubore inficere at mutare adulterinis coloribus crinem et expugnare omnem oris et capitis veritatem corruptelae suae impugnatione docuerunt.* God will not recognize you during the resurrection, *quando oculi tui non sunt, quos Deus fecit, sed quos diabolus infecit*[350].

Tertullian (3rd century) said: *illum ipsum nigrum pulverem, quo oculorum exordia producuntur* etc[351].

Commodianus (Africanus, fourth century) said: *oculos fuligine relinitis,* etc[352].

Painting of the eyes was only omitted as a sign of mourning. If a man's father-in-law or mother-in-law dies, he does not have the right to force his wife to apply cosmetics, but must mourn with her. Conversely, if the father or mother of a woman's husband dies, the woman may not use cosmetics[353]. The "earlier sages" had also decreed that a menstruating woman should not paint her eyes and rouge her face in order not to entice her husband; until Rabbi Akiba eliminated this custom[354].

It was considered to be particularly chaste to veil one eye, and to only paint the uncovered eye, as was the practice in large cities. In small towns, however, where both eyes were uncovered, they were both painted[355]. On the other hand, it was considered a sign of provocative coquetry to have both eyes uncovered and to paint only one of them. Even the worst prostitute would not be guilty of this. It is said that in Caesarea women blind in one eye used to paint only the good eye. This is probably incorrect[356].

Motherly vanity also treated the children in the same manner. If one finds a newborn anointed with oil, with an amulet hanging on him, and whose eyes are filled with *kuchla* (powder), one must assume that he is not a foundling left to die[357], as was the custom of the Romans and the Greeks.

The commonly used expression "to paint the eyes" is used in the same sense as our vulgar phrase "to color the eyes blue"[358]. In poetry, the glossy or reddish eyes of a wine drinker are also designated as "painted", as intimated in the *Midrash,* and as expressly stated by Nachmanides, and as recent writers have rediscovered[359].

In the *Midrash*[360], the expression "*shimshemin* of the eyes", or sun radiance, is used for the redness of the eyes of a drinker.

## XII    Dietetics for the Eye

Our dietetics for the eye is extremely scanty compared to that of antiquity. One need only consider the long list of collyria cited by Galen[361] for the strengthening of vision. I do not know of anything to report which could be considered to be "good for the eyes", and therefore I will limit myself to the warnings about certain detrimental things: draught, dust, heat, the use of the nasal handkerchief on the eyes. etc.

Among vegetable nutritional substances which are "good for the eye", the

---

350. Mignes. *Patrologie* Vol. 4 col. 467 & 469
351. *ibid* Vol. 1, 1420: *de cultu feminarum*
352. Instruct. 60. Migne Vol. 5:247
353. Kethuboth 4b
354. Shabbath 64b
355. *ibid* 80a
356. Jerushalmi Shabbath 8; 11b; the Talmud also states this is the meaning of Song of Songs 4:9 *thou hast ravished my heart with one of thine eyes*

357. Kiddushin 73b
358. Berachoth 58a and Yoma 69b. In both places, *Aruch* has a different textual reading.
359. Genesis 49:12; Proverbs 23:29; Genesis Rabbah 98:10; Nachmanides on Genesis: *chaklili* is equivalent to *kachlill*
360. Levit. Rabbah 12:1
361. Galen 12:738

Talmud mentions *thardin* (mangold or beta vulgaris), provided, according to Abaye, that it be well-cooked[362]; further, the Talmud mentions the fig, which the woman in Paradise (i.e. Eve) already recognized as being a delight to the eyes[363]; and according to Rabbi Akiba, also the various types of *pira*[364]. Wine prepared from cole sprouts (*asparagos* in Greek) should also be listed among the eye remedies[365]. Honey was also thought to have a propitious effect on the eyes, providing it was consumed after meals; if consumed before meals, it has the opposite effect[366]. Furthermore, three things do not produce diarrhea, give strength to the body, and give light to the eyes: white bread, fat meat and old wine[367]. The lung of a goose was considered to be extraordinary because it "brightens the eyes"[368]; it was therefore much in demand and cost four *zuzim,* whereas the remainder of the goose only cost one *zuz*[369]. According to Rabbi Gersom, the goose lung was dried and prepared as a medication. This was understood by very few ("only one in a thousand"), so that the high priest had to clarify whether or not a prepared lung was proper for use. According to Mar Samuel, a drop of cold water in the eye in the morning and bathing the hands and feet in hot water in the evening is better than all the collyria in the world[370].

The Talmud warns against Babylonian *kutach,* a pap made of whey, salt and stale crusts of bread, because of the Sodomitic salt which, as already mentioned, was considered to be harmful to the eyes[371]. Excessive walking destroys a small portion (1/500) of one's vision. Therefore, Rabbi Yochanan recommends that a person divide his time equally between standing, walking and sitting[372]. One is particularly warned against walking with large strides, even though zealous observance of a religious rite[373] can restore the damage to one's eyesight[374]. Samuel says that, "fish is poison to the eyes"[375] which, according to the discussion in the *Gemara,* is only applicable at the beginning of an eye illness. The Bible already mentions the harm done to the eyes by smoke[376].

Since the eye atrophies in the dark, in dark living rooms one used to make at least "a hole in the door, to nourish the eye"[377]; to which the commentaries add: "that light is for the eyes as nourishment is for the body". Even here one had to be careful because "parts of the sun[378] are more harmful than the sun itself". If individual rays of the sun shine into a dark room through a small opening, they can blind much more than if one looks at the sun in the sky, just as "drippings from the eaves" of a house are more damaging than the entire rain shower[379].

---

362. Berachoth 39a
363. Eccles. Rabbah 5:10:1 fol 15d
364. Sanhedrin 17a. The entire sentence is in Hebrew, so that the only Aramaic word *pira* cannot be understood to mean "fruit"
365. Berachoth 51a: "*Ispargus* is pleasant for the heart (stomach) and good for the eyes." *Ispargus* refers to young kale; the *kyma* of Galen (Löw. *Pflanzennamen.* p.51.) Concerning wine prepared therefrom see Plinius 13:19
366. Yoma 83b
367. Pesachim 42a. On the other hand "three things produce diarrhea, give strength to the body and take away 1/500 of a man's vision: coarse bread, fresh beer and raw vegetables"
368. there is a play on words: *reah* means "lung" and *meirah* means "to make bright"
369. Chullin 49a
370. Shabbath 108b. See also Deut. Rabbah

8:4 where it states "the commands of God are a collyrium for the eye and a compress for wounds". The community of Laodicea was given the following advice: *kollourion agchrisai tous ophthalmous son ina blepes,* meaning: he smeared collyrium on your eyes for you to see. Revelation 3:18
371. Pesachim 42a
372. Kethuboth 111a
373. drinking the sanctification wine of Sabbath eve
374. Berachoth 43b
375. Nedarim 54b. some interpret *nuna* to refer to a specific type of fish
376. Proverbs 10:26
377. Oholoth 13:4
378. *shabrire de shimsha*
379. Yoma 28b

Patients suffering from eye diseases and ill with fever should not go to the bath-house; blood-letting is dangerous for someone with very painful eyes[380]. Talking is also harmful to such patients and therefore one should refrain from visiting them[381]. Antyllus teaches the same thing[382].

Patients with eye disorders, together with their servants, are exempt from making use of the *Sukkah* during the Festival of Booths[383].

---

380. Abodah Zarah 28b & 29a
381. Nedarim 41a

382. Oribasius 6:7 ed. Daremberg 1:448
383. Tabernacles. *Tosefta* Sukkah 2:2

# CHAPTER VII

## *DENTISTRY*

### I

To the peoples of antiquity, the pathology of the teeth was the same as it is today. Other than toothaches, the peoples in those days, as well as those of the present, only knew of caries and loose teeth. *A broken (ro'ah) tooth is like confidence in an unfaithful man in time of trouble*[1]. Jeremiah laments: *God hath broken my teeth with gravel stones*[2]. Esau wept at the encounter with Jacob, because his teeth were loose and painful[3]. A priest who is lacking teeth is not fit for the Temple service because of his unsightly appearance[4].

Vinegar is harmful to the teeth, as is smoke to the eyes[5]. If there is a wound on the tooth or gum, however, vinegar heals; only when there is no wound does it cause loosening of the teeth[6]. It is thus good for that which is bad, and bad for that which is good.[7]. Sour fruit juice, on the other hand, is efficacious for toothache and is also not harmful to healthy teeth[7a]. In case of need, one may even utilize vinegar which was produced during the Sabbatical year (when fields must lie fallow); these fruits are otherwise only permitted[8] "for nourishment"[9]. The vapors of the bathhouse are also harmful to the teeth[10]. As a result of prolonged fasting, they become black[11].

Celsus enumerates toothache among the worst agonies[12]. When one reads of the accepted methods of alleviating toothache which he recommends, beginning with a red-hot iron, it becomes understandable that the Patriarch Rabbi Judah, in the *Aggadah,* was alloted unusual grace when the Prophet Elijah appeared and liberated him from his pain by placing his (Elijah's) finger on his (Rabbi Judah's) tooth[13].

A special remedy "for the teeth" *(kakka)* is that of Rabba Bar Rab Huna: one places a garlic root ground with oil and salt on the thumbnail on the side where the tooth aches, and puts a rim of dough around it, taking care that it not touch his flesh, for otherwise white (a white rash i.e. leprosy) would occur[14]. Long lists of remedies for toothache, containing the most blatant superstitions and repugnant things from the "dirt" dispensary, are found in Plinius[15].

---

1. Proverbs 25:19. Targum: *bischtha* (bad)
2. Lamentations 3:16
3. Genesis Rabbah 78:9. Targum Jonathan on Genesis 33:4
4. Bechoroth 7:4 and 44a; *nasheru* meaning fallen out; variant is *nittetu* meaning removed
5. Proverbs 10:26
6. Shabbath 111a
7. Jerushalmi Shabbath 14; 14c
7a. Shabbath 111a
8. *Tosefta* Shebiith 6:3
9. Levit. 25:12
10. Jerushalmi Abodah Zara 3; 42d
11. Jerushalmi Shabbath 5; 7c
12. Celsus 6:9 p.380. *Maximis tormentis annumerari potest.*
13. Jerushalmi Kethuboth 12; 35a
14. Gittin 69a
15. Plinius 28:49; 30:8; 32:26

Even today, tooth extraction is certainly not one of the pleasures of life. In antiquity, however, it was a most terrible operation. First the gums were incised around the tooth; then the tooth was shaken until it was freely movable; *nam dens haerens cum summo periculo evellitur,* and then one grasped the tooth with one's fingers, and when these were not sufficient, one extracted it with a pair of pliers[16]. These pliers resemble more closely the tools of the blacksmith than medical instruments. It is this fact that probably underlies the advice which Rab gave to his son: "do not have any tooth extracted", even if he was not at all averse to "polypragmasy"[17]. Rabbenu Chananel here explains as follows: "when an eye tooth (i.e. canine tooth) is painful, do not extract it, because your eyes might suffer from that." This is similar to the teaching of Celsus: *majore periculo in superioribus dentibus fit (extractio), quia potest tempora oculosque concutere,* which the people believe to this day.

# II

The Oriental people place great emphasis on beautiful teeth. Rabbi Yochanan teaches[18]: "The person who whitens the teeth of his neighbor is better than the person who gives him milk to drink". Lovers extol one another as follows: *Thy teeth are like a flock of sheep. . .which came up from the washing*[19]. The patriarch Jacob promised his son Judah "teeth whiter than milk"[20]. As already mentioned above concerning *foetor ex ore,* teeth and mouth care play an important role. Spleen was considered by the Rabbis to be "good for the teeth", and leek was considered harmful. However, the spleen should first be chewed and then spit out, since it is harmful for digestion[21]. Prolonged fasting causes the teeth to become black[22]; unripe grapes make them blunt[23]. "For dentures" *(ledor shinne),* a salt ball is recommended[24]. Plinius also advised people to allow a little salt to dissolve under the tongue every morning on an empty stomach in order to prevent tooth decay[25].

Often mentioned is the *kesem,* or splinter, hardly the toothpick[26]. It probably represents a toothbrush bitten up, in a hardly esthetic manner, as reported about Muhammed by his biographer Ibn Hischam[27], and as was customary among the Indians[28]. In addition, fragrant wood was probably used for this purpose[29]. Muhammed recommended rubbing the teeth with *Siwak* wood[30]. The Romans used mastic wood for this purpose[31]. One was only warned against the use of a reed, since it easily splinters and might injure the gums.

Thus explains *Rashi* in *Chullin* 16b. However, in the Jerusalem Talmud[32], the reason given is "because an evil spirit rests thereon". *Calamos* is not what is meant; rather it refers to a reed knife[33], for otherwise the prohibition of slaughtering[34] and of circumcising and of cutting meat therewith[35] would make no sense at all. Epiphanias (6:12) relates that Manes was killed with a reed; on the other hand, the Manichees made their beds with *epi kalamois* (reed or cane)[36].

---

16. Celsus 7:12 p.443
17. Pesachim 113a
18. Kethuboth 111b
19. Song of Songs 4:2 and 6:6
20. Genesis 49:12
21. Berachoth 44b
22. Nazir 52b
23. Jeremiah 31:19
24. Shabbath 65a
25. *Histor. Natur.* 31:45
26. Betzah 4:6; *Tosefta* Betzah 3:18; Jerushalmi Demai 3;23b
27. ed. Weil 2:348
28. *Das Kamasutram des Vatsyayana.* ed. Schmidt. Berlin 1907 p.62
29. *Tosefta* Shabbath 5:10
30. see Hammer. *Geisterlehre der Moslimen* p.20, from Sujuthi
31. Martial. Epigr. 3:28 and 6:72
32. Jerushalmi Shabbath 8; 11c
33. *Secare, incidere arundine.* Plinius 20:2 and 32:42
34. which is allowed in Tosefta Chullin 1:5
35. Chullin 16b
36. compare L. Löw *Graph. Requisiten* 1:193

In Ecclesiastes Rabbah (2 fol. 7 d) we find: "even reeds of *chiccim* were not lacking in Palestine". Kohut equates *chiccim* with the Syrian *chacina,* meaning toothpick. This seems rather unlikely in light of the above citation from the Jerusalem Talmud; more likely it means an arrow reed[37].

It appears that such a wood chip was constantly carried between the teeth[38], perhaps to achieve a better alignment of misaligned teeth. It is possible that the following expression has the same meaning: "If one says to another: take the chip out from between your teeth, the latter may reply: take the beam out from your eyes!"[39].

## III

The teeth also played a specific role in the legal sphere. On various occasions in the Bible, it is taught: *thou shalt give an eye for an eye, a tooth for a tooth*[40]. It is most unlikely that this so-called *jus talionis* in Judaism was ever to be administered in the literal sense. It is certain that the Talmud, in the discussions of bodily injuries other than murder and manslaughter, speaks only of financial punishments which the injured party is entitled to. That this interpretation is the one which the Bible meant to impart can be established with convincing proofs[41].

In the legislation of the heathens in antiquity, the *jus talionis* itself is dealt with the most stringent consequences. According to Solon, if someone blinds the good eye of a person who is already blind in one eye, the one responsible must lose both eyes. Hammurabi teaches[42] that if a man knocks out the teeth of another man, then the aggressor must have his teeth knocked out. Further[43], if he knocks out the teeth of a very poor man, he must pay one third *mine* of silver.

If someone knocks out the tooth of his man servant or maid servant, the servant is given his freedom as a substitute for the tooth[44]. This applies even if the tooth is already loose but still usable, and also if the tooth was not completely knocked out, but became loose and unusable as a result of the blow by the master[45]. This law does not apply, however, in the case of a baby tooth of a child servant[46]. Even a physician who was drilling the tooth of his servant, and caused it to fall out, must give his servant his freedom[47].

## IV

Dental technology in antiquity was already at a respectably advanced level. The Talmud speaks of the "drilling" of a tooth, *chathar*[47a], which the commentaries interpret as "poking and scratching around the seat of the tooth". This thus refers to the elimination of tartar, and is analogous to the rule of celsus; *dens scaber qua parte niger est, radendus est*[48].

Lost teeth were replaced by artificial ones. Surprisingly, the most ancient method of strengthening (or fortification of teeth) is a skillful job on an artificial dental bridge, as evidenced by the *truskic* prosthesis of Orvieto in the fifth century B.C.E.[49]. It seems to have been a more widespread practice to tie an artificial tooth to a healthy one with

37. Löw also explains it thusly: *Pflanzennamen* p.345
38. *Tosefta* Shabbath 5:1 where it states: "one may go out (on the Sabbath) with the chip in one's teeth". See also Mishnah Shabbath 6:6 where it states: "young girls may go out (on the Sabbath) with chips in their earlobes (to prevent healing of the pierced ear)
39. Arachin 16b. The parallel statement in Baba Bathra 15b has the following wording in most codices: take the chip out of your eye
40. Exodus 21:22 and Levit. 24:19
41. Concerning the assumption of the

Sadducees that the *jus talionis* is to be taken literally see Ritter, *Philo und die Halacha,* Breslau 1879 p.133
42. Paragraph 200
43. Paragraph 201
44. Exodus 21:17
45. *Tosefta* Baba Kamma 9:27
46. *Mechilta Mishpatim* Paragraph 9 p.85b
47. Baba Kamma 26b
47a. *ibid*
48. Celsus 7:12
49. Janus 1900 p.96

gold wire. This is already mentioned in the law of the Twelve Tablets[50]. In Rome during the epoch of the emperors, removable teeth were customary, and ladies only set them aside in the still of the night, as derided by Martial[51]. Such a tooth is referred to by the Talmud by the name *shen thothebeth* meaning an inserted (or extra) tooth (*thothab* is equivalent to *thoshab*)[52]. It may be lost by the woman on the street, and can also be removed[53] to be shown to a girl friend[54].

The substance of these artificial teeth was varied. Martial scoffs at the woman who considers herself "tooth-rich" because of "bought bones and their ivory"[55]. The *Gemara* speaks of a tooth of silver, the *Mishnah* of one of gold[56]. The commentaries also mention a tooth of wood[57]. Maimonides understands the gold tooth to be a gold case which the woman placed over a damaged (or defective) tooth in order to cover this beauty blemish[58]. Such cases made of silver for covering broken teeth are still utilized today in Tibet[59].

Teeth of mummies need not be considered here; they are covered with gold only after the death of their bearer. The replacement of missing teeth and the tying of loose ones were not known in Egypt[60].

Tooth replacement in antiquity seems to have been used only for cosmetic purposes. Therefore, Talmudic writings do not mention it at all in regard to a man, for whom all ornaments are forbidden. Furthermore, the Talmud and the Codes speak of it in the chapter of "women's ornaments"[61]. The golden tooth was expensive and hence accessible only to the well-to-do woman. On the other hand, even people of middle income could afford a *thothebeth* tooth[62]. Rabbi Ishmael had a golden tooth prepared for a young maiden who wore an ugly *thothebeth* (false) tooth. When her beauty blemish was thus removed, she was able to be married[63].

The preparation of artificial teeth was the craft of *naggara* or handworkers[64]. The treatment of diseases of the teeth, however, as already mentioned[65], lay in the hands of physicians.

50. Cicero leg. 2:24
51. *Epigr.* 9:37:3, *nec dentes aliter quam Serica nocte reponas*
52. "inserted hair" woven into the natural hair. Jerushalmi Shabbath 8b
53. See also *Tosefta* Kelim 3:16
54. Shabbath 6:5 and 65a
55. *Epigr.* 1:72. *Sic dentata sibi videtur Aegle, Emtis ossibus Indicoque cornu*
56. *loc. cit.*
57. *Korban Ha'edah* on Jerushalmi Shabbath 6; 8c

58. *Hilchoth Shabbath* 19:7
59. Laufer. *Tibetanische Medizin,* 1:38
60. George Ebers in Geist-Jacobi. *Geschichte der Zahnheilkunde.* Tübingen 1896 p.9
61. *Orach Chayim* 303
62. Jerushalmi Shabbath *loc. cit.*
63. Nedarim 66b
64. Jerushalmi Shabbath *loc. cit.*
65. see above Chapter 1, Part 1

# CHAPTER VIII

## DISEASES OF THE EARS
### (OTOLOGY)

### I

Only animals whose bodies are free of blemishes are suitable to be sacrificed in the Temple. Therefore, a lamb with a double ear may not be sacrificed, provided "that only one bone is present for both"[1]. The *Tosefta* is somewhat different: "an animal whose ears are rolled together over a single cartilage *(meguphaphoth bechasisa)* may be sacrificed; but not if there are two cartilages"[2]. Even an injury to the cartilaginous portion of the ear constitutes a body blemish, whether an entire portion is missing, or whether the shell is split (without loss of substance), or whether it has a hole the size of a pea, or is dry, that is, does not bleed when pierced, or crumbles to pieces between the fingers[3]. The Septuagint also interprets the *sarua* animal, which the Bible prohibits to be brought as a sacrifice[4], and the *sarua* priest[5], to be creatures with cut off ears, *ototmeton*.

A priest who is to offer a sacrifice must also be without a blemish. Noticeable abnormalities of the ears therefore make him unfit for Temple service. The exact designations of these abnormalities were unusually varied in the commentaries, and some of the terms, even at the time of the *Mishnah,* had vanished from usage and become unintelligible (if it was not a case of narrow usage of technical terms), so that an explanation had to be added: *tzima* is one who has small ears, and *tziman* is one whose ears resemble a sponge[6]; *tzometh* is one whose ears are obstructed (or obliterated)[7]. Also described are priests whose ears are pierced with an awl[8], and finally *tzimach,* which is a person whose ears are pendulous, as seen in some types of sheep[9].

### II

If a slave, because of love of his master or of his family, rejects his freedom to which he is legally entitled, his ear is pierced with an awl in formal court proceedings[10]; because the ear which heard the following words at Sinai *for unto Me (the Lord) the Children of Iṣrael are servants, they are My servants*[11], and still wishes to be a servant for a human being, must be branded forever[12]. According to

---

1. Bechoroth 6:9
2. *Tosefta* Bechoroth 4:13
3. Bechoroth 6:1
4. Levit. 22:23
5. *ibid* 21:18
6. Bechoroth 7:4; opposite in the *Tosefta*
7. *Tosefta* Bechoroth 4:15
8. *ibid* 5:3
9. Bechoroth 44a
10. Exodus 21:6
11. Levit 25:55
12. *Tosefta* Baba Kamma 7:5

Rabbi Judah, the piercing is done in the ear lobe, whereas, according to Rabbi Meir, in the ear cartilage[13], for only at the latter site does the opening not heal and close up again[14].

The teaching that a wound of cartilage does not heal was a type of dogma to the ancients. It is found in the writings of Aristotle[15] as an axiom of general pathology. Until Fabricius ab Aquapendente, this dogma prevented the use of a longitudinal incision for tracheotomy. I have already earlier mentioned[16] a teaching of the *Mishnah* which astonishingly emancipates itself from this viewpoint, and considers even large longitudinal wounds of the trachea not to be dangerous to life.

One of the miracles of Jesus was to heal the ear — just by touching it — of a slave of the high priest, which had been cut off by one near to him[17].

The judges of Sodom passed the following decree: "anyone who cuts off the ear of another person's donkey should keep the donkey until the ear grows back"[18]. This decree is cited as an example to caution one against sophisticated perversion of the law.

# III

If someone blows into another person's ear, he must pay one-half *zuz* for the insult; according to Rabbi Jose, 100 *zuz,* and he also pays for the pain involved[19], if any. Whether necessary medical expenses must also be restored is uncertain[20]. If one pulls *(tzaran)* on someone's ear, as a Sadducee once did to Rabbi Yochanan ben Zakkai[21], or on the hair, then the compensation amounts to 400 *zuz*. These normal (or maximal) payments could be modified according to the circumstances and conditions of the involved parties[22].

If a master strikes his slave on the ear, so that he is rendered deaf, then he must give the slave his freedom[23]. If someone screams in someone else's ear, so that the latter becomes deaf, then he is immune from punishment by an earthly court; if he also touches the deaf person, however, then the assailant is also sentenced by an earthly court[24], according to the general principles of bodily injury. A person who becomes deaf is always considered to be 100-percent unfit for work[25]. In this evaluation of a deaf person, it seems noteworthy that a vow in which he pledges his own value is valid[26]. The Lawgiver Himself obviously considers it correct to set the price of a slave who became deaf as zero, the value of such a person being used as a basis for all other evaluations.

Maimonides comments as follows on those rules: "it appears to me that if the assaulted person says: 'I have become deaf and cannot hear' or 'My eye is blinded and I cannot see', he is not believed automatically since we do not know whether he may be pretending. Thus he may not receive compensation *(nezek)* for damages until he has been observed over a long period of time and it is confirmed that he has indeed lost the sight of his eyes or has become deaf."[27]

According to Raba, he who makes his father deaf should be executed, for there is no sudden deafness without an associated wound. This occurs by virtue of the fact that

---

13. *Mechilta* Exod. 21:6 ed. Friedmann p.77a; Kiddushin 21b
14. Bechoroth 37a
15. *Hist. Anim.* 3 par.61
16. Chapter five, section 16
17. Luke 22:50
18. Sanhedrin 109a
19. I prefer this explanation to the other "he struck him on the ear" (which Maimonides also has in his *Hilchoth Chovel Umazik* 3:9), because otherwise I fail to see the reason why a blow on the ear should only cost half as much as a blow on the cheek, and why, in fact, pulling on the ear is punished four times as much
20. *Tosafoth Yom Tob -loc. cit.*
21. *Tosefta* Parah 3:8
22. Baba Kamma 8:6
23. Baba Kamma 98a
24. *Tosefta* Baba Kamma 6:16
25. Baba Kamma 85b
26. Arachin 1:1
27. *Hilchoth Chovel Umazik* 2:8

a drop of blood extravasates into the ear[28], and for wounding one's father, the death penalty is imposed[29].

## IV

Concerning pain in the ear, the physician Minyomi taught that any kind of fluid is bad except the juice of kidneys. One should take the kidney of a "bald-buck", cut it crosswise and place it on glowing coals, and pour the water which comes out of it into the ear, neither cold nor hot, but tepid[30].

Other recipes recommend the following[31]: take the fat of a large black cockchafer *(Melolontha vulgaris)*, melt it and drip it into the ear. This remedy reminds one of the ear remedy of Plinius[32] which recommends the use of fat obtained by tearing off the head of a cockroach.

Another remedy is to fill the ear canal with oil; then one makes seven wicks out of green blades of wheat stalks. One lights dry garlic leaves and some white thread at one end of the wicks while the other end is placed in the ear, and the latter is placed above the fumes. When one wick is burned through, it is replaced by another. One must protect against draughts in order not to get burned. Another version is that one dips seven wicks in balsam-wood oil, setting afire one end and placing the other in the ear, etc.... Similar procedures were employed by the Bosnian folk physician[33]. The use of fumes for a painful ear is today a well-known folk remedy.

Another remedy is to take blue wool which has not been combed and place it on the ear, near a fire (so that the fat of the wool drips into the ear?). One must be careful, however, to avoid draughts.

Another remedy is to take a tube of century-old cane and fill it with rock salt, then burn it and hold it close to the ear.

These remedies are not equally efficacious for all ear disorders. The mnemonic is as follows: in dry form for wet ear sores (draining ears?) and in liquid form for dry ear sores[34]. He who has an earache should place oil on his head and "whisper"[35].

For *schichala* which, according to the commentaries, is an ear affliction (perhaps buzzing in the ears), one placed a grasshopper egg in one's ear, a practice which the Sages prohibited as a superstitious custom[36]. Plinius recommends ant eggs for hearing loss[37].

If you desire not to suffer earache, "then incline your ears to the Torah, and come unto me and hear the word of the Lord; then you will recover"[38].

## V

The psalmist who laments: *But I am as a deaf man (cheresh), I hear not; and I am as a dumb man (illem), that openeth not his mouth*[39], considers a *cheresh* to be a deaf person and an *illem* a dumb individual. In the Talmud, the term *cheresh* mostly refers to a deaf and dumb person "who cannot hear and who cannot speak" — since in most cases dumbness is a consequence of deafness[40] — yet not as invariably as the *Mishnah* claims[41], as already noted in the *Gemara* by Rabbi Yonah[42]. According to the *Tosefta*[43], *cheresh* is someone who can speak but not hear, whereas *illem* is someone

28. Baba Kamma 98a
29. Exodus 21:15
30. Abodah Zarah 28b
31. *ibid*
32. *Hist. Nat.* 29:39
33. Stern. *Turkei.* 1:221
34. Abodah Zarah 28b
35. Jerushalmi Shabbath 6; 8c
36. Shabbath 6:10 and 67a

37. *Hist. Natur.* 29:39
38. Isaiah 55:3 and Deuter. Rabbah 10:1
39. Psalms 38:14
40. In Isaiah 56:10, the Targum translates the textual term *illmim* (dumb) with the word *chursha* (deaf-dumb)
41. Terumoth 1:2
42. Jerushalmi Chagigah 1:75d
43. *Tosefta* Terumoth 1:2

who can hear but not speak. Here, too, the dictum that *in foro* these people be considered as normal individuals in all respects led to restrictions to be discussed later.

Consequently, in many cases it remains doubtful whether the Talmud is speaking of a deaf person, or of a deaf and dumb individual[44].

# VI

No one may take unfair advantage of the weakness of a *cheresh*. *Thou shalt not curse the deaf*, bids the Torah[45], and if you believe that no one will know, then *thou shalt fear thy God, I am the Lord*[46], and I hear it. From the Aramaic Bible translation, tradition interprets deaf people to include anyone who cannot hear curses directed at him, for example, even because of great distances. The author of Proverbs admonishes: *open thy mouth for the dumb*[47]. In this phrase tradition sees an allusion to the obligation of a judge to make a shy person speak.

Even someone hard of hearing is not considered intellectually perfect[48]. The *cheresh* or deaf-mute, however, is certainly not in full possession of all his mental faculties *(lav bar de'ah)*[49], his understanding is weak *(kelishtha)*[50], so that he can perform physical labor, but cannot reflect[51]. Because of similar considerations, modern law also requires that in every case involving a deaf-mute, the secondary question of the necessary intelligence be posed[52], for if insight is lacking on the part of the accused, he is considered immune[53], and even his civil liability is abolished[54].

In the Talmud, there follow from this a large number of specific regulations, which in general correspond to the laws for the insane. Nevertheless, a charge that one insulted a *cheresh* is a valid one[55]. Promises made by a *cheresh* are legally invalid[56]. Deaf and deaf-mute individuals were specifically denied the ability to testify in ancient Roman courts, until Justinian narrowed this restriction to those born deaf[57]. Neither a mute nor a deaf person, and certainly not a deaf-mute, may testify in a Jewish court, the former because he cannot enunciate at all, and, in contrast to modern law[58], written testimony is not valid in Jewish courts. The deaf person cannot testify because he cannot follow the proceedings, and cannot hear the admonitions which must precede the interrogation of every witness[59].

In private law, for example, in the sale of movable objects, negotiations are conducted by the two parties with gestures with the hands and the head, and, according to Ben Bathera, through lip reading[60]. Moreover, the court may appoint a trustee *(epitropos)* to look out for the interests of a deaf-mute[61], but does not impose one by coercion, as is done for example by Prussian provincial law[62]. The Code of Civil Law[63] requires the acquiescence of the deaf-mute for the appointment of a guardianship. If one of the parents is mute or deaf-mute, proceedings to declare the son a "rebellious son" cannot be undertaken[64]. In spite of their intellectual inferiority, deaf-mutes can occasionally impart useful suggestions with their gestures[65].

---

44. Nowhere does the word *cheresh* mean a person who can hear but is dumb. In *Menachoth* 64b where *Rashi* gives this interpretation, the text is in error as evidenced by the Jerushalmi Shekalim 5:48d where *illem* is correctly mentioned. In the latter source, however, the interpretation of *Korban Ha'edah* is incorrect.
45. Levit. 19:14
46. *ibid*
47. Proverbs 31:8
48. In Sotah 13a, *Chushim,* the name of Dan's son (Genesis 46:23) is explained: he was hard of hearing.
49. Chagigah 2b
50. Yebamoth 113a
51. Machshirin 6:1
52. *Strafs P.O.* No. 298
53. *Strafgesetzbuch* No. 58
54. *Bürgerliches Gesetzbuch* No. 828
55. Baba Kamma 86b
56. Arachin 1:1
57. Dernburg. *Pandekten* Vol. 3:129
58. G.V.G. No. 188-189
59. Maimonides *Hilchoth Eduth* 9:11
60. Gittin 5:7 and 59a
61. *Tosefta* Terumoth 1:1
62. Part 2 title 18 No. 15
63. *Bürgerliches Gesetzbuch* No. 1910
64. Sanhedrin 71a
65. For example Menachoth 64b

The questions of marriage for deaf-mutes are also very difficult. Marriage is legally contracted when the groom gives his fiancée an appropriate object of value in the presence of witnesses, and makes known his intent by expressing his desire to marry her therewith. Although the deaf-mute cannot recite the appropriate formula[66], the Rabbis enabled him to enter into a marriage by considering that his affirmative gestures substitute effectively for the spoken word. The same applies to the dissolution of such a marriage[67].

# VII

The cause of deaf-muteness is thought to reside in the indecent behavior of the parents who are then punished in that their children are abnormal. Rabbi Yochanan ben Dahabai was told by the ministering angels: people are born·lame because their parents overturned their table (i.e. practiced *coitus recumbente viro*); dumb because they kiss "that place" (*locum illum* i.e. practice cunnilingus); deaf (mute) because they converse during cohabitation; and blind because they look at "that place" (*locum illum* i.e. the vulva)[68]. He who is familiar with the moral conditions of the heathen surroundings of the Jews in those days, even if only from Rosenbaum's *Geschichte der Lustseuche,* can understand how the Rabbis arrived at these threats of punishment. In general, only God can make a person dumb or deaf or intelligent or blind[69], as well as loosen (or unlock) the mouth of the dumb[70].

Among the miracles of Jesus is the healing of a deaf-mute. Jesus put his fingers on the patient's ears, spit, and touched his tongue, and spoke: *Ephatha; that is, be opened. And straightway his ears were opened, and the string of his tongue was loosened, and he spake plain*[71].

---

66. be thou consecrated unto me with this object according to the laws of Moses and of Israel
67. Yebamoth 14:1
68. Nedarim 20a
69. Exodus 4:11
70. Sanhedrin 100a
71. Mark 7:32-35

# CHAPTER IX

## *DISORDERS OF THE NOSE*

### I

Various noticeable abnormalities of the nose are included among the physical defects which exclude a priest from serving in the Temple. The Bible itself mentions a *charum* (flat-nosed) as being ineligible to serve[1]. The *Mishnah* interprets this term to mean a person "who can paint both his eyes at one time"[2] which, according to the explanation of the *Gemara*[3], is possible because his "nose is sunken between his two eyes" (so that the paint can run from one eye to the other). The word *charum* could also refer to a completely destroyed nose or a saddle-nose, *kolovorin,* as in the Septuagint, or *torto naso,* as in the Vulgate. The expression *charum-aph* (perhaps "turned-up or snub nose") even occurs as a proper name[4]. According to ancient sources[5], the ineligibility to serve in the Temple applies equally to a *salud,* or priest with a "leaping nose", that is which, either naturally or as a result of scarring and contracture, points upward (snub-nose); to a *balum,* one whose nasal passages are blocked (or obliterated); and to a *noteph,* one whose nose drops or hangs (ulcerated or cut up as opposed to snub-nose?).

I consider it likely that all these abnormal shapes refer to the numerous gross disfigurements of the nose that occur secondary to leprosy, as described and portrayed by Leopold Glück[6]. In addition, on the pre-Columbian tablets which Ashmead has reproduced[7], similar deformities of the nose are found.

Although it is only a legend, the following may refer to leprosy. It is the story of a priest from the sect of Sadducees who brought an offering in the Temple which he was not instructed to bring, as a result of which worms came forth from his nose[8]. There is also the case of another, upon whose forehead the image of a calf's foot (ulceration?) also appeared[9].

An animal whose nose is perforated cannot be used for an offering in the Temple[10]. Such perforations were made to fasten nasal rings into animals, as well as into humans. Since earliest times, the nasal ring, *nezem,* was considered by the Orientals to be an attractive adornment. Even today, Oriental women wear such rings

---

1. Levit. 21:18
2. Bechoroth 7:3
3. *ibid* 43b
4. Nehemiah 3:10
5. *Sifra* on Levit 21:18
6. *Mitt. U. Verh. d. Intern. Wiss. Lepra-konferenz zu Berlin* 1897 Vol. 1 p.22 ff
7. *ibid*
8. Yoma 19b
9. Jerushalmi Sukkah 4; 54d; in Yoma 19b, the Talmud substitutes "between the shoulders" for the forehead
10. Bechoroth 6:4

through the bottom of pierced alae nasi. Detailed accounts of this subject are found in the work of Hartmann[11], and in books dealing with Biblical archaeology.

## II

Among the cruel customs of war in antiquity was the mutilation of prisoners. The prophet warns the disobedient nation of Israel that the sons of the Babylonians and all the Chaldeans will act violently, and cut off the noses and the ears of the Israelites[12]. It is known that in the legal code of Hammurabi, such mutilations are prescribed as punishment in a variety of situations. This practice was never carried out by Jews, either on prisoners or on criminals. Only a single case is recorded, and that is from the fourteenth century, where one cut off the nose of a prostitute "in order to spoil her harlotry"[13], since she was producing a scandal because of her actions. In this case, the Jews were influenced by the customs of their surroundings. In their own laws, however, such practices were never condoned.

## III

Among diseases of the nose, *polypus* (Greek *polypous*) is repeatedly mentioned. Rabbi Muna used to say: if a hand touches the eyes, the mouth, or the nose, it should be cut off, because the fingers can produce deafness and blindness and cause a *polypus*[14]. The *Mishnah* prescribes that a marriage should be dissolved if either spouse develops a *polypus,* or leprosy[15]. The *Gemara,* however, limits this rule to leprosy. It makes no difference whether this affliction already existed at the time of the marriage or whether it occurred later; for the woman is allowed to protest, saying that she believed that she would be able to tolerate living with her husband[16]. A criminal who transgresses is compared to a hideous woman who brings forth nasal *polypus*[17].

The *Tosefta* interprets the word *polypus* to mean *foetor ex ore*[18], whereas Mar Samuel considers it to refer to (an offensive) nasal smell or *ozaena*[19]. The Indian physician (Susrutas) combines both opinions in his definition: *si cujus aer per humores combustos in gutturis palatique radice habitat et foetor ex ore nasoque prodit, foetorum nasi appellant hunc morbum*[20]. The nasal polyp in the sense used by Roman and Greek physicians is not mentioned in the Talmud.

A woman who claimed to have lost her sense of smell *(toteranith)* was found to be a malingerer when someone came into her room with a powerfully aromatic plant concealed under his coat[21].

Naturally, nosebleeds were known in ancient times. Squeezing the nose can produce nosebleeding[22]. According to Aristotle[23], it only occurs in human beings. According to folk medicine, it appears that there is universal validity in first resorting to therapy by magic or, if desired, faith healing, for any pathological condition involving "blood." Therefore, in the Talmud, in the often-mentioned collection of remedies listed systematically according to the organs of the body, amulets appear first in the listing, as follows, "for blood which flows from the nostrils"[24]:

One should bring a priest whose name is Levi and write Levi backwards to stop the patients's nosebleed; or any man should write backwards: "I, Papi Shila bar Sumki",

11. Hartmann. *Die Hebräerin am Putztische und als Braut* Amsterdam 1809. Vol. 2 p.166 ff.
12. Ezekiel 23:25
13. Asher ben Yechiel Chapt. 18 in *Eben Haezer* at the end of section 177
14. Shabbath 108b to 109a, probably a morbid growth in the nose.
15. Kethuboth 7:10
16. *ibid* 77a

17. *Midrash* Psalms 7:8. Buber p.346
18. *Tosefta* Kethuboth 7:11
19. Kethuboth 77a
20. Susrutas. *Ayurvedas.* 3:22, edit. Hessler p.42
21. Baba Bathra 146a
22. Proverbs 30:33
23. *Problem.* 10:2
24. Gittin 69a

meaning son of the red one, that is the blood demon; or, according to the Canaanite formula, one should write "the taste of the bucket in water of silver, the taste of the bucket in blemished water".

Then follow two other remedies[25]: clover root and the rope of an old bed and papyrus (*kurtam* or *charta*) and saffron and the red part of a palm branch are all burned together to ashes. Then one makes two threads from sheep's wool, steeps them in vinegar, rolls them in the ashes and places them in the nostrils. Or the patient with a nosebleed should look for a watercourse which flows from east to west and stand astride over it, so that one foot is on either side. Then he should pick up some mud with his right hand from under his left foot, and with his left hand from under his right foot, and twine two threads of wool, and rub them in the mud, and place them in his nostrils. Despite the mystical nature of these remedies, one can recognize the practical seed of tamponade, and possibly even the utilization of a medicinal hemostatic material, namely vinegar.

A final remedy reads as follows: the patient should sit under a gutter pipe while people bring water and pour it over him saying: "As these waters stop flowing, so may the blood of A, son of the woman B, stop flowing." Here too the douche of cold water on the head is a remedy also recommended by others. Aristotle advises people with nosebleeds to pour cold water on their faces, in order to stop internal warmth[26].

It was a widespread practice in the Orient to mention the name of the patient's *mother* in the incantation (recited over the patient praying for his cure)[27].

25. *ibid*
26. *Problem.* 33:6
27. Goldziher. *Zeits. Deuts. Morgenl. Gesel.*
   1894 Vol. 47 p.360

# CHAPTER X

## *NEUROLOGICAL DISORDERS*

### I  Epilepsy

The Midianite priest and prophet Balaam called himself *fallen down, (nophel), yet with opened eyes*[1]. Certainly the latter expression (opened eyes) refers to a clairvoyant soothsayer. I am equally certain that the term "fallen down" is the designation for epileptics; for in Hebrew and Arabic, the verb *naphal,* whose present participle is *nophel,* always means "fallen down". One should further be reminded that to the heathen peoples of antiquity, epilepsy was considered to be the *iere nousos*[2], the *morbus sacer et divinus.* In antiquity, not only the sickness itself, but also those afflicted by it, were thought to be envoys of God, and hence considered to be "holy". To the Jews, every illness is regarded as divinely ordained; therefore a corresponding designation of *morbus sacer* is unknown.

Who first offered this explanation (of the term *nophel* meaning "fallen down")?

I can certainly not be the first, for this explanation seems to be very obvious. However, I have looked in vain therefor in numerous translations and commentaries of ancient and modern times and in exegetic handbooks and dictionaries.

A parallel thereof is found in the story of Saul. Scripture uses the same expression *(vajipol)* in relation to Saul after he became "mantic": *and he fell down the entire day and the entire night*[3], that is, he had frequent epileptic seizures.

### II

Trusen[4] correctly considers some of the possessed mentioned in the New Testament to be epileptics. The description of a seizure in the Gospel[5] is quite clear: "when the spirit (*pneuma* in Greek, corresponding to the Hebrew *ruach*) seizes him, the patient suddenly cries out, falls to the ground and rolls around on the floor, foaming at the mouth and grinding the teeth. Often the spirit (demons) threw him into fire and water in order to destroy him"[6]. Coelius Aurelianus also remarks[7] that epileptics occasionally *in flumina vel mare cadunt.* Marcus calls this active demon *alalon* (mute), one who does not speak; perhaps, as Winer suggests[8], because the patient brings forth inarticulate sounds.

---

1. Numbers 24:4
2. sacred ailment in Greek
3. First Samuel 19:24
4. *Sitten, Gebräuche und Krankheiten der Alten Hebräer* p.239
5. Luke 9:39 and Mark 9:17
6. Matthew 17:15
7. Chronicles 1:4
8. *Bibl. Realwörterbuch* 1:191

The illness of the Apostle Paul has been most fully described by Max Krenkel and interpreted to be epilepsy[9]. The Apostle complains that he was given a thorn in the flesh *(skolops te sarki)* so that he should not become conceited[10]. He rejoiced that the Galatians did not scornfully spit at him[11] as was usually done to epileptics. "On the road to Damascus, there suddenly shined around him a light from heaven. And he fell to the ground and heard a voice speaking[12]. And he was three days without sight *(me vlepon en),* and did not eat nor drink[13]. Following the words of Ananias, something like scales *(osei lepides)* fell from his eyes, and he was able to see again, and he allowed himself to be baptized, and he ate food again"[14].

Undoubtedly, no one would state with certainty from the above description that the diagnosis is epilepsy. However, it is at least as reasonable a diagnosis as the others which have been proposed[15].

Since the time of Unzer and Bartholin[16], the moon sickness, somnambulism *(seleniazomenos),* of Matthew, who suffered badly in that he often fell into fire and into water[17], has been considered to be epilepsy. The ancients generally believed in the influence of the moon on the condition of health of a person, particularly on the psyche. Information on this subject can be found in the work of Bartholin and Mead[18]. To the English speaking peoples, even today, a lunatic is regarded as a person who is mentally ill. According to the words of the psalmist, someone protected by the Lord will not be smitten (harmed) by the sun during the day, or by the moon at night[19].

# III

During the time of the Talmud, the Jews referred to an epileptic as a *nikpheh* meaning one who writhes; perhaps also "one who is bent or forced over (by a demon)." A person who twists in his death throes is also identified by this term[20]. Curiously, indecent behavior during cohabitation is often stated to be the cause for epilepsy. It remains undecided, however, as so often happens in the Talmud, whether or not the warning intends to discourage indecent behavior, and whether or not the threat of severe illness in one's offspring only represents added emphasis. Thus, it is taught that someone who stands naked before a kindled lamp becomes epileptic, and someone who cohabits by the shine of a light will have epileptic children. If a child younger than one year of age[21] lies at the foot of the cohabitants, it becomes epileptic[22]. Similarly, children become epileptic[23] if their parents cohabit in a room which contains the handmill[24], and licentious if they do so on the floor.[25] Cohabitation immediately after defecation[26] or immediately after blood-letting[27] has the same result and produces epileptic children. A child can also become a *hapakpekan* as a result of coitus *recumbente marito*[28].

---

9. *Beiträge zur Aufhellung der Geschichte und der Briefe des Apostels Paulus* Braunschweig. 1890 p.47-125
10. Second Corinthians 12:7
11. Galatians 4:14
12. Acts 9:3 ff.
13. *ibid* 9:9
14. *ibid* 9:18
15. See also Kotelmann. *Die Ophthalmologie bei den alten Hebräern.* Hamburg 1910 p.178 Note 1215 ff.
16. *De Morbus Biblicis.* Francof. 1672 p.62
17. Matthew 17:15
18. *Medica Sacra.* London 1749 p.82ff.
19. Psalms 121:6

20. The dying Joseph writhed, *nikphe,* and fell on his attendant. Aboth de Rabbi Nathan 11:1
21. Is the textual reading correct? One would sooner expect the opposite
22. Pesachim 112b
23. Kethuboth 60b
24. Reason? Several women were always occupied at the handmill. *Odyssey* 7:104 and 20:105
25. See *Targum* on Ezekiel 23:20. I read *shemote,* not *shemute* as *Rashi*
26. Gittin 70a
27. Levit. Rabbah 16:1
28. Kallah Rabbah 1; 52a49

The Koran threatens with epilepsy those who live off usury; they will someday be resurrected "possessed", i.e. touched by Satan[29].

Evidence for the belief in the hereditary nature of epilepsy is the regulation that no one should marry a woman from a family with epileptics or lepers[30]. It is also significant for post-Talmudic times that *Rashi* (about the year 1050), in his commentary on the aforementioned citation, translates *nikpheh* by the general term "ill", whereas otherwise he equates *nikpheh* with *le mal de St. Jean* (the illness of St. Jean).

Naturally, the above regulation can also be interpreted to mean that families with epileptics and lepers were considered to be socially inferior, and therefore one avoided establishing ties with them.

The *Midrash* states that for an epileptic, one should call a skillful physician[31], and not an exorcist[32]. We learn nothing in the Talmud about his medications. This may, however, be a mere coincidence since Talmudic writings are not medical textbooks. Of medical value for epilepsy, and also recognized by the common people to be efficacious, is the amulet, the *kemiya,* both the written one and the one made from herbs, which one wears suspended from a chain or in a signet ring, "not only for someone who is already epileptic but also as a preventive measure"[33].

Whether or not the illness *kipha*[34] should also be discussed here was already undecided among the oldest commentators; they waver between pustules and epilepsy. The Talmud itself, aside from the name of the illness, only mentions an incantation which was used to treat this illness. I here describe this purely Canaanite incantation because the comparison of this formula with the corresponding Egyptian and Assyrian ones promises interesting results for the history of cultures. The formula states: "the sword quivers, the catapult has been let loose. His name is not *Yokhab;* illnesses are painful".

# IV

In the legal sphere, an epileptic seems not to occupy any special position. He is unfit to be a priest for all times, even if he only had a seizure once[35]. If a woman has epileptic seizures regularly (menstrual hystero-epilepsy?), it is considered to be a "hidden blemish" which the husband need not see before the wedding (since the woman conceals herself during her seizures), yet which makes the marriage invalid, if it is noted later. Seizures which occur at different intervals are classified as an "obvious defect" which the husband should have observed or inquired about before the marriage[36]. If during the sale of a maid-servant, the seller enumerates for the buyer a large number of defects from which she is supposed to suffer — she is feeble-minded *(she'iya),* epileptic, insane, (physically) ill — and if she is actually afflicted with one of these abnormalities, but the buyer becomes convinced by a spot-check that many of these blemishes are in fact not present and therefore believes that none are present, and that the maid-servant is completely healthy, the sale is invalid because it was consummated under deceitful conditions[37]. This law is also applicable in cases where maidens become engaged[38].

In post-Talmudic times, one was warned to be extremely careful concerning the testimony of epileptics. Maimonides, supported by examples from the Talmud[39],

---

29. Sura 3
30. Yebamoth 64b
31. Levit. Rabbah 26:5
32. Because of the uncertainity of the text, further interpretation of comparisons between physician and exorcist are questionable.
33. *Tosefta* Shabbath 4:9
34. Shabbath 67a; others have *kiba* or *kisa*
35. Bechoroth 7:5
36. Kethuboth 77a
37. *Tosefta* Baba Bathra 4:5
38. *Tosefta* Kethuboth 7:10
39. Kethuboth 20a

states: "as long as he has seizures, an epileptic is not admissable as a witness, irrespective of whether the seizures occur only at certain times or constantly, but without a specific type. On the other hand, he is qualified to testify when he is healthy, provided that his mind at that time (i.e. between seizures) is completely clear; for there are epileptics whose intellect is disturbed even when they are healthy". Therefore, "one must scrupulously examine the testimony of epileptic individuals"[40]. Later codes accepted this rule verbatim[41].

The post-Talmudic designation for epilepsy is *choli nophel,* which is the literal translation of *morbus caducus* or falling sickness.

# V

1) A type of spasm, according to the post-Talmudic commentaries, is the illness *avith.* Since *avah* in the Bible[42] already has the meaning contorted or writhing, the above interpretation should be accepted.

This sickness *(avith)* afflicts someone (as punishment) for cohabiting in a standing position, whereas someone who cohabits in a sitting position is threatened with the illness *alaria*[43]. It is a sad privilege of mankind to be chastised and afflicted with sufferings. Have you ever seen a donkey with *avith?* Or a camel with *avith*[44]? The *Aggadah* indicates from the (tribal) name *Avites*[45], that anyone who looked at them developed *avith*[46].

Therapeutically, it is not considered to be superstitious to frighten people ill with *avith* or *phikah* (trembling?)[47], perhaps in the same manner that, even today, one "instills a fright" into someone suffering from singultus.

2) Kohut has made an attempt to also identify the *ruach ben nephilim,* or demon "descended from giants", which makes priests unsuitable to serve in the Temple[48], as epilepsy, in that it reminds one of *Herakleia nosos* (disease of Hercules) and *morbus major.* However, the demons, *nephalim,* are listed *next* to the *nikpheh*[49], the latter undoubtedly referring to the epileptic, thus making the explanation of Kohut difficult to accept. According to Rabbi Gersom, *nephalim* means *shigga'on* or insanity.

# VI   Hysteria

Rabbi Judah in the name of Rabbi Chama from the village of Techamim relates the following parable in the *Midrash* in relation to the Biblical verse: *and the children of Israel sighed (in Egypt) by reason of the bondage, and they cried, and their cry came up unto God*[50], in order to make plausible the thought that the oppression by the Egyptians was not a punishment, but was ordained for the specific purpose of inducing the Israelites to call out to God for help (for their healing from hysterical muteness or dumbness): a king once had an only (mute) daughter whose idle chatter he wished to hear (again?). Therefore, he had the herald assemble the people on the palace grounds and, following a wink from him, the people suddenly pounced on the daughter like robbers; whereupon she began to cry out: father, father, save me! And the father

---

40. *Hilchoth Eyduth* 9:9
41. *Choshen Mishpat* 35:9
42. in the *Niphal* tense: writhing from fear or pain. Psalms 38:7; Isaiah 21:3
43. Gittin 70a; The *Aruch* considers *alaria* to be a fit of yawning, *s.v. pahak:* he explains it as a foreign word equivalent to *hilaria,* perhaps a laughing cramp. Others have *delaria* meaning delirium, which seems to correspond better to *avith,* but it is

immediately threatened as punishment for *coitus recumbente viro.*
44. Eccles. Rabbah 1 fol 6b
45. Joshua 13:3
46. Chullin 60b
47. *Tosefta* Shabbath 7:21
48. Bechoroth 44b
49. *Tosefta* Bechoroth 5:4
50. Exodus 2:23

replied: had I not done this to you, you would not have called out to me[51]! It appears that this story represents a case of hysterical dumbness. One must certainly assume that the above type of healing of mute individuals was already well known at that time, so that parables were utilized in sermons. Hippocrates already described the story of the illness of the hysterically dumb wife of Polemarch. As a result of *suppressio mensium,* she developed pain in the hips, her voice was completely suppressed the entire night until the following midday, but she heard, understood and showed where she had pain[52].

As far as I can see, the oldest example of hysterical dumbness concerns a man, the son of Croesus, who, though otherwise normal, *(epeikes)* was mute[53]. However, when he saw that a Persian was rushing towards his father to kill him, he "broke through the fear and terror of his muteness and called out: man, do not kill Croesus! That was the first time he spoke; thereafter, however, he spoke for the rest of his life." Valerius Maximus related that Echecles, an athlete from Samos, was mute[54]. One refrained from honoring and rewarding him when he achieved victories and *indignatione accensus vocalis evasit.* Perhaps the two *ilmim,* the disciples of the grandson of Rabbi Yochanan who concurred with his lectures by nodding their heads and moving their lips, were hysterically mute men. He prayed for them, and they were healed. Then it was revealed that they knew the entire Talmud[55].

The angel Gabriel speaks to Zechariah, the father of John (the Baptist): *thou shalt be dumb, and not able to speak, until the day that these things shall occur,* (namely the birth of the child)[56]. And when he came out of the Temple, he could not speak to the people. *And he beckoned unto them and remained speechless*[57]. When the child was born, his mouth was opened and his tongue loosened, and he spoke[58]. Here too, one cannot doubt the diagnosis of functional muteness.

Similarly "unhappy love" is today considered to be a type of hysteria and treated with potassium bromide and water. The ancients who, in relation to hysteria, always thought of *ystera* (uterus), attempted to treat the cause according to the categorical assertion of Plato: she should marry; then the sickness will vanish. Concerning the subject of love sickness, *de amore, qui hereos dicitur,* the physicians of antiquity and the middle ages wrote detailed expositions whose content has been assembled by Hjalmar Crohn[59]. The therapy of love sickness is a very complicated one, but essentially rests on the recommendations for the patient to travel and "speak freely". Even today, some intelligent people believe that they are able to heal psychic disturbances in this manner. From the writings of ancient Judaism, one should here mention two incidents not known to Crohn, both of which, just like the well-known story of Antiochus and the Stratonikes, involve men. Amnon, a son of king David, fell in love with his stepsister Tamar, and he was woeful and became love sick, so that his friend anxiously asked him: why are you so lean *(dal),* prince? He disclosed his anxiety to his friend. As a result of a concocted plan, he lured his sister to his room and raped her[60].

The Talmud relates[61]: "a man set his eyes upon a certain woman and *tina* came to

---

51. Song of Songs Rabbah 2:41. Much less beautiful is a similar parable on the same Biblical verse, Exodus Rabbah 21:15, where a king makes a shy beautiful maiden complaisant through the same trick, because then the lack of prayer on the part of the Israelites in Egypt was due to conscious apathy.
52. Epid. 5:91 Ed. Littré Vol. 5 p.255
53. Herodotus 1:85 *aphonos* meaning mute: and 1:34 *kophos* meaning deaf.
54. Book 1, Chapt. 8:4 Ed. Kempf. p.52. Both stories are also recorded by Gellius 5:9
55. Chagigah 3a
56. Luke 1:20
57. *ibid* 1:22
58. *ibid* 1:64
59. *Arch F. Kulturgesch,* Vol. 3, 1905, part 1 p.66-86. See also Lomer, *Liebe und Psychose* Wiesbaden 1907
60. Second Samuel 13:1 ff.
61. Sanhedrin 75a

his heart. The physicians were consulted and stated: there is no cure for his strong sexual desire, except to allow the woman to him. The Rabbis, however, replied to this request: let him die, rather than have the woman cohabit with him. The physicians made concessions asking that she stand naked before him[62] or that she at least be allowed to speak to him through the divided curtain of the harem window. But the Rabbis always gave the same answer: let him rather die unhealed.'' As regards the dispute as to whether the above case concerns a married woman (in which case the Rabbis' position would require no substantiation since it represents adultery) or an unmarried maiden whom the lovesick man could easily have married, the comment is made that legitimate bliss would not provide satisfaction to such a person as stated by the epigram: *stolen waters are sweet, and bread eaten in secret is pleasant*[63].

According to the Aramaic Bible translators, the word *tinea* from which our *tina* is probably contracted, is the usual term·for passion, envy and jealousy. The *Gemara* also speaks of an "eating worm" by the name of *tina* in whose nose fish crawl[64] and gill fins, *taenia,* so that romantically inclined exegetes see in that ancient story the equivalent of the modern "gnawing worm of passion"!

The Palestinian Talmud is much clearer[65] in that it calls the illness referred to above by the name *racham* (love), which is derived from *rechem* (uterus), and corresponds verbatim to hysteria in the ancient sense of the word.

## VII   Headache

Next to dysentery, headache *(michush rosh)* is the most frequent ailment in the Orient. Rab said: I can tolerate any illness but not intestinal disease, any suffering but not stomach (or heart) troubles *(ke'eb leb),* any pain but not headache, any evil but not an evil wife[66]! When Jabez prays to the Lord that He keep evil away from him[67], it is a supplication for health: that I not suffer from headache or earache or pain in the eyes[68]. The latter, as is known, is also one of the dreaded diseases of the Orient[69].

Rabbi Yochanan only wore both phylacteries in the winter, when his head was not heavy, but in the summer, he only wore the one on his arm[70]. When once the most eminent man of his time suffered from headache — it is thought to have been Rabbi Samuel bar Nachman — he cried out: behold what the generation of the deluge has brought upon us[71]; for only since that time do *cold and heat...not cease*[72]. Upon returning from a health resort, with his convalescing son, the king reminds him at individual rest stations: here you had heat, here frost, here headache[73]. Interesting is the opinion of Rabbi Judah of Siknin that if one of two twin sisters has a headache, the other feels it as well[74].

Concerning the underlying causes of this ailment, we only find the remark that blowing into the foam of beverages (such as beer or mead) is "damaging to the head"[75]. Naturally, headaches due to wine consumption were known, particularly affecting those who could not hold liquor. Thus, Rabbi Judah, after drinking the prescribed four cups of wine on the night of Passover, had to bind his temples (because

---

62. Perhaps because completely or only half covered women (*nudité gazeuse*) entice the mind most of all "It is completely erroneous to believe that in general the naked body or a bare part of the body stimulate erotic feelings as much as a clothed one. On the contrary, for very many men and women, a cooling influence is produced when their partner disrobes". See Hirschfeld in *Jahrbuch fur Sexuelle Zwischenstufen.* Vol. 8 p.146
63. Proverbs 9:17
64. Baba Bathra 73b

65. Jerushalmi Shabbath 14; 14d
66. Shabbath 11a
67. First Chronicles 4:10
68. Temurah 16a
69. trachoma? which may produce blindness
70. Jerushalmi Berachoth 2: 4c
71. Genesis Rabbah 34:11
72. this is the interpretation of Genesis 8:22
73. Numbers Rabbah 23:3
74. *Pesikta de Rabbi Kahana* on *Parshath Hachodesh.* Ed. Buber p.47a
75. Chullin 105b

of severe headache), from Passover to Pentecost[76]. In addition, the name of Ahasuerus is jokingly interpreted to mean "headache inducer" *(chasch berosh)*[77].

For the treatment of headache, one rubs the head with wine, vinegar or simply oil[78]. This therapy was already recommended by the heathen physicians of antiquity[79]. The universal remedy for any ailment, including headache, is to occupy oneself with the words of God[80], which, according to the expression of the epigram, are *an ornament of grace unto thy head*[81]. One should not visit people suffering from headaches, because speaking is harmful to them[82].

# VIII    Plethora and Migraine

Plethora plays a major role in the pathology of antiquity as well as in the Talmud. A Talmudic statement[83] teaches that "an excess of blood is the main cause of all illnesses", completely in the Galenic sense. People and animals "overcome by blood" are placed in cold water to cool off[84]. A first-born animal is bled for this reason, although one might thereby produce a bodily blemish which would render it unfit to be sacrificed[85].

If an animal is very hot because of an excess of blood, but later becomes cooled off, then its flesh is not harmful to man[86].

A special part of general plethora is probably "the blood of the head". In the listing of remedies according to the organs of the body, which we have already mentioned several times, the following prescription is found for the above ailment: take *schurbina* (a type of cedar) and *bina* (tamarisk?) and fresh myrtle and olive leaves and *chilpha* (willow) and clove and *jabla* (a certain herb, *cymedon*); cook these together and take 300 cups for each side of the head (as a liniment?). Or cook white roses with all the leaves on, on one side, and take 60 cups thereof for each side of the head[87]. Celsus (3:10) also recommended rose water, either alone or with vinegar, for head compresses: *si acetum offendit, pura rosa utendum est.*

Directly adjacent to this remedy there is another which is efficacious for *celichetha,* which perhaps more correctly should be *celochta:* one takes a wild cock[88] and slaughters it with a white *zuz* (piece of money) over that side of the patient which is painful (so that the blood flows on the head of the patient). One should be careful with the blood, however, in order not to blind the patient's eyes[89]. Then one hangs the slaughtered cock on the door-post. When the patient enters the house, he should rub his head against the bird, and he should do the same when he leaves[90]. Pine hearts are also useful for this ailment[91], perhaps to bring about suppuration, as recommended by Celsus: *resina tempora pervellere et exulcerare ea, quae male habent*[92].

One should therefore accept the interpretation of the commentators that one is here dealing with heterocrania or hemicrania of the ancients, from which the French have derived "migraine". The form of the word also does not mitigate against this

76. Nedarim 49b
77. Esther Rabbah 1:3. See also Megillah 11a
78. *Tosefta* Shabbath 12:11; Jerushalmi Maaser Sheni 2; 53b
79. Celsus 3:10; Coelius Aurelius. Chronicles 1 p.271
80. Erubin 54a
81. Proverbs 1:9
82. Nedarim 41a
83. Baba Bathra 58b
84. Shabbath 53b
85. *Tosefta* Bechoroth 3:7
86. *Tosefta* Chullin 3:19

87. Gittin 68b
88. It is difficult to accept heath-cock as suggested by Lewyson *Zoologie des Talmuds* No. 268, because its capture must have even then been extremely difficult.
89. In comparison, in *Tosefta* Shabbath 8:8, the blood of the same bird is recommended as a therapeutic remedy for the eye ailment *barkith.*
90. Gittin 68b
91. Shabbath 90a
92. Med. 4:2

interpretation, for since *calcha* refers to one part, then *celochtha* can mean a partial pain (i.e. pain in half the head).

The situation is similar in regard to the demon *palga,* which afflicts a person who deposits his feces on the stump of a palm tree[93]. *Palga* also usually means a part or a half, and the ancient commentaries[94] are probably correct in their interpretation: "pain of half the head". *Plegia,* which is what Löw suggests[95], does not exist; *plege* (in Greek) refers only to *vulnus* and is not identical with *makkah*[96].

On the other hand, the meaning of the simultaneously mentioned demon *cerada,* which afflicts a person who places his head on the stump of a palm tree, is completely uncertain. The illness produced by this demon, as so often, was considered to be a strange and separate entity. Even the mention of this same demon in another place sheds no light on the matter. Abaye related that he believed that the reason for the rule that one should not remove any dishes from the table while another person is drinking is because of the fear that in haste he may commit an act of clumsiness and spill something. However, Raba bar Nachmani taught him that the real reason is that the demon *cerada* may afflict him[97]. Also in Rome in those days, it was considered to be a bad omen for a table or a centerpiece to be cleared away while one of the guests was drinking[98]. Even the etymology leaves us in the lurch, and there is wide room for conjecture[99].

## IX   Tremor

The only tremor I find mentioned in the Talmud is the tremor of old age. The Levites may remain in service in the Temple until they grow old, which Rabbi Chanina explains: until they begin to tremble *(rathath)*[100].

On the other hand, trembling as a result of psychic anxieties such as fear and fright, is often mentioned. Furthermore, many women develop a shaking of their bodies *(rothetheth)* as an early sign of their menses[101].

## X   Paralyses

1) In the first book of Maccabees, the end of Alcimus is described: *his mouth became closed, and he was paralyzed and could no longer utter a word nor give orders about his household. So Alcimus died at that time, in great agony*[102]. The assumption that this was apoplexy is probably correct.

2) It is also possible to postulate that the seizure of Philopator was an apoplectic attack: *God jolted him hither and thither like cane in the wind, so that he lay on the ground motionless and with paralyzed limbs and justly punished, he was unable to make any sound*[103]. It is possible that the above episode consisted only of an epileptic seizure, in view of the fact that after he was carried out by his servants and withdrew

---

93. Pesachim 111b
94. *Aruch s.v. garad.* The explanation of *Rashi* which is found in our texts by the word *palag* probably belongs to the word *cerada* and vice-versa
95. *Pflanzennamen* p.82
96. Hebrew word for wound
97. Chullin 105b
98. Plinius 28:5 *Inauspicatissimum judicatur bibente conviva mensam vel repositorium tolli.*
99. Among the ancients, Rabbi Gersom explains our word *cerada* as epilepsy. *Rashi* once has *estourdisson* meaning *étourdissement,* and once *palazine* which, according to an old French dictionary, refers

to paralysis (Landau, in his *Marpé Lashon* transcribes the word of *Rashi* as *flux de sang* meaning golden vein! According to Löw (*Zeitsch. Deuts. Morgenl. Geselsch.* 1893 p.516), in spite of the authoritativeness of the manuscript, one should read *cedara.* According to Schönhak, it is *sardanion* (laughter) meaning *yelan* (laughing). Naturally, according to Kohut, it is a Persian word and refers to *zarda* which means jaundice; etc.
100. Chullin 24b
101. Niddah 63b
102. First Maccabees 9:55
103. Third Maccabees 2:22

from public view following vehement threats, nothing further is mentioned about his illness.

3) Some exegetes also consider the death of Nabal to have been caused by apoplexy. It is related[104] that he held a drinking feast in his house like the feast of a king, and he was very drunk. In the morning, when the wine was gone out of him, his wife told him of the imminent danger because of David, and *his heart died within him, and he became as a stone. And after about ten days the Lord smote Nabal and he died*[105]. It is certainly conceivable that such a violent fright experienced by a *churlish, brutal man*[106], coupled with a marked excess in *baccho,* might have deleterious consequences. It is not necessary to assume that his wife poisoned him, a thought which is certainly plausible. Whether the expression *and he became as a stone* refers to a cataleptic condition, as is occasionally observed in apoplectic coma, or refers only to the motionlessness of the paralyzed or unconscious individual, somewhat like our vulgar phrase "he is lying like a piece of wood", must remain undecided. Josephus[107] substitutes "his body resembled that of a corpse".

# XI

4) Concerning the *paralytikoi* (paralytics) of the New Testament, there already exists an entire literature. The authors, for the most part, have made their work more difficult in that they understand the term "paralytics" to entail either paralytics or cripples in the medical-clinical sense, whereas the paralysis of the ancients encompassed every type of important abnormality of movement. For example, according to Coelius Aurelianus[108], the physicians distinguished a paralysis *alia conductione effecta, alia extensione,* which perhaps corresponds to our "contracture" and "flaccidity".

The servant of the centurion of Capernaum was lying *paralytikos* at home, grievously tormented[109]. In Lydda there was a man named Aeneas who lay paralyzed (or crippled) in bed for eight years[110]. Many such "cripples", as well as those possessed with demons and lunatics, were brought to Jesus[111]. Some were carried on their beds[112]. As is known, they were healed by the word of Jesus. Many of the expounders of the New Testament consider a suggestive influence to have played a role. Therefore, these "paralytics" were probably hysterics or aggravators.

5) The "cripple" in John the Evangelist[113] is interpreted by Sir Ridson Bennet[114] to refer to a patient with chronic rheumatism. Bethesda in Jerusalem was a bathhouse in the modern sense with a "treatment house". Here, in five separate rooms, lay "many sick, blind, crippled and atrophic *(xeroi)* people, who waited for the water in the pool to move. The first person who entered the water was cured as soon as the water moved, no matter which contagious disease he was afflicted with". This cure was thought to occur because the priests washed the sacrificial animals in that pool, particularly at the time of a major holiday. For the patient, this would thus represent a type of mud bath, and as such was particularly suited for the healing of patients with rheumatism, as Sir Ridson conjectures, and as Richter had already stated 100 years earlier[115]. Furthermore, Eusebius[116] asserts that the efficacy of the sacrificial blood in

---

104. First Samuel 25:36
105. *ibid* 25:38
106. *ibid* 25:3
107. *Antiquities.* Book 6 Chapt. 13:8
108. Chronicles 2:1 p.342
109. Matthew 8:6 tortured: *vasanijomenos*
110. Acts 9:33
111. Matthew 4:24
112. Matthew 9:2; Mark 2:3
113. John 5:5

114. *The Diseases of the Bible* London 1887 p.93
115. George Gottlob Richter. *Opuscula Med.* Frankfurt & Leipzig 1780 Vol. 3 p.187
116. Onomasticon *s.v. vejatha. Die Christliche Schriftsteller der ersten drei Jahrhunderte.* Published by the Berliner Akademie des Wissenschaft. Leipzig 1904. Eusebius Vol. 3 p.59

the pool may perhaps be due to its miraculous effect and the reddish color of its water. The Talmud, which makes no mention at all of the pool called Bethesda, notes much more prosaically that blood from the altar flowed through an underground pipe *(ammah)* into a cesspool *(mechilla)* into which also flowed other wastes[117], and from there the blood was conducted into the channel of the river Kidron, which flowed very close to Jerusalem. These wastes were sold to the gardeners as fertilizer[118].

6) The story of the man in Jerusalem[119] seems to require a different explanation because he was *lame from his mother's womb*. Every day, he was carried and placed at the gate of the Temple, so that he could ask for alms. Peter saw him and spoke: rise up and walk! And he took him by the right hand and lifted him up; and immediately his ankles and leg bones became strong[120]. — Begging is an ancient evil of the Orient; particularly in places with heavy tourist traffic. Whereas originally only true cripples, the blind, and those maimed by leprosy begged, very early there blossomed the practice of fabricating lameness. One sees this very clearly from the threat of punishment enunciated in the *Mishnah*: "He who is neither lame (paralyzed) nor blind nor crippled, and feigns any of these, does not live to become old until he actually becomes like one of these"[121]. Similarly the *Tosefta* warns: "he who masquerades as if his eyes were blind, or his abdomen swollen, or his leg injured (or atrophic)[122], will not part from this world until he actually develops the abnormality he feigns"[123]. Therefore, the above case (of the man in Jerusalem) probably also concerned a man with such faked lameness whose malingering was recognized by Peter and unmasked. Such cures through "imperative suggestion" seem to have been not at all rare in those times. The *Midrash* relates that a servant of the Caesar Antoninus became very seriously ill. The Caesar asked Rabbi Judah to send one of his disciples "to make this dying man become alive again". The disciple, said to be Rabbi Simeon ben Chalaphta, addressed the patient imperiously: why do you lie in bed when your master is standing on his feet? Immediately the patient became terrified and stood up[124].

## XII  Hand Paralysis

Eleazar, a comrade in arms of (king) David, smote the Philistines, until his hand was weary and his hand clave unto the sword[125]. *Medizinal Rat* Huber from Memmingen called to my attention[126] that Oppenheim interprets this passage to represent a description of "occupational cramp"[127]. On the other hand, Ebstein demurs, stating that immediately at the beginning of the attack Eleazar should have developed cramps from the thrusting of the sword, similar to writer's cramp which seizes a person as soon as he *attempts* to write. He therefore considers that the ailment of Eleazar simply represented a passing cramp[128].

In the original text, there is no mention of the word *cramp*. Josephus interprets the situation in the following manner: Eleazar killed so many of the enemy that his sword stuck to his hand because of the adherent blood[129]. It is not astonishing, therefore, that his hand became weary therefrom.

In the Book of Judges[130], it is related as follows: among the Benjaminites there were 700 chosen men; every one could sling stones towards the enemy and not miss.

117. Jerushalmi Nazir 9; 57d
118. Yoma 5:6
119. Acts 3:2
120. *ibid* 3:6-7
121. Peah 8:9
122. Bechoroth 45b
123. *Tosefta* Peah 4:14
124. Levit. Rabbah 10:4
125. Second Samuel 23:10

126. *Munchen. Med. Wochenschr.* 1901 No. 12 Mitteilungun vom 6-6-1899 in a critique of Ebstein's *Medizin im Alten Testament.*
127. *Lehrbuch der Nervenkrankheiten.* p.881
128. Ebstein. *Die Medizin im Neuen Testament und im Talmud* p.34
129. *Antiquities* Book 7. Chapt. 12:4
130. Judges 20:16

They were all *itter yad yemino*[131]. The context alone indicates that this phrase cannot mean that their right hands were crippled, for would chosen troops be crippled on one side? A battalion of left-handed troops would perhaps be assembled for exhibition purposes, but not to go to war. The explanation of the Septuagint and the Vulgate, that they were *amphoterodexioi* and could wage battle with the left hand equally as well as with the right *(ita sinistra ut dextra proeliantes),* as we would say today ambidextrous, is clearly correct.

Ehud[132] was also such an *itter yad yemino,* an *amphoterodexious,* an ambidextrous individual *qui utraque manu pro dextera utebatur. For his special mission,* he girded his sword on his right thigh. Thus, his opponent (Eglon, king of Moab) did not think that he came armed with the intention of killing him and Ehud, without arousing the suspicion of the king, was able to reach for his sword and kill him.

In the Talmud, the simple term *itter* means a left-handed person. He writes with his left hand which corresponds to the right hand of other people[133]. Unless he is able to use both his hands equally, he places the phylacteries on the right arm, whereas most people place them on their left arm[134]. A priest who is an *itter* either with his hand or his foot[135] is not suited to serve in the Temple because he is abnormal; if he can use both hands equally well, then Rabbi Judah considers him to be unfit, but the Rabbis regard him to be fit to serve. The former believes that the equality of strength of the two hands results from the fact that the right hand is abnormally weak, so that it equals the left in strength; whereas the latter believe that the left hand is exceptionally strong[136]. Naturally, in actuality, both could be correct.

One should add here the reports of the Evangelists[137] about the man who had "a withered hand" *(heir xera)* and was healed by Jesus' summons: *stretch forth your hand!* And he stretched it forth and it was healed, just like the other hand. Höfler[138] interprets this as a case of paralytic atrophy (phthisis). However, it is different with the story of King Jeroboam[139] who stretched forth his hand in response to the command: *lay hold on the prophet!* As a result his hand became dried[140], and he could not pull it back to himself. The prophet prayed to the Lord and the hand of the king came back to him and was restored as before[141]. Was this a case of subluxation? Finally, another interpretation should be mentioned here, which Rabbi Joshua ben Levi provides in relation to Psalms 77:11: if there is only a disease of the hand, there is still hope; for one who still perceives pain can eventually recover. If a change in the right hand already occurred, however, (lepra anesthetica?), then there is no hope[142].

One should be reminded of the role of "pairs" in all of antiquity, including that of the Jews. The following story in the Talmud pertains to this matter: Rabbah bar Nachmani, after having been falsely accused, was pursued by a Roman officer. By chance the officer spent the night in the same inn as the pursued. They placed bread and *two* glasses of wine before him (the officer) and then removed the bread, whereupon his face was turned backwards by demons. The innkeepers, full of despair that such a misfortune befell the sergeant-major in their district, asked Rabbah for his

---

131. here incorrectly translated by some as "left handed"
132. Judges 3:15. The incorrect interpretation of Josephus is found in his *Antiquities* Book 5, Chapt. 2:10 and 4:2
133. Shabbath 103a
134. Menachoth 37a. In which case he places phylacteries on his left arm, like other people.
135. *Rashi* states: he who steps with his left foot, differently from other people
136. Bechoroth 45b
137. Luke 6:6; Matthew 12:10; Mark 3:1
138. *Janus* 1899 p.368
139. First Kings 13:4
140. Septuagint: *exeranthe;* so too Josephus *Antiquities* Book 8 Chapt. 15:4. He states otherwise, however, in Chapt. 8:5
141. First Kings 13:6
142. Lamentations Rabbah 1:23

advice. He advised them to set aside the "pair" and he was healed[143]. This case probably represented an example of an acute *caput obstipum rheumaticum*, for which a *medicus vulgaris* can occasionally effect a remarkable cure.

## XIII   Sciatica

It is generally accepted that the Talmudic term *shigrona*[144] refers to sciatica. Some people who read *shigdona* see in this word a transcription from the Greek *ischiadikos*. Since Hippocrates, however, the name of the illness is known to Greek physicians as *ischias,* and the *sch* never corresponds to the Hebrew *sh.* Anyhow, derivation from the Hebrew *shagar* or *shagran* seems more likely. When the author of the *Aruch* declares the illness to be gout, one should remember that Paulus of Aegina (3:77) also considered *ischias* to be a type of arthritis which has a special name only because it occurs in the hip joint, not because it has a separate pathologic basis.

The following report in the Talmud is most noteworthy: A ewe belonging to Rabbi Habiba was seen dragging along its hind legs. Said Rabbi Yemar, it is suffering from *shigrona.* Rabina demurred however saying: perhaps its spinal cord is damaged? *It was thereupon examined after having been slaughtered* and the opinion of Rabina was substantiated[145]. Here, therefore, we have a very modern method of establishing a diagnosis through an autopsy. In spite of this finding, there are many underlying causes for such abnormalities of gait, and *shigrona* is only one of them.

In the often-cited discourse concerning folk remedies[146], it is recommended that a patient suffering from *shigrona* should rub fish brine sixty times, that is very often[147], on each hip[148]. If one so desires, one can see in this recommendation a forerunner of the modern advocacy of rubbing trimethylamine on the painful hip. Judging from the prescription "on each hip", it appears as if the word *shigrona* also referred to lumbago. *Rashi,* with his general translation (of *shigrona*) as cramp, indeed comes very close to the truth.

"He who had pain in the loins" *(choshesh bemathenav)* used to rub himself with a mixture of wine and vinegar. Also for daily routine use, rubbing oneself with oil was considered to be propitious, especially if one could afford rose-oil[149].

---

143. Baba Metzia 86a. To drink an even number of glasses was believed to excite the ill will of certain demons.
144. Gittin 69b
145. Chullin 51a, see also 59a
146. Gittin 69b
147. The Babylonian sexagesimal system was also accepted by the Babylonian Jews. "Sixty times" would be comparable to "hundred times" in our decimal system
148. *metachta,* a word otherwise unknown, which, according to the commentaries means hips or loins.
149. Shabbath 14:4

# CHAPTER XI

## *MENTAL DISORDERS*

### I   The Madness of King Saul

In the Bible, two cases of mental aberration are generally well known. One concerns the Babylonian king Nebuchadnezzer; the other concerns the Jewish king Saul.

It is related of Nebuchadnezzer that the word of the Lord to him in an earlier dream became fulfilled: and he was driven from the company of men (probably his loyal subjects) and he ate grass like oxen, and his body was wet with the dew of heaven, until his hair became plentiful like that of eagles, and his nails became like the claws of birds. At the end of seven years he lifted up his eyes toward heaven, and his understanding returned to him, and he praised the Lord. He publicly informed his people of the story of his illness[1].

From time immemorial, this portrayal of Nebuchadnezzer has been interpreted as a psychosis, analagous to the lycanthropy of antiquity from which developed the werewolf of the Middle Ages. It remains uncertain today whether, according to modern nomenclature, the incident should be classified as melancholy or whether, as seems more likely to me, it was a case of paranoia, since a melancholic would simply have died of hunger.

It is harder for me to state with certainty that *Saul* suffered from mental illness. Year in and year out he had to wage a guerilla war with the neighboring peoples; when he tried to please his soldiers, he invited the reprimand of the prophet. He knew that his kingdom would be taken from him and given to another who was better than he[2]. He was rejected by the Lord, abandoned by his loyal friend Samuel, and discredited in the eyes of the people.

In view of these facts, which were not imaginary notions, it is no wonder that a depression set in, and *an evil spirit from the Lord suddenly terrified him*[3]. His servants did not consider him possessed by a demon, as suggested by Josephus[4], as evidenced by the therapeutic advice which they proposed to the patient, and which Saul at once accepted: one should seek out a man who is a skillful player on the harp, *and it shall be, when the evil spirit from God cometh upon thee, that he shall play with his hand, and thou shalt be well*[5]. Even in those days, music had a tranquilizing effect on the nerves, an effect which one has attributed to it, from antiquity until modern times.

---

1. Daniel 4:29 ff
2. First Samuel 15:28
3. *ibid* 16:14
4. "for all types of ailments and evil spirits

afflicted Saul, *pathe tine hai daimonia,* and tried to suffocate and strangle him." Josephus' *Antiquities* Book 6, Chapter 8:2
5. First Samuel 16:16

The king soon recognized, however, that in his harp player, he had taken into his palace a dangerous rival to the royal crown, whose superiority he felt. And the people rejoiced in David[6], the crown prince subjugated himself to David, Saul's court liked him, and Princess Michal loved him[7]. The king himself realized that David was very happy *(felix)*, and stood in awe of him[8]. Fear for his throne clearly began to come into prominence, and *an evil spirit from God came mightily upon Saul, and he raved in the midst of his house*[9], and, without being influenced by David's harp playing, grasped the spear (he was an Oriental sovereign!) in order to kill David. The intent failed, and in the failure, Saul saw a bad omen. Then ensued a desperate struggle for the crown — the king persecuted the pretendent who had already been crowned, and who was favored and concealed by his followers. When Saul met David, and the latter was magnanimous towards him, Saul had only one wish: *swear to me that you will not cut off my seed after me!*[10] Even this fear on the part of Saul was evoked or worsened as a result of true facts, and not because of insane notions.

In addition to the conflict with David, Saul's struggle with the Philistines certainly never abated. In the end, the battle went badly for the Israelites, and Saul's three sons were killed in battle, together with a large number of his army.

Saul himself was wounded and cornered. In order not to be pierced by his enemies and tortured to death, he took his sword and fell upon it[11]. Thus, even the suicide is psychologically understandable, motivated by the compelling situation[12].

Considering all of this, I would hesitate to designate Saul as a melancholic in the psychiatric sense. It does not necessarily follow from this, however, that *all* his actions, particularly his *sudden* affliction by the evil spirit and his raving, should be understood entirely in a physiologic sense. The true condition of his psyche was expressed when he sent messengers to fetch David from Naioth. They found a company of strange speaking people (prophets) and themselves succumbed to the psychic infection (and they also prophesied), as did the subsequent messengers sent by Saul[13]. Finally, Saul himself followed them *and he went on, and prophesied until he came to Naioth. And he also stripped off his clothes (as the others had done)... and he lay down naked all that day and all that night*[14]. Such frequent epileptic seizures (status epilepticus) would not occur without occasional previous seizures, or at least equivalents thereof. It is therefore highly likely that "the evil spirit of God which *suddenly* afflicted him" probably represented an epileptic equivalent, and that the raving (*mainesthai* in Greek) also portrayed an epileptoid condition. Naturally, we cannot know whether real epileptic seizures (grand mal) were also observed; the silence of the chronicler, a coreligionist, proves nothing. For a king, convulsions represent an illness which one does not mention without an overriding motive; for the seer, it is a matter of renown which one would just as soon exaggerate.

The fact that the palace officials were able to say that David healed the king proves that this illness was associated with long intermissions (remissions)[15].

If one accepts this interpretation — that Saul was an epileptic — then the portrayal of his illness bears an astonishing resemblance to that of Cambyses, as suggested by Herodotus. It is explicitly stated of Cambyses that he suffered from the sacred illness, and "it is therefore not surprising that when the body suffers from a serious illness, the mind also does not remain healthy"[16]. He too began to rave (*emane*

---

6. *ibid* 18:6
7. *ibid* 18:20
8. *ibid* 18:15
9. *ibid* 18:10
10. First Samuel 24:22
11. *ibid* 31:4. In Second Samuel 1:10, the story ends somewhat differently.

12. Genesis Rabbah 34:13 and *Yoreh Deah* 345:3
13. First Samuel 19:18 ff
14. *ibid* 19:23-24
15. Josephus' *Antiquities*. Book 6 Chapt. 11:2
16. Herodotus 3:33

in Greek, exactly like the *vayithnabe* of Saul), after not having been completely normal (*phreneres* in Greek) even before[17]. The more caustic Greek expressions used here derive from the fact that the Greek Herodotus is writing the history of barbarians, his sworn enemy. Cambyses can be differentiated from Saul in the unheard-of ferocity of the former, even for an Oriental despot, because of the absence of any political reason; it is strongly reminiscent of the insanity of the Caesars of the Roman empire.

It is not necessary to mention that to regard the appearance of the spirit of Samuel to the witch of Endor[18] as the hallucination of an insane person would contradict all the perceptions of antiquity concerning necromancy. Furthermore, the interpretation is not even objectively correct, for Saul himself did not see the spirit (or ghost) of Samuel. Saul only recognized Samuel's appearance from the description of the exorcist.

In modern times, Lomer has also placed the personality of Jesus under psychiatric scrutiny[19]. I must renounce writing a critique of his assertions and conclusions because of major dogmatic difficulties. The literary strife surrounding this question is presently being fought with great intensity[20].

## II   The Feigned Madness of David

A deliberate *simulation* of mental illness is described by the chronicler of David when he was with the king of Gath:[21] *and he changed his behavior before them, and feigned himself mad in their hands: he scratched* (Septuagint: thumped) *on the doors of the gate and let his spittle fall down upon his beard.* Then the king (Achish of Gath) spoke to his people: *behold you see a mad man, why did you bring him here? Have I a paucity of madmen that you brought this one to me, to act insane in my presence?* According to legend[22], he had a mentally ill daughter. The simulation of insanity was also known in heathen antiquity, as is described in the story of Bbutus[23].

The *Midrash* adds the following thought to the above story: David said to God: *God has created everything appropriately in its time*[24], meaning that everything which God created in the world is good. What purpose, however, does a madman serve? He runs around the street and tears his clothes; children run after him, and make a mockery of him. Even adults laugh at him. Do you consider that to be good? God answers by saying: you wish to contest the usefulness of insanity? By your life, you shall have need of it! During David's flight from King Saul to the king of Gath, the truth of the teaching became apparent.

Insanity *(shigga'on)* is one of the afflictions which first the Pentateuch[25] and later also the prophets[26] threaten as punishment for disobedience. The Israelites will become mad, when much misfortune befalls them[27], for not having obeyed the Lord. Noteworthy also is the speech and the conduct of a *nabi* (prophet). The Septuagint erroneously translates the *nabi* as *prophetes*, a "foreteller of the future", an *epitheton*, not at all suited to Moses and David who were also called *nabi*. A *nabi* is as different from an insane person as a superman is different from an inhuman creature, and as genius is different from insanity. It is no wonder that uneducated and evil people did not recognize this distinction, or did not want to do so. An arrogant scoffer once called a prophet *meshugga* or mad[28]. A man who is mad and makes himself a prophet is a

17. *ibid* 30
18. First Samuel 28:7 ff
19. *Jesus Christus vom Standpunkt des Psychiaters* by Dr. De Loosten (Dr. George Lomer). Bamberg 1905
20. See the writings of Rasmussen, Werner, Baumann, Schäfer and Rünze in *Zeitschrift fur Religionspsychologie* Vol. 3, 1909 Part 1. The literature grows daily.
21. First Samuel 21:14

22. *Yalkut op.cit.*
23. Livius 1:56
24. Eccles. 3:11. There is nothing extraordinary about David citing a teaching of Solomon
25. Deut. 28:28
26. Zechariah 12:4
27. Deut. 28:34
28. Second Kings 9:11

false prophet[29]. Once, however, the people of Israel will learn that the false prophet is only a fool, and the man of the spirit (*ish haruach* in Hebrew; *daimonijomenos* in Greek) is insane[30]. True prophets, however, according to a Talmudic statement[31], ceased to exist after the destruction of the Temple, and only "children and fools speak peculiarly".

One should also mention here that the Neoplatonists made use of children who were thought to be inhabited by demons. The latter expressed their views through the mouths of these children. The words of these children were thought to represent a direct proclamation of the demons, and were used to ban demons which provoked illness[32].

To the Turks even today, persons with mental illness are held in highest esteem[33], and are considered to be holy and inviolable throughout the Orient[34].

## III    Insanity, Demons and Exorcism

Thomas Bartholin, the well-known anatomist, in a monograph[35], first ventured to identify the *daimoniyomenoi* of the New Testament as epileptics and mentally ill. He also observed in Pavia that people who were thrashed (flogged) as "possessed" were treated by the famous physician Johann Dominik Sala as epileptics and melancholics, and healed[36]. Richard Mead enunciates the diagnosis in apodictic form: *insanorum sunt haec omnia. Nihil profecto hic sacrum, nihil, quod ex male affecta corporis sanitate oriri non possit, reperimus.* He adds that those people who do not believe that exorcism is nothing more than the healing of the insane are not very much at home in medicine *(in re medica nimis hospites sunt);* otherwise they could find numerous analogies, as for example, the illness of frenzy *(rabies canina)*[37]. Ever since that time, the literature concerning demons has increased enormously and represents a large portion of the history of civilization. The strife as to whether or not the *daimon* (demon) represents an actual being (the devil), was waged with unprecedented ferocity.

One should mention as a curiosity from antiquity the writings of the pastor from the village of Teichwolfram[38] whose name — what ironical coincidence — was Johann Gottlob Artzt[39] — German for physician — and who forcefully warned against the naturalistic perception of demons[40].

The Gospels portray "the possessed" as follows: he wears no clothes and resides in no one house[41]. Rather he spends his days and nights on the mountains and in the tombs, and cries and hits himself with stones[42]. And when he sees Jesus, he cries out: have you come to torment me before the time? (imaginary fear)[43]. He is extremely angry and no one can walk the same street with him. No one can bind him, not even with chains[44]. For he was often bound with chains and shackles, and threw off the shackles and crushed the chains, and no one could restrain him. Some are also dumb[45] or blind[46]. Other than Maria Magdalene[47], there is only one other woman afflicted with this illness[48]. Otherwise, only men are involved.

---

29. Jeremiah 29:26
30. Hosea 9:7
31. Baba Bathra 12b
32. Hugo Magnus. *Der Aberglauben in der Medizin*. Breslau 1903 p.59
33. Stern. *Turkei* 1:169
34. Riehm. *Handwb. des Biblisches Altertums* p.877a
35. *Paralytici N.T. medico et philolog. comment. illustr.* (Ed. 1?). Sec. Ed. Basel 1662; Third Ed. Leipzig 1685
36. *De Morbis Biblicis* (Ed. 1?) Second Ed. Frankfurt 1672 p.66. He considers flogging of the insane to be rational *(nec flagella damnentur)*
37. *Op. cit.* p.66 and 69
38. literally: wolf pond
39. literally: John — praise God — physician
40. *Soluti problematis hermeneut. de Daemoniacis periculum* Lips. 1763. 40 p. 4°
41. Luke 8:27
42. Mark 5:5
43. Matthew 8:28
44. Mark 5:3
45. Matthew 9:32
46. *ibid* 12:22
47. Luke 8:2
48. Matthew 15:22

The picture throughout corresponds to the type of person which the general populace even today considers "insane". Clinically, the picture was probably that of *melancholia agitata* or *furor melancholicus*.

To conjecture about the therapy used by Jesus to heal those "possessed" by demons[49] is useless, since the Gospels only assert that he drove the devil out, but are silent concerning the method used. The explanations concerning the entrance of the expelled devil into sows which threw themselves into the ocean and drowned can be found in the writings of the exegetes and do not belong here. It is true, Josephus asserts[50], that the exorcising of such a "possessed" patient through magic formulas, which were said to have originated with King Solomon, was practiced quite often among the Jews. In addition, in the story of the Apostles, it is related that several Jews expelled devils by the name of Jesus from "possessed" individuals[51]. However, Talmudic writings do not mention the concept of the "possessed" at all, and also not the skill of exorcists. Josephus probably fabricated his report, in order not to arouse the suspicion of his heathen fellow countrymen for whom his book was intended, that among the Jews there were lacking such prominent people to whom one attributed exorcism. Furthermore, Jews who treated patients in the name of Jesus, were certainly no longer considered to be Jews.

The noteworthy fact that whereas in the Old Testament there is no mention of the possessed, the Gospels describe them on numerous occasions, has already been commented upon by the *patres*. For example, in the sixth century, Anastasius Sinaita asks "why does one find *apud Christianos plures quam apud infideles manci... epileptici aliisque morbis distenti?*"[52] All answers are unsatisfactory. Tylor considers the marked religious excitement of that time to be the reason[53]. Edward V. Siebold complains that Christianity promoted belief in superstition as a result of its faith healing[54]. Magnus claims that an epidemic of mental illness developed from the belief in demons under the influence of Christian teaching[55]; etc. Adolph Harnack probably comes closest to the truth when he states that the belief in demons increased to such a large extent — it already existed for a long time — because "there no longer existed a strong naive public religion which could suppress it"[56]. For just at that time paganism was no more, and Christianity was not yet thought of as a religion.

## IV  Imbeciles

In the *Mishnah*, the name used exclusively for an imbecile is *shoteh*, which is derived from the root *shat* meaning to roam about. It is probably an alias for "absent-mindedness", or perhaps refers to a person who leads a vagrant life (i.e. roams about). Neither the *Mishnah* nor other law books define imbecility. From the fundamental principle that "the imbecile is not in full possession of his intellect" *(bar de'ah)* — very similar parallels are portrayed by minors and deaf-mutes — there follow a large number of individual regulations concerning the legal status of the imbecile. An enumeration of these regulations as far as ritual is concerned, is not of interest here[57]. However, from the fact that the mentally deficient person was considered *fit* to perform certain intellectual or physical skills — for example the slaughtering of cattle

49. as for example Renan. Apostel p.138
50. *Antiquities*. Book 8 Chapt. 2:5
51. Acts 19:13
52. *Quaestiones. Max. Bibl. vet. patr.* Vol. 9 Lugdunam 1677 Question 40
53. *Anfänge der Kultur* 2:139
54. *Geschichte des Geburtshülfe* Berlin 1839 Vol. 1:187
55. *Der Aberglauben in der Medizin*. Breslau 1903 p.61; and *Medizin und Religion in ihren Gegens. Beziehungen*. Breslau 1902 p.58
56. *Medizinisches Aus Der Altesten Kirchengeschichte*. Leipzig 1892 p.72
57. *Tosefta* Terumoth 1:1 and 10:18; Chagigah 1:1; Megillah 2:4; Rosh Hashana 8:8; Menachoth 9:8; Gittin 2:5; Niddah 2:1; Arachin 1:1; Machshirin 6:1; Zabim 2:1; Parah 5:4; Soferim 1:12

according to the Jewish ritual regulations, etc.[58] — one can conclude that he was not looked upon as an insane person according to the above portrayal of the Gospels or the general populace, which seems to nearly equate him with an animal. Nevertheless, it was natural that he was not entrusted with *official* functions, and was legally equated with a child. One must also assume that he was legally considered a minor in all other respects. However, in only an exceptional case of civil law is there mention made of the appointment of a guardian (or trustee), the *epitropos*[59].

An imbecile cannot function as a priest[60]. The court is obligated to initiate proceedings against the wife of an imbecile if she is suspected of being an adulteress, because of the deficient intellect of the husband[61]. It is clearly stated that a mentally deficient person who has caused physical injury is exempt from punishment[62]. I am not aware, however, of other regulations in the *Mishnah* concerning his responsibilities in criminal law.

Two legal questions are of special interest. According to Talmudic law, a person who injures another must pay for the medical expenses, for the loss of time from work, for depreciation of the worth of the injured person, for the pain incurred, and for the shame suffered because of the injury. It is undoubted that an injured imbecile is entitled to receive payment for the first four items. It is uncertain, however, whether restitution for degradation (*bosheth,* meaning shame) is applicable to an imbecile. The question is a special case of the principal difference of opinion in the Talmud, on the one hand, whether an insult is punishable *ipso facto,* without the insulted person having to be aware of it or perceive it (as for example insulting the Sovereign in modern times), and, on the other hand, whether the family of a person who has been put to shame is entitled to make a claim for punishment. The final decision states that claims for having insulted an imbecile are not admissible in court[63].

More important are the regulations concerning the marriage of an imbecile. Naturally, the marriage is invalid if both parties or even if only one of them is mentally deficient[64]. If the man recovers, however, he can legalize an already contracted marriage[65]. If the wife becomes mentally defective, dissolution of the marriage is forbidden in order that people (specifically men) not consider a sick helpless wife like a piece of ownerless property[66]; this rule prohibiting divorce is softened, because polygamy in the Orient was permissible. If the husband becomes an imbecile, according to Talmudic law, divorce is not possible. This results from the fact that a man must either personally, or through his designated representative, deliver the bill of divorce to his wife, and its writing he himself must have requested. An absolute prerequisite for these conditions to be fulfilled is full possession of one's mental faculties[67].

Furthermore, one should make reference to the above-cited regulations concerning the marriage of an epileptic.

A mentally deficient individual cannot testify in court. Even if he recovered, he can only testify about matters which *antedated* his mental illness[68]. On the other hand, modern legislation regarding testimony of witnesses allows a recovered patient to testify even about events which transpired during his mental illness[69].

If someone is at times healthy and at other times mentally ill, so that he suffers from periodic mental disturbances, then during the periods when he is healthy (during

---

58. Chullin 1:1
59. *Tosefta* Baba Kamma 4:4
60. Bechoroth 7:6
61. Sotah 4:1
62. Baba Kamma 87a
63. Baba Kamma 86b
64. Yebamoth 112b; *Eben Haezer* 44:2

65. *Tosefta* Kethuboth 1:3
66. Yebamoth 113b
67. Gittin 7:1
68. *Tosefta* Sanhedrin 5:4; Gittin 2:5
69. Prof. Aschaffenburg. *Mediz. Reform.* 1905 p.308

lucid intervals), he is considered perfectly normal, and during the periods when he is ill, he is regarded as totally sick[70]. A. Bumm, a Munich psychiatrist, has emphasized that "this perception of the Rabbis represents not only a nosologic but also a legal-psychiatric advance, (opposed to the teachings of the Greeks); all the more remarkable, the more one brings to mind the harmful influence on the administration of justice which was effected until the first half of the nineteenth century by the false doctrine of the partial soundness of mind of a mentally ill individual"[71].

It is noteworthy that mental illness is lacking among the listing of defects in the parents of a "rebellious son" which would constitute a mitigating circumstance, whereby the son would be immune from punishment in Jewish legal practice[72].

## V   Definition of Insanity

To this day, to have a useful definition of the concept of "mental illness" is the wish of all jurists and psychiatrists. The Rabbis also toiled to arrive at such a definition. They said: "Who is mentally ill? He who goes out at night alone, and he who spends the night in a graveyard, and he who tears his garments and destroys everything that is given to him". The inadequacy of this definition is immediately emphasized[73]: if he does them in an insane manner *(derech shetuth)* — a *petitio principii!*— then even *one* is proof of his imbecility; otherwise even all of them prove nothing. A person who goes out alone at night might be a *kynanthropos* (dog man) — and lycanthropy was not considered to represent insanity — or as *Rashi* explains more simply, he might go for a walk at night to cool off. Someone who spends the night in a cemetery might have done so (in order to conjure up evil spirits) for magical purposes, as happened often[74]. One who tears his garments might be a choleric or a cynic (both textual readings are known), and finally one who destroys everything that is given to him might be suffering from *morbus cardiacus,* and a broadening of the latter concept, Rabbi Bun explains, is inadmissible[75].

For the practice of law, however, the above is not helpful. It remains, as in today's legal proceedings, up to the "careful assessment of the situation by the judge"[76], who uses his discretion to consult with experts and utilizes their advice in arriving at a judgement. During the time of the great Sanhedrin, certain precautions were taken by the requirement that the members of this court of law possess some knowledge of all general sciences including medicine[77].

An example of auditory hallucinations, combined with mass suggestion, is related in the Book of Kings[78]: the king of Aram besieged the Israelite city of Shomrom. Four lepers who were at the entrance to the city wished to surrender to the enemy, came into the camp of the Arameans, but found no one there: *for the Lord had made the host of the Arameans to hear a noise of chariots, and a noise of horses, even the noise of a great host,* so that they thought that the king of Israel had hired neighboring kings to fall upon them from behind. So the Arameans arose and fled in the twilight, and left their tents and their horses, and their asses, *even the camp as it was, and fled for their life.* The entire route up to the Jordan was replete with clothes and weapons which the soldiers had discarded in their flight.

Mar Bar Rav Ashi did not permit a widow whose child died before the end of the usual suckling period of two years to remarry before the prescribed waiting period, for fear that another woman might kill her child in order to remarry expeditiously, as in

---

70. *Tosefta* Terumoth 1:3
71. *Spuren Griechisch Psychiatrie in Talmud.* Private printing. *circa* 1902 p.14
72. Maimonides. *Hilchoth Mamrim* 7:10
73. Chagigah 3b
74. Sanhedrin 65b; Niddah 17a

75. *Tosefta* Terumoth 1:3; Jerushalmi Terumoth 1; 40b; Jerushalmi Gittin 7; 48c
76. Maimonides. *Hilchoth Eduth* 9:9
77. *ibid. Hilchoth Sanhedrin* 2:1
78. Second Kings 7:6 ff

fact once happened[79]. The Rabbis retorted to him that the case which occurred involved a woman who was an imbecile. A sane woman would certainly not strangle her child, and the general rule is that "one cannot bring proof from the action of imbeciles"[80]. His opinion, however, is not accepted as the final ruling.

According to legend[81], King Solomon used to go around begging, saying wherever he went: *I, Koheleth, was king over Israel in Jerusalem*[82]. It was thought that he was mad. When he came to the Sanhedrin, however, the Rabbis said: "a madman does not stick to one thing only (but changes with his delusions)"! On the other hand, the epigrammatic poet teaches that a fool repeats his folly like a dog who returns to his vomit[83], a teaching which was well known to the *Midrash* in an Aramaic form[84].

It was naturally recognized that the picture of an intoxicated person is similar to that of a madman[85], as well as that of alcoholic amnesia. Philopater gave an order that the Jews should be trampled to death by elephants in the circus. When he awoke, following a long and extended drinking bout, "he completely forgot everything", and threatened with death those officials who reminded him of the execution of his order[86].

The loss of one's mental powers with aging is also known. Barzillai said: *I am this day fourscore years old, can I discern between good and bad*[87]? From here one can see, remarks the Talmud[88], that the intellect (or discernment) of an old man is altered. Sirach admonishes: honor your father even if his understanding weakens[89].

Rabbi Yochanan cried and wept so much for his deceased brother-in-law and colleague Resh Lakesh that "his mind was turned. The Rabbis prayed for him (Rabbi Yochanan) and he died", and was thus relieved of his grief[90].

One often comes across the teaching in antiquity which states that a criminal is ill in his soul. A talmudic proponent of this teaching is Resh Lakish who says: "A person does not commit a transgression until a spirit of folly enters into him"[91]. Thus a woman only commits adultery if she became mentally deranged[92]. Sexual excesses of the husband also only occur as a result of psychic abnormalities[93]. Similarly, the "rebellious son" who, according to the Bible, must be punished[94], is mentally deranged[95]; and it is only as a result of this perception that idolatry is considered to be a "mental disturbance".

The philosophers of Rome asked the Sages: if God derives no satisfaction from idolatry, why does He not destroy it? They answered: if people would only idolize useless things, then God would in fact destroy them. However, they also worship the sun, the moon and the stars. Should He destroy the world because of fools[96]? During a storm, the sailors cried out to their idols. A child said: how long will you be fools? Pray to the One who created the ocean[97]!

Kornfeld asserts that "in the Bible, crimes and psychic disturbances are fundamentally separated from each other"[98]. This can only mean that a law book does not, in general, deal with matters from the psychiatric standpoint.

79. Kethuboth 60b
80. Niddah 30b
81. Gittin 68b
82. Eccles. 1:12
83. Proverbs 26:11
84. Levit. Rabbah 16:9
85. Megillah 12b
86. Third Maccabees 5:27
87. Second Samuel 19:36
88. Shabbath 152b
89. Sirach 3:13
90. Baba Metzia 84a
91. Sotah 3a
92. The word *tishteh* in Numbers 5:12 is interpreted thusly in Sotah 3a through alteration of the diacritical points. In Jerushalmi Kethuboth 7; 31c, a woman who kisses a strange man is called a *shotah*.
93. Bechoroth 5b where the name *shittu'n* (Numbers 25:1) is combined with *shoteh*.
94. Deut. 21:18
95. *Sifre loc. cit.* ed. Friedmann p.114a and *Yalkut* No. 929 where the word *moreh* of the text is equated with (the Greek) *moros* meaning moron
96. *Tosefta* Abodah Zara 6:7
97. *Tosefta* Niddah 5:17
98. *Verbrechen und Geistesstorung im Lichte der Altbiblischen Tradition.* Halle 1904 p.35:5

Otherwise it would be superfluous.

Nothing is mentioned in the Bible concerning the management of such patients. It is probable that unruly or violent madmen were simply placed in chains, in addition to being starved and flogged. This seems to have been the customary manner of treatment from the time of antiquity until Pinel (1795), even among physicians[99]. The same can be surmised from the above-mentioned report of Mark the Evangelist (5:3), and also perhaps from the report in Jeremiah that Zephaniah had every madman *(meshugga)* and every prophesier *(mithnabe)* placed in prison and in the stocks[100]. The Talmudic writings, however, do not mention any of this, or any other treatment. They merely state: "we do not possess medications for madmen"[101].

In addition to the statement of Rabbi Reuben that *moria* (stupidity) is the Greek equivalent for *shoteh*[102], the Midrash relates the following story: a man who had a substantial income had an evil personality, and never gave the legally prescribed charities, such as the tithe for the poor, etc. One day he became mentally ill, and he took fire and hurled it into the houses which he possessed, and he took his silver and his gold and he cast them into the sea, and he took a hammer and smashed all the filled wine barrels which he owned. And all that because he did not honor the Lord whose grace he enjoyed[103].

In colloquial speech, the word *shoteh* has gradually lost its strict psychiatric sense; it refers to our "fool" and similar designations, and has a connotation which is equivalent to the expression: "to fool someone"[104].

The Talmud says that "he that presumptuously thrusts himself forward to render a legal decision is foolish, wicked, and of an arrogant disposition"[105].

Ibn Ganach adds thereto that he who thinks himself to be an expert judge in all areas is the worst type of fool.

The following story is amusing: a man wrote in his will that his son should only inherit him if he (the father) became a *shoteh* (fool). The commission before which Rabbi Joshua ben Korcha brought the case saw the man hopping around on his hands and feet with a rush in his mouth, and with his small son running after him. When the case was brought for adjudication, Rabbi Joshua laughed and said: you have just observed the answer to your question: a person becomes a fool as soon as he begets children[106].

# VI    Demons

As mentioned previously, the portrayal of demons in the Talmud differs from that of the Gospels. Whereas the latter interpret demoniacs to be madmen, the Rabbis only mention physical illnesses which are caused by the *ruach* (spirit) or *shed* (demon), and only rarely is madness identified with a *shed*[107].

We learn the following about the spirit which produces psychic disturbances: an idolater who ridiculed the ceremony of the red heifer[108] as a kind of witchcraft was asked by Rabbi Yochanan ben Zakkai: "Has the demon (or spirit) of madness *(thez-azith)* ever possessed you?" "No," he replied. "Have you ever seen a man possessed by this demon of madness?" "Yes," said he. "And what do you do in such a case?"

---

99. Celsus 3:18. *tormentis optime curatur... fame, vinculis, plagis coercendus est*
100. Jeremiah 29:26
101. Gittin 70b
102. Lamentations Rabbah. Foreword No. 31 fol 8c
103. *Pesikta Rabbah*. Ed. Friedman. *Piska* No. 25 p.127a
104. For example Baba Kamma 116a; Baba

Bathra 175a
105. Aboth 4:7. Other examples include Shabbath 121b; Erubin 53b; Jerushalmi Nazir 9; 57d
106. *Midrash* Psalms 92:13 p.206b; *Yalkut* No. 846
107. Rosh Hashanah 28a
108. Numbers 19:1 ff

"We (heathens) bring roots and make smoke under him; then we sprinkle water upon the demon and it flees", he replied[109].

I cannot as yet determine the identity of this "possessing demon"[110], which possessed a man so that, in a fit of rage, he smashed barrels of oil and wine and beat his grandson on the skull with a stick[111], and which appeared as a benefactor to the wild goats in labor[112], and which, according to the Babylonian Talmud, produces rabies in a dog[113].

A person pursued by heathens or by robbers or by the evil spirit should not fast, in order not to lose his powers[114]. One should attempt to help such individuals, even by desecrating the laws of the Sabbath[115].

## VII    Mental Illness

Concerning the "mentally ill" in the narrow sense, i.e. *shotim,* a distinction is made between several categories of psychic disturbances whose precise identification at the moment is also not possible. One situation of "confusion", called *sha'amumith*[116], is mentioned next to madness and epilepsy[117]. Does the tripartite Roman law *in furioisi, dementes* and *mente capti,* lie at the bottom of this condition? This type of confusion produces idleness[118], and also, according to the teaching of Mar Samuel, uncleanliness of one's clothes[119].

Temporary disturbances of the mind and the power of discernment *(teruph da'ath)* can also occur during the course of acute illnesses[120]. Physical ailments of the body also influence the psyche[121]; "one cannot break the cask without allowing any of the wine to spill"[122]. One intentionally induces a benumbing of the senses in a criminal who is being led out to execution, in that one gives him a goblet of wine containing a grain of frankincense[123], based on the words of the epigrammatic poet: *give strong drink unto him that is ready to perish, and wine unto the bitter in soul*[124]. Jesus also received this drink before the crucifixion[125]. The same expression for a disturbance of the mind is often used in the broadest physiological sense to refer to one whose unsoundness of mind results from an error on his part. Accordingly, the word *shoteh* (meaning "fool") is placed in opposition to the word *to'eh* (meaning "to be in error")[126].

## VIII    Kordiakos

If a man who is ill with *kordiakos* gives instructions that a bill of divorce be written for his wife, his words are of no effect[127], because the man is suffering from a disturbance of the mind and therefore a deficiency of insight. He is not, however, included in the legal definition of the mentally deranged *(shoteh),* because he shows none of the symptoms of the latter[128], even though, according to Rabbi Yochanan, he has many similarities to a *shoteh.* Resh Lakish compares the ability to act of a person seized with *kordiakos* to a person who is sleeping (semi-consciousness)[129]. According to Mar Samuel, this illness occurs when a person is overcome[130] by new wine from the

109. Numbers Rabbah 19:8
110. See Buber in his ed. *Pesikta de Rab Kahana* p.40 note 192
111. *ibid: asser,* p.97a; it is thus a fit of rage and not "possession" by a demon
112. Genesis Rabbah 12:9
113. Jerushalmi Yoma 8; 45b, according to *Aruch;* Aggadah: *chazazith*
114. *Tosefta* Taanith 2:12
115. *Tosefta* Erubin 4:8
116. from *amam,* to disguise the intellect, to confuse
117. Baba Metzia 80a and elsewhere
118. Kethuboth 59b
119. Nedarim 81a

120. Niddah 2:1
121. literally: soul
122. Baba Bathra 16a
123. Sanhedrin 43a
124. Proverbs 31:6 Regarding the psychology of women, it is interesting that the expenses for this wine and frankincense were borne by the noble women of Jerusalem who voluntarily provided it. See Sanhedrin 43a
125. Mark 15:23
126. for example Niddah 54a
127. Gittin 7:1
128. see above, section V of this chapter
129. Gittin 70b
130. literally: bitten

vat[131]. According to Rabbi Jose, a *kordiakos* is a *hamin*[132], or a confused person. Therapeutically, for a patient with *kordiakos*, red meat and diluted wine are recommended. This dietetic remedy is also helpful for *tertiana*[133].

Undoubtedly, *kordiakos* is an acute illness, and undoubtedly it is the *morbus cordiacus* of the heathen physicians. Unfortunately the meaning and the cause of this illness in the writings of these physicians are uncertain, and it is difficult from their portrayals of this sickness, even from the excellent description of Coelius Aurelianus[134], to arrive at a clear (or correct) picture thereof. The copious sweating and the insomnia[135] seem to suggest a state of delirium tremens with precordial anxiety. However, Celsus[136] specifically states that, in contrast to phreseny, in *kordiakos* there is no disturbance in the state of consciousness. His opinion that it refers to *nimia imbecellitas corporis,* is certainly not correct. Galen contradicts himself in his writings[137]. According to Maimonides[138], *morbus cardiacus* is one of the varieties of convulsive disorders in which there is unsoundness of mind as a result of overfilling of the chambers of the brain. Puschmann assembled a series of additional reports on *kordiakos* and agrees with the conclusion of Landsberg that we are dealing with situations which resemble those which occur in anemic and chlorotic individuals[139]. This explanation is hard to understand, as is the opinion of Ziegler (1843) that *morbus cardiacus* refers to *veterum nostra pericarditis exsudatoria sanguinolenta in homine scorbuto affecto,* and many others. Throughout, one develops the impression that the various authors interpret *morbus cardiacus* as many different illnesses, probably in part misled by the double meaning of the word *kardia:* heart and stomach.

In support of the interpretation of the Rabbis that their *kordiakos* refers to an alcoholic delirium — (even Coelius considers *vinolenta* to be one of the causes of *morbus cardiacus*) — in addition to the cause which they themselves mention[140], one can cite the following from the Palestinian Talmud[141]: Rabbi Jose had to adjudicate the ability of discernment of a weaver afflicted with *kordiakos.* "The latter was given red in black[142] and he babbled. Then he was given black in red, and he babbled. This is the *kordiakos* of which the Sages spoke (as written in the books)". "Babble" (i.e. to talk nonsense) is the translation of the word *le'i* of the text, and corresponds to the Arabic *laei* meaning *vana locutus est.* This word is already found in the Bible in relation to the babbling of the drinker, *shatu velua*[143], meaning they drink and they babble.

For the sake of completeness, one must still mention the *shuphtana,* who is not much different from the *shoteh*[144], and the *tippesh* or imbecile[145] or fool, in contradistinction to the *chacham* or wise person. The literature in the Bible concerning the *tippesh,* as well as that regarding the *kesil* (fool), belongs more appropriately in a history of psychology, and not here.

131. Gittin 67b
132. Jerushalmi Terumoth 1; 40b, probably corrupted. Is the Hebrew *hamam* synonymous with the above *'amam?* The Arabic *hami'm,* mentioned by Kohut, is, according to Freytag "naturally preserved milk". Should the work properly be *chami'm* meaning hot or fever?
133. The work *marka* cannot mean *meracum* or undiluted, for the opposite word is *chiya.*
134. *Acut.* 2:30 ff
135. neither symptom mentioned by the Talmud
136. Celsus 3:19
137. See Landsberg in Henschel's *Janus* 2:53 ff
138. Commentary on the Mishnah, Gittin 7:1
139. in his work *Alexander of Tralles.* Vol.1 p.214 ff
140. i.e. being overcome by new wine from the vat
141. Jerushalmi Gittin 7; 48c
142. ? diluted red wine or red thread while working with black thread. *Akim* meaning black, meaning diluted red wine, is deduced from the Babylonian Talmud, where the word *marka* appears. However, diluted red wine is not black!
143. Obadiah 1:16
144. Baba Kamma 85a
145. perhaps *shiphta* is a transposition of *tippesh!*

# CHAPTER XII

## *SKIN DISEASES*

### PART I
### The Illness Called Tzaraath

The number of books and treatises written about the thirteenth chapter of the third book of the Pentateuch, which deals with the illness called *tzaraath,* is nearly as large as the number of works written about circumcision. As a result, one might think that every detail would have been clarified and every linguistic and archaeological problem solved. However, just the opposite is the case. Every new work brings new (or old) hypotheses in which the authors often boast of being original, unconcerned as to whether or not they are truthful and honest in their claims. Many writers put forth a theory for which they then seek proof in the appropriate place in Scriptures. If the Scriptural text does not fit the theory, then they abruptly "revise" it. Other writers who insist on applying modern viewpoints to ancient writings, must also eventually give forced explanations to Biblical phrases. It is specifically the matters with which this chapter is concerned, as we will see shortly, that give the greatest difficulty in interpretation of all medical comments in the Bible.

I differ from all my predecessors in that I do *not* understand numerous details of the chapter on *tzaraath.* I even believe that the explanation of some of these details is impossible to elucidate. Therefore, in the main, I restrict myself to translating the respective Biblical citation from the original text and to adding what is necessary to understand every sentence or passage. A few preliminary general remarks seem appropriate.

### I Tzaraath

Above all, I must oppose the dogmatic opinion which is particularly advocated by Münch[1], that the Bible provides the depiction of a disease in all its stages. This would be without analogy in any law book, and the Bible is surely primarily a law book. One immediately notes from the Biblical text that the main concern is to determine who is clean and who is unclean, because when distinguishing marks of the latter are present, then the strict civil consequences of isolation are imposed on the person in question. If anyone thinks that formal proof is still required for such an interpretation, then one need only remember that the Lawgiver, in numerous places, is not satisfied with simply

---

1. Münch. *Die Zaraath (Lepra) der Hebräischen Bibel.* Hamburg & Leipzig 1893

stating: "it is a *tzaraath*", which would be sufficient for *medical* purposes, but always adds the phrase: "he is unclean". For this reason, Huth correctly speaks of a *lepra legalis*[2].

On the other hand, I would like to draw a different conclusion from the double expression of the text. Throughout the entire chapter, Scripture speaks only of that morbid condition whose precise identification is difficult, at least for a lay person, so that he seeks the counsel of an expert. Even the latter often only renders an opinion after prolonged observation of the lesion. One cannot assume that all cases are immediately brought to the priest for observation at the earliest stage. The text itself speaks of the case of a *"chronic tzaraath"*. In some cases — for example, where the involved person was away for a prolonged period — fully developed lesions were first examined, and these were most likely immediately correctly identified, even by lay persons. The advanced stages of the disease, in which the patient resembles one who is *dead, of whom the flesh is half consumed when he cometh out of his mother's womb*[3], were well known.

The constant repetition: "it is a *tzaraath*, he is unclean", is probably meant to impress upon us that where there is doubt as to the presence of *tzaraath*, not only in the diagnostically difficult cases enumerated in the Bible, uncleanliness is stipulated. The concluding sentence of the entire law recapitulates once more that "such and such restrictions are imposed upon the *tzarua*, who is afflicted with a *nega*"; referring to *everyone* who is undoubtedly suffering from that sickness. In view of the severe consequences of the diagnosis, final decision as to the precise diagnosis was nevertheless left in the hands of experts, i.e. the priests, to whom Scriptures elsewhere assigns this task; for *by their word shall every controversy and every nega be tried*[4].

I also wish to oppose another viewpoint, repeatedly enunciated by theologians, that the entire chapter on *tzaraath* is only to be understood in the allegorical sense, as if Scripture were only speaking of "leprosy of the soul". If one's intent is only to consider such an interpretation *next* to the correct literal one, then we would have no qualms. Everyone is free to interpret an illness into as many types of diseases as he wishes, but to offer the (allegorical) viewpoint as the only acceptable one so contradicts the clear flow of words of the text that it is (blatantly wrong, and it is) not necessary to speak much further thereof here. The situation is quite similar in the case of the Song of Songs which, since earliest times, has been considered to represent a dialogue between the Children of Israel and God, and, therefore, was adopted as part of the Biblical Canon. This interpretation of both Jews and Christians[5], however, cannot prevent archaeologists from considering it their duty to understand primarily the images, meaning that the Song of Songs is the antiphony between a pair of shepherd lovers.

## II

*Tzaraath* is an illness whose characteristics differentiating it from other harmless conditions are externally recognizable on the skin. This illness was thought to be so dangerous that an individual afflicted therewith was completely isolated from the company of healthy people. Such a patient was not bedridden; otherwise the priest would have been sent *to him,* as well as to the infected house. There also exist chronic forms of the disease. Among chronic skin diseases where there is good reason to be very concerned, only leprosy and syphilis need to be considered. Against the opinion that the Biblical illness referred to as *tzaraath* is syphilis, is the often-repeated symptom that the hair on the affected part of the skin becomes white. Furthermore, the

---

2. *ibid* p.48
3. Numbers 12:12

4. Deut. 21:5
5. literally: synagogue and church (F.R.)

entire description of *tzaraath* does not seem to depict a syphilitic skin eruption, not to mention the fact that there is no mention at all in the Bible of all the other symptoms of syphilis, particularly, the primary lesion. Therefore, we agree with the viewpoint which, until recent decades, was espoused by nearly all investigators[6], that *tzaraath* refers to *leprosy*.

I readily admit that this proof is far from conclusive, for it cannot be proven that persons afflicted with any other skin disease which *we* would consider to be harmless, were not also isolated. For the Bible does not at all mention the reasons for isolating the leper from the encampment. We *assume* that it was the fear of contagion, because today we no longer recognize any other reason for isolating a person with a physical illness. However, it remains only a supposition that the "unclean" of the Bible is really equivalent to "contagious". The reason might just as well be an ethical consideration, or perhaps esthetic repugnance, or possibly some other reason. There may be no compelling objections to the view of Kazenelson-Sack[7] that *tzaraath* is a trichophytosis (fungal infection). It would seem strange to us to "isolate" a person with *herpes tonsurans,* whereas the picture of isolated lepers is quite familiar to us.

In his already-mentioned monograph opposing the view that *tzaraath* means leprosy, Münch considers important the fact that, in spite of his careful attentiveness in Southern Russia, he never saw a case of leprosy that demonstrated the Biblically-described physical signs. On the other hand, among the Sarts in Turkestan, he found a skin sickness, which they call *pjesj,* with the identical symptoms of the Biblical *tzaraath.* It is an endemic vitiligo, and the people afflicted therewith are perfectly healthy and live to a ripe old age[8].

I consider it unacceptable, in principle, to draw conclusions from signs and symptoms of a disease that occur only in a single, limited district of a country. We must first be certain that local factors, related to that place, are not the cause of those signs and symptoms. One can further object to the comparison of people of Semitic ancestry that live in Palestine with Aryans of Central Asia. The distance, as the crow flies, is approximately 500 German miles. One cannot compare a people of shepherds and farmers, such as the Jews, with the hunters of the Turkestan mountains.

I would like to at least mention another possibility which was alluded to by Israels approximately 50 years ago, in a different context[9]. He attempts to explain that people of our times could well have diseases which were unknown in antiquity, and that the ancients may have had diseases which have since disappeared. He attempts to make his hypothesis more plausible by stating that with the passage of time, certain diseases might change their form and be associated with different symptoms, although the basic disease, in a certain sense, still remains the same. Just like a changed way of life can alter the entire body of an animal—for example, changing a short intestinal canal into a long one—so, too, changed conditions can also alter the abnormal manifestations of the body, i.e. illness. Taking this viewpoint into consideration, it is possible that *tzaraath* represents an illness which disappeared long ago, particularly if one considers the fact that the skin is especially susceptible to external influence. In point of fact, many authors probably adopted this viewpoint only because they were not able to explain many of the statements of the Bible, and were not yet sufficiently modern to hold the Hebrew author of the Bible responsible, instead of their own ignorance.

Thus, the interpretation that *tzaraath* is leprosy is at best a diagnosis of

---

6. A collection of authors and their opinions is found in Ebstein's *Die Medizin im Alten Testament.* Stuttgart 1901 p.85 ff
7. *Virch. Archives* 1896 p.201
8. Münch. *Die Zaraath (Lepra) der*

*Hebräischen Bibel.* Hamburg & Leipzig 1893 p.76
9. Israels. Nederl. Tydschr. voor Geneeskd. 1861. fol. 203. *De Geschiedenis der Diphtheritis.*

probability. Indeed it shares this lot with a large number of names of illnesses from antiquity. The most cautious approach is to consider *tzaraath* in the sense of a "collective name"[10].

# III

To understand the details of the Biblical law (concerning *tzaraath*), it is important, first of all, to explain the individual technical expressions. This is a very delicate task, however, for the Bible, which is not a medical textbook, here provides a guide for the priests as expert public health officials, and obviously assumes that these expressions and their conceptualization are well known. We are thus forced to use the form of the word to derive its meaning. It is not necessary to state how risky such an approach is. However, we have no other choice. Comparisons with related languages or with the usage of the word in later times is even more dangerous. The "oreillettes" and the "auricles" of the French and the English are not equivalent to the heart auricles of our anatomists, and the "frauenzimmer" of the time of Lessing is not equivalent to that in our language[11].

1) Pagel[12], and independently Kazenelson, conjectured that the word *tzaraath* is derived from *zara*, meaning to sow. *Tzaraath* is thus a sowing or dissemination (of lesions) on the skin. Against this interpretation is the fact that precisely this form of illness, which is characterized by the appearance of multiple spots, is not called *tzaraath* but *bohak*[13]. It is totally purposeless to enumerate here all the other innumerable derivations (of the word *tzaraath*).

2) *Bahereth* is derived from *bahar,* meaning shiny; i.e. a shiny pale spot. *Se'eth,* an infinitive of *nasa,* means to elevate; i.e. an elevation (on the skin). *Sappachath* is a desquamating illness, transposed from *chasaph,* meaning to peel off or to remove scales[14].

It seems obvious that we are dealing with three forms of leprosy: *bahereth* is the spotty leprosy; *se'eth* is the nodular leprosy; and *sappachath* is psoriasis or, as designated by Willan, *lepra vulgaris.* Thus, *tzaraath* is a "collective name", unless one accepts the assertion of Tobler[15] that it represents a true *lepra squamosa.*

3) The word *nega,* from *naga* meaning to touch, originates from the ancient viewpoint whereby a person who is "touched" by an external agent, becomes ill as a result. This agent itself is corporeal, most often a demon. In this manner of speaking, a person is still "touched" by apoplexy. To the Romans, the word *contagium,* and to the Greeks *e synapheia* have a similar meaning. *Our* concept of contagiousness, in which one person transfers a disease to another person, is also derived therefrom.

The opposite of *nega* is *machla,* "the illness according to the way of the world" (i.e. non-contagious). *Nega* must also be differentiated from *deber,* meaning plague, which is highly contagious and rapidly kills many people.

*Nega,* in and of itself, is a general concept: contagion. It is more precisely defined only when another word is added to it; for example, *nega tzaraath* is the contagion of leprosy, the infectious type of leprosy. To consider *nega* and *nega tzaraath* to be different entities, such as *nega tzaraath* representing an earlier stage than *tzaraath,* was already proposed by Nachmanides[16] and most recently by Sack (p.210). However, all such interpretations are frustrated by the wording of verse 25, where both expressions, *tzaraath* and *nega tzaraath,* obviously have the same meaning.

Sack, in order to save his theory, abruptly omits the second half. We do not know

---

10. Perhaps this approach is taken by Maimonides. *Hilchoth Tzaraath* 16:10
11. i.e. Preuss' German (F.R.)
12. Pagel. *Deutsche Mediz. Zeitung.* 1893 p.683
13. Levit. 13:38
14. cf. Exodus 16:14
15. *Medizinische Topographie von Jerusalem,* p.50
16. in his commentary on Levit. 13:3

whether or not the Biblical *nega* is also to be considered as a contagious illness (in our sense). This much is certain: it does not necessarily imply uncleanness, because *mispachath* is a *nega,* yet it is clean[17].

After these introductory remarks, I will now quote the Biblical text.

## IV    The Fundamental Law of Leprosy
## Leviticus - Chapter 13

*When a man shall have in the skin of his flesh a se'eth or sapachath or bahereth, and it become in the skin of his flesh nega tzaraath* (according to a lay opinion), *then he shall be brought unto Aaron the priest, or unto one of his sons the priests*[18]. A council (of judges), which is usually necessary for adjudication of civil matters, is not needed. *And the priest shall look on the nega in the skin of the flesh: and if the hair in the nega is turned white, and the appearance of the nega is deeper than the skin of his flesh, it is (truly) the nega tzaraath, and the priest shall look on him, and pronounce him unclean*[19].

Thus, in and of themselves, none of the three forms are even *suspected* of being leprosy. There has to occur some alteration in them — we do not know which — which raises the suspicion of the lay person. If this suspicion is corroborated by the expert, then it is confirmed to be *nega tzaraath.*

Whether *both* criteria, the hair becoming pale *and* the depth of the lesion, apply to all three forms, cannot be ascertained; they probably only apply to *bahereth.* For in the specific description of *se'eth,* the discoloration of the hair is indeed considered, but not the depth of the lesion. This would also be impossible, if we assume that *se'eth* represents nodular leprosy.

Tradition places considerable importance on the Biblical expression: *the appearance of the nega is deeper than the skin.* In reality, this is not necessarily so. This deeper appearance is explained by the lighter color of the spot when compared to the darker coloration of the skin of Semitic people. So, too, the shadow of an object appears to be lying *on* the flat surface which is exposed to the light. Against this hypothesis is verse 4 in Leviticus 13 which mentions a white *bahereth* whose appearance is *not* deeper than the skin, and a *se'eth* which *does* lie deeper.

The criteria for leprosy described in the Bible are in agreement with those adduced by Arabic physicians, particularly Avicenna, from personal observation. A white mole, *morphoea alba,* does *not* necessarily have to be an early stage of leprosy; it lies in the flat of the skin. In the case of leprosy, it is rougher, there are flakes and scales, and usually the affected site is *magis depressa.* The hair of a plain mole does not become discolored, whereas in leprosy, hair becomes thin and white[20]. Aristotle also states that in the case of the exanthem called *leuke,* all the hairs become gray[21].

## V    Tzaraath on Previously Normal Skin

### A)    *Bahereth*

During the observation: *although the bahereth is white in the skin of his flesh, the appearance thereof is not deeper than the skin, and the hair thereof is not turned white, then the priest shall shut up him that hath the nega for seven days*[22]. At the end of this time period, if the *nega* maintained its appearance in the eyes of the priest, and *did not*

---

17. Levit. 13:6
18. Levit. 13:2
19. *ibid* 13:3
20. Proof is found in Hensler. *Vom Abendländische Aussatze im Mittelalter.*

Hamburg 1790 p.104
21. Aristotle. *Hist. Animal.* Book 3 Chapter 2 No. 70
22. Levit. 13:4

*spread in the skin, then the priest shall shut him up seven days more*[23]. If, during the observation on the seventh day, the *nega* is dim (became pale or remained so) and *did not spread in the skin, then the priest shall pronounce him clean, it is a mispachath*[24]. *But if the mispachath (later) spread abroad in the skin, after that he hath shewn himself to the priest for his cleansing, he shall shew himself to the priest again*[25]. If the latter corroborates the spread in the skin, *he shall pronounce him unclean; it is tzaraath*[26].

Every *bahereth* is thus not *levana* or intensely white. A whitish-reddish one *(morphoea rubra)* is mentioned in verse 19. The white *bahereth* is the advanced stage of leprosy; the hair in it is usually also without pigment. If that is not the case, one must wait and observe whether or not spreading might occur, either *per continuitatem*, or by the appearance of new spots. If the spreading does not occur, and if the original intensely white spot loses its lustre, then it is a non-leprous *mispachath*. According to the word-formation, it is likely that *mispachath* is identical with the *sappachath* mentioned at the beginning of the chapter. Accordingly, *sappachath* is a variety of *bahereth,* perhaps an involutionary stage.

As a matter of fact, many leprous spots are covered with scales. On the other hand, we do not know of any skin disease, whether of a harmless or serious nature, where occasionally direct extension on the skin or dissemination does not occur. This sign, therefore, cannot be used by us as a determinant of the virulence of the illness. However, if the illness remains unchanged or if the skin rash improves, it is certainly benign.

## B)    *Se'eth*

A person is brought to the priest because of *nega tzaraath*[27]. There is a white *se'eth* on the skin, which turned the hair white, and in the *se'eth* there is a site of *live flesh*[28]. It is an old *tzaraath* of the skin of the flesh, and a further observation by the priest is not necessary[29].

*Live flesh* (or raw flesh), *basar chay* (in Hebrew), is usually the opposite of cooked flesh[30], and here probably refers to a red denuded area of the skin. In such cases, the popular usage of the German language speaks of "raw" flesh. If it proliferates, the granulation tissue bleeds easily. The "life" of "live flesh" may thus refer to "wild" flesh. (Compare *chaya,* the term for a wild animal.)

Scripture is thus here dealing with a leprous nodule which partially regressed, so that a pale protuberant spot with non-pigmented hair remains, and on the surface thereof is a leprous ulcer whose base, as usual, appears dark red and granular. Naturally, this type of illness occurs only if the illness is of long-standing.

*If the tzaraath blossoms on the skin and covers the entire skin of him that has the nega from his head even to his feet, as far as appeareth to the priest*[31]. *Then he shall pronounce him that has the nega clean; it is all turned white; he is clean*[32]. *But on the day when raw (or live) flesh appeareth in him, he shall be unclean*[33]...*raw flesh is unclean; it is tzaraath*[34]. *If the raw flesh turn again, and be changed into white,...then the priest shall pronounce him clean that hath the nega*[35].

This passage has to date no satisfactory explanation. The description of the illness, in which the entire surface of the body appears white, might represent vitiligo.

---

23. *ibid* 13:5
24. *ibid* 13:6
25. *ibid* 13:7
26. *ibid* 13:8
27. Levit. 13:9
28. *ibid* 13:10
29. *ibid* 13:11
30. First Samuel 2:15
31. Levit. 13:12
32. *ibid* 13:13
33. *ibid* 13:14
34. *ibid* 13:15
35. *ibid* 13:16-17

Nevertheless, one would certainly not use the expression "to blossom", as it is used concerning plants (efflorescences). In several narratives (which are not legal decrees, however), the Bible uses the term *leprous as snow*[36]. From this comparison, and from the fact that the persons afflicted therewith were healed in a short time, the conclusion has been drawn that these afflicted were not cases of leprosy, but a widely disseminated psoriasis which affected the entire body. These three instances, however, are exceptions from the normal and are described as miracles. Hence, under no circumstances can they be used to prove anything here. In addition, if Miriam's illness was universal leprosy, she should immediately have been declared unclean. In actuality, however, at the command of God, she was shut up for seven days.

Furthermore, the assumption that the above passage refers to psoriasis — even if one admits that in those days it was a rapidly healing illness — would be of no help to us in explaining why "live flesh", that is, an ulcerated area, should suddenly lead to a totally different conception of the illness. Only by coincidence could such an ulcer occur in psoriasis, and even then its secretions would not be contagious. And when it heals, is it again to be psoriasis? Furthermore, all specialists in leprosy admit that wounds on lepers heal very rapidly indeed.

Ancient authors describe an acute leprosy in which the entire skin suddenly turns white. This type of leprosy "is inclined to decide the critical stage of the illness and heal rapidly". Friedreich[37] is of the opinion that "in this case, Moses correctly assumed that such a patient is in the crisis stage and near recovery and, therefore, need no longer be declared unclean". Naturally, that is false; only a person who has recovered is clean, not one who is recovering. It seems uncertain to me whether or not any of those authors ever personally observed this acute form of leprosy, or whether they drew their conclusions solely from this Biblical citation. The ancients readily examined and supplemented their own observations with those of the Bible, not the reverse, as we do today.

As honest critics, we cannot extricate ourselves from the *non liquet* of this Biblical passage. In simple language: we cannot explain it. According to the *Gemara*[38], the situation depicted here is identical to the *bohak* mentioned in verse 39.

## VI    Leprosy on Previously Abnormal Skin

On the skin of a person, there occurred a *schechin* and it healed[39]. *And if in the place of the schechin there is a white se'eth or a reddish-white bahereth; then it shall be shewed to the priest*[40]. If the priest observes that *the appearance thereof is lower than the skin, and the hair thereof be turned white, then the priest shall pronounce him unclean; it is the nega of tzaraath, it has blossomed in the schechin*[41]. . . *but if there be no white hairs therein, and it is not lower than the skin, but is dim, then the priest shall shut him up seven days*[42]. *And if it spreads abroad in the skin, then the priest shall pronounce him unclean: it is a nega*[43]. *But if the bahereth stays in its place, and is not spread, then it is the tzarebeth of the schechin, and the priest shall pronounce him clean*[44].

*Schechin* in the Bible, as we will soon show, probably refers to eczema. If a white leprous spot occurs at a site where there previously was a (moist?) eczema, then it is looked at from the standpoint of the age of the scar, i.e. whether the scar is old and white, or whether it is still fresh and tender and red. Desquamation is not mentioned

---

36. Exodus 4:6; Numbers 12:10; Second Kings 5:27
37. *Zur Bibel* 1:218
38. Niddah 19a
39. Levit. 13:18
40. *ibid* 13:19
41. *ibid* 13:20
42. *ibid* 13:21
43. *ibid* 13:22
44. *ibid* 13:23

here at all, because scaling cannot occur on a scar which is connective tissue and not new epidermis.

It is also not necessary that these types of rashes should be deeper *(amok)* than the healthy skin; an eczematous scar does not sink in much. The site of illness is only somewhat flatter or *schaphal.* If both criteria are lacking, that is the spot is not shiny but opaque, and it stretches, then it is indeed also a *nega,* which renders one unclean (keloid?), but it is not leprosy for which isolation from the encampment of the Jews would also be required.

If the apparent *bahereth* in the scar does not stretch, then it is a special condition derived from the original eczema, and it is called *tzarebeth.* This word either means a fresh inflammation of the *schechin,* or refers to the development of a pseudomembrane (layer of fibrin, crust, *kerum*) on the healing eczema.

An eczematous scar is usually flat. A doubt can only arise in the case of *bahereth* which can be either flat or raised, not, however, in the case of *se'eth.*

*Or when the flesh of a person in the skin has a burning by fire, and the quick flesh of the burning becomes a bahereth, reddish white, or (pure) white*[45]. If the priest observes that the *hair in the bahereth is turned white, and the appearance thereof is deeper than the skin; it is tzaraath; it has blossomed in the burning, and the priest shall pronounce him unclean; it is nega tzaraath*[46]. But if the priest finds no white hair in the *bahereth, and it appears no lower than the skin, and is dim, then the priest shall shut him up seven days*[47]. If, when the priest observes him again on the seventh day, *it has spread, then the priest shall pronounce him unclean; it is nega tzaraath*[48]. But if the *bahereth stays in its place, and does not spread in the skin, but is dim, then it is the se'eth of the burning, and the priest shall pronounce him clean; for it is the tzarebeth of the burn*[49].

The Bible is not speaking of a healed fire burn, but "quick flesh of the burn", meaning a still granulating lesion within which a *bahereth* develops. This lesion, therefore, when it sinks into the skin, appears to be even more sunken *(amok).* If the discoloration of the hairs also occurred (a very deep burn could not therefore have happened), then the *bahereth* is a *tzaraath*-efflorescence, and the patient suffers from *nega tzaraath,* which is leprosy.

The appearance of a *se'eth* in the burn wound is obviously not suspected to occur in leprosy (as it does in eczema, as previously mentioned). A *bahereth* on such a base, which is pale, not shiny and white, and which does not spread, is an "elevation" *(se'eth)* in the burn wound, and has nothing to do with leprosy. It is a pseudomembrane (keloid formation?).

Concerning the various forms of leprosy described above, one waited until the lay person raised a suspicion as to whether the *bahereth* or the *se'eth,* in the opinion of that lay person, became *nega tzaraath.* On the other hand, a rash in a scar was immediately considered suspicious, as soon as one noticed it. The virulence of these forms must, therefore, have been known much earlier. In Avicenna, we find the remark that the *baras* (meaning *bahereth*) which occurs as a result of a burn which physicians inflicted for therapeutic purposes, cannot be smoothed or concealed[50].

## VII   Leprosy on the Head and Beard

*And if a man or a woman hath a nega upon the head or upon the beard*[51], and if the priest finds that the appearance of the *nega* is *deeper than the skin, and there is in it*

---

45. *ibid* 13:24
46. *ibid* 13:25
47. *ibid* 13:26
48. *ibid* 13:27

49. *ibid* 13:28
50. Hensler p.116. See note 20
51. Levit. 13:29

*yellow thin hair*, then it is unclean, it is a *nethek*, the *tzaraath* of the head or of the beard[52].

The signs of head and beard leprosy are thus the same as those for *bahereth*, except that the discoloration of the hair does not have to be as complete as for a *bahereth* elsewhere on the body; golden yellow suffices. The hair has to be *tzahob* and *dak;* the former, according to *Sifra* and *Tosefta*[53], refers to *zahab* meaning golden yellow. *Dak* ordinarily means "thin". However, since normal hair does not become thinner through discoloration, Nachmanides believes it refers to thinness where the hair fell out and is regrowing. According to the reliable explanation of the *Mishnah*[54], the Bible refers to "short" (broken off?) hairs. The depiction of this illness reminds one of crusted eczema (favus).

*But if the nega of the nethek is not deeper than the skin, and if there is no black hair therein* (but the normal hair fell out), *then the priest shall shut up him that hath the nega of the nethek seven days*[55]. *If on the seventh day, the nethek has not spread, and there is no golden yellow hair therein, and the appearance of the nethek is not deeper than the skin*[56], *then he shall be shaven* (so that any possible spread should not be covered by the hair), *but the nethek he shall not shave, and the priest isolates him again for seven days*[57]. *Then if the nethek has not spread on the skin, and if its appearance is not deeper than the skin, the priest shall pronounce him clean*[58].

*But if the nethek spread in the skin after his cleansing*[59], *then the priest need not look for the (characteristic) golden yellow hair; he is unclean*[60]. *But if in the priest's eyes, the nethek remained the same, and black hair is grown therein, then the nethek is healed, he is clean; and the priest shall pronounce him clean*[61].

Thus, in the legal sense, the *nethek* is very similar to the *bahereth*.

*And if in the skin of the flesh of a man or a woman there are beharoth, indeed white beharoth*[62], *then the priest shall look whether or not the beharoth in the skin of their flesh are dull white. Then it is a bohak; it has blossomed in the skin; he is clean*[63].

The multiple types of *bahereth* spots obviously represent a particular type of leprosy illness, whose benignity the Bible found it necessary to stress. There is no sign of uncleanness; on the contrary, the dull color in fact argues for cleanness[64]. Priests ill with *bohak* were not allowed to serve in the Temple, probably because of the conspicuous appearance of the skin lesion[65].

*And if a man's hair is fallen off his (entire) head, he is bald; yet he is clean*[66]. According to Plinius, baldness in a woman is rare[67] and, according to Aristotle, it never occurs[68].

*And if his hair is fallen off from the front part of his head, he is forehead bald, gibbeach; yet he is clean*[69]. The hairless head thus is the source of illnesses and the basis of judgements regarding the skin of the body. It cannot, however, show the *nethek* form of leprosy since, in the latter, at most, only partial alopecia occurs[70].

*But if there is in the bald head, or the bald forehead, a white-reddish nega; it is blossoming tzaraath on his bald head, or on his bald forehead*[71]. *If the priest beholds that the rising of the nega is reddish-white in his bald head, or in his bald forehead, as*

52. *ibid* 13:30
53. *Tosefta* Nega'im 1:4
54. Nega'im 10:1
55. Levit. 13:31
56. *ibid* 13:32
57. *ibid* 13:33
58. *ibid* 13:34
59. *ibid* 13:35
60. *ibid* 13:36
61. *ibid* 13:37
62. *ibid* 13:38
63. *ibid* 13:39
64. *ibid* 13:6
65. *Tosefta* Bechoroth 5:3 and Megillah 24b
66. Levit. 13:40
67. *Histor. Natur.* 11:47
68. *Histor. Animal.* 3:11; see also Ibn Ezra's commentary on Levit. 13:29
69. Levit. 13:41
70. *ibid* 13:30
71. *ibid* 13:42

*the appearance of tzaraath in the skin of the flesh[72], then he is a leprous man, he is unclean; the priest shall surely pronounce him unclean; his nega is in his head[73].*

Other than on this leprous man, only the *tzaraath* on a healed eczema is described as reddish-white[74]. Perhaps here, too, the Bible refers to a baldheaded person with a mildly inflamed skin (i.e. seborrhea).

## VIII   Leprosy in the Talmud

So much for the Biblical account (of *nega tzaraath*). The Talmud contains a large number of expositions on each of these Biblical decrees. The *Mishnah* comprises ten chapters on this subject[75].

The expression *tzaraath* is no longer used by the *Mishnah*; rather it only designates as *nega'im* the two major types of leprosy mentioned in the Bible: *bahereth* and *se'eth*. The *Mishnah* does not consider *sappachath* as a separate type, but each of the other two has a form of *sappachath* (or scaly lesion). The *tzaraath* illnesses of the head and beard are not even enumerated among the *nega'im*[76]. Thus we conclude:

The *bahereth* is intensely white[77] (shiny?) like snow[78] and has a second shade which is like the lime of the walls[79], that is to say, homogeneously glossy. According to the *Tosefta*[80], each of these types can transform into the other.

The color of *se'eth* is compared to white wool, and the second shade is compared to the skin in an egg. Both types of *se'eth* are thus dull-white, not shiny.

The difference between these two types of *nega,* therefore, does not lie in differences of flatness (or swelling), as we assumed above, but rather in the various qualities and shades of their white colors. However, because of its dull tone, the *se'eth appears* to be above the surface of the skin, just as a shadow appears on or above the illuminated level of the ground. The objections against this interpretation, which is the traditional one, have already been mentioned above.

The Bible also mentions a reddish form of *bahereth*. This color depends upon whether the basic color is the shade resembling snow or the one resembling lime. According to the depiction of Rabbi Ishmael, in the former case, the mixed color is like (red) wine mingled with snow, and in the case of the lime-like white, the mixed color is like blood mingled with milk. According to Rabbi Akiba, in both cases the reddishness is like wine mingled with water, but in the snow-like whiteness the color is more intense (deeper red), whereas in the lime-like whiteness, the color is lighter[81].

Individual interpretations describe many more color shades of leprosy, up to seventy-two types[82].

The observation that an intensely white *bahereth* spot appears dull on the skin of Germanic people, and a dull spot appears shiny on the skin of Ethiopians, is of significance[83], because it points out the importance of contrasting colors. The skin color of Oriental people is intermediate between these two and is compared to boxwood. In order to be safe, Rabbi Akiba suggests that a suspected leprosy spot should be encircled with a ring of paint of an "intermediate shade", which is not black and not white, and then the spot should be compared to this shade of color[84].

Leprosy symptoms may not be inspected early in the morning or at sunset, or within the house, or on a cloudy day, for then spots which are truly dull white would

72. *ibid* 13:43
73. *ibid* 13:44
74. *ibid* 13:19
75. Tractate Nega'im. There are actually 14 chapters. (F.R.)
76. Nega'im 6:8
77. Nega'im 1:1
78. or like lather
79. According to Josephus, *Antiquities,* Book 2 Chapt. 12:3, the hand of Moses was "white like the color of lime".
80. *Tosefta* Nega'im 2:6
81. Nega'im 1:2
82. *ibid* 1:4
83. *ibid* 2:1
84. *ibid*

appear intensely white (as snow); and no inspection may be made at midday because the opposite would occur (i.e. intense white would appear as dull white)[85].

A man is inspected standing as if he were hoeing or harvesting olives, that is with feet spread apart and hands held on high (whereby the epilated parts of the body with the depigmented hairs would be visible). A woman to be inspected stands as if working dough or as if suckling her child, or as if weaving, if the leprosy sign is within the right armpit, and as if spinning flax if it is within the left armpit (whereby the affected arm is held up)[86].

During the era of the *Sifra,* the terms *se'eth* and *bahereth* were still in common usage and, therefore, required no explanation. *Sappachath* meant "sub-variety" *(tephela)* and *se'eth* was a dull white, just like *bohak.* The *bohak* sickness was also evidently still known, but it referred to something other than the Biblical *bohak,* a term which was employed to designate multiple *shiny* spots.

According to the commentaries, not only is the patient with *tzaraath* himself sick, but others also suffer because of him, due to his perspiration[87].

The *Mishnah* does not consider the uncleanness of the leper from the standpoint of contagion. Among many proofs for this view is the statement that the rules of *nega'im* do not apply to non-Jews *(lepra legalis!)*[88]. The latter do not contract uncleanness. Furthermore, a child born with a *bahereth* is clean[89]. Did the Sages observe fetal leprosy or is the existence of the latter ruled out by this decree?

## IX

In Biblical law, the occurrence of "raw flesh" — which we interpret to mean an ulceration — is a double criterion for uncleanness, once combined with the decolorized hair in the *se'eth* making a diagnosis of chronic (or old) *tzaraath*[90], and once by itself in the universal *tzaraath*[91]. The *Mishnah* decrees that when the *michya* (raw flesh) occurs "at the tip of an organ", it cannot be used for the diagnosis of uncleanness (perhaps because these wounds are more easily exposed?). These "24 tips" are the tips of the fingers and of the toes, and the tips of the ears and the nose and the penis and the nipples of the breast[92]. According to Rabbi Eliezer, the same applies to the ulceration of warts *(yabeleth)* and the attached shreds of flesh *(dildulim* or wens). *Sifra* and *Tosefta* also add *masmeroth* meaning "nails", perhaps fungus tissue or molluscum.

A *bahereth* in the inside of the eye (i.e. the conjunctiva), inside the ear, inside the nose, or inside the mouth does not impart uncleanness[93]; for the Bible speaks only of the *skin* of the body, but not of mucous membranes. Also excluded from imparting uncleanness, are the soles of the feet and nails which, because of their hardness, are not considered "skin"[94].

*Sifra* points out that eczematous *(schechin)* leprosy does not mean oozing eczema *(schechin mored)* (which is not "healed"), nor does it refer to cicatrized leprosy (which has a *tzeleketh),* for the latter is not considered eczema any more. Rather, it refers to "healed and not healed" *(tzarebeth),* until there forms a skin thereon like an onion skin[95].

## X

Interesting are the rules concerning decolorized hair whose occurrence is considered by the Bible to be a sign of uncleanness. If the hair is black at the root but

85. *ibid* 2:2
86. *ibid* 2:4
87. *Sifra* fol. 60b. Weiss
88. Nega'im 3:1
89. *ibid* 7:1
90. Levit. 13:10

91. *ibid* 13:14
92. Nega'im 6:7
93. *ibid* 6:8
94. *ibid*
95. *Sifra* fol. 64b

white at the tip, it is of no significance, because this also occurs in healthy people, such as in old age. The opposite, however, (i.e. black at the tip and white at the root) renders a person unclean. It is also of no significance if *one* white hair splits at the tip so that it looks like two hairs[96].

It is further required in the inspection of a leprous spot for uncleanness that the hair in the *bahereth* became white, meaning the *bahereth* is the primary lesion. If a *bahereth* developed secondarily in a hair that had become white earlier, the person is clean[97]. Is it possible that the *Mishnah* is distinguishing between *morphoea alba* and vitiligo?

It is forbidden to pluck out the decolorized hair or to burn away the raw flesh in order to deceive the priest concerning the true nature of the skin lesion[98]. It is also prohibited to excise an entire *bahereth* lesion. If such a lesion occurs at the tip of the foreskin, however, it may be removed as part of ritual circumcision[99].

Although the Bible speaks of a *nega ha-nethek*[100], the *Mishnah* does not consider *nethek* lesions of the head and beard among the *nega'im,* but as a separate category of lesions. Certain statements again lead one to the supposition that some skin lesions observed in those days represent what we would today call favus or more likely *herpes tonsurans* (ringworm). The *Mishnah* speaks of two *nethek* spots side by side separated by a line of normal hair[101], or of two *nethek* spots, one *inside* the other, in which this separating row of normal hair was breached in one place[102]. The hair in the spot is short and pale golden in color, the spot itself is sunken in; a seemingly accurate depiction of ringworm.

Spreading of this skin affection over a large part of the head can then produce baldness of the crown to the back of the head or to the forehead[103]. Nevertheless, the Biblical terms *gabachath* and *karachath* should only be used for that type of baldness in which hair never regrows, in contradistinction to the baldness produced by *nethek.* The former type of baldness occurs following ingestion of *neshem* (a permanent depilatory agent) or if one smeared oneself with *neshem.* According to the commentators, this word is the dialect form of *sam,* which is the usual designation for any pulverized type of drug among Jews and other Semitic peoples (Babylonians and Arabs).

A bald-headed person (without any of the above skin lesions) is never unclean, even if the hair fell out as a result of a local or generalized disease[104].

## XI    Diagnosis of Leprosy

The role of the priest in diagnosing leprosy lesions in post-Biblical times became less and less conspicuous. Inspection of leprosy signs can be done by any person. Only the pronouncement of the deciding word "clean" or "unclean" must be made by the priest[105]. Nevertheless, the pronouncement of cleanness is not decisive if it occurs as a result of an error[106], for the Bible teaches: *if he is clean, the priest shall pronounce him clean.* A priest blind in one eye, or whose eyesight is weak, may not inspect leprosy signs[107]. A priest may also not inspect his own leprosy signs or those on a near relative[108].

In the *Sifra* book, the priest is only needed for the most external form of the verdict: the expert among the Israelites examines the *nega'im* and says to the priest,

---

96. Nega'im 4:4
97. *ibid* 4:11
98. *ibid* 7:4
99. *ibid* 7:5
100. Levit. 13:30
101. Nega'im 10:6
102. *ibid* 10:7

103. *ibid* 10:10
104. Sifra 67b
105. Nega'im 3:1
106. Sifra 67a
107. Nega'im 2:3
108. *ibid* 2:5

*even if the latter is mentally ill:* "declare unclean" and the priest need only repeat the word "unclean".

The *Tosefta,* at the beginning of its extensive discussion of this subject, decrees that only a person who has firm knowledge of all types and varieties of individual skin lesions is empowered to examine such lesions. An individual who undertakes to examine a case should remain with the same case in order to be able later to attest to spreading, etc. of the lesion, unless the examiner dies or becomes ill[109]. It seems likely that in this manner a type of expert gradually emerged, to whom people came to have their lesions examined, such as Rabbi Eliezer[110], Rabba[111] and others[112].

## XII    Treatment and Cure of Tzaraath

The sources do not speak at all about the treatment of *tzaraath.* We, therefore, do not know whether the healing of which the Bible speaks[113] occurred spontaneously or by human intervention. With greatest emphasis, one must object to the interpretation that Leviticus 14:1-32, and all the cleansing ceremonial of the *healed* leper depicted there, represent disinfectant measures. My reasons for this protest have already been presented above[114]. The procedure is divided into two parts; first is the seven-day period of seclusion. After this interval, the healed leper bathes and shaves his entire body: head, beard, eyebrows and the remainder of his body. Then he may return to the camp, but not yet to his own tent. In the Temple, there also existed a "Chamber of the Lepers" where the healed leper bathed again[115]. The *healed* leper was also brought to the priest (i.e. did not come on his own)[116], according to Ibn Ezra, because the leper tried to avoid the cost of the sacrifice he had to offer.

The bathing in the river Jordan seven times by the Syrian general to cure his leprosy, at the recommendation of the prophet Elisha, is certainly not intended by the Bible to imply healing in the natural sense[117]. The King of Israel, in fact, considered the healing of a leper to be as difficult as the revival of a dead person. And if bathing in the Jordan really had such a curing influence on leprosy, it would probably have been known to others besides the prophet.

On the other hand, the Bible demands the strictest isolation of the leper: *And the leper in whom the nega is, his clothes shall be rent, and the hair of his head shall go loose, and he shall cover his upper lip, and shall cry: "Unclean, unclean". All the days wherein the plague is in him he shall be unclean; he shall dwell alone: without the camp shall his dwelling be*[118].

The purpose of these rules naturally is to identify the leper to everyone else. Tradition suggests that the coiffure and the garb of the leper represent a sign of mourning for the Godless life of the leper, for which he was punished by being afflicted with leprosy. This is already the interpretation of the author of the Aramaic translation of the Bible. The purpose of covering the mouth up to the upper lip, according to some commentaries (Ibn Ezra), is to protect others from becoming ill as a result of the exhalation from his mouth.

The regulation of the loose hair is only applicable to a man, not to a woman, because her modesty would thereby be damaged[119]. For a man, there is no exception; even if the High Priest becomes a leper, he lets his hair loose, although ordinarily he is forbidden to let his hair grow and wear torn clothes[119a] because that is a customary sign of mourning.

---

109. *Tosefta* Nega'im 1:15
110. Sanhedrin 68a
111. Baba Metzia 86a
112. *Tanchuma Thazria* p.18b Buber
113. Levit. 14:3
114. At the beginning of Chapter 4
115. Nega'im 14:8
116. Levit. 14:2
117. Second Kings 5:7 ff
118. Levit 13:45-46
119. Numbers 5:18
119a. Levit. 10:6

The Talmud does not take the utterance "unclean" literally; because Rabbi Joshua ben Levi taught that one should never utter an offensive word[120] and the word "unclean" is offensive. It was, therefore, required that the leper rather call himself *parush,* meaning separated[121]. According to the *Gemara*[122], by his announcing his troubles to his friends, they will offer prayers for mercy to be vouchsafed for him; because the healing from this illness is requested of God through prayers[123]. Similar regulations were observed by lepers in all lands until modern times. They had to wear special clothes, and to ring bells which they carried in their hands to inform people from afar that they were approaching.

During the entire time of his isolation, a leper is not at all restricted in cohabitation with his wife. The leprous King Uzziah had a son Jotham during the time of his leprosy[124]. One must, therefore, assume that the woman is allowed to share the exile with her husband. Cohabitation is only prohibited during the seven days after the leper is already healed and has returned to the camp, but before he has immersed himself in the ritual bath, and while he is waiting "outside his house" (separated from his wife) for the definitive pronouncement of his cleanliness. The reason for this prohibition of cohabitation is given as follows: "he should be like a person who was excommunicated[126] and like a mourner"[127], for whom cohabitation is also forbidden. I am not clear as to why this prohibition is limited to these seven days.

The question of *leprosariums* during Jewish antiquity, establishments specifically constructed to receive a large number of lepers, must remain an open one. The Bible relates that King Uzziah (or Azariah) was a leper until the day of his death and he lived in a *beth ha-chophshith*[128]. It is possible to interpret this "house of refuge" as a leprosarium. One could equally well agree with the commentaries[129] that the expression is derived from *chophshi* meaning free of obligation; i.e. the King lived free of his royal duties. This much is sure: there is no other statement in the Bible or Talmud which speaks of the existence of a leprosarium. The Aramaic Bible translator states only that the King lived "outside Jerusalem", and is thus probably totally unfamiliar with the concept of a leprosarium. Naturally, one cannot conclude anything from the commentary of the *Sifra* that the leper had to be "solitary", i.e. not to live with other lepers; for it is possible to become "unclean" from a variety of causes.

The *Targum* translates *beth chophshith* as *beth segirutha* meaning the house of leprosy. The word *segirutha* is the usual Targumic translation for *tzaraath.* The same translation is given for the term *gibath gareb*[130] which the other ancient translators and commentators consider to be the name of a place (i.e. hill of Gareb). Even if *gareb* is equivalent to *garab,* and even if this meant leprosy, a "hill of leprosy" is still not a leprosarium. Either it simply refers to an "unclean place"[131] or any other site in the open fields where the lepers who were sent outside the city congregated.

It appears that during the time of the *Mishnah,* the exclusion of lepers was not handled quite as strictly (as in Biblical times). The leper was at least permitted to come to the house of study, but had to be separated from the other people present by a wall ten handbreadths in height and four cubits in width. He entered first and was the last to leave[132]. One must keep in mind how highly Judaism in all ages esteemed the studying and teaching of Torah.

120. Pesachim 3a
121. *Sifra* fol 64c
122. Niddah 66a
123. Josephus. *Antiquities.* Book 3 Chapt. 11:3
124. Moed Katan 7b; Kerithoth 8b
125. Levit. 14:8
126. *Sifra* on Levit. 14:8
127. *Yalkut* on Levit. 14:8
128. Second Kings 15:5 and Second Chronicles 26:21
129. on Horayuth 10a
130. Jeremiah 31:38
131. as in Levit. 14:40
132. Nega'im 13:12

Otherwise a leper is considered like a dead person[133]; he is not mentioned in any of the numerous ritual regulations. It was not considered necessary to further specifically exclude him from religious functions, as was done for the mentally deficient, or to provide him with special dispensations, as was done for the blind and the crippled.

Ordinarily, the lepers were found "at the gate of the entrance to the city"[134]. If such an unfortunate individual ever dared to enter the city, then even educated and pious people would throw stones at him and call out to him: "Go to your place and do not defile (infect?) the people"[135]. Since Jesus was able to enter the house of Simon the leper *(tou leproi)* in Bethany[136], it follows that the evangelist did not equate *lepra* with leprosy. On the other hand, the evangelist Luke[137] speaks of ten leprous men *(leproi andres)* who stood from afar and called out: Jesus, dear master, have mercy upon us. He sent them to the priests for examination and they declared them clean. Jesus was of the opinion that their faith caused the sudden healing.

When he died, the leprous King Uzziah was buried *in the field of the burial which belonged to the kings,* not in the grotto or *ma'arah, for they said: he is a leper*[138].

## XIII    Tzaraath As Punishment for Slander

Already in the Bible, *tzaraath* appears as a punishment, namely for speaking ill of a person. Miriam, the sister of Moses, suddenly became leprous as snow when she spoke slanderously about her brother. She was isolated but was healed after seven days as a result of her brother's prayer[139]. The priests *atone* for the leper with the latter's offering before God[140]. The *Midrash* explains that the spots on the skin of the snake represent signs of leprosy with which the snake was afflicted because of the slander it spoke[141]. The Hebrew word *metzora,* meaning leprous, is said to be derived from the words *motzi ra* meaning "who brings out evil"[142].

The question is raised as to why the leper, of all unclean persons, is singled out to receive a severe punishment in that "he must live apart". The answer given is that by virtue of the slander he speaks, he separates man from wife, and friend from friend[143]. When Israel stood at Mount Sinai, there was none among them with gonorrhea or with leprosy. However, because they cast aspersions on their neighbors, it was immediately decreed: send out from the encampment everyone with an issue and every leper[144].

It is because King Uzziah usurped the priestly functions that he was punished by the sudden occurrence of *tzaraath* on his forehead as he was burning incense. He was expelled from the sanctuary, and he ran out, because God had punished him. He remained a leper until the day of his death[145]. Legend attributes the refusal of the Persian Queen Vashti to come to the public banquet to the fact that leprosy had erupted on her body as punishment for her having completely undressed Jewish girls (tribady?)[146].

The Talmud[147] and *Midrash*[148] enumerate several other transgressions for which leprosy is inflicted as punishment: idolatry, blasphemy, incest, murder, theft, false testimony, robbery, perjury, trespassing, deceitful thoughts (atheistic philosophy?), arrogance, jealousy, etc... Examples and evidence from the Bible are cited for each of

---

133. Nedarim 64b
134. Second Kings 7:3
135. Levit. Rabbah 16:3
136. Matthew 26:6
137. Luke 17:12
138. Second Chronicles 26:23
139. Numbers 12:10
140. Levit. 14:18
141. *Tanchuma Metzora* 7 p.24a
142. *ibid* p.22b
143. Arachin 16b
144. Levit. Rabbah 18:4
145. Second Chronicles 26:18-21
146. Megillah 12b, commenting on Esther 1:12
147. Arachin 16a
148. *Yalkut* No. 563

these. According to the *Aggadah,* King David also became a leper as punishment for his sins[149].

Lewdness is particularly emphasized as a cause for leprosy. If a man cohabited with his wife during her menstrual period, the offspring of this coitus will be leprous. If the cohabitation occurred on the first day of the menstruation, then the child becomes ill at ten years of age; if on the second day, at twenty years of age..., if on the seventh day, at seventy years of age[150]. The prophet admonishes: *because the daughters of Zion are haughty... the Lord will smite with a scab (sippach) the crown of their heads*[151]. The *Midrash*[152] interprets this passage as an allusion to the *sappachath* of the head, which the Bible does not mention, but which is obviously the scaly eruption of the head called *pityriasis capitis.*

We have a strong indication of the cause of leprosy in the case of Gehazi, servant of Elisha. The thankful Syrian (general Naaman), healed of his leprosy by Elisha, wished to reward the prophet with gifts of gold and clothing. The latter, however, refused to accept them. On the other hand, the servant (Gehazi) obtained both by begging, and himself became leprous[153]. Naturally, I believe this was contracted by direct contact.

The assertions of heathen writers (Plutarch, Tacitus) that the Jews do not eat pork because it might produce leprosy, or aggravate already existent leprosy, find no support in Biblical and Talmudic writings.

Those who are of the opinion that leprosy can occur as a result of eating fish support their contention in that the Israelites bemoaningly remembered that they ate fish freely in Egypt[154], so that the possibility existed that they thereby contracted leprosy. On the other hand, the Egyptians, who abstained from fish[155], were free of this disease. However, the complaint of the Israelites was really directed against the monotony of the *manna:* they equally missed cucumbers and melons, leeks, onions and garlic, i.e. a variety of vegetables to which they were accustomed in Egypt. Although the latter were perhaps not freely available, it is difficult to attribute causation of leprosy to them. Furthermore, the fish theory of leprosy causation has today been generally abandoned.

By contrast, the *Midrash* considers plethora to be the cause of leprosy: the body of a normal person has equal quantities of blood and water; if the water gains over the blood, the person becomes hydropic; if the blood gains over the water, the person becomes leprous[156]. According to Rabbi Yochanan, there are no lepers in Babylon because the people there eat mangolds and drink beer and bathe in the water of the Euphrates[157].

## XIV

Things which were considered unesthetic or indecent were disguised, wherever possible, and not called by their real name but designated as *dabar acher, res alia.* This expression (*dabar acher* meaning something else) is used as a euphemism (or paraphrase) for the word cohabitation, as well as for the word leprosy, so that we sometimes cannot determine which interpretation is meant. For example, the Talmud states that it is dangerous for "the other" (i.e. cohabitation) if one does not eat immediately after one has had blood let, or if one encounters a pig[158]. For the same reason one should not eat fish and meat fried together[159].

149. Sanhedrin 107a. He prayed: *cleanse me with hyssop;* the latter belongs to items which purge a leper of his sins, Psalms 51:9
150. *Tanchuma Metzora* 3 p.22b
151. Isaiah 3:16-17
152. *Tanchuma Thazriya* p.21b
153. Second Kings 5:27
154. Numbers 11:5
155. Herodotus 2:37
156. Levit. Rabbah 15:2; cf Bechoroth 44b; Resh Lakish said: much blood produces much *schechin;* much sperm produces much *tzaraath.*
157. Kethuboth 77b
158. Shabbath 129b
159. Pesachim 76b

Only rarely does one find in Talmudic colloquial speech, but not in legal regulations, the word *sappachath* used as a synonym for *tzaraath*, as follows: "Rabbi Chelbo said: proselytes are as harmful to Israel as *sappachath*"[160]. We do not know the reason why this expression was specifically chosen here, whether for a specific purpose or whether it is just a dialectic peculiarity. On the other hand, another popular saying goes as follows: "an evil wife is a *tzaraath* to her husband. Wherein lies the cure? He should divorce her. Then he will be healed from his leprosy"[161].

# PART TWO

# THE ILLNESS SCHECHIN

## I   The Illness of Job

The Rabbis already considered the book of Job to be a poetical work and its principal character a fictitious personality[162]. The poet relates that Job was a very wealthy man and possessed large flocks of animals and many slaves; and he was blessed with ten children[163]. The latter were not, as today, an object of pity, but were a pride to the father and an object of envy for others. In order to test his belief in God, everything was taken away from Job, and in the end he himself was afflicted with *schechin ra, from the sole of his foot even unto his crown. And he took him a potsherd to scrape himself therewith; and he sat among the ashes*[164]. Three of his friends, who heard of this tragedy, each came from his abode (to visit Job); when they saw him from afar, they did not recognize him. They sat down on the ground with him, without speaking, because they saw that the pain was very severe. The unfortunate Job complained: *my flesh is clothed with worms and clods of dust; my skin closeth up and breaketh out afresh*[165]; *my skin is black and falleth from me*[166]; *my bone cleaveth to my skin and to my flesh, and I am escaped with the skin of my teeth*[167]. His sleep was disturbed by terrifying dreams[168]. He further complained: *my face is reddened with weeping*[169]; I convulse from the pain; and many other complaints of a similar nature.

Nothing is mentioned about the course or the duration of Job's illness and its eventual healing. The poet only tells us that, at the end, Job was restored to twice the prosperity he originally had, begat ten more children, and *died being old and full of days*[170].

Naturally, medical historians attribute all of Job's complaints to his illness, and closely examine all the details in order to find support for a diagnosis. They thereby overlook the fact that aside from his illness, the tormented Job had sufficient reason to complain, and that his complaints were not necessarily caused by his illness. One should observe[171] how Job himself depicts his aristocratic social standing; suddenly he became impoverished, so that each of his relatives gave him a small coin[172]. All his children were killed by a band of robbers in one day. Is it so surprising that he became so changed as a result of the emotional pains that his friends barely recognized him? Is it so astonishing that he became thin, that his face was reddened from weeping, and that his sleep was unsettled?

---

160. Niddah 13b
161. Sanhedrin 100a
162. Baba Bathra 15a
163. Job 1:2-3
164. *ibid* 2:7-8
165. *ibid* 7:5
166. *ibid* 30:30

167. *ibid* 19:20
168. *ibid* 7:14
169. *ibid* 16:16
170. *ibid* 42:17
171. in chapter 29
172. Job 42:11

The only statement which definitely refers to an illness is the remark of the poet that Job took a potsherd to scrape himself therewith[173]. One can only conclude therefrom that the illness in question was an itching affection of the skin which was serious but not life-threatening[173a], but which spoiled the enjoyment of life. One would not be far wrong to consider the illness of Job to have been *universal eczema*. This assumption would explain his various complaints, if one considers them to have been the result of the illness, because constant pruritis can very readily disturb one's sleep and consume the body's strength. The scratched-open lesions would be dark in color as they form scars; if they become infected, maggots might develop in the wounds. Alternatively, one can interpret these complaints as simple poetic exaggerations.

One can draw no conclusions at all from the name *schechin ra* meaning "bad *schechin*". The word *schachan* means to burn or to be hot. Thus, *schechin* would mean inflammation. In any event, the name does not mitigate *against* the assumption described above.

"Sitting in ashes" was interpreted as a therapeutic measure against pruritus in early antiquity and it is, in fact, an appropriate remedy[174]. One must, however, remind oneself that Oriental people sat on the ground in ashes *as a sign of mourning* and as a symbol of the transitoriness of life, and of death. In support of the latter interpretation is the fact that Job's friends who came to console him, sat with him silently on the ground for seven days and seven nights, for that is the duration of mourning for a close relative (i.e. children), and custom dictates that no one should speak a word unless the mourner initiates the conversation. This fact also dispels the theory that the ashes in which Job sat represented the *mizbele* of today's Arabs, the large dung piles outside every city where modern lepers congregate, the *kopria* of the Greek translation, and the *sterquilinium* of the Latin one.

The commentators on the Book of Job consider his illness to have been leprosy, not because they felt obligated to attribute to him the most serious illness known to them, but simply because the word "leprosy" was a large reservoir into which one cast all skin sicknesses, irrespective of whether or not they represented a nosologic entity. The Greek Bible translation renders the word *schechin* of the (Hebrew) text as *elkos*, which is even more difficult to identify than the otherwise usual term *lepra*. The latter is a difficult point of contention among medical historians. In the final analysis, all the attempts at explaining the term *schechin* do not leave us with anything but the conclusion that *lepra* was originally nothing more than the name of a scaly skin illness of any type; only much later did it become the designation for leprosy. Expressed differently: it cannot be proven from any place in ancient Greek writings that the author, using the word *lepra*, had in mind the disease we know today as leprosy. On the contrary, there can be no doubt that *schechin* to the Greeks, at least to the physicians, does not refer to *lepra*, but to elephantiasis. The translators of Arabic physicians first adopted the expression *lepra* for *schechin*, so that the *lepra* of the Arabs is identical with the elephantiasis of the Greeks. In point of fact, the church father Origenes, in the third century, also speaks of the elephantiasis of Job[175]. Naturally, he does not prove his contention. Therefore, a dispute as to whether Job suffered from leprosy or from elephantiasis is totally senseless.

All major changes in medical knowledge and opinions are reflected in the expositions of the Biblical narratives of illnesses. For every devout person, the Bible is the book of highest wisdom and of absolute truth, and every new doctrine must therefore already be contained in the Bible. Thus, when syphilis became known in Europe, traces thereof were immediately looked for in the Bible, and these were first found in the book of Job. The search was made so much easier because this illness has

173. *ibid* 2:8
173a. *ibid* 2:6
174. Ibn Ezra's commentary on Job 2:8
175. Contra Celsum 6

such polymorphic manifestations that one or another symptom thereof can eventually be found in *every* patient. As a rule, *one* symptom sufficed for the enthusiastic commentator. These commentators consider the complaint of the poet that he could not *sleep* because of pain to be particularly suspicious. The fact that emotional pain was probably the real cause of Job's insomnia seems not to matter to them and is judged by the axiom that *omnis syphiliticus mendax*. The poet explicitly states: *in the night my bones are pierced* (with pain)[176]. Since the word *atzamai* (bones) may be understood in the precise sense of "bones", the diagnosis of nighttime bone pain is established. When Job complains that the Lord does not grant him a single (pain-free) restful night: *till I swallow my spittle*[177], he is clearly referring to an inflammation of the throat, and mention of syphilis in the Bible has thus been "proven". It would not be worth the effort to even mention this point were it not for the fact that this is an example of innumerable other instances (of absurd Biblical interpretation), and were it not for the fact that the same nonsense is constantly repeated in modern times even by otherwise serious authors. Part of the responsibility rests with the bad translations which were utilized; however, wishing to be original, one also forgets the fact that poets in all generations speak in allegories and exaggerations.

Thomas Bartholin interpreted Job's illness as a case of Syrian throat pestilence, as described by Aretäus. Since today there is no more doubt that the illness depicted by Aretäus is diphtheria[178], the supposition of Bartholin, like many others, may be ignored.

We need only still mention the latest work on this subject, that of Ebbell[179]. He interprets the Biblical *schechin* to be variola, and considers Job to have been afflicted with black pox. At the end, he cautiously states that "the numerous complaints of Job *can* all be attributed to variola"[180]. It is possible that this interpretation is correct, but this is not probable[181].

## II   The Illness of King Hezekiah

Although in the description of the illness of Job, there is at least *one* reference point for the diagnosis, i.e. itching, there is no such clue at all concerning the illness of King Hezekiah, which is mentioned in the Bible three times[182]. King Hezekiah was deathly ill. Isaiah came to him and said to him: *set thine house in order, for thou shalt die and not live*. The sick King prayed to the Lord and, at the latter's command, Isaiah proclaimed: *I have heard thy prayer...behold, I will heal thee. On the third day, thou shalt go up unto the house of the Lord. And I will add fifteen years to thy days...* And Isaiah instructed that fig cakes be taken; these were placed on the *schechin* and Hezekiah was healed. In the "writing" which he wrote after he recovered, the King related: *I cried until morning like a lion, so did He break all my bones*[183]. It is uncertain whether he cried from pain or because of the anxiety that he would die: *in the noontide of his days he should go to the gates of the netherworld*[184]. Here in the Book of Isaiah, it is written: *let them take a cake of figs, and rub it over (or on) the schechin and he shall recover*[185], but in Chronicles it is only written: *he was sick to the death... and the Lord gave him a sign*[186].

---

176.  Job 30:17
177.  *ibid* 7:19
178.  See chapter 3 part 1:3 above
179.  Le Variole dans l'Ancien Testament et dans le papyrus Ebers. *Nord. Med. Arkiv* 1906. Inre Med. Section 2, part 4 p.30 ff
180.  p.40, emphasized by the author himself
181.  Kotelman also considers Job's illness to have been some type of pox eruption. See *Die*

*Ophthalmologie bei den Alten Hebräern.* Hamburg 1910 p.216 ff
182.  Second Kings 20:1 ff; Isaiah 38:1 ff; Second Chronicles 32:24ff
183.  Isaiah 38:13
184.  *ibid* 38:10
185.  *ibid* 38:21
186.  Second Chronicles 32:24

The Greek translators render the word *schechin* of the text as *elkos*. They translate the instructions of Isaiah to rub *(marach)* figs on the *schechin* as *tripson kai kataplasai epi to elkos*. From this translation there developed the general assumption that Hezekiah's illness was an abscess which became softened by the application of figs thereon. In the great debate of the court chaplains in the Prussian chamber of deputies concerning the paucity of knowledge of Biblical history by school children, Virchow spoke quite apodictically about the figs which King Hezekiah applied on his bubo. The text itself does not at all suggest such an interpretation. It seems much more reasonable to assume that Hezekiah had a skin sickness. Indeed, the use of figs as softening compresses in antiquity was well known[187], but one can certainly not draw any conclusions therefrom. The Rabbis, in fact, believed just the opposite, i.e. that figs are harmful for *schechin,* and their healing effect for this illness is quite miraculous.

Thomas Bartholin considered the illness of Hezekiah to be a throat abscess which spontaneously ruptured on the third day. Support for this contention comes from the lament of the patient himself: *like a crane or a swallow, so did I chatter; I did mourn as a dove*[188]. These bird sounds are said to resemble the voice of a person with an illness in the throat. If one wishes to explain the matter rationally, one should simply assume that the King was misled about the seriousness of his condition, and that his apprehension was due to the call of Isaiah: *set thine house in order, for thou shalt die*[189]. The *Midrash* already does not find that statement to be very humane, and this lack of complaisance increased considerably so that Isaiah was motivated to inform the patient of the truth, namely that there was no need for him to settle his affairs because the illness would shortly end favorably[190].

There is no dearth of other explanations of King Hezekiah's illness, but their foundation is as convincing as those of the others. The opinion of Friedreich and Winer[191] that Hezekiah contracted plague which, as already plainly described before, afflicted the Assyrian armies, seems worthy of mention. However, we have no reason to assume that this pestilence (the Hebrew word *deber* has the general meaning pestilence) was in fact bubonic plague; and even if this assumption is correct, we have no right to equate the word *schechin* in the text with a bubo.

According to the Talmud, King Hezekiah was afflicted with this illness as punishment for the fact that he remained unmarried. He made excuses for himself by saying that he foresaw that the children which would be his offspring would be worthless. Naturally, this excuse was not considered valid. Every person must first fulfill his obligation and then leave the rest in the hands of God[192]. It is unfortunate that modern syphilis historians were not familiar with this Talmudic assertion, for they would certainly have used it as evidence that the King remained unmarried solely because he feared offspring with hereditary (congenital?) syphilis!

## III   The Schechin of Egypt

The interpretation that *schechin* represents "boils" is perhaps based on the wording of the Biblical description of the sixth plague with which the Egyptians were afflicted:[193]

> *And the Lord said unto Moses and unto Aaron: take to you handfuls of ashes of the furnace, and let Moses sprinkle it toward the heaven in the sight of Pharaoh. And it shall become small dust in all the land of Egypt, and shall be schechin breaking forth with blains upon man, and upon beast, throughout all the land of Egypt. And they took ashes of the*

187. Plinius 23:63; Dioscorides 1:184
188. Isaiah 38:14
189. *ibid* 38:1
190. Eccles. Rabbah on 5:6

191. Friedreich. *Zur Bibel* 1:206; Winer. *Biblisches Realwörterbuch* p.588
192. Berachoth 10a
193. Exodus 9:8-11

*furnace and stood before Pharaoh; and Moses sprinkled it up toward heaven, and it became schechin breaking forth with blains upon man, and upon beast. And the magicians could not stand before Moses because of the schechin, for the schechin was upon the magicians, and upon all the Egyptians.*

The word *ababu'oth*, which is here translated as "boils", is not found elsewhere in the Bible. On the other hand, the term *bua* is encountered often in the Talmud to designate blisters or pustules which one opens on the lungs[194] or on the outside of the body[195]. Linguistically, both the Biblical and the Talmudic terms only mean "swelling". If *schechin* therefore refers to a skin rash (eczema), then the "eczema with sprouting blisters or boils" would mean either a situation in which these blisters or boils developed secondarily[196], or where they were present from the outset but progressed due to a strong inflammation of the skin. One might also think of furuncles which develop from infection in a scratch or surface wound.

If one tries to conceive of the words *schechin ababu'oth*[197] as a concept[198], then the translation "rash of blisters" seems likely, at least more likely than "pox". The latter was suggested by physicians in explaining this verse, in the beginning of the nineteenth century, and in modern times was repeated by Ebbell. In spite of Friedreich[199], for the above reason one should not think that (the Biblical *schechin ababu'oth*) refers to the granular illness of the Nile, because the latter illness is a pustular eczema which is endemic in Egypt[200]. Its occurrence should therefore not be such a curiosity, except for the fact that I find no mention at all of its occurrence in animals. The *schechin* of Egypt is a particularly virulent variety with which the people were threatened as a punishment (for sin)[201], and is probably identical with: *the schechin on the knees and in the legs that cannot be healed, from the sole of thy foot unto the top of thy head*[202].

The Vulgate speaks of *ulcera* (or *vulnera*) *et vesicae turgentes*. The Septuagint translates *elke phlyktides anazeousai,* and Josephus speaks of "ulceration of the body while the intestines degenerate" *(exelkounto ta somata ton entos diaphtheromenon).*

We do not know the significance of the sprinkling of the ashes (or the soot). It is possible that it produced a serious skin inflammation in the people standing nearby, i.e. the astrologers, so that they *could not stand before Moses*[203], and this inflammation was then transmitted to others.

According to the *Midrash,* the *schechin* plague was a punishment on the Egyptians because they forced the Jews to heat and cool water for their (Egyptian) baths[204]. The commentators explain that baths are harmful for *schechin* afflictions. The strongly criticized hydrophobia in eczema by modern physicians was thus already an ancient observation.

*Schechin* as punishment for sin is also mentioned in post-Biblical times. Thus, according to the Palestinian Talmud, a student was once afflicted with *schechin* because he ventured to explain the vision of Ezekiel[205]. According to Mar Samuel, a paucity of skin care *(arbrebitha)* leads to *schechin* afflictions[206].

---

194. Chullin 46b
195. Sanhedrin 84b
196. this is the interpretation of *Targum Onkelos*
197. Exodus 9:10
198. which is suggested by the accents. The Vulgate has: *ulcera vesicarum turgentium*
199. Friedreich. *Zur Bibel* 1:107
200. Pruner. *Die Krankheiten des Orients.*

Erlangen 1847 p.138; see also Scheube. *Die Krankheiten der warmen Länder.* p.582
201. Deut. 28:27
202. *ibid* 28:35
203. Exodus 9:11
204. Exodus Rabbah 11:5
205. Jerushalmi Chagigah 2; 77a
206. Nedarim 81a

## IV   The Illness Kiba

Often, *kiba* is mentioned together with *schechin*. Uncleanliness of the body, according to Mar Samuel, leads to *schichne* and *kibe*[207]. A Roman woman (matron) once urged Rabbi Chanina bar Pappi to immorality. He pronounced a certain (magical) formula whereupon his body became covered with boils and scabs *(schichna and kiba)*. But she did something (magical) and he was healed. So he fled and hid himself in a bath-house[208] .... Satan once appeared at the door of the pious Pelimo. Satan was disguised as a poor man and his entire body was covered with *schichna* and *kibe*[209]. It is said that the loss (or opposite) of beauty is *kiba*[210].

A magical incantation against *kiba*[211] is as follows: "the sword is drawn, the sling is prepared, his name is not Jokab. Illnesses are painful"[212]. Another incantation "to heal *schechina* and *kibin*" (probably more correct than *schechina keibin*) begins with names of demons and then continues "your appearance remains, your position remains, your seed is like an infertile *kalut* and like a mule that is not fruitful and does not increase. So be thou not fruitful nor increase in the body of so-and-so, son of so-and-so"[213].

According to Rashi, *kiba* is a skin pustule; perhaps *"schichna* and *kiba"* may refer to a form of impetigo.

## V   Therapy for Schechin

There is very little mention in the Talmud of the therapy of *schechin*. In the text of a purchasing document of a slave, as established by Rabbi Judah, there is the stipulation that the sale is invalid if *schechin* becomes visible on the slave within two years, whether the *schechin* is fresh or old[214]. During that time, a pre-existing *schechin* would probably manifest itself again. In order to avoid complications, the seller would also guarantee against the possible occurrence of a "new *schechin*". What was the remedy for such a *schechin* or boil? Abaye said: ginger, silver dross *(martheka),* sulphur[215], vinegar of wine, olive oil, and white naphtha *(natpik)* applied with a goose feather[215a].

Among the Assyrians, and perhaps also among the Egyptians and other nations of antiquity[216], there existed the custom of *aegrotos in viis exponendi exquirendique a praetereuntibus an morbo id genus norint remedia*[217]. A similar situation is related of Rab Huna. Whenever he discovered a new medicine *(miltha deasutha),* he would fill a water jug with it and place it on the doorstep and proclaim: "whosoever has need of it, let him come and take of it"[218]. The Talmud relates that in Rome during the time of Rabbi Joshua ben Hananiah (approximately 100 C.E.), every person with leprosy *(kol demenagga)* was given a spool and removed to the open square, and was given skeins to wind, so that people might see them and pray for their recovery. Even an emperor's daughter was said to have been treated like this[219]. It thus appears that these patients were thought to be incurable.

## VI   Garab, Cheres and Other Forms of Schechin

In the Biblical warnings of punishments for disobedience next to the *"schechin* of

---

207. *ibid*
208. Kiddushin 39b
209. *ibid* 81a
210. Shabbath 62b
211. *Aruch* has *kiba* but the Aggadah *has kipha. Rashi's* explanation covers both versions
212. Shabbath 67a
213. *ibid*

214. Gittin 86a
215. *kibritha* is sulphur according to *Rashi*. In Niddah 62a, the word is explained as *borith* or *soda*
215a. Gittin 86a
216. Sprengel-Rosenbaum p.73
217. *Strabo de Assyrus.* Book 3 p.415
218. Taanith 20b
219. Chullin 60a

Egypt,'' there are also mentioned *garab* and *cheres*[220]. These were also thought to be skin diseases. *Garab* is also a blemish which renders a priest unfit to serve in the Temple, and an animal unfit to be offered as a sacrifice[221]. The same is also true of the illness called *yalepheth*[222]. In the *Mishnah, chazazith* is also mentioned in this connection and all these individual forms of illnesses are included in the grouping *schechin. Yalepheth* is said to be identical to the "Egyptian *chazazith*". In addition there is a benign form called *chazazith vulgaris,* just as there are two types of *garab,* one which renders a priest unfit to serve in the Temple and the other which has a benign nature. The former, the Biblical *garab,* is dry both inside and outside; the *garab* of the *Mishnah* is moist both inside and outside. Finally, the *schechin* of Egypt is dry inside but "moist on the outside" since it gives rise to boils. The moist *garab* is curable, the dry one and the Egyptian one are not[223].

If one assumes that, according to tradition, *garab* is identical with *cheres*[224], one finds that the identification of the individual names of sicknesses is more than difficult. As so often, it seems likely that the Biblical designations gradually disappeared from active usage and were then explained or replaced by others.

According to the explanation of the *Midrash*[225], which is hardly to be taken seriously, *cheres* is derived from *charas* meaning to scratch and to be hot. Thus, *cheres* refers to a sickness which requires a potsherd (*cheres* meaning potsherd) with which to scratch oneself, i.e. an itching skin sickness. Alternatively, it refers to an illness produced by the sun (*cheres* meaning sun as in Job 9:7).

The collective source-word *chazza,* meaning to indent or to cut into, gave rise to the Arabic *chazaz,* meaning scab or scurf or mange, together with the scars that remain therefrom. *Chazaz* has the same meaning as the Hebrew and Aramaic *chazazith*[226].

A therapeutic regimen for *chazazitha* is as follows: take seven Arzanian wheat stalks and roast them over a new pan so that the juice exudes from them, and then smear the patient therewith. Rabbi Shimi bar Ashi used this remedy for a heathen against *dabar acher*[227], and it cured him[228].

The same uncertainty exists concerning the identification of the illness *chikkuk* which, according to the literal meaning of the word, refers to "scabies" (from *chakak* meaning to scratch; the *psora* of the Greeks). Here too, there is a more serious moist form and a more benign dry form. In its severity, it is in line with the afflictions caused by swarming creatures: locusts, flies, hornets, mosquitoes, serpents and scorpions, for which prayers are recited and repentance is solicited[229]. It must therefore refer to a situation of sickness which afflicts a large portion of the population simultaneously, without actually endangering their lives. Illnesses where danger to life exists were called *deber* meaning pestilence.

According to the *Midrash*[230], five scourges *(maglabin)* for man were preordained at the time of creation: *se'eth* (rising), *sappachath* (scab), *bahereth* (bright spot), *schechin* (boil) and *mikva* (burning); some say *tzaraath* (leprosy) and *nethek* (scall) as well.

Swine were especially afflicted with skin illnesses *(negaim)*. The Talmud states: ten measures of *negaim* descended to the world, nine were taken by swine and only one by the remainder of the world[231].

220. Deut. 28:27
221. Levit. 21:20 and 22:22
222. *ibid*
223. Bechoroth 41a
224. *ibid*
225. *Lekach tob* on Deut. 28:27
226. Fleischer. in Levy's *Neuhebräisches und*

*Chaldäisches Wörterbuch* Leipzig 1876-1889
227. literally: something else, i.e. leprosy (F.R.)
228. Gittin 70a
229. Baba Kamma 80b
230. Numbers Rabbah 13:4
231. Kiddushin 49b

Erysipelas can be considered among the *negaim,* but not trichinosis, as is explicitly emphasized in post-Biblical literature[232] where the term *negaim* is used exclusively for *skin* diseases.

# VII

We thus see that the term *schechin* is a collective name which comprises many individual types of skin illnesses. According to the definition of the *Mishnah*[233], the term *schechin* includes every inflammatory skin lesion[234], whether it occurs secondary to an injury by wood or by a stone or from a burn from olive peat or from the hot spring water of Tiberias or, as Maimonides adds, from any internal cause. This is perhaps what the "experienced Sage" from Jeruaslem had in mind when he said to Rabbi Jose that there exist twenty-four types of *schechin*[235], although we today do not recognize all these varieties any more.

Only two more types need still to be mentioned. The first is simply called *schechin* and the person afflicted therewith, *mukke schechin.* Such patients used to bury their arms in small earthen mounds. On the day before Passover, they would go to the physician and have their leprous limbs amputated. The physician would cut it and leave only a very small portion thereof and thrust it upon a thorn, and the patient swiftly tore himself from his severed limb. In this manner, neither the patient nor the physician touched "a severed limb from a live being", and both were able to bring their Passover offering in "cleanliness", as is prescribed[236]. *Mukke schechin* are thus patients with maiming leprosy, whose occurrence apparently was not rare. The famous story of Nahum Gamzu depicts a man with amputated arms and legs who was blind and deaf[237] and whose entire body was covered with *schechin*[238]. The unusual language of the Book of Judges[239], according to the *Midrash*[240], indicates that Jephthah was buried in the cities (plural) of Gilead because his limbs fell off one at a time and were buried in various cities. The same source also suggests that the men that Moses sent to scout the land of Israel and who brought back a bad report[241] died as a result of their limbs falling off, *neshilath ebarim*[242]. The same *Midrash* interprets the affliction of the people depicted by the prophet Zechariah in the same manner:[243] *and their flesh shall consume away while they stand upon their feet, and their eyes shall consume away in their sockets, and their tongue shall consume away in their mouth.*

The Talmud does *not* include the illness of the *mukke schechin* in the category of leprosy or, more carefully expressed, a *tzaraath* illness. The leper was in and of himself unclean, and therefore excluded from setting foot in the Temple or bringing his Passover offering. In addition, his body made a house into which he walked, and all its contents, unclean[244]. It would therefore not have helped the physician at all if he avoided touching the dead limb. The fact that the above *Mishnah* emphasizes this point specifically indicates that this *schechin* is, in principle, different from *tzaraath.*

Naturally, there is an alternate way of resolving this difficulty, namely, if one assumes that during the time of the *Mishnah* the *mukke schechin* was in fact considered to be suffering from a form of *tzaraath,* but the Biblical rules pertaining to this sickness were no longer observed. Since the *Mishnah* relates to the time of the Temple, such an assumption can be categorically rejected.

232. The *Bible* is indeed different. For example Exodus 11:1
233. Negaim 9:1
234. from *schadian* meaning to burn or to be hot.
235. *Tosefta* Kethuboth 7:11
236. Kerithoth 3:8
237. The *Gemara* does not state he was deaf.
Did Preuss err? (F.R.)
238. Taanith 21a
239. Judges 12:7
240. Genesis Rabbah 60:3
241. Numbers 14:37
242. Eccles. Rabbah 9:12
243. Zechariah 14:12
244. Kelim 1:4

A man who becomes ill with *schechin,* i.e. a *mukke schechin,* is *coerced* by the (Jewish) authorities to divorce his wife. According to Rabbi Meir, there is no difference whether the illness already existed at the time of the marriage or first became manifest later. In the former case, the wife might say that she believed she was able to live with her sick husband, but might later become convinced of its impossibility. The Sages, however, require the divorce in any event, even against the will of the wife, out of consideration for the husband, because through cohabitation with his wife, the man would decay[245]. Marriage with a female *mukka schechin,* at least according to the disciples of Rabbi Meir, is permitted *a priori.* The followers of this school of thought also require that under all circumstances a man marry a girl that he has raped, even if she is ill with *schechin*[246]. It is also mentioned in the *Midrash*[247] that a princess was once forced to marry such a person as a punishment. However, if a married man dies childless, the widow is not obligated to marry the brother of the deceased, as is ordinarily prescribed in the Bible, if this brother is a *mukke schechin*[248].

## VIII    The Ba'ale Rathan

According to the rule expressed in the *Mishnah*[249], if a married man develops leprosy, the court forces him *ex officio* to divorce his wife even if she is willing to remain married to him "because she causes him to dwindle". The usual explanation of this phrase is as follows: cohabitation accelerates the deterioration of the body powers of the patient. One of the elders in Jerusalem told Rabbi Jose (according to Rabban Simeon ben Gamliel, it was one of the elders from among the lepers of Sepphoris)[250] that there are twenty-four types of leprosy, and the Sages stated that coitus is harmful for patients with all types: the most harmful is coitus for *ba'ale rathan*[251]. The probable meaning is the premature loss of potency, for even Langerhans heard of confirmation of native leprosy in Jerusalem[252]. The discussion in the *Midrash*[253] also suggests that the *rathan* sickness is harmful to potency. For this reason, the *Aggadah* ascribes the illness of the Egyptian king who took Sarah into his harem[254] as being *rathan,* which hindered him in cohabitation[255].

The cause of this sickness is stated by tradition as follows: if a man has blood let from his arm and then cohabits, his children will be cachectic. If both partners are venesected prior to coitus, then the children will be afflicted with *rathan.* According to Rab, this is so only if the man eats nothing prior to the coitus[256].

What are the signs of this illness? His eyes tear, his nostrils drip, saliva flows from his mouth and flies swarm all over him[257].

And what is the cure? Abaye said: *polion,* ladanum, nut rinds, leather shavings, melilot and date peels. These are boiled together and the patient is brought into a house of marble. The latter is also mentioned elsewhere as an operating room[258]. And if no marble house is available, the patient may be carried into a house the walls of which are the thickness of seven and a half bricks[258a]. The same wall thickness was also required for venesection[259]. Three hundred cups of this mixture must then be poured upon the

245. Kethuboth 7:10
246. Kethuboth 3:5
247. *Midrash* Psalms 137:5 p.524 Buber
248. Yebamoth 4a
249. Kethuboth 7:10
250. *Tosefta* Kethuboth 7:11; Levit. Rabbah 16:1
251. Kethuboth 77b. According to Genesis Rabbah 41:2 ed. Theodor: "only for *ba'ale rathan* is coitus harmful"
252. *Virchow's Archiv.* Vol. 50 p.453
253. Levit. Rabbah 16:1
254. Genesis 12:17
255. Jerushalmi Kethuboth 7; 31d; *Yalkut* 1:68 fol 19a p.37; Josephus' *Antiquities.* Book 1 Chapter 12:1 speaks of a "serious illness, so that the physicians already gave up hope"
256. Niddah 17a, it was actually Rabbi Papa, not Rab (F.R.)
257. Kethuboth 77b
258. Baba Metzia 83b
258a. Kethuboth 77b
259. Shabbath 129a

patient's head until the base of his skull is softened and then his brain is cut open. Then four leaves of myrtle are taken and each foot (of the insect or tumor, *vide infra)* is lifted up in turn and one leaf placed beneath it. It (the insect or tumor) is then grasped with a pair of tweezers and burned; for otherwise it would return to the patient.

Rabbi Yochanan issued the announcement: beware of the flies of the man afflicted with *rathan*. Rabbi Zera never sat with such a sufferer in the same draught. Rabbi Ammi and Rabbi Assi never ate any of the eggs coming from the street where the patient lived (in isolation?). Rabbi Joshua ben Levi, however, attached himself to these sufferers and studied the Torah with them, confident that the Torah serves as a shield and protects those who study it.

Rabbi Chanina said: why are there no sufferers from *rathan* in Babylon? Because they eat mangold (or beet or tomatoes) and drink beer made from cuscuta of the *hizmi* shrub. Rabbi Yochanan states: why are there no sufferers from *tzaraath* in Babylon? Because they eat mangold and drink beer and bathe in the waters of the Euphrates[259a].

Today, we do not know of any illness that conforms to the clinical appearances and anatomical substrate described in the Talmud. In addition, I am unable to find any parallel thereto from antiquity. The symptoms suggest and probably refer to leprosy since, in the serious forms of leprosy, it is usual for the mucous membranes to become changed. The conjunctival membrane, the mucosa of the nose, the mouth and the throat develop leprous lesions, and the surrounding organs (eyelids, nose, lips) become stiff as a result of infiltration or tubercle development. To consider these very isolated lesions which, as a rule, were devoid of sensation to be particularly contagious is probably justified. The assumption that transmission of this disease can be effected by flies is probably also correct. In modern times, it became recognized that the virus for sleeping sickness and malaria is transmitted by flies, thus confirming the opinion of the ancients who in Kyrene worshipped a *Deum muscarum multitudine pestilentiam afferentem*, a *Zeus apomyeos* (Greek for god who chases away the flies), a *Deus miagros*[260].

In Asia Minor, during the time of the Jewish kings, we find *Ba'al Zebub* of Ekron, the god of flies, *theon myian,* in the land of the Philistines[261]. It is probably no coincidence that King Ahaziah sought an oracle of this deity to tell him whether he would recover from his sickness[262]. It is likely that Beelzebub was considered to be one of the healing or illness deities.

Concerning the flies of the gods, however, it must be pointed out with great emphasis that there is no mention at all in Bible or Talmud of the transmission of an illness such as by the anopheles mosquito or the tsetse fly. The postulation of direct injury by the bite of a poisonous insect ("dead flies")[263] seems at least as likely.

There is no dearth of other explanations of this noteworthy Talmudic passage. Although syphilis is not mentioned in the writings of the ancients, it is found everywhere in the works of historians. It is therefore natural that *rathan* was not spared the fate of being considered syphilis, notwithstanding the fact, as Peypers correctly points out[264], that only signs of antisyphilitic treatment — iodine and mercury — are described in relation thereto! Frizzi[265] thinks that "Italian leprosy" which is *scabbia* or *rogna,* moves internally, and he thereby also rescued *Rashi's* interpretation of "insect". Bergel[266] is of the opinion that the symptoms described in the Talmud refer to glanders; this is unfortunately incorrect. One might also consider that one type of

259a. Kethuboth 77b
260. Plinius 10:27
261. Josephus. *Antiquities.* Book 9. Chapt. 2:1
262. Second Kings 1:2
263. Eccles. 10:1
264. Peypers. *Nederl. Tydschr. voor Geneesk.* 1893 Part 2 p.397
265. Frizzi, Benedict. *Pethach Enayim.* Livorno 1878 Vol. 4 p.85 ff
266. Bergel. *Die Medizin der Talmudisten* p.50

glanders means "worms", perhaps according to the appearance of lymphangitic cords on the skin.

The meaning of the word *rathan* is unknown. Derivation from *ra'ah* meaning "to see" seems extremely unlikely, as does a grouping with the Greek *rytos, ryas,* etc.

Because of the uncertainty of the diagnosis, it must remain undecided whether the causes and hygienic factors mentioned in the Talmud are in fact correct. It is also possible that, aside from leprosy, we are dealing with ulcerating lupus. The assumption that the disease in question is leprosy would justify the rule that divorce is imposed upon the couple. This assumption, which is now generally accepted by most people, not only by all primitive races, includes the supposition that coitus is the cause of leprous contagion, even though, as Sticker points out, it can develop through the nose, or in another manner[267].

In regard to the sexual instincts of lepers, contrary to the above observation of Langerhans, Stern states that "this instinct (in the Jesus Help Asylum in Jerusalem) is very powerful; the patients defect from the asylum because of this"[268], perhaps because abstinence is demanded of them in order not to produce leprous children. This did not occur in Turkish asylums. Tobler could not perceive of lepers having a greater than normal desire for coitus[269]. Friedreich stated that lepers are "extremely lustful and have insatiable sexual appetites"[270], and Michaelis is of the opinion that the lack of a prohibition of the marriage of lepers in the Bible is motivated by the fact that the permissibility of marriage would hold back the voluptuous lepers from women other than their own wives[271]. Certainly, in these patients, as with healthy people, everything must be individualized and varies with the state of the disease.

Bathing in the Euphrates River enjoys great popularity among the Arabs even today. The water is opaque[272]; perhaps the contents exert a beneficial influence on the solid components of the body.

It is difficult to understand the recommended therapy (for *ba'ale rathan* described above). It would be the simplest thing to assume that the entire Talmudic passage, which is lacking in the more ancient sources (*Tosefta* and *Jerushalmi*), represents an insertion which originally pertained to a totally different illness, particularly since Abaye, the author of the therapy, lived approximately 200 years after the clinical report (100 to 150 B.C.E.). However, to the honest critic, the simplest explanation is often not the correct one, and so, at the moment, we must be content with ignorance about this matter.

The softening of the skull by complicated boiled concoctions, instead of the usual trepaning, certainly points to folk medicine, and, in general, Abaye can be regarded as the main spokesman for this in the Talmud. However, regarding the lexicographic difficulty of the "base of the brain", we cannot even be certain that an artificial opening of the skull is meant. If that were the case, one would have expected the word *gulgaltha*. The case might just as well refer to caries, meaning a tumor which bored through the skull, etc. *Rashi* states that the case involved an insect that was removed from the brain. The text, however, could be equally well understood as referring to a tumor whose outgrowths resemble "the feet" of a reptile, and whose removal must be accomplished with extreme caution. It is not worthwhile to debate whether or not the Talmud was referring to cysticercus or the like.

An astonishing similarity to our Talmudic source is found in a recipe which Oefele describes from the "Gotha pharmacopoeia" as follows: "for the worm which resides

267. Evidence can be found in Bloch. *Ursprung der Syphilis.* Jena 1901 Vol. 1 p.110
268. Stern. *Türkei* 1:120
269. Tobler. *Mediz. Topographie von Jerusalem.* Berlin 1855 p.49
270. Friedreich. *Zur Bibel* 1:220
271. Michaelis. *Moses Recht* No. 210
272. Rosenmüller. *Morgenland.* commentary on Jeremiah 2:18

in the head, cut the base of the cranium, lift up one foot of the worm with small vetches and place some cotton thereunder with a suitable instrument. Do the same under all its legs. Then take an appropriate forceps and pull it out as rapidly as possible. Grasp hold firmly and be careful that none escape; otherwise it will bore its feet and toes in another place in the substance of the brain and the patient will certainly die"[273].

## IX    Chatatin

If the years are bad (i.e. famine), then *chatatin* develop on human bodies[274]; the same occurs if people are negligent and do not dry their skin well after bathing[275]. Any animal poison (*eres* meaning virus), if accidentally imbibed in one's (drinking) water, gives rise to *chatatin,* except snake poison, which is lethal[276]. The preferred site of these *chatatin* is the head[277], but they also appear on the scrotum, where, because of scratching or softening, they might lead to destruction of the testicles[278].

Treatment of this illness consists of embrocations with wine and vinegar[279], and, in case of need, with oil[280]. In addition, bathing is absolutely essential for such patients, and omission thereof is considered to be dangerous to life[281]. Baths in the hot springs of Tiberias, in the dead sea, or in water in which flax was previously soaked are considered to be especially therapeutic[282].

The *Midrash* considers this illness to be one of the *tzaraath* group, meaning it is a severe skin illness[283]. I do not think further attempts at more precise identification of this illness would be productive. Linguistically, *chatat* means to pierce or to scratch, thereby making superficial broad depressions (for example chicken pecking on walls); from there the Arabs derive the words: to draw and to write; as opposed to *chaphar* which means to make deep holes or to perforate. One cannot seriously think that *chatatin* refer to the tracks of scabies mites, in spite of Buxtorf's explanation: *fossulae a scabie maligna erosae.*

## X    Other Skin Diseases

Finally, one should mention several additional names of illnesses, the identification of which is also quite difficult.

1) It is related that Rabbi Simeon ben Yohai and his son, out of fear of persecution by the Romans, lived hidden in a cave for thirteen years. In order to preserve their clothes and not to offend God by their nakedness, they buried themselves in sand up to their necks. They ate the fruit of a carob tree which was growing at the entrance to the cave and drank water from a well, until *chaluda* (or *chaludoth*) developed on their bodies[284]. When they emerged, the skin was covered with *pile* and when the tears of their friends fell on their skin, they cried out in pain[285].

The meaning is clear. Because of longstanding immersion in sand and poor nutrition, the skin became raw and cracked, and the salt of the tears evoked a burning pain in the cracks.

Usually the word *chaluda* means rust, as for example on a needle[286]. Thus it could here mean the development of a rusty crust on the skin. *Pila* is a crevice and hence means a skin crevice.

273. Oefele. *Arch. de Parasitologie* 1901 p.87
274. Genesis Rabbah 89:4
275. Levit. Rabbah 19:4
276. Jerushalmi Terumoth 8; 45c
277. Yoma 77b
278. Jerushalmi Yebamoth 8; 9b
279. *Tosefta* Shabbath 12:11
280. Jerushalmi Shebiith 1; 38a
281. Jerushalmi Berachoth 1; 5b
282. Shabbath 109b
283. Genesis Rabbah 85:1
284. Genesis Rabbah 79:6; Jerushalmi Shebiith 9; 38d; *Pesikta de Rab Kahana* p.88b Buber: *Midrash* Psalms 17:14
285. Shabbath 33b
286. Kelim 13:7

2) According to Mar Samuel, insufficient drying of one's face leads to *chaspenitha*. To heal it, he recommends a thorough washing with mangold water *(Beta vulgaris)*[287]. Warm water is helpful for *silwa*, the injury produced by thorns; and cold water is efficacious for *chaspenitha*. The reverse is dangerous[288].

Perhaps this condition is a milder form of the aforementioned *chaluda. Aruch* is of the opinion that *chaspenitha* refers to a desquamation or peeling of the skin.

3) A snake (its flesh?) is said to be efficacious against *chaphaphith*[289]. *Rashi* understands this illness to be "a type of *schechin*". According to the assertion of the Talmud, (the textual version of which is not absolutely certain), one should cook a black and a white snake together and rub the skin with the resultant mixture. The root-word *chaphaph* means to rub or to scratch.

4) In an inn, Rabbi Yitzchak bar Samuel bar Martha rubbed himself with oil (to cleanse his skin). *Tsimche* then developed on his face. The oil had been used for magical purposes (and was bewitched)[290]. Such *tzemachim* can also occur from a blow[291]. They are often found on the pleural membranes of slaughtered animals[292].

*Tzamach* means to blossom or to sprout. *Tzemach* or *tzimcha* thus refers to a "blossom", efflorescence. The term exanthem, which linguistically has the same meaning, is today used in a different sense.

5) According to Rabbi Huna, if one eats a large quantity of asafetida *(chiltith)*, one's skin becomes loose and it is dangerous to life[293].

6) The evangelist relates that Lazarus, the friend of Jesus, lay *elkomenos* (ulcerated) before the door of the rich. The Vulgate translates: *ulceribus plenus*. Luther translates that he (Lazarus) was full of sores and the dogs licked his sores[294]. We have already mentioned above that the Greek translators translate the word *schechin* as *elkos,* which we assume is the designation for chronic eczema. The poor (beggar) Lazarus surely did not have leprosy, for the rich person would certainly not have tolerated a leper at his door. The fact that the expression "Lazarus houses" and "Lazarette" originally referred only to leprosariums does not speak against the above interpretation.

7) An animal whose skin peeled off as a result of work or an illness is called *geluda*. If sufficient skin remains so that healing is possible, then the animal may be slaughtered and consumed[295]. Mar Samuel requires that a strip of skin remain along the entire backbone; others require the amount of skin as large as an Italian *issar* (coin) around the navel[296].

8) Flesh and skin do not regenerate. A scar *(tzeleketh)* develops there instead[297].

## XI   The Hair

A man whose hair has been plucked out is called bald-headed *(kereach)*[298]. Baldness in a woman is so rare that Aristotle totally denies its existence[299].

Baldness can occur:

1) as a result of an illness
2) by "an act of God", that is without recognizable cause[300].

3) as a result of a caustic substance, *nesa* or *nesam,* which permanently eliminates hair if one applies it thereto or, according to another interpretation, if one eats it[301].

287. Shabbath 133b
288. Abodah Zarah 29a
289. Shabbath 77b
290. Sanhedrin 101a
291. Baba Kamma 85a
292. for example Chullin 48a
293. Jerushalmi Shabbath 20; 17c
294. Luke 16:20

295. *Tosefta* Chullin 3:7
296. Chullin 55b
297. Niddah 55a; Maimonides. *Hilchoth Chovel Umazik* 2:6
298. Levit. 13:40
299. *Hist. Animal.* 3:11
300. *Sifra. Thazria* p.67b
301. *ibid* and Nega'im 10:10

If a person rubs *nesa* on another person, whereby the hair fails to regrow, then the former person is liable to pay the five types of damages, similar to the liabilities payable for any bodily injury[302]: a) the cost for pain; b) the cost for healing, because caustic substances cause inflammation of the skin of the head so that cracks or *kartuphne* develop which are painful and then require healing; c) the cost of lost time from work: If the injured person was a comedian by profession who danced and shook his hair *(dallaph rosho)* in wine houses, and is now naturally not able to do so because he is bald (he is recompensed by the injurer); d) payment for depreciation of his body, if he has to give up his profession permanently; e) payment for degradation, because the shame of this disfigurement (baldness) is certainly a major one[303]. This is how Maimonides interprets this Talmudic passage[303a].

4) as a result of severe emotional shock. A man once passed through a wilderness and accidentally stepped on a sleeping snake as one steps in a wine-press. Although the snake did not awaken, he became so terrified *(nithbahel)* from the sudden severe fright that his hair began to fall out, and they called him *meruta*, meaning baldhead[304]. Similar observations are recorded in modern times. Fredet described a seventeen-year-old girl who, following a sudden danger to life, lost all her body hair; even after two years, it had not regrown[305].

5) a widespread custom in antiquity was the shearing of a bald spot on one's head, *karach korcha*, as a sign of mourning for a deceased person — a "hair sacrifice". This was forbidden to the Israelites[306], and particularly to the priests[307], as a heathen custom. This tonsure was applied "between the eyes", that is on the forehead.

In spite of this prohibition, shaving of a bald spot as a sign of mourning is often mentioned during the time of the prophets, not only in relation to heathens[308] but also among the Israelites[309]. Jeremiah utters a curse that one will not make any cuts in one's skin[310] and not shave oneself bald[311].

In the ecstasy of mourning, one used to pluck out *(marat)* the hair of one's head and beard[312]. Rabbi Hamnuna found it necessary to admonish the Sages: "warn your women not to tear out their hair when they are in mourning, so that they not come to transgress the prohibition against baldness"[313].

## XII   Baldness

The bald-headed person, *kereach,* was the object of ridicule in ancient times. Little children—according to the Talmud, adults who were behaving like little children[314] — called out to the prophet Elisha: *go up, thou bald head*[315]. The Lord will smite the crown of the head of the daughters of Zion with baldness as punishment for their excessive indulgences[316]. This punishment is extremely severe in view of the fact, as already mentioned, that baldness in a woman is extremely rare. It is contested in the Talmud whether or not baldness in a woman is considered to be a physical blemish for the purpose of marriage laws, if she still had a strip of hair (on the back of her head) from one ear to the other[317]. Sorceresses, who are considered to be the embodiment of everything hateful, are also referred to as bald-headed[318]. "Bald-headed buck"

302. See chapter 1 above
303. Baba Kamma 86a
303a. *Hilchoth Chovel Umazik* 2:4. *Rashi's* interpretation is slightly different.
304. Exodus Rabbah 24:4
305. Samuel in Eulenburg's *R.E. s.v.* Trophoneurosen. Vol. 20:211
306. Deut. 14:1
307. Levit. 21:5
308. Isaiah 15:2; concerning Moab
309. Ezekiel 7:18; Amos 8:10; Micah 1:16
310. Levit. 19:28
311. Jeremiah 16:6
312. for example — Ezra 9:3
313. Jerushalmi Kiddushin 1; 61c
314. Sotah 46b
315. Second Kings 2:23
316. Isaiah 3:17
317. Jerushalmi Kethuboth 7; 31d
318. Pesachim 110a, in a magical incantation

(meaning beardless) is an abusive term for a castrate[319], and "the bald-headed person should become balder" is a curse[320].

A bald-headed priest is unsuited to serve in the Temple if he does not possess at least one strip of hair stretching from one ear to the other[321]; the bald spot itself would be covered by a turban. The exclusion of such priests from service is based solely on their unsightly appearance[322], not because one suspected any moral defect in these priests.

A bald person, however, does enjoy certain advantages. If a person with a thick head of hair and a bald person are standing together on a threshing floor, chaff would fly into the hair of the former and become entangled there, while the bald man need only pass his hand over his head to remove such chaff[323].

Concerning therapy, I can only mention the following: the *Midrash*[324] explains the proverb *all idle talk leads to weariness*[325] as follows: when Rabbi Jonathan's hair kept falling out, he went to the town of Magdala of Dyers[326] to be cured. There was a barber in that place who said to him, "Have you come here on account of your hair to be cured?" Rabbi Jonathan replied: "My hair is falling out, and I heard that there was a remedy for it here. I have journeyed here to hasten a cure." The barber arose, knelt at his feet and said to him, "I only spoke with Rab about this remedy last night"[327]. Unfortunately the "wearying idle talk" of the efficient Figaro and the entire narrative ends here.

## XIII   Full Head of Hair

The opposite of baldness is *kivvetz*, the man with thick and long hair. He was not allowed to serve as a cashier for fear lest he embezzle money in his hair[328]. A case of excessive development of hair (hypertrichosis) is described in the Bible as the case of Esau who, at birth, came out like a hairy garment[329], and even later was still called a "hairy man"[330], as opposed to the smoothness of his brother Jacob. Gebuhr has written a very serious monograph concerning the question of *rufus ac pilosus Esau fuerit monstrum*[331]. A beard is an ornament for a man, but a blemish for a woman[332].

God sent the Prophet Elijah who had wavy hair to the Israelites. They ridiculed him and called him *ba'al se'ar*, a hairy man[333]. He then sent a man without hair, the prophet Elisha; he was insultingly called "baldhead"[334]. Thus, the Israelites can never be satisfied[335]!

---

319. Shabbath 152a
320. Jerushalmi Shabbath 20; 17d. Concerning Rabbi Akiba's surname *karcha*, see *Rashi* and *Tosafoth* in Bechoroth 58a.
321. Bechoroth 7:2
322. Bechoroth 43b; Jerushalmi Yoma 2; 40a
323. Genesis Rabbah 65:15
324. Eccles. Rabbah 1:8
325. Eccles. 1:8
326. Preuss has town of Otterturm; literally: tower of otters (F.R.)
327. Preuss erroneously has: this morning (F.R.)
328. Jerushalmi Shekalim 3; 47c
329. Genesis 25:25
330. *ibid* 27:11
331. Regiomonti 1687; 12 p.40
332. Jerushalmi Kethuboth 7; 31d
333. Second Kings 1:8
334. *ibid* 2:23
335. *Pesikta Rabbati* 26. ed. Friedmann p.129a

# APPENDIX   I

## I   GONORRHEA

Every flux from the genitalia is called *zob* or *effluvium;* the male person afflicted therewith is a *zab,* the female *zaba* — and the condition is called *ziba.* The juxtaposition of the law of *ziba* with that concerning pollution and menstruation proves that we are only dealing here with discharges from the genitalia, as is explicitly deduced in the *Sifra*[336]. The hypothesis of Beyer that the situation concerns hemorrhoids, may be disregarded[337]. Common language usage reserves the term *zaba* for abnormal genital *bleeding* in a woman. For this reason, Leviticus 15:18, which is juxtaposed to the law of the *zob* of a man, has the additional phrase "*blood* is her flux from the genitalia" as an allusion that here only the *blood* efflux of a woman is meant.

The Biblical law concerning the *zab* is as follows:

*Every man, from whose flesh (penis) there issues a flux, is unclean*[338]. He is unclean irrespective of whether the flux drips from his flesh or whether the flesh becomes obstructed from the flux (diminution of the secretion as occurs, for example, in epididymitis). The bed that he lies upon, and items upon which he sits, and riding equipment which he uses, are all unclean. He who touches either his bed or the *zab* himself[339], or he who sits on the bed which had been used by the *zab,* or touches or carries his saddlecloth, must wash his clothes, and is unclean until evening. The same applies to someone upon whom sputum of a person with a flux fell, and for everything that the patient has touched without having first rinsed his hands in water. Earthen vessels that he touches must be broken, and wooden ones are rinsed in water.

During the time of the wandering of the Jews through the desert, such patients were sent completely out of the encampment[340]. During the time of the *Mishnah,* such patients were permitted to remain only in the outermost of the three concentric "camps"[341]. When the flux ceases, he counts seven days for his cleansing, washes his clothes, bathes in running (literally: living) water, and is clean. On the following day, he brings two turtledoves to the priest who offers them as atonement[342].

It is clear forthwith that the only illness we know of that can be referred to here is gonorrhea. Even if rare cases of spermatorrhea and of benign catarrh of the urethra occurred in antiquity, it would still not have been necessary to make exceptional laws for them. The hygienic value — the intent is unclear to us — of these regulations is obvious. One can even attribute such a meaning to the offering which follows the cleansing process, but only insofar as it was dependent on the proof of healing (i.e.

---

336. ed. Weiss. fol 75a
337. C.A. Beyer. *De Haemorrhoid. ex lege mos. impuris.* Leipzig 1792. "The author was indeed a theologian and deacon in Leipzig". Rosenbaum, *Lustseuche* p.307. Notes
338. Levit. 15:2 ff
339. in the text it states "his flesh" to which Ibn Ezra states: "in any body part". Thus *basar* here does not refer to penis. As a

result, the supposition of Winer (*Biblisch. Realwörterbuch* p.373) that according to modern circumstances the case concerns the examining physician, is untenable. Healing does not have to be attested to by a priest as in the case of leprosy.
340. Numbers 5:2
341. Kelim 1:8; Taanith 21b
342. Levit. 15:2-15

seven clean days) and the preceding bath. On the other hand, we consider it inadmissible in the ceremony of the offering to involve the most modern theories of disinfection.

It seems quite justified, in view of the clothing of those days, that everyone who used the chairs upon which the patient previously sat, must bathe. This is because priests who served in the Temple were repeatedly instructed to wear trousers and hence, one must assume that, as a rule, they only wore one *chiton*.

The transmission (for example on the eyes) of this disease by utensils soiled with secretions is also not inconceivable. It is not clear why the sputum of a patient with gonorrhea was thought to be harmful. If one considers the abhorrence which the Oriental person has for sputum in general, so that, for example, he considers being spat upon as an insult for which the law requires a stronger revenge than for a blow on the ear[343], then one can perhaps imagine that to him the sputum of such a patient appears to be so unclean that he believed only a complete bath can cleanse him. According to our present knowledge of gonorrhea, the Biblical (and, juxtaposed thereto, the Talmudic) law is lacking in not prohibiting coitus for the *zab*. However, the knowledge concerning the contagiousness of venereal diseases in general was lacking in antiquity. The reason for this, as correctly pointed out by Notthafft, is the fact that the liver was considered to be the seat of diseases and that gonorrhea was thought to represent flow of semen. The concept of infection is first mentioned in the 13th century.

It is not necessary to mention that, in view of all the above, the Talmud is certainly not recommending cohabitation, as was otherwise suggested in antiquity, as a cure for gonorrhea. Unfortunately, that superstition has not yet been eliminated, even today.

## II

The *Tosefta*[344] first mentions the difference between *zob* and sperm: "*zob* issues from a flabby (literally:dead) penis whereas sperm flows from an erected (literally:alive) penis. *Zob* resembles the water of barley dough; it is pale[345] and resembles the white of incubated eggs. Sperm is 'bound'[346] and resembles the white of non-incubated eggs". In spite of the uncertainty of the textual reading in the last part of this citation, it is at least undoubted that the efflux of a patient with gonorrhea — if otherwise our interpretation of *ziba* is correct — is not considered identical with *gonos* or sperm flow, but is regarded as something distinct from it. This recognition is not found even among physicians for centuries thereafter.

The *Mishnah*[347] is mainly concerned with the diagnosis of *ziba*. A single efflux from the urethra is considered to be pollution (even from an already flabby penis). If the flux, however, occurs two or three times within a twenty-four hour period, then the individual becomes a *zab*[348]. Even the mentally defective, deaf and dumb people, and castrates can render unclean through *ziba; today* we would not argue with the fact that, since they are capable of cohabitation, they can also acquire gonorrhea. Nevertheless, certain causes must be excluded, that is, it must be certain that the patient did not in fact have repeated sperm effluxes[349]. Among these causes are all those reactions which

343. Baba Kamma 8:6
344. *Tosefta* Zabim 2:4
345. Aruch and Vilna edition of the Talmud have *diha* (Niddah 35b) meaning dull, that is less opaque. *Tosefta* Zabim 2:4 has *dohah;* Maimonides *Hilchot Mechusar Kapparah* 2:1 has *kehah* meaning weak, extinguished, etc.

346. see Niddah 56a: the stream does not emerge as globules (balls), as does sputum or *rok*
347. Zabim 2:3
348. Baba Kamma 24a has: three times in one day or once on each of three consecutive days
349. Nazir 9:4

are independent of the patient's will[350] such as cohabitation — which makes the twenty-four hour period of observation for *zob* uncertain and therefore makes the principle *in dubiis pro reo* impossible —[351] certain foods and beverages, carrying heavy objects, jumping, and illness[352]; furthermore, sexually arousing thoughts and the looking at things which might lead thereto[353] such as: "if he saw animals that were copulating, or even only women's clothing *(fetishism)*". According to Rabbi Akiba, only a flux from an absolutely empty-stomached man is conclusive that the flux is *zob*. His colleagues retorted: then there would never be any *zabim*[354]!

Among the things which lead to *ziba*[355], Rabbi Judah ben Betheyra mentions: milk and cheese, fat meat, bean gruel and fish soup[356] and, in general, excessive eating and drinking[357]. In a child, illness of the mother must also be excluded (before calling the child a *zab*). In the case of a proselyte, one attempts to attribute a flux to the circumcision, as long as he still has pain as a result thereof (painful erection?)[358]. When the day to take the cleansing bath arrives, the convalescent patient may do so even on the Day of Atonement[359], because it is a ritual bath.

Not only is the *zob* discharge unclean, but also the urine and the sperm of the patient, because both these liquids are constantly mixed with *zob*[360]. This is not the case for blood which flows from the urethra, however[361]. A chamber pot which he used must be rinsed three times[362]. Scripture also mentions the uncleanness of the sputum of a patient with gonorrhea; so too bloody sputum because it contains spittle, as well as nasal secretions. However the uncleanness does not extend to foul-smelling mucus (?), perspiration and feces[363]. The Talmud also describes a sack to collect the secretion[364], a sack made either of leather or of metal[365]. The constant use thereof, however, was abandoned "in order not to excite a person's flesh and cause pollution"[366].

As already mentioned, definite declarations concerning the permissibility of a *zab* to cohabit are lacking in the *Mishnaic* writings. It is, however, decreed that during the seven days after the discharge of a *zab* has ceased (before he has bathed and given his offering), he is allowed to cohabit without fearing that these "clean days" would be invalidated[367]. However, one can draw no conclusion from this regulation about the earlier time. Equally inconclusive is the other Talmudic statement that the uncleanness of the *zaba* or abnormally bleeding woman is greater than that of the *zab*, since she communicates uncleanness to her cohabitant for seven days, whereas he only transmits uncleanness to the woman that copulates with him until the evening (of the same day) just like a healthy person[368]. Finally, also inconclusive is the commandment: a *zab* should not eat with a *zaba* because it offers an occasion for transgression[369].

It is questionable whether or not the *Tosefta* speaks of *ziba* out of its own experience; at least the introduction of this tractate seems to suggest such a doubt.

---

350. although the causes referred to are subject to the patient's will, the result thereof is not, i.e. ejaculation
351. Maimonides' commentary on Zabim 2:3 states that people who cohabit frequently often tell their physician of an efflux following cohabitation
352. No commentary explains which type of "illness" is meant. Maimonides only states that it refers to a generalized illness of the body as opposed to an illness limited to the genitalia.
353. I cannot explain *Rashi's* comment: if he saw a demon and was frightened thereby
354. Zabim 2:2
355. perhaps pollution is meant here, not *ziba*?

356. *Tosefta* Zabim 2:5
357. Kiddushin 2b
358. *Tosefta* Zabim 2:6-7
359. *Tosefta* Yoma 5:5
360. Nazir 66a
361. In the Orient, hematuria due to filaria was probably more common than bleeding or blood admixtures due to gonorrhea
362. *Tosefta* Tohoroth 5:3
363. *Sifra parshath Zabim* fol 75a ff
364. Shabbath 53a
365. Niddah 13b
366. *Tosefta* Niddah 2:9
367. *Tosefta* Zabim 1:9
368. Kelim 1:4
369. Shabbath 1:3 and 13a

Then the interesting observation would emerge that an illness whose existence at the time of the Bible is proven by the legal regulations pertaining thereto completely disappeared one thousand years later.

On the other hand, there is no doubt that the *distillatio* about which the Catholic moral theologians speak, and which they correctly distinguish from *pollutio*, does not refer to spermatorrhea, as claimed by Capellmann[370], but to gonorrhea.

## III

Gonorrhea and leprosy are already considered in the Bible to be evil sicknesses, even though they are not found in the Pentateuch in the warnings of punishment for transgression. The general who treacherously[371] killed Abner was cursed by David as follows: *let the blood of Abner rest on the head of Joab, and let there not fail from the house of Joab a zab or a metzorah, anyone with gonorrhea or with leprosy*[372]. The *Gemara*[373] is of the opinion that if a father has lived deservingly, then he will live to experience five pleasures from his son: handsomeness, strength, wealth, wisdom and long life. Otherwise, he will experience five anguishes: leprosy instead of beauty and *zob* instead of strength, for nothing weakens like the latter[374]. One might perhaps conclude from a *Midrash* that the main cause for gonorrhea, *coitus cum immundis,* was already known at that time at least, for it states[375] that if a young person sins, he is punished with *zibuth* and leprosy. That is why Moses warns against sin.

Also noteworthy is the fact that one of the two bird offerings is brought as a sin offering, and then Scripture adds[376]: *and the priest shall make an atonement for him* (the convalescent patient) *before the Lord for his issue.* Of further noteworthiness is the fact that both illnesses, gonorrhea and leprosy, were later designated with the collective name *negaim* which is derived from *naga* meaning to touch, and can only refer to *contagia* or contagious illnesses.

# APPENDIX    II

## COSMETICS

### I   Haircutting Instruments

It is totally incorrect to assert that "among the ancient Hebrews, the men had long flowing hair". On the contrary, it is absolutely certain, as will become clear without question from what follows, that during the times about which we have information,

---

370. *Pastoralmedizin* p.97
371. literally: from behind (F.R.)
372. Second Samuel 3:29
373. Jerushalmi Kiddushin 1; 61a
374. Thus the interpretation in the *Yalkut* where *zab* means *thachish* or weak. The story continues as follows: when Solomon killed Joab, the above-spoken curse of David was taken over by the house of Solomon as punishment for this murder, although, as David's son, he was duty bound to do so. For

Scriptures states of his (Solomon's) son Rehoboam: *he made speed to get him up to his chariot, to flee to Jerusalem* (First Kings 12:18). According to some commentaries, he was suffering from *zab* and, according to others, he was weak in general. The explanation in Sanhedrin 48b, which is the same as Numbers Rabbah 23 fol 95b, appears to be much more strained.
375. Levit. Rabbah 18:1
376. Levit. 15:15

short hair was the general custom. The misogynists speak contemptuously about women who let their hair grow like a night demon[377]. The Bible already mentions a professional barber, *gallab*[378]. In post-Biblical writings, he is mentioned often by the term *sappar*.

There existed a large number of instruments used to remove the hair. In the Bible, the following are mentioned:

1) The *mora,* translated by the Septuagint as *sideros* and by the Vulgate as *novacula,* is the usual designation for a razor[379].

2) The *taar*[380]. Since there also exists a "*taar* of writers"[381] (used to make a point on a writing quill), *taar* may refer to a knife. Tradition is also in agreement with this interpretation, namely that *taar* is a razor. This term is mentioned very often in the *Gemara.* The Septuagint translates *taar* as *xyros* (sharp edge) and the Vulgate again uses the term *novacula* or *radere.*

3) The Arameans translate both terms, *mora* and *taar,* as *maspera,* which is also a designation for the razor.

4) A knife is naturally the oldest instrument used to cut hair. Scissors are not mentioned until much later. According to Pollux, in the second century, hair shears are called *diple machaira* (double knife) and also *psalis* (scissors)[382]. An exact analogue is found in the *Mishnah* where a dual *mispereth* is called *misparayim,* which also means double knife, in the sense of a scissor. The expressions *zug shel sapparim*[383], "the pair of the haircutter", or the abbreviated *zug*[384], *zuga* or *zava*[385], also meaning "a pair (of scissors)" are also used. Such "pairs (of scissors)", in which one differentiates a top part from a bottom part[386], were found not only at the barber but also in (wealthy) private homes. Scissors were also called *mispereth shel perakim*[387] meaning scissors of (two) sections, as opposed to simply *mispereth* or *misparayim* which refer to the scissors of dressmakers which were made from one piece. If the explanation of Hai Gaon and the depiction of Lippman Heller[388] are correct, this scissors would look just like our sheep-shearing scissors, that is made from a single piece of resilient steel, bent like a staple, and whose ends are sharpened like a knife.

According to the report of Hai Gaon, the scissor made of two segments had a spike on one segment, and a hole in the corresponding location of the other segment. During use, the spike is placed in the hole thus forming a hinge.

If one wished only to "make the hair lighter", but for special reasons did not wish to use these cutting instruments exclusively for this purpose, one would employ a *sakkin,* or regular knife, instead of a *taar,* and a *maspereth* instead of *misparayim*[389].

I am unable to describe how a razor differed from other knives. Perhaps it was curved in the form of a crescent. At least Martial speaks of the *curva novacula*[390].

Shearing or *gillach* was only carried out with the *taar.* The *zug* only "removes" *(natal)* hair[391] or "pinches off" *(karatz)* hair[392].

An instrument case, *theke* (Greek), is also mentioned in the Talmud in regard to cutting scissors, hair shears and razors[393]. The Romans also used the name *theca* for

377. Erubin 100b
378. Ezekiel 5:1
379. Judges 13:5; First Samuel 1:11 and the exceptional *Targum;* compare Numbers Rabbah 10:5
380. Numbers 6:5 and 8:7; Isaiah 7:20
381. Jeremiah 36:23
382. *Onomast.* Amsterdam 1706. Book 2 Chapt. 3, 31 fol 166-167
383. Kelim 13:1
384. for example Shabbath 94b
385. Megillah 16a. *Zuza* is a printing error;

Esther Rabbah *loc. cit.*
386. Kelim 13:1
387. *Tosefta* Kelim 3:2
388. in their commentaries on Kelim 13:1
389. Jerushalmi Moed Katan 3; 82a; *Rashi* has the same intent with his expression *derech shinnuy,* Taanith 13a
390. Martial 11:58
391. Niddah 6:12
392. Nega'im 4:4
393. Kelim 16:8

the barber's pouch[394]. There also exists a *"tharbus* for the scissors"*, which is a leather box which is so large that one can sit on it, if the need arises[395].

5) According to some commentaries, the *schachor*[396] is a small hair shears which can also be dismantled.

6) The *rehitani*[397] is also a folding instrument for removing hair. It is also the name of a carpenter's instrument[398] which, according to some commentators, is identical with the Biblical axe or *maatzad*[399], with which one can probably remove the end of a beam[400]. The *izmal shel rehitani*[401] must, therefore, refer to the iron of the axe. I do not know what shape the corresponding hair (cutting) instrument had.

7) *Malket* (or *malkat*) and *malketeth*[402] are forceps with which to pull the hair out (epilation). One can also use as a hair forceps two teeth which broke off from a carding-comb[403]. *Malket* corresponds to the forceps or *forfex* of the Roman barber or the *volsella* ("tweezers"). The term *melkachayim* is translated by the *Targum* as *malketa*[404]. These were thought to be forceps which served as candle snuffers for the candelabra in the Temple.

8) The *negustre* or *genustre*[405] (according to Mussaphia equivalent to *knesterion*), also *angistor*[406], is undoubtedly a nail knife. Scissors to cut nails were not used by the ancients[407]. Manicure at that time played a greater role than it does today. Such care was rendered by barbers in barber shops.

## II  Haircuts

One took a haircut if one had to appear before an important official, as did Joseph when he was summoned to see the Pharaoh[408], "in order to show respect to royalty"[409]. If someone dreams that he is having a haircut, he should consider it a good omen and hope for a successful career similar to that of Joseph[410].

Cutting one's hair is one of the preparations for the Sabbath and for Holy Days. To this end "one sat before the *sappar*"[411]. For this reason, even in the places where people refrained from work on Passover eve, the barber was permitted to conduct his professional activities[412].

The act of haircutting, *tisporeth*, begins when one places the *"maaporeth* of the barber" on the knees[413]. This "covering", perhaps a hairdressing apron, is different from the often-mentioned *"mitpachoth* of the barber". The latter probably refer to hand towels or napkins because they are usually mentioned together with the *"mitpachoth* of the hands"[414].

During the haircutting, well-to-do men look into a mirror. Every person who has a haircut done by a heathen should also look into a mirror, unless it is done on the open street[415], in order to observe all the movements of the heathen, although ordinarily looking into a mirror for a man, as well as any other "womanly" practice, was prohibited[416]. A separate prohibition existed on the Sabbath against the use of small

394. Becker-Göll. *Gallus* 3:240
395. Kelim 24:5
396. *ibid* 13:1
397. *Tosefta* Makkoth 4(3):10
398. Baba Kamma 119a; Shabbath 97a
399. Isaiah 44:12 and Jeremiah 10:3
400. *Tosefta* Kelim 2:2
401. Shabbath 48b
402. Makkoth 3:5
403. Kelim 13:8
404. Exodus 25:38 and 37:23
405. Moed Katan 18a; Niddah 17a
406. *Tosefta* Kelim 3:12; also *agnister* (onychisterion) etc.
407. Böttiger. *Sabina* 1806 1:320 and 516
408. Genesis 41:14
409. Genesis Rabbah 89:9
410. Berachoth 57a
411. Shabbath 1:2
412. *Tosefta* Pesachim 2:18
413. Shabbath 9b
414. The *mitpachoth* which are adorned with pictures (Kelim 28:4) are book covers. In Kelim 9:3, "*mitpachoth* of books" and "*mitpachoth* of the barber" are mentioned side by side.
415. Abodah Zarah 29a
416. cf. *Tosafoth opus cit.*

metal hand mirrors which were not fastened to the wall, because one employed them to cut off loose-hanging hair, *nimin ha-meduldalim*[417].

The king should have his hair cut daily, because *thine eyes shall see the king in his beauty*[418]; the High Priest, only on Fridays, because the Temple watches were changed on that day[419]; and ordinary priests, only every 30 days. The people who are offering sacrifices in the Temple, *anshe mamad,* and those who are on the priestly watches, *anshe mischmar,* may not leave their service position to obtain a haircut except on Thursdays, in honor of the Sabbath[420].

One may not look at a king when he is receiving a haircut or when he is naked or when he is bathing[421], because *thou shalt in any wise set him king over thee*[422], meaning you shall revere him[423]. The same applies to the High Priest[424].

## III   Omission of Haircutting

Only for exceptional reasons was the cutting of hair omitted.

1) As a result of vows of abstention (Nazarite vows). He who makes such a vow may not consume any grapes or products made therefrom (i.e. wine), nor may he drink beer (palm wine or *shechar*). All the days that he is a Nazarite, no razor, *taar,* is allowed to come on his skin, *until the days be fulfilled, in which he separateth himself unto the Lord, he shall let the locks of the hair of his head grow*[425]. At the end of this period, he brings a sacrifice, cuts his hair and burns it under the kettle of the peace offering. A vow need not be articulated *expressis verbis;* it suffices for someone to simply state: (from today on) I wish to curl *(mesalsel)* or cultivate *(mekalkel)* my hair[426].

The possible reasons for such a vow are manifold. As a freewill offering (pleasing to God), such a vow is just as undesirable as any other. Simeon the Just only experienced *one* case in which he was pleased: a young shepherd once went to draw water from a well. He gazed upon his own reflection in the water: beautiful eyes, handsome appearance and thick locks of resplendent hair. In order to avoid killing himself (because of the evil desires which rushed to his head), he made a Nazarite vow and offered his hair[427]. This seems to be the Jewish version of the legend of Narcissus.

A "Nazarite for life" was differentiated from a *nazir* of short duration — at least 30 days[428]. In the latter case, the vow is removed (after a set time period). In the former case, he is permitted to "lighten his hair with a razor" if his hair becomes too heavy for him. As a rule, this could occur only once a year[429]. Since in the cases of Samuel and Samson it was determined prior to birth that "no razor shall come on their heads", and they themselves did not make Nazarite vows, it is questionable whether or not they were true Nazarites. By contrast, it is stated that Absalom, the son of David, was "a Nazarite for life". It is also possible to conclude from the Biblical text that he let his hair grow long purely out of conceit[430]. When he polled his hair once a year[431] because it was too heavy on him, the hair weighed *two hundred shekels after the King's weight*[432]. It is generally assumed, probably on the basis of the report in Josephus[433],

417. Shabbath 149a
418. Isaiah 33:17
419. and it is appropriate that the people of the watch see their superior in proper attire; *Rashi*
420. Taanith 17a
421. Sanhedrin 2:5
422. Deut. 17:15
423. Sanhedrin 22a
424. *Tosefta* Sanhedrin 4:1
425. Numbers 6:12-21
426. Nedarim 1:1
427. Nedarim 9b
428. Nazir 1:3
429. Nazir 4b
430. *Kimchi's* commentary on Second Samuel 14:26
431. see the various opinions in *Tosefta* Sotah 3:16 and *Mechilta* p.36a
432. Second Samuel 14:26
433. *Antiquities.* Book 7 Chapter 10:2

that his *hair* was caught in a tree as he rode under it and he remained hanging there, while the mule that was under him rode away. The text, however,[434] only speaks of his *head* (getting caught in the tree, not the hair), and this seems more likely.

A husband has veto powers over his *wife* who makes a Nazarite vow, just as he has that same right over any other vow she might make that involves asceticism[435], as soon as he becomes aware of the vow. It is disputed whether or not he is able to exercise this right if the offering of the sacrifice, which is included in the shaving of the hair, has already begun. Most Sages answer in the affirmative. The man could say: I cannot tolerate a disfigured wife, *menuveleth!* To be sure, she could later wear a wig, *peah nochrith*. However, according to Rabbi Meir, the husband could still say: I cannot tolerate a shaven woman, and I do not like a wig because it is dirty and unappetizing[436].

2) A person omits cutting his hair if he anticipates a fright: "it is natural for a person upon whom judgement is to be pronounced shortly, to wear dark clothes and allow his beard to grow, for he doesn't know how the trial will end"[437]. In general, a person omits haircutting if he is anxious.

When Palestine was divided among the Children of Israel, the tribes of Reuben and Gad went with them, and then returned to the area of the Transjordan, but allowed their children to remain in Palestine[438]. According to legend, the children let their hair grow until they saw their fathers again fourteen years later, and their fathers did the same until they saw their children again[439].

3) Rabbi Joseph relates of the Persians that they let their hair grow like that of a bear[440].

4) Cutting of the hair, *tigalachath,* is one of the ten things which causes a patient to suffer a relapse, and the relapse is worse than the original illness[441]. The patient should, therefore, omit it.

## IV   Hair Styles

1) Cutting one's hair is forbidden on the Sabbath and on Holy Days. Exceptions are made for half holidays (the intermediate days of Passover and Tabernacles) when the following individuals may have their hair cut: he who returns from a business trip from across the sea, or comes out of prison, or was released from excommunication[442], and he who developed an illness *(makka)* on his head[443].

According to Samuel, a child that is born on a half holiday may have its hair cut because it is considered as one who comes out of prison (i.e. out of the mother) if, as *Rashi* asserts, the hair is so long that it bothers the infant[444]. It would be a very rare occurrence indeed that a newborn child, at birth, would have such long hair that one could not wait the few days until after the holiday to cut it off. Therefore, it appears that the Talmud is referring to the "first haircut" which many people celebrate as a festive occasion[445]. This law concerning the cutting of the hair of an infant probably refers to another Talmudic passage which states the following: "one is permitted to cut a child's hair on a half holiday, whether it was born on the half holiday or earlier"[446]. In general, the celebration of the first haircut occurs on the first birthday. If the birthday is earlier, one is even permitted to postpone the first haircut until the half holiday.

---

434. Second Samuel 18:9
435. Numbers 30:14
436. Nazir 28b
437. Jerushalmi Rosh Hashana 1; 57b
438. Numbers 32:16
439. Genesis Rabbah 98:15
440. Megillah 11a

441. Berachoth 57b
442. Moed Katan 3:1
443. *Tosefta* Pesachim 2:18
444. Moed Katan 14a
445. Ploss, *Das Kind.* Vol. 1. p.290ff
446. Moed Katan 14b

This "celebration of the first haircut" is mentioned by Jewish writers as late as the eighteenth century as a custom of the people of Jerusalem. It was celebrated with music and dancing in the synagogues or at the graves of especially pious people[447].

2) Cutting one's hair is also forbidden during the time of mourning for close relatives[448]. The High Priest is specifically forbidden to let his hair grow or to rend his garments during his period of mourning[449]. The same prohibition was issued to the sons of Aaron when their brothers died[450]. Thus, the abstention from cutting the hair as a sign of mourning was a general practice and, as far as I can see, there is no argument at all with the Talmudic phrase "the suffering person may not cut his hair". Apparently, this formal rule is the result of the establishment of the observation that the person in mourning has no sense for any comforts: for washing or anointment[451], for nice clothes[452], or for his coiffure. The law is simply the codification of a practice of custom.

However, there was also a time when the opposite practice prevailed. Job cut his hair when he learned from the messengers of evil tidings of the death of his own children[453]. A prophet admonishes the people to cut their hair as a sign of mourning[454]. As can be readily proven, haircutting was a heathen custom of many nations of antiquity and even present times, a type of the already-mentioned hair sacrifice. So, too, a female war captive shaved her head as a sign of mourning for her relatives killed in the war[455].

3) The Bible prescribes[456] that *ye shall not round the corners of your heads,* meaning one should not shave the head all around so that, as the Talmud explains, the temples are as bald as the skin behind the ears and on the forehead, while in the middle of the head a tuft of hair remains[457]. The ancient commentaries explain that the hair was left on the neck like a tail[458] and braided like a chain[459]. It thus refers to a pigtail. These hair styles were probably related to certain cultic notions which the Biblical prohibition of imitation (of the heathens) attempts to counter. As a result, the growing of such a long lock of hair *(belorith)* is expressly designated as a "heathen practice"[460], for anyone who grows his locks does so specifically as an act of idolatrous worship[461]. The sons of David, who were raised with heathen war captives, also let their locks grow[462], as did the Israelites in Egypt to imitate the Egyptians[463].

When God gives a son to a heathen, the latter makes the foreskin long and allows locks of hair to grow. When the son grows up, the father brings him into the idolatrous temple and enrages the Lord[464]. Jeremiah calls the heathens "people with polled hair"[465]. If a Jew cuts the hair of a heathen, as soon as he reaches the locks, he (the Jew) should remove his hand[466] in order not to assist the heathen in his idolatry.

The day on which the heathen shaves his beard and polls his hair is considered by him to be a festive occasion[467].

The *belorith* of a heathen *woman* is also mentioned as follows: Zimri grasped the Midianite woman by her hair and brought her to Moses exclaiming: if you forbid this woman to me, then how could you marry the daughter of Jethro who was also a heathen?[468].

447. Evidence is found in the Commentaries on *Orach Chayim* 531:3
448. Moed Katan 14b
449. Levit. 21:10
450. *ibid* 10:6
451. Second Samuel 14:2
452. Ezekiel 26:16
453. Job 1:20
454. Micah 1:16
455. Deut. 21:12
456. Levit. 19:27
457. Makkoth 20b
458. *Rashi* on Abodah Zara 11b
459. *Rabad* on *Sifra* p.86b
460. *Tosefta* Shabbath 6:1
461. Deut. Rabbah 2:18
462. Sanhedrin 21a
463. Levit. Rabbah 23:2
464. *Pesikta de Rav Kahana* 30 p.190a
465. Jeremiah 9:25
466. *Tosefta* Abodah Zara 3:6
467. Abodah Zarah 1:3 and 11b
468. Sanhedrin 82a

*Mesapper koma* is different from *belorith* or *tzitzith*[469]. Whereas the growing of locks *(giddul belorith)* is considered to be a direct heathen cultic practice which involves the prohibition of idolatry and for which no dispensation can be granted under any circumstances, the cutting of the *koma* is only a heathen *custom* which is only forbidden and punishable as such[470]. The *koma* is a coiffure in which the corners of the head were shaven and only at the back of the head a line of hair was left[471], but not a lock[472]. Only in exceptional cases were people "who were close to the government" such as Abtolos bar Reuben[473], or "related to the government" such as the family of the Prince Judah[474] permitted "to cut their hair in the form of a *koma*". Reuben Ben Astrobolus once tried to have a Roman decree which was hostile to the Jews abrogated. In order not to be recognized as a Jew, he cut his hair in the form of a *koma,* and went and sat among the Romans[475].

The first type of coiffure, the *belorith,* is reported by Herodotus to be a custom of the Macers: they let the hair grow in the middle of the head, but shaved clean down to the skin all around. The other type of coiffure is the *ektoreia kome* (Hector's hair), where the hair in the front is cut off, whereas the hair in the back falls freely over the neck. According to the report of Plutarch, when young people became of marriageable age, they went to Delphi and there cut their hair in front and offered it to the gods[476].

4) The Bible further states: *neither shalt thou mar the corners of thy beard*[477]. In the decree for the priests, however, it states "they shall not shave off the corners of their beards". Tradition deduces therefrom that the former law, which applies to every Israelite, only forbids the removal of the beard with a razor. The hair-removing tweezers *malket,* and the depilatory substance *nasha,* both mar the beard but do not cut it and the razor does not mar it.

Five corners of the beard were identified, two at each jaw (point and angle) and one at the chin[478], so that the prohibition refers to the beard in its totality. It is probably as a result of this law that the Jews were and still are a beard-wearing people.

There are only three exceptions to this prohibition of shaving off the hair: a healed leper must shave his entire body including the head, beard and eyebrows, at the beginning and at the end of the eight day final quarantine period[479]. The same applies to the Levites at their first consecration for Temple service[480], and to the Nazarite; however, the latter only shaves his head[481].

The razor is specifically prescribed for these three types of people[482].

It is quite understandable that of all these rules of the Jews, who lived among nations which embraced other customs, some evoked ridicule and others evoked enmity. Yet the Jews followed these rules with the same pride as they did rules for circumcision and the like[483].

# V   The Beard

The *beard* is a beauty blemish on a woman but an ornament for a man[484]. The beard of the high priest reached down to the seam of his garments[485]. Only a castrate is

469. *Sifra Acharey* per. 13 p.86a
470. Deut. Rabbah 2:18
471. *Sapha,* as is found in a gloss to *kome* in *Sifra, loc. cit.* It is lacking in *Rabad.* Maimonides' interpretation (*Hilchoth Abodah Zarah* 11:1) is probably identical
472. as *Rashi* states in Meilah 17a; for the Romans never had locks
473. Baba Kamma 83a
474. Jerushalmi Shabbath 6; 7a
475. Meilah 17a
476. Evidence in Dionys. Vossius.

Maimonides. *De Idololatria liber.* Amsterdam 1642 p.144
477. Levit. 19:27
478. *Sifra.* Levit. 19:27 fol. 90c
479. see above chapter 12
480. Numbers 8:7
481. *ibid* 6:18
482. Nazir 40a
483. Lamentations Rabbah 2:13
484. Jerushalmi Kethuboth 7; 31d
485. Psalms 133:2

beardless[486]. It was thus an insult for Hanun to cut the beards[487] — or, according to some commentaries, half the beards —[488] of David's servants and to send them back in that manner. David instructed his servants to remain in Jericho until their beards grew back.

To the Spartans, cutting half the beard off was punishment for cowardice[489]. If someone admires someone else's beard, it is impertinent for the latter to reply: I will cut it off (just to spite you)[490]. A grave robber, caught in the act, held Abaye's beard so tightly that he had to bring scissors and cut off his beard[491].

Cutting off the beard is a heathen sign of mourning[492]. It was probably also practiced by individual Israelites[493]. The already-mentioned prohibition for the priests to cut off the corners of their beards expressly refers to this usage of beard-cutting as a sign of mourning. In Rome, one also let the beard grow as a sign of mourning[494].

For the *beard around the lips* (i.e. moustache) the separate expression *sapham* is used in the Bible and Talmud. When Mephibosheth went to greet King David, he had neglected his personal hygiene and had not even arranged his lip beard[495]. During mourning, one covers the moustache[496]. According to tradition, a leper must also cover his moustache[497], in order not to endanger others by his exhaled breath. One hundred haircuts cost one *zuz* each, but one hundred moustache trimmings cost nothing — it was done as a free extra. If the students missed a day of Torah study, it was said: "this is a day of moustaches"[498].

## VI   Men's Hair Styles

*Doth not even nature itself teach you that if a man have long hair (ean koma), it is a shame (atimia) unto him?*[499] This statement of the Apostle was probably the general attitude of the Jews in those days. A vain courtier was ridiculed because he "turned *(mehappek)* his hair"[500], i.e. he curled it. The name Pethuel, father of the prophet Joel, is said to be derived from the fact that Pethuel used to curl his hair *(mesalsel)* like a young woman[501], probably a ridiculing of contemporary indecency. Otherwise, there is no mention (in the Bible or Talmud) of coiffures in relation to men.

We must still mention the haircut as prescribed for the priests by Ezekiel. He said: *neither shall they shave their heads, nor suffer their locks to grow long; they shall only poll their heads (kasom yiksemu)*[502]. According to tradition, this rule only applied to the High Priest. Most ancient and modern commentaries explain that he should wear his hair at medium length, i.e. "half length". The *Gemara* considers it to be a unique coiffure, *thispartha yechidta,* namely the *lulyanith* coiffure[503], in which the hair is cut in such a way that the tips of the lower hairs touch the roots of the upper hairs, so that the entire haircut looks like a *kussemeth,* in the form of steps[504]. Barbers charged a lot of money for such coiffures, because they required a considerable amount of time[505], so that only very rich people such as Ben Elasah could afford them[506]. As a result, such a haircut also bears his name[506a].

---

486. see above chapter 5
487. First Chronicles 19:4-5
488. Second Samuel 10:4-5
489. Plutarch — *Agesilaos* 30: *meros tes ypenes xerontai*
490. Berachoth 11a
491. Baba Bathra 58a
492. Isaiah 15:2; Jeremiah 48:37
493. Jeremiah 41:5
494. Liv. 27:34
495. Second Samuel 19:25. *Targum* has "trimmed" his mustache
496. Ezekiel 24:17-22

497. Levit. 13:45
498. Shabbath 129b
499. First Corinthians 11:14
500. Megillah 18a
501. *Midrash* Psalms 80:1
502. Ezekiel 44:20
503. Rabbenu Chananel's and Rabbi Nissim's commentaries on Shabbath 9b
504. Hence, Mussaphia combines the name with *lul* meaning step
505. Shabbath 9b
506. Nedarim 51a
506a. Shabbath 9b

## VII   Women's Hair Styles

For a *woman,* beautiful hair is an adornment. The young lover gives the following compliment to his beloved: *thy hair is as a flock of goats, that appear from Mount Gilead*[507].

It is natural that a woman is careful in the care of her hair. Before Judith came to Holofernes, she braided her hair *(dietaxe tas trichas tes kephales),* washed herself and anointed herself[508]. The well-to-do people hired a permanent coiffeuse, *gadeleth*[509] or *megadeleth*[510], who made the hair into a skillful weaving *(oregeth)* or a form. The hairdressers placed the young girls in a *yam napha* or type of flour-sifter (so that the hair does not fall on the floor while their hair is being dressed)[511].

A beautiful hairdo makes a woman more attractive. Legend relates that God Himself "built" (literal meaning of the Biblical word *vayiben*) a hairdo for Eve, adorned her like a bride[512], and then brought her to Adam[513]. It is a special renunciation for a woman to cut off her beautiful hair. Rabbi Akiba bought his wife a golden mural crown as a head ornament. When the wife of Rabban Gamliel was jealous because of it, he said to her: "did you do what she did? She sold her hair braids *(keliatha)* and gave her husband the proceeds so that he could learn Torah undisturbed"[514]. The hair magic which women practiced is also well known[515].

If the hair (of a woman) exerts an attractive influence on a man, it is likely that it would also distract the thoughts of a worshipper and would arouse prurient thoughts in him. Since a covetous look is considered more reprehensible than consummated adultery, it was prohibited to pray in the presence of a married woman whose hair was uncovered[516]. The Apostle preaches that a woman with uncovered head *(akathakalypton)* should not pray to God even alone, without the presence of others[517]. It was a general custom for Jewish women to cover their hair, not only while praying, but at all times. Only heathens failed to cover their hair[518].

A man marries a woman with the understanding that she live "according to the laws of Moses and of Israel". A woman who walks around with uncovered hair must be divorced for that reason, for she is not living according to this law[519]! Chaste women maintain their hair covering not only in the presence of strangers. The wife of Kimbeth had seven sons all of whom became high priests in succession. When she was asked why she merited such unusual joy from her children, she replied: "never did the beams of my house see the plaits of my hair!" To be sure, they retorted to her, many other women did likewise yet without such wondrous results[520].

Concerning a suspected adulteress, the priest shall uncover her hair before he begins the offering ceremony[521]. People retreat from a woman who stands in the doorway with uncovered hair[522]. If someone uncovers a woman's hair on the street (i.e. in public), he must pay, according to the accompanying circumstances, up to 400 *zuz* penalty for the insult he inflicted on her — more than for a slap on the face. Once Rabbi Akiba fined a man the highest allowable penalty of 400 *zuz* for having uncovered a woman's hair on the street. At the defendant's request, he was granted time to pay. He watched out for her, and when she was standing at the entrance of her house, he broke a jug in front of her wherein there was a few pennies worth of oil. Immediately the woman took off her shawl (uncovered her hair) and scooped up the oil

507. Song of Songs 4:1
508. Judith 10:3
509. Shabbath 94b and Kiddushin 49a
510. Shabbath 104b
511. Kelim 15:3
512. Genesis Rabbah 18:1
513. Berachoth 61a
514. Jerushalmi Sotah 9; 24c

515. Jerushalmi Sanhedrin 7; 26d
516. Berachoth 24a
517. First Corinthians 11:13
518. Numbers Rabbah 9:16
519. *Tosefta* Kethuboth 7:6
520. Yoma 47a
521. Numbers 5:18
522. Sanhedrin 110a

with her hand and then laid her hand on her head. The defendant had prepared witnesses to the event and he then came to Rabbi Akiba: "Do I have to pay 400 *zuz* to such a woman who uncovered her hair for such a trifle of oil?" Rabbi Akiba replied: "Your protest is to no avail. If someone wounds himself, even though he is not permitted to do so, he is exempt; but if others inflict a wound on him, they are liable"[523].

Only unmarried women do not cover their hair. A young virginal bride also moves into her marriage house with her hair uncovered[524], and a dead bride is, therefore, buried with her hair uncovered and loose[525].

If a woman requests that, after her death, her hair be cut and given to her daughter, this request cannot be honored, because one is not permitted to derive any benefit from the dead[526].

# VIII   Hair Hygiene

To arrange the hair, one employed a *masrek* or *masreka*[527], which is a comb. The more precise term is *masrek shel rosh* meaning a comb for the head[528]. It once happened that a tooth, *shen,* broke off from a comb and this tooth was then replaced with one of metal[529]. In general, a comb in antiquity was made of box-tree or of ivory. Individual hairs which the hairdresser had not arranged *(nimin meduldaloth)* were also removed with this comb[530]. In its appearance, it resembled a curry-comb, and for this reason, the same term is used for a horse curry-comb[531]. The Romans used iron combs as instruments of torture with which they tore the flesh from the body of delinquents[532]. They did the same to Rabbi Akiba[533].

Combing was part of the toilette of both men[534] and women.

To cleanse the head, one used *nether* (soda), soapwort *(ahala)* and *adama.* It was said of carbonate of soda that it tears the hair loose *(mekatteph),* and of soapwort, that it makes the hairs so treated stick together *(masrik).* It is also practical to exclusively use warm water, even if it is only warmed in the sun, but not cold water, for the latter makes the hair stick together[535].

*Adama,* a type of earth which is used for the same purpose, has a similar effect[536]. The use of soda and sand, a combination that was also employed, resulted in hair being torn out[537].

This cleansing of the head, *chaphipha,* was customary among both men[538] and women. For women, it was explicitly prescribed before they take their ritual bath at the end of their menstrual period[539]. This ordinance is considered to be one of the decrees of Ezra[540]. Naturally, a thorough combing of the hair is done in association with this *chaphipha,* although, strictly speaking, *chaphipha* and *serika* are two separate concepts[541].

Hairs which are stuck together, *kilkim* or *kilkelim*[542], from perspiration or dust, on the breast, on the head, in the beard or elsewhere on the body[543], are plucked apart

---

523. Baba Kamma 8:6
524. Kethuboth 2:1
525. Semachoth 7 fol. 47b
526. *Tosefta* Arachin 1:4
527. Berachoth 18b
528. Kelim 13:7
529. *ibid*
530. Nazir 42a
531. Moed Katan 10b
532. Gittin 57b
533. Berachoth 61b
534. Berachoth 18b and Levit. Rabbah 5:8

535. Niddah 66b, according to the correct textual reading of Alfasi
536. Nazir 6:3
537. Shabbath 50a
538. for example Hillel in Shabbath 31a
539. Niddah 66b
540. Baba Kamma 82b
541. Nazir 42a: *chopheph* but not *sorek;* Jerushalmi Pesachim 1; 27b: *chopheph* and *sorek*
542. Sifra *Zabim.* per. 3., par. 5, fol. 76c
543. Mikvaoth 9:2-3

with the fingers, *pispes* or *siphseph*[544]. In healthy people, the hairs are so firm that they are not thereby torn out[545].

Because of his extreme poverty, Rabbi Akiba, together with his wife, slept on plain straw (on the floor) even in the winter. In the morning, he removed the stubble from her hair[546].

It was forbidden for men to "pick out"[547] or to "separate out"[548] white hairs from among the black hairs because this was considered to be a womanly custom.

## IX   Wigs

If her own hair is insufficient to achieve the desired coiffure, a woman supplements it with foreign hair. Sometimes individual strands of hair *(chuté se'ar)* are used, either one's own[549] or those from another woman *(chaverta)* or from an animal, even though it might be unappetizing. The woman whose hair is now being used might have suffered from a fox-illness (alopecia), as a result of which her hair fell out, remarks Maimonides. Alternatively, a woman would wear a *peah nochrith* or wig[550]. Since this wig is mentioned as an aid for bald-shaven women[551], it probably represents a complete wig which was hung on a peg when not in use[552]. It was made of foreign hair (*nochrith* meaning *peregrina*) which one obtained from outside of the country, just as the Roman ladies obtained their *capillamenta* from Germania. Men's hair was also bought[553].

To fasten the coiffure, a woman wore "needles without perforations" in her hair[554].

The coiffure is part of the toilette or ornament of a woman (*takshit* or *tachshit*). In this manner, there is no "old" woman; even if she is already a grandmother, or even if she is already on her deathbed, she still wishes to look beautiful[555].

The description of a wig for men (in the Talmud) is not certain. There is mention of *pekorin* and *cipha* which were dyed (with oil) and bound together with a thread[556]. *Rashi* interprets this to refer to hackled flax and flocked sheep's wool, both of which are applied on wounds as a protection against the rubbing of the clothes. This explanation was adopted by Rabbi Joseph Karo[557]. Rabbi Chananel, however, states: "it is *peah nochrith*[558]; it is a cap which a bald-headed person puts on his head, and it looks as if he has real hair". Maimonides considers it to be a type of protective covering which was worn by people with a rash on their heads *(baale chatatin)*[559].

## X   Pubic Hair

Throughout the Orient, pubic and axillary hair were and still are removed. For Mohammedan women, this is a religious ordinance. Men also, in general, followed this practice in order to be better able to carry out the prescribed washings of the genitalia following any excretion. Plinius laments the destruction of the hair *itemque pectines in feminis quidem publicati* through resins among the Romans[560]. This practice probably also existed among (married) Jewish women, although it was never a law. The

544. Nazir 6:6
545. *ibid* 42a
546. Nedarim 50a
547. Shabbath 94b: *melaket*
548. *Tosefta* Shabbath 10:12: *haborer*
549. those which fell out from the combing
550. Shabbath 6:5 and 64b
551. Nazir 28b
552. Sanhedrin 112a
553. Nedarim 9:5
554. Shabbath 60a and Jerushalmi Shabbath 1; 3b

555. Moed Katan 9b
556. *Tosefta* Shabbath 5:2 and Shabbath 50a; *pakorin* equivalent to the Greek *pokarion* meaning wool flakes
557. *Orach Chayim* 308:24
558. thus in the text of Rabbi Chananel. In the citation in *Tosafoth* this phrase is lacking.
559. *Hilchoth Shabbath* 19:16
560. Plinius 29:8. Additional proofs in Rosenbaum's *Lustseuche* p.333 and 424 (India).

daughters of Zion enjoyed renown for beauty[561] because, as the *Aggadah* states, they had neither pubic nor axillary hair[562] and, therefore, did not constantly have to remove them. It was considered to be the greatest lewdness for women to "make their openings (vulva) like a forest"[563].

It was thought that during cohabitation the penis might become entangled in the woman's pubic hair. According to legend, this was the case in the sad incident of the concubine of Gibeah[564]. She had to leave her husband for that reason[565]. This, too, is the reason which legend offers to explain the sudden conversion of Amnon's love toward his step-sister Tamar into fiery hatred[566] after he attempted to seduce her[567]. This custom is no longer practiced among Jewish women, even in the Orient[568].

For men, this epilation of pubic hair was always forbidden[569]. It was considered to be a transgression of the Biblical command: *neither shall a man put on a woman's garment*[570], nor practice womenly customs[571].

# XI    Depilatories

For the "hair removal" which was known as *maabir* for short[572], all the above-mentioned instruments were used including the razor, scissors and *epilatorium,* and even a regular knife *(sakkin)*. As a rule, however, use was made of *sid* or lime which, even today, other than auripigment, is the major ingredient of *rhusmas,* which were used in enormous quantities in the Orient. Lime also serves as a modern depilatory. The paste is applied *(taphal)* to the skin and is scraped off *(kalaph)* together with the hair, and causes pain[573].

Rabbi Yochanan said: young girls in whom pubic hair develops before the usual age (of 12 years) remove this sign of precociousness. Poor girls use lime for this purpose; rich girls use *soleth* or *psilothron*[574]; and princesses employ oil of myrrh *(shemen hammor,* the resin of Balsamodendron Myrrhae)[575] which, according to some people, refers to *stakte*[576] and, according to others, refers to oil of unripe olives. On the other hand, Rabbi Judah correctly points out that oil of green olives is called *anpikinon* or *omphakinon,* i.e. *elaion* by the Greeks. Myrrh resin was used because it not only removes the hair but also makes the flesh soft *(meadden)*[577].

*Aruch*[578] remarks: "instead of *maschschir* meaning to remove, one should read *maschchir* meaning to blacken". The last reference would then signify: "resin of myrrh blackens the hair".

According to the *Midrash*[579], when the prophet admonishes the carefree Israelites because they *anoint themselves with the best oil*[580], he is also referring to *stakte* or *omphacinum.*

Rabbi Bibi treated his daughter limb by limb (with large intervals in between) with lime[581], and she made a brilliant match. A jealous heathen in the vicinity thereupon

---

561. Ezekiel 16:14
562. Sanhedrin 21a
563. Shabbath 62b
564. Judges Chapter 19
565. Gittin 6b
566. Second Samuel 13:15
567. Sanhedrin 21a
568. Tobler. *Med. Topographie Von Jerusalem* p.19.
569. Nazir 59a
570. Deut. 22:5
571. The remark of the *Gemara* in Yebamoth 103a concerning Mephibosheth and the explanation of *Rashi* thereto are, therefore, noteworthy.
572. Moed Katan 1:7

573. Moed Katan 1:7
574. This *soleth* is not fine flour because the latter is not a depilatory; rather, it refers to the *psilothron* or *rhusma* which is also mentioned by Galen and which appears as *saltha* in the Syrian translation of Gloponica. see Löw's *Pflanzennamen* p.263
575. Löw. *Pflanzennamen* p.246
576. The *Targum* always translates the Biblical *stakte* as *smyrna*
577. Pesachim 43a
578. Kohut 1:153b
579. Levit. Rabbah 5:3
580. Amos 6:6
581. *Rashi* on Shabbath 80b

painted the entire body of his daughter at one time (with lime). The girl died as a result of the treatment. The heathen said: Bibi killed my daughter!— Rabbi Nachman explained: the daughter of Rabbi Bibi required the pasting *(taphla,* tincture) only because her father drank palm wine *(shikra* i.e. beer); since we do not drink palm wine, our daughters do not need the lime pasting. This is because palm wine produces an increase in hair growth and makes the flesh thick[582].

Whosoever wishes to make his daughter white (i.e. to provide her with a tender skin color) should give her milk to drink and young fowl to eat during her developing years[583].

The above-mentioned *neshem*[584], whose composition is unknown to us, was scarcely used as a cosmetic material because of the possible corrosion of the skin that it might produce.

Axillary hair has a shorter lifespan than hair on the head. In elderly, obese men it gradually falls out[585].

## XII    Facial Make-up

It is debatable whether or not *facial make-up* was used by Jewish women in Biblical times[586], although during the time of the *Mishnah* it was already a general custom. "To fix one's hair" *(godeleth),* "apply make-up" *(pokeseth),* and "paint the eyes" *(kocheleth)* are the usual expressions used to denote the various parts of toilette, particulary for a festival[587]. *Pakas* in Babylon is an expression for hair coiffure, and was employed to denote spinning (hair braids) and constructing (hair locks)[588]. On the other hand, in Palestine, it is an expression for coloring (or painting, reminiscent of *phykoo)*[589].

A man should not force his wife who is in mourning to paint her eyes or her face — both being part of normal toilette — and if a man is in mourning, his wife should also abstain from using make-up[590]. It was an ancient custom that menstruating women would neither paint their eyes or their faces, so that they not entice their husbands, until Rabbi Eliezer also permitted it during the time of the menses so that a woman not become repugnant to her husband[591]. The rouge, *scharak* or *sarak* or *sikra,* was either applied directly with the hand or "a woman would wipe her face with a cloth upon which there is paint"[592].

Concerning eye painting, see above, chapter 5.

Any vow made by a woman that entails an element of asceticism can, according to Biblical law, be invalidated by the husband as soon as he hears it. If a woman vows that she renounces the use of make-up *(kashat)* and the husband is silent, then he must divorce her and pay her the stipulated amount of money of the marriage settlement or *kethubah.* Then, if the woman is poor, she must abstain from using cosmetics for one year (unless she specified a different time in her enunciated vow); but if she is rich, she abstains for only 30 days[593]. According to some Sages, both (rich and poor women) need only abstain until the next festival[594].

## XIII    Cosmetics

One cannot in any way protest a woman's striving to create a beautiful appearance by using all sorts of cosmetic materials, as long as the intent is not to deceive.

582. Moed Katan 9b
583. Kethuboth 59b
584. Part one, Section X of this chapter
585. Nazir 59a and *Tosafoth s.v. gebul*
586. see Isaiah 3:16
587. for example Moed Katan 9b and *Tosefta* Shabbath 9:13
588. Shabbath 94b
589. Jerushalmi Shabbath 10; 12d
590. Moed Katan 20b
591. Shabbath 64b
592. Shabbath 95a
593. Kethuboth 7:3
594. *ibid* 71a–b

Otherwise it becomes a *pirkes* or *pirges,* a "decoration". The same prohibition applies to anything that is sold, whether it is an object or a slave[595]. Thus, if one wishes to sell a slave, one may not say to him: *tzur garmek,* "make yourself pretty"[596]. Once an elderly slave colored his head and beard in order to look young and then presented himself for the sale. However, when his new master asked him to serve him, the slave removed the coloring and said: "I am older than your father!"[597]

If a widow applies cosmetics and adorns herself, yet does not wish to remarry, she loses her right of support by the heirs of her husband, because she thereby shows that she is not excluding remarriage because of attachment to her previous husband[598].

Even prostitutes adorn each other in order to conceal small blemishes; how much more so should learned people do so[599].

# XIV   Embrocations

*Oil embrocations* of the body are among the daily requirements of Oriental people. Captives were given clothing and shoes and food and drink and embrocations[600]. Only during mourning, when all comforts are omitted, is embrocation also discontinued. Thus did King David, when his child died[601]; and Daniel mourned for three weeks, ate no meat, drank no wine and did not anoint himself[602]. The disobedient Israelites were warned with the following curse: *thou shalt have olive trees, but thou shalt not anoint thyself with the oil; for the olive tree shall cast off its fruit unripe[603].*

These circumstances, which were already fully developed in the Bible, did not change in later times; omission of embrocation was perceived of as a penance or *innuy[604].* Since the Bible prescribes penance for the Day of Atonement[605], anointing oneself on this day[606] as well as on the Ninth Day of Ab (a fast day) is prohibited, as is eating and drinking[607]. The same prohibition exists during the time of mourning for a close relative[608], as well as in times of general calamity[609].

# XV

The most commonly used oil is olive oil: one either maintains it ready made in stock, or one presses the olives directly on the body[610] and then embrocates oneself. The King proudly showed his guest his stocks of herbs and precious oils[611]. The oil is ordinarily used warm, in that one either warms it in the flask or one holds the oil-impregnated hands near a flame[612]. There were many types of ointments, *miné sikoth[613],* which we do not know any longer.

The use of fragrant oil, *shemen areb,* for embrocation, is also mentioned[614]. Olive oil in which rose leaves were macerated, or which was perfumed in another way, was also known[615].

Holy anointing oil, as used in the Temple, was forbidden to be used for profane purposes: *Upon man's flesh shall it not be poured, neither shall ye make any other like it[616].* It was made with choice herbs and compounded expertly by the apothecary,

---

595. Baba Metzia 4:14
596. Jerushalmi Baba Metzia 4; 9d
597. Baba Metzia 60a
598. Kethuboth 54a
599. Shabbath 34a
600. Second Chronicles 28:15
601. Second Samuel 12:20
602. Daniel 10:2-3
603. Deut. 28:40 and Micah 6:15
604. Yebamoth 73b
605. Numbers 29:7
606. Yoma 8:1
607. *Tosefta* Taanith 4:1
608. Taanith 13b
609. *ibid* 1:5
610. Maaseroth 4:1
611. Isaiah 39:2
612. *Tosefta* Shabbath 3(4): 5
613. *ibid* 3(4): 6
614. *Tosefta* Shebiith 6:13
615. Löw. *Pflanzennamen* p.132; Goldmann. *Der Oelbau in Palästina* 1907 p.66:9 and 67:1
616. Exodus 30:32

*rokeach*[617]. For this reason, it was also not used to anoint priests or kings. Nevertheless, for this symbolic anointing, the expression *maschach* was used (from which is derived *maschiach,* the Messiah or anointed one), whereas the anointings for profane purposes are called *sika* in the Bible and Talmud (from *suk*).

As far as I am aware, the reason why these embrocations were performed in antiquity is not mentioned anywhere. Since they are accompanied by massages, we assume they had therapeutic intent. Rabbi Chanina said: the warm water and the oil with which my mother rubbed me during my youth stand me in good stead now in my old age[618]. A tired traveler had his feet washed and anointed by his host as a sign of special honor[619]. Hands soiled by food are rubbed clean with oil[620]. The epigrammatic poet states: *oil and perfume gladden the heart*[621]; that is, they are amenities.

According to an expression of the Psalmist, it appears as if one assumed that oil directly penetrates the body (when rubbed on the skin), whereas the Talmud explicitly teaches that an embrocation does not enter the body, but the body nevertheless derives a benefit (or enjoyment) therefrom[622]. The parallel expression is: *like water in my bowels, koilia*[623].

We will discuss embrocations following a Turkish bath in the chapter concerning bathing.

Oiling of the hair was also quite customary. It is a sign of exceptional good fortune if the Lord *anointeth my head with oil*[624]. Jesus criticized Simon directly because the latter did not anoint Jesus' head with oil[625]. At weddings, among the Babylonian Jews, it was customary to pour oil on the heads of the learned men to honor them[626].

Other embrocations were also used for various reasons (exclusive of the enumerated healing reasons). Wine and vinegar were used[627]. Children who were dirty were rinsed *(duach)* in wine[628]. Malodorous perspiration was neutralized with *kiyuha de chamra,* wine vinegar[629].

## XVI  Soaps

In the Bible, the strongest washing materials for the body are *nether (nitrum)* which is neutralized with vinegar[630], crystal soda which is extracted from the earth, and *borith*[631], the alkaline plant salt which is prepared from burned plants which are rich in potash and which are also used by washerwomen[632].

The root of *leontopetalon*[633] and its use as an ordinary soap is first mentioned in the *Midrash* as *eschlag,* and in the *Gemara* as *shalga*[634]. However, its usage appears to be even more ancient, since I believe the use of both the root and the plant are already mentioned in the Bible. Job complains that "even if I wash myself with *me scheleg* and cleanse my hands with *bor,* the Lord would again plunge me in the ditch so that my garments become soiled"[635]. Since *scheleg* is undoubtedly a parallel to *bor,* the latter unquestionably refers to *borith,* and since one cannot attribute any special cleansing effect to "snow water", which is the usual translation of *me scheleg,* then the Hebrew word *scheleg* here probably more correctly designates the Aramaic *schlaga,* and

617. Exodus 30:25
618. Chullin 24b
619. Luke 7:38; John 12:3
620. Berachoth 53b
621. Proverbs 27:9
622. Berachoth 57b
623. Psalms 109:18
624. Psalms 23:5
625. Luke 7:46
626. Kethuboth 17b

627. Jerushalmi Maaser Sheni 2; 53b
628. *ibid* 66
629. Kethuboth 75a
630. Proverbs 25:20
631. Jeremiah 2:22
632. Malachi 3:2
633. Löw *Pflanzennamen* p.304
634. Shabbath 9:5; Niddah 9:6; Shabbath 90a
635. Job 9:30-31

should, therefore, be translated as "soap root". In support of this premise is the original textual reading *bemo scheleg,* which was first transformed to *me scheleg* by the Masoretes.

For the needs of more refined toilette, one used perfumed soap powder which, however, mostly contained soapwort *(ahala)* or Salsola[636], as a base. Wax powder, *barda,* was composed of equal parts of soapwort, myrtle *(asa)* and violet *(sigle).* Also used were frankincense powder and *kruspa de jasmin.* The latter, according to the commentaries, refers to sesame residue which is soaked with jasmin roses, then dried and pulverized. Pepper powder is also mentioned (as a soap-like material). These powders are mild and do not loosen the hair[636a], as does *nitrum*[637].

That which the ancients call "soap" is a mixture of fat and ashes and only serves to bleach dark hairs. It is only since the fourth century that this mixture is also being used as a washing material for body and clothes.

# XVII    Perfumes and Cosmetics

The use of real *perfumes* was very great so that when this nuisance also became widespread in Rome, Lucian was able to correctly state: "women squander their entire husband's wealth and allow the entire good fortune of Arabia to emit fragrance from their hair!" Crito, the personal physician of Empress Plotina, composed a two-volume work on cosmetics and described therein alone twenty-five different types of hair oils.

The *Mishnah* decrees that, as part of the dowry, a husband must pay his wife ten *denars* for her *kuppa,* the perfume basket, *kuppa shel besamim*[638]. Rabban Gamliel imposes the restriction that he must pay her only according to the usual cost of such cosmetics in the city in which they reside[639]. It is disputed as to whether the affixed amount must be paid as a lump sum or whether it is continuously paid as an addition to the household money[640]. The *Tosafoth* decided according to the former, although the husband may pay the sum according to his wife's need.

The following perfumes are mentioned in the Talmud: *kobeleth* or *kokeleth,* "beads of *phyllon*" which is malabathrum, which were traded in the form of charm beads, and *pholyaton, foliatum i.e. unguentum*[641], an anointing oil made of nard and other fragrant leaves. *Folium* was simply the explanation for nard, as *radix* was considered to refer to costus root[642]. In Bethany, a woman poured a bottle of precious *morou nardou pistikes* on the head of Jesus in order to honor him[643]. According to Rabbi Judah ben Baba, since the destruction of Jerusalem, as a sign of national mourning, women should no longer use this expensive perfume[644]; for this *folium* is considered to be an "expensive oil", *shemen tob*[645]. Even in a place of refuse, the fragrant aroma of a phial of spikenard imparts a good scent[646].

The beads of *phyllon* were suspended from the neck in a small container made of silver or gold[647], perhaps like the fragrant cushions on the bosoms, analogous to the shepherdess who carried a bundle of myrrh "between her breasts"[648], and occasionally showed it proudly to a friend. The oil of nard was kept in a bottle, *tzeluchith,* of transparent glass which was made of *bolos* or *bolus*[649]. This bottle had a neck which

---

636. Löw *op. cit.* p.43
636a. see footnote 634
637. Shabbath 50a
638. Niddah 66b
639. Kethuboth 66b
640. *ibid* 6:4
641. Shabbath 6:3 and 62a
642. Böttiger, *Sabina* 2:145

643. Mark 14:3
644. *Tosefta* Sotah 15:9
645. *Tosefta* Demai 1:26
646. Sanhedrin 108a
647. Maimonides Commentary on Sanhedrin 108a
648. Song of Songs 1:13
649. *Tosefta* Shabbath 8:20

occasionally broke off[650]. Only when the bottle was opened did the aroma escape[651]. The Greeks called these oil bottles *alabastros*[652].

Among the pleasant fragrant aromas, one should also include the holy frankincense of the Temple. It was, however, prohibited to prepare it as prescribed in the Bible for profane use. If anyone compounds it in order to smell therefrom, he shall be cut off from his people[653]. The house of Abtinas were expert in preparing the incense but closely guarded the secret. In order not to be suspected of making and using incense for profane purposes, they forbade their women[654] from using any kind of perfume. If they married a woman from another place, where this practice was not known, they made an explicit agreement that this woman was not allowed to use perfumes. Nevertheless, the Sages did not approve of keeping this a secret[655].

The preacher in the *Midrash* sees a need for women to perfume themselves because of their nature: "why must a woman use perfume *(lehithbassem)* while a man does not need perfume? Because man was created from earth, and earth never putrefies. A woman, however, was created from bone (Adam's rib). If you leave meat three days unsalted, will it not rapidly putrefy?"[656] This *(Midrash)* is not exactly polite and probably had as little effect as the efforts of the church fathers against the painting of the lips and cheeks, the piercing of ears, and the sprinkling of the hair with gold dust in order to attain the appearance of Germanic women. These were customs practiced by women of early Christian communities[657].

# XVIII

Ezra mentioned that peddlers *(rokelim)* were peddling their wares directly in private homes[658], not, as was usual, offering their wares in the bazaars. These spice peddlers also had other merchandise such as fruit[659]. However, when a peddler came into a house with his basket, the first question was: do you have fine oil or folium or balsam?[660] Serious men were quite displeased with these house peddlers because "they caused innumerable moral injuries, because they enticed to lewdness"[661]. This occurred either because of their persons, or their procurement function, or perhaps indirectly through the perfumes which they sold. For the stimulation of sexual sensations through aromas was widely known. Cloqet[662] and, more recently, Ivan Bloch[663] have written whole books on this subject.

The Sages expressly prohibit smelling any perfume which the woman may have on herself[664]. According to the description in the Book of Esther, the maidens who were to sleep with the Persian King were perfumed in a particularly refined manner: *according to the law for the women, twelve months — for so were the days of their anointing* (cleansing, polishing) *accomplished, to wit, six months with oil of myrrh, and six months with sweet odors*[665] *and with other ointments of the women — when then the maiden came to the King*[666]. The sweet spices with which one filled the grave

---

650. Kelim 30:4
651. Abodah Zarah 35b
652. Matthew 26:7 and the Septuagint on Second Kings 21:13
653. Exodus 30:34-38
654. *Tosefta* Yoma 2:6 and Jerushalmi Yoma 3; 41a; However *Babli* Yoma 38a has *kalla* or bride instead of women
655. Yoma 3:11
656. Genesis Rabbah 17:8
657. Cyprian. *De Habitu Virgin;* Tertullian, *De Cultu Feminis;* Migne. *Patrol.* Vol. 1, col. 1417ff

658. Baba Kamma 82a
659. Maaseroth 2:3
660. Aboth de Rabbi Nathan 18:1 fol. 25c
661. Yebamoth 63a
662. *Osphrésiologie* Paris 1821
663. Alb. Hagen. *Sexuelle Osphresiologie.* Charlottenburg 1901. See also Krafft-Ebing. *Psychop. Sex.* p.17; Havelock Ellis, *Gattenwahl.* p.111 ff
664. Shabbath 62b; Maimonides. *Hilchoth Issurey Biah* 21:2; *Eben Ha'ezer* 21:1
665. Preuss translates herbs (F.R.)
666. Esther 2:12-13

of King Asa were called *zenin*[667] because, according to the commentaries, they excite one to licentiousness, *zenuth*.

The Talmud describes a cunning practice of prostitutes which must have been considered offensive because it is mentioned quite often. Rabbi Yitzchak, who lived in the first or second century, already ascribes this practice to the maidens of the corrupt era under Isaiah[668]: "They took myrrh and balsam and placed them in their shoes between the heel and the sandal; when they saw a group of young men, they would step on the spices and splash them on the young men, and the aroma (of the perfume) would penetrate them and arouse their evil inclination"[669]. Since coquettes usually walk on the tips of their feet, the above *modus* is quite conceivable. In later sources[670] it is mentioned that perfume was enclosed in a chicken maw, *zephek,* or in a chicken uterus, *schalphuchith,* or in an eggshell[671].

# XIX

Perfume is only intended for women. It is not honorable[672] but, in fact, offensive[673] for a man, particularly a learned man, to stroll around perfumed *(mebussam).* It is, therefore, surprising that when a woman poured expensive spikenard oil on the head of the young Jesus, he was only indignant about the waste: *this oil could have been sold for much and the proceeds given to the poor*[674]. Nevertheless, in some places it seems to have been customary that on the *Sabbath,* even men used perfumes and wore beautiful clothes[675].

667. Second Chronicles 16:14
668. Isaiah 23:15
669. Yoma 9b and Shabbath 62b
670. Lamentations Rabbah 4:18; Pesikta de Rab Kahana 17 p.132b; *Yalkut* Lamentations 2:1033; Levit. Rabbah 16:1
671. Ehrentreus' interpretations *schalphuchith*

*shel betza,* a reed tube of egg, in Isaiah 42:3 (*Jahrbuch d. Jüd. Lit. Ges.,* Frankfurt 1901, p.68) should be rejected.Löw
672. *Tosefta* Berachoth 6(5): 5
673. Berachoth 43b
674. Matthew 26:9
675. Soferim 20:1

# CHAPTER XIII

## *GYNECOLOGY*

### I Menstruation

The *Zaba,* or woman with a flux, is fundamentally different from the normal menstruating woman.

*And if a woman have an issue of her blood many days not in the time of her impurity, or if she have an issue beyond the time of her impurity; all the days of the issue of her uncleanness she shall be as in the days of her impurity: she is unclean*[1]. And when she is cleansed of her issue, then she counts to herself seven days, and only then is she clean. On the eighth day she brings an offering to the door of the Temple, one is sacrificed as a sin offering and one as a burnt offering, and the priest makes atonement for her for the issue of her uncleanness[2]. Since the *zaba: shall be as in the days of her impurity* (menstruation), a separate prohibition against cohabitation would be superfluous, since, as in the case of menstruation, it is a *peccatum mortale.*

It is rather astonishing that the Catholic moralists permit copulation under these circumstances of *zaba* without reservation, on the one hand because the woman cannot conceive because of her weakness, and hence will not bear leprous or monstrous children, as was feared to be the result of *copula menstruationis tempore*[3], and on the other hand because one couldn't expect the husband to abstain for such a prolonged period[4].

We are thus dealing with two abnormal types of bleeding, the protracted and the atypical. In both cases, the uncleanness does *not* cease with the end of the bleeding, as in the case of menstruation, but a full week without bleeding is required, perhaps to see whether the bleeding has actually stopped. Then the woman must bring sacrifices which are not required of a normal menstruating woman and, as already stated above, a full bath is probably necessary. The entire procedure clearly indicates that *these* bleedings were considered to be abnormal and *pathological,* and they were fundamentally separated from menstruation, as already asserted in the *Midrash*[5].

One must constantly stress that we know absolutely nothing about the reasons for *this* commandment, as is true of so many others. We do not even know whether this law was given for health reasons. Although it is written that *ye shall warn the children of Israel from their uncleanness, that they not die in their uncleanness*[6], one can draw no conclusions therefrom. Conjectures with the widest latitude are many, but it seems useless to repeat them here. I only wish to point out two facts. First, the discomfort of the prolonged uncleanliness, and for some perhaps also the cost of the sacrifices

---

1. Levit. 15:25ff
2. *ibid* 15:28-30
3. See chapter 2 above, section on menstruation
4. Liguori. book 6:925, cited according to Capellmann
5. Exodus Rabbah 1:34
6. Levit. 15:31

required at the end of this period, motivate the "bleeding" woman to seek rapid relief from her ailment, in order to obviate recurrence of a similar condition. Thus, in fact, strict adherence to this law provides great health advantages. From the statement in the *Mishnah* that during the time of Rabban Simeon ben Gamliel a pair of turtle doves in Jerusalem cost a golden *denar*[7], one sees that, at least during certain times, one also had to be concerned about the cost of the sacrifice. Moreover, one should not underestimate the advantage of sexual abstention for the healing of diseased female genitalia.

In addition to the above-mentioned reasons for a man to separate himself from his menstruating wife, other important factors might perhaps include the health of both partners, as well as national-economic considerations. Naturally, it is sheer folly to assert that "Moses had to prevent the birth of a large number of children in his capacity as physician, in addition to his position as statesman"[8]! A lawgiver who decrees laws with this tendency certainly does not earn a place in history, but in a lunatic asylum, particularly if his intentions are to make an entire land dependent upon, and subjugated to, his small group of Israelites. And why does he not first prohibit polygamy? The exact opposite is in fact the case. The increased capability of conception after the cessation of menses was already known in ancient times, at all events already during Talmudic times[9]. This increased capability is even greater, for obvious reasons, if a more or less lengthy separation of the marriage partners precedes the cessation of menses. This is probably what the Talmud means when it states that a menstruating woman is held in physical separation from her husband so that he not develop a loathing towards her by constant contact with her. Through the separation, she again becomes beloved by her husband as the time of her first entry into the bridal chamber[10].

*Every* period of uncleanness, as already mentioned, ends with a bath. Even after the destruction of the Temple, a full bath was required before one could indulge in marital intercourse after menstruation, or after any other uterine bleeding. This law — both the separation of the husband from his bleeding wife as well as the bath — is strictly adhered to by Jews to this very day. Every Jewish community today possesses its own ritualarium (or bathhouse or *mikveh*). We will describe it in a later chapter in greater detail.

To us modern, cultured people of the large cities, who have bathing facilities even in our private homes as part of the requirements of our daily life, the existence of such ritualariums does not seem to be extraordinary. However, in the eighteenth and nineteenth centuries when the use of baths, at least in Germany, nearly ceased, "the Jewish bath" was often the only bathing facility in small towns[11]. Even today, I could name villages, not just in darkest Africa, in which the collective inhabitants have never taken a full bath since they were infants. The religious character of "the Jewish bath" naturally does not change its therapeutic value.

## II   Vaginal Bleeding

Bleeding which occurs *following cohabitation* is especially important. A man can easily fall into danger if he has coitus with a woman who is bleeding "from the source" (i.e. uterus). He thereby commits a serious sin, and the laws pertaining thereto are especially strict. However, this danger cannot be excluded in the case of any woman whose menses are irregular, and there must have been other considerations — perhaps certain practical experiences — which motivated the Rabbis to the Draconian reprimands described below. Today, we can conjecture with some degree of accuracy

---

7. Kerithoth 1:7
8. Landau. *Geschichte der Jüdischen Aerzte.* Berlin 1895 p.12
9. Niddah 31b and Levit. Rabbah 14:5
10. Niddah 31b
11. Baumer. *Geschichte des Badewesens* p.18

as to what type of considerations these are, in view of our knowledge of the symptoms and consequences of uterine carcinoma.

If bleeding occurs following cohabitation on three successive occasions, the marriage must be dissolved. To be sure, the woman is permitted to marry again, but if the same misfortune occurs again, and even with a third marriage — "because the penis and the power of cohabitation is not the same for all men" — the woman is obligated to undergo an examination.

"How does she examine herself? She takes a tube (i.e. speculum) within which there is a painting stick, *makchol,* which has absorbent cotton attached to its tip, and inserts this tube into the vagina. If blood is found at the tip of the absorbent, then it is known that the blood emanated from the source (i.e. uterus) and is unclean. But if no blood is found on the absorbent, it is known that the blood seen after coitus emanated from the sides and is clean"[12]. The *Tosefta*[13] asserts that if the blood is found on the sides of the tube, it is known that the blood has only been wiped off. In order that the tube itself should not produce a wound, Mar Samuel requires that it be made of lead, and its edge (literally: mouth) should bend inwards. According to the wording of the aforementioned *Tosefta,* it appears that this examination is not performed by the woman herself, but by someone else, although perhaps not always.

If a woman has a wound in the genitalia, then the blood can be attributed to the wound, since it may not have originated from the uterus, provided that the blood of this wound has a different appearance than the blood which occurs following cohabitation. According to Rabban Simeon ben Gamliel, however, any blood which flows from the *makkor,* meaning uterus, is unclean, even if it is known that the blood originates from a wound in the uterus. Hence, under all the above-mentioned circumstances, the marriage must be dissolved. The other Sages of the Talmud, however, do not agree with him[14].

Medical or health considerations are not mentioned in the Talmud as the basis for these regulations either. However, it is precisely here that one is struck with the advantageous consequences of strict observance of these laws. The most common reason by far for bleeding through coitus is erosions of the *portio,* and these may result from a catarrh of the cervix or, more importantly, the beginning stages of a carcinoma. Since married people know that the law prescribes dissolution of the marriage in case of repeated bleeding following coitus, and that in such a case, divorced women have great difficulty in finding another marriage partner, it is quite certain that in such cases medical opinion is promptly sought. No matter which reason the physician ascertains to be the cause for the bleeding, it is undoubted that in serious cases, therapy can be expeditiously instituted, and carcinoma in its early stages can thus be uncovered.

Mention of a *speculum* is quite remarkable. Ordinarily, Aetius in the sixth century[15], and later Paulus of Aegina, are considered to be the earliest authors to mention a *dioptron* (tube or speculum) which was used to dilate the external uterine os, i.e., the vaginal orifice, and to visualize the vagina. Undoubtedly, however, the mention of the speculum in the Talmud occurred much earlier, for Mar Samuel, who provided a detailed description of the speculum[15a], died as early as 257 C.E. The uterine speculum for the use described in the Talmud (i.e. to determine the ritual cleanliness or impurity of a woman) was totally unknown in antiquity[16].

From practical experience, the Talmud relates the following two cases: a certain woman who saw blood occasioned by intercourse once came to Rabbi Judah. He instructed his assistant Abdan to go and frighten her. He did as he was instructed and

12. Niddah 66a
13. *Tosefta* Niddah 8:2
14. Niddah 66a
15. *Tetrabibl.* 4, sermo 4, c.108

15a. Niddah 66a
16. See D. Haussmann. *Zeitschrift. für Geburtshilfe und Gynecologie* 3 p.366

"a clot of blood dropped from the woman." Rabbi Judah declared: she is now cured[17]. Perhaps this was a loose fibroma which bled during cohabitation and which was expelled following the sudden fright.

Another case is that of a woman with a similar complaint who came to Mar Samuel. He dealt with the case as above and tried to frighten her, but nothing dropped from her. Then Samuel declared: "This woman is one whose uterus is full of blood which she scatters as a result of intercourse. Such an illness is incurable"[17a].

## III    Castration

There is no doubt at all that *castration* of female animals was already practiced in antiquity. Soranus reports in the year 100 C.E. in Galatia, that the pigs became fatter following removal of the uterus[18]. Galen asserts the same thing, but speaks of the excision of the female testicles (i.e. ovaries)[19], and the Talmud, in several places, mentions "Theodos the physician" who reported that in Alexandria every cow and sow to be exported from Egypt had its womb removed, in order to prevent breeding of these highly rated animals outside the mother country[20]. Soran, in the above-mentioned citation, declared that Themison did not consider the extirpation of the uterus of women to be fatal. The same was later affirmed by Paulus of Aegina[21]. It is doubtful whether, at least for antiquity, the often-cited assertion that the excision of the testicles in the Orient for the purpose of maintaining one's youthful beauty is of historical interest. In support of this opinion is the Talmudic recommendation that the prohibition of castration, which is specifically stated in the Bible[22] for men, should also be applied to woman[23]. The debate concerning the case of "the uterus of a woman which became detached (i.e. extirpated, literally: rotted) and fell to the ground"[24] gives one the impression of a merely theoretical discussion.

## IV    Treatment of Vaginal Bleeding

The Gospels describe a case of blood flow which corresponds to the Talmudic concept of *zaba;* they do so in generally similar terms. Matthew speaks of *a woman who was diseased with an issue of blood for twelve years*[25]. Mark relates that *she had suffered many things of many physicians . . . and was nothing bettered, but rather grew worse*[26]. Luke — himself a physician[27] — states that she had *spent all her living upon physicians,* but could not be healed by any of them[28]. This woman came behind Jesus from among the crowd and touched his garment, and immediately her issue of blood ceased. *And she felt in her body that she was healed from that plague*[29].

Most commentators assume that the above case was one of chronic uterine bleeding, but a few even consider hemorrhoids[30]. It is senseless to discuss this matter, as well as the anatomic source of the blood, for metrorrhagia can have many causes. All commentators unanimously agree that the therapy was of a purely psychic nature. The healing powers of Jesus were already widely known. The Mesmerists naturally interpret the words of Jesus: *I perceive that virtue is gone out of me*[31] in this sense.

In the Talmud are described a long list of remedies which were employed by the general populace, as well as by physicians of that time, for vaginal blood flow. One can

17. Niddah 66a
17a. *ibid*
18. Ed. Ermerius p.15; Oribasius, 24:31. vol 3:377
19. Oribasius, *ibid* 22:2. vol 3 p.45
20. Bechoroth 4:4 and 28b
21. *Chirurg.* chapt. 88
22. Levit. 22:24
23. Shabbath 111a
24. Niddah 41b
25. Matthew 9:20
26. Mark 5:25
27. Colossians 4:14
28. Luke 8:43
29. Mark 5:29
30. Friedreich. *Zur Bibel* 1:279
31. Luke 9:46

anticipate in advance that for such a chronic ailment, the list of remedies will not be small, and the "sympathetic remedies" will not be of minor consequence.

Among these remedies are the following:[32]

The "cup of the unfruitful", *kos shel akarin,* or perhaps more correctly the "cup of roots", *kos shel ikarin.* According to Rabbi Yochanan, it consists of a ground mixture of the weight of one *zuz* of Alexandrian gum, alum[33] and garden crocus. The powder is then prepared by mixing the above with grape wine or beer, *shechar*[34]. The *zaba* is given three cups thereof mixed with wine, and she does not become barren therefrom. For someone with *yerakon*[35], one gives two cups mixed with beer; the patient is healed of his (or her) illness but simultaneously becomes infertile. There also exists an "oil of *ikarin*"[36], but no details of its ingredients are mentioned.

Another remedy is as follows: take three measures of Persian (large) onions, boil them in wine, make her drink it and say to her "Cease your discharge"!

Another remedy: place the woman at a crossroads, give her a cup of wine in her hand, have a man come up from behind and frighten her and exclaim: "Cease your discharge"!

Another remedy: take a handful of cumin, a handful of safflower and a handful of fenugreek. Boil these in wine, make her drink it, and say to her: "Cease your discharge"!

Another remedy: take six drops of sealing clay from a vessel, smear her therewith, and say to her: "Cease your discharge"!

Another remedy: take a *pastina*[37], boil it in wine and smear her with it, and say to her: "Cease your discharge"!

Another remedy: take Loranthus Acaciae[38], burn it and gather the ashes in linen rags in the summer and in cotton rags in the winter.

Another remedy: dig seven holes and burn therein young shoots of *orlah* (whose vine is not yet three years old); then put a cup of wine into the woman's hand, make her rise from one hole and seat her on the next, make her rise from that one and seat her on the third one, and so on, and at each hole say to her: "Cease your discharge"!

Another remedy: take fine flour (or *psiothrum*) and rub her from the middle part of her body downwards, and say to her: "Cease your discharge"!

Another remedy: take an ostrich egg, burn it and wrap the ashes in a linen rag in the summer or a cotton rag in the winter.

Another remedy: open a barrel of wine specially for her sake. According to the explanation of *Rashi,* "she should constantly drink wine". This seems to be the most inappropriate remedy imaginable for a bleeding woman.

Another remedy: take barley grain which is found in the dung of a white mule; if the woman holds it one day, her discharge will cease for two days; if she holds if for two days, it will cease for three days; but if she holds it for three days, it will cease for - ever.

---

32. The entire list is found in Shabbath 110ab
33. Löw. *Aramaische Pflanzennamen* p.83
34. The cup or "potion of roots" thus contains no "roots". The term "root" is probably used to designate any plant remedy. Rhizotomes also do not only refer to roots.
35. anemia or jaundice. See above in chapter 4
36. Shabbath 14:3
37. a low-spreading plant
38. a thistle growing among Roman thorns

# CHAPTER XIV

## *OBSTETRICS*

### PART I
### PHYSIOLOGY

#### I  Pregnancy

The *Aggadah* provides a particularly rich literature concerning the miracle of pregnancy and birth. If one turns a keg of water over so that its opening is facing downwards, all the water contained therein would be spilled out[1]. Similarly, if one holds a filled money bag with the opening facing downwards, do not the coins scatter? The embryo, however, lies in the mother's womb whose orifice is turned downwards, and God guards it so that it should not fall out. An animal walks in a horizontal position, and its embryo lies in its womb, as in a sack; whereas a woman walks erect with the embryo in her womb, and God guards it so that it should not fall out and die[2]. God built a woman like a storehouse; just as a storehouse is narrow at the top and broad on the bottom so as to hold the produce, so, too, a woman (is narrower above and broader below) so as to hold the embryo[3].

Menses cease with the beginning of pregnancy; the blood is changed and is converted to milk[4]. But pregnancy may occur even prior to the onset of menses (menarche). Justinia, the daughter of Aseverus, told the Rabbis that she was married at the age of six and bore a child at the age of seven[5]. Bathsheba, the wife of King David, also gave birth at six years of age[6]. Even today young mothers are not a rarity in the Orient. Nevertheless, the Rabbis considered pregnancy in such young individuals to be very undesirable because parturition could easily result in the mother's death. They could not, however, outrightly prohibit such marriages, which were common practice in the Orient, and they, therefore, recommended the use of a contraceptive absorbent tampon[7]. Rabbi Huna teaches that a woman who becomes pregnant before puberty will die together with her child during parturition[8]. Soran asserts that conception before the occurrence of menses is impossible, *pseudos estin,* "without menstruation, there is no conception"[9]. Aëtius, as always, agrees with Soran[10]. As is well-known, he is incorrect.

---

1. Niddah 31a
2. Levit. Rabbah 14:4; Midrash Psalms 103:6
3. Berachoth 61a
4. Niddah 9a
5. *ibid* 45a

6. Sanhedrin 69b
7. Yebamoth 12b
8. Jerushalmi Pesachim 8; 35c
9. Soran. Chapt. 6, p.32 and 34, ed. Ermerins
10. Aëtius. Book 16 Chapt. 51. ed. Zervos

Pregnancies after the cessation of menses are miracles. One is reminded of the Biblical narration of the birth of Isaac: *Abraham and Sarah were old* (not through *senectus praecox,* but truly old), *and well stricken in age; it had ceased to be with Sarah after the manner of women* (menses)[11]. When she was told that she would yet give birth to a son, she laughed within herself, or, as the *Aggadah* states, concerning her insides: "can these internal organs perchance carry a child, and can these wrinkled breasts suckle him? The entire world would say: they picked up this child from the street and assert that it is theirs! That is how unbelievable the fact would appear to everyone". A miracle occurred to Sarah in that the breasts of this 90-year-old woman[12] opened like two fountains, so that she was able not only to suckle her own child, but also the children of the women who came to the banquet to celebrate the weaning of Isaac[13]. Rabbi Chisda said: a woman who marries before she is twenty years of age begets children until age sixty; if she marries at age twenty, she begets until age forty; if she marries at age forty, she does not beget any children anymore[14]. A miracle happened to Jochebed, the mother of Moses, who married at 130 years of age.

Cessation of menses during pregnancy, according to the Talmud, is not invariable,[15] however. Aristotle even teaches that, in *most* women, menstruation continues for a certain time after conception[16].

# II

Pregnancy results in various difficulties. The Biblical phrase *I will greatly multiply thy pain and thy travail* is, according to the usual understanding, the curse which the Lord spoke unto the woman (i.e. Eve) in Paradise[17]. When a woman is pregnant, she becomes repulsive and loathsome[18], her head and limbs become heavy[19], and she has fancies of the mind[20]. Only pious women are exempt from this curse of Eve[21].

Frequently, a pregnant woman might have unusual "cravings" — the *kissan* of the Greeks — which, if not satisfied, are thought to constitute a danger to her life. People still believe that this is true. Since pregnancy in and of itself is a purely physiological condition, there is no reason to provide a pregnant woman with a dispensation for the Biblically prescribed total abstinence from food on the Day of Atonement. A problem arises if these "cravings" occur on the Day of Atonement; however, if they persevere in spite of mentioning the Holy Day, one gives her food as stated in the Talmud: "If a pregnant woman smelt a dish and became faint because of a morbid desire for it on the Day of Atonement, she must be given it to eat until she feels restored"[22]. If the craving is for a food whose consumption is prohibited (for example, pork), one should first try to satisfy the craving by offering something that was dipped in the juice of this prohibited meat. If this does not suffice, the prohibited meat itself is given to the pregnant woman, for all ritual laws are set aside in the face of danger to life. It was assumed that these "cravings" originated from the fetus, and it was believed to represent an evil sign concerning the religiosity of the child[23]. Thus, according to legend, Esau eagerly struggled to get out of his mother's womb when she passed idolatrous temples, and Jacob struggled when she passed by religious schools[24]. The baby of the pregnant Elizabeth leaped in her womb, when Mary, pregnant with Jesus, came near[25]. When the mother of Elisha ben Abuya, the apostate, was pregnant

11. Genesis 18:11
12. *ibid* 17:17
13. Baba Metzia 87a
14. Baba Bathra 119b
15. Niddah 10b
16. *Hist. Anim.* 7:2:20
17. Genesis 3:16
18. Song of Songs Rabbah 2:14:8; incorrect in

Genesis Rabbah 45:4; see Luria *op. cit.*
19. Niddah 10b
20. Sirach 34:5
21. Sotah 12a
22. Yoma 8:5
23. Yoma 82a-b
24. Genesis Rabbah 63:6
25. Luke 1:41

with him, she passed an idolatrous temple and "smelt" the aroma of an idolatrous sacrifice. This aroma spread throughout her body like snake poison[26], and infected the delicate fetus with the desire for the prohibited.

Movements of the fetus can be quite painful to the mother. When the twins "struggled" in the womb of Rebecca[27], she asked the other women whether they had similar experiences. When she received an affirmative reply, she said: if such pains occur from having children, then I would be better off not having become pregnant[28].

A person should always be thankful for the protection of the womb. It was considered to be a sign of unusual unkindness that Edom (Esau) "spoiled the womb from which he and his brother were born"[29].

## III    Recognition of Pregnancy

Symchos quotes the teaching of Rabbi Meir that a pregnancy is first *externally* recognizable after three months[30]. The twin pregnancy of Tamar was also first recognized at the three-month stage[31]. The pregnancy of the aged Elizabeth, mother of John the Baptist, however, was first recognized after the fifth month because she hid herself for that period[32]. The pregnancy of a young primigravida is most difficult to recognize; whereas in the case of all other women, the Bible uses the expression: "and she conceived" (i.e. was overtly pregnant) and "bore a child", the former phrase is lacking in the case of Zilpah, the handmaid of Leah[33].

A widow or divorced woman shall not marry before a period of three months elapses after the death of her husband or the divorce, in order to make a distinction between the seed of the first husband and that of the second[34]. The German Code of Civil Law requires ten months[35], but grants exemptions. How and by whom the woman is to be examined for signs of pregnancy is not mentioned in the Talmud. It is mentioned, however, that remarried women were "scrutinized as to their gait". The ancient commentators[36] explain this to mean that a pregnant woman, walking on soft soil or loose earth, leaves a deeper impression than a non-pregnant woman! It is much simpler to assume that "the gait of the woman" was observed. In advanced pregnancy, this type of walk is commonly quite characteristic. If the Sages were able, in general, to recognize a three-month pregnancy by external observation, then the latter assumption is not so improbable. The Sages were fully aware of the frauds that women could perpetrate, such as, for example, a divorced and then remarried pregnant woman trying to conceal her pregnancy in order that her child might inherit his share of her second husband's estate[37]. Nevertheless, I was unable to find any precautionary measure mentioned in the Talmud to obviate such a fraud. Perhaps it was assumed that the woman would not risk the possibility of being discovered.

Naturally, if one sees "the abdomen of a woman between her teeth" (i.e. reaching up to her teeth), this is an undoubted sign of pregnancy[38]. This was, in fact, a proverbial expression[39].

## IV    Duration of Pregnancy

The normal duration of pregnancy in a woman is nine solar months. Mar Samuel, the Babylonian physician-sage of the Talmud, states it is 271 to 273 days[40]. According

---

26. Jerushalmi Chagigah 2; 77b
27. Genesis 26:22
28. Genesis Rabbah 63:6
29. Amos 1:11. See Commentary of Ibn Ezra; also Rahmer in Frankel's *Monatschrift* 1898 p.6.
30. Niddah 8b
31. Genesis 38:24
32. Luke 1:24
33. Genesis Rabbah 71:9
34. Yebamoth 42a
35. *Bürgerliches Gesetzbuch* No. 1313
36. Responsa of the Geonim. Cf. *Rashi* a.1.
37. Yebamoth 42a
38. *Tosefta* Kethuboth 1:6
39. Rosh Hashana 25a
40. Niddah 38a

to the Palestinian tradition[41], it is up to 274 days. This calculation begins from the first cohabitation and, according to the law of the Bible, this cohabitation cannot occur before seven days after the beginning of menstruation, at the earliest[42]. Hence, the calculation coincides precisely with our current computation of 280 days. The interval between 271 and 273 days is flexible, according to the amount of time elapsed between cohabitation and conception. The difference cannot be more than three days, because after that, if the sperm has not fertilized an egg, it disintegrates[42a]. "The ancient pious people", therefore, only cohabited with their wives on a Wednesday, Thursday or Friday, in order to avoid a delivery on the Sabbath[43].

Exceptionally, a longer period of pregnancy is mentioned. Thus, Raba Tosfa'ah (in the year 200 C.E.) declared the child of a woman whose husband had gone to a country beyond the sea and "remained there for a full year of twelve months" to be legitimate[44]. If one assumes that in this case the fetus was dead — there is no mention of this in the Talmud — then one can readily accept the possibility of retention of this fetus even up to three months after the normal time of delivery. Recently, E. Fränkel reported on twelve similar incontestable cases of missed labor[45]. But even if one assumes the fetus to be alive, the matter is not so shocking. One can assume that of the "twelve months", only one day of the first and last month need be counted and since, in the Talmud, months were either 29 or 30 days long (lunar months), the duration of the pregnancy calculates to be 297 days, which is five days less than the maximum allowable number cited in the Code of Civil Law[46], and considerably less than the maximum figure reported by Winckel concerning 30,000 births. The latter found that for heavy children the pregnancy may last up to 336 days[47].

Hippocrates[48] and Aristotle[49] both speak of an eleven-month pregnancy; the latter does so with skepticism, however.

The shortest duration of pregnancy following which a viable child can be born, according to Mar Samuel, is 212 days. The catchphrase, therefore, (*harbeh* whose letters in Hebrew add up to 212; and *arbeh* meaning "I will cause to increase") is a play on words which is untranslatable[50]. The Code of Civil Law[51] gives 181 days as the minimum figure.

The possibility of a child crying out while still in the mother's womb, the *vagitus uterinus,* is strongly denied by the Rabbis. If one heard the child crying, then it is certain that the head was already outside the antechamber[52]. Aristotle teaches that the child would not cry out in such a case until the *entire* body is born[53]. This is an assertion which is less in agreement with the truth of the matter than is the teaching of the Rabbis.

The not infrequent expressions found in the sermonizing sections of the *Midrash* such as "the children began to sing hymns in their mother's wombs, and they praised the Lord, etc." are naturally not to be taken literally.

## V   Diet and the "Preserving Stone" during Pregnancy

There is very little mention in Bible and Talmud about dietetics during pregnancy. During the first three months of pregnancy, cohabitation is thought to be harmful to both mother and fetus; during the next three months, it is harmful to the mother, but

41. Jerushalmi Niddah 1; 49b
42. Levit. 15:19 and 18:19
42a. Shabbath 86a
43. Niddah 38a
44. Yebamoth 80b. The same expression is used in Abodah Zarah 35a
45. Volkmann's *Sammlung Klinische Vorträge*. 1903 N.F. 351

46. *Bürgerliches Gesetzbuch* No. 1592
47. *ibid* 1901 No. 282 to 293
48. *De Septim. Partu.* Ed. Foes. fol. 255 p.48
49. *Hist. Anim.* Book 7, Chapt. 4 No. 31-34
50. Jerushalmi Niddah 1; 49b
51. *Bürgerliches Gesetzbuch*
52. Niddah 42b
53. *Hist. Anim.* Book 7 Chapt. 10 No. 61

beneficial for the fetus; and during the final months, it is beneficial for both, because the child becomes white (light complexion) and fast (speedily born)[54]. Aristotle has already mentioned that women who cohabit often with their husbands prior to delivery, *ai plesiazousai tois andrasi,* have more rapid deliveries[55]. Soran considers copulation at any time during pregnancy to be dangerous, both because of the vigorous body movement *(dia ton salon)* as well as the fact that the uterus thereby produces contractions which are opposed to the conception. In addition, during the later months of pregnancy he is fearful of tearing of the amniotic membrane with premature outflow of amniotic fluid[56]. Cohabitation *intra partum* was still recommended in the medical literature of the seventeenth century as an ecbolic[57], and is still today held in high regard by elderly midwives. This does not apply to Jews, since at that time the woman is impure and forbidden to her husband.

Light foods were always considered to be indicated for pregnant women. When God commanded Moses to take the Israelites out of Egypt, Moses retorted: the provision of food for the masses will entail difficulties. Have You (God) also prepared soft foods *(rekikin)* for the pregnant women, provisions *(anonas)*[58] for the nursing mothers, and nuts and roasted corn for the children[59]? I do not know what the *zrd* is, which pregnant women ate together with barley groats[60]. Egyptian *zythos* was thought to be dangerous for both pregnant women and ill people[61] because, as the commentaries explain, it is a powerful purgative.

The prohibition of alcohol in the case of the mother of Samson has nothing to do with either the conception or the pregnancy, as has been asserted by prominent medical authorities in recent times[62]. The expected child (Samson) was to be "a *nazir* of God from the womb". *For this reason,* his mother was instructed: *drink not wine nor (other) strong drink, and eat not any unclean thing*[63]. Both things are prohibited to the nazarite[64]. Furthermore, the same prohibition is found at the announcement of the birth of John the Baptist[65].

As a protection against miscarriage, a pregnant woman wore an *eben tekuma,* a preserving stone. And not only did women who had already miscarried wear such a stone to prevent a recurrence, and women who were already pregnant, to protect against a miscarriage, but also women who wished to become pregnant[66].

It is probable that it is the *aetites* or eaglestone which is here referred to. These "rattling stones" have an inner hollow space within which there is a loose pebble. The *aetites,* according to Plinius[67], is found in the nest of the eagle, and protects the embryos from the danger of a premature birth. If it is not removed at the appropriate time, however, then no birth occurs at all[68]. Plinius attributes its use[69] to the fact that the stone itself may be said to be pregnant; if one shakes it, one hears the rattling sound, similar to that which occurs in the womb. The same is mentioned by Dioscorides[70] and Aëtius[71]. In ancient French it was called *contenant (Rashi)* and in Germany *sternschuss.*

---

54. Niddah 31a. Alternate translation: the child becomes well-formed and of strong vitality.
55. *loc. cit.* Chapt. 4 No. 30
56. Soran. Chapt. 16 p.79, ed. Ermerins
57. Johanus Eleri Ulyssi. *Philosophi ac Medici Libellus de Partu.* Lunaeberg 1626. Cited according to Osiander
58. Exodus Rabbah 3:4; "foods"
59. Song of Songs Rabbah 1:7
60. Yoma 47a
61. Pesachim 42b
62. Ebstein. *Die Medizin im Alten Testament* p.168
63. Judges 13:4
64. Numbers 6:4
65. Luke 1:15
66. Shabbath 66b
67. Plinius 30:44
68. *ibid* 36:39
69. *ibid* 10:4
70. Dioscorides 5:90
71. Book 16:21 ed. Zervos p.26 to carry *kata tes gastros* meaning against the abdomen.

The "genuine" stone was probably very rare, and one, therefore, wore other stones with an allegedly similar quality, *mishkal eben tekuma*[72].

The author of *Shilte Gibborim*, Abraham Portaleone, who was a physician in Mantua (1542-1612), specifically identifies the preserving stone with the *aetites*. He, however, states that it was a dark green stone[73], which is the green jasper of our modern mineralogists[74]. This stone, too, which is not identical with the *aetites,* was surely worn as a birth amulet by the Assyrians, and perhaps already much earlier by the pre-Semitic inhabitants of Southern Mesopotamia, for the purpose of hastening birth[75]. For the same purpose, the Greeks tied it to the thighs of women in labor[76]. In Northern Germany during the Middle Ages, a woman wore it on her finger[76a].

I do not know of other examples in the Talmud of such useless regimens to preserve a fetus or hasten birth. In modern times, one can find a large collection of superstitions, particularly in the monastic obstetrical armamentarium, in Osiander's *Handbook of Obstetrics*[77].

## VI   Superfecundation

The legitimacy of a child is one of the prerequisites for its claim to inherit the parent. The Talmud has numerous discussions on this subject. Within narrow limits, the Palestinians admit to the possibility that one woman can be pregnant at one time from two men, i.e. superfecundation. Since conception occurs within three days of cohabitation, if the woman copulates with another man during this time period, then mixing of the sperm may occur and the child may, in fact, have two fathers. If she copulates with another after a longer interval, then either a conception has already occurred, or the sperm of the first partner became putrefied (disintegrated and, therefore, incapable of fertilization); and, therefore, a conception which follows the second cohabitation must be attributed to it[78].

Today, judgement in such a case would depend upon whether or not one accepts the supposition that several spermatozoa can simultaneously penetrate a single egg. If one accepts this — and there are prominent modern embryologists who do — then one should not by any means promote an objection against the Talmud.

Another aspect of this question concerns the possibility of an already pregnant woman becoming pregnant again from a later cohabitation, the much-talked-of, much-discussed problem of superfetation. The ancients assumed that a human uterus has two horns, analogous to that of animals, and, therefore, it was a simple matter for them to assume that one horn would first become pregnant and then the other horn at a later time, as is explicitly stated by Aristotle[79] and Hippocrates. Such an occurrence is unquestionably possible in the very rare case of a complete duplication of the entire genital tract of a woman. For a normal uterus, however, various stages of pregnancy must be differentiated. During the first month, the possibility of superfetation is certainly a real one. During the second and third months, the probability is also still great. Only from the twelfth week onwards is it impossible for the sperm and egg to meet. This is the opinion of Schröder[80] and other obstetricians, but is strongly opposed by Kleinwächter, who denies even the possibility of a second pregnancy occurring in the other uterine horn[81].

In the Talmud, one finds proponents of both opinions. The Babylonians totally deny the possibility of superfetation: "a woman does not conceive and conceive

---

72. Shabbath 66b
73. *Marpé Lashon* p.126
74. Fühner, *Lithotherapie.* Berlin 1902 p.110
75. See Oefele. *Allgemeine Medizinische Centralzeitung* 1899 No. 20
76. Dioscorides. Book 5:89; Kühn 1:818

76a. see above note 75
77. *Handbuch der Entbindungskunst.* 2 p.81
78. Jerushalmi Yebamoth 4; 5c
79. *De Generatione* 4:87-88
80. *Lehrbuch des Geburtshilfe* p.79
81. Eulenberg's *Real-Encyclopedia s.v.*

again"[82]. In spite of this, if, as once happened, a child is born and three months later another is born and both survive, then, according to Abaye, the explanation is that one drop of sperm was divided into two sections; the features of one of these were completed at the beginning of the seventh month, and those of the other were completed at the end of the ninth month[83]. Nevertheless, Rabbi Bibi advised a pregnant woman to use an absorbent tampon so that her fetus not degenerate into a *sandal (foetus compressus)*[84].

On the other hand, the Palestinians are of the opinion that a pregnant woman probably can become pregnant again, but only within the first forty days[85].

## VII   The Fetus[86]

The name "fruit of the womb" for the fetus is derived from the Bible[87]. The abbreviated term "fruit" is also used[88]. The Talmud also occasionally uses this expression[89] although, in general, the term used for embryo and fetus in the Talmud is *ubbar.*

The author of the book of Job, who is generally credited with having considerable knowledge of natural science, compares the generation of the fetus with coagulation: *Hast thou (Lord) not poured me out as milk, and curdled me like cheese*[90]? The *Midrash* asserts that the uterus is full of blood, some of which ordinarily comes out as menstrual flow. When it is the will of the Creator, a drop of white (sperm) falls therein and immediately the fetus begins to form. It may be compared to milk in a basin: if one puts *meso* into it, it congeals and becomes solid, if not, it continues to be liquid[91]. The same thought is found in the Apocryphal book Wisdom of Solomon where it states: "I, too, am a mortal man...The body is shaped into flesh in the mother's womb, solidified in blood in ten months, from man's seed and the pleasure of marriage"[92]. The same teaching is also found in Aristotle[93].

There first develops a *golem,* a mass of substance, as stated by the Psalmist[94]. Aristotle designates it as *anarthron kreodes,* meaning flesh without limbs[95].

To this theory of procreation, one should add the remark of the Talmud that each of the father's limbs does not engender the corresponding limb in the child, for if this were so, a blind man should beget blind children and an amputee should beget children without legs[96]. The Talmud thus subscribes to the theory, strongly promulgated in antiquity primarily by Pythagoras, that the semen which is produced from all parts of the body generates a type of extract similar to it. Aristotle, as is well known, strongly opposed this theory[97].

In a moral teaching of the Talmud, it is stated that there are three partners in the creation of a human being: God, the father and the mother. The father provides the white (sperm) from which are derived the child's bones and sinews, his nails, the marrow in the head (brain) and the white of the eye. The mother provides the red (menstrual blood) from which are derived skin and flesh and blood and hair and the black of the eye. God gives the spirit and the soul, beauty of features, sight of the eyes, hearing of the ears, speech of the mouth, the ability to move the hands and walk with the feet, understanding and discernment. When the time arrives for a person to depart from this world, God takes His portion back and leaves the portions contributed by the

82. Niddah 27a
83. *ibid*
84. *ibid* 45a
85. Jerushalmi Yebamoth 5c
86. Literally: the fruit
87. for example Genesis 30:2
88. Lamentations 2:20
89. Chullin 114b; Shabbath 135b
90. Job 10:10
91. Levit. Rabbah 14:9
92. Wisdom of Solomon 7:1-2
93. *De Generatione* 1:88
94. Psalms 139:16
95. *Hist. Anim.* Book 7 Chapt. 3:23
96. Chullin 69a
97. *De Generatione* 4:36 ff

parents before them[98]. Then both father and mother cry. When God speaks: "Why do you cry? I have only taken back My own portion", they answer: "As long as Your portion was combined with ours, our portion was protected from maggots and worms; now, however, our portion is cast away and given to the maggot and the worm".[99]

# VIII   Fetal Development

The *Aggadah* speaks at length about the question as to the part of the body from which the fetus begins to develop. According to some Sages, development begins from the head; according to Abba Saul, it begins in the navel, and the latter spreads its roots in all directions[100]. Rabbi Abahu states that it is an extreme kindness of God, that He commences the development of the embryo with the skin and the flesh, rather than with the sinews and bones; otherwise, the child would break through the mother's womb and come out[101]. As long as the child is in the mother's womb, it receives its nourishment only through the navel[102].

According to Aristotle, the heart develops first, and it is also the last part of the body to die[103]. Plutarch asserts that the teaching of Alcmaeon is that the head develops first because it is *to egemonikon;* the physicians assume that the heart, in which are the large arteries and veins, develops first; others state that the large toe develops first, and yet others are of the opinion that the navel develops first[104]. According to Galen, the liver develops first[105]; and according to Plinius, the heart develops first; then the brain, and the eyes develop last. Dying, however, occurs in the reverse order[106].

The answer to the question as to the time when the soul enters the body, has no meaning in Talmudic law. Nevertheless, it is discussed as follows: King Antoninus asked Rabbi Judah: when does God place the soul in man; at the time of conception or when the embryo is actually formed? He replied: from the moment of formation. Antoninus objected: is it possible that a piece of meat should remain unsalted for three days — as already mentioned, the longest interval between conception and impregnation — without becoming putrid? Therefore, it must be that the soul is implanted by God from the moment of conception[107]. In the same Talmudic discussion, it is taught that, according to the teaching of Emperor Antoninus, the evil inclination of man first holds sway over a person from the time of birth. If it came earlier, the child would rebel in its mother's womb, tear the womb and go forth[108].

There is a rather voluminous literature, from the earliest of times in the writings of the church fathers and until the present time, concerning this question of *de animatione foetus.* Plutarch has collected the opinions of the ancient philosophers on this matter[109]. It only has practical significance for the legislative system which considers a fetus with a soul to be a human being, and intentional abortion to be punishable as murder. Inasmuch as physicians are supporters of the stoic teaching *partem ventris, non animal foetus,* they would certainly easily decide to dismember the living fetus. The concept of the "evil inclination" has generated, in the various religious sects, all those passionate disputations concerning original sin — a doctrine rejected by Judaism.

---

98. Niddah 31a
99. Eccles. Rabbah 5:10
100. Sotah 45b
101. Levit. Rabbah 14:9
102. Song of Songs Rabbah 7:3
103. *De Generatione* 2:78
104. Plutarch. *De Placitis* 5:17
105. *De Formatus Foetus* 5:292

106. *Histor. Natur.* 11:69
107. Sanhedrin 91b
108. *ibid* and Genesis Rabbah 34:10
109. *De Placitis Philos.* Book 5 Chapt. 15. There is also a rich literature in the work of Hansen *De Termino Animationis foetus hum.* When the child receives its soul in the mother's womb. Halle 1724

# IX

The position and appearance of the fetus *in-utero* is pictured as follows: Rabbi Eleazar states that the embryo in its mother's womb resembles a nut floating in a bowl of water. If someone puts his finger on it, on this side or on that side, it would sink[110].

Rabbi Simlai states that the embryo in the mother's womb resembles a folded writing tablet *(pinax);* its hands rest on its two temples[111]; its two elbows are on its hips, its two heels are against the buttocks, its head is between the knees, the mouth is closed, and the navel is open. It eats what its mother eats and drinks what its mother drinks, but produces no excrement, because otherwise it might kill its mother. As soon as it sees the light (i.e. is born), the closed (mouth) opens and the open (navel) closes; otherwise the fetus could not live even one single hour[112].

Abba Saul says: in the beginning of its development, a fetus resembles a locust, its eyes are like two drippings of a fly, abnormally far removed from one another; its two nostrils also resemble two drippings of a fly but are abnormally near one another. The mouth of the fetus is stretched as a hair-thin thread, its membrum is the size of a lentil and, in the case of a female, the genitalia have the appearance of the longitudinal slit of a barley grain; but it has no shaped hands or feet[113]. In order to definitively establish the sex of the fetus, one takes a splinter with a smooth tip and moves it to-and-fro in "that place" (i.e., the genitals). If it gets caught, it is proved that the fetus is a male, and, if not, it is a female. This splinter test must be done only in an upward direction, however, for if it is done sideways, it is possible that the obstruction encountered is due to the sides of the vulva (i.e. the labia). The objection of Rabbi Nachman that it (the presumed female organ) might be the thread of the testicles (spermatic cord?) is countered by Abaye who states that since the testes themselves are not yet discernible, the testicular thread is certainly not yet recognizable[114].

According to Rabbi Amram, the thighs of the early fetus resemble two thick or thin purple threads, and the arms likewise. Mar Samuel said that the sex of the fetus can only be decided with certainty if it has hair[115].

# X

The determination of the sex of the fetus occurs at the moment of cohabitation. In agreement with Aristotle[116], the Rabbis teach that if a woman emits her seed first, she bears a male child, and if the man emits his seed first, she bears a female child[116a]. It is, therefore, a vain prayer for a man to supplicate that God grant that his wife bear a male child, if his wife is already pregnant[117]. Some Rabbis, however, are of the opinion that such a prayer might avail before 40 days of conception have elapsed, and before the sex has differentiated. This would be true in the case where man and woman emitted their seed simultaneously, so that the fetus is originally sexually neutral.

In these remarks one can easily recognize the respect which the Rabbis had for the laws of nature.

According to the teaching of Rabbi Ishmael in the *Mishnah*[118], a male fetus is fully formed after 41 days, whereas a female fetus is not finished until 81 days. The Sages, however, state that the formation of a fetus of either sex is of the same duration; namely, 41 days. They told Rabbi Ishmael that Cleopatra, Queen of Alexandria, once

---

110. Niddah 31a
111. This assertion is more correct than that of Aëtius 16:22 p.28 who states: *paratetamenon ton charon tois merois,* meaning its arms stretched across the thighs; which corresponds exactly to Soran, Chapt. 62 p.271 in Ermerin's edition
112. Niddah 30b
113. Niddah 25a
114. *ibid* 25b
115. *ibid*
116. *De Generatione* 4:25
116a. Niddah 25b
117. Berachoth 60a
118. Niddah 3:7

provided her handmaids, who were sentenced to death, to the physicians for study. They had been made pregnant by slaves on a certain day, and were later examined postmortem. It was found that in one handmaid, a male embryo was fully fashioned on the forty-first day of the pregnancy, and in another handmaid, the same was the case with a fully fashioned female embryo. In opposition to this "proof", Rabbi Ishmael correctly replied that it is possible that the handmaid with the female embryo might have already been pregnant forty days earlier, to which the Sages retorted that at the beginning of the experiment, every handmaid was given an abortifacient potion *(samma de naphtza)*. Rabbi Ishmael rejoined by saying that some bodies are insusceptible to such a potion and are refractory to its effect.

On his side, Rabbi Ishmael related that when the handmaids of the Grecian Queen Cleopatra were sentenced to death by the government, they were examined, and it was found that a male embryo was fully fashioned on the forty-first day and a female embryo on the eighty-first day. The Sages retorted that one does not adduce proof from such foolishness, since it is possible that the handmaid with the female embryo became pregnant forty days later. The eighty-first day was, therefore, in reality, the forty-first day. And even if she had been placed in the charge of a prison warden so that cohabitation after the day of the experiment could be prevented, "there is no guardian against unchastity"; the warden himself might have had intercourse with her! If a surgical operation had been performed on the forty-first day, the female embryo might also have been found in a fully-fashioned condition like the male, continued the Sages, in countering Rabbi Ishmael.

Abaye, the proponent of folk medicine in the Talmud, states that an 81-day-old female embryo has features identical to that of a 41-day-old male one[119].

The belief in a slower development of female embryos was widespread in antiquity. It is found in the works of Aristotle who teaches that a 40-day-old aborted male fetus already has many limbs clearly recognizable, including the genitalia. On the other hand, if a female fetus is aborted during the first trimester, it is mostly limbless. Fetuses which reach the fourth month then develop very rapidly, so that they soon catch up with the males[120]. Hippocrates also teaches that a male fetus takes form after 30 days, but a female not until 42 days[121].

# XI   Sex Determination

Since time immemorial, man has tried to discern the origin of the formation of sex. According to Hippocrates and Galen, the right ovary gives rise to boys and the left ovary to girls. Anaxagoras is of the same opinion[122]. However, Bischoff removed one ovary from guinea pigs, and yet observed that the oophorectomized animals gave birth to fetuses of both sexes. In modern times, extirpation of one ovary in women has produced the same result, so that the above theory of the ancients can be definitively discarded. Proponents of this theory only have the two above-mentioned Talmudic discussions to support their contention; the determination of sex at the moment of conception, and the somewhat later differentiation of the originally neutral genitalia. There is not even a remote certainty in this matter.

According to the causes relating to the determination of the sex of the fetus, advice is given about the voluntary production of either boys or girls. Rabbi Kattina is of the opinion that anyone who desires to beget male children should contain himself (i.e. his sperm) during intercourse, so that his wife ejaculates first. If that is not possible, he should cohabit twice in succession since orgasm in the woman occurs more

---

119. Niddah 30b
120. *Histor. Anim.* 7:3

121. *De Nat. Pueri.* ed. Foes. Sect. 3 fol. 239 p.57
122. Aristotle. *De Generatione* 4:9

slowly than in a man[123]. Galen, and not Baas's "lustful Rabbis", recommends that one compress and hold fast to the right testicle if one wishes to beget girls[124]. This follows from his theory that boys are derived from the right testicle and girls from the left[125], analogous to the above-cited statement regarding the ovaries. Remarkably, the same practice was utilized by Hindu peasants in British East India, except that the woman compressed the testicles[126].

Abba Benjamin teaches that if one wishes to beget male children, one should position one's bed so that it faces north and south[127]. This reminds one of the ancient pastoral experience that animals which are facing north when they copulate give birth to female offspring[128]. Baron Reichenbach, in his "Od"[129], and recently Harrison Mettler[130], have discovered that sleeping with one's head facing north contributes to the strengthening of the body. Such advice, which belongs to the moral sphere, is not lacking in the Talmud. What must a man do that he may have male children? He should marry a wife that is worthy of him and conduct himself in modesty[131] at the time of marital intercourse. To be sure, many acted in this manner, but did not achieve the desired result[132]. Many such recommendations are promulgated (in the Talmud). Only the expression of the *Midrash*[133] remains correct, that "no man knows what a woman is bearing, for it is written: *nor how the bones do grow in the womb of her that is with child*"[134].

## XII    Psychic Maternal Influences on the Fetus

Not only is the sex of the fetus determined at the time of cohabitation, but it is also established at the time of reproduction whether the child will be strong or weak, wise or foolish, poor or rich. However, righteousness or Godlessness is not predetermined, but is dependant upon a person's own will[135]. Individual conceptualizations which a man or a woman have *ipso actu,* or external impressions which influence them, can play a role in the outward appearance of the offspring. The oldest example of this phenomenon from the animal world is the famous Biblical story of Jacob: *and he took him rods of fresh poplar, and of the almond and of the plane tree, and peeled white streaks in them, making the white appear which was in the rods. And he set the rods which he had peeled over against the flocks in the gutters in the watering troughs where the flocks came to drink; and they conceived when they came to drink. And the flocks conceived at the sight of the rods, and the flocks brought forth streaked, speckled and spotted*[136], as desired. In the Talmud, Rabbi Kahana reported that in order to produce the necessary ceremonial red heifer[137], one held a red cup before the eyes of the mother cow while she was copulating[138]. Even in heathen antiquity, such devices are not unknown, as evidenced by examples in the writings of Soran[139] and Oppian[140]. Discussions on the above Biblical citation by church fathers probably belong to the realm of fantasy.

Human experiments of this sort are unknown in the Talmud. Nevertheless, it is related that Rabbi Yochanan used to sit at the gates of the ritual bathhouse with the

123. Niddah 31b
124. Kühn 17:2 p.212
125. *Comment. ad lib. 6 Epid.- Hippocratis Comment.* 4:27; Kühn 17:2 p.212
126. *Münch. Mediz. Wchschr.* 1906 No. 12 fol. 561
127. Berachoth 5a
128. Aristotle. *De Generatione* 4:32
129. Rahmer's *Litteratur Blatt.* 1883 p.119
130. *Deutsch. Medizinische Zeitung* 1894 fol. 109b
131. literally: sanctify himself
132. Niddah 70b-71a
133. Genesis Rabbah 65:12
134. Eccles. 11:5
135. Niddah 16b
136. Genesis 30: 37-39
137. Numbers 19:2
138. Abodah Zarah 24a
139. Soran. Chapt. 10, ed. Ermerin p.51
140. Oppian. *Kynegetikon.* Book 1 Sp. 358. *Poët Buc. et Did. Rec. Leñrs.* Paris 1846 Vol. 1 p.7

expressly declared intent that the women coming out from bathing would see him and, from looking at his renowned beauty, beget children as handsome as he[141]. We are not here talking of sensuous thoughts in regard to the personage, for no person cohabiting with his wife should think of another woman, lest the children be like bastards[142]. And when a divorced man marries a divorced woman, there are four minds in the marital bed[143], a double adultery. Goethe cites an analagous case in the same sense as that of the Talmud[144]. The *Midrash* states that a woman would go out into the market place, see a young man and conceive a passion for him, cohabit with her husband, and give birth to a child that resembles the young man[145].

The *Midrash* relates another story pertinent to our discussion. A king of Arabia once asked Rabbi Akiba: I am black and my wife is black, yet she gave birth to a white son. Shall I kill her for having played the harlot? Rabbi Akiba retorted: Are the figures (statues) in your house black or white? The king answered white. Then Rabbi Akiba assured him: when you had intercourse with her, she fixed her eyes upon the white figures and bore a child like them[146].

This matter has achieved literary notoriety in that a large number of authors have written about this "anticipation of pregnant women", a concept which is cited as originating from the writings of Hippocrates, but which, in reality, is not found in his works, as proven by Huber[147], and independently by me. I base my presumption on the fact that some authors were satisfied with quoting Hieronymus as an authority, and thus provide second-hand quotes. However, I say that due to the knowledge of Hebrew on the part of Hieronymus thanks to Rabbi Chanina and other Talmudic Sages[148], he probably also heard the above *Midrashic* story from Jews and erroneously attributed it to Hippocrates[149]. But even this presumption would be untenable if the assertion of Migne is correct, i.e. that this citation does not exist in the manuscripts of Hieronymus[150]. In that case, it would represent an addition and an oversight on the part of the publisher, Erasmus of Rotterdam[151].

Furthermore, Heliodorus, the author of amatory stories, in his *Ethiopian Stories,* describes an anecdote which is quite similar to the above-mentioned story from the *Midrash*[152].

In all the foregoing, the only point is the psychic influence of the mother on the child at the moment of conception. The Talmud only rarely admits to such an influence on the pregnancy itself. For example, the *Midrash* states that one must not suppose that the features of the infant resemble those of the adulterer only when the woman conceives from the adulterer. No! Even if she conceived from her husband, and the adulterer then cohabited with her, God transforms the features of the child into those of the adulterer[153]. Perhaps, another story in the same *Midrash* is pertinent to our discussion: a she-ass was sick and was taken to the veterinary surgeon who cauterized her. She bore an offspring with a flame-mark. Why? Because the mother was cauterized[154].

Only in recent times has the teaching relating to psychic influence of the mother on the body of the child during all stages of pregnancy been propounded. In my aforementioned monograph on the subject, I have provided numerous proofs thereon.

---

141. Berachoth 20a
142. in the figurative sense. Nedarim 20b
143. Pesachim 112a
144. Goethe *Wahlverwandtsch.* Vol. 1. Chapt. 11
145. Genesis Rabbah 26:7
146. Numbers Rabbah 9:34
147. Friedreich's *Blätter* 1886 p.321; cf. Wolff. *Deutsche Medizinal Zeitung* 1894 No. 59
148. Graetz. *Geschichte der Juden.* Vol. 4

p.459; Bardenhewer, *Münch. Rektoratsrede* 1905
149. Preuss. Vom Versehen der Schwangeren. *Berliner Klinik* 1892 No. 51 note 6
150. Migne *Patrologie* Vol. 23 p.1035
151. S. Hieronymi *Quaest. Hebr. in Genes.* Chapt. 30. Basel 1526 Vol. 3 fol. 222c
152. Heliodori. *Aethiopic.* Book 4 Chapt. 10
153. Numbers Rabbah 9:1
154. *ibid* 9:5

## XIII   Multiple Births

In general, a woman only carries *one* child. Twins occur as a result of the drop of sperm dividing into two parts[155]. Whether or not the Talmud agrees with Hippocrates that each of these portions came into one of the two uterine sinuses, *kolpoi*[156], is very doubtful, because the Talmud has no mention at all of the concept of the two horns of the human uterus, a concept which was otherwise accepted throughout antiquity. The twins either lie within the same amniotic membrane *(shephir)* or in two separate fetal membranes. In either case, one of the fetuses may be born dead, the other alive[157]. The umbilical cord of twins must be cut quickly, for otherwise they would pull upon each other endangering their lives[158].

In an after-dinner speech, Rabbi Jose the Galilean deduced that the wife of Obed-edom, as well as each of her daughters-in-law, gave birth to sextuplets, as a reward for having attended to the Ark of the Covenant[159]. Legend reports the same to have occurred to the Children of Israel in Egypt (i.e. they begat sextuplets) in its explanation of the Scriptural verse *and they were fruitful like reptiles (sherazim) and increased abundantly*[160]. These cases are, therefore, not meant to be understood literally, but only as figures of speech in the discussion. Aristotle has already mentioned that, in reality, multiple births greater than quintuplets do not occur[161].

## XIV   Premature Births

Normally, birth occurs at the end of nine months. Nevertheless, births of live children occurring after a lesser duration of pregnancy are not rare.

Concerning the viability of such prematurely-born infants, the Talmud states that a child born after six and a half months of pregnancy, but not less, is viable[162]. This corresponds with modern experience. Furthermore, in all of antiquity, it was widely accepted that an infant born after eight months of pregnancy cannot survive, whereas a baby born after seven months of pregnancy is viable. This is stated by Hippocrates, affirmed by Galen, and taught by all subsequent authors in antiquity. Only Aristotle reports that, in Egypt, babies born after eight months of pregnancy, even malformed babies *(teratode),* are viable[163]. Plinius copied this assertion of Aristotle and magnified it out of his own fantasy[164]. The verse ''a baby born after eight months of pregnancy is non-viable'' is nearly accepted as dogma by the Rabbis[165].

However, the Rabbis were apparently better observers than theoreticians. Contrary to all expectations, one observed babies born after eight months of pregnancy that survived. People were not ready to give up what everybody believed in. Therefore, it was assumed that there are two types of ''creations'' in the modern sense, one of nine months' duration, and one of seven months' duration. One type of fetus is planned at the outset to be a nine-months' creation; the other a seven-months' creation; both are potentially viable. If an infant is created as a seven-months' creation, it is fully developed after seven months, and if it is not born until the eighth month, it naturally remains alive. If an infant is created as a nine-months' creation, however, and if it is born one month earlier, then it will certainly die[166].

Another explanation of the non-viability of an eight-month fetus is the teaching that a nine-months' birth can also occur following ''chopped off'' months, if for

155. Yebamoth 98b
156. *De Nat. Pueri.* ed. Foes. Sect.3 fol. 248 p.10ff
157. Oholoth 7:5
158. Shabbath 129b
159. Berachoth 63b (It was in fact Rabbi Eliezer the son of Rabbi Jose, F.R.)
160. Exodus Rabbah 1:8
161. *Hist. Anim.* Book 7 Chapt. 4: 36
162. Yebamoth 42a
163. *Hist. Anim.* Book 7 Chapt. 4:33
164. Plinius 7:4
165. for example, *Tosefta* Shabbath 15:5 and elsewhere
166. Jerushalmi Yebamoth 4;5d

example, only a small part of the ninth month has elapsed[167]. The Greeks simply assumed that the woman had made an error in the calculation of the duration of pregnancy[168]. Among the Greeks of later times, however, and perhaps among the Alexandrian Jews, there must have existed doubters of *this theory*.

In a jesting manner, Rabbi Abahu vindicates the Greek linguistic usage of the theory. The Greek letter *zeta* has the numerical value of 7 (although it is the 6th letter of the Greek alphabet), and, as the word *zeto*, means "shall live"! The letter *eta* has the numerical value of 7, and, as the word *etta*, means "destruction", or the like. This narrative is found very often in Biblical and Talmudic literature with numerous variations[169].

According to Rabbi Jose, one can recognize an eight-month premature birth by the lack of development of the hair and nails of the fetus[170].

## XV    Parturition

During the first three months of pregnancy, the fetus occupies the lowest chamber (of the mother's womb?), during the middle three months it occupies the middle chamber, and during the last months it lives in the uppermost chamber; and when its time to emerge arrives, it turns downwards and then emerges, and this is the cause of the woman's labor pains[171].

The Bible uses the expression *chabalim* for *labor pains,* corresponding to the Assyrian *habal,* from the root *chaval,* meaning "to tie together". It is probably so named because of the subjective feeling of the woman in labor, and not because of the objective finding of the contracting uterus. It is probably only coincidence that this term is only found in the poetic books of the Bible.

The picture of a woman in labor is very often depicted in the discourses of the prophets: *and they shall be affrighted; pangs (tzirim) and throes shall take hold of them; they shall be in pain as a woman in travail*[172]; and *like a woman with child, that draweth near the time of her delivery, is in pain and crieth out in her pangs, so have we been...*[173]. The moaning and the crying, particularly of a primigravida *(mabkira)*[174], is often portrayed (in the Bible). The prophet says: *I have long time held my peace, I have been still, and refrained myself, now will I cry like a travailing woman, gasping and panting at once*[175]. A secret makes a fool suffer such pangs, as a woman in childbirth suffers to bear a child[176].

A woman having labor pain is called *cholah*[177], labor itself being called *chul;* actually "to turn oneself in a circle". As correctly stated, it is the behavior of *a woman with child, that draweth near the time of her delivery*[178]; or, as we would define it, the preliminary labor pains and the period of dilatation. In actuality, Nägele has already proven by precise observations — and every physician can confirm it — that parturient women left alone will restlessly walk to and fro during the preliminary labor pains, and later, during the period of dilatation, encircle the bed or some other object in their room during the interval between pains. The "circling"[179] of the Hebrew linguistic usage is, therefore, not identical with the "turning or twisting in labor"[180] of our language; the latter is a derivative of the shrieking (in labor of pregnant women)[181].

---

167. *ibid* 5c
168. Aristotle. *loc. cit.*
169. Jerushalmi Yebamoth 5d; Numbers Rabbah 4:3; Genesis Rabbah 14:2; Genesis Rabbah 20:6; *Tanchuma Bamidbar,* ed. Buber p.9b
170. *Tosefta* Shabbath 15:7
171. Niddah 31a
172. Isaiah 13:8

173. *ibid* 27:17
174. Jeremiah 4:31
175. Isaiah 42:14
176. Sirach 19:11
177. Jeremiah 4:31
178. Isaiah 26:17
179. *kreisen* in German
180. *kreissen* in German
181. *kreischen* in German

In order "to give birth", i.e. at the actual time of delivery, the woman kneels down. The expression *kara* is always used to denote kneeling, and it means, as expressly stated in the Talmud and proven from the Bible[181a], "to bend one's knee". When a woman kneels down to give birth, she presses her heels against her thighs and thus gives birth, says Abaye[182]. She also presses her hands against her hips (during labor pains)[183]. This kneeling position of both humans[184] and animals[185] is mentioned both by the Bible as well as the Talmud[186]. It is likely that this position, at least for the beginning of delivery, is a natural one, in that a woman sinks to her knees at the first labor pains; she is "confined", or as is popularly said, she "buckles under". Greek mythology also describes a goddess of birth, Eileithyia *en gonasi* (on the knees)[187]. Sambon saw a marble relief given as a votive offering in an ancient Roman temple, portraying a parturient woman in a knee-elbow position[188].

Only mountain goats complete parturition in this manner. They kneel down, allow the offspring to emerge, and are free of labor pains[189]. It is exceptional, however, for a woman to give birth to a child before she has any labor pain at all[190]. According to later legend, the curse on Eve: *in travail shalt thou bring forth children*[191] was not decreed on righteous women[192]. As a result, at least according to Josephus[193], the delivery of Jochebed, mother of Moses, occurred without strong labor pains. The Christian dogma that the Virgin Mary, as the most righteous of all women, had no labor pains at all, is an extension of the aforementioned assertion.

## XVI

The Talmud says that if a woman goes into labor in a strange house, she will naturally try to return to her own house; either she is able to walk on her own, or she is carried by both arms, *gappayim*. As soon as the uterus opens, she is no longer able to walk[194]. Today we know that it might well be possible.

In general, during the delivery, a woman is not alone. The obstetricians Moschion and Soran[195] consider three women to be necessary, in addition to the midwife; one supports the back of the woman in labor, and the other two stand on either side, and upon them the (sitting) woman in labor can lean[196]! The bad habit of "women visiting with women in labor" was already in vogue at that time[197]. However, those onlookers were at least sensible enough to encourage the woman in labor, in that they spoke to her: "the Lord who answered your mother in her time of need will also answer you in your time of need"[198]!

At the beginning of the birth, the woman's friends carry her on their arms and she sits on the *mashber*[199]. The term *mashber* is already used in the Bible in the lament of the prophet: *the children are come to the mashber, and there is not strength to bring forth*[200]. The meaning of the word in the Bible is not clear; it could refer equally well to either a part of the maternal genital passage, or a utensil used by the woman in labor (i.e. a birthstool). The latter interpretation, namely that *mashber* even in the Bible refers to a birthstool, is espoused by the *Targum* and *Rashi*.

In the *Mishnah* and *Gemara*, it is undoubted that *mashber* is, in reality, a

181a. Berachoth 34b
182. Yebamoth 103a
183. Jeremiah 30:6
184. First Samuel 4:19
185. Job 39:3
186. Shabbath 54b; Niddah 31b; animal kneeling is cited in Baba Bathra 16a
187. Pausanias. *Descr. Graec.* Book 8, Chapt. 48
188. *British Medical Journal* 1895, Vol. 2:147
189. Job 39:3
190. Isaiah 66:7
191. Genesis 3:16
192. Sotah 12a
193. *Antiquities.* Book 2 Chapt. 9:4
194. Oholoth 7:4
195. Soran. Chapt. 21 p.103
196. Moschion. Chapt. 51
197. Jerushalmi Kethuboth 5; 30a
198. Deut. Rabbah 2:11; Midrash Psalms 20:4
199. Shabbath 129a
200. Isaiah 37:3; cf Hosea 13:13

birthstool. Here (in the Talmud), the *"mashber* of women in labor" is explicitly enumerated among the utensils which are ordinarily not used to sit upon[201]. The Talmud also speaks of a woman who died in childbirth on the *mashber*[202]. Of a hundred shrieks that a woman emits while sitting on the *mashber,* ninety-nine are for death and only one is for life[203].

On the other hand, the *Midrash*[203a] cannot be translated as Buber does: "Pharaoh said: While the children are still under the birthstool, I will destroy them"; rather "under the *wombs* of their mothers"; for the word *kursia,* which is found there, means "stool" or "seat", but never "birthstool". The *Targum* always uses the term *mithbar* which means *mashber.* The more correct textual reading is found in Leviticus Rabbah 27:11.

The expression "to sit on the *mashber"* gradually came to be used for "parturition", so that the literal meaning of the phrase became forgotten. One even speaks of an animal "that sat on the birthstool"[204]!

The meaning of the Biblical term *obnayim* is quite uncertain. Pharaoh spoke to the midwives saying: *when ye do the office of a midwife to the Hebrew women, and look on the obnayim; if it be a son, then ye shall kill him; but if it be a daughter, then she shall live*[205]. At the time of the Talmud, the word had already disappeared from common usage, and, hence, was subject to interpretation by the Rabbis. Most of them consider *obnayim* to be a "birthstool", as *Onkelos* translates *mithbar.* Rabbi Chanina explains the decree of Pharaoh as follows: "when you deliver the Hebrew women, you will already observe on the *obnayim* whether it is a boy"; because when the woman kneels down to give birth, her thighs become cold as stone (*obnayim,* from the word *eben* meaning stone), if she delivers a male infant. Other commentators state that the word *obnayim* is also used to designate a potter's wheel[206]: *as the potter sits, one thigh to each side and his turning wheel in the middle, so, too, the woman in labor.*

Probably in order to refute the immediate objection that one can only, with difficulty, recognize the sex of the infant when the vaginal orifice of the parturient woman is stretched circularly, since head presentations were the rule even in those days, Rabbi Chanina remarks that Pharaoh entrusted the midwives with an important sign, viz. if the child lies face downward, it is a boy, but if the face is turned upward, it is a girl[207]. The *Midrash* notes another meaning for the word *obnayim,* from the verb *bana,* to build, viz. "the place where the child is built", that is, the genitalia[208]. The *Mechilta* on Exodus 15:5 cites yet additional meanings.

A number of modern explanations for the Biblical *mashber* are found in the work of Friedreich[209]. Rawitzki found the already-mentioned Midrashic derivation of *obnayim* from *bana,* meaning to build, all by himself[210]. According to Pagel, in German, the meanings of *Geschoss* and *Geschösse* are analogous thereto[211]. Schapiro points out that, according to Ploss, some primitive races have the custom that a woman in labor supports herself over two stones to deliver her baby; he is of the opinion that *obnayim* too were two such stones[212]. Sarsowsky also reads *abanim* (stones) in the text, instead of the traditional *obnayim,* and considers them to be the magic birthstones, or *aban aladi,* of the Babylonians[213]. This magic birthstone was actually an amulet, and

---

201. Kelim 23:4
202. Arachin 7a
203. *Pesikta de Rab Kahana* 77b
203a. Midrash Psalms 2:4
204. Midrash Psalms 42:1
205. Exod. 1:16
206. Jeremiah 18:3; Sirach 38:29
207. Sotah 11b
208. Exodus Rabbah 1:14

209. *Zur Bibel* 1:117 ff
210. *Ueber die Kephalotrypsie.* Dissertation. Berlin 1871 p.7
211. in Virchow's *Jahresbericht für 1904*
212. *Revue des études Juives* Vol. 40 p.37, 1900; and *Obstétrique des Anciens Hebreux.* Paris 1904 p.108
213. Sarsowsky, in his periodical *Hakedem,* Year 1, 1907, Part 1 p.23

certainly was not able to indicate the sex of the child at the moment of birth.

The birthstool, *diphros maieutikos,* was a necessary prerequisite for the midwife for every delivery, at least in Greece. Antyllus already mentions it[214]. Exact descriptions thereof are those of Soran[215] and Moschion[216]. A religious poem by Benjamin ben Serach (presumed to have lived in Southeastern Europe in the year 1058)[217] mentions that "the Hebrew letter *shin* has three stems, just like the birthstool or *kise ha-mashber*"[218]; he obviously is referring to the two armrests and the back support.

Delivering a baby on the birthstool is a relatively recent institution, and was probably first derived from the confinement on the lap of the husband or another woman. The latter method is still employed today by certain Asian peoples, and was earlier often utilized in Europe[219]. Soran[220] and Moschion also mention it: "If, because of poverty, a birthstool cannot be provided, then the woman should sit on the thigh of another woman, be firmly held there and give birth there"[221]. It was also customary among the ancient Teutons "to give birth on the husband's knees"[222].

In the Talmud, there is no trace of this method of delivery, but in the Bible it is demonstrable. When Rachel saw that she bore no children to Jacob, she gave her maid Bilhah to him as a mistress, so that *she shall bear upon my knees that I may also have children by her*[223]. The same source also states that the great-grandsons of Joseph *were born on his knees*[224].

It is, however, certain that, at least in the Bible, this confinement on the knees also has symbolic meaning, whereby the person on whose lap the confinement takes place has a claim to the newborn. Otherwise, Rachel would not have easily consented to serve as the birthstool for her handmaid, no more so than Sarah, who gave her maid to Abraham as a mistress[225]. The Aramaeans consider both Biblical citations to mean "raise" (or rear the children).

# XVII

In Egypt, although midwives were in attendance, the Israelite women delivered their babies more easily than the Egyptian women: *the Hebrew women are not like the Egyptian women; for they are lively and are delivered ere the midwives come in unto them*[226]. Accepting the validity of this report, many of the birth stories in the Bible and especially the much greater detail in the *Mishnah* and *Gemara* indicate that this was not due to a special racial characteristic of the Hebrews.

In general, if a girl is being born, labor pains are stronger and the labor more difficult than for a male birth. The reason is that each sex assumes the same position during birth as during intercourse, the male face downwards and the female face upwards. In a female birth, the girl must thus turn her face downwards in order to be born in the normal manner, thus intensifying the labor pains, whereas a male fetus need not effect such a turn[227]. It is possible that some people assume that this turning first takes place in the vaginal outlet when the fetus is already visible to the eye, as must have been presumed to be the case in the above-cited teaching of Rabbi Chanina

214. in Oribas. 10:19; ed. Daremberg 2:425
215. Chapt. 21 p.100, Ermerins
216. Chapt. 44 p.133, Dewitz
217. Zunz, *Literaturgeschichte der synagogische Poesie* p.121
218. Recited in the *yotzer* poetry on the Sabbath prior to Pentacost. Baer erroneously has *umashber*
219. Ploss. *Das Weib* 2:180
220. Chapt. 21
221. *De Mul Pass.* Chapt. 44. ed. Dewitz p.133
222. Höfler in Neuburger-Pagels *Handbuch der Geschichte der Medizin* 1:474
223. Genesis 30:3
224. *ibid* 50:23. Perhaps Job 3:11 should also be mentioned here. Compare Stade, *Zeitschift für alttestamentischen Wissenschaft* 1886 p.143-156
225. Genesis 16:2
226. Exod. 1:19
227. Niddah 31a

concerning the *obnayim*. Seventeenth-century German physicians still believed that the male is born with his face *ad podicem matris conversi* and the female *facie ad partes obscoenas*[228].

Normally, every birth is accompanied by bleeding, which is due to small or large tears of the birth passageways. Rarely, a "dry birth" or *leda yebeshta*[229], which is the *partus siccus* of the ancients, may occur. It is not clear from the Talmud where only ritual purifications are discussed, whether or not such an occurrence was considered to be dangerous for the woman.

*Oil* was utilized for every delivery, and it is permitted to procure it on the Sabbath for a woman in labor[230]. It was probably used by the midwife to lubricate the birth passageways, as was specifically prescribed by ancient obstetricians[231], and as is still in our times recommended by scientific obstetric practice.

## XVIII    The Placenta

The placenta is already mentioned in the Bible by the name *shilya*. In the warnings concerning starvation, the Bible states: *the tender and delicate woman among you, who would not adventure to set the sole of her foot upon the ground for delicateness and tenderness, her eye shall be evil against the husband of her bosom, and against her son, and against her daughter; and against her afterbirth (shilya) that cometh out from between her feet, and against her children whom she shall bear; for she shall eat them for want of all things secretly...*[232].

In the Talmud, Rabbi Simeon ben Gamliel compares the *shilya* to the craw (stomach) of a hen out of which the small bowels issue (the umbilical cord)[233]. The Rabbis compare its beginning, that is the umbilical cord, to a thread of the woof, and its end (or head[233a]), that is the placenta, to the flat form of lentils. In actuality, the roots of the umbilical cord look as if they were the placenta. The *shilya* is hollow like a trumpet[234]. A portrayal of this ancient trumpet is still preserved in Rome on the Arch of Triumph of Titus. It resembles our fanfare and has a very long and very thin blow pipe[235].

Maimonides understands the *shilya* to be the amniotic membrane, and considers the words "beginning" and "end" in the aforementioned Talmudic quote to refer to the stages of its development. This interpretation is impossible to understand[236].

Rarely, the placenta can be expelled twenty-three days after the birth of the child[237]. It also happens that part is expelled on one day and the remainder is not expelled until the next day[238].

There is no *shilya* without an accompanying baby. According to Rabbi Simeon, if such is found, it might represent a case where the fetus may have dissipated and become resorbed before the birth[239]. The other possibility is the presumption that the woman aborted a small fetus during defecation or during an episode of vaginal bleeding, without being aware of it, and is now apparently only expelling a placenta.

I do not know of any procedure which could accelerate the expulsion of a "hesitating" placenta. "One ties the navel and cuts it"[240]. Some Rabbis consider this

228. Joh. Eleri Ulyssei. *Philosophi Libellus de Partu.* Lunaeburg 1626, cited according to Osiander. *Lehrbuch der Geburtshilfe* Vol. 2 p.24
229. Kerithoth 10a
230. Shabbath 128b
231. for example, Soran. Chapt. 21 p.99
232. Deut. 28:56-57
233. *Tosefta* Niddah 4:9
233a. *ibid*
234. Niddah 26a

235. Description in Josephus' *Antiquities.* Book 3, Chapt. 12:6. A picture thereof is found in Benzinger & Frohnmeyer. *Bilderatlas zur Bibelkunde,* Stuttgart 1905 Fig. 386
236. Maimonides. *Hilchoth Issure Biyah* 10:13
237. Niddah 27a
238. Baba Kamma 11a
239. Niddah 3:4
240. *Tosefta* Shabbath 15:3

cutting to be prohibited on the Sabbath, and thus left the child attached to the umbilical cord and placenta until after the Sabbath[241]. If any serious consequence to either mother or child had ever been observed, there would certainly have been recorded an energetic objection against leaving the baby attached to the placenta until after the Sabbath. Such is not the case, however. Nevertheless, the former opinion, that it is permissible to cut the umbilical cord on the Sabbath immediately after birth, is codified as law[242].

Soran also considers the rule to be that after the birth the child remains attached to the placenta until the latter is expelled; only "if the placenta is still withheld, one has to doubly tie the umbilical cord"[243].

## XIX

According to the general national custom[244], the expelled placenta was brought out[245] and preserved in a bowl, perhaps a night pot[246], "so that the child becomes warmed". Princesses used to hide it in bowls with oil, wealthy women in wool fleeces, and poor women in oakum[247]. The *Tosefta* also states: one hides the placenta in bowls with oil, cushions (?), a straw basket and the like, so that the child does not become cold[248]. Finally, the Palestinian Talmud asserts that rich people preserved the placenta in oil, poor people in straw and sand; but all later preserved it in earth (i.e. buried it) to pledge to it[249] that the person who was attached to it will himself someday be preserved in the earth.

It was forbidden to bury the placenta at the crossroads, or to hang it from a tree, because this was considered to be a heathen superstitious custom[250]. It is noteworthy that this custom of placing the placenta on trees is still practiced today by many primitive races[251].

Nevertheless, such heathen customs, which are here and elsewhere[252] strongly prohibited, found their way into the folk medicine of the Jews even during the time of the Talmud. The placenta was then always referred to by the name *silyatha,* which is the Aramaic dialect which the people spoke at that time.

Abaye's nurse once told him: if a newborn infant does not cry or does not breathe, his afterbirth should be rubbed and he will cry (i.e. breathe easily)[253]. The same should be done for a newborn infant that is too thin, that is the placenta should be rubbed over him from the thin part of the infant to the thick part (i.e. from his feet to his trunk). If the infant is unnaturally fat, the rubbing should proceed in the opposite direction[254].

If one slaughters an animal and finds therein a placenta — if he is not fastidious — he may eat it, for as long as it is still in the animal, it is considered to be a part thereof. If the placenta had emerged, however, before the mother was slaughtered, it is forbidden to eat it. Rather, it should be thrown to the dogs or buried[255]. We learn from Ploss[256] that on the island of Java, even human placentas are eaten.

The placenta of a black cat was once used for a demonic exorcism[257].

## XX Maternity

In general, a woman who had just delivered a baby lay in bed. However, it also occurred that her poor husband had to go searching for a little straw: "for my wife is in

---

241. Shabbath 128b; Numbers Rabbah 4:3; *Tanchuma Bamidbar* 9b.
242. *Shulchan Aruch. Orach Chayim* 330:7
243. Soran. Chapt. 26 p.118
244. Numbers Rabbah 4:3
245. Niddah 27a
246. Niddah 9:2
247. Shabbath 129b
248. *Tosefta* Shabbath 15:3; also Numbers Rabbah 4:3

249. Jerushalmi Shabbath 18; 16c
250. Chullin 77a
251. Ploss. *Das Weib.* 2: 251
252. *Tosefta* Shabbath 7
253. Shabbath 134a
254. *ibid*
255. Chullin 4:7
256. *loc. cit.* p.248
257. Berachoth 6a

confinement, and I have nothing for her to lie on"[258]. In that case even people who slept on straw because of their poverty deprived themselves of their own "wealth".

The lying-in woman should be kept warm. If she felt cold, one prepared a fire for her on the Sabbath, even at the height of the summer[259]. Rabbi Yochanan decreed that one should provide her on the Sabbath with the same warm beverages (probably tea) that she was accustomed to drinking on weekdays[260].

The newly-delivered woman is ritually unclean. Biblical law states as follows: if a woman conceives and gives birth to a male child, she shall be unclean for seven days, just as she is unclean during the time of her menstruation. *And she shall continue in the blood of purification three and thirty days; she shall touch no hallowed thing, nor come into the sanctuary, until the days of her purification be fulfilled.* If she delivers a female child, she is unclean for two weeks, just as during her menstruation; she remains in the blood of purification for sixty-six days. After fulfillment of these days, she brings a lamb as a burnt offering and a young pigeon as a sin offering *unto the door of the tent of meeting,* unto the priest. If she is not wealthy enough to purchase a lamb, it is sufficient to bring two turtle doves or two young pigeons[261].

The uncleanliness of a woman in child-bed was also adopted by other peoples of antiquity, Arians as well as Semites. In Greece, a woman in child-bed did not enter the Temple for forty days. Even today, a large number of people consider a parturient woman to be unclean. In accordance with the aforementioned Biblical law, the Christian religion established February 2 as the "purification of Mary day". It is the fortieth day after December 25, the day of her confinement. The evangelist specifically declares — and for a Jewish woman of that epoch this was obvious — that Biblical law was observed in the purification of, and offering brought by, the newly-delivered woman[262].

We do not know why the period of uncleanness is longer following a female birth than that following a male birth. This opinion was also widely accepted by physicians in antiquity, as is already known from the pseudo-Hippocratic book *De Natura Pueri.* The author sets a time period of purification of forty-two days for a female birth and thirty days for a male birth[263]. It is not worth the effort here to repeat the immense number of hypotheses that have been proposed to explain this matter, and even less so in view of the fact that the meaning of "cleanness" or, as one usually translates it, "purification", in our Biblical citation is quite uncertain. In general, it is said that during the first seven days, the pure blood flows out; there then follows a more or less blood-colored fluor. It might be grammatically correct when the text speaks of the "blood *(dam)* of purification", but can we really accept the suggestion that women in those days normally bled, or even had a colorless discharge, for forty or eighty days, that is *nearly three months,* after a birth? The Bible is certainly speaking of the normal situation. Those women were closer to a primitive state than our modern women, and suckled their children themselves; should all of them have suffered from subinvolution of the uterus to explain the prolonged bleeding? The above Biblical observations are obviously based upon certain principles with which we are not familiar.

Among the Rabbis, Rab is of the opinion that both types of blood, the clean blood during the first seven or fourteen post-partum days, and the unclean blood during the subsequent thirty-three or sixty-six days for a male and female birth, respectively, emanate from the same source, and the Bible declares the one to be clean, the other unclean, without providing us with any apparent reason therefor. Another Sage is of

258. Nedarim 50a
259. Shabbath 129a
260. Jerushalmi Shabbath 9; 12a
261. Levit. 12:1-8
262. Luke 2:22
263. Ed. Foes. Vol. 3 p.239:29

the opinion that there are two sources, the one is opened only after the other closes[264].

The question as to why a new mother is obligated to bring a sin offering is naturally raised in the Talmud. Rabbi Simeon ben Yochai answers that when the woman kneels to give birth, she swears impetuously that she will never again have intercourse with her husband[265], and later she does not uphold her oath.

During the first seven or fourteen days post-partum, the woman is unclean "just like a menstruating woman", that is, she is not permitted to touch her husband nor anything hallowed. At the end of this time period, however, only the latter restriction remains. This practice, however, was soon changed. The Rabbis, as already mentioned[266], began to consider every menstruating woman as a *zaba*. They also required of every new mother that not only should the bloody discharges completely cease after the delivery, but in addition seven "clean days", that is completely blood-free days, had to elapse before marital intercourse was again permissible. Often, even if no colored discharge was present anymore, people waited a full seven plus thirty-three or fourteen plus sixty-six days[267] which, according to modern concepts of hygiene, conforms to the female body's needs. Catholic moralists, for the most part, consider copulation during the lying-in period to be permitted, *nisi ex concubitu gravis morbus vel notabilis aggravatio morbi immineat;* such would occur on the day of delivery or the following day[268].

Concerning the laws of the Sabbath, every newly-delivered woman during the first three days is considered to be dangerously ill, and, hence, one must desecrate the Sabbath for her, even if she herself feels very well. During the next seven days, one desecrates the Sabbath only if she says "I need it"; after that, all the general rules which apply to all sick people apply to her as well[269].

Before the thirtieth post-partum day, no woman should bathe in the bath, in order that she should not catch a cold, unless her husband is with her and the possibility exists that he can shortly thereafter warm her through cohabitation[270]. In order for the husband of a parturient woman to touch his wife, the ritual bath is a prerequisite.

## XXI   The Newborn

A normal newborn is one and a half cubits in length (*amma geduma,* also translated: a little less than a cubit)[271]. The signs of maturity are: hair and nails which are fully developed[272].

The infant emerges from the mother's womb dirty and besmirched, full of mucus and blood. Nevertheless, everyone embraces it and kisses it, particularly if it is a boy[273]. This high esteem in which a male infant is held is expressed in many places in the Talmud, and can also be shown to be so by nearly all peoples to this very day. The reason is that the male is more often (than the woman) engaged in business and, as a result, enjoys a higher social standing. Rabbi Amin states that when a male comes into the world, he holds his bread (i.e. provision) in his hand[274]. Legend describes a "town of males" called *Kfar Dichraya,* where all women bore only male offspring, and to which people who wished to have male children moved. People who desired to have a daughter moved away from that town[275].

---

264. Niddah 11a
265. Niddah 31b
266. See above chapter 2
267. *Yoreh Deah* 194:1; Maimonides considers this to be a Karaitic custom
268. Capellmann p.178
269. Shabbath 129a

270. *ibid*
271. Genesis Rabbah 12:6
272. Yebamoth 80b
273. *Pesikta de Rab Kahana* 9 p.77b
274. Niddah 31b
275. Lament. Rabbah 2:4 fol. 21c. In abbreviated form: Gittin 57a

A daughter, on the other hand, is an object which produces anxiety, as is gloomily depicted by Sirach: "a daughter is a secret cause of sleeplessness to her father; his concern for her robs him of his rest; in her youth, for fear she will pass her prime; and when she is married, for fear she will be hated; when she is a girl, for fear she will be profaned, and be with child in her father's house; when she has a husband, for fear she will transgress; and when she is married, for fear she will be childless"[276]. However, if the firstborn child is a daughter, it is a good sign for the boys, in that she aids her parents in rearing her brothers[277].

## XXII    Treatment of the Newborn

We learn certain details concerning the handling of a newborn in Biblical times from the portrayal of the prophet Ezekiel:... *in the day thou wast born thy navel was not cut, neither wast thou washed in water for cleansing; thou wast not salted at all, nor swaddled at all. No eye pitied thee, to do any of these unto thee, to have compassion upon thee; but thou wast cast out in the open field in the loathsomeness of thy person...*[278].

The Talmud deals with these matters when it discusses the laws of the Sabbath, and decrees that one should carry out all the measures mentioned in the above words of the prophet, which are in general necessary for the newborn infant[279]. These measures were evidently still in use and generally known, so that more details thereof are not mentioned, and we have to rely on the reports of the contemporary heathens.

In addition to the knife, Greek obstetricians also mention the use of shards, hard bread crusts, sharp stones and reed stems to cut the navel[280]. Some of these items are also mentioned in the Talmud as cutting instruments, but not necessarily for cutting the umbilical cord[281].

The "salting" was an indispensible part of the treatment of the newborn. Galen states it is for *symmetrois aloin peripattomenon;* so that the skin will become thicker and harder than the inner parts of the body[282]. Soran has a separate chapter entitled *peri alismou.* Since he is a specialist, his recommendations are complicated, and his measures sophisticated[283]. Moschion writes that the ancients used to wash the baby with saltwater and wine[284]. We specialists (!) carefully apply finely powdered salt and sodium carbonate on the baby[285]. This procedure is supposed to simultaneously cleanse and act as an astringent, so that the skin becomes hard and able to withstand rashes or *exanthemata*[285a]. The Arabs copy from Galen: *ut cutis dura fiat*[286]. Rashi gives the same explanation for the "salting". This procedure is absolutely not a religious ceremony.

Osiander presumes that the "salt" of the Biblical text refers to "*natrum subcarbonicum crudum, or soda nativa,* which to this day is excavated from the salt lakes in Egypt, and which is then used as a soap, when combined with fatty slime"[287]. Although this soda was well-known during Biblical times, it was called *nether,* meaning *nitrum,* whereas in our citation, the original text has the word *melach,* which usually refers to cooking salt.

Plutarch, in his *Leben des Lykurg,* relates that the lace-demons (?) used to wash their newborns with wine, in order to strengthen their healthy children[288]. This custom

276. Sirach 42: 9-10
277. Baba Bathra 141a
278. Ezekiel 16:4-5
279. Shabbath 129b
280. Soran. Chapt. 26 p.117; Oribas. 3:117
281. Chullin 1:2
282. *De Sanit. Tuend.* 1:7; Kühn 6:32; Oribas. 3:118
283. Soran. Chapt. 27 p.120

284. Moschion Chapt. 66
285. *Aphronitron. Natr. Carb. Depur;* see Puschmann, *Alexander of Tralles* 1:308
285a. Soran. Chapt. 27 p.120
286. Avicenna. Book 1, fen. 2, doctr. 1, chapt. 1
287. Osiander. *Handbuch der Entbindungskunst.* Tübingen 1820, 2:213, notes
288. Ed Reiske Vol. 1 p.197

was also practiced by Jewish mothers during the time of the Talmud. They also bathed their children in wine, and not only for health reasons[289].

After the salting, the child is "wrapped in wrappings". This bad habit, which even today is in general widely practiced, is supposed to have the effect of making the child's limbs become and remain straight. The Greeks also wrote special chapters concerning this *sparganosis* (wrapping of the baby)[290]. It is also known as *lafaf* in the Talmud[291]. One can obtain a mental image of the horrifying nature of this "wrapping" when one reads how Antigenes prescribed that the newborn be tied to a board equipped with rings (or hooks). The ostensibly considerate method of Soran is not much more humane[292]. The Aramaeans state the actuality of the situation when they translate the Hebrew word *chathulla* for the baby's binder with the word *isurin* meaning shackles[293]. It is a regular bandaging of every part of the body, for which Soran and Moschion[294] provide detailed instructions.

A preliminary act or act performed simultaneously with the binding was the "adjusting of the limbs". The feet and other individual limbs were so arranged that that which should be curved was compressed, and that which should be straight was stretched. Finally, the entire body was supposed to be stretched and relaxed[295].

The form of the head was also part of the "adjustment". Moschion requires that the head be made round, *stroggulen poiesai*. Hippocrates asserts that the midwives of Asiatic peoples made the heads of newborns long through binding and other appropriate methods: *longissima enim habentes capita generosissimos existimantur*[296]. This practice of midwives is also mentioned in the Talmud. Hillel answered the question "Why are the heads of the Babylonians round?" by saying, "because they have no skillful midwives"[297] who could stretch the heads.

Part of the swaddling procedure was apparently first carried out when the child was already a few days old. Thus, the Talmud uses the expression *katan,* rather than *velad* or *tinok,* which are the usual expressions for the newly-born infant. Also, the performance of this procedure is prohibited on the Sabbath, in contrast to the other acts such as salting or washing, which are permitted. It is stated in the Talmud that this *me'atzbin*[298], which is prohibited on the Sabbath, refers to *chumre de shedra* or manipulation of the spinal column[299]. Soran describes that this pleasant procedure is performed so that the child's ankles are held fast, so that the head hangs down in order for the vertebrae to stretch, so that the spinal column becomes flexible: *diatasin tous spondylous kai aukampe ten rachin apoteleisthai*[300].

An *asube januka* serves the purpose of "causing a newborn to vomit"[301]. This was obviously done to fulfill the requirement of ancient obstetrics that the mouth of a newborn be cleansed to rid it of the mucus.

The Talmud states[302] that, according to Abaye's mother, a child that doesn't breathe[303] should be moved to-and-fro[304]. If the infant does not cry, it should be rubbed with its own placenta. Wunderbar surmises that, in this manner, if the child was still attached to the placenta, one was able to lead more placental blood to the baby to revive it[305].

289. *Tosefta* Shabbath 12:13
290. Soran. Chapt. 28 p.123ff
291. Shabbath 147b
292. Soran. *loc. cit.*
293. *Targum* on Ezekiel 16:4
294. Moschion. Chapt. 91
295. *ibid*
296. *De Aere et Locis.* ed. Foes 3:289
297. Shabbath 31a
298. Straightening the limbs by manipulation: Shabbath 22:6
299. but other swaddling is permitted even on the Sabbath. Shabbath 147b

300. Soran. Chapt. 34 p.156
301. Shabbath 123a
302. Shabbath 134a
303. *Rashi:* gives no sign of life; *Aruch* interprets "that does not urinate"; supported by the textual reading reported by Levy (*Neuhebräisches und Chaldäisches Wörterbuch.* Leipzig 1876-1889) to be *velinashtin maja*
304. *Rashi:* one should place the fan one level above the child and fan him
305. Wunderbar. *Biblisch-Talmudische Medizin* 1:3:52

In the town of Gabath Shammai, it was customary to smear the head of newborns with a dough made of unripe grapes *(adamdemane),* so that insects should not bite it[306]. I am not familiar with any non-Jewish source that refers to this custom. In Jerusalem, a rooster was once stoned because it picked out the brains of a newborn infant, thinking that the pulsating fontanel was a moving insect[307]. The statement of Rabbi Simeon ben Eleazar concerning the worthlessness of human beings is more poetic than true: "an infant, even only one day old, need not be guarded from snakes and weasels to prevent them from picking out his eyes; a lion sees him and flees — so great is the power of the living. However, when a person dies, then his corpse must be guarded from weasels and mice, even if it is the corpse of Og, King of Bashan[308], because animals have no fear of the dead"[309].

Legend relates that under Egyptian bondage, when the time to deliver the baby was at hand, a woman would go out into the field and deliver that child under an apple tree. God would then send someone, an angel from heaven above, who cleansed and manipulated the child, in the manner of the midwife[310], and who cut his navel, bathed him and anointed him[311]; or the mother herself would cut the navel with a sharp stone[312].

The child used to be in a small bed or *arisa* in which it was rocked *(nidned)*[313]. At night, however, it would not sleep in its own bed, but would sleep with its mother. The small bed was quite low so that it was possible for a person to inadvertently sit on it and crush the baby[314].

## XXIII    Lactation and Suckling

As soon as a woman becomes pregnant, her blood (the menses) becomes muddy and turns to milk[315]. According to the opinion of many Sages, this milk formation first begins during the third month of pregnancy[316]. During lactation, the menstrual blood flow ceases because of the milk formation[317]. Milk drips from the breasts of some women while they perform household tasks[318]. If the child does not suck forcefully, then drops of milk may remain on the nipple[319].

This teaching that the menstrual blood rises to the breasts and is there converted to milk was preached throughout all of antiquity. Aristotle already mentions it: *eis tous mastous trepetai kai ginetai gala* (it goes to the breasts and becomes milk)[320]. It is also found in the works of Moschion[321] and Galen[322], and in great detail in Arabic writings. Ali Ibn Abbas writes that until birth the infant is nourished from menstrual blood. After birth, it requires a nourishment which corresponds as much as possible to the menstrual blood, i.e. milk, for milk is produced from menstrual blood[323]. Avicenna states that there is a direct venous connection between the uterus and the mammary gland[324]. Some primitive peoples think that there is an even more intimate connection between the breast and the uterus, and for this reason forbid a woman suckling a baby to have sexual intercourse, because they believe that the baby might imbibe sperm together with the milk[325].

306. Genesis Rabbah 34:15
307. Jerushalmi Erubin 10; 26a
308. Deut. 3:11
309. *Tosefta* Shabbath 17:19; Shabbath 151b; Genesis Rabbah 34:12
310. Sotah 11b
311. Exodus Rabbah 23:8
312. Levit. Rabbah 5:1; Midrash Psalms 8:5
313. Genesis Rabbah 53:10
314. Jerushalmi Makkoth 2; 31c
315. Niddah 9a
316. Jerushalmi Sotah 4; 19c; Kethuboth 60b
317. Jerushalmi Niddah 1; 49b; *Tosefta* Niddah 2:1

318. Kelim 8:11
319. Kerithoth 13a
320. *Hist. Anim.* 7:3:21
321. Moschion. Chapt. 12: the *katharsis* (cleansing) is the nourishment of the fetus in utero
322. *De Sanit. Tuend.* Vol. 1 Chapt. 8. Kühn 6:36; *ex aimatos e tou galaktos genesis* (the formation of milk from blood)
323. *Trois Traités d'Anatomie Arabes.* Ed. Koning. Leiden 1903 p.419
324. *ibid* p.640
325. Ellis. *Gattenwahl* p.31a

For the suckling babe, the breast is of prime importance, everything else being secondary; he can suckle all day with impunity[326]. He must suckle every hour of the day. So, too, Israel must always occupy itself with God's teachings[327]. The night has three "watches"; during the third watch, towards morning, the child suckles from the breast of his mother[328]. Naturally, there is nothing indecent about this sucking at the mother's breast[329]. If one of two twins stops sucking, so does the other, and the breast runs dry[330].

It is considered to be the norm for the newborn to be placed at the mother's breast immediately after birth, but in any event before 24 hours have elapsed, even if the navel has not yet been cut, the reason being that a delay in easing the mother of her milk might constitute a danger to the mother[331]. Soran allows the newborn to go hungry for two days, and then to be suckled by a wet nurse. If a wet nurse is unavailable, the baby is given honey water, possibly enriched with goat's milk. The child is not given the mother's breast until the twentieth day of life and onwards, because earlier the milk is not suitable[332]. Moschion is of a similar opinion[333].

In general, a woman suckles a babe for twenty-four months. If she suckles it longer, it is as (harmful?) as if the child sucks on excrements, so says Rabbi Eliezer. According to Rabbi Joshua, the time for suckling is unlimited, even up to five years[334]. A suckling period of three years is mentioned in the Book of Maccabees[335]. The disciples of Hillel consider eighteen months to be the normal suckling[336].

Moschion cites one and a half to two years to be the normal suckling period. The latter period was also the customary one in Greece, as evidenced by the yet to be discussed Alexandrian wet nurse contracts. In ancient Babylon and Egypt, three years seems to have been the normal period[337]. The law of Confucius also has a three-year time period for the suckling of infants[338]. From a remark in the story of Hannah[339], Schubart incorrectly concludes that the period of suckling of babes by the Jews in Biblical times was three years[340]. The Prussian code decrees that "a mother is obligated to suckle her own baby herself. The duration of suckling is dependent upon the stipulation of the father. However, if the health of the mother or the child would suffer as a result of his stipulation, he should submit to the advice of experts"[341].

These regulations had great practical significance. If the husband of a woman who is suckling a baby dies, she is not allowed to remarry until 24 months or 18 months have elapsed, for fear that she become pregnant again, and, thereby, stop the production of breast milk. To be sure, this possibility of pregnancy exists in any suckling woman who cohabits even with her own husband. Even in such a case, the real father would "provide money for eggs and milk, in order to sustain the child who would be deprived of its mother's milk". A stepfather, on the other hand, might not provide for the sustenance of the child in this situation[342]. If someone marries a widowed or divorced pregnant or suckling woman, then the admonishment of the epigrammatic writer[343] is infringed upon: remove not the ancient landmark (legal title), and enter not into the fields of the fatherless[344].

In order to prevent a pregnancy in a woman who is suckling a baby, lest the baby

326. Tosefta Sotah 4:3
327. Jerushalmi Berachoth 9; 14d
328. Berachoth 3a
329. Numbers Rabbah 4:20
330. Song of Songs Rabbah 4:5:2
331. Shabbath 135a
332. Soran. Chapt. 29 p.130
333. Moschion. Chapt. 73 and 94
334. Tosefta Niddah 2:3
335. Second Maccabees 7:27
336. Kethuboth 60b

337. Schubart. Die Amme im Alten Alexandrien. Jahrbuch für Kinderheilkunde 1909 p.93 Vol. 70 Part 1
338. Mayet. Mediz. Reform 1905 p.414
339. First Samuel 1:23. She offered three animals, not a three-year-old animal
340. loc. cit. p.84
341. Thema 2, title 2 No. 67-69
342. Yebamoth 42b
343. Proverbs 23:10
344. Tosefta Niddah 2:7

starve to death, some Sages recommend the use of an absorbent tampon during cohabitation. Rabbi Meir even advises the use of *coitus interruptus* during the twenty-four months of suckling[345]. According to Rabbi Simeon ben Gamliel, the marriage may already take place three months before the end of the period of suckling, since milk does not become bad in less time than three months[346]. The modern popular belief that lactation exerts a contraceptive effect was apparently not subscribed to in antiquity, although it is explicitly stated about the wife of the prophet Hosea that: *when she had weaned her daughter, she conceived and bore a son*[347]. The Prussian code, in a separate paragraph, gives a married woman who is suckling a babe the right to refuse cohabitation[348]. The Catholic moralists allow her to cohabit as usual during lactation[349].

If one has already weaned a child, according to the opinion of Rabbi Joshua, one should not again allow it to suckle; provided that it was weaned when it was completely healthy. If it occurred during an illness, however, the child may again be suckled[350].

# XXIV

Suckling of an infant was the mother's *obligation*[351]. It was questionable whether a vow of the woman not to suckle her own child had any validity. The school of Shammai, which urges the literal fulfillment of the Biblical phrase: *he shall do according to all that proceedeth out of his mouth*[352], is of the opinion that the woman must withhold her breast from the baby. On the other hand, the school of Hillel considers such a vow to be totally invalid, and forces the woman to continue to suckle her baby. If the woman becomes divorced from her husband, this coercion ceases; however, if the infant knows the mother and refuses to suckle from the breast of a wet nurse, then the mother must continue to suckle the child; otherwise, the child would be in danger. The husband, however, must then pay for the suckling[353].

The intelligence of the child determines the age at which he can differentiate the mother from a stranger; some infants already refuse a strange breast at thirty days of age, others at fifty days of age, yet others not until three months of age.

An infant that already knows its mother may not be given to another woman to suckle because of danger to the baby's life[354]. It is not clear from the Talmudic sources whether the danger is related to the change in milk or to the child's refusal to suckle from a strange breast. A blind infant recognizes its mother's breast by the smell and the taste[355].

Mar Bar Rav Ashi wanted to prohibit a widow from remarrying before 24 months had elapsed, even if her suckling babe had died, because a woman once killed her baby in order to be able to remarry. It was rejoined that that woman was undoubtedly mentally ill, since a sane woman would not strangle her own child, and laws are only made for sane people[356].

No man can coerce his wife to also suckle the child of his friend, and no man needs to tolerate his wife suckling the baby of her friend[357]. If a woman has twins, she cannot be forced to suckle both children; rather, she suckles one child herself, and a wet-nurse is hired to suckle the other one[358].

345. *ibid* 2:6
346. *ibid* 2:2
347. Hosea 1:8
348. *loc. cit.* No. 180
349. Capellmann p.180
350. Jerushalmi Niddah 1; 49b
351. Kethuboth 5:5

352. Numbers 30:3
353. *Tosefta* Kethuboth 5:5
354. *Tosefta* Niddah 2:5
355. Kethuboth 60a
356. *ibid* 60b
357. *Tosefta* Kethuboth 5:5
358. Jerushalmi Kethuboth 5; 39a

According to the opinion of Rabbi Meir, if a woman suckles her baby in the street, the husband should divorce her, because such is shameful behavior[359].

If the woman herself wishes to suckle the baby, but the husband refuses to grant permission therefor, then the wishes of the mother prevail, because she suffers the pain[360], either from the suckling itself (through cracking of the nipple, back pain, etc.) or from congestion of milk, due to the lack of suckling, or from the separation from her baby ...In the reverse case, that is if the *woman refuses* to suckle, the usual practice of the family from which the mother is derived is followed. These laws are naturally only applicable to those women in whom the possibility of suckling their children exists.

In those days, there must already have existed women in whom the suckling of their own children would have been considered to be a "denigration" of their position. These women must have totally disregarded the natural feelings of a mother's heart, as the Bible depicts and as the Talmud states: "more than the calf wishes to suck does the cow desire to suckle"[361]. The mother who refuses her breast to her suckling babe is — even if she is near death from hunger — considered cruel, and she, "the daughter of my people", is guilty of a heinous act: *even the jackals draw out the breast, they give suck to their young ones; the daughter of my people is become cruel, like the ostriches in the wilderness. The tongue of the sucking child cleaveth to the roof of his mouth for thirst, the young children ask bread, and none breaketh it unto them*[362]. We do not know why there was a wet-nurse in the royal family of King Ahaziah[363], nor why Rebekah had one called Deborah[364].

In antiquity, there also certainly existed women who were incapable of nursing their babies. The men of the priestly watches fasted every Thursday for nursing mothers, so that they should be able to suckle their infants. Perhaps, the aforementioned were only undesirous, but not incapable, of nursing.

Catholic moral theologians also require mothers to suckle their infants. However, the mother is excused not only because of *etwaiger necessitas* or *notabilis utilitas,* but also because of a *consuetudo apud familias nobiles vigens*[365].

On his deathbed, Jacob blessed his son Joseph with: *blessings of the breasts and of the womb*[366], which, according to the *Midrash,* refers to the love of the wife of his heart i.e. Rachel: "blessed be the breasts that suckled thee, and the womb which gave birth to thee"[367].

The mother of the seven martyred sons whom Antiochus put to death admonished her youngest son to be steadfast when confronted with the executioner: "my son, have pity on me, who carried you nine months in the womb, and nursed you for three years"[368]. A certain woman called out to Jesus: *blessed is the womb that bore thee, and the breasts which thou has sucked*[369]! On the other hand, breasts which suckled a villain were cursed[370].

## XXV   Wet-Nurses

If the mother could not, or did not want to, nurse her own baby, then another woman substituted for her. If a father had a son, he gave him to a maid servant that she suckle him; if he had no servants, then he provided a wet-nurse for the baby. How

---

359. Gittin 89a
360. Kethuboth 61a
361. Pesachim 112a
362. Lamentations 4:3
363. Second Kings 11:2
364. Genesis 24:59

365. Capellmann p.57
366. Genesis 49:25
367. Genesis Rabbah 98:20
368. Second Maccabees 7:27
369. Luke 11:27
370. Jerushalmi Kilayim 1; 27b

long does the latter suckle him? For two or three years. With God, however, it is not so: *even to old age, I am the same, and even to hoar hairs will I carry you*[371].

A wet-nurse is ordinarily engaged for two years. During this time, she may not accept any other employment, nor nurse another child[372], not even her own[373]. According to the "humane" law of Hammurabi, in such a case, the breast of the wet-nurse would be cut off. Conventional punishments are provided for in the Alexandrian wet-nurse contracts, which were ordinarily written for a two-year duration[374].

There is great controversy among the Sages concerning the permissibility of using heathen wet-nurses. Their opinions were probably arrived at on the basis of the circumstances of the time and place. The *Tosefta* allows this practice unconditionally[375]. Although it was usual to give the child to the wet-nurse in her own house, the *Mishnah* requires that the heathen wet-nurse suckle the baby in the domain (house) of the baby's father[376], for safety's sake. According to Rabbi Meir, no amount of watching is sufficient to prevent her from harming the baby; for the wet-nurse may, unnoticed, rub some poison on her breast beforehand, and thus kill the baby[377]. The Palestinians, who apparently lived in a less hostile environment, had none of these fears. In fact, in the suckling of their children by heathen wet-nurses, they saw the fulfillment of the prophetic vision of Isaiah: *and Kings shall be thy foster fathers, and their Queens thy nursing mothers*[378].

Gellius reports[379] that in Rome, wet-nurses *externae atque barbarae nationis* were preferentially employed. The reason is probably the same as to why the urban woman of our times preferentially seek out "rural" wet-nurses, because the latter were thought to have natural strength, as opposed to the effeminate condition of the urban women. In any case, this reason only played a minor role for the Jewish women of Talmudic times.

Just as in Alexandria[379a], both single girls as well as married women were hired as wet-nurses[379b]. Legend relates that when Pharaoh's daughter found Moses, she had him carried to all the Egyptian women, but he would not suck from any of their breasts. "Shall a mouth which will once speak with God suck that which is unclean"![380] According to Josephus, the refusal of Moses to suck was motivated by the fact that the wet-nurses were not of the same race as he[381].

Rabbi Achai said: he who buys grain in the market can be compared to a suckling babe whose mother has died, and who is then taken to other nursing mothers but is not satisfied. However, a person who eats of his own produce can be compared to a suckling babe who was reared at his own mother's breast[382].

Wet-nurses often occupied a position of prominence in the families in which they served. Thus, the Bible describes the death of Deborah, the wet-nurse of Rebekah, as that of an important personality[383]. On the other hand, the wet-nurse is always anxious and afraid, even while the little darling sleeps peacefully in his cot, because she knows that for any disturbance of his condition, she will be held responsible[384]. A grandchild of Hiram is said to have been killed by the four sons of his wet-nurse[385]. In ancient Egypt, even after the nursing, a wet-nurse was regularly incorporated into the royal household[386].

371. Deut. Rabbah 7:12 on Isaiah 46:4
372. *Tosefta* Niddah 2:4
373. Kethuboth 60b
374. Schubart *loc. cit.* p.84,91,93,89
375. *Tosefta* Niddah 2:5
376. Abodah Zarah 2:1
377. Abodah Zarah 26a
378. Jerushalmi Abodah Zarah 2; 40c on Isaiah 49:23
379. Gellins 12:1

379a. See above n.374
379b. Abodah Zarah 26a
380. Sotah 12b
381. *Antiquities.* Book 2, Chapt. 9:5
382. Aboth de Rabbi Nathan 31:1
383. Genesis 35:8
384. Genesis Rabbah 2:2
385. Josephus. *Against Apion* 1:18
386. Schubart p.83

As long as a woman nurses, she is required to work less, and she is fed more[387]. If she enters into an agreement whereby she is only to receive a small allowance for food, then she must still eat well but pay for it out of her own means[388]. Later judicial Sages, however, ruled that such an agreement is legally invalid; and they obligate the father of the child to provide the wet-nurse with additional expenditures for food[389].

What "additional sustenance" should one provide for her? According to Rabbi Joshua ben Levi, wine, which increases the mother's milk[390], or which is at least "good for the milk"[391]. A nursing woman must not eat things which are injurious to the milk, such as hops, *chaziz* (green vegetables), small fishes, and earth; according to Abaye, even pumpkins and quinces (*chabusha,* perhaps a type of apple); according to Rabbi Papa even a gourd and unripe dates; according to Rabbi Ashi, even *kamak* (curdled milk) and fish-hash. Some of these cause the flow of the milk to stop, while others cause the milk to become turbid[392]. This is probably what the Greek-Egyptian wet-nurse contracts have in mind when they speak of "pure, unadulterated milk", which the wet-nurse is supposed to provide from her breasts to the suckling babe.

Even nursing women are not exempt from the legally enacted fast days[393]. No harm has ever been done to either the mother or the infant.

## XXVI    Nursing From an Animal or Bottle

I know of no mention in the Talmud of artificial feeding of suckling infants. We hear often of the nursing of an infant by an animal. In most cases, it is decided that the child can even suckle from an unclean beast, i.e. one that is prohibited to be eaten. Most often, the donkey and the camel are the animals referred to. According to Rabbi Huna, every child's life would be in danger if he were deprived of milk. It is quite certain that the Talmud refers to direct sucking from the animal's teats, and not to the use of animal milk from a utensil. Even adults suck milk directly from the udder[394]. Throughout antiquity, those who were ill with breast sicknesses benefited most in this matter, from the highly esteemed "warm animal" milk[395].

To be sure, women also milked the milk from their breasts into a glass or a bowl, and thus nourished their children, but this was considered nothing more than frivolous play[396]; one also gave the baby milk to drink from an animal horn[397]. If a woman had to stop nursing because she became pregnant again, the father would buy milk and eggs for the sustenance of the child[398]. However, in the latter case, the baby was probably no longer a newborn, even if one were to assume, as reported by Oribasius, that the Alexandrian teaching of exclusively nourishing infants with milk during their first two years of life and only then introducing a mixture of other foods, was ever put into practice[399].

Nursing of humans on the breasts of animals is already mentioned in Roman and Greek mythology; the former in the fable of Romulus and Remus, who were suckled by a she-wolf, the latter in the story of the goat of Amalthea who was the wet nurse of Zeus. Ploss correctly sees in these fables a portrayal of the real situation as it occurred in Italian pastoral populations[400].

It remains undecided whether or not the vessels portrayed by Sambon in his collection of ancient Roman Temple oblations as sucklings' bottles[401] were actually used for newborns.

---

387. Kethuboth 5:9
388. Kethuboth 60b
389. *Be'er Hetev* on *Eben Ha'ezer* 80:11
390. Jerushalmi Kethuboth 5; 30b
391. Kethuboth 65b
392. Kethuboth 60b
393. Taanith 14a
394. Yebamoth 114a

395. *Tosefta* Baba Kamma 8:13
396. *Tosefta* Shabbath 9:22
397. *ibid* 13:16
398. Yebamoth 42b
399. Oribasius. *Synops.* Book 5:5 Vol. 5:202
400. *Das Weib* 2:429
401. *British Medical Journal* 1895, Vol. 2
        p.147 and 216

Aristotle already observed lactation from the mammary glands of men[402]. Albrecht V. Haller collected many similar cases[403], in which not only serum, but real milk was expressed from the breasts of males. The Talmud also mentions an example thereof: it once happened that a man's wife died and left a child to be suckled. He could not afford to pay a wet nurse — giving a bottle was as yet unknown — whereupon a miracle occurred to him and his teats opened like the two teats of a woman, and he suckled his infant himself. This case is expressly denoted to represent a "change in nature"[404].

Rabbi Abbahu, in a discourse, explained the Biblical phrase: *And Mordecai was the omen of Esther*[405] to mean that Mordecai suckled Esther; perhaps he had in mind the fact that in ancient Egypt, the one who raised the prince was given the title "wet nurse"[406]. The congregation laughed at Rabbi Abbahu for his interpretation[406a], although the *Mishnah* already speaks of the "milk of a male"[407]. As a legal code, the *Mishnah* considers even the rarest case, as long as it enters the realm of possibility. Furthermore, the commentator Rabbi Simson notes that the milk of a male in the *Mishnah* is not equated with the milk of a female, but is considered to represent an exudation from the body of the male. Accordingly, another *Midrash* is of the opinion that the *wife* of Mordecai suckled Esther, and that he himself was only the male nurse[408].

During Biblical times, at least during the time of the Bedouins, a feast was made to celebrate the weaning of an infant[409]. We do not know how later generations conducted themselves in regard to this feast. The interpretation of the Biblical story of the weaning feast for Isaac, as described in the Talmud[410], supports the contention that its usage was no longer customary in Talmudic times.

# PART II
# PATHOLOGY

## I   Sterility

The Prussian law code has the following rule among its marriage regulations: "the main reason for marriage is the procreation and rearing of children"[411], corresponding to the definition of the Roman law: *matrimonium est societas liberorum procreandorum et educandorum causa*. Such a phrase, or at least the essence thereof, is also found in Jewish marriage laws: every person is obligated to take a wife, in order to fulfill the Biblical commandment *be fruitful and multiply*[412]. That which emanates from the state laws as a *raison* of the state, is, in fact, an expression of the Divine will, and represents a moral obligation. He who does not engage in the propagation of the race is as though he sheds blood[413]. For only two purposes may one sell a Torah scroll: to obtain means with which to study the Torah, and in order to be able to marry a wife[414].

---

402. *Histor. Anim.* Book 3 Chapt. 20 No. 102
403. *Elem. Phys.* Vol. 7, Book 28, Sect. 1 No. 13 p.18
404. Shabbath 53b
405. Esther 2:7
406. Schubart p.83
406a. Genesis Rabbah 30:8
407. Machshirin 6:7

408. Midrash Psalms 22:23 p.96b
409. Genesis 21:8
410. Pesachim 119b
411. *Allgemeines Landrecht.* Thome 2 title 1 No. 1. Hinschius
412. *Eben Ha'ezer* 1:1
413. Yebamoth 63b
414. Megillah 27a

Theoreticians may take issue with this prosaic definition of the purpose of marriage; the law of the state can have no other decisive purpose than the preservation of the race. Therefore, a person correctly sang a hymn at a wedding with the following refrain: "Alas for us that we are to die"[415]! We marry because we are mortal. Nevertheless, the Talmud describes a large number of regulations concerning the contracting of marriage and the reasons for marriage which, according to the modern concept of moral laws, might be considered to be "good advice", in spite of the fact that they actually represent Divine commandments. For whereas modern lawmakers can or should only decree such laws whose fulfillment can be enforced, the Talmud, as a religious code, also deals with transcendental matters, and hence can also contain laws whose transgression might be punished by God, and not by a human court.

If the purpose of marriage is the rearing of children, then a childless marriage has failed to fulfill its purpose. Despondent, the childless Rachel calls out to her husband: *give me children, or else I die*[416]. Four types of people are accounted as dead: a poor man, a blind man, a leper, and one who is childless[417]. According to the law of the *Mishnah*[418], a man who lives with his wife for ten years, and she is childless, should pay her the prescribed widow's jointure and divorce her, or take an additional fertile wife. The first wife after the divorce is, however, permitted to marry another man and to live with him for ten years, even if she had as yet no children from the latter, because it is possible that she was only unable to have children from the first husband. Thus, Sarah only bore no children to "Abraham"[419], but she did bear children to another husband[420]. If the woman aborts, the ten years are computed from the time of the abortion. If the husband or the wife is ill, or if both are in captivity, this time does not count.

It is uncertain whether or not a man who refuses to fulfill the commandment of procreation is coerced by the authorities to do so[421]. According to Rab, the ten-year waiting period only applies to earlier generations who lived many years. With respect to the later generations whose years of life are few, the waiting period is much shorter[422]. Thus, contrary to Catholic teaching, Jewish marriage laws in general require of the marriage partners not only *potestas coeundi* but also *facultas generandi*.

Children are a blessing from God, and are dependent upon His will. Three keys are in the hand of the Holy One, blessed be He, and are not entrusted to the hand of any messenger: the key of childbirth, the key of the revival of the dead and the key of rain[423]. In the agricultural country of Palestine, the material existence of the inhabitants is dependent upon the latter. In a very rare exception, an especially pious person, such as the prophet Elisha[424], is entrusted to be such a messenger[425].

Sarah said that *the Lord hath restrained me from bearing*[426]; therefore, there is no purpose in people telling me: "you must have an amulet *(kemiya)*, you must wear a charm (*himos* meaning *haematis* or blood stone)"[427]! Only on the tree of the future, the prophet announces, the *leaf will be for healing*[428], to loosen the mouth of the dumb and the mouth of the womb of barren women[429]. Both are considered to be closed by spasms. The *Aggadah* states that our ancestors mostly lived in barren marriages because the Holy One, blessed be He, longs for the prayers of the righteous[430]. An

---

415. Berachoth 31a
416. Genesis 30:1
417. Nedarim 64b
418. Yebamoth 6:6
419. Genesis 16:1
420. Genesis Rabbah 45:1
421. Kethuboth 77a
422. Yebamoth 64b i.e. two and a half years

423. Taanith 2a
424. Second Kings 4:16
425. Midrash Psalms 78:21
426. Genesis 16:2
427. Genesis Rabbah 45:2
428. Ezekiel 47:12
429. Menachoth 98a
430. Yebamoth 64a

extension of this thought concerning the Divine blessing of a large family is the statement of the *Midrash* which considers part of the happiness of Paradise to be the fact that a woman will there give birth to a child every day[431]. Laws against infanticide and child abandonment do not exist in Judaism.

## II  Oral Contraception

A woman who remains unmarried for ten years after the death of her husband and then remarries, bears no more children, unless she had the intention of remarrying all along. Exceptions, however, do occur[432].

A woman "who is not suited to bear children" is distinguished from an *akara* or barren woman. The former category also includes the woman with malformation or inadequate development of the genitalia, the *aylonith,* whom we have discussed before[433].

Whereas a man is prohibited from imbibing the "cup of roots" in order not to procreate, this temporary sterilizing medication is permitted to a woman so that she not conceive[434]; for the *obligation* of procreation is only incumbent upon the man; for in all of nature, the male is the more aggressive partner, and thus the obligation rests upon him, irrespective of the fact that otherwise the danger of encouraging prostitution would be real. On the other hand, the law cannot mean that for a *married woman* artificial sterility is sanctioned; for, as Rabbi Yochanan ben Baroka points out in the *Mishnah*[435]: *And God blessed them both and He said to them, Be fruitful and increase*[436]. Only where pregnancy would constitute a danger to the life of the mother or the life of her suckling infant through the milk drying up is the woman permitted to use a *mukh* (sponge, diaphragm?) during coitus[437]. In an actual case, Judith, the wife of Rabbi Chiya having suffered agonizing pains during childbirth, drank a sterilizing potion called *samma di'akartha,* without her husband's knowledge. When her husband learned of it, he was strongly upset[438]. In post-Talmudic times, this law was made considerably more restrictive.

We have already discussed the ingredients and preparation of this "cup of roots"[439]. There probably existed several varieties.

According to the *Aggadah,* it is this type of sterilizing potion that Er gave Tamar[440] in order to preserve her beauty by not disfiguring her through a pregnancy[441]. This is also what the men of the generation of the flood did: each took two wives, one to bear children, the other for sexual gratification. The former was neglected like a widow throughout her life, while the latter was given to drink the potion of roots, so that she should not bear, and then she sat before him made up like a harlot[442]. Er was killed by God, and the men of the generation of the flood perished in the flood. The intent of these stories is easily recognizable. They are a protest against the morals or immorality of maintaining a concubine in addition to the *walide* (*walad* equals *yalad* meaning to bear children), a practice still in vogue today among Oriental royal households, even though today the *walide* might be the more influential and more esteemed of the two women.

Barrenness of a marriage may also be due to the infertility of the husband. The Bible promised: *there shall not be male or female barren among you*[443]. According to legend, Manoah and Hannah disagreed among themselves as to who was the infertile

---

431. Kallah Rabbathi 2;52b 14
432. Yebamoth 34b
433. Chapter 5 above
434. *Tosefta* Yebamoth 8:4
435. Yebamoth 6:6
436. Genesis 1:28
437. *Tosefta* Niddah 2:6

438. Yebamoth 65b
439. Chapter 13, section 4
440. Genesis 38:7
441. Yebamoth 34b
442. Genesis Rabbah 23:2
443. Deut. 7:14

partner of their childless marriage[444]. Rabbi Acha bar Jacob stated that many scholars became impotent because of the long discourses of Rabbi Huna[445].

Contrary to the analogous regulation concerning a woman, sterility of the husband is not a reason for divorce. Considering the whole attitude towards a man in the Orient, one would not have expected otherwise. Thus, Isaac, who married at forty years of age, impatiently looked forward to heirs for twenty years, because he was infertile[446].

Specific discussions concerning castrates are found elsewhere in this book[447].

## III    Abortion

Most women carry their babies until the end of the pregnancy; a minority aborts. An equal number of male and female fetuses are aborted[448].

Among the causes of spontaneous abortion, the following are mentioned: a fright sustained by the woman when a mad dog jumps on her[449], the strong aroma of a large amount of burnt meat[450], and the blowing of the south wind[451]. The latter is considered to constitute a danger in this regard. Only a scoundrel throws cut-off fingernails or toenails into a public thoroughfare, because a pregnant woman stepping over them might miscarry because of the fright! A considerate person burns them or buries them[452]. In the vicinity of Jericho there was bad water, so that the land predisposed women to miscarry; through the prophet Elisha, the water was healed at its source, so that no more death and miscarriages ensued as a result thereof[453]. If two men accidentally strike a pregnant woman during a fight, she can miscarry as a result[454]. In such a case, the deceitful judges of Sodom (probably the Sophists) sentenced the claimant husband to give his wife to the guilty person so that the latter restore the *status quo ante,* that is make her pregnant[455].

A moral teaching states that a woman miscarries as punishment for groundless hatred[456]. "No miscarriages and no infertility in the land" is a Divine promise to those who fulfill the laws of God[457]. The men of the priestly watch fasted on Thursdays and prayed that pregnant women not lose the fruits of their wombs[458].

Women buried their aborted fetuses in small mounds of earth near the town[459], whereas heathen women also buried theirs in their "menstruation rooms"[460]. The maid servant of an oil-pressor in Rimmon once threw her fetus into a cistern from which it was said a polecat and weasel can easily drag it off[461].

## IV

Every fetus which is aborted before it is viable, that is one which "never sees the light of the world"[462], is called a *nephel* in both Bible and Talmud. The Psalmist compares it to a snail which melts away[463]. This is analogous to the teaching of Aristotle in which he speaks of a "secretion", *ekrysis,* if the fetus is aborted before the seventh day after conception, and of a premature birth, *ektrosmos,* if the fetus is lost before forty days after conception[464]. In the Talmud, the term "secretion"[465] is used

---

444. Numbers Rabbah 10:5
445. Yebamoth 64b
446. Yebamoth 64a
447. Chapt. 5
448. Bechoroth 20b
449. Shabbath 63b
450. Aboth 5:5
451. Gittin 31b
452. Niddah 17a; Moed Katan 18a
453. Second Kings 2:19
454. Exodus 21:22
455. Sanhedrin 109b

456. Shabbath 32b
457. Exodus 23:26
458. Taanith 27b
459. *Tosefta* Oholoth 16:1
460. Niddah 7:4; see also above Chapter 2, and Rosenzweig, *Das Wohnhaus in der Mishnah.* Berlin 1907 p.84, note 1
461. *Tosefta* Oholoth 16:13
462. Job 3:15
463. Psalms 58:9
464. Aristotle. *Histor. Anim.* 7:3:21
465. or "mere fluid", *maya be'alma*

up to forty days after conception. The woman is first regarded to be pregnant if the pregnancy lasts longer than forty days. At the other extreme, the *juridical* concept of *nephel* extends even to thirty days after birth, at which time the infant will have proved its viability[466]. A blighted ovum (amniotic sac) is called a *schefir*. Rabbi Chanina once saw a calf embryo like a bean in a *schefir*[467].

The Bible and Talmud never use the expression "to give birth" in the case of the birth of a normal child before the normal end of the pregnancy, or in the case of the birth of an abnormal child but at the normal time; rather, it is always stated "the woman loses" her fetus, or she "lets drop" a *nephel,* or a *schefir;* or has a miscarriage; perhaps because it was assumed that true labor pains *(kushi)* are lacking in the case of an abortion[468].

Concerning the question of ritual uncleanness, it is of extreme importance to distinguish whether a bloody issue from a woman is due to menstruation or due to an abortion, because the decision in an actual case as to whether the Biblical laws for the menstruating or the parturient woman shall be applied and followed depends on the above distinction. For the Talmud, only the desire that these laws of the Bible, just as all others, be fulfilled, is decisive, and determines the outcome of all its innumerable discussions and judgements; the intent is not "to penetrate the most intimate matters of married life".

If a woman loses a *schefir* full of water or full of blood or full of *genunim* (multicolored matter), one need not assume necessarily that there is, or was, a fetus there; but if the *schefir* is "fashioned" (*merukam,* meaning formed or organized), i.e. a cohesive mass of tissue surrounded by a membrane, then the woman is to be considered as one who gave birth, and the expressed material is considered to be an aborted fetus[469].

However, uncertainties exist even in the case of the sac filled with multi-colored matter, as to whether a fetus existed there and became squashed or putrefied. Abaye considers the thought that a fetus becomes squashed to be an impossibility[469a]. Raba is of the opinion that if a fetus were squashed, the amniotic sac would not be full (and the *Mishnah* states "full of"). Rabbi Ada asserts that if a fetus were squashed, one would expect a sac full of uni-colored matter, not multi-colored[470]. Mar Samuel considered all these artificially constructed differences (between a valid birth, i.e. a fetus) and expression of menstrual blood (i.e. no fetus) to be invalid. Only where the content of the sac was so clear that if one placed a hair on one side of the sac one could see it right through on the other side, does he admit to the possibility that a fetus was not absorbed[471]. He is thus of the opinion that only the transparent amniotic sac, that is one which probably originates from an hydatidiform mole, never contained a fetus. All other moles and amniotic sacs, however, comprise dead and more or less squashed or dissolved fetuses.

A more difficult question arose when only a "piece of tissue", *chaticha,* was expelled from the vagina and was under consideration; not a *schefir* which is an entire sac or amniotic membrane. If a woman "loses" such a piece of flesh, she is ritually unclean if there was blood with it[472]. For these pieces of flesh are considered to be growths in the womb (tumors which later might even develop into pseudo-moles), which eventually can be expelled even without bleeding. According to Rabbi Judah, *every* woman who expels a piece of flesh is ritually unclean because, as a rule, these are blood cots. If they are truly tumoral growths, then the uterus will not open in order to expel such growths without there being some accompanying bleeding[473]. According to

---

466. Shabbath 135b
467. Jerusalmi Nazir 7; 56b
468. Niddah 38a
469. Niddah 3:3
469a. literally: comical

470. *ibid* 24b
471. *ibid* 25a
472. Niddah 3:1
473. see *Tosafoth* on Niddah 21a

Biblical law, any woman with vaginal bleeding is ritually unclean. These aborted pieces can be red, black, yellow or white; that is, more or less changed during the bleeding. They can also assume various shapes and resemble fish, locusts, reptiles or worms. If a bone is found in a "piece" of aborted tissue, then all doubts are eliminated and it certainly represents a human fetus.

According to Rabbi Meir, if the woman aborts something which looks like a beast, or a wild animal, or a bird, she is considered like a parturient woman and must abide in uncleanness according to the sex of the fetus, i.e. seven days for a male child and fourteen days for a female child[474]. The Sages, however, make the general statement that an abortus which does not have features of a human being is not considered to be a "human child". They so ruled, for example, in the case of a woman in Zidon who three times gave birth to the form of a raven[475].

These rules of the *Mishnah* are discussed in great detail in the *Gemara,* whereby is demonstrated the enormous difficulty which exists even to this day, of distinguishing pieces of menstrual decidua from an early abortus. This difficulty must have been even greater in those days because the ancients could not identify microscopic chorionic villi. It was well-known that a woman could emit "pieces of menstruation" rather than liquid blood[476]. It is also possible that the woman aborted a piece of disintegrating tumor, or possibly thick clots, since no gynecological examination was performed. On the other hand, it was also recognized that not every vaginal bleeding — apart from puerperal bleeding — is due to menstruation.

It once happened that a woman aborted objects like red (onion) rind, and the Sages consulted the physicians, who explained to them that the woman had an internal sore *(makka),* the crust of which she cast out in the shape of pieces of rind[477]. Perhaps this was a case of dysmenorrhea membranacea.

Another incident occurred in which a woman was aborting objects like red hairs. The Sages consulted the physicians who stated that the woman had a wart (or nevus) in her internal organs from which she was aborting these hairs. The Sages, however, manifestly more intelligent than the physicians, advised that the rinds and the hairs be soaked in luke-warm water for 24 hours. If they dissolve, this proves they are blood clots and not hairs[478].

Did the Rabbis think that a woman could give birth to animals? There was not a shadow of a doubt in all of non-Jewish antiquity, not excluding even the great Plato[479], and through the late Middle Ages, that this, in fact, was possible. It was explained to occur either as a result of a woman becoming pregnant from an animal through a type of sodomy or — and this seems most likely to be the accepted view — a woman became pregnant from a man but then "saw" (or "was frightened by") an animal, so that she gave birth to a fetus with the shape of that animal. In the Talmud, sodomy with animals is said to be completely unfruitful: "no animal can become pregnant from a human being, and no human being can become pregnant from an animal"[480]. A similar expression states *cattle and beasts cannot become one flesh with man*[481], as do man and wife[482], for only creatures whose manner of copulation is the same and whose period of gestation is the same can bear young from each other[483]. I have already shown how narrowly limited was the belief in this "seeing an animal", and, therefore, giving birth to an infant with that form.

After all this, it is not surprising that the Talmud never speaks of the birth of an

474. Niddah 3:2
475. *Tosefta* Niddah 4:6
476. Niddah 21b
477. Niddah 22b
478. *ibid*
479. Kratylos 393 C ed. Wohlrab. Leipzig

1887, I p.19
480. *Tosefta* Bechoroth 1:9
481. Genesis 2:24
482. Sanhedrin 58a
483. Chullin 127a

animal to a human being and vice versa. On the contrary, Rabbi Jeremiah, who raised the question as to whether or not a beast in a woman's body is considered to be a valid birth, only did so in jest to try and make the earnest Rabbi Zera laugh[484]. Also, all good editions of the *Mishnah* speak only of a woman who aborts a fetus which *resembles* an animal or a bird. The Sages only differ from Rabbi Meir in that they state that a fetus which does not have the features of a human being is not considered to be a valid birth. The consequences are that the woman need not abide by the rules for a parturient woman. It is doubtful whether or not one used as a basis for this rule the assumption that such a malformed fetus is non-viable.


# V   Monster Births

The definition of "features of a human being" is discussed repeatedly. The Catholic moralists, who are particularly interested in this question because of the baptism of newborns, consider a child to be "human" if it has a human head and chest[485]. We can learn a considerable amount of the teratology of antiquity from the Talmud. We must, however, make the observation that the Talmud only speaks of malformations which we know exist even today. Where a specific identification of a malformation mentioned in the Talmud cannot be made, the fault almost certainly lies in an inability to understand the technical terms. In the Middle Ages, when observation of nature had to yield to speculation, scholars went as far as to picture and portray with bold fantasy the most unbelievable and complicated malformations. This was amply shown in the pictorial works of Lykosthenes[486] and Finzel[487]. Even the physicians are no more reliable than the chroniclers and the theologians[488], as shown by the pictures of Ambroise Paré[489] and Casper Bauhin[490].

"Human features", according to the Rabbis[491], refers to a case when the face is that of a human being, even if the rest of the body resembles a he-goat. What is decisive is fully developed forehead, eyebrows, eyes, cheeks and chin (*gabboth hazakan* or jawbone). The development of the mouth, nose and ears seems not to be of decisive import in this regard[492].

Among the malformations of individual parts of the body mentioned in the Talmud is disfigurement of the face *(panav musmasin),* or a severer form, *panav tuchoth,* in which none of the normal facial features are recognizable[493]. The sons of Rabbi Chiya knew of such a case.

The infant may also have only one eye, either in the middle of the head, as in a cyclops, or on the side, known as monops[494].

The skull may be "stopped up", that is, unrecognizable *(atuma),* which, according to the commentaries, means "missing", i.e. anencephalus[495].

The entire lower portion of the body, from the navel down, may be missing (tied off by the umbilical cord). Fingers and toes on hands and feet may be inadequately separated[496].

The fetus can be born resembling a palm leaf in the botanical sense or *afikta*

484. Niddah 23a
485. Capellmann p.129
486. *Wunderwerck...durch Johann Herold verteutscht.* Basel 1557
487. Job. Fincelins. *Wunderzeichen.* Jena 1556
488. Luther. *Tischreden* No. 2290. ed Irmischer
489. Paré. Book 19. ed. Malgaigne Vol. 3 p.24

490. Casper Bauhini *de Hermaphrodit...natura.* Chapt. 11. Oppenheim 1614 p.115
491. Niddah 23b
492. *ibid*
493. *ibid* 24a
494. *ibid*
495. *ibid*
496. *ibid*

*dedekla,* meaning a palm twig, with a strong base below and with leaves ramifying above, like a siren pelvis, or with fusion of the lower limbs[497].

If a single foot or a single hand is born, the mother is subject to the uncleanness of birth, because then the existence of a complete human child is certain[498].

If a woman aborts the form of a head without any indentation, or a complete fetal body without any indentations (i.e. separation of limbs), the mother is *not* considered to have given birth. This case probably refers to tumors of the uterus which are aborted, and which are *not* considered by the Talmud to represent human malformations, as some later authors claim[499].

A child can look like the night ghost Lilith which, according to Samuel, means it is a normal child that also has wings[500], and, according to others[501], means a demon with very long hair.

The fetus can look as if it had two backs and two spinal columns[502]. Some interpret such a creature to be the Biblically-prohibited animal *shesua*[503], whereas others state it refers to the Biblically-mentioned *gibben* priest[504], who is unfit to serve in the Temple because of his double-backed physical deformity[505]. Rabbi Shimi considers that it refers to a child with a crooked spinal column[506]. This case is obviously one in which the spinal column is split, or one in which a severe hunchback develops in a fully-grown man or animal, so that it appears as if there are two spinal columns, one straight and one crooked.

A person with six fingers and six toes is already mentioned in the Bible[507] and an animal with five or three feet is described in the Talmud[508]. Furthermore, a thirty-day-old child with two heads is the object of juridical discussion[509].

We have already discussed hermaphrodites and certain other malformations of individual body parts[510].

# VI  *Sandal*

A malformation known in the Talmud as *sandal* requires a separate discussion.

The Rabbis teach that a *sandal* is a fetus which resembles the sea fish with the same name; namely, the sole (i.e. flat). Originally, such a child was normal in utero but then became flattened. Rabbi Simeon ben Gamliel compares it to the large ox tongue, probably the *bouglossos* of the Greeks, which is the name of the aforementioned sea fish. Both explanations thus denote the same concept[511]. Sometimes the neck is twisted so that the fetus looks like someone whose face is twisted backwards following a slap in the face.

Such a flat *sandal* fetus only occurs in association with the simultaneous birth of a normal child. During birth, according to some Sages, both are born "intertwined in one another", that is, the normal child is lying on half of the *sandal* (perhaps with his head on the navel of the *sandal*) and thus, in the case where both are lying head down, presses the *sandal* out with his feet, in order to immediately follow it out. Alternatively, if both are positioned feet first, then the normal child is born first. Even if one assumes that both fetuses are fully covered with amniotic membranes in utero, it is possible that during birth, the normal child remains attached because of its life's

---

497. *ibid*
498. *ibid*
499. Fortunatus Licetus. *De Monstris* Amstelod 1665 p.56; Hufeland. *Harles Journal für die praktische Heilkunde.* April 1816
500. Niddah 24b
501. Erubin 100b
502. Niddah 24a

503. Deut. 14:7
504. Levit. 21:20
505. Bechoroth 7:2 and 43b
506. Niddah 24a
507. Second Samuel 21:20
508. Bechoroth 40a
509. Menachoth 37a
510. Chapter 5, above
511. Niddah 25b

strength, whereas the *sandal* fetus simply slides out. Nevertheless, it is obviously only a theoretically constructed mechanism of birth; the law only considers the more or less widely separated birth of both fetuses[512].

In order to prevent the occurrence of such a *fetus papyraceus* or *compressus,* the Talmud recommends that a pregnant woman use a *moch* or absorbent tampon during cohabitation, so that her fetus not become a *sandal* by superfetation[513]. It was obviously assumed that another fetus might develop as a result of cohabitation, which, because it was conceived later than the first fetus, is weaker than the earlier one and dies, and then gradually becomes flattened; for "a *sandal* occurs only when a live child presses on it". The Palestinian Talmud states that the child born together with the *sandal* is also non-viable[514].

## VII   False Pregnancy

From all the preceding, it is evident that the Rabbis did not subscribe to the collective understanding of the "mole", which played such a major role in non-Jewish antiquity. One can especially appreciate the concept of the mole in the minds of heathen physicians from a statement of Aristotle in which he considers stone children to be moles *(myle)*[515], and also from a statement of Oribasius, whose source is unknown, in which he clearly describes a *mola* or *myle* to be a suppurated extrauterine pregnancy which perforates through the rectum and which leads to the exhaustion and death of the woman. He surmises that the "mole sickness" occurs as a result of the woman conceiving from a type of wind egg, *osper ypenemion,* producing a shape which is not formed through fertilization with male sperm[516]. The expression "wind eggs" *(enemos* or *anemos)* or "zephyr eggs" is also used by Aristotle for the unfertilized eggs of birds[517]. Today, at least in my native country, one uses this name for chicken eggs without shells. Osiander also mentions wind eggs, *ovum inane putidum,* in regard to human beings[518].

Wind eggs also play a role in the Talmud, where they are called wind or *ruach,* for short. The Talmud mentions the case of a woman who was thought to be pregnant, but who gave birth to a *ruach* or the like — which has no substance[519]. A wind egg is distinguished from a *nephel* or abortus[520]. A pregnancy with a wind egg is recognizable at three months, just like a real pregnancy[521]. The prophet, portraying his futile efforts, complains: *We have been with child, we have been in pain; we have as it were brought forth wind*[522].

It is not possible to determine whether or not the Rabbis considered this *ruach,* as did the Greeks with their *son ypenemion,* to be a product excreted from the uterus without there having been a pregnancy. Since we do not know which signs were needed to establish a definitive diagnosis of pregnancy, we cannot say whether the above refers to a new growth of the uterus or of the chorion.

## VIII   Difficult Labor

A protracted, painful birth is distinguished from a normal birth. It is not unlikely that the expression used to describe the former, *hamekasha,* is to be taken quite literally: *(piel* causative tense) "the woman hardens her uterus during birth", in that

512. *ibid* 26a
513. *Tosefta* Niddah 2:6. That which Rawitzki states (*Janus* 1901) concerning this citation is certainly not consistent with the facts.
514. Jerushalmi Niddah 3; 50d
515. Aristotle. *De Generat. Animal.* Book 4, Chapt. 7 No. 107
516. Oribasius 22:6; Vol. 3 p.66

517. *Hist. Anim.* 6 No. 8 and 10
518. *Handbuch der Entbindungskunst.* 1.T. p.793
519. Niddah 8b
520. *ibid* 16a
521. Jerushalmi Yebamoth 4; 6a
522. Isaiah 26:18

one can externally *feel* the abnormally hard uterus which represents the spasms of the contracting uterus (as for example in a small pelvis). Furthermore, in the case of Rachel, where this expression is used[523], a live child was born.

Such a parturition can last for several days with bleeding and pain; pain and bleeding may also cease for one day or longer and then recur; or the pains may cease while the bleeding continues[524]. In the latter case, it is possible that the woman no longer feels pain, because of exhaustion and stupefaction[525].

## IX    Sorcery in Obstetrics

It is self-evident that in Talmudic antiquity, the use of *sorcery* in obstetrics was known to the populace. The *Midrash* relates that a woman once used witchcraft *(keshafim)* in order not to bear children. When the physicians came to heal her, she said: you are not capable of healing me for I afflicted it upon myself[526]. Such a sorceress who was "a misfortune for the world" was Yochani, the daughter of Ratibi[527]. According to the explanation of the commentaries, *(the Talmud itself does not mention the story*!), she was a widow who practiced witchcraft. When a woman went into labor, this sorceress closed the womb through sorcery, and when the woman (in labor) suffered greatly, the sorceress, giving the impression of piety, would offer to pray for her in her private chamber! In reality, she released the witchcraft, and the child was born. Once she gave lodging to a day-laborer in her house. The latter heard the noise of an elf in her coffer, like the child moving in the mother's womb. He lifted the lid of the coffer, the elf escaped, and it was recognized that the pious widow was in fact a witch.

A person who is knowledgeable in folklore will recognize not only the superstition of antiquity in this sorceress-widow, but also that of many peoples.

## X    Embryotomy

The *Mishnah* states: "if a woman is having difficulty in birth (and her life is in danger), one cuts up her fetus within the womb and extracts it limb by limb. However, if the major portion were already born — according to some Rabbis the head[528] —, then one may not touch it, for one may not set aside one person's life for that of another"[529].

It is self-evident that the *Mishnah* is speaking of the dismemberment of a *live* infant, for in the case of a baby that was already dead, only the prohibition of the desecration of the dead would be involved. It is also evident that the *Mishnah* gives a *judicial,* and not an obstetrical ruling, that one may not always destroy the fetus in every case of difficult labor. From a rational point of view, the law does not specify under what circumstances the fetus should be dismembered and when a different type of intervention should be undertaken, but leaves the decision to the conscientious judgement of the surgeon (i.e. physician or midwife), limited, however, to purely medical considerations. The Talmud has no other reasons for discussing such cases. If someone licensed by the authorities to practice obstetrics dismembers the fetus in the mother's womb and, because of negligence, also kills the mother, then he must be exiled, just like any person who kills another accidentally without having had intent to harm him[530].

For the purely practical activities of the surgeon, the introduction of the above legal ruling is certainly adequate. If no major limb is yet born (for example if only one

---

523. Genesis 35:16
524. Niddah 4:4
525. Niddah 37b
526. *Yalkut* 1 No. 845

527. Sotah 22a
528. *Tosefta* Yebamoth 9:4
529. Oholoth 7:6
530. *Tosefta* Makkoth 2:5

arm fell out) then the obstetrician is not at all limited in his actions by the law. If the head is already born, then dismemberment of the remaining fetus would only be invoked extremely rarely (i.e. for ascites, abdominal tumor, malformations). In such a case, however, during the futile attempts at extraction, much time elapses, as a result of which the fetus suffers so intensely, that, as a rule, it dies, and the above regulation would no longer be applicable. The same is also valid if one accepts the reading in the *Mishnah:* "the major portion". Also, in cases of pelvic presentation, when the major portion of the fetus has already been born and the extraction of the head is not readily accomplished, the child rapidly dies, even if one doesn't tear off its head. The additional phrase in the *Tosefta:* "even if (after the birth of the head) two days should pass", is thus an exaggeration.

The Catholic Church did not adopt this regulation. As reported by Capellmann, a prohibition against craniotomy was enunciated by the Holy See in the year 1884. Recently in the Rhineland, a midwife was sentenced to pay a fine because she abode by this decree for religious reasons and refused to assist in an embryotomy. "The physician can thus do nothing but wait for the death of the infant, and even of the mother, for he cannot do anything permissible by the Church to save either life"[531].

Moral justification for embryotomy is already mentioned in the Talmud in that the child (because of whose birth the mother's life is in danger) is considered like a criminal who is attempting to destroy another person. In such a case, not only is the pursued party (i.e. the mother) in self-defense allowed to repulse and render the pursuer harmless (i.e. the unborn fetus), but a third party (i.e. the physician) may also act in this manner[532]. The Talmud, however, rejects this reasoning, since the child cannot be held responsible, because it is forced to act in this way. Maimonides, about 1200 C.E., on the other hand, accepts the view that the child is considered to be a "pursuer" *(rodeph)*[533]. We have already previously alluded to the lack of logic in this position; for if the child were to be considered a "pursuer", then this criminal status should also apply *after* the major portion of the baby is born, because prior to that time the baby is not considered to be a "soul" (independent person)![534]

Surprisingly, in the non-Jewish juridical and theological literatures, embryotomy of the live fetus is first mentioned by the church father Tertullian in the year 200 C.E.[535], although all surgeons in antiquity describe it in great detail.

## XI    Cesarian Section on the Dead

Performing a cesarian section on a dead pregnant woman is decreed by law by nearly all peoples. The oldest example thereof is the famous *Lex regia* of Numa Pompilius[536]. Only a few Oriental peoples make an exception thereof[537]. Traces of this operation are already found in Greek mythology. After portraying the dangers of miscarriages, Plinius states: fortunate are those who are born after their mother died in childbirth, such as the first of the Caesars, who was so named because he was extracted from the cut-open abdomen of his mother[538]. If, as it appears, he thought that Julius Caesar was cut out of his dead mother's abdomen, he is in error, for Aurelia was still alive when Caesar moved to Gaul. The "first Caesar" must therefore be the forefather of the Roman emperor *ex gente* Julia[539]. A Talmudic commentary also asserts

531. Capellmann p.25
532. Sanhedrin 72b
533. *Hilchoth Rotzeach* 1:9
534. Yet, after the major portion is born, one may no longer perform an embryotomy. See Rabbi Meshullam Weibs (Phöbus?) in *Gutachten der Spaeteren Geonim,* Turkey 1764 No. 45 p.51a; cited by Rabbi Akiba Eger on the Mishnah Oholoth 7:6

535. Siebold. *Geschichte der Geburtshilfe.* p.202
536. Digest. 1:11 tome 8
537. Ploss. *Das Weib.* 2:327
538. Plinius 7:7
539. Siebold. *Geschichte der Geburtshilfe* 2:135; Osiander. *Handbuch des Entbindungskunst* 2:279; notes.

(according to Josippon) that the name Caesar is derived from the fact that the first Roman Caesar was cut out *(caesus)* from the abdomen of his dead mother[540].

A Talmudic law states the following: if a woman who is sitting on the birthstool dies, one brings a knife even on the Sabbath, incises her abdomen, and takes out the fetus. Usually the child dies before the mother, as soon as the "drops of poison" of the Angel of Death enter her body, because his vitality is less than hers. It is possible, however, that such a child might twitch up to three times. To be sure, some Sages believe that this "twitching" is comparable to that of a lizard tail, which still moves even after it has been cut off from the animal[541]. Thus, twitching is not proof of the life of an entire individual; nevertheless, the above rule remains law. Naturally, it was known that excision of the fetus must be undertaken immediately after the death of the mother; otherwise it would not be required on the Sabbath. Noteworthy is the fact that none of the Rabbis finds it necessary to mention the fact that this is a clear example of what would otherwise be a strongly prohibited act of desecrating the dead *(nibul-hameth)*. We see here too how valuable a human life is, no matter how small the chance of saving that life. Catholic moral theologians even wished to *obligate priests* to undertake cesarian sections on dead women in order to be able to baptize the fetus[542].

The following case concerning the legal procedure to be followed for a pregnant woman sentenced to be executed is discussed in the Talmud. Appeals do not exist in Talmudic law. Amnesty does not exist in Talmudic law either, since all people, without exception, are subject to the law, and in order to spare the convicted person the agony of a long wait before the execution, the sentence must be carried out immediately. Therefore, according to the decree of the *Mishnah,* in the case of a pregnant woman, one should not wait until she gives birth before executing her, unless she is already sitting on the birthstool[543], or, according to another tradition, if the child already stretched one hand out[544]. For as long as the fetus is still in the mother's womb, it is legally considered to be an appendage of the mother; as soon as it becomes separated from her, it is considered as a separate being. Mar Samuel was of the opinion that one intentionally kills the child by striking the woman against her abdomen before taking her out to be executed, so that she not become embarrassed (disgraced) if the child would be born after her death by post mortem vaginal bleeding. The above teaching that, as a rule, the fetus dies before the mother, not as in this case, following the violent death of an otherwise perfectly healthy pregnant woman[545].

It is doubtful whether this rule of Mar Samuel, although sanctioned by Maimonides[546], was ever carried out, because, during the era of Mar Samuel in the second century, the Jews no longer had their own system of criminal justice. We are thus only dealing with a purely theoretical teaching. In addition, because of all the Jewish legal requirements and technicalities, the imposition of a death sentence was such a rarity that a court of Jewish law that imposed a death penalty once in seven years — according to some Rabbis, once in 70 years — was called a murderous court. In fact, Rabbi Tarfon and Rabbi Akiba were of the opinion that *they* could never have voted for a death penalty[547].

## XII   Yotze Dophen

A variety of legal regulations are mentioned in the *Mishnah* concerning an abnormal type of birth called *yotze dophen* (delivered by cesarian section) which is not more precisely defined because it was obviously well-known in those days.

540. *Tosafoth* in Abodah Zarah 10b
541. Arachin 7a
542. Capellmann p.34 ff
543. Arachin 1:4
544. *Tosefta* Arachin 1:4
545. Arachin 7a
546. *Hilchoth Sanhedrin* 12:4
547. Makkoth 1:10

It is known that, according to Biblical law, a first-born is entitled to a double portion of inheritance in relation to his brothers[548]; and that the first-born of man and beast is considered to be holy to God. The first-born of man must be redeemed by a payment to a priest[549]. We have already mentioned above that a parturient woman was first unclean for seven or fourteen days for a male or female birth, respectively, and then had to observe thirty-three to sixty-six days of purification. The following rules of the *Mishnah* pertain to these laws of the Bible.

Neither a *yotze dophen* nor the male infant born after him is considered to be a first-born in regard to inheritance and in regard to the obligation of redemption of the first-born. To qualify as a first-born in regard to inheritance, according to the wording of the law, the baby must have been *"born"* in the normal manner[550], which is not the case for a *yotze dophen*. For the priest's claim of redemption money, it is required that the baby be the *peter rechem* or "opener of the mother's womb" in the normal manner[551], which is also not the case for a *yotze dophen*. The next child born is neither the "beginning of the father's strength"[552], nor is it the "first-born", because another child was already born before him[553].

In order for a woman to be subject to the obligation of a parturient woman, she must also have "given birth" in the normal manner, according to the wording of the Biblical law. This expression was, therefore, not applied to a *yotze dophen*[554]. Circumcision takes place on the eighth day if it falls on a Sabbath only if the woman "gave birth" in the normal manner[555], but not in the case of a *yotze dophen,* when it is postponed to the ninth day[556].

The rules for a *yotze dophen* in the case of an animal are derived in a similar manner. It is always emphasized that the expression "was born" is not applicable to a *yotze dophen,* and it refers to an animal that was not born by way of the *rechem,* i.e. through the genitalia, but was delivered by way of the *dophen* (or abdomen).

Nevertheless, the word *olid* (born) is found in relation to *yotze dophen* in the Talmud[557]. Otherwise the correct term for every abnormal birth is *hamappeleth*[558].

Traditionally, Jews understand *yotze dophen* to refer to a child delivered by *cesarian section.* Since the above-mentioned laws were decreed in regard to the mother and her live child delivered in this manner, a successful outcome of the operation is assumed for both mother and child. There is no further definition or explanation of the aforementioned Talmudic decrees. At the time when the expression *yotze dophen* was written down in the Talmud, in the second century, it was obviously in common usage; for, whereas other terms relating to this law were explained in the law itself, the text is satisfied to use the expression "as is known", in relation to *yotze dophen*[559]. Thus, the always uncertain *linguistic* argument seems to be the only valid one.

*Dophen* is otherwise the designation for a certain type of wall, especially that of the Tabernacle[560] — a thin wooden wall as opposed to *kothel,* a wall made of bricks. Concerning living creatures, the term *dophen* is used to denote a rib, perhaps the chest wall which lies over the lungs of the animal[561]. According to the Biblical story, Abner pierced Asahel in the *chomesh,* so that the spear came out behind him[562], which the *Gemara* interprets to be "the fifth *dophen*" (i.e. fifth rib, from *chomesh* meaning five), where the gall and liver are situated[563]. Naturally, it could only mean the soft

548. Deut. 21:17
549. Exodus 13:13
550. Deut. 21:15
551. Exodus 13:2
552. Deut. 21:17
553. Bechoroth 8:2
554. Niddah 5:1
555. Levit. 12:2

556. Shabbath 136a
557. Niddah 41a
558. Kerithoth 1:5
559. *Tosefta* Bechoroth 7:6
560. Sukkah 6b ff
561. Chullin 48a
562. Second Samuel 2:23
563. Sanhedrin 49a

space between the ribs, which is actually what probably occurred. If one assumes that, in general, not just in the above citation, the word *dophen* refers to the Biblical *chomesh* or rib, then one must understand the term *dophen* to mean the entire "wall" of the body, including the abdominal wall. When Joab killed Amasa, it is stated: *he pierced him in the chomesh, and shed out his bowels to the ground*[564]. This could not have happened by piercing the *chest* wall. Therefore one can translate *yotze dophen* to mean "delivered through the abdominal wall", and, without constraint, equate it with a cesarian section.

At least equally as difficult as the linguistic justification is the archaeological justification. We have no other reports from antiquity concerning the performance of cesarian section on live people. All assertions to date attribute the first operation of this kind to the beginning of the sixteenth century. This argument cannot be decisive, however. In many places, the Talmud mentions an epidemic throat illness in children called *askara,* which is also unknown in heathen writings of antiquity, and whose existence in those days one might have questioned, were it not for the writing of Aretaeus concerning acute illnesses which fortuitously came to our attention, in which he not only portrays the Syrian throat plague, but also calls it by its name *eschara,* which is equivalent to *askara.* This name must have been so fluent in the mouths of the Greek populace, that it crossed over into the language of another people, namely the Jews, and is mentioned in a variety of contexts in their writings; whereas the enormous Greek literature, both medical and lay, other than this single citation of Aretaeus, does not mention any illness called *eschara,* or any Syrian throat plague[565].

Could not a similar situation apply to *yotze dophen*? An *extensive* use of this operation is not presumed anywhere, not even by the Jews. It suffices that certain positive information in the sphere of legal regulations concerning that surgical operation should be available, which would be followed, whether the operation is performed only once, or for all times. The operator also need not have been a methodical, obstetrical surgeon; perhaps he was a simple lay person such as Nufer the pig cutter who, as related by the entire world since Bauhin, cut open the abdomen of his pregnant wife in labor; or perhaps it was a despondent woman who, with the best of results to herself and her baby, cut open her own abdomen and extracted her baby, as reported from England in our own times[566].

In order to make more plausible the assumption of the use by Jews in antiquity of cesarian section, it has been alleged that the Jews witnessed the "slitting open" of their women[567] by their heathen enemies during wartime. However, this outrage has been practiced by brutal, coarse and animalistic soldiers throughout the ages, and yet none of the heathens hit upon the idea of cesarian section! It is true that Israels refers to a report of Wise in which it is alleged that the Indians undoubtedly performed cesarian sections[568]. I cannot verify the report of Wise according to the Sanskrit text, which alone would be reliable. However, even if we accept its accuracy, the legend of the early age of Sanskrit medical writings has long been destroyed. Nobody today still believes that which Nork once asserted in many books and essays, namely that the Bible and Talmud only represent plagiarisms of Indian sources; the opposite is more likely the case. The legend that Buddha entered his mother on her right side and, similarly, came out from his mother on the right side, without a tear, without a wound, and without using the unclean genital passages, is a clear reference to "Immaculate Conception".

It was also emphasized that the Jews, as already mentioned[569], did not consider

---

564. Second Samuel 20:10
565. See above Chapter 4
566. *Lancet* 1886 No. 8, May 22
567. Second Kings 8:12

568. *Nederl. Tydschrift Voor Geneeskund* 1882 p.128
569. Above chapter 14, section 22 in part 1

removal of the uterus to be a life-threatening situation, and therefore certainly ventured to make a simple incision therein. Now the Talmudic discussion only relates to the extirpation of a non-pregnant organ and, in addition, only those of animals; however, one can also counter this objection by the fact that the castration of female animals was as well known to the other peoples of antiquity as it was to the Jews; yet, even with this knowledge, no one ventured to perform cesarian sections on live human beings.

There remains the possibility that the Rabbis constructed their laws concerning cesarian section on live women on purely theoretical grounds, according to their knowledge of the implementation of this operation on the dead. Fulda, in particular[570], assumes that this is the only acceptable explanation, and does so, without obvious reason, in an extremely passionate manner.

One must forthwith admit that nowhere in the Talmud where this subject is mentioned, is there a sentence such as: "It once happened *(ma'aseh)* that a living woman in labor had her abdomen incised and the baby extracted". If such a statement existed, then all other discussion on the matter would be superfluous. It is also undoubted that the *Gemara* not infrequently theorizes; that is, it invents a theoretical case in a certain matter under discussion, inasmuch as a legal principle can be deduced therefrom which might be important for other cases; or a law may be more precisely defined; or a different viewpoint might be developed therefrom, just as occurs today in a well-run juridical seminar. The best example is the discussion concerning the applicability of the laws of the first-born in the case of a pregnant animal whose vulva was placed next to that of another animal, so that the fetus slides into the uterus of the latter animal and is then born normally[571]. The oldest commentators on the Talmud, the *Tosafoth,* have already mentioned repeatedly that this case has purely didactic intent since in nature such an event does not occur[572]. Another purely theoretical case concerns the question asked about the ritual impurity of a mother whose child was born one-third through the abdomen and two-thirds through the normal birth passageway[573]. There are many other examples. Nevertheless, Maimonides quotes these two examples as actual occurrences in his *corpus juris judaici*[574].

All these examples are derived from the *Gemara* which comprises the discussions concerning all the laws. In the *Mishnah,* however, which is admittedly not a legal code, but a source for laws, it would be difficult to cite an example which is based on pure fiction to prove a point.

# XIII

*Rashi,* one of the oldest commentators on the Talmud, makes the remark that the abdomen of a woman was opened "by means of a *sam*", and the fetus thus came out[575]. *Sam* is the name of a medicament; often it is more precisely identified as a caustic substance[576]. During the time of *Rashi, cauterium potentiale* was used instead of a knife, particularly where there was fear of bleeding, in which case it was used throughout. It was thus easy for him to conceive that during a cesarian section the abdominal wall and the uterus were divided by means of a caustic substance. He, naturally, never personally witnessed such an operation, since there were certainly no cesarian sections performed during his lifetime (he died in the year 1105). In another place in the Talmud[577], *Rashi* speaks of the opening of the abdomen by means of *sam* and *sakkin,* a caustic and a knife.

---

570. Siebold. *Journal für Geburtshilfe. . . .*
    1826 Vol. 6, part 1
571. Chullin 70a
572. *Tosafoth* on Sanhedrin 47b; Kethuboth
    4b; Shabbath 152b; Yebamoth 102b

573. Chullin 69b
574. *Hilchoth Bechoroth* 4:18
575. *Rashi* on Niddah 40a
576. Abodah Zarah 28a
577. Chullin 69b

Another Talmudic commentator, Rabbi Gersom (died in the year 1040) states the following[578]: the child was not born through the normal birth passageways, but the woman was cut open, and the child came out from the side. Then the uterus healed and later became pregnant again. Most unique and certainly not correct is the opinion of Rabbi Levi from the seventh century that *yotze dophen* means a birth through the rectum, via the anus[579]. This interpretation is refuted by invoking peculiar reasons[580].

Maimonides is plainly in a dilemma. He considers it bizzare that the "preachers", in their interpretation of the above *Mishnah*, speak of the rights of the *yotze dophen* and the fetus born after him, since they assume that a woman recovers after her abdomen is cut open and later may bear another child. It seems much more self-evident to him, that a woman dies following such an operation, because, according to his opinion, a cesarian section is only performed on a woman who is already near death[581]. The same argument is advanced by the author of *Aruch*[582]. Even Ambroise Paré considered it impossible for such an operated-upon woman not to bleed to death[583]. In order to explain the birth of the second son in the above *Mishnah*, Maimonides has to invoke a most colossal assumption; namely, the case involves a twin birth, in which the abdomen of the woman is opened (or splits open), and one of the children comes out in this manner. Then the second twin is born spontaneously or is extracted! After both children are born, the mother dies[584]. It remains unexplained, according to Maimonides, why the *Mishnah* exempts a woman who gave birth to a *yotze dophen* from all the laws pertaining to the first-born; this would obviously only make sense if the woman is still alive. Perhaps, he assumes that the death of the mother does not occur immediately.

In modern times, Rawitzki[585] has made the assertion that *yotze dophen* is a child born through a central perineal tear in the mother. He defends this assertion with an unusual display of acumen against dialectic opponents of equally high stature. I can only take exception, in that such an "abdominal birth" was not considered to be something other than *peter rechem* (by way of the uterus, even if this word is translated in the most precise sense of "uterus"). There were also no misgivings in calling a perineal birth a real *"birth"*, whereas, as already mentioned, all places (in the Talmud) consider a *yotze dophen* to be the *opposite* of a normal *"birth"*. The understanding of the ancients was that a "birth" occurred when a child came into the world as a result of its own and its mother's strength, whereas a *yotze dophen* is helped by outside intervention. He is, therefore, not *"born"*, but "extracted" or "evolved", as we say today in the case of a cesarian section. Children who lie transversely in the womb, as well as those with other abnormalities, are also not said to be "born", since such fetuses are dismembered, unless the baby turns by itself or the birth occurs *conduplicato corpore* if the child "helps itself". The fact that *linguistically yotze dophen* means "a child that *comes out* through the abdominal wall" thus encompassing the concept of "activity", bears no weight against the above facts. As far as I can see, no one agrees with Rawitzki. Both physicians[586] and Talmudists[587] dispute his assertion in a similar manner, without placing any weight upon the aforementioned argument which I consider to be convincing.

In his already-mentioned work, Fulda[588] asserts that in ancient Judaism, the unborn fetus was not considered to be of such value that one would allow the mother's

578. Bechoroth 19a
579. *Tosafoth* Kerithoth 7b
580. *ibid*
581. literally: reached the gates of death. Bechoroth 2:9
582. Kohut. *s.v. dophen*
583. Osiander. *Handbuch der Entbindungskunst.* Vol. 1 p.21

584. Maimonides on Bechoroth 8:2
585. *Virchow Archiv.* 1880 to 1884
586. *ibid* and Israels-Pinkhoff. *Nederl. Tydschr. voor Geneeskund* 1882 No. 8
587. *Magazin für das Wissenschaft des Judentums* 1881 No. 4
588. *opus cit.* p.29

life to become endangered for its sake. This opinion was also accepted by all other peoples of antiquity who considered correct the teaching of the Stoics that the fetus is not a person with a soul. He forgets, however, that even today, we perform cesarian sections in some cases in the interest of the mother, for example, in absolute pelvic contraction.

## XIV

From the foregoing, it is evident that "cesarian section" always means the opening of the abdomen *and* the pregnant uterus. There is, however, nothing which obviates the possibility of an *abdominal pregnancy*[589] for which an operation was certainly already risked in ancient times, for here one could directly see the fetus moving under the abdominal wall. Nor is it any longer doubtful that from antiquity until the sixteenth century, laparotomies performed on far-advanced pregnancies were done in the mistaken belief that these were abdominal pregnancies. The fact that this operation (laparotomy) performed *today* on a mature fetus because of the danger of placental bleeding carries a worse prognosis for the mother than a routine cesarian section performed under the same circumstances, is no proof at all for antiquity.

In any event, with this supposition, it is possible to explain a case in the Talmud which otherwise might be considered to be a purely theoretically constructed example: namely, the case of a woman who gives birth to *one* child through the abdomen and a *sandal* fetus through the normal birth passageway[590]. One can, in this case, assume that there were simultaneous extra- and intra-uterine pregnancies, but the concept of the *sandal* must be extended more than usual.

One might therein perhaps find support for *Rashi's* statement cited above that this operation was carried out with a corrosive substance.

I can summarize all the above as follows:

*It is certain that the Talmud mentions a type of birth other than by way of the normal birth canal, with a happy outcome for both mother and child (i.e. both remain alive). It is likely that laparotomy for an abdominal pregnancy, and perhaps also cesarian section on a living woman, is what the Talmud is referring to. There is no conclusive evidence, however, that either of these two operations was ever actually carried out during the time of the Talmud.*

## XV    Abnormal Animal Births

Among *animals*, there are three types of abnormal births:

1) The orphan, *yathom*, an animal which was born an orphan. According to the explanation of the *Mishnah*[591], this refers to an animal whose mother died or was slaughtered and then gave birth. The mother animal thus died in childbirth or was slaughtered (forced slaughter), and then the birth was completed through the natural birth canal, either spontaneously or with the help of some substance.

2) The *ben pekua*, the "young of a cut-open animal". The pregnant mother animal is slaughtered and, during the dissection, one finds a live baby in the uterus[592]. This case might be considered analogous to a cesarian section on the dead. Galen also reports an observation of this kind.

3) The *yotze dophen*. Here we must assume that a live animal was subjected to laparotomy for reasons which are unknown to us. Perhaps, the case involved an unusually valuable animal that became pregnant contrary to the owner's wishes, and which he did not wish to have slaughtered. The *Mishnah* explicitly speaks of a mother

---

589. This opinion was already stated by Wunderbar in his *Biblisch-Talmudische Medizin* Part 1, Section 3 p.54

590. Niddah 26a
591. Bechoroth 9:4
592. Chullin 74a

animal that was cut open *(kara)*. The living and viable baby removed from the uterus requires ritual slaughtering if one wishes to eat it, "since its mother was not slaughtered"[593].

The *yotze dophen* of animals is mentioned very often in regard to the laws of sacrifices and tithes. One cannot draw any conclusions concerning the frequency of its occurrence from the frequency with which it is mentioned. It is characteristic of Talmudic law to mention even rare occurrences at every opportunity. One need only think of the constantly repeated rules in ceremonial law for the deaf-mute and the mentally ill.

The doe has a very narrow womb *(rechem)*[594]; therefore, at the time of delivery, God sends her a serpent *(drakon)* which bites her, and she then delivers her offspring[595]. The difficulty that a doe has in copulating is also mentioned by Aristotle; he is motivated, however, by the rigidity of the penis of the male[596]. In order to expedite the birth, one presses on the flesh (i.e. abdomen) of the animal and catches the offspring, so that it should not fall on the ground[597]. In the case of a lamb, the lips first appear in the vulva, but in the case of a kid, the ears appear first[598].

The *Mishnah* also assumes that during a difficult delivery, the baby may even put its foot or even its head out of the vagina and then withdraw it. Where the delivery cannot otherwise be completed, the fetus of the animal may be dismembered in the womb of the mother[599].

One blows air into the nostrils of the newborn animal[600], and places the teat in its mouth, so that it can suckle. If the mother animal pushes the baby away, then one places a clump of salt in the mother's vagina; thereby she develops the desire to nurse her offspring. One also sprinkles the "water of the afterbirth" on the newly born animal so that its mother will smell it and have pity upon it. Furthermore, an unclean (i.e. prohibited for human consumption) animal does not spurn its young, and if it does, it does not take it back[601].

All animals have a slimy discharge from their genitalia during birth, or one day beforehand[602].

One cannot compare the process of labor and midwifery of man to that of animals[603].

## XVI    Puerperal Illness

Because of the delivery, a woman's limbs are disjointed and her natural strength does not return before 24 months[604], whereas the child is not harmed by passing through the womb[605].

The only *puerperal illness* that I am familiar with in the Talmud is the sickness called *kuda* which, according to the commentaries, is the "sickness of a lying-in woman that caught a cold on the birthstool". To the Syrians, the word means "blood flow during and after the birth"[606]. The remedy for it consists of cumin (Carum carvi), caraway (Cuminum cyminum), ammi (mint), asafetida, Satureia capitata, and a type of thyme, cooked in beer[607].

The death of the woman during the delivery or during the lying-in period is often mentioned in the Talmud. It serves as punishment for a woman who did not happily

593. Chullin 4:5
594. cf. Erubin 54b
595. Baba Bathra 16b
596. Aristotle. *Hist. Anim*: Book 6:29 p.99
597. Shabbath 128b
598. Bechoroth 35a
599. Chullin 4:1
600. according to some authorities: wine
601. Shabbath 128b

602. Niddah 29a
603. Chullin 68a
604. Niddah 9a
605. Chullin 51a
606. Fleischer in Levy's *Neuhebräisches und Chaldäisches Wörterbuch*. Leipzig 1876-1889. Part 3: 448b
607. Abodah Zarah 29a

fulfill her religious obligations[608]. "Three types of people die even while they are conversing", teaches the Talmud, "viz. one who suffers from bowel diseases (dysentery), a woman in confinement, and one afflicted with dropsy; so that one should prepare their burial shrouds for them."[609]. From the juxtaposition of the parturient woman to the patient suffering from dysentery or dropsy, it is apparent that what is meant here is not the *sudden* death of the woman in confinement by obstruction of the pulmonary artery, but rather "death while fully conscious", as one might observe frighteningly in a parturient woman who dies because of sepsis. The next section will describe in detail three cases from the Bible in which women died while in confinement, following difficult deliveries[610]. According to some sources, these women died in childbirth[611].

## XVII     Birth Stories in the Bible

### 1) The Confinement of Rebekah[612]

*And when her days to be delivered were fulfilled, behold, there were twins in her womb. And the first came forth ruddy, all over like an hairy garment* (fur); *and they called his name* (therefore) *Esau. And after that came forth his brother, and his hand held onto Esau's heel, and his name was called Jacob* (perhaps by his father?); *and Isaac was three score years old when she bore them.* According to the Talmud, Rebekah was 23 years old at the time.

The diagnosis of a twin pregnancy was already established and known to the mother during the pregnancy[613]. There was thus no reason for the expression of surprise: *behold!*[614] Esau is a child with marked hypertrichosis. It is undecided whether the *admoni* of the text really means *red* or *blond*. In any event, it must refer to the color of the hair (not the skin) which was *noticeably* different from the usual hair color of the Semites, namely, black[615].

*Adom* is the color of lentil; *adama* is the name of the earth, and *adamu* is the Arabic color designation of ripe wheat. Whereas, according to the Bible, Rebekah went to question God "because the children were fighting within her womb", Josephus asserts that Isaac was the one who inquired of God, because he was afraid for her because her womb became so hard.

The expression "to hold onto the heel" is said to be so unusual in obstetrics that it was not interpreted in the literal sense. It was said to refer to what we today call "to be hard on a person's heels" i.e. to be pursuing someone. This meaning is found in Genesis 27:36 and Jeremiah 9:3. In the birth story of Esau and Jacob, however, it is possible to accept the literal translation, if one assumes that the first child was born in the normal manner, head first, and immediately after the egress of his feet, a hand of the second twin fell out, so that it appeared as if it were holding onto the heel of the first child. It seems evident, therefore, that the amniotic membranes of the second child were already ruptured at the time of birth of the first child, an assumption which Ibn Ezra states is "a most unusual occurrence"[616]. This assumption, however, is totally unnecessary, since twins might be born from a *single* amnion. A common chorion is not at all unusual if both children derive from a single egg, so that the words of Hosea can be interpreted literally: *he took his brother by the heel in the womb (ba-beten)*[617].

### 2) The Confinement of Tamar[618]

608. Shabbath 2:6
609. Erubin 41b
610. Genesis Rabbah 82:7
611. *Yalkut* 2 No. 103
612. Genesis 25:24-26
613. Genesis 25:23

614. *Rashbam's* commentary on Genesis 25:24
615. Levit. 13:31
616. *Ibn Ezra's* commentary on Genesis 25:25
617. Hosea 12:4
618. Genesis 38: 27-30

*And it came to pass in the time of her travail, that, behold,* (the midwife recognized that) *there were twins in her womb. And it came to pass, when she travailed, that one put out a hand; and the midwife took and bound upon his hand a scarlet thread, saying this came out first. And it came to pass, as he drew back his hand, that, behold, his brother came out; and she* (the mother or the midwife) *said: wherefore hast thou made a breach for thyself? Therefore, his name was called Peretz. And afterward came out his brother, that had the scarlet thread upon his hand; and his name was called Zerach.*

The portrayal of this birth allows two possible interpretations.

(a) Both children lay in the womb in head presentations. The arm of one twin was situated next to the head of the other. When the head of the latter pressed forward, however, the arm of the former was pushed aside, and only later did this arm come out, together with its appropriate head, after the path was clear and the birth canal was wide open. In modern times, this interpretation is espoused by V. Winckel[619].

(b) The first twin lay in a shoulder presentation and one arm fell out. Then, however, the other twin pressed forward so that the first, together with his fallen-out hand, retreated into the uterus. The second twin was thus born first, and only then did the first twin egress.

Thus, either a self-turning of this twin occurred within the uterus, or, it was born in the original presentation *conduplicato corpore*. The latter seems more likely if one agrees with the Talmud that the confinement of Tamar occurred before the normal end of pregnancy, so that the birth involved premature infants. The Talmud derives this supposition from the fact that concerning the confinement of Rebekah, it is expressly stated *when her days to be delivered were fulfilled,* whereas, in the case of Tamar, the general expression *in the time of her travail* is used[620].

The text precisely indicates the two unusual aspects of this birth, the presence of twins and the pressing forward of the second twin to be born first, with the repeated exclamation: *behold*!

The diagnosis of a twin pregnancy was probably made much earlier by the midwife, but certainly no later than the beginning of the confinement. Otherwise, the recognition sign (i.e. the scarlet thread) applied to the infant whose hand protruded first would be senseless. It is known that according to Biblical law, the first-born is entitled to a double portion of inheritance, so that the establishment of the identity of this first-born had great import in civil law. Here, therefore, the testimony of the midwife can be decisive[621]. Furthermore, the Talmud discusses whether or not the falling out of one arm is considered a valid "birth".

Concerning the rupture of the amniotic membranes, the remarks made concerning the previous case (i.e. the confinement of Rebekah) apply equally well here.

It is difficult to explain the exclamation in Genesis 38:29. The above translation follows the usual interpretation, which had already been adopted by the Aramaic translators. According to the accents (or notes), the translation should be: *what breachest thou? May there be a breach upon you,* i.e. in retaliation of your breaching, I wish such a breach upon you! This type of accent-separation is also supported by the *Midrash* where it states: *"The breaker* (Messiah), *poretz*[622] *is gone up before them"*[623]. Grammatically, the exclamation can only be directed toward the child, and not toward the midwife. It is also not possible to say who expelled him from the uterus, the mother or the midwife. What type of breach is referred to? Certainly not, as is often claimed[624], a tear in the amniotic membranes; for such a tear is not seen by the

619. *Handbuch der Geburtshilfe.* Wiesbaden 1903 Vol. 1:19
620. Genesis Rabbah 63:8
621. Kiddushin 74a
622. Michah 2:13
623. Genesis Rabbah 85:14
624. first by Siebold. *Geschichte der Geburtshilfe* p.36

midwife, or perceived by the mother. Furthermore, it is a normal phenomenon, without which no birth can take place. There remains only the supposition that it was a tear in the perineum, as suggested by Slevogt in a separate work on this subject[625]. Then the exclamation would emanate from the midwife, since a pregnant woman, as is known to every obstetrician, does not perceive such a wound as a tear, but as a burning or cutting sensation.

However, it is not absolutely necessary to assume that our case refers to a "tear" in the precise sense of the word. The expression *paratz peretz,* "to tear a tear" (or "breach a breach"), only entails a use of language frequently employed in antiquity. In Latin, one says *bellum bellare,* "to war a war", etc. The object *peretz,* therefore, need not have a precise meaning. The sentence could simply mean: why do you spread out so much (or make yourself so spread out)? Or why do you press forward so much? The Bible not infrequently uses the word *peretz* in the sense of "spreading out"[626] or "to be plentiful[627]. In this manner, the name of the child Peretz seems more logical, for certainly no father in antiquity would name his son "tear" or "tearer" in the evil sense, because a name was then considered to be an omen, much more so than in our times[628].

3) The Confinement of Rachel[629]

*And they journeyed from Beth-el; and there was still some way to come to Ephrath; and Rachel travailed, and she had hard labor. And it came to pass, when she was in hard labor, that the midwife said unto her: fear not, for now thou shalt have another son. And it came to pass, as her soul was in departing, for she died, that she called his name Ben-oni (son of my sorrow), but his father called him Benjamin (son of the days or son of my old age). And Rachel died, and was buried on the way to Ephrath, the same is Beth-lehem.*

Whereas the first confinement of Rachel seems to have had a normal course, the second confinement, which occurred about ten years after the previous one, resulted in her death. We know absolutely nothing about the cause of death. We have already alluded to the possibility that the term *kashi* (in the *piel* and *hiphil* Hebrew tenses) should be understood quite literally: "she became hard", referring to the uterus. This can even be determined by the hand of a lay person, and thus the case of Rachel may have involved unusually strong labor pains. There seems to be no point in arguing as to the reason for this: whether it was due to *tetanus uteri,* or an abnormal presentation of the baby, or the like. Usually the expression *kashi* is translated: "she had hard labor".

Kotelmann suggests that Rachel died of exsanguination as a result of uterine atony. She was predisposed thereto because of her advanced age (approximately forty years) and because of exhaustion following the long trip[630]. We have no right to blame the midwife for limiting herself to consoling the pregnant Rachel, because we cannot state what else she might have done. She comforted the mother, who believed in the adage of the Talmudists and others in antiquity that the labor pains when a girl is born are stronger than those for a boy, saying that this baby would also be a boy, just as she (Rachel) had wished it[631]. The fact that she was *afraid* of having a girl is perhaps based on the high esteem in which male offsprings were held, as we have previously described.

4) The Wife of Phinehas[632]

*And...the wife of Phinehas was with child, near to be delivered. And when she*

625. *De Partu Thamaris Difficili Et Perineo Inde Rupto.* Jena 1700; Winckel also agrees with him.
626. Genesis 30:43
627. Proverbs 3:10
628. In another sense, the word *peretz* means "to be killed". See Second Samuel 6:8
629. Genesis 35:16-19
630. Kotelmann. *Die Geburtshülfe bei den Alten Hebräern.* Marburg 1876
631. Genesis 30:24
632. First Samuel 4:19-21

*heard the tidings that the ark of God was taken, and that her father-in-law and her husband were dead, she kneeled down and gave birth;* (or bowed herself and travailed) *for her pains came upon her. And about the time of her death, the women that stood by her said unto her: fear not, for thou hast born a son* (or better: you are giving birth to a son)! *But she answered not, and set not her heart* (to the promise). Rather she bemoaned the death of her relatives and the loss of the glory of Israel in the taking of the ark by the Philistines. *And she named the child Ichabod* (meaning "where is glory"?) and died, lamenting the above losses.

It is a daily observation that a tremendous shock can elicit labor pains even prematurely. It is hopeless to attempt to list the possible reasons for the immediate cause of death. According to Josephus[633], this case was a premature birth in the seventh month of pregnancy. The mother named the child, because it appeared to be viable.

5) Michal, (wife of King David)

When King David brought the ark back from the land of the Philistines, he danced in joy before it[634]. His wife, a daughter of King Saul, criticized David's behavior which she thought was inappropriate[635]. *Therefore, Michal, the daughter of Saul, had no child unto the day of her death*[636], to which the Talmud states: "but on the day of her death, she had a child", i.e. she died in childbirth[637].

6) The Mother of Queen Esther

According to legend, the mother of Queen Esther also is said to have died in childbirth[638].

633. *Antiquities.* Volume 5, Chapter 11:4
634. Second Samuel 6:14
635. *ibid* 6:20
636. *ibid* 6:23
637. Sanhedrin 21a
638. Megillah 13a

# CHAPTER XV

## *MATERIA MEDICA*

One must be unusually careful in describing the pharmacology of antiquity. In the last several decades, chemistry has made enormous progress and has synthesized a large number of medications. As a result, our entire dispensing of drugs has been revolutionized and simplified. One need only compare a prescription of today to one of a hundred years ago to immediately recognize the difference, even by considering only the length of the prescription. The difference in the content of the ingredients becomes more marked the further one reverts back into history. Even into the sixteenth century, the apothecary was *legally* required to maintain the following in stock: wood lice, rain worms, ants, vipers, scorpions, frogs and crabs; also the skull of a dead person who was not buried, the bone from the heart of a hart, sparrow brains and hare brains, teeth of wild pigs and elephant skin, frog hearts, fox lungs, wolf intestines, human fat, and so on[1].

In a regulation promulgated in the year 1585 by a commission of physicians at the request of a Berlin magistrate, the following was recommended for the "ripening and opening of an abscess":

Although the pains are severe when one fleeces a live black or reddish cock or hen or even pigeons and ties them onto the abscess and frequently changes them, this method draws out the poison. The same is true if one uses frogs or the like[2].

Mummies were still brought to Austrian pharmacies as internal medicaments until 1843[3]. They thus belonged to the *official* stock. Accordingly, one can well imagine what could be found in folk medicine.

## I   Plant Remedies

The medications described in the Talmud are mostly derived from the flora. Among the trees that grow on the banks of the rivers of the future, *the fruit shall be food and the leaf thereof for medicine*[4]. One often used the tree (i.e. drug) in its entirety; from some only the leaves, and rarely the roots or the barks. Plant oils were also used as therapeutic agents; for example, olive oil was used as a gargle for pain in the throat[5]. Mostly, the drugs were cooked, either individually or together. Such a liquid remedy was called *shikyana*. The most efficacious time to imbibe the liquid remedy, according to Mar Samuel, is the springtime, between Passover and Pentecost[6].

---

1. Ferd. Winkler. *Wiener Med. Pr.* 1904, No. 51

2. Kurtzer Bericht wie menniglich...die Ertzney...in dieser Seuche der Pestilenz gebrauchen sol. Von einem Erbarn Rath doselbst in Druck verfertiget. Berlin 1585

3. Wiedemann, *Ztschr. d. V.f rhein. u. westfal. Volkskd*

4. Ezekiel 47:12

5. Berachoth 36a

6. Shabbath 147b

The wise King Solomon had already stated that everything has its time, and also that there is a time to heal[7]. In folk medicine, one took these medications for three, seven or twelve days, and all on an empty stomach[8].

Sometimes the drugs were pulverized and then taken internally, either as the dry powder, or suspended in water. In this manner the *samma de naphtza,* an abortifacient remedy, was imbibed[9]. So too, did Rabbi Chiya advise his sons: drink no *samma*[10]. For an abscess of the mouth, the remedy was blown in with a blade of straw[11]. A powder of that type was called *sam,* and in Aramaic *samma.* It can either be a "powder of life", *sam chayim,* which is a healing remedy, or "a powder of death", *sam mitha*[12] or *sam maveth*[13] or *sam hamaveth*[14], which is a poison. In post-Talmudic usage,[15] the term *sam* without addition of prefix or suffix is mostly used in the latter sense (i.e. poison). The reason is that in the *Mishnah*[16], the term *sam* also refers to a writing material which is thought to be orpiment[17]. There is nothing in the word *sam* to indicate its true meaning and derivation[18]. Also, in the cuneiform tablets, the word *sam* is used in this broad sense[19].

Dry *sam* applied to normal skin does not harm, but is of no use[20]; if there is a wound, it penetrates and goes to the depths thereof (i.e. cauterizes)[21]. The sectarian Jacob applied a *samma* on the wounded thigh of Rabbi Abbahu, and if his disciples had not rapidly scratched it off, the thigh would have been destroyed[22]. If someone sprinkles "a sharp powder" *(samma charipha)* onto another, as a result of which the latter's skin becomes white (corroded), then the one responsible must provide another powder to restore the skin to its previous condition[23]. In addition, the seven substances which are employed to determine whether a stain is menstrual blood or only a dye stain[24], and the dyes of dyers[25], are called *samemanim* and *sammanim,* respectively.

A *sam,* whose precise ingredients are not listed, is the emetic *aphiktephizin*[26], obviously a Greek word. Cultured plants were probably also used as emetics, because the use of produce of the Sabbatical year for this purpose was specifically prohibited[27]. The simplest method of inducing vomiting was to place one's finger in the mouth. During the times of the Roman Caesars, after having enjoyed a large meal, gluttons had the custom of tickling the throat with a peacock feather to induce vomiting, in order to be able to assimilate further courses of food at the feast. Rabbi Nehemiah probably had this detestable practice in mind when he prohibited the induction of vomiting, because, as a result, food would be squandered[28]. To do so on the street was considered improper[29]. During a discussion of obscene matters, a person may become nauseated to the point of vomiting[30].

A medication with an unusually efficacious therapeutic potency is *samthar,* which the commentaries consider to be a type of herb. A hind leg from which the *nervus ischiadicus* and all its branches had been removed[31], healed and grew back together again when it was placed on *samthar*[32]. Sometimes a person may be struck by an arrow

---

7. Eccles. 3:3
8. Gittin 70a
9. Niddah 30b
10. Pesachim 113a
11. Gittin 69a and Yoma 8:6
12. for example Shabbath 88b; Erubin 54a; Taanith 7a; Yebamoth 72b
13. Chullin 58b
14. Baba Kamma 47b
15. perhaps even earlier: a wet-nurse might rub poison, *sam,* on her breast in order to kill the child (Abodah Zarah 26a)
16. Shabbath 12:4
17. arsenic sulfide
18. See also *Rashi* on Sanhedrin 49b. Seven substances *(samim)*....

19. Oefele. *Südd. Apothekerzeitung* 1902, p.33
20. Sotah 7b
21. Tosefta Sotah 1:6
22. Abodah Zarah 28a
23. Baba Kamma 85a
24. Niddah 9:6-7
25. Niddah 31a
26. Shabbath 147b
27. Sukkah 40b
28. Shabbath 147b
29. *ibid*
30. Sanhedrin 55a
31. see Genesis 32:33
32. Baba Bathra 74b

or a spear, and one assumes that he will certainly die; yet if someone applied *samthar* on the wound, he can survive[33]. It was even thought that the head of an executed (decapitated) individual could be made to grow together with the rest of the body by the use of this herb, were it not for the action of a certain wind which plays or blows upon the wound[34].

A further type of remedy is the *salve* (or ointment) for whose base tallow and wax were used[35]. For the needs of the ophthalmologist, one prepared pastes which were traded in the form of loaves (*kollyra* in Greek) and were called collyria. In cases of need, they were rubbed into a salve, possibly with some liquid, to which one ascribed exceptional healing power. Plasters and poultices were also commonly employed.

Among *plasters,* the following are mentioned and considered to be different one from the other: *retiya, ispelanith* and *melugma*[36].

1) A *retiya* is only applied to a wound, never on healthy flesh[37], or at most on a healed wound for protection[38]. When a person falls from the roof, his whole body is injured, and the physician comes and places a *retiya* on his head, as well as on his hands and feet and on all his limbs, so that the patient is completely covered with plaster[39]. A wound which is inflicted with an *izmel* can be healed with *retiya*[40]. We do not know what *retiya* consists of, except that wheat flour is said to be one of its ingredients. This is mentioned in a discussion of the prohibition of sour dough on the Passover holiday[41], and elsewhere[42]. *Retiya* can move out of place so that it has to be applied evenly[43]. Sometimes it even falls off completely[44].

2) It is no longer possible to ascertain how *ispelanith*, or *siphlani*, differs from *retiya*. Perhaps, as the dictionaries suggest, it refers only to the Greek *splenion* (cloth), which is identical to the Hebrew *retiya*. Perhaps they are different in their consistency, similar to the *emplastrum* and *pastillum* (pasta) of contemporary heathendom; the former is applied *(imonitur)*, the latter is painted on[45]. The *ispelanith,* which one opens from the side in order to cleanse the wound[46], could only refer to *emplastrum*. If new wounds which one has plastered begin to hurt, then the plaster must be cut off[47]. The plaster was made either of leather or material[48], or linen or wool rags[49]. It is within the sphere of forbidden superstitions to consider the fat of an ox who was stoned because he killed a human being to be exceptionally efficacious when used in a therapeutic poultice[50].

A poultice recommended by a wise woman for all types of pain consisted of seven parts of fat and one part of wax[51].

3) *Melugma* is undoubtedly the *malagma* of the Greeks, the cataplasm of later generations. Its preparation is similar to the mixing of dough[52] on a wound. There are some made of plant materials, such as wheat or figs[53]. If one lets it (the *melugma*) stand for a long time, it becomes foul smelling[54]. King Hezekiah also placed a fig-cake on his *schechin*[55].

## II   Animal Remedies

From the *fauna* the most important item is honey: "with sweet a person heals the

33. Yebamoth 114b
34. Baba Metzia 107b
35. Shabbath 133b
36. *Tosefta* Kelim 6:9 and *Tosefta* Kilayim 5:25
37. *Tanchuma Mishpatim* p.41b
38. Jerushalmi Shabbath 6; 8b
39. Exodus Rabbah 24:9
40. *Mechilta* on Exodus 14:24
41. *Tosefta* Pesachim 2:3
42. *Tosefta* Demai 1:25
43. Shabbath 75b
44. *Tosefta* Shabbath 5:5
45. Celsus 5:17
46. *Tosefta* Shabbath 5:6
47. Jerushalmi Abodah Zarah 2: 40d
48. Kelim 28:3
49. Jerushalmi Kilayim. End 32d
50. Pesachim 24b
51. Shabbath 133b
52. Jerushalmi Shabbath 7; 10b
53. Shebiith 8:1
54. *Tosefta* Pesachim 2:3
55. Second Kings 20:7

bitter"[56]. Honey was also utilized in the Bible to revive a person who fainted; and in the Talmud it plays a role in the treatment of bulimia, "so that the eyes sparkle again". If wounded people eat honey, it is harmful to the wound, as are all sweet things[57]. A sick person, perhaps one who is coughing, according to the recommendation of physicians, should suck goat's milk directly from the udder of the animal[58]. Someone bitten by a rabid dog was given liver from that animal to eat[59], as recommended by physicians in antiquity, and as practiced by primitive races even today. The gall of a white *dayah* (stork?) in beer was given to a child bitten by a scorpion[60]. The juice of the kidney of a goat was recommended by the physician Minyami for earache[61]. Squashed gnats were applied on snake bites[62].

The pearl should be included in the animal remedies because in antiquity it was very costly and, as today, was therefore quite efficacious. In the Talmud, the legal consequences are discussed in the case of a man who crushed a pearl that was worth one thousand *zuz* and gave it to drink to his future son-in-law. *Rashi* accepts the usual interpretation that a rich man was able to afford such a beverage for medicinal purposes[63]. It is evidently not considered remarkable that Cleopatra, in order solely to mock Antonius, dissolved a pearl worth millions in vinegar and swallowed it[64].

It is noteworthy that very little attention is devoted in the Talmud to the *"filth pharmacy"* which is extensively described by the Greeks and Romans. This observation is obviously related to the general repugnance of Orientals against anything unclean and unesthetic. I am only aware of the following citations thereon in the Talmud: Rabbi Chanina said: forty-day-old urine taken in an amount of 1/32 of a *log* is helpful for the sting of a wasp; a quarter thereof is efficacious for a scorpion bite, one half of a *log* for water left uncovered into which an animal may have injected poison, and one *log* is even useful against witchcraft[65]. It is not possible to ascertain whether the remedy is to be taken internally or applied externally. Children's feces are an ingredient of a remedy for scurvy, which Rabbi Chanina learned from a Roman woman[66]. Pigeon dung is found in a remedy for *ruschchatha*[67]. White dog excrement is the *ultimum refugim* against *barsam,* which is pleuritis. Here, however, the Talmud adds: if he can possibly avoid it, he should not eat the excrement of the white dog, as it is too strong[68]. *Album graecum,* dog excrement, was still considered to be a worthwhile medicament by German physicians of the last century, as opposed to *album nigrum* or mouse exrement.

Finally, let me say a word about the *theriac,* which is the remarkable mixture of antiquity and modern times, and which was originally prepared as an antidote for animal bites. It contained everything which the fantasy could possibly think of. The Talmud took over the name and the evaluation of the theriac from the Greeks. Rabbi Yochanan said: *oenogaron* and *koloquint* and theriac are antidotes against water that was left uncovered which was suspected of being infected with snake poison, and against witchcraft[69]. It was prohibited to purchase theriac from heathens[70], probably because one did not feel secure that poison was not added thereto.

The commentaries take great pains to explain a Midrashic story related by Rabbi Joshua ben Levi of Siknin. In Jerusalem (or Alexandria) there were two families of priests, one of whom had a cold temperament, the other warm. Physicians

56. *Tanchuma Beshallach* 18 p.33a
57. Baba Kamma 85a
58. *Tosefta* Baba Kamma 8:12
59. Yoma 8:6
60. Kethuboth 50a
61. Abodah Zarah 28b
62. Shabbath 77b
63. Baba Bathra 146a
64. Plinius. *Hist. Natur.* 9:58
65. Shabbath 109b
66. Jerushalmi Shabbath 14;14d
67. Gittin 69b
68. *ibid*
69. Shabbath 109b
70. Jerushalmi Abodah Zarah 2; 40d

once sent to have something brought from them in order to prepare a theriac with which to heal snake bites[71]. The commentator Math. Kehunna has an ancient textual reading *cibonim* meaning snakes, instead of "priests"; and David Luria amends *kohanim* (priests) to *chachinim* (snakes), so that the original art of preparing theriac was to cook snake extract — *fiunt e vipera pastilli, qui theriaci vocantur*[72]. Those who retain the textual reading "priests" assume that one excised excess fat from the priests and made theriac therefrom, as once happened to Rabbi Eleazar[73]. Israel Einhorn is of the opinion that this is not so unbelievable; he in fact heard that physicians used the urine of a patient which was excreted in large amounts and was sweet, and they healed therewith!

## III    Perfumer and Apothecary

It is not easy to ascertain who *prepared* the medicines. The preparation of the incense which, as long as the Temple was in existence, was burned on the altar, was an act of the *roke'ach*[74]. In the Chronicles[75] it was considered to be the work of the priestly race; this seems very likely during the time of Nehemiah[76]. The *roke'ach* was therefore perhaps the perfumer. Wherever perfumes were used in large quantities, such as in palaces, one also probably employed maidservants to aid in the production[77].

The place where *roke'ach* (perfume) was sold is the *beth merkochayim*. Whosoever enters (a *beth merkochayim*), even without purchasing or selling anything, takes some of the pleasant aroma with him[78]. Similarly a man who associates with wise men becomes wise[79]. We also always hear of the pleasant aroma of the occupation of the *bassam* (perfumer) of the Talmud, who is equivalent to the *roke'ach* of the Bible *(Targum)*, as opposed to the (bad smell of the) tanner: the world cannot exist without a perfume-maker and without a tanner; happy is he whose craft is that of a *bassam* (perfume-maker)[80]. A marriage at whose onset the man asserts that he is a *bassam* whereas in reality he is a tanner is invalid (and vice-versa)[81]. He utilizes "the small mortar of the perfume-makers", with the pestle called *ker'a*[82] or *regel*[83], as opposed to the "large one found in the kitchen"; he purchases old debt bills for use as wrapping paper[84]; he no longer has a herbal cellar, but rather a "perfume bazaar" called a *chanuth*[85]. Whether in addition to providing the needs of the *toilette,* he also cared for the sick, is not known.

It is also not certain how much *the physician* simultaneously served as an apothecary, according to the custom of the remainder of antiquity.

## IV    Non-Medicinal Remedies

Over and above medicaments, non-medicinal remedies of various types are mentioned in the Talmud. For abdominal pain, one applies warm cloths on the abdomen[86], or places a hot cup on the navel[87], whereby one seeks to obtain the effect of a dry cupping-glass. One also uses a flat lens-shaped hot water bottle called an *adascha*[88] — *vasa fictilia, quas a similitudine lenticulas vocant*[89]. On the other hand, it

---

71. Song of Songs Rabbah 4:5
72. Plinius, *Histor. Natur.* 29:21
73. Baba Metzia 83b
74. Exodus 30:35
75. First Chronicles 9:30
76. Nehemiah 3:8
77. First Samuel 8:13
78. *Pirke de Rabbi Eliezer* 25
79. Proverbs 13:20
80. Kiddushin 82b

81. *Tosefta* Kiddushin 2:4
82. Shabbath 81a
83. Jerushalmi Shabbath 8; 11c; according to Rabbi Chananel
84. Baba Metzia 56b
85. *Tosefta* Berachoth 6:8 and *Yalkut* 950
86. Shabbath 40b
87. *ibid* 66b
88. *Tosefta* Shabbath 3:7
89. Celsus 2:17 p.95:21

is forbidden to place a kettle, *kumkumos* (Greek *koukoumion*)[90], or a bowl, *ariba,* with hot water on the abdomen to soothe a stomachache, because it is considered dangerous[91].

To put sick patients to sleep, one raises water into the air from a container with a spout which has a double siphon, and allows the water to slowly trickle out from the other siphon[92], probably in a manner similar to that of Alexander of Tralles[93], who "let water flow from one container into another, because the moderate noise of the water induces sleep." Music serves to sedate the mentally ill. In order to allow a seriously ill patient to sleep on the Sabbath, one may extinquish a burning light[94].

Bread soaked in wine serves for eye compresses[95], green leaves were applied on inflamed eyes[96]; and ripe as well as unripe gourds were placed on the forehead to cool the patient[97].

Sunbaths were known to all of antiquity, not just to the Greeks[98], but also to the Teutons[99]. The Talmud, too, recognizes the healing effect of the rays of the sun[100] which, according to the words of the prophet, "carries healing in its wings"[101]. The narration in the Bible in the story of Jacob: *and the sun rose upon him as he passed over Peniel*[102], is commented upon by Rabbi Berachya as follows: "the sun shone on him in order to heal him"[103]. Through experience, one became convinced of the efficacious effect of rain (in the Orient!) on sick people. Rabbi Chiya ben Abba is of the opinion that their limbs become supple, and even lepers are relieved therewith[104].

The Babylonian Mar Samuel considers cool water for eye compresses to be the best collyrium in the world. His fellow countrymen, as did the Galileans, used pure water, without the addition of any medications, as an expedient for poor people[105]. Human beings and animals "overcome by blood", who suffer from blood congestion, were placed in cold water in order to cool off[106]. Children were bathed in wine "for healing purposes"[107]. Water was used throughout the Orient in very large quantities, mainly in the form of Turkish baths. These serve for body cleanliness and body care but, in addition, comprise an important component of religious usage (i.e. the ritualarium or *mikvah*). However, I have nothing to report concerning their use for healing purposes. The water "treatment" of Hazael, which the exegetes interpret imaginatively in the Books of Kings, is in actuality a common assassination, as was a frequent and unending occurrence in the history of royal households, particularly in the Orient: King Benhadad was ill and Hazael *took a thick cloth and dipped it in water and spread it on his face so that he (Benhadad) died; and Hazael reigned in his stead*[108]. Josephus states very clearly: he threw a moist blanket over him and suffocated him[109]. It is naturally not possible to know whether the blanket was moistened to apply it more tightly to the face to accelerate the suffocation, or to thereby give the impression of helping the patient with a cool compress. Both are likely.

On the other hand, the use of natural waters and springs for healing purposes is undoubted. In the laws of the Sabbath, "bathing for healing purposes" in the Great (Mediterranean) Sea and in the waters of Tiberias is mentioned, and is explicitly

90. Shabbath 40b
91. Jerushalmi Shabbath 9; 12a
92. *Tosefta* Shabbath 2:8
93. Ed. Puschmann. Vol. 1 p.361
94. Shabbath 2:5
95. Shabbath 108b
96. *ibid* 109a
97. Yoma 78a
98. Marcuse. *Diaetetik im Altertum* Stuttgart 1809 p.13 and 25
99. Höfler. in Neuberger-Pagel's *Handbuch* 1:477

100. Nedarim 8b
101. Malachi 3:20
102. Genesis 32:32
103. Genesis Rabbah 78:5
104. *ibid* 13:16
105. Shabbath 78a
106. *ibid* 53b
107. *Tosefta* Shabbath 12:13
108. Second Kings 8:15
109. *Antiquities.* Book 9 Chapt. 5:6

permitted. Bathing in a wash-basin in which flax, laundry, etc. is soaked, and in the Sea of Sodom (the Dead Sea) is permitted, but with certain restrictions[110]. The law does not speak about the illnesses which are supposedly helped by these baths. The *Midrash* provides evidence for the healing power of river water[111]; in the words of the prophet: *wherever the waters cometh, they shall be healed, and everything liveth whither the river cometh*[112].

It seems uncertain whether or not one can explain by natural means the efficacy against leprosy of bathing in the Jordan River, a practice which the Syrians followed with success at the suggestion of the prophet Elisha[113]. In later times, one hears no more about these baths, although leprosy is mentioned in many places. Therefore, one is forced to either assume that supernatural infuences played a role (which verse 8 seems to imply), or that the *tzara'ath* of the field generals was a different skin disease from leprosy, against which the waters of the Jordan were efficacious. Rabbi Yochanan explains the absence of people ill with *tzara'ath* in Babylon on the basis of the utilization of bathing in the Euphrates River[114].

We will later discuss the therapeutic efficacy of drinking water from the Siloa Springs.

Also famous and well-tried is *climatotherapy*. Among the things which "avert misfortune" are changes of one's place of residence[115]. A king who travels with his ill son to a health resort is described not infrequently in the parables of the *Midrash*. Rebbe lived in Beth Shearim; when he became ill, he moved to Sepphoris, which is situated at a high altitude and whose air is fragrant, *bassim*[116]. Rationalistic Bible commentators are also of the opinion that the lions which slew the foreign settlers in Samaria because *they knew not the manner of the God of the land*[117] did so because of the unaccustomed climatic conditions. Furthermore, "the God of the people", into whose hand the Lord wishes to give the Pharaoh and the Egyptians[118] can supposedly be understood in the same manner[119].

We have already spoken above about the "sympathetic remedy"[120] as well as about bloodletting[121].

## V   Diet

The regulation of one's entire mode of life, particularly the nourishment for a sick patient about which we are first beginning to learn again in our time, was one of the principal duties of the physician in antiquity. Out of humaneness, the Talmud requires that for a patient in whom the illness is considered to be hopeless the physician prescribe: "eat this, but not that." The physician should not, however, as once the prophet did to King Hezekiah, abruptly state: *set thine house in order, for thou shalt die*[122]. One can inform the next of kin that meticulous compliance with the physician's dietary instructions will probably not help the incurable patient and he can really eat whatever he wishes. Others are of the opinion that such patients should be allowed to eat whatever they desire[123]. An indication for the *practical* handling of such a situation by the physician is provided by the following: the *Torah* introduces the laws concerning the priests with the allusion that the sons of Aaron died because they offered sacrifices contrary to the Divine instructions[124]. Rabbi Eleazar ben Azariah compared this to a

110. *Tosefta* Shabbath 12:13
111. Exodus Rabbah 15:21
112. Ezekiel 47:9
113. Second Kings 5:14
114. Kethuboth 77b
115. Genesis Rabbah 44:12
116. Kethuboth 103b
117. Second Kings 17:26
118. Ezekiel 31:11

119. Levi Ben Abaham ben Chayim; Frankel's *Monatschrift* 1900 p.66
120. Chapter 3, Section 9
121. Chapter 5, Appendix 2
122. Second Kings 20:1
123. Exodus Rabbah 30:22; Eccles. Rabbah 5:6
124. Levit. 16:1

sick patient to whom the physician comes[125] and says: do not drink anything cold and do not sleep in a damp place. Another physician then comes and says to the patient: do not drink anything cold and do not sleep in a damp place lest you die as so and so died. The latter physician makes a much greater impression on the patient than the former[126].

Concerning those patients in whom recovery is still anticipated, it is said that a healthy person eats whatever he happens to have, whereas a patient requests all types of delicacies[127]. Particularly desirable among these delicacies are apples "whose aroma is pleasant"[128], and which were craved by the love-sick Shulamith[129]. In a legal regulation, the manner of payment for a worker who was hired to bring grapes, apples and plums for a patient is determined, whether he finds the patient dead or well[130]. People who try to conceal their baseness by performing pious acts, or who attempt to justify the means by the end, are compared to a harlot who prostitutes herself for apples and then distributes them to the sick[131]. Also useful for sick patients is "an egg laid on the same day"[132] and fish[133].

Sick people should avoid eating gourds *(kara)*. A physician came to heal the ill Rabbi Jeremiah. When the physician saw a gourd in the patient's room from which he had eaten, the physician abruptly left the bedside of the patient saying: "he has the angel of death in his house, and I should heal him"! On the other hand, patients may eat the very delicate kinds of *hatriyoth*[134] as a side dish[135].

The food called *arsan* is "good for sick patients". According to Rabbi Jonathan, it consists of old peeled barley from the bottom of the sieve (i.e. heavy, large kerneled barley) and according to Rabbi Joseph, it consists of fine flour made from such barley. It should be cooked like beef[136]. *Arsan* is thus good old *ptisane* whose original name is found in the *Midrash:* "*Tisane* which is prepared for the sick"[137]. Pregnant women eat it in order to have strong children[138].

*Schathitha* also belongs to the dietetic remedies. It is prepared in both "thick" and "thin" forms; the former is used as a nourishing food and the latter as a medication[139]. According to the commentaries, it consists of corn flour which is dried in the oven while still unripe[140], and admixed with honey[141]. The "thin" type was also probably used as a beverage for a traveler who arrived at an inn and requested water. He was given *schathitha*[142]; it could therefore not refer to a thick pap. Another type of *schathitha* is prepared from lentil flour to which vinegar has been added. Barzillai sent both types to David[143] when the latter arrived hungry and tired with his entourage[144]. *Schathitha* also serves as a remedy for *achilu* fever[145].

About the therapeutic beverage *keruretin,* we only know that it was also imbibed for pleasure[146]. Dictionaries identify the word with Late Latin: *claretum,* medicated wine, which seems to be unlikely.

Hadrian once decreed that for three days no one should kindle a fire. During the

125. *Yalkut* and *Rashi* substitute: who comes to the physician
126. see also *Sifra* on Levit. 16:1
127. Song of Songs Rabbah 2:5
128. Soferim 16:4
129. Song of Songs 2:5
130. *Tosefta* Baba Metzia 7:4
131. Exodus Rabbah 31:17
132. Sanhedrin 64a
133. *ibid* 98a
134. The meaning meal-pap for *hatri* has already been excluded. In addition, the transcription *athare* for *hatri* is unacceptable.
135. Nedarim 49a
136. *ibid* 41b
137. *Tanchuma Shemoth* 22 p.7b and *Beshallach* 22 p.34a
138. Yoma 47a
139. Berachoth 38a
140. *Rashi. loc. cit.*
141. *Rashi* on Erubin 29b
142. Sanhedrin 67b
143. Abodah Zarah 38b
144. Second Samuel 17:28
145. Gittin 70a
146. Jerusalmi Shabbath 14; 14c

evening of the same day, he noticed the glow of a light and learned that an official was ill and the physician told him that he would not recover unless he ate warm food[147].

A type of dietetic treatment practiced by Roman physicians is described from the time of Vespasian. It is related that Rabbi Zadok, in order to ward off the fall of Jerusalem, abstained from all nourishment for forty years. He lived only on figs which he sucked and then threw away. He became so emaciated that when he ate something one could see it externally. Before the surrender of Jerusalem, Vespasian was asked to send physicians to heal Rabbi Zadok. On the first day, they gave him water in which bran had been soaked *(paaré)*; on the second day, they gave him water in which there was *sipuka* or *sipuska* (coarse bran mixed with flour); on the third day, they gave him water in which there had been coarse flour, until his intestines gradually expanded[148].

Many items pertinent to our discussion are found in a form which leads one to suspect that they deal with ancient academic regulations or utterances of folk medicine. They are presented in such a form specifically to be more easily remembered.

Ten things bring a man's sickness back, and in a severer form, namely; the consumption of beef, fat meat, roasted meat, poultry, roasted eggs, cress, milk and cheese, and shaving and a Turkish bath. Some Sages also add nuts and large cucumbers.

Six things heal a man of his sickness with a complete cure, namely: cabbage, mangold, camomile, the maw (or fourth stomach of a ruminant), the womb, and the (large lobe of the) liver. Some also add a small fish[149].

## VI    Geriatrics

King David was old and getting on in years (not through *senectus praecox*). They covered him with clothes, but he did not become warm. Then his servants suggested that a young maiden sleep next to him, so that he should become warm. And Abishag of Shunam was selected, and she ministered to the king as directed. The king knew her not, however (i.e. did not have coitus with her)[150], because of his senility, as the *Aggadah* adds, as Abishag expresses it in the malicious phrase: if the thief lacks the strength to commit a theft, he becomes an honest man[151].

The King was seventy years old at the time. His clothes no longer fulfilled their function, as a punishment for the fact that once he conducted himself contemptuously with the clothes of another[152], that is he cut off the corner of King Saul's skirt[153].

We know nothing concerning the mode of action of this treatment and the results thereof. The physician Johann Heinrich Cohausen of Muenster has proposed numerous possibilities to which the interested reader is referred. He also cites parallels from heathen antiquity [154].

Reports from modern times concerning geriatrics were compiled by Iwan Bloch, who also coined the term Shunamitism for this method (of warming an aging person)[155].

## VII    The Visiting of the Sick

The care of the sick (i.e. visiting the sick, known as *bikkur cholim*) is one of the holy duties; it is a charitable deed or *gemilath chesed*. Its first explicit mention is found

---

147. Eccles. Rabbah 9:4
148. Gittin 56a
149. Berachoth 57b
150. First Kings 1:1 ff
151. Sanhedrin 22a; see also the commentary of Rabbi Chananel thereon.
152. Berachoth 62b

153. First Samuel 24:5
154. Der Wieder Lebende Hermippus oder...sein Leben durch das Anhauchen Junger-Magdchen bis auf 115 Jahr zu verlängern... 1753 8°.
155. Albert Hagen. *Die Sexuelle Osphresiologie*, Charlottenburg 1901 p.191 ff

in the book of Sirach[156]. The Rabbis, however, derive this obligation from various places in the Bible. They interpret the phrase *ye shall walk after the Lord, your God*[157] to mean: attempt to emulate Him. God visited Abraham when he was ill following his circumcision[158]; a person should therefore follow this Divine example[159]. God says that *I know him, and he will command his children and his household after him that they shall keep the way of the Lord*[160]. *The way of the Lord* refers to the visiting of the sick[161]. Jethro admonishes Moses to show the Children of Israel the path they should follow and the deeds they should perform[162], namely charitable deeds, visiting the sick and burying the dead[163].

The Psalmist tells us: *happy is he that considereth the poor*[164]; only the sick are truly poor for they cannot earn a living[165]. In Talmudic times, it was the "custom of the world" that the sick who were lying ill in bed were visited by others[166].

We are told very little concerning the obligations of those who visit the sick. Since these obligations are in fact charitable deeds, no specification can be set in any individual case. The Psalmist does not say "blessed is he that *giveth* to the poor (i.e. the sick)" but "he that dealeth wisely with (i.e. is considerate of) the poor" (from the Hebrew word *sechel*), that is he observes (from *sakal*) the special circumstances and considers how best he can help the patient[167]. As the prototype of one who cares for the sick, God supports the sick patient on his bed of illness and turns his bed completely around in his sickness[168].

When one of the disciples of Rabbi Akiba fell ill, he (Rabbi Akiba) went to visit him and, because the people caring for the patient swept and sprinkled the ground before him, following orders from Rabbi Akiba who found the room neglected, the disciple recovered. He said, "My master, you have revived me", following which Rabbi Akiba taught: he who does not visit the sick disciple can be like a shedder of blood. Rabbi Dimi similarly taught: he who visits the sick causes him to live, whilst he who does not causes him to die[169]. The *halacha* deduces therefrom that concern for the cleanliness of the chamber in which the patient lies is among the obligations incumbent upon the one who visits, as well as the one who cares for the sick[170]. If necessary, one lets a light remain kindled near the patient. Oil of *terumah* which became ritually unclean and should therefore properly be burnt, may be used as kindling oil for the lighting of synagogues, houses of study, dark alleys and chambers of the sick[171]. In the latter case, according to the opinion of some Sages, one does not even need the permission of the priest to whom the oil belongs[172], further proof of the importance which one attributes to the care of the sick.

Where it seems appropriate, one exhorts the patient to take care of his financial affairs, since he perhaps has outstanding debts or obligations. One should not, however, allude to the imminent death of the patient[173].

There is no measure for visiting the sick; even a prominent person must visit a simple person, if necessary "even a hundred times a day"[174]. Even the religion of a patient should make no difference[175]. Even one's affinity *(ben gilo)*[176] must visit the

---

156. Sirach 7:35
157. Deut. 13:5
158. Genesis 18:1
159. Sotah 14a
160. Genesis 18:19
161. Genesis Rabbah 49:4
162. Exodus 18:20
163. *Mechilta, loc. cit.*
164. Psalms 41:2
165. Nedarim 40a
166. *ibid* 39a

167. Jerushalmi Peah 8; 21b
168. Psalms 41:4
169. Nedarim 40a
170. *Yoreh Deah* 335:8
171. Terumoth 11:10
172. Jerushalmi Terumoth 11; 48a
173. *Yoreh Deah* 335:7
174. Nedarim 39b
175. Gittin 61a
176. a person born at the same hour and under the same planetary influence

sick, although he himself becomes afflicted with 1/60 of the illness by his visit[177]. It is customary that relatives and friends first visit a patient. After three days, even the more distant acquaintances come to visit. If one is dealing with an illness that occurred suddenly, then all visit immediately[178].

One should not visit the sick either early in the morning or toward evening[179], in order not to be deceived by the patient's appearance: in the morning the sick appear better — as the day begins, the illness lightens[180] — in the evening, they seem worse. Mar Samuel says that one should visit a sick person only after his fever has subsided[181]. One should also not visit those suffering from diarrhea, or eye diseases or headaches; the first because of embarrassment, and the latter two because speech is injurious to the eyes and to people with headaches, and their fever increases[182]. Rather one should inquire outside the patient's room about his situation and about his needs[183].

One who visits the sick takes away 1/60 of the patient's illness. It might thus appear that if sixty people visited him simultaneously, the patient would be immediately cured and could then go out into the street with them! However, the Talmudic statement is to be understood as follows: every visitor takes away 1/60 of the illness which remains after his predecessor had visited the patient and taken away 1/60 of the illness. Hence the patient would not be completely cured by sixty visitors[184]. And even to achieve this result, it is necessary that every visitor love the patient as himself[185].

One of the duties of every visitor is to pray for the sick; if one does not do so, one has not fulfilled the obligation of visiting the sick in all its aspects[186].

Visiting the sick is one of the things, the fruit of which man eats in this world, while the principal remains for him for the world to come[187]. Rab teaches that he who visits the sick will be delivered from the punishments of Gehenna[188], for *the Lord will deliver him in the day of evil*[189]. Also in this world, *God will preserve him and keep him alive*[190]. Jesus also teaches that on the Day of Judgement, the Lord will give special recognition to the sheep on His right side because they visited the sick, and the goats on His left side to be sent to the devil because they neglected this duty[191].

In the Bible we already find municipally regulated care of the poor, whereby the provision for the needy is not left to the "good hearts" of the wealthy. This public care of the poor seems to have been built into a firm legal system in the *Mishnah* and the *Gemara*. In many towns, already during the time of the Temple[192], there existed a "town brotherhood" known as *chaber ir,* whose function was to collect and distribute funds to the poor. Brotherhoods or societies also concerned themselves with charitable deeds in the narrow sense, namely the burial of the dead — such a *chaburetha* is explicitly mentioned in the Talmud[193] — and the visiting of the sick. It is related that Abimi, a member of a sick-visiting society or brotherhood, used to visit the sick[194]. Here there was no municipal organization as there was for the provision for the poor. Even the Essenes, who ordinarily did nothing without an order from their leaders, had a free hand in two matters, in the *epikouria* (assistance) and in *eleos* (mercy)[195].

177. Baba Metzia 30b
178. Jerushalmi Peah 3; 17d
179. Nedarim 40a
180. Baba Bathra 16b
181. Nedarim 41a
182. *ibid*
183. *Yoreh Deah* 335:8
184. Nedarim 39b
185. Levit. Rabbah 34:2
186. Shabbath 12a-b
187. *ibid* 127a

188. Nedarim 40a
189. Psalms 41:2
190. *ibid* 41:3
191. Matthew 25:36 and 43
192. Kohler in *Festschrift zum 70 Geburtstage A. Berliners.* Frankfurt a.M. 1903 p.197
193. Moed Katan 27b
194. Genesis Rabbah 13:16
195. Josephus. *The Jewish War.* Book 2 Chapt. 8:6

In every "old-fashioned" Jewish community, there exists such a society even today. It has the name *chebra kadisha,* and its meritorious deeds are the visiting of the sick and the burial of the dead. In addition, there exist numerous separate *bikkur cholim* (visiting the sick) societies, whose history regretfully has not yet been written.

On the other hand, the Jews did not have hospitals during the time of the Talmud. This fact cannot be denied by any apologetics. The *beth chophshith* of King Uzziah was, at most, a home for lepers[196], but more likely only a place of refuge which the leprous king had built for himself away from residential areas, whereas his less fortunate co-sufferers had to terminate their miserable lives in huts.

The lack of hospitals can, from the medical point of view, be considered to represent a serious deficiency of insight into hygiene. For the Orient — not only for the Jews — the establishment of such a hospital would have signified a complete reversal of understanding, and an alienation of the deep-rooted concept of hospitality which was practiced without reservation and was actually considered to be a holy duty. If one took in the healthy traveler without question, how could one lock out a sick person from one's house? A person who became ill while traveling was brought to the nearest guesthouse as must still be done today; if the patient can reach the city, then every house is open to him.

For passing strangers, particularly however for the poor, there undoubtedly existed special lodging homes in which one made provision for all necessities, even if the temporary inhabitants were ill. These special houses were used in order to practice hospitality in a grand manner where there were an insufficient number of available rooms in private homes. Legend relates that Abraham had already built such a lodging place for strangers[197], *a tamarisk which he planted in Beer Sheba*[198]. It is this legend which Hieronymus had in mind when he stated that Fabiola, the foundress of the first Christian hospital in Rome, transplanted a twig of the terebinth of Abraham on the banks of the Auson[199] — in other words, the hospital is an imitation of a long familiar establishment of the Jews. For everything in antiquity that is understood to be included in the term "hospital" is nothing more than the hospitality houses[200] in the ancient Jewish sense, copied from both the object itself and the name: *geruth*[201], from *ger* meaning *hospes.* Leprosariums were first built in the Middle Ages and the *Charité,* at the time the only hospital in Berlin (more correctly "in the vicinity" of Berlin), was originally founded in the year 1703 as a plague hospital. The truly modern hospital dates first from the 19th century.

The Roman *valetudinaria* for slaves and soldiers have nothing in common with these humanitarian institutions, and even less so with a hospital. One can most appropriately compare them in principle with the grazing paddocks of horse owners of modern times. I would like to temporarily leave undecided into which category to place the Buddhist hospitals of King Asoka and the corresponding institutions of the pre-Columbian Mexicans[202].

The designation *hekdesh,* meaning sacred or sanctuary, for a hospital, can first be attributed to the Jews in the eleventh century, in Cologne[203]. In Berlin the first Jewish hospital existed even before the expulsion of the Jews from Brandenburg in 1573. After their return under the Great Elector, the newly founded *chebrath bikkur cholim* (society for the visiting of the sick) established a new *hekdesh* in 1703.

---

196. Second Kings 15:5 and Second Chronicles 26:21
197. Genesis Rabbah 54:6
198. Genesis 21:33
199. Kohler. *loc. cit.*

200. from *hospes* meaning guest or stranger
201. Jeremiah 41:17
202. Block in Pagel-Neuberger's *Handbuch* 1:498
203. Kohler *loc. cit.*

In Talmudic times, it appears that a room on the uppermost floor, the *aliya*[204], was preferentially used as a sick room, probably because up there, the noise from the ground floor of people entering and leaving is least disturbing (to the patient). For this reason "one goes up" to visit a patient[205] and the physicians "go up" in order to treat him[206].

204. Shabbath 1:4; Josephus' *Antiquities* Book 18 Chapt. 8:2

205. Shabbath. *loc. cit.*

206. Numbers Rabbah 18:13

# CHAPTER XVI

## *LEGAL MEDICINE*

## INTRODUCTION

With complete justification I could have divided the entire content of this book into two large sections — legal and folk medicine — whereby the first section would contain the pertinent halachic passages and the second the corresponding aggadic passages. For well-considered reasons, I chose to subdivide the material in a different manner and, therefore, much of that which is usually considered under the heading of "legal medicine" has already been discussed, particularly body injuries and mental illnesses. Therefore, only the questions concerning the sexual sphere remain.

Even among these, the signs of puberty and the uncertain sexual symptoms have previously been discussed.

### I

For most of us, the unhappy remembrance of the news of the Mariaberger trial first brought to our attention the existence of a "moral theology" and "pastoral medicine". Nevertheless, the literature on this subject is extraordinarily extensive and already quite ancient. Individual themes such as the influence of the fantasies of the mother on the embryo are already found in the writings of the church fathers. In the Middle Ages, the Jesuits are represented by exceptionally numerous writings, and in modern times, we have a work from a physician's pen, frequently reprinted — the already often-referred to book of Capellmann. As far as I can see, all these works are written from the Catholic viewpoint.

A relatively large portion of these books is devoted to consideration of questions of sex, and it was, therefore, thought that these should be simply considered among pornographic writings. Schürer also speaks of "the obscene casuistry of the Jesuits"[1]. One can only have arrived at this undoubtedly false conclusion if one overlooks the milieu from which these writings originate. One should only call obscene those books which aim, either in form or in content, to elicit lewd thoughts *in the readership for whom they are intended*. Without this qualification, every *medical* book which deals with sexual or gynecological questions would have to be classified as pornographic. Obscene books in the usual sense of the word would certainly not have been allowed to pass by the church censors.

---

1. *Geschichte d. jüd Volkes im Zeitalter Jesu Christ* 3, II, 494

The truth of the matter is essentially different, however. Only the uninformed or the hypocrite would deny the fact that in the individual the *vita sexualis* plays an inordinately important role. As much as the physician would wish that one bring to *him* all questions pertaining to this subject, one must reckon with the reality of the situation, i.e. that the public is accustomed to seek a physician only for matters which have a connection with *health*. Questions of morality and ethics, however, are brought to a different forum. For a large section of mankind, morality and ethics are synonymous with religion, and, therefore, it is understandable that the theologian is often in the position of offering advice in this area, particularly if one can question him or be questioned by him without bashfulness, as in the confession box. Even where religious and medical precepts actually or seemingly conflict, the clergyman is approached in the decision of an individual where a sin was committed and he confesses to the priest, in order to receive forgiveness. In this manner the confessional priest acquires a richer knowledge of sexual perversions than some physicians. Many collected this practical knowledge and adapted it in book form with their own reflections and with the interpretations from other books which confirm the decisions of the author, and provided such books to their less informed colleagues in the priesthood, but not to laymen. Therefore, these writings should certainly not be considered obscene since, in addition, most are written in a scholarly Latin which is unintelligible to the layman.

At this point, one should draw attention to a similar situation in India. According to the Hindu religion, if a man dies without leaving any male offspring, he is not accepted in Paradise and must suffer a disgraceful metempsychosis. For this reason, the goal of every faithful Hindu is the raising of male children. There exists a large number of writings concerning the *ars amandi* from antiquity, which, to the Europeans, seem to be obscenely pornographic, but which the Hindus view as scientific and moral, because they provide the Hindu with methodological instructions to help him attain his life's wish. Accordingly, people took serious offense and, in fact, couldn't comprehend why the French government prohibited and confiscated some of these writings[2].

I also wish to take into consideration the possibility that the Egyptian Papyrus Turin, which is usually considered obscene, perhaps served a similar purpose.

## II

The above statements are certainly barely applicable to Talmudic medicine, primarily because in Judaism there is no clergy, and all concepts of auricular confession, dispensation, pardon and absolution of sins through human beings are totally foreign. All people, without exception, are subject to the same *law*, and when the "clergyman" (i.e. rabbi) is called to render a decision in a religious matter, he does it not by virtue of a direct Divine inspiration, but rather on the basis of his extensive and in-depth knowledge of the law. This knowledge of the law is his only consecration, and distinguishes him from the laymen only by degree, and not in principle. The highest title in ancient Judaism which one could bestow upon someone was the promotion to *Rabbi,* and this word means simply "teacher" or doctor.

The entire law of the Jews is based on the Bible; the latter also regulates sexual relations in a detailed manner. Concerning marriage and fornication, as well as concerning many things which we today consider as hygiene, the Bible contains regulations, just as do all other law books, up to our times. The Mishnah and the Talmud provide the explanatory discussions thereto and the practical appreciation of certain situations, such as the delineation of the practices of daily living. The Jewish

---

2. See *La France Médicale* 1905 No. 11 p.212

"clergyman" cannot demand a confession from anyone, nor is anyone obligated to confess to him. Only where a special religious law is involved, such as in divorce cases, where sexual matters such as impotence and the like are the reasons given for the divorce, can one not avoid investigating these allegations. But in such a circumstance it is not a single judge that officiates, but a council of rabbis that supervises the observance of the law, just as is done by a municipal court. When the Jews still had their own system of criminal justice, cases of capital crimes, adultery, incest, etc. were also naturally debated in the courts of law, in order to be able to arrive at a final judgement. Moreover, in all ages in cases where a doubt existed about the law, one asked advice from those learned in the law, so as not to conflict with the law.

If one here wishes to speak of "lewdness", then one must logically equally so designate all modern legal decisions which discuss such cases with all the details. I do not believe, for example, that there exists in Talmudic literature a parallel to the decision of the German Reich's court which very seriously speaks of the question as to whether the penetration of the penis into the mouth of a sleeping person is considered "fornication"[3]. On the other hand, if such a case were to come before a Talmudic court of law, then the court could not avoid a discussion thereof. For to no jurist could it or should it make any difference whether the accused transgressed and committed a crime against a human life or against morality, or any other legal matter; for the reputation of the accused and the damage done to the legal conscience of the people are always involved. The judge should, therefore, not be held responsible for this; rather the persons or the circumstances which gave rise to such deplorable trials.

# III

According to the aforementioned statements, it might in fact appear that people such as E. Schürer who assert that the Jewish "ethic and theology is resolved in jurisprudence"[4], are correct. One could only arrive at this undoubtedly false conclusion if one saw in Judaism, as represented in the Bible and Talmud, a "religion" in the modern sense of the word. The religion of modern times, however, encompasses only the relationship between man and his God, all according to how the individual religious denominations perceive Him, and, therefore, primarily regulates only transcendental matters. Concerning most matters of life in any community, there exists the public law *in addition* to religion, but one rarely gives an accounting for this sphere of activity. For example, in Germany we have a book of civil laws with 2000 paragraphs excluding the introductory material thereto, a penal code, civil and penal lawsuit proceedings, commercial and military penal codes, etc... To these must be added the various church laws, the thousands of laws and decrees such as the individual edicts of local and police authorities, and for every law, the interpretations and the decisions of the highest law tribunals.

The content of all these laws can also be found in the Talmud, for the simple reason that, possibly unlike any other country at any time, in the Jewish state, government and religion were completely identical. The Jewish state was a theocracy in which no state law existed other than the Divine law or, expressed differently, each governmental law was simultaneously a religious law. If *every* law on the earth has, as it should have, the reasonable purpose of promoting universal morality, then, in our times, we could affirm with the same, and perhaps greater, justification that the ethic of jurisprudence is also resolved in it.

Naturally, the ancient Sages of the Talmud knew, as well as or even better than the Sages of modern times, that legal regulation is not the aspiration of man, but is only an

---

3. See the decision in *Strafsgesetzbuch* Vol.     4. *Loc. cit.* p.491
20, 1890, p.225

expedient. For that reason, they teach that when the Messiah arrives, that is, at the time of the highest level of man's moral perfection, all laws will be suspended[5]. And they also recognized that all laws do not suffice to genuinely make man good and to raise him to that lofty height of moral perfection which is the final goal he strives for. Therefore, they stated in a beautiful allegory[6] that the ink which remained in the pen of Moses *after* he recorded all the laws was responsible for the rays and the Divine brilliance of his face, of which the Bible speaks[7]. In addition, in many matters of which they disapprove, they emphasize that although there is no punishment by the earthly court, the action involved is liable to Divine punishment. *These* laws, which are unwritten, represent that which is today called morality, as opposed to laws.

# PART I

## I    Chastity

For the unmarried, chastity is an obvious requirement[8] which is therefore not explicitly stated in either the Talmud or the Bible. However, Rabbi Eliezer finds this precept of chastity already articulated in the Bible. That is, the Bible teaches: *and thou* (as the father) *shalt not profane thy daughter, to cause her to be a prostitute, lest the land* (i.e. its inhabitants) *fall to prostitution, and the land become full of fornication*[9]. Since sexual intercourse with a married woman is specifically prohibited[10] and punished as adultery with the death of both partners, therefore, the above legal precept can only refer to the unmarried, and of both sexes, as is the opinion of Rabbi Eliezer[11].

Many *admonitions* of this type occur. Three are mentioned (praised) daily by God: an unmarried person who lives in a large city and doesn't sin, a poor person who finds an object of value and returns it to its owner, and a rich person who gives his tithe secretly. When these teachings were recited in the presence of Rabbi Safra, who as a young bachelor lived in a large city, his face shone from joy. However, Rabbah said to him: not someone such as you is meant, but rather such as Rabbi Chanina and Rabbi Oshaya who live in a street of prostitutes, repair shoes for them, and whom the prostitutes come and look at, but who in spite of this do not lift their eyes to look at the prostitutes[12]. He who yields to prostitution is afflicted with premature senility or *senectus praecox*[13]. That sexual abstinence brings no damage to the health of either young girls or young men is most emphatically stressed by Soran in ancient times[14].

The overall position of the Talmud on the question of illegal sexual intercourse seems to be clearly enunciated in two theses. Rabbi Yochanan teaches: "there is a small organ in man; he who satisfies it goes hungry and he who allows it to hunger is satisfied"[15]; and Rabbi Ilay teaches: "if a man realizes that his evil instinct is stronger than he is, he should go to a place where he is not known, dress in dark clothes, wrap his head in a dark turban and do that which his heart demands, but he should not openly profane the name of God"[16]. This can only mean that lust in general only governs one who has tasted the fruit, and that the most reliable remedy against carnal appetite is abstinence. Where, however, in spite of this, the instinct occasionally threatens to become overpowering, then a person is obligated to struggle against it, and in any case not to immediately submit thereto.

---

5. Niddah 61b
6. Exodus Rabbah 47:6
7. Exodus 34:35
8. cf. Job 31:1
9. Leviticus 19:29
10. *ibid* 20:10
11. *Tosefta* Kiddushin 1:4

12. Pesachim 113a-b
13. Shabbath 152a
14. *de mul. pass.* chap. 7 p.35, Ermerins
15. Sanhedrin 107a
16. Moed Katan 17a; see also *Tosafoth* Kiddushin 40a

An important supportive measure in the struggle against carnal lust and against temptation is a strong moral foundation, especially also the remembrance of a strong moral code in one's parents' home. A Roman woman found it remarkable that Joseph, "a young man of seventeen years, with his full vital energies", withstood the seductive demands of the wife of Potiphar. However, the Rabbis explain, when he *came into the house to do his work* (i.e. to lie with her)[17], a vision of his father's face appeared to him, and his blood cooled, and his sperm came out through his finger nails[18], in that he bored his hands into the earth, or more simply, because he pressed his fingernails into his hand and thus forcibly distracted himself. Also, in another place in the Talmud, for the same purpose, it is recommended "to bore the ten nails into the ground"[19].

The above narrative is more valuable ethically than the one transmitted by Johannes Moschus, in which a monk from the Penthukla cloister who could no longer withstand the demands of the flesh went into a brothel in Jericho, and when he entered there, was suddenly stricken with leprosy, whereupon he rapidly returned to his cloister[20].

Bloch is correct in designating the above-mentioned teaching of abstinence as the most worthwhile goal to aspire to, until there develops the possibility of a permanent satisfactory hygienic sexual traffic, whether this is based on medical or moral grounds[21]. Naturally, this demand of chastity applies to both sexes, not only to the female.

## II  Marriage

The ancient Sages recognized that the most effective measure against the prevalence of the evil instinct is prophylaxis. He who loves his wife as himself but honors her more than himself, and leads his sons and daughters along the straight path, and *marries them off shortly after* (literally: near) *their puberty, before they fall prey to sin*[22] — concerning him can one state together with Job[23]: "Know that your house is peace"[24]. The knowledge of how to satisfy carnal appetite at any time is the best protection against it. For the one who has bread in his basket, even if he once has to go hungry therewith, is not comparable to the one who suffers hunger because his basket is empty[25].

Only one who has a wife can occupy himself with the study of the Torah with purity of thoughts[26]. For the sake of avoiding adultery, says the apostle[27], everyone should have his own wife. This early marriage of even adolescents certainly builds a powerful factor in the prevention of illicit intercourse, for in this market, too, the supply depends on the demand. To be sure, even in antiquity, circumstances led the Rabbis to teach that it is sensible *(derech eretz)* that one first build a house and then plant a vineyard and only then bring home a bride[28]. But Rav Huna is correct when he stated that he who is still unmarried at twenty years of age spends his life in sin or even worse[29], in sinful thoughts. In this matter, I am better off than my comrades, said Rav Chisda, in that I already married at age sixteen[30]. Even so, marriage with a young lad less than thirteen years of age was considered lewdness[31]. In the Mishnah, the normal age for marriage for a man is considered to be the eighteenth year of life[32]; later, however, some Sages extended the upper limit to twenty years[33] or to twenty-four

---

17. Genesis 39:11
18. Genesis Rabbah 87:6-7
19. Shebuoth 18a
20. in Rosenbaum's *Lustseuche* p.417
21. *Das Sexualleben Unserer Zeit.* Berlin 1907 p.730
22. Derech Eretz Rabbah 2; 56b, 10
23. Job 5:24
24. Yebamoth 62b

25. Yoma 18b
26. Yoma 72b
27. First Corinthians 7:2
28. Sotah 44a
29. Yoma 29a
30. *ibid*
31. *Even Ha'ezer* I, 3
32. Aboth 5:24
33. Kiddushin 29b

years[34]. In even later times, one is taught, according to the "usage of the world" *(noheg she'beolam)*, to marry at age thirty or forty[35]. This occurred under the heavy burden of those times in Palestine when the economic conditions and the religious persecutions under Diocletian made independence very difficult[36].

He who has no wife is considered as if heaven has excommunicated him[37], and he does not want to be called "human"[38], since it states *man and wife God created them and called their name "man"* (Hebrew: *adam*)[39]. He lives without joy, without blessing, without goodness and without peace[40]. One of the reasons why the sons of Aaron died prematurely was their celibacy[41]. *Nadab and Abihu died before the Lord, and they had no children,* states the Bible[42], which the Talmud interprets "because they didn't want any children". Similar statements can be extracted from the Talmud in great numbers[43].

He who becomes engaged to a girl should marry her as soon as possible[44], because "a hope which becomes protracted makes the heart sick, but the tree of life is a fulfilled wish"[45]. For a virgin, the normal period of engagement is twelve months, for a widow four weeks, as required to provide the dowry[46].

## III   Procreation

The words with which the Creator addressed the first pair of human beings: *be fruitful and multiply*[47] are perceived as a transmission for all times of a divine command, and its validity for all generations should be preserved. It therefore follows that, unless restricted by considerations to be mentioned later, such as incest and the like, cohabitation in and of itself is not thought to be immoral. However, strictly speaking, this only applies if the cohabitation serves the purpose of procreation.

As far as we know, only one branch of the Essenes drew this stringent conclusion. Whereas the major part of this sect on the whole did not marry[48] or, in fact, scorned marriage *(gamou hyperopsia par' autois)* without rejecting it in principle *(ton gamon ouk anairountes)*[49], that branch was of the opinion that the striving for descendants is the most important goal in life. They did not cohabit with pregnant women in order to demonstrate that they married not out of lasciviousness, but for the purpose of having children[50]. This is the account of Josephus concerning that sect, whose ascetic attitudes makes one believe them to be the forerunners of Christianity. Plinius also recorded their celibacy[51].

However, even to the Christians, monasticism and priestly celibacy is only a later institution. Originally nobody among them apparently found anything objectionable in marriage[52]. Paul explicitly writes: "it is better to marry than to suffer lust"[53]. When Rabbi Judah teaches that every cohabitation which does not serve the purpose of expanding humanity is considered to be the same as lust[54], he only has in mind, as is apparent from the context of his discussion, a marriage in which this possibility is excluded from the outset.

In Judaism, celibacy never existed. It could not be legally applied to a special

34. Kiddushin 30a
35. Song of Songs Rabbah 7:3,2
36. Funk, *Frankels Mtschr.* 1905 p.541
37. Pesahim 113b
38. Yebamoth 63a
39. Genesis 5:1
40. Yebamoth 62b
41. Leviticus Rabbah 20:9
42. Numbers 3:4
43. See *Yalkut* to Deut. 23:14 No. 934
44. Pesikta de Rav Kahana *Ha-Chodesh* p.44a, Buber

45. Proverbs 13:12
46. Kethuboth 5:2
47. Genesis 1:28
48. Josephus. *Antiquities* No. 18 Chapt. 1,6
49. Josephus. *The Jewish War* II, Chapt. 8, 2
50. *ibid* No. 13
51. *Hist. Nat.* 5,15
52. See First Timothy 4:3
53. First Corinthians 7:9
54. Yebamoth 61b

group because such a decree would contradict the earlier-mentioned Biblical words of *be fruitful and multiply*, which apply to *all* people without exception, least of all to the priests who were specifically assigned the supervision of the law[55]. In the special regulations which the Mishnah describes for the High Priest, it is stated as a prerequisite that he be married, and indeed to only *one* woman[56]. The praises of the infertile and of eunuchs[57] can at best only be considered as a consolation to these unfortunate individuals, as is already found in the Bible[58].

The question as to whether the *prophets* lived in celibacy should altogether not be raised, because Judaism sees no sign of distinctive holiness in celibacy and, even more, regards it as a constant enticement to sinful thoughts. On the contrary, legend reports[59] that when the prophets were detained for a lengthy period of time in a strange place, they would marry an additional woman — polygamy was not prohibited — because the Talmud specifically instructs a learned person, meaning a religious scholar, never to be without a wife[60]. In fact, the Bible also mentions the wives and children of the prophets Samuel[61], Isaiah[62], Ezekiel[63] and Hosea[64]. Long *after* Talmudic times did Jewish religious philosophers first raise the question of the celibacy of the prophets. Saadia rightfully denies it; others contradict him[65].

Non-Jewish influences obviously provided motivation for the erroneous attitude toward this question, particularly the internal strife within the Roman Church which ended, as is well known, after a duration of nearly 700 years, through the decree of Gregory VII in the year 1074 with the triumph of the opponents to marriage. A detailed refutation of the teaching of the alleged immorality of marriage was written by Nachmanides, who died in 1260[66].

The Talmudic literature describes only a single bachelor among all the Rabbis, namely Ben Azzai. He excused his celibacy: "What can I do? My soul is attached to the Torah. Let the world be preserved by others"[67]! Such an exception, however, is only allowed for one who truly, as Ben Azzai, constantly studies the Torah and devotes his entire life to it; and then only if his instincts do not arouse him. Otherwise he should take a wife, even if he already has children, in order not to develop sinful thoughts[68]. Our modern renowned orators of *Uranismus,* who have discovered that "all important thinkers carefully avoid becoming attached to a loving wife"[69], will certainly hasten to claim that Ben Azzai was one of them.

## IV   Genealogy In Marriage

In contracting a marriage it is natural that the economic situation is not the only factor to be considered. In the selection of a spouse, there exists a large number of suggestions in the moral sphere, but their enumeration here is inappropriate. Thorough consideration is recommended not only to the individuals getting married, but also to their families. Especially welcome was the connection with (i.e. marrying into) the family of a scholar. Since children mostly resemble the brothers of the mother[70], one should pay careful attention thereto. One should not take a wife from an epileptic or leprous family[71], since the hereditary nature of both these diseases was firmly believed in.

55. Deut. 21:5
56. Yoma 1:1
57. Wisdom of Solomon 3:13
58. Isaiah 56:4
59. *Yalkut* 2, No. 209
60. See Yoma 18a
61. First Samuel 8:2
62. Isaiah 8:18
63. Ezekiel 24:18
64. Hosea 1:2

65. *Frankels Mtschr* 1900, p.215, notes
66. Graetz. H. *Geschichte Der Juden* 1894 Vol. 7 p.41
67. Yebamoth 63b
68. Maimonides,*Hilchoth Ishuth* 15:3
69. Freimark, *Der Sinn des Uranismus.* Leipzig 1906 p.27
70. Baba Bathra 110a
71. Yebamoth 64b

# V   Conjugal Duties

Among the duties whose fulfillment is prescribed for both parties in a marriage is *cohabitation,* even when, because of physiological reasons (pregnancy, menopause) the intent of raising children is not applicable. All ancient and most newer law books contain very precise instructions in this regard. One might have a difference of opinion as to the value of such detailed laws, but he who is desirous of eliminating as much as possible the personal perceptions of the judge in the passing of the sentence, will certainly approve of them. Subjective experiences of individuals play a large role in our topic of conjugal duties. This is most clearly seen in the commentary of Albrecht V. Haller, who proclaimed the following as a scientific teaching with very general application: *Homini adeo modicae sunt vires, ut non multo plus, quam bis in septem diebus coire possit*[72]. In the year 1766, when this volume of the *Elementa* appeared, Haller was 58 years old! Completely wrong is the indignation of Hinschius concerning the corresponding regulations of the Prussian general provincial law[73]. For even if it is true that the fulfillment of this conjugal law cannot be coerced by an officer of the law, the refusal to engage in one's conjugal duty and the constant impossibility of its fulfillment represent grounds for divorce in the eyes of all legislators. It, therefore, seems only logical that, as much as possible, what is meant by "conjugal duty" should be precisely described.

# VI   Cohabitation

According to the account of Niebuhr[74], the Arabs are obligated to cohabit once weekly with each of their wives. Solon's law requires three cohabitations per month *(tris ekastou menos entygchanein)*[75].

"The practical Luther stated that the normal rule for marriage is to practice cohabitation two or three times a week"[76]. The Prussian provincial law spoke only of "continuous refusal of the conjugal duty. This duty cannot be demanded if the performance thereof would be detrimental to the health of one or the other marriage partner. In addition, married women who are nursing may legally refuse cohabitation"[77]. The civil law book does not mention this any more at all.

The Talmud discusses this question when it speaks of a Biblical law. In the Bible it states that if someone sells his daughter as a maidservant[78], she is not liable to the regulations of male slaves. If her husband and master takes himself another wife, he cannot decrease her sustenance, her clothing and her cohabitation. Concerning the execution of the stipulations of this law, the Mishnah describes more precisely these three rights of the woman. Concerning the *debitum conjugale,* the Mishnah determined as follows: idle (unemployed) men without a trade should cohabit daily; workmen who do not labor away from their place of residence should cohabit twice a week; donkey drivers, once a week; camel drivers, once a month; sailors, once every half year. Scholars without the consent of their wives are permitted to sojourn away from their place of residence, separated from their wives, for the purpose of study of the Torah for thirty days[79]. According to other Sages, scholars may even stay away for two or three years, and with the consent of their wives, they may remain as long as they wish[80]. In later times one finds the additional statement that in all these cases the husband should be healthy and strong[81].

---

72. *Elem. Physiol.* Vol. 7, Section 3, Book 27 No. 14, p.571
73. to part 2, title 1, No. 174 in the Koch edition, volume 3, p.128
74. *Beschreibg. von Arabien.* Copenhagen 1772 p.74
75. Plutarch, *Solon.* Chapt. 20,6

76. Forel, *Die Sexuelle Frage.* p.81
77. Part 2, title 1, No. 178 to 180
78. Exodus 21:7
79. Kethuboth 5:6 and Genesis Rabbah 76:7
80. Kethuboth 62b
81. *Even Ha'ezer* 76:3

A vow through which a man denies cohabitation to his wife is only valid for two weeks according to the School of Shammai, and only for one week according to the School of Hillel. If it is of longer duration, the woman is entitled to demand her bill of divorce and her *donatio propter nuptias (kethubah)*[82].

Therefore, even though the wife has a *right* to marital cohabitation, she should not demand it. For it is a good characteristic of the woman that she maintain her desires in her heart, while the husband expresses it[83]. *For thy husband shall be thy desire, but he shall rule over thee*[84], thus spoke God at the expulsion from Paradise[85].

The husband should also not make indecent demands of his wife. If he asks "that she draw water and pour it out on a dunghill", then she should request a divorce from him[86]. What is meant are violent movements such as jumping and turning in circles[87] and the like, as a result of which the woman provokes the expulsion of the *sperma viri statim post cohabitationem*. These tricks were already practiced by prostitutes in antiquity[88], and were recommended by physicians as a preventive to conception[89]. Many women today are quite familiar therewith[90]. The Catholic moral theologians teach: *peccat mortaliter mulier, quae statim post copulam mingit, surgit, vel quid aliud facit animo semen expellendi*[91]. The Talmud correctly states that this procedure is completely identical in principle to *coitus interruptus*[92], since both measures prevent conception.

It is also considered improper to have sexual intercourse while fully clothed, as the Persians do[93]. Among the things which God abhors is someone who has sexual intercourse while naked, and openly discusses that which transpires between him and his wife[94]. Equally despised is cohabitation under the open sky. A man was once caught as he was having sexual intercourse with his wife under a fig tree. He was brought before the court and the latter sentenced him to "the flogging of chastisement". Although he did not directly violate any law, the circumstances of the time required this punishment[95], because general morality was thought to be in danger and an example had to be enacted.

A very important concept, which is appropriate to modern times, is "the children of drunkenness", that is those children which are sired during a drunken frenzy. The prophet[96] calls them "rebellious and sinful"[97]. These children resemble drunks, that is they are mentally ill, and their behavior has many similarities to that of the intoxicated[98].

A woman who refuses to copulate with her husband is punished in that the husband is entitled to deduct seven dinars from her *kethubah* weekly until the entire *kethubah* is exhausted. According to Rabi Jose, a further deduction may result on account of a possible future inheritance which she might fortuitously receive. A similar procedure takes place in reverse in the case of a husband who refuses to fulfill the marital duty. Then he has to add seven dinars weekly to his wife's *kethubah*.

According to the Sages, the procedure is different. When the case is brought to the attention of the court, "one proclaims the sin of this woman for four consecutive Sabbaths", that is her case is publicized in the usual manner, somewhat as we do, either by affixing a note on the court bulletin board or by public delivery of the

82. Kethuboth 5:6
83. Erubin 100b
84. Genesis 3:16
85. Aboth d' Rabbi Nathan 1:7
86. Kethuboth 7:5
87. Niddah 42a
88. Kethuboth 37a
89. Saliceto, in the *Dissertation of Oscar Basch*. Berlin 1898, p.25
90. Bumm., *Deutsch. Med. W.* 1904, p.1757b
91. Scavini, Vol. 4 p.575
92. Jerushalmi Kethuboth 7; 31b
93. Kethuboth 48a, an exception for an unusual reason is found in the Jerushalmi Yebamoth 1; 2b
94. Leviticus Rabbah 21:8
95. Sanhedrin 46a
96. Ezekiel 20:38
97. Nedarim 20b
98. Kallah Rabbathi 1, fol. 52a,25

message[99]. She is also personally threatened by an official of the court — according to some even before the publicizing of her misconduct — that her continual refusal to cohabit with her husband would result in her forfeiture of the *kethubah* at the expiration of four weeks[100].

The apostle Paul demands that the husband of a woman and the wife of a man both fulfill the *debitum conjugale (ten opheilen)*. They should not avoid each other, unless it occurs by mutual consent; and after some time, they are required to fast and pray and then reunite, so that Satan should not tempt you[101].

# VII   Impotence

If the husband becomes ill or, because of diminishing body strength, cannot adequately fulfill his conjugal duty, then one should wait for six months to see whether his health is restored. Otherwise he should dissolve the marriage, unless the wife is contented even without cohabitation[102].

If the woman refuses the conjugal duty because her husband is repugnant to her, not only out of temper, but to anger him, then the husband should be coerced to execute a separation[103]. For the woman is not like a war captive, adds Maimonides, who must offer herself to her detested captor[104]. In general, no cohabitation should take place without the consent of the woman[105].

Difficult for the legal decision-making even today are divorce proceedings concerning *impotence* of the husband. Concerning this, we find the following in the *Mishnah:* if the wife states: "Heaven is between you and me"[106], (meaning: only Heaven knows that we cannot have sexual relations) then the husband should be forced by the court to divorce his wife and pay the *kethubah*. Later, however, one became fearful of believing her accusations, because the wife could cast her eyes upon another man and attempt to scorn her husband by declaring him impotent in order to rid herself of him, and therefore refuse cohabitation. For that reason, one should attempt an amicable reconciliation, and possibly persuade the husband to voluntarily divorce his wife without coercion from the court[107].

For those, such as Rabbah, who were of the opinion that polygamy is permissible, an expedient existed in that the court consented to the husband's request to take another wife and to prove his potency with her. For Rabbi Ammi and his school, who only allow monogamy, this possibility is eliminated[108].

In such cases, the non-Jewish courts of the Middle Ages found support for their judgements in the so-called investigations of states of wedlock; that is, they demanded that the marital partners engage in coitus in the court of law to provide a *demonstratio ad oculos*. Such an expedient was rejected by the Jewish court because cohabitation in the presence of other people, and according to some, even in the presence of any living creature, is absolutely prohibited in the Talmud[109]. Perhaps Maimonides specifically alludes to this practice of the non-Jewish court[110].

Where one suspects psychic causes for the impotence, one should invite the marital partners to the same table, according to Rav Huna[111]. During the meal, they will once again become accustomed to one another.

In a case of denial of conjugal rights, according to Rabbi Yochanan, the man

99. *Bürgerliches Gesetzbuch* No. 1567, 2
100. *Tosefta* Kethuboth 5:7; Kethuboth 63b
101. First Corinthians 7: 3-4
102. Yebamoth 64a
103. *ibid*, 63b
104. *Hilchoth Ishuth* 14:8
105. Erubin 100b
106. namely, only Heaven knows, but no

mortal, that no cohabitation between us is possible
107. Nedarim 11:12
108. Yebamoth 65b
109. Niddah 17a
110. *Mishneh Torah. Hilchoth Ishuth* 14:16
111. Jerushalmi. Nedarim 11; 42d

suffers more than the woman. When Delilah offended Samson by such a denial, as the legend has it[112], *his soul was vexed unto death*[113], but not hers. Some, who do not believe in the physiological frigidity of the woman, maintain that she found compensation by seeing other men[114]. This can be observed in the street of harlots: who hires whom?[115] The man naturally hires the woman because he suffers more from sexual abstinence than the woman. In the Middle Ages, one taught the opposite, namely, that the woman finds abstinence more difficult than the man[116].

In spite of the above, the man should not coerce cohabitation and should not surprise his wife while she is sleeping[117]. "The children of a woman seduced while asleep become sluggards"[118].

## VIII   Unnatural Coitus

There was a tendency among the teachers of law to punish each *situs in cohabitatione praeter situm naturalem,* even those used in wedlock. Nevertheless, this point of view is not prevalent; for it is the nature of people that one person eats meat from the slaughterhouse and fish from the angler's house salted, another person fried, a third individual cooked and a fourth simmered[119]. This is also the viewpoint of Catholic moral theologians. Gury teaches as follows: *situs qui solus possibilis est, qualiscunque demum sit, nullatenus damnatur;* and Capellmann states: *Omnis situs, etiamsi innaturalis in copula (vel stando vel sedendo vel more pecudum vel a latere vel viro succumbente) per se non excedit culpam venialem, dummodo actus conjugalis satis perfici possit*[120].

The refusal of the Rabbis to enact a formal prohibition is obviously legislative prudence, and does not represent looseness of moral viewpoint. For in the Talmud there is a large number of comments about these unnatural intercourses which were well known to the Jews because of the actions of the Greco-Roman environment. Rabbi Yochanan ben Dahabai was told by the ministering angels — probably by the Rabbis themselves — that children born of such an unnatural coitus[121] are lame (deformed) because the parents "overturn their tables" and act like animals[122] i.e. *more pecudum;* such children are born dumb because their parents kiss "that place" (the vulva) i.e. *cunnilingi;* such children are born deaf because their parents converse about them during intercourse and hence sin through speaking and hearing; such children are born blind because their parents gaze at "that place"[123]. He who cohabits while in a sitting position is afflicted with delirium, *vir succubus,* that is wantonness, *azzuth,* and a child easily becomes *hapakpekan* therefrom, i.e. one who turns himself (epileptic?); *duobus simul concumbentibus,* that is the path of moral perversity, *ikkesh.* When marital partners cohabit on a bed on which an awake infant child is lying, then this child will become epileptic[124]. He who has coitus near a kindled light is worthy of abhorrence[125]; his children become epileptic[126]. He who has coitus in a standing position will be afflicted with the convulsive disorder *avith*[127]. Rabbi Yochanan says that he who has coitus during the daytime is worthy of detestation[128], for the time of cohabitation is only the nighttime[129], and particularly during the middle

112. Sotah 9b
113. Judges 16:16
114. Jerushalmi. Kethuboth 5; 30b
115. Kethuboth 64b
116. Petrus de Sancho Floro, in the *Amand. Concordance in Pagel, Neue Literatur; Beitrage zur Mittelalterlischen Medizin,* Berlin 1896 p.30
117. *Tosafoth* in Niddah 12a; see also the commentary of *Ransburg* thereon
118. Kallah Rabbathi Chapt. 1 fol. 52a 16
119. Nedarim 20b
120. *Pastoral Medicine* p.175
121. Kallah Rabbathi Chap. 1 fol. 51b 13
122. Kallah 50b 9
123. Nedarim 20a
124. Kallah Rabbathi Chapt. 1 fol. 52a 23
125. Niddah 17a
126. Pesachim 112b
127. Gittin 70a
128. Genesis Rabbah 64:5
129. Shabbath 86a

portion of the night[130]. It is even so recorded about the maidens of the heathen Persian king Ahasuersus: *in the evening she went, and on the morrow she returned*[131].

Mohammed, in his Koran, in precise opposition to the teachings of the Jews[132], records only the following general principle: "your wives are your fields, go into your fields in any way you desire"[133]. There are no restrictions of any kind.

The concept of the Rabbis concerning coitus is best revealed by their portrayal of the hereafter. Mohammed uses the expression of the general Oriental concept which repeatedly speaks of "unblemished young women"[134], whose skin and flesh is so delicate that the edges of the bones protrude[135]. On the other hand, the Talmud teaches[136] that "in the future world all earthly matters do not exist. There is no eating nor drinking, no fecundity nor propagation (a usual expression for coitus), but the righteous sit and feast on the brightness of the Divine presence," just like the angels[137]. This Jewish concept is then also found in the pronouncements of Jesus: "in the resurrection they neither marry nor are given in marriage, but are as the angels of God in Heaven"[138].

## IX   Coitus Interruptus

Already in the times of the Bedouins, there existed among the Jews a practice, which was later adopted into law[139], that when a man dies without leaving offspring, his brother shall marry the widow, and the firstborn of this marriage shall be considered as the child of the deceased, and accordingly shall be regarded as his universal heir. Thereby is accomplished, as is explicitly stated in a similar instance[140], that the family (ancestral) property remain together and not be transferred to another lineage if a woman perchance marries a man from a different tribe.

From those ancient times the following is reported: the firstborn of Prince (or Sheik) Judah, Er, was married to a woman called Tamar. However, Er was wicked in the eyes of God, and God slew him without his having left any male offspring. At the command of Judah, his second son, Onan, was supposed to marry the sister-in-law and to raise offspring for his brother. Onan, however, knew that the offspring would not be his[141], so he spilled his sperm on the ground when he had coitus with his brother's wife, so as not to give offspring to his brother. In the eyes of God, however, what he did was displeasing, and He slew him too. Judah hesitated to give Tamar the third son, for he feared that he too would die, like his brothers[142].

The ancients explained the act of Onan with an analogy which is derived from their agricultural occupation: "he threshed within (the vagina) and winnowed without"[143]; or "he ploughed in the garden and poured out on manure piles"[144]; that is he practiced *coitus interruptus*. This act, and not masturbation, is what is known as *"onanism"*, for it is unreasonable to accept that, in order for Onan to masturbate, he "came to his brother's wife". The Catholic moral theology also defines onanism correctly: *Onanismus in eo consistit, quod vir post inceptam copulam ante seminationem se retrahat et semen extra effundat, ut generationem impediat*[145]. It cannot be determined with certainty from Scripture whether the act in itself, that is

---

130. Kallah Rabbathi Chapt. 1 fol. 52a 15
131. Esther 2:14
132. see Hammer's *Fundgruben des Orients* I, 460
133. *Sure* 3 p.25 in Ullmann's translation
134. *Sure* 2 p.3; 3:36; 4:61 etc.
135. *Fundgruben* I, 364
136. Berachoth 17a as cited by Rab
137. Chagigah 16a
138. Matthew 22:30 and Mark 12:25

139. Deuteronomy 25: 5-10
140. Numbers 36:7
141. i.e. as *Onkelos* translates: would not be named after him
142. Genesis 38:6 ff
143. Yebamoth 34b
144. Genesis Rabbah 85:4
145. Gury, *Comp. Theol. Mor.* 3rd ed., vol. 2, p.915; cited according to Capellmann

even without the goal of purposefully transgressing the law as in the case of Onan, is punishable by God, or if Divine retribution occurs only in the aforementioned special social circumstances. In the laws of the Bible, there is nothing else that deals with this subject. For our tradition, the explicit statement of the Bible that "what he did was displeasurable in the eyes of the Lord" suffices to strictly prohibit the "expulsion of sperm for naught". Included in this prohibition are both *coitus interruptus* as well as masturbation, since both are equally a *peccatum mortale*[146].

Rational-thinking physicians can accept the proposition that the death of the man occurred through the constant practice of *coitus interruptus*. A possible damaging effect on the health of both partners, as in every perversion of nature, cannot be lightly dismissed.

Scripture states that "the Lord slew him (Onan) *too*" which the Sages explain "with the same death and for the same transgression as his brother Er[147]. The motivating force behind Er's practice of onanism was a different one, namely, the fear that the beauty of his wife might be compromised by the occurrence of a pregnancy[148].

According to the teaching promulgated by Rabbi Judah the Patriarch in Talmudic times, the Biblical Judah was correct in not giving a third husband to a woman who has already had two husbands that died. The cause of the mortality of the husbands of a woman is in dispute in the Talmud[149]: some are of the opinion that it lies in the body of the woman[150], whereas others disagree and state that this cause is certainly not applicable *in general*, as for example, if the man died as a result of falling off a palm tree. The latter believe that the woman's fate or her evil star or her ill luck are responsible for the death of successive husbands.

In the Apocryphal book of Tobit, it is reported that the daughter of Raguel in Ecbatana had been married to seven husbands; "Asmodeus, the wicked demon, had killed them all before they had cohabited with her as is customary with wives"[151]. When Tobias went to her, he took the ashes of incense and put the heart and the liver of the fish on them and made smoke, whereupon the demon fled to Upper Egypt[152].

## X   Abstention From Procreation

Even if it is better, according to the words of the wise Sirach[153], to be childless, rather than to have Godless children, no one should refrain from the obligation of having children because of such a fear. It is told that the prophet Isaiah came to King Hezekiah and declared that his (Hezekiah's) death was near because he did not apply himself to the propagation of his race. When Hezekiah answered that he foresaw that the children that he would have would not be virtuous, Isaiah countered with: "what have you to do with the secrets of God? You should have done what you were commanded"[154]. According to the description of Josephus, the King (Hezekiah) was not voluntarily sterile but, on the contrary, was afflicted with a deep depression *(athymia deine)* when he became ill because of the thought of his childlessness. The prophet promises him recovery and offspring[155], with which he was later endowed. Whether the King was already married before he became ill cannot be determined. The fact is that Hezekiah's son, King Manasseh, who was born when his father was 43 years old, did not follow in the footsteps of his religious father. Rather, he sinned through idol worship, even if one considers in his favor the fact that he began to reign when he was only twelve years old[156].

146. Niddah 13a
147. Yebamoth 34b
148. Yebamoth 34b
149. Yebamoth 64b
150. the "source" i.e. some malignant disease in the womb
151. Tobit 3:8
152. Tobit 8:2
153. Sirach 16:3
154. Berachoth 10a
155. *Antiquities* Vol. 10, chapt. 2: 1
156. Second Kings Chapt. 21

## XI   Times When Coitus is Prohibited

Copulation during the week of mourning for one's parents or siblings is prohibited. A person who, in his crudeness, did not abide by this rule, had his abdomen torn open (or his penis torn off) by swine[157]. Before a healed leper can be reaccepted into the community of the healthy, he must *live outside his tent for seven days*[158] which, according to tradition, refers to a prohibition of cohabitation[159]. On the Day of Atonement, copulation is prohibited, together with other earthly pleasures such as eating, drinking, bathing, etc.[160]. Concerning copulation during the menstrual period *(kopula menstruationis tempore),* as well as during genital bleeding of the woman and during the puerperium, we have already spoken earlier (in the second chapter of this book in the section dealing with the genital system).

Travelers lodging at an inn should, because of common decency, not indulge in coitus[161].

Copulation is also prohibited in order to preserve body strength (and, perhaps, also as a sign of mourning) in times of famine, as is described in the Bible concerning Joseph: *And unto Joseph were born two sons before the years of famine came*[162]. Only the childless are allowed to take exception to this rule[163]. When you see that dearth and hunger come upon the world, consider your wife to be segregated from you (i.e. as if menstruating)[164]. Therefore[165], before the flood, Noah was commanded *come thou and thy sons* apart, *and thy wife, and thy sons' wives* apart, into the ark[166]. However, when the flood had passed, it states *go forth from the ark, thou and thy wife and thy sons and thy sons' wives*[167]. Three individuals who nevertheless transgressed the prohibition against coitus in the ark were punished therefor: Ham became black (negro), the dog is doomed to stick firmly during coitus, and the raven expectorates his seed into his mate's mouth[168].

The month during which *one* body receives the greatest pleasure from another body is the month of Tebeth[169]. For that reason did the Persian king have Esther brought to him during that month[170].

## XII   Cohabitation and Sexual Desire

According to a popular saying, cohabitation is one of the three things which, unlike food and beverage, is not absorbed by the body yet the body still derives pleasure therefrom[171]. The other two things are bathing and anointing. Nevertheless, since the destruction of the Temple, the real pleasure of sexual intercourse has been lost due to constant worries and anxieties[172]. According to another popular saying, coitus is one of the eight things which are beneficial in small amounts but harmful in large quantities. The other things are: walking, wealth, work, wine, sleep, warm water (to bathe and to drink) and bloodletting[173].

It is advisable from the standpoint of health, that one maintain a certain time for coitus, either before or after sunrise[174]. Excessive coitus weakens[175], and Zimri, through his repetitive intercourse with the Midianitish woman[176], completely

---

157. Moed Katan 24a
158. Levit. 14:8
159. Nega'im 14:2
160. Yoma 8:1
161. Kethuboth 65a
162. Genesis 41:50
163. Taanith 11a
164. Genesis Rabbah 31:12
165. *ibid* 34:7
166. Genesis 6:18
167. Genesis 8:16
168. Sanhedrin 108b
169. approximately December (Megillah 13a)
170. Esther 2:16
171. Berachoth 57b
172. Sanhedrin 75a
173. Gittin 70a
174. Levit. Rabbah 4:3
175. Berachoth 57b
176. Numbers 25:6ff

destroyed his body[177]. Excessive indulgences during our youth cause our countenance to become black and our strength to become weak during the time of our old age[178]. Even death can occur thereby, and "when women cause the death of a man", explained by the commentaries to mean that the man died *intra copulam*, "then there is no court nor judges"[179]. Two cases of death during sexual intercourse are already mentioned by Plinius[180].

The following case in the Talmud is found in a discussion of a suit: someone rented a cat to catch mice. Because of excessive eating of mice, the cat died. Is the renter liable?

Even the viewing of obscene pictures can stimulate sexual desire in some people. Legend tells us that Jezebel painted pictures of harlots on King Ahab's chariot that he might look upon them and become sexually aroused[180a], since he had a frigid nature. After the battle in which the king was killed, the blood on these pictures of the harlots was washed off[181]. According to the tradition of Josephus, prostitutes bathed in the fountain into which the king's blood had flowed[182].

The viewing of animals "who are occupied with each other", as well as the mere viewing of women's garments, can excite sexual passions[183]. The latter is exemplified by the clothing fetishes frequently mentioned in our time. In spite of the danger which is entailed in the viewing of mating animals, the farmer is permitted to assist his breeding cattle by bringing them together in the closest manner[184]. If necessary, he is even allowed to place the penis of the male animal into the vagina of the female, for the great care with which he devotes himself to this task is of sufficient weight to counterbalance the sexual excitation which he may experience.

# XIII   Aphrodisiacs

Among the *aphrodisiacs* used by the Aryans and the Semites even today throughout the Orient is garlic. It has the reputation of increasing sperm[185], just as fish consumption stimulates propagation[186]. This property is specially commented upon in the recently discovered (1890) ancient Indian (Sanskrit) song of praise of garlic[187].

Noteworthy is the fact that *milk* is also considered as a sexual inciter[188]. Indeed it was forbidden to the High Priest before the Day of Atonement[189]. According to the legend, in Deborah's song of praise to Jael concerning the fleeing Sisera, it states *he asked for water, but she gave him milk*[190]. She did this to entice him to cohabitation in his weakened condition, in order to bring him to complete exhaustion and thereby to deliver him more easily into the hands of his pursuers[191]. According to the explanation of Josephus, she gave him spoiled milk *(gala diephtorosede)* which put him to sleep[192].

Actually feared in this respect was wine, particularly for women. An ancient saying proclaims: one glass of wine is becoming to a woman, two are somewhat degrading, and if she has three glasses she solicits coitus, but if she has four, she solicits even an ass in the street and forgets all decency[193]. One is here reminded that the Jews as well as the Romans, in those days, did not drink wine at all at the table (i.e. during meals), and the women left the table as soon as the drinking began. This was an

177. Sanhedrin 82b
178. Shabbath 152a
179. Baba Metzia 87a
180. *Hist. Nat.* 7:54
180a. Sanhedrin 39b
181. First Kings 22:38
182. *Antiquities* 8 Chapt. 15:6
183. Yebamoth 76a
184. Abodah Zarah 20b

185. Baba Kamma 82a
186. Berachoth 40a
187. Aschoff, in *Janus* 1900 p.493 ff
188. *Tosefta* Zabim 2:5
189. Yoma 18a
190. Judges 5:25
191. Yebamoth 103a
192. *Antiquities* 5 Chapt. 5:4
193. Kethuboth 65a

exclusive right of the men, perhaps analogous to the present-day stag party. But wine is damaging for a man too. If he is drunk, he will not refrain from cohabiting with his wife even if she explicitly tells him that she is "blossoming like a rose" (i.e. menstruating)[194]. The most injurious of wines in this respect (i.e. inciting to coitus) is that from Pethugta[195].

"He who does not understand the manner of the world", that is he who is impotent, should take three measures of safflower seeds *(qurtemi)* which grow on fertilized soil, pound them and boil them and drink them in wine. Rabbi Yochanan extols this remedy, claiming it restored his youth.

Eight things cause a diminution of sperm[196], namely salt, hunger, leprosy, weeping, sleeping on the ground, oleander (lotus), Cuscuta out of season[197], and bloodletting from below, which is as bad as any two. Bloodletting from above, however, is as good as any two, and Rabbi Papa states the testicle to be the border (between "above" and "below"). "In season" for Cuscuta means July (Tammuz), when they have an opposite effect, namely beneficial; "out of season" means January (Tebeth)[198].

At four times it is harmful to cohabit: on returning from a journey, after bloodletting, on rising from an illness, and on being released from prison[199].

It is certainly credible that the fear of immediate danger in war has on more than one occasion prevented erections in men[200]. Here, too, one should mention the relative impotence that occurs through weakness following inadequate nutritional intake. In a legal case which came before the court of Rabbi Judah in which he observed that the faces of the young people were black from hunger, he instructed that they be taken to bathe, and he gave them food and drink, and then had them brought into the bed chamber. There they reached their goal[201].

There is little to be found in the Talmud of the unending list of remedies against impotence which are contained in the writings of antiquity and the Middle Ages. The recommendations of Plinius[202], in which horse and donkey testicles, donkey penis, bull urine and similar ingredients play a role, are mild in comparison with the "experiences" of other authors.

## XIV   Duda'im

Much has been written about the *duda'im* (mandrakes) mentioned in Genesis 30:14. These are universally considered to be aphrodisiacs without, I believe, sufficient reason.

After Leah gave birth to four sons of Jacob, *she ceased giving birth*[203]. No reason is mentioned in Scriptures but it is quite clear that the preference of Jacob for her sister Rachel was behind it. At the time of the wheat harvest, Reuben, the firstborn of Leah, found *duda'im* (mandrakes) in the field and brought them to his mother. The latter gave them to Rachel when she asked for them, on the condition that Jacob cohabit with her, Leah, during that night. Jacob agreed. *And God hearkened unto Leah, and she conceived, and bore Jacob a fifth son*[204]. This one was followed by a sixth, and also a daughter. Only then God remembered Rachel, and hearkened unto her and opened her womb and she gave birth to Joseph.

Perhaps the *duda'im* brought the favor of her husband back to Leah; for the one night which Rachel conceded to her must have been followed by many more, as the

194. Leviticus Rabbah 12:11
195. *ibid* 5:3
196. Gittin 70a
197. so according to Löw, *Pflanzennamen*, p.230. *Rashi* has hops
198. Gittin 70b
199. Aboth d'Rabbi Nathan 34:7
200. Zebachim 116b
201. Kethuboth 10b
202. Plinius *Hist. Nat.* 28:80; 30:49
203. Genesis 29:35
204. Genesis 30:17

subsequent births demonstrate. The mandrakes, however, did not provide her with fertility, for she had never lost her ability to conceive. The correction of the infertility of Rachel as a result of the use of the *duda'im* is similarly difficult to accept. For a medication to act only after nearly three years — such a period must be considered for the three births of Leah — is a difficult concept for the public to endorse. The fact that in the text, the pregnancies of both women resulted from the hearkening by God to their prayers cannot be used as evidence for or against the efficacy of the mandrakes, because according to religious interpretation, no medication is effective without God giving His blessing thereto, and, on the other hand, even God employs natural means to effect healing.

As a result, I cannot accept the adoption by exegetics of the hypothesis that *duda'im* represent a remedy against infertility. I am also not disconcerted by the Song of Songs in which it states "the mandrakes emit an aroma"[205]. For it is a long way from the efficacy of an aroma as a sexual excitant, an action which is undisputed since time immemorial, to the presupposed influence on the sterility of a woman.

Very difficult to understand is the *botanical* identification of *duda'im*. It is usually accepted that it is a *plant* which grows or blossoms or ripens "in the days of the wheat harvest". The post-biblical Jewish writings already make no more mention of this word, and so the conjectures began early. In the Talmud[206], one Sage considers *duda'im* to be *yabruchi,* another says *sabiski,* both expressions referring to mandrakes (or mandrake flowers), whereas a third Sage identifies *duda'im* as *sigli* which is cypress. In the Midrash, there is an additional interpretation of *duda'im* as "barley", and another as fruits of *mayishim*[207] meaning hackberry (or myrtle berry)[208]. There is thus no certainty at all as to the precise identification of *duda'im*. Others, including Josephus[209], have mandrakes, and a number of modern commentators also endorse this meaning, primarily because the root of the mandrake, since time immemorial, not only in the Orient, served as an aphrodisiac and also healed infertility. The Arabs also believe the fruit of the mandrake has similar powers. Friedreich has assembled literature on this subject[210].

The prudent J. Chr. Huber explains the identification (of *duda'im*) as mandrakes to be "highly problematical"[211].

# XV    Conception Sine Concubito

In order for cohabitation to be fruitful, there is the requirement that the whole body of the man "feels" (the emission of seed i.e. orgasm) and that the sperm shoot forth like an arrow[212]. No impregnation can occur through spermatorrhea. This at least is the teaching of Mar Samuel the physician. For that reason, a large number of teachings explain that men with mutilations or abnormal openings of the penis (hypospadius or epispadius) are incapable of procreation[213]. These questions which have occupied medical jurisprudents and marriage jurists during all eras, cannot even today be definitively explained in all their details.

Another question discussed throughout the centuries concerns the possibility of a pregnancy *utroque stante*. In the Talmud, this possibility is thought to be extremely unusual[214]. In general, this type of cohabitation is said to be dangerous, since it markedly weakens the body[215]. In our times, a single coitus performed in a standing

205. Song of Songs 7:13
206. Sanhedrin 99b
207. Löw p.269, 250
208. Genesis Rabbah 72:2
209. *Antiquities* Vol. 1 Chapt. 19, 7
210. Friedreich. *Zur Bibel.* Vol. 1 p.158 ff

211. *Münch. Med. Wchnschr.* 1901 No. 12, in the review of Ebstein's book
212. Niddah 43a
213. See above. Chapt. 5, Section 25
214. Sanhedrin 37b
215. Gittin 70a

position is incriminated as being the cause of acute hyperemia of the spinal cord[216].

On the other hand, it was believed that a woman could become pregnant by bathing in a tub in which shortly before a man had bathed and ejaculated[217], even though this belief is contradictory to the above teaching of Samuel. This probably occurred in antiquity more than just rarely, to both laymen and physicians alike. For Averroes (died 1198), in his *Kitab el-Kollijjât* in the Middle Ages, was nearly of the same opinion as the Canon of Avicenna, in which a story is found which supports the same opinion as that enunciated in the Talmud (i.e. that pregnancy *sine concubito* is possible). He reports that *vicina quaedam mea de cujus sacramento confidere multum bene poteramus, juravit in anima sua, quod impraegnata fuerat subito in balneo lavelli aquae calidae, in quo spermatizaverunt mali homines, cum essent balneati in illo balneo.* In the book of Avemcladis[218] *De Spermate,* the author described a similar finding. He asserts that this method of pregnancy induction is possible, *quia vulva trahit sperma propter suam propriam virtutem.* Ibn Ruschd concludes[219] *"ô quam bene placet mihi"*!

From the famous *Colliget,* the legend found its way into the writings of the physicians of the Occident who devoted several chapters thereto, until the eighteenth century. It then wandered to Portugal where Amatus Lusitanus in 1550 used it to exonerate a nun who gave birth to a mole, from a disgraceful suspicion. This was even contrary to the opinion of Galen, who stated that moles can only occur through cohabitation[220]. Amatus relates a story of robbers which was told to him by someone as a "Legend of the Rabbis". Several people had masturbated in a bath. When the prophet Jeremiah rebuked them for this, they dragged him into the bath and forcibly ejaculated him. Shortly thereafter, his daughter came to bathe there and became pregnant from her own father's sperm and later gave birth to Ben Sira. Amatus also quotes Avicenna and Algazar[220a] as authorities. To be sure, there are also skeptics concerning the possibility of conception *sine concubito.* Thus, Paolo Zacchia (died 1659) disputes this possibility, although he does not doubt for a moment that the devil is an *incubus*[221]. In fact, Schurig sides with him[222].

According to Stern[223], this belief in conception in a bath is still widespread in Turkey today.

That which the Middle Ages have contributed to this subject is known. Thus, Thomas Aquinas (died 1274) relates that a woman became pregnant from lying in a bed into which sperm was previously discharged. The above-mentioned Amatus also describes a case in which a woman who had cohabited with a man shortly thereafter became pregnant from another *(sine concubito).* In the year 1637, in the courts of justice in Havre, a child was declared legitimate, after the mother said she *dreamed* that she was embraced by her husband who was absent for four years *eadem conceptionis et ingravidationis accidentia*[224]!

In modern scholarship, naturally, all such stories of *de foecundatione absque consuetudine viri* are denied. Haller[225] already called them *dubias historiolas.*

---

216. Pick. in *Eulenberg R.E.* 17:22
217. Chagigah 15a
218. an otherwise unknown physician; not even mentioned by Wüstenfeld
219. *Colliget.* Vol. 2 Chap. 10 fol. 14b of the Junten edition, Basel 1553
220. A. Lusitanus., *Cent. 3,* Curat 36, fol. 352, ed. Froben. Basel 1556
220a. an otherwise unknown physician, not even mentioned by Wüstenfeld.
221. P. Zacchias. *Quaest. Med. Legales.*

Amsterdam 1651, liber 3, tit. 1, quaest 8, fol. 145ff
222. Schurig *Spermatologia.* Francof 1720 p.223
223. Stern, *Medizin, Aberglaube und Geschlechtsleben in der Türkei.* Berlin 1903, 2:289
224. Th. Bartholin. *Hist. Anat. et Med. Rar.* Cent. 6 Hafniae 1661 Hist. 61 p.296
225. Haller. *Elem. Phys.* Liber 29, Sect. 2 p.92

According to the teaching of Rabbi Eleazar, a woman does not become pregnant from the very first cohabitation[226]. Exceptions to this are only the legends of Hagar[227] and the daughters of Lot[228].

# PART   II

## I   Proscribed Marriages

*And the Lord spoke unto Moses, saying; speak unto the Children of Israel, and say unto them, I am the Lord your God. After the doings of the land of Egypt, wherein ye dwelt, shall ye not do; and after the doings of the land of Canaan, whither I bring you, shall ye not do; neither shall ye walk in their statutes. My judgements shall ye do, and my statutes shall ye keep, to walk therein. I am the Lord your God. Ye shall therefore keep my statutes, and my judgements, which if a man do, he shall live by them* (or: by which he shall live); *I am the Lord*[229].

After this solemn introduction to the passage in question, the Bible enumerates the individual degrees of kinship where the "uncovering of nakedness", cohabitation, and naturally also matrimony, is forbidden.

1. The wife of one's father, whether it is the real mother or the stepmother, whether the father's marriage is still in existence or after the death of the father or dissolution of matrimony by divorce;
2. One's sister, whether a full sister or a half sister;
3. One's granddaughter;
4. The sister of one's father or mother (aunt);
5. One's brother's wife;
6. One's daughter-in-law;
7. One's mother-in-law as well as the stepmother of one's wife.

The intimacy with first order blood relatives or a stepdaughter is not explicitly prohibited in the Bible, perhaps because the milieu in which these laws were given was such that such a prohibition would seem to be superfluous. Perhaps the same reason applies for the absence of a specific prohibition against patricide because, according to the well-known statement of Cicero's, Solon, the lawgiver did not consider any son[229a] capable of such hideousness. The Talmudic legal discussion derives the prohibition of intimacy with one's daughter from a simple conclusion *ad majus* from the granddaughter. Sexual intercourse with one's daughter, therefore, is not only a Rabbinic prohibition, but is also Biblically interdicted[230].

## II   Rabbinically Proscribed Marriages

The Talmudic Sages added additional remoter grades of kinship, the so-called *shniyyoth,* to the above *Biblically prohibited* marriages. These *rabbinic* prohibitions extend partially along the entire lineage of kinship without regard for degree, and partially one grade further than the Biblically proscribed relationship.

The entire lineage without regard for degree includes the following:

1. The mother of one's mother (and also her mother etc.);
2. The mother of one's father (and also his mother etc.);

226. Yebamoth 34a
227. Genesis Rabbah 45:4
228. *ibid* 49:8
229. Levit. 18: 1-5

229a. The original has 'father' instead of 'son', probably an error (F.R.)
230. Maimonides. *Hilchoth Issurei Biyah* 2:6

3. The mother of one's parental grandfather;
4. The wife of one's grandson (and also the wife of one's great-grandson etc.);
5. The granddaughter of one's son or one's daughter etc.;
6. The greatgrandmother of one's wife etc.;
7. The greatgranddaughter of one's wife, etc.

One degree further than the Biblical prohibition, either (A) extending out from that relative, or (B) a new but homologous degree, includes the following:

A.  1. The mother of the father of one's mother;
    2. The mother of the father of one's father;
    3. The wife of the father of one's mother; (one's mother's stepmother);
    4. The wife of one's paternal grandfather's brother;
    5. The sister of one's maternal or paternal grandfather;
    6. The sister of the mother of one's mother;
B.  1. The wife of one's mother's brother;·
    2. The wife of one's maternal father's brother;

Completely permissible is the marriage of first cousins, of uncle and niece, and of complete stepsisters with stepbrothers.

The latter is only prohibited by the Palestinian Talmud. The regulations of the German civil law books (paragraph 1310) and the penal code (paragraph 173) differ somewhat from the above enumerated prohibitions, in that they consider intimacy and, of course, also matrimony between nephew and aunt, whether blood aunt or by marriage, to constitute incest.

The Roman and Canon laws are more complicated than the above regulations. Contrary to Catholic practices, Talmudic law remains firm and does not recognize any *dispensation* for possible reasons mentioned in the introduction above. The power to lift the ban on *any* grade of prohibited kinship *for anyone,* is unthinkable in Judaism[231].

# III   Punishment for Incest

The punishments for individual transgressions are varied, all according to whether it is a Biblical or Rabbinic prohibition, and according to the specific punishment which the Bible has determined for that case. Most of the Biblical prohibitions are threatened with the death penalty. In fact, incest with blood relatives or with one's stepmother or with one's daughter-in-law is punished by stoning, the most severe of the death penalties. This is the meaning, according to tradition, of the Biblical expression *their blood shall be upon them*[232]. Incest with one's granddaughter or mother-in-law or grandmother or daughter is punished with death by burning. The solemn curse enunciated at Mount Ebal[233] is said to have reference to those who have sexual intercourse with their father's wife, their sister or their mother-in-law. In the other cases, Scripture only threatens with *and they* (the sinners) *shall be eliminated from among your midst.* The implementation of this threat, however, is fulfilled by heaven; the court does not pronounce the death penalty, but must inflict forty lashes[234].

For Rabbinic prohibitions, the above-mentioned *shniyyoth,* "the flogging of chastisement" or *makkath marduth* is inflicted. This differs from the Biblically enunciated scourging[235] or *malkoth,* in that the number of lashes (in *makkath marduth*) is not limited, but stripes are inflicted until the delinquent pledges improvement[236].

---

231. According to Frankel. *Grundlin d. Mos. Eherechts.* Breslau 1860 p.17ff
232. Levit. 20: 11-12
233. Deut. 27:20
234. Makkoth 3:1
235. Deut. 25:2-3
236. Shabbath 40b

We do not know the reason for the various types of death penalty (stoning or burning) which the law demands for the various types of incest, nor do we know why the punishment for incest with one's daughter-in-law is more severe than with one's own daughter. We also do not know why the Bible refers to incest with a daughter-in-law and copulation with an animal as *thebel*[237], incest with one's daughter as *zimma*[238], with one's sister as *chesed*[239] and with one's sister-in-law as *niddah*[240]. For every reason that one might propose, there are as many counter-arguments.

## IV   Rarity of Punishment Infliction

These apparently extraordinarily severe punishments present a totally different picture in their practical application. According to tradition, without exception, these punishments could only be ordained if the act was performed with premeditation. The premeditation, however, only serves as evidence if the perpetrator, prior to the performance of the transgression, was warned with reference to the specific type of punishment. Ignorance of the law protects. Where an error *de jure* and certainly an error *de persona* occurred, no verdict could be rendered. During the time of the Temple, the culprit was only required to bring a sin offering.

To this must be added the individuality of the Talmudic legal process which exclusively recognizes the evidence of witnesses and rejects the use of circumstantial evidence or even the confession of the accused in the judgement of the case. In the very strict interpretation of this regulation, as already enunciated in the *Mishnah*[241], in the case of an accusation of incest, one must ask the witnesses (at least two are required): "did you observe the *conjunctio membrorum* as the kohl-flask and its probe?" (a euphemism for carnal intimacy). Thus a sentence of capital punishment could never be imposed[242]. To be sure, most cases did not go so far as to totally absolve the guilty party, but the death penalty was so seldom imposed that a Jewish court *(Sanhedrin)* which effected an execution once in seven years, or according to some even *once* in seventy years, is branded a murderous tribunal[243]. And the death penalty was not only imposed for incest.

## V   Reasons for Proscribed Marriages

A reason for the prohibited marriages is not found anywhere in the Bible. It is not true that the reason is in accord with the general laws of nature, since one glance at the animal kingdom demonstrates just the opposite. Nor is it an expression of the perception of every cultured individual, since Egypt was a highly civilized country and yet sister marriages were the order of the day[244]. Persians and Phoenicians also lived in legal matrimony with sisters and daughters. We are also reminded from Greece, that Cimon, as stated by Corn. Nepos[245], took his sister Elpinice for his wife. In contrast to the Egyptian practice, the laws of the Bible are explicitly the opposite. In fact, the introduction to this chapter in the Bible states *after the doings of the Land of Egypt ye shalt not do*[246]. In Russia today, it is customary that the father sexually misuses the wives of his sons[247]. If the Biblical laws do not seem to add anything new to our *modern* discoveries, and if copulation with one's sister and even with one's mother seems to us to be a ghastly unnatural act, notwithstanding the law of the Arabs which

237. Levit. 20:12 and 18:23
238. Levit. 20:14. The verse actually reads: and if a man take with his wife also her mother, it is wickedness, *zimma* (F.R.)
239. Levit. 20:17
240. Levit. 20:21
241. Makkoth 1:9-10

242. Makkoth 7a
243. *ibid*
244. Erman, *Aegypten* p.221 ff
245. Nepos. *Cimon,* Chapt. 1
246. Levit. 18:2
247. Forel. *Die Sexuelle Frage.* Munich 1906, p.174

requires the son of a widowed mother to marry her[248], then the educational influence of the Bible throughout the centuries is again manifest.

It is questionable whether the potentially harmful influence of incest on the descendants was already known. The Bible certainly warns only that matrimony with one's brother's wife and with one's aunt results in childlessness. In the former case, the couple is *childless*[249], that is will have no offspring at all, and in the second case, they will *die childless*[250], that is children engendered through incest die early. However, in a later place, the Bible speaks of the *tenth generation,* i.e. descendants in the tenth degree, of a *mamzer* (bastard) from *e coitu damnato procreatus*[251], in order to exclude them from entering into a legal marriage. Thus a rapid degeneration of this line of offspring is not obviously presupposed. For the children derived from adultery, this is self-evident.

## VI    Additional Proscribed Marriages

It is not the intent here to write a history of the Biblical and Talmudic marriage laws. However, it should be briefly stressed that marriage with a woman of the Canaanite peoples who served the *Moloch,* or with an Egyptian or an Edomite woman, is also prohibited. No one is allowed to remarry a woman whom he had previously divorced, if she was married to another man in the interim[252]. In direct contradistinction to this is the law of the Koran in which a man who wishes to remarry his divorced wife can only do so if she was married to another man in the interim[253]. It is difficult to understand how the wondrous use of "a preventive measure of the lawgiver causes petitions for divorce to be very rare"[254].

Additional regulations exist for a priest: he is forbidden from marrying a divorced woman, or any woman who has lived as a partner in a prohibited marriage[255]. The High Priest is also prohibited from taking a widow for a wife[256].

In all these cases, however, there is no question of incest. The death penalty can, therefore, never be invoked even when the law is violated.

The remainder of the proscribed marriages will be discussed in other contexts.

## VII    The Incest of Lot And His Daughters

A case of incest with one's daughters is the story of the daughters of Lot[257].

Only Lot and his family survived the destruction of Sodom and Gomorrah. His wife was turned into a pillar of salt during their flight, and he lived with his two daughters in a mountain cave which was known to them from an earlier time. The girls thought that the entire world had perished, such as occurred at the time of the deluge, and then feared the most terrible fate that an ancient Hebrew woman can imagine, to die childless. They were not prostitutes who demand sexual activities *coûte que coûte* (i.e. at all costs). They did not dare approach their father to ask that he cohabit with them. The older one spoke to the younger one: our father is old — we must, therefore, carry out what lies before us, very soon — and there is no other man on this earth who could come unto us — after the manner of the whole world. Come then, let us give our father wine to drink — the national custom was to store wine in mountain caves (grottos) so that it could be found in abundance[258]— and we will sleep with him and

248. Ploss. *Das Weib* I: 373
249. Levit. 20:21
250. Levit. 20:20
251. Deut. 23:2
252. Deut. 24: 1-4
253. Koran. *Sure* 2 p.25 d. in the translation of Ullmann

254. Nork. *Etym-mythol.-symb. Realworterb.* Stuttgart 1843, I:432
255. Levit. 21:7
256. Levit. 21:13-14
257. Genesis 19: 30-38
258. *Sifré, Eqeb* 84a:24

preserve seed from our father. And they gave their father wine to drink that very night, and the older daughter went in and lay with her father, and he perceived not when she lay down nor when she arose.

The next day the younger sister was induced by the older one to perform the same deed with the explicit motivation *that we may preserve seed of our father*[259]. And they gave their father wine to drink that night as well, and the younger one lay with her father without his perceiving when she lay down or when she arose. Both daughters became pregnant from their father and each gave birth to a son. The children became the ancestors of both Canaanite tribes, the Moabites and the Ammonites, whose hatred of the advancing Israelites is well known[260].

The school of De Wette interprets the whole story to be "a popular saying obviously originating from national hatred". The fact of the matter is just the opposite, in that the Talmud, as already mentioned above, although not sanctioning the Biblically described deed of the girls, seeks to examine more closely their motives, and does not simply consider the ancestresses of enemy nations to be debased prostitutes. In addition, modern Bible commentators, including even the most liberal ones, acknowledge this interpretation[261].

We are here also interested in other questions. Lot is obviously considered as a "senseless drunk" — the Talmudic expression, therefore, is "Lot's drunkenness"[262]. There is no doubt that such drunks are capable not only of cohabitation but of procreation as well. In fact, alcohol is a stimulant for sexual activity[262a], as was already known to the Talmudic Sages, and does not only act by removing the normal moral restraints. Therefore, in our case, particularly since the drunk Lot was not aggressive, one might postulate a rather strong type of intoxication. However, one cannot assume that there was complete alcoholic narcosis, for then all reflexes would be suppressed, and the statement that Lot perceived nothing of the entire event would be looked upon with skepticism by the Rabbis. In the transmitted Biblical text, the word *bekumah, when she rose*[263], is accentuated with a punctuation mark, perhaps a question mark. For the Talmud means that even if he didn't perceive *when she lay down*, he must have perceived *when she arose*, because he must have become somewhat aroused by the orgasm of the ejaculation (similar to nocturnal pollution). Even if he couldn't undo that which was already done, he should at least have been on guard against the use of alcohol the following evening[264]. The Talmud is, therefore, not sparing in its criticism of Lot.

A second question arose from the general Talmudic teaching that a woman cannot become pregnant from the first cohabitation (defloration)[265]. Here, however, although apparently there was only one coitus (with each daughter), nevertheless, pregnancy resulted therefrom. One, therefore, assumes that the girls had assaulted themselves and torn their hymens so that the cohabitation with their father was equivalent to their second[266].

## VIII    Amnon And Tamar

An exception to the above-mentioned prohibited sister marriage is apparently contained in a remark in the narratives of the kings.

It is related[267] that Absalom, the son of King David, had a beautiful sister called Tamar, who was loved by Amnon, a son of David from another mother. And Amnon

259. Genesis 19:32
260. Genesis 19:30 ff and the Talmudic supplementation thereon
261. Gunkel, in Nowacks *Komm. Zu. St.*
262. Erubin 65a
262a. Today there is medical evidence to the contrary (F.R.)
263. Genesis 19:33
264. Nazir 23a
265. Yebamoth 34a
266. Genesis Rabbah 51:9
267. Second Samuel 13:1 ff

was so vexed that he became ill, for she was a virgin who could not leave her house, according to Oriental custom, so that it seemed impossible for Amnon to do anything to her. Upon the advice of a clever friend who remarked that the prince, due to sleepless nights, was becoming leaner from day to day, Amnon lay down in bed, pretended to be ill and asked the King that Tamar care for him. Although under ordinary circumstances women were completely secluded from men, for nursing the sick an explicit exception was made. Tamar came and, as depicted in great detail, prepared several foods before his eyes. And when she brought them to him to eat, he took hold of her and said: *Come lie with me, my sister!* But she answered him, *Nay, my brother, do not force me; for no such thing ought to be done in Israel, do not thou this shameful deed! And I, whither shall I carry my shame? And as for thee, thou shalt be as one of the base men in Israel. Now, therefore, I pray thee, speak unto the King; for he will not withhold me from thee.* He, however, would not listen to her and, being stronger than she, forced her, and lay with her.

And Amnon hated her with a great hatred. In fact, the hatred was greater than the love wherewith he had loved her. And he called unto her: *Arise, begone!* She, however, said unto him: *do not do this great wrong in putting me forth, for it is worse than the other thing that you did unto me.* But he would not listen to her but called his servant and instructed him: *Put now this woman out from me, and bolt the door after her!* Although the servant must have recognized by her clothes that she was a princess, he still did as he was told. As a sign of mourning, Tamar put ashes on her head, rent her garment and went her way lamenting. She remained desolate in her brother Absalom's house. The latter brought about an opportunity later to kill Amnon in revenge.

The remark by Tamar that the King would not withhold giving in marriage his daughter to her stepbrother if the latter so desires, has occupied the Bible commentators ever since, since the Mosaic code prohibits any type of sister marriage. The modern expositors make the matter easy in that they assume that the Mosaic law is younger than the Books of Kings, and, therefore, the prohibition of matrimony — at least with a stepsister[267a]—did not yet exist, especially since elsewhere there was never any objection thereto[268].

The Talmudic tradition states as follows: During the war, the Bible gives a soldier the right to have coitus once with a beautiful woman that he sees among the captives if he has a desire for her; (individual Talmudists indeed speak strongly against this permissibility). As stated, the intent was to make a concession to the evil instinct in order to prevent massive excesses of illicit coitus[269]. If the soldier, however, wanted to keep the woman for his wife, he was obligated to give her one month's period of time to bewail her parents who died in the war. Then he marries her and she is entitled to all the privileges of a married woman in that, if the man wishes to divorce her, he cannot sell her as a slave[270].

Children born from such a legal marriage are naturally considered on an equal basis with the other children of the father. This does not apply to children who are conceived before the time of captivity, even if they are born after the marriage, because in these cases the woman was already pregnant at the time of the single coitus of war captives, as above. Besides, the legitimate ancestry can be in doubt, because, as a war captive, the woman was the property of the whole division of troops and, therefore, could have also cohabited with other soldiers besides her future husband.

Tradition, therefore, assumes that Maacah, the mother of Absalom[270a] and of Tamar, was one of the captives that David proferred during his many military

267a. Preuss erroneously has "stepdaughter" (F.R.)
268. See part 2, section V above
269. Kiddushin 21b
270. Deut. 21:10-14
270a. Preuss erroneously has Amnon (F.R.)

expositions. Absalom was her real son, whereas Tamar was her daughter born previously whose paternal ancestry was at least very doubtful, so that she should in any event legally not be considered his sister, even though she lived in the house of David as one of his children[271].

The entire Biblical narration provides a series of interesting psychological moments, which we will not delve into here, except to emphasize that the Talmud's explanation of Amnon's sudden change to exceedingly great hate is that when the perpetrator thought he had achieved his goal, and found himself impotent, he let out the anger of his "shame" on the innocent object[272].

## IX   Levirate Marriage

Whereas Biblical law in *one* place specifically forbids marriage with the wife of one's deceased brother, as mentioned above, in another place it is so commanded, but only under specified circumstances[273].

If brothers live together and one of them dies without offspring, then the widow should not marry outside (the family) unto a stranger; rather she should marry her husband's brother. The firstborn son of this marriage should be given the name of the deceased brother so that his name should not be put out of Israel. If the man does not wish to marry his sister-in-law, then she has to notify the elders of the court. The latter should try to persuade him, but if he formally persists in his refusal, then the woman, in the presence of the elders, should remove his shoe, and spit in his face, and cry out: so shall it be done unto that man that will not build up his brother's house!

We have already indicated in the discussion on onanism[274] that the practice of marriage to the brother-in-law already existed among the Israelites in the times of the Bedouins. One thus might get the impression that its insertion into the law was only a concession to an ancient popular custom. In favor of the antiquity of this practice is the fact that the ancient expression used for this act of sister-in-law marrying, *yabam*, has been preserved as a *terminus technicus,* and also that the brother-in-law and sister-in-law are designated by the names *yabam* and *yebama*, names not used in any other context in the Bible.

The sense of the entire law is openly an agrarian-political one. It is an attempt to prevent the dispersal of land ownership and its transfer to another lineage or another tribe. This is explicitly stated in the exceptional case of the daughters of Zelophechad[275] and in a similar manner in the case of Ruth.

The Talmud deduces certain restrictions from the wording of the Biblical text. If the woman is subject to a man who is incapable of procreation because of malformed genitalia, then levirate marriage would obviously be useless. The law is also not applicable if the name of the deceased was already extinguished during his lifetime, that is if he was *impotens generandi*. The law can also not be fulfilled if the widow is related to the brother-in-law in one of the relationships which prohibits matrimony, such as if she is his daughter or his mother-in-law[276], or if there exist reasons in the previous marriage which would have required that the woman be divorced. Among these is included an affliction of leprosy in the husband[277]; also included is an occupation which is of such a nature that the woman under normal circumstances cannot be expected to live with her husband who practices that profession, such as tanning[278].

271. Sanhedrin 21a
272. *ibid*
273. Deut. 25:5-10
274. See part I, section IX above

275. Numbers 36:9ff
276. Yebamoth 1:1
277. *ibid* 4a
278. Kethuboth 77a

In general, the entire institution of levirate marriage is not very congenial to the Talmud and *"chalitzah kodemeth le-yibbum"*, the obligation of *chalitzah* precedes the obligation of levirate marriage[279], is the rule of conduct. This was motivated by the fact that previous generations had religious intent, namely, the fulfillment of the law of levirate marriage, which was not the case in later generations. Abba Saul was of the opinion that he who marries his sister-in-law because of her beauty or to acquire her property or for any other incidental reason is guilty of incest; opinions were divided, however[280].

The Karaites teach that since agrarian-political considerations no longer apply to the Jews, the entire institution of levirate marriage is untenable, and the other Biblical command which considers such a marriage as incest is now applicable[281]. This is also the present viewpoint of the Occidental Jews; for them, the possibility of levirate marriage is excluded in all cases where the surviving brother is already married.

# X   Adultery

Each of the above-mentioned transgressions and sins (incest etc.), juridically speaking, can occur in conceptual opposition to adultery, rape and seduction.

*Adultery* can only be committed with the wife of another man or by a married woman. Sexual intercourse between a man and an unmarried woman, although prohibited as immoral, can never be punished as adultery because of other reasons which will be discussed presently (*s.v.* polygamy).

Adultery is already prohibited in the Ten Commandments[282]. In a later place in the Bible, the death penalty is prescribed for both partners[283]. According to tradition, execution is to be carried out by strangulation[284], and the remark in John[285] that "Moses commanded us in the law, to stone an adulteress" *(lithoboleisthai)* is, therefore, incorrect. Here, too, one should note that which was remarked above, namely, that a death penalty is only imposed when premeditation is proven, and that the act itself must be verified by the testimony of eye witnesses. If both conditions, that is prior warning and the proof of eyewitnesses, are not fulfilled, then a death penalty is not possible.

At the time of the Temple, if a man seriously suspected his wife of adultery, he could subject her to the Biblically described ordeal[286]. With the destruction of the Temple, this procedure was abrogated. However, it became the duty of a husband to divorce his wife if she gave him grounds to suspect her loyalty. Thereby the woman lost the right to the allowance of the *donatio propter nuptias (kethubah)* which she would otherwise be entitled to in the case of the death of her husband, or divorce for other reasons. The husband is not allowed to pardon his wife for marital disloyalty. In addition, if the marriage is dissolved for this reason, then reconciliation and remarriage are out of the question.

Adultery is also punished in modern law, but only where a claim is made and only when the marriage is dissolved because of it[287]. Whereas, therefore, in Biblical law the state punishes for the infringement of morality *qua talis,* our time protects the legal sphere of the husband. Indeed, according to Biblical law, not only the husband (as in our law), but anyone, had the right to bring an accusation or charges about the moral offense. In Rome, relatives were also permitted to bring charges.

A legal connection between an adulterer and a divorcée is also prohibited in our German state law, as well as in Talmudic law. However, in state law on this matter, it

---

279. Bechoroth 1:7
280. Yebamoth 39b
281. L. Löw. *Ges. Schr.* 3:76
282. Exod. 20:13 and Deut. 5:17
283. Levit. 20:10

284. Sanhedrin 11:1
285. John 8:5
286. Numbers 5:12ff
287. *Strafgesetzbuch* No. 172

is possible to grant exemptions[288], which is not possible in Judaism because of the aforementioned reasons. Also, according to state law, no one can hinder a divorced couple from living together in permanent concubinage, which, according to Jewish law, must be punished as immoral.

# XI    Lustful Thoughts

Not only is adultery in the true sense prohibited, but even only "coveting one's neighbor's wife" is forbidden in the Ten Commandments[289]. Rabbi Shesheth teaches us in the Talmud[290] that whoever looks only upon the little finger of a woman in order to derive sensuous pleasure therefrom is no different morally than an adulterer. This is the same teaching which is found in the Gospel in the famous form: *whosoever looketh on his neighbor's wife to lust after her hath committed adultery with her already in his heart*[291].

One who thinks of another woman while he is cohabiting with his own wife is also guilty of adultery even though not in the punishable sense. Children born from such an intimacy are nearly comparable to bastards[292]. For this reason some people dissuade marriage with a widow; if the man is a widower (and marries a widow) it is possible that "there are four minds in the marital bed"[293].

# XII    Sotah (Suspected Adulteress)

The above-mentioned proceedings in the case of a woman suspected by her husband of adultery, a *sotah*, can only be understood as a Divine judgement. The husband brings his wife to the priest who places her before God. He then places holy water in an earthern vessel and adds thereto some dust from the floor of the Temple. Then the priest uncovers the woman's head and charges her by an oath saying: *if no man have lain with thee, and if thou hast not gone aside to uncleanness, being under thy husband, be thou free from this water of bitterness that causeth the curse. But if thou hast gone aside, being under thy husband, . . . the Lord make thee a curse and an oath among thy people, when the Lord doth make thy thigh to fall away, and thy belly to swell. And this water that causeth the curse shall go into thy bowels, and make thy belly to swell, and thy thigh to fall away. And the woman shall say: Amen, Amen!*[294] And the priest then writes these curses in a book and blots them out in the water of bitterness. And he makes the woman drink this water. Then follows the offering. And if the woman was defiled and had committed a trespass against her husband, then the water of bitterness enters her and becomes bitter, her belly swells, her thigh falls, and she becomes a curse among her people. But if the woman is innocent, then she remains unhurt and conceives seed from her husband.

Much effort has been expended attempting to rationally explain these threatened punishments and their causation. Michaelis guessed at *hydrops ovarii*[295]. Saalschütz thinks that the "bitter waters" might represent "a specifically designed remedy which is harmful to an already initiated pregnancy, but which is otherwise without consequences"[296]. This explanation is unacceptable because not every cohabitation is necessarily immediately followed by a pregnancy. Ebstein, on the basis of an incorrect Bible translation[297], makes the observation that this drink was "holy water in which

---

288. *Bürgerliches Gesetzbuch* No. 1312
289. Exod. 20:14
290. Shabbath 64b
291. Matthew 5:28
292. Nedarim 20b; Yalkut 2:305 to Jeremiah 23, fol. 413d
293. Pesachim 112a

294. Numbers 5:11-31
295. *Mos. Recht,* T.V. p.272
296. *Das Mos. Recht* p.574
297. The word *mishkan* in the text, which Kautzsch translates as "residence", always refers to the residence of God, that is the Temple

the only foreign ingredient was a little dust from the floor of the residence of the woman suspected of having committed adultery"! He cannot decide whether "we are dealing with a swelling of the abdomen secondary to the expansion of the uterus or a form of dropsy which incidently complicates the pregnancy or some other condition"[298]! Josephus states: "the right thigh will *fall out of its joint*"[299] *(tou skelous ekpesontos and exarthrorgenesthai).* It is pointless to restate here all the other clarification attempts since none is convincing.

It seems quite certain that the entire procedure with all its unusual and exciting details, not the least of which being the fear of the threatened physical consequences, served to have the woman admit her possible guilt. Then it was obligatory upon the husband to divorce his wife. Criminal proceedings against the woman, however, could not take place because, according to the word of Scripture, the entire proceedings were only possible in the absence of witnesses. Punishment, without the proof of witnesses, as repeatedly stated, cannot result from a lawsuit, even if the accused plead guilty.

Nothing can better characterize the position of the Talmud in giving equal rights to the woman than the statement of the *Gemara* that the "bitter water" only takes effect if the husband was never unfaithful to his wife[300]. Since, in later times, when men no longer were strict in their marital fidelity, the water ceased to be fully effective, Rabbi Yochanan ben Zakkai abolished this law of *Sotah* entirely[301].

## XIII   Rape

If a married woman or a woman of the prohibited marriages is forcibly violated (i.e. raped), the perpetrator receives the death penalty appropriate for that particular transgression, assuming that the above-mentioned conditions (warning and witnesses) have been fulfilled. An intensification of the death penalty, perhaps execution by stoning instead of strangulation, does not occur. Also, if a criminal punishment hangs over the offender, the rape victim cannot bring a lawsuit in the civil court. The latter is a general principle in Talmudic law (i.e. that he who is liable to two penalties receives only the severer one). Where adultery occurs concomitantly with incest, such as incest with one's married mother-in-law, the stronger punishment is applied. In this case, death would be through burning rather than through strangulation[302].

The raped woman obviously is not punished. Nevertheless, the assumption is that her body itself has been violated. If, however, she was only *threatened* with "danger to life or limb" if she does not accede to the assailant's demands, then she should rather endure death than submit to his bidding[303]. The Talmudic law in this case is thus more stringent than modern law[304].

Rape only applies to a woman. A man can never use the excuse that he was forced into coitus with someone forbidden to him. For Rabba has already remarked that erection depends entirely on "the will"[304a]. On the other hand, the *Gemara* also takes exception to this by pointing out that erections can also occur while a person is sleeping[305].

## XIV   Rape And Seduction

If the rape victim was a "betrothed virgin" *(na'ara bethula meorasa),* that is already betrothed but still a virgin, it makes a difference whether the rape occurred in the city or in the field[306]. In the former case, both man and woman are stoned, because

298. Ebstein. *Die Medizin im Alten Testament.* Stuttgart 1901 p.137
299. *Antiquities,* 3 Chapt. 11:6
300. Sotah 28a
301. Sotah 9:9
302. Sanhedrin 9:4
303. Sanhedrin 73b-74a
304. *Strafsgesetzbuch* No. 177
304a. Yebamoth 53a
305. *ibid*
306. Deut. 22:23ff

it is assumed that the cohabitation took place with the willing consent of the damsel; otherwise one of her neighbors would have heard her screams and come to her rescue. In the latter case, only the man is executed, because it is assumed that the damsel cried out but there was none to save her. *For this matter is just like when a man riseth against his neighbor and slayeth him, without another coming to his aid.*

If the case concerns a virgin damsel who is not betrothed, then the rapist must pay fifty pieces of silver to her father, and must marry the damsel and loses forever the right to divorce her[307]. According to Talmudic law, the obligation of marrying her occurs under all circumstances, even if the damsel is lame or blind or leprous. The only exception is if she is one of the grades of relatives forbidden to him. On the other hand, the damsel and her father have the right to refuse.

In addition to the fifty pieces of silver which is called a "fine", the rapist has to pay reparation for the disgrace he inflicted, for the physical pain endured, and for the deterioration of the personal value of the damsel[308]. There is no doubt also that, if need be, he will also have to pay medical bills and "sick benefits", since rape must be restituted according to the normal procedures in bodily injuries.

The penal regulations for seduction are very similar indeed. According to Biblical law, the seducer must marry the maiden he enticed if she and her father both agree. If the father refuses, the seducer must pay a fine according to *the dowry of virgins*, namely, fifty pieces of silver[309]. However, here the man has the right to divorce her. According to the Talmud, he also has to pay for the disgrace and for the devaluation whereas he does not have to pay for the physical pain he inflicted upon her because, in contrast to one who is raped, a virgin who is seduced experiences no pain, as the Rabbis asked of their wives[310]. The upper limit for a seduction is 12 ½ years of age, which conforms with the conditions of the Orient[310a].

I believe that this ancient law of the Bible was the best and most practical of all "motherhood assurances".

The moralists in the Talmud added the point to these laws that not only is their transgression a sinful act, but their observance is a praiseworthy thing. Thus, in the prohibition of imbibing blood, we are told: *Thou shalt not eat it, that it may go well with thee, and with thy children after thee*[311]. The *Mishnah* tells us[312] that if a man who refrains from eating blood which a person naturally abhors receives a reward, then all the more so in the case of someone who refrains from forbidden intercourse which a person lusts after and covets. Therefore, too, these laws precede and serve as an introduction to the sentence *these are mine statutes which if a man do he shall live by them*[313].

A further clause of the Talmudic moralists, namely that lewdness of a person, in the broadest sense of the word, is punished both in this world as well as in the next world[314], is stated in detail by the Apostle Paul, in that neither fornicators (*pornoi* in Greek) nor Sodomites (*arsenokoitai* in Greek) will inherit the kingdom of God[315].

## XV    Definition Of Coitus

We have already mentioned above that our civil law does not give a definition of "coitus". The lack of such a definition is felt even more in the penal code. Our *Strafsgesetzbuch* speaks only of "cohabitation" (No. 173, 177, 179) or simply of "immoral conduct" (No. 174, 176) since the context of this expression presupposes

---

307. *ibid* 22: 28-29
308. Kethuboth 3:4
309. Exod. 22:15
310. Kethuboth 39b
310a. The original has a sentence here indi-
    cating that in German law, the age is 16

years.
311. Deut. 12:25
312. Makkoth 3:15
313. Levit. 18:5
314. Aboth deRabbi Nathan 40:1
315. First Corinthians 6:9; First Timothy 1:10

sexual intercourse, just as does the phrase "professional prostitution" (No. 361,6). One observes, however, that doubts still existed before the court in that the Reich's courts often produced their own definitions[316].

The Talmudic administration of justice was also occupied with this question. It distinguishes between ha'arajah and the real biyah, in that the former is understood to mean the introduction of the glans penis until the digitus (penis) reaches between the sephiyoth (labia)[317], known as coitus inter labia to modern jurists. The latter is understood to mean regular coitus. The full punishment of the law is incurred even for the former (partial coitus)[318]. Whether or not ejaculation occurred is of no importance[319]. The Reich's court makes a similar decision, namely, that for the concept of coitus, immissio seminis is meaningless[320]. According to Austrian law, copula vulvaris is only considered "attempted coitus"[321].

Just as in penal law, so too in civil law there is no difference between coitus inter labia and immissio perfecta. Even through the former method, where no anatomic lesion is produced, the maiden ceases to be considered a virgin, and a High Priest is not, therefore, allowed to marry her[322]. In a case dealing with attempted rape by a soldier who only arrived at ejaculatio inter genua feminae, the legitimate conclusion was, however, neglected[323].

According to some authors the meaning of the word ha'arajah is identical to that of the word neshika. The latter word describes every coming together of two things and is used extensively in the Bible and Talmud to denote the meeting of the lips, or a kiss. Therefore, ha'arajah would represent any appositio membrorum genitalia. Baas makes the uncomplimentary remark: "the lascivious Rabbis" called coitus a kiss of limbs.

A requisite for punishability is the presence of the possibility of cohabitation, that is the erection of the penis. Where this was lacking for any reason whatsoever, such as in a castrate, a conviction for incest was not possible[324]. However, punishment by means of flogging could be inflicted because an immoral act was committed[325].

It is all the same in terms of culpability whether the immissio penis took place in vaginam sive in anum, since the Bible nowhere makes a distinction between natural (i.e. per vagina) and unnatural (i.e. per anus) coitus[326]. This means, therefore, that paedicatio feminae ad coitum vetitae is also included: for example, the married wife of another is punished in an identical manner (in the precept of the death penalty) as with normal cohabitation[327]. I am not familiar with the modern penal code in this matter.

He who injures his wife during coitus — defloration is obviously not included — is punishable, because he neglected the care and consideration which he was obligated to observe[328]. The punishment (monetary punishment) is realized as in the general cases of bodily injury[329].

## XVI   Virginity

Virginitas laesa for all civilized peoples is a ground for dissolving the marriage, if the groom was not aware of this deficiency, or should have known of the situation. If the man asserts: I took this woman and when I came nigh to her for coitus, I found not in her the tokens of virginity (bethulim)[330], then the parents have the obligation of

316. Entschliessung. in Strafsrecht. Vol. 20 p.225 and Vol. 4 p.23
317. Jerushalmi Yebamoth 6; 7b
318. Jerushalmi Sanhedrin 7; 24a
319. Yebamoth 54a
320. Entschliessung. in Strafsrecht Vol. 20 p.225 and Vol. 4 p.23
321. Haberda, in Casper Liman. Vol. 1:182
322. Kiddushin 10a

323. Jerushalmi Nedarim 9; 42d
324. Shebuoth 18a
325. Maimonides. Hilchoth Issure Biyah 1:11
326. Kethuboth 46a
327. Tosefta Kerithoth 1:16 p.562:17
328. Baba Kamma 32a
329. Be'er Hetev on Choshen Mishpat 421:12
330. Deut. 22:14

defending the honor of their daughter. The expression which the father uses in his defense capacity is: *these here* (demonstration) *are the tokens of my daughter's virginity (bethulim)*[331]. The law's requirement of the simultaneous presence of the mother — a most unusual necessity in the administration of justice in antiquity — as well as the appearance of the accused *woman* before the court ("this woman here")[332], might evoke one to think that the intent is to demonstrate the facts directly on the *body* of the accused. However, the directions "and the parents should bring forth the tokens of the damsel's virginity unto the elders of the city" and "they shall spread the cloth before them" speak strongly against such an interpretation. It obviously means that they exhibit the blood-stained bed sheet as a *demonstratio ad oculos*. Such is still the custom today among many primitive races.

Even in the Talmud, only the *bethulim* are spoken of continually, without there being an absolute indication in any place as to whether it refers to an organ or the *sanguis virginitatis*. The latter is by far the more likely.

The meaning of the Biblical rule "and they shall spread the cloth" is already in dispute in the Talmud[333]. According to Rabbi Eliezer ben Jacob the law is to be taken literally in order to encompass the aforementioned. According to Rabbi Ishmael and others[334], it means "they shall explain the matter clearly" (as clear as a new garment). For the opinion that defloration must *always* be followed by bleeding, and that the absence of such bleeding is evidence for *virginitas laesa,* is strongly contradicted by the Talmud. The most definitive statement is that of Mar Samuel, the Babylonian physician, who asserts that even repeated sexual connections with a *virgo intacta* are possible without any bleeding. The question is then raised as to whether a High Priest, who, according to Biblical law, is only permitted *a virgin of his own people*[335], is allowed to marry a pregnant maiden[336]. Certainly, in modern times, it is incorrect to find an allusion to the birth of Jesus in this matter, since Ben Zoma, to whom the question was addressed, was a disciple of Rabbi Akiba who lived in the first century after Christ, that is at a time when the dogma of the Immaculate Conception was not yet known.

The opinion of Mar Samuel, however, is not the legal one. The Sages think that that case of repeated coitus with a virgin without her losing her virginity was a rare exception with an extremely capable man *(rob gubreh),* or there were no real cohabitations, but rather an "inclination (of the penis), *hattaya,* as many understand it"[337], or perhaps only *coitus inter labia*[338]. Legal medicine of our times recognizes the opinion of Mar Samuel to be correct. With an extensible hymen, a not too forceful penis, and careful *immissio,* there can undoubtedly result an absence of blood of virginity, although a "strong man" would normally not be so careful.

*But if this thing be true, that the tokens of virginity were not found in the damsel, then they (the elders) shall bring out the damsel to the door of her father's house, and the men of her city shall stone her with stones, that she die, because she hath wrought a wanton deed in Israel, to play the harlot in her father's house; so shalt thou put away the evil from the midst of thee.* Thus speaks the Biblical law[339]. In the Talmud, the absence of defloration bleeding *alone* has no civil or criminal consequences any longer. Only if the young groom states "I found an open opening" (i.e. lack of virginity) and authentically proves his accusation, then the marriage is annulled, and the woman is stoned as a prostitute or as an adulteress.

If the accusation cannot be proved, the husband is a slanderer for which the Bible prescribes punishment: he is flogged, has to pay 100 pieces of silver as a fine to the

---

331. *ibid* 22:17
332. *Sifre, opus citum*
333. Kethuboth 46a
334. should be Rabbi Abbahu (F.R.)
335. Levit. 21:14

336. Chagigah 14b
337. Kethuboth 6b
338. Niddah 64b
339. Deut. 22:20-21

father of the damsel because he brought an evil name upon a virgin of Israel, and loses forever his right to divorce his wife[340]. Rabbi Nachman instructed that a young newly married man who came to him with the accusation of the "open opening" be immediately flogged, because Rabbi Nachman correctly assumed that the knowledge of this young groom must have stemmed from previous illegal cohabitations[341]. He who was "secluded" with his fiancee before the marriage completely forfeits his right of accusation of *virginitas laesa*[342].

The proper adjudication of these kinds of cases is among the most difficult tasks to legal medicine even today, and the disputes concerning marriage and the legal and penal interpretation of *virginitas laesa* fill many volumes among the casuistry of marriage law of all peoples. For the Rabbis, the decisions must have been even more difficult, since they prohibited the physical examination (of the accused virgin), as already mentioned. From their details, one gains the impression that lawsuits of this type were not very appealing to them, and one recognizes everywhere their endeavors to strongly oppose immorality, frivolousness and fraudulent accusations of a woman's morals, as was otherwise customary in the Orient.

An ancient folk remedy through which one was able to verify a maiden's virginity consisted of sitting the woman on the opening of a wine barrel. In the case of one who is no longer a virgin, "the aroma goes through"[343]; but not so in the case of a virgin[344]. This is the same method employed by the Greek physicians when they wished to determine the possibility of conception in a woman. Euenor and Euryphon would place the woman on a birth stool and fumigated (under her) with powerful aromatic substances. If the aroma came out from the mouth, then one assumed the woman was fertile[345]. Aetius has a similar account[346]. The critical Soran explains the reliability of these diagnoses to be a lie (*aper pseudos* in Greek), although Hippocrates had already mentioned it earlier[347]. One again finds these and similar expedients in the writings of Albertus Magnus[347a] and later authors. Philippus Neri is also said to have been able to recognize abstinent men by their aroma[347b].

According to military custom, the virginal women belonged to the soldiers as booty. Legend relates that these (virgins) were differentiated from already deflorated women in the above-mentioned manner[347c]. One also employed it as an aid in cases where the man raised the accusation of *virginitas laesa,* but the women asserted that no copulation had as yet taken place[347d]. Later law teachers explain that "we are no longer skilled in the performance of any of these types of investigation"[347e]. In a few areas of the world, one allowed witnesses to sleep in the bridal chamber[347f], such as in the testimony of Ploss concerning the Catholic Christians in Egypt and concerning the Abyssinians, where copulation before witnesses is still customary[347g].

# XVII

An unusual difficulty arose if a woman had been raped in earlier years or if she had an antecedent injury. Do the *bethulim* (tokens of virginity) destroyed in childhood later return, or is it possible that they cannot be completely destroyed until after the third year of age ? Both questions are answered affirmatively. It is like putting a finger

340. Deut. 22:13-19
341. Kethuboth 10a
342. Kethuboth 1:5
343. *Rashi:* one can smell the wine from the mouth
344. Kethuboth 10b
345. Soran. Chapt. 9 ed. Ermerins p.45
346. Aetius 16:7, ed. Zervos, Leipzig 1901 p.10
347. *De Nat. Mul.* ed. Foes. Section 5, fol.

565:30
347a. *De Secretis Mulierum* p.108
347b. Ellis, *Gattenwahl* p.77
347c. Yebamoth 60b
347d. Kethuboth 10b
347e. *Be'er Hetev* on *Even Ha'ezer* 68:4
347f. Kethuboth 12a
347g. *Das Weib* I, 306

in the eye; it tears and tears again[347h]; so, too, with each new cohabitation before age three, blood appears again[347i].

A woman whose virginity was "injured by a piece of wood", *mukkath etz,* is a regular expression of forensic medicine. The one upon whom it is incumbent to bring proof in a concrete case[347j] is in dispute[348]. Rabbi accepted as the truth the declaration of a woman that she lost her tokens of virginity because of the high steps of the staircase in her parents' house[349]. Also related is the story of women of a family in Jerusalem who were accustomed to taking unusually large steps (when they walked) so that "their tokens of virginity *(bethulim)* were destroyed". They were advised to wear decorative bracelets on their knees with a chain connecting the two so that they would be forced to take smaller steps[350].

Whether the hymen can be torn by bruskly spreading the legs wide apart or through jumping, etc. is a disputed question which has not been settled to this very day, but which is answered in the negative by most people. The following legal case seems to be much simpler: a young newly wedded couple came to Rabbi. The man said "I found no *bethulim*" (that is, no *sanguis virginitatis*). The woman assured him that she was a virgin, but it was a period of years of famine. The judge saw that their faces were black from hunger and gave no verdict. He commanded that they be brought to a bath and given food and drink and then sent them to the bridal chamber. Then the young groom had his wish fulfilled (i.e. he found blood following intercourse with her)[351]. It is likely that the hunger had weakened them so that they lacked bodily strength.

Destruction of the *bethulim* (tokens of virginity) can also occur following digital manipulation[352].

An accusation of *virginitas laesa* is not allowable against a deaf-mute, a mentally ill woman and, according to Rabbi Meir, against a blind woman[353]. They are explicitly considered to be mentally inferior, in that their moral fortitude against temptation is diminished, and the husband must count on the possibility of an earlier defloration. In the case of a blind woman, one must take into consideration the greater ease with which she can be violated.

Finally, families were known in which the female descendants have no bleeding at all; they have no blood of virginity and no blood of menstruation[354]. This is a bad characteristic for the married man who is counting on offspring, for the *bethulim* (tokens of virginity) of women are compared to vines, some give red wine, some black wine, some have abundant wine and some have little. Rabbi Judah says: "every (normal) vine has wine; that which has none is *dorkati*[355] or *terukti*"[356]. So, too, is a woman. The *dorkati* represent a "cut-off generation", *dor katua,* that is they are barren and the generation ceases with them[357].

The Arabs also describe women without any bleeding[358]. In earlier times, there was known a fraud which women practiced in order to be able to show a bloody bed sheet *post primam noctem*. Casuistry mentions the case where a man asserted that the exhibited stain was actually bird blood[359]. Naturally, it is incumbent upon him to bring evidence. Bloch has assembled a large number of methods used to date for the re-establishment of the *signa virginitatis*[360].

---

347h. Niddah 45a
347i. i.e. the features of virginity disappear and reappear again
347j. i.e. the man or the woman
348. Kethuboth 13a
349. Jerushalmi Kethuboth 1; 25a
350. Shabbath 63b
351. Kethuboth 10b
352. Jerushalmi Kethuboth 1; 25b
353. *Tosefta* Kethuboth 1:3

354. Kethuboth 10b
355. Niddah 9:11
356. Jerushalmi Kethuboth 1; 25a
357. Niddah 64b
358. Niebuhr. *Beschreibung von Arabien* p.37
359. Jerushalmi Kethuboth 1; 25a and *ibid* 4; 28c
360. Duhring, Eug. *Gas Geschlechtsleben in England*. Chartlottenburg 1901 Vol. 1:370

Rabbi Meir is of the opinion that the blood following defloration can be distinguished from menstrual blood by the color. The latter is red, the former is not, but is rather pale, opaque, *diha*[361]. Menses are dirty, *zihum,* whereas defloration blood is not. Menses arise from the source, the uterus, whereas defloration blood comes from the sides. In contrast, the Sages consider there to be no difference in the color[362].

# PART   III

## I  Prostitution

There is no explicit prohibition in the Bible against *prostitution* of unmarried girls. However, such a prohibition is clearly implied in the commandment *you* (the father) *shalt not profane thy daughter, to make her a harlot, lest the land fall into harlotry, and the land become full of lewdness*[363]. Since sexual intercourse with a married woman is separately forbidden, the punishment for adultery being the death of both partners, the aforementioned scriptural regulation must necessarily refer only to an unmarried girl. So, too, does Rabbi Eliezer deduce in the *Tosefta*[364].

A separate threat of punishment in the Bible is only pronounced against a priest's daughter: *And the daughter of any priest, if she profane herself by playing the whore, she profaneth her father; she shall be burnt with fire*[365]. But every maiden who at the time of her marriage is found not to be a virgin should be stoned, unless her innocence can be unquestionably established, perhaps by proving an earlier episode of rape[366].

According to tradition, other than for adultery, the death penalty is imposed only on a "betrothed woman", that is one who is already betrothed but not yet deflorated, and not on a single girl[367]. The latter is flogged[368]. When Philo reports that prostitutes were stoned, he is probably referring to a regulation of the Alexandrian Jewish courts of justice, as Ritter conjectures[369].

A further method of protection from prostitution was early marriage: "if your daughter has attained puberty, (and you cannot find a suitable husband for her), free your slave and give him to her"[370]. Naturally, one is not talking of a marriage at all costs. Prior to marriage, a young maiden is particularly warned against marrying an old man[371]. The Biblical command *do not profane thy daughter to cause her to be a whore*[371a], according to Rabbi Akiba, refers to one who delays marrying off his daughter who has already reached puberty. Rabbi Eliezer states it refers to one who marries off his daughter to an old man[372]. Both the above situations, as well as the case of a man who takes a wife for his infant son[373], are displeasing to God and are referred to in the Scriptural phrase *The Lord will not be willing to pardon him*[374].

A third prophylactic measure against adultery and prostitution was work, in particular, physical toil. Even if a woman brought a hundred slaves to her husband when she married him, according to Rabbi Eliezer, she is still obligated at least to help work in wool, for idleness leads to lewdness[375]. A man had a son; he bathed him and

361. *Tosefta* Niddah 9:10
362. Niddah 65b
363. Levit. 19:29
364. *Tosefta* Kiddushin 1:4
365. Levit. 21:9; according to tradition, only a married priest's daughter
366. Deut. 22:21
367. *Rashi's* commentary on Deut. 22:20
368. Maimonides. *Hilchoth Na'ara Bethulah* 2:7
369. *Philo und die Halacha,* Leipzig 1879

p.92; in opposition see Buchler, *Frankels Mtschr.* 1906 p.673
370. Pesachim 113a
371. Sanhedrin 76a. Since she may not willingly accept him, she may commit adultery.
371a. Levit. 19:29
372. Sanhedrin 76a
373. Sanhedrin 76b
374. Deut. 29:19
375. Kethuboth 5:5

anointed him, gave him plenty to eat and drink and hung a purse with money around his neck and set him down at the door of the whore house — how could the boy help himself and *not* sin? asks Rabbi Yochanan[376]. In this case, in addition to idleness there was also superabundance leading to lewdness.

A further important consideration is the fact that Biblical law prohibits in the strongest terms prostitution in honor of a deity, as was practiced in antiquity, not only in the Orient. Therewith, the notion that extramarital sexual traffic is not always lewd falls by the wayside. One must also take into consideration that polygamy was not forbidden in Biblical law, and entering into a legal bond was naturally easier for a girl than in the monogamous situation. Solon is even said to have *legally* sanctioned the profession of prostitution, because he thereby hoped to keep the men away from other married women.

To this must be added the Oriental custom of secluding women, both married women as well as young girls, from the outside world. One finds it quite natural that Dina, the daughter of Jacob, was violated by the son of a heathen Nomadic sheik, because she *went out to see the daughters of the land*[377]. In fact, one even reproached her mother Leah for *going out to meet her husband*[378]. The mother is exactly like the daughter, both are "outgoing". This is why the Bible calls Dina "the daughter of Leah" and not also the daughter of Jacob[379]. "She who goes outside", *naphkath bara*, is the technical expression for a prostitute used by the Aramaic Bible translators.

These customs and laws, together with a very generous posture in laws for the poor, must have sufficed in Biblical times to prevent the advent of prostitution among Jewish girls. Prostitution did exist, of course, as evidenced by the numerous warnings, particularly those of the epigrammatic poets. Even so, however, it has long been pointed out that the Bible designates a prostitute as a *nochriya* or foreigner *(peregrina): Prudence will deliver thee from the strange woman, even from the alien woman that maketh smooth her words*[380]. *Why then wilt thou be ravished with a strange woman, and embrace the bosom of an alien?*[381] *For a harlot is a deep ditch, and an alien woman is a narrow pit*[382]. It is thought that these strange women refer to immigrant Syrian or Phoenician prostitutes, since Syrian harlots were also prevalent in Rome at the time of the emperors[383].

In the Talmud, Arabia is regarded as *the* land of lewdness: "Of the ten measures of immorality that descended to the world, nine were taken by Arabia, and one by the rest of the world"[384]. Even Egypt did not enjoy a good reputation: "it was steeped in immorality". Some say that Pharaoh did not have the newborn Jewish girls drowned as he did to the boys in order to allow them to live so that fornication could be practiced with them[385]. It is also evident from the research of Rosenbaum[386] that, in actuality, Egypt and Syria must be regarded as the training places of lewdness in antiquity. To the Apostle, Babylon is the mother of harlots (*e meter ton pornon* in Greek) and all abomination on the earth[387]. At Persian banquets, if the desires of those assembled reached a high point, then "women" were summoned, as we know from the Book of Esther[388], and as is reported by Herodotus[389]. At the court of kings, there was an ample supply of concubines: the king kept 360 wives, corresponding to the days of

376. Berachoth 32a. The questioner was actually Rabbi Hiyya bar Abba. (F.R.)
377. Genesis 34:1
378. *ibid* 30:16
379. Jerushalmi Sanhedrin 2; 20d
380. Proverbs 2:16
381. *ibid* 5:20
382. *ibid* 23:27
383. Hartmann *Die Hebraerin am Putztische und als Braut.* Amsterdam 1809 Vol. 2:494;

Winer. *Biblisch Realwörterbuch* 1:612, note 1
384. Kiddushin 49b; Aboth de Rabbi Nathan 28:1
385. Exodus Rabbah 1:18
386. Rosenbaum, *Geschichte der Lustseuche im Altertum.* Berlin 1904, p.226
387. Revelation 17:5
388. Esther 1:11
389. Herodotus, 5:18

the year[390]. This is explicitly reported concerning Darius the Second[391]. Later, Alexandria took the place of Arabia[392].

Judaism in antiquity did not preach asceticism, but held in high esteem the human desire for wine and music[393]. Yet "women" have never been included in these pleasures of life. Even sexual intercourse with *slaves,* which the Koran permits without question[394], is prohibited in the Talmud and punishable[395].

The Apostle explicitly enjoins converted *heathens* through decree to abstain from fornication[395a] *(porneia* in Greek). For converted Jews, this command was considered self-evident.

The relationship between idolatry and lewdness is well known, and is just another reason for the Rabbis to combat the former. It is known that some cultures in antiquity consisted only of the most shameless fornication. "For the devising of idols is the beginning of fornication" asserts *The Wisdom of Solomon*[396]. The Talmud considers the opposite situation to be the normal one. When Israel camped in Shittim, the people began to behave lewdly with the daughters of Moab. And these girls lured the people to bring sacrifices to their gods; the people ate and bowed down to these gods, so that it became necessary to resort to the Draconian method to hang all the chiefs of the people[397]. The legend, which is obviously influenced by contemporary *Roman* circumstances, more accurately pictures the temptation: in Midian they set up booths for the sale of pastries — even the Roman pastry shops were a type of brothel[398]. Outside stood an old woman who demanded the real price, and inside was a maiden who offered the wares cheaper. If a man entered unto her, she served him a glass of *amoni* wine, which incites the body to lewdness. If he drank and then asked for her body, she would extract the picture of her idol from her bosom and demand that he honor it as a precondition for her surrender. Instead of "pastry shops" one also finds the expression *qinqelin,* which is supposed to correspond to the Roman word *cella*[399].

A large role in political history was played by the relationship of the kings with heathens. King Solomon was led astray by "alien women" to introduce idolatry[400]. The same occurred during the kingdom of Israel under King Ahab through the influence of the Zidonian princess Jezebel[401].

## II   Biblical and Talmudic Terminology for Harlots

The generally used Biblical expression for a prostitute is *zona,* meaning "the clinging one". The Aramaic translators, as already mentioned, usually employ the term *naphkath bara,* meaning "the one who walks about outside". This Aramaic expression is translated back into Hebrew in the Mishnah as *yotzeth chutz*[402]. Less often the Aramaic translation uses the term *mat'aja,* or *mat'itha,* meaning "the seductress". Where the Hebrew text speaks of an *ishah zona,* the Aramaists often use the term *pundeqitha (pandokissa* in Greek), meaning "who receives everybody, as an innkeeper or procuress". So is Rahab in Jericho called when she provided lodging for Joshua's spies[403]; so too is Jephthah in Gilead called[404]; so too, the wife whom Samson took in Gaza[405]; and so too, the two women concerning whose quarrel King Solomon pronounced his famous judgement[406]. In yet other places, they also translate

390. Diodorus 1:97
391. Plutarch. *Artax* 27
392. Esther Rabbah 1:17
393. For example Sirach 35:5-6
394. Sure 23:5
395. Sanhedrin 82a and *Halachoth Gedoloth* p.253:25
395a. Acts 15:20 and 21:25
396. Wisdom of Solomon 14:12
397. Numbers 25: 1ff
398. Rosenbaum, *loc. cit.* p.103
399. Jerushalmi Sanhedrin 10; 28d
400. First Kings 11:4ff
401. *ibid* 16:31
402. Kelim 28:9
403. Joshua 2:1 and 6:17
404. Judges 11:1
405. *ibid* 16:1
406. First Kings 3:16

*isha zona* as *naphkath bara*[407].

The difference in this matter is certainly not very significant. Rabbi David Kimchi is probably correct when he states that an innkeeper's wife serves her guests not only food and beverages[408]. Her reputation is also not faultless in the Mishnah[409]. In the inn (*pandokeion* in Greek) where Balaam sought lodging, he found harlots who ate and drank with him and fulfilled his wishes[410]. The Septuagint and the Vulgate make no distinction at all in their translation. They ordinarily speak of *porne, meretrix* or *scortum*. This bespeaks the circumstances which were tendered by Greece and Rome in which all the landlords legally considered their wives to be on the same level as whores and brothel mistresses[411]. Josephus explains a *zona* with whom a priest is forbidden to marry to be a woman who procures herself a wine-tavern (*kapeleia* in Greek) as a business or a guesthouse as a means of livelihood[412] (*pandokeuein* in Greek).

Concerning the lodging of Rahab, Josephus uses the expression "shelter" *(katagogion)*, which designates a "decent place"[413]. In the New Testament, this Rahab is considered to be an ancestor of Jesus[414] and enjoys a good reputation[415], although she maintained her nickname "whore" (*e porne*). Even the Jews count her among the religious proselytes[416].

Whether or not she was married is uncertain. She bargains for the rescue of her parents and siblings, who do not live with her[417], but does not speak of her husband; but neither does she speak of herself.

## III    Street of Harlots

When the Talmud speaks of a "street of harlots"[418], one should not conclude that this represents barracks of whores. Even today, it is an Oriental practice that individual branches of professions live together on individual streets. Thus the Talmud speaks of a street of butchers, of leather workers[419], of Rabbis[420], of Aramaeans[421], of circumcisors[422]. A street of bakers is already mentioned in the Bible[423].

In heathen Canaan, the prostitute lived *in* the town wall[424], which in Roman times, is where the brothels were located, so that often the expression *fornix* for prostitute is considered identical with the word *fornix* which means arch of the wall[425]. From the apartment a window led directly to the field[426].

On the other hand, the existence of brothels, the *qubbah* of whores, is certain. The word is already used in the Bible for *whorehouse*[427]. But it is not a Jewish, but rather a Roman, institution with all its well known details. The Talmud relates that the Roman government once forbade the Jews to occupy themselves with the Torah. Rabbi Chanina ben Teradion who persisted therein was sentenced to die, but his daughter was condemned to live in the *qubbah* of the whores[428]. Captured maidens were also placed in brothels and ransom was demanded for their freedom[429]. Under Diocletian, a young Christian girl was sentenced to live in a brothel[430]. After the death of Agrippa, the inhabitants of Caesaria and Sebaste rapidly forgot the kindness he extended to them,

---

407. Jeremiah 3:3; Ezekiel 23:44 and 16:30. In the Targum of Proverbs, neither expression is found. Levit. 21:7 does not belong here at all.
408. *Radak* on Joshua 2:1
409. Demai 3:5; even better Yebamoth 16:7
410. Targum Jonathan on Numbers 24:14
411. Rosenbaum, *opus cit.* p.102
412. Josephus' *Antiquities* Section 3 Chapt. 12:2
413. *ibid.* Section 5 Chapt. 1:2 and 1:7
414. Matthew 1:5
415. Hebrews 11:31 and James 2:25
416. *Yalkut* 2:9

417. Joshua 2:13 and 2:18
418. Pesachim 113b; Genesis Rabbah 91:6
419. Chullin 48a
420. *ibid* 48b
421. Jerushalmi Nedarim 4; 38d
422. Jerushalmi Erubin 5; 22d
423. Jeremiah 37:21
424. Joshua 2:15
425. Rosenbaum. *opus cit.* p. 96, note 1
426. Joshua 2:15
427. Numbers 25:8
428. Abodah Zara 27b
429. Aboth de Rabbi Nathan 8:7
430. Rosenbaum, p.404, note 4

robbed the statues of his daughters, and brought them into the brothel *(porneia)*. Thus reports Josephus[431].

Legend also sees whores in the name of the place *chiroth* at the Red Sea[432], "who diverted their eyes"[433] from the Israelites.

The late Greek expression *mimurion* for *lupanar* is perhaps found in the Midrash[434].

Even a brothel owner, *moger zanjatha,* is mentioned. His activities are specifically designated as sinful. He also furnishes theaters, brings clothes to whores in the bathhouse, and dances and plays the flute before them[435].

## IV    Harlotry in Biblical Times

The Scriptural narrative that Joseph, during his first encounter with his brothers *spoke harshly to them*[436], is explained by legend as follows: when the brothers of Joseph came to Egypt, they had the intention of immediately searching for their brother Joseph, whose position of power, however, they did not know. They said to one another: "our brother Joseph has a beautiful face and figure, perhaps he is in the *qubbah*" and, therefore, looked for him in the street of harlots. When the messenger of Joseph, who already knew of their arrival, found them there, Joseph was quite enraged, and angrily addressed them and rebuked them[437]: *you came to see the nakedness of the land*[438], that is, its lewdness. It is likely that we are dealing with a Kynaden brothel[439] which flourished at the time of the Roman Caesars. According to the custom of the preachers of morality not to take into account the time or the place of incidents, this immorality is without question considered to have occurred in Biblical times; or, more correctly, the Biblical narrative serves as a text and pretext for censuring immorality at the time of the preachers and one is warned against it.

During the times of the Bedouins, the prostitute sat on the street of the caravan, *at the source or entrance*[440]; that is where travelers rested and where she would most likely find patronage. That is, we are dealing with a "holy source", as she functioned as a hierodule. The Jews had no holy sources. The name of the place *baalath be'er* meaning Goddess of the well[441], no doubt originates from heathen times. David's command, reported by Josephus[442], that Solomon should be anointed with holy oil at the well (*epi ten pegen* in Greek) is not mentioned in the Bible.

## V    Skills of a Harlot

Many of the skills of harlots are related. Just like Ambubaja of Horatius[443], and the famous Gaditan maidens in former Rome[444], as well as the later Greek harlots[445] (*etairai mousikai*), the Oriental prostitutes also understood music. The prophet compares the sinful people to a prostitute when he calls to them: *take an harp, go about the city, thou harlot that hast been forgotten; make sweet melody, sing many songs, that thou mayest be remembered*[446]. Otherwise, the "song of a harlot" serves as a picture of seduction[447]. Sirach admonishes: "Do not associate with a woman singer, or you may be caught by her wiles"[448].

On the other hand, I do not at all find mention in our sources of erotic dances which were quite customary among the harlots.

431. *Antiquities,* Section 19; Chapt. 9:1
432. Exodus 14:2
433. Kallah Rabbathi 7; 54b
434. Song of Songs Rabbah on 7:9 fol. 38b
435. Jerushalmi Taanith 1; 64b
436. Genesis 42:7
437. Genesis Rabbah 91:6
438. Genesis 42:9
439. see *Mathnas Kehunna* on Genesis 42:9

440. Genesis 38:14
441. Joshua 19:8
442. *Antiquities* 7 Chapt. 14:5
443. First *Satyr.* 2:1
444. Nork, *Wörterbuch s.v.* Hierodule
445. Rosenbaum, *opus cit.* p.88 and 102
446. Isaiah 23:16
447. *ibid* 23:15
448. Sirach 9:4

An exceptional craftiness of harlots has already been described above[449].

The misconduct in which a woman places into the vagina of another woman a piece of meat from a fallen animal is mentioned *en passant*[450].

## VI    Clothing of Prostitutes

There is nothing in the Bible concerning special clothing worn by prostitutes. Attempts have been made to interpret the veiling of Tamar[451] as a characteristic of harlots. This is certainly erroneous, for even the *virtuous* Oriental woman does not show herself unveiled on the streets. The *Mishnah* mentions "the shirt, *chaluk,* of the runabout (i.e. harlot)" which is woven like a hair net, *sebacha,* and is, therefore, perforated so that the body is visible through it[452]. Greek harlots walked about in the same manner *(en leptomenois hymesin)*[453]. Three types of such head nets were known: those of children, old women and harlots[454]. The differences among these were evidently generally known at the time of the *Mishnah,* but later became forgotten, so that the commentaries were no longer able to provide satisfactory explanations. Perhaps, the head cover of prostitutes was often torn so that it no longer held the major portion of her hair[455].

Whether harlots hated each other[456] or decorated each other[457] would depend on the circumstances of the times.

Not infrequently even today, some harlots have been observed to perform noble and altruistic deeds. Thus it could happen even today that a harlot commits prostitution for apples — a delicacy in antiquity[458] — and then distributes them to the poor[459]. In the Talmud, this example is used to teach the lesson that the goal does not justify the means. Some were driven to lewdness out of noble motives. Thus, an account is given of a woman who wished to sell herself in order to be able to ransom her husband from captivity with her earnings[460].

The harlot gradually becomes accustomed to the prostitution so that "when she no longer receives payment (because of her age, etc.), she pays herself recompense"[461]; or as the Talmud states, the harlot who first allows herself to be hired will at the end have to hire some man[462].

## VII    The Hire of Harlots

Through Diogenes Laertius we know of the state of a prominent Roman who, just as some distinguished people even today, only had one drachma for his physician but who, on the other hand, paid his mistress one talent of silver. It seems certain that only exceptionally desirable women could command such high honoraria as Phryne and Lais in Greece[463]. Even the Talmud[464] describes the moralizing case of a harlot who lived in "a town by the sea" who took 400 gold denars for her hire and asked for payment in advance. She let her guests wait in the antechambers to be announced by her maid. When the visitor was finally admitted, she prepared for him seven beds, six of silver and one of gold — an allusion to Roman immorality where the beds and couches of the women were draped with gold and silver[465]. This was a luxury which naturally

---

449. in Chapter 12, section XVIII where Preuss speaks of perfume used prior to cohabitation (F.R.)
450. Niddah 42b
451. Genesis 38:14
452. Kelim 28:9
453. Rosenbaum *op. cit.* p.88
454. Kelim 24:16
455. cf. *Tosefta* Kelim 2:10
456. Pesachim 113b

457. Shabbath 34a
458. Song of Songs Rabbah 2:5
459. Exodus Rabbah 31E
460. Jerushalmi Taanith 1; 64b
461. Ezekiel 16:34
462. Abodah Zarah 17a
463. Rosenbaum *op. cit.* p.86 and 97
464. Menachoth 44a
465. Plinius *Hist. Nat.* 33:51

only the richest people could afford[466]. She placed a ladder of silver[467], whose top rung was of gold, between the beds, and went and sat naked upon the top bed. The visitor, however, beheld at the deciding moment the Divine law[468] and he withstood the tempting seduction.

Another prostitute, also from "a town by the sea", took a purse of denars for her hire and had men cross seven rivers in order to come to her[469]. Even ordinary harlots are given *nedeh,* a generous gift[470]. Everyone scorns the hire which she receives called *ethnan,* for it is found to be too meager[471]. He who chases after harlots will spend a fortune[472] until eventually *he is brought to a piece of bread*[473], which is his only nourishment. When the money is used up, they give their son for a harlot and their daughter is sold for wine and drink[474].

Marriage with a harlot was never looked upon favorably, and Josephus even speaks of a direct prohibition[475] *(etarmenes einai gamon)* which in general is only applicable to the priests.

Fornication is the only sin for which God inflicts immediate punishment. When one finds harlotry, war also comes to the world and the good and the bad are both killed[476]. Immorality in a house is like a worm in a sesame seed[477]: it always destroys it.

## VIII   The Jus Primae Noctis

In the "Book of Fast Days", the following is related concerning the occasion of the rise of the Maccabees under Antiochus Epiphanes (165 B.C.E.):

"On the seventeenth of the month of Elul, the Greeks were driven out of Jerusalem and Judea. The kings had placed *qastriaoth*[477a] in the cities who were to violate all newly married women *(kalloth);* only then could they be taken home. As a result, no one wished to marry out of fear of the *qastriaoth*, or it was done in great secrecy. When the daughter of Mattathias, the son of Johanan Hyrcanos, was to marry (because of the prominent position of her father the marriage could not readily be concealed), the *qastrin* came in order to defile her by cohabiting with her. It was not permitted, however; rather Mattathias and his sons were. seized with zeal and conquered the Greek state"[478].

More detailed is the description in several later reports in which the appearance of the young woman is dramatically depicted:

"At the time of the wicked Greek government, it was decreed that as soon as a woman marries, she must first cohabit with a *hegemon* and then may return to her bridegroom. This occurred for three years and eight months, until the marriage of the daughter of the High Priest Jochanan Hyrcanos. When it was attempted to take her to the *hegemon,* she bared her head and tore her clothes, so that she stood naked before the people. Judah and his brothers were immediately stirred by feelings of anger and called out: take her out to be burned to death, for she conducted herself shamelessly and immorally. Whereupon she answered: What? Should I shame myself before my brothers and my ancestors but not shame myself in the eyes of an uncircumcised and

466. Aboth de Rabbi Nathan 6:2E
467. see the picture of such a bed in Benzinger
     & Frohnmeyer. *Bilderatlas zur Bibelkd.*
     Stuttgart 1905, fig. 296
468. the four fringes of his garment struck him
     across the face
469. Abodah Zarah 17a
470. Ezekiel 16:33
471. *Radak's* commentary on Ezekiel 16:31
472. Proverbs 29:3

473. *ibid* 6:26
474. Joel 3:3
475. *Antiquities,* Vol. 4 Chapt. 8:23
476. *Yalkut* No. 585 p.367a in the Warsaw
     edition
477. Sotah 3b
477a. Officers of the army or prominent
     leaders who served as *hegemonim.*
478. Megillath Taanith. Chapt. 6 ed. Meyer.
     Amstelod 1724 p.50

defiled individual to whom you were faithlessly taking me in order that he cohabit with me? When Judah and his relatives heard this, they resolved to jointly kill the *hegemon*''[479].

In another report it states that it was decreed that every newlywed must spend the first night in the home of the local *hegemon* . . . when the brothers saw her naked, they were ashamed and lowered their eyes to the ground, tore their clothes in mourning and jumped up in order to kill their sister[480]. A third work has a similar account[481]. The latter originates from a Munich manuscript from the year 1435; the two former, from manuscripts of the municipal library of Leipzig, whose catalog does not list a date of origin.

The time of the composition of *Megillath Taanith* is uncertain. Whereas Graetz[482] and Derenbourg[483] attribute it to early antiquity, others consider it more recent. There can be no doubt, however, that it was composed prior to the eighth century of the Common Era. According to Schuerer[484], it was edited in the first century C.E.

The *hegemon* is naturally the *hegemon* of the Greeks, the commander in chief or city commandant; *qastrin* corresponds to the Roman designation derived from *castra*.

It is correct, as strongly emphasized by Herzfeld[485], that the Books of the Maccabees[486] give a different cause of the rebellion, as does Josephus[487]. The Talmud also does not contain this cause for the rebellion of the Maccabees. However, one should not refute these accounts of the legend in their entirety as does Karl Schmidt in his hypercritical book[488]. Perhaps the author of the Books of the Maccabees meant to include such immorality as the hegemonian coitus in the "blasphemies" *(blasphemias* in Greek) which Mattathias saw in Judah and in Jerusalem[489]. The silence of the assimilated Josephus proves absolutely nothing. And when Schmidt is in doubt whether we are really dealing with the later so-called "seigneurial rights", the fault certainly lies in the erroneous translation of the word *kalla*. This word does not refer to a betrothed woman but to a just-married one. Schmidt in fact admits that the accounts have at least a kernel of historical fact as their basis.

# IX   Hegemonian Coitus

Concerning these, in our opinion, historically true facts, there are perhaps several remarks which are found in the Talmud.

We have already mentioned that every groom had to presume the *virginitas intacta* of his fiancee, and when the presumption proved to be incorrect, the young maiden became liable to the death penalty, under Biblical law. Later, however, when the criminal justice system of the Jews ceased, he was expected to divorce her. The possibility of such an accusation of loss of virginity naturally fell away when a cohabitation already occurred prior to the marriage. As an example of such an occurrence is the following report:

Once the heathen overlords decreed a persecution of Judah because they had received the tradition from their forefathers that Judah killed Esau, the latter being considered the ancestor of Rome. Other atrocities were also motivated by the same misconception[490]. Therefore, they subjugated the Jews, violated their daughters and

479. Jellinek. *Beth Hamidrasch* Vol. 1. Leipzig 1853 p.133
480. *ibid* Vol. 6 p.2 and 3 ·
481. Berliner. *Magazin für die Wissenschaft des Judentums. Hebr. Beil. Otzar Tob* 1878 p.400
482. *Geschichte der Juden.* Vol. 3 p.561
483. *Essai sur l'histoire de la Palestine* 1867 p.439
484. *Geschichte des Jüdischen Volkes* Vol. 1 p.156
485. *Geschichte des Volkes Israel* Vol. 2 p.239
486. First Maccabees Chapt. 2 and 3
487. *Antiquities.* Vol. 12 chapt. 6
488. *Das Jus Primae Noctis.* Freiburg 1881 p.169
489. First Maccabees 2:6
490. For example; Jerushalmi Gittin 5; 47b

decreed that the general (*stratiotes* in Greek), who is designated in the Talmud as the *highest ranking* soldier, first cohabit with her. To be sure, the woman was then "innocent and coerced", for whom divorce was not prescribed. However, the door to fornication was thereby opened, since the head lord would take no notice of a previous defloration. Naturally, there were also some chaste women, who would have rather suffered death[491].

In the *Tosefta,* an ancient source of Jewish law which runs parallel to the *Mishnah,* it is reported that "from the time of danger and subsequently", it became customary among the people to arrange weddings on Tuesdays[492]. This "time of danger" is explained by Rabba (in the year 250 C.E.) to be that period during which the heathen overlords had decreed that every newlywed must first cohabit with the *hegemon*[493].

The matter itself was generally known. Rabbi Judan interprets the Biblical phrase *when the sons of God saw the daughters of men that they were fair; and they took them wives of all that they chose*[494] as follows: "when these coercers (*theoi*) saw that a woman was being made beautiful (i.e. adorned) for her husband, one of them went unto her and cohabited with her first"[495]. The author himself naturally does not wish to proclaim that those primitive times of which the Bible speaks are historical fact; it is the practice of the *Midrash,* as in all sermons in which the speaker wishes to rebuke people in *his* time, to use a Biblical verse without regard to the time or place of the occurrence. The citation here is also only given as evidence that the matter of *jus primae noctis* was already known at the time of Rabbi Judan.

A final note must here be conveyed. It is already very briefly mentioned in the "Tractate Soferim"[496], more fully in the *Yalkut,* which is also a *Midrash* collection, and is connected with the Bible. When the messenger of Abraham came to Padan Aram, to fetch a wife for Isaac, at first Laban and Rebekah's father Bethuel took an interest in the conversation[497] and gave their approval to the proposed marriage. Very shortly thereafter, however, only "her brother and her mother" spoke[498], but not the father anymore. From this the legend concludes that Bethuel was the king of the land and every young girl was forced to cohabit with him at her wedding. His vassals tried to coerce him to do the same with his own daughter, Rebekah. They gathered together and said: if he behaves with *his* daughter as he does with ours, good; otherwise, we will kill him. Bethuel died during the night, so that Rebekah remained trustworthy and was not defiled[499].

He who believes this baseness, in which an overlord practices his seigneurial right even with his own daughter, to be a product of a grisly fantasy, should see that which Ploss quotes as a popular custom among several peoples. It is possible that for these tribes the underlying thought is "that the father has to deliver his daughter to the marriage in a serviceable state"[500].

From all the statements on this subject, it is evident that the contention of Rosenbaum[501] that the weak Asiatic would renounce his personal *jus primae noctis* and would gladly give it over to another for the sake of convenience is, as far as the Jews are concerned, absolutely erroneous.

# X   Masturbation

The "evoking of sperm emission for naught" (not for procreation) is considered

---

491. Jerushalmi Kethuboth 1; 25c; cf *Tosafot* Gittin 55b. *s.v. bi-yehuda*
492. *Tosefta* Kethuboth 1:1
493. Kethuboth 3b
494. Genesis 6:2
495. Genesis Rabbah 26:5

496. Tractate Soferim 21:9
497. Genesis 24:50
498. *ibid* 24:55
499. *Yalkut* 1:109
500. Ploss. *Das Weib* I, 555
501. *op. cit.* p.331

by the Rabbis, as already mentioned[502], as a transgression. They include under this phrase both *coitus interruptus* and masturbation. According to Rabbi Yochanan, one who masturbates like Onan deserves death. He is compared to a shedder of blood[503], a murderer[504], and an idolater; the latter probably because masturbation is also part of the heathen cult. The rebuke of the prophet *your hands are full of blood*[505] is interpreted to refer to "those who are lewd with their hands"[506]. The hand with which a person excessively examines his penis (to see whether perhaps sperm are present and hence ritual uncleanliness) is worthy of being cut off[507]. The deluge came upon the world because "everyone expended his sperm on the ground"[508].

Rabbi Eliezer states that one who only holds his penis during micturition can be the cause of a similar catastrophe. Indeed, drops of urine will fall on his clothes and his feet, and he will be considered to be incapable of procreation. People will think he has hypospadius, and that his children are illegitimate; but it is better that he and his children thus become the target of gossip than to sin before God for one moment. According to Rabbi Yochanan, there is nothing objectionable for a married man to hold the *shaft* (but not the glans) of his penis during micturition[509]. However, it was a sign of extraordinary "holiness" for a married man, as related about Rabbi Judah the Prince[510], never to place his hand below his belt. Rabbi Tarfon describes this requirement in a general sense: "if a thorn is stuck in the abdomen ("below the navel"), one should not remove it (in order to avoid touching that area of the body), even if the abdomen bursts." Some people even considered prohibiting the wearing of tight-fitting trousers under the *chiton*[511].

According to Rab, a man who intentionally evokes an erection through licentious thoughts should be placed under a ban, and Rabbi Joshua ben Levi cursed a man who sleeps lying on his back. One is here reminded of the remark of Aristotle that animals have no nocturnal pollution because they do not sleep on their backs[512]. Perhaps, the physician should be thinking of the danger of masturbation when considering "the sword which hangs over young people who *sit alone* and study and thereby not only become stupid but also sin"[513]. Camel riders were generally excluded from enjoying the heave offering, since they mostly rode without saddles and were constantly, therefore, exposed to "the danger of the warming of their flesh"[514].

A popular saying states: "he masturbates with a pumpkin, his wife with a cucumber"[515], when one wishes to designate a *par nobile fratrum* (depraved couple, each in his own way). According to the explanation of the *Aruch*, this means that when the man cannot find a woman for cohabitation, he makes a hole in a pumpkin and masturbates therewith. So, too, the woman masturbates using a cucumber as a phallus[516]. In actual life, such manipulations are probably not so rare. For among the questions which Catholic priests pose at the confession is the following: *fecisti fornicationem, ut quidam facere solent, ut tuum virile membrum in lignum perforatum aut in aliquod hujusmodi mitteres et sic per illam commotionem et delectationem semen projiceres*[517]?

As far as I am aware, there does not exist in the Talmud a prohibition *for a woman* against masturbation. It seems quite certain that women are not easily excited

502. see above under *coitus interruptus*
503. *Shophech Damim.* Niddah 13a
504. *Horeg Nephashoth,* Kallah Rabbathi 2, beginning of 52b
505. Isaiah 1:15
506. Niddah 13b
507. Niddah 2:1; s.a. Sabbath 108b, Rabbi Muna
508. Genesis 6:13
509. Niddah 13a

510. Sabbath 118b
511. Niddah 13b
512. *Problem.* Sect. 9:16
513. Berachoth 63b
514. Niddah 14a
515. Megillah 12a
516. *Aruch. s.v. qar* ed. Kohut 7:183a
517. According to Forel in *Die Sexuelle Frage.* Munich 1906 p.371

*(benoth hargasha)* in this manner, so that one unhesitatingly required that a woman should often examine herself by dabbing a cloth into her vagina to see whether unexpected bleeding has occurred as a result of which she would be ritually unclean for her husband[518]. Since only married women are involved in this procedure, one does not need to exaggerate the possible danger therein.

This question is thoroughly debated by the Catholic moral theologians. They proceed from the correct axiom that pollution in a woman, similar to that which occurs in a man, does not exist because an *effusio seminis* does not take place, *quia verum semen in mulieribus non datur*. They consider masturbation in a woman in the framework of *tactus impudici*. Capellmann speaks exhaustively about how far this is permitted[519].

## XI   Pederasty (Homosexuality)

Pederasty is considered in the Bible among the *doings of the land of Egypt, wherein ye dwelt, and after the doings of the land of Canaan, whither I bring you. Ye shalt not do as they do, neither shall ye walk in their ordinances. Rather, ye shall do My judgements and keep My ordinances ... which if a man do, he shall live in them: I am the Lord*[520]. After a series of interdicted marriages, copulation with a menstruant, with the wife of one's neighbor and the prohibition against *Moloch* worship, Scripture continues: *thou shalt not lie with mankind, as with womankind; it is an abomination*[521]. Somewhat later, in a similar sense but without the simultaneous mention of *Moloch* worship: *and if a man also lie with mankind, as he lieth with a woman, both of them have committed an abomination; they shall surely be put to death; their blood shall be upon them*[522].

Since in both places, indeed even in the original text which alone should be completely reliable, the expression is stated in the plural *mishkebei isha, copulae*, the Rabbis in the Talmud deduce that thereby Scripture indicates not only coitus, *immissio penis (in anum)*, but also *appositio membri*, or any other similar practice in cohabitation. They state that for such occurrences, the perpetrators are put to death, and indeed death is inflicted by stoning[523].

The modern defenders of homosexuality[524] were of the opinion that only *paedikatio* is forbidden in Scriptures inasmuch as it served for purposes of cult or worship. They cite as evidence that the above-mentioned initial Biblical citation concerning the prohibition of pederasty is immediately followed by the prohibition of *Moloch* worship. By contrast, one can oppose such an opinion because in the second citation there is lacking the apposition of pederasty with idol worship, the prohibition is found much more among the prohibitions of incest and adultery, and most importantly the prohibition of fornication with animals is immediately adjacent thereto. The eradication of fornication in *all* its forms, even without the references to cult, is the duty of the Mosaic legislation. While in Egypt, the land of fornication, Israel was *the rose among thorns*[525], so, too, Israel was to remain in Canaan[526].

For those individuals of either the male or the female sex who prostitute themselves for the purposes of cult, particularly in the worship of Persian deities, the Bible has ordained the special designation of *kadesh* or *kadesha,* respectively (for male

518. Niddah 13a
519. *Pastoral Medizin.* Aachen 1892 p.88ff
520. Levit. 18:3-5
521. *ibid* 18:22
522. *ibid* 20:13
523. Sanhedrin 55a
524. *Homosexualität und Bibel. Von einem katholischen Geistlichen. Jahrb. f. sexuelle Zwischenstufen.* Vol. 4, 1902; Wirz. *Der*

*Uranier vor Kirche und Schrift. ibid* Vol. 6, 1904
525. Song of Songs 2:2
526. Levit. Rabbah 23:7. The explanation of Wirz is rejected by Numa Praetorius, his otherwise comrade-in-arms, in *Jahrbuch für Sexuelle Zwischenstufen.* Vol. 8, 1906 p.826 ff

and female). Even in the Hammurabic law, there is mention of male and female temple prostitutes as an institution of Babylonian cult[527]. These are also prohibited, but separately from *paedikatio*[528]. But as soon as the Children of Israel again began *to do according to all the abominations of the nations which the Lord cast out*[529], as for example King Rehoboam, then the homosexual reappeared; King Asa banished them[530], but the remnants were finally destroyed by his son Jehoshaphat[531]. Nevertheless, 100 years later, the prophet Hosea again zealously rebukes them for *hiding with whores, and sacrificing with Temple harlots (kedeshoth)*[532].

When Jerusalem stood under Greek dominion, the Temple was replete with voluptuousness and debauchery from *the heathens* who fornicated with whores and who copulated with women in the holy places[533]. It is specifically this Temple prostitution which the Apostle had in mind, according to Wirz[534], when he criticized the heathens as follows: the men left the natural use of the woman and burned in their lust one toward another; in that men with men performed that which is unseemly[535].

Many prostitutes brought the payment for their fornication as an offering to their temple[536]. The hierodule herself received no direct payment; rather the price was paid to the temple. In the Bible, directly after the commandment: *There shall be no harlot (kadesha) of the daughters of Israel, nor shall there be a sodomite (kadesh) of the sons of Israel*[537], we find the additional commandment — *thou shalt not bring the hire of a harlot (zona,* not *kadesha) or the price of a dog (keleb) into the house of the Lord thy God, for any vow, for even both these are an abomination unto the Lord thy God*[538]. This refers not only to the hierodule herself, but also leaves no doubt that *no* offering which is acquired through immorality is acceptable to God. The Talmud states[539] that not even to build a lavatory for the officiating High Priest in the Temple could the payment for harlotry be used (filth for filth). The statement by Ploss[540] that "Priests were permitted to accept money or other gifts which were acquired through prostitution for the Temple" is, therefore, exactly the opposite of the truth.

The expression *keleb,* which is used in the above citation from the Bible for pederasty and which usually means "dog", is also found among the Greek-speaking Jews at the time of Jesus as *kynes*[541]. It is hardly to be taken in the ancient Homeric sense, since the word *keleb* elsewhere in the Talmud has the meaning of insolence. The dog in the Orient is not man's friend and companion. It is more likely that the Biblical expression refers to the ownerless dogs that roam the streets, *quo modo canis coeat cum cane.* The word *skylax,* which usually denotes a young dog, was used by the Greeks for cunnilingus. Concerning the Talmudic legend of the family of Goliath[542], where the word *keleb*[543] clearly is to be taken in our sense, see Lewysohn[544].

The Talmud, moreover, in the above citation, considers the word *keleb* to literally refer to "dog", and, therefore, forbids the proceeds of the sale of a dog (an exchange object) to be used as a contribution to the Temple[545]. Even according to Josephus, the use of the proceeds of the breeding of a hunting dog or a sheep dog *(ep'ocheusei kynos)* is prohibited[546].

Peter Hamecher asserts that the abhorrence against homosexuality is a consequence of the fact that the Christian world outlook is towards the poor and

527. Paragraph 181:2
528. Deut. 23:18
529. First Kings 14:24
530. *ibid* 15:12
531. *ibid* 22:47
532. Hosea 4:14
533. Second Maccabees 6:4
534. *loc. cit.* p.38
535. Romans 1:27
536. cf. Micah 1:7
537. Deut. 23:18

538. *ibid* 23:19
539. Abodah Zarah 17a
540. Ploss. *Das Weib* p.486
541. Revelation 22:15
542. Sotah 42b
543. First Samuel 17:43
544. *Zoologie des Talmuds.* paragraph 511
545. Temurah 6:3; *Tosefta* Temurah 4:6-9; *Sifre op. cit.*
546. *Antiquities* Section 4, Chapt. 8:9

the oppressed, and that homosexuality is among the shameful activities of the rich, which the early Christians, with their moral outlook, punished[547].

Marcuse's belief that Christianity annihilated homosexuals[548] is to me incomprehensible.

From the fact that the Bible does not mention lesbianism at all, yet imposes the death penalty for infidelity of a wife and thus has laws which do not correspond to our own moral concepts, one can conclude absolutely nothing. For every law must be explained in the context of the time and milieu in which it was given. For even *our* own penal code does not impose punishment for lesbianism or, as we have recently learned in horror, for fornication with corpses[549]. On the other hand, we must agree with the "Catholic clergymen" that the expression "abomination" — in the original text the term is *tho'eva* — leaves no ground "to conclude anymore than the usual sinfulness"; just as the warning of the death penalty for pederasty means "support for any type of internal sinfulness". As an analogy from *our* times, we could cite that, according to our penal code, the same penalty can be imposed for treason as for murder.

Equally to the point is the conclusion that "the Bible obligates homosexuals to abstinence and nothing more than the same extramarital obligations which are incumbent upon sexually normal people and in the same amount and in the same manner". A marriage between individuals of the same sex is not found in the Bible, however, and probably also not in other sources. One should extend this and say that according to Biblical teaching every desire for the prohibited, even without "participation", but just the "sensation" alone, although not "dishonorable", is nevertheless sinful, and its suppression is a religious obligation.

## XII

According to the Rabbis, pederasty is among the crimes for which, in self defense, it is not only permissible but even obligatory to kill the attacker if no other means of saving the attacker from sinning is successful[550]. In fact, not only the victim but any third person who observes such a pursuit has the obligation of incapacitating the attacker. Homosexuality is among the things which causes the sun to be in eclipse[551].

It is precisely at the time of the origin of the Talmud that the Rabbis had ample opportunity to observe that the practice of "favorite love" commenced to be proper form in the highest circles and that the emperors themselves set the most abominable example[552]. Alexander, the son of Herod, through large gifts, practiced pederasty with his chamber servants (eunuchs) *(eis ta paidika upegeto)*[553]. It is therefore, easy to understand why the Rabbis see an allusion to the sovereigns of their time in the *kings of the nations, even all of them be in glory, lying every one in his own house*[554] of which the Prophet speaks[555].

When Potiphar bought Joseph who *was of beautiful form and fair to look upon*[556], his intention was to use Joseph for pederasty. God, however, castrated Potiphar so that he became harmless. This may be compared to a she-bear that wrought havoc (literally: tore) among her master's children, whereupon he ordered her fangs to be broken[557].

Rabbi Jehuda ben Pazi once observed from the roof that two men "were

547. "Entrechtet" (deprived). Leipzig 1906, Cited from *Jahrbach für sexuelle Zwischenstufen* Vol. 8, 1906 p.757
548. *Sexuelle Fragen und Christentum.* Leipzig 1908, p.40
549. so too a theoretical deduction. Yebamoth 55b
550. Sanhedrin 73a
551. Sukkah 29a

552. Rosenbaum, *op. cit.* p.119
553. Josephus. *The Jewish War.* Book 1 Chapt. 24:7
554. Isaiah 14:18
555. Shabbath 149b
556. Genesis 39:6
557. Genesis Rabbah 86:3; cf. Sotah 13a

occupying themselves with one another". They intimidated him by saying: "ponder that you are one and that we are two"[558].

At the time of the famine, the Egyptians came to Joseph: *only our bodies and our lands do we possess; buy us and our land for bread*[559]. Josephus explains that they were thus forced to immorality *(aschemona)* in order to stay alive[560]. He, therefore, clearly takes the word *geviya* in the text to mean penis, although the usual translation is "body". The Greeks also use the word *soma* in both meanings. I am not familiar with such a Scriptural interpretation from Hebrew sources.

According to Wirz, Jesus and John are said to have been a homsexual pair. The interested reader is referred directly to his writing for more details[561].

# XIII   Avoidance of Homosexuality

The prevention of such immorality is certainly the basis of the rules in the Mishnah that two unmarried men not sleep under the *same* cloak (i.e. quilt)[562], and further than an unmarried man should not teach young children[563]. From the latter, Löw draws a comparison to the law of Solon that a school principal or a grammar school headmaster who gives permission for adults to have access to school children should be punished with death[564]. Indeed the *Gemara* believed that the Biblical laws against *paedikatio* exerted such an educational influence on the Jews that *this* danger was no longer to be feared, and therefore based the last mentioned rule in the Mishnah upon the fact that a young teacher could easily stumble into sin through contact with the *mothers* who brought their children to school[565]. Regarding the heathens, however, one could never be sure about pederasty, especially where individual instruction was concerned[566].

# XIV   Transvestism

Interesting in many respects is a report which Josephus cites in *History of the Jewish War*. Military discipline among the troops in Galilee weakened; to murder men and to rape women served as amusement for the soldiers. Still dripping with blood, out of boredom, they conducted themselves unabashedly as women in that they shaved their hair, dressed in women's clothing, anointed themselves with fragrant oil and decoratively painted their eyes. However, not only did they try to imitate women in terms of attire, but also engaged to excess in lewd practices and monstrous lusts *(athemitous edonas)*. They ran around the city as if in a brothel and tainted it with many acts of immorality[567].

Perhaps the origin of the "prominent sanitary measures" regarding the establishment of a brothel in the German colonies[568] is based on similar experiences.

# XV   Sodom and Gomorrah

In the Biblical narrative of the destruction of Sodom and Gomorrah, recent writers on homosexuality have placed more weight on the mention of pederasty than the ancient Bible commentators ever dreamed of.

The Biblical account is as follows:

God speaks: Although the cry of Sodom and Gomorrah is great and their sin is exceedingly grave, I will go down there and see whether they have done, altogether,

---

558. Jerushalmi Sanhedrin 4; 23c
559. Genesis 47: 18-19
560. *Antiquities.* Section 2, Chapt. 7:7
561. *loc. cit.* s.a. p.32; 2nd ed. 1905 p.78
562. Kiddushin 4:14
563. *ibid* 4:13
564. *Ges. Schr.* 3:19, notes

565. Kiddushin 82a
566. *Tosefta* Abodah Zarah 3:2
567. Josephus. *The Jewish War,* Book 4 Chapt. 9 and 10
568. Representative Held, in the 81st session of the Reichstage on March 31, 1906

according to the cry of it which is come unto Me[569]. Then I will find them corrupt; but if not, not; I wish to know. In the evening the two angels of God came and turned in unto Lot. But before they lay down, the men of the city, the men of Sodom, both young and old, all the people from every quarter, encircled the house. And they called unto Lot, and said unto him: Where are the men that came in to thee this night? Bring them out unto us, that we may know them. And Lot went out unto them to the door, and shut the door after him. And he said: I pray thee, my brethren, do not so wickedly. Behold now, I have two daughters that have not known man; let me, I pray you, bring them out unto you, and do ye to them as is good in your eyes; only unto these men do nothing; forasmuch as they are come for protection under the shadow of my roof. And they said: Stand back. And they said: this one fellow came in to sojourn, and he plays the judge; now will we deal worse with thee than with them! And they pressed upon Lot and tried to break the door open. God, however, smote them with blindness, so that they could not find the door. After Lot and his family were brought to safety, Sodom and Gemorrah were destroyed by a rain of brimstone and fire[570].

In the Bible and also in post-Biblical writings, Sodom serves as the prototype of all depravities, particularly, however hardheartedness against the poor[571]. *Sodomite grapes* is the poetic expression for the fruits of immoral, debased conduct[572]. The *rulers of Sodom* means the hardhearted[573]. The lack of any altruistic sentiment exemplified by "one who says what is mine is mine and what is yours is yours" is designated by the *Mishnah* as a Sodomite characteristic[574]. It was thus only logical that, in addition to all other depravities, pederasty was ascribed to them, in that the phrase "that we may know them" is taken to mean "coitus". This, however, was only incidental[575], at most it was as if the premeditated immoral assaults of the Sodomites brought the measures of the abomination to overflowing[576].

Only the Alexandrian Philo seems to place greater emphasis on the sexual perversion, in that he reports that the Sodomites were affected with feminine afflictions (Greek: *nousos theleia*)[577]. If this interpretation was already the prevailing one in *early* antiquity, then the Prophets, who so strongly fought against immorality, would not have failed to use Sodom as an example. However, this occurs nowhere, as often as Sodom is mentioned by them. The unbiased reader more rapidly develops the impression that the disdain of hospitality, which ordinarily is one of the holiest obligations for the Orientals, and the entire conduct of the Sodomites represent unusual acts of brutality against the individual dissenters who appeared in their midst. They considered such visits with jealousy and mistrust in that they themselves wished to become acquainted with the visitors. Had Lot seen homosexual intentions among his fellow citizens, he would surely have offered his sons-in-law and his sons, who were also with him[578], instead of his virgin daughters. Moreover, the notion that an entire city, "both young and old", was comprised only of pederastic inhabitants is difficult to accept, totally exclusive of the fact that if this were so, then during the destruction of both cities, the *women,* although totally innocent, were punished. Or should we maintain that Sodom had no female inhabitants at all, because Scripture doesn't mention them?

Therefore, the assertion that the Bible considers the sexual perversions to be the basis for destruction of the two cities should be completely rejected and requires no

---

569. Genesis 18:20-21
570. Genesis 19:4-24
571. Ezekiel 16:49-50
572. Deut. 32:32
573. Isaiah 1:10
574. Aboth 5:13

575. for example, Genesis Rabbah 50:5 and Josephus *Antiquities.* Book 1, Chapt. 11:3
576. *Yalkut loc cit.* No. 585
577. *De Abrahamo* p.20; see also Rosenbaum *op. cit.* p.175
578. Genesis 19:12 and 14

further refutation. Therewith is also eliminated the further assertion, which in itself is highly unlikely, that immorality was only intended for purposes of cult.

On the other hand, it is self-evident that Lot's offer to surrender his daughters was violently opposed: "from his good deed in being concerned for the safety of his guests, we also learn his bad attribute, his frivolity in the valuation of prostitution"[579]. Although the Apostle calls Lot a just person[580], Jewish writings are less complimentary about his character[581].

Medical linguistic usage considers *sodomy* to be fornication with animals; that is, however, historically incorrect as is evident from the above. Only *paedicatio* should in all instances be the interpretation of this term, as it in fact occurs in England. Indeed, female *paedicatio* is also called sodomy. As is well known, the penalty for *paedicatio* in England, even today, is death, and for sodomy (fornication with animals) the penalty is life imprisonment[582].

## XVI    The Outrage at Gibeah

There are some similarities to the story of Sodom in a narrative found in the Book of Judges.

A Levite who lived in the mountains of Ephraim took a concubine, who fled from him and returned to her father's house. After one and half years the man brought her back. On the return journey they had to spend the night in Gibeah, a Benjamite city. Yet no one offered them hospitality to spend the night although they carried sufficient provisions for themselves and for their donkey. Finally, "an old man" came from the field — it could have been an elder — who was not one of the native inhabitants of the city, and he brought them unto his house. Then behold, the men of the city, certain base fellows, surrounded the house and beat on the door and called unto the master of the house: bring forth the man that came unto thy house, *that we may know him.* Instead of this, the master of the house went out unto them and pleaded: do not do anything wicked, my brethren, seeing that this man came unto my house, do not do this wanton deed. I will bring my young virgin daughter and his concubine to you. Violate them *('annu)* and do with them what you wish, but unto this man do not do this wanton thing.

But the men would not hearken to him, so the stranger himself seized his concubine and brought her forth unto them. And they knew her (i.e. cohabited with her) and abused her all night until the morning. When the day began to dawn, they let her go. She came to the house in which her master was and fell down at the door (with cramps?) till it was light. When her master opened the door in the morning, he found his wife dead at the door with her hands upon the threshold.

Between the tribe of Benjamin and the other tribes of Israel there occurred a war as a result of this atrocity, during which nearly the entire tribe of Benjamin was exterminated[583].

Even in this narrative, the question as to whether the demand of the "base fellows" to "know" the strangers was a desire for *paedikatio* must remain open. It is probably not so, because for such a purpose they had a more convenient opportunity, when the man was camped on the street with his wife. Much more likely here, too, is the hatred of strangers, and the theme, although not identical to that in Sodom, is concerned with hatred for those who believe differently. As long as the small caravan of three people was camped on the street, it aroused no interest in the townspeople.

579. Nachmanides, *loc. cit.*
580. Second Peter 2:7
581. For example *Tanchuna loc. cit.* Ed. Buber p.49b
582. *Jahrbuch für sexuelle Zwischenstufen.* Leipzig 1899, Vol. 1 p.142
583. Judges Chapter 19

Only when the travelers were taken into the house of a "foreigner" was suspicion aroused which then led to brutality. The man also only states to the war council: *they thought to have me slain*[584]. The women were offered to them to divert their anger, not to satisfy their sexual desires. That the *promise* did not appease them is understandable, but when one of the women was delivered to them — and the second is not mentioned anymore — all was forgotten. Assuredly it is not the manner of true homosexuals to be satisfied with a woman!

When recent commentators, particularly Wirz, here, too, attempt to explain the intent of the Gibeonites to have been to drag the man to temple prostitution, they overlook the fact that this incident, like the events in Sodom, did not occur in a heathen village but in an Israelite city, and that in the latter there did not exist any such temple procedures.

It is very clearly seen from the description of this event in Josephus that, according to the Sages, it was out of the question to consider that pederastic desires are referred to. A desire of the Gibeonites for men is not at all mentioned. They only coveted a woman. The old man offered them his daughter "for their sin would be smaller if they satisfied their desires with her than if they forsook the right of hospitality"[585]. The infringement upon the right of hospitality, which is so holy to the Oriental, is the factor which is of the utmost importance.

Furthermore, a comparison of this story with that of Sodom provides additional evidence that the reason for the destruction of the city of Sodom was not sexual assault — if there was such! For also in Gibeah an identical attempt was made, and even if it did not involve "the entire people", the actively disinterested people should also have been liable to punishment, because they tolerated abomination; yet there is no word promulgated in the Bible about any *Divine* judgement against them! The author of the Book of Judges, who was undoubtedly familiar with the popular story of Sodom, never gave serious credence to this inconsistency.

# XVII  Sodomy (Bestiality)

Immorality with animals, which, although historically incorrect, we call sodomy, like pederasty, is considered in the Bible to be among the depravities of Egypt and of the native Canaanites, and prohibited under penalty of death. According to tradition, the execution is by stoning, and the judgement is passed by a gathering of twenty-three judges, as in all cases of criminal offenses[586]. The animal which is either actively or passively involved in this shameful act is also killed, although one cannot speak of its "being responsible for its act". However, other people should thereby be prevented from being lured to sin with this same animal. Others are of the opinion that the killing of the animal is carried out in order that when the animal passes through the street people should not say: this is the animal because of which so-and-so was stoned[587]. Through the death of the guilty party, his sin is totally expiated. It is accordingly self-evident that one cannot use such an animal for a Temple sacrifice[588].

The killing of the animal is also still prescribed by general provincial law[589]; our German penal code (no. 175), however, has no mention thereof.

The Bible cites this prohibition in three places: *Whosoever lieth with a beast shall surely be put to death*[590], and twice in the "Priestly Code" as follows: *And thou shalt not lie with any beast to defile thyself therewith; neither shall any woman stand before a beast, to lie down thereto; it is perversion (tebel)*[591], and *And if a man lie with a*

---

584. Judges 20:5
585. *Antiquities*. Section 5, Chapter 2:8
586. Sanhedrin 1:4
587. *ibid* 7:4

588. Temurah 6:1
589. Volume 2:20 No. 1070
590. Exodus 22:18
591. Levit. 18:23

*beast, he shall surely be put to death; and ye shall slay the beast. And if a woman approach unto any beast, and lie down thereto, thou shalt kill the woman, and the beast; they shall surely be put to death; their blood shall be upon them*[592]. Finally, on Mount Ebal, the Levites called out a solemn curse on *he that lieth with any manner of beast. And all the people shall say: Amen*[593]. I do not know why pederasty is not mentioned and forbidden by the first and last of these passages as it is by the other two.

The commentators are not unanimously in agreement as to whether the *rebiyah* mentioned here refers to a true act of sodomy on the part of the woman or whether it refers to the shameless denuding of the women, as practiced by the cult of the Bull of Apis or the Ram of Mendes in Egypt[594].

In order not to become guilty of aiding such an immoral act, it was forbidden to give cattle to a heathen shepherd or to leave cattle in a stable of heathens[595]. Rabbi Judah was fundamentally opposed to hiring unmarried shepherds to care for small livestock[596]. The righteous in general remained distant from animals[597]. It was also commanded that a widow not rear dogs, lest she be suspected of immoral practices[598]. This seems not at all absurd in view of the role that some of our modern chase dogs play. An assault by a hunting dog[599] or an ape[600] on a young girl once gave rise to lawsuits. A righteous person once fortuitously observed two men occupied with a bitch; they tried to forestall him in that they accused *him* of sodomy[601]. A combination of sodomy and sadism is probably represented in the case observed by Rabbi Chanina. He saw a heathen take a goose from the market, sodomize it, then strangle it, roast it and eat it[602]. Rabbi Jeremiah of Difti once saw an Arab take a side of meat from the market, bore a hole in it, act immorally with it (i.e. masturbated with it), then roast it and eat it[603].

According to the *Aggadah*, Balaam committed sodomy with his ass[604]. King Artaxerxes had a bitch, *shegel*, next to him on the throne[605]. Already in antiquity, *the sons of God took unto themselves wives from whatever they chose*[606], even animals. The *Midrash* is of the opinion that the generation of the Flood even wrote formal marriage contracts between men and beasts[607]. Preachers attributed the worst immorality that they observed in their times to the behavior of people in antiquity, and provided as a warning the example of the destruction of the world through the sins of the generation of the Flood.

Endless was the contempt in which the "ignorant", the *am ha'aretz (profanum vulgus)*, was held. It was said that they are no better than beasts, and of he who marries the daughter of an *am ha'aretz,* the Scriptural expression *cursed be he that lieth with any manner of beast*[608] can be applied[609]. The same applies to the daughters of nomadic shepherds, who are also considered like animals, probably because of the easy opportunities for sodomy. Ulla said: because they have no bath houses, and Rabbi Yochanan is of the opinion that they easily fall prey to prostitution with male heathens or with wanderers.

A cow, less than three years of age, is thought to become sterile as a result of sodomy[610]. On the other hand, directly opposed to the other teachings of antiquity and

592. *ibid* 20:15-16
593. Deut. 27:21
594. Saalschuetz. *Mos. Recht.* p.584, Note 743
595. for they are suspected of using beasts for carnal relations. Abodah Zarah 2:1
596. *Tosefta* Kiddushin 5:10
597. Kiddushin 81b
598. Abodah Zarah 22b
599. Yebamoth 59b
600. Derech Eretz 1 fol. 55 d

601. Jerushalmi Sanhedrin 6; 23b
602. Abodah Zarah 22b
603. *ibid*
604. Sanhedrin 105a
605. Rosh Hashana 4a on Nehemiah 2:6
606. Genesis 6:12
607. Genesis Rabbah 26:5
608. Deut. 27:21
609. Pesachim 49b
610. Abodah Zarah 24b

the Middle Ages[611], the Rabbis strongly denied the possibility of a pregnancy in an animal from a human being and vice-versa. In the Middle Ages, it was believed that monsters occur from such sodomy and bring bad luck, and these had to be prevented by burning the sodomized animal together with the human perpetrator[612]. From *this* belief is derived the cited regulation of the Allgemeines Landsrecht[613].

## XVIII    Tribady (Lesbianism)

Fornication between women is considered by the Sages to be equivalent to the *doings of the Egyptians*[614], although the Bible itself makes no mention thereof nor does it mention a punishment therefor. The usual expression, therefore, is *soleleth* or, in the Jerusalem Talmud, *soledeth*[615], copulation in which they move about forcefully one against the other. Only a few individuals, such as Rabbi Huna[616] and the School of Shammai, consider such women as true prostitutes and hence forbidden to marry priests. Others consider lesbianism between women to be mere obscenity, *peritzuth,* but without legal consequences[617].

In the post-Talmudic period, Maimonides decreed that a man should prohibit his wife from associating with women "known to indulge in such practices". However, he is not obligated to divorce his wife if she is a lesbian[618].

The father of Samuel did not permit his grown-up daughters to sleep together so that "they not become accustomed to a foreign body"[619], obviously to prevent lewdness.

It is also likely that the Apostle meant tribady when he spoke of "their women that did change the natural use into that which is against nature"[620].

## XIX    Ba'al Peor Cult

In the portrayal of lewdness in the Bible by modern authors, the cult of *Ba'al Peor* is usually also considered. The Bible relates:

When Israel abode in Shittim, the people began to commit harlotry with the daughters of Moab. These called the people unto the sacrifices of their gods; and the people ate and bowed down to their gods. And Israel joined himself unto the *Ba'al Peor,* and the anger of the Lord was kindled against Israel. The chiefs of the people were all hanged according to martial law, and the judges sentenced to death all the others that honored *Ba'al Peor*. A plague ensued, a *magepha,* which killed 24,000 people[621].

It is impossible to conclude from the Bible what the practice of this heathen cult actually was. It is not true that "the Rabbis use the name *Peor* to refer to *aperire sc. hymenum virgineum"*, as Rosenbaum claims. Even in his citation from Targum Jonathan[622], there is no mention of this interpretation. As far as I can see, there is considerable unanimity throughout the Talmud that the cult consists of *aperire anum,* that is the practice of exposing oneself in the nude and *defecating* in front of the graven image of their god. This practice is used as an example to indicate that any type of idol worship is prohibited, even if, as in this case, most intelligent people would consider such a practice to be a mockery rather than an adoration[623]. When Sabta ben

---

611. *Tosefta* Niddah 4:6
612. Petermann in *Deuts. Zeitschr. für Sexualwiss.* 1908 p.291
613. Preuss' repeated references to German civil and criminal law have little meaning to the English reader but are retained in the translation for the sake of completeness (F.R.).
614. Levit. 18:3
615. Jerushalmi Gittin 8; 49c
616. Shabbath 65a
617. Yebamoth 76a
618. *Mishneh Torah. Hilchoth Issure Biyah* 21:8
619. Shabbath 65a-b
620. Romans 1:26
621. Numbers 25:1 ff
622. *op. cit.* p.71
623. Sanhedrin 7:6

Alas once practiced this "adoration" to the point that after the defecation he wiped his anus on the nose of the pagoda, the community of *Peor* jubilantly called out to him: no one has ever performed the adoration so well[624]! This is most likely an exaggeration.

Moreover, it is well known that defecation can be perceived as an expression of *sexual* perversion[625]. One first finds in the writings of the church father Hieronymus the opinion that *Peor* is identical to the *priapus*. Women adored him *ob obscoeni magnitudinem* (because of his obscene size). His name *Peor* was derived from the fact that *idolum tentiginis* (the penis) *haberet in ore*, that he was pictured as having the penis in his open mouth[626], just as the Hindus portray their Siva, namely, with the *lingam* in the mouth.

## XX   The Plague Following the Peor Cult

If one does not wish to accept the Rabbis' interpretation of the *Peor* cult, one will at least find a basis, admittedly weak, for the name of the idol. We must, however, attempt to more precisely identify the relationship of the epidemic to the *Peor* cult. Even if we totally dispense with the help of the name *Peor*, we are dependant on "mere guesswork". It is a characteristic of all enthusiastic specialists in any field, not only literature, to find some explanation within their specialty for any matter which comes to their attention, even if the patient is incidentally sent to the wrong outpatient clinic. So, too, in the story of *Ba'al Peor*, the syphilis specialists argued with each other so much that they finally happily declared the plague to have been syphilis[627]. The pathfinder in this matter was Sickler (1797), and the systematic analyzer was Rosenbaum (1839)[628]. They argue as follows: the seduction to idol worship came from the women; therefore, the disease must have been venereal.

In the war against Midian, the Israelites killed all the men, but allowed the women to remain alive. Moses was angered: "It was specifically the women who were the cause of your sin against God concerning the *Peor*, and so the plague — syphilitic infection — came into the congregation of Israel. Now kill all women who have known a man by sleeping with him, since they are to be considered as being infected with syphilis. Only the women children may you leave alive. And encamp outside the camp for seven days — for disinfection (perhaps for clinical lubrication treatments) — whosoever has killed any person, or whoever touched any slain person. And purify yourselves on the third day and on the seventh day, you and your captives. And you shall purify every garment, all that is made of leather (i.e. skin) or goats' hair, and all things made of wood"[629].

In the time of Joshua, Phinehas, a witness to that epidemic, complained that *we are not cleansed of the iniquity of Peor until this day*[630]. Thus, in spite of all the cures, the illness was not yet eradicated. Even the author of the Apocalypse speaks thereof, that one there practiced prostitution *(porneusai)*[631]. The danger of syphilitic infection was especially great because the generation born in the desert was uncircumcised.

It would certainly not have entered the mind of the non-specialist to construct the picture of syphilis from these statements. That the seduction to idol worship originated from the women is certain, since *cherchez la femme* has validity during all eras. In order to prevent any further seduction once and for all, all the seductresses were exterminated (the men were already killed). Anyone who touched a corpse, according to Mosaic law, is ritually unclean and must purify himself. This offense is so severe, that when the Jews began illegally to build altars, Phinehas considered them not to be

---

624. *Sifré, Balak* ed. Friedman p.74b E; Sanhedrin 64a
625. See Krafft-Ebing. *Psychop. Sex.* p.28
626. Commentary to Hosea 9:10 — in Mignes,
*Patrologie*, Vol. 25, col. 940

627. probably *lues maligna endemica*
628. *op. cit.* p.70ff
629. Numbers 31:15-20
630. Joshua 22:17
631. Apoc. 2:14

morally healthy yet. The name of the illness in the text, *magepha,* means nothing more than epidemic (plague, pestilence). It arose out of the anger of the Lord[632]. The number of people who *died* in the epidemic amounted to 24,000. This would be an unusually large number for syphilis. Through the braveness of the intervention of Phinehas, who struck down a distinctly insolent pair of lovers, the pestilence was halted, and the epidemic can be considered to have died out.

Pinkhoff, in his polemic against Peypers, has already demonstrated that the affidavits of Rosenbaum, Philo and Josephus prove nothing[633]. Philo speaks of a plague (*miasma* in Greek) and Josephus of a pestilence *(loimos)*[634]. The exact nature of this plague, which infested a large portion of the wandering people, cannot be decided. The assumption that it was a syphilis epidemic is probably the least likely possibility.

632. Numbers 25:3                           Vol. 2 .782
633. *Nederl. Tijdschr. voor Geneeskd.* 1893    634. *Antiquities.* Book 4 Chapt. 6:12

# CHAPTER XVII

## *REGIMEN OF HEALTH*

### PART I
### DIETARY LAWS

The Biblical dietary laws are included in the chapter on "Hygiene" solely because *we* can conceive of no reason other than sanitary for their ordination. It must be emphasized, however, that the Torah gives no reason at all for these laws, and the later sources do so only rarely. Thus, nearly everything which one alleges to be the reason for the dietary laws is only a hypothesis and is read into the sources. One can assume with certainty that considerations of physical health are at least part of the reason. At the same time, however, were it not for higher grades of other motivations, whether of a cultic or ethical nature (such as, for example, the prohibition of the slaughtering of a female animal and its offspring on the same day), then these hygienic considerations would be the determining ones to explain the dietary laws.

### I

In order for meat to be consumed, according to Jewish law, the following conditions must be fulfilled:

1. The meat must be derived from an animal whose consumption is permitted by the Torah: the animal must be ritually *clean* (i.e. kosher). "Clean" according to the law of the Torah includes:

(a) three types of domesticated animals: cattle, sheep, and goats; and seven types of deer (according to the usual translation): the hart, the gazelle, the roebuck, the wild goat, the pygarg, the antelope and the mountain sheep[1]. Common signs of clean animals are that they chew the cud and have completely split hoofs. Specifically excluded therefore are the camel, the rabbit (or badger), the hare and the swine[2], which are obviously animals that were generally eaten by heathens. Additional signs of cleanness of an animal are described in the Talmud for the case where the entire animal is no longer available for examination.

(b) Among birds, the prohibited varieties are enumerated in Leviticus 11: 13-19. Their precise zoological identification, however, even today, poses insurmountable difficulties. Even the meaning of the criteria given in the Talmud for cleanness is uncertain; so that the following principle applies: a bird can only be considered clean

---

1. Deut. 14:5
2. Levit. 11:3-7; Deut. 14:4ff. See also D.

Hoffmann. *Das Buch Leviticus*. Berlin 1905–1906

**501**

and, therefore, eaten on the basis of positive (more or less local) knowledge (or tradition). In general, the only undoubtedly clean birds are the goose, hen, duck, turkey and dove.

(c) Eight small animals which crawl on the ground, *sheretz,* whose identification is also not certain[3]. According to Hoffmann, they are the weasel, the mouse, the toad, the hedgehog, the chameleon, the lizard, the skink and the mole. They are all unclean.

(d) Only those fish which have fins and obviously visible scales are permitted. Other criteria for cleanliness (i.e. permissibility for consumption) are mentioned in the Talmud; the shape of the spinal cord, the head, the bladder etc. On such grounds, the eel is an example of a forbidden fish.

(e) All amphibia (frogs, turtles, crabs and lobsters) and all molluscs (snakes, mussels and oysters), as well as all worms, are forbidden[4]. Because of the latter, every raw grain, as well as raw products prepared therefrom (grits, groats, flour), upon which are found worms or maggots or mites, is forbidden. Therefore, every fruit suspected of containing a worm must be thoroughly examined.

(f) Among insects, only a few types of grasshoppers are permitted[5]. Here, too, their identification poses serious difficulties. On the other hand, all beetles without exception are prohibited, so that legumes, prior to their preparation for consumption, must be examined for the presence of parasites.

2. Quadrupeds and birds must be slaughtered in the prescribed manner. Therefore, the consumption of any meat derived from animals which died naturally *(nebelah),* or which were strangled by other animals *(terefah),* or which were shot or slain by man, or which were killed in any manner other than that prescribed in the Torah is prohibited.

The "prescribed manner" means that the animal's throat must be slit below the larynx with a knife that is absolutely free of notches, without the application of any pressure, and without interruption, by a simple to-and-fro movement of the knife. With this incision, the windpipe (trachea) and the foodpipe (esophagus), as well as the major arteries of the neck, are severed, and the death of the animal occurs due to exsanguination. The slightest notch in the slaughtering knife, or any type of pressure applied therewith, or even the slightest pause in the making of the incision (for example, if the slaughterer injures himself, and because of his alarm hesitates for a moment) renders the slaughtering invalid, and the consumption of the meat from that animal is prohibited. The knife should be of an appropriate size, according to the type of animal that is to be slaughtered. Every type of material is permissible: stone, reed[6], and so forth[7]. The only requirement is that the instrument fulfill all the other requirements, particularly that it is, and remains, absolutely free of notches. For not only before, but also after, every slaughtering, the knife must be examined for notches. If notches are found *after* the slaughtering, it is surmised that these were present even before but were overlooked. In practice, steel knives exclusively are used for slaughtering.

From the Scriptural text: *then thou shalt kill . . . as I have commanded thee*[8], tradition concludes that even the method of slaughtering originated at Sinai.

3. The animal may not have any external wound or internal change in an organ from which, if it were not slaughtered, it would die spontaneously in a short period of time. In the evaluation, it makes no difference if the wound of the animal occurred immediately prior to the slaughtering. Therefore, any animal whose cervical spinal cord (medulla) is pierced in order to facilitate the slaughtering, or whose skull is

---

3. Levit. 11:29
4. Levit. 11:41
5. Levit. 11:22

6. see *Secare Harundine.* Plinius 20:2
7. Chullin 1:2
8. Deut. 12:21

crushed, or in whom a bone or a rib breaks when the animal is thrown to the ground, is forbidden for consumption. Every animal, without exception, must be examined for the presence of such wounds or changes before it can be released for consumption. If such wounds are detected in advance, then the slaughtering has to be cancelled.

In the *Mishnah* are mentioned those wounds which animals inflict upon one another which render them unusable for consumption i.e. *terefah*. The list of such wounds is evidently a type of guidance for the meat inspector. It gives a general picture of the knowledge of surgical veterinary pathology among the *Tanna'im*[9]. Since the list contains not a single expression in a foreign language, one should no doubt exclude pertinent material from foreign sources.

*Terefa* is an animal with perforation of the esophagus, severance of the windpipe, perforation of the membrane of the brain, perforation of the heart as far as the cavity thereof, breaking of the vertebral column with severence of the spinal cord, complete absence of the liver, perforation or defects of the lung, perforation of the gallbladder, and perforation of the stomach or intestinal system, so much so that feces or quantities of fodder may be extruded in that vicinity[10].

Not life-threatening are: simple perforation or a lengthwise slit in the windpipe, wounding of the skull but without damage to the membrane of the brain, non-penetrating wounds of the heart, breakage of the spinal column without damage to the cord, partial absence of the liver, a fistulous communication between the omasum and the reticulum[11], and removal of the spleen[12], the kidney, the lower jawbone, or the womb[13].

A detailed accounting of these individual regulations, together with the explanatory rules found in the *Gemara,* has already been given in earlier chapters.

4. For every animal, whether *terefah* or *kosher,* consumption of the following is prohibited:

(a) Blood. This prohibition is enjoined upon Jews in many places in the Bible, with great emphasis[14]; *it shall be a perpetual statute for your generations*[15]; *no blood may be eaten in any of your dwellings, whether it be of fowl or of cattle*[16]; *you should pour it on the ground like water*[17]; *whoever eats it shall be cut off*[18]. The prohibition of blood is found in the Bible long *before* the law at Sinai[19]. Also, concerning the heathens that converted to Christianity, in spite of the dispensation of other ritual duties, the Apostles demanded abstention from strangled (that is, not slaughtered) animals and from blood[20]. For converted Jews, such a prohibition was superfluous.

Large arteries (i.e. blood vessels) which still contain a large quantity of blood, even in an already slaughtered animal, must be removed before the meat of that animal is used. These include especially the large veins of the thigh and the shin bones, the veins of the tongue, the large veins in the neck, the veins of the heart and the mesentery, as well as the entire membrane of the brain[21].

The following regulation best illustrates how exact one is with the prohibition of blood: he who ate hard bread and injured his gums so that they bleed should cut away and discard the bloody piece of bread, in order to avoid even the appearance of having eaten blood[22].

---

9. Sages in the *Mishnah*
10. Chullin 3:1
11. the second and third stomachs in ruminants
12. Preuss erroneously has "liver" (F.R.)
13. Chullin 3:2
14. particularly Deut. 12:23-25
15. Levit. 3:17
16. *ibid* 7:26

17. Deut. 12:16
18. Levit. 17:14
19. Genesis 9:4; according to tradition this phrase refers to a "limb (severed) from a living animal" and the "blood from a living animal".
20. Acts 15: 20 and 29
21. *Yoreh Deah* 65:1 with the sources
22. Kerithoth 21b

One can appreciate how strong the educational influence of the Torah laws is for those who observe them, from the fact that Rabbi Simeon bar Rabbi was able to declare: "man's soul has a loathing for blood"[23], although the existence of the often-repeated Torah prohibition of blood seems to indicate the opposite, and, even today, many normally sensitive people consume black vinegar[24] and black pudding[25] without aversion.

(b) *Cheleb.* This, too, is a Biblical commandment as a *perpetual statute*[26]. This prohibited "fat", according to the *Gemara,* refers to that type which lies like a covering on organs without being fused to them, and which can be easily peeled off[27]. Intended are the fat of the large omentum, and the mesentery, and the fat in which the kidneys are embedded.

(c) The prohibition against eating the *sciatic nerve,* based on the Biblical narrative, was a custom which became law[28]. The removal of this nerve, together with all its ramifications, from the flesh is extraordinarily difficult, requires very great skill and conscientiousness, and finally results in shredding of the meat in such a way that this meat, that is the entire hind quarter of the animal, is nearly universally not eaten at all.

(d) The prohibition of eating "a limb (severed) from a *living* animal" is also one of the pre-Sinaitic laws[29]. Raw pieces of meat, excised from a live animal, represented a delicacy to many peoples in antiquity[30].

5. The Biblical command prohibiting the cooking of a kid in its mother's milk[31] is understood by tradition[32] to be a general prohibition against cooking together or consuming meat and milk (butter, cheese). It is also prescribed that after the consumption of meat, one should not consume any milk or milk products for several hours. On the other hand, it is assumed that milk which comes into an empty stomach passes therefrom quickly, so that meat consumed shortly after milk no longer meets the milk in the stomach.

6. A mother animal and her young may not be slaughtered on the same day[33].

7. Before meat can be cooked, it must be soaked in water for half an hour to remove any adherent blood. Afterwards, it is sprinkled on all sides with coarse salt, to bring out the blood. The meat remains thus in a vessel with holes (so the blood can run off) for one hour, and is finally well rinsed and washed, in order to remove the blood-impregnated salt.

Among all these laws, a reason is given only for the prohibition of blood: *for the soul (or the life, nefesh) of the flesh is in the blood, and I the Lord have given it to you upon the altar, to make an atonement for your souls*[34]; and in another place: *for the blood is the life, and thou mayest not eat the life with the flesh*[35]. However, why this should not occur is not stated.

For all other regulations, as already mentioned, there is no reason at all given, either in the Torah or in the later legal sources. Everything which is mentioned as a reason by later writers can only lay claim to be a more or less probable hypothesis. A compilation of all these hypotheses would certainly fill many volumes, and still hardly advance our understanding, so that we will limit ourselves here to calling attention to a few selected points.

Concerning the differentiation between clean and unclean animals, which we will

23. Makkoth 23b
24. translation uncertain
25. literally: blood sausage
26. Levit. 3:17
27. Chullin 49b
28. Genesis 32:33
29. Chullin 101b

30. For example the Abyssinians. Noldeke. *Zeitschr. Deut. Med. Gesel.* 1895 p.715
31. Exodus 23:19 and 34:26; Deut. 14:21
32. Chullin 8:1ff
33. Levit. 22:28
34. Levit. 17:11
35. Deut. 12:23

discuss in the next section, such a differentiation was undoubtedly made by many peoples in antiquity. The main distinction, however, consists in the fact that to them clean animals were considered holy, and were, therefore, protected, cared for and honored, whereas unclean animals were considered to be creatures hated by God, and hence exterminated. The Torah teaches exactly the opposite: clean animals may be slaughtered for human consumption. We do not know which concepts were of influence here and in the arranging of the individual animals in the "clean" or "unclean" category. One should make this frank admission honestly.

Concerning the prescribed methods of slaughtering, exact investigations in modern times have demonstrated that this Judaic method of slaughtering is in fact the best to exsanguinate the flesh. These investigations have also shown that such exsanguinated meat endures longer than other meat, so that this method must be spoken of as the most hygienic[36].

The specific laws dealing with *terefoth,* that is the rules concerning wounds, the presence of which would prohibit the consumption of such animals, according to the Talmud, are "laws given to Moses on Sinai", and are propagated by transmission from generation to generation *without further explanation.* These laws thus belong to the "oral tradition". Nowhere is it mentioned that the consumption of an animal which exhibits one of the aforementioned wounds is detrimental to human health. Major emphasis is only placed on the requirement that the animal be viable, that is, it should not be "torn" by another animal — the narrowest (i.e. literal) meaning of the word *terefah.* The entire questioning, therefore, is in principle different than that raised by modern veterinary pathology, and everything that was written about the sanitary character of these laws, from the time of Maimonides on[37], is pure supposition.

The final sentence in the chapter in the Torah dealing with the dietary laws proclaims: *Ye shall not make yourselves abominable...For I am the Lord, your God, ye shall, therefore, sanctify yourselves, and ye shall be (or become) holy; for I am holy; neither shall ye defile yourselves*[38]*...*If one assumes that this sentence refers to the dietary laws, then one should also probably assume that it was thought that the more blemish-free (healthier, stronger) the animal, the less likely the possibility of a detrimental influence on the psychic functions (i.e. emotions) of the human body.

However, even this assumption does not explain, for example, the laws concerning the individual *classes* of animals permitted for human nourishment. It is not true that the animal considered to be at the highest level in each class in question is "clean". Also, for certain designations of *terefoth,* another interpretation seems necessary. When an animal with recent bone fractures which perhaps occurred only minutes before its planned death by slaughtering is declared prohibited, the intent of this ruling may perhaps be: to take into consideration the shackling and the knocking down of the animal which is required as part of the slaughtering; that is, to avoid inflicting any unnecessary torment upon the animal. This can also be presumed to be the reason why pausing during the slaughtering is prohibited. This purely psychic reason is accepted to be the correct one for the prohibition of slaughtering a female animal and its calf on the same day.

No matter what the reasons for these dietary laws, and even if our understanding of the importance of a potentially fatal pathologic finding in the slaughtered animal were very different than that described in the Talmud — about which there is no doubt at all — just the thought and the existence of *obligatory meat examination,* which

36. Dembo. *Das Schächten im Vergleich zu Andern Schlachtmethoden.* Leipzig 1894 p.38

37. *Guide for the Perplexed* 3:40
38. Levit. 11:43-44

applies without exception, even to animals slaughtered at home, is for that time a phenomenon exceedingly worthy of note, which has almost no analogy even in our times.

In only one respect is the Talmudic meat examination fundamentally different from that practiced today. A differentiation into "spoiled, badly spoiled, and unhealthy meat" as we have it today does not exist in the Talmud; nor does the latter mention the destruction of individual organs which, for example, could be considered "spoiled" because of disease (sold on the open market, etc.?). In Jewish law, the *whole* animal is either healthy *(kosher)* and then permitted for consumption, or it shows anatomic marks of a dangerous illness in any organ, in which case it is *terefah* and forbidden. We cannot decide as yet which viewpoint serves health interests better, nor do we know any longer which one is better from the standpoint of economics.

Fundamentally different from the dietary laws discussed until now is the following:

An animal which has ingested a poison which would be fatal to man *(sam hamaveth),* or an animal which was bitten by a snake or a mad dog, is prohibited, not because it is *terefah,* since such a notion is inapplicable here, but because its consumption would constitute a danger to life. On the other hand, it is not harmful if the animal ingested things which are not detrimental to man, even though they may be harmful to the animal, for example, rododaphne (oleander), hen feces, asafetida, crowfoot or pepper cabbage[39]. There can be no doubt as to the sanitary character of *this* law.

# PART 2
## LAWS OF PURITY (CLEANNESS)

In the teaching of Biblical-Talmudic hygiene, the meanings of the terms *tahor* and *tameh,* respectively translated as "pure" and "impure", have produced much confusion. Since the Torah gives *no* reason for any of its laws of purity, the fantasy of the commentators has covered the greatest latitude imaginable.

One must first distinguish two types of impurity:[40]

1. The above-discussed impurity of forbidden, unclean (i.e. non-kosher) foods. To consume these foods is an unequivocal Biblical prohibition, transgression of which is punished with flogging, unless a more stringent punishment is inflicted, as in the case of someone who consumed blood or forbidden fat. A purification from this type of uncleanness does not exist.

2. The impurity of the external body, which can be lifted by an act of purification. Such uncleanliness is contracted through contact with a human corpse or an unclean animal, where different grades of impurity prevail, through physiologic or illness-related fluxes from the genitalia of men and women, through the illness called *tzora'ath,* and finally through the water of separation[41], and the scapegoat[42].

Without here discussing or repeating details, one should note in general that impurity contracted through any of the manners listed in this second category occurs as a rule by simple contact therewith. The consequences are that an unclean individual cannot set foot in the Temple, and is not permitted to touch objects which are designated for use in the Temple. In some cases, his uncleanness is transferred to other people or chattels, and thus he may be an undesirable fellow-citizen to his neighbors. A

---

39. Chullin 3:5 and *Tosefta* Chullin 3:19
40. see D. Hoffman *Loc. cit.*
41. Numbers 19:21
42. Levit. 16:26

prohibition against becoming unclean did not exist, except for priests under certain circumstances. On the contrary, it was obligatory to become unclean in relation to a corpse. These circumstances have already been discussed earlier[43]. One was also allowed to confidently enjoy foods and beverages which had become "unclean"[44].

Also, there was no obligation to "cleanse" oneself. He who wished to renunciate contact with the Temple and to tolerate the above-mentioned inconvenience to his fellow-citizens — a person is in fact a "political animal" — was allowed to remain unclean without being punished. However, every individual was obligated to slaughter his Passover offering in the Temple and to eat it in purity[45]. He, therefore, had to make sure that he was "clean" at that time. In addition, he had to bring Second Tithe to Jerusalem every year and to consume it there in purity[46]. In the *Gemara,* Rabbi Yitzchak also considers it obligatory to be pure for the other two pilgrimage festivals[47] so that, in practice, at least the pious Jews saw to it that they remained "clean" at all times or became so as rapidly as possible.

As a rule, part of the act of purification for an individual, according to the Torah, includes a prescribed sacrifice. He who becomes unclean through contact with a corpse requires the ashes of the red heifer[48] for purification. Every unclean person, however, without exception, had to immerse himself completely in a (ritual) bath before he became completely clean. We will speak in greater detail later concerning this ritual immersion. We do not know whether and how, by law, one controls uncleanliness and purification, or whether one leaves both up to the conscientiousness of the individual.

Naturally, philosophers of religion and Bible commentators since time immemorial have attempted to find a reason for those Torah regulations. However, no solution to this problem that has been attempted can withstand sober criticism. It is, however, certain that the expressions "pure" and "impure" do not have moral connotations[49], perhaps as we say[50]: "everything is pure to the pure person". It is also certain that these expressions "pure" and "impure" are not identical with "clean" and "unclean" in the physical sense. It is entirely ridiculous to say that impure means infected and pure means aseptic, although the non-physician might easily take such a suggestion seriously; notwithstanding the fact that this hypothesis is shown to be untenable by virtue of the law concerning semen ejaculation which, although considered to represent impurity by many peoples in antiquity, was not thought by any of them to be contagious. My own opinion concerning the Biblical "method of disinfection" has already been enunciated earlier with sufficient clarity[51]. One cannot but comprehend the meaning of "purity" in the Torah in the purely spiritual, metaphysical, transcendental or similar sense.

According to the tradition that impurity and purity should be understood in the correlative sense of holiness, then to that extent where there is no holiness, there can also not be any impurity[52]. Thus with the cessation of holiness, the Temple and its service, the laws concerning *tumah* and *tahara* (purity and impurity) have lost their practical significance. Accordingly, the *Mishnah* and the *Tosefta* which extend back into that time period, discuss a considerable number of expositions of regulations on this subject matter in separate treatises (*Negaim, Zabim,* etc.). The *Gemara,* on the other hand, although mentioning most of these regulations in passing, does not give a comprehensive or continuous commentary, as it customarily does for other laws.

43. see above chapter 2
44. Maimonides' *Mishneh Torah. Tumath Ochelin* 16:12
45. Deut. 16:2; see also Second Chronicles 30:17 and John 11:55
46. Deut. 14:22
47. Rosh Hashanah 16a
48. Numbers 19:17

49. as suggested by Goldstein. *Neue Med. Press* 1901, number 24; see also *Ralbag* on First Samuel 20:26
50. in the source *Ep. Pauli ad Titum* 1:15, the sense is somewhat different
51. see above chapter 4
52. *Kusari* 3:49 p.261 Cassel; see also Numbers 19:20

The rules regarding the *consumption* of forbidden foods and *copula cum femina impura* were naturally not abrogated[53] following the destruction of the Temple.

The grade of impurity and the manner of purification differ according to the various objects in question. The highest grade of impurity (or uncleanness) is that contracted through a human corpse. Whoever touches a corpse, whether the deceased died a natural death or was killed with a sword on the open field, or whoever only comes into a tent (or house) in which the corpse is lying, becomes unclean for seven days, and must be sprinkled with the water of expiation on the third and the seventh day[54]. Every open utensil that has no cover is unclean. Whosoever touches the bone of a man, or a grave, is unclean. The purification ceremony consisted in the sprinkling of the "atonement water"[55]. The latter was prepared in the following manner: a red heifer was slaughtered and burned to ashes, together with cedar-wood, hyssop and scarlet. Some of these ashes were dissolved in fresh water (i.e. well water). This material was then sprinkled by means of a hyssop stalk on the object or person to be purified. Then the unclean person had to wash his clothes and take a bath.

Katzenelson, on the basis of a work by a Russian physician which was inaccessible to me because of the language in which it was written (i.e. Russian), concocted the following theory: the law of ritual purification has the intent of restricting the spread of bubonic plague, which "prevailed in Egypt and Syria since antiquity", and which is considered to be one of the miasmatic illnesses. The incubation period is seven days, and hence the requirement for seven days of uncleanliness. For lifeless objects, the same time period is required, in order "to provide more uniformity to the norm", and it is securer to prohibit more rather than less[56]. For this reason, the person killed with a sword is treated in the same manner as one who died of plague, although in the former case, the only danger is the poison of a corpse. Moreover, bodies of soldiers who died in battle were rapidly buried for this same reason. The water of purification was effective by virtue of its content of alkaline substances which disinfect, and because of "the not completely burnt resinous substances and the small quantity of creosote contained in the ashes"[57].

It is not necessary to comment even one word concerning all these arbitrary and fantastic theories which were perpetuated and expanded by later writers. It borders on insult to maintain, as a result of such interpretations, that the Lawgiver considered plague victims (corpses) to be infectious, yet declared a person ill with the plague to be harmless and allowed the infected individual to roam free for three days, instead of at least putting him into quarantine. It must again be reiterated *with strong emphasis* that no mention at all is found either in the Torah or in any of the other legal sources, that one might be able to disinfect a person afflicted with plague or other infectious illness, through the *sprinkling* of any type of liquid, even if it is the most concentrated corrosive potion, even if it were used immediately after exposure, as would be done by intelligent people.

3. The cadaver of a deceased quadruped, whether it itself is clean or unclean, or the cadaver of any of the above-mentioned eight small animals, conveys uncleanness, but only until the evening of the same day. He who carries the cadaver must, moreover, wash his clothes. Anything upon which one of these animals falls as it dies becomes unclean, whether it be a wooden utensil or a skin or a garment. Every utensil with which any work is done must be put into water, remains unclean until the evening and

---

53. literally: touched
54. Numbers 19:11 ff
55. literally: water of separation
56. "Die Rituellen Reinheitsgesetze in der

Bibel und im Talmud" *Frankel's Mtschr.*
1899 p.111
57. *ibid* p.112

then becomes clean. Concerning any earthenware utensil, if anything unclean falls therein, then everything that is already in this utensil becomes unclean, and the utensil itself should be smashed. Every consumable food upon which water falls becomes unclean, and every drinkable beverage can become unclean in any utensil. Anything upon which carrion falls becomes unclean. Ovens and hearths (both of which are earthen cooking-stoves) must be broken; they are unclean and shall be unclean unto thee. However, a well and a cistern, a gathering of water (which is not in utensils), remains clean. If some carrion fell on sowing seeds and saturated them, they remain clean; if water was first applied to the seeds and then the carrion fell on them, they are unclean[58].

This is the Biblical law. It applies to all Israelites; it was, however, enjoined more strongly upon a priest[59], because if he violated it, he was dismissed from carrying out his profession of serving in the Temple.

Certainly, in reading these laws, the thought comes to mind as to their sanitary appropriateness, particularly if one arbitrarily assumes that one is dealing not only with the cadaver of an animal that died of a non-contagious disease, concerning which the only concern is the poison of a corpse, but also with those that died of anthrax and, perhaps, also of cattle plague or of septicemia; and then one observes that any person who carries such an animal also has the obligation of washing his clothes. Earthenware utensils must be destroyed, evidently because the poison is absorbed therein; accordingly, tradition explicitly excludes stone utensils. The contagious material does not attach as easily to, nor germinate, on dry plant seeds as on moist ones.

One can easily find more such remarkable specifics (to support the hygienic hypothesis of explaining the Biblical laws of purity). I only wish to emphasize that, according to tradition, the power of a cadaver to impart uncleanliness ceases when a high degree of putrefaction has already set in[60]: ptomaine disappears at high temperatures, which we surmise are the rule in the Orient, after eight to ten days, as demonstrated by Brieger. I have also heard an enthusiastic apologete show that, according to the *Mishnah*[61], only seven types of liquids can become unclean: wine, blood, oil, milk, dew, bees' honey and water. All of these give a neutral or alkaline reaction, and are, therefore, an excellent fertile medium for bacteria!

However, the more one becomes enraptured with the "infection theory", the more astounding the demeanor of the Lawgiver must appear. The latter declares a cistern to be clean; that is, He allows water to be drunk therefrom without any concern, notwithstanding the fact that a cadaver of an animal lies therein. One can thus see to what absurdities one is led if one has to explain the Biblical law of impurity at all costs!

4. *Tzora'ath on clothing.* If there appears a *nega tzora'ath* which is deep yellow (green) or deep red on an article of clothing made of wool or linen, or on the warp or the weft-yarn of flax or wool, or on leather or on a leather utensil, it must be shown to the priest. The latter must lock the article up and examine it again after seven days. If he observes a spreading of the *nega,* then the afflicted object must be burned, because the *nega* is virulent, *mamereth.* If the *nega* does not spread, then the priest has the affected object washed, and locks it up again for seven days. If after this time the appearance of the *nega* is unchanged, and it has not spread (but it has remained completely as it was), then the object is likewise unclean and must be burned; the eruption is *pecheseth.* If the eruption, however, became paler after the washing, then the priest should tear it out from the material. If it recurs, then it is "sprouting"

---

58. Numbers 31:20 (should be Levit. 11:37-38, F.R.)
59. Levit. 22:8
60. Bechoroth 23a

61. Machshirin 6:4, according to the interpretation of Maimonides. *Hilchoth Tumath Ochelin* 1:4

(florid, *porachath*), and the material must be burned. If the spot, however, disappeared after the washing, then the article of clothing is washed again and is clean[62].

Whereas the human *tzora'ath* can at least be identified with a certain probability, the meaning of the *tzora'ath* of clothing is completely uncertain. Some people believe that human leprosy can attach itself to clothing and utensils and then again infect human beings. Others think of mildew stains, which is just as absurd. Maimonides renounces every natural explanation and considers this *tzora'ath* to have been a miraculous occurrence, which happened only at that time, and only in Palestine.

5. *House Tzora'ath*. And God spoke unto Moses and Aaron (during the desert wandering): when you come into the land of Canaan, and I put a *nega tzora'ath* in a house, then the owner of the house shall come and tell the priest saying: it looks to me that something like a *nega* is present in my house! And the priest, before he comes for an observation, instructs that the house be emptied out, so that not everything which is in the house should become unclean. If he finds a *nega* on the walls in the form of dark yellowish (or greenish) or dark reddish indentations, then he goes out of the house and locks it up for seven days. If after this time, the *nega* has spread, then he instructs that the stones on which the *nega* is seen be torn out, that the house be scraped within and round about, and the mortar and the stones cast off outside the city in an unclean place. The removed stones are replaced with others, and the house is freshly plastered. If the *nega* is then found again, and remains in spite of the removal of the stones and in spite of the scrapings, then the *tzora'ath* is virulent, *mamereth:* the house is unclean. The whole house must be torn down, and its stones and timber and all the mortar thereof must be carried outside the city to an unclean place. Whoever goes into that closed house is unclean until the evening. Whoever lies down or eats there must also wash his clothes. If after the removal of the stones and the scraping, the *nega* did not spread, then the priest declares the house clean; for the *nega* is healed. — Then follows the purification ceremony, similar to that described for human leprosy[63].

The exact identification of this house *tzora'ath* has been unsuccessful up to the present time. Some people have suggested corrosion by saltpeter on the dry-rot of houses; others believe that human leprosy could be transferred to the walls of houses; yet others have proposed unlikely meanings which need not be mentioned.

The *Mishnah* states that the introduction of this law of *tzora'ath* in the Torah explicitly declares: *when you (Israelites) come into the land of Canaan;* and the entire law is only applicable as a ritual to those over whom this law extends its sphere of influence. Therefore, it is taught that this law has no application to the houses and clothing of non-Jews[64]. Perhaps conditions of this sort did not occur anymore in the post-Biblical period in Palestine, so that the *Tosefta* in fact ventures to teach that house leprosy does not exist at all. At the time of Rabbi Eliezer ben Zaddok, a ruin was observed that was thought to have originated from such a house[65]. In any event, the exclusion of non-Jews from this law is the strongest proof against the infectious theory.

Although we cannot identify *tzora'ath* any more — even the interpretation that human *tzora'ath* is leprosy is not certain — we can at least say that in order to combat this abnormal situation, certain precautionary measures which seem appropriate can be implemented. Even today, we are of the opinion that the most expedient measure is to isolate patients with leprosy, to burn clothes which are suspected of being harmful to man, to order the removal of the plaster and the affected masonry of such buildings, and if that does not suffice, to demolish the buildings.

---

62. Levit. 14:47
63. Levit. 14:33 ff

64. Negaim 11:1 and 12:1
65. *Tosefta* Negaim 6:11

The other sources of impurity — menstruation and the puerperium, ejaculation and gonorrhea, as well as *tzora'ath* of humans — have already been discussed in earlier chapters.

# PART 3
# THE DEAD and their BURIAL

## I   A Dying Person

One may not perform certain acts on a dying person that are carried out for a person who is already dead: one does not tie up his cheek bones, or stop up his apertures (anus and nose), or place a metal vessel or anything which chills on his navel, until he is definitely dead[66], and, in the words of the preacher, until *the golden bowl is shattered*[67]. According to the explanation of the *Gemara*[68], the latter represents a poetic allusion to the distention of the abdomen after death. One may not move a dying person or place him on sand or salt, until he has actually died. One may not close the eyes of a dying person. Whoever touches him or moves him is a murderer, for Rabbi Meir used to explain this matter by an analogy: he who touches a flickering lamp extinguishes it[69].

Already in the Code of Jacob ben Asher (in 1340) we find the prohibition of removing the pillow from under a dying man's head to alleviate his dying. On the other hand, Abraham Portaleone, physician in Mantua in 1612, complained bitterly that, in spite of energetic pleas, he was unable to abolish the erroneous custom of those who removed the pillow from below the patient's head, in accordance with the belief that bird feathers contained in the pillow prevent the soul from departing. In fact, Rabbi Nathan of Igra sanctioned this practice, notwithstanding the fact that he thereby transgressed the above Talmudic rule that one may not touch a dying person[70]. In addition, Joseph Karo (1575) found it necessary to reiterate this prohibition[71]. On the other hand, Maimonides makes no mention thereof[72]. That this custom does not merely represent a specifically Jewish superstition is apparent from the fact that already in 1678, Casper Questel, in fifty quarto pages, without ever mentioning the Jews, angrily denounces it, *ex moralibus, divinus, juris item ac artis medicae principiis,* and considers it to represent a hastening of death[73]. It was customary in those times to remove the beds from under the *dead*[74].

The "stopping up of apertures" was to prevent air or *ruach* from penetrating the body, unless the word *ruach* refers to a demon[75]. Corpses were placed on sand in order to preserve them[76]. He who wishes to prevent a corpse from beginning to give off a bad smell should place it face down[77]. If one desires that a dead man's eyes should close, one should follow the advice of Rabbi Simeon ben Gamliel and blow wine into his nostrils, and apply oil between his two eyelids, and squeeze together his two big toes; then the eyes will close of their own accord[78].

---

66. Semachoth 1:2
67. Eccles. 12:6
68. Shabbath 151b
69. Semachoth 1:3-4
70. see *Alfasi* Moed Katan. Chapt. 3 fol. 164b ed. Pressburg
71. *Yoreh Deah* 339:1
72. *Hilchoth Abel* 4:5

73. *De Pulvinari Morientibus Non Subtrahendo.* Jenae 1678
74. Shabbath 23:5
75. Shabbath 151b
76. Jerushalmi Shabbath 4; 6d
77. Abodah Zarah 20a
78. Shabbath 151b

## II  Apparent Death

I found no mention in the Bible or Talmud of the signs which indicate that death has taken place. Nevertheless, the following statement of the *Mishnah* should be noted: men and women who suffer from discharges, and menstruant women, and women after childbirth, and lepers who have died, are not considered dead (in regard to imparting ritual uncleanness) until their bodies begin to decay[79], because, as Rab indicates, one must consider the possibility that they only fainted (apparent death, *yith'alpha*). Rabbi Eliezer even demands that one wait until the abdomen of the deceased bursts. This was one of the questions posed by the "Sages of Alexandria"[80]. Who these people were is uncertain, as is the reason why one had to be concerned with the possibility of apparent death only in the above categories of individuals. Plinius[80a] has already reported on circumstances in hysterical women which mislead one to believe that they have died (catalepsy). In addition, in people with *lepra mutilans,* death occurs imperceptibly after a long, dreadful agony.

A case of apparent death is described by the Sages: one goes out to the cemetery and examines the dead for three days and one is not suspected of practicing heathen cults of the dead. It once happened that a man who was buried was "examined" and found to be living, and he lived for an additional 25 years, raised five children and only then really died[81]. One can also cite a case of apparent death from the Bible. Elisha the prophet was buried, and shortly thereafter another man was being carried out to the cemetery for burial. A band of enemy Moabites was sighted. Frightened, the people carrying the deceased threw him into the sepulchre of Elisha (which was only sealed with a stone placed in front of it). The corpse rolled therein and touched the bones of Elisha. As soon as this occurred, the man revived and stood up on his feet[82]. Also, the revival of Lazarus on the fourth day after burial in a sepulchre[83] is enumerated by the exegetes. On the other hand, there is certainly only an ethical intent behind the teachings of Abahu that the deceased hears everything until the gravestone is closed, and, according to Rabbi Chiya, until the corpse is decayed[84]. Conversations with long deceased individuals are naturally part of legend.

## III  Perfuming and Embalming the Dead

A dead person is washed and anointed[85]. A practice of antiquity, which was and still is widely practiced in the Occident, is to pour water over a deceased person. The reason given by Servius is that one might thereby be able to reawaken an apparently dead person. The anointing of the body was performed with pleasantly smelling spices, as the evangelist describes: *there came Nicodemus and brought a mixture of myrrh and aloes, about one hundred pounds weight; and they took the body of Jesus and wrapped it in linen clothes with the spices*[86].

On the other hand, *embalming* bodies in order to mummify them and thereby protect them from decomposition was a custom of the Egyptians. Joseph had his father's body embalmed according to Egyptian practice, not according to the rules of his own people. This procedure was needed in that case specifically because of the necessity to preserve the body during its long transport from Egypt to Canaan. We are not told in the Bible in what manner the preservation of the body was carried out. *And Joseph commanded his servants the physicians (rophim) to embalm his father; and*

---

79. Niddah 10:4
80. Niddah 69b
80a. Plinius 7:53
81. Semachoth 8:1
82. Second Kings 13:21; Josephus.

*Antiquities,* Book 9 Chapter 8:6
83. John 11:17
84. Shabbath 152b
85. Shabbath 23:5
86. John 19:30-40

*they embalmed Israel. And forty days were fulfilled for him; for so are fulfilled the days of those who are embalmed. And the Egyptians mourned for him for threescore and ten days*[87]. Also, when Joseph died, he was embalmed and placed in a coffin in Egypt[88].

We are thankful to Herodotus 2:85 and Diodorus 1:91 for details concerning the method of embalming. The brain is pulled out through the nose with hooks, the abdomen is opened, the skull and abdominal cavity are filled with palm wine and spices, and the entire body is placed in saltpeter brine for seventy days. At the end of this period, the body is wrapped in linen clothes which are smeared with gum. In addition to this expensive procedure, there were two simpler and, therefore, cheaper modifications. Which method was used for Jacob and for Joseph can, of course, not be decided.

The Talmud relates about Herod[89] that he preserved the body of the daughter of a Maccabee, who committed suicide by throwing herself from a roof-top, in honey for seven years. Honey was a preservative substance also used in Mycenae and Babylon. According to one opinion, his purpose was that people might say that he had married the daughter of a king of Judea. Others say that he had intercourse with her in order to gratify his own evil desires. One does not necessarily have to consider this to be a case of hideous fornication with a corpse if one remembers the advice of Democritos who said that if one preserves bodies in honey, they come back to life again. Plinius states: *mellis natura talis est, ut putrescere corpora non sinat*[90]. He considers this advice to achieve eternal life to be foolish[91]. It must, however, have been believed by his contemporaries. In addition, the body of the poisoned Aristobulus lay in honey for a long time, until Antonius sent it to the Jews for burial[92].

## IV  Suicide

The Bible describes five cases of suicide, all of which involve prominent people. King Saul saw his three sons killed, together with a large part of his army, in the battle against the Philistines. He himself was wounded and pressed hard. In order not to be abused by the enemy, he took his sword and thrust it through himself[93].

Ahithophel, a faithless counsellor of King David, joined the rebellious camp of Absalom and recommended that David be attacked. *And when he saw that his counsel was not followed, he saddled his ass and arose, and gat himself home to his house, to his city, and put his household in order, and hanged himself*[94].

During the rebellion of Zimri against King Elah, the people would not allow him to execute the entire royal family. They, therefore, elected Omri in his stead to be king, because Zimri was besieged in the city of Tirzah. When Zimri saw that the town was about to fall, he went into the citadel of the royal palace and burned the palace over himself with fire, and he died[95].

The fourth case of suicide concerns Razes (or Ragesh). A company of soldiers was sent by King Demetrius Soter to arrest him. When Razes saw that he could not escape, he fell on his sword[96].

Ptolemy Macron was accused by Eupator and, in general, was considered to be a traitor. As he could not maintain the dignity of his office, in desperation, he took poison and so ended his life[97].

---

87. Genesis 50:2-3
88. *ibid* 50:26
89. Baba Bathra 3b
90. *Hist. Nat.* 22:50
91. *ibid* 7:56
92. Josephus. *Antiquities*. Book 14, Chapt. 7:4; *The Jewish War*. Book 1, Chapter 9:1

93. First Samuel 31:4
94. Second Samuel 17:23
95. First Kings 16:18
96. preferring to die nobly rather than to fall into the wretches' hands. Second Maccabees 14:41
97. *ibid* 10:13

In his misery, Job considered "strangulation, death by my own hands, but I reject it"[98]. The seven husbands of the daughter of Raguel died, and she was so distressed that she wished to hang herself[99].

Concerning the judgement of suicide in the eyes of contemporary people one must be very careful indeed in drawing conclusions from the above-cited instances[100]. Firstly, all these cases, if one can so state, are psychologically understandable. Each knew exactly what lay ahead for him if he remained alive, and one can readily *comprehend* that each preferred a rapid death to lengthy torture at the hands of the enemy. Furthermore, in all cases, we are dealing with very prominent people, and perhaps modern times are not the only eras which are lenient in their outlook towards suicides of sovereigns. The description of Razes and Ptolemy in the book of Maccabees, which was written in Greek, was definitely influenced by Greek thought, for these suicides are considered to be *noble* deeds. In no case are we dealing with suicide "during an attack of temporary insanity". In fact, Ahithophel even first set his house in order before he took his own life. The personality of Saul, as already previously clearly expounded, was mentally abnormal, but he was not induced by any mad notion to slay himself with the sword. An explicit sanctioning of his action, motivated by the circumstances he found himself in, is first found in the *Midrash*[101].

In the New Testament, one should mention the suicide of Judas Iscariot, who, according to the statement in Matthew[102], hanged himself. According to the story of the Apostles, he flung himself down from a roof[103]. He burst asunder in the midst, and all his intestines gushed out.

There is no doubt at all as to how the *Mishnah* views suicide. As a law book, it naturally does not engage in moral and philosophical considerations, but gives specific rules concerning the handling of the corpse of a person who committed suicide: "We do not occupy ourselves at all with the funeral rites of one who has committed suicide willfully." Rabbi Ishmael said: "we exclaim over him: Alas for a lost life[104], alas for a lost life"[105], to which Rabbi Akiba[106] retorts: "leave him unmourned; do not honor him but also do not curse him". One does not rend garments for him, nor do we remove our shoes for him, nor do we hold a wake for him, i.e. the remainder of the mourning ceremonial. However, we do comfort the bereaved relatives, for this shows respect for the living. The general rule is: the community occupies itself with him only in things which are considered respect for the living[107].

No distinction was made concerning the burial place. Ahithophel was buried in his father's grave. Judaism is thus more considerate than the Romans, who denied any kind of burial to a person who committed suicide. The Greeks buried their suicides in secrecy outside the cemetery, and chopped off the right hand of the corpse.

However, even the above rules of the *Mishnah* require certain qualifications: "who is considered to be in the category of having committed suicide willfully? Not the one who climbed to the top of a tree or to the top of a roof and fell down and died. (It may have been an accidental fall.) Rather one who calls out: 'Look, I am going to the top of the tree or the top of the roof, and I will throw myself down that I may die', and before the eyes of the onlookers (witnesses) climbs to the top of the tree, falls down and dies. If a person was found strangled, hanging from a tree, or lying dead on a sword, then he is considered to have committed suicide, but not willfully, and none of the rites

---

98. Job 7:15
99. Tobit 3:10
100. Preuss omits mention of the suicide of Samson (Judges 16:23-31)(F.R.)
101. Genesis Rabbah 34:13
102. Matthew 27:5
103. Acts 1:18

104. Probably a song of mourning and its refrain.
105. The Gaon Elijah of Vilna amends the phrase "lost life" to "hanged"
106. Preuss erroneously has Rabbi Eleazar (F.R.)
107. Semachoth 2:1

are withheld from him"[108]. Here, too, we use the principle of the courts in that a conviction can only be arrived at on the basis of testimony of witnesses, and, in cases of doubt, the accused receives the benefit of the doubt *(in dubiis pro reo)*.

The aforementioned section of the *Mishnah* also discusses child suicide which is usually considered to result from excesses in modern civilization: the son of Gornos of Lydda ran away from school and his father "pointed to his ear"[109]. In fear of his father, he went and "destroyed himself" with a garment[110]. Another child from Bene Berak broke a glass on the Sabbath; for the same reason as the above lad, he "destroyed himself" in a pit. From this the Sages learn that a man should not "point at the ear" of a child, but either punish him immediately or remain silent and say nothing[111].

It is noteworthy that the expression "he destroyed himself" is constantly used in regard to suicides, and not "he killed himself". Does one by these *words* mean to articulate *permanent* destruction, including the loss of one's portion in the world to come?

The *Gemara* has a rather rich casuistry on suicides: A certain student of the Sages once left his phylacteries in a niche while he went to the privy. A harlot passed by and stole them. She came to the house of learning and showed the phylacteries which she claimed the student gave her as payment for her hire. The student threw himself down from the roof of the house of learning and died[112].

Herod was a slave of the Maccabees. He wanted to marry the remaining daughter of the Maccabees after all the members of the family were murdered. She, however, threw herself down from the roof, and preferred self-inflicted death[113].

When Turnus Rufus destroyed the Temple, Rabbi Gamliel was sentenced to death. In order to prevent this calamity, the officer who was sent to arrest Rabbi Gamliel (obviously a secret follower of Gamliel) threw himself down from a roof and died. The others saw a bad omen in this act and annulled the decree[114].

During a time of famine, a man had only three pieces of meat which he set before three guests. His small son entered and each of the guests gave him their piece of meat. When the father entered the room and saw that the lad had all the food in his mouth and his hands, he angrily picked him up and flung him to the ground so that he died. When the mother saw her child dead, she threw herself down from the roof. The father, who only then came to an understanding of what he had done, committed the same act[115].

A woman waited vainly for her husband; she sat on the roof, "the roof collapsed, and she died"[116].

A man who had invited guests wished to serve them wine. When he saw that a barrel of oil rather than wine was sent to him, he hanged himself in anger[117].

Furthermore, Valeria (or Beruria), the wife of Rabbi Meir, is said to have hanged herself out of shame, because she was enticed by one of her husband's disciples[118].

Once four hundred Jewish boys and girls were on a ship. They were prisoners and were to be used for immoral purposes. When they recognized what lay ahead for them, the girls and then, following their example, the boys jumped into the sea and drowned[119].

---

108. *ibid* 2:2-3
109. i.e. threatened to punish him
110. or more correctly: in a pit
111. Semachoth 1:4-6
112. Berachoth 23a
113. Baba Bathra 3b
114. Taanith 29a
115. i.e. suicide. Derech Eretz Rabbah 9 fol.

57c
116. Kethuboth 62b. Others interpret that *he* was on the roof when it collapsed and *he* died.
117. Chullin 94a. The actual story is slightly different (F.R.)
118. *Rashi* on Abodah Zarah 18b
119. Gittin 57b

A palace eunuch, when reproached for his useless existence, struck his head against a wall until he died[120].

Finally, the story is told of Jakim, nephew of Rabbi Jose ben Jo'ezer, who subjected himself to all four modes of execution that the courts can inflict: he placed a post in the ground, to which he tied a rope, placed wood round about it and put stones thereon. In front of it he built a pile of logs[121] and fixed a sword in the middle. He kindled the wood under the stones and hanged himself on the post. When the rope was burned through, he fell into the fire, and the sword caught him, and the pile of stones fell on him simultaneously[122].

From Josephus, one can cite the following cases: an aged robber killed his son and then threw himself off a precipice[123]. Hyrcanus, the son of Joseph, killed himself in order not to be executed[124]. The suicide of Phasael[125]. The wife of Pharaoh threw herself from the roof but remained alive, for she landed on her feet[126]. Simon first killed his entire family, including parents, wife and children, and then pierced himself in the abdomen with the sword[127]. Soldiers killed themselves so as not to fall into the hands of the Roman enemy[128]. Finally, one should mention the suicide of the Roman general Otho[129].

Concerning the moral judgement about suicide, one should remember that when Job's wife demanded of him that he "curse God and die", he answered: *thou speakest as one of the foolish women*[130]. In the Talmud, even the Sage who allows self-wounding disallows suicide[131]. The *Midrash*[132] understands an explicit prohibition in the Biblical phrase: *and surely your blood of your lives will I require* (if you commit suicide)[133]. When Rabbi Chanina ben Teradion stood on the pile of logs at his martyrdom, his disciples called out to him: open your mouth so that the fire will enter your body more quickly! He answered: it is better for the One who gave me life to take it away from me, rather than I should bring about (i.e. hasten) my death[134].

Josephus speaks beautiful words against suicide[135]. To be sure, the entire discussion has the purpose of saving one's own life.

# V   Coffins

It is very doubtful whether bodies which were not transported to distant places (for example to Palestine) in ancient times were carried in coffins. The expression *aron,* which in the Bible[136] refers to the coffin of a mummy, is used in the *Mishnah*[137] to denote a section of graves in rocks (i.e. in caves). On the other hand, at the time of the *Gemara*, an *aron* of boards[138] or of stone[139] was known. According to legend, the Egyptians placed Joseph in a bronze coffin and sank it in the Nile[140]. Burial was carried out either in an *aron* of marble or wood; or on a base, *ritzpa* or *tabula*[141], made of stones or bricks or earth[142], whereby the body was either unclothed or clothed with a raiment. In the former case, and with the exclusive use of marble or stone, the

120. Eccles. Rabbah 10:7 fol. 26d
121. contrary to the usual interpretation of serepha
122. Genesis Rabbah 65:22; Midrash Psalms 11e p.52b
123. *Antiquities* Book 14; Chapt. 15:5
124. *ibid* 12; Chapt. 4:11
125. *ibid.* 15; Chapt. 2:1
126. *ibid.* 17; Chapt. 4:2
127. *The Jewish War.* Book 2; Chapt. 18:4
128. *ibid* 3; Chapt. 8:34
129. *ibid* 4; Chapt. 9:9
130. Job 2:9-10
131. Baba Kamma 91b
132. Genesis Rabbah and *Rashi* on 34:12; also Maimonides. *Hilchoth Rotzeach* 2:2
133. Genesis 9:5
134. Abodah Zarah 18a
135. *Antiquities.* Book 3; Chapter 8:5
136. Genesis 50:26
137. Oholoth 9:15
138. Moed Katan 8b
139. Jerushalmi Moed Katan 1; 80d
140. Sotah 13a
141. Jerushalmi Nazir 7; 56b
142. *Tosefta* Oholoth 2:3

decomposing matter, the *rakkab*, is exclusively derived from the corpse[143] (since no foreign matter can mix with the decaying corpse to neutralize it).

According to the most probable tradition, as expounded in the Palestinian (or Jerusalem) Talmud, corpses were first placed in caves; as soon as the soft parts putrefied, the bones were gathered and placed in a box of cedar wood[144]. This "gathering of bones" is frequently mentioned in Talmudic writings, and is also considered to be one of the holy duties[145].

Rabbi Yochanan, whose only surviving child fell into a cauldron filled with boiling water and died, carried a bone[146] of this child with him, which he showed to people whose fate had dealt them equally hard blows to console them[147]. Is this bone an analogue of the Roman *os reservatum?*

## VI  Graves

Two types of interment are described in the Bible: burial in natural or artifically produced caves, and burial in the earth. Abraham acquired a cave of volcanic limestone from the Hittites and adopted it as a family burial site[148]. Besides him, it is also the resting place of Sarah, Isaac, Rebekah, Leah and the mummy of Jacob. These graves were disturbed by friars from Hebron in the year 1119 who sold the remaining bones as religious relics in the Occident[149]. Already in the time of Isaiah "one hewed oneself a sepulchre during one's lifetime"[150]. The body of Jesus was also brought to the sepulchre which Joseph of Arimathias had hewn out of a cliff for himself in order to be buried there one day[151]. Occasionally, imposing monuments were found over such tombs, as in the case of the Maccabees[152] and Queen Helena[153].

This type of grave is not specifically Jewish, but was the custom of the land. The Hittites offered Abraham that he bury his spouse *in the choice of our sepulchres; none of us shall withhold from thee his sepulchre*[154].

A grave in the ground, as we understand it today, is not mentioned at all in the Bible. Although Deborah, Rachel, Miriam and many others died during the wanderings of the Jews, so that sepulchres could not be readily procured for them, there is no statement in the Bible that would indicate that a tomb was placed in the earth and the corpse lowered into it and then covered with earth. It is probable that, in these cases, sand was poured over the body as it lay *on* the ground, or, as was once done for the slain Absalom, a great heap of rocks was erected[155]. The same was applicable in normal times. Nowhere do we find an expression which refers with certainty to an earthen grave. The original meaning of the word *keber,* as shown in the Syrian, has the sense of "heaping up", and could refer equally to a heap of wheat as to the heap of earth poured on a corpse which is lying on the ground. However, such graves were the exceptions. Concerning the "earth mounds, *teloloth,* near the city", it is explicitly stated that "women and lepers, respectively, buried their aborted fetuses and their leprous limbs there"[156].

It is first in a recent *Midrash* that a grave, according to our present concept, is mentioned. The parents of the slain Abel sat near the body, not knowing what to do with the corpse. They beheld a raven burying its dead comrade by digging *(chaphar)* in the earth, and they did the same with the body of their son[157]. He

143. Niddah 27b and Nazir 51a
144. Jerushalmi Moed Katan 1; 80c
145. Semachoth 12:49c
146. some say a tooth
147. Berachoth 5b
148. Genesis 23:1-20
149. if this commerce was not a swindle
150. Isaiah 22:16

151. Matthew 27:60
152. First Maccabees 13:27
153. Josephus. *The Jewish War.* Book 5 Chapt. 4:1
154. Genesis 23:6
155. Second Samuel 18:17
156. *Tosefta* Oholoth 16:1
157. *Yalkut* 38 on Genesis 4:10

who wishes to express this type of burial uses the phrase *kabur ve chaphur*[158].

The entrance to a sepulchre was sealed, as is well-known from the story of Jesus[159], and as often indicated in the *Mishnah* by the word *golal,* an object that can be rolled away (*galal* means to roll), usually a large stone which is at all times prevented from rolling away by a wedge stone, the *dophak,* which is placed underneath the stone to support it. The wedge stone itself is held in place by a buttressing stone, *dophek dophekim*[160]. Instead of a stone, a leaning or standing beam could be used to close a tomb, and where necessary, even a barrel was placed in front of the tomb, or an animal was tied there[161].

As a rule, such sepulchres were established as a family burial place. In fact, civil law arranged standards therefor. If someone buys a place from another to make a *keber* (grave site) for himself, or accepts from his fellow the mandate to prepare such a burial ground for others, then the following implied conditions prevail: he must make the inside of the vault, *me'ara,* 4 by 4 by 6 cubits, and open therein eight crypts, *kukin,* three on each long side and two opposite the entrance. Each crypt *(kuk)* must be four cubits long — the average length of a person —, seven handbreadths high, and one cubit wide. At the entrance to the vault, there should be an anteroom in which the bier, the *mittah,* could be put down. According to Rabbi Simeon ben Gamliel, there are no general rules regarding the size of the anteroom, or for the number and size of the individual graves; all depends on the character of the *rock*[162]. Thus, here too, the word *keber* or grave is understood without question to mean a vault (literally: rock grave) with crypts in which the bodies are pushed in lengthwise; that is, *keber* is the all-encompassing term, whereas *kuk* only represents one part thereof, namely, the crypt. Later, at the time of the *Gemara,* the term *kuk* meant a grave hewn out of rock, and *keber* designated a tomb built above ground[163].

A. Berliner describes such Jewish vaults (catacombs) which are still extant in Rome[164].

The *Tosefta* also describes a "field of *kukin* within which a family burial site was lost"[165]. Apparently, as a rule, the underground passageway was lined with bricks, but not the crypts. Therefore, it was possible that later, if the upper level of the crypt collapsed, a ploughshare, in tilling the land, would grasp the bones and break them. Such a ploughed area was called *beth-haperas,* an area of pieces[166]. It could also happen that one might purely by accident discover a mortar with bones in it in such a vault[167], or fall into a vault because of ploughing above it[168]. For a graveyard, the name *beth ha-kebaroth* (place of graves) was considered more appropriate.

One looked with favor upon a grave that was placed under a tree[169], just as Deborah, the wet-nurse of Rebekah, was buried under a tamarisk tree[170], so that occasionally the tree grew through the body, and when a storm overturned it, unexpectedly a skull would be hanging from the roots[171].

Burial sites had to be 50 cubits distant from the wall of the city[172]. For walled cities (literally: fortresses), there existed a specific prohibition against burying the dead within the walls of the city[173]. Especially strict regulations existed for Jerusalem. One

158. Aboth de Rabbi Nathan 31:1
159. Matthew 27:60
160. Oholoth 2:4; see particularly *Yoreh Deah* 373, note 8 of *Be'er Hetev*
161. Oholoth 15:8-9
162. Baba Bathra 6:8
163. Moed Katan 8b
164. *Geschichte der Juden in Rom.* Frankfurt a. M. 1893 p.51 ff
165. *Tosefta* Oholoth 17:11
166. Oholoth 17:1. According to Löw in Krauss' *Lehnwörter* 2:492: *forum,* anteroom
167. *Tosefta* Niddah 8:6
168. Niddah 24b
169. *ibid* 57a
170. Genesis 35:8
171. *Tosefta* Niddah 8:5
172. Baba Bathra 2:9
173. Kelim 1:7

is not permitted to keep a corpse there overnight, nor pile up[174] human bones, nor erect monuments. Since the time of the prophets, only the royal house of King David and the family of the prophetess Huldah were privileged to have ancestral burial places in Jerusalem itself[175]. Below that site, there were vaults from which streams flowed to the brook of Kidron[176]. The grave was thus drained. On the other hand, it was strictly forbidden to course a stream of water through a burial site, or to place water pipes there, or to allow cattle to graze there; nor should grass be plucked from there[177]. A water channel that comes from a burial site is unclean[178]. Among the eighteen things which are harmful to one's mind is the drinking of water from a channel that flows through a cemetery[179].

The Talmud also mentions "The Sepulchre of the Pious" and "The Sepulchre of the Judges". For burial in either of these places, certain conditions had to be fulfilled; unless the whole story is only a legend[180].

For the executed, there was a separate burial site. After the decomposition of the body, one gathered the bones, and brought them to the family plot[181]. As already mentioned, for suicides there were no corresponding separate regulations.

It is uncertain whether an exception to the rule for lepers is implied in the story of King Uzziah. It is told that the deceased leprous king was buried *in the fields of the burial which belonged to the kings* (and not in the *me'ara*), *for they said: he is a leper*[182]. The leprosy of the king occurred under such unusual circumstances that even the burial might be a continuation of the punishment.

The burial site is inviolable forever; it is a *beth olam,* a house of eternity[183]. A limited "cemetery repose" does not exist in Jewish law. A vault is only opened in order to add a new body or to transfer the bones to a place of honor. In addition, a grave which is harmful to society may be moved to another place[184]. Other reasons are not decisive. In an inheritance dispute, the disinherited family protested, saying that the deceased had not yet reached puberty (and, therefore, could not legally disinherit them) and was not capable of testifying. They demanded that the grave be opened and the body be examined for signs of puberty. The court ruled that to exhume the body was not allowable to obtain evidence, because a body may not be moved from its place once the tombstone *(golal)* has closed the grave[185].

The Persians considered earth and fire to be holy, and, therefore, set out their bodies as booty for jackals. In their fanaticism, they opened the vaults of strangers in order to discard the bodies and to use the coffins as cribs for their horses[186]. Their King Shapur (beginning of the 4th century) asked the Jews whether there existed a Biblical commandment to bury in the ground or whether it was purely a custom which they could readily abandon for the sake of amity. The answer obviously was the former of these two possibilities[187]. When Samuel warns that *the Lord will be against you, and against your fathers*[188], he is referring to the "exhumation of the dead"[189].

During an epidemic or during a war, the ownership rights to a family burial site need not be respected. Bodies are buried wherever it is possible[190]. If it was at all possible, however, one attempted to bury even those fallen in war in the burial sites of

---

174. ma'amidim: Tosefta Negaim 6:2; so too Maimonides. Beth Habechira 7:14; variant tzoberin; Aboth de Rabbi Nathan 35:2 has ma'abirin. The entire passage is missing in Baba Kamma 82b
175. Tosefta Negaim 6:2 and Semachoth 14:10
176. Tosefta Baba Bathra 1:11
177. Megilla 29a
178. Yadayim 4:7
179. Horayoth 13b
180. Moed Katan 17a

181. Sanhedrin 6:6
182. Second Chronicles 26:23
183. Eccles. 12:5
184. Sanhedrin 47b
185. Semachoth 4:12; also Baba Bathra 154a
186. Sanhedrin 98b
187. ibid 46b
188. First Samuel 12:15
189. Yebamoth 63b
190. Semachoth 14:4 ff

their relatives[191]. The corpses of the enemy were at least thrown into a pit[192]. Even those executed were buried, as already mentioned[193]. Only rarely does one not hinder a dog from licking the blood of a criminal[194]. However, the criminal is not excluded from burial. The assertion of Josephus, that a person who committed suicide is left unburied until after sundown[195] is simply not true.

# VII

Anyone who touches a grave is considered by the Bible to be unclean[196]. The consequences of this ritual uncleanness were that the affected person was not permitted to enter into the Temple, nor was he allowed to touch any object which was destined to be used in the Temple. It was, therefore, important, particularly for those who made the pilgrimage to Jerusalem for the three pilgrimage festivals[197], to scrupulously avoid graves. This was extremely difficult because, scattered throughout the entire country, there were grottos and sepulchres from the outside of which it was not possible to recognize whether or not a corpse was contained therein. Therefore the necessity arose to identify burial sites prior to the festivals[198]. This was accomplished by white-washing them. The white color was also reminiscent of the color of the bones[199]. Another coat of paint was even applied during the intermediate days of the festival, just in case the first coat was washed away by rain[200]. A disinfection, as suggested by some zealous exegetes, was naturally not intended or accomplished by this painting.

# VIII   Burial Delay

If the corpse of a person stoned to death by court decree is then hanged to emphasize the punishment, one may not under any circumstances leave it on the post overnight, but one must bury it the same day, for "a hanged person is painful to God"[201]. The hanging of a live person "as was practiced by the Roman government"[202] does not exist in the Jewish penal code. If the sight of even an unburied criminal is already painful for God, how much more so an unburied righteous person. Therefore, no body should remain unburied overnight, except if one still has to make certain necessary arrangements for its honor[203], or if one wishes to transport the body to Palestine, as was done in the cases of Jacob and Joseph. Let he who takes offense at this haste in burying the dead reflect on the following: that decomposition of bodies occurs more rapidly in the Orient than in our latitude, that the customary "interment" is hardly comparable to our transfer of the body to the mortuary (for their bodies were probably not placed in coffins), and that finally, as already stated, the dead were observed for an additional three days for possible signs of life.

Only for one's father's or mother's burial should one not unduly hurry, unless pressing causes are present, such as, for example, to remove the body from the rain[204]. It is difficult to accept as historic fact the story that the body of Rabbi Eleazar, son of Rabbi Simeon, according to his own wish, was kept in an upper chamber for more than

---

191. Second Maccabees 12:39
192. Jeremiah 41:9
193. See also Josephus. *Antiquities*. Book 4 Chapt. 8:24 and Book 5 Chapt. 1:14
194. Second Kings. 9:36: Jezebel; Jerushalmi Terumoth 1; 45c
195. *The Jewish War*. Book 3 Chapt. 3:5
196. Numbers 19:18
197. Exodus 23:17
198. Shekalim 1:1

199. Baba Kamma 69a
200. Jerushalmi Shekalim 1; 46a
201. This is the interpretation of the Mishnah of *killelath hashem* of Deut. 21:23. The usual translation is *he that is hanged is accursed of God*. See also Josephus. *The Jewish War*. Book 4, Chapter 5:2
202. Sanhedrin 46b
203. Sanhedrin 4:5
204. Semachoth 9:9 and fol. 48a

twenty years[205]; or the story of Rabbi Chiya ben Abuya who wrapped the skull of King Jehoiakim in silk, and preserved it in a chest[206].

Also among the Greeks, speedy burial was the rule. Already in Homer the burial of Patroclus was requested by his friend as follows: "bury me as soon as possible"[207]. Additional quotations are cited by Becker in his *Charikles,* Leipzig 1840, 2:178 ff.

# IX    Cremation

Numerous other reminiscences for the above-depicted customs are found in Greece and in Rome. Even here, every owner of a field originally had his burial place prepared in that field. Only for the ownerless and for foreigners did there exist common graves *(puticuli)* outside the city walls. Those who owned houses in the city of Rome were buried in the garden of their property, until the Law of the Twelve Tablets prohibited any burial within the city. Even here, the graves were only laid out as trenches, as most clearly demonstrated by archeological excavations.

In the aforementioned Law of the Twelve Tablets, there is found the custom of cremation next to the discussion of burial: *hominem mortuum in urbe ne sepelito neve urito*[208]. According to the assertion of Plinius (7:54), the above was the origin of the custom of cremation, which was only established later as a result of numerous wars. In Greece, both forms of burial were no doubt customary during all epochs. The cadaver was first burned on a funeral pile, either over a grave or at a special crematorium; then the smouldering cinders were extinguished, the bones were collected and dried and placed in an urn. Only several days later was the latter secretly buried in a grave or in a burial monument. The Talmud also presumes that the Romans practiced cremation when it quotes Titus as having said: "burn me and strew my ashes over the sea"[209].

The Jewish writer explains that graven images originated from the godless custom of making a picture of the deceased carved in wood[210].

# X    Cremation in the Bible

The accounts of cremation in *Jewish* antiquity are mostly based on an erroneous interpretation of the Biblical passage in question. It was prophesied for King Zedekiah: *thou shalt die in peace, and with the burnings of thy fathers, the former kings which were before thee, so shalt they burn for thee*[211]. King Asa was laid in a bed which was filled with herbs and spices prepared according to the apothecary's art; and they made a very great burning *for him*[212]. On the other hand, for Jehoram, they made no burning, like the burnings they made for his fathers[213]. One, therefore, burnt *for* the king, but not the king himself. That which was burned for the king we learn from the *Tosefta:* his bed and his utensils[214]. This burning originated as a heathen custom, and one made no secret of the fact that one would never again have permitted it, had not the Bible mentioned it without any critical comment, thus giving it silent approval. One thus allowed it as a national honor *(chaschibutha),* and, in fact, even furnished it for the Jewish Princes of the Exile, but not unanimously[215]. When Rabban Gamliel the Elder died, the proselyte Onkelos burned spices worth seventy talents[216].

The entire establishment of kingship in Israel is only a concession to the wish of the people: *and when thou shalt say: I will set a king over me, like as all the nations that*

---

205. Baba Metzia 84b
206. Sanhedrin 82a
207. *Iliad* 23:71
208. Cicero, *De Lege* 2:23
209. Gittin 56b
210. Apocrypha. Wisdom of Solomon 14:15

211. Jeremiah 34:5
212. Second Chronicles 16:14
213. *ibid* 21:19
214. *Tosefta* Shabbath 7:18
215. Semachoth Chapt. 9
216. Abodah Zarah 11a

*are about me; then thou shalt in any wise set him king over thee*[217]. One should also compare First Samuel, Chapter 8 and Judges 8:23. However, once this concession was made, one simultaneously adopted various practices for the king from heathendom, by which one thought to honor him and his position. Among these are ceremonies relating to the dead. Indeed, the burning of a fortune of spices involves a great squandering of money and is prohibited by the Bible[218]. It is also an abominable cruelty against animals — the prohibition of which is likewise deduced from the Bible[219] — to sever the sinews of the king's horse so that no one else can make any further use thereof[220]. However, one overlooked this prohibition, if done for the king. King Solomon is supposed to have placed untold treasures in the grave of King David[221], so that Johanan Hyrcanus, who broke open the grave, was able to remove 3000 talents of silver therefrom[222]. In spite of this, the *Tosaphoth*[223] specifically state that this is all a frivolous and absurd practice. For private people, it was specifically prohibited[224].

Such a prohibition was obviously necessary for there was an early propensity toward the development of luxurious practices during burial[225]. Gradually, the expenses of the funeral became more difficult for the relatives of a deceased person than the death itself, so that some people let their dead lie and ran away, until Rabbi Gamliel made an example of himself in arranging for a simple funeral, which then all the people emulated[226]. He is said to have been buried in a single garment (shirt), according to his own wish, for he intended to convey thereby the fact that a person does not arise again in the clothes with which he leaves this world[227].

Extraordinary is the case of Saul. His sons were killed in battle, and he threw himself upon his sword, as did his armor bearer. In a search of the battlefield, the Philistines found his corpse, cut off its head, and nailed it to the wall of the city with the other corpses[228]. Men from Gilead learned of it, marched a whole night in order to steal the corpses and burn them at that very place (where ?). And they took the bones of the dead and buried them under the palm tree in Jabesh[229]. Here the burning was no doubt motivated by the fact that the corpses had already markedly decomposed through prolonged lying (unburied), so that to transport them *in toto* was not possible *(Kimchi)*. Moreover, neither the report of Chronicles[230] nor Josephus mentions this. The other commentaries and translations consider here, too, the burning of spices, or even embalming[231].

Two other places in the Bible are frequently quoted. The prophet proclaims that God will punish Moab because he burned the bones of the King of Edom to lime[232]. King Josiah, who energetically cleared away all idolatry, saw the sepulchres that were there in the mountain, and had the bones removed from the graves and burned them upon the altar[233]. And he also slew all the idolatrous priests that were still alive, and burned their bones on their altars[234]. The first case is not at all concerned with Jews, and the second is an exception and based on the reasoning of officials, which proves nothing for normal times.

217. Deut. 17:14-15
218. *ibid* 20:19, according to the Talmudic interpretation
219. Baba Metzia 31a
220. Abodah Zarah 11a
221. Josephus. *Antiquities.* Book 7 Chapter 15:3
222. *ibid* Book 13, Chapter 8:14
223. *loc. cit. s.v. wei'*
224. *Tosefta* Shabbath 7:18
225. See the teaching of Rabbi Yannai in Niddah 61b
226. *Tosefta* Niddah 9:17
227. Jerushalmi Kilayim 9: 32b
228. Josephus. *Antiquities.* Book 6, Chapt. 14:8
229. First Samuel 31:1-13
230. Second Chronicles 10:12
231. See *Tosafoth Yom Tov* on Pesachim 4:9
232. Amos 2:1
233. Second Kings 23:16
234. *ibid*

## XI   Cremation in the Talmud

It is not easy to give a precise answer as to the status of cremation in the Talmud. Apparently in specific places and at certain times the influence of the neighboring Greeks was dominant. On the occasion of a pure ritual decision, Rabbi Shabthai mentions a body which was burned, but in such a manner that the skeleton *(scheled)* remained intact. In the discussion, there is even a controversy over whether one is dealing with cremation on a *katabla* or on an *ephodrin,* expressions which obviously belong to the Greek language, although I cannot identify them yet *(katavolé and ephedron* have different meanings)[235]. The Talmud also speaks of a singeing (slight burning) of the abdomen[236]. In a related question, the *Mishnah* speaks of the "ashes of burned corpses"[237]. Furthermore, there is a discussion of the decision in an inheritance dispute, where the testator made the specific request: "burn me"; or where he said:"perform a certain task with my body"[238].

This narrative has no analogue in the entire Talmud, and is strongly incompatible with other statements concerning the burial of the dead. No commentator has been successful in clarifying this matter. (That which Rabbi Asher teaches on the above-cited *Mishnah* is not to be taken seriously). One should also not think that the Talmud, in reality, constructed a hypothetical or impossible legal case, as it often does, in order to sharpen the mind through the controversy of the Sages; for it explicitly speaks of an actual case *(ma'aseh).* Perhaps it refers to the case of a criminal who was burned on a funeral pile, contrary to the traditional teaching concerning execution through death by fire[239]. Sadducees and unlearned judges, in fact, are said to have proceeded in this manner[240]. Also, in the earlier-mentioned case of the suicide of Jakim[241], this type of punishment and execution is presupposed. It certainly does not refer to the accidental burning of a person during a conflagration. However, it follows from the above inheritance law, that cremation was not a general custom.

A not uncommon curse for evildoers states that even their bones should be burned[242] or pulverized[243].

## XII   Decomposition of Bodies

During the course of decomposition of a corpse, the soft parts disintegrate *(nithakel),* in that they become *nakal.* According to the explanation of the *Gemara,* this means that the flesh of the dead becomes coagulated *(karash,* like blood), whereas the juice *(mohal)* simmers; that is, it allows air bubbles to develop[244]. Or it turns to *rakab,* i.e. disintegrates into a powder[245]. Even the hair changes its consistency[246]. The bones last the longest. It is in them that the grave digger Abba Saul tried to recognize the owner's mode of life: "the bones of he who imbibed undiluted wine during his lifetime look burned; if he diluted the wine too much, his bones look black (or fatless, dried). If the mixture of wine and water was appropriate, the bones look fatty. The bones of someone who drinks more than he eats appear burned; if he eats excessively, they appear fatless; if he eats normally, they look fatty"[247].

Gradually, even the bones disintegrate *(dikdek)*[248]. Only the *luz* bone of the vertebral column is indestructible. The legends on this matter have already been described above[249].

---

235. "origin" and "reserve", respectively
236. Niddah 28a
237. Oholoth 2:2
238. Jerushalmi Kethuboth 11; 34b
239. *Serefah* see Sanhedrin 52a, where execution by fire is described
240. Sanhedrin 52b
241. see part 3, section IV, above

242. Jerushalmi Shebiith 8; 38b
243. for example Genesis Rabbah 28:3
244. Nazir 50a
245. Oholoth 2:1
246. Semachoth 4:12
247. Niddah 24a
248. Oholoth 2:7
249. see above chapter 2, part 2

# PART   4
# ABLUTIONS AND BATHS

## I

In the mode of life of the Orientals, ablutions and baths play a much greater role than in ours. They are, by virtue of the climate, a necessity. Particular attention is devoted to care of the feet, which, protected at best by sandals, suffer the most from walking on the hot sandy ground. 'Modes of transportation other than one's own feet did not generally exist for the average person, even for distant journeys. If a man owned a donkey or even a camel, he would probably let his wife and children ride thereon. He would also load his possessions and his cargo thereon, but would himself walk on foot. The same was true of the usage of wagons; they, too, served only to transport loads, women and children[250], or at most for the journeys of princely people[251]. The use of litters, in which one was carried, first became customary in post–Biblical times. For the general public, naturally, even these were out of the question.

The custom of offering water to travelers to wash their feet is characteristic of the entire Orient. According to the Biblical account, not only did Abraham[252] and his brother's son Lot[253] invite their guests to wash their feet and remain overnight, but also the Egyptians[254] and the heathen Gibeonites[255] indulged in this practice of hospitality. Jesus reproached Simon as follows: I came into your house and you gave me no water for my feet. The sinful woman washed his feet with her tears and dried them with her hair[256]. Upon returning from a journey[257], and every evening before retiring[257a], the feet are cleansed. A "millionaire", upon returning home from his fields, has his maidservant bring him a kettle of hot water with which he washes his hands and feet. Then one brings him a golden utensil with oil in which he immerses his hands and feet[258].

According to Rabbi Huna, it is the obligation of every woman to wash the face, hands and feet of her husband, even if she maintains four domestic servants which she brought to the marriage with her dowry, and even if she is accustomed to giving orders from the cathedra, the elevated family seat in the woman's chambers[259]. A master may not have his feet washed or his shoes put on by his Hebrew slave, nor support himself on the latter's haunches when he (the master) climbs stairs; for he (the slave) is "your brother". However, one is certainly permitted to have these services performed by one's son or by one's disciples[260]. Abigail volunteered herself to the lowest form of servitude, to wash the feet of the slaves[261]. Even in Egyptian slavery, each woman placed a pot of hot water for a footbath on the hearth, every day, for her husband[262]. A special tub for footbaths, arebath ha-raglayim, is mentioned in the Mishnah[263].

"Foot washing" as a sign of humility is still today a prescribed and observed ceremonial of the Catholic church.

---

250. Genesis 45:19
251. First Samuel 8:11
252. Genesis 18:4
253. ibid 19:2
254. ibid 24:32
255. Judges 19:21
256. Luke 7:44
257. Second   Samuel   11:8;   Jerushalmi Berachoth 2; 5b
257a. Song of Songs 5:3

258. Menachoth 85b
259. This name is the same in Rome; to the Greeks it is thronos (throne) or thiphrax (seat). Böttiger, Sabina. Szenen aus dem Putzzimmer einer Römerin. Leipzig 1806, 1:35
260. Mechilta Mishpatim 1, p.75 a–b
261. First Samuel 25:41
262. Sotah 11b
263. Yadayim 4:1

The *hands* must be washed first every morning upon arising[264]. For the ritual obligatory hand washing, the expression used is always *netilath yadayim*, whereas ordinary washing is called *rechitzah*. There is also an obligation to wash one's hands before meals. According to the tradition of the Talmud, this obligation originally existed only for the consumption of sacrifices and priestly dues[265]. Only later was it extended by analogy *(serek)* from the former decree to also include, for sanitary reasons[266], the consumption of profane (non-holy) foods. As far as one conceived of this obligation of hand washing as being a religious rite, it remained limited to the consumption of bread, which constituted the major part of the meal. For reasons of cleanliness, however, it was practiced even prior to the consumption of other foods, such as fruit[267].

The guests present at a banquet given by the master of the house would each wash the hand with which they intended to touch the customary goblet prior to the meal, for sanitary reasons[268]. Then everybody would be seated at regular seats for the meal, and then everyone would again wash his hands before one began eating[269].

Some people wanted to give the appearance of exceptional holiness by repeated washings, so that Rabbi Nachman said: "he who (ritually) washes his hands before eating fruit does it only out of arrogance"[270].

As is well known, Jesus and his followers, to the vexation of the Jews, did not observe the law concerning hand washing. From the reprimand with which Jesus rebuked his host in discussing this matter, one cannot conclude with certainty whether Jesus neglected this hand washing ritual in principle[271]; nor can we conclude it from the answer of the scribe[272].

The habit of eating with one's fingers probably led to the custom of washing the hands *after* the meal. Whereas the washing before the meal, however, was (and is) only considered a religious obligation *(mitzvah)*, the washing after the meal is regarded as a *chova*, an obligation motivated by the consideration of one's health. The rule of "after the meal water" was motivated by the assumption that there existed "Sodomite salt", which blinds the eyes if someone to whose fingers such salt adheres rubs his eyes. Although only one kernel of such salt is found in a bushel of salt, this kernel might just be the one to remain adherent to the fingers. For washing after the meal, *cold* water was recommended; warm water makes the hands soft and cracked, so that the dirt is absorbed[273]. One also used to rub one's hands with oil after the meal[274].

According to popular belief, the demon *shibbetha* rests on hands which have not been washed[275]. Whenever he possessed any medicinal substance, Rabbi Huna was accustomed to hang a pitcher of it at the end of his house and say: "he who has need of it may come and take it." According to another interpretation, he believed in the *shibbetha,* and hung a pitcher with water over his door so that everyone who entered his house would first wash his hands, so as not to be harmed[276].

When water was difficult to obtain, one used to wrap the hands in a napkin; particularly sensitive people, *astheneis*[277], did the same, although they had washed their hands[278].

In order to stress and emphasize the importance of these washings, the following two stories are related, which can here simultaneously serve as examples of how one

264. Shabbath 109a
265. *ibid* 14b
266. *Tosafoth* Chullin 106a
267. Chullin 106a
268. *Tosafoth* Chagigah 18b *s.v. hanotel*
269. Berachoth 43a
270. Chullin 106a
271. Luke 11:37 ff
272. Matthew 15:2
273. Chullin 105a–b
274. Berachoth 53b
275. Yoma 77b; see Abaye
276. Taanith 20b
277. Jerushalmi Berachoth 8; 12a
278. Chullin 107a–b

attempted to impress the people with health regulations. Firstly, during the persecution of Jews under Hadrian, a Jewish innkeeper, in order not to be recognized as a Jew, also sold pork meat. If someone did not wash his hands before he ate, the innkeeper assumed he was a heathen and served him pork. If someone washed his hands first, the innkeeper recognized him as a Jew and served him other foods. Once a Jew lodged at the inn and sat down at the table to eat without having washed his hands. The innkeeper, assuming he was a heathen, served him pork. While the guest was paying his bill, he learned of what he ate; his hair stood on end and he was terribly frightened. He exclaimed: "you served me pork"! Whereupon the innkeeper rebuked him (for not having washed his hands before the meal)[279].

The second story concerns a man who ate peas at lunchtime and left the table without washing. A swindler noticed the food remnants on his fingers and went to his wife with an alleged request of the husband to obtain money. As a legitimation he declared: "you ate peas for lunch", whereupon the woman handed him the money. When the husband returned and learned of the deception, he chased his wife away in anger. According to another more terrifying interpretation, he killed her on the spot[280].

One is reminded of these stories by the brief expressions: because of the "water before the meal" a person ate pork, and because of the "water after the meal" a woman was expelled[281]. Since no Sodomite salt exists in our times, the custom of washing after the meals ceased[282].

He who has blood let and then does not wash his hands will be frightened for seven days without knowing why. He who has a haircut and does not wash will be frightened for three days. He who cuts his nails and does not wash will be alarmed for one day[283]. These rules, although quite rational themselves, obviously owe their primitive warnings to the influence of Persian demon teachings. In post-Talmudic times, particularly in the Middle Ages, numerous regulations concerning the washing of hands were promulgated, all of which had justifiable reasons: following removal of one's boots with one's hands; after touching naked feet; after scratching one's head; after coitus; and after touching the body[284]. Here, too, rinsing one's mouth in the morning is prescribed[285].

Mar Samuel teaches that the skin of one who washes his *face* without drying it well will crack open and become covered with scales. To heal such a person, one must wash diligently with mangold water[286]. Mar Zutra correctly conjectures that a person who washes his hands and then wipes them in someone else's coat is in other matters also not particular with "mine" and "yours"[287].

Cleanliness in general is constantly alluded to with great emphasis, for external cleanliness leads to internal purity[288].

## II    Ritual Baths

*Full ritual baths* in the Bible are nearly exclusively mentioned in connection with ceremony. The High Priest bathed on the Day of Atonement[289]. Also, anyone who ate of forbidden foods[290] or touched a corpse or one of the eight "unclean" small animals[291] took a full "ritual" bath. Often we find the regulation requiring a bath in

279. Numbers Rabbah 20:21
280. Yoma 83b
281. Chullin 106a
282. *Tosafoth* Berachoth 53b; *Tosafoth* Chullin 105a *s.v. mayim*
283. Pesachim 112a
284. *Orach Chayim* 4:18

285. *ibid* 4:17
286. Shabbath 134b
287. Baba Metzia 24a
288. Abodah Zarah 20a
289. Levit. 16:24
290. *ibid* 17:15
291. *ibid* 11:32

relation to corporeal conditions: after cohabitation, for both partners[292], as well as after involuntary ejaculation[293]. A person with gonorrhea bathes at the onset of his healing[294], and a person with leprosy after he is healed, twice in seven days[295].

For a menstruating woman and, in general, for any bleeding woman, and for a parturient woman after the conclusion of her puerperium, the Bible, although not explicitly, prescribes a cleansing bath. It was certainly in usage since the earliest times, possibly already alluded to in Zechariah 13:1; and it is undoubtedly stressed in the numerous accounts thereof in the *Mishnah*. Moreover, it would be most unusual to require a full bath for someone who touched a bleeding woman or her bed, if this obligation for the woman herself (the "source of the infection") were not self-evidently presupposed. In these rules, one cannot resist the impression that these baths in general served the purposes of cleanliness and body hygiene. One must constantly, however, keep in mind that none of these reasons are found in the ancient writings. These rules of ritual baths were established without further motivation.

The regular expression for these "ritual" baths in the Talmud is *tevila,* an immersion bath, as opposed to *rechitza* which is a bath for other purposes, such as for bodily hygiene. The former is usually a cold bath, the latter warm, although there are exceptions to both, which will be discussed later.

Tradition teaches that these baths, as with all rules concerning "cleanliness"[296], only had application with respect to Temple activities. He who wished to enter the Temple or touch objects destined for Temple use had to be "clean"; and to achieve this cleanliness, in case anyone became affected by any one of the aforementioned impurities, a ritual bath was required. With the destruction of the Temple, therefore, all these regulations concerning baths lost their practical significance. However, two exceptions exist.

1. Adjacent to the *Biblical* precept to bathe after every *ejaculatio seminis*[297], which, as already stated, was only prescribed for activities related to the Temple, there also existed another requirement, which dates back to Ezra, in which a *man* must bathe after every ejaculation, whether *intra coitum* or not, before he again occupies himself with the study of the laws of the Torah. This study of the Torah is among the most important obligations of the daily life of every person. This "decree of Ezra" had the specific purpose of restraining people from all too excessive cohabitation, through the inconvenience of (repeated ritual) bathing. The result, however, was .not the desired one, in that some people neglected the study of the Torah and some people refrained longer from cohabitation; whereas the desirable goal was the propagation of the people[298].

During the time of Rabbi Joshua ben Levi, the women in Galilee remained barren because the men refused to bathe in the severe cold[299]. Rabbi Huna, therefore, said that for this purpose a bath in a Turkish bath (literally: steam bath) is sufficient, an opinion which Rabbi Chisda strongly opposed. Rabbi Zera sat in a warm water basin in the steam bath and had his servant pour nine measures of water over him. The majority of the Sages, however, still required the ritual immersion bath discussed above. This interpretation must, at least for a certain time, have been the prevailing view. It is related that a man wanted to force a girl "to act sinfully with him". When she called out to him "where will you later get water for the prescribed bath?", he let her go[300]. Even more drastic is the story in the Palestinian Talmud: a vineyard

---

292. *ibid* 15:18
293. Deut. 23:12
294. Levit. 15:13
295. *ibid* 14:8
296. see above part 2 of this chapter

297. Levit. 15:18
298. Berachoth 22a
299. Jerushalmi Berachoth 1:6c
300. Berachoth 22a

watchman wanted to meddle with a married woman; while they were looking for an immersion bath, people came upon them and the sin did not take place[300a]. Simultaneously, from this story one observes how seriously the people took this "decree of Ezra", in that they were more concerned with it than with the Biblical law which for adultery prescribes the death penalty for both partners[301]. Some people, who perhaps formed a separate sect, bathed regularly *every* morning, probably for moral reasons, so as not to draw attention through a morning immersion to the fact that they had become unclean "by virtue of a nocturnal emission".

The "decree of Ezra" is not at all concerned with the bath that *women* take after cohabitation which is required by the Bible[302]. However, even this bath for men was not preserved. Rabbi Zera speaks of a formal abolition thereof in the Talmud[303], whereas Maimonides asserts that this bath was never in general use, and, where it was practiced, its use gradually ceased [304].

2. The condition of "impurity" in which a woman is placed because of bleeding from the genitalia, whether physiological (menstruation, parturition) or due to illness, represents a hindrance not only in regard to Temple activities, but also in regard to her husband. For cohabitation with a woman "during the impurity of her blood flow"[305] is, according to Biblical law, a crime punishable with the death penalty, even though the conviction and execution of sentence was not to be carried out by an earthly court. This "impurity" does not disappear by itself with the cessation of the blood flow, but requires a ritual bath to set it aside. The validity of this bath naturally remained even after the destruction of the Temple; it occurs after the very end of a period of bleeding. Only after the woman has taken the ritual bath does cohabitation become permissible again.

Because of the severity of the threatened punishment, this bath was always meticulously observed. The Biblical precept which applies only for pollution: *he shall wash his entire flesh in water*[306], is extended to *every* ritual bath. It is only valid if there is no separation *(chatzitzah)* between the body and the water. For this reason, not only must all clothing and jewelry be removed, but the body must *first* be rid of all dirt (even under the nails), accidentally adherent blood, etc.[307]. From time immemorial, one, therefore, took a (warm) cleansing bath *before* entering the ritual immersion bath. One must remain cognizant of this fact, if one wishes to take offense at the observation, about which we will speak more later, that often many women make use of the same immersion bath. One wonders how infrequently the water is changed even in our own comfortable baths, and in what condition the numerous bodies are which simultaneously or consecutively bathe in larger numbers than is the case in ritual baths[308].

The regulation that *every* part of the body surface come in contact with the water has the result that one must also give consideration to the maintenance of the cleanliness of the *water*. Otherwise, if any object, no matter how small, accidentally adheres to the skin (for example, a hair floating in the water), it serves as a separation between the body and the water and thus renders the immersion invalid. The daughters of Mar Samuel, for this reason, when the river bed was loosened during the rainy

---

300a. Jerushalmi Berachoth 1; 6c
301. *Tosefta,* Yadayim; end
302. Levit. 15:18
303. Berachoth 22a
304. *Hilchoth Keriyath Shema* 4:8
305. Levit. 20:18
306. *ibid* 15:16

307. Mikvaoth 9:2
308. Remarkably it was told to me in 1905 that in Johannisbad in Bohemia, the general basin was completely emptied daily, and even so not only did the multitude of regular bath customers bathe there, but also the innumerable tourists.

season, would place a mat underneath themselves in order to avoid a "separation" by some possibly suspended sand, etc.[309].

## III   Ritualariums

For certain specific categories of impurity (*zab* and *metzorah*), the Bible prescribes the requirement to bathe in "live (i.e. flowing) water", which tradition considers desirable for *every* ritual bath. "Live water" is that which flows from wells, but also the water of rivers (other than during the rainy season and during the time when the snows melt) and the seas[310]. A substitute for it is offered by the rainwater which gushes forth from the *fountains of the great deep (mayenoth tehom rabba)*[311], in case it collected in a reservoir[312], and if at least 40 *seahs* (approximately 800 liters) were present; that is as much as is required for a full-grown person to immerse himself in. The column of water should be three cubic cubits, that is cover a floor area of one square cubit and have a height of three cubits. The basin (or reservoir) itself must naturally be large enough to hold not only the water but also the bather. From the reservoirs which are ordinarily found under the open skies, the rainwater can be led through a pipe, *tzinor,* which may not be made of metal, however, into the true bathing basin, the *mikveh*[313]. Drawn water in and of itself is absolutely unusable; however, one may add therefrom to well water or to the minimally prescribed quantity of rainwater. It is similarly not permissible to bathe in a utensil such as a bathtub. Scripture states: *Only a well or a cistern, a gathering of water (mikvey mayim) is clean;* that is, cleanses[314].

"The gates of the immersion bathhouse", which indicate that the bathhouse was secluded, are already mentioned in the Talmud[315].

The ritual immersion bath was naturally required not only in summer, but also in winter, and for that season the temperature of the water was of utmost importance. For the High Priest, one warmed a bath on the Day of Atonement, in case he was old or weakly, by adding hot water[316], or according to another interpretation, by placing pieces of iron, which were made red hot, into the water[317]. This is thus the opposite of the old Germanic stone baths, in which the hot water was poured on the glowing stones in order to produce steam[318]. Since a bath in well water was not always available, and even where available not usable in the cold of winter, the communities in which no well (underground) water was obtainable, or was obtainable only with difficulty, used to place basins under the open sky to collect rainwater, and warm the contents thereof by pouring hot water therein. But even rainwater is not always available in the desired amount — every bath, as already mentioned, requires approximately 800 liters of water — so that, *for this reason,* the basins could not be pumped dry as often as one would have liked.

This is the much spoken of *"Jewish bath",* as it is in use even to this very day. It was usually located in the cellar, for the simple reason that one wanted to utilize underground water (well water). The accommodations were rather primitive, partially due to a paucity of understanding, but mostly due to a lack of financial means of the communities (with which to build elegant ritualariums). Where both were adequate, there existed immersion baths which

309. Shabbath 65a
310. Parah 8:8
311. Genesis 7:11
312. Mikvaoth 5:5
313. *ibid* 4:1
314. Levit. 11:36

315. Berachoth 20a
316. Yoma 3:5
317. *ibid* 34b
318. Höfler in Neuberger-Pegel's *Handbuch der Geschichte der Medizin.* Vol. 1 p.465

were hygienically and esthetically faultless[319]. Here the community basins did not exist anymore.

The immersion bath, as is evident from all the aforementioned, cannot be equated with a bathing establishment, even if the latter fulfills all the requisites. For the bathtubs, which are used in the same manner in both, as elsewhere too, are only considered secondary and are not an integral part of the ritualarium, but in fact are only placed there for the convenience of the bath users, so that they can immediately proceed from the cleansing bath to the immersion bath without having to get dressed in between. There might otherwise easily result a small dirtying of the body which would render the immersion bath invalid. In the immersion bath, the woman completely immerses her faultlessly clean body three times, and then leaves. In modernly constructed establishments, there are individual compartments containing both bathtub and immersion bath, *both* of which are emptied after every usage.

The immersion bath is thus a *religious* institution (one's health is naturally not impaired thereby). Accordingly, any person who jumps into a *mikveh* (ritualarium) exactly as he would into a regular bath is considered abominable[320]. The immersion itself is a symbolic act, and is reflected in the immersion of the christening of some Christian sects, which was customary, in general, until the thirteenth century.

In the Temple, there were several such ritual baths, one for the High Priest on the Temple Mount, the *Har Ha-Mischcha*[321]. On both sides lighted steps descended thereto; a fire burned in front of it at which the priests warmed themselves after the cold ritual bath[322]. A second ritual bath existed for lepers in a room specially designated for them, the *lischkath ha-metzoraim*[323]. Prior to that, the lepers used to bathe in "wells and brooks which God provided"[324].

The *drying* after the bath, *sippug,* is done with an object which soaks up the moisture; a type of sponge, *sephag*[325], which one also puts on wounds[326].

## IV   River Bathing

Concerning river bathing for non-cultic purposes, in the Bible we only come to know the case of the Egyptian princess who descended to the Nile to bathe while her maidservants patrolled along the river's side[327]. Legend relates that she suffered from a serious skin sickness, *negaim kashim,* so that she could not tolerate any hot baths, and therefore sought out the cold river for bathing[328]. This legend obviously originated at a later date, in which one already considered hot baths to be the norm. Concerning the use of river bathing for *therapeutic purposes,* the only incident in the Bible is the story of the Syrian general Naaman who was healed of his leprosy by bathing in the Jordan river[329]. It remains undecided, however, whether the healing should be regarded as having occurred as a result of this bathing.

During the reconstruction of the Temple, people remained in their clothes day and night, undressing only at the water[330], which probably refers to cleansing baths. In post-Biblical times, baths in wells are often spoken of, at which one washed and also carried out other needed functions[331]. Whether these concern cold or hot wells cannot be ascertained.

---

319. for example in Berlin and Frankfurt a. M. etc.
320. *Tosefta* Mikvaoth 5:14
321. Parah 3:7
322. Tamid 1:1
323. Negaim 14:8
324. Midrash Psalms 104:9
325. Zabim 1:4; Parah 3:8
326. *Tosefta* Shabbath 5:3
327. Exodus 2:5
328. *Yalkut op. cit.*
329. Second Kings 5:14
330. Nehemiah 4:17
331. *Tosefta* Erubin 8:6

It is related about Vespasian that he bathed *behada giphna* during the siege of Jerusalem[332]. This could not mean "in the river", because there was no river in the vicinity of Jerusalem; rather "in *guphna*" refers to a suburb of Jerusalem, often mentioned in the Talmud, as already correctly noted by David Luria.

## V   Well of Siloa and Hot Springs

The well of *Siloa,* in whose history Jesus played a role, originates at the foot of the Temple Mount in Jerusalem and flows into a pool. A man blind from birth came to Jesus who spat on the ground, made a dough from the spittle, stroked it over the blind eyes and spoke to him: go and wash in the pool of Siloa. He went there, washed himself and came back able to see[333]. The role of spittle in the treatment of blindness is well known[334]. It is often asserted[335] that washing the eyes with well water has an extraordinary influence on that affliction, but the exegetes are in dispute about the method.

Tradition maintains yet another efficacy of this pool of Siloa. When the priests had eaten much meat from sacrifices at the time of the Temple, they drank of the waters of Siloa and digested thereby the meat like normal food[336]. *This, therefore, was one, and to the best of my knowledge, the only account in Talmudic literature concerning the internal use of mineral water with medicinal intent.* From a religious viewpoint, to the Jews, the waters of the well of Siloa were endowed with an extraordinary cleansing power: "Even if someone bathes in the water of Siloa or in the source water, he does not become clean if he is holding a reptile in his hand; so, too, we can lift our hearts in praise of God, only if there is no ill-gotten gain in our hands"[337].

The name Emmaus is considered to be a Greek distortion of the Aramaic *chamtha,* which generally means "hot springs". That place does not have a good name in the Talmud. Rabbi Chelbo said: the grove of Perugitha (Phrygien) and the water of Emmaus destroyed ten tribes of Israel. As an example of this destructive influence, the following is told: Rabbi Eleazar ben Arach, the talented disciple of Rabbi Yochanan ben Zakkai, came to Emmaus, a place with pleasant water and pleasant residences *(nawah),* and remained there — according to the *Midrash* at the urging of his wife — until he forgot all his knowledge, so that he was unable to correctly read even a well-known verse of the Bible.

On the other hand, Emmaus is "a site of pleasant water and a pleasant sojourn"[338]. It is also related that when Rabbi Yochanan suffered from bulimia (a ravenous hunger), he went to Emmaus, sat there under a fig tree, and became healthy[339].

The regular course of treatment (or baths) lasted three weeks. The season was between Passover and Pentecost[340].

In Shabbath 147b and Aboth de Rabbi Nathan 14e there is written *diomeseth* instead of Emmaus. Rabbi Chananel also explains it as the name of a place. He may have read Emmaus. *Rashi* and David Kimchi *(Radak)* cite Isaiah 28:1 with the word *durmaskith,* which probably refers to Damascus. Maimonides *Hilchoth Shabbath* 21:28 has "*dimusith* in the land of Israel".

Among the hot springs, the ones in *Tiberias* are the most famous. They are so hot that irritations of the skin, *schechin,* can develop therefrom[341]. Pipes with cold water

332. Lamentations Rabbah on 1:5 fol. 14d
333. John 9:1-7
334. See above chapter 6 part 9
335. Friedreich, *Zur Bibel* 1 p.59
336. Aboth de Rabbi Nathan 35:5
337. Jerushalmi Taanith 2; 65a

338. Eccles. Rabbah 7:7, 2 fol. 19a
339. *ibid* 7:11 fol. 20b; see above chapter 8 part 3; perhaps the figs are the active therapeutic substance
340. Shabbath 147b
341. Negaim 9:1

were led through the springs in order to warm them for household use, for the well water itself, because of its taste, was not suitable for kitchen use[342]. "Bathing in the waters of Tiberias for healing purposes" is explicitly mentioned[343]. The troop commander John asked Josephus to allow him to use the hot baths in Tiberias to heal his body[344]. Rabbi Yochanan and Resh Lakish were also described as users of such baths[345]. Taken internally, the waters of the springs produce watery stools[346]. Since the Talmud mentions cups from Tiberias as a specialty because of their exceptionally clear and transparent nature[347], one concludes that these were cures of mineral springs, according to the modern method. Had God created hot springs in Jerusalem similar to those in Tiberias, then people would certainly not make the pilgrimage to Jerusalem for the festivals with the proper intention of fulfilling God's commandment, but to use the hot springs[348].

Enumerations of many other springs in the Bible and Talmud are found in the writings of Wesseley[349] and Rappaport[350]. However, since their use for bathing is nowhere mentioned, we can here pass over them.

The only two places in the Bible that describe *full baths* (i.e. bathtubs) in the house are concerned with women, namely Bath Sheba[351] and Susanna[352]. Since these bathing women were both observed from the roof of a neighbor's house, the bathtubs were probably in an enclosed structure in the courtyard, as is still the case in the Orient today.

## VI   Swimming In A Bath

It appears that during bathing a very pleasant form of physical exercise was swimming. To learn how to swim one used "a barrel (for the support of those practicing to be) swimmers"[353], which the commentators explain was braided from leaves of paper bushes and shaped into the form of a barrel, and naturally closed on all sides[354]. Some Sages considered it an *obligation* upon the father to arrange for swimming lessons for his son[355]. However, in general, one used to swim differently than we do today, namely, alternating one hand up and one hand down[356].

## VII   The Warm Bath

Although *warm* baths were occasionally employed even during the times of the Bible, the regular use thereof, particularly the utilization of *bathhouses,* belongs to the time of the Talmud, that is the Greco-Roman epoch. Nowhere in the entire Talmudic literature is there to be found an overall cohesive description of this type of bathing establishment. Nevertheless, one can construct a picture from the many individual Talmudic notations which are in accord with and derived from Greek, and especially also Roman, sources. I will here only quote the citations from ancient Hebrew writings, and refer the reader to handbooks of Greek and Roman archaeology for discussions of bathhouses of heathendom. A usable handbook of Biblical-Talmudic archaeology still awaits an author[357].

---

342. Shabbath 3:4
343. *Tosefta* Shabbath 12:13
344. *Vita* No. 16
345. Jerushalmi Peah 8; 21b
346. Machshirim 6:7
347. Jerushalmi Niddah 2; 50b
348. *Sifré.* Chapt. 89 or Numbers 11:9 p.25a
349. *Des Eaux Salutaires et des Bains des Hébreux.* in Carros' *Almanach de Carlsbad.* Munich 1844 p.66
350. *Bicc. Haitt.* 1830 p.18; Dechent. ZDPV

Vol. 7 p.173-210, 1884
351. Second Samuel 11:2
352. Susanna 15
353. Betzah 36b
354. Kelim 2:3
355. *Tosefta* Kiddushin 1:11
356. Midrash Psalms 114:7
357. During the printing of this book, the long advertised *Outline of Talmudic Archeology* by S. Kraus had not yet appeared.

# VIII   The Bathhouse

For a warm bath, the general term *merchatz* is used; for a bathhouse *beth ha-merchatz,* less often *bé bâne*[358] or *bé bané*[359], both contractions of the Greek *balaneia,* according to the dictionaries. Quite rare is *balne*[360] or *bane*[361]. In the Palestinian Talmud the word *sachi* is used mostly for "bathing", from which are said to be derived the terms *mis'chuta*[362] or *bé mesutha*[363] for a bathhouse. Otherwise, one attempted to connect *bé mesutha* with *assi,* to heal. As already mentioned, for a ritual bath, the terms *tebila* (immersion) or *mikveh* (collection basin) are used exclusively.

The bathhouse consisted of three rooms, one in which everyone stood naked, the true bathing room; a second room in which some people were naked and others clothed, the dressing room; and a third room in which everyone was clothed, in which people rested after the bath[364]. The second room corresponded to the *apodyterion* of the Greeks and Romans. The latter is actually a later development which was not known to Aristotle, for example. The presence of individual clothing-room attendants in Jewish bathhouses, on the other hand, cannot be authenticated even later. The clothes were given to the house attendant who gave them to an agreed-upon *olearier*[365], or he put them in the "window of the *olearier"* where they could be locked and the door bolted[366]. In spite of this, robberies occurred. In a parable in the *Midrash,* the son of a prominent citizen stole clothing and valuables in a bathhouse. The bath attendant hesitated to identify him by name, but designated him very clearly "the young man with the white clothes", so that everyone recognized him[367].

At least in the luxuriously equipped bathhouses of the heathens, the anteroom was fenced in by colonnades, basilics, so that it resembled a basilica *(basileké),* as seen in royal palaces[368]. In the bathhouses of Pompeii, the large courtyard was constructed with a row of Doric columns on both sides.

The bath water was drawn from ponds, *berechoth,* which conveyed the water both in summer and in winter, less during the summer and more during the winter; or from *meguroth,* water basins, from which the water was led through pipes[369]. In later times in the Orient, as well as in Rome, there were conduits in which the waters were led in lines which were exactly the opposite of the "straight paths of God", that is, the pipes were curved[370]; they twisted *(nimschakin)* through fields and gardens, through lavatories and bathhouses[371].

In the storehouses for wood, *otzeroth* or *beth ha-kneseth shel etzim,* the fuel was stored[372]. In general, wood was used, but straw and stubble were also employed. Rich people also had fragrant herbs added to the fire[373]. The latter fuel was thrown onto the fire by the bath attendant with a shovel[374].

On the other hand, additions to the baths themselves, as far as I can see, are not mentioned. Raba found the lascivious Persian Bar Schleschach sitting in a bath of roses up to his neck and surrounded by naked prostitutes[375]. Children were bathed in

358. Shabbath 41a
359. Berachoth 60a
360. Jerushalmi Maaser Sheni 4; 54d
361. Jerushalmi Taanith 1; 64b
362. Kiddushin 33a
363. Baba Metzia 6b; Shabbath 140a; Berachoth 22a; Chullin 45b
364. *Tosefta* Berachoth 2:20
365. Jerushalmi Berachoth 2; 4c (The meaning of this word *olearier* is not clear to me. It may refer to the person who gives an oil rub after a bath. F.R.)
366. *Tosefta* Tohoroth 8:8
367. Numbers Rabbah 13:5
368. Abodah Zarah 16a
369. Baba Bathra 4:6
370. Characteristically the channels only extremely rarely are completely straight for a long distance; rather throughout their length they are curved. Schick in *ZDPV* 1787 Vol. 1 p.138
371. Song of Songs Rabbah on 1:6; fol. 6b
372. Baba Bathra 4:6 and Jerushalmi Baba Bathra 4; 14c
373. Shebiith 8:11
374. Kelim 17:1
375. Abodah Zarah 65a and *Rashi op. cit.*

wine, if one wished thereby to effect extraordinary healing[376]. God will someday allow the pious to bath in streams of milk[377]. Job is so rich that he bathes in cream[378].

Occasionally there existed in the bathhouse a residential room, *beth dira*[379], perhaps for the bath attendant.

# IX

The specific immersion pool (literally: bath basin) in Hebrew writings is ordinarily called *ambate* or *embate,* which is derived from the Greek *emvati* (anteroom). However, the Greeks called their basin a *loutér* (tub) or *pyelos* ( basin) or less frequently *emvasis* (vestibule)[380]. Only once was I able to find the term *sephalim,* wash basins[381], probably referring to the *luteiros* (bathtub) which stands on feet and which is the norm in pictures on Greek vases; also the term *agana de maja,* a tub in which one sat, is only mentioned once in the Talmud[382]. For prominent people, there were small individual tubs; otherwise, several people bathed simultaneously in the communal immersion pool[383]. Rabbi Abahu even *swam* in an *ambate*[384]. Generally, however, the immersion pools were so flat that one could only sit therein. One should not, however, put one's feet in the bathtub and then crouch down, for this is indecent. One should not say to another: "press your hand on me in the bathhouse"; he who utters it does not leave the bathhouse unscathed. If there is a lot of water, on the other hand, it is to be recommended[385]. The last passage is already incomprehensible to the commentaries.

We learn much about the *inventory* of a bathhouse from a regulation concerning civil law: if someone sells another a "bathhouse", he has not sold the boards or the benches or the curtains[386]. According to other views, the kettles, *yekamin,* and *migdalin* are also excluded[387]. If the buyer also wants these, then he must buy "the bathhouse including the inventory". If he also wants the water containers (or reservoirs) and the wood stores, then he must acquire "the bathhouse including all its accessories".

1. The bath water was warmed by the bath attendant with a portable oven, the *tannur,* through a pipe, *abik,* which led into the bathing pool[388], and was here mixed with cold water, *meziga*[389], and then flowed out of the pool after it was used into a trench under the *merchatz*. The trench was covered with boards, *nesarim*[390]. It once happened to Rabbi Abahu that the bathhouse became defective under him, that is, the boards gave way. A miracle occurred to him that he came to rest on a pillar which supported the floor, and he was thus able to save not only himself but a large number of other people[391]. In such a bathhouse heated by an oven, one had to pray to remain protected from being burned by the oven, or scalded by the water, and from collapse of the wooden floor[392]. Cautious people would refrain from using a new bathhouse until its safety was established by prolonged use[393].

In addition to this ordinary type of bathhouse, which is not much different from our own bathrooms, there also existed bathing establishments with *aqueducts,* excavated floors and hollowed walls, as in Pompeii, so that beneath them and within them, the hot air and even the flame from the fire places could distribute itself. They were directly connected with the real bathing rooms. These openings could be sealed, if

---

376. *Tosefta* Shabbath 12:13
377. Numbers Rabbah 13:2 fol. 51a
378. Job 29:6
379. Mezuzah 1
380. Daremberg. on Oribas. Vol. 2 p.870
381. Baba Bathra 67b
382. Berachoth 22a
383. Machshirim 2:5
384. Shabbath 40b

385. Derech Eretz 10
386. Baba Bathra 4:6
387. *Tosefta* Baba Bathra 3:3
388. Mikvaoth 6:10
389. Levit. Rabbah 28:6
390. ibid
391. Berachoth 60a
392. Jerushalmi Berachoth 9; 14b
393. Pesachim 112b

one desired to prevent further heating of the bathing room[394], or if one wished to maintain the temperature of the room without further fire. For this purpose, there were cloths of specified sizes[395].

The floor in the bathing rooms were made of stone, perhaps of mosaic or smooth marble plates. If one wished to prevent chilling of the feet or slipping, one even covered the stone floor with boards. Where these board coverings were lacking, the prudent tried to help themselves. Thus it is related about Rabbi Abahu that when he bathed, he supported himself on two boards which he alternately placed on the ground and picked up, thus moving them forward. He used to say: "I want to save my strength for my old age"[396]! Perhaps it was in one of the boardless bathing institutions that a man once fell and suffered a cerebral concussion[397].

2. *Benches, saphselim* (late Greek *subsellia,*), are known in various forms and shapes from heathen edifices. The seat is made of stone, the feet either likewise of stone, or one of stone and the other of wood[398]. In the Aramaic dialect they are called *itztaba*[399], which cannot be equivalent to the Greek *stoa,* because there also exists an "*itztaba* for the pillars"[400].

3. The *curtains, wilaoth* or *balnioth,* are probably substitutes for doors. The dictionaries derive the term from the Latin *velum.* That the word should mean "chastity cloth" (Maimonides) is excluded for a great variety of reasons.

4. The word *yekamin* in the dictionaries is thought to be derived from the Greek *kaminos* (furnace), which must thus mean bath oven. The *kamin* was filled with wood prior to use[401]. Perhaps, the *migdalin* were boxes for the bath laundry. They must have been portable, as part of the "inventory". More precise archaeological discoveries go even further: the *kinkillin* (fumigators) either had a receptacle for clothes or resembled a beehive, and, according to the commentator Rabbi Obadya, a wire basket. Below it one lit sulphur, in order to fumigate the clothes[402]. The loan-word *kinkilin,* according to I. Löw, is a fusion of *kaguellon* and *kigulis*[403]. I cannot derive either word from Greek bathing establishments. The "*dakkon* of the *olearier*", which sometimes was used as a seat, *pitput,* perhaps like our tripod[404], was probably a *duchan,* an elevated seat or stand *(estrade).*

# X    Bathhouse Personnel

Bathing establishments were originally private enterprises. The *merchatz* is one of the things which always brings a profit. If someone is in undisputed possession of such a bathhouse for three consecutive years, he is considered to be the legal owner thereof[405]. Only later did cities or communities begin to build public bathhouses, and the names *demosia* or *velanea* were adopted therefor in the *Gemara.* In the *Mishnah* we do not yet find this expression[406]. Where the text differentiates between community baths and those of private enterprise, the former is called *demosia* (public), whereas the latter retains its ancient name *merchatz* or *merchatzaah*[407], and is only rarely called *privata*[408]. The hot springs of Tiberias are also called *demosia* (public)[409]. There were no separate establishments for cold baths; bathing in cold water is not considered a bath, *rechitza*[410].

---

394. *Tosefta* Shabbath 3:3
395. Kelim 28:2
396. Jerushalmi Betzah 1; 60c
397. Chullin 45b
398. Kelim 22:10
399. Niddah 9:3
400. Shabbath 7a
401. Jerushalmi Shabbath 3; 6a
402. Kelim 22:10

403. in Krauss. *Lehnwörter* 2:534a
404. *Tosefta* Kelim 5:8
405. Baba Bathra 3:1
406. The term *demosia* in Abodah Zarah 1:7 is false
407. Shabbath 33b
408. Jerushalmi Shebiith 8; 38b
409. Jerushalmi Sanhedrin 7; 15d
410. Jerushalmi Berachoth 2; 5b

The proprietor of the bathing establishment is the *ballan,* corresponding to the Greek *valanes;* in community or private bathhouses, he is the manager or director, and receives his salary from the leaseholder, *aris,* or from the landlord, unless he is the tenant[411]. Otherwise, a bathing fee was naturally collected from every bath user[412]. For this bathing fee, one received a token, *siman,* which the *olearier* accepted as payment. Such bathing tokens, which were probably valid for the large baths in Jerusalem, could also be used or exchanged in the rural districts[413].

The *ballan* belongs to the class of people who must professionally also deal with women, and whose natural inclinations are therefore evil. Otherwise, profession and genealogy are not considered decisive in the acquisition of even the highest offices. However, types of professions which are associated with such serious dangers to morality are in principle excluded. Therefore, a *ballan,* as well as people with similar professions, cannot be elected to become king or High Priest; not even to become a community leader or an *epitropos*[414]. One should, however, not assume that such individuals are always of a low moral standard[415].

In addition to the *ballan,* there often existed the *olior* or *orior.* Rappaport first stated that this name referred to the late Greek *olearios.* He was followed by all later writers, who assume the term refers to the Latin *olearius*[416]. An oil rub was part of every bath, as will be shown later on. This was done by another person, and it was conjectured that the *bath attendant* received his name from this task, although it was also his responsibility to bring the bath laundry into the bath[417] and to take the clothes of the bathers[418]. His position in the bathhouse is different from that of the *ballan*[419]; he had a *korah* or a rafter, which he used as a seat[420].

The name of the *olior* is found in all parts of the Talmud: *Mishnah, Tosefta* and both *Gemaras.* Mostly, it is mentioned in the plural. The reason why the Greeks and Romans in classical times do not mention him still requires explanation. Sometimes the *Mishnah,* under personnel, also mentions the *sappag,* the orderly who attends to the drying of the bathers, *sippug*[421].

Hairdressing after the bath was not attended to by the *valanes* as among the Greeks, but by a separate barber, *sappar*[422], or hairdresser, *chappan*[423]. Ordinarily, people took care of their own hair with the comb, *masrek,* that they brought with them[424].

## XI    The Bathing

Some people, for reasons of convenience, or perhaps also out of consideration for their health, renounced a hot water bath, and were satisfied with a stay in the damp warm air, so that the steam (or vapors of the bathing room) bring out the vapors (of the body), as taught by Mar Samuel[425]. This vapor *(habel)* is not identical with perspiration; it develops together with perspiration following useful body movements, as the Greeks state: *idrota thermon atmo symmige* (sweat and hot vapor together)[426]. Furthermore, it was an Oriental custom to drink hot water while bathing in a hot bath; otherwise one would be like an oven which is heated from the outside but not from the inside[427]. Three types of perspiration, according to an ancient tradition, are good for

411. *Tosefta* Baba Metzia 9:14
412. Shebiith 8:5
413. *Tosefta* Maaser Sheni 1:4; Baba Metzia 47b; Jerushalmi Maaser Sheni 1; 52d
414. Derech Eretz Zutta 10 fol. 59b 24
415. Kiddushin 82b
416. Proofs in Krauss. *Byzant. Ztschr* 2, 1893 p.507
417. Shabbath 147b
418. Jerushalmi Berachoth 2; 4c
419. Jerushalmi Baba Bathra 4; 14c
420. Zabim 4:4
421. Kilayim 9:3
422. Esther Rabbah 10:4
423. *Tosefta* Baba Metzia 9:14; See also *Chaphipha* in Chapter 12, 2:8
424. Shabbath 41a
425. Shabbath 40b
426. Oribas.6:15. Ed. Daremberg 1 p. 480
427. Shabbath 40b

the body: the critical sweat of illness, that of toil, and that of bathing. The sweat of the illness heals; and nothing can compare with the sweat of a bath[428].

Weakly people would easily become faint during perspiration and require prolonged periods to recuperate[429].

The vapor of the bathhouse is harmful to the teeth; for this reason some people even avoid speaking in a bathhouse, even about profane matters[430].

Every hot water bath or hot vapor bath was followed by the pouring of cold or temperate water *(mischthatphin)* over the bather[431]. He who does not do so is compared to an iron which was reddened in a fire, but then not placed in cold water, according to the opinion of the same Mar Samuel[432]. Either one used the concavity of the hand for this or a bucket, a *deli*[433]; or one allowed the pouring to be done by the *parkhita,* who was simultaneously employed for the cleansing of the bathing room[434], and who was probably identical to the Greek *parachytes.* Alternatively, one could stand under a drain, a *tzinnor,* to cool off or to be rinsed off[435]. Ordinarily, there were two such douche pails, *metahereth,* one above the other, which were filled with water of different temperatures[436]. Three such water troughs are represented on the famous picture of the baths of Titus. True showers, on the other hand, probably did not exist[437]. Such sprinkling of water after a warm bath was also practiced on young infants[438]. It was considered robbery of the public if one bathed in cold water and then sprayed oneself with hot water[439], probably because one thereby wasted the hot water which was alloted for many people.

In the bath, one used to soap oneself, and for this purpose one brought *nether* along. We have already spoken about this *nether,* as well as about other chemical cleaning substances[440].

## XII    The Oil Rub

The actual bath was followed by a series of manipulations, the most important of which is the *oil rub.* A bath without an oil rub is compared to the pouring of water *on* a barrel without penetrating the inside thereof, teaches Mar Samuel[441]. One brought the oil in a flagon, a *celuchitha*[442], or in a Galilean pitcher[443], unless one's slave carried it to the bathhouse. Thus, Susanna had her maidservant bring oil and soap (or salves) to the bath[444]. One is not permitted, however, to have a Hebrew slave give one a rubdown, or to have him anoint oneself[445]. In addition, in the bathing establishment itself, there was oil prepared for sale in a jug[446]. At the entrance, olives which had become softened were also sold[447]; from these the oil was squeezed directly onto the body. The bottle was placed on a supporting base, an *agaltha*[448], and allowed to become warm on the fireplace, the *ashuna,* probably the *hypokaustum*[449].

One should not bring the oil in a glass bottle, because it might be dangerous if the bottle should break. One should also not spit on the ground, because one could then easily slip on the stone floor[450]. Some people poured the oil on their heads at home, thus using their hair as an oil receptacle[451]. In times of wealth, fragrant oils, *besamim,*

428. Aboth de Rabbi Nathan 41:4
429. Shabbath 9b
430. Jerusalmi Abodah Zarah 3; 42d
431. *Tosefta* Shabbath 3:4
432. Shabbath 40b
433. *Tosefta* Shabbath 3:4
434. Genesis Rabbah 63:8
435. Machshirin 4:4
436. Mikvaoth 6:11
437. Oribas. 2:877
438. Shabbath 19:3
439. Derech Eretz 10

440. see above Chapter 12, part 2:16
441. Shabbath 40b
442. Jerusalmi Shebiith 8; 38a
443. *Tosefta* Kelim 2:9
444. Susanna verse 17
445. Abadim beginning of Chapt. 2
446. *Tosefta* Kelim 10:4
447. *Tosefta* Niddah 4:8
448. Jerusalmi Shabbath 3; 6a
449. Jerusalmi Shebiith 8; 38a
450. Derech Eretz 10
451. *Tosefta* Shabbath 16:6

were also utilized[452]. If the commentary of *Peneh Moshe* is correct, then the anointing of Rabbi Jeremiah was effected with sesame oil perfumed with wild jasmine[452a].

According to Krauss, *zusima udjatha* means a "Zosimos heater"; according to Levy[453], *zusima* is "the servant who prepared the waistband" and *udjatha* is the bathhouse. Kohut considers the Arabic *sadad* which means "watchman". All are improbable.

It seems that there was an additional type of rubbing in which oil was poured on a marble slab or on a *katablia,* and upon which a person rolled[454], or, as others state, "upon which a person broke himself", *mishtabar.* It appears that this type of rub required less exertion, particularly for sick people, and hence was more desirable. Nevertheless, at least for healthy people, it was not considered respectable. Rabbi Simeon ben Gamliel said: he who breaks himself on the marble floor is the companion of a donkey (his behavior is like that of a donkey); he who eats on the street behaves like a dog[455].

Anointing is connected to the "*mishmesh of the bnei meayim*"[456], probably a massage of the abdomen, whose purpose was to produce defecation[457]. It is evident from the statements in Becker-Rein[458] how the arrangements for lavatory facilities were made. In the *Mishnah,* we only find the allusion that "all people in a bathhouse urinate"[459].

The embrocation was followed by the *mith'amel,* the tiring of oneself by physical exercise. For example, one placed the head between the legs[460]. Rabbi Chananel, an Arabic commentator of the eleventh century, explains: "one bent and stretched the arms forwards and backwards, as well as the legs on the haunches, so that one became warm and perspired"[461]. The introduction of gymnastics was never opposed by the Jews[462]; only those institutions in which, in addition to the physical activity, immorality was often practiced, as is known.

The conclusion of the bathing procedure is the *mithgared,* "scraping oneself". For this purpose, one used a *magredeth* or *magrereth* (Aramaic *migreda* or *maghradeta*) which belonged to the *olearier*[463] and which were hung on specially shaped pegs *(taliy)* for the use of the bathers[464]. On the famous pictures of Mercuriali, four such *strigiles* (for the Greeks *steleggis*) are hanging on a ring; three are in use. They serve the purpose of scraping off the sweat, the oil and the skin dirt from the body. One either performed the scraping oneself, or had one of the attendants do it. A *migreda* made of silver for use on the Sabbath is mentioned[465]. It is not certain whether or not the separately occurring "scratching", *mepharkin,*[466] is identical to the bathhouse scraping.

He who perspires first leaves the bath first[467]; he who has already put his coat on and then returns to the steam bath robs the public, in that he takes away someone else's place[468]. The use of a scale in the bathhouse is well-known; as a result thereof, it was believed established that in spite of the loss of perspiration body weight did not decrease[469]. This could only be explained by the fact that bathers used to *drink* hot water during the bath (which compensated for the water loss of perspiration).

452. *Tosefta* Berachoth 6:8
452a. Jerushalmi Shebiith 8; 38a
453. *Neuhebräisches und Chaldäisches Wörterbuch.* Leipzig 1876-1889
454. Jerushalmi Shebiith 38b; *Tosefta* Demai 1:19; *Tosefta* Shabbath 16:14
455. Derech Eretz Rabbah 10:2
456. Shabbath 22:6
457. Berachoth 62a
458. Gallus 3:112
459. Abodah Zarah 3:4
460. Kallah Rabbathi 9:54d
461. Rabbi Chananel on Shabbath 22:6
462. as claimed by Ewer. See Pagel-Neuburger's *Handbuch* 3:342
463. *Tosefta* Kelim 2:12
464. Kelim 12:6
465. Shabbath 147b
466. *Tosefta* Shabbath 3:18
467. Leviticus Rabbah 14:9
468. *ibid*
469. Genesis Rabbah 4:4

To dry oneself after the bath, one used a *mappa*, a napkin[470], or *mitpachoth*, hand towels, which were woven of wool and linen[471]; in Greco-Roman times, *aluntioth*, linen towels *(lintea)*[472] which were employed exclusively by the Romans. For women, a *saknitha*, perhaps a bathrobe with a cape, is also mentioned[473]. The bathing linens of men are called *antitaya*[474], whose meaning is uncertain[475]. The bath linens are among the requisites of a bath, the *balneré*, abbreviated *balré*[476], *balnearia*, and differ for men and for women. He who can afford it lets his things be carried for him by his servant or the *olearier*. That is a universal custom[477]. One may not require one's Hebrew slave to perform this task[478]. Rabbi Yochanan, in one of his usual manners of speech, promises that he would carry into a bathhouse the clothes of a person who would explain to him the meaning of a certain Biblical expression[479].

Propriety demands a certain sequence of dressing and undressing. Before one steps into a bath, one takes off the shoes, removes the head covering, takes off the coat, loosens the belt, sets aside the shirt, *chaluk*, and lastly slackens the *phorkas* (underwear). After the bath, one first dries the head, and then the limbs. If oil is brought, one first embrocates the head and then the limbs, and one gets dressed in the opposite order of the aforementioned disrobing[480].

After the bath one drinks a glass of wine[481]. It is called *diplé potirin*[482] or *pijali potirin*[483]. The former is thought to be *diplaun* (in Greek i.e. double), the latter *phiale poterion* (glass bottle); whether this is correct is uncertain. Rabbi Joseph, who was not accustomed to drinking wine, felt it "from the hair on his head to the tips of his toes". Alternatively, one drinks *alunthith* "to cool off"; this is a beverage made from aged wine, clear water and *apharsemon*, which is balsam[484].

One should not bathe in the bathhouse before the fourth hour of the day[485]. At this time, one usually ate the meal and, therefore, as in Rome, one bathed before this time. "To run to the bath keeper in the midday heat on a July day" is a figure of speech used for exaggerated zeal[486].

# XIII   Mixed Bathing

According to Germanic[487], Roman and Greek custom, men and women bathed together. Juvenal and Martial speak frequently about this. "Warm baths for women" are indeed mentioned[488], but at all events constitute a rare exception. Hadrian tried to put an end to the mischief in that he *lavacra pro sexibus separavit*[489]. However, later repeated prohibitions and ordinances[490] demonstrate that this evil could not be eliminated. Even among the Jews, this misconduct threatened to become ingrained[491], and one was dependent on the Draconian law that a man is obligated to divorce a woman who bathed together with any other man, and he is not compelled to pay her the stipulated widow's monetary settlement, the *kethuba*, because she did not fulfill the condition of her marriage contract to live "according to the laws of Moses and of Israel"[492]. This ordinance seems to have originated even *before* the time of Rabbi

470. Derech Eretz 10
471. Kilayim 9:3
472. Shabbath 20:6
473. *ibid* 147b
474. Jerushalmi Kilayim 9; 32a
475. Löw, in Krauss, *Lehnwörter* 2:70a
476. Shabbath 147b
477. *Tanchuma, Beshalach* p.29b Buber
478. *Mechilta, Mishpatim* p.75a, Friedmann
479. Erubin 27b; Sanhedrin 62b
480. Derech Eretz Rabbah 10:1
481. Genesis Rabbah 10:7
482. Jerushalmi Pesachim 10; 37c

483. Genesis Rabbah 51:2
484. Shabbath 140a
485. Derech Eretz Rabbah 7:3
486. Jerushalmi Maaser Sheni 4: 54d
487. *Promiscue in Fluminibus Perluuntur.* Caesar. *Bell. Gall.* 6:21
488. *Tosefta* Niddah 6:15
489. *Dio Cass.* 49:8 and Spartian's *Hadrian* 18
490. in Becker-Rein. *Gallus* 3:89
491. for example in Gedara, Dechent in *ZDPV* 7:192
492. *Tosefta* Kethuboth 7:6; *Tosefta* Sotah 5:5

Meir, who lived in the year 150 of the Common Era, and is, therefore, older than the law of Quintilian with a similar intent: *signum est adulterae, lavari cum viris*[493]. Also, the zealousness of the church fathers is shown from the Christian era[494], in that the puritanical tendencies of the young Christian communities could not prevent the common (i.e. men and women) use of the baths.

In the *Gemara,* one finds the thought of a decent woman bathing together with strange men so shocking that one has to search for another exegesis of the law of the above *Tosefta.* For in such a case, the woman gives the strong impression of committing adultery, and it is, therefore, self-evident that the man is obligated to divorce her. The *Tosafoth* comment differently: it is not possible to think that Rabbi Meir intended to forbid a woman from bathing with strange men, for this would not be tolerated by any man, completely exclusive of the fact that even the most frivolous woman would not indulge in such a practice. The prohibition is intended to refer to bathing in places where the woman could be *observed* by other men[495]. The *Midrash* also expresses this law in this form[496]. In the post-Talmudic collections of laws, this regulation is no longer found. It seems probable that, because of its rigorousness, it was successful in its intent and, therefore, became superfluous.

It is likely that it was the reaction against this immorality in the baths[497] which "induced many of the most prominent holy men of early Christianity to intentionally cultivate bodily uncleanliness". Augustine teaches: *munditia corporis atque vestitus animae est immunditia.* This "Christian glorification of dirt", as it is called by Havelock Ellis[498], did not last long, however, and, in the Middle Ages, the collective tub bath was again in general use[499]. Benjamin Osiander relates that even in his time in Germany, in many warm baths community bathing was practiced[500]. In Japan, community bathing of both sexes is customary even today[501]. In Holland and Belgium such baths are called *bains mixtes* (mixed baths) and in Germany *familien-baden* (family baths).

These *bains mixtes* seem to be especially indecent because no bathing clothes at all are worn. The Greek writers indeed speak of *loutrides* which the women wore, but on the vase pictures and, particularly clearly on the already often-mentioned pictures of Mercurialis, all bathers, men and women, appear completely naked; only the bath attendant is wearing an apron. It appears that the use of bathing trunks by the Jews in male bathing establishments was not looked upon with favor, because in the company of people of other faiths, some Jews probably used the trunks as a pretext to hide their circumcision, that is their association with Judaism. Some people already took offense at the fact that Rabbi Abahu placed his hand over his genitalia in the bath for reasons of propriety[502].

Probably because of the consideration of naked bodies, it was especially forbidden for a teacher and his disciple, a son and his father or stepfather, or a son-in-law and his father-in-law to bathe together, unless the father was ill and old and required assistance[503]. There was no objection to brothers bathing together. Only in the place called Kabbul did the entire community consider such a practice scandalous. In those places where people take offense at brothers bathing together, it should be omitted[504]. No one should be present when the king bathes, because it would damage the public awe of the king[505]. The same is true of the warm bath of the High Priest.

493. Inst. 5:9
494. for example, Cyprian *de habitu virginum.* in Mignes Patrol. Vol. 4 Col. 471
495. Gittin 90b
496. Numbers Rabbah 9:12
497. Details in Rosenbaum. *Lustseuche* p.350
498. *Gattenwahl* p.47
499. See Ploss. *Das Weib* 1:416 ff

500. *Handbuch d. Entbdgskunst.* Tubingen 1819 Vol. 1 p.250, notes
501. *Baln. Centralztg* No. 7, 1902
502. Shabbath 41a
503. Semachoth 12:49c
504. Pesachim 51a
505. Sanhedrin 2:5

Even if he requests that others bathe with him, he has no right to forego the honor and dignity of his position[506]. In every place one should and must reflect about the Torah[507], except in the bathhouse and in the toilet[508].

The *Mishnah* prohibits the use of a bathhouse which was built to honor an idol if a fee must be paid to the idol[509]. On the other hand, even the pious did not take offense if a statue of Aphrodite was present in the bathhouse as an adornment, as apparently was often the case in Palestine[510]. Nevertheless, Rabbi Yochanan broke all the idols in the Demosia of Tiberias[511]. Jews and Gentiles used the same warm bath[512]; such establishments were probably built with public funds[513]. On the other hand, one should not lease to a Gentile a bath which is owned and operated by a Jew, because the Gentile would not interrupt the business on the Sabbath, and the Jew would thereby fall under suspicion of desecrating the Sabbath[514]. One was advised against bathing together with only a single Gentile for reasons of personal safety[515].

## XIV   Warm Baths

The high esteem in which hot baths are held is evidenced primarily by the arguments concerning their permissibility on the Sabbath. As is well known, the Torah prohibits the kindling of a fire on the Sabbath[516], so that a hot bath on the Sabbath would be impossible. One, therefore, heated the bath on Friday and then, at nightfall, locked the place where the fire was burning. In spite of this, soon thereafter the owners of the baths began to secretly make fires on the Sabbath, and it became necessary to totally forbid a water bath, to cover the tubs with boards, and to only allow staying in the hot air to perspire. In order to at least be able to thoroughly accomplish this goal of bathing, on holidays people brought their own glowing coals and gave them to the *olearier*[517]. The bathing fanatics, however, removed the boards, and then even visiting a bathhouse on the Sabbath was totally forbidden. However, the use of natural hot springs was permitted. When deceitfulness occurred even here, the natural hot springs were also closed, and only a cold bath was allowed. Shortly thereafter, one became convinced that "the people cannot bear it", that people could not forego a hot bath even for one day, and, therefore, at least the hot springs were again opened[518].

In addition, there are innumerable proofs for the high esteem in which warm baths were held. A mourner should not take a warm bath during the seven days of mourning, although some Sages allow it, because they consider a bath to be as essential as eating and drinking[519]. A similar thought is already found in the Talmud in the interpretation of Deuteronomy 14:26. There it is prescribed that if the quantity of second tithe is too heavy to transport to Jerusalem *in natura,* it should be exchanged for money, and the money spent for food and beverage, as the heart desires. The Talmud interprets this Biblical regulation to include the permissibility of buying bathing tokens with this money[520].

In times of great droughts, where there was fear of a bad harvest and famine, one established fast days as a sign of penance, and finally it was decided to close the warm baths[521]. A guest was invited to accompany his host to the bathhouse[522]. When Simeon ben Yochai left his hiding place in the cave for the first time after thirteen years, his

506. *Tosefta* Sanhedrin 4:1
507. literally: Divine teaching
508. Berachoth 24b
509. Abodah Zarah 4:3
510. *ibid* 44b; Jerushalmi Shebiith 8: 38a
511. Jerushalmi Abodah Zarah 4; 43d
512. Machshirin 2:5
513. Abodah Zarah 1:7
514. *ibid* 1:9
515. *Tosefta* Abodah Zarah 3:4
516. Exodus 35:3
517. Betzah 32a
518. Shabbath 40a
519. Jerushalmi Berachoth 1; 5b
520. *Tosefta* Maaser Sheni 1:4
521. Taanith 1:5
522. Kallah Rabbathi 9 fol. 54d 78

father-in-law immediately took him to the bathhouse[523]. The landowner who hopes for good business, goes happily to the *beth ha-merchatz*[524]. Someone who arrives in the vicinity of a city with a caravan, hurries over a shortcut to the bathhouse and bathes[525]. A prince left his city and went into the desert; the sun burned on his head so that his face became crocus-colored; he returned to civilization and with a little water from, and a little bathing in, the warm baths, his body became white and beautiful as before[526]. When King Solomon says that he procured for himself "all conveniences of people"[527], he is referring to warm baths[528]. The complaint of the prophet that he must forget "prosperity"[529] mourns the loss of warm baths in captivity[530]. Among the recommended accommodations which should be found in a city before a scholar sets up residence there is a bathing establishment[531].

All vows of a woman which end in asceticism can be forthwith declared null and void by the husband[532]. Included in this rule are vows whereby she renounces the use of a warm bath[533], in addition to the fact that the omission of bathing is damaging to the beauty of a woman[534]. The life of shepherds who live in sheep pens, and that of desert wanderers, is no life at all because, states Ulla, they take no warm baths[535]. If the bath does not enter the body, the bather nevertheless has the same benefit as from an embrocation and from cohabitation[536]. It is related about the land of Shinar that the people there suffocated in the dirt, because they had no light and no warm baths[537]. When Hillel the Elder went to bathe, he declared: "I wish to fulfill a Divine obligation"[538]. If a person dies without heirs, his wealth reverts to the public treasury and the king builds bathhouses for the poor therewith[539]. If the king goes into his land and the people pay homage to him, he promises to build them baths and water conduits[540]. According to the way of the world, the king extols his country, although he has not yet done anything for it, not even built a single bathhouse — first comes his name and then his deeds. The reverse is true of God: at the beginning of the Bible it states "He created" and only then is the name of God mentioned[541].

## XV

This general requirement of warm baths naturally gave rise to the creation of a large number of bathing establishments. Very early, each tribe had thirteen public baths, and jointly owned the springs of Tiberias[542].

Ulla in the year 300 C.E. extolled the large city of Rome, where there were said to be 3000 bathhouses and 500 windows which led the smoke to the outside of the city walls[543]. This apparently exaggerated number is only in accord with the assertions of the contemporary writers. Agrippa alone built 170 public baths whose use was free. "Since then the number of baths in Rome has increased immensely", states the critical Plinius[544]. This gratuitousness is naturally, as always, only apparent; in reality the costs are borne by the taxpayers. The statement of Rabbi Gamliel has this in mind: "the Roman Empire eats us (ruins us) with its tolls, its baths, its theatres and its taxes"[545].

---

523. Shabbath 33b
524. Aboth de Rabbi Nathan 6:3 fol. 21a 12
525. Abodah Zarah 5:4
526. Song of Songs Rabbah 1:6 fol. 9b
527. Eccles. 2:8
528. Gittin 68a
529. Lamentations 3:17
530. Shabbath 25b
531. Sanhedrin 17b
532. Numbers 30:14
533. Nedarim 11:1
534. *ibid* 80a

535. Erubin 55b
536. Berachoth 57b
537. Genesis Rabbah 37:4
538. Levit. Rabbah 34:3
539. Exodus Rabbah 31:11
540. Levit. Rabbah 26:1
541. Genesis Rabbah 1:12
542. Levit. Rabbah 5:3
543. Megillah 6b
544. *Histor. Natur.* 36:24
545. Aboth de Rabbi Nathan 28:4

The bath was always ready for use, and thus did not have to be ordered in advance; as soon as the bath manager received the entrance fee, he would declare: "the bath is open, enter and bathe"[546]. Only at night was it closed, and one could use it as a hiding place[547].

## XVI

The bath was not only considered to be an amenity, but most importantly a means for the maintenance of health. Yet, serious people reproached the Romans for having built their baths only for pleasure[548]. The "watching over one's body" is a religious obligation which the Bible already enjoins. Although the use of a warm bath is forbidden to a healthy mourner, Rabbi Gamliel believed he could not bear abstaining therefrom even on the day that his wife died, because he was of feeble health[549].

Whether many baths are, in fact, necessary for the preservation of health cannot be decided by the prejudiced views of Plinius. He is of the opinion that the detested Greek physicians "ostensibly recommended them for the preservation of health; in reality, however, no one comes out of the bath healthier, and the most obedient patients may come out as corpses"[550]. One should not forget that one did not take *warm* baths but *hot* ones. The *embate* could be so hot that if a violent person jumped therein, he would scald himself[551]. Plinius himself[552] speaks of "burning hot baths", and Celsus describes a *fovens balneum*[553]. Agathinus declares that nurses used to first cook the children soft in hot bath water (*takerothenta* in Greek i.e. soaked in wax) so that they would sleep well[554]. Soran, too, rebukes the scalding of newborns[555]. That these *hot* baths are, in fact, beneficial to health we first learn from the writings of Bälz from Tokyo. Only recently does a medical report indicate that in Japan people consider it important to bathe above 30°C. and to heartily scald oneself[556]. One cannot, however, speak of a pampering of the Japanese. Bälz even asserts that a hot bath protects from a cold.

We often encounter warm baths in civil law. The following law should be appended here: if a man discovers physical defects in his wife after the wedding, which he could not have known about before, he can declare the marriage invalid. If, however, there is a warm bathhouse in that town, then he cannot lodge any complaint about "hidden defects" because he could have had her observed by his female relatives[557]. It is thus assumed to be self-evident that even young girls bathed in warm baths, and indeed together with other women.

## XVII

It is generally accepted that hot baths originated in the Orient, and were then transplanted from there to the West, first to Greece and from there to Rome. Nevertheless, from the foregoing discussions, one notices the large number of Greek names used for details in the arrangements of steam baths. This observation can only be explained as follows: the hot bath itself is a discovery of the Orientals, but the arrangement and refinement of details, so to speak, ensued from the Greeks. There were many occasions, particularly in Alexandria, for this melting of cultural elements, so that the bath, which to a certain extent was a raw material exported out of the

546. Meilah 5:4
547. Kiddushin 39b
548. Shabbath 33b
549. Berachoth 2:7
550. *Histor. Natur.* 29:8
551. *Pesikta de Rav Kahana, Zakor*, p.27a. Also cited by *Rashi* on Deut. 25:18
552. loc. cit.
553. *De Medicina* 1:3; additional citations in Becker-Rein. *Gallus* 3:85
554. in Oribas. *Coll.* 10:7; Vol. 2:396
555. Chapt. 34 p.154
556. *Baln. Centralztg* No. 7, 1902
557. Kethuboth 7:8

Orient, reverts back to its place of origin, but in refined form. Many of the aforementioned details are not provable from Greek writings. This certainly is due to the fact that, as all archaeologists decry, reports concerning Greek baths are altogether very sparse.

# PART  5

## I  Circumcision

The reasons which the religious sources give for *circumcision* have already been enumerated above. Many attempts have been made to represent circumcision as a sanitary expedient; even recent times have produced long series of such attempts. These, however, only presuppose the sanitary consequences of the operation, but do not reveal the reason for it.

In the year 1902, Breitenstein reported that only 0.8 percent of 15,000 native (i.e. circumcised) soldiers of the Dutch-Indian army became ill with syphilis, compared to 4 percent of 18,000 European (i.e. uncircumcised) soldiers of the same army. In spite of the "identical local social and hygienic conditions", one should not forthwith attribute this difference to circumcision, as does Breitenstein. One must also first know the attitude of the Malayans towards the satisfaction of illegal libido (and body cleanliness), either for religious or other reasons. One must also take into consideration that all Europeans are inclined to indulge in sexual excesses as soon as they arrive in the Tropics.

It appears to me that the statistics of Loeb in Mannheim provide stronger evidence[558]. He reports on 2000 uncircumcised and 468 circumcised patients with venereal disease. The circumcised patients were not always Jews, and the uncircumcised patients were not always Christians (exact numbers are lacking). He found syphilis and canker sores in 40 percent of the uncircumcised and 15 percent of the circumcised patients, and attributes this difference to the circumcision.

I would like to note here that a comparison of the number of illnesses among circumcised and uncircumcised Jews does not provide absolute proof of the value of circumcision; for, by experience, the neglect or omission of circumcision by the Jews was accompanied by the abandonment of other precepts and customs of their people, and the influence of such deviations from the Torah on the acquisition of venereal disease cannot be disputed.

Various authors describe a large number of other sicknesses which can be prevented by circumcision: a complete list of such illnesses is found in the work of Remondino[559]. As with some physicians before him, he is, therefore, a champion of the introduction of compulsory *universal circumcision,* similar to smallpox vaccination.

These are the fanatics to the right. The fanatics to the left, among which particularly belong G. Lewin, Pott[560] and Herbert Snow[561], emphasize primarily the dangers which might occur to the child as a result of the circumcision act, but overlook the fact that a large number of these dangers cannot be attributed to the operation itself, but to the operator, particularly when the latter does not strictly observe the precepts of ritual circumcision, as for example, if he performs circumcision on a child two of whose siblings from the same mother died following circumcision (as a result of

---

558. *Monatsschrift für Harnkrankheit* 1904 No. 6
559. *The History of Circumcision.* Philadelphia 1891
560. *Münchener Medizinishe Wochenschrift* 25:1, 1898
561. *The Barbarity of Circumcision.* London 1890

hemorrhage)[562]. The law also prescribes that only "an especially pious and especially capable man should be allowed to perform circumcision"[563].

## II   The Weekly Day of Rest (Sabbath)

Whether any nation of antiquity other than the Jews had a *weekly day of rest* is not being investigated here. It is certain, however, that no nation perceived it in the manner that the Jews did. If one wishes to rationalize, then one can say with Winer: "it was an obvious thought for an agricultural nation to celebrate by resting the last day of the week, since people and animals were exhausted from work"; and then at the same time conclude with his later remark: "why must all Mosaic institutions have a foreign prototype? Why must such simple observances be founded upon such farfetched explanations?"[564].

The Torah commands: *six days shalt thou labor and do all thy work; but the seventh day is the Sabbath of the Lord thy God; in it thou shalt not do any work, thou, nor thy son, nor thy daughter, nor thy manservant, nor thy maidservant, nor thy cattle, nor thy stranger that is within thy gate. For God created the world in six days and rested on the seventh day*[565].

Everything which needs to be said concerning the Jewish Sabbath is contained in these words: one is commanded to work, and work is dignified, with the proof that the Lord God Himself worked. A day of rest should follow exhausting work, and, in fact, for everything that worked, which therefore includes cattle and slaves. The latter stood on the same level as cattle in the eyes of heathen antiquity. The day of rest should be dedicated to God, that is to spiritual matters, and the principal thing leading thereto, the teaching and learning of Torah. For this reason, the Torah is always read at Sabbath synagogue services[566]. Thereby, on the one hand, one is far removed from sadness but, on the other hand, physical pleasures also come into their own: three meals on the Sabbath were prescribed at first hand. One should not consider the Sabbath to be a lost day of work, nor suggest that it gives rise to a "blue Monday"; rather one should contemplate it as a "delight", or *oneg*[567].

Exceptions for individual businesses or professions did not exist. The farmer, concerning whom the question first arose, is specifically commanded to "rest in sowing time as well as in harvest time"[568].

Post-Biblical times brought a large number of explanations of this commandment, particularly in the definition of the term "work". He who herein wishes to ridicule the "micrology" and the "Talmudic sophistry" should compare these with legal decisions which relate to our Sunday rest-day law in Germany, which is only 20 years old.

Today one need not speak any more concerning the health (and also the national economic) value of the Sabbath rest.

## III   Water Supply

The provision of water occurred in three ways:

1. Through wells, *be'eroth,* which were privately owned by individuals or publicly owned[569]. Their great importance often gave rise to disputes and hostility between individual tribes[570]. Naturally, it was extraordinarily fortunate if one discovered a

562. as in the case of Karewski
563. *Yoreh Deah* 264:1
564. *Biblisches Realwörterbuch* 2:410
565. Exod. 20: 9-11
566. literally: collective Sabbath worship

567. Isaiah 58:13
568. Exodus 34:21
569. Erubin 2:4
570. Genesis 21:25

"well of living (i.e. flowing) water"[571]. One also rented them for use for a certain finite time period[572].

2. By far the most common sources of water were cisterns in which rainwater was gathered. There were two types:

(a) The usual one, which alone is mentioned in the Bible, is the cistern, *bor,* which is dug in loose earth or hewn in rocks. The ideal is *"bor sud"*, a limed (cemented) cistern which does not allow the loss of any drop of water[573].

(b) First mentioned in the Talmud is the *duth* or *chaduth,* which is a water basin standing above the ground which has borders and sconces[574]. A *bor* is dug whereas a *duth* is built[575].

In the courtyards of large houses, both types were found[576]; they are not, however, a component of *every* house. If someone sells a house, the *bor* and *duth* are not considered to be included in the sale, even if the buyer bought "the depth and the height"[577].

The large Alexandrian ships, which served the commerce of the Mediterranean Sea, had a *bor,* a tank for sweet water[578].

Cisterns used to be covered with a stone[579] to protect the water from becoming dirty and warm[580]. In the cities, there were also public cisterns or *bor-ha-rabbim*[581]. Some were very large, so that once Ishmael ben Natanya was able to cast seventy dead bodies therein[582]. Joseph was thrown into a dried-out cistern by his brothers[583]. A girl who had aborted threw the fetus into a cistern[584].

"In general, cistern water is good and cool, and to a person who is accustomed thereto, it often tastes better than some well water, primarily because when it is directly drawn, it is fresher than water which was drawn from a well and which became tepid from even a very short transport"[584a].

3. Jerusalem, situated on limestone rocks, possesses only a single well, which was already named *Gichon* in the Bible[585]; even this well was situated outside the city wall. However, under Hezekiah (700 B.C.E.), its water was led through a 535 -meter-long canal to the Siloa pool, and from there to the city. In 1880, an ancient Hebrew inscription was discovered at the southern exit of the canal which provides information about its construction[586]. Moreover, however, there existed another large water conduit which provided the city with water from the south, and its collecting basins were in the Solomonite pools which are still in existence today. Thereby, and by means of numerous cisterns, Jerusalem never suffered from lack of water.

# IV    Lavatories

The usual expression for the lavatory is *beth ha-kisse,* "the place (or site) of the seat or the chair", and not "the place of concealment".

The Biblical *kese,* which people ordinarily refer to, probably has a totally different meaning. In support of the first meaning is the Jerusalem Talmud[587] where it speaks of the "feces under the *kisse*". Rarely is the expression *beth-ha-mayyim,* site of the water (i.e. *urinary),* used.

---

571. *ibid* 26:20
572. Aboth De Rabbi Nathan 6:3 fol. 21a 7
573. Aboth 2:8
574. Oholoth 11:8
575. Baba Bathra 64a
576. *bor:* Second Samuel 17:19; *duth:* Oholoth 11:8
577. Baba Bathra 4:2
578. Shabbath 35a
579. Genesis 29:2
580. Baurat Schick. Die Wasserversorgung der Stadt Jerusalem, in *ZDPV* 1,1878 p.132-176
581. Erubin 2:4
582. Jeremiah 41:9
583. Genesis 37:24
584. *Tosefta* Oholoth 16:13
584a. See note 580 above
585. Genesis 29:2
586. Portrayed in Benzinger-Frohnmeyer. *Bilderatlas zur Bibelkund.* Stuttgart 1905. Pictures 151 and 348
587. Jerushalmi Pesachim 3; 30a

The Biblical *macharaoth*[588] is considered to refer to lavatory — in fact, "the site of defecation", *charaim*. Both expressions are replaced by the Masoretes by dysentery, *motzaoth* and *tzoah*[589]. It is, therefore, a double outrage when the Assyrian general speaks of people who eat their feces, *chorehem,* and drink their urine, *shenehem;* for even the latter word is indecent and is replaced by *me reglayim.*

One must conceive of the lavatory facilities in antiquity as having been quite primitive, as we still find today in rural areas. As a rule, however, one retired quite a distance from the vicinity of an inhabited city and relieved oneself in the open field, up to one mile away (*circa,* a 20 minute walk)[590]. Here there was a designated place therefor; nearby were stones (bricks *or lebena*) placed together upon which one sat[591]. The Persian lavatories were extolled in that they had ditches between or behind the stones[592]; these ditches could not be provided in Babylon because of the swampy ground[593]. These sites were probably surrounded by a fence; this was the *beth ha-kisse kabua*[594], the permanently designated lavatory, which one probably built for that purpose, and concerning whose existence one must take heed before one settles in a city[595].

A rich man lends money for usury, and in this manner amasses a fortune. If he died without heirs, his entire fortune is taken over by the royal (or public) treasury. What is done with this money? Bathing establishments and rest homes and lavatories for the poor who cannot afford to build these by themselves are constructed[596], exactly according to the words of the poet: *he that by usury and unjust gain increaseth his substance, he shall gather it for him that will pity the poor*[597]. It is a formal law that a lavatory may only be sold on the condition that the purchasers will return it to the vendors if they so desire and not keep it permanently[598].

A special regulation existed for time of war. *When your host goeth forth against thine enemies, then keep thee from every wicked thing…Thou shalt have a place (yad), also without the camp, wither thou shalt go forth abroad. And thou shalt have a paddle upon thy weapon, and it shall be, when thou wilt ease thyself abroad, thou shalt dig therewith, and shalt turn back and cover that which cometh from thee (excrements). For the Lord thy God walketh in the midst of thy camp…therefore, shall thy camp be holy*[599]. In this commandment, we observe for time immemorial a national camp hygiene, a prophylaxis against the spread of contagious disease. The Essenes strictly observed this commandment even in time of peace[600].

The opposite of the *beth ha-kisse kabua* (the permanent lavatory) is the *beth ha-kisse ar'ai,* the occasional, random lavatory, any place outside the range of vision of people. No one should urinate at (or on) the wall of a neighbor[601]. One must remain three handbreadths distant from clay walls and two handbreadths from stone (or brick) walls. If the wall is made of boulders, it is permitted to urinate on it[602]. In Babylon, one was not even allowed to urinate on solid ground or in an earthenware vessel, firstly because, according to Rab, the slopes of Babel would carry the water to the well called *Etham* in which the High Priest bathed on the Day of Atonement[603]; and secondly,

---

588. Second Kings 10:27
589. Isaiah 36:12 and Second Kings 18:27
590. Berachoth 62a, Raba
591. *ibid* 61b
592. *ibid* 26a
593. *ibid* 8a; *Rashi*
594. *ibid* 23a
595. Sanhedrin 17b
596. Exodus Rabbah 31:11
597. Proverbs 28:8
598. Megillah 3:2 *beth ha-mayim;* Orach

Chayim 153:9 *beth ha-kissé*
599. Deut. 23: 10-15
600. Josephus. *The Jewish War.* Book 2, Chapt. 8:9
601. perhaps from here is derived the scornful ring of the ambiguous Biblical phrase *mashtin bekir* meaning "he who urinates on the wall". First Samuel 25:22 and in the Book of Kings
602. *Tosefta* Baba Bathra 1:4
603. Yoma 31a

because one might empty the vessel at the nearest convenient place, possibly into a river[604]. Only a heathen urinates in the middle of the road; a Jew is supposed to proceed to one side or go to a corner to urinate in semi-privacy[605]. A horse stands still when it urinates and can thereby endanger its rider during a battle[606].

The custom of women of urinating before the hearth so that the food will be cooked more rapidly was forbidden as a heathen superstition[607]...Abaye said to his colleagues: when you walk through the small streets of Mechoza to reach the field (i.e. the *beth hakisse kabua*), do not look either to the right or to the left; perhaps there are women sitting there, and it is not proper to gaze at them[608]. Particularly preferrred for defecation and urination were corner nooks, *keren zavith,* and the backside of a fence[609].

It was considered proper before entering a *beth ha-kisse* to clear one's throat or to blow one's nose *(nachar)* in order to discover whether or not the lavatory is free[610]. He who occupies it should hurry up to make room for the person who is coming, exactly the opposite of a bathhouse where the new arrival has to wait[611]. One was advised against staying alone in a water house *(urinary)* with a Gentile[612], probably because of the fear of a surprise attack. It once happened that a Persian dragged away by force Rabbi Eleazar who was sitting on the lavatory; it was the latter's good fortune, because immediately thereafter a snake came crawling along and bit the Persian in the hindquarters so that he died[613]. Particularly emphasized is the fact that in the vestibule of the Temple there was a "dignified (decent) lavatory". Its "dignity" consisted in the fact that it could be locked. If it was locked, it meant that it was occupied[614]. Later there seem to have been many such "dignified" lavatories[615]. There existed lavatories for public use, *shel rabbim,* and others which were privately owned[616].

Little fuss was made at night. Then one sought a place on the street which was free of people, and one sat down[617]. Therefore, the advice that Rab Chiya and Rabbi Huna gave their sons was: take care of your needs morning and evening; then you will not have to go so far[618].

# V

These conditions, namely the inconvenience of having to search for the lavatory at a more or less considerable distance, make it understandable why one ascribes such great importance to its existence and particularly its easy access. "Every pious person shall pray to God that he find the toilet in time"; thus does Mar Zutra[619] interpret the words of the Psalmist[620]. The Biblical phrase *Blessed shalt thou be in the city*[621] refers to a person who has a *beth ha-kisse* near his table[622], which to us modern people appears to border on blasphemy. Rabbi Jose says that a person is rich if he has a toilet near his table[623] which he can easily reach when he is plagued by Oriental dysentery. The *Midrash* states: if God gave understanding to fools, they would rejoice with toilets, theatres and bathhouses[624].

---

604. Bechoroth 44b
605. Lamentations Rabbah 1:12 fol. 11d; Sanhedrin 104b has *niphna,* he defecated instead of "urinated".
606. Jerushalmi Pesachim 4; 31a
607. Shabbath 67b. However, it is not a superstition to place a chip of mulberry wood or glass shards into the pot for the same purpose; nevertheless the shards were forbidden because of danger.
608. Berachoth 62a
609. Tohoroth 10:2
610. Berachoth 62a
611. Derech Eretz Rabbah 10:2 and Rabbi

Jacob Naumburg *loc. cit.*
612. *Tosefta* Abodah Zarah 3:4
613. Berachoth 62a
614. Tamid 1:1
615. Tefillin fol. 63a
616. Eccles. Rabbah 1:8 fol. 4a
617. Berachoth 62a
618. Tamid 27b
619. Berachoth 8a
620. Psalms 32:6
621. Deut. 28:3
622. Baba Metzia 107a
623. Shabbath 28b
624. Eccles. Rabbah 1:7 fol. 3a

A Roman matron ridiculed Rabbi Judah ben Illay when she said: you look as well-nourished as if you were a pork fattener or a money lender for usury. He, however, retorted: both are prohibited in Judaism, but on the road from my house to the house of study there are 24 lavatories, and at each I can think whether nature is calling and, if so, I can relieve myself immediately[625]. One sees from here the importance one ascribed to the unhindered ability to relieve oneself for the body's wellbeing.

With great emphasis, it is required that discreet conditions, *tzniuth,* exist in the lavatory. One should not disrobe when one is still standing, but first when one is seated[626]. Rabbi Gamliel extolled the Persians for such modesty[627]. Rabbi Tanchum ben Chanillay teaches: he who behaves modestly in the toilet is protected from three dangers: snakes, scorpions and demons. In Tiberias, there was a *beth ha-kisse* in which people were harmed, even if they entered in pairs during the day. Only Rabbi Ammi and Rabbi Assi were not harmed, because they knew the antidote: modesty and silence. One should not deviate from this modesty even at night[628].

It is considered damaging to one's health to "suspend" oneself in the *beth ha-kisse,* and to markedly lower the seat, because one feared that injury to the intestines might thereby result[629]. One should also not sit down too hastily nor press down too hard; because the large intestine, the *karkashta,* lies on three teeth, and these "intestinal teeth" might become loosened, and the person in question might become endangered (rectal prolapse?)[630].

The toilet is a dirty place; one should, therefore, not only refrain from speaking on Torah matters there, but not even reflect on them. Yet, nevertheless, Rabbi Zera said: "whenever something was difficult for me to understand, I understood it there (in the toilet)"[631], a noteworthy experience which one can even today hear confirmed by many people. Before one entered that dirty place, one used to solemnly take leave of the angels which constantly accompany every person in his life's pathways[632]. The above-mentioned dangers of snakes and scorpions to which one was exposed on a swampy floor make it appear understandable that one thought that toilets were inhabited by demons. The same is still a popular belief among the modern day Arabs who do not utter the name of Allah in the *beth el-ma* where all types of demons live. The pious protects himself from this by reciting upon entering the lavatory the following saying from the Koran: "peace upon *Nûch* in the worlds"[633].

We also have in this regard a totally unexplained magical incantation against the demon of the lavatory: "On the head of a lion and on the snout of a lioness did we find the demon Bar Shirika Panda; with a bed of leeks I hurled him down, and with the jawbone of an ass I smote him"[634]. It was thought this demon had the form of a ram (or goat). It is related about Abaye that he took a goat into the lavatory for this reason, to deflect the goat from his person. One used to rattle "with a nut in the basin", or someone behind the wall placed his hand on the head of the person sitting on the toilet[635]. The demon used to accompany a person for a little while longer; for this reason one should avoid cohabitation immediately after using the lavatory, because otherwise one begets epileptic children[636]. Upon leaving the lavatory, one should say: "Lord of the Universe. You know that if one of the orifices which You have created in man were to become unduly opened or closed, it would be impossible for the person to remain alive. Therefore, I thank Thee, wonderful healer of all people"[637].

625. Berachoth 55a; very characteristic is the parallel in Jerushalmi Pesachim 10; 37c
626. Berachoth 62a
627. *ibid* 8b
628. *ibid* 62a
629. *ibid* 55a
630. Shabbath 82a

631. Jerushalmi Berachoth 3;6b
632. Berachoth 60a
633. Hurgronje Snouck. *Mekka* 2:41
634. Shabbath 67a
635. Berachoth 62a
636. Kallah Rabbathi 1:52 a 29
637. Berachoth 60a

Probably only in case of necessity did one defecate in the house using a *Leibstuhl* ("body chair"). The name used by the Romans for this chair is *sella* (in full *sella pertusa* or *familiarica*), and this term is also found in the *Mishnah*. According to the commentaries, it was an iron seat with a leather covering, below which stood a bucket[638]. This leather covering is also mentioned in the *Gemara*[639]. In addition, the following are mentioned: the *beth ha-rei*[640] or *graph shel rei*[641], meaning a chamber pot (or feces pot); the *gasteriyoth* (or *natzriyoth*)[642], according to the *Aruch* derived from the Arabic *gazriya*, usually referring to night pots[643]; *cheres*, the earthenware night pot[644]; *sephel*, a urine basin (bowl)[645]; in the Gemara: *abith shel mémé raglayim*, the urine utensil[646]; also *kankan*[647] or *karun*[648].

From the time of the Judges, we have the report that the King of Moab was stabbed by Ehud. His servants found the door of the winter garden, *mekera* (parlor), which was located on the roof (in the *alliya*), locked and bolted, and they presumed that: *surely he covereth his feet* in the designated room of the winter garden, and they tarried until they were ashamed that they didn't investigate earlier[649]. Josephus modestly notes that the servants thought the king fell asleep[650], probably because he couldn't believe that a sovereign should answer the call of nature in the house. The *Midrash* is also of the opinion that it was not customary for kings to have a lavatory, a *beth ha-rei*, in the palace. For this reason, Belshazzar, who suffered from diarrhea the entire night out of fear concerning the meaning of *mene thekel,* had to leave his house[651]. It was a popular fiction of Egyptian kings that they, as gods, had no human excretory needs: For this reason Moses was commanded to go to Pharaoh when he *goeth out unto the water*[652], and to catch him at the critical moment, for a king does not have a lavatory in his house[653]! Even modern master builders are of the same opinion. The *Palazzo Pitti* has no lavatories, just as Klenzer, the builder of the royal buildings in Munich, forgot them[654]! In the playhouse in Frankfort a.M., the forgetfulness of the builder was later rectified.

# VI    Defecation

To cleanse the anus after defecation, as in antiquity in general[655], little stones were used; *abanim mekortzaloth,* of varying sizes. These were eventually carried in a small sack, *chaphisa*[656]. One also used shards, particularly the upper, smooth edges of broken jugs, since other shards are dangerous. A virgin can even damage her hymen[657]. One is warned against the use of reed skin, *krum shel kana,* because of the danger of splinters. One should also not use things which are affected by light, such as fresh grass (dry grass would be acceptable); for otherwise "the teeth of the *inferiores*" tear *(shinnay ha-tachtoniyoth)*[658]. One is probably here referring to hemorrhoidal bleeding[659]. One should not cleanse the anus with water from which a dog has licked,

---

638. Kelim 22:10
639. Erubin 10b
640. Kelim 17:2
641. *Tosefta* Shabbath 3:12
642. Machshirin 2:3
643. Fleischer on Levy's *Neuhebräisches und Chaldäisches Wörterbuch*. Leipzig 1876-1889, 1:435b
644. *Tosefta* Toharoth 5:3
645. Niddah 9:2
646. Berachoth 25b; Baba Bathra 89b
647. Genesis Rabbah 19:11
648. Numbers Rabbah 20:6

649. Judges 3:24-25
650. *Antiquities*. Book 5. Chapt. 4:2
651. Song of Songs Rabbah 3:4 fol. 19d
652. Exodus 7:15
653. Exodus Rabbah 9:8
654. Döpler in a *feuilleton*
655. For the Greeks: Aristophanes. Friede 1232; Pluto 818; for the Arabs: Relandus, *De Relig. Mohammed* p.59, no. 5
656. Shabbath 81a
657. Yebamoth 59b
658. Shabbath 82a
659. see above Chapter 4, Part 8:6

nor with the snout of a dog or in the face of a dog. The water with which one washes the pipes[660] or the tub is harmful for the anus[661].

One should only wipe oneself with the left hand, not with the right, for one eats with the latter[662]; the hand which touches the anus is worthy of being chopped off[663]. It is probable that all ancient nations utilized their left hand[664], but I could find no reason given for this habit.

If one touches any part of the naked body, one is obligated to wash the hands; in the Temple it was, in fact, the general rule that "whoever covered his feet" required a full bath[665], a phrase already usually used in the Bible for "defecation"[666]. The *chiton* (tunic?) was free of feet and only covered the feet when one crouched.

To the Rabbis, the embodiment of filth is the *pig,* and some modern scholars attribute the Biblical prohibition of eating its flesh to its habit of constantly wallowing in dung. Its snout was compared to a wandering or strolling toilet[667]. It was also said that contagious diseases *(nega'im)* mostly crop up from the pig[668].

# VII   Dung Heaps

Dung heaps, *ashpoth,* in the Talmud *ashpa,* were present next to houses and on the street[669]. All wastes from the house were also brought there[670]; some people even threw dead poultry there. The odor of this dung heap was naturally not very pleasant[671]. The construction of dung heaps was forbidden in Jerusalem. The reason given was the prevention of *tumah*[672], but the value of this precept for hygiene is naturally not to be overlooked. In Jerusalem there was a Dung Gate, *sha'ar ha-ashpa*[673], probably the one through which the dung was removed from the city.

Dung, salt, lime and stones must be stored three handbreadths distant from a neighbor's wall or the wall must be limed[674].

Noteworthy is a remark which is found in the Talmud quite incidentally in a discussion of the laws concerning the found money of Shemaya bar Sira in the year 200 C.E.: "the streets of Jerusalem were cleaned (swept) daily"[675]. It is noteworthy in that, even today, a daily cleaning of the streets of the large cities in the Orient is unknown. Road construction in Jerusalem is probably already spoken of in the Bible[676]. According to Josephus, the city was paved with white marble under Claudius *(katastoresai leuko litho)*[677].

Four weeks before the festival of Passover, they began to repair the streets and highways leading to Jerusalem, as well as the baths and the water reservoirs which became loosened or dirty during the rainy season, to alleviate the pilgrimage to Jerusalem prescribed in the Bible[678].

Even street lighting was known. It was decreed that oil of priest's due which became unclean and, therefore, would ordinarily be burned be utilized to light dark streets[679], probably because they were a publicly used utility. To my knowledge, this is

---

660. Jerushalmi Shabbath 8; 11c; edit. Krotoschin 1866 *bibne,* Pietrikow 1897 *bubne; Korban Ha'edah: bibna* or *bibin,* plural of *bib; Pne Moshe; bebé bané;* "in the bathhouse; the water with which one rinses oneself after perspiring"
661. *ibid*
662. Berachoth 61b; Rabbi Eliezer
663. Shabbath 108b
664. Rosenbaum. *Lustseuche* p.344, footnote 7
665. Yoma 3:2
666. Judges 3:24; First Samuel 24:4; see also Jerushalmi Shabbath 8; 11c

667. Jerushalmi Berachoth 1; 4c
668. Kiddushin 49b
669. Chullin 12a
670. Jerushalmi Shabbath 2:4 d 69
671. Berachoth 25a
672. *Tosefta* Negaim 6:2
673. Shabbath 15a
674. Baba Bathra 2:1
675. Baba Metzia 26a
676. Nehemiah 3:8
677. *Antiquities.* Book 20, Chapt. 9:7
678. Shekalim 1:1
679. Terumoth 11:10

not mentioned elsewhere in the Talmud. In general, one made use of torches by night especially on a highway[680].

# VIII

If a person has a business involving blood or animal cadavers, as a result of which crows gather and disturb the neighbors, with their croaking, even if only one of the neighbors declares: "my nature is weakly[681], I am nervous *(kapdan)* or physically ill; I cannot tolerate it", then he must give up that business or remove it so far that it does not disturb anyone anymore. The same applies to smoke nuisance (or pollution) and the odors from open lavatories. The business proprietor cannot claim the benefit of prescriptive law[682]. Similarly, in a common courtyard, any tenant can prohibit any other tenant from establishing a shop with the assertion: I cannot sleep because of the noise of those who enter and those who leave. The sale must take place in the market or on the sides of the street[683].

The general rule is as follows: for everything which is known to be intolerable to some, there exists no prescriptive law even if it is tolerable to other people[684].

There was thus greater concern for tranquility (not only sleep) in those days than today where German law requires no consideration for any individual.

---

680. for example Sotah 21a
681. Baba Bathra 23a
682. *Choshen Mishpat* 155: 39-40

683. Baba Bathra 2:3
684. Choshen Mishpat 155:41

# CHAPTER XVIII

## *DIETETICS*

Dietetics is the hygiene of the individual; it provides the rules which a healthy person should follow in order that he not become ill. However, "diet" in the sense of the ancients does not refer only to nutrition as in modern usage, but includes the entire mode of life of an individual. Therefore, in order to pass proper judgement on the dietetic rules of a people, it is first necessary to be familiar with its entire *normal* way of life, the errors of which the dietetic rules seek to avoid. In other words, one must describe an entire archaeology; for residence and clothing and sport and work and many other things have certain influences on health and belong in the word "diet". For obvious reasons, I have resigned myself to not presenting such an all encompassing picture. As much as is required for the understanding of specific rules will be provided.

### I   General Health

Praises of *health* are sung by the Sirachites[1]. "A poor man who is well and has a strong constitution is better off than a rich man who is afflicted in body. Health and a good constitution are better than any amount of gold, and a strong body, than untold riches. There is no greater wealth than health of body". The high esteem in which health is held finds expression in the law in that, as already mentioned, all laws concerning the observance of the Sabbath or a Holy Day or dietary laws and the like are set aside in the case of a possible danger to life.

### II   General Rules of Nutrition

First of all, the following general rules concerning nutrition should be enumerated:

1. *Eat moderately! More numerous are the people that die at the cooking pot than are victims of starvation*[2]. Rabbi Chiya taught: in a meal which you enjoy, indulge not excessively[3]. Elijah once said to Rabbi Nathan: eat a third and drink a third and leave a third empty so that you can exist (and not explode) when your abdomen is full of anger[4]. Cases of sudden death following marked excitement after opulent dinners are well known.

2. *Eat simply!* Two men entered a shop. One ate coarse bread and vegetables while the other ate fine bread and fat meat and drank old wine. The one who ate fine food suffered harm, while the one who had coarse food escaped harm. Observe how simply animals live and how healthy they are as a result[5]. The Talmud relates[6]: when one can eat barley bread, but eats wheaten bread, one violates the Biblical precept of *thou shalt not destroy* (your wealth and your health)[7].

---

1. Sirach 30:14-16
2. Shabbath 33a
3. Gittin 70a
4. *ibid*

5. Ecclesiastes Rabbah 1:18
6. Shabbath 140b
7. Deut. 20:19

If someone says: "with what shall I eat my bread", take the bread away from him too[8]. Rabbi Judah bar Ilai said: eat onions *(bazel)* and dwell in the protection *(bezel)* of your house (i.e. do not overspend on food and you will be able to afford your house); and do not eat geese and chicken, lest your heart pursue you (i.e. do not cultivate a greedy appetite); reduce your food and drink and increase expenditure on your house. When Ulla came, he said: in the West (Palestine) a proverb is current: He who eats the fat tail *(allitha)* must hide in the loft *(alitha)* (i.e. he who squanders his money on costly dishes must hide from his creditors), but he who eats cress *(kakule)* may sit in front of his door *(kikle)* (afraid of none, not being in debt)[9].

3. *Eat slowly!* The Talmud states: Chew well with your teeth and you will find it in your steps[10], and the drawing out of a meal prolongs a man's life[11].

*Rashi* interprets the latter Talmudic statement in a moral sense: in time, poor people will come and join in the meal, and, as a result, the host will receive Divine reward by having his life prolonged.

4. *Eat regularly!* Alteration in one's way of life leads to disturbances of digestion, teaches Mar Samuel[12]. A source of difficulties for this rule is the Sabbath, for which richer food is prescribed. Thereby, *all the days of the poor are evil*[13], because even his Sabbaths and festivals, which require a change in his way of life, lead to evil (i.e., indigestion)[14]. It is necessary to be satisfied with cold food on the Sabbath because on this day there is a prohibition against kindling a fire[15].

Rabbi Chanina teaches: hot water to drink and bathe in after the termination of the Sabbath is therapeutic (i.e., soothing); so, too, warm food. For Rabbi Abbahu, a three-year-old calf was prepared at the termination of the Sabbath, of which he ate a kidney[16]. The members of the lay division of the priesthood fasted on four days of the week, from Monday to Thursday; but they did not fast on Friday out of respect for the Sabbath, nor on Sunday in order not to suddenly change over from the rest and delight of the Sabbath to weariness and fasting and so, perhaps, die[17].

5. He who wishes to derive the greatest pleasure from his food should eat during the day; for *better is the sight of the eyes than the wandering of the desire*[18]. For this reason, the blind also eat, but are not satiated[19], and do not have full gratification.

## III Bread

The main nutrition of people was bread, and it was so predominant a part of the diet that "eating bread" was said to be the same as "consuming food". We also speak of our "daily bread". Caravans of old took bread as food for the journey and wine in bottles[20]. A rich man ate wheat bread and a poor man ate barley bread[21], possibly even mixed with coarse bran[22]. Bran bread, *path qibar*, was completely black and was sold outside bakeries[23]. Prisoners received this type of bread as their daily ration[24]. Bread was also made out of rice and millet and lentils[25]. The taste of the *manna,* which God gave to the Israelites in the desert as nourishment, varied according to the individual nutritional needs of each person and its taste varied accordingly. Young men ate it as bread, old men as honeywafers. To the babies it tasted like the milk from their mother's breasts, and to the sick it was like fine flour mingled with honey[26].

---

8. Sanhedrin 100b
9. Pesachim 114a
10. Shabbath 152a
11. Berachoth 54b
12. Sanhedrin 101a
13. Proverbs 15:15
14. *ibid*
15. Exodus 35:3
16. Shabbath 119b
17. Taanith 4:3

18. Eccles. 6:9
19. Yoma 74b
20. Joshua 9:5
21. Josephus. *The Jewish War.* Vol. 5. 70:2
22. Shabbath 76b
23. Song of Songs Rabbah 1:6
24. Jeremiah 37:21
25. Ezekiel 4:9 and Erubin 81a
26. Exodus Rabbah 5:9

The Talmud teaches[27] that three things increase movement of the bowels, bend the stature, and take away one five hundredth part of a man's eyesight. These are coarse black bread (i.e. bran bread), fresh date wine (i.e. beer), and raw vegetables (if consumed excessively). Three things decrease movement of the bowels, straighten the stature and give light to the eyes. These are clean (i.e. white) bread, fat meat and old wine. White bread means made of fine meal; fat meat means from a goat which has not yet given birth to young; old wine means very old. Everything which is beneficial for one body organ is detrimental to another, except for moist ginger, long peppers, white bread, fat meat and old wine, which are beneficial for the whole body.

Samuel took the recently arrived seasick Rab into his house, gave him barley bread and a fish pie to eat and date wine to drink, in order that Rab develop diarrhea[28].

An infant doesn't learn to say father and mother until it has tasted of wheat[29].

## IV    Bread Seasoning

A poor person is satisfied with dipping his bread in salt[30] or vinegar, particularly as a refreshment in hot weather[31]. Accordingly, the worst curse is: you should have neither vinegar nor salt in your house[32]! Salt is a necessary seasoning for every food. Rabbi Dimi says that a meal without salt is no meal, and Rabbi Yochanan says that a meal without *saraph* (either gravy or vegetable juices or something sharp) is no meal[33]. A proverbial expression is the following: "(without taste) like a food without salt"[34]. Salt is cheap; pepper is expensive. People can exist without pepper, but not without salt[35]. However, it must be used in the proper proportions. Three things are harmful in large amounts, but beneficial in small amounts: yeast, salt and humility[36]. Different concentrations of salt water were employed. The strongest mixture consisted of two parts salt and one part water. Salt water in which an egg floats is called *halme*[37]. An expert cook was required for its preparation[37a].

Important for dietetics is the following rule of Rabbi Chiya: after every food eat salt, and after every beverage drink water, and you will come to no harm. And another rule is as follows: if one ate any kind of food without taking salt after it, or drank any beverage without taking water after it, by day he is liable to suffer from an evil-smelling mouth and by night he will suffer from *askara* (croup?)[38].

In time of war, when the enemy cut off the water supply, people were content with a drop of vinegar or date wine[39]; for vinegar envigorates[40], even though it is harmful to the teeth[41].

## V    Cabbage and Turnips

As a rule, bread was eaten with a relish, *lipthan*[42]. Whether this relish was usually turnips (Brassica rapa), as one could conjecture from the name *lepheth,* remains uncertain. Opinions were greatly divided concerning the wholesomeness of this relish. Some considered it harmful: woe to the house (stomach) through which turnips are passing![43] Others considered turnips beneficial if they were well cooked, and yet others only when they were prepared with meat; and others still only when wine was imbibed after their consumption. Raba said to his servant: if you see turnips in the market, you

27. Pesachim 42a-b
28. Shabbath 108a
29. Sanhedrin 70b
30. Berachoth 2b
31. Ruth 2:14
32. Aboth de Rabbi Nathan 20:1
33. Berachoth 44a
34. *ibid* 34a; Kallah Rabbathi 3:52d 11
35. Jerushalmi Horayoth 3; 48c
36. Berachoth 34a
37. Shabbath 108b
37a. Jerushalmi Shabbath 14; 14c
38. Berachoth 40a
39. Aboth de Rabbi Nathan 20:1
40. Jerushalmi Shabbath 14; 14d
41. Proverbs 10:26
42. Nega'im 13:9
43. Berachoth 44b

need not ask me what relish I would like to eat with my bread[44]. He could probably afford to have them prepared in any desired manner.

*Lepheth* is a type of cabbage. Only the stalk of another type of cabbage, the *kerub* (Brassica oleracea)[45], was ordinarily used for eating. For sick people, the plant itself (the leaves) is also useful[45a].

## VI   Meat

*Meat* represents another very important nutrient. The general prerequisites which must be fulfilled before one is allowed to eat meat at all have been discussed in the previous chapter. When we speak simply of "meat", we refer only to meat of domesticated ruminant animals, and even there only if all the other aforementioned conditions have been met.

During the wandering of the Jews in the desert, every slaughtering was an act of offering; that is, every ox, lamb or goat that was to be slaughtered and was deemed fit therefor had to be brought as an offering in the Tabernacle, and the owner only received his portion. This rule in the desert was an expedient in order to prevent offerings to idols[46]. This restriction was not lifted until after the conquest of Canaan and the dispersal throughout the land, whereby there were great distances between the masses of the people and the sanctuary in Jerusalem. *When thou wilt say: "I will eat flesh", because thy soul desireth to eat flesh; thou mayest eat flesh after all the desire of thy soul. (If the place which the Lord thy God choose to put His name there be too far from thee) then thou shalt kill of thy herd and of thy flock (which the Lord hath given thee), and thou shalt eat within thy gates after all the desire of thy soul*[47].

Concerning this the Talmud remarks: from this law one can learn the following rules of life:

1.  a person should only eat meat when he has a special desire (or need) therefor.

2.  *of thy herd* means that a person should eat only if he himself owns cattle, but should not purchase meat in the market (admonition to breed cattle oneself[48]!)

3.  *of thy herd* means not "all" your cattle.

On this basis, Rabbi Eleazar ben Azariah taught that a man who has one *maneh*[49] should buy a pound of vegetables for his stew; if he has ten *maneh,* he may buy a pound of fish for his stew; if he has fifty *maneh,* he may buy a pound of meat for his stew, and if he has a hundred *maneh,* he may have a pot set on the hearth for him every day. Rabbi Yochanan added that this only applies to extremely healthy people, "but as for us, whosoever amongst us has a penny in his purse should hasten with it to the shop-keeper". Rabbi Nachman said: "as for us, we must even borrow to eat"[50].

The commentary of *Tosafoth* calls attention to the thought that in the time of Rabbi Eleazar, fish must have been cheaper than meat. However, in the *Midrash*[51], the following is taught: guests were fed geese and chickens on the first day, fish on the second day, meat on the third day and legumes on the fourth day; the longer they stayed, the simpler the foods. Here, *meat* must have been cheaper.

The author of Proverbs teaches us: *Be not among winebibbers; among riotous eaters of flesh. For the drunkard and the glutton shall come to poverty*[52].

*Attend to the life of your young ones (your young offspring)*[53]. From here, says Mar Zutra, learn that *you should not teach your child to eat meat or drink wine.*

---

44. ibid
45. Löw. *Pflanzennamen* p.213
45a. Berachoth 44b
46. Leviticus 17:3-7
47. Deut. 12:20-21
48. Chullin 84b

49. a coin equal to 100 *zuz*
50. Chullin 84a
51. *Tanchuma Pinchas* 78b and *Pesikta de Rav Kahana* 195b. Buber
52. Proverbs 23:20-21
53. Proverbs 27:27

During the sojourn in the wilderness, the Jews naturally ate very little meat — hence the surprised question of Moses in Numbers 11:22 — since the existing cattle were needed as beasts of transport and for breeding. It was, therefore, natural that after their entrance into Canaan when the *manna* ceased, the Children of Israel next turned to the *fruit of the land, mithebuath ha'aretz*[54], and no doubt nourished themselves with vegetables.

## VII    Meat at Festive Occasions

Meat is, therefore, not part of the normal nutrition of man. Sirach enumerates the following elements as essential for man's life: water, fire, iron, salt, wheat flour, honey, milk, grape blood, olive oil and clothing[55] — meat is not among them. Meat and wine belong only to joyous occasions where one eats out of joy.[56] Meat should also not be lacking on the Sabbath table, and the same applies to the meal that we prepare for a beloved guest. Abraham set meat from a tender and good calf before the messengers of God who were his guests[57]. Rabbi Hamnuna used to say: What does a good guest say? How much trouble my host has taken for me! How much meat he has set before me! How much wine he has set before me! How many cakes he has set before me! And all the trouble he has taken was only for my sake! But what does a bad guest say? How much after all has my host put himself out? I have eaten a piece of bread, I have eaten a slice of meat, I have drunk a cup of wine! All the trouble which my host has taken was only for the sake of his wife and children[58].

According to the opinion of Rabbi Simeon ben Gamliel, if meat and wine only belong at festive occasions, then it would be appropriate that we not eat meat or drink wine, since our Holy Temple has been destroyed. However, the authorities do not impose a law by which most people could not survive[59].

## VIII    Vegetarian Diet

According to the text of the Torah, which is also confirmed in the tradition[60], the first people on earth ate no meat at all. Only after the deluge were they permitted *every moving thing that liveth as food for you, even as the green herb*[61]. On the other hand, according to one legend, the angels roasted meat and cooled wine for Adam in paradise[62].

If anyone wishes to draw a conclusion in this matter, it cannot be "that God decreed that people exclusively eat fruit", as the extreme vegetarians propound[63]. It is nearly self-evident that primitive man was not familiar with the killing of animals and their consumption, but rather first learned it when he did battle with them.

Equally prejudiced is the application of the narrative in the book of Daniel.

After the conquest of Jerusalem, Nebuchadnezzar instructed that four young men from the conquered city be brought to the palace, in order to prepare them to become attendants in three years. They were supposed to eat from the king's table and drink his wine. Daniel, however, purposed in his heart *that he would not defile himself* through the king's food and beverage and, therefore, requested of the chief of the officers a trial period for ten days during which he and his three companions should only be given *zer'oi'm* (peas or legumes; pulse) and water. Then one would look to see if their countenances were any worse than those of the other pages (or attendants). The result

54. Joshua 5:12
55. Sirach 39:26
56. Pesachim 109a
57. Genesis 18:7
58. Berachoth 58a
59. *Tosefta* Sotah 15:10
60. Sanhedrin 59b

61. Genesis 9:3
62. Aboth de Rabbi Nathan 1:8. The same dispute occurs in Church writings. See Fraenkel's *Mtschr.* 1899 p.461
63. Baltzer. *Vegetarianismus in der Bibel,* Nordhausen 1872 p.5

was that they appeared fairer and were fatter in flesh than the youths who ate of the king's food[64].

It is as clear as can be stated that the refusal of Daniel to accept the food offered was for religious reasons and was not intended to represent an experiment to document the efficacy of vegetarianism. On the contrary, the success of a meatless and wineless diet is an unnatural and wondrous outcome, and the intent is obviously to strengthen the belief of faithful Jews that they should do the same if they find themselves in similar distress. That the author of the book of Daniel placed little weight on the type of diet is clear from the fact that he makes no more mention of this diet in the later life of his heroes. In fact, much later, he himself states: *In those days I, Daniel, was mourning three whole weeks. I ate no pleasant bread, neither came meat nor wine in my mouth, neither did I anoint myself*[65]. It is hardly plausible that during that interval, Daniel was in a position to enjoy ritually prepared meat[66].

## IX   Excessive Meat Consumption

From the law of the "rebellious son"[67] where the parents accuse their son before the court, we learn how much is the normal quantity of meat consumption. He was a *zolel* and *sobeh,* usually translated as a "glutton and a drunkard", who intoxicates himself at banquets. The Talmud explains[68]: he eats one *tartemar* (or 197 grams) of meat, and drinks half a *log* of wine. Rabbi Jose says a *maneh* of meat[69] and a *log* of wine, one *log* being equivalent to one quarter liter of Italian wine. The meat is prepared in an unusual manner, only half roasted, like a thief who doesn't take the time to fully cook it, and consumed in an unusual way, like a glutton who gormandizes it. In order to be liable to the Biblically prescribed punishment of stoning, a rebellious son must fulfill an additional large number of requirements which are enumerated in the Talmud[70].

That meat is more nourishing than a vegetable dish is well known: porridge (of wheat or of barley) nourishes up to one parasang, but beef up to three parasangs[71].

An excess of meat is harmful. This is proven from the health condition of the priests, concerning whom it is explicitly stated that they suffered from diarrhea because they constantly ate meat from Temple offerings and walked barefoot on the stone floor, and for whom it was necessary to appoint a special physician "for those with bowel sicknesses"[72], and to provide spa cures with the waters of Siloam[73].

With the Talmud and *Midrash,* one can understand all the illnesses depicted in the Bible[74] as representing an acute severe damage to the body from meat consumption: the "mixed multitude" and also the Children of Israel complained about the continual nourishment of *manna.* They yearned for the *fish which they were wont to eat in Egypt for naught, and the cucumbers, and the melons, and the leeks, and the onions*[75], but they did not ask for these (whose procurement in the wilderness would also have been difficult), but for meat. Moses threatened them: *you will eat meat for an entire month, until it comes out at your nostrils, and it be loathsome unto you*[76]. And a large swarm of quails came down which the Israelites gathered in large numbers for two nights and one day uninterruptedly[77], and they spread them out (arranged them in heaps to be "cured" in the sun) round about the camp. While the flesh was yet between their teeth,

---

64. Daniel Chapt. 1
65. Daniel 10:2
66. Hence, Daniel was certainly *not* a vegetarian.
67. Deut. 21:18-21
68. Sanhedrin 8:2
69. one *maneh* equals three *tartemar*
70. Sanhedrin Chapt. 8

71. Nedarim 49b
72. Shekalim 5:1-2
73. Aboth de Rabbi Nathan 35:5
74. Numbers Chapt. 11
75. *ibid* 11:5
76. *ibid* 11:20
77. the text actually has two days and one night (F.R.)

before it was chewed, the anger of the Lord was kindled against the lustful people, and He smote them with a very great plague. And there they buried the lustful people.

It is quite plausible that the sudden transition from a heretofore vegetable diet to a rich meat diet, the consumption of meat which had been lying around a long time in the heat of the Orient, and, because of fear that it might rot or be stolen, the hurried swallowing of the meat — that such a diet might have resulted in serious harm to one's health, even with fatal outcome. Perhaps the expression *until it come out at your nostrils* signifies much vomiting. *Ibn Ezra* explains "it was a pestilence"[78] and the Septuagint has "cholera".

# X

He who, for any reason, vows not to eat "meat" is also forbidden to eat the head, the feet, the windpipe, the liver and the heart. Rabbi Simeon ben Gamliel is of the opinion that "meat" only includes (muscular) flesh; the entrails are not meat, and do not at all constitute nourishment for man[79]. In spite of this, "entrails" were consumed by some people.

*Liver* substitutes in nutritional value for blood which is forbidden[80]. However, only the substance of the liver is permitted, not the blood contained in the large vessels thereof. Before being prepared, a liver must therefore be cut lengthwise and breadthwise, in order to avoid consuming the blood therein[81]. In addition, the opinion of Rabbi Yochanan ben Nuri, that liver only exudes blood during cooking, but does not absorb (juice from other meat cooked together with it), is incorrect[82]. If liver is roasted on a spit, the blood which drips therefrom floats at the top of the vessel, whereas the blood of flesh settles at the bottom, and the fat floats at the top[83].

Concerning the preparation of goose *lung,* see above.[84].

Concerning the *heart:* five things make one forget one's studies: eating something from which a mouse or a cat has eaten, eating the heart of a beast, frequent consumption of olives, drinking the remains of water that was used for washing, and washing one's feet one above the other. Some also say he who puts his clothes under his head forgets his studies[85].

A special food was "the chicken of Rabbi Abba". Concerning its preparation, there is a divergence of opinion in the commentaries. It was assumed that it was prepared in such a way that after it was cooked, it was soaked in warm water for a long time until it completely dissolved. Rabbi Abba is said to have consumed this fowl as a remedy. It was not, however, to everyone's taste. Rabbi Safra said that he was once given some of it to eat; only hasty drinking of old wine saved him from vomiting[86].

*Fat meat, bassar shumen,* is a special strengthening remedy. It straightens the stature and gives light to the eyes[87], and appears in some recipes as an emetic (analeptic). However, it also has its disadvantages: it returns a convalescent to his illness[88], it brings healthy people to *ziva,* that is, it is an aphrodisiac[89]. Rabbi Judah ben Bathyra said that the following are also aphrodisiac: milk, cheese, old wine, soup of pounded beans, eggs and fish brine. Therefore, on the eve of the Day of Atonement, the High Priest was forbidden to consume the above as well as *ethrog,* eggs and heavy wine[90]. Rabbi Simeon ben Gamliel said: for three things I like the Orientals, they do not tear meat with their teeth and eat, but cut it and eat it; and they only cut the meat

---

78. Numbers 11:23
79. Nedarim 54b
80. Chullin 109b
81. *ibid* 111a
82. *ibid* 110b
83. *ibid* 111b
84. See above chapter 6, part 12

85. Horayoth 13b
86. Shabbath 145b
87. Pesachim 42a
88. Berachoth 57b
89. *Tosefta* Zabim 2:5
90. Yoma 18a

on the table (not on the hand); and they kiss (not on the mouth but) on the hand; and they take counsel only in a field[91]. Rabbi Eleazar[91a], lauds the Medes for the same thing[92].

## XI    Fish

*Fish* was eaten salted, roasted, cooked or seethed *(shaluk)*[93], and also roasted on coals[94]. The honoring of the Sabbath includes each worker being sent home before nightfall in order that he be able to fill a cask of water and to broil a fish[95]. Rab teaches: one who regularly eats small fish does not suffer from intestinal disorders. Moreover, they have the property of stimulating propagation, and they strengthen a man's whole body[96]. They are beneficial for the sick[97], and in river-rich Babylon they belonged to the usual diet of sick people[98] (as flounder served in Hamburg).

Abaye declares that only for the eyes are fish detrimental. Before phlebotomy one should abstain from fish, fowl and salted meat[99].

Mar bar Rav Ashi is of the opinion that fish and meat should not be salted together, for this food produces a foul aroma in the mouth, and leads to a skin sickness *(rel alia,* which is leprosy)[100].

A small salted fish is sometimes deadly if eaten on the seventh, seventeenth or twenty-seventh day after it was salted. Some say also on the twenty-third. This is the case only if it is incompletely roasted. If one drinks date wine (i.e. beer) after it, then it is not harmful[101].

Rab teaches: a fish that has holes in it or is chewed up is forbidden, for one must assume that the chewed up places are the result of snake bites, and that the poison is still in the fish. Others are of the opinion that the prohibition only applies to a live fish which is chewed up or a salted fish in which the poison of a snake disseminates by virtue of the salting. Only in the case of a dead fish is it sufficient to only cut away the chewed out portions[102], for in such a fish the poison does not spread anymore.

Pharaoh did not want to let the children of Israel emigrate; finally he was forced to agree and also had to withstand all ten plagues. Thereto the *Midrash* relates the following parable: a king once sent his servant to market with money to buy a fish. The servant brought a rotten fish, whereupon the king said to the servant: make your choice, either eat the fish or pay for it, or you will receive one hundred lashes. The servant replied: I will eat the fish. As soon as he ate the first bite, he thought he would die and cried out: I would rather get the lashes. After 50 lashes, however, he thought he was near death and called out: I would rather pay for the fish. So he ate a rotten fish and received a thrashing and also had to pay money[103].

## XII    Eggs

Rabbi Yannai said in the name of Rabbi[104]: an egg is superior in food value to the same quantity of any other food. Rabin said: a lightly cooked egg *(megulgeleth)*[105] is better than six measures of fine flour. Rabbi Dimi said: a lightly cooked egg is better than six measures of fine flour, a hard boiled one, *mithvatha,* is better than four.

91. Genesis Rabbah 74:2
91a. It was actually Rabbi Akiba (F.R.)
92. Berachoth 8b
93. Nedarim 20b
94. Kallah Rabbathi I fol. 52a 5
95. Genesis Rabbah 72:4
96. Berachoth 20a
97. Berachoth 57b
98. Sanhedrin 98a

99. Nedarim 54b
100. Pesachim 112a
101. Berachoth 44b
102. Jerushalmi Terumoth 8; 46a
103. *Mechilta, Beshallach* 1 p.26b; *Tanchuma* p.29a
104. Berachoth 44b
105. so *Rashi* in Shabbath 38b; others translate lightly roasted

Concerning cooked food, an egg is better than the same quantity of any other boiled food except meat.

The mother of Abaye said: the proper way to raise a child is to bathe him in warm water and rub him with oil. If he has grown a bit, give him an egg with *kutah*[106]. If he is grown even more, give him clay utensils to break. Thus did Rabbah buy clay vessels in damaged condition for his children to break[107] — in order to satisfy the destructive instinct of the children and to simultaneously make them harmless.

Five things restore one's learning if one has forgotten it: bread roasted on coals, and certainly the coals themselves, a soft-boiled egg[108] without salt, the regular use of olive oil and wine and spices, and the drinking of water which remains from kneading. Others say: dipping one's finger in salt and eating this is also included[109].

The following things have life-threatening consequences and a person who does them is taking his life in his hands: eating peeled garlic, a peeled onion or a peeled egg that were kept overnight without their peels, or drinking diluted liquids that were kept overnight, or spending a night in a graveyard, or removing one's nails and throwing them away in a public thoroughfare, or having sexual intercourse immediately after bloodletting[110].

Foods made from fine flour and eggs soften the stool but, as already mentioned, stimulate the sexual sphere[111].

Addled eggs (i.e. eggs upon which the hen has brooded but out of which no chicks can develop) may be eaten by those who are not squeamish. If a blood spot is found on the egg, then the entire egg may not be eaten. This is so if the blood is found on the knot (i.e. the stringy portion of the egg white), but if the blood spot is on the white, then only the blood spot is forbidden[112]. The controlling factors here are not dietary considerations but restrictions related to the general prohibition of eating blood.

Eggs were eaten either very soft, so that they could be sucked out; or hard boiled, *sheluka,* so that the peel had to be broken off[113]; or fried, *tzeluya,* without any water. For frying, an egg was placed in sand heated by the sun, or in the dust of the road (heated by the sun), or one cracked it upon a hot cloth and allowed it to roast in the sun[114]. Whether one also ate raw eggs is not certain[115].

## XIII   Milk

It must be noticeable to the reader that although the fact that Canaan is a land flowing with milk and honey[116] is so often mentioned as one of its advantages, very little fuss is made about milk. Even in the nourishment which God gave to the people as a sign of His special kindness are enumerated fine flour, oil and honey, but not milk[117]. Nevertheless it is considered a sign of wealth if the vessels are full of milk[118], and a sign of luck if wine and milk can be procured free[119].

A particular delicacy seems to have been goats' milk[120]. The Romans also considered it to be the most easily digestible type of milk, because the goat lives more from foliage than from plants[121]. A remark of Galen which asserts the opposite, but which allows the combination of "milk and honey" to be also considered in the

106. a preserve consisting of sour milk, bread crusts and salt
107. Yoma 78b
108. others translate: lightly roasted egg
109. Horayoth 13b
110. Niddah 17a
111. Yoma 18a
112. Chullin 64b
113. Uktzin 2:6
114. Shabbath 3:3
115. *Tosefta* Sotah 1:2

116. e.g. Exodus 3:8; Joshua 5:6; (also Exodus 3:17; 13:5 and 33:3; Levit. 20:24; Numbers 13:27; 14:8; 16:13 and 16:14; Deut. 6:3; 6:11; 9:26; 9:15; 27:3 and 31:20; Jeremiah 11:5 and 32:22; Ezekiel 20:6 and 20:15.F.R.)
117. Ezekiel 16:19
118. Job 21:24
119. Isaiah 55:1
120. Proverbs 27:27
121. Plinius 28:33; cf Bochart *Hierozoic* 1:629

medical-dietetic sense, will only be conveyed here but not commented upon. He teaches that one should always give goats' milk together with honey because it curdles in the stomach, is distressing to a person, and can lead to death by suffocation[122].

The milk of a clean animal is white, that of an unclean animal is yellow; the former curdles, the latter does not[123]. The same is mentioned by Plinius: the milk of animals who are fully teethed in both jaws produces no cheese, for it does not curdle[124]. Nevertheless, he himself speaks of mare's cheese, *hippace*[125].

It was already mentioned above that the Rabbis considered milk to be a sexual stimulant, whereas physicians specifically prescribe milk as part of a "bland diet" for irritating conditions of the urogenital apparatus. If both opinions are correct, that of the Rabbis and ours, then one must assume that their cattle breeding, and in particular their fodder, was basically different from ours. The difference of opinion cannot relate to a difference in the species of animal, for the Rabbis only spoke of milk derived from ruminant animals (which chew their cud), for all other animals (camel, donkey, mare, pig) are unclean, and "that which is derived from an unclean animal is unclean". Since milk was also considered to be an intoxicant[126], it is possible it was imbibed in the form of a *kumys* or *kefir*.

Young girls who drink milk and eat fowl during their years of maturation develop a bright complexion[127]. Warmed animal milk is beneficial for people with illnesses of the chest [128].

## XIV    Butter

It is quite uncertain whether the Biblical term *chem'ah* means butter, cream or buttermilk. Butter first became known in the Occident much later, so that Plinius[129] found it necessary to precisely portray its production. He also only knows that "*among foreign nations* it is considered one of the most praiseworthy of foods, and it distinguishes a rich man from a common person". He apparently recognizes its utility in Rome only as a liniment for children, but not as a food[130].

In Proverbs we find the following: *For the churning of milk bringeth forth "chem'ah"; and the wringing of the nose bringeth forth blood; so the forcing of wrath bringeth forth strife*[131]. When David and the people that were with him were languishing from hunger and thirst, they were brought honey and *chem'ah* and cheese of kine, *schephoth bakar,* in addition to flour and vegetables[132]. Thus they seem to be solid substances, either butter or curd. However, in the song of Deborah, when the exhausted Sisera asked for water, Jael gave him *chem'ah* instead, in a lordly dish[133]; and concerning Job, it is related that during the time that he was wealthy, he bathed his feet in *chem'ah*[134]. Thus Scriptures seem to be referring to liquid substances. The Septuagint and Vulgate use the term *butyrum* throughout.

According to a remark by Rabbi Chanina[135], the best butter is made from a sixtieth part of the milk; medium quality is from a fortieth part; and inferior butter is from a twentieth. What is undoubtedly meant is that the larger the amount of water, the poorer the quality of the butter. According to Rabbi Yonah, the numbers should be one hundredth, one sixtieth and one twentieth. Today we estimate, on the average, fifteen liters of milk for one pound of butter.

122. see also Oribas. 3:29 (Vol. 1:242)
123. Abodah Zarah 35b
124. Plinius 11:96
125. *ibid* 28:34
126. Maimonides. *Hilchoth    Biyath    Ha Mikdash* 1:3
127. Kethuboth 59b
128. *Tosefta* Baba Kamma 8:13

129. *Hist. Nat.* 28:35
130. *ibid* 11:98
131. Proverbs 30:33
132. Second Samuel 17:28-29
133. Judges 5:25
134. Job 29:6
135. Genesis Rabbah 48:14

# XV   Cheese

Cheese, *gebina,* was prepared by curdling milk with rennet[136], or by coagulating the milk directly in the stomach of a calf[137]. Casein was also precipitated with vinegar or fruit ciders. The surface of cheese was smeared with lard by the heathens[138]. Cheese made from fresh milk is said to be difficult to digest[139], and serves as a sexual stimulant[140].

The excess water that drains off milk in the preparation of cheese (i.e. whey) is called *mey chalab*[141]. The *nisjube de chalba* is said to refer to the same thing[142].

This *nisjube de chalba* is considered to be one of the ingredients of *kutach* or *kameka,* which is a "sour spicy side dish" used by many Oriental peoples[143]. For example, to the Persians it consisted of milk, *oxygala* and salt. In the Talmud, Babylonian *kuthach* is mentioned as a distinctive specialty and the following is related concerning it: it closes up the stomach (or the heart) because of its content of whey, *nisjube de chalba;* it blinds the eyes because of its salt content (into which Sodom salt might easily have become admixed); and it weakens the entire body because of the mould of the flour, *kumurtha de uma,* which is also contained therein[144]. Occasionally, it also incorporated small pieces of sour dough[145]. It is possible that in the depiction of the action of *kuthach,* there emerged a certain jealousy between Palestine and Babylon. The Palestinian Rabbi Yochanan vomited at the mere thought of this mash; said Rabbi Joseph the Babylonian: in revenge we vomit at the "fowl of Rabbi Abba". But it was further faithfully related that when Rabbi Gaza came to Palestine and prepared some Babylonian *kuthach,* all the invalids from Palestine asked him for it[146].

# XVI   Honey

Honey, which to the ancients was a substitute for sugar, is enumerated by Sirach as one of the essential elements for life[147]. Kings and wicked people derived benefit therefrom for their health[148]. Only a satiated person steps on a honeycomb with his feet[149]. *Hast thou found honey, then eat so much as is sufficient for thee, lest thou be filled therewith, and vomit it*[150], because it is not good to eat too much honey[151]. He who eats one-quarter measure of honey at one time will have his stomach (or heart) torn out; according to Rabbi Joseph, this only applies if one consumes it on an empty stomach[152]. Faint people delight therein[153]. Next to butter, it serves as an extraordinarily efficacious nourishment for children[154]. As an accompaniment to meal offerings, honey and leaven are both forbidden[155], because they lead to souring. Honey after a meal satisfies, before the meal it stimulates the appetite[156].

Rancid honey was applied to the wounds of camels caused by the chafing of the saddle[157]. Barley flour in honey was consumed for stomach pains[158] and for weakness of the stomach or heart[159]. White honey is found in a recipe against *barsam*[160]. Wax

136. Abodah Zarah 2:5
137. Chullin 8:5
138. Abodah Zarah 35b
139. Berachoth 57b
140. Yoma 18a
141. Machshirin 6:5
142. Baba Metzia 68b
143. Fleischer. in Levy's *Neuhebräisches und Chaldäisches Wörterbuch.* Leipzig 1876-1889, 2:452b
144. Pesachim 42a
145. Jerushalmi Pesachim 3; 29d
146. Shabbath 145b
147. Sirach 39:26
148. Septuagint in the paraphrase from Proverbs 6:8
149. *ibid* 27:7
150. *ibid* 25:16
151. *ibid* 25:27
152. Kallah Rabbathi 1 fol. 52a 41
153. First Samuel 14:27
154. Isaiah 7:15
155. Levit. 2:11
156. Yoma 83b
157. Shabbath 154b
158. Yoma 83b
159. Gittin 69b
160. Chullin 105b

was used in plasters; the dead were preserved in honey[161].

The term "honey" alone refers to bees' honey. The bee, like all insects, is an "unclean" animal, and everything that stems from something unclean is itself unclean. Nevertheless, the honey of bees is permitted because it is thought that the bee only gathers in its body and expels unchanged that which it sucks out of blossoms and leaves, and does not add anything "from its own body". On the other hand, the honey of the wasp and the hornet is a type of saliva, *ri'r*, of the animal, and hence is considered to be a product of the body[162].

A second meaning of *debash* is the sticky juice of sweet fruits (syrup), such as date honey[163] and fig honey. Rabbi Jacob ben Dostai saw so much fig honey flowing from fig trees, that he waded up to his ankles therein, and literally saw fulfilled the promise that the land flows with milk and honey[164].

A very thorough treatise on this subject, with parallels from heathen classicists, is found in Bochart, Hieroz. lib. IV, chapt. 12, col. 517ff. Creigh amuses himself by considering *debash* to be hashish.

## XVII   Honey Foods

Among the honey-containing foods and beverages, the following are mentioned:

1. *Schathitha*[165] (pearl barley) a food made from honey[166] and coarse flour from incompletely ripened, roasted corn. One distinguished a thick and a thin type; the former was a nutriment, the latter a medicine[167]. As such, *schathitha* is mentioned as a therapy for the illness called *achilu*[168].

2. *Inomilon*, sometimes also *jenomalin* (*yayin* means wine) This substance, according to Rabbi Yochanan[169], consisted of wine, honey and pepper[170], where "pepper" refers to "seasoning" in general[171], such as our "pfefferkuchen"[172]. This *oenomeli* is probably identical with the *konditon, vinum conditum,* which is often mentioned in the Talmud and which has the same ingredients[173]. It was always prepared fresh, even on the Sabbath, and, when necessary for a large number of guests, by the barrel[174].

## XVIII   Oil

Oil is a component of food in both hot and very cold countries. A variety of oils was known[175], but for food only olive oil was used, for it was considered the best of all. There was a debate as to whether oil, in addition to the enjoyment it gives, is at all nourishing; the answer given, however, is affirmative. On the other hand, "it does not delight the soul", as does wine[176].

In general, oil is used as an adjunct to other foods[177]. When consumed alone, it is harmful. However, if it is mixed with mangold juice, then not only is it not harmful, but it even heals illnesses such as a sore throat[178].

Maimonides evidently does not believe in the harmfulness of pure olive oil. He only states that its taste is not pleasant[179].

---

161. Baba Bathra 3b
162. *Tosefta* Bechoroth 1:8 and Bechoroth 7b
163. Berachoth 38a
164. Kethuboth 111b
165. Löw. *Pflanzennamen* p.240
166. *Rashi* on Erubin 29b
167. Berachoth 38a
168. Gittin 70a
169. Jerushalmi Shabbath 20; 17c
170. Abodah Zarah 30a
171. see the Commentaries on Soferim 15:7
172. gingerbread; literally: pepper cake
173. Pesachim. *bachodesh* 102b
174. Shabbath 20:2
175. Shabbath 2:2
176. Berachoth 35b
177. Goldmann. *Der Oelbau in Paelestina.* p.62
178. *Tosefta* Terumoth 9:12; Berachoth 36a
179. *Hilchoth Berachoth* 8:2

Mangold broth, according to Rabbi Bar Samuel, is the often-mentioned beverage *ingaron* or *anigaron,* which served as a vehicle for using oil in gargling. As far as I am aware, it is nowhere explicitly stated that it regularly also contained wine, from which the Greek name *oinogaron* (wine potion) is derived. However, one can surmise that it did from a remark[180]. *Rashi* also mentions this often. Ground pepper root was also added thereto, which was first recognizable by virtue of its taste and not from the color[181].

Generally, next to *anigaron, aksigaron* is mentioned, according to Rabbi bar Samuel, a broth of all types of cabbage[181a]; conceptually, therefore, not identical with the *oxygaron* (in Greek, sour potion), which is a beverage of vinegar and fish broth.

## XIX   Legumes

Legumes, *kitnith* or *kitniyoth* — perhaps the word refers most specifically to peas — were placed before a lowly guest[182]. Beans and lentils are already mentioned in the Bible as nutritional substances[183]. The eating of lentils was a mourning custom among the Jews[184]. Beans were considered for *venerem excitantes*[185]. It is known that Pythagoreans prohibited beans, and that the Egyptian priests and Brahmins also did not eat beans. Many reasons are given for this prohibition. According to Plinius, it was related to the Pythagorean teaching of the transmigration of the soul[186]. The fantasy of the Egyptians is said to have seen a resemblance between the shape of the bean and the vulva[187].

When Joseph promised his brothers: *and I will give you the good of the land of Egypt*[188], according to the *Midrash*[189], he meant pearl barley beans. It is not very probable that one believed that "they are efficacious against spiritual torment", *ayakath nefesh*[190].

## XX   Vegetables

The "living green", *yerek chai,* raw cabbage, indeed comparable to our salads, was often spoken of in antiquity. "Every living (i.e. raw) green vegetable makes the face green" (pale), according to Rabbi Yitzchak, only applies if one derives benefit therefrom as one's first meal after bloodletting. Prior to the fourth hour of the day, that is before the main meal (on an empty stomach), one should not eat any green vegetables because of the odor *(fötor ex ore);* and one should not speak with someone who has eaten thereof. "Everything small (unripe) makes small"[191], even if it is a young billy goat for two *zuz* (which is already good and fat; *Rashi*). This only applies, however, if it has not yet grown one quarter of the adult size. "Living beings restore vitality", even tiny fishes from among the reeds[192]. "That which is near the vital organs restores vitality". Rabbi Acha bar Yitzchak says: that is meat from the neck (or nape, *unka*), near the site of slaughtering[193], where the seat of life was presumed to be.

Even the poor used to purchase from the vegetables which the gardeners brought to market on Friday, in order to eat vegetables on the Sabbath[194].

A learned man should not live in a city in which vegetables are not available. The

180. Jerushalmi Erubin 6; 23c
181. Jerushalmi Betzah 2; 61d; *Tosefta* Betzah 2:16
181a. *Tosefta* Terumoth 9:12; Berachoth 36a
182. *Tosefta* Peah 4:8
183. Second Samuel 17:29; Ezekiel 4:9
184. Genesis Rabbah 63:14
185. Yoma 18a
186. *Histor. Natural.* 18:30
187. Nork. *Etym. - symb. - mythol.* WB

Stuttgart 1843. *s.v. Bohnen*
188. Genesis 45:18
189. *Yalkut* 1:152
190. *Tosefta* Niddah 8:9; Genesis Rabbah 94:2; Niddah 9:9; *chalukath nefesh*
191. things not fully grown retard growth
192. Löw. *Fischnamen* no. 4
193. Berachoth 44b
194. Taanith 20b

reason for this, explains the commentary, is that vegetables are wholesome to eat and cheap, so that he can occupy himself with his studies without having to be disturbed by financial worries of providing nourishment for himself[195]. Even so, in an already-mentioned place[196], green vegetables are considered harmful! However, it is said that only garlic and leek *(keresha)* are harmful; not, however, other vegetables. So, too, it was taught: "garlic is a vegetable, leek is only half a vegetable; if radish *(tzenon)* appears, a life-giving drug *(sam chayim)* has appeared". Others, however, teach that radish is a poison! Both are correct: the leaves are harmful, but the roots (or main bulb) are useful — efficacious in the summer, but harmful in the winter[197].

The apostle advises that he who is weak should eat cabbage[198].

## XXI   Garlic, Onions, Leeks, Radishes

In the entire Orient, sharp green vegetables were and still are today particularly popular, especially leeks, and among these the most coveted is *garlic, schum.* It is not only a favorite food of Semites, but also of Aryans, as best demonstrated in the recently (1890) discovered love song of Bower on garlic, written in Sanskrit (from the 5th century)[199].

Garlic and onions were eaten as vegetables; however, one should not eat them from the bulbs outwardly (literally: from the head), but from the leaves. He who does eat from the bulbs is called a glutton, just like the drunkard who drinks his entire glass in one gulp[200].

Five things were said of garlic: it satiates, it keeps the body warm, it brightens the face, it increases semen, and it kills worms in the bowels[201].

Rabbi Eleazar ben Pedath was very poor; once he had nothing to eat after a phlebotomy; he placed a rib of garlic in his mouth and became faint.

*Onions, Allium cepa,* are injurious to the stomach (or heart); only the species called "wild onion" is efficacious[202]. They stimulate a strong expectoration of spittle[203], and should be avoided after bloodletting[204]. He who is easily satisfied is content with an onion[205].

As already mentioned, leek, because of its own characteristics, was only partially considered a vegetable. According to some Sages, it is good for the bowels and bad for the teeth; (others say it is good for the teeth and bad for the bowels); therefore, one should chew it well and spit it out[206].

Among the types of onions, *bazel,* is included the *kaplut* or Syrian leek[207], which is added to fish[208], but which is served in restaurants with poppy and plums[209].

The juice of sharp raddish, *pugla charifa,* is healthy, according to Samuel; therefore it is useful not to salt it after it is cut into slices[210].

Round radish, *chazereth* (lettuce, garden salad) and cucumbers were never lacking on the table of Antoninus and Rebbe, either in the summer or winter[211]. The reason, as the commentator explains[212], is that the table was so richly endowed with food that substances such as the aforementioned were necessary to help digestion. So, too, the

195. Erubin 55b
196. above in section 3; from Pesachim 42a
197. Erubin 56a
198. Romans 14:2
199. Aschoff in *Janus* 1900 p.493; see also Grunwald in *S.Milt. z. Jüd. Volkskd* Section 5 (1900) p.65, note 221
200. Betzah 25b
201. Baba Kamma 82a
202. Nedarim 26b
203. Yebamoth 106a
204. Abodah Zarah 29a
205. Pesachim 114a
206. Berachoth 44b. The Talmud here speaks of spleen, not leek(F.R.)
207. Chullin 97b
208. Jerushalmi Betzah 2; 61b
209. Jerushalmi Berachoth 6; 10c
210. Shabbath 108b
211. Berachoth 57b
212. *Tosafoth* Abodah Zarah 11a

"officers of King Solomon provided victual...they let nothing be lacking"[213], as they supplied him with beets *(thardin)* in the summer, and cucumbers in the winter[214]. Only the small cucumbers, however, are healthy; the large ones are as dangerous as swords[215]. An unknown Sage taught: "radish helps the food to dissolve, lettuce helps the food to be digested, and cucumbers make the intestines expand"[216].

A person once made many people ill with a type of cucumber, the sugar melon, *cucumis melo.* He gave some of this melon which had been partially eaten by a snake to ten people to eat, and they all died as a result[217].

## XXII    Food Poisoning

Relevant here is a Biblical story which illustrates what is purported to be an example of poisoning by plants. One of the pupils of the prophet Elisha went out into the field[218] to gather herbs, *oroth* (green cabbage), according to the *Targum,* or *Eruca sativa*[219] to eat. He found a wild vine and gathered wild gourds therefrom *(pakkuoth, Cucumis agrestis),* and shred them into the cooking pot, for they knew them not. And they poured them out for the men to eat, but as they began to eat of this pottage, they cried out "there is death in the pot", and they could not eat thereof. When they added meal to the pot, according to the instructions of Elisha, they ate and there was no harm in the pot[220].

The wild gourd is intensely bitter. Since poison and bitterness are considered to be correlated in the minds of the people, if one were not to interpret the cry "death is in the pot" as referring simply to this bitter taste, the thought of poisoning could easily arise. The *Vulgate* translation of the Bible led to the opinion that *pakkuoth* were colocynths. Colocynth by itself, as is well known, is a drastic purgative which rapidly induces bloody stools, but there is no mention in the text of this or other signs of poisoning. It only states "they could not eat thereof". A further consideration against this assumption is the fact that the addition of meal made it edible; and, at the time of the *Mishnah,* fruit which was steeped in wine or vinegar was eaten[221].

There, therefore, simply occurred a mix-up among different fruits, which, however, had no consequences on one's health, and which did not affect one adversely when one partook of them.

## XXIII    Gourds, Asafetida and Mustard

A pumpkin (or gourd), *kara, Cucurbita pepa,* is very difficult to digest. Rabbi Huna teaches: one must never expectorate before one's teacher, except after eating a pumpkin (or gourd) or porridge, because they are like lead pellets in the body[222].

Asafetida, *chiltith,* in spite of its dreadful aroma ("devil's dirt"), is still eaten today in Central and Eastern Asia[223], and not only used as a seasoning as in the time of Maimonides[224]. Among the Rabbis, opinions are divided: according to Samuel, *chiltith* is a nutritional substance (food for the healthy), but according to Rabbi Huna, it is a poison. He who eats the weight of a *zuz* thereof becomes dangerously ill and his skin dissolves. When Rabbi Ba ate the above amount, he plunged into the river to cool himself from the heat[225]. Asafetida ground in water[226] or vinegar is a remedy for weakness of the stomach (or heart)[227].

213. First Kings 5:7
214. Deut. Rabbah 1:5
215. Berachoth 57b
216. Abodah Zarah 11a
217. Jerushalmi Talmud. Terumoth 8; 46a
218. Second Kings 4:39
219. Yoma 18b
220. Second Kings 4:40-1

221. Uktzin 3:4
222. Nedarim 49b
223. Brunnhofer. *Ostasiat.* Lloyd. 1901 p.579
224. Maimonides' Commentary on Uktzin 3:5
225. Jerushalmi Shabbath 20; 17c
226. Shabbath 20:3
227. Shabbath 140a

Among the characteristic *spices,* in addition to the already-mentioned salt and pepper, one should add *mustard.* Rabbi Yochanan teaches: he who becomes accustomed to eating mustard every thirty days keeps illnesses out of his house (abdomen). He who eats mustard daily, however, weakens the stomach[228]. Whether mustard refers to the seeds or the greens from the leaves and the stalks is uncertain[229].

Hedge mustard, *gargir, Eruca sativa,* was used by the ancients as a substitute for pepper, of which they had none[230]. To the heathen writers of antiquity, it served as an aphrodisiac[231].

It was utilized against scurvy[232], and in macerated form against intestinal worms[233], and for compresses on the eye[234].

# XXIV  Fruit

Among the tree fruits, apples, *tappuchim,* are considered a particular delicacy[235]. Cherries, *godganiyoth*[236], enter the body but do not provide it with any benefit[237]. Nuts are considered harmful to one convalescing from illness[238], particularly the hazelnut, *pundak.* This plays a role in the following legal case: if a sick person gives a bill of divorce to his wife on the condition that it should only be valid if he, the ill husband, dies of this illness — and if the sick man recovers and goes out on the street, but later falls ill again and dies — then it must be decided whether death occurred as a result of the first illness; otherwise, the bill of divorce is not valid[239]. For example, if the man ate a considerable amount of barley groats during the time of his improvement, then his death can be attributed to his first illness, because these groats, even when consumed in excess, do not produce death. However, if he ate hazelnuts without any other food, and then did not recover again from his state of illness, then one must assume that death was produced by the hazelnuts and not the original illness[240].

However, the most important fruits by far are *dates* and *figs.* At the table, dates and pomegranates were served as a separate course, and figs and grapes as dessert[241]. In the teaching that dates are nutritious, the Rabbis[242] agree with Plinius[243]. Unripe, bitter dates eaten on an empty stomach, however, are harmful. Mar Samuel said: for all things I know the cure except the following three: eating bitter dates on an empty stomach, girding one's loins with a damp flaxen cord, and eating and not walking at least four cubits after it[244]. Only date grapes *(rispe), paphniyoth*[245], and unripe dates are assimilated in the body without giving it any benefit[246]. Dates warm the body, satiate, act as a laxative and strengthen, without adversely affecting the stomach. Another teaching states that dates are wholesome if consumed morning and evening; in the afternoon they are bad, and at noon they are incomparable (i.e. extremely good). They remove three things: bad thoughts, intestinal illnesses and hemorrhoids, *tachtoniyoth*[247]. A dried date or fig is sufficient to revive a person who has fainted[248].

Dates were also thought to be intoxicating. Therefore, no one who has eaten dates should teach[249]. Therefore, too, a person who cannot afford to buy wine after

---

228. Berachoth 40a
229. Löw. *Pflanzennamen.* p.178
230. Erubin 28b
231. Löw p.93
232. Shabbath 65a
233. Gittin 69b
234. Shabbath 109a
235. Song of Songs 2:5
236. see particularly Löw. *Pflanzennamen.* p.95, Gittin 70a. *Rashi* translates "oleander"
237. Berachoth 57b
238. *ibid*

239. Gittin 7:3
240. Jerushalmi Gittin 7; 48d
241. Berachoth 41b
242. *ibid* 12a
243. *Histor. Natur.* 23:51
244. Baba Metzia 113b
245. Löw. *Pflanzennamen* p.118
246. Berachoth 57b
247. Kethuboth 10b
248. Lamentations Rabbah 1:2
249. Kethuboth 10b

blood-letting can eat seven black dates as a substitute[250]. Plinius also teaches that fresh dates intoxicate and induce headache[251]. Oribasius also enumerates them among the stimulating foods[252]. I cannot decide whether this is, in fact, correct or whether the matter of considering dates intoxicating is derived from a conclusion by analogy from date wine, about which we will speak more later.

Date pits, *sophele,* are an ingredient of a fumigation remedy against external fever *(cimra bara)*[253]. If one drinks the juice of such cooked pits, it induces barrenness[254].

The *fig tree* was cultivated in Palestine in large quantities and was considered among the most eminent products of the land[255]. Its fruit was a common nutritional substance, especially in the form of fig cakes, which were composed of dried and pressed summer figs[256]. It is for this reason that Noah took fig cakes into the ark—according to some commentators, as the main provision, because it is a nourishing substance for man and beast[257]. A man who does not live with his wife, must deliver the following natural products to her weekly for her sustenance: at least two *kab* of wheat or four *kab* of barley; further, half a *kab* of peas (or beans), half a *log* of oil, one *kab* of dried figs or one *maneh* of fig cake; if he doesn't have these, he must substitute other types of fruits[258]. The fig cake was also used as a cataplasm[259].

According to the *Midrash,* a fig was the fruit which Adam ate in paradise. Three things were, therefore, said of the fig: it is good to eat, it is pleasurable for the eyes to behold, and it increases wisdom[260].

Dried figs, *gerogeroth,* were distributed to the poor at the time of famine[261].

Among the varieties of figs are *belofesin,* "a type of fig of which pap is made"[262], which are overripe[263], and which Rabbi Simeon said never pass out of the intestines[264].

## XXV   Beverages

Naturally, among beverages, *water* is the most important. We have spoken about the fear of drinking water that was left uncovered since a snake may have discharged poison therein[265]. There we already mentioned the statement of Mar Samuel, that he had no fear of such water because he only drank it after boiling it. Rabbi Yochanan similarly teaches: it is better to drink a glass of bewitched water than a glass of warm water (he probably means lukewarm cistern water, which easily develops fungi). This is only so, however, if the water is in a metal vessel, but in an earthenware vessel, it does not harm. Moreover, even in a metal vessel it is harmless, if spice roots were thrown into it or if it was boiled[266].

It is dangerous to drink water from rivers and streams at night[267]. Also, river water in and of itself can be harmful. As long as the Jews were in Palestine, they drank only rain (i.e. cistern) water and well water. When they came to Babylon, they drank water from the Euphrates, and many of them died[268].

*Snow* is neither a food nor a beverage. Yet it was found on the table, but, perhaps, only on a king's table[269]. Snow mixed with red wine is also mentioned[270].

Among ancient beverages which were not used for medicinal purposes, in addition to milk about which we have already spoken, are apple wine, *yen tappuchim*[271] and

250. Shabbath 129a
251. *Histor. Natur.* 23:51
252. *Coll.* 3:31 (vol. 1:249)
253. Gittin 69b
254. *ibid*
255. For example Numbers 13:24
256. First Samuel 15:18 and 30:12; Kelim 8:10
257. Genesis Rabbah 31:14
258. Kethuboth 5:8
259. Hezekiah-Second Kings 20:7
260. Eccles. Rabbah 5 fol. 15d
261. Jerushalmi Erubin 4; 22a
262. Nedarim 50b. Perhaps Lesbian figs
263. *Rashi* on Nedarim 49b
264. Nedarim 49b
265. see above chapter 5 section 4
266. Chullin 84b
267. Pesachim 112a
268. Midrash Psalms 137:3
269. Niddah 17a
270. Nega'im 1:2
271. Berachoth 38a

fruit juices, *may peroth.* Several others are also mentioned which are prepared from
cereals: the Babylonian *kutach*[272] and Edomite vinegar, prepared with the addition of
barley water[273]. According to *Rashi,* whole barley grains are added thereto so that the
wine becomes sour. It is the seasoned Roman vinegar, *bassima*[274], the Medean beer,
*shechar* "into which one places barley meal"[275], and the Egyptian *zythos,* a type of
barley beer[276], which were used as universal remedies[277]. Plinius states that *zythos* is
prepared from legumes and also from *cerevisia*[278].

Barley beer is also mentioned elsewhere[279]. It was prepared for every meal[280].
*Keshuta* was added thereto; these are not hops but rather *cuscuta* or "devil's
twine"[281]. However, in Babylon, the most commonly used beverage was date-palm
wine, which was, therefore, called *shechar* for short, and only rarely "*shechar* of
dates"[282].

There were most likely many such beverages, made from figs, blackberries etc.[283]
The following was taught of an asparagus brew, made from certain roots soaked in
wine[284]: it is good for the stomach (or heart), it is good for the eyes, and certainly for
the bowels. If one uses it regularly, it is good for the whole body, but if one gets drunk
on it, it is harmful for the whole body[285].

# XXVI  Wine

The most esteemed of all alcoholic beverages, however, was wine, the fruit of the
vine, the red blood of grapes, as the Bible calls it[286]. There exist a large number of
varieties — one speaks of sixty! The worst is *tilia*[287]; the most fiery is *amoni* wine,
which incites to lewdness[288]. Palestinian wine was so strong that one was only to drink
it after diluting it with water[289]. "It is offensive to us to drink pure (undiluted) wine as
well as pure water; however, wine mixed with water is sweet to us, and assures a
pleasant taste"[290]. A recommendable mixture was two parts of water for one part of
wine of Saron[291]. Every good wine must be capable of tolerating this dilution ratio[292].
Romans and Greeks usually diluted two parts of wine with three parts of water. The
customary expression for "pouring wine" is "to mix the cup", and the word "wine"
used alone always refers to diluted wine[293]. The word "wine" always refers to red
wine[294]; boiling it improves it; that is, makes it more durable[295].

It is not true that "the grape vine was a *Ba'al* plant (i.e. a plant that was
worshipped) and, therefore, distasteful to the Jews". The principle of our ancestors was
not the fight against the pleasures of life or low spirited asceticism, but the restraint of
carnal lusts and their control to reasonable proportions. The fact remains, as already
explicitly expounded by Erich Harnack[296], that wine in Palestine was considered a
nutriment, as it still is today in France, Italy and all real wine countries. Special
attention is drawn to the remarkable fact that for forty years of wandering in the

272. above section xv
273. Pesachim 42b
274. Jerushalmi Pesachim 3; 29d
275. *ibid*
276. Pesachim 3:1
277. Shabbath 156a
278. *Histor. Natur.* 22:82
279. Baba Bathra 96b
280. Abodah Zarah 8b
281. Löw. *Pflanzennamen* p.232
282. Baba Bathra 96b
283. Pesachim 107a
284. Löw p.52
285. Berachoth 51a

286. Genesis 49:11
287. Gittin 70a
288. Jerushalmi Sanhedrin 10; 28d
289. Berachoth 7:5
290. Second Maccabees 15:19. (incorrect reference, F.R.)
291. Song of Songs Rabbah 7:3 fol. 36c
292. Shabbath 77a
293. Rabbi Eleazar Hakappar. Numbers Rabbah 10:8 fol. 38c
294. Nega'im 1:2
295. Terumoth 11:1
296. *Die Bibel und die alkoholischen Getränke.* Berlin 1894

desert, the Israelites drank no wine or date beer[297], and yet felt quite well. Even if it were not explicitly proven, it is quite self-evident that even Jesus drank wine[298], and that he also celebrated the festival of Passover according to Jewish custom with wine[299].

The main abstainers from wine are the sect of the Rechabites, who also advocated other strange views[300]. A wine prohibition is only found in reference to a priest who is forbidden to drink wine before the start of his service in the Temple and for the duration thereof[301]. A person who wishes to make a vow as a Nazarite and, as a result, to refrain from drinking wine may do so[302]; but later he must bring a sacrifice, because by refraining from wine, he sinned against himself[303]. It is recorded in the year 50 C.E. that Queen Helena of Adiabene converted to Judaism and remained a Nazarite for very many years[304]. According to the legend, Joseph drank no wine during the entire twenty-two years of separation from his brothers. The brothers, too, refrained from drinking wine as a manifestation of repentance[305]. Only when they were reunited did they drink with him[306].

Otherwise, there is no talk at all of abstinence in Judaism. On the contrary, at every joyous occasion, meat and wine are served, and every Sabbath and every festival began, and still begins today, with a benediction over a cup of wine. The Preacher states: *eat thy bread with joy, and drink thy wine with a merry heart*[307]; and Sirach teaches: *wine and music gladden the heart*[308].

## XXVII

Whether wine was considered to be a nutriment or not was debated. Raba drank wine the entire evening before he began the festival of Passover in order to make his stomach hungry, and in order to eat unleavened bread with a greater appetite. From this, one concluded that wine consumed in large quantities makes one hungry, but in small amounts is nourishing. It, therefore, has an advantage over bread which only nourishes, in that wine not only nourishes, but simultaneously, as the Psalmist states[309], *gladdens the heart*[310]. The wanderers in Canaan, in addition to bread, carried wine in leather bottles with them[311]. Harnack also accepts the nourishing characteristic of Southern wine, and refers to its high sugar content[312]. Wheat and wine are also mentioned as food for children[313].

It once happened that a person stated that he could not exist without wine.[314] This can occasionally occur in an individual, but not to the general public: water is cheap and wine expensive; the world could exist without wine but not without water[315]. Wine is one of the eight things which are beneficial in small amounts but harmful in excess. The others are work, sleep, wealth, cohabitation (or movement), warm water and bloodletting[316]. One should only drink it during the meal; after the meal it intoxicates[317]. However, late morning sleep, wine at midday, chatting with children, and sitting in the meeting houses of the ignorant drive a man from this world[318]. Only

297. Deut. 29:5
298. Matthew 11:18
299. *ibid* 26:27-29
300. Jeremiah 35:1 ff
301. Levit. 10:9
302. Numbers 6:11
303. Taanith 11a
304. Nazir 3:6
305. Shabbath 139a
306. Genesis 43:34
307. Ecclesiastes 9:7
308. Sirach 40:20

309. Psalms 104:15
310. Berachoth 35a
311. Joshua 9:4
312. *loc. cit.* p.12
313. Nedarim 8:7
314. Nazir 2:4
315. Jerushalmi Horayoth 3; 48c
316. Aboth de Rabbi Nathan 37:5. Preuss omitted "business" (F.R.)
317. Jerushalmi. Pesachim 10; 37d
318. Aboth de Rabbi Nathan 21:1

Rabbi Chanan bar Papa expounds that it is a sign of prosperity if wine flows like water in a house[319].

Aged wine is good for the intestines; fresh wine is harmful[320]. Therefore the apostle Paul writes to Timothy: *drink no longer water but use a little wine for thy stomach's sake and thine often infirmities*[321]. Ben Achiya was especially well familiar with the effect of individual types of wine on the function of the stomach and intestines[322]. After bloodletting, one should drink undiluted wine[323]. It was also used for compresses[324].

A "collector of human bones" in Sepphoris remarked: the bones of those who drink water are black, and of those who drink wine, red; the bones of people who have only imbibed warm water are white[325].

# XXVIII  Drunkenness

The amount of wine that a person can tolerate is dependent upon many factors. It is taught that even a quarter *log* which is one sixth of an Italian liter, intoxicates, but walking cools the inebriated[326]. Some people need only drink a little wine and they feel it from the top of the head to the tips of the toes[327]. Some people who drink the four prescribed cups of mixed, that is diluted, wine on the night of Passover suffer from headaches until the Pentecost seven weeks later, because they are not wine-drinkers[328]. Mar Samuel was made giddy solely by the aroma of wine which was stored in a certain house[329].

Harnack has already emphasized that the effects of wine are already very accurately described in the Bible. It gladdens the heart of man and makes his face shine more than oil[330]. Therefore, give wine to drink to one with a bitter soul so that he forget his affliction and not remember his poverty anymore[331]. As famous as the stimulating property of alcohol is its crippling effect. The latter is first of all noted in a clouding of one's power of judgement. It is not becoming for a king to drink wine, nor should a sovereign consume an intoxicating beverage, so that he not forget the law and distort the rights of the oppressed[332]. It is assumed that the fear of this type of action underlies the prohibition of wine to priests. The *Aggada* ascribes as one of the reasons for the premature death of two sons of Aaron the fact that they were drunk when performing the Temple service[333], for in the Scriptural text, the prohibition of wine to the Aaronites immediately follows the report of their death[334]. Not only are priests forbidden to drink wine according to Talmudic law, but so are judges when they officiate in court[335].

Pertinent is the description which the author of Proverbs depicts concerning drunkenness: *thine eyes shall behold strange things, and thy heart shall utter confused things. Yea, thou shalt be as he that lieth down in the midst of the sea, or as he that lieth upon the top of a mast. They have struck me, and I felt it not; they have beaten me, and I knew it not; when shall I awake? I will seek it again*[336]. These are the psychic consequences of intoxication: the action on one's visual faculty, hallucinations, loquacity, the feeling of seasickness and finally apathy[337]. Also very instructive is the

---

319. Erubin 65a
320. Nedarim 9:8 and 66b
321. First Timothy 5:23
322. Jerushalmi. Shekalim 5; 48d
323. Shabbath 129a
324. *ibid* 109a
325. Genesis Rabbah 98:2
326. *Tosefta* Pesachim 1:28
327. Shabbath 140a
328. Ecclesiastes Rabbah 8:1

329. Erubin 65a
330. Psalms 104:15
331. Proverbs 31:6-7
332. *ibid* 31:4
333. Levit. Rabbah 20:9
334. Levit. 10:9
335. Sanhedrin 5:5
336. Proverbs 23:33-35
337. Harnack p.15

description of inebriety in the Apocrypha[338].

A well-known property of alcohol is that it sets aside certain restraints which are very important for a moral life: if wine goes in, secrets go out. A person's character is recognized by three things: by his cup[339], by his purse[340] and by his anger. Some say also by his jokes[341]. A description in the *Midrash* of the megalomania which occurs from the loss of one's power of judgement and the resulting acts of violence on the part of the intoxicated person is given as follows: a drunken palace soldier beat up the guard and allowed the prisoners to escape. He also threw stones at the bust of the governor of the city, cursed the magistrate, and cried out: "show me where the governor of this city lives and I will give him a piece of my mind". However, when he came face to face with the governor, he suddenly became meek[342]. Not always does the famous "angel" shelter the intoxicated person: a butcher became drunk, plunged from the roof and died[343].

In the sexual sphere, one observes both the stimulating and crippling effects of alcohol side by side in a frightening manner, in that the restraints of the sense of shame are removed. The drunken Noah denuded himself in his tent[344], and Lot, in a state of drunkenness, committed the dreadful incest with his daughters[345]. *Look not thou upon the wine when it is red*[346], means he is not even frightened away by *sanguis feminae menstruationis tempore*[347].

In this respect, wine is especially dangerous for a woman. The Talmud relates that one glass of wine is becoming to a woman, two are degrading; and if she has three she solicits coitus, but if she has four she solicits even an ass and is not ashamed[348]. Therefore, if a man is not with his wife, he must provide her with all types of natural products to eat but not wine[348]. A drunken wife evokes great shame; her shame cannot be disguised[349], and only rarely can a woman drunk with wine restrain herself if another cup of wine is poured for her[350].

# XXIX

Warnings about the consequences of excessive wine consumption are found not infrequently in the Bible; these are collected by Reinelt in his booklet: *Was Sagt die heilige Schrift vom Weine und von der Abstinenz?* Hamm, 1908 p.27 ff. Here I will quote a few additional Talmudic sayings.

Rabbi Judah bar Ilay said: the tree in Paradise was a vine; it brought everything unhealthy into the world: Noah uncovered himself and cursed Canaan (Ham) — one third of the world![351] The sons of Aaron died, because they were drunk when they performed Temple service[352]. During the seven years that King Solomon built the Temple, he drank no wine. However, when the construction was completed, and he

---

338. 1 Esdras 3:17-24. "Gentlemen. how supremely strong wine is! It leads the minds of all who drink it astray. It makes the mind of the king and the mind of the fatherless child alike; the mind of the menial and the freeman, of the poor and and rich. It turns every thought to mirth and merrymaking, and forgets all grief and debt. It makes all hearts rich, and forgets kings and governors, and makes everybody talk in thousands. And when they drink, they forget to be friendly to friends and brothers, and very soon they draw their swords. And when they recover from their wine, they cannot remember what they have done. Gentlemen, is not wine supremely strong, since it forces them to act so?"

339. i.e. the amount he drinks
340. the amount he gives to charity
341. Erubin 65a-b
342. Exodus Rabbah 30:11 fol. 54a
343. Jerushalmi. Terumoth 1; 45c
344. Genesis 9:21
345. *ibid* 19:32 ff
346. Proverbs 23:31. Preuss has: *look not thou upon the wine for it evokes a desire for blood* (F.R.)
347. Levit. Rabbah 12:1
348. Kethuboth 65a
349. Sirach 26:8
350. Nazir 2:3
351. *Tanchuma, Shemini* p.13a
352. Levit. Rabbah 12:3

married an Egyptian princess, he arranged for two drinking bouts, one for the consecration of the Temple, and one in honor of the new Queen. In that night, God immediately decided to destroy the Temple again.

Wine leads to blood, to the shedding of blood, and to crime for which the death penalty is invoked. Wine was created for the punishment of evil people, so that they cannot acquire eternal bliss (i.e. salvation)[353]. As the drunkard looks to his cup of wine, so does the storekeeper look at his purse[354]. The drinker says to himself: why do we need brass pots, earthenware pots can do the same. So he sells the former and drinks wine with the proceeds. In the end, he will even sell his other household articles and drink wine with the proceeds[355]. The drinker has wounds and boils[356], damage and shame; he defiles himself with feces and urine, and he doesn't know what he says or what he does[357]. When wine enters the body, understanding leaves[358]. Nothing brings lamentation to man other than wine[359].

Let the drunkard run, he will fall by himself[360]. He who sings Biblical verses in an inn has no share in the world to come[361]. The Lord loves three: he who does not display temper, he who does not become intoxicated, and he who does not insist on his full rights[362] of retaliation[363]. He who allows himself to be appeased with wine has characteristics similar to his Creator's[364]. The following is related as a "proverb of Ben Sira": there are three that I hate, yea, four that I do not love: a scholar who frequents wine shops[365], a person who sets up a college in the high parts of town[366], one who holds his penis during micturition, and one who suddenly enters his friend's house unannounced[367].

## XXX   Chronic Alcoholism

Conclusions about *chronic* alcoholism cannot be proven with certainty from either the Bible or the Talmud. Harnack (p.16) believes that chronic alcoholic poisoning first arose with the use of burnt (i.e. distilled) beverages, whereas here in the Bible and Talmud one spoke of fermented *alkoholicis*. The word delirium, however, is already mentioned in the Talmud[368]. It is just as unlikely that it refers to alcoholic delirium, as is the assumption that the Greek *kordiakos* refers to alcoholic delirium.

Juridically, there is a distinction between a *shattuy* (tipsy or fuddled) and a *shikkor* (drunk or intoxicated). A person who is tipsy can still speak before the king, whereas one who is drunk is unable to speak before the king. One who is tipsy can still pray, whereas the prayer of the latter is an abomination[369]. People in both categories, however, are responsible for all business matters and all liabilities for punishment: the purchase or sale by an intoxicated person is valid. For a crime he is flogged or executed just like a sober person. Only if he was as drunk at Lot[370] is he exempt from all responsibilities[371]. A marriage contracted while the man is in such a condition is obviously legally invalid[372]. He is then considered in the same category as someone who is mentally ill[373].

---

353. Numbers Rabbah 10:3 fol. 35c
354. Proverbs 23:32. Play on words: *kos* means cup and *kis* means purse.
355. Levit. Rabbah 12:1
356. Proverbs 23:29
357. *Tanchuma. loc. cit.*
358. Numbers Rabbah 10:8 fol. 38c
359. Sanhedrin 70b
360. Shabbath 32a
361. Sanhedrin 101a
362. Pesachim 113b
363. *Rashi* in Megillah 28a
364. Erubin 65a
365. literally: a house of drinking
366. a manifestation of arrogance
367. Niddah 16b. See also Eccles. 21:23 and Proverbs 19:16
368. Kallah Rabbathi 1 fol. 52a and Pesachim 112b
369. Erubin 64a
370. Genesis 19:30 ff, a state of complete unconsciousness
371. Erubin 65a
372. *Even Ha'ezer* 44:3
373. *Choshen Mishpat* 235:22

## XXXI    Mealtimes

Concerning the relationship between eating and drinking, the following is recommended: just as in the case of offerings solid foods outweigh beverages by far, so, too, a person should consume more solid food than liquid[374]. On the other hand, one is protected from intestinal illnesses if one lets one's food float in water, that is, if one drinks abundantly[375]. And he that eats without drinking eats his blood, the vitality of his body[376]. We, therefore, have here the forerunners of the most modern remedies: the promotion of normal defecation by the provision of water, and the reduction of obesity by withdrawal of fluids.

As a rule, one ate only once a day. The time of this meal for the *ludi'm*[377] is the first hour of the day[378]; robbers eat during the second hour, laughing heirs (who have nothing to attend to and need not prepare any meals) during the third hour, laborers during the fourth hour, and all other people normally eat during the fifth hour of the day. According to Rabbi Papa, the normal mealtime for most people is at four o'clock. In other places, laborers eat at five o'clock and scholars, who do not wish to interrupt their studies, at six o'clock. Eating later than that is as harmful as "throwing a stone into an empty tube", which is damaged as a result. According to Abaye, this is only applicable if one has eaten nothing at all in the morning; otherwise, there is no objection to eating later. However, he who has a weak stomach had better eat twice a day and not overfill his abdomen at one time[380]. The house steward of King Agrippa relates of himself that he was accustomed to eat only once a day[381].

## XXXII    Defecation

Evacuation of the intestines is for the Orientals a matter of great importance, not only because they live in constant fear of dysentery, but also because the lavatory facilities were quite primitive. Evacuation of urine and stool early in the morning is good for the body as hardening is to iron[382]. He who holds back his "openings" transgresses the Biblical command: *ye shall not make your souls detestable*[383]. He who fails to heed the call of nature for four or five days will die[384]. A saying which Bar Kappara used to sell for money propounded that: when you are hungry, eat; when you are thirsty, drink; when your pot is boiling, empty it out[385] (i.e. the feces). Only the fetus in the mother's womb does not excrete feces; otherwise, it would cause the death of the mother[386].

Diarrhea *(shilshul)* is among the favorable prognostic signs for a sick person[387], provided that, according to Rabbi Chaggai, a sick person does not suffer from dysentery[388]. The Rabbis of Cesaria, on the other hand, only considered "the normal motion of the bowels" to be propitious[389]. It is a good sign if one dreams that one is defecating[390].

If the time for defecation has arrived but the person's efforts are unsuccessful, according to Rabbi Chisda, one should repeatedly stand up and sit down on the toilet. Rabbi Hamnuna recommended that he should rub that place (the anus) with a shard.

374. Megillah 12a
375. Berachoth 40a
376. Shabbath 41a
377. Jastrow: gladiators; *Rashi:* gluttonous cannibals
378. the "hours of the day" were determined by dividing into twelve equal parts the time between sunrise and sunset. An "hour" thus changes depending on the time of year, i.e. shorter in winter, longer in summer.
379. Shabbath 10a
380. *Be'er Hetev* on *Orach Chayim* No. 157
381. Sukkah 27a
382. Berachoth 62b
383. Levit. 20:25 see Makkoth 16b
384. Numbers Rabbah 16:24
385. Berachoth 62b
386. Levit. Rabbah 14:8
387. Berachoth 57b
388. *Pesikta Rabbah* 33 Ed. Friedmann p.152a
389. Genesis Rabbah 20:10
390. Berachoth 57a

The Rabbis advised that he distract his thoughts, whereas Rabbi Ashi suggested just the opposite, namely, concentration of one's thoughts will lead to successful defecation[391]. Also, a severe fright can occasionally act like a laxative[392]; the same is true of great fear[393].

A flogging which is in progress is interrupted if the culprit defecates during the procedure[394].

The dietetics of the intestines have already been discussed[395].

## XXXIII    Fasting

By *fasting*, the Jews mean the complete abstention from food and beverage. The Torah only lists one general fast day, the Day of Atonement[396], but four others were added later. Extraordinary fast days were declared after military defeats and after calamities[397]. Thus, later, whole cities and provinces fasted after a generalized misfortune[398]. And when the rainy season was markedly delayed, thereby causing fear of bad harvests and famine, the *Sanhedrin* used to decree generalized fasts[399].

The law does not decree anything about private fasts although such fasts were frequently held. However, these did not meet with general approval. On the contrary, in many instances, they were specifically discouraged: a city surrounded by hostile troops or by an overflowing river, the crew of a ship which is sailing on the seas, as well as an individual who is fleeing from heathens or other enemies or from an evil spirit may not torment themselves through fasting, so as not to weaken their strength. Rabbi Jose said: an individual is altogether not allowed to castigate himself by private fasts lest he damage his health and thereby become a burden on his community, which would have to provide for his sustenance[400]. For similar reasons, fasting at the time of an epidemic was later discouraged[401]. Indeed, because of such considerations, Mar Samuel declared that private fasts represent transgressions[402], further proof that Judaism does not consider asceticism very highly and strongly refuses to see a God-pleasing act in self-inflicted abstention from the permitted pleasures of life.

The duration of a fast was usually twenty-four hours, as is explicitly prescribed in the Torah for the Day of Atonement[403], "from evening to evening". There are, however, examples of longer abstinences. Queen Esther asked of her co-religionists that they fast for three days before she went to the king[404]. Rabbi Huna and Rabbi Chisda each fasted forty days because they were falsely suspicious of each other[405]. Rabbi Jose and Resh Lakish fasted eighty and one hundred days, respectively, in order to see once more the spirit of their deceased teacher Rabbi Chiya[406]. Legend relates that Rabbi Zadok fasted for forty years in order to ward off the downfall of Jerusalem. Whenever he ate anything, one could recognize it externally, so emaciated had his body become[407].

Fasts of the above type only lasted during daytime; after sundown, food was consumed. The *Midrash* is of the opinion that if the Jews at the time of Esther had really fasted for three days without interruption, they would have died[408]. This is, therefore, similar to the fast month of Ramadan of the Mohammedans, except that, in

391. Shabbath 82a
392. Megillah 15a
393. Song of Songs Rabbah 3:4
394. Makkoth 3:14
395. Above chapter 4, section 8:1 and chapter 17, section 5:4
396. Levit. 16:29 and 23:27; see also Acts 27:9
397. Joel 1:14
398. Josephus *Vita* 56
399. Taanith 1:5
400. *Tosefta* Taanith 2:12
401. *Be'er Hetev* on *Orach Chayim* 576:2; also see Isserles *(Ramah)* on *Yoreh Deah* 374
402. Taanith 11a
403. Levit. 16:29. Josephus *Antiquities*. Book 3 Chapter 10:3
404. Esther 4:16
405. Baba Metzia 33a
406. Jerushalmi Kilayim 19; 32b
407. Gittin 56a
408. Midrash Psalms 22:1

contrast to the latter, the Jews did not spend the nights in revelry, but contented themselves with modest, light snacks. When Rabbi Zadok ended his fast every evening, he only sucked on a dried fig, *grogereth,* and then threw it away. The Day of Atonement is not celebrated for two days as are all other festivals outside Palestine, in order to avoid the risk of danger to the health of weak people[409].

Concerning the intrinsic value of fasting, that is, insofar as it is not a means to repentence nor considered to produce a change of heart in a person, reference should be made to the beautiful words of the prophet[410]. These words should serve as a guiding principle for all times and are, therefore, read aloud to the congregation on every Day of Atonement.

# XXXIV

Through fasting, the fat and the blood of a person become diminished[411] and a bad odor emanates from his mouth[412]. If the fasting is of long duration, his teeth become black[413], and his face becomes as pale as polished horns[414]. The body of hungry people evokes *thappuchey ra'ab*[415] (hunger pangs), gradually delirium develops, and finally death ensues as a result (literally: sign) of exhaustion. From a strictly medical point of view, one can only interpret the laughter and the crying of the exhausted Rabbi Eleazar ben Pedath and the resultant visions which he experienced[416], as well as the vision of the fasting Rabbi Jose[417], as fantasies due to inanition.

An intelligent preventive measure during a time of famine is the voluntary restriction of food intake. He who remains hungry during a time of famine is protected from the occurrence of unnatural death, *mitha meshunna.* One should also be sparing in the use of one's body strength, and, hence, should particularly restrict cohabitation[418].

A repetitive criminal who killed a person without witnesses — whose guilt is unquestionable but the death penalty cannot be imposed because of legal procedural reasons — is put into a prison cell, *kippa,* and is fed with *sparing bread and scant water*[419] and then barley until his stomach bursts[420].

The appropriate amount of nourishment varies from person to person. One can also get used to hunger. "The poor man is hungry and does not know it"; he no longer realizes it[421].

Among the laws regarding the poor, the following are noteworthy: a repeatedly enjoined decree in the Bible is the feeding of the hungry[422]. The Talmud expounds on this saying: the poor man who wanders from place to place should be given oil and peas. For the Sabbath, he should be given food for three meals consisting of oil and peas and fish and green vegetables. One is not concerned about the habitual beggar "who goes from door to door"[423]. In every community, there existed a *kuppa,* "a basket" (public poor box) with natural products, and a *tamchuy,* "a bowl" (public poor kitchen). From the former, the poor were supplied once weekly, and from the latter, they received cooked foods daily[424]. In general, one should try to provide the poor with that to which they were formerly accustomed.

A person who was accustomed to eat fat meat and drink good wine once applied for maintenance. Rabbi Nehemiah, as the officer in charge of the poor, came to terms

409. Berachoth 8b
410. Isaiah 58:3ff
411. Berachoth 17a
412. Aboth de Rabbi Nathan 6:3:24
413. Nazir 52b
414. *Chiwi,* in opposition to *Ibn Ezra* on Exodus 34:29
415. Sanhedrin 63b
416. Taanith 25a
417. Jerushalmi Kilayim 9; 32b
418. Taanith 11a
419. Isaiah 30:20
420. Sanhedrin 9:5
421. Megillah 7b
422. For example, Isaiah 58:7
423. *Tosefta* Peah 4:8
424. Peah 8:7

with the man that he be satisfied with peas, but the man died. It was said: Alas to Rabbi Nehemiah, who has killed a man[425]. Where a man and a woman are both in need of sustenance, the woman takes precedence.

# XXXV   Combined Rules of Nutrition and Decency

The following rules relate to both dietetics and to common decency: rinse a wine glass before you drink, and rinse it again before you put it away. And when you drink water, pour some out over the rim where your mouth touched before you give the glass to your disciple. It once happened that a teacher forgot to pour off some water and handed the cup to his thirsty disciple. The latter was squeamish, did not himself wish to pour from the rim of the glass out of respect for his teacher, and died of thirst[426].

The difference in the treatment of wine and water is suggested by the following commentary: sticky sweet wine, which conceivably comes into contact with the mouth of the first drinker, sticks to the glass; however, it is too expensive to simply avoid contact with the second drinker by pouring some out, as is possible in the case of water. Hence, a wine glass is wiped or rinsed, but no wine poured out.

One should not act contemptuously towards food: one should not throw foods from one place to another, and one should not sit on a basket of dates or dried figs lest they be crushed, but one may sit on a basket of legumes which a woman is to sell at the market[427], and on a cake of pressed figs, because it is customary to do so; the latter are not spoiled by sitting on them[428].

He who wishes to be a scholar (i.e. refined) should not eat standing, nor lick his fingers[429].

Rabbis Jose and Judah were once eating porridge from the same bowl. One ate with his fingers, the other with a prick (spoon). The one who was eating with the spoon said to the other: how long will you make me eat the filth of your fingers? The other replied: how long will you feed me your saliva (which adheres to the spoon)[430]?

We have already mentioned[431] that it was an obligation to wash one's hands before and after meals.

Our Rabbis taught: he who eats in the marketplace (i.e. street) is like a dog; and some say he is unfit to testify as a witness because he has no self-respect[432].

It was an important custom in Jerusalem that at a banquet all the courses were placed on the tablecloth simultaneously. The reason for this is so that those who were fastidious with their food should not be forced, out of respect for the host, to eat foods which might be harmful to themselves[433].

Rabbi Ammi said: one must pay attention to the habits of the people: one should not place coins in one's mouth — which may have been done to relieve thirst —[434] nor place food under one's bed, nor take bread under one's arms[435], nor place a knife in a radish or in a citron (ethrog). All perspiration that emanates from a person is a fatal poison, except the sweat from the face; so states Rabbi Jose bar Rabbi Bun; it is probably the reason for the prohibition of carrying bread under the arms[436].

Equally instructive from a pedagogic and dietetic standpoint is the following proverb: "if you give a morsel of bread to a child, inform his mother"[437], so that she can act accordingly.

---

425. Kethuboth 67b
426. Tamid 27b
427. Kallah Rabbathi 2 fol. 52a 68
428. Soferim 3:14
429. Derech Eretz Zuta 5:1
430. Nedarim 49b
431. Chullin 106a
432. Kiddushin 40b

433. Lamentations Rabbah 4:4 fol. 28a
434. Kelim 8:10
435. another version: nor place the hand in the axilla. Yoreh Deah 116:5
436. Jerushalmi Terumoth 8; 45d
437. Semachoth. Foreword. See also Betzah 16a

## XXXVI Exercise

Rabbi Yochanan says: do not sit too much, for sitting provokes hemorrhoids; do not stand too much, for standing is harmful to the stomach (or to the heart, *leb*); do not walk too much, for excessive walking is harmful to the eyes. Rather divide everything into equal amounts (i.e. sit one third of the time, stand one third and walk one third)[438]. One should not take long strides when walking; one long stride diminishes one's eyesight by a five hundredth part[439]. After meals, one should perform some exercise; if one eats without walking at least four cubits thereafter, the food rots *(rakab)* in the intestines, and is not digested[440].

Rabbi Judah teaches that in a town where there are ascents and descents (hills and valleys), people and beasts die in the prime of their lives, and if they do not die, they age prematurely[441].

Ben Azzai teaches: lie on anything but not on the ground for fear of snakes; sit on anything but not on a beam lest you fall off[442]. Rabbi Ishmael bar Rabbi says: the stones which we sat upon during our youth wage war with us (i.e. are harmful) during our old age. Rabbi Yonah warned his colleagues: do not sit on the stone benches in front of the learning hall of Bar Ulla, because they are cold. Rabbi Judah delivers the same warning[443] in regard to the learning hall of Assi[444].

It is likely that his lectures lasted as long as those of Rabbi Huna[445], so that the students were happy to sit on the benches outside the school.

Anxieties are also damaging to one's health: "a groan breaks half a man's body". Rabbi Yochanan says: "the whole body"[446]. Fear, errands (i.e. toil) and sins weaken the strength of man[447].

Also *much study is a weariness of the flesh*[448]. For this reason, we also observe that people who work with their minds become leaner, as the Roman physician said: *studentium corpora fieri tenuiora*[449]. From the time that the strength of people began to diminish, the strength of scholars also weakened. From the time of Moses until the time of Rabbi Gamliel, scholars stood when they learnt the Torah; after the latter's death, sickness came on the world and they had to sit when they learnt Torah[450].

## XXXVII Domicile

It is healthiest to live in an open city and it is harmful to live in a fortified city[451]; therefore, *the people blessed all those who (in spite of this) willingly offered themselves to dwell in (the fortified city of) Jerusalem*[452]. Rashi adds the following comment: "in a fortified city people become settled and build houses very close to each other; in an open city, however, there are gardens and parks near the houses, and the fresh air is good. It was considered particularly unhealthy to live in the vicinity of Gerar.[453].

A woman was obligated to follow her husband from poor living quarters to better ones, but not vice versa. According to Rabbi Simeon ben Gamliel, she is not even obligated to tolerate a move from poor living quarters to better ones, because even the better living quarters may be harmful *(bodek)*[454] or may test the adaptability of the body to the new environment so that illnesses may easily occur[455], as may happen

---

438. Kethuboth 111a
439. Berachoth 43b
440. Shabbath 41a
441. Erubin 56a
442. Berachoth 62b
443. Jerushalmi Betzah 1; 60c
444. without the title "Rabbi" as in the other statement of Rabbi Judah. Pesachim 113a
445. Yebamoth 64b
446. Berachoth 58b
447. Gittin 70a
448. Eccles. 12:12
449. Coel Aurel. *Chron.* 5 Chapt. 4 p.600
450. Megillah 21a
451. Kethuboth 110b; see also *Kimchi* or *Radak* on Micah 5:10
452. Nehemiah 11:2
453. Genesis Rabbah 64:3
454. Kethuboth 13:9 like the Biblical *bedek*
455. *Rashi— loc. cit.*

through any change in one's customary life pattern[456]. It is for this reason that Lot declined the request of the angel to flee to the mountain: *lest some evil take me and I die*[457]. He declined, although he lived in the valley[458] and living on a hill is much healthier. So Sepphoris was extolled for its situation on high ground and its salubrious air[459].

On the other hand, a change in one's residence is one of the things which has the property of being able to ward off a threatening evil destiny[460], as was commanded to Abraham: *get thee (for thy benefit) out of thy country and from thy kindred*[461].

Finally, the value of comforts is well-known. Three things enlarge a man's spirit: a beautiful dwelling, a beautiful wife and beautiful clothes (or furniture)[462].

# XXXVIII    Macrobiosis (Longevity)

Many theories have been proposed to explain the long lifespan of man before the deluge. It is not worthwhile to repeat them here. The ancients have already called attention to the fact that lifespan diminished rapidly in the ten generations from Noah to Abraham[463], so that Abraham only reached the age of 175 years. Concerning Moses, who died at 120 years of age, Scripture considers it noteworthy that his eyes did not dim and his strength did not wane[464]. Caleb mentions that at age 85 he felt as strong to wage war and to come and to go as he did 40 years earlier, and he, therefore, asks for mountainous land for a dwelling site[465]. At the time of Sirach, people lived for a maximum of 100 years[466]. The Psalmist considers 70 years to be the normal lifespan and 80 years if one is strong[467].

To the question of their disciples: "to what do you attribute your longevity?", the Rabbis answered by recommending and teaching an ethical, faultless and strongly moral life. Thus did Rabbi Zera (or Rabbi Adda bar Ahaba) answer[468]: I never displayed any anger in my house, and I never walked in front of any man greater than myself, nor did I ever meditate over the words of Torah in dirty alleys, nor did I ever walk four cubits without musing over the Torah, nor did I ever sleep in the *Beth Hamidrash* (house of learning) in which one spends the day and night, nor did I ever rejoice at the disgrace of my colleagues, nor did I ever call my colleague by his nickname. Rabbi Joshua ben Korcha answered the question about his longevity as follows: never did I gaze upon the countenance of a wicked man[469].

In various places, the Torah promises as a reward for a faithfully dutiful life: that you will have a good and long life on this earth. Among these duties belong those rules which we have already described and noted as having hygienic connotations, and the fulfillment of which we would still today consider to have a beneficial effect on health and on the lifespan of man. Particularly important in this regard is the influence on longevity of performing charitable acts. Rabbah, who devoted himself only to the Torah, lived for 40 years; Abaye, who devoted himself both to the Torah and to charitable deeds, lived for 60 years, although both were descended from the same ancestors[470].

It is related[471] that there was a family in Jerusalem whose members used to die at the age of eighteen. Rabbi Yochanan (ben Zakkai) advised that they occupy themselves

---

456. *Peneh Moshe* and *Korban Ha'edah*— loc. cit.
457. Genesis 19:19
458. Jerushalmi Kethuboth 3; 36b; Genesis Rabbah 50:11
459. Kethuboth 104a
460. Eccles. Rabbah 5:6 fol. 14d
461. Genesis 12:1
462. Berachoth 57b

463. *Rashi* on Genesis 17:17
464. Deut. 34:7
465. Joshua 14:10-12
466. Sirach 18:8
467. Psalms 90:10
468. Taanith 20b
469. Megillah 28a
470. Rosh Hashana 18a
471. *ibid*

with the Torah and they would remain alive[472]. For the Torah is magnificent in that it provides life in this world and the world to come to those who practice it, as it is written: *for the (teachings of the) Torah are life unto those that find them, and health to all their flesh*[473], and the Torah is a *tree of life to them that lay hold upon her*[474], and *through me,* says the Torah, *thy days shall be multiplied, and the years of thy life shall be increased*[475]. If even Tacitus, who is certainly not biased in favor of the Jews, and is, therefore, all the more a credible authority, states of them *corpora hominum salubria et ferentia laborum*[476], then one should certainly not explain this favorable condition as merely a "peculiarity of the race".

---

472. Aboth 6:7
473. Proverbs 4:22
474. *ibid* 3:18

475. *ibid* 9:11
476. *Hist.* 5:6 ed. Helm. Lips. 1907 p.206

# CHAPTER XIX

## *WRITINGS ON MEDICINE IN THE BIBLE AND TALMUD*

For a variety of reasons, I have *not* attempted to make the following bibliography exhaustive. Completely omitted are theological writings concerning demoniacs. Concerning leprosy, only a small selection of works is presented; and from the literature on circumcision, dietary laws and other laws still observed by Jews today, the intention of this book is to cite only those works which are specifically concerned with Biblical and Talmudic material. However, I did digress from custom somewhat and have included essays from periodicals, because I fail to see why a writing just because it is separately published (for example, as a dissertation) should lay claim to a greater value (than an article in a journal). As much as was possible, I sought to personally examine the various works.

## GENERAL

1. Gross, Joh. Georg: *Compendium Medicinae ex Scripturâ Sacrâ depromtum.* Basil. 1620. 8°.
A type of compendium of medicine with allusions to appropriate Biblical places. Forerunner of Schmidt's *Biblischer Physicus.*
2. Ader, Guil. *medici Enarrationes de aegrotis, et morbis in Evangelio.* Tolosae 1623. 458 p. 8°.
3. Mussaphia, Benjamin. Alias Dionysii dicti: *Sacro-Medicae Sententiae.* Hamburg 1640. 72 double p. 12°.
The author was a physician in Hamburg from 1606-1675, famous for his glossary to the Talmudic dictionary of Nathan ben Yechiel *(Aruch).*
4. Major, Joh. Dan.: *Summaria medicinae Biblicae.* Kilon. 1672 fol.
5. Bartholinus, Th., *de morbis biblicis.* Francof. 1672. 133 p. 8°. — Ed. sec. Francof. s.a. (1672) 100 p. 8°. — Ed. tert. Francof. 1692. 119 p. 8°. — Francof. 1705. 69 p. 4°.
Choulant mentions another edition, Hafnee 1671. Also in *Ugolini Thesaurus* Vol. 30. col 1522 ff.
6. Vogler, Valent. Henric.: *De rebus naturalibus ac medicis quarum in scripturis sacris fit mentio commentarius. Accessit Ejusdem physiologia historiae passionis Jesu Christi.* Helmstadi 1682. 2nd part 1693. 472 + 63 p. 4°.
7. Wedel, George Wolffgang, *Exercitationum medico-philol. decades duae.* Jenae 1686. *Decas tertia ib.* 1687. *Decas quarta ib.* 1689. *Decas quinta ib.* 1691. For the latter two, the title is *...phil. sacrarum et profanarum.*
8. Schultz, Georg Petrus, praes. Conrad Johren: *de morbis biblicis* N.T. Francof. ad Viadrum 1704. 16 p. 4°.

9. Antonius, Hermann: *Abhdlg. über d. Krankheiten und die Aerzte derer Jüden, so in der Heyligen Schrift vorkommen.* Greifswald 1707. 8°.

10. Calmet, Augustin, Benedictin: *Dissertations qui peuvent servir de prolégomenes de l'Ecriture Sainte.* Paris 1720. 3 vol. 4°. — Latin by Mansi, Venet. 1734 fol. Wirceburg 1789. 8°. French extract. Amsterdam 1723.
Containing numerous treatises on medical subjects.

11. Kerersztési, Paul: *Diss. med. theolog. complectens historiam gentis Hebraeae ex libris. V.T., nec non personas praxin medicam exercentes maxime subinitiis* N.T. Franequerac 1725. 4°.

12. Mieckisch, Gottfried. autor, Hieron. Ludolff praesid.: *Diss. med. inaug...Medicinam in S. Script. fundatam.* Erford 1726. 24 p. 4°.

13. Colmar, Paul: *üb.d. Arzneigelahrtheit der Juden, so in dem alten Testamente enthalten ist.* Gera 1729. 8°.

14. Götz, Georg: *Variae celeber. medicorum observationes, quibus multa loca Novi Testamenti docte illustrantur.* Fascic. prim. (the only one). Altorph. 1740 223 p. 8°.
Reproduction of 22 essays by various authors.

15. Csernansky, Samuel, Hungaricus, praes. D. Michaele Alberti, *de medicinae apud Ebraeos et Aegyptios conditione.* Halae Magd. 1742. 22 p. 4°.

16. Schmidt, Johann Jacob, prediger: *Biblischer Medicus.* Züllichau 1743. 761 S. 8°.

17. Mead, Richard, med. regius: *Medica sacra: sive, de morbis insignioribus, qui in Bibliis memorantur.* Londini 1749. 108 p. 8°. Amstelaed. 1749. 76 p. 8°. Lausannae 1760. 75 p. 8°; further in: *Opera medica* tom. secund., III. Götting. 1749. 85 S. 8°. — German: *Abhandlg. von den merkwürdigsten Krankheiten deren in der heil. Schrift gedacht wird...Lpz.* 1777. 90 S. 8°.

An original English version of the *Medica Sacra,* although suggested by the title of the total work *(ex anglico in latinum conversa),* does not exist. The author himself, in the foreword, admits he wrote in Latin because it is the language of physicians and theologians, and it is only for these types of people that the book is composed. An English translation by Strack, London 1755. 8°. is mentioned by Choulant.

18. Börner, Frider, praeses, defens. Wagner, Sam. Aug.: *de statu Medicinae apud veteres Ebraeos.* Witteberg 1755. 82 S. 4°.

19. Michaelis, Christ. Bened. praes., Schleunitz, Joach. Daniel: *Ad medicinam et res medicas pertinentia, ex ebraea et huic adfinibus orientalibus linguis decerpta.* Halae Magd. 1758. 54 S. 4°.

20. de Albertiz, Anton. German, Albert: *An etiam gens hebraea olim medicinam de industria coluerit, ac promoverit?* (Diss.). Vindobonae 1765 16 unpag. S. 4°.
The question is answered negatively.

21. Reinhard, Christian Tobias Ephraim, der Arzneygelahrtheit und Wundarzneykunst doctor. *Bibelkrankheiten, welche im alten Testamente vorkommen, erster u. anderer Theil.* Together with Augustin Kelmet's Benedictiner-Ordens *Abhandlung von dem Aussatze der Juden.* Frankfurth u. Lpz. 1767. 282 + LI S. (Kalmet). 8°. Third and Fourth Book *ibid.* 384 S. 5th and last book (New Testament) *ibid.* 1768. 244 S.

22. Frommann, Erh. Andr. Prof. theol. *Disquisit. de legibus mosaicis climatis contagiones reprimentibus.* In his *Opusc. philol. atque hist.* Coburg. 1770. tom. I p.150-160.

23. Lindinger, Jo. Simeon, Prof. theol. *De Ebraeorum veterum arte medica, de Daemone, et Daemoniacis.* Servestae et Leucoreae 1774. 188 S. 8°.

24. Eschenbach, Christ. Ehrenfried: *Scripta medico-biblica.* Rostoch. 1779. 134 p. 8°.

Seven revised lectures.

25. Frizzi, Benedetto: *Polizia medica sul pentateuco in riguardo alle leggi, e stato del matrimonio.* (Pars I:) Pavia 1788. 140 S. 8°. (p. II:)...*alle leggi spettanti alla gravidanza, al parto, puerperio...ib.* 1788. 128 S. 8°. (p. III:)...*al cibi proibiti...* Cremona 1788. 135 S. 8°. (p. IV:)...*in istato di malattia, e ceremonie funebri...*Pavia 1789. 166 S. 8°. (p. V:)...*formalita sacerdotali* ...Cremona 1790. 124 S. 8°.

26. Levin, Meyer, praes. Curt Sprengel. *Analecta historica ad medicinam Ebraeorum.* Halae 1798. 60 S. 8°.

27. Carcassonne, David: *Essai hist. sur la médecine des Hébreux anciens et modernes.* Montpellier & Nismes 1815. 83 p. 8°.
Minor changes from his dissertation. Montpellier 1811.

28. Shapter, Thomas M.D., *Medica sacra.* London 1834. 191 p. 8°.

29. Frensdorf, Maximilian: *Ueber d. Medizin d. alten Hebräer.* Inaug.-Diss. Bamberg 1838. 18 S. 8°.
Biblical only, and even this only from secondary sources.

30. Brunati, Giuseppe Sacerdote: *della medicina degli antichi Ebrei.* Diss. II of his *Dissertazioni bibliche.* Milano 1838. p.37-52.

31. Trusen, Garnison-Staabsarzt in Posen: Erläuterung einiger Stellen der heiligen Schrift, die auf die Medicin Bezug haben. — *Caspers Wochenschr. f. d. ges. Heilkunde.* Berlin 1842. S. 545, 566, 587, 600, 619.

32. Trusen, J.P.: *Darstellung der biblischen Krankheiten.* Posen 1843. 199 S. 8°. 2nd edition with the title: *die Sitten, Gebräuche und Krankheiten der alten Hebräer.* Breslau 1853. 288 S. 8°.

33. Goldmann, Heimann: *de rebus medicis vet. test.* Vratislav. 1845. 8°. Diss. inaug. 36 S.

34. Oppler, Einiges aus der altjüdischen Medizin. *Rohlfs' Arch. f. Gesch. d.Med.* Vol. IV. p.62.
"I am indebted to my father who diligently occupied himself with Talmudic studies and who in Jewish circles was known as a prominent Talmudist, for kindly calling my attention to several Talmudic citations."

35. Friedreich, J.B. (Prof. der gerichtl. Medizin in Würzburg:) *Analekten zur Natur- und Heilkunde.* 3 Vol. Anspach 1846.

36. idem: *Zur Bibel. Naturhistorische, anthropol. u. medicin.* Fragmente. 2 Parts. Nürnberg 1848.

37. Geoffroy, J.: Les sciences médicales chez les Hébreux. — *L'Union médicale.* Paris 1880, vol. XXX p.697-701; 757-761; 769-772.

38. Bergel, Joseph: *Die Medizin der Talmudisten.* Lpz. 1885. 88 S. 8°.

39. Grünbaum, A.: Medycyna w talmudzie, akuszerya i ginekologia. — *Medycynie* 1886. No. 41/42.

40. Bennett, Sir Ridson, M.D., F.R.S.: The diseases of the Bible. *By-Paths of Bible Knowledge* IX. 1887 (Oxford). 143 p. 8°. — 1891. 1896.

41. Ebstein, Wilhelm: *Die Medizin im alten Testament.* Stuttgart 1901. 177 S. 8°.

42. idem. *Die Medizin im neuen Testament und im Talmud. ibid.* 1903. 338 S. 8°.

43. Piassetzky, Dr. A.A.: *Medizin in Bibel und Talmud.* 2 parts *(Med. der Bibel).* St. Petersburg 1902. 1903. 203 p. 8°. Russian.
More did not appear. The author died in 1903.

44. Seuffert. Ernst Ritter von: *Welche Krankheitszustände kennt die Bibel und was berichtet sie über deren Bekämpfung.* Inaug.-Diss. Munchen 1905. 100 S. 8°.

45. Gintzburger, Benj. Wolff. Judaeus, natus Polonus, praes. Georg Gottlob Richter: *Disp. inaug. med., qua Medicinam ex Talmudicis illustrat.* Goïting. 1743. 23 p. 4°.
Also in: G.G. Richter: *opusc. med. Francof. et Lips.* 1780/1 tom. I no. 7. pg. 142/6. Here the author's name is written Ginzburger. The word "Judäus" is missing, but not "Polonus". In the index it is Gintzburger again.

46. Cohn, Sigismund: *De medicina Talmudica.* Diss. inaug. Vratislav. 1846. 28 p. 8°.

47. Wunderbar, R.J.: *Biblisch-talmudische Medizin.* Riga und Leipzig 1850-1860. 8 installments. Together 485 p. 8°.

48. Rittmann, Dr. Primararzt in Brünn: Die talmudische Medizin im Mittelalter. *Alg. Wiener med. Ztg.* XIII (1868) p.123 and 131.
A small number of citations (from another collection?) with often arbitrary interpretations, e.g., uterine probes in the Talmud, *choli r'a* in the Bible is said to refer to cholera, etc.

49. Rabbinowicz, Israel-Michel: *la médecine du Thalmud.* Paris 1880. 176 p. 8°. German introduction in: *Einleitung in die Gesetzgebung und die Medicin des Thalmuds*...translated by Sigmund Mayer. Lpz. 1883, p.237-268.

50. Magil, Rabbi Julius M.: Medicine and Physicians among the Jews — from Bible, Talmud and Ancient History. *Fort Wayne med. Journal-Magazine.* vol. XVIII (1898) No. 2. p.33-43.

51. Weiss, M.: Die talmudische Medicin. *Wiener med. Presse* 1898. No. 36 and 37. Offprint. 16 p. 8°.

52. Stern, A.: *Die Medizin im Talmud.* Frankfurt a. M. 1909. 24 S. 8°.

# THE PHYSICIAN

1. Lautenschläger, Joh. H.: de medicis veterum Hebraeorum eorumque methodo sanandi morbos. *Gratulationsschrift für Jo. Christ. Gottl.* Ackermann. Schleiz 1786. 14 p. 8°.

2. Fein, M.: *Die Stellung der Aerzte im jüd. Alterthume.* Ben Chananja III (1860) p.539-44. Additional notes by L. Löw *ibid.* p.544-549. Also found in: *Ges Schr.* Vol. III, 370-375.

3. Preuss, J.: Der Arzt in Bibel und Talmud — *Virchows Arch.* Vol. 138 (1894) p.261-283. Hebr. translation by Kahan in *ha-m'asseph* ed. Rabbinowitz. Vol. I p.79-91.

4. Delius, Heinr. Friedr.: *Prüfung einiger Stellen aus den siebenzig Dolmetschern worin die Auferstehung der Aerzte geläugnet wird. In einem Schreiben an Herrn M. Christian Gottl. Kratzenstein*... Halle 1746. 16 p. 8°.
The "book" of Chr. Reinecke is a funeral oration concerning Prof. Otto: *Hebraeorum Dictum talmudicum ... optimum medicum dignum esse Gehenna ... non ferire optimum medicum ... Joh. Georg Otto ... 1724 ... defunctum ... ostendit ... Christ. Reineccius.* Title one page, Text *(Vita panegyrica)* 3 p. fol. Owner: Univ.-Bibl. Jenna. Bud. var. 382. No. 158.

5. Schultz, Georg Petrus, praes. Conr. Johren: *Diss. inaug. med. de Christo medico.* Francof. ad Viadr. 1703 unpag.

6. Christ, am Ende resp..Mich. Alberti praes.: *De Medicina Christi divina et miraculosa.* (Halle) 1725. 54 p. 4°.

7. Gutsmuths, Hieron. Christ.: *Diss. inaug. med. de Christo medico. Jenae 1812.* 54 p. 8°.

8. Baudouin, Marcel: Jésus médecin et la médecine des Esséniens. — *Gaz. med. de Paris* 1903. No. 19 and 20.

9. Knur, K., Christus medicus? *Ein Wort an die Kollegen und die akademisch Gebildeten überhaupt.* Freiburg 1905. 74 S. 8°.

10. Winckler, Jo. Dieter., resp. C. Chr. Woog: *de Luca Evangelista medico.* Lips. 1736. 39 p. 4°.

11. Clausewitz, Bened. Gottlob: *de Luca Evangelista medico.* Hal. 1740. 4°.

12. Harnack, Prof. Adolf: *Lukas der Arzt. der Vf. des dritten Evangeliums in der Apostelgesch.* Lpz. 1906. V. 160 p.

13. Pagel, Prof. Dr. J.: Dr. Esra, praktischer Arzt? — *Allg. Ztg. d. Judent.* 26. III. 98. No. 12

14. Hervorragende Aerzte aus der talmudischen Epoche. Ein Beitrag zur Geschichte der Medizin. Signed: Wien. (Dr. — 1). *Wiener med. Wochenschr.* XXIX (1879) col. 177.
Cursory notes concerning several Talmudic physicians.

15. Krochmal, Abraham: *tholedoth Schemuel jarchinaj.* Schorr's *Hechalûtz* I (1852) S. 66-89. Hebrew.

16. Hoffmann, D. *Mar Samuel.* Lpz. 1873. 79 S. 8°.

17. Fessler, Sigmund: *Mar Samuel, der bedeutendste Amora.* Breslau 1879. 68 S. 8°.

18. Schapiro: Les Connaissances médicales de Mar Samuel. *Revue des ét. juives* Vol. XLII. No. 83 (1901). p.14-26.

# ANATOMY

1. Schagen, Petrus, rector Jo. Freder. Reitzius: *Specimen anatomes biblicae.* Traject. ad Rhenum 1750. 15 S. 4°.

2. Reinhard, Chr. T.E.: *Untersuchung d. Frage: ob unsere ersten Urältern, Adam und Eva einen Nabel gehabt?* Hamburg 1752.
Satire on positive theology. Choulant (by a different title) cites additional editions. Berlin 1753. Frankf. & Lpz. 1755. 8°.

3. Stock, Joh. Christ...*de sudore Christi sanguineo prolusio I inaug. diss...Wistinghausen, Sim. Henr. Ernest., praemissa.*Janae 1756. 4 S. 4°. id: prolus. II, *inaug. diss. de cerevisiae salubritate suspecta a Joanne Ad. Magen...praemissa.* Jenae 1756. 4 S. 4°.
Additional ancient writings on this theme are found in Choulant p. 112-13.

4. Hirsch, Dr. med. Marcus: Die pathol. Anatomie des Talmud. *Jeschurun* ed. S.R. Hirsch, XIII (1866) S.83-91 und 187-198. XV (1869) S.270-278.
Pathologic anatomy of the lung and chest cage. 1. Structural abnormalities.
2. Color alterations. 3. Wounds of the lung

5. Katzenelson, L.: Die Osteologie der Talmudisten. Offprints from *Haiom.* St. Petersburg 1888. 138 S. 8°. Hebrew.

6. Kazenelson, L.: *Die normale und pathol. Anatomie des Talmud.*Ins. Deutsche übersetzt (aus der russ. Inauguraldissert.) von N. Hirschberg. Koberts *histor. Studien.* Bd. V (1896). S.164-296.

7. Löw, Immanuel: Die Finger in Literatur und Folklore der Juden. *Gedenkbuch für David Kaufmann.* Breslau 1900. S.61 ff. (Separate offprint. p.I-XXV.)

8. Preuss, J.: Die Mundhöhle und ihre Organe nach Bibel und Talmud. — *Deutsche Mediz.-Ztg.* 1897. No. 16-18.
As with all other works of this author, this one contains also pathology and surgery.

9. Preuss, J.: Materialien z. Gesch. d. talmud. Medicin. Die Organe der Brusthöhle. *Allg. med. Central-Ztg.* 1899. No. 61 ff.

10. Preuss, J.: Materialien z. Gesch. d. alten Medicin. Die Organe der Bauchhöhle nach Bibel und Talmud. *Allg. med. Central-Ztg.* 1898. No. 39 ff.

11. Moore, George F.: ha jothereth 'al ha-kâbêd, Lobus caudatus and its Equivalents, lovos..., *Orientalische Studien. Theodor Nöldeke zum siebzigsten Geburstag.* p.761-769.

12. Preuss, J.: Materialien z. Gesch. d. talmud. Medizin. Das Nervensystem. *Deutsche Medizin.-Ztg.* 1899. No. 37 f.

13. Rosenbaum, Emanuel: *une conférence...sur l'anatomie et la physiologie des organes génitaux de la femme...*Francfort 1901. 89 S. 8°.

14. Preuss, J.: Materialien z. Gesch. d. bibl.-talmud. Medicin. XVI. Die weiblichen Genitalien. *Allg. med. Central-Ztg.* 1905. No. 5 ff.

# PATHOLOGY and THERAPY

1. Moles, Vinc.: *Pathologia morborum, quorum in sacris scripturis mentio fit.* Madrid 1642. 4°.

2. Rittmann (Brünn): Moses und die Volkskrankheiten seiner Zeit. *Allg. Wiener med. Ztg.* 1867. No. 6 S.41 und 7, S.49.

3. *Bibel und Naturwissenschaft. Apologetische Studien eines Naturforschers.* Part One: *Die biblischen Krankenheilungen (Jesu) im Lichte der modernen Medizin.* Gütersloh 1896. 45 S. 8°. Offprint from Zöckler-Steude's: *"Der Beweis des Glaubens".*

4. v. Oefele: Die pneumatische Anschauung des J. wisten und die humorale Anschauung des Elohisten in der Genesis. *Prager m. W.* 1900. No. 10.

5. Preuss, J.: Bibl.-talmud. Pathologie u. Therapie. — *Ztschr. f. klin. Medicin.* Vol. 45 Part 5/6.

6. Peters (Goslar): Die Pathologie der Bibel. Eine med.-histor. Skizze. *Medizin. Woche.* 1907. No. 49, 50, 51.

7. Johren, Conr. praes., Georg. Kuppermann autor: *de Philistaeorum plaga, I. Sam. V. verse 6.* Francof. ad Viadr. 1715, 24 p. 4°.

Hemorrhoids is the illness referred to.

8. Kanne, Joh. Arnold: *Die goldenen Aerse der Philister.* Nürnberg 1820. XII und 101 S. 8°.

9. Aschoff, L.: Die Bedeutung der Ratten auf dem Bilde Poussins "les Philistins frappés de la Peste". 1630. *Janus* 1900. Heft 10.

10. Preuss, J.: Die Askara-Krankheit im Talmud. *Jahrb. f. Kinderkrkht.* N.F. XL (1895) S.251-257.

11. Wedel, George Wolffgang: *Proempticon inaug. de morbo Jorami regis Judae.* Jenae (1717) 8 S. 4°.

12. Küchenmeister, Med.-R. in Zittau: Ueber die angeblichen Fälle von Lausesucht in der Bibel und bei Josephus. Göschen's *Deutsche Klinik.* 1857. No. 36 & 38.

Where is the concluding article mentioned in number 38 which is supposed to be concerned with the alleged vermin in the second book of Moses?

# SURGERY

1. Halpern, Joachim: *Beitr. z. Gesch. der talmudischen Chirurgie.* Inaug.-Diss. (Breslau 1869) 25 S. 8°.

2. Preuss, J.: Chirurgisches in Bibel und Talmud. *Deutsche Ztschr. f. Chirurgie.* Vol. 59 (1901) S. 507-534.

3. Higier, H (einrich): Zur Geschichte der Medizin bei den Juden. Einiges über die Chirurgie des Talmud. *Medycyna.* Warschau 1904. Polish.

4. Grünbaum, A.: czy nasza nowoczesna chirurgia istotnie jest nowa? (Is our modern surgery really new?) *Krytyka lekarska,* Rok VIII (1904) p.16-18.

5. Kühn, W.: Etwas vom Verbinden aus alter Zeit. *Ztschr. f. Samariter- u. Rettungswesen* XII (1906). No. 7.

6. Bartholinus, Thomas: *De latere Christi aperto.* Lips. 1685. 144 p. 8°.

7. Preuss, J.: Die männlichen Genitalien und ihre Krankheiten nach Bibel und Talmud. *Wiener med. Wochenschr.* 1898. No. 12 ff.

8. Brecher, Gideon: *Die Beschneidung der Israeliten.* Wien 1845. 78 S. 8°.

9. Glassberg, A.: *Die Beschneidung in ihrer geschichtlichen, ethnographischen, religiösen und medizinischen Bedeutung.* Berlin 1896. 335 S. 8°.

10. Preuss, J.: Die Beschneidung nach Bibel und Talmud. *Wiener klin. Rundschau.* 1897. No. 43/44.

11. Löw, L.: Aderlassen und Schröpfen. *Ben Chananja* V (1862) 314-315; *Ges. Schr.* III, 375-379.

12. Brecher (Eichwald): Der Aderlass im Talmud. *Prager med. W.* 1876. p.228-230; 257-260.
From the legacy of his father Gideon Brecher.

13. Preuss, J.: Zur Geschichte der Aderlasses. *Wien. klin. W.* 1895. No. 34 & 35.

# THE EYES

1. Friedmann, M.: *Der Blinde in dem biblischen und rabbinischen Schriftthume.* Das Blinden-Institut auf der hohen Warte bei Wien. Wien 1873, S .81-139.

2. Rosenzweig, Adolf: *Das Auge in Bibel und Talmud.* Berlin 1892. 36 S. 8°.

3. Preuss, J.: Das Auge und seine Krankheiten nach Bibel und Talmud. *Wiener mediz. Wochenschr.* 1896. No. 49 ff.

4. Creighton, C.: Antiquity of tattooing for corneal opacities: the case of Leucoma in the book of Tobit? Peypers' *Janus* VI (1901) p.357/8.

5. Kotelmann, L.: *Die Ophthalmologie bei den alten Hebräern.* Hamburg und Leipzig. 1910. 436 S. 8°.

6. Nobel, Gabriel. Zahnarzt: *Zur Gesch. d. Zahnheilkunde im Talmud.* (Inaug.-Diss.) Lpz. 1909. 66 S. 8°.

7. Preuss, J.: Materialien z. Gesch. d. talmud. Medicin. Nase und Ohr. *Allg. med. Central-Ztg.* 1899. No. 76 ff.

# NERVOUS and MENTAL DISORDERS

1. Naschér, S.: Psychiatrisches in der Bibel. *Allg. Ztg. d. Judenth.* 1898. No. 30. p.356.

2. Preuss, J.: Nerven- und Geisteskrankheiten nach Bibel und Talmud. *Ztschr. f. Psychiatrie* etc. Vol. 56 (1899). S .107 to 134.

3. Bumm, Prof. Dr. A. (Direkt. d. psychiatr. Klinik) in München: *Spuren griech. Psychiatre im Talmud.* (Private printing 1902.)

4. Kornfeld, Dr. Herm.: *Verbrechen u. Geistesstörg.im Lichte der altbiblischen Tradition.* Halle a. S. 1904. 36 S. 8°.

5. Wulfing, M.: *Pathologie nerveuse & mentale chez les Anciens Hébreux et dans la Race juive.* Thèse de doctorat en med. Paris 1907. 124 p. 8°.

6. Bartholin, Thom., *Paralytici N.T.* ed. sec. Basil. 1662. 105 p. 8°. Ed. tert. Lips. 1685. 103 p. 8°. Also in *Ugolini thesaurus* vol. 30 col. 1459 ff.

7. Pipping, Henric., praes. Casp. Loescher, *De Saule per musicam curato.* Wittenberg 1713 Ed. IV. 64 S. 4°. Also in his: *Exercitat, acad. juveniles.* Lips. 1708. p.99-223.

8.  Sharp, Granville: *The case of Saul* (1777). London 1807. 187 p. 8°.
9.  Binet-Sanglé, *les prophètes juifs. Etude de psychologie morbide.* Paris 1905. 324 p. 18°.
10.  Dieulafoy, Saul et David. *Acad. des inscript. et belles lettres,* séance du 19. VII. 1895. *Comptes rend.* p.311.
Saul's attacks were grand hysteria of demoniacal form (hysterodemonopathy).
11.  de Loosten (Dr. Georg Lomer): *Jesus Christus vom Standpunkte des Psychiaters.* Bamberg (1905) 104 S. 8°.
12.  Werner, Hermann: *Die psychische Gesundheit Jesu. Bibl. Zeit- und Streitfragen* IV. ser. Part 12. Gr. Lichterfelde 1909. 64 S. 8°.

# SKIN DISEASES

1.  Crugot, Martin, praes. Nic. Nonnen: *Diss. theol. de Leprae Aedium Mysterio.* Bremae 1744. 60 S. 4°.
Symbolic meaning of the chapter on *tzora'ath.*
2.  Lehmaier, J.: *Ueber den in der Bibel erwähnten Aussatz.* Inaugural-Abhdlg. Nürnberg 1838. 8°. 30 S.
3.  Essinger, David, praes. Autenrieth, H.F.: *Ueb. den Zaraath des Moses oder den weissen Aussatz.* Diss. Tübingen 1843. 50 S. 8°.
4.  Blanc, Henry William: Anthrax, the Disease of the Egyptian Plagues. *New Orleans med. and surg. Journ.* July 1890. p.1-25.
5.  Münch, G.N.: Der Aussatz in Egypten zu Moses Zeiten. *Dermatol. Ztschr.* Vol. I, Heft 3. S. 242-257.
6.  idem: Die Zaraath (Lepra) der hebr. Bibel. *Dermatol. Studien* ed. Unna. Heft 16. Hambg. u. Leipz. 1893. 167 S. 8°.
7.  Kazenelson, J.L.: *schemôth ha-negâ'îm bekithbe ha-qôdesch.* Names of skin diseases in the Holy Scriptures. *Ha-jeqeb,* Petersburg 1894. S. 41-79. Hebrew.
8.  Sack, Arnold, Dr. med. et phil. in Heidelberg: Was ist die Zaraath (Lepra) der hebräischen Bibel? *Virchow's Archiv. f. path. Anat.* 1896. Suppl. –Bd. S.201-223.
9.  Cohn, Naphtali: *Die Zarâath-Gesetze der Bibel nach dem Kitâb alkâfi des Jûsuf Ibn Salâmah.* Frankf. a. M. 1899. XVIII und 54 S. 8°.
10.  Pogorelsky, Messala: *Was ist die biblische Zara'ath?* St. Petersburg 1900. 221 S. 8°. Russian.
11.  Preuss, J.: Materialien z. Gesch. d. bibl.-talmud. Medicin. Die Erkrankungen der Haut. *Allg. med. Central-Ztg.* 1903 No. 21ff.
12.  Grünbaum, A.: Jaka wlasciwie postac chorobna nalezy rozumiec pod nazwa biblijna "zoraath"? (Which type of illness is to be understood by the Biblical term *zoraath?) Krytyka lekarska.* Warschau 1905. No. 5. p.206-210.
13.  Lagowski, St. Critical comments thereto. *Ibid.*
14.  Higier, H.: Was findet man über Lepra und Lues in der Bibel, im Talmud und in neuen Testament? *Medycyna* 1906. No. 3. Polish.
15.  idem: Was lehren uns die Bibel, der Talmud und das Evangelium über Lepra und Syphilis? *St. Petersbg. med. W.* 1907. S.67-70.
16.  Withof, Frider. Theod.: *De leprosoriis vet. Hebraeorum.* Duisburg 1756. Also in his *Opusc.* No. IX p.295-304.
17.  Feige, Sam. Gottfr., praes. Fr. Hoffmann: Diss. inaug. *med. chir. de morbo Lazari.* Halae-Magd. 1733. 29 S. 4°.
18.  Rogers, Daniel: *Naaman the Syrian his disease and cure.* London 1642. 898 p. fol.
19.  Reiske, Joh.: *de Morbo Jobi difficillimo...* Helmstadii 1685. 4°.

20. Wedel, Ge. Wolffgang: *De morbo Hiobi*. Jenae 1689. 8 p. 4°.

21. Hoffmann, Joh. Nic., praes. Benj. Ewaldt: *Scrutin. med. Ezechiae morbi per ficum curati*. Regiom. 1708. 16 p. 4°.

22. Ebbell, B.: La variole dans l'Ancien Testament et dans le papyrus Ebers. *Nord. Med. Arkiv*. 1906. Vol. II, part 4. No. 11 p.1-58.

23. Pinkhof, H.: antieke lues? *Nederl. Tijdschr. voor Genesskd*. 1893 deel I p. 130 ff (*Raathan* in the Talmud is said to refer to lues.) However: Peypers *ibid*. deel II p.397. Further controversy *ibid* p.781, 1894 deel II p.152 u. 443.

24. Gebuhr, Christophor. Henr., praes. David Bierfreund: *Utrum rufus ac pilosus Esau fuerit monstrum*. Regiomonti 1687 (12 p.) 4°.

25. Pascal, Nicol. Bened.: *quaestio an Esau fuerit monstrum*. Viteb. 1671. 4°.

26. Beyer, Carol. Aug.: de haemorrhoidibus ex lege mosaica impuris ad Levit. XV commentatio. *Gratulationsschrift für Degenkolb*. Lips. 1792. 12 p. 4°.

27. Löbl, Jos. M.: Ueber die venerischen Krankheiten bei den alten Israeliten. *Wiener med. Wochenschr*. 1895. No. 15/16.

28. Goldstein, Ferd.: Ueber eine merkwurdige "Krankheit" in der Bibel (and commentary thereon by J. Preuss). *Neue medizin. Presse*. 1901. No. 24.

The *Zab* in Levit. 15 is said to be a passive Mexican pederast with chronic spermatorrhea. Preuss doubts the evidence presented by Goldstein.

29. Kroner, Kirchenrat Dr.: Ein Blick in die Geschichte der Bekämpfung der Geschlechstkrankheiten. *Ztschr. f. Bek. d. Geschlechtskrkht*. Bd. V. Heft 5 S. 179-197.

# GYNECOLOGY and OBSTETRICS

1. Sachs, Aron, Arzt: *Die Gynäkalogie in der Bibel und im Talmud*. Inaug.-Diss. Leipzig 1909 30 S. 8°.

2. Israels, Abr. Hartog: *Diss. hist.-med. inaug. exhibens collectanea gynaecol. ex Talmude babylonico*. Groningae 1845. Title for the bookdealers: *Tentamen hist.-med., exhib. coll. gynäc. quae ex Talm. bab. depromsit*. 189 S. 8°.

3. Redslob, Gustav. Maurit.: *de Hebraeis obstetricantibus*. Lips. 1835. 14 S. 4°.

4. Mattei, *la maternité et l'obstétrique chez les Hébreux*. Paris 1857. 37 S. 8°.

5. Kotelmann, L.: *Die Geburtshülfe bei den alten Hebräern. aus den alttestamentlichen Quellen*. Marburg 1876. 50 S. 8°.

6. Schapiro, D.: *Obstétrique des anciens Hebréux*. Paris 1904. 162 p. 8°. Also in *La France Médicale*. 49th Year (1902) No. 1-9.

7. Preuss, J.: Schwangerschaft, Geburt und Wochenbett nach Bibel und Talmud. *Ztschr. f. Geburtsh. u. Gynäk*. Bd. 53 (1904) Heft 3.

8. *ibid:* Die Pathologie der Geburt nach Bibel und Talmud. *Ztschr. f. Geburtsh. u. Gynäk*. Bd. 54 (1905) Heft 3.

9. Wyss, Joh. Franc., praes. Henr. Philiponei de Hautecour: *Diss. philolo-theol. in qua demonstratur obstetrices illas Aegyptiacas Siphra & Phua veritatem Pharaoni tradidisse*. Franequer. 1706. 19 p. 4°.

10. Gudius, Gottlob Friedr.: *de Hebraica obstetricum origine*. Lips. 1724. Also in *Ugolini Thesaurus* vol. 30 vol. 1061 till 1066.

11. Kraft, Fridr. Guil.: *De pietate obstetricum, qua Deus domos aedificasse dicitur Israelitis*. Jena 1744. 4°.

12. Kall: *De obstetricibus matrum Hebraeorum in Aegypto*. Hamburg 1746. 4°.

13. Goguel, L.: accouchements chez les Hébreux et les Arabes. *Gaz. hebdomad. de med. et de chir*. Paris 1877. No. 23 p.363.

He observed two Arabic women in Tunis who died while sitting on the birth stool.

14. Schapiro: Attitudes obstétricales chez les Hébreux d'aprés la bible et le talmud. *Revue des étud. juives.* Vol. 40 (1900) p.37-49.

15. Slevogt, J.H.: *De partu Thamaris difficili et perinaeo inde rupto.* Jena 1700. 4°.

16. Rawitzki, M., weiland prakt. Arzt in Berlin: Ueber die Lehre von der Superfötation und der Entstehungsursache des Fötus compressus im Thalmud. Peypers' *Janus* VI. 8.9.10; 1901 p.410-418, 461-470, 542-546. Offprint 23 p. 8°.

17. Lippe, K.: *Thorath ha-'ubbarin beme'ee immân.* (Talmud. Embryology). Jassy 1900. 12 p. 8° Hebrew.

18. Finalyson: On the care of infants and young children according to the Bible and Talmud. *Med. Magazine* Oct. 1893 and *Glasgow med. Journ.* Dec. 1893.

# CESARIAN SECTION (YOTZE DOPHEN)

1. Tobia ha- Kohen: *Ma'ase Tobijja,* Vol. III pereq 18. p.138a–b ed. Venet. 1705. Hebrew.

2. Mansfeld, *Ueber d. Alter des Bauch- und Gebärmutter-Schnittes an Lebenden.* Braunschweig 1824. 2nd edition 1825. 24 p. 8°.

3. Fulda, L.: Beytrag zur Geschichte des Kaiserschnitts mit besonderer Beziehung auf die Schrift des Herrn Mansfeld... E.v.Siebolds *Journalf. Geburtshülfe* etc. Bd. VI, 1. Stück. 1826.

4. Levysohn, Joce dophen. *Littbl. des "Orients".* 1849 (X) No. 24 p.378.

5. Wunderbar, R.J.: Die im Talmud erwähnte chirurg. Operation *joce dophen.* *Littbl. des "Orients"* XI (1852) 102-105. Later reprinted in his "Biblisch-Talmudische Medizin".

6. Reich, B.: Ueber einige Andeutungen des Kaiserschnittes an Lebenden nach dem Talmud. *Virch. Arch.* Vol. 35 (1866). p.365-368 and *Aerztl. Literaturblatt d. Wiener med. Ztg.* 1866. p.18/19.

7. Spiegelberg. Der Kaiserschnitt im Talmud. ibid. p.480.

8. Israëls, A.H.: Der Kaiserschnitt im Talmud. ibid. Vol. 36 (1866[II]) p.290.

9. Löw, L.: Der Kaiserschnitt (nach dem Talmud). *Ben Chananja* IX (1866). 681-700; *Ges. Schr.* III. 379-406.

10. Rawitzki, M.: Die Lehre vom K. im Thalmud. *Virch. Arch.* Vol. 80 (1880) p.494-502.

11. (Hildesheime)r: Rezension. *Berliner-Hoffmanns Mag. f.d. Wiss. d. Judenth.* VIII (1881) p.48-53.

12. Kotelmann, L.: Kritische Bemerkungen zu dem Aufsatz... *Virch Arch.* Vol. 84 (1881). p.164-176.

13. Rawitzki, M.: Erwiderung...*ibid.* Vol. 86 (1881). p.240-262.

14. Kotelmann, L.: Noch einmal die Lehre vom K. im Talmud. *Virch Arch.* Vol. 89. (1882) p.377-382.

15. Israëls, A.H.: De keizersnede bij levenden, volgens den babyl. Talmud. *Ned. Tijdschr. voor Genesskd.* 1882. II. p.121-130.

16. Rawitzki, M.: Ueber den K. im Talmud. (Replik mit Bemerkungen des Rezensenten.) *Berliner Hoffmans Mag.* XI (1884) p.31-42.

17. Rawitzki, M.: Wiederum über die Lehre vom K. — *Virch Arch.* Vol. 95 (1884). p.485-526.

18. (Hildesheime)r: Rezension. *Berliner-Hoffmanns Mag.* XI (1884) p.43-45.

19. Pinkhoff, H.: Bijdrage tot de jotze dofen-quaestie. *Nederl. Tijdschr. voor Geneesk.* 1888. p.158-164; see also

20. *ibid: Janus* IV (1889) p.447-448.

# LEGAL MEDICINE

1. Bergel, Joseph: *Die Eheverhältnisse der alten Juden.* Lpz. 1881. 33 p. 8°.
2. Schvob, Alexandre: *Sur la médecine légale chez les Hébreux.* Thèse. Strasbourg 1861. 80 p. 4°.
3. David und der heilige Augustin, zwei Bisexuelle. *Jahrb. f. sex. Zwischenstufen* II (1900). p.288-294.
4. Homosexualität und Bibel. Von einem katholischen Geistlichen. *Jahrb. f. sex. Zwischenstufen* IV (1902) offprint 47 p. 8°.
5. Wirz, Caspar, Prof.: Der Uranier von Kirche und Schrift. Eine Studie vom orthodox-evang. Standpunkt. *Jahrb. f. sex. Zwischenstufen* VI (1904) p.63-108. offprint Lpz. 1904. 44 p.; 2nd edit. Lpz. 1905. 112 p. 8°; without the subtitle and with V.D.M. as the title of the author.
6. Rejtö, Sandor: *A mózesi törvényekröl.* (of the Laws of Moses.) Budap. orvosi ujság. 1905. off-print 9 p.

The prohibition of cohabitation during and after the menses is said to protect against abdominal pregnancies which would occur during that time (of the woman's cycle).

7. Preuss, J.: Sexuelles in Bibel und Talmud. *Allg. med. Central-Ztg.* 1906. No. 30 ff.
8. Preuss, J.: Prostitution and sexuelle Perversitäten nach Bibel und Talmud. *Monatshefte f. prakt. Dermatol.* Vol. 43 (1906).
9. Sickler, Wilh. E. Christ. Aug: *Diss exhibens novum ad historiam luis venereae additamentum.* Jenae 1797. 32 p. 8°.

The plague during *Baal Peor* worship was lues.

# HYGIENE

1. von der Hardt, Herm.: *Officia Judaeorum antelucana pro sanitate et studiis.* Helmstad 1706. 114 p. 8°.
2. Gumprecht, Ignaz: *De religionis Judaicae in sanitatem influxu.* Götting. 1800. 8°.
3. Schneider, Dr. P.J., Amtsphysicus zu Ettenheim im Breisgau: Medizinisch polizeiliche Würdigung einiger Religionsgebräuche und Sitten des israelitischen Volkes, rücksichtlich ihres Einflusses auf den Gesundheitszustand desselben. *Henke's Ztschr. f. Staatsarzneykd.* Vol. X (1825) p.213 ff.

1. Circumcision. 2. Observance of general and specific cleanliness. 3. Order of food and lifestyle (a) food habits (b) holidays and festivals (c) business. 4. Death and burial.

4. Kahn, Ignaz: *Ueber den medicinisch-polizeylichen Sinn der mosaischen Gesetze.* Inaug.-Abhdlg. Augsburg 1825. 56 p. 8°.
5. idem: *Medizinisch-polizeiliche Abhandlung über die Mosaischen Sanitats-Gesetze.* Augsburg 1833. 54 p..12°.
6. Manson, Salom. Ludov.: *Diss. med. de legislatura mosaica, quantum ad hygieinen pertinet.* Hagae Comit. 1835. 84 p. 8°.
7. de Sola, Abraham, L.L.D.: *The sanitary institutions of the Hebrews, as exhibited in the scriptures and rabbinical writings, and as bearing upon modern sanitary regulations.* part 1. Montreal 1861. (74 p.)
8. v. Klein, Carl H.: Jewish hygiene and diet. *Journ. of the Americ. med. assoc.* 1884. off-print. 22 p. 8°.

9. Borchard, Marc: *l'hygiène publique chex les Juifs.* Paris 1865. 39 p. 8°.

10. Guardia, J.M.: Preceptes de Moîse touchant l'hygiene. *Gaz. med. de Paris.* 1865. No. 43. p.657-660.

11. Adler, Marcus N.: the health laws of the Bible, and their influence upon the life-condition of the Jews. *Imperial and Asiatic quarterly Review.* Jan. 1892. offprint. 11 p.

12. Loebl, Jos. M.: Die Hygiene der alten Juden. *Mitt. d. österr.-israel. Union.* Wien 1894. No. 58. offprint. 15 p. 8°.

13. Gillespie, C.G.K.: The sanitary code of the Pentateuch. (*By-paths of Bible Knowledge* XXI.) (London) 1894. 96 p. 8°.

14. Nossig, Dr. Alfred: *Die Sozialhygiene der Juden und des altoriental. Völkerkreises.* Suttg. etc. 1894. 152 p. 8°.
Offprint from *Einführg. in das Studium der sozialen Hygiene ib. ib.* (Juden: p.31-end).

15. Baginsky, Adolf: Die hygienischen Grundzüge der mosaischen Gesetzgebung. *D. Vierteljahrsschr. f. öff. Gesundheitspflege* XXVII, part 3. offprint 2nd edit. Braunschweig 1895. 27 p. 8°.

16. Rattray, Alexander, M.D.: *Divine hygiene. Sanitary science and sanitarians of Sacred Scriptures and Mosaic code.* 2 vols. London 1903. 655 and 748 p. 8°.

17. Wolzendorff, Dr. Gustav: *Gesundheitspflege und Medizin der Bibel.* (Christ as a physician.) Wiesbaden 1903. 63 p. 8°.

18. Medvei Béla: *Az ó-testamentumi egészségügy jelenkori világitásban.* (The hygiene of the Old Testament in the light of modern times.) Gyógyászat 1904. offprint. 23 p.

19. Steinthal, S.: *Die Hygiene in Bibel und Talmud.* Berlin 1907. 31 p. 8°.

20. Hagemann, E.: Zur Hygiene der alten Israeliten. *Janus* XII (1907) p.369-381, p.449-461.

21. Piazza, L.: *Sul valore della igiene Mosaica.* Lentini 1908. 23 p.

22. Warliz Christ.: *De Morbis Biblicis, e prava diaeta animique affectibus resultantibus.* Vitembg. 1714. 390 p. 8°.
Dietetics with parallels from the Bible.

23. Troppaneger, Chr. Gottl., praes. Fr. Hoffmann: *de diaetetica sacrae script. med.* Hal. 1728. 59 p. 4°. Also in Hoffmanni *Opuscula theol.-physico-medica.* Hal. 1740. 4°. German: Ulm 1745. 8°.

24. Aronstam, N.E.: The jewish dietary laws from a scientific standpoint. *The med. Age* 1904. offprint 10 p. 8°.

25. Wolfsheimer, Salom. Bernh.: *De causis foecunditatis Ebraeorum, nonnullis sacri Codicis praeceptis intuentibus.* Halae 1742.

26. Worms, Simon Wolf, natione Ebraeus: *De causa immunditei spermatis humani apud Ebraeos...loco speciminis inauguralis.* Gissae 1768. 28 p. 4°.

27. Burgheim, Salomo Hirsch, praes. Adam Michael Birkholz: *De studio munditiei corporis penes Judaeos morbis arcendis atque abigendis apto.* Lipsiae 1784. 36 p. 4°.

28. Katzenelson, L.: Die rituellen Reinheitsgesetze in der Bibel und im Talmud. *Mtschr. f. Gesch. und Wiss. d. Judent.* 1899 p.1-17; 97-112; 193-210. 1900. p.385-400; 433-451.

29. Nicolai, Joh.: *de sepulchris Hebraeorum.* Lugd. Bat. 1706. 285 p. 4°.

30. Gakenholz, A.C.: *programma de immunditie ex contrectatione mortuorum secundum legem Mosaicem.* Num. XIX. *cum anatomen corporis feminini institueret.* Helmstadii 1708. (22 p.) 4°.

31. Perles, Dr. J.: Die Leichenfeierlichkeiten im nachbibl. Judenthume. *Frankel's Mtschr. f. Gesch. u. Wiss. d. Judenth.* X (1861). p.345-55 and 376-94.

32. Preuss, J.: Materialien z. Gesch. d. talmud. Medicin. Der Tote und seine Bestattung. *Allg. med. Central.-Ztg.* 1902. No. 25 ff.
33. Locard, Edmond: La mort de Judas Iscariote, étude critique d'exégèse et de méd. légale sur un cas de pendaison célèbre. *Arch. Anthrop. Crim.* 15 June 1904.
34. Küchenmeister, Fr.: *Die Totenbestattungen der Bibel und die Feuerbestattung.* Stuttg. 1893. 163 p. 8°.
35. Stössel, Bezirks-Rabb. in Stuttgart. Die Feuerbestattung. *Allg. Ztg. des Jud.* 1894. 32/33.
36. Leufstadius, Andreas, praes. Olaf Celsius: *De lotionibus Ebraeorum.* Upsalae 1727. 32 p. 12°.
37. Spitzer, Sam.: Ueber Baden und Bäder...bei den Hebräern, Griechen und Römern. *Grünwalds Studien und Kritiken.* 1883. offprint. 43 p. 8°.
38. Wessely, Wolfgang. Ueber die Heilquellen und Bäder bei den alten Hebräern. *Oesterr. Blätter f. Litt. & Kunst.* March-April 1844. French. in de Carro's *Almanach de Carlsbad.* Munich 1844. p.66-133.
39. Löw, L.: Dampfbäder in der talmud. Zeit. *Ben Chananja* IX (1866) p.23-25; *Ges. Schr.* III, 367-369.
40. Beugnies, Ablutions et bains chex les Sémites. Peypers' *Janus* I (1896) p.202-215.
41. Preuss, J.: Waschungen und Bäder nach Bibel und Talmud. *Wiener mediz. Wochenschr.* 1904. No. 2 ff.
42. Krauss, Samuel: Bad und Badewesen im Talmud. offprint from *Hakedem* I. II. (Frankfurt a. M.) 1908. 65 p. 8°.

# DIETETICS

1. Formstecher (Offenbach): Beiträge zur rationellen Erklärung einiger mos. Vorschriften mit bes. Beziehung auf d. Speisegesetze. *Israelit d. 19 Jahrhdt.* 1847. No. 31-34.
2. Garrault, P.: Die Rindertuberkulose und der Talmud. *Rev. scientifique* 1902. 3/4; *Medizin. Woche* 1907. No. 39-48. off-print. 29 p. 8°.
3. Rubinstein, Mátyás: A mózesi talmudi húshigiene (Fleischhygiene). *Jubelschrift für Moses Bloch.* Budapest 1905. p.187-197. Hungarian.
4. Baltzer, Eduard: *Vegetarianismus in der Bibel.* (Die natürliche Lebensweise. IV.) Nordhausen 1872. 2nd, 3rd edit. Lpz. o. J. 131 p. 8°.
5. Wawruch, Andr. Ign.: *Diquis. med. cholerae, cujus mentio in sacris bibliis occurrit.* (Num. cap. XI) Wien 1832. 8 p. 4°.
6. Delitzsch Franz: Die Bibel und der Wein. *Schriften des Institut. Judaicum* No. 7. Lpz. 1885. 18 p. 8°.
7. Harnack, Erich: Die Bibel und die alkoholischen Getränke. *Festschr. . . . z. Jubelfeier d. Univ. Halle* 1894. offprint. 18 p. fol.
8. Asmussen, G.: Die Bibel und die Alkoholfrage... Erwiderung an Prof. Dr. E. Harnack. *Tages- und Lebensfragen* No. 19. Bremerhaven 1895. 32 p. 8°.
9. Boas, Kurt. W.F.: Trunksucht in der Bibel. *Zeitschr. f. Religionspychol.* Bd. I. p.345-351.
10. Reinelt, Paul: *Was sagt die hl. Schrift vom Weine und von der Abstinenz?* Hamm 1908. 42 p. 8°.
11. Kohler, K., New-York: Zum Kapitel der Jüdischen Wohltätigkeitspflege. *Festschrift zum 70. Geburtstage A. Berliner's.* Frankf. a M. 1903. p.195-203.

12. Cassel, Dr. D., *Offener Brief eines Juden an Herrn Prof. Dr. Virchow.* Berlin 1869. 38 p. 8°.
Virchow thought ("Ueber Hospitaler u. Lazarette", Sammlg. gemeinverständl. wiss. *Vorträge v. Firch. und von Holzendorff* Third Series Part 72, p.6) that the Jews had no hospitals at all. On the other hand, Cassel criticizes Virchow's reply in his *Archiv.* Vol. 46 p.470. See *Beth Chophschith* II Reg. 15,5.

13. Schervier, C.G., Religionslehrer: *Ueber die hohe Lebensdauer der Urväter des Menschengeschlechts. Progr. d. Höheren Bürgerschule zu Aachen.* 1857. 19 p. gr. 4°.
Previous writings on this subject are found in Choulant p.107.

14. von Seelen, Joh. Henr.: *de medicorum meritis in S. Scripturam diatribe hist.- crit.* Lubec. 1719. 48 p. 4°.
This is not a complete bibliography of writings on Biblical medicine.

15. Steinschneider, Moritz: Schriften über Medizin in Bibel und Talmud und über judische Aerzte. *Wiener klin. Rundschau* 1896. No. 25/26.

16. Preuss, J.: Schriften über Medizin in Bibel und Talmud. Ein Nachtrag nebst einigen Berichtigungen zu Steinschneider's Artikel. . .*Brody's Ztschr. f. hebr. Bibliographie* II (1897) Part 1. p.22.

# INDEX

## Compiled by Robert J. Milch, M.A.

### I. PASSAGES CITED

#### HEBREW BIBLE

*Genesis*

| | | | | | |
|---|---|---|---|---|---|
| **1:14** | 160 | **15:20** | 15 | **21:8** | 410 |
| **1:28** | 412, 452 | **16:1** | 411 | **21:14** | 49 |
| **2:7** | 58, 74 | **16:2** | 397, 411 | **21:19** | 270 |
| **2:21** | 58, 64, 202 | **17:5** | 60 | **21:25** | 545 |
| **2:24** | 415 | **17:7** | 241 | **21:33** | 444 |
| **3:15** | 237 | **17:10-15** | 240 | **22:3** | 134 |
| **3:16** | 382, 395, 455 | **17:13** | 109 | **22:4** | 224 |
| **4:10** | 517 | **17:17** | 382, 580 | **22:6** | 48 |
| **5:1** | 452 | **17:23** | 103 | **23:1-20** | 517 |
| **5:2** | 227 | **18:1** | 133, 442 | **23:6** | 517 |
| **6:2** | 281, 488 | **18:4** | 524 | **24:9** | 57 |
| **6:4** | 201 | **18:7** | 557 | **24:15** | 49 |
| **6:7** | 65 | **18:11** | 122, 382 | **24:32** | 524 |
| **6:12** | 497 | **18:19** | 442 | **24:50** | 488 |
| **6:13** | 489 | **18:20-21** | 494 | **24:55** | 488 |
| **6:18** | 460 | **19:2** | 524 | **24:59** | 407 |
| **7:11** | 529 | **19:4-24** | 494 | **25:23** | 59, 113, 114, 428 |
| **8:16** | 460 | **19:11** | 263, 269, 270, 273 | **25:24** | 428 |
| **8:22** | 304 | **19:12** | 494 | **25:24-26** | 428 |
| **9:3** | 557 | **19:14** | 494 | **25:25** | 81, 353, 428 |
| **9:4** | 503 | **19:19** | 580 | **26:20** | 546 |
| **9:5** | 516 | **19:30** | 183 | **26:22** | 383 |
| **9:21** | 573 | **19:30 ff** | 469, 574 | **27:1** | 72, 73 |
| **9:22 ff.** | 57, 109 | **19:30-38** | 468 | **27:11** | 353 |
| **9:23** | 49 | **19:32** | 469 | **27:16** | 47 |
| **12:1** | 580 | **19:32 ff.** | 573 | **27:36** | 173, 428 |
| **12:17** | 347 | **19:33** | 469 | **28:27** | 113 |
| **14:22** | 51 | **20:18** | 114 | **29:2** | 546 |
| **15:4** | 114 | **21:4** | 35, 240 | **29:11** | 83 |

## John

| | |
|---|---|
| 5:5 | 307 |
| 7:22 | 244 |
| 8:5 | 472 |
| 9:1-7 | 531 |
| 9:2 | 271 |
| 9:6 | 277 |
| 11:12 | 135 |
| 11:17 | 512 |
| 11:44 | 170 |
| 11:55 | 507 |
| 12:3 | 371 |
| 19:30-40 | 512 |
| 19:34 | 209 |

## Acts

| | |
|---|---|
| 1:18 | 514 |
| 3:2 | 308 |
| 3:6-7 | 308 |
| 5:15 | 150 |
| 5:36 | 20 |
| 8:27 | 222 |
| 9:3 ff. | 300 |
| 9:9 | 300 |
| 9:18 | 300 |
| 9:33 | 307 |
| 9:37 | 170 |
| 12:23 | 184 |
| 13:11 | 273 |
| 15:1 ff. | 241 |
| 15:20 | 482, 503 |
| 15:29 | 503 |
| 19:12 | 150 |

| | |
|---|---|
| 19:13 | 315 |
| 19:17 | 276 |
| 20:9 | 170 |
| 21:25 | 482 |
| 27:9 | 576 |
| 28:6 | 198 |
| 28:8 | 160, 180 |

## Romans

| | |
|---|---|
| 1:26 | 498 |
| 1:27 | 491 |
| 3:13 | 209 |
| 14:2 | 566 |

## I Corinthians

| | |
|---|---|
| 6:9 | 475 |
| 7:2 | 451 |
| 7:3-4 | 456 |
| 7:9 | 452 |
| 7:18 | 246 |
| 11:13 | 365 |
| 11:14 | 364 |
| 12:17 | 74 |
| 14:34 | 101 |

## II Corinthians

| | |
|---|---|
| 6:5 | 134 |
| 11:27 | 134 |
| 12:7 | 300 |

## Galatians

| | |
|---|---|
| 4:14 | 300 |

## Colossians

| | |
|---|---|
| 4:14 | 20, 378 |

## I Timothy

| | |
|---|---|
| 1:10 | 475 |
| 4:3 | 452 |
| 5:23 | 572 |

## II Timothy

| | |
|---|---|
| 2:17 | 195 |

## Titus

| | |
|---|---|
| 1:15 | 507 |

## Hebrews

| | |
|---|---|
| 11:31 | 483 |

## James

| | |
|---|---|
| 2:25 | 483 |
| 3:5 | 87 |

## II Peter

| | |
|---|---|
| 2:7 | 495 |

## Revelation (Apocalypse)

| | |
|---|---|
| 2:14 | 499 |
| 3:18 | 283 |
| 13:16 | 79 |
| 14:1 | 79 |
| 17:5 | 46, 481 |
| 22:15 | 491 |

# TALMUD

## Note to Talmud section

The arrangement of the index of talmudic passages is alphabetical and includes appended tractates such as *Soferim, Gerim,* etc. Within each sequence, the abbreviations *M., Tos., Bab.,* and *Jer.,* stand for Mishnah, Tosefta, Babylonian Talmud and Jerusalem Talmud respectively.

Although occasionally confusing, Preuss' original citations have been preserved wherever possible. For example, *Derekh Eretz Rabbah* is sometimes cited by Preuss simply as *Derekh Eretz; Kallah Rabbathi* is sometimes referred to as *Kallah Rabbah;* and *Yoma* is used interchangeably with *Yom Hakippurim.*

Even more confusing are the three different systems of citation used by Preuss for the Midrashic sources: by *sedrah,* by Biblical chapter and verse, and by folio. All three have been preserved in the text of the book but folio numbers are listed in the index only when they are the sole indication of the source.

The editions of the various Biblical, talmudic, and Midrashic sources used by Preuss are listed in his introduction and the reader is advised to refer there, and also back to the reference in the text itself, in order to be sure of the citation.

| | |
|---|---|
| 14:4 | 239, 310 |
| 17:1 | 192 |
| 18:3 | 37 |
| 19 | 242 |
| 19:1 | 241, 248 |
| 19:2 | 238 |
| 19:3 | 537 |
| 19:4 | 227 |
| 20:2 | 564 |
| 20:3 | 567 |
| 20:6 | 539 |
| 21:24 | 171 |
| 22:6 | 193, 194, 403, 538 |
| 23:5 | 511, 512 |

## Tos. Shabbath

| | |
|---|---|
| 1:8 | 78 |
| 2:8 | 136, 438 |
| 3:3 | 535 |
| 3:4 | 537 |
| 3(4):5 | 370 |
| 3(4):6 | 370 |
| 3:7 | 437 |
| 3:12 | 550 |
| 3:18 | 538 |
| 4:5 | 146 |
| 4:9 | 146, 301 |
| 5:1 | 287 |
| 5:2 | 367 |
| 5:3 | 530 |
| 5:3-4 | 238 |
| 5:5 | 435 |
| 5:6 | 435 |
| 5:10 | 286 |
| 6:1 | 362 |
| 6:7 | 137 |
| 6:12 | 51 |
| 7 | 399 |
| 7:5 | 76 |
| 7:11 | 149 |
| 7:18 | 521, 522 |
| 7:21 | 302 |
| 7:23 | 145 |
| 7:25 | 75 |
| 8:8 | 265, 278, 305 |
| 8:20 | 372 |
| 8:23 | 193 |
| 8:28 | 74 |
| 8:30 | 183 |
| 9:1-2 | 80 |
| 9:13 | 369 |
| 9:22 | 409 |
| 10:12 | 367 |
| 10:13 | 281 |
| 12:2 | 239 |
| 12:8 | 171 |
| 12:10 | 172 |
| 12:11 | 305, 350 |
| 12:13 | 438, 439, 532, 534 |

| | |
|---|---|
| 13:16 | 409 |
| 14:14 | 11 |
| 15 | 242 |
| 15:3 | 398, 399 |
| 15:5 | 393 |
| 15:7 | 394 |
| 15:8 | 165 |
| 15:14 | 198 |
| 16:6 | 537 |
| 16:14 | 538 |
| 17:19 | 72, 404 |

## Bab. Shabbath

| | |
|---|---|
| 7a | 535 |
| 9b | 359, 364, 537 |
| 10a | 179, 575 |
| 11a | 179, 180, 304 |
| 11b | 78, 236 |
| 12a-b | 443 |
| 13a | 356 |
| 14b | 525 |
| 15a | 551 |
| 25b | 542 |
| 26a | 267 |
| 28b | 548 |
| 31a | 55, 207, 231, 267, 366, 403 |
| 31b | 253 |
| 32a | 27, 231, 574 |
| 32b | 413 |
| 33a | 157, 166, 167, 189, 553 |
| 33b | 71, 350, 535, 541, 543 |
| 34a | 370, 485 |
| 35a | 546 |
| 36a | 93 |
| 38b | 560 |
| 40a | 541 |
| 40b | 181, 437, 438, 466, 534, 536, 537 |
| 41a | 170, 533, 536, 540, 575, 579 |
| 42a | 180 |
| 48a | 109 |
| 48b | 359 |
| 49a | 131 |
| 50a | 238, 366, 367, 372 |
| 53a | 356 |
| 53b | 239, 305, 410, 438 |
| 54b | 46, 186, 206, 395 |
| 60a | 367 |
| 62a | 372 |
| 62b | 344, 368, 373, 374 |
| 63a | 90 |
| 63b | 121, 413, 479 |
| 64a | 121, 147 |
| 64b | 52, 282, 367, 369, 473 |
| 65a | 171, 286, 288, 498, 529, 568 |
| 65a-b | 598 |

| | |
|---|---|
| 66a | 73 |
| 66b | 149, 161, 181, 385, 386, 437 |
| 67a | 136, 145, 162, 194, 212, 291, 301, 344, 549 |
| 67b | 548 |
| 75b | 54, 124, 435 |
| 76b | 554 |
| 77a | 47, 570 |
| 77b | 69, 199, 239, 272, 278, 351, 436 |
| 78a | 266, 277, 438 |
| 80a | 282 |
| 80b | 368 |
| 81a | 87, 185, 437, 550 |
| 82a | 549, 550, 576 |
| 86a | 384, 457 |
| 86b | 119 |
| 88b | 434 |
| 89b | 127 |
| 90a | 80, 128, 171, 305, 371 |
| 94b | 81, 358, 365, 367, 369 |
| 95a | 281, 369 |
| 97a | 359 |
| 98b | 226 |
| 103a | 309 |
| 104b | 80, 365 |
| 105b | 144 |
| 107b | 193 |
| 108a | 181, 262, 555 |
| 108b | 109, 251, 271, 277, 278, 283, 438, 489, 550, 555, 566, 572 |
| 108b-109a | 296 |
| 109a | 69, 235, 239, 270, 276, 280, 438, 525, 568, 572 |
| 109b | 186, 187, 199, 277, 350, 436 |
| 109b-110a | 166 |
| 110a | 187 |
| 110a-b | 379 |
| 110b | 225, 265 |
| 111a | 285, 378 |
| 118b | 180, 489 |
| 119a | 20 |
| 119b | 554 |
| 120a | 247 |
| 120b | 80 |
| 121b | 319 |
| 123a | 403 |
| 127a | 443 |
| 128b | 398, 399, 427 |
| 129a | 50, 120, 152, 253, 254, 255, 347, 395, 400, 401, 569, 572 |
| 129b | 35, 249, 250, 253, 254, 338, 364, 393, 399, 402 |
| 130a | 34 |
| 130b | 36 |

**MIDRASH**

(See Note at Head of Talmud Section, p. 607)

# 2. SUBJECT INDEX

Spiegelberg (medical
writer), 592
Spikenard, 372, 374
Spinal column, 65, 403, 523
dislocation of, 230
defects of, 417
hyperenia of, 464
Spinal cord, 130, 131-32,
203, 310
injuries of, 207-08, 230
Spinal fluid, 204
Spine, 62
Spitting. *See* Expectoration
Spittle. *See* Saliva
Spitzer, Sam., 595
Spleen, 91, 98-99, 181, 255,
269, 286
disorders of, 188
of animals, 112
prolapsed, 216
excision of, 216
Splinters, 192
Splints, 239
Split lip, 85, 208
Sponges, 238, 530
Spoons, 578
Spotty Leprosy, 326
Sprains, 194, 202, 309
Sputum, 86, 173, 354, 355,
356
bloody, 86, 174, 356
Stab wounds, 192, 209, 210,
215, 422-23, 508, 513, 514,
516
Stags, 194
Stammering, 89, 230
Standing, 579
Starvation, 271, 319, 398,
441, 479, 576, 577
Status epilepticus, 312
Steam baths, 371, 438, 441,
527, 538, 543
Steatopygia, 232
Steinschneider, Moritz, 596
Steinthal, S., 594
Stephanus, Henry, 172
Sterility, 114, 124, 162, 199,
203, 410-11, 412, 459, 463,
471. *See also* Childlessness
Stern, A., 252, 349, 464, 586
Sternum, 107
Stibium, 265, 270, 280, 281
Sticker (medical writer), 156,
349
Sties, 262
Stimulants, 192
Stock, Joh. Christ., 587
Stoics, 23, 24, 68

Stomach, 91, 92, 94, 105,
135, 180, 183, 212, 213,
256, 555, 563, 566, 568,
570, 572, 579
cancer of, 105
disorders of, 178, 563,
567, 575
Stomatitis, 172. *See also*
Aphthae
Stoning, 227, 466, 467, 472,
474, 477, 480, 490, 520,
558
Storks, 436
Stössel (rabbi), 595
Strack, Hermann
Leberecht, 124
Strack (medical writer), 584
Strangulation, 157, 227, 472,
474, 514
Stranguria, 163, 229. *See
also* Urination
Street cleaning, 551
Strength, 104
Strigilation, 538
Strongiloidae, 176
Stunted growth, 226
Stuttering, 88, 230
Suckling, 129, 274, 317, 333,
385, 404, 405, 408, 409,
412.
of animal, by human, 409
*See also* Mother's milk
Suffocation, 188, 438, 562
Suffusion, 193
Sugar, 563, 571
Sugar melons, 567
Suicide, 214, 215, 513-16,
519, 520, 522
Suidas, 19
Sulphur, 344
Sunbaths, 438
Sunstroke. *See* Heatstroke
Superfecundation, 386
Superfetation, 386, 418
Supernumerary fingers, 233
Supernumerary toes, 233
Superstitions, 51, 137, 139,
147, 150, 162, 285, 386,
399
Surface wounds, 343
Surgeons, 34, 38, 419, 420
Surgery, 11, 14, 28, 32, 33,
191, 215, 216, 219, 233,
241, 242, 248, 276, 390,
587, 588-89
Surgical instruments, 11, 12,
191, 192, 205, 251
Surgical operations, 423. *See
also names of operations*

Susak, 120
Susanna, 532, 537
Suturing, 31
Swaddling, 402, 403
Swallowing, 91, 92, 159
Sweat. *See* Perspiration
Swelling, 154, 155, 231, 235,
343
Swimming, 532
Swine. *See* Pigs
Symchos, 383
Symmachos, 165
Synanche, 159, 211, 249
Syphilis, 155, 185, 186,
324-25, 340, 341, 342, 348,
499, 500, 544, 591, 593
Syrian leek, 566
Syrian throat plague, 423

Tacitus, 580
Tail, human, 58
Talipes calcaneus. *See*
Clubfoot
Talmud, medicine in, 448,
449-50
Tam, Jacob b. Meir, 50
Tamar (Absalom's
sister), 303, 368, 469-70,
471
Tamar (Er's wife), 37, 383,
412, 428-29, 458, 485
Tamarisk, 305
Tampons, 381, 387, 406, 418
Tanchum b. Chanillay, 549
Tapeworms, 187, 199
Tarfon (tanna), 233, 421,
489
Tartar, 287
Taste, sense of, 87, 88, 274
Tattooing, 80, 239, 266
Tea, 400
Tears, 70-72, 263, 350, 524
tearing eyes, 347, 479
*See also* Lacrimal
glands; Weeping
Teeth, 11, 47, 60, 61, 84, 86,
89-91, 120, 150, 172, 181,
285, 286, 287, 537, 554,
555, 559, 566, 577
cleaning of, 171, 286
misaligned, 287
extraction of, 286
toothache, 52, 88, 173, 285
Telescopes, 280
Temples (anat.), 46, 362
Tendons, 132
Tenesmus, 71, 155
Teratology, ancient, 416

# ABOUT THE AUTHOR

Julius Preuss (1861–1913) was born in Gross-Schoenebeck (Saxonia). A practicing physician and medical historian in Berlin who was also an active member of the Orthodox Jewish community, he was renowned for his writings on medicine in biblical and talmudic literature.

# ABOUT THE TRANSLATOR/EDITOR

Dr. Fred Rosner is a respected hematologist and renowned medical ethicist. He is director of the Department of Medicine at Mount Sinai Services at Queens Hospital Center, Jamaica, New York, and professor of medicine at the Mount Sinai School of Medicine, New York, New York. Dr. Rosner is the author, editor, or translator of many works, including *Medicine and Jewish Law, The Existence and Unity of God, Six Treatises Attributed to Maimonides,* and *Moses Maimonides: Physician, Scientist, and Philosopher.*